The Colorado Guide

The Colorado Guide

LANDSCAPES, CITYSCAPES, —— ESCAPES ——

Bruce Caughey
Dean Winstanley

with additional accounts by
Vince Bzdek and Mark Eddy

Fulcrum, Inc.
Golden, Colorado

The information in *The Colorado Guide* is accurate as of February 1989. However, prices, hours of operation, phone numbers and other items can change rapidly. If something in the book is incorrect or if you have some ideas for the next edition, please write the authors at Fulcrum, Inc., 350 Indiana Street, Golden, CO 80401.

The Colorado Guide provides many safety tips about weather and travel, but good decision making and sound judgment are the responsibility of the individual.

Library of Congress
Cataloging-in-Publication Data

Caughey, Bruce, 1960–
    The Colorado guide : landscapes, cityscapes, escapes!! /Bruce
Caughey, Dean Winstanley.
        p.   cm.
    Includes index.
    ISBN 1-55591-039-4
    1. Outdoor recreation—Colorado—Guide-books. 2. Colorado—
Description and travel—1981– —Guide-books. I. Winstanley, Dean,
1960– . II. Title.
GV191.42.C6C38   1989
917.88—dc19   88-31726
                                                        CIP

Fulcrum, Inc.
Golden, Colorado

CONTENTS

ACKNOWLEDGMENTS

If we could name, individually, all the people who assisted us during the past year, we'd have another manuscript on our hands. We'll attempt to keep it brief without offending anyone. First, we must thank our parents who instilled in us the love of Colorado from the beginning. They also helped greatly by conducting some research and by reading stacks of chapters during the past year. Thanks also go to other readers who patiently scoured our work: Sher, Barb, Simon, Collette, Martha, Ron and Vince.

David French's unfailing encouragement and advice helped focus our efforts and were instrumental in getting the project off the ground. We thank Margaret Sillstrop for her early assistance. David C. Holloway provided the striking photos of Colorado for the initial proposal and, eventually, the photos on the cover and the back of this book. Doug Jonas created the Colorado maps.

We acknowledge the people at Fulcrum, Inc., especially Betsy Armstrong and Pat Frederick, whose contagious energy made this project a joy from the start. We greatly appreciate the honing and tightening of our manuscript by Margaret Terrell-Morse, Carmel Huestis, Cindy Thompson and Karen Groves, and the excellent composition work by Jay Staten. We thank Maxine Benson for ensuring our history was on track and for providing the list of top 10 historic Colorado sites.

Thanks are due to Mark Asimus, Jim Bolick and Ron Catterson for their help in putting major pieces together for a few specific chapters and to Andy Darr of Silverton for use of his pen-and-ink sketches. We are grateful to the Colorado Tourism Board for providing all of the uncredited photos within these pages.

The folks at the Western History Department of the Denver Public Library helped in our research. While on the road, offices of the National Forest Service and Bureau of Land Management as well as many chambers of commerce provided us with an invaluable base of information. The public relations staffs at the ski areas, particularly Aspen, Vail, Breckenridge and Telluride, were a huge help. To all those people who assisted us when we needed it most—THANKS!

Finally, to Sheila and Naomi, who endured many late-night edits and a constant preoccupation with the project—your support, advice and comfort meant everything.

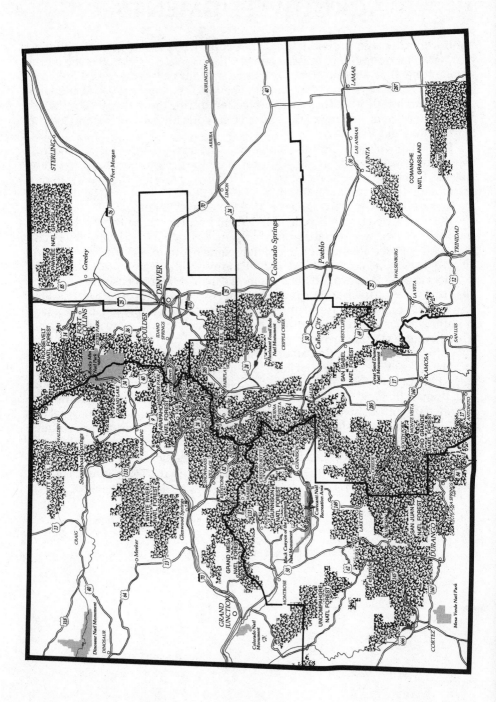

Introduction

BACKGROUND INFORMATION

No one summed up Colorado better than former US President Teddy Roosevelt when he said, "The scenery bankrupts the English language." Dominating this striking scenery are the Rocky Mountains that run through the middle of the state, constituting a mountainous area three times as large as the Swiss Alps. Colorado's peaks are legendary—over 1,140 of them are 10,000 feet or higher (54 top off at over 14,000 feet).

The state's colorful history comes alive at the cliff dwellings of Mesa Verde National Park and in the former mining boom towns of Leadville and Central City. Woven into the historic fabric are the unmistakable impacts of Anglo, Hispanic and Indian culture, all indelibly etched into Colorado's character. Colorado is a rich and varied land; its three million residents appreciate the healthy mix of recreation and culture, coming together with a dash of the Wild West.

More than 20 million visitors make their way to the state each year, not only for personal adventure and wilderness travel, but to enjoy some of the best powder skiing in the world. As "Winter Sports Capital of the Country," Colorado offers 27 major ski areas.

Colorado is a place with so much to do that up-to-date, accurate advice is a precious commodity. As native Coloradans, we enjoy sharing tips about the state with friends who come to visit—this is the intent of our guidebook. With an insider's perspective of Front Range cities, small mountain towns and areas far from civilization, we unlock some of Colorado's best-kept secrets. Included are specifics that guide the way to many popular activities, such as hiking, downhill skiing, fly-fishing and whitewater rafting. We also offer information about luxurious mountain resorts, the arts and museums of Denver, and the region's many hot springs.

We spent over a year building on an already well-established knowledge of Colorado, doing research in musty libraries and traveling the state to discover exciting, out-of-the-way places. The result is a complete, easy-to-use and unbiased guide, which we hope will get years of use while imparting some of the fascination and love we feel for the state. Now get out there and enjoy!

HISTORY

This land called *Colorado*, to which so many people come for rest and relaxation, was anything but that to its first inhabitants. Nomadic hunters of bison and woolly mammoth may have roamed the state as far back as 15,000 years ago. Archaeologists continue to learn more about these prehistoric residents (Folsom Man) from their stone spear heads and other artifacts. Close on the heels of Folsom Man was the more advanced Anasazi civilization—Colorado's first farmers. They inhabited the mesa tops and cliffs of southwestern Colorado from approximately AD 1 until their mysterious disappearance in AD 1300. The Anasazi were initially known for their basketmaking and later for pottery and stone masonry (the latter is witnessed in the stunning cliff-hanging citadels at Mesa Verde National Park, near Cortez).

In centuries following the disappearance of the Anasazi, family bands of nomadic tribes (most notably Utes and Comanche in the mountains and Arapaho and Cheyenne on the plains) wandered the state in search of game. To these tribes, the buffalo was an integral part of their way of life. By the late 1500s the arrival of white men forever changed the Indians' lifestyle in Colorado. These newcomers brought horses, enabling the Indians to travel greater distances and to hunt more effectively.

By many accounts, the first European to enter Colorado was the Spanish explorer, Francisco Coronado. In 1540 he and other conquistadors made their way north from Mexico City in search of the mythical "Seven Cities of Cibola," where it was said the streets were paved with gold. No such luck for Coronado, who arrived in northern New Mexico only to find Pueblo Indians living in poverty. Probably to get rid of him, they suggested he head to what is now Kansas . . . there he would find the riches he sought. Many historians believe he traveled through southeastern Colorado on his way to Kansas. Alas, he never found his gold. At about this time, the Spanish gave Colorado its name, which means "reddish" or "ruddy."

Over the next few hundred years, as the Spanish moved north and settled in the Rio Grande Valley of New Mexico, they played a major role in the history of Colorado. Although they never established any permanent settlements in the state, Spain claimed all the land south of the Arkansas River and west of the Continental Divide. One of the first written accounts of Colorado was provided by the Spanish friars Dominguez and Escalante. These men left Santa Fe (northern New Mexico) in the summer of 1776, looking for a route to the new Spanish settlement in San Francisco, California. Their journey took them through much of southwestern Colorado. Poor relations with the Indians persisted throughout Spain's colonization of the New World—perhaps stiff taxes and enslavement had something to do with it! This disregard for Indian culture on the part of the Spanish was repeated in later years by Americans.

After the Louisiana Purchase in 1803, the United States doubled in size. This largely uncharted land was acquired from Napoleon Bonaparte, ruler of the French empire, in one of the best real estate deals of all time. Expeditions were sent west to explore the new territory, which included northeastern Colorado. In 1806, Zebulon Pike led the first expedition to Colorado via the Arkansas River. Though a rather inept pathfinder, Pike did manage to explore much of southern Colorado before being captured in Spanish territory along the Rio Grande River in the San Luis Valley (he thought he was on the Red River of Texas).

Another significant expedition was conducted in 1820 by Maj. Stephen H. Long. Entering Colorado on the South Platte River, Long explored much of the Front Range of the Rockies before leaving along the Arkansas River. Unimpressed with the land along the Front Range, Long called it the "Great American Desert" and "unfit for cultivation." He was wrong, though, as eastern Colorado went on to support some of the most productive agricultural land in the western US. Later expeditions in the 1840s by John C. Fremont and in 1853 by Capt. John Gunnison added knowledge about the complex geography of Colorado.

In the 1820s the trading and trapping era began. Beaver hats were the rage in Europe and the eastern US. The high prices paid for beaver pelts swayed a number of adventurous trappers to venture into the wilds of Colorado. These men were the real pioneers and they included Jim Bridger, Jim Beckwourth, Jedediah Smith and Kit Carson. After Mexico achieved independence from Spain in 1821, trade between this new country and the US blossomed. To facilitate trade, the Santa Fe Trail was established between St. Louis, Missouri, and Santa Fe. In the late 1820s traders William and Charles Bent and Ceran St. Vrain built Bent's Fort along a section of the Santa Fe Trail that passed through southeastern Colorado. For almost 20 years, the fort served as a base for western trade with Mexico and the Pacific Coast.

When beaver hats fell out of fashion in the 1830s, trappers looked around for an alternative income and found it in hunting buffalo. The Plains Indians were concerned, and rightly so, that the buffalo slaughter threatened their way of life. Short-term relations were soothed by trading guns and liquor. Within a few short decades, the buffalo were almost hunted to extinction.

By 1846 relations between the US and Mexico deteriorated to such a point that the Mexican War broke out. Two years later, Mexico ceded its land in present-day Colorado to US victors in the Treaty of Guadalupe Hidalgo. The US, however, agreed to honor Mexican land grants in extreme southern Colorado. These grants had been given by the Mexican government to individuals who agreed to establish settlements in remote northern areas of the Mexican frontier. In 1852 Hispanic settlers, moving into what is now southern Colorado, established San Luis, the first permanent town in the state. A number of other settlements followed;

today, this area is still dominated by Hispanic culture.

Colorado's most glorious era kicked into gear in 1858 when William Green Russell and his party from Georgia discovered gold along Dry Creek near present-day Denver. Hundreds of anxious miners made their way to the mining camps of Denver City and Auraria in the Pikes Peak Gold Rush. Many returned east in disgust calling the strike a hoax, but gold strikes by George Jackson near Idaho Springs and by John Gregory near Central City in the spring of 1859 proved the early rush was well founded and thousands more streamed into the territory. Publicity in eastern newspapers also prompted fortune seekers to head west, and in the early 1860s, towns sprang up along the Front Range and in the mountains at Breckenridge, Fairplay and Georgetown, among others. Denver quickly grew as a supply town for the mining camps.

In February 1861 the Colorado Territory was established, which was a step toward statehood and self-rule for the new residents. When the Civil War broke out in 1862, however, the Colorado Territory fell on hard times. Many miners left to fight, and the Plains Indians used this preoccupation with the war to begin a series of raids on white settlers. Angered by the whites' encroachment on their hunting grounds and their disregard for Indian culture, Arapaho and Cheyenne intensified their strikes between 1862 and 1864. The conflict reached a bloody climax when over 100 innocent Indians, including women and children, were slaughtered by volunteer troops at the Sand Creek Massacre (see the **Southeast Plains** chapter). Although there were a few more uprisings, Sand Creek was really the death knell for the Indians of Colorado's eastern plains.

By the late 1860s, most of the easily obtainable gold from stream beds in the territory had been snatched up. Miners were now forced to dig shafts into the mountains to get at the gold ore. The problem was that gold proved difficult to extract from the ore—a cheap processing method was badly needed. In 1868, Prof. Nathaniel Hill solved the ore reduction problem and opened his Boston and Colorado smelter in Black Hawk.

In the 1870s and 1880s Colorado mining really boomed. Prospectors pushed further west into the mountains, discovering new mining areas. Silver was mined and soon became more dominant than gold. After Colorado achieved statehood in 1876, the state received the nickname "Silver State." Georgetown and Silver Cliff were large silver-mining towns, but nothing could compare to the deposits near Leadville. When silver was discovered in Leadville in 1877, the population soared from less than 100 to more than 24,000 within a few months. Many fortunes were made, including that of H.A.W. Tabor (see the **Leadville** chapter).

The quest for new mining areas created a conflict with another of Colorado's Indian tribes—the Utes. A tough, stocky tribe, the Utes roamed the mountains of Colorado following herds of deer, elk, buffalo and antelope. At first they were friendly with the white settlers, especially since these strange-looking newcomers made war on the Arapaho and Cheyenne, the Utes' bitter enemies on the plains. Under the guidance of Chief Ouray, the Utes accepted a series of treaties with the US government, which continued to reduce their territory. Finally, after a band of northern Utes killed Indian agent Nathan Meeker in the Meeker Massacre of 1879, the tribe was relocated to Utah and a small reservation in southwestern Colorado. White settlers now had reign over the whole state.

Another major factor contributing to Colorado's development was the arrival of the railroads. In 1870, the Denver Pacific spur was completed, connecting Denver to the Union Pacific's transcontinental line at Cheyenne, Wyoming. Soon after, other railroads snaked through the state, including the Denver & Rio Grande Railroad. Well-engineered narrow-gauge railroads chugged along to out-of-the-way mountain mining towns, providing an inexpensive means of shipping ore to the smelters and supplies to the towns.

In addition to the mining industry, cattle ranching on the eastern plains helped fuel the state's economy for a couple of decades before homesteaders began farming much of the land. Ambitious irrigation projects turned the arid land along the lower Arkansas River Valley and the South Platte Valley near Greeley into lush farmland by the late 1880s. This diversification of Colorado's economy came not a moment too soon, as troubling times for the mining industry were just around the corner.

In 1893 the US government abandoned the silver standard, causing silver prices to plummet. Colorado's economy was hit heavily—mines shut down and in a span of a few days, 10 banks closed in Denver. Despite a large gold strike at Cripple Creek that produced through the 1890s and into the 1900s, Colorado's glory days of mining were over. With the new century came an increased emphasis on agriculture and a new industry—tourism.

During the Great Depression of the 1930s, projects by the Civilian Conservation Corps (CCC) and the Work Projects Administration (WPA) helped develop Colorado's national forest land and highway system, making it easier for visitors to enjoy the beauty of the state. Irrigation projects, including the enormous Big Thompson diversion in north central Colorado, brought water from the state's Western Slope through tunnels in the mountains to the more heavily populated Eastern Slope.

With World War II came an interest in Colorado by the Air Force. High altitude and good weather made Colorado an ideal training area for pilots. Numerous military facilities were built that continue to be important in Colorado—most notable is the Air Force Academy in Colorado Springs. The extremely cyclical oil and gas industry has put a damper on the state's economy in recent years. Steady growth in transportation, light manufacturing, ranching, agriculture and the high-tech industry, however, keep residents optimistic about the future. But none of these is as exciting as the ever-growing sport of downhill skiing and other components of the tourism boom.

TOP TEN HISTORIC SITES IN COLORADO*

1. **Bent's Old Fort National Historic Site, on Hwy. 194, 8 miles east of La Junta and 15 miles west of Las Animas—**
    This reconstructed 1833 fur-trading post and Santa Fe Trail way station first served as headquarters for trappers and Indians and later as a military rendezvous for American troops during the Mexican war.
2. **Central City–Black Hawk National Historic District—**
    At the site of John H. Gregory's 1859 gold discovery, the historic buildings include the Opera House and the Teller House. Also of interest are the colorful Victorian homes perched on the steep hillsides—note the "Lace House" in Black Hawk.
3. **Colorado History Museum, 1300 Broadway, Denver—**
    The museum of the Colorado Historical Society features exhibits on Colorado archaeology and history, including a timeline and a detailed model of 1860 Denver.
4. **Cripple Creek–Victor National Historic District—**
    This once-booming mining area is dotted with abandoned mines and mills. The Cripple Creek and Victor Narrow-Gauge Railroad takes visitors into the center of the district. The Imperial Hotel in Cripple Creek provides melodrama in a historic atmosphere.
5. **Durango–Silverton Narrow-Gauge Railroad—**
    Victorian passenger cars pulled by steam locomotives travel along the Animas River from Durango to the mining town of Silverton.
6. **Georgetown Loop Historic Mining and Railroad Park, in the Georgetown–Silver Plume National Historic District—**
    The narrow-gauge train travels the reconstructed Georgetown Loop between Georgetown and Silver Plume. Along the way is the Lebanon Mine and Mill Complex.
7. **Leadville National Historic District—**
    The silver-mining town of Leadville is situated over 10,000 feet high in the Colorado Rockies. The H.A.W. Tabor Home, the Tabor Opera House, the Healy House and Dexter Cabin are among its notable buildings.
8. **Molly Brown House Museum, 1340 Pennsylvania, Denver—**
    Located in downtown Denver is the restored Victorian home of the "Unsinkable Molly Brown," who survived the *Titanic* disaster. Her

---

* This list was compiled by Maxine Benson, former state historian for Colorado.

story has been portrayed in stage and screen musicals.

9. **Silverton National Historic District—**
   Silverton lies in the heart of the rich San Juan mining district. The 1882 Grand Imperial Hotel evokes images of boom-town days.

10. **Telluride National Historic District—**
    Another former San Juan mining town, Telluride is now a noted ski resort. The New Sheridan Hotel is an elegant town landmark.

Suggested Reading—

A Colorado History (Pruett, 1988), edited by Carl Ubbelohde, Maxine Benson and Duane Smith, is the best complete history we've been able to find. While driving through the state, carry along James McTighe's well-organized and lively *Roadside History of Colorado* (Johnson, 1984).

GEOGRAPHY AND GEOLOGY

Some residents say if Colorado were to be ironed out flat, its area would be larger than Texas. This may be an exaggeration, but it does draw attention to Colorado's most distinctive feature—the Rocky Mountains. The Rockies slice north/south through the state with more than 54 peaks rising higher than 14,000 feet, including the highest "14er," Mt. Elbert at 14,433 feet. Covering the eastern third of Colorado, the Great Plains extend east to Kansas and Nebraska and north into Wyoming. On the western side of the Rockies, the Colorado Plateau is characterized by beautiful canyons and valleys.

Along the spine of the Rockies lies the Continental Divide, which acts as a watershed for North America. All waters on the Western Slope drain into the Pacific, while Eastern Slope waters eventually drain into the Atlantic. Colorado encompasses the headwaters for more than 10 major rivers, including western giants such as the Colorado, Rio Grande, Arkansas and Platte. The state has been called the "Father of Rivers," an apt nickname.

Looking at the rugged peaks, deep, beautiful canyons and wind-swept plains of Colorado, one doesn't have to be a scientist to guess that the state has had a long, active geologic past. This history began 300 million years ago with the uplift of the Ancestral Rockies. These mountains consisted of two ranges similar to the present-day Rockies, located 100 miles west of today's Front Range. After 20 million years, the uplift ceased and erosion began. A million years of exposure to water, wind and ice eroded away the Ancestral Rockies to small hills similar to the Appalachian Mountains of the eastern US. Remnants of these ancient mountains can be seen in the red formations throughout the mountains of Colorado (Red Rocks, Garden of the Gods and the area around Vail are good examples).

During this period of erosion, a shallow inland sea covered most of North America, including Colorado. The water level of this sea varied greatly, causing the formation of huge coastal plains, which, due to a very dry climate, sometimes resembled a desert with windblown sand and dunes. This was especially true in western Colorado.

Later the climate became more humid. Rivers meandered over the coastal plains and the "desert" was transformed into a lush, green, sometimes swampy environment. This period, between 200 and 65 million years ago, was the age of the dinosaurs. Fossils of more than 70 dinosaur species have been found in the Morrison Formation of Colorado, including the bones of the largest Brontosaurus ever excavated. Near the end of this period, the inland sea once again engulfed most of Colorado, depositing thick layers of shale over most of the state.

The present-day Rockies began to form 65 million years ago and continued for 20 million years during an event called the Laramide Orogeny. Forces within the earth pushed up the Precambrian "basement" rock by 15,000 to 25,000 feet. The previously deposited layers on top of the much older Precambrian rock folded, buckled and cracked. Today these soft layers have been eroded away to expose the harder, more resistant Precambrian rock. Evidence of this monumental event can be seen throughout Colorado, where layers that had once lain flat have been violently forced up to almost vertical positions.

Forty million years ago in southwestern Colorado, volcanoes erupted over and over again, expelling immense amounts of gas, lava and ash. This period continued for 30 million years. Before some of the magma could reach the surface, it solidified into dikes, sills and laccoliths. Today, erosion has exposed these features. Sleeping Ute Mountain near Cortez is a good example of a huge laccolith; the dikes radiating from the Spanish Peaks near La Veta are hard to miss. This highly volcanic area includes the San Juan Mountains, the West Elk Mountains and the Flat Tops Plateau. Beginning 28 million years ago (and lasting 23 million years), Colorado land was uplifted by 5,000 feet, yet the overall makeup of the region really didn't change.

From 75,000 to 10,000 years ago, glaciers helped carve and shape the mountains of Colorado. Many glaciers in the higher mountains created cirque valleys, characterized by the U-shaped walls and floor instead of the normal V shape of a stream-formed valley. This U shape forms because the glacier scours out the bottom of the valley.

Suggested Reading—

One of the best sources for geological information is *Roadside Geology of Colorado* (Mountain Press, 1980) by Halka Chronic.

FLORA AND FAUNA

Colorado's varied terrain (grassland, mountains, arid plateaus) provides habitat for diverse plant and animal life. Throughout the book we have tried to include relevant information about the predominant flora and fauna in different parts of the state, but you may want more. The state of Colorado maintains more than 220 wildlife areas, which serve as excellent observation locations, especially for birdwatchers. The **Colorado Division of Wildlife** at **6060 Broadway, Denver, CO 80216, (303) 297-1192,** has a *very* friendly staff; they will be happy to answer your questions about Colorado wildlife or to send you brochures and pamphlets.

Suggested Reading—

An excellent source for information on the flora and fauna of Colorado is *From Grassland to Glacier: The Natural History of Colorado* (Johnson, 1984) by Cornelia Fleischer Mutel and John C. Emerick. This highly readable book describes various ecosystems of Colorado in easy-to-understand terms.

CLIMATE

It depends on what you're looking for, but certainly there is weather to suit anyone's tastes in Colorado. Skiing rules the high country from November through April; Colorado is a playground for hikers, campers, anglers and sightseers the rest of the year. The Rocky Mountains cut through the middle of the state, creating their own uncertain weather patterns and making forecasting a nightmare. Colorado's mountains can attract snow flurries almost any time of year, but it isn't until November that large quantities of fluffy, powder snow stick around for winter. Snowcover remains at the highest locations until early summer. Driving in the mountains during or after a snowfall can be treacherous; for road conditions call **(303) 639-1111.**

One thing you can count on all year is cool nights as the thin mountain air loses its heat. The dry climate takes some of the swelter out of summer and some of the bite out of winter. Denver, at the eastern foot of the Rockies, is almost a desert, with only 15 inches of precipitation annually. The city enjoys more than 300 days of sunshine each year, but afternoon rainshowers are commonplace in summer.

The spectrum of weather will affect your decisions on what to wear and when to drive. In Colorado, you can experience all four seasons in one day, so dressing for unpredictable weather is something of an art— a good rule is to be prepared for anything by wearing layers. In summer be prepared for cool mornings and evenings, hot midday temperatures and afternoon rainstorms. Winter requires a warm jacket, hat and gloves.

When you're exploring the high country, summer or winter, be sure to take along sunscreen.

VISITOR INFORMATION

GENERAL INFORMATION

Many sources of visitor information are just waiting to be tapped. The **Colorado Tourism Board** is perhaps the best place to begin. Offering a wealth of general information about the state, they can put you in touch with many clubs and organizations for more specifics. Contact them at **1625 Broadway, Suite 1700, Denver, CO 80202; (303) 592-5410.** They also operate four Welcome Centers at major access points into Colorado. These centers, located in Burlington, Cortez, Fruita and Trinidad, are great resources for the whole state (and you can leave swamped with pamphlets).

For information about specific destinations, start with the area's chamber of commerce (see the Services section of each chapter). One of the largest organizations offering a breadth of knowledge on the entire state is the **Denver Metro Convention & Visitors Bureau, 225 W. Colfax Ave., Denver, CO 80202; (303) 892-1112.**

Telephones—

There are two area codes in Colorado that serve as a prefix for long-distance telephone numbers; the northern region is (303) and the southern region is (719). When calling within each region, there is no need to dial the area code—just dial 1 before the number if it's a long-distance call. For long-distance directory assistance, call **(303) 555-1212;** within Denver dial **1-411.** The operator will answer if you dial "0." For emergency assistance, dial **911.**

GETTING THERE

Colorado is virtually at the geographic center of the United States, and Denver is the largest city in the Rocky Mountain region. Therefore, it's natural for the city to be an important transportation hub. Denver's **Stapleton International Airport** is the fifth busiest in the world, with American, Continental, Delta, Mexicana, TWA and United airlines making frequent flights. From Stapleton you can make connecting flights to smaller destinations in Colorado, including Aspen, Colorado Springs, Grand Junction, Durango, Steamboat Springs, Telluride, Gunnison and Crested Butte.

Upon arrival, the vast concourses and sprawling layout of the airport can be intimidating. Thankfully, there are many information booths and services within the complex. To arrange ground transportation (van, bus, taxi, ski-area shuttle) to almost anywhere in the state, be sure to stop in at the **Information and Ticketing** booth on the lower level near the baggage carousels; **(303) 270-1750**. In addition, a long line of car rental companies, including Avis, Budget, Dollar and Hertz, is nearby. Upstairs on the ticketing level of the main terminal, you'll find a smile and a helping hand at **Travelers Aid**—a nonprofit resource center with information on just about anything you might need; **(303) 398-3873**. Another excellent source of statewide information is the booth operated by the **Denver Metro Convention & Visitors Bureau**.

Trains are no longer a way of life in the West, but the **Amtrak** East Coast to West Coast route, passing through Denver and Glenwood Canyon, is one of the prettiest rides imaginable. For information, stop in at downtown Denver's **Union Station; (303) 893-3911**.

From virtually any point in the country, you can take a **Greyhound Trailways** bus into Denver. From there you can take a bus to most towns in the state. **1055 19th St., Denver; (303) 292-6111**.

GETTING AROUND

To really experience the back roads of Colorado away from the major highways, you should have your own vehicle; many rental companies at Stapleton can help you. If you are on a tight budget, consider renting at **Cheap Heap**. These folks will rent you a late-model American car (with snow tires and ski racks if necessary) by the day, week or month. They will pick up and drop you off at the airport for no extra charge. **4839 E. Colfax Ave., Denver; (303) 393-0028**. A sidenote: hitchiking in Colorado is legal, but rides come v-e-r-y infrequently.

Other ways of getting around include catching a connecting flight from Stapleton to mountain resorts. **Greyhound Trailways Bus Lines** makes daily runs to many Front Range and mountain towns. There are frequent buses from the airport to the downtown bus station. **1055 19th St., Denver; (303) 292-6111**. The Ski Train makes runs from Denver to Winter Park Ski Area every Sat.-Sun. in winter. **555 17th St.; (303) 296-ISKI**.

INFORMATION FOR THE HANDICAPPED

Colorado is finally reacting to the long-existing needs of handicapped travelers by offering them more and more accessible public facilities and improved services. Many organizations throughout the state do exemplary jobs providing outdoor recreation for people with special needs. **Winter Park** has the largest handicapped ski program in the country. **Wilderness on Wheels** (see the **South Park and 285 Corri-**

dor chapter) offers a system of wide, wooden boardwalks along a trout-filled creek. The US Forest Service and National Park Service have worked hard to create accessible campgrounds and facilities. For organized group tours, contact **Accessible Tours, Directions Unlimited, 720 N. Bedford Rd., Bedford Hills, NY 10507; 1-800-533-5343.**

Suggested Reading—
   Access Denver is an informative guide from a handicapped perspective. It goes into detail on the facilities of restaurants, stores, museums, churches and lodging. To obtain a copy, contact the Sewell Rehabilitation Center, 1360 Vine St., Denver, CO 80206; (303) 399-1800. A donation of $2.50 is requested. Another useful source of information is the *National Park Guide for the Handicapped* from the US Government Printing Office, Washington, DC, 20402.

TIPS FOR VISITORS

Drinking Laws—To purchase or drink hard liquor, wine or 6 percent beer, you must be 21 years old. But if you look under 25, have a photo identification ready (a passport is fine). Bars are normally open until 2 am, Mon.-Sat; 12 am on Sun. Colorado strictly enforces laws against drunk driving—*do not drive while impaired.*

Driving—To rent a car in Colorado, you will need a national driver's license or an International Driver's Permit. Once you're on the road, remember that wearing a seatbelt is law in Colorado. One hint for driving in the city: After coming to a complete stop, it is permissible to turn right at a red light when traffic is clear.

Money—
Credit Cards—Our society has become almost entirely dependent on credit. Major credit cards (American Express, Mastercard and Visa) are accepted nearly everywhere except the grocery store. You may need one to put a security deposit on a rental car. They are also extremely handy for getting emergency cash from banks and Automatic Teller Machines (ATMs).

Travelers Checks—Visitors from abroad should be sure to get travelers checks in US dollar denominations because most banks don't have the capability to exchange foreign currencies.

Student and Senior Discounts—In Colorado seniors can find discounts at movies, motels and restaurants as well as on buses and airplanes. Students seeking discounts are not quite as well received, but with an

International Student Identification Card (ISIC), you may find some price breaks.

Time—Mountain Standard Time (Colorado) is two hours earlier than Eastern Standard Time (New York) and one hour later than Pacific Standard Time (California).

Tipping—Porters and bellboys expect 50 cents per bag. Taxi drivers, barbers, hairdressers and bartenders expect 15–20 percent. Unless you are part of a large group, service charges are not normally included in restaurant bills. When the service has been pleasant, figure a 15 percent (up to 20 percent) tip based on the price of the meal excluding tax.

———— HOW THE BOOK ————
IS ORGANIZED

"Visitor friendly," *The Colorado Guide* is arranged in six geographic regions: Northwest, North Central, Northeast, Southwest, South Central and Southeast. Each region, with a map pinpointing its location in the state, is divided into "destinations"—40 in all. Background information about each destination sets the scene: general introduction, history and directions. Specific information is then provided on the major attractions, festivals and events, outdoor activities, sightseeing highlights, lodging and camping, restaurants and services. Profiles of some fascinating people or a unique aspect of a specific area of the state add an extra dimension to the guide.

The format of this introduction generally parallels the arrangement of the destination sections. Within each chapter, you will find all you need to plan a terrific trip. The index is an added help.

FESTIVALS AND EVENTS

A full calender of festivals and events takes place throughout Colorado; from these, we have selected some of the most outstanding to include in each chapter. Several are worth planning your vacation around, while others may merit only a detour. **Telluride** is well known for its wide array of artistic events and, of course, the renowned Bluegrass Festival. Any mention of music must include **Aspen**, which is the best place for a summer's worth. Rodeo is another Rocky Mountain favorite—the National Western Stock Show in **Denver** should not be missed. Colorado is known for a number of active, sporting events, including marathons, triathalons and bike races. Events are listed each month in *Rocky Mountain Sports & Fitness Magazine*, available for no charge at sporting goods stores throughout the state; (303) 893-6667. For a complete listing of Colorado's festivals and events, contact the **Colorado Tourism Board, 1625 Broadway, Suite 1700, Denver, CO 80202; (303) 592-5410.**

OUTDOOR ACTIVITIES
BALLOONING

The oldest form of airborne travel (excluding Icarus's wax wings) is the balloon—it's also the safest. Climb into the basket beneath a colorful hot-air balloon and float into rarified air high above the Rockies. The tranquil sensation is impossible to compare. Many of Colorado's mountain towns have companies that offer flights by the hour, but they are not cheap. A catered breakfast often accompanies the voyage and, upon landing, the traditional bottle of champagne is uncorked.

BIKING

Mountain Biking—

This relatively new sport has found a welcome home in Colorado, with its maze of backcountry logging and mining roads. Mountain bikes, equipped with 15 gears, a sturdy alloy frame and wide, knobby tires, are perfectly suited for rough rides. Some adventurous souls prefer "single-track" riding, which essentially involves riding on hiking trails. As long as mountain bikers respect the rights of people on foot, this is fine. Mountain bikes are allowed on national forest land, but remain strictly prohibited in wilderness areas. Since "fat-tire" riding has become so popular, several extensive trail systems have been developed, and rentals are available in many towns. **Crested Butte, Winter Park** and **Steamboat Spings** in particular have become well-known centers for the sport. For an extended ride from alpine to desert terrain, consider the San Juan Hut System between **Telluride** and Moab, Utah.

Touring—

With a good road map you can tour anywhere in the state. Of course, there are some outstanding rides, especially in the Colorado National Monument (see the **Grand Junction** chapter) and along the maintained bike path between Breckenridge and Vail (see the **Summit County** chapter).

Suggested Reading—

For a selection of mountain bike rides across the state, complete with topographical maps, pick up a copy of William Stoehr's *Bicycling the Backcountry* (Pruett, 1987).

FISHING

Colorado, with more than 7,000 miles of streams, nearly 2,500 cold-water lakes and 360 warmwater reservoirs, provides a kaleidoscope of fishing opportunities. Getting away from it all, clearing your brain of every thought except landing a big brown trout, is what Colorado angling is all about—no matter if you are into fishing with a miniscule dry fly or with a No. 6 hook and a worm. We have carefully selected better-than-average public waters to include in each chapter—this is not a guarantee of good fishing, but you can always catch a few by the tale!

We mention the following special designations throughout: **Gold Medal Water**, the highest-quality trout water in Colorado, offering the greatest potential for catching large numbers of fish, including trophy-sized trout, and **Wild Trout Water**, which supports self-sustaining trout populations. A Colorado fishing license is a must for fishing on all public water; resident and nonresident licenses are available at most sporting goods stores. These stores are also a great source of information—as long as you keep in mind that they would love to sell you armloads of tackle. When buying your license, be sure to pick up a copy of *Colorado Fishing and Land and Water Use Information* for specific details on restrictions and regulations throughout the state. For information, contact the **Colorado Division of Wildlife, Central Regional Office, 6060 Broadway, Denver, CO 80216; (303) 297-1192.**

Suggested Reading—
Tim Kelly's Fishing Guide (Hart Publications, 1985) is as complete an almanac of fishing in Colorado as you'll find.

FOUR-WHEEL-DRIVE TRIPS

Jeeping in the Colorado Rockies is *very* big. Logging and mining roads built as far back as the late 1800s provide access to ghost towns and some of the most spectacular scenery in the country. Jeep tour and rental companies are scattered throughout the mountain towns. No matter whether you take to the back roads on a guided trip or are driving your own vehicle, be sure to pack out all your trash. Please don't drive off existing roads, as this promotes erosion. This is especially important above treeline—the alpine tundra, which is very fragile, will quickly die if driven on. A number of standout four-wheel-drive trips are discussed in the chapters of this book, especially around **Ouray, Telluride, Silverton** and **Creede**. Information about jeeping on public land is available from the **US Forest Service, PO Box 25127, 11177 W. 8th Ave., Lakewood, CO 80225; (303) 236-9431** or the **US Bureau of Land Management, 2850 Youngfield, Lakewood, CO 80215; (303) 236-2100.**

Suggested Reading—
One of the best guides to the ghost towns of Colorado is *Jeep Trails to Colorado Ghost Towns* (Caxton, 1963) by Robert L. Brown. For a more in-depth look at the state's ghost towns and mining camps, as seen through the eyes of artist Muriel Sibell Wolle, read her classic, *Stampede to Timberline*, 2nd revised edition (Swallow, 1974).

GOLF
Some of the courses in Colorado rival any in the country for challenge and beautiful scenery. If you plan to play golf in the mountains, practice your putting ahead of time—the difficult break in mountain greens continues to baffle pros and amateurs alike. Also keep in mind that at this high altitude the ball travels *much* farther than at sea level—you may want to club down. Although the mountain courses are only open in summer and early fall, many courses on the Western Slope and along the Front Range (including Denver) are open year-round. Greens fees for 18 holes can vary anywhere from $10 to $50; the mountain resorts tend to charge much more than city courses. Due to the constantly changing fees, we do not list specific prices in this book. But don't worry—we'll warn you if the greens fees are steep.

A number of celebrity and PGA tournaments take place throughout the state. For specific information about tournaments or anything else connected with golfing in Colorado, contact the **Colorado Golf Association, Suite 101, 5655 S. Yosemite, Englewood, CO 80111; (303) 779-GOLF or 1-800-228-4675** in Colorado.

HIKING AND BACKPACKING
For our money, one of the best ways to experience the varied and beautiful country of Colorado is by getting into the backcountry for a hike. The state is set up for it. Public lands include 11 national forests (comprising a fifth of Colorado), more than a dozen wilderness areas, Bureau of Land Management (BLM) land, two national parks, five national monuments, two national grasslands and numerous state parks and recreation areas.

The national forest land is administered by offices scattered throughout the state. Destinations bordering on national forest land will have the local address for the ranger office. These folks provide a wealth of information for hiking and other outdoor pursuits. They also offer printed material, including the useful *Recreational Opportunity Guide* (*ROG*) and forest service maps. For general information about the different national forests in Colorado, contact the **US Forest Service, PO Box 25127, 11177 W. 8th Ave., Lakewood, CO 80225; (303) 236-9431**.

Wilderness areas, located within the national forests, are so designated to retain their pristine nature. They differ primarily from the rest of the national forest land in that no motorized vehicles or mountain bikes are allowed. Aside from that, a few extra rules apply as well as some very important *wilderness ethics*. Maintaining the unspoiled beauty of these areas is a monumental task; everyone needs to help. Here are a few suggested wilderness practices that you should apply to any outdoor trip, whether it's in a wilderness area or at a roadside picnic table.

1. While hiking, stay on existing trails. Straying off the trails kills vegetation and promotes erosion, especially on the alpine tundra.
2. Camp at least 100 feet from trails, streams and lakes. Choose a site in the woods rather than in an open meadow, for your own privacy as well as that of other hikers.
3. Use existing campsites to protect unused areas.
4. Use gas stoves, especially at high altitudes where firewood is scarce and slow to replenish itself. If you absolutely need a fire, use an existing fire-ring.
5. Wash at least 100 feet from water sources; use biodegradable soap.
6. Carry a small shovel or trowel to bury human waste 6-8 inches below the ground.
7. Pack out all other trash—don't bury it!
8. Please leave pets at home—they disturb the wildlife.
9. Take only pictures and leave only footprints . . . leave your camp in better shape than you found it.

Colorado's ever-changing weather conditions can be a real problem for unprepared hikers. Warm clothing and waterproof raingear are two essentials you should always have with you in the high country. Speaking of the high country, altitude sickness (pulmonary edema) can be a problem for people accustomed to lower elevations. Take time to adjust to the high altitude—don't go out and climb a 14,000-foot peak the day after arriving from sea level. Afternoon thunderstorms frequent the mountains in summer; lightning strikes above treeline are common. Another precaution involves the hundreds of old abandoned mines scattered throughout the state. It's very likely that you'll come across one or two of them. If you do, *stay out!* They are very dangerous and can contain toxic gases, hidden shafts and rotten timbers, among other hazards.

One of the most exciting things to happen in Colorado in recent years was the opening of the **Colorado Trail** in the summer of 1988. The 469-mile trail stretching from Denver to Durango was 15 years in the making. It crosses national forest and private land, winding through low-lying valleys and over high passes along the Continental Divide. Sections of the trail are mentioned in appropriate chapters throughout the book. Quite impressive, the trail is the product of a lot of hard work by volunteers, supplemented by funds from the Colorado Lottery. If you want more information about this trail or are considering hiking the entire distance, contact the US Forest Service. Pick up a copy of the excellent *A Colorado High: The Official Guide to the Colorado Trail* (FreeSolo, 1988) by Randy Jacobs—an official guide (240 pages) complete with maps.

For topographical map quadrangles of Colorado, stop in at sporting goods stores around the state or visit the **US Geological Survey** in downtown Denver, located at **1961 Stout St., Denver, CO 80294; (303) 844-4196.**

Suggested Reading—
The Hiker's Guide to Colorado (Falcon, 1984) by Caryn and Peter Boddie offers details on many hikes around the state. *A Climbing Guide to Colorado's Fourteeners* (Pruett, 1989) by Walter R. Borneman and Lyndon J. Lampert provides interesting information about Colorado's highest peaks. A large number of quality hiking books deal with specific regions of the state.

HORSEBACK RIDING
Colorado is horse country, and you'll feel comfortable wearing cowboy boots and a hat in most towns. We have listed stables in each chapter where applicable—most offer trail rides, breakfast rides and overnight pack trips. If you want a chance to ride every day for a week, consider a dude ranch vacation (see page 22). For more information about horseback riding, you may want to get in touch with the **Colorado Outfitters Association, Inc., PO Box 31438, Aurora, CO 80041; (303) 751-9274.**

LLAMA TREKKING
In South America llamas have been domesticated beasts of burden for more than 1,000 years; now they've become the rage in Colorado. You can't hop on the back of a llama and ride off into the sunset, but these lovable cousins of the camel can carry up to 100 pounds of gear on their backs. Just drape a tether over your shoulder and start hiking up a trail— your llama will follow wherever you go. It's an exotic way to spend an afternoon or, better yet, a few days of vacation. Many llama packers in the state offer first-class excursions to base camps far into the wilderness; in the evening you'll be treated to a catered dinner of lobster brochette, halibut steaks or teriyaki chicken accompanied by a bottle of fine wine. We have listed many llama packers in destinations around the state. If you need additional information, contact the **Colorado Llama Outfitters and Guides Association, PO Box 1394, Carbondale, CO 81623.**

RIVER FLOATING

There you are, paddling through a stretch of calm water within a beautiful rock-walled canyon. Suddenly you hear the roar of the approaching rapids. Charging furiously down through the white water and maneuvering over a small waterfall, you finally reach calm water once again and have time to catch your breath. If you have the chance, a raft trip down one of Colorado's rivers promises to be an unforgettable part of your vacation, if not the highlight.

From the high Rocky Mountains of Colorado, more major rivers begin their long journeys to the ocean than in any other state in the country. When the snow begins to melt each spring and the water levels in the rivers swell, almost 400,000 rafters and kayakers take to the frigid waters for calm floats and hair-raising runs down some of the most challenging rivers in the world. Desert canyon sections of the **Dolores** and action-filled floats down the **Upper Arkansas** and **Green** rivers are definite highlights. Descriptions of rivers and a few outfitters are listed in appropriate chapters of this book.

Although some people take their own rafts down the rivers, most trips are run through private outfitting companies. Outfitters vary greatly, offering different types of trips, so it's important to decide ahead of time what kind of river experience you are looking for. Colorado's rivers offer the full gamut, whether it's a leisurely float (Class I—easy) or a demanding (Class IV—very difficult) multiday expedition. A particularly good source of information about planning a river float is the **Western River Guides Association, Suite 114, 7600 E. Arapahoe Rd., Englewood, CO 80112; (303) 771-0389.** They can provide information to help you choose the best river and best outfitter to suit your particular needs. Another source is the **Colorado River Outfitters Association, PO Box 1805, Vail, CO 81658; (303) 369-4632.**

Suggested Reading—

If you are planning to arrange your own rafting or kayak trip or just want further information about rivers in Colorado, we strongly suggest two books: *The Floater's Guide to Colorado* (Falcon, 1983) by Doug Wheat and *The Rivers of Colorado* (Falcon, 1985) by Jeff Rennicke.

SKIING

Cross-Country Skiing—

Gliding across freshly fallen snow, away from crowds and expensive lift tickets, is becoming an attractive alternative for many people. Partly because of this surge in popularity, there has been an increasing number of serious accidents due to avalanches. Before heading into the backcountry, find out about avalanche conditions by calling **(303) 236-9435.**

There are many groomed trail systems throughout the state that usually charge a small trail fee. All the mountain resorts have cross-country rental shops, which also can be gold mines of valuable advice. Check in at the local forest service office for additional information, but remember they are usually closed on weekends in winter. Extended backcountry trips can be taken on the 10th Mountain Trail Association Hut System (see the **Aspen** chapter). For more general information, contact the **Colorado Cross-Country Ski Association, PO Box 169, Winter Park, CO 80482; (303) 887-2152.**

Downhill Skiing—

Very few places in the world can boast the abundance of light powder snow, vertical drop and striking views that Colorado provides. With 27 ski areas to choose from, you should plan your winter getaway with these factors in mind: size and difficulty of the mountain, base village amenities and cost. **Vail** and **Aspen** are world-class resorts in every respect. The four ski areas in **Summit County** are fast approaching that status. If you are in search of a low-key atmosphere in a destination with as much mountain as you'd ever desire, make arrangements at **Steamboat Springs, Winter Park, Crested Butte** or **Telluride.** Smaller family areas such as **Ski Cooper, Sunlight** and **Monarch** offer low-cost vacations.

We have written about all the major ski areas in the state. Turn to the table of contents to find out if there is a full chapter covering the area; otherwise, check the index. With expanded snowmaking capabilities, Colorado's ski season is well underway in November. It peaks during Christmas week and lasts into April (Arapahoe Basin usually stays open until late May). Almost every area has discounted lift tickets early and late in the season. Quite often, reduced-price tickets can be purchased at Front Range grocery stores and gas stations throughout the season. It's usually less expensive to rent downhill equipment in Denver before heading into the mountains.

Sometimes all-inclusive vacation package deals offered through travel agents are quite a bargain. For more information about downhill skiing, contact **Colorado Ski Country USA, One Civic Center Plaza, 1560 Broadway, Suite 1440, Denver, CO, 80202; (303) 837-0793.** Call **(303) 831-SNOW** if you would like a complete snow report; **(303) 639-1111** for mountain road conditions.

SNOWMOBILING

This sport is becoming extremely popular in Colorado. We have not gone into any depth of coverage on snowmobiling because of our emphasis on cross-country skiing (quite often, they are in conflict). Each year, however, an excellent trail guide is put out by the **Colorado Division of Parks and Outdoor Recreation.** To obtain a copy, contact them at **13787 S. Hwy. 85, Littleton, CO 80125; (303) 791-1954.** For more information, contact the **Colorado Association of Snowmobile Clubs, 10950 W. Bear Creek Dr., Denver, CO 80227; (303) 985-9192.**

SEEING AND DOING

DINOSAURS

More than 60 million years ago, dinosaurs roamed all over Colorado, eating plants and each other. Some of the world's most significant dinosaur fossils have been found in Colorado. It's not that the state had more dinosaurs; it's just that the geologic upheaval that formed the Rockies exposed many dinosaur remains. Some of the best places to learn about dinosaurs are in **Grand Junction, Dinosaur National Monument** and the **Denver Museum of Natural History.**

HOT SPRINGS

The Indians would find spiritual well-being in Colorado hot springs. Then came the spas for well-to-do tourists in the late 1800s. Colorado is home to many natural hot springs—some are highly developed, while others present a more natural setting. We have tried to uncover the best places to take a relaxing soak. See Hot Springs in the **Glenwood Springs, Ouray** and **Steamboat Springs** chapters for some great ideas.

MUSEUMS AND GALLERIES

We have included most museums (worth their salt) in the appropriate chapters. With our firsthand descriptions, you should be able to decide if you want to stop by for a visit. As far as galleries are concerned, we have covered only those that are truly outstanding. In places like Aspen or Denver, it would be absurd to list the scores of possibilities for viewing and buying art. Stop in at the chamber of commerce in each destination, as the staff will be happy to help you get in touch with galleries and antique shops in that area.

WHERE TO STAY

ACCOMMODATIONS

We have gone out of our way to select unique accommodations that you'll remember (fondly, we hope) well into the future. No one has paid for inclusion in the book and, while our narrowed-down list of selections may be subjective, we have given honest evaluations. Each write-up should provide you with enough information to decide whether a particular hotel, motel or bed and breakfast is for you. Whenever possible, we have avoided national chains—not because these places are bad, but simply because most people already know what to expect when checking into a Hilton, Holiday Inn, Best Western or Motel 6. To find the toll free reservation numbers for these chains, call 1-800-555-1212. If you would like a complete listing of what is available in an area, give the chamber of commerce a call (listed under Services in each chapter). They will be more than happy to answer your query. The larger resorts offer toll free central reservations numbers (also listed under Services in each chapter).

Because prices are constantly changing, we have used a price guideline throughout the book that shows approximately how much a night's lodging (double occupancy) will cost:

$	less than $25
$$	$25 to $50
$$$	$50 to $100
$$$$	$100 and up

For those of you who have never stayed at a **bed and breakfast**, it's time to step in from the cold. This European idea is catching on in Colorado, and a number of wonderful "escapes" are scattered throughout the state. Since a bed and breakfast is generally on a smaller scale than other lodging establishments, the owner's personal touch is always evident; you can stay in a small, immaculate Victorian, a sprawling mansion, a fantasyland castle or a rustic lodge. In the morning, you'll have the chance to meet and talk with other guests during a complimentary breakfast.

Historic hotels provide another unique getaway. During their boom days, many of the mining towns built grandiose hostelries that eventually fell into disrepair. Quite a few have now been beautifully refurbished—for example, you might stay at the Peck House in **Empire**, the Imperial Hotel in **Cripple Creek** or the Hotel Boulderado in **Boulder**. Perhaps the best-known hotel in Colorado is the Brown Palace Hotel in **Denver**. Not quite as many people know about the impressive Strater Hotel in **Durango**, the Hotel Jerome in **Aspen** or the Hotel Colorado in **Glenwood Springs**. The central reservations number for the **Association of Historic Hotels of the Rocky Mountain West** is **1-800-888-4886** nationwide; **(303) 759-1918** in Denver.

Guest (dude) ranches can be found throughout the state. Normally guests stay for a week and everything (including meals) is provided. If you have ever had a longing for the Wild West (riding horses each day, singing around the campfire . . .), but also like sleeping on a firm mattress, you should consider a ranch vacation. Families seem to take very well to the wide list of activities and somewhat structured environment. Some ranches also specialize in fishing, cross-country skiing and outdoor skills vacations. For specific information on some of Colorado's best, turn to the Home Ranch or Vista Verde in the **Steamboat Springs** chapter, Latigo Ranch in the **North Park** chapter, Skyline Ranch in the **Telluride** chapter or the C-Lazy-U in the **Winter Park** chapter. You may also want to contact the **Colorado Dude and Guest Ranch Association, PO Box 300, Tabernash, CO 80478; (303) 887-3128.**

When on a budget, there is no better place to find shelter than at a **youth hostel.** Hostels are also great places to meet other travelers. Sometimes, restrictive rules are enforced and a quick morning chore is required, but the price is right. Despite the name, people of all ages are welcome. Though the American Youth Hostel (AYH) system is not as developed as its European counterpart, several accommodations are available in Colorado. For a complete listing and membership information, write the **American Youth Hostel Association, Inc., National Campus, Deleplane, VA 22025.**

People over 60 years of age (companions 50 or older) may want to inquire about **Elderhostel** programs, which flourish in Colorado. For a complete brochure, contact **Elderhostel, 80 Boylston St., Boston, MA 02116; (617) 426-8056.**

CAMPING

Camping opportunities in Colorado are diverse and numerous. Variations in terrain, amenities and price are all key considerations. Within the chapters of this book, we have listed most campgrounds in the national forests, monuments and parks, state parks and recreation areas as well as many private campgrounds. Most of the listings are designated sites that can be reached by a regular passenger car or RV.

Remember that whether you're camping in the wilderness or just off the highway, minimum impact camping ethics should always be practiced. *Leave your campsite in better shape than you found it.* The following is a brief explanation of possible camping experiences in Colorado.

In the National Forests—

Not everyone realizes this simple fact about camping in the national forest: you can camp anywhere you want to unless it's posted otherwise. Most designated campgrounds charge a fee between $5 and $8 per site per night. Amenities usually include picnic tables, fire pits, pit toilets, pump water and trash cans. Campsites that don't charge a fee usually don't supply drinking water. Most campgrounds have a maximum-stay limit of two weeks; sites are given away on a first-come, first-served basis. Some of the most popular areas of the national forests get extremely crowded in summer—advance reservations are taken for some of these campgrounds at the district offices. For more information about camping in the national forests, contact the **US Forest Service, PO Box 25127, 11177 W. 8th Ave., Lakewood, CO 80225; (303) 236-9431.**

In the National Parks, Monuments and Recreation Areas—

Camping in these areas is usually allowed only at designated sites; most charge a fee and offer the same amenities as national forest campgrounds. An entrance fee to these areas is also required. With the exception of two campgrounds in Rocky Mountain National Park that are available with advance reservations, all campground sites are available on a first-come, first-served basis. For additional information about camping in the national parks, monuments and recreation areas, contact the **National Park Service, PO Box 25287, Denver, CO 80225; (303) 969-2000.**

In Colorado State Parks and Recreation Areas—

These areas have some very civilized campgrounds that often include restrooms with hot showers. An entrance fee is usually required as well as a fee for camping. Reservations can be made in advance by calling **MISTIX** at **1-800-365-2267.** For further information about camping in the state parks and recreation areas, contact the **Colorado Division of Parks and Outdoor Recreation, 1313 Sherman St., Suite 618, Denver, CO 80203; (303) 866-3437.**

Bureau of Land Management (BLM) Land—

Camping on land supervised by the BLM is possible in many places throughout Colorado. Here and there are some relatively primitive campgrounds that often include picnic tables and outhouses; only a few charge a fee. Some of these campgrounds have been mentioned in the book. For additional information about camping on BLM land, contact the **US Bureau of Land Management, 2850 Youngfield, Lakewood, CO 80215; (303) 236-2100.**

Private Campgrounds—

When possible, each camping section ends with a listing of at least one private campground. These are the plush places with all the amenities you could ask for, including shower rooms, laundry facilities and **RV hookups.** If you require further information about private campgrounds in Colorado, try contacting the **Colorado Campground Association, 5101 Pennsylvania Ave., Boulder, CO 80303; (303) 499-9343.**

WHERE TO EAT

The restaurants we've listed in each chapter constitute what we consider to be an accurate representation of price ranges and styles available around the state. We narrowed down the list of restaurant choices in each destination by asking locals about their favorite places to eat. We personally visited each of the establishments to see if they were worthy of mention; we accepted no payment for inclusion in the book. If there was a particular specialty in an area, we have given it more play: Mexican food in the San Luis Valley, for instance. You may also notice that we have an aversion to chains—does anyone need to explain what's in store for you under the "golden arches"?

Most people like to know about how much their meal will cost. So we have enacted the following price guideline based on the price of an entrée per person.

$	Under $5
$$	$5 to $10
$$$	$10 to $20
$$$$	$20 and up

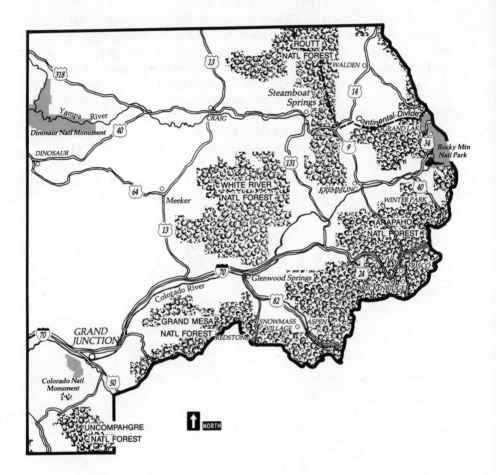

NORTHWEST REGION

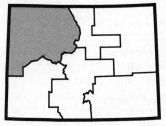

Aspen

Colorado's premier ski resort town, Aspen sits mountain-locked at the head of the beautiful Roaring Fork Valley. Historic mining town, laid-back mountain retreat, cultural mecca, elitist playground for the super rich: Aspen's images vary greatly, quite often in what would seem to be direct conflict. It's a complex town with many levels to be uncovered, offering something of interest for everyone.

Aspen's allure comes in part from its intriguing and tumultuous history. Beginning as a remote mining camp in 1879, the town quickly prospered and grew to be one of the richest silver-producing areas in the world, until the crash of the silver market in 1893. Today, remnants of Aspen's Victorian-era prosperity make up a large part of its personality. Reminders of Aspen's past range from the many beautifully restored homes to restaurants and bars named after famous mines and residents.

The visionaries who developed Aspen as a winter ski resort and summer intellectual/cultural retreat in the late 1940s set the tone for what exists today. Winter activities revolve around the four distinctive ski areas that uphold an international reputation for fine powder skiing and runs suited to everyone's ability. Cross-country skiing is excellent, and the après-ski partying is unmatched. In summer, the town comes alive with the Aspen Music Festival, theater, ballet and other events that attract people from around the world. With many wilderness areas nearby, hiking, backpacking and fishing opportunities are limitless. In autumn, the area is a spectacular draw, as the aspen trees are transformed into a burnished coat of golds and reds. Aspen virtually shuts down in the spring (mud season) and late fall (after the leaves have fallen), though these can be perfect times for a quiet visit.

Over the years Aspen has drawn a very educated and sophisticated group of residents. Add to this a lively mix of values and lifestyles, and the result is explosive. The vast majority of political issues hinge on the long-running conflict between development and slow growth. Aspen politics are a heated and very serious part of life for many locals who have their own vision of what Aspen should or should not be. In the early 1970s, as liberals began to make their presence known, the "hippies" were pitted against the "redneck" establishment. This conflict climaxed when gonzo journalist Hunter S. Thompson ran his nearly successful campaign for sheriff.

Aspen's image as a hangout for jet-setters is valid, though it has been blown out of proportion. Money is very important here. As a destination for celebrities and other well-heeled clientele, the town naturally provides unlimited ways for vacationers to part with large stacks of cash. However, you don't necessarily need to take out a loan to eat at many of the restaurants, because Aspen offers some affordable vacation options for budget travelers. Summertime offers the best deals—hotel rates are lower, many of the festivals are free and you can stay at the campgrounds around the area for practically nothing.

HISTORY

In addition to first-rate scenery and great skiing, Aspen draws a lot of people for another reason: its interesting past. Like its beautiful surroundings, Aspen's economic history has a generous share of peaks and valleys.

For centuries, the Roaring Fork Valley had been a prime hunting ground for the Ute Indians, who tenaciously fought to keep the area off-limits to white settlers. But a treaty in 1868 forced the Utes to move west, out of the valley they loved so dearly. It wasn't until more than 10 years later that significant settlement (prospecting) began in the area.

In June 1879, Walter Clark and three others made their way over Independence Pass from Leadville. For more than a year they had studied geologic maps that had led them to believe the remote Roaring Fork Valley might contain as much silver ore as the rich Leadville area. They weren't disappointed, as silver was found in abundance. Word of the silver strikes quickly spread, and other anxious miners arrived to stake their claims (mainly on Aspen Mountain) before winter set in. As snow fell that first winter, three camps had already been established: Independence, Ashcroft and Aspen, which was originally called Ute City. While the first camp leader, H.B. Gillespie, was away in Washington, DC, petitioning for postal service for Ute City, a newcomer named B. Clark Wheeler arrived. Wheeler proceeded to organize the miners and rename the town Aspen. When Gillespie returned, the dispute was settled peacefully.

By the summer of 1880 the town of Aspen had a population of more than 1,000. The Mollie Gibson, the Chamberlain, the Venus and the famous Smuggler mines began producing (over time) some of the richest silver ore ever found. One big obstacle remained between the miners and fantastic profits: the lack of a nearby smelter for the silver ore. Transporting the ore by pack mules over Independence Pass to the smelters in Leadville, Pueblo and Denver was costly and inconvenient. Aspen needed someone with very deep pockets willing to finance the building of a smelter. In 1883 the answer to the miners' dreams materialized in the form of eastern capitalist Jerome B. Wheeler (no relation to B. Clark Wheeler). This one-time partner in Macy's department store in New York City came to Aspen, bought up some mining claims and built the much-needed smelter. This spurred Aspen's growth, and things started to boom.

The arrival of the Denver & Rio Grande Railroad in 1887 was another milestone. A year later the Colorado Midland Railroad also began service to Aspen. (Unfortunately, Colorado Midland's depot location—on brothel-strewn Fanny Hill St.—left a bit to be desired; "nice" women of the town stayed away, thereby saving themselves from the embarrassment of being confused with the "soiled doves.") The railroads provided the vital link with the outside world, thereby helping Aspen turn into a hopping town of 12,000 inhabitants by 1893, the third largest in the state.

From 1887 to 1893 Aspen was the richest silver-mining area in the US. It boasted six newspapers, two banks, a waterworks, telephone service and the distinction of being one of the first towns in America to run on electricity. During this heyday, Jerome Wheeler built the Wheeler Opera House and the magnificent Aspen showpiece, the Hotel Jerome. The hotel opened on Thanksgiving Eve 1889 with Aspen's biggest social event to date. Guests came from as far away as Europe; for perhaps the first time in their lives, miners spruced up with starched shirts and top hats—and bay rum. This soirée helped bring Aspen into the national spotlight, but the attention was short lived.

In 1893 the demonetization of silver caused silver prices to plummet. Within a week the mines had closed and people were moving out. The Smuggler II Mine on Smuggler Mountain managed to stay open for a while longer, and in 1894 produced the largest silver nugget in the world, weighing in at over a ton. But not even the richest silver mine in the world could afford to stay open. Aspen was on the skids and would not see the end of economic hard times for decades.

By 1930 the population had dwindled to 700. But before long the Aspen area began to draw attention as a potentially great wintertime resort. Ironically, Aspen Mountain was not the first slope to be eyed for development. Alpine ski experts initially decided on nearby Ashcroft as the best location for the resort they envisioned. On December 26, 1936, Billy Tagert, a local, began charging skiers 50 cents for a sleigh ride up the mountain. But the short run down Little Annie Basin was as close as Ashcroft ever came to being a world-class ski area. In the meantime, the

Works Progress Administration (WPA) had constructed a lift on Aspen Mountain in 1936. The lift was actually a boat tow, consisting of a half-inch cable, two mine hoists and a gas motor. The fee was 10 cents per ride, and the tow carried 20 people at a time.

World War II put Aspen's ski area development plans on hold. As America was drawn into the war, the 10th Mountain Division ski troops, stationed at Camp Hale, held maneuvers near Aspen. Many fell in love with the town and its skiing, vowing to come back after the war. When the war was over, a number of these men returned to help transform Aspen into a winter resort.

Raising the money needed to develop Aspen into a major ski resort proved difficult. In 1947 Walter Paepcke, founder of Container Corporation of America, arrived with his checkbook open to save the day. Ironically, Paepcke was initially drawn to Aspen for the purpose of establishing a summer retreat for business leaders to "revitalize body and soul." He thought the retreat would make money, but was eventually convinced by a local businessman, Austrian Friedl Pfeiffer, that the winter resort idea would be even more lucrative. So Paepcke helped locate investors, and soon Aspen was a year-round attraction.

Very quickly Aspen gained worldwide recognition. The 1949 Goethe bicentennial festival lured more than 2,000 people, including many celebrities. The following winter, Aspen Mountain hosted the World Ski Championships and was catapulted into the league of world-class ski resorts. Aspen Highlands Ski Area opened in 1958, soon followed by the opening of Buttermilk, the teaching mountain. The last piece fell into place when the Snowmass area was opened in 1968.

GETTING THERE

Fly Continental Express or United Express from Denver's Stapleton International Airport to the Aspen/Snowmass Airport. Direct service is available from Los Angeles and San Francisco. Taxis are available for the 4-mile jaunt into town (see the Services section).

From Denver's Stapleton Airport it is also possible to rent a car, hire a limo or take a Greyhound Trailways bus. The shortest route from Denver to Aspen (162 miles) can only be taken in summer. Take Interstate 70 west for 79 miles to Copper Mountain, then follow Hwy. 91 south past Leadville to the junction with Hwy. 82. Turn right and drive on the narrow, winding road over Independence Pass to Aspen. (For more information about the pass, see the Scenic Drives section.) In winter closure of Independence Pass makes it a longer trip (200 miles) to Aspen via Interstate 70 to Glenwood Springs and then south on Hwy. 82.

You can also take an Amtrak train into Glenwood Springs (40 miles from Aspen) from Chicago (via Denver) or from San Francisco. Call Amtrak for reservations and information at 1-800-872-7245. From Glenwood take a bus or rent a car for the ride into Aspen.

FESTIVALS AND EVENTS

Wintersköl

mid-January

Since 1952 Aspen and Snowmass locals have staged a dead-of-winter party that is fun for all. Visitors and residents are welcome to get involved in five days of events in a carnival atmosphere. Sample a potent concoction at the bartenders' drink-mixing contest before moving along to the canine fashion show. Colorful hot-air balloons fill the dawn sky at Snowmass for an annual balloon race. Ski races and hot-dog skiing competitions are a highlight of the festivities. After dark there are fireworks and torchlight descents on Snowmass and Aspen mountains. For more information call the Aspen Resort Association, **(303) 925-1940.**

Anderson Ranch Arts Center

all summer

At one time a working ranch, the property has gained quite a reputation in the arts community as a place to come and learn from the best. Each summer, photographers, woodworkers, furniture designers and painters, among others, enroll in one- or two-week courses taught by visiting masters. During the rest of the year, the ranch houses 10 to 15 artists who trade work around the place for studio space. The ranch offers self-guided tours of the galleries and grounds between 9 am and 5 pm daily; during weekdays, visits to the studios are permitted after 3 pm. **PO Box 5598, 5263 Owl Creek Rd., Snowmass Village; (303) 923-3181.**

Aspen Music Festival

late June through August

For the past four decades music has drifted across the summer hills of Aspen. Styles range from jazz to symphonic, chamber to avant-garde. Music comes not only from formal concerts but from intense rehearsals, informal sessions and private practice. The festival helps provide a perfect learning environment for students at the Aspen Music School. An idyllic summer afternoon at the music tent might feature a famous guest artist such as Itzhak Perlman on violin or James Galway on flute. The concerts are reasonably priced and most people prefer to see as well as hear the musicians, but the unique tent-enclosed setting also allows the music to reach nonpaying patrons seated comfortably on the grass outside. For more information call **(303) 925-3254.**

Snowmass Balloon Festival

second weekend in July

Billed as the largest high-altitude balloon festival in the world, the Snowmass Balloon Festival has attracted increasing numbers of spectators since it began in 1975. More than 50 balloonists compete in this series of races and maneuvers. An added attraction for spectators is the champagne breakfast served at the launch site to the accompaniment of classical music. **1-800-421-7145.**

Colorado Mountain Fair in Carbondale

end of July

More than 10,000 people cut loose each summer at this very popular festival in Carbondale, which is 30 miles northwest of Aspen on Hwy. 82. Since 1971, the fair has offered many kinds of food, music and booths with everything from massage to jewelry making. Music and special contests like log splitting keep the valley locals and outsiders flocking here each summer. For more information call the Carbondale Chamber at **(303) 963-1890.**

OUTDOOR ACTIVITIES

BIKING

MOUNTAIN BIKING

Need you ask? When the snow melts off the surrounding mountain trails and jeep roads, locals put away their skis and bring out their mountain bikes. Actually, a few fanatic bikers start riding around town before the snow has even melted. Great trails await riders of all abilities.

Government Trail—

This is a demanding route that traverses the Snowmass Ski Area and leads eventually to Buttermilk Ski Area. Mountain meadows and panoramic views make it worth the effort. Inquire at Blazing Pedals in Snowmass Village for exact trail directions.

Maroon Lake Road—

This paved road climbs 1,000 feet in 9 miles (18 miles round trip). It's an easy ride, and the view of the Maroon Bells from Maroon Lake is outstanding. To reach Maroon Lake Rd., take Hwy. 82 out of Aspen for 1 mile north and turn left at the Aspen Highlands sign.

Owl Creek Road—

This ride offers an alternative to Hwy. 82. From Aspen, head northwest on the bike path along Hwy. 82 to the Owl Creek Rd. turn-off just before the airport. Owl Creek Rd. is a well-maintained dirt road that climbs up and around a ridge for about 3 miles to Brush Creek Rd. When you reach Brush Creek Rd., turn left and ride up into Snowmass.

Pearl Pass—

This is a tough ride. Pearl Pass crosses over into the Crested Butte area to the south. The road was built as a freight route to ship silver from Ashcroft to the nearest railroad down the valley from Crested Butte. To reach the pass, head up Castle Creek Rd. to Ashcroft, 13 miles from Aspen. From Ashcroft, at 9,500 feet, the road follows the river up 3,200 vertical feet and 8 miles to the pass. You need to be in good shape to do this ride. From the pass you can head back to Aspen or proceed down to Crested Butte 12 miles away.

Rentals and Tours—

Hub of Aspen provides rentals and trail information. 315 E. Hyman Ave.; (303) 925-7970.

Blazing Pedals offers downhill bicycle tours, a unique option for those who want to enjoy the scenery and the thrill of mountain biking without the huffing and puffing. Two trips leave daily for group rides down Castle Creek Rd. from Ashcroft and down Maroon Creek Rd. from Maroon Lakes. Take your time and relax. There are two Blazing Pedals locations—one in Aspen and one in Snowmass. Box 5929, Snowmass Village, CO 81615; (303) 923-4544 in Snowmass, (303) 925-5651 in Aspen.

DOG SLEDDING

Authentic Alaskan sled-dog teams in Colorado? That's right. At **Krabloonik's Kennels**. Actually, dog sledding has been a long tradition in the Aspen area. In 1947 Stuart Mace, who handled sled dogs for the 10th Mountain Division during World War II, began offering sled rides from Toklat, his lodge up in the nearby ghost town of Ashcroft. Raising and training the dogs was a strenuous job. When Mace realized he was getting too old to handle the rigorous routine, he offered 50 dogs as a gift to Dan MacEachen. MacEachen accepted them and began an intense 4.5-year apprenticeship, proving to Mace and himself that he had what it took to raise and mush sled dogs.

MacEachen moved the kennel to its present site at the edge of the Maroon Bells–Snowmass Wilderness Area and named it Krabloonik, after the first lead dog he worked with up at Toklat. *Kra-*

bloonik, meaning "bushy eyebrows" in the Eskimo language, is also a term for "white man." As the largest working dog kennel of its kind, Krabloonik's has increased its ranks over the years to the present 300 dogs. The dogs are husky mixes of Malamute, Eskimo and Siberian, three of the original sled-dog breeds.

Running a sled-dog kennel isn't cheap. With each dog costing $3 a day, MacEachen helps make ends meet by offering full- and half-day sled rides up the valley toward Mt. Daly and the towering 14,130-foot Capitol Peak. Pulled by teams of 13 dogs, the sleds are designed similarly to those made by Eskimos from bone and rawhide.

Full-day trips begin at 9 am and last until 4 pm. Services include lunch in a tent up in the wilderness area. Half-day Alaskan adventures leave at 9 am and 1:30 pm daily. The trips last two hours and include a complimentary "peasant" lunch at Krabloonik's restaurant, which specializes in wild game. Caution: the rides are quite pricey, so bring a well-padded wallet. For more information about the restaurant, see the Where to Eat section.

Reservations are highly recommended during the busy winter months (especially around Christmas). Krabloonik's requires a 100-percent advance deposit.

The kennels can be reached by car year-round. Follow Brush Creek Rd. past the Snowmass Ski Area for about a half mile to the parking lot. The walk down to the restaurant and lodge is a pretty raucous experience, with 300 dogs yipping and howling. Skiers can reach the restaurant via Dawdler Trail and after lunch can ski down to the Campground Chairlift. Call **(303) 923-3953** for reservations and information.

FISHING

Fryingpan Lakes—

Follow Forest Rd. 105 until it turns into Forest Rd. 505. From the end of Forest Rd. 505, a 5-mile hike is required to reach the three small lakes at 11,000 feet. The reward is not only the beautiful scenery, but a chance at the multitude of small brook trout. This unstocked natural habitat yields many fish over its sum total of only two acres of water.

Fryingpan River—

This river is legendary for large browns and rainbows from Ruedi Reservoir down to Basalt. Due to its "legend" status and Gold Medal designation, you can expect crowds, especially on weekends. The river never gets muddy, thanks to a controlled water flow from the dam. Use artificial flies or lures only. Catch and release all trout on the **Upper Fryingpan** (beginning at Ruedi Dam and continuing downstream 4 miles). You can keep two fish over 16 inches on the **Lower Fryingpan** (beginning at Basalt and continuing upriver 9 miles). For solitude, try fishing the Fryingpan in winter and early spring. Use nymphs in spring and dry flies in summer. In late Aug. lots of top action results from the green drake mayfly hatch.

Hunter Creek—

This smallish creek flows into the Roaring Fork on the northeast edge of Aspen. Catch small brook, brown and cutthroat trout with small flies in the evening hours. Access can be difficult, but a dirt road (Hunter Creek Rd.) from Aspen loosely follows the creek 6 miles to the boundary of the Hunter–Fryingpan Wilderness Area.

Ivanhoe Lake—

To reach this moderately fished lake, head 5 miles up the rough dirt road (Forest Rd. 105 and 527) that follows Ivanhoe Creek from east of Ruedi Reservoir. Ivanhoe Lake is pushed up against the Continental Divide in a beautiful setting. The lake is stocked with rainbows, and rainbows are what you'll catch.

Roaring Fork River—

After the spring runoff calms down, fishing within the city limits can be good. Be aware of the mix of public and private land on the river. Just to the north of town is a good area to catch both rainbow and brown trout. Downstream from the Woody Creek Bridge to Carbondale there is premium trout fishing water with beautiful scenery.

There is also a Gold Medal water designation from Carbondale, at the merging of the Crystal River, down to the Roaring Fork's confluence with the Colorado. This is a heavily fished stretch with high yields and a two-fish limit; only artificial lures and flies may be used from Apr. through Oct. Catch large browns, rainbows and whitefish.

Willow Lake—

This alpine lake is above treeline at an altitude of 11,705 feet. The fishing is good for brook and cutthroat; most are around 12 inches, some much larger. A longtime Aspen fishing expert saw a dozen bighorn ewes on his last trip to this area. Willow Lake is a 5-mile trek from Maroon Bells Lake, high in the Maroon Bells–Snowmass Wilderness Area.

FOUR-WHEEL-DRIVE TRIPS

See the **Gunnison and Crested Butte** and the **Redstone and Crystal River Valley** chapters.

GOLF

Aspen Golf Course—

Although it's a municipal course, unlike the privately owned Snowmass Club course, the Aspen Golf Course has a higher rating, and the green fees are cheaper! It's a fine 18-hole course that poses a pretty good challenge, even to scratch golfers. The holes are laid out fairly flat, making some of the hazards difficult to see. Watch out for irrigation ditches and lakes on this course, as there are more of them than seems fair. If the golf gods will it, snow in the valley clears enough to open the course by May 1. Restaurant and pro shop. Carts available. **22475 W. Hwy. 82; (303) 925-2145.**

The Snowmass Club Golf Links—

If you want to play golf in Snowmass, take a sizeable roll of cash or a major credit card. The course is situated in the valley down by Brush Creek and offers reduced greens fees for guests of the Snowmass Club. Like the Aspen Golf Course, the Snowmass Club course is fairly treeless. Of the two, the Snowmass course is rated lower. Pro shop, carts and club rentals available. **239 Snowmass Club Cir., Snowmass Village; (303) 923-3148.**

HIKING AND BACKPACKING

The Aspen area is a mecca for hikers and backpackers. White River National Forest surrounds Aspen, tempting lovers of the outdoors with three wilderness areas: Collegiate Peaks, Hunter–Fryingpan, and Maroon Bells–Snowmass. Within the jagged Elk Mountains are no fewer than six 14,000-foot peaks, including the "Deadly Bells," a name given to the Maroon Bells for all of the climbers who have died on their treacherous slopes. Mountaineers, backpackers and daily strollers converge on Aspen's mountains each summer. Although this creates some congested spots, it is possible to get away from the crowds.

Wilderness ethics continues to be a crucial part of preserving the fragile alpine ecosystem of Colorado's mountains. There is no better example of a fragile alpine area than the Maroon Bells–Snowmass Wilderness Area. Minimum-impact camping is essential for overnight trips in this area. The old cliché "Take nothing but pictures and leave nothing but footprints" is very appropriate here. Be sure to pick up a copy of the wilderness area regulations from the ranger station in Aspen.

It's difficult to condense a list of the trail opportunities in the Aspen area; the ideas included here are but a sampling. For more trail ideas, contact the **Aspen Ranger District Office, 806 W. Hallam St., Aspen, CO 81611; (303) 925-3445** or the **Sopris Ranger Office at 620 Main, PO Box 309, Carbondale, CO 81623; (303) 963-2266.**

For maps, equipment and informed advice, visit the **Ute Mountaineer, 308 S. Mill St., Aspen; (303) 925-2849.** If you want a very detailed, knowledgeable hiking book for the Aspen area, pick up a copy of *Aspen Snowmass Trails: A Hiking Trail Guide* (W. Ohlrich, 1988), by Warren Ohlrich, which provides 30 trail ideas.

American Lake—

This day-long, 7-mile round-trip hike is steep but worth the trouble. The lake is beautiful and the fishing for rainbow trout can be surprisingly good. Views of surrounding peaks are also stunning. Plan on about 5 hours hiking time. Camping is not permitted on the east end of the lake. To reach the trailhead, turn left onto Maroon Creek Rd. from Hwy. 82 just west of Aspen. Take another quick left onto Castle Creek Rd. and drive 10 miles to the trailhead, which is on the right side of the road across from the Elk Creek Lodge.

Braille Trail—

Approximately 2 miles farther up Hwy. 82 from the Grottos turn-off (10 miles east of Aspen), the quarter-mile-long Braille Trail offers blind hikers a chance to experience the beautiful surroundings. Guiding themselves by a nylon cord, hikers can decipher the more than 20 signs, which are in both Braille and print. Look for the turn-off on the right side of Hwy. 82.

Conundrum Creek—

See the Hot Springs section for specifics on this 9-mile (18 miles round trip) hike.

Four Pass Loop—

This is a very well-known route passing through the heart of the Maroon Bells–Snowmass Wilderness Area. It's a beautiful and demanding 28-mile loop taking you over four major passes (West Maroon Pass, Frigid Air Pass, Trail Rider Pass and Buckskin Pass), all of which are about 12,500 feet in elevation. Allow four to five days for your journey and don't hurry. Enjoy some of the most memorably scenic valleys in the state. The loop takes you by Maroon Lake, Crater Lake and Snowmass Lake. The trail begins and ends at Maroon Lake (see Maroon Lake Scenic Trail below for directions). Parts of the trail are usually snow covered until July. *Get a topographical map for this hike.*

Grottos—

The Grottos are located about 8 miles up Independence Pass (east on Hwy. 82 from Aspen), just a short walk along the Roaring Fork River from the parking area. It's a popular picnic and suntanning spot in the summer, drawing a large number of people on sunny days. Grottos gets its name from its interesting rock formations, including the granite "ice caves" that were carved out when the river flowed through here. The area is close to town and very scenic. Look for the dirt road on the right side of Hwy. 82 about a half mile past milemarker 50. There is a footbridge over the river at the parking area.

Maroon Lake Scenic Trail—

Bring your camera on this easy 1.5-mile hike at the most photographed spot in the state—Maroon Lake. Follow the trail up along the creek that flows into Maroon Lake. Or just enjoy the beautiful lake with its stunning backdrop—the Maroon Bells (North and South Maroon peaks). In summer, the multicolored wildflowers above the lake are stunning; during autumn the golden aspen make for quite a sight, especially if there is a light snowcover on the Bells.

To reach the trail, head west from Aspen on Hwy. 82 for a half mile and turn left on Maroon Creek Rd. Nine and a half miles past the turn you will arrive at the Maroon Lake parking lot. In summer you will need to take the free shuttle bus that departs from near the Aspen Highlands Ski Area (just a mile or so up Maroon Creek Rd.).

Midway Pass to Hunter Creek—

Located in the Hunter–Fryingpan Wilderness, this long hike (allow three days) is less known than the trails in the

Maroon Bells–Snowmass Wilderness Area. Both elk and deer make their homes here in summer. Start at about 10,000 feet and enjoy views to Independence Pass as you work your way northwest into the Hunter Creek drainage, which leads back to Aspen. The trail begins 14 miles east of Aspen on Hwy. 82, on the left side of the road across from Lost Creek Campground. There is a fork about half a mile up the trail. Take the left fork up Midway Creek Trail. After crossing Midway Pass, the trail drops and snakes through marshy areas until it intersects Hunter Creek Trail. Take a left onto Hunter Creek Trail and proceed down to the outskirts of Aspen for the completion of this 20-mile route. *Snow remains on the upper part of this trail until July. Get a good map for this hike.*

HORSEBACK RIDING

With so much national forest land around the Aspen area, horseback riding possibilities are extensive. Fully equipped guest ranches and stables can provide what you are looking for. Here's one outfit that offers it all.

T-Lazy-7 Ranch—
The T-Lazy-7 has been around for years. Located up Maroon Creek Rd., horses can be rented by the hour. Or perhaps you'll want to go on an overnight pack trip. Guides are not required for hourly rentals. For information about the ranch, see the Sleigh Rides section. **3129 Maroon Creek Rd.; (303) 925-7040 or (303) 925-4625.**

ICE SKATING

The **Ice Garden,** a public indoor ice rink, has skating throughout the week. Special events may preclude public use of the ice. Call to be sure of open ice. Skate rentals are available for a nominal fee. **233 W. Hyman Ave.; (303) 920-5141.**

LLAMA TREKKING

From July through Sept., **Ashcroft and the Pine Creek Cookhouse** offers daily llama treks up into White River National Forest. Treks begin at the cookhouse at 10:30 am and return at 3 pm. The cost is $35 per person and includes a gourmet lunch. The treks are a bit pricey, but if unique is what you seek—do it. Overnight trips are available on request. Be sure to call for reservations and information. Located 12 miles up Castle Creek Rd. from Hwy. 82. **PO Box 1572, Aspen, CO 81612; (303) 925-1044.**

RIVER FLOATING

Crystal River—
See the **Redstone and Crystal River Valley** chapter.

Roaring Fork River—
The upper Roaring Fork River is one of the most popular kayak rivers in Colorado, and parts of it can be treacherous. This well-named river angrily surges out of the Sawatch Range east of Aspen. Just before reaching town, the river mellows, providing good beginner stretches all the way through Aspen. Above the Maroon Creek convergence (just west of Aspen), expert kayakers put in at Slaughterhouse Bridge for a 5-mile stretch down to Woody Creek Bridge that includes a portage around a severe set of waterfalls that have killed a number of people.

From Woody Creek Bridge down to Basalt (12 miles), the water is not so dangerous, but novices are warned to keep out. Class II and Class III rapids are especially challenging at high water. Kayakers (no rafters) should take warning of the Toothache section near Snowmass Bridge. The 12-mile section below Basalt to Carbondale is much easier. For information about floating the lower section of the Roaring Fork from Carbondale to Glenwood Springs, see the River Floating section of the **Glenwood Springs** chapter.

Outfitters—
Blazing Paddles—407 E. Hyman Ave., Aspen; (303) 925-5651. They offer trips on the Roaring Fork, Colorado, Gunnison and Arkansas rivers.

SKIING
CROSS-COUNTRY SKIING

Aspen serves as a mecca not only for downhill skiers but for cross-country skiers as well. This town always has its fingers firmly on the pulse of the winter recreation consumer. As cross-country skiing has increased in popularity in the US, Aspen has been quick to provide creative opportunities for cross-country skiers of all abilities. Everything from groomed trail systems to demanding backcountry trails are to be had here. Roughing it overnight in a unique backcountry hut is a peaceful alternative to the town's highly charged atmosphere. For those of you headed off on your own to do some backcountry skiing, remember to call **Avalanche Information** at **(303) 920-1664.** For more backcountry ski ideas and information, contact the **Aspen Ranger District Office, 806 W. Hallam St., Aspen, CO 81611; (303) 925-3445,** or **Ute Mountaineer, 308 S. Mill St., Aspen, CO 81612; (303) 925-2849.**

Backcountry Trails—

Braun Hut System—This series of six high-mountain huts, stretching as far south as Pearl Pass, is accessible via Ashcroft (12 miles up Castle Creek Rd. from Aspen). The trail continues over a summer jeep road leading to Crested Butte. Isolation, difficult trail conditions and avalanche danger make it necessary for skiers to have advanced skills. Guides are available through **Elk Mountain Guides, PO Box 10327, Aspen, CO 81612; (303) 923-6131.**

These huts are a bit more spartan than the Tenth Mountain huts (see entry below). Fred Braun, an Austrian ski trooper in the early 1920s, has lived in Aspen since 1951. Braun remembers that when he arrived in the US in 1928, he could find skis only in Minnesota and he had to send to Norway for boots! He began working on the huts in the mid-1960s and has been renting them out since the early 1970s. The huts are built to accommodate from six to 18 people and are open year-round. They are not part of a connecting hut-to-hut system and can be reached only from separate trails. A 20-percent deposit is required when making a reservation; the balance is due before departure. For more information and reservations, call or write **Braun Hut System, PO Box 7937, Aspen, CO 81602; (303) 925-7345.**

Tenth Mountain Trail Association Hut System—For more adventurous and experienced skiers, there is an impressive series of European-style backcountry ski huts. The Tenth Mountain Trail Association (TMTA) operates the hut system ($$ to $$$). Beginning just northeast of Aspen, this hut system was started in 1980 by Fritz Benedict (a 10th Mountain Division veteran) and a group of volunteers. There are now more than 100 miles of trails with six overnight huts and four private lodges stretching north by northeast through the spectacular Hunter–Fryingpan and Holy Cross wilderness areas. More trails and huts are planned in the near future.

The huts offer many conveniences and supplies, such as mattresses, stoves and other kitchen necessities. Two of the private lodges along the trail (Diamond J Ranch and the Polar Star Inn) provide more creature comforts, such as running water and saunas. The **Diamond J Ranch** is a full-blown ski touring resort that can be reached via Forest Rd. 105 from Basalt.

The Tenth Mountain hut system is very popular and attracts people from all over the world who want to experience the beauty of Colorado's high country in winter. These trails are not for beginner skiers! Intermediate to advanced skills are needed as well as heavy-duty backcountry equipment. Guides are available for hire around the area. The huts are open Nov. through Apr. Full payment is required at the time reservations are made. For more information and reservations, contact the TMTA at **1280 Ute Ave., Aspen, CO 81611; (303) 925-5775.** Contact the **Diamond J Ranch** directly for information and reservations. **26604 Fryingpan Rd., Meredith, CO 81642; (303) 927-3222.**

The Toklat Chalet—This Swiss-style chalet is perched above Ashcroft in the Castle

Creek Valley and accommodates backcountry skiers. At 11,000 feet, it was a destination for Stuart Mace's sled dogs from the 1950s into the 1970s. (For more information see the Dog Sledding section.) These days it is a year-round high-country hostel offering a bedroll, dinner and breakfast to those staying the night. The Toklat Chalet can sleep eight people. Skiers who are in the area for the day can use the hut and stay for lunch.

For information and reservations ($$$$), contact full-time resident Julie Mace at the **Toklat Chalet, c/o Toklat, PO Box 1048, Aspen, CO 81612; (303) 925-7345.** Knowledgeable guides are available through **Elk Mountain Guides, PO Box 10327, Aspen, CO 81612; (303) 923-6131.**

Groomed Trails—
Ashcroft Ski Touring Center—For a relatively remote groomed trail system, try this one, which starts in Ashcroft 12 miles up Castle Creek Rd. south of Aspen. The center offers warming huts and 30 kilometers of groomed trails. How about a gourmet lunch or dinner at the Pine Creek Cookhouse? For details, see the Where to Eat section. For more information about the Ashcroft Ski Touring Center, call **(303) 925-1971.**

Aspen/Snowmass Nordic Trail System—This fine nordic system offers a 48-mile (80K) network of groomed cross-country trails within a 15-mile area in the valley. Coordinated by the nonprofit Aspen/Snowmass Nordic Council to facilitate ski connections between the two towns, the trail system is easily accessible from many points in and around town. Use of the trails is free. Pick up a map of the trail system at the Aspen Visitors Center in the Wheeler Opera House (see the Services section) or at a sports store. For more information, contact the **Aspen/Snowmass Nordic Council, PO Box 10815, Aspen, CO 81612; (303) 925-2145.**

Telemarking Lessons—
At Buttermilk Ski Area, telemark les-

sons are offered each Tues. and Thurs. during ski season. Classes last from 9 am–noon. For information, call **(303) 925-1220, ext. 281.**

Ski Rentals—
Aspen Cross-Country Center in Aspen has what you need. Half-day to multiple-day rentals are available. Located along the Aspen/Snowmass Nordic Trail System. **22475 W. Hwy. 82, Aspen, CO 81611; (303) 925-2145.** Another choice for equipment, including heavy-duty backcountry gear, is the **Ute Mountaineer, 308 S. Mill St., Aspen, CO 81612; (303) 925-2849.** In Snowmass try the **Snowmass Club Touring Center, 0239 Snowmass Club Cir., Snowmass Village, CO 81615; (303) 923-3148.**

DOWNHILL SKIING
Life in Aspen still revolves around downhill skiing, despite the wealth of peripheral activities. Since 1936, when trees were cut to make room for Roch Run on Aspen Mountain, the ski industry has flourished. Today there are four ski mountains and more than 3,000 skiable acres to choose from. Each mountain has a personality of its own. The key to having an enjoyable ski day is to correctly match the mountain with your ability and mood. Three of the four—Aspen Mountain, Buttermilk and Snowmass—are jointly owned and operated by the Aspen Skiing Co., a division of 20th Century Fox. Aspen Highlands is separately owned. Skis can be rented at dozens of places in Aspen and at each ski area. Following is a brief description of each area.

Aspen Highlands—
Aspen Highlands is an all-around ski area with what many consider the ideal division of terrain: half is intermediate, the rest is split between advanced and beginner. Since the mountain is privately owned and operated, there is more flexibility in money-saving lift ticket options, including multi-day tickets for all four mountains. Highlands is one of the few places in the

country to learn how to ski by the Graduated Length Method (GLM), which was pioneered here in the 1960s. The 3,800-foot vertical drop at the main area is surpassed at Highlands Bowl—a walk-in, guided, experts-only powder mecca that boasts the longest vertical drop in North America: 4,300 feet. **PO Box T, 1600 Maroon Creek Rd., Aspen, CO 81611; (303) 925-5300.**

Aspen Mountain—

This mountain was designed for the enjoyment of expert and strong intermediate skiers. Since there are no "green" runs, there are also no worries about novice skiers making tentative tracks across your fall line. The Silver Queen gondola whisks skiers from the base to the 11,300-foot summit of Aspen Mountain in a mere 13 minutes. Locals call the mountain Ajax, after a now-defunct silver mine. By whatever name, it is steep, challenging and fun. For more information, call **(303) 925-1220.**

Buttermilk—

Two miles west of Aspen, Buttermilk is widely known as a great teaching mountain, thanks to endless miles of novice and easy intermediate terrain. Families (especially the kids) will enjoy cruising smooth trails; advanced skiers can head for the more difficult Tiehack Parkway and Tiehack Trail runs on powder days. Telemark lessons are available to cross-country skiers. For information, call **(303) 925-1220.**

Snowmass—

A staggering variety of slopes for every ability is just 12 miles from Aspen in a perfect family environment. There is no need to ski the same run twice with four contiguous peaks and more than 1,500 skiable acres. Intermediate runs comprise 62 percent of the total. The most notable of these is the Big Burn—a mile-wide swath of white space, broken only by occasional stands of evergreen trees. Supposedly, the Big Burn is the result of an 1870s fire set by the Ute Indians to spite white settlers. Slope names provide more than a hint of what's

to come: take your pick from, say, the steep challenge of Hanging Valley Wall or the gentle incline of Fanny Hill. You can enjoy fine dining on this mountain. Or, for a truly interesting lunch, make a reservation and ski into Krabloonik's restaurant by way of Dawdler Trail (see the Where to Eat section). For information about Snowmass contact **PO Box 5566, Snowmass Village, CO 81615; (303) 923-2000.**

New snow means hit the slopes early to ski the new powder (courtesy of Breckenridge Ski Area).

SLEIGH RIDES

The Pine Creek Cookhouse—

This restaurant offers a mellow, intimate sleigh-ride dinner, ending at the Pine Creek Cookhouse near Ashcroft. See the Where to Eat section for details.

T-Lazy-7 Ranch—

The T-Lazy-7 offers sleigh rides up the Maroon Creek Valley in winter. Day or evening—you choose. If you really want to do it right, reserve a Wed. or Thurs. evening for a sleigh ride to a cabin in the woods that features a steak dinner and live music. A honky-tonk piano player entertains during the meal; afterwards, a country-western band gets everyone dancing. This sleigh ride/dinner dance is extremely popular, so get reservations far in advance. **Box 858, Aspen, CO 81612; (303) 925-4614.**

SNOWSHOE WALKS

The Aspen Center for Environmental Studies (ACES) organizes two-hour walks in the Hallam Lake Wildlife Sanctuary (see the Wildlife section). Learn about the winter ecology from a naturalist-guide. Mon.–Fri.; self-guided tour. Call **(303) 925-5756** for details.

SWIMMING

Iselin Park Complex—
An outdoor swimming pool. Fee charged. **450 Maroon Creek Rd.; (303) 925-8214.**

TENNIS

Aspen Meadows Tennis Courts—
Six courts and a pro shop are open to the public for a fee. **25 Meadows Rd.; (303) 925-7218.**

Iselin Park Complex—
Four outdoor tennis courts. Fee charged. **450 Maroon Creek Rd.; (303) 925-8214.**

WINDSURFING

Aspenites and other folks in the Roaring Fork Valley who windsurf go to **Ruedi Reservoir.** Bring a wet suit, because the water in this high-mountain reservoir is cold! Most folks surf from the shore at Freeman's Mesa, located about mid-lake on the north side. Camping is allowed only at the designated national forest campgrounds. Some sports shops in the valley rent boards by the day. To get to the reservoir from Aspen, head northwest on Hwy. 82 for 18 miles to Basalt. Turn right and drive along the Fryingpan River for about 18 miles to the reservoir.

SEEING AND DOING

BALLOONING

Lifting off in a balloon is the fantasy excursion of a lifetime. Not every high alpine area is suited to ballooning, but in Aspen it's a popular adventure. The panorama of 14,000-foot peaks takes on a new dimension from the hanging basket of a hot-air balloon. Most ballooning companies depart shortly after sunrise and stay aloft for an hour or two; the traditional bottle of champagne is uncorked at the end of the flight. Balloons accommodate up to eight passengers—just enough for a small wedding party. Warning: the flights are a bit pricey. For additional information and reservations, call the following places.

Aspen Balloon Adventure, Ltd.—PO Box 4995, Aspen, CO 81612; (303) 923-5749.

Unicorn Balloon Company of Colorado—300B, Aspen Airport Business Center, Aspen, CO 81611; (303) 925-5752.

GHOST TOWNS

Ashcroft—
Memories are fading of this town that once rivaled Aspen in importance. In the summer of 1882, Ashcroft had two main streets, three hotels, a jail and a newspaper. Horace Tabor plowed millions of his Leadville silver profits into Ashcroft's Tam O' Shanter and Montezuma mines, with modest success. It is said that when he brought his young bride, Baby Doe, to Ashcroft, a 24-hour holiday ensued, with all drinks on Tabor. Though Tabor made a number of friends in Ashcroft, he poured more into the mines than he ever got back out.

Once Aspen found its place on the map in 1883, Ashcroft started to wane. The transport of silver ore was far easier for Aspen, due to its location in the Roaring Fork Valley. Ashcroft's only route was over Pearl Pass on a rough road to Crested Butte. When the D&RG Railroad puffed into Aspen in 1887, the quiet fate of Ashcroft was secured. Today only nine buildings remain of the town that once boasted a population of 2,500. However, it is still nestled in a beautiful location surrounded by the peaks of the Elk Mountains.

To get to Ashcroft, follow Hwy. 82 west to Castle Creek Rd. Turn left and continue up Castle Creek Rd. for 12 miles until reaching the sign for Toklat gallery. Ashcroft is in the valley east of Toklat.

HOT SPRINGS

Conundrum Hot Springs, in the Maroon Bells–Snowmass Wilderness Area, receives visitors year-round. Most people show up in mid-summer. To avoid crowds, the best time to make the fairly long but not overly steep hike is in spring and fall. Wintertime sees ambitious (and skillful) cross-country skiers visiting for a quick soak before returning in the afternoon.

Conundrum Hot Springs is located on Conundrum Creek, a couple of miles down the valley from Triangle Pass, which leads over into the Gunnison/Crested Butte area. There are two pools, one about 3 feet deep and the other 5 feet deep. Conundrum is overused, and the vegetation directly around the hot springs has been trampled and the tree branches stripped. If you must camp up here, remember to do it at least a quarter mile below the hot springs at designated campsites only. There are a number of good sites available.

To reach the trailhead from Aspen, head about 5 miles up Castle Creek Rd. toward Ashcroft. Turn right onto Forest Rd. 128 and drive about a mile to the trailhead parking lot. The 9-mile (one-way) trail is very level for the first 3 miles and then begins its gradual climb.

MUSEUMS AND GALLERIES

Aspen Art Museum—
The museum features exhibits from local artists as well as nationally acclaimed touring shows. Fine arts, sculpture and crafts are on display. A performing arts series brings in emerging and well-known talent from the fields of music, theater, dance and multimedia performance art. The museum is situated in a park area near the Roaring Fork River, complete with picnic tables and a view to Red and Aspen mountains. It is a great place to stop and relax for a while. Open Tues.–Sun. noon–6 pm, Thurs. until 8 pm. No admission charge on Thurs. evening after 5:30 pm; closed Mon. **590 N. Mill St.; (303) 925-8050.**

Aspen Galleries—
Paintings, sculpture, Eskimo art, gemstones, photography, jewelry, pottery, weavings . . . Aspen's galleries run the gamut. This town is one of the best places to gallery-hop this side of Rodeo Drive. *Aspen* magazine has a rundown of galleries that belong to the Aspen Fine Arts Association. Or pick up a free copy of *The Gallery Guide to Aspen*, with map and descriptions, at the Aspen Visitors Center in the Wheeler Opera House. (See the Services section for directions.) Get to know the town and numerous galleries by embarking on a leisurely window-shopping excursion.

Rocky Mountain Institute (RMI) (in Snowmass)—
Amory and Hunter Lovins are living in an energy-efficient experiment. With the help of more than 100 volunteers they built a 4,000-square-foot, $500,000 research center near Old Snowmass. In keeping with RMI philosophy, their showpiece is built with passive solar, super insulation and an earth-sheltering design, but without a conventional heating system. Low energy appliances are used whenever possible. Showers rely on compressed air to drastically reduce hot water consumption. Since construction was begun in 1982, more than 6,000 people have toured this unique structure, which offers a visual example of energy sources that may be common in the not-too-distant future. For more information, contact RMI at **1739 Snowmass Creek Rd., Snowmass, CO 81654; (303) 927-3851.**

Toklat—

The Toklat gallery is located up in Ashcroft and is run by Stuart and Isabel Mace. Local and Indian arts and crafts are on display in the Maces' cabin. Just let yourself in the front door and browse your way back past folding snowshoe chairs, wooden bowls, vases, sculptures and even agatized dinosaur bones. Traditional Zapotec Indian weavings and Navajo sand paintings are offered for sale. This very unique gallery reflects the colorful history of Toklat and its owners (see the Dog Sledding entry in the Outdoor Activities section for more information on Stuart Mace). To reach Toklat, drive west on Hwy. 82 to Maroon Creek Rd. and turn left. Turn left again onto Castle Creek Rd. and continue for 12 miles. **11247 Castle Creek Rd., PO Box 1048, Aspen, CO 81612; (303) 925-7345.**

Wheeler Stallard House Museum—

The Aspen Historical Society is located in the spacious house Jerome B. Wheeler built in 1888 in a futile effort to entice his wife to Aspen from Manitou Springs. (She never budged.) Inside are authentic Victorian furnishings that have been donated by various families. On the main floor are a re-created living room, dining room and kitchen. Upstairs are collections of photos, clothing and children's toys. The museum gift shop sells books and other items of interest. The staff is an interesting bunch, adding life to an otherwise quiet and musty museum. On one visit we heard incredible stories about the Aspen of old, Joe Boland played songs he knew by heart on an antiquated Hammond organ in the living room, and Hilder Anderson reminisced about growing up on her ranch in Snowmass: "Back in 1914 a Swedish classmate taught me how to ski. And we took some ribbing at school from kids who said that only a dumb Swede would ski!" The times have changed a bit. Open 1–4 pm daily. Small admission fee. **620 W. Bleeker St.; (303) 925-3721.**

Windstar (in Old Snowmass)—

This nonprofit, educational foundation is committed to making an impact on current and future global social problems by exploring new ideas and solutions. It strives to facilitate informed action at the individual level. Windstar nurtures individual growth and excellence, and provides research, education and demonstrations that encourage people to take responsibility for themselves and the planet. Programs include the annual Choices Symposium, hosted by John Denver in late Aug.

Tours of Windstar are offered each Fri. at 3 pm. Visitors can examine many of their projects, including the 50-foot diameter Biodome, a solar-heated greenhouse integrating horticulture and agriculture. Founded in 1976, the Windstar Foundation is located on 1,000 acres. The turn-off for the road to Windstar is 14 miles northwest of Aspen on Hwy. 82. For more information on the programs offered, write **2317 Snowmass Creek Rd., Snowmass, CO 81654; (303) 927-4777.**

NIGHTLIFE

The nightlife in Aspen is not to be missed. Whether you want a quiet night in a piano bar or an all-night binge, you'll find it here. For those who sample a bit too much "local flavor," Aspen provides a free ride service called Tipsy Taxi. Since the Aspen Police Department enforces DUI laws zealously, the free taxi service should be used. The phone number for the **Tipsy Taxi Service is 925-3232.**

André's—

Pulsating music and strobe lights, complete with a spinning mirrored ball on the ceiling, set the tone for what is perhaps Aspen's trendiest night spot. Rub elbows with celebrities, the very rich and the genetically perfect. The ceiling has retractable skylights that offer dancers a view of the stars on clear nights and snow showers on nights when things get a bit steamy inside. The decor is a mix of styles with original red brick walls, mirrors, stained glass and Greek pillars. Downstairs, on the main floor, you can escape the frenetic group in a quieter bar offering live acoustic music. **312 S. Galena St.; (303) 925-6200.**

Bentley's—

Looking for a quiet, classy atmosphere? Crystal and brass chandeliers ornament a narrow room bordered by a long mirrored bar. One of J.B. Wheeler's personal safes is at one end. Rimmed by windows, the bar is located in a restored corner of the historic Wheeler Opera House. Heineken and Bass Ale on tap. Full restaurant menu available. Bentley's fills with theatergoers before and after shows. **221 S. Mill St.; (303) 925-2240.**

Crystal Palace Dinner Theatre—

The Crystal Palace has been an Aspen institution for 30 years, thanks to owner-creator-performer Meade Metcalf. This original cabaret revue, performed by waiters and waitresses, pokes satirical fun at up-to-date subjects. A longtime Aspen resident assured us that the restaurant could "stand on its own" by virtue of its good food alone. Backlit stained glass, a mammoth chandelier and a balcony railing formed from wrought-iron bedsteads whimsically decorate the Crystal Palace. The central bar area is dominated by a 1908 Maxwell and a 1914 Ford Model T. This theater succeeds on the high energy of multi-talented performers. Two seatings nightly; reservations strongly recommended. **Crystal Palace, 300 E. Hyman Ave.; (303) 925-1455.**

The Jerome Bar—

Located in the historic Hotel Jerome, built in 1889, this bar goes back a few years. It attracts a diverse crowd of elbow-benders ranging from locals to out-of-towners wealthy enough to stay in the hotel. In Aspen's early ski days, John Wayne brawled here and playwright Thornton Wilder impressed local ranchers with his legendary drinking capacity. The ceiling is decorated with pressed-tin designs, and there is a great old wooden bar. Belly up to the bar for an après-ski drink or stop in after dinner when things pick up. Appe-

tizer menu items available. **330 E. Main St.; (303) 920-1000.**

Paradise Club—

Top-notch, nationally recognized live music can be heard in this small club setting. A well-placed dance floor just in front of the stage draws an energetic and diverse crowd to its feet. The cover charge is usually fairly minimal, but a recent New Year's Eve bash featuring Stevie Nicks required a $250 entrance fee (the concert sold out). **450 S. Galena St.; (303) 925-5886.**

The Paragon—

This fairly casual Aspen night spot offers a dance floor with an impressive 8-foot by 24-foot screen showing music videos and eight smaller monitors scattered about. Music is varied and controlled by a DJ. Occasionally there is live music by nationally known performers. This fun bar is an easy place to mingle and meet people. Two enormous Victorian-style rooms (one an oyster bar) are connected by two large walk-throughs. Appetizers are available until midnight. **419 E. Hyman Ave.; (303) 925-7499.**

Ute City Banque—

A central location and a century of history have created a unique, clubby atmosphere at the Ute City. The lively bar draws a mature cross-section of Aspenites and tourists. Popular both for après-ski and late-night crowds. Minks are seated next to T-shirts, champagne next to beer (only in Aspen). See the Where to Eat section for more information. **501 E. Hyman Ave.; (303) 925-4373.**

Wheeler Opera House—

Jerome B. Wheeler built this three-story Victorian showpiece in 1889. For many years the opera house languished in disrepair, a burned-out reminder of better days. A multi-million-dollar restoration was completed in 1984, returning the Wheeler to its former glory. Today it is home to Aspen's artistic and cultural community. Natural wood is used lavishly throughout, contrasted by plush velvet stage curtains, red carpeting and gold stars painted on the ceiling; an elegant chandelier dominates the interior. Orchestra or balcony seating and side boxes are available. Today the opera house is much more than a museum—thanks to a year-round program of music, theater, dance and film. Check with the ticket office at **(303) 925-2750** for the performance schedule, or call **(303) 920-2268** for a historic tour. **320 E. Hyman Ave.**

SCENIC DRIVES

Independence Pass—

One of the best known "white knuckle" drives in the state is the narrow paved road over Independence Pass. The winding route, braced on one side by a stone guardrail, provides a bit of excitement for flatlanders unaccustomed to mountain driving. It is unquestionably at its colorful best during autumn and is impassable in winter. The pass, with its barren summit at 12,500 feet, provides the best route through the Sawatch Range; when the pass is closed, the drive to Aspen from the east is substantially longer.

The story goes that the pass is named Independence because of a gold strike on July 4, 1879, 4 miles west of the pass. A town quickly grew on that site. In the early 1880s, Independence had daily stage service to Leadville. (Reportedly, the population of only 2,000 supported ten saloons!) The treacherous road over Independence Pass fell into disuse soon after the arrival of railroads into the lower valleys. Going over the pass required 10 to 25 hours, several changes of horses and payment at three tollgates. Since no railroad ever made its way to Independence, the town was all but a memory by the turn of the century.

An interesting place to pull off is at the Grottos, a series of large, granite caverns 8 miles east of Aspen. See the Hiking and Backpacking section for more information.

To reach Independence Pass, follow Hwy. 82 east from Aspen. About 15 miles from Aspen, but before reaching the summit, look to your right. You will see the remains of Independence down below the road. At the summit there is a parking area and a short walking trail. Hwy. 82 to the pass is closed in winter.

WILDLIFE

Aspen Center for Environmental Studies—

In 1968, Elizabeth Paepcke founded this nonprofit foundation in order to preserve Hallam Lake, on the north edge of town. The Aspen Center for Environmental Studies (ACES) provides environmental programs for local school kids and offers a series of summer programs aimed at enhancing awareness of the environment around Aspen. The ACES facilities at the Hallam Lake Wildlife Sanctuary and the 175-acre Northstar Wildlife Preserve (located just east of Aspen), offer indoor and outdoor classrooms for environmental education. Year-round tours of Hallam Lake and Northstar are available. In winter, the tours are made on snowshoe. ACES has programs for everyone, from youngsters to environmentally conscious adults. **PO Box 8777, Aspen, CO 81612; (303) 925-5756.**

WHERE TO STAY

ACCOMMODATIONS

The array of lodging choices in Aspen runs the gamut from ritzy full-service hotels to small European-style ski lodges to luxury condominiums. You will not, however, find many large chain hotels, because of strict zoning requirements in this historic town. Staying overnight in Aspen is generally more expensive than in other parts of the state, especially in high season when rooms are at a premium. We have listed some of the more outstanding accommodations in Aspen to suit a variety of tastes and budgets. For a more complete listing, call the **Aspen Resort Association** locally **925-9000**, toll free in Colorado **1-800-421-7145**, or toll free outside Colorado **1-800-262-7736**.

Hotel Jerome — $$$$

If you want to stay in a fine, historic hotel, the Hotel Jerome is the place. This Victorian monolith is Aspen's great reminder of an age gone by, when Aspen basked in the limelight of being one of the world's richest silver mining towns. A grand hotel in its day, the Hotel Jerome fell into years of disrepair until recent renovations put it back in a league with the finest historic hotels in the country.

Jerome B. Wheeler, the one-time president of Macy's department store in New York City, was Aspen's major benefactor. He donated the land on which the hotel sits and loaned money to the developers. Hopelessly overbudget, the developers skipped town after receiving a number of death threats from unpaid workers. Wheeler eventually took over the unfinished project and opened the hotel on Thanksgiving Eve 1889.

The lavish hotel enjoyed some glory years but began a downward spiral in 1893, as did Aspen itself, when silver was demonetized. Through Aspen's economic drought, which lasted until the late 1940s, the Hotel Jerome remained a social focal point for the town. Locals would meet at the hotel on Sun. nights for 50-cent chicken dinners and live music. In the 1950s, as more people became attracted to Aspen for its skiing, the Hotel Jerome continued its important role in the community.

The hotel was purchased in 1984 by Dick Butera, who began an expensive restoration and reconstruction. Interior designer Zoe Compton was called in to spearhead the restoration done in the style of 1880s Eastlake-Gothic. Layers of paint were stripped, revealing sandstone and beautiful wood that had not seen daylight for the better part of 60 years. Furniture was restored and priceless tile and solid-iron door fixtures were polished for reuse. The resurrection is now complete.

Today the original hotel offers 27 rooms, including seven guest suites. The new wing offers an additional 67 guest rooms (no two rooms are the same). The rooms include wall-to-wall carpeting, private bathrooms, brass and black-iron beds and other period pieces.

The original gathering rooms all remain, including the Ladies' Ordinary. Back in the 1890s it was one of the first places in the country where unescorted women could go for a sarsparilla or, if they wanted, a shot of whiskey and a beer. The hotel lobby is stunningly plush with restored furniture. An open core in the center of the building rises three stories to a glass-covered ceiling. The original bar, restaurant and ballroom are worth visiting. A pool on the west side of the building is a great après-ski venue, with poolside service. Airport shuttle and 24-hour concierge service are available. Reserve far in advance for the ski season and the summer music festival. 330 E. Main St., Aspen, CO 81611; 920-1000 local, 1-800-331-7213 toll free nationwide, 1-800-423-0037 toll free in Colorado.

Hotel Lenado — $$$$

Nowhere will you find a better combination of elegance and rustic charm in a luxury-class hotel. Contrasts abound, yet the overall result is one of extreme comfort. Once inside, you can't help but notice the soaring 28-foot-high lobby. A slow look around reveals bent-twig furniture topped with enormous down-filled pillows, a contemporary cement-and-flagstone fireplace and a well-stocked library that opens onto a park. An upper terrace has a protected sun deck and a hot tub with views to Aspen and Shadow mountains.

The rooms are everything you would hope for in a hotel of this caliber. Most unique are the beds of either hand-carved applewood or bent-twig ironwood topped with thick down comforters. A hearty breakfast is served in the sunny breakfast room. After a day on the slopes, return for an après-ski gathering featuring complimentary drinks and hot hors d'oeuvres. The Lenado is the perfect environment for a romantic getaway. **200 S. Aspen St., Aspen, CO 81611; (303) 925-6246.**

Sardy House — $$$$

Bordered by two towering blue spruces, Sardy House is a Victorian mansion steeped in history and beautifully restored to its former glory. As you pass the red brick Sardy House on Main St., its gables, turrets and French-cut balcony will provoke you into taking a second look. Once inside, oak staircases lead to well-appointed guest rooms and suites. Televisions and VCRs are hidden away in cherrywood armoires, Laura Ashley prints overlay the feather comforters and many of the hardwood ceilings are vaulted and multiangled. White-tiled bathrooms have new fixtures done in the old style—and heated towel racks! Don't worry about the driveway icing up; it's heated as well. Outside is a heated swimming pool and a jacuzzi. Gourmet breakfast is included, and dinners are served in a subdued, intimate atmosphere. **128 E. Main St., Aspen, CO 81611; (303) 920-2525.**

Alpine Lodge — $$

Hans and Sharon Reiger have a caring outlook, which is warmly reflected in their small, family-run *gasthaus*. About half of the comfortable lodge rooms have private baths, as well as balcony views to Aspen Mountain. Though the lodge rooms are rather small, each guest is made to feel at home in the large downstairs common area. Hans's Bavarian heritage is obvious from the collection of beer steins and the *stammtisch* table (reserved for repeat guests). Even though Sharon is from Colorado, she cooks authentic German dinners of goulash, wiener schnitzel, bratwurst and other specialties during the winter. Dinners are available six nights a week for an extra price (BYOB). Full breakfast is included with a room in winter. Guests are apt to mingle in front of the large ceramic wood stove during après ski or, in summer, over a game of outdoor ping-pong.

There are also four cottages placed around a grassy interior courtyard with easy access to an outdoor hot tub and a barbecue. Each unit has a TV, a kitchenette and a private bathroom. Unless you reserve far in advance, you'll be lucky to find space at the Alpine Lodge during high season. It's a place where guests commonly reserve rooms for next year as they check out. A great value! Located a short walk from the slopes. No credit cards. **1240 E. Hwy. 82, Aspen, CO 81611; (303) 925-7351.**

The Little Red Ski Haus — $$

Referred to by locals and past guests as a "mini-museum," the Little Red Ski Haus is a small bed and breakfast with a lot of character. It was built by a miner in 1888. Back then the street was called Fanny Hill St., which leads owner Marge Riley to suspect the house was once a brothel. In 1951 Marge and her husband, Jim, bought the place and decided to open a bed and breakfast. Marge fell in love with the house while walking down the street. "It looked like a little red schoolhouse," she recalls, "so, being school teachers at the time, we decided to call it the Little Red Ski Haus."

From the beginning the Rileys worked like dogs, first refurbishing the existing house and later adding on rooms. All the while, Jim collected antiques, which now fill the house. Today there are 21 guest rooms, some with baths and some without. There are no TVs or telephones, so visitors tend to strike up friendships with other guests. A large number of guests at the Little Red Ski Haus are repeat customers. Breakfast is served every morning in the main lounge; there is a wine and cheese party every Mon. evening in winter so guests can get to know one another. It's only a few minutes' walk to the ski slopes. Rates are lower in the summer. Reservations are encouraged, especially for the Christmas season. **118 E. Cooper Ave., Aspen, CO 81611; (303) 925-3333.**

St. Moritz Lodge — $ to $$$

This is a reasonably priced, loud and lively lodge offering a variety of accommodations. Stay in a shared dorm room that serves as Aspen's unofficial youth hostel, or sign up for a private lodge room or apartment. For après ski, everyone heads to the oversized hot tub in front of the lodge. The well-worn common room looks onto the deck. A small library, grand piano, TV room and morning coffee/tea round out the amenities. In high season make early reservations. Weekly and monthly rentals available. **334 W. Hyman Ave., Aspen, CO 81611; (303) 925-3220.**

In Snowmass—

There are a number of reasons (besides the skiing) to venture into Snowmass, but unique, interesting lodging opportunities is not one of them. Condominiums dominate the Brush Creek Valley, reflecting the era of Snowmass' recent boom, which was quite different from Aspen's. But the condos are a good option for families and people who want to escape the hurly-burly of Aspen. For condominium reservations, contact the **Snowmass Resort Association; (303) 923-2000.**

CAMPING

In White River National Forest—

In the Aspen area there are 15 forest service campgrounds equipped with a variety of facilities ranging from primitive to plush. Please remember to pack out your own trash from the sites without garbage pickup. Campsites are assigned on a first-come, first-served basis.

Up the Fryingpan River—Although a bit far from Aspen, the drive may be worth it if you seek solitude and great fishing. From Aspen drive northwest on Hwy. 82 for 18 miles to Basalt. From Basalt, head upriver on Fryingpan Rd. (County Rd. 105) to Ruedi Reservoir. There are four campgrounds at Ruedi, which all charge a fee: Mollie B (26 sites), Little Maud (22 sites), Little Mattie (20 sites) and Dearhamer (13 sites). A few miles above the reservoir are two other campgrounds: Elk Wallow (eight sites, no pump water, no fee) and Chapman (42 sites, fee charged).

Toward Independence Pass—Up the valley on Hwy. 82 there are five campgrounds to choose from before you reach the pass. **Difficult Campground**, with 47 sites, is the closest to Aspen (5 miles). Reservations for groups of up to 90 people are taken with at least two weeks' advance notice. Farther up Hwy. 82 you'll find **Weller** (11 sites, no fee), **Lincoln Gulch** (seven sites, no fee) and **Lost Man campgrounds** (nine sites, no fee), located 9 miles, 11 miles and 14.5 miles, respectively, from Aspen. Up Hwy. 82, 11 miles from Aspen, turn south up Lincoln Creek Rd. for 7 miles to reach **Portal Campground** (seven sites, no fee) on Grizzly Reservoir. This road is not maintained and may be tough going for trailers and passenger cars.

Up Maroon Creek Road—The view of the Maroon Bells from Maroon Lake is world famous. It is easily the most recognizable mountain view in the state. Consequently, it is very hard to find a campsite in this valley during mid-summer. Four campgrounds: **Maroon Lake** (44 sites), **Silver Bar** (four sites), **Silver Bell** (four sites) and **Silver Queen** (six sites) are open from early June until mid-Sept., depending on the snowpack. Travel up the road from early July until after Labor Day is restricted to shuttle buses (small fee) from 9 am–5 pm. During this time, private vehicles need to secure a camping permit at the entrance station before heading up the road. Maroon Lake Campground checkout time is 11 am during summer when the bus system is in operation. Silver Bar and Silver Bell do not accommodate trailers; there is a fee charged at all four sites.

If you are expecting a man (or woman)-in-the-wilderness experience, this is not the place. For more isolation, a suggestion is to take the shuttle bus up to the lake, enjoy the incredible scenery and camp elsewhere.

Private Campgrounds—

For top-notch RV park facilities in the Aspen area, you need to head down the valley to Basalt. Here's what you'll find.

KOA Campground—3096 Hwy. 82, Basalt; (303) 927-3532.

Pan & Fork Trailer Park—123 Hwy. 82, Basalt; (303) 927-3266.

For More Information—
Call, write or visit the **Aspen Ranger District Office, 806 W. Hallam St., Aspen, CO 81611; (303) 925-3445.** Open Mon.–Fri. year-round.

WHERE TO EAT

As a playground for the rich and famous, Aspen fills the demand for top-quality restaurants. But there are also places to get decent food at reasonable prices. There are more than 100 restaurants in the Aspen area, ranging from five-star master-pieces to dive diners. The following are some of the best of the different dining categories.

Chez Grandmère — $$$$

Located in Snowmass, this intimate Victorian house specializes in French cuisine. This is unquestionably one of the finest restaurants in the area, and the fixed price for the meal reflects this. The menu changes nightly. There is one seating per evening and reservations are a must. **16 Kearns Rd., Snowmass; 923-2570.**

Pine Creek Cookhouse — $$$$

Imagine a light-falling snow under a full moon. . . . Place yourself on cross-country skis or in a horse-drawn sleigh in the Castle Creek Valley, 12 miles from Aspen, and head off to an intimate dining experience. Starting at the ghost town of Ashcroft, the 1.5-mile jaunt through the woods heightens your senses and creates a certain camaraderie among guests. Bernard Moffoid, one-time personal chef for Brigitte Bardot, puts together a choice of three entrées each evening. Cornish game hen, herbed Rocky Mountain trout and roast leg of lamb were the choices during our visit. One word of caution for people who ski to the cookhouse and plan on having a few drinks: you've got to ski back out! The set dinner price includes a guide and cross-country ski rental. A sleigh ride is an extra $10. Lunch ($$$) is served noon–2:30 pm. In summer it is possible to drive to the

cookhouse. Dinner seating is once per evening; reservations are a must. **Ashcroft Touring Center, Ashcroft; 925-1044.**

Krabloonik's — $$$ to $$$$

As a working sled-dog kennel, Krabloonik's has to be one of the most unique places to dine in the Aspen area, if not in the entire state. Located up the road from Snowmass Ski Area, this atmospheric log cabin boasts the honor (?) of being the only restaurant ever written up in *Sports Illustrated*. Large picture windows offer a spectacular view up the valley to Mt. Daly and 14,130-foot Capitol Peak. The decor is Alaskan rustic, but white tablecloths and fine crystal immediately clue you in to the fact that you are not going to be eating Spam and beans. Krabloonik's fare is indeed gourmet caliber. The wild mushroom soup is fantastic and their most-requested recipe. The wild game selections include moose, caribou, elk and wild boar shipped in from as far away as New Zealand. Selections change daily. Choose from more than 200 wines and a European beer list.

Walk down to the cabin from the parking lot to the sound of 300 dogs yipping and howling. Playful pups may approach for some attention. Open for lunch 11 am–2 pm and dinner from 5:30 pm daily in winter (dinner only in summer). Skiers at Snowmass can reach the restaurant via Dawdler Trail. After lunch ($$$), ski down to the Campground Chairlift. Reservations are recommended; the place is booked months in advance for the three-week period around Christmas. Krabloonik's also offers sled-dog rides in winter. For more information about Krabloonik's, see the Dog Sledding entry in the Outdoor Activities section. To get there, drive a quarter mile above Snowmass Ski Area on Brush Creek Rd. to the parking lot. **PO Box 5517, Snowmass Village; 923-3953.**

Ute City Banque — $$$ to $$$$

Ute City offers fine dining and a great bar scene in the classy atmosphere of an 1880s bank. Brass-barred teller windows proclaiming Discounts, Savings and Bank Collections are inlaid into wooden restaurant booths; the bank's original Diebold safe is built into the bar; an extensive wine list is written in a thick bank ledger. The food is innovative and pricey. Delve into appetizers of steak tartare, graved ahi, or broiled scallops wrapped in bacon. Entrées include duckling Marguerite, New York sirloin served with Cajun bourbon sauce, and swordfish topped with parmesan-fried oysters. A less expensive bar-cafe menu is offered in a separate section. Lunch ($$) is served daily 11:30 am–2:30 pm, dinner nightly from 6 pm, reservations suggested. **501 E. Hyman Ave.; 925-4373.**

The Grill on the Park — $$ to $$$$

Great outside seating in summertime for suntanning and people-watching. Oh yeah, the food is good too. Open for lunch 11:30 am–4:30 pm; dinner from 4:30 pm. Located next to Wagner Park. **307 S. Mill St.; 920-3700.**

Asia — $$ to $$$

An unusual combination: Chinese cuisine served in an old Victorian home. The house features a 100-year-old bar and woodwork throughout. Asia's cuisine is a favorite with Aspen locals (one reason being the *free delivery* service). The restaurant offers Mandarin and Szechuan menu items with a few Hunan and Cantonese dishes thrown in for good measure. Seafood, vegetarian and duck dishes are of particular note. Lily Ko, the manager, came to the US from Beijing a few years ago, so rest assured the Peking duck is done to perfection. Outside seating in summer. Dinner is served 5–11 pm. Located at **132 W. Main St.; 925-5433.**

André's — $$

This is where a very devoted following goes for brunch, including both non-partygoers and those who boogie late into the night upstairs in the disco. André's has a reputation for the best Bloody Marys in town. Open daily 8 am–2:30 pm. **312 S. Galena St.; 925-6200.**

Home Plate — $$

Home-cooked meals are served up at this family-style restaurant. Located in the basement of the Mountain Chalet on the south end of Wagner Park, Home Plate offers dinner specials prepared from scratch each night. Vegetarian items are available, as well as fresh trout. An all-you-can-eat spaghetti dish attracts the summer rugby tournament players (or is it the cold beer?). Sandwiches are available for take-out from 2–10 pm. Dinner served from 5:30–9:30 pm daily. Call after 3 pm for information about the nightly specials. **333 E. Durant Ave.; 925-1986.**

La Cocina — $$

Over the years many Aspen eateries have bitten the dust, but La Cocina has been a consistently great place to eat since 1971. A favorite among locals, La Cocina offers creative New Mexican-style food. The owners, Nick and Sarah Lebby, work seven days a week, Sarah in the kitchen and Nick greeting and seating guests. A local in the bar told us Nick never forgets a name. This personal touch and La Cocina's good value make it a highlight of dining out in Aspen. Menu favorites include the Cocina bean dip appetizer, any enchilada plate and the blue corn tortilla dinner. Don't miss the Chocolate Velvet dessert. The decor is New Mexican, and the atmosphere is friendly and down-to-earth. Hours are 5–10 pm daily. Highly recommended. **308 E. Hopkins Ave.; 925-9714.**

Little Annie's — $$

Rough wood walls, throwaway antiques and a well-worn floor provide the set for this local stomping ground. The handwritten menu describes a generous assortment of dishes at most reasonable prices (especially considering the quantity of food on every plate). Giant half-pound hamburgers, Greek salads, Poncho's pizza, barbecue ribs and sautéed rainbow trout are only a few of the favorites; nightly specials are served. By the way, a shot and a beer at Little Annie's are still only $1.50—cheapest in town! Kitchen open from 11:30 am–11:30 pm, bar stays open till 2 am. **517 E. Hyman Ave.; 925-1098.**

The Village Smithy — $ to $$

If you are driving into or out of Aspen, stop in at the Village Smithy. This is without a doubt one of the finest, if not the finest, breakfast place in the valley. Located down the valley from Aspen in Carbondale, this restaurant is in an old blacksmith's shop. Eggs Benedict are the house specialty, but the huevos rancheros are a favorite with regulars. Liquor is served; try a Bloody Mary or a Mimosa. Breakfast is served 7–11 am on weekdays; until 2 pm on weekends. Located at **3rd and Main in Carbondale; 963-9990.**

Hickory House — $

You'll find no quiche served here. Located in an old, rickety wooden structure at the west end of town, Hickory House is the place to go for a good old bacon-and-egg breakfast. Standard breakfast fare is offered at reasonable prices. This spot is packed with budget-conscious locals and a few out-of-towners. Lunch ($) and dinner ($$) are also served; full bar. Breakfast served 6–11:20 am Mon.–Fri. (until 11:45 am on weekends), lunch and dinner are served 11:45 am–2:30 pm and 5–10 pm, respectively. **730 W. Main St.; 925-2313.**

Paradise Bakery — $

The Paradise has two major things going for it: a superb assortment of homemade muffins (cinnamon apple spice, pumpkin nut, bran ...) and a perfect corner location at Cooper and Galena. Plenty of outside benches are available in the warmer months—ideal for people-watching. Small counter space inside. The bakery also serves cookies, ice cream and fresh-squeezed lemonade. Open daily from 7 am–midnight. **320 S. Galena St.; 925-7585.**

Wienerstube — $

A couple of talented Austrian chefs opened the Wienerstube in 1965. Breakfast at this popular restaurant has become something of an Aspen tradition. A light garden setting is complemented by lots of stained glass. There is even a *stammtisch* table reserved for regular customers. Breakfast choices include eggs Benedict, crêpes, Belgian waffles with fruit and homemade Viennese pastries. Open for breakfast from 7–11 am. Or stop in after 11 am for a look at the six-page lunch menu ($ to $$). Dinner ($$$) is served after 5 pm. Closed Mon. **633 E. Hyman Ave.; 925-3357.**

Woody Creek Tavern — $

If the glitz of Aspen starts to get to you, stop in at the Woody Creek Tavern for a game of pool, a burger and a cheap beer on tap. This out-of-the-way spot is a hangout for many unpretentious locals, including journalist Hunter S. Thompson. Assorted outrageous announcements and paraphernalia cover the walls. Mexican food, burgers and chicken make up the menu. To get there take Hwy. 82 west from Aspen for a few miles and turn north on Woody Creek Rd. Follow the road across a bridge and turn left at the fork. The tavern is just down the road from there. **2 Woody Creek Plaza, Woody Creek; 923-4585.**

The Brown Bear

SERVICES

Bus Transportation—

Frequent free shuttle buses begin their route at Rubey Park (on Durant Ave. between Mill St. and Galena St.), before whisking skiers to each of the surrounding ski mountains. The buses run every 15 minutes during the morning and afternoon skier rush; during midday the buses operate on a more leisurely schedule, leaving every half hour or so. With buses leaving for many destinations from Rubey Park, you will want to be careful that you catch the right one.

In addition to the free shuttle buses, there are free city buses serving the city of Aspen. The buses run four different routes from 7 am–1 am. All bus routes originate at Rubey Park. For schedule and route information, call **(303) 925-8484.**

Central Reservations—

Aspen Resort Association, 700 S. Aspen St., Aspen, CO 81611; call locally **925-9000,** toll free in Colorado **1-800-421-7145,** or toll free outside Colorado **1-800-262-7736.**

Snowmass Resort Association, 45 Village Sq., PO Box 5566, Snowmass Village, CO 81615; call locally **923-2010,** toll free in Colorado **1-800-237-3146** or toll free outside Colorado **1-800-332-3245.**

Day Care—

Aspen Child Care Center at **(303) 925-9364, Aspen Sprouts** at **(303) 920-1055** or **Big Burn Bears** at **(303) 925-4444, ext. 4570.**

Public Parking—

Free parking can be found in the lot on N. Mill St. just behind the County Courthouse, near the Hotel Jerome. There is a pay lot at the corner of Hyman Ave. and Original St. that is closer to the mountain.

24-Hour Taxi Service—

High Mountain Taxi—specializes in luxury four-wheel-drive vehicles and limousine service, **(303) 925-TAXI.**

Visitor Information—

Aspen Visitors Center, 328 E. Hyman Ave., Aspen, CO 81611, in the Wheeler Opera House; or call **(303) 925-1940.**

Dinosaur National Monument

Remote and often overlooked, Dinosaur National Monument is a recreationist's mecca and a stunning geological exhibit. Located in the unforgiving, arid Colorado Plateau country in the extreme northwestern corner of the state, this three-pronged, 325-square-mile monument straddles the Utah-Colorado border. In its southwestern corner, where an ancient river once flowed, lies the dinosaur quarry, representing one of the highest concentrations of fossilized dinosaur bones in the world. Sprawled across the monument, the Uinta Mountains are one of just a few mountain ranges in the western hemisphere that run east-west. At the center of the monument at Echo Park lies the confluence of two of the West's mightiest rivers: the Green and the Yampa.

Dinosaur is a land of plateaus and deep canyons that are deceptive from a distance. Like other western canyon country, the monument's parks and side gorges are best viewed and discovered from within. By far, the best way to see the monument is from the river. Rafters and kayakers spend days floating through the narrow rock canyons, carved as deep as 3,300 feet over millions of years. Tranquil for a few miles, then violent and angry, the river pinches together for steep drops down the narrow rapid sections. Driving the back roads and hiking the backcountry of Dinosaur are other ways to experience the canyons, plateaus and mountains. If you make the effort to reach Dinosaur National Monument, you won't be disappointed.

HISTORY

More than 140 million years ago, during the Jurassic period, dinosaurs and other creatures roamed around the area that today is Dinosaur National Monument. Many of these beasts' bones were covered and preserved over the eons until discovered in August 1909 by paleontologist Earl Douglas. On a search for large fossils for the Carnegie Museum in Pittsburgh, Douglas was shocked, to say the least, when he discovered eight brontosaurus vertebrae imbedded in what was once a sandbar along an ancient river. The dinosaur bones had collected in the silt of the river and had been covered up by accumulating sand and mud.

Over the next 15 years, 350 tons of dinosaur bones were excavated from this area and taken to the Carnegie Museum and other institutions around the world. Today, more than 14 different species have been unearthed in what has proven to be one of the world's most prolific dinosaur digs. In 1915 President Woodrow Wilson proclaimed the dinosaur dig and 80 acres around it a national monument. President Franklin Roosevelt expanded the monument land by adding 326 square miles in 1938.

At least as far back as 6000 BC, primitive man was making his way over the plateaus and through the canyons of northwestern Colorado. More recently (AD 1–AD 1200), Fremont Man, the prehistoric hunter/gatherer, left his mark throughout the area in the form of rock art. Petroglyphs are etched into scores of canyon walls in the form of humans, sheep, lizards and numerous other renderings of life seen through the eyes of these ancients. Whether these etchings are a form of written language or of art is still not known.

Modern man's first recorded ventures into the area began in 1776 with the Franciscan friars Dominguez and Escalante, who traveled just south of Dinosaur on their search for a safe route to the West Coast from Santa Fe. When the beaver pelt business was booming in the early 1800s, trappers who fanned out in the Wyoming, Utah and Colorado area met annually at a rendezvous spot along the Green River called Brown's Park. This area is just north of the monument boundary.

With men entering the area to trap and later to search for gold, it was only a matter of time before someone's search led him down the canyons on the Green and Yampa rivers. In 1825, Gen. William H. Ashley, a fur trader from Missouri, floated through perhaps the most treacherous section of the Green River—Lodore Canyon. The group of men he assembled in Missouri for one of his many trips west read like a *Who's Who* of mountain men, including Jim Beckworth, Jim Bridger, John Colter and Jedediah Smith. In 1869, Maj. John Wesley Powell brought news of the Dinosaur area and its river to the world through his compelling journal entries, written during his much publicized survey and exploration trip west. A few years later, he again floated the upper Green River down through its narrow canyons in northwestern Colorado. These accomplishments become even more significant given the fact that Maj. Powell had only one arm.

Due to Dinosaur's remote location and rough terrain, sections of the area remained wild and unexplored until well into the 1900s. At the turn of the century, some settlers entered the region to homestead the remote canyons and parks. Cattle rustlers, highwaymen and bank robbers also found the remote area a perfect place to hide out between jobs while the heat wore off. Butch Cassidy and his Wild Bunch frequented Brown's Park (then called Brown's Hole).

Dinosaur National Monument has the distinction of being one of the few sites in the country where an environmental battle was won by conservationists. From about 1950 to 1955, intense debates raged over two proposed dams that would have flooded the beautiful canyons and covered up forever a multitude of ancient rock art. Largely due to efforts by the Sierra Club to increase public awareness, the proposed site was canceled. Today the rivers in the northwestern part of the state remain free flowing, though there is a dam proposed on the Cross Canyon section of the Yampa, just upriver to the east of Dinosaur National Monument.

FACTS ABOUT THE PARK

Dinosaur Quarry Visitors Center—
Come and visit the place where the first dinosaur bones were discovered in 1909. *This is the only place in the park to see dinosaur bones!* A structure encloses the quarry, where technicians continue to uncover the bones—not for removal, but just enough for visitors to see. Watch them work, browse through the displays and ask questions of the knowledgeable park ranger on duty. The entrance is 7 miles north of Jensen, Utah. From the parking lot, a shuttle bus, which operates from Memorial Day to Labor Day, takes you up to the quarry. You can drive up yourself during the rest of the year. The quarry visitors center is open 8 am–7 pm daily, early June to early Sept.; 8 am–4:30 pm during the rest of the year. Admission fee is charged. Jensen, Utah, is located 20 miles west of Dinosaur, Colorado, on Hwy. 40; **(801) 789-2115.**

Park Headquarters—
The park headquarters is located 2 miles east of the town of Dinosaur at the intersection of Hwy. 40 and Harper's Corner Rd. There is an audio-visual program as well as exhibits. Free admission. Obtain backcountry camping permits and any other information you need here. Open daily, 8 am–4:30 pm, June through Aug.; Mon.–Fri., 8 am–4:30 pm, the rest of the year; **(303) 374-2216.**

Services—
Gas, food and lodging are not available within Dinosaur National Monument. The towns of Dinosaur and Rangely offer the closest services in Colorado; Jensen (no lodging) and Vernal have what you need on the Utah side.

Weather—
The Dinosaur area is arid, but this doesn't necessarily mean hot. In the summer it can get very hot during the day and cool at night. Thunderstorms are common during June, July and Aug. Snow usually falls by Oct., and cold weather continues into the spring. Temperatures below 32° are common. Dress accordingly.

GETTING THERE

The two main entrances to the monument are located at Dinosaur, Colorado, and at Jensen, Utah. To reach Dinosaur (295 miles west of Denver), head west via Hwy. 40 through northern Colorado. From the south (Grand Junction), head west on Interstate 70 for 16 miles and turn north on Hwy. 139 to Rangely and then northwest on Hwy. 60 to Dinosaur. The northern end of the park at the Gates of Lodore can be reached via Hwy. 318, which heads northwest out of Maybell.

Green River flowing into the Gates of Lodore at Dinosaur National Monument.

OUTDOOR ACTIVITIES

FOUR-WHEEL-DRIVE TRIPS

Exploring the back roads in the Dinosaur area is a great way to experience the country. But be forewarned that when rain starts to fall in canyon country, some of the roads are not even passable with a four-wheel-drive vehicle. If you get stuck at the bottom of a muddy hill you may have a long wait while the road dries—or an even longer hike out. Be sure to have plenty of gasoline, food, water and tools along with you.

For road ideas in and around Dinosaur National Monument, visit the rangers at park headquarters near the town of Dinosaur. Bureau of Land Management (BLM) land surrounds practically the entire monument, offering some fascinating country just waiting to be explored. For more information about backroad BLM possibilities, contact the BLM Office in Craig. **Little Snake Resource Area, 1280 Industrial Ave., Craig, CO 81625; (303) 824-4441.**

Crouse Canyon—

Although Crouse Canyon can be driven in a passenger car in good weather, it is a very rough road for the first few miles. The road begins in Colorado, then quickly curves over into Utah for the duration of the 25-mile, dirt road trip. The Crouse

Canyon Rd. begins dramatically by crossing a swinging bridge over the Green River. Once across, the road follows the river upstream for a while, on the southern edge of Brown's Park National Wildlife Refuge. Suddenly the road turns southwest and propels you into a beautiful, narrow canyon. Towering rock walls and a cool stream lined with cottonwood groves await. The road eventually climbs up onto a plateau.

Be on the lookout for some of the most memorable residents of the area, the Mormon crickets. These huge wingless grasshoppers swarm across the road, devouring their comrades who've been tragically crushed under the wheels of passing cars. When the Mormons first settled in Utah, their crops were set upon by these creatures. By "divine intervention," a flock of California seagulls came to the rescue, gorging themselves on these tasty insects. The Mormons were so thankful to the birds that the California seagull was made the state bird of Utah.

To reach Crouse Canyon, head northwest from Maybell on Hwy. 318 for 62 miles to the turn-off to Brown's Park National Wildlife Refuge. Turn left and proceed on the dirt road down to and over the swinging bridge. After 25 miles, you hit a paved road which goes to Vernal, Utah, or to the dinosaur quarry.

Yampa Bench Road—

This rough dirt road bumps and bounces its way for 42 miles through the monument and adjacent BLM land. Through canyons and over open country covered with sage, juniper and pinon, Yampa Bench Rd. offers a rugged look at the area. To reach Yampa Bench Rd., head north from park headquarters on Harper's Corner Rd. for 25 miles to Echo Park Rd. Turn right and drive 8 miles down to the fork in the road. The right fork is Yampa Bench Rd. It comes out on Hwy. 40 at Elk Springs, 32 miles northeast of park headquarters.

HIKING AND BACKPACKING

Although the number of established hiking trails within the monument is rather limited, routes into side canyons are endless. Backcountry camping is allowed in the monument, but you need to obtain a free permit issued at either the quarry, park headquarters or some of the field ranger stations. Be very careful if you venture out on your own. Take plenty of water and consult the rangers about the area where you intend to backpack. Below are a few hiking and backpacking ideas.

Irish Canyon—

This is a beautiful, multicolored canyon not more than 150 feet wide. Steep walls with green, red and gray layers tower above the pinon pines in the canyon. An exhibit, petroglyphs and three campsites are at the entrance to the canyon. Side canyons beckon to hikers. Near the north end of the canyon are two natural ponds known as Irish Lakes. You need to bring your own drinking water for camping or hiking in this area. This is a very secluded place, considering it is accessible by road. To reach Irish Canyon, head northwest from Maybell on Hwy. 318 for 41 miles and turn right on County Rd. 10N. Proceed 4 miles to the canyon entrance.

Jones Hole—

Follow this 4-mile trail down through the Jones Hole Creek Gorge into Whirlpool Canyon, one of the few remote parts of the Green River accessible on foot rather than by water. There are plenty of trees and steep rock walls (some with petroglyphs) along the way to keep you somewhat cool in the summer heat. The trailhead is located on the north side of the river, 40 miles east of Vernal. For directions and a map, stop in at park headquarters or the quarry.

Nature Trails—

There are short, interpretive nature trails at the following spots: Split Mountain Campground, Gates of Lodore and

Harper's Corner. The trail at Harper's Corner is 2 miles round trip and offers a fantastic view.

Willow Creek Canyon, Skull Creek Canyon and Bull Canyon—

These three areas are located on BLM land and are accessible from Plug Hat Picnic Area, 4 miles north on Harper's Corner Rd. from park headquarters. Bull Canyon, characterized by many draws and creeks, is west of the road. Willow Creek and Skull Creek canyons, to the east, contain higher cliffs. For specific information and maps pertaining to these beautiful, secluded canyons, contact the BLM office in Craig or talk to the ranger at park headquarters.

RIVER FLOATING

Some of the best floating in the state can be had on several sections of the Green and Yampa rivers, namely, Cross Mountain and Split Mountain gorges, Whirlpool, Lodore and Yampa River canyons. Each year, commercial and private rafters and kayakers submit applications to obtain the limited permits. The best way to experience the monument is definitely from the water. Floating allows access to many places inaccessible by any other means.

Green River—

The Green River flows peacefully into northwestern Colorado below Flaming Gorge, then turns south and enters the magnificent, colorful **Gates of Lodore** at the northern tip of the monument. It's here that the Green cuts through the Uinta Mountains, exposing 3,300-foot-deep **Lodore Canyon**. Once inside the 17-mile-long canyon, the river picks up speed, crashing down through the narrow passageway that has frightened and captivated so many boatmen over the years. In 1869 Maj. John Wesley Powell described the scenery of Lodore Canyon as "even beyond the power of pen to tell." The Gates of Lodore, like most of the landmarks along the river, was named by Powell. It refers to a passage from a 19th-century poem by Robert Southey that Powell liked to recite

to his crew as they started down the rapids in their stiff wooden boats.

Once through Lodore Canyon, the Green is met in **Echo Park** by the meandering Yampa River from the east. The swollen Green then snakes its way around Steamboat Rock and heads southwest through Whirlpool Canyon and Split Mountain Gorge, before emerging onto the desert plateau.

Yampa River—

Intersecting Hwy. 318 at Sunbeam, 7 miles northwest of Maybell, the Yampa River meanders west for 15 miles until it reaches the treacherous **Cross Mountain Gorge**. An incredibly demanding stretch of river for kayakers, Cross Mountain Gorge is only for rafters with a death wish. For 3.5 terrible miles, a virtually unending maelstrom eats rafts as it continually scours the rock canyon. The gorge comes out in Lily Park and continues to Deerlodge Park, a put-in point at the east end of Dinosaur National Monument. This is where most rafters put in for the Yampa River trip down through the beautiful **Yampa River Canyon**. Past alcoves and overhangs of canyon walls rising 1,000 feet, Yampa River Canyon twists and turns its way farther west. Along the banks in sheltered spots under rock overhangs, ancient campsites still show signs of fire pits, food caches and cryptic rock art. Downriver, Warm Springs Rapids shakes, rattles and rolls river mariners down to the confluence with the Green River at Echo Park. From here on it's a relatively relaxing ride down the Green.

Outfitters—

There are more than 10 commercial outfitters offering float trips on the Green and Yampa rivers through Dinosaur. Trips vary from one to five days in length. If you just want a day trip through Split Mountain Gorge, check with the park headquarters to see which outfitters have been granted that concession. For extended multiday trips, be sure to book far in advance, because the trips fill up. Listed below are some of the better-known outfitters.

Adrift Adventures—1816 Orchard Pl., Fort Collins, CO 80521; (303) 493-4005 year-round, 1-800-824-0150 summers only.

Don Hatch River Expeditions—First out-fitter in the area. Bus Hatch, the father of the current owner, began running trips for "dudes" back in 1936. PO Box 1150, Vernal, UT 84078; (801) 789-4316, or 1-800-342-8243.

Holiday River Expeditions—544 E. 3900 S., Salt Lake City, UT 84107; (801) 266-2087, or 1-800-624-6323.

Mountain Sports Kayak School—Barry Smith has begun taking kayakers down the treacherous Cross Mountain Gorge section of the Yampa River. Only expert kayakers should consider this trip. PO Box 1986, Steamboat Springs, CO 80488; (303) 879-8033.

Further Information—
For more information about the rivers and obtaining permits, write the superintendent at Dinosaur National Monument, PO Box 210, Dinosaur, CO 81610; (303) 374-2216.

—————— SEEING AND DOING ——————

SCENIC DRIVES

Although some of the dirt roads around the area can be driven in a regular passenger car, if it rains heavily, the desert clay becomes very slick and can make the roads impassable, even for four-wheel-drive vehicles.

Cañon Pintado—

Located in Douglas Creek Valley, just south of Rangely, Cañon Pintado is one of the finest areas in the state for observing the rock art left on the canyon walls by ancient cultures. More than 50 sites throughout the valley display rock art created by people who lived here as far back as 11,000 years ago. Most of the work was done by the Fremont people.

The canyon gets its name ("painted canyon" in Spanish) from friars Dominguez and Escalante, who admired the artwork while riding through the canyon. To reach the canyon from Dinosaur, head south from park headquarters on Hwy. 64 to Rangely. From Rangely, head south into the canyon on Hwy. 139. For more information about the canyon, contact the BLM White River Resources Office, PO Box 928, Meeker, CO 81641.

Cub Creek—

From the entrance to the dinosaur quarry 7 miles north of Jensen, Utah, begin

this scenic 12-mile drive to Josie Morris's Cabin. Morris moved to this homestead nestled at the foot of Split Mountain in 1914 to raise livestock, crops and fruit. For 50 years she lived here, visited only occasionally by friends and relatives.

On the drive in, the view of Split Mountain is as spectacular as the rock formations along the way. About 10.5 miles from the entrance, stop and inspect the impressive array of petroglyphs. A small road guide can be purchased at the entrance or at park headquarters.

Echo Park Road—

This is a highlight of the monument, offering beautiful canyons, panoramic views, rock art, history and even a cave. To get there, head north from park headquarters on Harper's Corner Rd. for 25 miles, then turn right on Echo Park Rd. Almost immediately, this dirt road begins a steep climb down into the canyons; many rocky side gorges head off from it. This section is impassable when the road is wet. After 8 miles on the dirt road there is a fork. Turn left. After a mile or so there is a place on the left side of the road where you can pull off and inspect the petroglyphs, which are chiseled into the rock at least 15 feet above the ground. You have to wonder how ancient people were able to get up there, but it seems likely they used ladders; also, the creekbed has since eroded at least a few feet. After another mile or so down the road, there is a turn-off at Whispering Cave. Once inside the arch-shaped entrance, the cool air of the cave may keep you there awhile. A crack in the rock at least a hundred feet high—and just wide enough to squeeze through—extends into the dark for a long distance. Bring a flashlight and see how far you get.

Another 2 miles down the road, you reach the confluence of the Green and Yampa rivers at Echo Park. The park gets its name from Maj. John Wesley Powell, who was the first to notice the incredible echoing qualities of the rock walls. Echo Park was better known at one time as Pat's Hole, named after the old Irish hermit who lived here until the early 1900s. Pat Lynch, who died in 1917 at the ripe old age of 98, was a loner who lived in the caves along the river until some local ranchers finally built him a decent cabin. According to many stories, Lynch made pets of wild animals in the area, including a mountain lion, which he would screech at—and then get a far-off reply. Perhaps the original

conservationist of the Dinosaur area, Lynch left these words scribbled on a piece of paper found by a local rancher's wife in a nearby cave:

If in these caverns you shelter take
Plais do to them no harm
Lave everything you find around
Hanging up or on the ground

Harper's Corner Road—

The view from the overlook at Harper's Corner is considered by many to be the most scenic in the state. A 2-mile round-trip hiking trail follows a knife ridge to an overlook perched 2,500 feet above Echo Park. Harper's Corner is named after a rancher who used to keep his herd in this natural corral. Steep cliffs served to enclose most of the corral, and all he needed was a short stretch of fence to contain his herd. The 31-mile drive on Harper's Corner Rd. begins at park headquarters. At the headquarters, be sure to pick up a copy of *Journey Through Time*, a guide to interesting points along the road.

WHERE TO STAY

There are no accommodations within the monument other than campsites, but there is a small motel in the town of Dinosaur and a few in Rangely. For a bigger selection, try Vernal, Utah, 13 miles northwest of Jensen, Utah, on Hwy. 40.

CAMPING

There are some great places to camp within the monument. All campgrounds are available on a first-come, first-served basis. There is usually no problem finding a site, except on holidays. The seven campgrounds can accommodate up to 200 people. Although some of these provide drinking water (none in the winter months), you should pack in your own to use for washing. RVs can use some of the campgrounds, but there are no hookups. Fires are allowed in the designated fire rings only. If you don't want to stay in one of the

designated campgrounds, talk to the rangers at park headquarters for other car-camping and backpacking ideas.

Deerlodge Park Campground is located just above the Yampa River Canyon. There are no individually designated sites. Most Yampa River floaters put in here for the trip downriver. No fee. To reach Deerlodge Park, head northeast on Hwy. 40 from park headquarters for 39 miles and turn left on Deerlodge Park Rd. Proceed 14 miles to the campground. From Maybell, head southwest on Hwy. 40 for 16 miles and take a right onto Deerlodge Park Rd.

Echo Park Campground (14 sites) is a primitive campground located in Echo Park at the confluence of the Green and Yampa rivers. This small meadow borders the river and is surrounded by sandstone walls and Steamboat Rock, a monstrous fin of sandstone around which the river flows. No fee. Echo Park Campground is reached by following Harper's Corner Rd. 25 miles from park headquarters. Take a right onto Echo Park Rd. (dirt) and go 13 miles. Echo Park Rd. is very steep in spots and impassable when wet. Big RVs and trailers should not try to drive it. For more information about Echo Park see the Scenic Drives section.

Gates of Lodore Campground (17 sites) is located at the north end of the park at the entrance to Lodore Canyon on the Green River. Most rafters put in here for a float down through the monument. To reach the campground from park headquarters, head northeast on Hwy. 40 for 55 miles to Maybell. At Maybell, turn northwest on Hwy. 318 and proceed 41 miles to a turn-off, heading left on a dirt road for 10 more miles to the campground. No fee; open year-round.

Rainbow Park Campground (four sites) and the primitive **Ruple Ranch Campground** (camping is allowed, but there are no designated sites) are located on the north side of the Green River, 26 miles and 31 miles respectively from the dinosaur quarry. The road in to these campgrounds is rough and impassable when wet. No fee. Both campgrounds have put-ins for rafters taking day trips through Split Mountain Gorge and the famous S.O.B. Rapids.

Split Mountain Campground (35 sites) and **Green River Campground** (100 sites) are the only modern campgrounds, located 4 and 5 miles east of the dinosaur quarry, respectively. Fee charged. This is where many rafters take out after a trip downriver. Split Mountain itself is quite a geological wonder. Waters of the Green River have somehow scoured and scraped away at the rock, splitting the mountain down the middle and baffling geologists at the same time. Interpretive campfire talks are given by rangers during the summer months. Split Mountain Campground is open all year; Green River Campground is open from Memorial Day to Labor Day.

SERVICES

Park Headquarters—
Superintendent, Dinosaur National Monument, PO Box 210, Dinosaur, CO 81610; (303) 374-2216.

Glenwood Springs

Indians, prospectors, gamblers, health nuts—throughout the years Glenwood Springs has attracted many types of souls, giving the area a colorful history matched only by the surrounding natural beauty.

Located at the confluence of the Colorado and Roaring Fork rivers, Glenwood Springs is best known for its hot springs pool. Originally used by the Ute Indians, the hot mineral springs began attracting wealthy miners and aristocrats from around the world when the resort was built in the 1880s. These bluebloods who came to "take the waters" received first-class service at the famous Hotel Colorado. For over 100 years, people have come to Glenwood Springs to get out and enjoy the surrounding mountains. Outdoor recreational possibilities here are endless. Great downhill skiing is nearby at Sunlight and Aspen. The surrounding White River National Forest offers backcountry paradise. The Colorado River running through the spectacular Glenwood Canyon to the east of town has some pretty good whitewater stretches for rafters. The list goes on.

Today tourism still dominates the local economy. In contrast to its up-valley neighbor, Aspen, Glenwood is a resort town characterized by affordable prices and friendly, down-to-earth people. Quaint lodging and memorable dining make Glenwood Springs a highly recommended destination for Coloradans and out-of-staters alike.

HISTORY

Long before the first white man entered the Glenwood Springs area, the Utes returned to the hot springs each season to bathe in the waters and enjoy the rejuvenating steam of the vapor caves. The Utes called the hot springs *Yampah*, meaning "Big Medicine," and jealously protected them from other tribes. The site held religious significance for the Utes, and they believed the waters had magical healing powers. Isolated from the white settlements to the east, the springs were not officially discovered until 1860. Capt. Richard Sopris was in the area to prospect, survey and explore. When a member of his party was hurt in a fall, the Utes welcomed the group to the hot springs and helped nurse the injured man back to health. Sopris named the spot Grand Springs.

It was not until 20 years later that the first permanent settler appeared. In 1880 James Landis, from Leadville, arrived and claimed the hot springs as his property. This took a lot of guts (or stupidity), because, at the time, the Glenwood area was still part of the Ute reservation. But the Utes were soon driven out. The land in the valley was rich and could be easily irrigated. Settlers began to trickle in, as well as frustrated miners from camps in the Flat Tops area. The town's name was changed to Glenwood Springs in honor of an early pioneer's hometown, Glenwood, Iowa.

In 1885 Walter Devereux began his effort to put Glenwood Springs on the map as a hot springs resort. Devereux was an engineer, educated at both Princeton and Columbia universities, who had been sent to Aspen to work for silver magnate and town benefactor Jerome B. Wheeler. He made his fortune quickly in the silver strikes at Aspen and then turned his attention to Glenwood Springs. Devereux incorporated the town and purchased the hot springs along with 320 acres on the south side of the Colorado River. Then, with the help of some English investors, he began to build the resort he hoped would bring a little class and culture to the area.

The influx of big money into Glenwood attracted a lot of questionable characters, and by 1887 there were no less than 22 bars within a two-block area. Among these high-profile low-lifes was Doc Holliday, the card-dealing, gun-toting dentist of Wild West fame.

Development was rapid. In 1887 the Denver & Rio Grande Railroad arrived in Glenwood Springs to much celebration, after blasting its way through the last 20 miles of Glenwood Canyon. The town now had contact with the outside world. By 1888 the world's largest hot springs pool was completed. Measuring 615 feet by 75 feet, the brick-lined pool was created by diverting the Colorado River. This unenviable task was given to the local jail inmates, who pounded away at "jailbird rock" in order to earn meals. The bathhouse was completed in 1890; it featured, among other things, a beautiful casino upstairs (used today as offices).

The icing on the cake was the completion of the Hotel Colorado in 1893, two months before the demonetization of silver and the onset of nationwide economic troubles. However, the hotel did not suffer much, as many of the guests were foreigners or the super-rich Astors and Vanderbilts. For more about Hotel Colorado history, see the Where to Stay section.

In the late 1800s a strange phenomenon developed in Glenwood Springs—the "dude cowboy." Many European aristocrats visited the resort and thought it only fitting to take a trip into the wilderness before returning home. Local cowboys made good money as guides and quite often tried to play tricks on these rich "city slickers." Sometimes the tricks backfired. Al Anderson, a famous local guide, tried to trick his customer, Lord Rathbone, by losing him in the wilderness. Miles from nowhere, Anderson took off on his horse through some impossibly thick brush. To his great surprise, Lord Rathbone kept up with him, saying only, "By jove, that was a lively canter!" Today, of course, dude ranches exist all over the West.

Glenwood Springs was well known for its polo teams at the turn of the century. The Glenwood Polo and Racing Association won the National Championship in 1903, 1904 and 1912. However, on more than one occasion, club members were trounced by a team of local cowboys riding cow ponies instead of thoroughbreds.

After World War I, hot springs resorts went out of fashion and Glenwood's glamorous days faded into a memory. Things weren't necessarily quiet, though. During Prohibition, the town achieved a questionable distinction by becoming a haven for Al Capone and other Chicago mobsters on the run.

History is everywhere in Glenwood Springs, and the town makes a great effort to keep historical buildings intact and renovated. The hot springs are *still* one of the best places in the state to visit for a relaxing vacation.

GETTING THERE

Glenwood Springs lies conveniently along Interstate 70, 160 miles west of Denver. It is easily accessible by car or train. Amtrak trains stop in Glenwood twice a day: one headed east and one headed west. Call Amtrak for more information at **1-800-USA-RAIL**. Greyhound Trailways Bus Lines has service to Glenwood Springs. Road construction on Interstate 70 in Glenwood Canyon, east of Glenwood Springs, can cause delays of up to a half hour on weekdays.

Aspen's airport, 40 miles up the Roaring Fork Valley, has daily flights from Denver year-round.

——— MAJOR ATTRACTIONS ———

GLENWOOD HOT SPRINGS POOL

Completed more than 100 years ago, this facility has been soothing everyone from saddle-sore cowboys to skiers ever since. You'd be foolish not to come and relax at the "world's largest outdoor mineral hot springs pool." Open year-round, visitors suntan on the grassy area in summer; in winter, the pool provides a steamy haven from the surrounding snow. There are two pools: the large one is heated to 90 degrees, and the smaller, therapeutic pool is maintained at 104 degrees. The hydrotube water slide is a kick. Towels and swimsuits can be rented. Also available is an athletic club, bathing suit shop and restaurant. The pools are closed the second Wed. of each month during Sept. through May. Hours are 9 am–10 pm in winter and 7:30 am–10 pm in summer. Located on the north side of the river. **401 N. River St., Glenwood Springs, CO 81601; (303) 945-7131.**

VAPOR CAVES

For hundreds of years before the white man "discovered" Glenwood Springs, the Utes brought their sick and ailing to utilize the healing qualities of the vapor caves. These caves, formed by hot mineral water percolating up through fissures in the rocks, have curative powers that supposedly alleviate a variety of ailments, from asthma to constipation. The original Ute cave was on the south side of the river. Last used in 1887, it was sealed over and now lies under the railroad tracks. Though such equipment is standard today, the caves were quite luxurious when first developed in the 1880s with marble benches and electric lighting. Back then, men and women had separate bathing times and wore linen bags with a drawstring at the neck as suits. Today, the Vapor Caves are privately owned and, in addition to the soothing steam, offer other services such as massages, facials and foot reflexology. Three caves are heated to a piping hot 115 degrees. Open every day of the year 9 am–9 pm, except Thanksgiving and Christmas. Located next to the hot springs pool at **709 E. 6th St., Glenwood Springs, CO 81601; (303) 945-0667.**

FESTIVALS AND EVENTS

Strawberry Days
mid-June

Since 1898, the residents of Glenwood Springs and the surrounding area have celebrated what is now the oldest civic festival in the state—Strawberry Days. The festivities have been expanded over the years to include such things as a pony express ride, western band performances, a 5K and 10K footrace and a mountain bike race. One thing that hasn't changed over the years is the free strawberries and ice cream. For more information, call **(303) 945-6589.**

Doc Holliday Poker Party and Dance
November

This off-the-wall celebration is a wake for Doc Holliday, the deadly gun-slinging dentist of Wild West fame. He died in Glenwood Springs in November 1887. The festivities include poker games with great prizes and a country-western dance. For more information, call **(303) 945-6589.**

OUTDOOR ACTIVITIES

BIKING
MOUNTAIN BIKING

Many of the trails listed as cross-country skiing and hiking routes are also fine for mountain biking. The possibilities are limitless. One area worth checking out is located northwest of **Dotsero.** Head east 18 miles on Interstate 70 to Dotsero and head north. Two roads, Coffee Pot Rd. and Sweetwater Rd., both head off to the left within a few miles, providing access to the Flat Tops area of the White River National Forest. According to an avid Glenwood mountain biker, "The Flat Tops is like a little northern Michigan plopped down at 10,000 feet, man." This translates roughly to "It's a great place to mountain bike." If you do head up to the Flat Tops, remember that no bikes are allowed in the wilderness area.

TOURING

The construction currently going on in Glenwood Canyon will benefit not only the motorist but also the bicyclist. A bike path, running the entire length of the canyon (about 20 miles), will trace the pathway of Interstate 70 and the Colorado River. Already the trail goes a few miles out of Glenwood and is definitely worth a ride.

To reach the bike path from the north side of town, head east on 6th St. past the Vapor Caves and keep going.

Rentals and Information—

Alpine Bicycle rents just about everything you need to get going, including touring bikes, mountain bikes and accessories. They can also give trail ideas. Open in summer only. **109 6th St.; (303) 945-6434.** Information and rentals also available at **BSR, 210 7th St.; (303) 945-7317.** Talk to Scratch and the boys.

CAVES AND SPELUNKING

The Glenwood Springs vicinity has the highest concentration of caves in the state, as well as what may be the largest underground river in the country. For years, cave explorers (spelunkers) have probed the vast, labyrinthine depths of these caves. Iron Mountain, just north of town, boasts a number of these caves, including Fairy Cave, Cave of the Chimes and Cave of the Clouds. Across the river to the southeast is Hubbards Cave, one of the state's largest, awaiting experienced spelunkers. Trips are organized monthly by

Timberline Grotto. For more information about these caves, contact: **Timberline Grotto, 508 9th St., Glenwood Springs, CO 81601; (303) 945-5053.**

FISHING

Colorado River—
Fishing in the Colorado River—west of Glenwood Springs for 19 miles to the small town of **Silt**—can be quite good for large brown and rainbow trout. West of Silt, the river becomes muddy and poor. In the deep water closer to Glenwood, large boulders alter the flow of the water; there are also some long riffles. Since the river is too deep for wading, fishing with lures and bait from the bank is the preferred method. Seven miles west of Glenwood Springs, Hwy. 6 breaks off from Interstate 70 and parallels the Colorado River, providing easy access.

Colorado River Cutthroat

Elk Creek—
This small stream flowing south out of the Flat Tops is a good place to catch smaller rainbows. About 13 miles west of Glenwood Springs on Interstate 70, Elk Creek flows into the Colorado River at the town of New Castle. From **New Castle**, head northwest on Buford Rd. which parallels Elk Creek. After 2.5 miles, turn right (north) on Forest Rd. 603. This road follows Elk Creek for 7 miles into the White River National Forest. There are plenty of places along the road to access the river.

Rifle Gap Reservoir—
No question this is a pretty place to throw a line. Clear blue water is hemmed in by sandstone and shale cliffs. At the north-shore midpoint, there are several camping spots and a boat ramp. Browns, rainbows and bass are all caught here. Keep an eye out for underwater spear fishermen, who like this area for the exceptionally clear water. It would be an ugly scene to accidentally snag one of those guys. To

reach Rifle Gap Reservoir from Glenwood Springs, take Interstate 70 west for 26 miles to Rifle. At **Rifle**, head north on Hwy. 13 for 5 miles to a junction with Hwy. 325. Turn right and continue 11 miles to the recreation area.

FOUR-WHEEL-DRIVE TRIPS
Climbing the mountains toward the Flat Tops to the north of town is **Transfer Trail.** From Glenwood Springs drive north on Forest Rd. 602. The views from the top of the mountain are fantastic.

See the **Aspen** and **Redstone and Crystal River Valley** chapters for other nearby roads.

GOLF
Glenwood Springs Golf Club—
A mature nine-hole course that enjoys a commanding view up the Roaring Fork Valley to Mt. Sopris. Pro shop, restaurant and driving range; carts available. **193 Rd. 131; (303) 945-7086.**

Johnson Park Miniature Golf—
That's right, miniature golf. This place, boasting two 18-hole putt-putt courses, is definitely worth a visit if you are with the family or just want to kill a couple of hours. Water cascades down a waterfall, winding its way through the only naturally landscaped putt-putt courses in the country. The rock and grass landscaping is well done and the creative holes are impressive. Skee-ball, picnic tables and snacks are available. Open Memorial Day to Labor Day, 9 am–10 pm; the months of May and Sept., noon–9 pm; Apr. and Oct., Fri.–Sun., noon–9 pm. **51579 Hwy. 6 (between Glenwood and west Glenwood); (303) 945-9608.**

Westbank Ranch Golf Course—
This nine-hole course has a pro shop and restaurant. Motorized and pull carts available. Par is 70, and the course plays 6,264 yards from the men's tees. **1007 Westbank Rd.; (303) 945-7032.**

HIKING AND BACKPACKING

Up the Roaring Fork Valley from Glenwood Springs, no less than four wilderness areas can be reached for day hikes and extended overnight trips within White River and Gunnison national forests. Possible trails in these areas are discussed in the **Aspen** and **Redstone** chapters. Contact the **White River National Forest Headquarters** in Glenwood Springs for maps, trail ideas, etc.: **901 Grand Ave., Glenwood Springs, CO 81601; (303) 945-2521.** **Summit Canyon Mountaineering,** located at **1001 Grand Ave., (303) 945-6994,** has rental equipment available as well as information you may need.

In the immediate vicinity of Glenwood Springs there are a number of memorable day hikes. Here are a few.

Boy Scout Trail—

This is a relatively short, easy hike that offers great bird's-eye views of the town, the Roaring Fork Valley and Glenwood Canyon. Near the turn of the century, an observatory was built at the top of the hill, and in 1910 the trail got much use as people flocked to the observatory at night for a view of Halley's Comet. The observatory burned shortly thereafter and was never rebuilt. The 1.5-mile trail begins at the dead end at the east end of **8th St.** Follow the signs.

Doc Holliday's Grave—

This is an easy half-mile hike that just about anyone can do. Linwood Cemetery lies on a promontory overlooking the town from the east. The view from the cemetery is great. Supposedly, the second person to be buried here was Doc Holliday, famous gambler and shootist from the Old West. Holliday came to Glenwood Springs in the spring of 1887 to relieve his tuberculosis. It didn't help. Holliday died in November of that year at the young age of 35. Friends pitched in to buy a casket and bury him in the cemetery on the hill. Controversy still rages about whether or not he was really buried in the cemetery or in a plot in town. At any rate, a stone marker in the cemetery commemorates Doc Holliday and says he "died in bed," a sentiment Holliday would have been proud of.

Few people know that another famous (infamous, perhaps) character from the Old West is also buried in the cemetery. In the pauper grave section, a stone with the name *Harvey Logan* marks the resting place of Kid Curry. He was a noted bank robber and a one-time member of Butch Cassidy's legendary Hole-in-the-Wall Gang. The trail to the cemetery begins at **12th St.** and **Palmer Ave.** A sign marks the trailhead. The hike takes about 15 minutes.

Hanging Lake—

An extremely popular hiking destination, Hanging Lake is both scenic and easily accessible. It was formed by a geologic fault that caused the lake to drop down from the valley floor above. It's fed by cascading waterfalls. The 1.2-mile trail climbs 930 feet from the floor of Glenwood Canyon, taking about one hour. It's worth the climb. Due to the large number of visitors to the lake, it is important to help preserve the beauty of the surrounding environment by sticking to the designated trails both on the way to the lake and once you are there. To reach the trailhead, head east for 10 miles on **Interstate 70** from Glenwood Springs. There is a pull-off parking area on the left side of the road.

No Name Creek Trail—

The No Name Creek Trail can be as long or as short as you want. Starting from the bottom of Glenwood Canyon and heading up the steep creek valley to the north, this trail follows the same tracks of some of the first pioneers who headed into the Flat Tops area seeking their fortune. For a day hike, the views of the valley below are quite scenic. Longer trips allow you to get rather creative. After about 11 miles the trail splits, one fork heading up East No Name Creek. The other trail bears left, heading up No Name Creek. At the top of the drainage, 3,700 feet above the valley floor, a loop back to Glenwood Springs is possible by meeting up with the Mitchell Creek Trail, which eventually reaches the fish hatchery just north of town on Mitchell Creek Rd.

There is good camping near the top of the trail. Water is fairly plentiful, but be especially careful on the first few miles of the trail not to contaminate the water, as it is the town's drinking water supply. To reach the trail, drive east from Glenwood Springs on **Interstate 70** to the first exit at **No Name**. The trailhead is on the north side of the highway.

HORSEBACK RIDING

Centennial Stables—

Ride your horse up the mountain on the north side of town to get a sweeping early-morning view of the town, the Roaring Fork Valley and looming Mt. Sopris to the south. These one- to two-hour rides are not a total wilderness experience but are quite pleasant and reasonably priced. The trail guides know their stuff about the outdoors and are interesting to talk with. Ask about the barbecue dinner ride and the Sierra brunch ride, both of which include a meal. Reservations are recommended. **1515 Donegan Rd.; (303) 945-1078.** For longer, multi-day pack trips and guided hunting trips, contact: **Larry Darien** at **Twin Pines Outfitting, 2880 County Rd. 3, Marble, CO 81623; (303) 963-1220.**

RIVER FLOATING

Colorado River—

As you probably know by now, the Colorado River flows right through Glenwood Springs, paralleling the highway on its way west. A 20-mile stretch of river that is very popular for floating goes from just below Shoshone Power Plant (in Glenwood Canyon), down through the canyon, through Glenwood Springs and downriver to New Castle. The Glenwood Canyon stretch has some fun rapids, petering out at the mouth of Grizzly Creek. The water down through town is nothing to worry about. Below Glenwood Springs, the river enters South Canyon, which offers some exciting rapids for the remainder of the way to New Castle.

Roaring Fork River—

The 13.5-mile stretch from Carbondale on down to Glenwood Springs along the Roaring Fork River is popular with many kayakers, rafters and canoeists. The rapids are fairly mellow (Class I and Class II), offering little unexpected surprises, especially for people just out for a leisurely float. The river drops an average of 27 feet per mile along this stretch, with many good places to take out on the north end of Glenwood Springs.

Outfitters—

Although many outfitters closed up when the construction activity in Glenwood Canyon began a few years ago, a number are still operating in the Glenwood Springs area. Consistently, locals have high praise for **Rock Gardens Rafting, 1308 County Rd. 129; (303) 945-6737.** Located at the No Name exit in Glenwood Canyon, they offer trips on the Colorado and the Roaring Fork.

SKIING

CROSS-COUNTRY SKIING

As with hiking and mountain biking in the Glenwood Springs area, the cross-country skiing possibilities are plentiful. Whether it's track skiing or a backcountry adventure, you'll find it close by.

For further information about trail possibilities, maps and avalanche danger, contact the White River National Forest Headquarters in Glenwood Springs at **9th** and **Grand, Glenwood Springs, CO 81601; (303) 945-2521.**

Backcountry Trails—

West Elk Creek, located about 16 miles northwest of Glenwood Springs, has a number of good trails on White River National Forest land. The trails head north, eventually reaching the Flat Tops Wilderness Area. To get to the trails, head west on

Interstate 70 from Glenwood Springs for 11 miles and turn northwest on Elk Creek Rd. at New Castle. Drive a few miles to **West Elk Creek Rd. (County Rd. 244)** and take a right. Trails leading to the right off this road begin after a mile or so.

Sunlight Peak and **Four Mile Park** snow trails are two other close possibilities. From the 10,603-foot summit of Sunlight Trail, views up and down the Roaring Fork Valley are fantastic. Four Mile Park snow trails are well maintained in winter for snowmobile use. If you don't mind sharing the trails with machines, you may like the area. The Four Mile Park trails extend to Grand Mesa, about 30 miles to the west. Both are located near the Ski Sunlight ski area. Take the right fork just below the ski area onto Forest Rd. 300. From the fork go about 2 miles to the Forest Rd. 318 turnoff to the right. Sunlight Trail begins here. About 2 miles farther up Forest Rd. 300, Four Mile Park snow trails begin.

Groomed Trails—

The **Ski Sunlight Nordic Center**, located at the ski area, has an extensive trail system that is well integrated with the downhill facilities. Cross-country trails can be reached from the Ski Sunlight base, as well as from the top of the Primo and Segundo chair lifts. Equipment rental and cross-country skiing lessons (including telemark) are available. Track fee. **10901 County Rd. 117 (Four Mile Rd.), Glenwood Springs, CO 81601; (303) 945-7491; toll free 1-800-445-7931.**

Spring Gulch Trail System is located 19 miles south of Glenwood Springs. Head south for 12 miles on Hwy. 82 to Carbondale and then west for 7 miles on County Rd. 108. See the Skiing section of the **Redstone and Crystal River Valley** chapter.

Rentals and Information—

Sturdy backcountry cross-country skiing equipment can be rented at **Summit Canyon Mountaineering** in Glenwood Springs at **1001 Grand Ave.; (303) 945-6994.**

DOWNHILL SKIING

Aspen—

Forty-two miles south of Glenwood Springs on Hwy. 82. See the Skiing section of the **Aspen** chapter.

Ski Sunlight—

"We are not high-tech ... we're high-touch," explains Tom Jankovsky, general manager of this family-oriented ski area just 10 miles out of Glenwood Springs. Offering good value in a laid-back atmosphere, Ski Sunlight is a great alternative to the larger resort areas on the western slope. Besides, where else can you ski all day and then soak your sore muscles in the world's largest hot springs pool?

Ski Sunlight's vertical drop is 2,010 feet. Runs are primarily intermediate, but there is something for everyone. Reasonably priced package deals include a lift ticket, lodging in town and a pass to the hot springs pool. Ski lessons and rentals are available. If you're tired of the glitz and high lift rates at bigger resorts, try Ski Sunlight. **10901 County Rd. 117 (Four Mile Rd.), Glenwood Springs, CO 81601; (303) 945-7491; toll free 1-800-445-7931.**

SWIMMING

Glenwood Springs Pool—

See the Major Attractions section.

———— SEEING AND DOING ————

MUSEUMS AND GALLERIES

Frontier Historical Museum—

Actually, this is a pretty good place to get a feel for the history of Glenwood Springs and the surrounding area. Information and artifacts about the development of Glenwood's Yampah Hot Springs, coal mining in the area and Teddy Roosevelt's visits highlight the displays. Upstairs in the Tabor Room is a hand-carved bed and dresser that once belonged to H.A.W. and Baby Doe Tabor of Leadville silver-boom fame. A small fee is charged for visitors over 12. Hours are Thurs.–Sat. 1–4 pm in winter, and Mon.–Sat. 1–4 pm during summer. The museum is located in a house built in 1905 at **1001 Colorado Ave.; (303) 945-4448.**

The Watersweeper and the Dwarf—
Local handcrafts that are unique and fun. Take time to browse. If you are interested in trains, especially the history of trains in Colorado, be sure to talk with Robert. **717 Grand Ave.; (303) 945-2000.**

NIGHTLIFE
Club Car Lounge—
Located in the Hotel Denver, this fairly upscale night spot offers jazz. **402 7th St.; 945-7160.**

Mother O'Leary's—
Live rock-n-roll nightly. **914 Grand Ave.; 945-4078.**

SCENIC DRIVES
Glenwood Canyon—
Although it's heavily used by trains,

bikes, rafts and cars, Glenwood Canyon is one of the most beautiful canyons in the state. This 15-mile-long, 1,800-foot-high canyon was carved by the Colorado River through layers of sedimentary rock, the oldest being 600-million-year-old Precambrian granite. The canyon is just east of Glenwood Springs on **Interstate 70.** Currently, the road is under construction, causing delays of up to half an hour on weekdays. In spite of the activity and change going on in the canyon, the scenery is still stunning.

Rifle Falls—
Located 39 miles northwest of Glenwood Springs, Rifle Falls stands out in this semi-arid part of the state. At the base of the 50-foot falls, lush green ferns, flowers and moss flourish. It's a beautiful place to visit. Near the falls are a number of caves ideally suited for novices (no pits or brain-twisting labyrinths).

To reach Rifle Falls from Glenwood Springs, head west on Interstate 70 for 26 miles to Rifle. At **Rifle,** head north on Hwy. 13 for 5 miles to a junction with Hwy. 325. Turn right and continue 11 miles to a sign that reads Entering Rifle Gap and Falls State Recreation Area. Turn right on this road to the campground where you will find a good map of the area. From here, it is a short hike to the falls.

——— WHERE TO STAY ———

ACCOMMODATIONS
Sweetwater Creek Guest Ranch — $$$$
Sweetwater Creek Guest Ranch near Gysum provides an excellent base for enjoying the nearby Flat Tops Wilderness Area. Streams rush down from the Flat Tops and are full of rainbow, German brown and cutthroat trout. Nearby Sweetwater Lake and dozens of smaller lakes on the Flat Tops plateau also provide outstanding fishing. The wildlife in the area includes herds of elk and deer as well as an occasional black bear.

Originally homesteaded by Jimmi and Mary Boni, the ranch has served as a post office and a stage stop. In the 1920s and 1930s, notorious New York gangster Diamond Jack owned a spread nearby.

The main lodge was built in 1904 and many additions have been made, making it a very comfortable guest ranch. Surrounding the lodge, with its kitchen and fireside meeting area, are five guest cabins. The ranch has many horses for short day rides or pack trips into the wilderness area. After a day in the saddle, relax in the swimming pool or the hot tub. The current host at the ranch, John Atwater, stresses that although the summer and fall are fine times to visit, the ranch is also open in winter for cross-country skiing and snow-mobiling on nearby trail systems.

Guests are required to stay at least one week in summer and fall. Winter guests can stay on a daily basis. The ranch is located 34 miles northeast of Glenwood Springs. For reservations and information, contact Atwater at **Sweetwater Creek Guest Ranch, 2650 Sweetwater Rd., Gypsum, CO 81637; (303) 524-9518.**

Hotel Colorado — $$$ to $$$$

If the walls could talk at this still-elegant old Colorado resort, the famous names it could drop would be mind-boggling. Since its grand opening in June 1893, Hotel Colorado has lodged and entertained notables from all over the world, including six US presidents.

Walter B. Devereux opened the hotel as the final stage of his dream of a world-class spa in the mountains. The hotel, which cost $850,000, was built Italian Renaissance style. Rooms went for $5 per night ($200 by today's standards). No detail was overlooked in making this a hotel for royalty. Devereux and the management thought the local labor market was a bit too unrefined and might offend the sophisticated clientele, so the front-desk crew was brought in from London and the restaurant waiters from Boston. A tunnel was built between the employee housing and the hotel laundry room to help guests avoid the uncomfortable and unpleasant possibility of running into the hired help. However, Devereux wouldn't tolerate distasteful behavior from any of his guests. Colorado steel magnate J.C. Osgood was at the hotel entertaining out-of-town industrialists when his wife, Lady Bountiful, consumed a bountiful amount of booze. The rowdy behavior that ensued got them a quick invitation to leave the hotel.

In 1905 the hotel became the White House of the West when Teddy Roosevelt came and stayed while bear hunting in the surrounding mountains. One day he returned empty handed from his hunt. The hotel maids sewed some old rags together and made a stuffed toy resembling a bear. They presented it to the president while he was giving a press conference in the hotel's Devereux dining room, and the newspaper people had a heyday with the bear, as did the public. The result was the birth of the teddy bear! At least that's the most common version of the story.

President William Howard Taft visited the hotel a few years later and greatly enjoyed the accommodations—especially the over-sized bathtubs. Just prior to his arrival in Glenwood Springs, this portly president had gotten stuck in a bathtub at the Brown Palace hotel in Denver.

As the 20th century pushed on, economic constraints forced the hotel to relax its decorum and admit the common man. Gangsters of the late 1920s were frequent guests. Mike Reilley, the present bell captain, said he recently talked to an old-timer who delivered illegal booze to the hotel during Prohibition. The man reported delivering a case of bathtub gin to Al Capone and Baby Face Nelson, who were staying in the Bell Tower Room. Capone tipped the man $100—enough to pay for his tuition and books at the University of Colorado for one semester!

During World War II the navy turned the hotel into a naval hospital. Wide hallways, therapeutic waters and good rail connections to the coast made it an obvious choice. The navy updated the wiring and plumbing—but also took most of the antique furniture and sent it to admirals' quarters around the world.

Today, this large hotel has been fully restored. No two rooms are alike. Take note: the deluxe rooms and suites, although a bit more expensive than the regular rooms and suites, are worth it. They are exquisitely decorated with antiques, while many of the regular rooms and suites tend to be a bit dreary. For history, ask for Room 230, where presidents Taft and Roosevelt both made speeches to the people in the courtyard below. The Bell Tower Room at the top of the hotel contains a spiral staircase and a sun deck. Guests in the Bell Tower Room are encouraged to carve their names in the bricks, a tradition started back in the 1890s. The hotel also offers dining in the Devereux Room and the outdoor courtyard cafe. **526 Pine St.,Glenwood Springs, CO 81601; (303) 945-6511; toll free from Denver, 623-3400.**

Hotel Denver — $$$

Conveniently located across the street from the Amtrak station, this recently restored hotel offers modern, comfortable rooms. Built in 1906, the Hotel Denver features art deco styling, lounge, restaurant and three-story New Orleans-style glass atrium. It is a plush and popular spot to get away in Glenwood. **402 7th St., Glenwood Springs, CO 81601; 1-800-826-8820 toll free in Colorado or (303) 945-6565.**

Adducci's Inn — $$

Opened in November 1986, this old Victorian home is a quiet stay. Gourmet breakfasts prepared each morning by Virginia Adducci. Candlelight dinners on request. Private bath in one room; others share shower. Located at **1023 Grand Ave., Glenwood Springs, CO 81601; (303) 945-9341.**

Sojourner's Inn — $$

Well-restored old home with great wooden porch. The rooms are tastefully decorated and spacious. The owner's arrowhead collection, which lines the walls upstairs, is quite impressive. Full breakfast is highlighted by homemade granola. **1032 Cooper Ave., Glenwood Springs, CO 81601; (303) 945-7162.**

Sunlight Inn Lodge — $$

A nice option in the winter when skiing at Sunlight, this out-of-town bed and breakfast is very reasonably priced and in a great location. During summertime, get out in the hills and explore the surrounding White River National Forest. Breakfast included. Hot tub on the deck; restaurant and lounge. Rates in winter slightly higher than in summer. For more information, contact: **10252 County Rd. 117,Glenwood Springs, CO 81601, (303) 945-5225, or toll free 1-800-445-7931.**

Talbott House — $$

"I don't care as much about the guests remembering my breakfast . . . I want them to remember me," explained Cherry Talbott, proprietor of the Talbott House. No problem. She really makes this place work.

Built about 1900 by a local miner, this home was fixed up and opened for business in 1985. Antiques and collectibles from Talbott's trips to various countries make up a large part of the decor. Upstairs there are four bedrooms (shared baths). On the back porch is a solar-heated hot tub. In the late afternoon, lounge in the living room or on the back porch and enjoy a drink and good conversation. By the time this book goes to press, the house next door (with private bathrooms) will be open to accommodate additional guests.

Talbott's dogs (two boxers) are very friendly—perhaps too friendly for many people. The female, Salem, thinks she's a boy, but her behavior can be discouraged by a firm "Down." Full breakfast served each morning. Smoking permitted downstairs only. Open year-round. **928 Colorado Ave., Glenwood Springs, CO 81601; (303) 945-1039.**

CAMPING

White River National Forest
Northeast of Glenwood Springs—

Drive east on Interstate 70 for 18 miles to **Dotsero.** Head north for 2 miles and take a left on Forest Rd. 600 (Coffee Pot Rd.) and proceed about 16 miles to **Coffee Pot Spring Campground.** Coffee Pot has 15 sites, no water and no fee. On up at the end of the road (another 15 miles) are **Supply Basin Campground** (six sites), **Kline's Folly Campground** (four sites) and **Deep Lake Campground** (21 sites). None of these has drinking water or charges fees. Supply Basin and Kline's Folly campgrounds are located on Heart Lake, Deep Lake Campground on the shore of Deep Lake.

About 8 miles north of Dotsero, take a left on Sweetwater Lake Rd. and drive 10 miles to **Sweetwater Lake Campground.** There are nine sites, drinking water and a fee charged.

White River National Forest Northwest of Glenwood Springs—

About 7 miles north of Rifle Falls State Recreation Area (see Scenic Drives for location) are Three Forks Campground (four sites) and Little Box Canyon Campground (four sites). No fee.

Private Campground—

The Hideout—For cushy camping, this place offers seclusion, close proximity to town, RV hookups and tent sites. Rental cabins with maid service are just the thing for people who can't decide whether they want a weekend in town or a wilderness experience. Winter sites and cabins also. 1293 County Rd. 117; (303) 945-5621.

WHERE TO EAT

Penelope's — $$$

Penelope's is, quite simply, a very pleasant place to eat. Located near the south end of town overlooking the Roaring Fork River, this restaurant is a dining highlight in Glenwood Springs. According to the manager, Randall Parsons, the restaurant "intimidated the locals at the beginning. They thought it might be too fancy." The building is Cape Cod-like, with a sun deck looking out on the river. Inside, the atmosphere is bright and cheery—wooden floors, picture windows with window boxes, floral watercolors on the walls and lots of hanging plants. The menu is varied, offering a large selection of fish and beef dishes. One menu standout is the pasta scampi. Daily fish specials; full wine list. Dinner hours are 5:30–10 pm nightly; Sun. breakfast served 9 am–1:30 pm. Bar opens at 5 pm. 2525 Grand Ave.; 945-7003.

Sopris Restaurant and Lounge — $$$

Perhaps the finest restaurant in the Roaring Fork Valley. Owner and chef Kurt Wigger spent 17 years tickling customers' tastebuds at the Red Onion Restaurant in Aspen before opening the Sopris in 1974. Originally from Lucerne, Switzerland, Wigger has professional chef credentials that include membership in the elite *Confrerie de la chaine des rottisseurs* of France. After serving celebrities such as Clint Eastwood, George C. Scott, Cybill Shepherd and Vince Bzdek, Wigger surely must have felt his life was complete when Jill St. John announced, "Kurt, I love your crazy cooking." It is impressive fare. Specialties include oysters Rockefeller, lobster Newburg, veal piccata Milanese and pepper steak flambé. The restaurant is a bit dark, unfortunately, with no view up the valley to Mt. Sopris. The dress code is wide open— some patrons wear jeans, others tuxedos or evening dresses. Located about 7 miles south of Glenwood Springs on Hwy. 82. Open 5 pm–midnight daily. 7215 Hwy. 82; 945-7771.

The Bayou — $$

"Food so good you'll slap your mama," declares the ad. Diving dinosaurs, Gary Hart Night, frog legs limboing under the flame of a Bic lighter and a zillion other twisted gimmicks helped this establishment get voted by the *Aspen Times* as "The best place to go down valley." Cajun food and wild drinks like the Woo Woo and Blue Bayou keep locals coming back for more. Asked why he came to Glenwood Springs in the first place, owner and New York transplant Steve Beham replied, "Tourist women." The sun deck is at the perfect angle for afternoon rays. Beham reminded us, "It's not the size of the deck ...it's how you use it." For guaranteed fun, check out the Bayou. Be sure to ask for the "abuse room." Open 4–10 pm daily. 52103 Hwys. 6 & 24; 945-1047.

Los Desperados — $$

The best all-around Mexican restaurant in town, Los Desperados is very popular, especially at lunchtime. Margaritas are good but not world-class. Very spacious, with a patio. House specials include the macho burrito, Jaime's biftec platillo and the relleno royale. It's best to keep Glenwood's Mexican dining opportunities in perspective. When asked where the best Mexican food was in town, more than one person responded, "At my house." Open Tues.–Sat. 11:30 am–10 pm, Sun. 4:30–9:30 pm, Mon. 5–10 pm. **0055 Mel-Rey Rd.; 945-6878.**

Rosi's Bavari Inn — $ to $$

What started as a dream for Rosi, a Bavarian, and her husband, Jim, evolved over eight and a half years into one of Glenwood's most popular breakfast spots. Recently sold to Kim and Mike Legge, the tradition of delicious pastries and breakfast/lunch cooking continues. For breakfast try the strawberry waffle or biscuits and gravy. Lunch notables include Reubens, quiches and bratwurst. After either meal, stroll over to the pastry showcase for turnovers, chocolate whipped-cream cheesecake or apple-raisin strudel, just to name a few. Pastries are available to go. Space is tight at Rosi's, and you can expect a long wait for a table during the busy summer season. Open Memorial Day–Labor Day, Mon.–Fri. 7 am–2 pm, Sat. and Sun. breakfast only 7 am–1 pm. Closed Mon. in winter. **131 W. 6th St.; 945-8412.**

Daily Bread Cafe and Bakery — $

Home-cooked meals with large portions characterize this popular breakfast and lunch spot. Each day, all of the breads and delicious pastries are made from scratch. Along with traditional breakfast fare, special items like granola and Huevos Extraordinaire are served. For lunch try their monstrous salads and bowls of homemade soup. Top off your meal with one of their famous chocolate chip cookies or a slice of cheesecake. Wholesome food, welcome atmosphere. Open Mon.–Fri. 7 am–2 pm, Sat. 8 am–2 pm. **729 Grand Ave.; 945-6253.**

The Devereux at the Hotel Colorado — $

A semi-formal yet affordable place o grab breakfast. This spacious room oozes h story. Chandeliers hang from high, arched eilings, and antique hutches are plac d throughout. Daily specials; also a g eat Sunday brunch ($$). Open for breakfast 7–11 am. Also open for lunch and dinner on a limited basis ($$ to $$$). **526 Pine St.; 945-6511.**

19th Street Diner — $

The atmosphere and most of the food is a blast from the past. 19th Street Diner, with its black and white checkered floors, booths and counter seating, serves up Americana with its blue plate special, chicken fried steak, honey-dipped southern fried chicken and hamburgers. Updated items such as fettucini Dinaldo and mozzarella sticks please the modern palate. Prices are very reasonable at this casual eatery. Full bar at the back. Dining area open Mon.–Sat. 6:30 am–10 pm, Sun. 7:30 am–3 pm; bar is open Mon.–Sat. 6:30 am–1:30 am, Sun. 7:30 am–8 pm. **1908 Grand Ave.; 945-9133.**

SERVICES

Central Reservations—
Toll free **1-800-221-0098.**

Glenwood Springs Chamber Resort Association—
1102 Grand Ave., Glenwood Springs, CO 81601; (303) 945-6589.

Grand Junction

It's difficult to explain why more visitors aren't aware of the Grand Junction area; it has so much to offer. Located in the fertile Grand Valley of western Colorado, Grand Junction is surrounded by diverse, rugged country just waiting to be explored. To the southwest is the stark beauty of Colorado National Monument and the canyon country of the Colorado Plateau. Grand Mesa, with its many forests and lakes, towers to the east. To the north, the bleak allure of the Book Cliffs captures your attention. There are so many enticing sites—yet the Grand Junction area remains an underrated vacation destination.

Exposed strata of the surrounding canyons and buttes attract geologists from around the country—but these layers of shale, sedimentary rock and red slickrock sandstone are so riveting, they catch everyone's eye. From within these layers, fossilized dinosaur bones have been unearthed since the turn of the century. Discoveries continue almost daily, giving paleontologists more work than they can handle.

To fully appreciate Grand Junction you'll want to get out and get involved in the natural surroundings. The whitewater kayaking and canoeing are outstanding in the area, while the wind- and water-scarred plateau country is perfect for mountain biking and hiking.

HISTORY

The Northern Ute Reservation occupied most of the Grand Valley until 1881, when the Utes were forcibly expelled from their lands and pushed into Utah to allow white settlers into the valley. Ironically, the town of Ute was established in 1881, only three months after the Utes moved west. The town's name soon changed to West Denver—a mere 258-mile commute to downtown Denver. The town eventually settled on a name taken from its location at the junction of the Grand and Gunnison rivers. In 1921 the Grand River was renamed the Colorado, and to this day Grand Junction remains a misnomer.

In 1881 settlers were initially drawn to the valley for the semi-arid land, which was perfect for pasturing cattle. By the end of that year, however, irrigation of the valley caused the rich red soil to spring to life. With new emphasis placed on agriculture, cattle ranchers were soon relegated to the high mesas. The young town began carving a niche as a trade center for western Colorado when the Denver & Rio Grande Railroad's main line started service in 1887.

Over the years, apricots, cherries, grapes and peaches have provided an economic mainstay for the town. Even though the economy has diversified over time, Grand Junction has gone through several boom-bust cycles. In the last 40 years, nearby uranium and oil-shale mining promised to turn Grand Junction into a major city. Hopes and regional pride ran high. (During the uranium boom of the 1950s, one travel writer even referred to the uranium mining as "a radioactive icing" on your "vacation cake.") Neither the uranium or oil-shale development, however, panned out. Both went bust, leaving Grand Junction with little more than dreams about what might have been. Having been burned twice by the economic fickle finger of fate, nowadays locals talk, hopefully but warily, of Grand Junction's becoming a major tourist destination. Maybe they're being too pessimistic.

GETTING THERE

Conveniently located on Interstate 70, 258 miles west of Denver, Grand Junction is serviced by Greyhound Trailways Bus Lines. Amtrak rolls through Grand Junction on its way to the west and east coasts. Walker Field Airport is becoming very popular with out-of-state visitors who are worried about air traffic and snow closures at Stapleton Airport in Denver. With Grand Junction's fine weather, Walker Field has not had a closure in five years. Direct flights can be booked from many locations around the country.

———— MAJOR ATTRACTIONS ————

COLORADO NATIONAL MONUMENT

Thousand-foot-deep red canyons and solitary rock monoliths characterize this beautiful monument and serve as an example of the force of wind and water erosion. Sheer sandstone cliffs and wide vistas have created a unique patchwork of colors, textures and shapes. To fully appreciate the muted contrasts of this national treasure, it's better to visit during low sun—in early morning or late afternoon. Once within the canyons, civilization seems light years away, even though Interstate 70 is only a few miles in the distance.

History—

We can thank a dedicated hermit for the creation of Colorado National Monument. For many years in the early 1900s, John Otto lived alone in the canyons while waging a one-man letter-writing campaign urging the creation of a national park in the area. The rest of his time was spent cutting trails and guiding adventurous tourists over the rugged terrain. Many of the trails Otto created are still in use today. Finally, in 1911, President William Taft proclaimed the area a national monument, and John

Otto was made the first superintendent. Later the same year, he was married at the base of 501-foot-high Independence Monument.

Getting There—To reach the east entrance to the park from the center of Grand Junction, head west on Broadway (Hwy. 340). Cross the bridge over the Colorado River and turn left at the monument sign. The west entrance of the monument can be easily reached from Interstate 70 by taking the Fruita exit and following the signs. Pick up a map of the monument and its hiking trails at either entrance. Open year-round; small entrance fee is charged per car.

Biking—

Rim Rock Dr. became known to professional and novice cyclists thanks to the Coors International Bicycle Classic, which until recently used the road during its race. It is an ideal touring ride, especially in the early morning when road traffic and heat are at a minimum. The smooth asphalt road draws cyclists fit enough to handle the severe change in elevation—2,300 vertical feet during the 35-mile loop from Grand Junction. For an easier 10-mile ride, start at the visitors center, ride to Artist's Point and return. Off-road mountain biking is not permitted in the park, but several adjoining areas are ideal for it. See the Biking section in Outdoor Activities.

Camping—

Next to the visitors center there is a first-come, first-served campground (81 sites) and a picnic area. A fee is charged in summer from Memorial Day to Labor Day; the campground is open year-round. Backcountry camping is permitted throughout the monument; register (no fee) at the visitors center.

Hiking—

A hike down into the deep canyons to soak up the sights and sounds of this place is something you will not soon forget. The desert is alive in small ways that require a closer look and more patience than city dwellers are used to. There are many trails snaking their way down into the inner sanctum of Colorado National Monument.

Short trails such as **Coke Ovens, Window Rock** and **John Otto's Trail** offer good views in an hour or less. A hike down popular **Monument Canyon Trail** requires 4 hours of your time. It is a well-maintained 5.5-mile trail that descends 600 feet and provides a close look at massive cliff walls and looming rock monoliths. Another long walk is **Serpent's Trail**. Located near the east entrance, the trail follows an old roadbed around 54 switchbacks in only 2.5 miles. The steep trail allows for sweeping views to Grand Junction and beyond.

Bring your own water for hikes into the canyons. In summer carry at least a gallon per day for each person. Do not drink the water you find in the canyons. No pets or fires are permitted in the backcountry.

Rim Rock Drive—

In the 1930s the Civilian Conservation Corps (CCC) shoveled dirt and blasted rock for 23 miles through the park to form Rim Rock Dr. Today the road offers motorists, bicyclists and even an occasional roller skater dramatic views from the northern edge of the Uncompahgre Plateau. The road, with its many turnouts, descriptive plaques and scenic overlooks, is a worthwhile and easy way to see the broad expanse of desert canyon terrain. There is a 35-mile circuit over Rim Rock Dr. from Grand Junction and back.

Visitors Center—

Located 4 miles from the west entrance, the center has exhibits and a slide show on the geology, history, plants and wildlife in the area. Knowledgeable rangers are here to answer any questions you may have. Restrooms and water fountains are available. Open 8 am–4:30 pm daily, year-round. For more information about the monument, contact the **Superintendent of Colorado National Monument, Fruita, CO 81521; (303) 858-3617.**

GRAND MESA

Located east of Grand Junction, 10,000-foot-high Grand Mesa rises more than a mile above the valley floor. Its 53 square miles make it one of the largest plateaus in the country. Lava flows, 400 feet thick, helped form the flat surface and protected the underlying sedimentary rock from the erosion so evident in this area of the state. Dotted with more than 200 lakes and covered with thick pine forests and aspen groves, Grand Mesa attracts a lot of visitors in summer. With its magnificent views and many recreational opportunities, it's easy to see why.

The entire mesa is part of Grand Mesa National Forest. Heavy snow in winter closes all roads except Skyway Dr., which runs north-south across the mesa. In summertime after the snow melts, activity on Grand Mesa reaches "grand" proportions. As one Grand Junction local says, "It turns into one big Winnebago parking lot." Al-

View from Rim Rock Drive within Colorado National Monument.

though that's an exaggeration, an autumn visit will avoid crowds while providing a look at the changing aspen.

History—

To the Ute Indians, Grand Mesa was known as *Thigunawat*, meaning "Home of Departed Spirits." Ute legend says the many lakes on the mesa were created by vicious thunderbirds that lived along the rim. Apparently, an irate Ute pitched several baby thunderbirds out of their nests and into the waiting jaws of a giant serpent in the valley below. The vengeful thunderbirds reacted by ripping the serpent to pieces and dropping the remains from high over the mesa. These falling chunks of serpent caused indentations, which filled with water and created the lakes. A more scientific explanation suggests the lakes were formed by erosion.

In 1879, following the nearby massacre of Indian Agent Nathan Meeker and some of his men, the Utes took five hostages up onto the mesa. Shortly thereafter, the US Cavalry arrived to negotiate the hostage release. The Utes surrendered and none of the hostages were harmed.

In 1881, when significant numbers of settlers began to arrive in the valleys below Grand Mesa, farmers realized irrigation was necessary to grow crops. A need for a summer-long water supply led to the building of many reservoirs on the mesa top. Nowadays these reservoirs and lakes not only supply water to the thirsty valley below, but also double as fishing holes. The mesa has developed into a cool summer retreat from the hot, arid valley below.

Getting There—To reach Grand Mesa from Grand Junction, drive northeast on Interstate 70 for about 20 miles and then east on Hwy. 65 for approximately 25 miles to the mesa. Another way to get up on the mesa from Grand Junction is via **Land's End Rd.** (open only in summer). See the Land's End Road write-up in this section for more information.

Camping—

There are 15 campgrounds with more than 300 sites on the mesa equipped with a variety of amenities. Those with more of the comforts of home charge a small fee; the more primitive campgrounds without water are free. All the campgrounds open in late June and close for the winter Oct. 15, except for Valley View Campground, open May 1–Sept. 30.

Hiking—

Crag Crest Trail is a 10-mile circular trail that is ideal for short day trips or full day hikes. The trail winds its way past lakes and through fir, spruce and aspen. The northern section of Crag Crest is the highest part of the trail. On a clear day you'll have great views in all directions: the Book and Roan cliffs to the north, the West Elk and San Juan mountains to the south and the La Sal Mountains far to the west in Utah.

Crag Crest Trail is restricted to foot and horse travel. Be sure to bring your own water or a means for purifying what you find along the trail. Camping is allowed at least 300 feet off the trail. Be sure to keep a close eye on children when approaching the northern section of the trail, as there are a number of sheer drop-offs on both sides. The west trailhead parking lot is located just off Hwy. 65 next to Island Lake; the east trailhead can be reached by taking Forest Rd. 121 from Hwy. 65 near Island Lake and driving to Eggleston Lake (about 5 miles). For maps and more information, go to the visitors center at Carp Lake, which is open in summer 9 am–6 pm daily.

Land's End Road—

In the summertime, a drive on Land's End Rd. can be spectacular as well as hair-raising. Land's End is located on the western edge of Grand Mesa, where it snakes its way down a sloping cliff on a series of seemingly endless switchbacks.

To reach the road from Grand Junction, head south on Hwy. 50 just past the town of Whitewater and turn left on the road marked as an access to Land's End Rd. The pavement ends after about 7 miles as you reach the Grand Mesa National Forest boundary. Follow the road as it winds its way up the side of the mesa. Eventually you'll reach an observation site, just to the left of the road as you reach the rim. From here the view down to the valley floor, thousands of feet below, is dizzying. Once on top of the mesa, continue on to the Hwy. 65 intersection.

From Hwy. 65 you can either re-trace your 53-mile route back down Land's End Rd. to Grand Junction or turn left and head north across the mesa and down the north rim. This route takes you past Powderhorn Ski Area, eventually hitting Interstate 70 about 23 miles northeast of Grand Junction. It offers some great views of the Book and Roan cliffs to the northwest and Battlement Mesa to the north. Both routes back to Grand Junction are about the same length.

Lodging—

There are several lodges on the mesa, but most of them are open for only a short time during the summer and early fall. The two listed below are open all year.

Grand Mesa Lodge is located on the shore of Island Lake, offering cabins that accommodate up to six people apiece. A tackle shop, a grocery store and a restaurant are on the premises. Boats and horses can be rented. For more information contact Kevin Swenson at **Star Rt. 205, Cedaredge, CO 81413; (303) 856-3211.**

JJCC Tuttle Ranch Bed and Breakfast sits just below the north rim, just off Hwy. 65, 3 miles south of Mesa. This 48-acre ranch offers full breakfasts and a large community room where you can mingle and meet other guests. Powderhorn Ski Area is a short 4 miles to the south. **865 Hwy. 65, Mesa, CO 81643; (303) 268-5864.**

Winter on the Mesa—

The mesa virtually closes up in winter. Hwy. 65 (Skyway Dr.) stays open, but Land's End Rd. is closed and doesn't reopen to cars until June. You can cross-country ski on most parts of the mesa, but be warned—there are a lot of snowmobilers. A cross-country trail system is maintained on the north side of Hwy. 65, about a half mile east of the junction with Land's End Rd. Powderhorn Ski Area offers cross-country as well as downhill skiing. For more information, see the Skiing section in Outdoor Activities. In winter, ice fishing on the lakes is very popular, not to mention successful.

For More Information—

Visit the **Grand Junction Ranger District, 764 Horizon Dr., Room 115, Grand Junction, CO 81506; (303) 242-8211.**

EVENTS

International Bike Classic

mid-August

For the past few years the best bicyclists in the world have sped through Grand Junction and Colorado National Monument every summer. Racers haven't forgotten the grueling ascent into the monument or the 1,000-foot drop-offs along Rim Rock Dr. Reaching speeds of up to 60 mph, cyclists have jockeyed for position on a road with a legal speed limit of only 25 mph. Spectators have been allowed into the monument before the intense road race begins. A French journalist dubbed this stage of the classic the "Tour of the Moon" because of the sculpted desert setting. Because the main sponsor of the race recently pulled out, the future of "Tour of the Moon" is uncertain. Race coordinators hope it will continue. For up-to-date information, call **(303) 442-7300.**

OUTDOOR ACTIVITIES

BIKING

MOUNTAIN BIKING

The area around Grand Junction is perfect for mountain biking, offering open spaces and unlimited BLM land for exploring. Little Park Rd. is a popular ride, with its canyons and many junipers. To reach Little Park Rd., take the road into Colorado National Monument from the east side. Turn left onto Little Park Rd. For more information about possible trails, contact the **Cycle Center, 616 North Ave.; (303) 242-2541** or the **BLM Office at 764 Horizon Dr.; (303) 243-6561.**

Rentals—

Try a mountain bike for a half day or a few days. Rentals are available at **Cycle Center,** but a $350 deposit is required. **616 North Ave.; (303) 242-2541.**

TOURING

See the Biking section, Colorado National Monument, in Major Attractions.

FISHING

Unfortunately, the fishing near Grand Junction is not something you should go out of your way for. Even though two of the state's largest rivers converge at the city, fishing is much better elsewhere. Tailings from the mines have altered the fertility of the fish and have killed off many.

There are more than 200 lakes on Grand Mesa. The fish begin feeding as soon as the ice melts from the perimeter of the lakes. Unless you fish early or late in the season you will have plenty of company on these waters. In winter, ice fishing is popular as well as productive.

FOUR-WHEEL-DRIVE TRIPS

John Brown Canyon/Moab Loop—

For a mellow day's drive, this is a bit ambitious. But for someone fascinated with the canyon country of the Colorado Plateau, it's time well spent. John Brown Canyon is a steep-walled slickrock canyon that winds its way to the Utah border. This area is *remote* and closed in winter. Make sure your gas tank is full and that you bring plenty of water; once in the canyon, there are no facilities for car or driver. For the necessary details, visit the **BLM** office in Grand Junction at **764 Horizon Dr.; (303) 243-6561.** *We strongly recommend that you use BLM and/or USGS topographical maps!*

To reach the canyon from Grand Junction, head south on Hwy. 50 for 9 miles to Whitewater, and take a right on Hwy. 141. Drive 44 miles to the town of Gateway and take a left after crossing the Dolores River. The canyon road is just upriver on the right. A four-wheel-drive dirt road leads west into Utah, following the north slope of the La Sal Mountains and providing a dramatic view of the spectacular Wingate sandstone of Fisher Towers to the north. The road eventually comes out on Hwy. 128 along the Colorado River northeast of Moab. Take a left to Moab or just turn right, following the road along the river to where it turns northwest and rejoins Interstate 70. Turn east on the interstate and return to Grand Junction, about 60 miles down the highway.

Rattlesnake Canyon—

See the Hiking and Backpacking section for details.

GOLF

Grand Junction's mild climate and beautiful views make it one of the best places in the state for year-round golfing. Winter snowfall is minimal and usually melts quickly. In the summertime, the town can really heat up, making early-morning or late-afternoon tee times a good idea. Here are two places to play.

Lincoln Park Golf Club—

A mature, nine-hole course with pro shop and driving range. Located in Lincoln Park at **14th St.** and **Gunnison Ave.; (303) 242-6394.**

Tiara Rado Golf Course—

This 5,907-yard, 18-hole course is fairly young but challenging. It's located on the west end of town near the entrance to Colorado National Monument. The views are spectacular. Pro shop, driving range and restaurant. Motorized and pull carts are available. **2063 S. Broadway; (303) 245-8085.**

HIKING AND BACKPACKING

There's no question about it: the Grand Junction area is the place to come in Colorado for desert canyon hiking and backpacking. Many of these remote canyons are as beautiful as Canyonlands and Arches national parks in Utah; there are just fewer people. For hiking among pines in the mountains try the **Crag Crest Trail** on Grand Mesa (see the Hiking section, Grand Mesa, in Major Attractions).

Rattlesnake Canyon—

This is one of the best-kept secrets in Colorado. Rattlesnake Canyon offers the second largest concentration of natural rock arches in the world, next to Utah's Arches National Park. At least 12 arches await you, carved by erosion in the Entrada sandstone of the canyon walls. The largest is about 80 feet by 120 feet. The canyon's remote location, underdevelopment (no marked trails, fire pits, etc.) and intimidating name keep most people away, so if you make the effort you may not see anybody. *Be sure to take water with you. Lots of it.*

To get to the area from Grand Junction, head west on Interstate 70 to Exit 19 (the Fruita exit). Head south to the west entrance of Colorado National Monument. Enter the monument and go about 11 miles. Turn right on a dirt road marked with the sign Glade Park Store 5 Miles. Proceed 0.2

Natural arch in Rattlesnake Canyon near Grand Junction.

miles, cross a cattleguard and turn right at the Black Ridge Hunter Access Road sign. From there, continue 11 miles and park your vehicle. Begin hiking the last mile to the canyon rim. From the canyon rim, walk south along the rim to the southernmost arch and descend through it. At the lower level, head down the canyon.

The road to the canyon should be attempted only by four-wheel-drive vehicles and only during good weather. When it rains the road becomes a slippery, muddy mess. For more information and maps, contact the **BLM** office in Grand Junction at **764 Horizon Dr.; (303) 243-6561.**

Other Canyon Hiking Possibilities—

To many people who have hiked and backpacked in canyon country, the scenery and positive overall experience are unparalleled. However, this deceptive country can quickly turn hostile and deadly to even the most experienced desert rats. The following backpacking trips should be undertaken only by seasoned hikers familiar with desert camping.

Mees Canyon, Knowles Canyon and **Jones Canyon** offer miles of remote hiking. Red sandstone walls and cottonwood groves characterize this desert canyon terrain, currently under consideration for wilderness area designation. The trailhead for Mees Canyon can be reached from the

Black Ridge Hunter Access Rd., on the way to Rattlesnake Canyon (see previous hike). Knowles and Jones Canyons are approached by taking the Glade Park Store Rd. out of Colorado National Monument. Pass the Glade Park Store and continue west on BS Rd. for 20 to 30 miles. *Obtain BLM or USGS topographical maps, directions and other important information from the BLM office in Grand Junction,* **764 Horizon Dr.; (303) 243-6561.**

RIVER FLOATING

Colorado River—

Though the Colorado River runs through Grand Junction, for the most part the stretches are very calm.

Upriver (northeast of town), **DeBeque Canyon** offers calm water with cliffs on either side. From the town of DeBeque, put in for a 32-mile stretch downriver. Be sure to get out before reaching the Grand Valley Diversion Dam with its 15-foot drop-off.

Downriver from Grand Junction the Colorado turns northwest near Loma and enters **Horsethief Canyon** (9 miles long), then heads southwest through **Ruby Canyon** (6 miles long) to the Colorado-Utah border. Both of these canyons are fairly calm and are rimmed by gigantic slickrock cliffs. Be looking for the Anasazi *mochi* steps carved in a rock cliff on the north side of the river near the border. Once in Utah, **Westwater Canyon** offers one of the wildest stretches on the Colorado River. A permit is required for Westwater Canyon. It may be obtained at the **Moab District BLM Office, PO Box M, Moab, UT 84532; (801) 259-8193.**

Gunnison River—

The lower Gunnison offers some good stretches of water as it flows northwest to Grand Junction before emptying into the Colorado River. For more information, see the River Floating section of the **Black Canyon Country** chapter.

Outfitters—

For trips down the Colorado River

near Grand Junction, contact **Adventure Bound River Expeditions, 2392 H Rd., Grand Junction, CO 81505; (303) 241-5633.**

SKIING

CROSS-COUNTRY SKIING

The lifts at Powderhorn take cross-country skiers to the rim of Grand Mesa, where an organized trail system heads into the backcountry. The Powderhorn Nordic Center grooms about 15 kilometers of trails within ski area boundaries. Gentle ski area slopes are excellent for telemark skiing. Rentals and instruction are available. Grand Mesa is a snowmobilers paradise, but many good cross-country trails exist and are kept fairly separate. For trail locations, see Grand Mesa in Major Attractions.

DOWNHILL SKIING

Powderhorn—
Logic would have it that downhill skiing near an area called Grand Mesa would be less than thrilling. Yet, surprisingly, there is a generous vertical drop of 1,650 feet at this ski mountain, only 35 miles east of Grand Junction. If you are looking for an area with a majority of intermediate runs, Powderhorn is perfect. While skiing, the stunning views from anywhere on the mountain are completely different than from any other area in Colorado. The ski area boasts far more trees, primarily spruce and aspen, than either the barren plateau in the distance or the valley below. Ski rentals and lessons are available. Base lodging remains limited, with most units being sold on a time-share basis. There are plans for a major resort in the coming years. It is also possible to stay near Powderhorn at lodges and motels, two of which are on Grand Mesa.

SWIMMING

Lincoln Park—
This outdoor pool is open daily from late May until Labor Day from 1:30–8 pm. Locker rentals are available. Small fee charged. **12th St. and Gunnison Ave.; (303) 244-1548.**

Orchard Mesa—
This indoor pool is open Mon., Wed., Fri. and weekends 1:30–8 pm; Tues. and Thurs. 1:30–5 pm. Admission fee. Open year-round. **2736 C Rd.; (303) 244-1485.**

TENNIS

Lincoln Park—
Eight outdoor courts are available on a first-come, first-served basis. No charge. Located in Lincoln Park at **14th St. and Gunnison Ave.**

SEEING AND DOING

DINOSAURS

Dinosaur Valley—
Enter the world of scientifically re-created dinosaurs with moving bodies, roving eyes and terrifying roars. There are eight half-sized replicas, including an Iguanodon, a Tyrannosaurus rex and a Stegosaurus. You'll come face to face with aggressive beasts that ripped their opponents' flesh with knife-edged teeth, as well as more docile vegetarians. Also featured are several dinosaur skeletons in the "death pose," exactly as paleontologists found them.

A working paleontological laboratory on the premises shows the painstaking work of scientists and volunteers on recent finds in the area. The lab has worked on some of the world's smallest dinosaurs (about the size of a rugby ball) to one of the world's largest, the Supersaurus, weighing in at 80 tons and standing 90 feet high. The Grand Junction vicinity is so rich in fossils that new discoveries come in almost daily. Dinosaur Valley is a special exhibit of the Museum of Western Colorado. Open May–Sept., Sun.–Tues. 9 am–5 pm, Wed.–Sat. until 7 pm; open Tues.–Sun. the rest of the year 10 am–4:30 pm. Small admission fee. **362 Main St.; (303) 243-DINO.**

On-Site Digs—

Here is your chance to go out in the field and do some work at an actual dinosaur dig. The Museum of Western Colorado organizes field trips, classes and workshops for interested parties. Call **(303) 242-0971.**

Walk down the Trail through Time at **Rabbit Valley Dinosaur Quarry,** located west of Grand Junction. Many sites en route feature uncovered dinosaur bones; several areas are under current excavation by professionals. Pick up a tour brochure at Dinosaur Valley Museum before heading out. Rabbit Valley is located 24 miles west of Grand Junction. Take a marked turn-off north from Interstate 70.

MUSEUMS

Museum of Western Colorado—

This museum offers a rare treat: free admission. Inside you'll learn about the history of western Colorado and, more specifically, of Grand Junction. The history begins with the woolly mammoth-spearing Folsom Man of 15,000 years ago and ranges to the present-day fruit farmers. Other interesting displays include the beetle/butterfly collection and a gun section that includes flintlocks from the early 1800s. The museum also has managed to get most of the pistols used by Mesa County sheriffs dating back to 1883. Dinosaur digs at nearby archaeological sites are organized and run from the museum. Open May 1–Sept. 30, Tues.–Sat. 10 am–4:45 pm, Mon. 1–4:45 pm; open the rest of the year, Tues.–Sat. 10 am–4:45 pm. **4th St. and Ute Ave.; (303) 242-0971.**

NIGHTLIFE

Gladstone's—

This is Grand Junction's where-to-see-and-be-seen spot. Gladstone's is a reasonably good restaurant, but is perhaps better known for its active nightlife. The bar section has booths, tables and plenty of barstools. Everything imaginable lines the walls and hangs from the ceiling, including old signs and a kayak. Behind the bar several TVs offer a nonstop look at the day's televised sporting events (even if the only thing on is the World Croquet Championships). A bar menu is available. Mingling is easy here. Be sure to ask about the bar's namesake, G.B. Gladstone. **2531 N. 12th St.; 241-6000.**

SCENIC DRIVES

Dolores Canyon—

From the town of Gateway (see following paragraph for directions), Hwy. 141 takes a swing south and begins winding its way up along the Dolores River in one of the state's most beautiful sandstone canyons. Over the years the Dolores has cut its way down through sedimentary rock, sandstone, mudstone and shale, revealing many-colored layers—a geologist's dream. The looming bulk of the slickrock and Wingate sandstone walls is a monument to time and weather.

Head south from Grand Junction on Hwy. 50 to the junction of Hwy. 141 at Whitewater. Turn west on Hwy. 141 and head to Unaweep Canyon. About 14 miles west of Whitewater, a dirt road (Divide Rd.) heads off to the left, leading up to the rim of the canyon for a good view. Continuing west on Hwy. 141 you'll eventually hit the town of Gateway.

Twenty-nine miles south of Gateway is a turnout on the right side of the road where you can get a bird's-eye view of the **Hanging Flume.** Constructed from 1889 to 1891, the Hanging Flume was built into the canyon walls to carry water to Mesa Creek Flats for hydraulic gold mining. During construction, workers clung to swinging ropes lowered as much as 400 feet from the canyon rim above. The 6- by 4-foot, 6-mile-long flume was an engineering success but a financial disaster.

Continuing south on the highway leads you into uranium country. Beginning in the late 1800s, the world began to see a use for uranium ore. In 1898 an order came from France for several tons of ore, which was then refined into radium by Pierre and Marie Curie. At Uravan, 6 miles south of the Hanging Flume turnout, ore was mined during World War II to supply the Manhattan Project, the US government operation to develop the world's first atomic bomb. Mining boomed in Uravan during the 1950s but died out in 1962, with the town soon following suit. Other abandoned mines can be seen in the vicinity.

From Uravan there are two ways to return to Grand Junction. The shortest way is to turn around and retrace your 88-mile route. Another possibility is to continue south through Norwood, Placerville, Ridgeway, Montrose and Delta. Though scenic, this route tacks on an additional 63 miles, for a total of 151.

Land's End Road—

See the Grand Mesa write-up in the Major Attractions section.

The Orchards—

The roads in eastern Grand Junction can be something of a nightmare if you are attempting to follow directions. Road names such as B, C 1/2, F and D 7/8 are common. To reach the graded dirt roads that plot their way into the orchards, head east on F Rd. out of central Grand Junction toward Clifton and Palisade. Driving into the orchards on virtually any secondary road, you will be able to view the rich peach, apricot, grape and cherry orchards. The fields are especially active during the harvest season: mid-July through Aug. Spring is particularly beautiful when the trees are blossoming. You really can't get lost because of the visible landmarks all around. Mt. Garfield and the desolate Book Cliffs lie to the north, Grand Mesa to the east and Colorado National Monument to the west.

Rim Rock Drive—

See the Colorado National Monument write-up in the Major Attractions section.

Unaweep Canyon—

If you have some time on your hands, this trip is well worth your while. It was through Unaweep Canyon (44 miles long and 2,500 feet deep) that the waters of the Gunnison and Colorado rivers once flowed. When the Uncompahgre Plateau began to push up through the shale about 8 million years ago, the water found a new course, leaving Unaweep high and dry. The canyon's steep rock walls and groves of cottonwood and pine make it a pleasant drive.

To reach Unaweep Canyon, follow the directions to Gateway in the Dolores Canyon write-up.

———— WHERE TO STAY ————

ACCOMMODATIONS

In the early 1880s the two most noteworthy hostelries in Grand Junction were called The Pig's Ear and The Pig's Eye. No wonder they went out of business. Thankfully, things have come a long way since the early days, and now there are 2,000 motel rooms to choose from. Just off Interstate 70 there are a number of easily identifiable and accessible chain motels and hotels. To reach most of these establishments from Interstate 70, take the exit for Horizon Dr. or North Ave. For an alternative, there are a few bed and breakfast inns that have recently cropped up around town. Listed below are a couple of the better choices.

The Orchard House — $$$

Quiet. If you really want to get away from it all, this is the place. Peach orchards surround this country home just 20 minutes east of Grand Junction. Get there in Aug. and you may be able to pick fruit from the trees in the owners' private orchard. Smokers welcome; dinners available. **3573 E. 1/2 Rd., Palisade, CO 81526; (303) 464-0529.**

The Gate House — $$

Drive under the stone archway and into a sanctuary of comfort, elegance and history. Carefully tended grounds surround the former gatehouse to Redstone Castle (for more information see the **Redstone and Crystal River Valley** chapter). The Gate House was built as part of the castle by coal baron John Osgood for his wife, Lady Bountiful, in the early 1900s. Some 40 years later it was moved, stone by stone, to its present location in Grand Junction. In 1988 the large, Tudor-style home was remodeled and given new purpose as a bed and breakfast.

The four guest rooms (two with private baths) are tastefully decorated with many personal touches. Each room is named Abbott and Costello style: are you staying in *My* room; is she in *His* room or *Her* room? You'll understand when you get to *Your* room at the Gate House. The downstairs common area has a small library and several sofas placed around a fireplace. A full breakfast is served in the dining room. We had a wonderful concoction of French toast with a cream cheese, peach and pecan filling. They also served fresh fruit, scrambled eggs, coffeecake, bacon, coffee and juice. The atmosphere is light and airy, and the innkeepers will make you feel at home. Children over 10 years OK; no smoking inside; reservations recommended. **2502 N. 1st St., Grand Junction, CO 81501; (303) 242-6105.**

CAMPING

For information on campgrounds, see Colorado National Monument and Grand Mesa in the Major Attractions section.

———— WHERE TO EAT ————

The Winery — $$ to $$$$

The Winery is a place where residents go to celebrate special occasions. Low lighting, interior walls of weathered wood and comfortably spaced tables provide an intimate setting. The menu is limited, yet carefully chosen. Dinners of freshly cooked prime rib, shrimp tempura, sirloin steak, mahi mahi or even lobster are prepared in an open kitchen. Wine is available by the carafe or bottle, though the list is not as extensive as you might expect. Open daily 4:30–10 pm; **642 Main St.; 242-4100.**

Los Reyes — $$

This small Mexican cafe isn't flashy, but is that ever a true measure of a good restaurant? Somehow, the plastic interior brickwork, fake Aztec artifacts and Mexican music blend well with the good food. Chips with three kinds of salsa (green tomato, chunky red tomato and onion, and taco sauce) go perfectly with a cold *cerveza Mexicana.* Los Reyes offers nine choices of Mexican beer. The large combination dinners are filling but not cheap. Most menu items may be ordered à la carte—for something different, try a stuffed sopapilla. **811 S. 7th Ave.; 245-8392.**

Panda Inn — $$

Fairly new to the Grand Junction area, Panda Inn is already at the top of the heap among Chinese restaurants. Szechuan and Mandarin seafood dishes are the specialty. The Taiwanese owners have kept the menu fairly un-Americanized, which is refreshing. Luncheon specials ($) come with soup, wonton, egg roll and rice. The booth seating is very comfortable and the service is great. Takeout orders are available. Open Sun.–Thurs. 11:30 am–9:30 pm, Fri. and Sat. until 10 pm. **1037 North Ave.; 242-1099.**

Sweetwater's — $$

Sweetwater's is a very popular restaurant serving northern Italian cuisine. It's located on the attractive Main Street Mall downtown, which resembles a scaled-down version of Denver's 16th Street Mall. The restaurant offers a small patio facing the mall that attracts a loyal lunchtime and cocktail-hour crowd. Menu items include pasta (especially fettucini), veal and pizza. A full bar includes house wine specials and a good selection of bottled and draft beer. Open Mon.–Thurs. 11:30 am–9 pm, Fri. and Sat. until 10 pm. **336 Main St.; 243-3900.**

W W Peppers — $$

Innovative New Mexican cuisine is featured in this extremely popular restaurant. Shredded beef or crab enchiladas, Santa Fe burritos and chimichangas keep the locals coming back. Also available are sandwiches, burgers and chicken dishes. A light southwestern decor is enhanced by skylights and many plants. Be prepared for waits of up to an hour during prime dinner hours. Open Mon.–Fri. 11 am–10 pm, Sat. and Sun. 5–10 pm. No reservations. **759 Horizon Dr.; 245-9251.**

Starvin' Arvin's — $

As you may have guessed by its name, Starvin' Arvin's is the place to deal with serious hunger. The prices are reasonable and the portions ample. Don't be surprised if the owner stops by your table to shoot the breeze. Arvin's biscuits and gravy are well known around town. In addition to breakfast items, sandwiches, salads, seafood and steaks are available. Service is fast. The restaurant is located just off Interstate 70 on Horizon Dr. Open daily 6 am–10 pm. **752 Horizon Dr.; 241-0430.**

SERVICES

Grand Junction Chamber of Commerce—

360 Grand Ave., Grand Junction, CO 81501; (303) 242-3214.

Transportation—

Greyhound Trailways Bus Lines, 655 Rood Ave.; (303) 242-6012.

Sunshine Taxi Service, 1000 N. 9th, Bldg. A, Suite 3; (303) 245-9013.

Grand Lake

Bordered by Rocky Mountain National Park, Routt National Forest and Arapaho National Forest, this attractive alpine village has little room for growth, but the 400 full-time residents seem to like it that way. Because of its location at the west entrance to Rocky Mountain National Park, Grand Lake sees an average of 3,000 visitors daily pass through in summer, its peak season. But the boardwalks, log-front stores and rustic homes speak of a quieter, more relaxed approach to life than do many other tourist towns. Indeed, the gem that is Grand Lake remains somewhat unknown and unpolished, but precious to those who want to escape the hassles of the city.

Located on the shores of Grand Lake, the largest natural lake in Colorado, the town also has two reservoirs, two national forests and a national park nearby. For those who prefer to look at rather than venture into the wilderness, Grand Lake, at an elevation of 8,369 feet, affords impressive views of the Continental Divide as well as a number of other peaks, especially the massive, bald Mt. Craig.

In winter, the closure of Trail Ridge Rd. (which winds through Rocky Mountain National Park) turns Grand Lake into a town at the end of the road. The crowds of summer have disappeared and winter sports are king. Snowmobiles share the streets with cars and four-wheel-drives. Though most of the stores in town are closed in winter, Grand Lake may be at its pastoral best then. Only 30 minutes from Winter Park and Silver Creek ski resorts, Grand Lake village is days away in atmosphere.

HISTORY

Ute Indians living near Grand Lake used trails along the North Inlet and Tonahutu Creek to travel east across the Continental Divide on hunting expeditions. At the same time, the Arapaho and Cheyenne came to Grand Lake from the plains to hunt elk and deer and to fish in the lake. Every once in a while the two tribes would run into each other and fighting would break out. It was after one of these legendary fights that the Utes began calling the lake "Spirit Lake."

The Utes were camping by the lake when a group of Arapaho attacked them. Greatly outnumbered, the Utes put their women and children on a fishing raft and told them to paddle to the middle of the lake, where they would be safe. During the fight, a storm blew up, the water turned choppy and capsized the makeshift raft, drowning all aboard. The Utes on shore were badly beaten; most were killed. From that time on, the Utes, believing the spirits of their dead haunted the lake, would not camp on its shores. Legend has it that the early morning mists seen rising from the lake are the spirits of the dead Utes.

The first resident of Grand Lake was Joseph (Judge) Wescott. He settled here in 1867, living in an abandoned trapper's cabin while building his own. Homesteading 160 acres on the shore of the lake, Wescott made a living by trapping and fishing. Supposedly, each morning he caught about 100 trout, which he kept alive in boxes; periodically, he packed them off to hotels in Georgetown for sale or traded them for supplies.

Except for an occasional hunting party or bands of Utes (with whom he was on friendly terms), Wescott had Grand Lake to himself. In 1877 a Denver businessman moved there with his wife and eight children. Several other families followed and the area began to grow.

In 1879 gold was discovered on the Colorado River about 15 miles north of Grand Lake. To reach the gold fields, well-provisioned prospectors crossed the Continental Divide from the east, along present-day Trail Ridge Rd. Those needing supplies followed a trail into Grand Lake, where they could load up before continuing their search for riches. By the end of 1879 Grand Lake had a hotel, a general store, a sawmill as well as many commercial buildings and residences. Along with this progress came gambling, prostitution and gunfights. A reputation for lawlessness kept many people away.

The boom was short-lived as the gold soon played out. By fall 1883, mining camps such as Lulu City were almost deserted. In Grand Lake, with bankruptcies the order of the day, only a handful of people remained. Only one business, James Cairn's general store, survived Grand Lake's depression.

There might not be any gold left in the mines, but according to legend, a treasure is buried just east of Grand Lake near Adams Falls. Three miners, on their way east from the gold fields of California, were carrying a small fortune in gold. Upon hearing an Indian war party approaching their camp at Adams Falls, they placed the gold in a Dutch oven and buried it by a large boulder and a spruce tree. The men then slipped away with plans to return for the gold, but all three were killed in the Civil War. One of the men left a map with his son, who came back and dug for the gold without success. To this day the gold has never been discovered.

Gradually, word spread of the area's beauty and its excellent fishing and hunting. As the 1880s drew to a close, Grand Lake prospered. By 1902 the area was attracting wealthy families from Colorado and surrounding states, who built summer homes along the shores of the lake. In 1905 the highest (at 8,369 feet) registered yacht club in the world was formed.

The biggest boost to tourism came in 1952 when the Colorado–Big Thompson Project was dedicated. The project created a series of dams, reservoirs, channels and a 13.1-mile-long tunnel beneath the Continental Divide to deliver much-needed irrigation water to the plains. In addition to smaller reservoirs, the project created Shadow Mountain Lake and Lake Granby, making the Grand Lake area an ideal water sports playland.

Ute scouting party crosses the Los Piños in 1899 (courtesy of the Denver Public Library, Western History Collection, photo by H. S. Poley).

GETTING THERE

Grand Lake is located 100 miles (about two hours) northwest of Denver on all-weather roads. Take Interstate 70 west to Hwy. 40 and turn north. Just past Granby head north on Hwy. 34 toward Rocky Mountain National Park. A highly recommended alternative, in summer, is a drive through Rocky Mountain National Park on Trail Ridge Rd. (see the Major Attractions section in the **Estes Park** chapter).

———— FESTIVALS AND EVENTS ————

Western Weekend Buffalo BBQ
mid-July

Patterned after old-time celebrations, the Western Weekend features a buffalo barbecue, as well as a parade down the 100-foot-wide Grand Ave., a fish fry and a lighted boat parade on Grand Lake. For more information, call **(303) 627-3402.**

Lipton Cup Regatta
early August

Shortly after the founding of the Grand Lake Yacht Club in 1905, English tea baron, Sir Thomas Lipton, was wined and dined by several of the club's members. They convinced him their annual regatta needed a trophy. He donated a solid sterling silver cup which today is worth $500,000. Each year members of the Grand Lake Yacht

Club compete for the prestigious Lipton Cup while spectators cheer them on. For information, call **(303) 627-3402.**

Annual Fishing Derby
all summer
Each spring a number of tagged trout are released in Grand Lake and Shadow Mountain Lake. When a fisherman catches a tagged fish, he takes it to "Peper," at the Stagecoach Inn in Grand Lake. He redeems the tag for a gift certificate worth about $25 from a local merchant. Each winner is then eligible for prizes drawn at the end of the summer. The grand prize is usually a fishing boat.

——— OUTDOOR ACTIVITIES ———

BIKING
MOUNTAIN BIKING
Although there are plenty of places to ride in the Grand Lake area, no organized mountain biking trail systems exist. In nearby Winter Park, however, there are more than 500 miles of marked trails, making it one of the top mountain-bike centers in the state. For more information, see the Biking section in the **Winter Park** chapter.

Rocky Mountain Bikes—
These folks rent mountain bikes, helmets and child carriers if needed. Familiar with the area, they can suggest many good trails. If you own a bike, the shop will watch it while you eat lunch or wander around the village. Open Memorial Day to mid-Sept. **1137 Grand Ave., Grand Lake, CO 80447; (303) 627-8327.**

FISHING
The Grand Lake vicinity is famous for its fishing. With Grand Lake, Shadow Mountain Lake and Lake Granby, the angler has a large area from which to choose. Arapaho National Recreation Area, which encompasses several lakes, provides 340 overnight campsites as well as public boat access. The recreation area headquarters is located in **Shadow Mountain Village, Grand Lake, CO 80447; (303) 627-3551.** Though there are many streams and the Colorado River nearby, the best fishing is in the lakes. Some experts believe state record fish are cruising the cold depths of these lakes. The possibility of trophy fish and the majestic views make these lakes a paradise. The local fishing expert is "Peper," co-owner of the Stagecoach Inn in Grand Lake (see the Nightlife section). He can tell you where the fish are hitting and what you'll need to bring in the big ones. There are several good tackle shops in Grand Lake.

Colorado River—
The stretch from Granby Dam down to the juncture with the Fraser River offers good fishing for brown and rainbow trout. Some browns up to 15 pounds have been taken in this area, but nearly all of the surrounding land is private.

Grand Lake—
As the largest natural body of water in Colorado, this 300-foot-deep lake offers rainbow trout, kokanee salmon and some of the largest mackinaw in the state. Mackinaws weighing more than 20 pounds are taken almost every year. Because most of the shoreline is private property, a boat is recommended here. Rainbows are more active in spring. Trolling and inlet fishing usually produce the best results, especially from early spring through mid-July. Wet flies and lures are good for brown and rainbow while sucker meat can tempt those mackinaw. Spear fishing can be good, if you don't mind cold (64°) water. When the lake freezes over in winter, ice fishing is popular.

Lake Granby—

The largest of the three lakes, Granby offers 41 miles of shoreline when full. Mostly rainbow, kokanee and an occasional big brown trout are caught. Mackinaw fishing has picked up in recent years and some over 30 pounds have been caught by lucky trollers.

Shadow Mountain Lake—

This shallow reservoir offers rainbow, kokanee and some mackinaw as its prizes. Because of its 20-foot depth, it is often choked with weeds in late summer but the fish are there. The reservoir is best for rainbows and browns through July with kokanee hitting later in the summer. The most popular areas for fishing are the submerged Colorado River channel and the shoreline. Ice fishing is often good.

GOLF

Grand Lake Golf Course—

At an altitude of 8,420 feet, this 18-hole course offers a challenge even to the best duffers. Carved out of aspen and pine forests and surrounded by the rugged peaks along the Continental Divide, the course has tight, tree-lined fairways. An errant shot will leave you with a lost ball, an unplayable lie or little chance of chipping back into play. Leave the driver in the bag at this course. Don't expect to putt well the first time out. The break of the greens is very confusing. Be sure to bring a sweater and rain gear, as seasonal storms can appear without warning. Greens fees are moderate. From Grand Lake, take Hwy. 34 north about a quarter of a mile. Turn left on County Rd. 48 and follow it about a mile to the course. **PO Box 590, Grand Lake, CO 80447; (303) 627-8008.**

HIKING AND BACKPACKING

Grand Lake, surrounded by Routt and Arapaho national forests and Rocky Mountain National Park, offers some of the most accessible and magnificent hiking in the state. Almost any trail here is sure to be a winner.

For more information, backpacking supplies and maps, check with Tim Randall at **Never Summer Mountain Products.** An experienced outdoorsman, he has lived in the area most of his life. Open year-round, daily in summer and Fri.–Mon. in winter. **919 Grand Ave., Grand Lake, CO 80447; (303) 627-3642.** The **Sulphur Ranger District Office** can also be of help. **62429 Hwy. 40, Granby, CO 80446; (303) 887-3331.**

East Inlet Trail—

This trail offers the day hiker several alternatives. Those wanting a short hike can stop at Adams Falls (0.75 miles one way). The falls offer beautiful scenery with awesome mountain backdrops. Those who continue along the relatively flat trail another 15 minutes will find themselves in a beautiful high-country meadow. It's a great place for a picnic and for photographing Mt. Craig. Those who can handle more uphill hiking can take the trail to Lone Pine Lake, 4.5 miles one way from the trailhead, or to Lake Verna, another 0.75 miles. To get to the trailhead from Grand Lake, follow W. Portal Rd. to the end, about a mile and a half from the Grand Ave. junction.

Rocky Mountain National Park—

A written permit is required for all backcountry overnight stays in the national park. These free permits, limited in number, are available at the **West Unit Office** all year (located at the west entrance to the park on Hwy. 34). The permits are given out on a first-come basis, but may be reserved by writing ahead of time. (See the Major Attractions section of the **Estes Park** chapter.) The following are three standout trails within the national park.

Colorado River Trail—The Colorado River Trail is an easy "up and back" hike that can be as long or as short as desired. It's a 2-mile walk to Shipler Park and 4 miles to Lulu City, an early mining town. When the national park was established, all the structures were removed as part of an effort to restore the area to its natural state. To get to the trailhead from Grand Lake, take Hwy. 34 north 8 miles into the park. Park at the Timber Lake trailhead sign. The Colorado River Trail begins on the left side of the road.

Timber Lake Trail—The 5.5 mile hike to Timber Lake is a little more challenging than the Colorado River Trail. This area is the only place in the United States where the Continental Divide makes a horseshoe, thus surrounding the Kawuneeche Valley, including this trail and the Colorado River Trail. For directions to the trailhead, see the Colorado River Trail (previous entry). The Timber Lake trailhead is on the right side of the road.

Tonahutu Creek/North Inlet Loop—A challenging 27-mile, three-day hike (down-right difficult in two days) is the Tonahutu Creek/North Inlet Loop, which takes you deep into Rocky Mountain National Park. The best way to hike it is to head east up North Inlet Trail. Proceed over Andrews Pass (in the neighborhood of 12,000 feet) to Ptarmigan Pass and Ptarmigan Point (12,363 feet) through Bighorn Flats to the Tonahutu Creek Trail and then back to the trailhead. The hike from Andrews Pass through Bighorn Flats (all above 11,000 feet) takes you along the Continental Divide for spectacular views. This trip definitely is not for the beginner. Camp in designated areas only. The trail leaves from the north end of the town of Grand Lake at the national park boundary.

In Indian Peaks Wilderness Area—
Since the Indian Peaks Wilderness Area receives heavy use from Front Range visitors, a backcountry permit is required for overnight camping. They are available at the **Sulphur Ranger District Office** in **Granby**. Call for reservations or check in to see if there are any last minute permits available. Many trails leave from Monarch Lake into the wilderness area. For more hikes in the Indian Peaks, see the Hiking

and Backpacking sections of the **Winter Park** and **Boulder** chapters. Here are two good hikes near Grand Lake.

Buchanan Creek Trail—A 9- to-10-mile hike of intermediate difficulty, the Buchanan Creek Trail parallels the north shore of Monarch Lake, then follows Buchanan and Cascade creeks to Crater Lake. You can camp and fish at Crater Lake, making the trip back the next day. Several opportunities exist for side trips off this trail. If you care to go to the top of the divide you can take Buchanan Pass Trail (veer north at the confluence of Buchanan and Cascade creeks) to 12,304-foot Buchanan Pass. It's about an 8-mile trip (*not* an easy hike) from the trailhead to the top of the pass. Another way to the top of the divide is Pawnee Pass Trail. Instead of turning south to Crater Lake, continue east 3 miles to the top of the 12,541-foot pass. To get to the trailhead from Grand Lake, take Hwy. 34 south to County Rd. 6. Turn left and follow the road about 10 miles to the trailhead at Monarch Lake.

Arapaho Pass Trail—This relatively easy trail follows Arapaho Creek to the top of the pass (approximately 11,900 feet). It's about 10 miles one way: The first 8 miles are easy hiking, with the last two uphill. This trailhead is also at Monarch Lake (see directions to Buchanan Creek Trail).

HORSEBACK RIDING
Sombrero Stables—
Horses are rented by the hour, day or week for trips into Rocky Mountain National Park. Special breakfast and dinner steak-fry rides are available as well as all-day Continental Divide trips. Reservations are necessary. Pony rides are offered for the kids. Open from the week before Memorial Day to mid-Sept. **304 W. Portal Rd., Grand Lake, CO 80447; (303) 627-3514.**

RIVER FLOATING
Although the headwaters of the Colorado River begin on the Continental Di-

vide just north of Grand Lake, there is really no rafting in the immediate area. Downriver, less than 50 miles away, is one of the most popular trips anywhere. As many as 40 outfitters make the trip from Pump House to State Bridge on the Colorado. You can make reservations with Rapid Transit Rafting in Grand Lake.

Rapid Transit Rafting—
Rapid Transit Rafting offers trips of moderate difficulty: perfect for the beginner but exciting enough to keep the experienced rafter interested. Though not mandatory, reservations are recommended. PO Box 1368, Grand Lake, CO, 80447; (303) 627-3062 or toll free at 1-800-367-8523.

SKIING
CROSS-COUNTRY SKIING
When covered with a thick blanket of snow, undiscovered in winter, the Grand Lake area offers outstanding cross-country skiing. Numerous trails into Rocky Mountain National Park and Indian Peaks Wilderness Area provide serene backcountry opportunities. Groomed trails in Grand Lake are readily accessible along with many other fine trail systems in the Winter Park area. Before heading into the backcountry, be sure to check with an expert about the latest snow conditions. Call or visit the **Sulphur Ranger District Office** in Granby at **(303) 887-3331.**

Backcountry Trails—
Green Mountain Trail—For this one-way trail, you may want to use two cars to shuttle between the beginning and ending points. Take one car to the Green Mountain Trail, about 3 miles north of Grand Lake on Hwy. 34 into Rocky Mountain National Park. Ski along Green Mountain Trail east (uphill) about 2 miles. When you hit the Tonahutu Creek Trail, turn right (south) for a nice 4-mile downhill run. Total distance one way is 6 miles. Pick up your other car at the Tonahutu Creek/North Inlet trailhead. To reach the trailhead, take West Portal Rd. about 0.75 miles to the Shad-owcliff Lodge turn-off. Turn left; the road dead-ends at the trailhead in less than a mile. If you want a longer, more strenuous trip, start at the Tonahutu Creek trailhead and do the trip in reverse and then return (6 miles each way).

Groomed Trails—
Ski Touring Center—Based at the Grand Lake Golf Course, this center features 25 kilometers of groomed trails on and around the course. In addition, a connecting trail leads to Soda Springs Ranch and more trails. Rentals and lessons are available. For information contact the **Metropolitan Recreation District, PO Box 590, Grand Lake, CO 80447; (303) 627-8008.**

Rentals and Information—
Never Summer Mountain Products—Talk to Tim Randall about rentals and guided backcountry trips. Open Fri. through Mon., but Randall tends to vary hours and days in winter. **919 Grand Ave., Grand Lake, CO 80447; (303) 627-3642.**

DOWNHILL SKIING
See the Outdoor Activities section of the **Winter Park** chapter.

SNOWMOBILING
Come winter, snowmobiles take to the streets of Grand Lake with the same rights as conventional street vehicles—so don't be surprised. Grand Lake boasts the largest groomed trail system in the state with approximately 130 miles of trails, in addition to deep powder riding. The system provides everything from simple trail riding to hill climbing. Numerous shops in the area that rent snowmobiles can give you information on where to ride.

TENNIS
Town Park—
Several public courts are located at Town Park in downtown Grand Lake. No fee.

Grand Lake Golf Course—

The Metropolitan Recreation District operates several tennis courts at the Grand Lake Golf Course. No fee; call **(303) 627-8328** for reservations.

WATER SPORTS

In addition to fishermen, the lakes attract many other water sports enthusiasts. Public boat ramps and marinas are spread out on all major lakes in Grand County, providing access for boaters and waterskiers. Along Hwy. 34, there are numerous rental outfits on the shores of Shadow Mountain Lake and Lake Granby. Lake Granby, with its constant afternoon winds, is a favorite of windsurfers and sailors.

**Whale Watch Tour
(Spirit Lake Marina)—**

You won't see any whales, but this tour of Grand Lake is still fun. As Tom Phillips and Walt Henderson regale you with tall tales, you'll learn a lot about the history of the area. There's really no other way to see the luxurious but rough-hewn homes built on the lakeshore. Take a sweater because it can get windy: even in the height of summer you may get cold. Tours leave daily at 10:30 am and 2 pm. If you want to take off on your own tour, the marina also offers boat rentals. Open from mid-May through mid-Oct. **1244 Lake Ave., Grand Lake, CO 80447; (303) 627-8158.**

SEEING AND DOING

MUSEUMS

The Kauffman House—

The Kauffman House in downtown Grand Lake, built in 1892 by Ezra Kauffman, was run as a hotel until his death in 1921. It was made with logs from the Kauffman homestead and constructed in parts; the first was a square, two-story building. Sections were added until it gained its present appearance. The restored house features displays depicting life in late 19th and early 20th centuries. Open in summer for free tours. Contact the **Grand Lake Chamber of Commerce** at **(303) 627-3402** for tour information.

NIGHTLIFE

Stagecoach Inn—

Founded in 1923, this rustic bar is one of the local favorites. With a warm, friendly atmosphere, it features live country and western music on summer weekends. The Stagecoach Inn boasts the only dance floor in Grand Lake. The bar also serves food. Open all year from 11 am–2 am. **920 Grand Ave.; (303) 627-9932.**

The Lariat Saloon—

Another local favorite is the Lariat Saloon. Occasionally, cowboys ride their horses to town, tie up right in front of the saloon and step in for their favorite drink. The saloon also serves food. Open year-round from 11 am–2 am; grill from 11 am–1 am. **1121 Grand Ave.; (303) 627-9965.**

SCENIC DRIVES

Trail Ridge Road—

This incredible 48-mile road through Rocky Mountain National Park crosses the Continental Divide at a lofty 12,183 feet. Driving over during the short summer season is an absolute must! See the Major Attractions section of the **Estes Park** chapter.

WHERE TO STAY

ACCOMMODATIONS

Grand Lake offers a multitude of places to stay—from rustic cabins and 80-year-old lodges to modern condominiums. Those listed below we feel have a special significance, but are by no means the only good places to stay.

Grand Lake Lodge — $$ to $$$$

This picturesque lodge, constructed from lodgepole pine in 1925, is situated on a wooded hillside overlooking Grand Lake and Shadow Mountain Lake. Guests can relax and enjoy the spectacular view from the long, open porch or plunk down in a lounge chair at poolside. Simple but comfortable two-room cabins are located around the main lodge. Larger families or groups are invited to stay in a cabin once used by Henry Ford. Continental breakfast served in the open dining room is included in the room rate (see the Where to Eat section). The lodge entrance is located a quarter-mile north of the Grand Lake turn-off on Hwy. 34. Open from Memorial Day through Labor Day week. For summer reservations, contact the Grand Lake Lodge, PO Box 569, Grand Lake, CO 80447; (303) 627-3967. Off-season, try 4155 E. Jewell, Suite 104, Denver, CO 80222; (303) 759-5848.

Lemmon Lodge — $$ to $$$$

Set on the banks of Grand Lake, Lemmon Lodge offers a private sand beach, access to the North Inlet stream and 21 cabins on five wooded acres. Each of the cabins is unique. Some have a full kitchen and cable TV; others are more spartan. This private hideaway is an ideal spot for quiet getaways and family vacations. Bring your boat along and slip it into the private dock. As the lodge is an extremely popular place, cabins are usually booked a year in advance. Open from the end of May through mid-Sept. For reservations (minimum stay requirement) contact the Lemmon Lodge, PO Box 514, Grand Lake, CO 80447; (303)

627-3314 in summer, and (303) 595-3733 in winter.

Rapids Lodge — $$ to $$$

Completed in 1910, the Rapids Lodge is the oldest existing lodge in Grand Lake. On the shore of Tonahutu Creek, this charming lodge is sure to be a favorite. A historic marker at the entrance to the parking lot gives information about the lodge. Owners Lou and Toni Nigro have worked hard to restore the lodge to its original appearance. Some rooms feature four-poster beds and claw-footed bathtubs. If so inclined, guests can step right out the door to do some fishing in the stream. In addition to the historic lodge, cabins and modern condominiums are available. Open all year. For reservations, contact the Rapids Lodge, PO Box 1400, 209 Rapids Ln., Grand Lake, CO 80447; (303) 627-3707.

Motel Waconda — $$

Mike and Leatrice Tacha own and operate this 1940s whitewashed, Tyrolean-looking motel that features 10 newly refurbished rooms. All rooms come with queen-size beds, cable color TV (one room has a VCR with rentals available in the lobby), and several have private fireplaces. The Waconda (a Sioux name for running water) is well known for its outstanding pancake house. Open year-round. 725 Grand Ave., Grand Lake, CO 80447; (303) 627-8312.

Shadowcliff Lodge — $ to $$

Operated by Warren and Pat Rempel, the Shadowcliff Lodge is perched on a cliff overlooking Grand Lake and the North Inlet stream, affording magnificent views. The lodge offers a comfortable, friendly atmosphere for the lone traveler as well as families. Many religious groups use the lodge for summer retreats; some dorm rooms are set aside for youth hostel members. Open Memorial Day through Sept. To get to the lodge from Grand Lake, take

W. Portal Rd. about 0.75 miles. Turn left at the Shadowcliff Lodge sign, then turn right at the next sign. Continue for a quarter-mile. For reservations contact Shadowcliff Lodge, PO Box 658, Grand Lake, CO 80447; (303) 627-9966 in the summer and (303) 355-1012 in winter.

CAMPING

In Rocky Mountain National Park—
To reach Timber Creek Campground from Grand Lake, go north on Hwy. 34 about 7 miles into the park. There are 100 sites and a fee is charged.

In Arapaho National Recreation Area—
Nearly 350 campsites are located within the recreation area and all charge a fee. From Grand Lake go south on Hwy. 34 about 3 miles to County Rd. 66. Turn left and go another mile to Green Ridge Campground (80 sites) next to Shadow Mountain Lake. Stillwater Lake Campground (145 sites) is located 6 miles south of Grand Lake on Hwy. 34, just off the highway on the shores of Lake Granby. Another mile south from Stillwater Lake Campground, turn left on County Rd. 66 and proceed 10 miles to Arapaho Bay Campground. Also on the shores of Lake Granby, this campground has 77 sites. To reach Willow Creek Campground (35 sites) from Grand Lake, head south on Hwy. 34 for 8 miles and turn right on County Rd. 40. Proceed 3 miles to the shores of Willow Creek Reservoir.

In Arapaho National Forest—
From Granby, head 3 miles northwest on Hwy. 40 and turn right on Hwy. 125. Proceed 10 miles to Sawmill Gulch Campground; five sites and a fee is charged. Another 2 miles up Hwy. 125 leads to Denver Creek Campground. It has 25 sites; no fee.

—————— WHERE TO EAT ——————

The Red Fox Restaurant and Lounge — $$ to $$$$
Although it has a reputation for inconsistent service, most locals agree the Red Fox Restaurant and Lounge has a wide variety of fine food. Chef Ron Kays oversees a kitchen that prepares such specialties as escargot, scampi, veal marsala and chateaubriand. Children's menu offered. Dinner is served at this hilltop restaurant from 5–10 pm. After dinner, patrons can go downstairs to the lounge and let that delicious food settle. Both the restaurant and lounge sport magnificent views of the lake and town. Open from May 15 through Nov. 1. 411 W. Portal Rd.; 627-3418.

Corner Cupboard Inn — $$ to $$$
Built in 1881 as the Grand Central Restaurant, the Corner Cupboard remains one of Grand Lake's historic landmarks. Owners Frank and Marianne Moulton and Allen and Jean Miller have taken great pride in keeping the history of the building alive. Specialties range from prime rib of beef to Alaskan salmon steak. In addition, the restaurant boasts a 28-item salad bar and an extensive selection of wines. Children's menu offered. After dinner, patrons can visit the adjoining Pub Room for some nightlife. Open for dinner Mon.–Sat. 5-11 pm, Sun. from 2–10 pm. 1028 Grand Ave.; 627-3813.

Grand Lake Lodge Restaurant — $$ to $$$
Located in the Grand Lake Lodge (see the Where to Stay section), the Grand Lake Lodge Restaurant offers a spectacular view of Grand Lake along with fine dining. The restaurant serves breakfast, lunch and dinner as well as a Sun. champagne brunch. A rough-hewn interior and the mesquite-grilled specialties will have you imagining that you are indeed back in the Old West. Talented waiters and waitresses perform

songs in between serving your dinner courses. Children's menu offered. Breakfast is served from 7:30–10:30 am; lunch from 11:30 am–2:30 pm, dinner from 5:30–10:30 pm. Sun. champagne brunch is served from 9:30 am–1:30 pm. Open from Memorial Day through Labor Day week. Located just off Hwy. 34 north of Grand Lake; 627-3967.

The Mountain Inn — $$ to $$$

When the urge hits for a meal like Grandma used to make, head for the Mountain Inn. Locals consider the Mountain Inn one of the best spots in town for down-home, country-style cooking. Specialties include real mashed potatoes, country gravy, chicken fried steak and biscuits. Top off your meal with a dish of old-fashioned ice cream. Open daily all year from 5–10 pm. 612 Grand Ave.; 627-3385.

The Rapids Restaurant — $$ to $$$

Part of the historic Rapids Lodge (see the Where to Stay section), the Rapids Restaurant offers fine Italian dining in a picturesque setting overlooking Tonahutu Creek. Big picture windows in the dining room allow you to watch the creek rush by while enjoying the house specialties.

There's also a piano, so if you can play (even just a little) don't hesitate to sit down and treat everyone to a tune. Favorite dishes among patrons include lasagna and manicotti (all pasta is imported from Italy) as well as prime rib of beef. Children's menu offered. Open year-round from 5–9:30 pm. 209 Rapids Ln.; 627-3707.

Scandinavian Kaffee House — $ to $$

This quaint breakfast spot, owned by Ed and Ginger Chadwick, is widely known for its popular specialty—Swedish pancakes with lingonberries. Although primarily a breakfast place, a few lunch items are on the menu. Hours are from 7 am–2:30 pm. Open Memorial Day through Labor Day week. 917 Grand Ave.; 627-3298.

Waconda Pancake House — $

Part of the Motel Waconda (see the Where to Stay section), the family-owned and operated Waconda Pancake House is a favorite among Grand Lake locals. Specialties include homemade cinnamon rolls, strawberry, blueberry and buttermilk pancakes and French toast. Children's menu offered. Summer hours are 7–11:30 am. The restaurant closes at the end of Sept. 725 Grand Ave.; 627-8312.

SERVICES

Grand Lake Chamber of Commerce—

The chamber of commerce visitors center is located at the intersection of Grand Ave. and W. Portal Rd. as you enter town. PO Box 57, Grand Lake, CO 80447; (303) 627-3402.

Meeker

Every autumn elk and deer hunters crowd into Meeker before setting off into the Flat Top Mountains to the east. The rest of the year, with the exception of July 4th weekend, this small town in the White River Valley is quiet. The only conceivable traffic jams occur when ranchers move large herds of cattle and sheep to new pastures along the local roads. Meeker is an offbeat vacation destination. Nearby there are several guest ranches. Camping, fishing and hiking opportunities are limitless in the White River National Forest and Flat Tops Wilderness Area.

Meeker's apparent resistance to change adds to its charm. Most ranchers in this wide valley enjoy a way of life similar to previous generations. This continuity, coupled with the fact that Meeker is in a rather remote location, has caused a rich local flavor to emerge. There is no question that residents are proud of their rock-solid community.

HISTORY

Meeker was named after the unfortunate Indian agent Nathan C. Meeker, who was killed on the afternoon of Sept. 29, 1879, during a Ute uprising at the White River Indian agency. The incident was not solely the result of a local problem; rather, it was the culmination of inevitable conflict between Indians and whites.

Nathan Meeker accepted the job as White River Indian agent in the spring of 1878. An idealist, he had been, at various times, a Greenwich Village poet, war correspondent, columnist and founder of a Colorado agricultural cooperative named Greeley. He wanted the Utes to stop their migratory hunting expeditions and to adopt the plow. The Utes, of course, had a different opinion about the sedentary life of farming. Distrust and resentment simmered as Meeker imposed his will during the first growing season. The next year he made a fatal mistake when he ordered an irrigation channel built through the racetrack where the Utes ran their horses. He also had some of their best horse pastures plowed under.

War clouds gathered over the White River Indian agency in the late summer of 1879. Meeker finally understood that his safety was in peril when his favorite Ute chief, Johnson, threw him against the wall of his cabin for his offensive suggestion that some of the Utes' ponies be killed to free more farmland. After this assault, Meeker sent a formal request for troops. A detachment of army troops, led by Maj. Thomas T. Thornburgh, moved in to support the agency. They were ambushed at Milk Creek by a small band of Utes, who swiftly killed Thornburgh and many of his men.

The Utes' anger turned on Meeker; they felt he was responsible for the advance of troops. In a blind rage, the Indians descended on the agency later the same day. They set fire to the buildings and killed all of

98

the men at the post. Meeker was found stripped and mutilated. The women, including Meeker's wife, Arvilla, and daughter, Josephine, were kidnapped and made captive for nearly a month on Grand Mesa. During this time they were raped, according to Ute custom, but eventually released. As a result, all Utes in Colorado suffered: the southern bands were relocated to reservations in extreme southwestern Colorado, while the northern Utes were banished to a barren wasteland in Utah.

The massacre took place 3 miles west of present-day Meeker by way of Hwy. 64. A roadside marker points the way to the exact location of the White River Indian agency. A military camp was established at the present site of Meeker after the massacre. The army maintained order until 1883, when it closed the post and sold its buildings to settlers coming into the valley.

GETTING THERE

Meeker is 227 miles west of Denver. Drive west on Interstate 70 for 185 miles to the Rifle exit. Turn right on Hwy. 13 and continue 41 miles north to Meeker.

—— FESTIVALS AND EVENTS ——

Range Call
July 4th weekend

More than a century ago cowboys started competing in the rodeo at Meeker. The annual tradition continues during the July 4th weekend as professionals prove their skills in riding and roping events. The final day is reserved for competition among local ranch hands. In addition to the rodeo, Range Call offers dances, concerts, footraces and, most importantly, the Meeker Massacre pageant.

History comes alive during the historical reenactment of the Meeker Massacre. Since 1938 the people of Meeker have dressed the parts of Ute Indians, Indian agency workers and the Meeker family. The pageant brings to life the painful clashing of the Indians with the intruding white settlers. Played out in the rodeo arena, the pageant ends with the Indians torching the White River Indian agency (with real flames), killing the male employees and kidnapping the women. The evening ends with a massive fireworks display. For more information, contact the Meeker Chamber of Commerce at **(303) 878-5510**.

—— OUTDOOR ACTIVITIES ——

FISHING

The best fishing in the Meeker area is east of town. Nearly all the lakes and streams discussed in this section are located in the Flat Tops Wilderness and other parts of White River National Forest. Meeker offers easy access to the Flat Tops, which encompass some of the finest fishing territory in the state. This 9,600-foot plateau is laced with many high-country lakes and streams. Since there are no roads in the wilderness, getting to the best fishing requires some effort on foot or by horseback. One word of caution: the fish in the Flat Tops are well fed by multitudes of insects that flourish in the waterlogged environment. From spring through fall, be prepared to encounter thick clouds of mosquitos.

We have chosen to include bodies of water that provide good fishing year after year. Remaining are countless fisheries in the backcountry, known only to longtime residents and guides. While many hidden lakes and ponds provide excellent fishing, some are unstocked and others face a yearly winterkill.

Since the terrain is virtually devoid of readily identifiable landmarks, it is easy to get lost or confused. *Maps and a compass are essential.* If you have ever considered hiring a guide or an outfitter, this is the place for one.

Bailey Lake—

If you want a smaller lake in the backcountry, this is an excellent choice. A 5-mile hike from Buford is required to reach Bailey Lake. It is another half mile to **Swede Lake.** Both lakes are considered good fisheries for brook and rainbow trout. To reach the trailhead, take Hwy. 13 for 2 miles east of Meeker. Turn right on River Rd. (County Rd. 8) and head 21 miles to Buford. The trail leads south from the community center in Buford.

Lake Avery—

We actually heard some complaints about catching too many fish at this large lake 20 miles east of Meeker. If you fish Lake Avery as soon as the ice melts, chances are you will load up on some good-sized rainbows. Fishing from the bank is possible, but trolling from a boat is the best method. There are campsites and a boat ramp located at the north end of the lake. Motorboats are allowed. Take Hwy. 13 east of Meeker for 2 miles. Turn right on River Rd. (County Rd. 8) and head 18 miles to the parking area below the dam. Or continue a mile farther to the turn-off for the Lake Avery Recreation Area.

Marvine Creeks—

Eight miles northeast of Buford, Marvine Creek flows into the White River on private land. County Rd. 12 follows the creek upstream 7 miles to the Flat Tops Wilderness boundary at Marvine Campground. Below the campground much of the creek flows through private land. Above the campground the creek splits into West, Middle and East forks with good trails following each. The West Fork of Marvine Creek provides ideal water for catching small brook, rainbow and cutthroat trout on small flies. The Middle Fork is wider and therefore easier to fish. The East Fork can be good, if you can put up with the brush along the narrow banks. From Meeker, take Hwy. 13 east for 2 miles. Turn right on River Rd. (County Rd. 8) and continue for 28 miles. Turn right on Marvine Creek Rd. and travel 7 miles to the campground.

South Fork of the White River—

Flowing into the White River near the town of Buford is the South Fork. A road parallels the river for 11 miles to the Flat Tops Wilderness boundary at South Fork Campground. From the boundary a good trail follows the river 16 miles to its origin. The farther you hike, the more beautiful the water and the better the fishing. Though the river is fast, there are many deep pools with lunker cutthroat and rainbows. Six miles of the upper section are limited to flies only. Stop in at the Buford Store and talk with Harry about his selection of small dry flies. He suggested we use a size 24 hook on the upper South Fork. Take Hwy. 13 for 2 miles east of Meeker. Turn right on River Rd. (County Rd. 8) and proceed for 18 miles. Turn right on South Fork Rd. and continue to the campground.

Trappers Lake—

Located near the northeast Flat Tops Wilderness boundary, this beautiful and easily accessible lake remains one of the best fisheries in the state. A pure strain of cutthroat trout reproduces naturally in the deep water of Trappers Lake. Boats without motors are allowed and may be rented at the Trappers Lake Lodge (see the Where to Stay section). Due to heavy fishing pressure, there are some special rules: the inlets (several) and the outlet (only one) to the lake are closed to fishing from Jan. 1 to July

31 to allow native trout to safely spawn; only flies and lures with one hook are allowed; any trout caught between 11 and 16 inches must be released. Four campgrounds with a total of 53 developed units are located near the lake. To get to Trappers Lake, take Hwy. 13 for 2 miles east of Meeker. Turn right onto River Rd. (County Rd. 8) and proceed 39 miles to Trappers Lake Rd., which ends at the lake 10 miles away.

White River—

This river's headwaters are at Trappers Lake (see previous entry), then it flows west through Meeker and eventually into Utah. The upper portion of the river, for 6 miles from Trappers Lake to Himes Peak Campground, offers good fishing for brook, rainbow and cutthroat trout. **Big Fish Creek** flows into the White River at the campground and can be excellent for small rainbow trout. Below Himes Peak Campground, the river enters a long, narrow swath of private property. The next stretch of public fishing is located on the river near North Fork Campground. West of Meeker, fishing on the White River is poor, and whitefish are the only catch. To reach the upper portion of the White River, take Hwy. 13 for 2 miles east of Meeker. Turn right onto River Rd. (County Rd. 8) and travel 39 miles to Trappers Lake Rd., which ends at the lake 10 miles away.

HIKING AND BACKPACKING

To the east of Meeker is one of the most underrated recreation areas in the state—the northern section of the White River National Forest. If you hope to hike and backpack among the state's tallest peaks, this isn't the place. It's a land of rolling hills surrounding the vast plateau known as the Flat Tops Wilderness Area, which never rises above 12,000 feet. It offers instead: few people, plentiful wildlife, excellent fishing and beautiful scenery. Thick stands of aspen and pine are interspersed with fields of wildflowers.

Just after the turn of the century, Teddy Roosevelt came to the Meeker area on a hunting expedition in country that is still home to herds of deer and elk as well as mountain lion and black bear. If you plan a multi-day backpack trip in this area, it would be foolish not to pack a fishing rod. Some of the streams and lakes in the national forest are what fishing dreams are made of.

Vegetation is lush and for a very good reason—it rains a lot here in the summer. Be sure to pack adequate rain gear. The mosquitos and flies can get thick, so bring some effective insect repellent. In autumn this is a popular hunting area, so it would be wise to dress in bright clothing.

You will notice the large number of dead Engelmann spruce trees on many of these hikes. A pine beetle epidemic a few decades ago wiped out whole stands of these beautiful trees. The dead trees that remain are not only a fire hazard, but they quite often fall down, especially in high wind. Try to camp clear of them. Also, there are a lot of sheep grazing in the Flat Tops area, so be sure to boil and/or purify all of your drinking water. Once up on the Flat Tops, the trails crisscross, making route possibilities endless. Here are a few of the standout hiking trails in the area. For more information about trail ideas, contact the **Blanco Ranger District Office, PO Box 358, 361 7th St., Meeker, CO 81641; (303) 878-4039.**

Chinese Wall Trail—

This trail begins at about 10,000 feet and runs south by southeast for 18 miles along the northwest border of White River National Forest. It then loops back around north for 7 miles to Trappers Lake. Along the way, enjoy far-reaching views into the White River drainage to the west and the Williams Fork drainage to the east. The trail winds its way through a few trees and quite a bit of high plateau tundra and meadows. Quite a few trails branch off from the Chinese Wall along the way. *Be sure to bring along a topographical map.* To reach the trailhead from Meeker, drive east

2 miles on Hwy. 13 and turn right on County Rd. 8. Drive 44 miles to the trailhead on the right, 0.2 miles from the summit of Ripple Creek Pass.

Marvine Trail—

This is a fairly long hike (11.5 miles), giving you a good sample of the Flat Tops Wilderness Area: good fishing, the rolling hills of the Flat Tops plateau and lots of pine and aspen groves. The hike up Marvine Creek is a very gradual climb, rising from 8,000 feet up to about 10,800 feet. There are a couple of stream fords necessary on the hike, and they can be tricky during spring runoff. This highly popular valley is also a good place to cross-country ski in wintertime. To reach the trailhead from Meeker, head east 2 miles on Hwy. 13, then turn right onto County Rd. 8 and drive 28 miles to Marvine Creek Rd. (County Rd. 12). Turn right, cross the bridge and take a left; proceed 6 miles to Marvine Campground and the trailhead.

Mirror Lake—

Located in a basin below some 1,000-foot cliffs, Mirror Lake, with its blue water and fantastic brook trout fishing, is one of the best short hikes in the area. The 2.5-mile trail climbs from 8,500 feet up to 10,000 feet, crossing private land in the process (stay on the trail). After about 2 miles you reach a lake with green water. This is Shamrock Lake. Continue on up the trail to Mirror Lake. To reach the trailhead from Meeker, drive east 2 miles on Hwy. 13 and then turn right onto County Rd. 8. Drive 39 miles to Trappers Lake Rd. (Forest Rd. 205). Turn right at Trappers Lake Rd. and drive half a mile to the Mirror Lake Trailhead access road. Turn right and drive a quarter mile to the trailhead.

Peltier Lake Trail—

This 6.5-mile trail (one way) climbs through oak brush and aspen groves as it rises to about 9,000 feet. After 3.5 miles, the trail passes Peltier Lake and after another 3 miles, Bailey Lake. Both lakes offer good fishing for brookies and rainbow trout. To reach the trailhead from Meeker, head east on Hwy. 13 for 2 miles and then right on County Rd. 8 for 18 miles. Turn right on South Fork Rd. and drive 10 miles to the Peltier Lake Trailhead on the left.

Skinny Fish Lake/ McGinnis Lake Trail—

This short 2.5-mile trail (one way) branches to the two lakes half a mile below Skinny Fish Lake. Located in the Flat Tops Wilderness Area, these lakes get heavy use from horse packers and hikers because the fishing is good. Either of the lakes makes for a great day hike. There are a lot of beetle-killed trees in the area. Also, be on the lookout for aspen trees that have been written on. In the late 1940s a Greek shepherd named Nick "Theo" Theopolis killed time (and maybe a few trees) by writing a daily diary entry on the aspen. ("Today I saw a coyote ... but not a problem ... looks like rain.") To reach the trailhead from Meeker, drive east 2 miles on Hwy. 13. Take a right at County Rd. 8 and drive 39 miles to Trappers Lake Rd. (Forest Rd. 205). Turn right and continue 8 miles. Pull in at the Skinny Fish Lake Trailhead parking area on the left. Walk a mile up the Lost Lakes Trail to the Skinny Fish Lake Trail intersection, which heads off to the right.

Spring Cave Trail—

A short half-mile hike from South Fork Campground leads to Spring Cave, the second largest cave in Colorado. From the campground the trail crosses the White River through blue spruce and climbs into aspen about halfway to the cave. Exploring the cave (spelunking) is definitely not suggested unless you are experienced! It's easy to get lost. To reach the trailhead from Meeker, drive 2 miles east of town on Hwy. 13 and take the right fork onto County Rd. 8. Proceed 18 miles to South Fork Rd. (County Rd. 10) and turn right. Drive 12 miles to the South Fork Campground. The trailhead begins here.

Trappers Lake Trail—

This trail begins at Trappers Lake. It

follows the pine forests along Fraser Creek up into the alpine tundra of the Flat Tops plateau, about 5.5 miles from the lake. The trail extends about 16 miles (one way), and there is good camping along most of the way. You can make your trip as long or as short as you want. There are numerous trails intersecting the Trappers Lake Trail, so a good map of the area can let you play it by ear and take side trips. Fishing in the endless potholes on the plateau is worth your while because the fish are often biting. To reach the trailhead from Meeker, drive 2 miles east on Hwy. 13 and turn right onto County Rd. 8. Drive 39 miles to Trappers Lake Rd. (Forest Rd. 205). Turn right and drive 10 miles to Trappers Lake and the trailhead.

HORSEBACK RIDING

White River National Forest has over 250 miles of maintained trails that are perfect for riding. Many outfitters can take you into the backcountry for hunting and fishing expeditions as well as for shorter rides. Consider staying in a local guest ranch if you want to experience western

hospitality and saddle sores. Rental horses are available from each of the following:

Fritzlan's Guest Ranch—
1891 County Rd. 12, Meeker, CO 81641; (303) 878-4845.

Bill Krimmel—
13246 County Rd. 8, Meeker, CO 81641; (303) 878-5370.

Sleepy Cat Guest Ranch—
Trappers Lake Lodge—
Both are described in detail in the Where to Stay section.

SKIING
CROSS-COUNTRY SKIING

You will be more apt to find a rental snowmobile than a pair of touring skis in the Meeker area. Even so, there is some beautiful and remote cross-country skiing in the Flat Tops Wilderness Area just east of Meeker. For trail ideas, see the Hiking and Backpacking section.

——— SEEING AND DOING ———

MUSEUMS
White River Museum—
A visit to this museum is far better than climbing up into Grandma's attic. The museum is housed in a former US Cavalry garrison. Inside is a hodge-podge of artifacts and memorabilia from the long history of the area. The friendly museum curator said truthfully, "We've got a little bit of everything." You'll see a can of carrots from 1938, a bottle collection, a bear coat and a copper still from the 1920s. Prominently displayed is the plow that Nathan Meeker used to destroy the Ute Indians' racetrack. Don't miss the Spanish war ax or the carving in aspen bark of a pretty woman by local sheepherder Pacino Chacon. In the back room are a bright-red fire truck, horse-drawn carriages and a

mounted two-headed calf. No fee charged, but donations are accepted. Open in summer Mon.–Sat. 9 am–5 pm, Sun. by special appointment. Winter hours: Mon.–Sat. 10 am–4 pm.

WHERE TO STAY

ACCOMMODATIONS

7-Lakes Ranch — $$$

Locked away in the woods, in the midst of rolling hills, this ranch offers its guests plenty of peace and quiet. Fishing on private lakes spread throughout the property can be very productive. Only flies and single-hook lures are allowed. Horses are saddled for guests at an additional charge. Five cabins and a maximum of 16 guests make this quiet getaway a very personal experience. "Meals like you'd expect at Mom's house" are served three times daily in the main lodge. In winter many guests bring their cross-country skis; others bring their snowmobiles. The host, Rick Wilson, will meet you at the road with his snowmobile because the ranch road is not plowed. Seven-Lakes is located several miles south of Buford on private property surrounded by White River National Forest. Reservations only. **738 County Rd. 59, Meeker, CO 81641; (303) 878-4772.**

Sleepy Cat Guest Ranch — $$

Located 18 miles east of Meeker in the White River Valley, Sleepy Cat has been putting up families and sportsmen for the last 50 years. Twenty-one cabins with kitchenettes are rented by the night or by the week. The restaurant attracts people from miles away for great food and drink (see the Where to Eat section). Unlike some guest ranches, Sleepy Cat does not have an organized plan of activities for the week. The ranch sits near the edge of the Flat Tops Wilderness Area and offers outstanding fishing, hunting and cross-country skiing. Horses can be rented from an outfitter a half mile away. The people running Sleepy Cat are friendly, and the price is a pittance for what you are getting. The only drawback, if you want a secluded mountain experience, is that Sleepy Cat is fairly close to a main road. From Meeker, take Hwy. 13 east for 2 miles. Turn right on County Rd. 8 and continue for 16 miles to the ranch. **16064 County Rd. 8, Meeker, CO 81641; (303) 878-4413.**

Snow Goose Bed and Breakfast — $$

Built in the 1890s, this small, brick house on a corner lot in residential Meeker offers a unique kind of comfort. Three upstairs bedrooms are decorated with the kind of detail you would expect to find between the pages of a glossy decorating magazine. Little touches make the whole experience stand out: on the bed you will find a hand-crocheted linen cover or a plush down comforter; quilts hang on the wall. Three rooms share two spotless bathrooms. Guests are welcome in the downstairs common room except late in the evening. Breakfast is served in your room, in the breakfast nook or, weather permitting, outside on the covered porch. One recent guest said the Snow Goose has a "dreamlike quality." That just about says it all. No smoking; older children considered. **687 Garfield St., Meeker, CO 81641; (303) 878-4532.**

Trappers Lake Lodge — $$

Tired of modern comforts? This collection of 14 rustic cabins offers no indoor plumbing. Each cabin has a coal stove for cooking and heating. The owner pointed out, "They're not modern, but they're clean." A central bathhouse has modern restrooms and hot showers. The cabins are located near the banks of one of Colorado's most beautiful and productive fisheries (see page 100). Rowboats, canoes and horses are available to rent by the hour or by the day. Ranch-style meals are served with advance reservations. The Trappers Lake Lodge is located near the northeast Flat Tops Wilderness boundary. Open from June through mid-Nov. To get there, take Hwy. 13 for 2 miles east of Meeker. Turn right at River Rd. (County Rd. 8) and head 39 miles to Trappers Lake Rd., which ends near the lodge 10 miles away. For more information write: **7700 Trappers Lake Rd.,**

PO Box 1147, Meeker, CO 81641; (303) 878-3336.

Meeker Hotel — $ to $$

Even if you are just passing through, stop off at this 90-year-old hotel and take a look around the lobby. Once inside, your every move is watched by 30 pairs of glass eyes from within the stuffed heads of elk, buffalo, deer and bighorn sheep. On one side of the room the Meeker Massacre is depicted by a mural-sized oil painting. Asked about the gruesome art work, the elderly woman behind the desk said, "Let's face it, Mr. Meeker was out on a limb when he did what he did." Velvet wallpaper is covered along one wall with framed yellowed newspaper articles and photos from the turbulent past. One article recounts a bank robbery just up the street from the hotel. It begins, "A gang of three highwaymen try to rob the bank of Meeker and are now sleeping beneath the sod as a consequence of their daring."

The hotel once offered high-class accommodations; it had a bar, a restaurant and even a barbershop. Teddy Roosevelt stayed here while on a bear hunting expedition. The old hotel still fills up during hunting season. There are many different rooms available, from suites with private baths to small rooms with a bath down the hall. Don't be startled by the garish wallpaper and the multicolored striped carpet in one upstairs hallway. The rooms are adequate but not plush. You can even stay in Teddy's two-room suite, with its bright red wallpaper and canopy bed. 560 Main St., Meeker, CO 81641; (303) 878-5061.

CAMPING

In White River National Forest—

Several campgrounds are spread out near the White River Valley east of Meeker. To reach all of the listed camping areas, drive east on Hwy. 13 for 2 miles. Turn right on River Rd. (County Rd. 8) and proceed to the campground turn-off.

South Fork Campground: drive 18 miles east on River Rd., turn right on South Fork Rd. and head 12 miles to the campground; 17 sites; fee charged. **East Marvine Campground**: take River Rd. 28 miles east and then turn right onto Marvine Creek Rd. and proceed 6 miles; seven sites; fee charged. Another mile up Marvine Creek Rd. is **Marvine Campground**: 16 sites; fee charged. **North Fork Campground**: drive 33 miles east on River Rd. (County Rd. 8) to the campground; 46 sites; fee charged. **Himes Peak Campground** is 39 miles down River Rd.; turn right on Trappers Lake Rd. and continue 6 miles to the campground; eight sites; no fee. **Bucks, Shepherds Rim, Trapline** and **Cutthroat campgrounds** are all located near Trappers Lake; fee charged. To reach the lake, drive 39 miles on River Rd., turn right onto Trappers Lake Rd. and proceed 10 miles. The campgrounds are located past Trappers Lake Lodge.

——— WHERE TO EAT ———

There are a few restaurants in Meeker, but nothing in town was outstanding. If you just want a quick burger, try **Clark's Big Ol' Burger ($)** at 858 Market St. For a sit-down meal, go across the street to **The Last Chance Restaurant ($ to $$)** at 975 Market St.

Sleepy Cat Ranch — $$ to $$$

Nearly everyone we talked with in Meeker raved about the good food and atmosphere at Sleepy Cat. *It's definitely worth the short and scenic trip 18 miles east of town.* The restaurant is divided into several small dining rooms. Some tables look out over a grassy meadow to the White River. The heavy pine walls of the old restaurant are lined with the requisite hunting and fishing trophies. The menu dwells on steaks and chops; on weekends there are specials of prime rib, baby back pork ribs and barbecue beef ribs. Some seafood and chicken entrées are served, along with lighter meals ($), such as hamburgers and a salad and soup bar. A separate bar area fills up with ranch hands from the surrounding area and can be a fun place to spend some time before or after a meal. Dancing to tunes from the jukebox or occasional live bands often takes place on weekends. From Meeker take Hwy. 13 east for 2 miles. Turn right on County Rd. 8 and continue 16 miles to the ranch. Open in summer 6–10 pm nightly and winter Fri.–Sat. only 6–10 pm. **16064 County Rd. 8, Meeker, CO 81641; 878-4413.**

SERVICES

Meeker Chamber of Commerce—
    PO Box 869, 710 Market St., Meeker,
CO 81641; (303) 878-5510.

North Park

The most striking impression for most visitors to North Park is the limitless view around the basin to sharply uplifted peaks of various ranges. This vast expanse of grassland is rimmed on three sides by the Medicine Bow Range to the east, the Rabbit Ears Range and Never Summer Mountains to the south and the Park Range to the west. It is the smallest, most isolated of the three Colorado parks (North, Middle and South). Located in north central Colorado, North Park opens north toward Wyoming. Ranches cover much of the wide valley floor with irrigated plots of hay, interrupted here and there by copses of sagebrush. What a relief to be away from flashy billboards, six-lane highways and congestion. Instead of neon, you look west to an unspoiled array of spectacular peaks rising to over 12,000 feet in the Mt. Zirkel Wilderness Area.

With a population of less than 1,000, the ranch supply center of Walden is the only town in North Park offering accommodations and meals. Within a few miles of Walden, several spring-fed lakes and a number of meandering streams, including the North Platte River, provide excellent fishing. Fishing and hunting remain the primary sporting activities within the park, but the surrounding mountain ranges also beckon avid hikers away from the flat basin.

HISTORY

Prior to 1820, Ute Indians migrated to North Park during summers to hunt buffalo and an abundance of other wild game. Beginning in the 1820s, trappers made sojourns into North Park because of the easy game. Despite their presence, life for the Indians was relatively routine until whites began settling to the east, near present-day Fort Collins. Utes made raids on the new settlements, stealing horses and stashing their plunder back at North Park. They often returned from their expeditions over Ute Pass in the Medicine Bow Range. The Anglos were afraid to follow them into the mountains.

When John Fremont visited the valley on his second expedition in 1844, he called it a "paradise to all grazing animals." But it wasn't ranching that drew the first wave of settlement in North Park—it was prospecting. James O. Pinkham, a short Canadian old-timer, began panning for gold in the early 1870s. Other men followed but never struck the rich placer gold they were searching for. By 1880 silver was the draw, and in only two years the new town of Teller City had a population of 1,300. The miners, however, soon learned that transporting the ore was too expensive and by 1885 Teller City was deserted. Many of the men who gave up on mining eventually settled in North Park and began raising livestock. John Fremont had been on the mark back in 1844: the future of the valley was to be found in ranching. Today the economy is still based primarily on ranching, as well as lumbering and oil.

GETTING THERE

The center of North Park is at Walden, which is located about 150 miles from Denver. You can take a number of routes from the Front Range, including a scenic drive on Hwy. 14 west of Fort Collins. From Denver, perhaps the best way is to drive west on Interstate 70 for 42 miles to Hwy. 40. Turn right and continue past Winter Park and Granby before heading north on Hwy. 125, which drops into North Park from the south.

——— OUTDOOR ACTIVITIES ———

FISHING

Fishing is the major tourist attraction in North Park. Not only is the angling good on the dozens of streams flowing out of the mountains, but there are many popular lakes in the bottomland. So take your time and enjoy the mixture of plains and mountains while fishing in North Park. Don't hesitate to pursue some of the smaller tributaries and beaver ponds, for they sometimes offer the best fishing. Although much of the land in the park is privately owned and posted against fishing, miles of streams are open, due to leases made with land owners. These areas are marked; if you need more information on public water, stop by **Sportsman's Supply in Walden, 466 Main St.**, and talk with Russ Bybee. Or call him at **(303) 723-4343** for an update on local conditions.

Delaney Butte Lakes—

Cold spring water feeds this series of three lakes, and ample hatches of insects help the brown and rainbow trout grow to large sizes. The fishing tends to be better in spring and fall, especially early and late in the day. In Aug. the moss and weeds can get to be a problem for fishermen. Motorboats are allowed at Delaney Butte but are unavailable for rent. Camping is permitted around the lakes, but it's not the most scenic setting and there is no protection from the often gusty wind. To reach the lakes head west 9 miles from Walden, past the southern end of Walden Reservoir, until the road reaches a T. Turn right on the well-marked road to Delaney Butte and drive north to the lakes.

Lake John—

A local favorite, this lake is very shallow but seemingly full of good-sized cutthroat; also caught are some brown and rainbow trout. This 550-acre lake is easier to fish from a boat. There is camping on the west shore. To reach Lake John drive about 4 miles north of Delaney Butte Lakes on well-marked roads.

Michigan River—

Locals seem to prefer the conditions and setting of the Michigan River to those of the North Platte. About 30 feet wide, the Michigan offers many good holes as it flows just to the east of Walden toward its confluence with the North Platte. Many lunker browns can be caught on the Michigan with lightweight fly or spin tackle. Three forks of this river flow into North Park from Colorado State Forest and Routt National Forest to the south. Much of the river southeast of Walden is parallel to Hwy. 14, with many access points along the way.

North Platte River—

This meandering stream, flowing north into Wyoming, presents many deep pools and riffles where the predominant population of brown trout feeds. Most of the fish are about a foot long, but there are some really large trout pulled from the North Platte every year. Spinners and bait can be effective early in the year, despite muddy water during the spring runoff; casting toward the banks is very good as long as you hunker down low enough to avoid showing yourself to the fish. The

North Platte is a good river to wade with fly-fishing gear. At times in late summer, irrigation demands severely reduce the flow. To get through irrigated plots, be sure to bring your waders and some mosquito repellent. Private land is interspersed with public access fishing. Just north of Walden, below the confluence with the Michigan River, is a good public fishing area. Ten miles north of Walden, a narrow canyon off Hwy. 127 is designated Wild Trout water; 1 mile after crossing the North Platte on Hwy. 127, turn right on a public access road to reach this stretch of river.

HIKING AND BACKPACKING

If your goal is to get away from crowds and enjoy some of Colorado's best mountain scenery, then North Park provides seldom-used access. Many roads run west out of North Park and butt up against the boundary of the Mt. Zirkel Wilderness Area. Encircled by Routt National Forest, this wilderness area offers an expanse of beautiful terrain for hikers. Stop by the **Walden District Ranger Office** for information and maps: **612 5th Street, Walden, CO 80480; (303) 723-4707.** For more information on trails from the other side of the Mt. Zirkel Wilderness Area, see the Hiking

section of the **Steamboat Springs** chapter.

Colorado State Forest forms the eastern boundary of North Park. For more information on hikes in this area, see the Hiking section of the **Fort Collins and West** chapter.

RIVER FLOATING

North Park is close to one of the most popular river floating areas in the state. The Upper Colorado River, downstream from Kremmling, offers a 14-mile day trip from Pump House to State Bridge that attracts crowds of floaters on weekends. The periodic rapids and canyon scenery along the way add greatly to the trip. Several other lesser-used stretches of the river downstream from State Bridge offer leisurely floats virtually devoid of people, but without any exciting rapids. Kayaking and canoeing are also great ways to glide down the water. The best rafting outfitter in the area is located in Kremmling.

Colorado Whitewater Yacht Club—
This outfit has more than 17 years of experience in guiding raft trips. With reasonable prices and a variety of trips including half-day, full-day and evening steak floats, you can't miss. **309 Park Ave., Kremmling, CO 80459; (303) 724-9333.**

—— SEEING AND DOING ——

MUSEUMS

North Park Pioneer Museum—
This museum, located in the center of Walden, keeps going and going.... Every time we thought we'd seen it all, another room, chock-full of historical items, would open up. Take your time wandering through the Pioneer Museum and you'll gain a better understanding of the ranch heritage of Jackson County. Guns, saddles, carriages, kitchen items and antiques fill the museum. Open in summer only; small fee. Open mid-June through mid-Sept.;

Tues.–Sun. noon–5 pm; by appointment in winter, call **(303) 723-4379. 365 Logan St.** In Walden, follow the signs from Main St. to the courthouse block.

SCENIC DRIVES

See the **Steamboat Springs** chapter for information on Buffalo Pass and Rabbit Ears Pass, which cut through Routt National Forest south of the Mt. Zirkel Wilderness Area. This is a beautiful loop trip, especially in fall.

WHERE TO STAY

ACCOMMODATIONS

North Park is not a place you'll be able to find a restful bed and breakfast or a historic hotel. But if you want to stay in the area, a basic motel room can be found in Walden or to the south of the park in Kremmling. Many camping areas in the surrounding mountains lie in wait. If you would like an extended stay near North Park, consider the following guest ranch.

Latigo Ranch — $$$$

The drive up into the heavy woods of Arapaho National Forest northwest of Kremmling hardly gives an indication of the spectacular open setting at Latigo Ranch. With tremendous views of the Indian Peaks and unlimited trails for horseback riding and hiking, this small ranch is a perfect secluded getaway. Riding is emphasized and guests are paired with compatible horses for the duration of their stay. All the wranglers have a wealth of experience, and after a week under their instruction, you will have improved your riding technique and your knowledge of horses. Every day you can take off on morning and afternoon trail rides. Other activities include swimming (in a pool) and fishing (in a private pond or nearby rivers), but there is also plenty of time to just relax.

The family atmosphere at Latigo is warm and friendly, encouraging people from around the country to get to know one another. One return guest commented, "They make you feel as though you were a guest in their own home." She went on to confess that she had been saving to bring her family here again ever since their visit last summer. The food is gourmet-ranch style—if there is such a thing. Two entrées are served each evening in the cozy dining room; breakfast and lunch are served buffet-style. Latigo is also open in winter, attracting cross-country skiers and snowmobilers alike. Adjacent to the ranch are more than 15 kilometers of groomed ski trails and some of the best backcountry terrain you'll ever encounter. **PO Box 237, Kremmling, CO 80459; (303) 724-3596.**

CAMPING

In Routt National Forest—

To reach **Grizzly Creek Campground** from Walden, drive southwest on Hwy. 14 for 24 miles. Located on the edge of the national forest, this campground has 12 sites and a fee. Four miles south of Grizzly Creek Campground on Hwy. 14 you'll come to **Hidden Lakes Campground** with nine sites and a fee. Don't worry about fishing in the lakes—it's lousy.

Aspen Campground (in the southeast corner of North Park) is 1 mile southwest of the town of Gould on Forest Rd. 740. It has 12 sites and a fee. **Pines Campground** is 2 miles farther south on Forest Rd. 740. It has 11 sites and a fee.

Colorado State Forest—

There are more than 70 campsites located within Colorado State Forest to the east of North Park. See the Camping section of the **Fort Collins and West** chapter for more information.

SERVICES

North Park Chamber of Commerce—
Box 227, Walden, CO 80480; (303) 723-4600.

Redstone and Crystal River Valley

The Crystal River Valley is an ideal mountain retreat. Away from large resort towns, it offers exactly what many people hope to find while visiting the mountains of Colorado. It's a pristine valley flanked by reddish cliffs and hemmed in from the east by peaks reaching above 14,000 feet. The small towns of Redstone and Marble and the ghost town of Crystal bring an enduring past to light. Something for everyone exists here in a lode of year-round activities, including hiking, cross-country skiing, jeeping and fishing.

After turning onto Hwy. 133 at the town of Carbondale, the scenery along the Crystal River becomes more beautiful as the valley narrows. The lower part of the valley is completely dominated by the broad shoulders of Mt. Sopris (12,953 feet). Ten miles upriver is Redstone, a one-street community of about 100 residents. Many former miners' homes are now refurbished summer homes, painted in pastels. Redstone is also home to a number of fine art galleries and antique shops. At the south end of town is the distinctive Redstone Inn, looking much as it did in the early 1900s. Two miles south of town, the magnificent Redstone Castle (Cleveholm) stands exactly as it did at the turn of the century. Following the course of the Crystal River beyond Redstone soon provides a panorama of the Elk and Ragged mountains. In fall, enjoy the spectacular contrast of golden aspen with a sheer backdrop of rocky red cliffs.

HISTORY

For many hundreds of years nomadic Ute Indian tribes spent summers hunting in the Crystal River Valley. They were later promised by treaty that this land would be theirs forever. However, by 1872 prospectors began trickling into the southern end of this secluded valley from the towns of Gothic and Crested Butte. The land was officially opened to settlement in 1881 when the Utes were forced to depart for distant reservations in Utah. Small ranches and farms began to flourish, especially in the wide northern end of the valley near the confluence of the Crystal and Roaring Fork rivers.

In 1882 John Osgood, founder of Pueblo's Colorado Fuel & Iron (CF&I), purchased coal claims in the area. Two decades later he founded the model coal village of Redstone with mixed success. In an attempt to avoid the labor problems of other coal towns, Osgood provided a rather luxurious setting for every worker. But the miners resented their loss of independence, as they were forced to join in the community and obey Osgood's rules. For instance, the men were to shower before appearing on the streets after work, and a "no treating" rule prevented workers from buying drinks for their friends.

111

The Redstone Inn was created as an upscale community hall and bachelor rooming house. Miners with families were put up in small houses, each built slightly differently from the next. A couple of miles up-valley Osgood built his opulent $2.5 million, 42-room dream palace, called *Cleveholm* (from the first part of his middle name, Cleve, and *holm*, which in Old English means a grassy place with a stream running through it). Rooms were paneled with solid mahogany woodwork, gold leaf, silk brocade and elephant hide; imported chandeliers, rugs and furniture were placed throughout. There, Osgood entertained industrialists, celebrities and even President Theodore Roosevelt. But by 1903 Osgood was virtually forced out of business by economic difficulties and the incursions of Eastern tycoons J.P. Morgan and John D. Rockefeller. Although Osgood resigned, he remained a millionaire until his death in 1926.

In the late 1800s marble was quarried with some success at the southern end of the Crystal River Valley. The marble, with its glistening white color veined with pale browns, rivaled the best Italian varieties. With the opening of the Yule Marble Quarry in 1905, the entire valley underwent an economic revival. Trains of 40 mules brought the marble to the railhead in the town of Marble until 1908, when an electric train first made it to the quarry. The town grew quickly and by 1916 boasted a population of over 1,500. The largest piece of marble ever quarried at Marble was a 100-ton block for the Tomb of the Unknown Soldier; it took one year to pare it down to a weight of 56 tons. Other huge pieces were used in the construction of the Lincoln Memorial in Washington, DC. In 1941 a flood and resultant mudslide destroyed much of the town and caused the railroad to stop service.

Over the years, many developers have come into the Crystal River Valley with new ideas to promote tourism. For a while there was a golf course on the front lawn of Cleveholm, and a working 1,000-foot T-bar ski lift nearby. Although these ventures faltered, the area still draws many visitors. Most people seem to come to this isolated valley because it's a relatively undeveloped haven that offers peace and quiet along with some of the most striking scenery in the state.

GETTING THERE

From Denver, take Interstate 70 west for 166 miles to Glenwood Springs. Turn onto Hwy. 82 and go 10 miles southeast to Carbondale. Turn right onto Hwy. 133 and head up the Crystal River Valley.

Fly Continental Express or United Express from Denver's Stapleton International Airport to the Aspen/Snowmass Airport. (Direct service is available from Los Angeles and San Francisco.) Redstone is located 42 miles from the airport.

For a change of pace, take an Amtrak train into Glenwood Springs from Chicago (via Denver) or from San Francisco. Call Amtrak for reservations and information at **1-800-872-7245**. From Glenwood, rent a car for the 27-mile ride to Redstone.

——— FESTIVALS AND EVENTS ———

See the Festivals and Events sections in the **Aspen and Glenwood Springs** chapters for information on nearby happenings.

——— OUTDOOR ACTIVITIES ———

BIKING

MOUNTAIN BIKING

Two-wheeled, non-motorized transportation is enjoying a surge of popularity in the valley. Many jeep roads and single-track trails are ideal for mountain bikes. The best rides leave from Marble. There is a great 4-mile ride to the historic marble quarry and another 5-mile ride to the ghost town of Crystal (see the Four-Wheel-Drive Trips). Adventuresome riders can continue over Schofield Pass, eventually dropping into Gothic and then Crested Butte, the mountain biking capital of Colorado.

For rentals and backcountry information, contact the **Redstone Country Store**, located across from the Redstone Inn; **(303) 963-3408.**

TOURING

The 31-mile ride up the Crystal River Valley from Carbondale to Marble has long been a favorite of bicyclists. Not only is the scenery fantastic, but the narrow valley protects you from the wind and the road is paved. It's a great way to experience the mountainous beauty along Hwy. 133.

FISHING

Beaver Lake—
Located in the town of Marble, this small, heavily fished lake is filled by the Crystal River. More importantly, it is stocked with plenty of rainbow and brook trout each year. It's a great place for a canoe or a small rowboat, but no motors are allowed.

Crystal River—
At the ghost town of Crystal, the north and south forks converge and the fast-running Crystal River begins its 35-mile tumble down the valley. The river eventually flows into the Roaring Fork River a couple of miles below Carbondale. The heavily stocked river is a good place to catch pan-sized rainbow trout. Since the river is within such a scenically stunning valley and because it is easily accessible from the road, it's a very popular place to fish. There are fewer people as you move up-valley toward Marble, and chances are you'll get more action from brook trout there.

Dinkle Lake—
Rainbow and brook trout are frequent catches at this high-country lake situated near the edge of White River National Forest northeast of Redstone. It's a good place for a leisurely picnic. A 3.5-mile hike from Dinkle Lake, with a 1,600-foot elevation gain, will land you at **Thomas Lakes.** There you'll be challenged by feisty cutthroat trout. The two lakes are about a quarter of a mile apart and have several primitive campsites on their perimeters. The marked turn-off to Dinkle Lake is located a mile south of Carbondale, near the fish hatchery on Hwy. 133.

Gold Medal Waters—
The highly rated Roaring Fork and Fryingpan rivers are discussed in the **Aspen** chapter.

Yule Creek—
Yule Creek flows into the town of Marble from the south. It's quick and narrow and can provide good fishing for cutthroats. Cascading over remnants of white marble, the creek takes on a translucence even in some deep spots. The four-wheel-

drive road to the marble quarry parallels the creek for 4 miles. After the quarry a hiking trail follows the creek southeast toward Yule Pass. To reach Yule Creek from Marble, turn right on 3rd St. and drive to a parking area for the mill. Walk or drive across the one-lane bridge for a short distance until you see the little creek by the road.

FOUR-WHEEL-DRIVE TRIPS

Jeep Tours—

Seven different trips are available from **Crystal River Jeep Tours,** including daily tours to the Yule Marble Quarry and the Crystal Mill. All leave from the town of Marble. Call for reservations. **116 Main St.; (303) 963-1911.**

Schofield Pass—

Beginning in Marble, a rough dirt road heads west to the ghost town of Crystal before a treacherous ascent to the top of Schofield Pass (10,707 feet). A mile past Beaver Lake, turn right on Forest Rd. 314 and continue 4 miles to Crystal. The first man-made structure you will see is the photogenic Sheep Mountain Mill; since 1892 it has been clinging to its rocky perch above the Crystal River. Just beyond the mill, over a slight rise, are the wood-frame houses of "Crystal City." In 1881 Crystal was a bustling town of 650 residents, who used the town as a jumping-off point for prospecting in the area. It had its own newspaper, hotel, general store and post office. Today a dozen original buildings remain as summer homes. From Crystal, the narrow road becomes perilous; *please use extreme caution.*

After Crystal, Forest Rd. 317 leads southwest on a precipitous road toward the pass. At the top of the steep grade a lush meadow marks the site of the abandoned town of Schofield. It was founded in 1879 by a group of men who didn't seem to care that they were inside Indian territory. After the summit, wind down the other side to Gothic and eventually to Crested Butte. If you are staying in Redstone or Marble, try a scenic loop trip from Crested Butte: return over Kebler Pass, then over McClure Pass, and drop back to the Crystal River Valley.

Yule Marble Quarry—

From the town of Marble, an easy 4-mile jeep road begins at the remains of the marble mill, where it crosses a one-lane bridge over the Crystal River. At the mill you'll see massive chunks of quarried marble and tall supporting columns built of white marble. The road parallels Yule Creek on its southern route toward the slopes of Treasure Mountain (13,462 feet). The deep quarry pits bear the scars of the process that removed huge slabs of the crystalline rock. One such 30,000-square-foot "room" could produce 3,000 cubic feet of marble per day. The quarry is a great place to explore, as long as you are aware of the inherent dangers of being around deep holes in the ground. Scattered about are riggings and wooden supports used to bring the marble up to the surface. Please leave all the pieces of marble for the next person to enjoy.

HIKING AND BACKPACKING

The hiking in this area is surprisingly diverse. There are little-used access points to the Maroon Bells–Snowmass Wilderness Area and hikes into historic locales. You'll always be accompanied by a vista of tall peaks. Since most hikes lead into high elevations, beware of altitude sickness. For more information and maps, contact the rangers at the **Sopris District Office, Main and Weant** streets, **Carbondale, CO 81623; (303) 963-2266.**

Avalanche Creek—

This trail leads from Avalanche Campground on a southwestern route into the Maroon Bells–Snowmass Wilderness Area. Hike in as far as you wish for a day trip. This is also a good choice for a two-day backpack trip, since the elevation gain is fairly gradual. The trail merges with East Creek Trail after about 6 miles. East Creek Trail eventually heads west back to Redstone. If you continue on Avalanche Creek Trail, you'll end up in the heart of the Maroon Bells–Snowmass Wilderness Area near Capitol Peak, Capitol Lake and Avalanche Lake. These are gorgeous hikes, especially when the wildflowers are at their peak, starting in mid-July. Good maps are essential. To reach the trailhead, drive south on Hwy. 133 for 12 miles from Carbondale. Turn left (east) and continue for 3 miles on a rough dirt road to Avalanche Campground.

Crystal—

Bring your camera on this easy 4-mile walk over a jeep road to the ghost town of Crystal. The walk is shaded by aspen and evergreens most of the way. In summer you'll enjoy the cooling effect of walking beside the rushing waters of the Crystal River. Before long you'll see the famous mill, waterfall and the dozen remaining buildings of the old town. See the Four-Wheel-Drive Trips section for more information. To reach the road from Marble, head east from Beaver Lake for a mile to a junction in the road. Park near the junction, unless you have a four-wheel-drive vehicle, and walk down the right fork (Forest Rd. 314) to Crystal.

Thomas Lakes—

From Dinkle Lake the 3.5-mile hike to Thomas Lakes is a beautiful introduction to hiking trails in the area. The two lakes are located on the northwestern side of the massive twin peaks of Mt. Sopris (12,953 feet). The hike can be done easily in a day; you'll want to bring along your fishing pole. Many hikers spend the night at primitive campsites near the lakes before making the 2,700-foot climb from the lakes to the top of Mt. Sopris. The hike to the summit is non-technical, but you must be in good shape. The trail leads due south from the southeast side of Thomas Lakes. Both of the Sopris summits are the same elevation. The marked turn-off to Dinkle Lake is

located a mile south of Carbondale, near the fish hatchery on Hwy. 133.

Yule Marble Quarry—

This is a perfect day trip on an easy four-wheel-drive road. The walk from the marble finishing mill to the quarry is 4 miles each way. This hike is not only extremely beautiful, but is historic as well. See the Four-Wheel-Drive Trips section for more information and directions.

HORSEBACK RIDING

It doesn't matter what kind of equestrian training you have, because rides for all abilities are provided by **Twin Pines Outfitting** in Marble. You can arrange anything from a five-day wilderness pack trip to an hour's walk on horseback through the woods. Larry and Dana Darien have been renting horses and guiding trips for over a quarter of a century. Breakfast, lunch and barbecue dinner rides are available. **2880 County Rd. 3, Marble, CO 81623; (303) 963-1220.**

RIVER FLOATING

Crystal River—

The fast-running Crystal is a great river for experienced kayakers with enough sense to portage at a Class VI section known affectionately as the "meatgrinder." The river is free flowing and is therefore a very high run in June before slacking off in mid- to late summer. To have a successful trip, you must either know the river or spend some time along its banks scouting suitable stretches.

Roaring Fork—

See the **Aspen** chapter.

SKIING

CROSS-COUNTRY SKIING

The Crystal River valley offers a range of cross-country skiing in fluffy powder snow. Many nordic skiers come to this peaceful valley to make tracks on old forgotten roads, mountain trails and organized trail systems. The only conceivable drawback about skiing in this narrow valley is that sunshine is extremely short-lived in winter. There are, however, many trails that climb above the valley and provide plenty of sunshine.

Backcountry Trails—

Marble Quarry—Beginning in Marble at the 3rd St. bridge is an easy 4-mile (one way) tour. The trip up to the quarry is quite safe, but it would be wise to begin your return from there. Beyond that point the trail becomes difficult to find and crosses many avalanche paths. For more information see the Four-Wheel-Drive Trips section.

McClure Pass—From the top of McClure Pass (8,755 feet), enjoy spectacular views of the Ragged Mountains and back to the Crystal River Valley. While skiing un-groomed trails far above the valley floor, you'll have a chance to bask in the sun. A moderately easy forest road sets out to the south from the summit. Dogs are allowed. Check with the US National Forest Service Headquarters in Carbondale for current avalanche conditions. **Main and Weant sts.; (303) 963-2266.**

Town Trail—Starting at the Redstone Inn is an easy 2-mile round-trip tour past the historic homes of this mountain hamlet. The trail follows along behind town, providing a route by the old schoolhouse as well as many former miners' homes. The Town Trail is perfect if you are interested in skiing the flats with the opportunity for a warm cup of hot chocolate at the end of the trail.

Groomed Trails—

Redstone Inn Ski Touring Center—Miles of groomed trails leave not far from the front door of the historic inn. The trails lie to the west of town and, for the most part, have moderate elevation gains. Also available are rentals and instruction. Small trail fee. **0082 Redstone Blvd., Redstone; (303) 963-2526.**

Spring Gulch Trail System—Near Carbondale a 10-mile nordic system of groomed trails is open to the public at no charge. There are advanced, intermediate and beginner trails. Pick up a map and a descriptive brochure at many locations in Carbondale. Spring Gulch is located 7 miles west of Carbondale on **County Rd. 108.**

Rentals and Information—

The **Redstone Country Store** rents an array of cross-country equipment. Guided tours and instruction available; open daily. Across the street from the Redstone Inn; **(303) 963-3408.**

DOWNHILL SKIING

Aspen and Snowmass—

Skiing at four world-class mountains is only 46 miles away. See the **Aspen** chapter for more information.

Sunlight—

Consider a day of skiing at this un-crowded mountain. It's an excellent choice for families and anyone who wants to stay on primarily intermediate and beginner terrain—at bargain prices. From the Crystal River Valley, Sunlight is about half as far as Aspen. See the **Glenwood Springs** chapter for more information.

—— SEEING AND DOING ——

HOT SPRINGS

Hot Springs Pool at Glenwood Springs—

Only 27 miles away is the world's largest hot springs pool. See the Major Attractions section of the **Glenwood Springs** chapter.

Penny Hot Springs—

Long used by Ute Indians and later by settlers, Penny Hot Springs is still bubbling forth. An unofficial caretaker has made a couple of shallow pools that mix cold water from the Crystal River with the boiling source water: the result is a soothing 104° soak. Lately though, the springs have become mired in conflict. Some people want to bathe stark naked, which has infuriated the landowners across the river (even though they would need powerful binoculars to see any bathers from their houses). A couple of indecent exposure charges have been filed, and unknown vigilantes keep pushing huge boulders into the hot pools when no one is looking. Our advice is to ask locally about the status of Penny Hot Springs and, if you decide to soak, wear a suit. The springs are located below Hwy. 133, 1.5 miles north of Redstone, along a wide bend in the road.

MUSEUMS AND GALLERIES

Redstone Blvd. is lined with many fine galleries. It is worthwhile to walk down the street and peer into as many windows as you can. Among other things, you'll see stained glass, original oils and watercolors, and even wearable art. The aesthetically pleasing valley has long inspired artists; well-known painters such as Frank Mechaw and Ben Turner have spent time here.

Elk Mountain Gallery—
The theme of this gallery is wildlife and mountain art. The work of 35 artists is displayed in a pleasant setting throughout the year. 0385 Redstone Blvd., Redstone; (303) 963-1769.

Marble Museum—
This small museum gives you an idea of the town's good years, when the quarry was operating at full tilt. Artifacts and photos follow the interesting history of Marble from the early 1900s. Donations accepted; open 2–4 pm, Memorial Day to Labor Day. 412 Marble St., Marble.

Redstone Art Center—
Don't miss this gallery. Nationally known sculptor Eric Johnson works marble into incredible art forms that are displayed in quantity at this location. He often can be seen transforming huge pieces of local marble into remarkable human forms just outside the front door. In addition to sculpted marble, there is pottery, jewelry, woodwork and other media. 0173 Redstone Blvd., Redstone; (303) 963-3790.

SCENIC DRIVES
Crystal River Valley—
The extreme beauty encountered while driving up the Crystal River Valley to Marble will remain in your memory for a long while. Follow Hwy. 133 south past the coke ovens of Redstone for 5 miles to a marked turn-off for Marble. Once in the town of Marble, turn right on 3rd St. and go a block to the remains of the marble mill. At the site are tons of rejected pieces of the gleaming stone and white marble support columns reminiscent of classical Greek ruins. The mill is located next to the Crystal River. Four miles south, on the slopes of Treasure Mountain (13,462 feet), is the Yule Marble Quarry. The quarry is a pleasant 4-mile walk on an easy four-wheel-drive road; some make the trip with only two-wheel-drive. (See the Four-Wheel-Drive Trips section for more information.)

McClure Pass—
Head south on Hwy. 133 past Redstone and toward the top of McClure Pass (8,755 feet); near the summit be sure to pull off and take a long look south to the Ragged Mountains and back north to Mt. Sopris at the head of the valley. The highway eventually drops into the quiet orchards of Paonia. Instead of ending in Paonia, you could easily continue to Crested Butte by way of Kebler Pass. Either of these options would be a brilliant choice in autumn.

WHERE TO STAY

ACCOMMODATIONS

Redstone Castle — $$$

Recently, the castle started offering its spacious 42-room interior as a bed and breakfast from Sun. to Fri. each week (group bookings are available on Sat. night). The $2.5 million castle was built by John Osgood in 1903 to impress his friends and enemies alike. Osgood and Teddy Roosevelt used to sit on the front lawn while the game-keeper let loose captive deer, one at a time, for them to shoot down! Other guests included John D. Rockefeller, J.P. Morgan, Jay Gould and John "Bet a Million" Gates. John Osgood's second wife, Alma, was known as Lady Bountiful. Each Christmas she asked the children of Redstone to write letters to Santa. She then collected the mail, left on her private railcar for a New York City shopping spree and returned with armloads of presents for the kids.

Relive the castle's history as you walk around the library, the armory and the main living room with its massive fire-place. The 16 enchanting bedrooms are carefully appointed with antiques. Views from the windows across the well-tended grounds to the Crystal River are fabulous. Staying in the castle is somewhere between living in a museum and living out your wildest dream. If you want only to tour the castle, reservations are essential. Located 1 mile south of Redstone at **0058 Redstone Blvd., Redstone, CO 81623; (303) 963-3463.**

Redstone Inn — $$ to $$$

Nestled beside the Crystal River on the south end of town, this distinctive Tudor-style inn is a perfect getaway. You can't miss the four-faced clock tower that is an exact replica from a Dutch inn at Rotter-dam. The inn was built in 1902 by John Osgood as a place for his unmarried coal workers to live. Today it is widely known as a relaxing getaway. Reserve rooms well in advance for summer weekends, as the inn tends to fill up.

The rooms vary quite a bit in size, with some on the small side. The large bridal suite is a honeymoon fantasy. For people on a tight budget, inexpensive dormer rooms with half-baths are available; showers are down the hall. All rooms are furnished tastefully in antiques, and the rest of the decor is subtle and classy. The large outdoor hot tub beckons and there are tennis courts for guests. Though much of the interior decor is new, it has that old European feel: rich oak paneling, a comfortable lobby, reading rooms and a small, sophisticated bar. The elegant restaurant is a place you will want to visit for breakfast, lunch or dinner. Don't miss the Sun. brunch. See the Where to Eat section for more information. **0082 Redstone Blvd., Redstone, CO 81623; (303) 963-2526.**

Beaver Lake Lodge in Marble — $$

Offering basic accommodations in the midst of the charming little town of Marble, the two-story lodge is clean and comfortable. It wouldn't be all that special if not for the friendly owners and the wonderful location. There are also a few cabins for rent. In winter, many people stay here as a base for cross-country excursions in the area. Hank and Pat Kimbrell will also prepare your meals, to be served inside or out depending on the season. **201 E. Silver St., Marble, CO 81623; (303) 963-2504.**

CAMPING

There are a number of excellent White River National Forest campgrounds in the Crystal River Valley.

Bogan Flats Campground enjoys a beautiful setting near the Crystal River south of Redstone. From Redstone, take Hwy. 133 for 5 miles, turn left at the turn-off to Marble (Forest Rd. 314) and continue 1.5 miles to the campground. Drinking water; 37 sites; fee charged.

Janeway Campground is located 12 miles south of Carbondale on Hwy. 133. Turn left (east), cross a bridge and continue for half a mile to the campground. 10

campsites; no water; no fee. It's another 2.5 miles to **Avalanche Campground** down the same dirt road, which is so rough that trailers over 20 feet long are not allowed. 10 sites; fee charged.

Redstone Campground is located a mile north of the town of Redstone. It offers shaded campsites next to the Crystal River and is very popular. Drinking water available; 24 sites; fee charged.

WHERE TO EAT

There are only a few restaurants in Redstone. If you want to find a better variety in dining, there are many nearby options. A local favorite for breakfast and lunch is in Carbondale, only 10 miles away: the **Village Smithy** at 3rd and Main. A wide selection of restaurants can be found by heading to Glenwood Springs or to Aspen (see Where to Eat in those chapters).

Redstone Inn — $$$

The classic setting of the inn matches the excellent food. In the gracious dining room you can enjoy carefully prepared continental cuisine and first-class service. Linens adorn the tables and mouth-watering aromas fill the air. The dinner menu includes roast duckling with an orange and Grand Marnier glaze, crab and shrimp crêpes under a delectable white sauce, and a tempting filet mignon. Open from 5:30–9 pm each evening. The restaurant is also open for breakfast ($, 7:30–11 am) and lunch ($$, 11:30 am–2 pm). If you are lucky enough to be staying at the inn over a weekend, make certain you stay for the champagne brunch buffet (Sun. from 9 am–2 pm). People from all around the area make a special trip to Redstone for this brunch. Located in the Redstone Inn at the south end of town. **0082 Redstone Blvd., Redstone; 963-2526.**

Steamboat Springs

Surrounded by sprawling cattle ranches, Steamboat Springs remains a major ranch-supply center in the midst of some of the best skiing in the world. The imposing ski mountain is the reason people flock to Steamboat Springs in winter. It offers the pinnacle of Colorado skiing: deep powder, aspen glades and the second highest vertical drop in the state. Thanks to the massive mountain, lift lines are usually short.

Lincoln Avenue, the 12-block main street of Old Town, is the perfect place to buy a bridle for your horse or get a hot wax for an old pair of skis. Staid Western-wear stores share space with an occasional T-shirt shop. The blending of old and new gives Steamboat a permanence and personality beyond many other ski resorts. Three miles south of the town center, Steamboat Village—a planned development of hotels, condos and boutiques—has sprung up at the base of the ski mountain. A diversity of restaurants and lodging opportunities awaits you both at the mountain and back in town.

Steamboat's 6,000 year-round residents seem to appreciate the stunning natural environment and laid-back attitude of the town. In 1987, *Rolling Stone* magazine rated Steamboat's Colorado Mountain College as one of the nation's "Cool Schools." No doubt its 1,500 students would agree.

Steamboat has a long tradition of skiing and somehow maintains a competitive advantage over other ski towns. Since the Winter Olympics began in 1924, Steamboat has provided 24 competitors for the US team. At the 1988 winter games in Calgary, six participants and two coaches were from Steamboat.

Cross-country skiing is less touted here, but no less spectacular. The trails are virtually unlimited in the surrounding valleys, on top of Rabbit Ears Pass and at an organized nordic center beginning near the mountain village. Be sure to take a plunge in the steaming hot spring pools after a day in the cold. There is a large pool right in town, and the more natural Strawberry Park Hot Springs pools are just a few miles away.

The long days of a Steamboat summer can be filled with any number of activities. It's a lousy place to sit on your duff and a great place to get out into the surrounding country. Set out on foot, horse or mountain bike. Bring along a picnic lunch or your fishing rod. If you are inclined to take part in a guest ranch vacation, this is an excellent area. The experience can range from the cushy to the rustic.

Beware of the "Yampa Valley curse": according to Ute Indian legend, the valley casts a spell over all visitors, compelling them to return year after year. Legend or not, Steamboat Springs is a place that will become embedded in your memory, and it will be difficult to stay away. Ask short-term locals how they came to live in Steamboat, and the answer will begin, "We were just passing through on vacation and . . . . "

HISTORY

With more than 150 hot springs and bountiful game in the Steamboat area, the northern Utes (*Yampatika*) began summering here as early as the 1300s.

According to most accounts, Steamboat Springs got its name in 1865 when three French trappers riding horseback along the Yampa River heard a chugging sound they thought was a steamboat. It turned out to be a hot spring that continued to chug until 1908 when the railroad blasted out the rock chamber over it.

In 1875 James Crawford, the first white settler in the valley, built his homestead. Although a treaty in 1868 took away the land around Steamboat from the Ute Indians, they still made frequent trips to the valley. Soon Crawford was good friends with the Utes. In the summer of 1879 when the Meeker Massacre took place southwest of Steamboat and the Utes attacked settlers in northwest Colorado, Crawford's homestead remained unscathed. By 1880 the Utes were forced onto a reservation in Utah. This was followed by a sharp increase of white homesteaders flocking to the Steamboat area. Farms and ranches started to fill the valley.

At about the same time, a late mining boom was in full swing 30 miles to the north at Hahn's Peak. Although the area produced a meager $4 million in gold, eager miners scoured the hillsides and creeks until the early 1900s.

During this period miners and ranchers would converge on Steamboat Springs for a good time. Proper residents of the town objected to their rambunctious behavior and passed an ordinance prohibiting alcohol in town (it lasted until 1940). The rowdy visitors had to go across the river for drinking and hell-raising.

Although the locals relied on skis in winter as a means of transportation, it was not until a wiry Norwegian came to town in 1913 that people started to ski for fun. Carl Howelsen, a champion jumper and cross-country skier from Norway, organized Steamboat Springs' first Winter Carnival, during which he amazed the townsfolk by heaving himself more than 110 feet off a jump he had built. It was not long before locals were trying it themselves. Howelsen Hill, just west of town, became the jumping hill. Many of the early jumpers would land among a startled herd of elk wintering in the vicinity. By the 1940s, downhill skiing had also become a passion for the townsfolk—so much so that it became part of the school curriculum in 1943. During the late 1940s and into the 1950s, Steamboat Springs produced more downhill champions and Olympic team members than any other town in the country. Among them were Gordy Wren, Skeeter Werner and her brother Buddy Werner.

In the late 1950s, many locals, particularly Jim Temple, began scouting out Storm Peak, the mountain south of town, as a possible site for a new ski area. In January 1963 the mountain opened for business. It was Temple who coined the often-used phrase "champagne powder" to describe the light fluffy snow the mountain is known for. In 1964, when Buddy Werner died tragically in an avalanche in Switzerland, the mountain was renamed Mt. Werner. Since the early days of the ski area, expansion of the facilities has been dramatic.

GETTING THERE

Located 166 miles northwest of Denver, Steamboat Springs takes longer to drive to than you would think. Due to two-lane roads for much of the way and blowing snow in winter, you should allow between 3.5 and five hours. Greyhound Trailways Bus Lines services Steamboat.

About 22 miles from Steamboat Springs, the Yampa Valley Regional Airport has non-stop flights from many large cities in the country (during ski season only). Closer to town, the smaller Bob Adams Airport accommodates Continental Express, which flies daily from Denver year-round.

—— FESTIVALS AND EVENTS ——

Winter Carnival
early February

Like many snowbound communities that get "cabin fever" about mid-winter, Steamboat has a remedy: Winter Carnival. In early February the town lets loose with a week-long celebration highlighted by traditional and not-so-traditional events and activities. Ice-sculpture competitions, a hockey tournament and ski jumping are some of the more predictable activities. Some of the more unusual things happen when Lincoln Ave. is blocked off and covered with snow. Thrill seekers sit on snow shovels that are pulled down the street by galloping horses while the crowds cheer them on. The Diamond Hitch Parade features the high school band, who are all on skis. The famous (at least locally) All Broads Kazoo Band makes an annual appearance. Winter Carnival goes back to 1914, a tradition that attracts many visitors to town. At night, fireworks explode and the "lighted man" skis down Howelsen Hill. After hours, the bars are packed and hopping. For more information, call the **Steamboat Springs Winter Sports Club** at **(303) 879-0695.**

Weekly Rodeo
mid-June through mid-August

Since the late 1800s, Steamboat-area ranch hands have been pitted against one another in rodeo competitions. The tradition continues at Colorado's oldest weekly rodeo. Every Friday and Saturday night the Steamboat Rodeo Grounds fills up for this genuine exhibition of talent and luck. Most cowboys would be considered unlucky if they drew "Mr. T," the Professional Rodeo Cowboy Association's bucking bull of the year in 1986, for the ride of a lifetime. For more information, call **(303) 879-0880.**

Rainbow Weekend
mid-July

A hot-air balloon rodeo and an arts and crafts fair highlight Rainbow Weekend. One of the ballooning events demands that the balloonists negotiate their crafts close enough to a mock steer to rope it. Good luck. Dance to polka and folk music with teachers available to show you the steps. For more specifics, call **(303) 879-0880.**

Vintage Auto Race

Labor Day weekend

Imagine 175 classic automobiles speeding around a specially designed 2-mile race course or displayed for close inspection during the Concours d'Elegance. It's a thrill watching vintage race cars such as AC Cobra, Ferrari and Maserati pitted against each other. The weekend is a flash of Monte Carlo in Steamboat! For more information, call **(303) 879-0880.**

─── OUTDOOR ACTIVITIES ───

BIKING

MOUNTAIN BIKING

Mountain bikers have found a welcome home at Steamboat. There are an infinite number of ride possibilities spreading out from Steamboat like bent spokes from a hub. This relatively new sport has caught the area by storm. Many of the popular rides are on seldom-used dirt roads in the rolling hills of ranch country; some riders, however, seek out the steepest grade possible. Mountain biking is a perfect way to experience the stunning beauty of the country surrounding Steamboat.

Diamond Park Trail—
A 10-mile round trip begins at Seedhouse Rd. just north of the town of Clark. This graded dirt road leads east up the Elk River Valley to Seedhouse Campground. From there an unmaintained jeep trail tracks off to the left, providing perfect, if rough terrain for mountain bikes. Steep ups and downs are interspersed with some fairly level cruising terrain. Along the way, views to the Continental Divide and the Mt. Zirkel Wilderness Area are fantastic. To reach Seedhouse Rd., take County Rd. 129 north of Steamboat for 18 miles.

Fish Creek Falls—
This rather short ride is a steady 3-mile climb up a twisting road to the falls. Once at the falls, the reward is in the beauty of the rushing water and in the knowledge that the return trip is all downhill. From Lincoln Ave. (Hwy. 40), turn north onto Third Ave. and drive one block to the four-way stop at Oak St. Turn right and continue 3 miles until the road ends in the parking area for Fish Creek Falls.

River Road—
This cruising ride is on a fairly flat, improved gravel road that follows the Yampa River south of Steamboat. Great views! You can ride as far as 9 miles from town on the road, or as short a distance as you like. The return is via the same route or on Hwy. 131. To reach River Rd. cross the 5th St. Bridge in town and turn left.

Rentals and Information—
There are two full-service mountain bike shops in town. Both shops offer repairs, rentals and advice to anyone willing to hop on a two-wheeler.

Ski Haus—Located in front of Safeway at **Hwy. 40** and **Pine Grove Rd.; (303) 879-0385.**

Sore Saddle Cyclery—1136 Yampa St.; (303) 879-1675.

FISHING

Dumont Lake—
Each year, plenty of catchable rainbows are stocked at Dumont. The lake offers good fishing and the kind of beauty that makes any fishing trip worthwhile. Your best bet is with bait or spin gear. Dumont Lake is the first in a series of small backcountry lakes that reaches north from Rabbit Ears Pass all the way to Fish Creek Reservoir on Buffalo Pass. If you decide to walk to any of the backcountry lakes, *be sure to carry and know how to use a map and compass.* Dumont Lake is located near the top of Rabbit Ears Pass. Take Hwy. 40 east of Steamboat for 24.5 miles and watch for a white sign on the north side.

Elk River—

The Elk flows out of the northwest side of the Mt. Zirkel Wilderness Area, and its upper portions are excellent for small rainbows and some brooks. The best fishing is in late summer after the runoff. To reach the upper Elk, take County Rd. 129 north of Steamboat for 18 miles to the small town of Clark. A couple of miles north of Clark turn right on Seedhouse Rd. and parallel the Elk River into Routt National Forest. After turning on Seedhouse Rd., the best fishing is 5 miles upriver between Hinman Campground and Seedhouse Campground.

The smaller tributaries flowing into the Elk River in the Routt National Forest are normally quite good for brooks, rainbows and mountain whitefish. The North Fork of the Elk is brimming with small brook and rainbow trout, especially in its upper portions. From Seedhouse Campground, head north on Forest Rd. 431 (four-wheel-drive) along the North Fork to the boundary of the Mt. Zirkel Wilderness Area. There are a number of even smaller creeks flowing into both the North and South forks that are worth pursuing with light fly gear. Even on the smaller streams the fishing is better in late summer.

Flat Tops Wilderness Area—

A maze of lakes, ponds and streams is spread throughout this high plateau only a short distance from Steamboat. Since the backcountry terrain is confusing, many people prefer hiring a guide for trips away from the roadside. The entire area is a superb trout habitat. For more information see the **Meeker** chapter.

Mount Zirkel Wilderness Area—

Remote and wonderfully beautiful are the many backcountry lakes and streams of the Mt. Zirkel Wilderness. The farther you hike, the better the fishing tends to be. A few ideas for backcountry lakes are Three Island Lake, Mica Lake and Gold Creek Lake. These lakes are not affected by winterkill and tend to offer excellent fishing for small (better eating!) brooks and rainbows. To reach the Mt. Zirkel Wilderness from Steamboat, travel north on County Rd. 129 for 18 miles to Clark. A mile or so north of Clark, turn right on Seedhouse Rd. and continue until the road forks. A right turn on Forest Rd. 443 takes you to the trailhead for Three Island Lake; continue on Seedhouse Rd. and you'll be at the trailhead for Mica and Gold Creek lakes.

Pearl Lake—

Several small streams flow into Steamboat Lake, but are not worth your time. However, Pearl Lake, only 3 miles east of Steamboat Lake, is well worth the minimal effort of getting there—especially if you prefer a smaller lake that is restricted to flies and lures only. To get here from Steamboat, take County Rd. 129 north 24 miles to the marked right turn for Pearl Lake.

Steamboat Lake—

This popular and scenic fishery is stocked with hundreds of thousands of fingerling rainbow each year. The average size catch is about 12 inches, but much larger fish are taken regularly. Some brooks and Snake River cutthroat are also taken. Both shore and boat fishing often result in good catches on the large lake. You may want to talk with the lake manager, Dennis Scheiwe, about where the fish are biting. His office is located at the northwest end of the lake. Steamboat Lake is open to fly, lure and bait fishing; a limit of eight fish each is imposed on all fishermen. From Steamboat Springs, drive north on County Rd. 129 for 27 miles to reach the lake.

Mike's Marina at Steamboat Lake dabbles in a little bit of everything, including big game safaris in Zimbabwe. Back at Steamboat Lake they rent a variety of boats and sailboards. They also have fishing supplies and licenses, groceries and pontoon dinner cruises on the lake. Located northwest of **Steamboat Lake; (303) 879-7019.**

Yampa River—

The Yampa flows east out of the Flat Top Mountains, but eventually changes course and passes directly through Steamboat Springs. Due to heavy runoff, the river stays murky well into July. Spin and bait casters do quite well in spite of the brown water. The fishing near Steamboat has been improved by a kayak course just south of town; pools and eddies provide a good habitat for rainbows, browns, natives and whitefish. Recently there have been a number of large northern pike caught within the town limits.

FOUR-WHEEL-DRIVE TRIPS

Four-wheeling in the Steamboat area is not quite as spectacular as in other parts of the state, mainly because there are not as many old roads available for exploration. The lack of roads can probably be attributed to the fact that the mining in the area was not very successful, so roads just didn't get cleared. Nonetheless, there are some good places to explore.

Many jeepers head up Elk River Rd. (County Rd. 129) well past Steamboat Lake and the town of Columbine to County Rd. 550. Turn right at this junction and head up into Red Park about 3 miles up the road. Here there is another fork in the road. The right fork (County Rd. 500) heads up to Big Red Park, then winds its way north to Hog Park on the Encampment River at the Wyoming border. The left fork goes up through Crane Park and Whiskey Park before reaching the Wyoming border.

Another popular four-wheel-drive road begins at the old mining town of Hahn's Peak (near Steamboat Lake). County Rd. 409 snakes its way east for about 10 miles to the North Fork of the Elk River. From here you can proceed downriver to the south, eventually reaching Seedhouse Campground on Seedhouse Rd.

GOLF

Sheraton Steamboat Golf Club—

Designed by Robert Trent Jones, Jr., this 18-hole golf course is one of the finest and most challenging mountain courses in the state, with a rating of 71. Groves of aspen and pine combine with far-reaching views of the Yampa River Valley and Mt. Werner. Guests staying at the Sheraton Hotel get a break on the greens fees. Walk-ons are welcomed seven days a week, but reservations 24 hours in advance are strongly recommended. The course is open mid-May to mid-Oct., so long as the weather cooperates. Cart and club rentals available; pro shop and restaurant/bar with a great outside patio. Golf clinics are offered. This course is first class and charges accordingly. Carts are required. Call **(303) 879-1391** for reservations and tee time. To reach the course, drive south of town on Hwy. 40. Turn left toward the ski area on Mt. Werner Rd. and take another left onto Steamboat Blvd., then right onto Clubhouse Dr. Follow the signs.

Steamboat Golf Club—

For a course with more down-to-earth prices, try the nine-hole Steamboat Golf Club, located just west of town on **Hwy. 40.** Greens fees are higher on weekends. **(303) 879-4295.**

HIKING AND BACKPACKING

Tree-covered ridges of aspen, lodgepole pine and spruce, meadows packed with colorful wildflowers and quiet streams meandering through scenic valleys: these are the characteristics of Routt National Forest near Steamboat. Though it hasn't nearly the rugged terrain or soaring peaks other parts of the state possess, Routt National Forest, with its ample wildlife and great fishing, has its own allure. Some of the peaks rise above 12,000 feet, but overall the forests and mountain meadows are closer to 10,000 feet. Within the national forest, directly east of Steamboat Springs, lies the Park Range. Extending more than 50 miles, this range runs north from Rabbit Ears Pass all the way to the Wyoming border. Straddling the Continental Divide for much of the way, the beautiful Mt. Zirkel Wilderness Area beckons many hikers and backpackers. Those who take the trouble to hike up to the divide are rewarded with spectacular views of the Yampa River Valley to the west, North Park and the Medicine Bow Range to the east.

Access to the wilderness area is fairly easy from a number of points. Trailheads into the wilderness area branch off from Buffalo Pass Rd., which cuts east from Steamboat over the divide and into North Park. Seedhouse Rd. (Forest Rd. 400), north of Clark, provides the most popular access to the backcountry. Unfortunately, many of the popular campsites at the nearby lakes are used quite heavily. If you plan to be out overnight, please comply with the minimal impact camping suggestions listed in the Introduction to this book or available at the ranger station in Steamboat.

Make sure you have good topographical maps with you in the backcountry. Maps are sold at a number of stores in the Steamboat area, including **Ski Haus**, located in front of Safeway at **Hwy. 40** and **Pine Grove Rd.; (303) 879-0385.** In Clark pick up a map at the **Clark General Store; (303) 879-3849.** You can't miss it. When you're at the Clark store, either before or after your backcountry trip, be sure to get a "Clark single" ice cream cone. It's the best deal in the state.

If you have any more questions about hiking in the Steamboat area, contact the **Hahn's Peak Ranger Office, PO Box 1212, 57 10th St., Steamboat Springs, CO 80477; (303) 879-1870.**

Fish Creek Falls—

Fish Creek Falls and the trail heading east from there are good areas for day hikes and extended backpack trips. This has to be the most popular tourist spot in the Steamboat area, and with good reason. Each year thousands of people drive the 3 miles up Fish Creek Falls Rd. to the recreation area and look in awe at the 283-foot waterfall. During the late spring and early summer, when the snow melt-off is particularly high, the falls are torrential.

Originally homesteaded in 1901 by the Crawford family, the falls were aptly named for the whitefish and brook trout spawning here in autumn. The townspeople used to have a picnic each year during the spawn. Using pitchforks, hooks and gunnysacks, they would collect the fish to be salted and stored for winter. In the early 1980s, after a threat by California developers to turn the area into residential housing, locals began an effort to purchase the land and turn it over to the forest service. In 1984 Fish Creek Falls became part of Routt National Forest.

Because the walk to the falls from the parking lot is less than a quarter of a mile, it gets a lot of use. Picnic tables, restrooms and interpretive signs make things easier for visitors. The Fish Creek Falls Trail leads to an overlook above the falls and then continues east up to a second set of falls, eventually reaching the Continental Divide. About 5 miles above the lower falls is Long Lake. The camping around Long Lake is good. For a longer hike, stay on the trail (No. 1102), which eventually turns southeast, reaching Dumont Lake Campground on Rabbit Ears Pass, 10.5 miles from Fish Creek Falls.

The Flat Tops—

For information about fishing and hiking in the Flat Tops Wilderness Area, see the Hiking and Backpacking section in the **Meeker** chapter.

Lake Dinosaur—

This lake is close to Steamboat and doesn't get a lot of visitors. It's less than a mile's walk to the lake, and the wildflowers are bountiful in summertime. To reach the trail from Steamboat Springs, head 4 miles northeast on Strawberry Park Rd. to the Buffalo Pass Rd. Turn right, go 12 miles to Buffalo Pass and turn right on Fish Creek Reservoir Rd. (Forest Rd. 310). Proceed about 3 miles. Park your car on the right side of the road and begin hiking west up the faint old road, which leads through a meadow to the lake.

Luna Lake—

You won't find many people at Luna

Lake, as it's a bit secluded. And the fishing is pretty good. To reach the lake, head north on Hwy. 40 for 2 miles, turn right on Elk River Rd. (County Rd. 129) and proceed to Mad Creek, about 5 miles up the road. Park near the buck and rail fence on the right and hike 7 miles up into Swamp Park near the lake. For an alternate access route, begin at Buffalo Pass and head 6 miles north on the Wyoming Trail to the intersection with Trail No. 1168. Turn left and hike a mile or so to the lake.

Mount Werner (the ski area)—

Many people who visit Steamboat overlook one of the most obvious places to hike in the area: Mt. Werner. Not only are there cut trails and great views, but gondola rides are available up the mountain for less ambitious hikers. From the top of the gondola you can continue to the top of Storm Peak. A number of trails can get you back down to the bottom of the mountain. There is a fee for gondola rides; kids under 5 and adults over 70 ride free. The summer season is from July 4th–Labor Day 9 am–3 pm. For ticket information call **(303) 879-6111.**

Seedhouse Road Trails—

Just north of Clark, Seedhouse Rd. (Forest Rd. 400) turns northeast, following the Elk River 13 miles to the old mining camp of Slavonia. From this road, many people begin day hikes and backpack trips into the beautiful lakes and mountains of the Mt. Zirkel Wilderness Area. Because the road provides such easy access for hikers and horseback riders, many of the most desirable destinations, especially **Gilpin Lake, Gold Creek Lake** and **Three Island Lake,** are overused. Damage from camping has taken its toll, and backpackers should not camp any closer than a quarter mile from the lakes. Day hikes into these lakes for fishing and sightseeing are a better idea. Up above Gilpin and Gold Creek lakes, **Ute Pass** crosses the Continental Divide at a low spot that the Utes used to frequent when traveling back and forth between the Yampa Valley and North

Park while hunting buffalo and deer.

One good possibility for backpacking in this area is a trip up to **Dome Lake,** about 8 miles up the South Fork of the Elk River. At 10,100 feet, the lake is snowed in until July. Directly in back of the lake to the south is the impressive 11,739-foot granite monolith known as the Dome. It can be scrambled up fairly easily from the southwest ridge. To reach the trailhead, head south on Forest Rd. 443 from the intersection on Seedhouse Rd. Continue about 3.5 miles. Allow some extra time for the hike due to a landslide on the trail that takes some effort to walk over.

Walton Peak—

This peak in the Rabbit Ears Pass area provides great views of the nearby Flat Tops, Never Summer and Rabbit Ears mountain ranges. The 4-mile hike is on a rarely used four-wheel-drive road. From Steamboat Springs, head east on Hwy. 40 up Rabbit Ears Pass to the Dumont Lake turn-off. Across the highway to the south (right) is the trailhead (Forest Rd. 251).

Wyoming Trail—

Feeling ambitious? How about a trail that follows the Continental Divide for 40 miles along rolling hills, past lakes, through forests of ponderosa and lodgepole pine? The Wyoming Trail (No. 1101) begins on Buffalo Pass near Summit Lake Campground and heads north through the Mt. Zirkel Wilderness Area and on up to Medicine Bow National Forest just over the Wyoming border. Views down into North Park and the Yampa River drainage are spectacular from the trail, which is above treeline for much of the way.

The trail can be indistinguishable in spots and difficult to follow, due to late snowpack and boggy areas. Much of the trail is still used by the local ranchers as a stock driveway. If you just want to hike part of the way, it's possible to get back out on Seedhouse Rd. near Slavonia, about 15 miles from Clark. To reach the trailhead on Buffalo Pass, take Strawberry Park Rd. 4 miles out of Steamboat Springs, turn right on Buffalo Pass Rd. and proceed 9 miles to the pass.

HORSEBACK RIDING

In case you've forgotten, here's a reminder: Steamboat Springs is one of the best areas of the state for horseback riding. Cowboys and the western persona that the ski area associates with are for real. The Yampa River Valley and nearby Elk River Valley are packed full of working ranches, dude ranches and some that are a combination of both. The ranching way of life is vital to the Steamboat area. Even the ski area used to be part of a ranch. Many dude ranches and riding stables provide the opportunity to get out on the trail for an overnight trip or a short hour-long ride.

Dude Ranches—

For extended stays at the **Home Ranch** and the **Vista Verde Guest Ranch**, see Where to Stay.

Steamboat Stables—

"A lot of changes over the years," pondered Steamboat Stables' proprietor Pat Mantle, "a lot of changes." Born in Dinosaur National Monument at his father's homestead, Mantle has spent his life in northwestern Colorado, and horses have been a big part of it.

In 1959 Mantle began raising horses near Estes Park to supply to dude ranches, riding stables and boys' camps. Since coming to Steamboat in 1970, the business has done well and now, with more than 1,000 horses, Mantle owns the largest herd in the state. Objecting to being called a horse rancher, Pat took a drag off his cigarette and admitted, "I'm more of a horse renter." Steamboat Stables is, obviously, only a small part of his operation, but it offers visitors the chance to take a trail ride on a gentle horse broken by an outfit that knows what they are doing.

Located on the west side of town at the base of Howelsen Hill, Steamboat Stables is open from mid-June through Labor Day for trail rides up the hill, from an hour up

to a full day. Breakfast rides and evening steak-dinner rides may be of interest. Horses can also be reserved for overnight pack trips, fall hunting trips, etc. Just give the stables some advance notice. For more information, contact: **PO Box 770885, Steamboat Springs, CO 80477; (303) 879-2306.**

Windwalker Ranch—

For more secluded trail riding, try the Windwalker Ranch. They offer a variety of riding possibilities, including breakfast rides, wagon dinner rides, moonlight rides and overnight pack trips into the Mt. Zirkel Wilderness Area. Half-day rides are very affordable. Discounts are available for children under 12 years and senior citizens. Reservations would be very wise. **PO Box 5092, Steamboat Springs, CO 80477; (303) 879-0595.**

LLAMA TREKKING

Elk River Valley Llama Company—

"Dogs bite, horses kick and, yes, llamas spit," answered Peter Nichols of Elk River Valley Llama Company when asked to verify the stories we had heard about the defense mechanisms of these cousins to the camel. "But llamas spit only if they are severely abused." In 1981 Peter Nichols began offering pack trips with these docile animals as the first commercial outfitter in the state. Since small beginnings, business for Peter and other packers around Colorado has really taken off. Recently Peter and one of his llamas, Hahns, landed themselves on the capitol steps in Washington, DC, during a promotional tour. Their visit to the steps of the capitol "drew more stares than a presidential motorcade," according to the *Denver Post*.

The Elk River Valley Llama Company is located near Clark, about 25 miles north of Steamboat Springs near the edge of the Mt. Zirkel Wilderness Area of Routt National Forest. Trips with Nichols's llamas are tailored for guests, whether they want a hard hiking trek, a relaxing one or something in between. These four- to five-day trips are first class, and include gourmet trail meals, such as steak and lobster brochette and grilled halibut steaks. How about a cocktail by the campfire? No problem. The llamas pack in all of the creature comforts. For details, including prices, etc., contact Peter Nichols at **PO Box 674, Clark, CO 80428; (303) 879-7531** and toll free 1-800-562-LAMA .

RIVER FLOATING

The water in the Steamboat Springs area is primarily of interest to kayakers. Sections with good rapids are located on rivers too small for larger rafts and canoes. The two largest rivers, the Yampa and the Elk, tend to be dominated by gentle stretches that don't give the adrenaline rush so many people look for. In addition, both rivers run through vast acreages of ranch land, quite often owned by hostile characters unwilling to grant permission to float through their property. As a matter of fact, some river floaters have been sent running after being threatened with a shotgun blast of rock salt.

Elk River—

Kayakers flock to the Elk River in late May through June to float a stretch currently under consideration for Wild and Scenic River status. From Box Canyon Campground down to Glen Eden, 8 miles away, the river drops an average of 70 feet per mile, with mainly Class III rapids. This is a beautiful area located in Routt National Forest. Thick stands of pine and aspen line the banks. Be sure to take out at Glen Eden, because the river is closed for 10 miles below that point.

At a park 2 miles above the town of Mad Creek, the national forest protects the water, and a short float featuring Class I and II rapids is possible. Take out at Mad Creek.

Yampa River—

The Yampa River flows through the town of Steamboat Springs before turning west and building steam on its way to the spectacular canyons carved in Dinosaur National Monument. Originally called Bear River by early settlers, the Yampa got its present name from the potato-like root that grows along its banks. The Utes relied greatly on it as a food source.

In Steamboat Springs, local kayakers and canoeists, with the help of city money, have fixed up a section of the river. From the south end of town to the city park on the west end of town, boulders have been placed in the river, forming a kayak course. Kayakers, canoeists and inner-tubers float this stretch all through the late spring and summer.

Outfitters—

Barry Smith, owner of the **Mountain Sports Kayak School**, has been kayaking for years and has built a national reputation. Smith led an expedition of handicapped people on a first-ever run down a river in Iceland that was filmed for a National Geographic special. So if you want to learn how to kayak, this is the guy to teach you.

Mountain Sports Kayak School offers lessons on the river from three hours up to five days. His two-day class on the Yampa is perhaps the most popular. Anyone 8 years and older is welcome. Open from mid-Apr. until as late as the water permits. Kayaks and inner-tube rentals are available. Located at **435 Lincoln Ave., PO Box 1986, Steamboat Plaza, CO 80488; (303) 879-8033.**

Buggywhip's offers one- to four-day, guided raft-floating trips. Fishing while floating is high priority for these guys. Located at **903 Lincoln Ave., PO Box 770479, Steamboat Springs, CO 80477; (303) 879-8033** and toll free **1-800-759-0343.**

SKIING
CROSS-COUNTRY SKIING

The cross-country skiing in the Steamboat area is ideal from a nordic skier's perspective and is perhaps the best area in the state. Rolling hills make it easy to do circle tours, as opposed to skiing up a steep river canyon and out the same way. Heavy snowfalls make for a long touring season, which attracts the US Olympic nordic team in early fall and late spring.

Tradition and local enthusiasm have also contributed to the quality and quantity of cross-country skiing opportunities in the area. As in many Colorado mountain towns, Steamboat's pioneers were well acquainted with skis, relying on them to get around in deep winter snows. For years locals have been skiing for sport. People like Sven Wiik, the "Guru of American cross-country skiing" (see Colorado Profile section), have been instrumental in fueling the enthusiasm for cross-country skiing in the area. Volunteers gather in wintertime to stake out trails in Routt National Forest. Whether you are looking for a groomed, tracked trail or a backcountry experience, it's here in Steamboat.

For trail maps and other information, contact the **Hahn's Peak Ranger Office, PO Box 1212, 57 10th St., Steamboat Springs, CO 80477; (303) 879-1870.**

Backcountry Trails—

Rabbit Ears Pass—People from all around the state who enjoy cross-country skiing are familiar with the Rabbit Ears Pass trail system. Rolling hills at 10,000 feet offer beautiful views and miles of circuitous, marked trails through the pine and aspen. The terrain is great for everything from gliding to telemarking.

Volunteers from the Steamboat Springs area help maintain the staked markers on the trails. Stay on the trails, as it's deceivingly easy to lose your way in the forest, and there are not many distinguishable landmarks except the Rabbit Ears. Rabbit Ears Peak, with its two crumbly, rose-colored granite spires, is one of Colorado's most well-known landmarks. In winter, you can ski to the base of the rocks from the top of the pass. All trailheads lie along **Hwy. 40** on Rabbit Ears Pass, about 10 miles southeast of Steamboat Springs.

Seedhouse Road—This road follows the path of the Elk River down from the Mt.

Zirkel Wilderness in a beautiful mountain valley. Routt National Forest has a marked trail system that begins 4.5 miles northeast of Clark in the Hinman Park area. You may also follow Seedhouse Rd. up from Hinman Park, as it remains unplowed. The trails are mostly of the rolling hill variety, with views to Mt. Zirkel in the distance. For information and maps, contact the forest service office in Steamboat. To reach Seedhouse Rd., take County Rd. 129 north of Steamboat for 18 miles to Clark. A couple of miles north of Clark turn right on Seedhouse Rd. and parallel the Elk River into Routt National Forest. There is also a trail system in and around Clark.

Groomed Trails—

Steamboat Ski Touring Center—At the beginning of each winter, the Steamboat Sheraton Golf Course undergoes a transformation. The course, with its rolling fairways and panoramic views, becomes the Steamboat Ski Touring Center. Twenty-eight kilometers of trails (both tracked and skating) wind along Fish Creek and the golf course, offering something for beginners to experts. Tickets can be purchased at the clubhouse. Lessons on the trails as well as backcountry guided trips are available, and rest assured that the instructors are qualified. The center is operated by Sven Wiik and his daughter, Birgitta, of the Scandinavian Lodge. Rentals are available, and the Picnic Basket sandwich shop offers warm drinks, Danish open-faced sandwiches, soups and salads. For directions see the Sheraton Steamboat Golf Club in the Golf section. For more information, contact: **PO Box 772297, Steamboat Springs, CO 80477; (303) 879-8180.**

Nearby Trails at Dude Ranches—

Home Ranch—This full-service guest ranch offers daily cross-country packages and longer stays. See the Where to Stay section.

Vista Verde Guest Ranch—See the Where to Stay section.

Rentals and Information—

Ski Haus—The Ski Haus rents a full selection of track and backcountry equipment. They can also provide you with good trail ideas. Located in front of Safeway at **Hwy. 40** and **Pine Grove Rd.; (303) 879-0385.**

The Clark Store—Located 20 miles north of Steamboat on **County Rd. 129**, the store rents equipment throughout the winter. There is also a trail system. **(303) 879-3849.**

DOWNHILL SKIING
Howelsen Hill—

You can be sure that locals were impressed when, in 1914, Carl Howelsen jumped 119 feet at Steamboat's first Winter Carnival. The "Flying Norseman" was responsible for teaching Steamboat residents the pleasures of skiing. No longer were the heavy wooden boards used only for transportation around the snow-covered streets—skiing could be fun!

Howelsen Hill offers a vertical drop of only 470 feet and is served by a poma lift and a rope tow. In addition to downhill skiing, the hill now has five different ski jumps that are used for Olympic-level qualifying meets and training. Perhaps you remember "Eddie the Eagle," the fledgling ski jumper from England who participated in the 1988 Winter Olympic Games. He practiced on the 90-meter Howelsen Hill ski jump just prior to the Olympics. The hill is open to the public each day; night skiing Tues.-Fri. 6–9 pm. Located across the 5th St. bridge from downtown; **(303) 879-4300.**

Steamboat—

From the base of Steamboat, you have only an inkling of what kind of mountain exists beyond the visible 1,000-foot rise of Christie Peak. As you come over the first hill, in an eight-passenger gondola, you are on the verge of discovery. Each year an average of 324 inches of Colorado powder drops on 2,500 skiable acres. The area is spread out among four interconnected mountains offering a wide diversity of terrain for all abilities. Storm Peak is the choice of experts, with its long bump runs and, after a storm, deep powder skiing. On Sunshine Peak, picking a route through the aspen-studded glades of Shadows and Twilight is a thrill you won't soon forget. Another beauty about Steamboat is the simple fact that you will rarely be kept waiting in a long lift line.

The legacy of champions continues as Billy Kidd, 1964 Olympic silver medalist and 1970 world champion, serves as the Director of Skiing at the Steamboat Ski Area. Most days at 1 pm sharp, you can meet Kidd at the top of Thunderhead Mountain for an informal ski clinic and a ski down from the top of Thunderhead Mountain. **2305 Mt. Werner Circle, Steamboat Springs, CO 80487; (303) 879-6111.**

Steamboat Powder Cats—

This is a service for powder lovers (with spare cash) who want to get away from the world of groomed runs and lift lines. Enter a new dimension of skiing by taking a snow cat into the high country and cutting the first tracks. For more information: **PO Box 2468, Steamboat Springs, CO 80477; (303) 879-5188.**

SLEIGH RIDES

Riding through the crisp winter air in the back of a sleigh is a lot of fun, but it can also be disappointing and overpriced. What follows is a run-down on a couple of the reputable companies in the Steamboat area and what they offer.

All Seasons' Ranch—

This company has been offering sleigh rides longer than anyone in the area. Cover up with elk robes while the horses whisk your sleigh up Walton Creek Canyon to a secluded tent where a family-style western meal is served. Departs 5 and 7:30 pm nightly. Call **(303) 879-2606** for reservations.

Windwalker Elk Tours—

This is one of the more unique sleighing opportunities. At 1 pm daily, Windwalker Ranch loads up its sleighs with passengers and rides into a large herd of elk during feeding time. The photo opportunities are fantastic, so be sure to bring your camera. Allow two hours and dress warmly. Transportation to the sleighs is provided and reservations are required. **(303) 879-8065.**

SWIMMING

Steamboat Springs Health and Recreation Association—

Several large pools and a hydro water slide are available for a fee. See the Hot Springs section for more information. **136 Lincoln Ave.; (303) 879-1828.**

TENNIS

More than 30 tennis courts are available for play in the Steamboat area. Most are located at large hotel or condominium complexes. A couple of options for public courts are at the Howelsen Hill Recreation Complex or at the Steamboat Springs Health and Recreation Association (see the Hot Springs section).

SEEING AND DOING

BALLOONING

Pegasus—

Owned and run by Tom and Karen Fox, Pegasus has been providing year-round balloon rides in the Yampa River Valley since 1983. They also offer rides from Hinman Park in the Upper Elk River Valley and a spectacular trip up and over Mt. Werner (the ski area) to the Continental Divide. In summer, rides are offered in the morning; winter rides are given both in morning and afternoon. Wear warm layers of clothing for the early morning rides, especially in winter. Rides last 15 minutes, half an hour or a full hour. It all depends on how much you want to spend. Of course, flights conclude with the traditional champagne toast and a balloonist's prayer. Reservations required. Call **(303) 879-9191.**

HOT SPRINGS

Beginning with the Ute Indians, hot springs around Steamboat have been used for medicinal and recreational purposes. Indians believed their strength would be rejuvenated by the Great Spirit who lived below the surface of the earth. In addition to using the mineral springs for health reasons, the Utes may also have used a sulphurous vapor cave across the river for torturing prisoners. Stories indicate that enemies of the Utes, especially captured Arapaho and Cheyenne, were put in the cave and slowly asphyxiated.

In 1875, James Crawford, the first white settler in Steamboat, shoveled out a hole in the sand so his family could enjoy a good hot soak at Heart Spring—now the location of the Steamboat Springs Health and Recreation Association. Crawford counted more than 150 springs in the Steamboat vicinity. Though many of the natural springs have disappeared as the town has grown, you'll likely smell an occasional burst of sulphur gas emitted from thermal waters coming up from faults deep in the earth. Iron Spring, Steamboat Spring, Lithia Spring, Soda Spring and Sulphur Spring are the names of a few that still bubble to the surface. A couple of great soaking opportunities remain at year-round swimming holes.

Steamboat Springs Health and Recreation Association—

Starting with James Crawford, many bathers have enjoyed bathhouses and pools at this location. Today there are several concrete and tile pools, a hydro water slide, a snack bar and workout facilities. The hot mineral soaking pool is kept at a steady 100 degrees. Though this site has been heavily developed, it is a great place for families to come and enjoy an in-town soak. Open year-round. Summer and winter hours 7 am–9 pm daily; fall and spring hours 7 am–8 pm daily. An admission fee is charged. **136 Lincoln Ave.; (303) 879-1828.**

Strawberry Park Hot Springs—

Longtime Steamboat residents bemoan the recent changes at Strawberry Park Hot Springs. Only a few years ago the springs were known by locals as a great place to ski in to for a private soak. Now the road is plowed in winter and admission is charged, but the rock-lined pools remain a fine place for those in search of a natural location. Three knee-deep pools are fed by source water of 150 degrees and mixed with cold creek water to an ideal temperature of about 104 degrees. On hot summer days the water is kept cooler. The owners have made the pools a bit larger than before and have imposed as few rules as possible. The important rules are: bring no glass, bring no pets unless you are camping and please wear a bathing suit during daylight hours. Bathing suits are optional after dark. There are a couple of cabins ($$) for rent and nine campsites ($) spread around the property for those interested in staying overnight. Open daily 10 am–midnight. To reach Strawberry Park Hot Springs, drive 7 miles north of Steamboat on **County Rd. 36** (Strawberry Park Rd.). The road ends at the gate; **(303) 879-0342.**

MUSEUMS AND GALLERIES

Depot Art Center—

The historic railroad depot, built in 1906, now serves as a hub for the artistic community. Special dance programs, music programs, plays and continual gallery displays are featured. For more information and a schedule of year-round events, call **(303) 879-4434.** Open Mon.–Fri. 9 am–5 pm. Located across the 12th St. Bridge from Lincoln Ave.

Tread of Pioneers Museum—

With the exception of the Indian room, nearly all of the items in this museum came from pioneer families in Routt County. It is a worthwhile stop for those interested in

the early history of the area. The living room is filled with worn furniture and old photos; check out the piano that was shipped around Cape Horn on a voyage beginning in New York City in 1868 and ending in Steamboat Springs 18 years later. You will gain a new respect for the origins of ski jumping when you look at the heavy leather ski-jumping boots that Carl Howelsen (alias the Flying Norseman) used in the early 1900s. The stockman's room still smells like it. It's filled with saddles, traps, spurs and guns. The Indian room displays a collection of arrowheads, Navajo rugs, baskets and pottery from around the country. Just next door is a small room showing the eccentric waste of the white man—with furniture created from the horns of moose, elk and bighorn sheep. From Memorial Day to Labor Day the museum is open noon–8 pm daily. The rest of the year it is open by appointment only; call Jim Stanko at (303) 879-0825. At the corner of **8th St.** and **Oak St.; (303) 879-2214.**

NIGHTLIFE

In keeping with other ski resort towns in Colorado, it's very easy to have a good time after hours in Steamboat. Those wishing to make their way from the mountain to town, or vice versa, for an evening of partying can take the town bus, which goes about every 20 minutes. For late-night trips back to your lodge, ask the bartender about the **Tipsy Taxi Service, 879-2800,** which offers free rides for those who have had a bit too much to drink.

Antlers Cafe and Bar (in Yampa)—

Mike Benedict and his wife, Emily, have been tending bar for over half a century—and they've been married even longer! When I asked Mike if he was considering retirement, he looked me in the eye and said, "I don't mind this business. After all, I have more fun than my customers do." The Antlers Bar, in business since 1898, is a snapshot from the past. Game trophies hang from the walls, two paintings of nude life-sized Rubensesque ladies gaze down from one side of the long room and the original oak back bar still gets plenty of use. The Antlers Bar was recently chosen as the set for a Henry Weinhard TV commercial, and now the Benedicts sell Henry's extra cheap. Mike is a crotchety old guy who likes to recall obscure liquor laws (just try to walk away from the bar with your beer). He has put up every sarcastic sign imaginable, including one that reads, Hungry? Eat an Environmentalist. Some regular customers call him Groucho. He doesn't mind, but goes on to remind us, "I'm not quite as dead as he is . . . yet." The Antlers Bar is located on **Main St.** in Yampa; **(303) 638-9986.**

Club Majiks—

The glitz and glitter of Broadway has taken up residence in a small second-floor dinner theater at the mountain in Steamboat. Guests are treated to a "gourmet American" meal in a plush setting complete with linens and candlelight. Dinner is served by the actors in costume and in character. The carefully rehearsed show is done in the style of a cabaret. It is definitely not the garden variety show you might expect in such a small community. Mark Schwartz, the owner/producer of Club Majiks, has a long line of Broadway hits to his credit. He has produced well-known plays such as *La Cage Aux Folles* and *Zorba the Greek*, winning five Tony Awards along the way. Compared to similar venues, Mark says his show is "unequivocally the most spectacular live show in the country." Dinner is served at 7 pm and the show begins at 9 pm. Reservations are essential, whether for dinner and the show, or just the show. **The Clock Tower; 879-5848.**

The Inferno—

A wild après-ski spot on the mountain, just to the right of the gondola in a ski-in, ski-out location. The Inferno is a great place to take the edge off after a day on the slopes. Their famous shot wheel is spun periodically (à la Wheel of Fortune) to determine special drink prices for the next few minutes. Live music Mon.–Sat. On the mountain. **2305 Mt. Werner Rd.; 879-5111.**

Old Town Pub—

This is a casual, local hangout with wooden floors, a long bar and lots of friendly conversation. It's the people who make the Old Town Pub a great place to visit. In summer, the outdoor patio has the spirit of a Bavarian beer garden. Inside, one large room is split down the middle with a bar on one side and a restaurant on the other. The restaurant serves standard American fare at reasonable prices (lunch $, dinner $$; Sun. brunch $$). Live bands rock the house on most weekends. Open daily 10 am–2 am. Located in town at **6th St.** and **Lincoln Ave.; 879-2101.**

Steamboat Yacht Club—

Located down on the bank of the Yampa River across from the ski jump at Howelsen Hill, Steamboat Yacht Club is a great place to go for an outside wooden deck and bands that play on the lawn in summer. The inside is broken up into many rooms for no particular reason. Mostly a younger crowd. Full menu and bar. Open 11:30 am–2 am. In town. **811 Yampa St.; 879-4774.**

The Tugboat—

This place, a local favorite, has been around forever and is an integral part of "The Triangle" of popular restaurants and bars at Ski Time Square. The Tugboat is a casual sports bar, offering live music on weekends and big crowds. A recent expansion that was the talk of the town should offer a bit more elbow room. Skiers flock here for lunch and après ski. Burgers highlight the menu. For a rowdy night of dancing to rock and blues, try the Tugboat. Après ski from 4–7 pm daily; live entertainment from 9:30 pm–1:30 am Mon.–Sat. in winter and Thur.–Sat. in summer. On the mountain. **1860 Mt. Werner Rd. (Ski Time Square); 879-7070.**

SCENIC DRIVES

Buffalo Pass—

This is the only road crossing the Continental Divide through the Park Range just east of Steamboat Springs. It offers great views of the Yampa River basin and North Park. Buffalo Pass gets its name from the time when Ute Indians used to wait in ambush for the herds of buffalo migrating between North Park and the Yampa Valley. In fall, the aspen groves are a spectacular sight. The dirt road is pretty rough but passenger cars can make it. Snow usually prohibits crossing the pass until after the Fourth of July. Hiking trails branch off to the north of the road into the Mt. Zirkel Wilderness Area. To reach Buffalo Pass, take Strawberry Park Rd. 4 miles out of Steamboat to the intersection of Buffalo Pass Rd. The summit of the pass is about 12 miles up the road. Continue on down into North Park and return to Steamboat over Rabbit Ears Pass, southwest of Walden.

Elk River Valley—

It's hard to match the beauty of this valley as it traces the path of the Elk River down from the Mt. Zirkel Wilderness. In July the wildflowers create a patchwork of colors in the high meadows. Routt National Forest encompasses much of the valley, where you may enjoy camping, fishing and hiking. (See the appropriate sections for more information.) After about 13 miles, at Slavonia, the road ends at a wilderness access point, with views of snowcapped peaks along the Continental Divide. To reach the Elk River Valley, take County Rd. 129 north of Steamboat for 18 miles to Clark. A couple of miles north of Clark, turn right on Seedhouse Rd. and proceed into Routt National Forest.

Fish Creek Falls—

Only 3 miles east of Steamboat Springs, a torrent of water cascades over a cliff and descends 283 feet to the rocks below. When runoff is at its peak in July, the thundering falls are at their most spectacular. Of course, the falls remain a beautiful sight throughout the year. A small footbridge crosses just in front of the falls, and six picnic tables are nearby. The viewing and picnic areas are accessible to the handicapped. If you are interested in hiking to a second set of falls or up to Long Lake, see page 126. From Lincoln Ave. (Hwy. 40), turn north onto Third Ave. and drive one block to the four-way stop at Oak St. Turn right and continue 3 miles until the road ends in the parking area for Fish Creek Falls.

——— WHERE TO STAY ———

ACCOMMODATIONS

Home Ranch — $$$$

In a spectacular natural setting just 20 miles north of Steamboat is a secluded ranch with an international reputation. This spacious spread, located in the Elk River Valley at the edge of Routt National Forest, offers guests the chance to enjoy a mountain lifestyle without giving up any comforts. Each cabin has a private jacuzzi on a secluded porch and is furnished with handmade furniture, Indian rugs and a wood stove. Down comforters overlay the beds and terrycloth robes are hanging in the closet. Daily maid service and a nightly turndown make it feel as though you were staying in a five-star hotel. Carefully prepared gourmet food is served three times daily. The heated pool is open year-round as a further inducement to guests.

Summer or winter there are enough activities to fill anyone's appointment book, but "no one is pushed or obligated to do things...." Horseback riding is the emphasis in summer; "you can do as much or as little riding as you want." By the time you leave you'll be able to groom and saddle your own horse. Fly-fishing in their private pond and llama trekking are also options. In winter, cross-country skiing takes over. Instruction and rentals are available to guests. Unlimited powder trails exist on the adjacent public lands. On the ranch property there are 40 kilometers of groomed tracks, with some set aside for skating. The trails are open to day skiers who are bused from Steamboat each morning. If you're staying at the ranch, you can catch the bus to Steamboat for a day of downhill skiing.

In July and Aug., guests must reserve their stays on a weekly basis or for a three-night stay, with all meals included. The rest of the year is a bit more flexible. For more information, write: **Ken Jones, PO Box 822, Clark, CO 80428;** or call **(303) 879-1780.**

Vista Verde Guest Ranch — $$$$

Winter or summer, this rustic hideaway attracts guests from around the country who enjoy the perfect combination of activities and pure relaxation. Frank and Winton Brophy have been taking on "dudes" since 1974. Located 25 miles north of Steamboat, their 600-acre ranch is bordered by 1.2 million acres of Routt National Forest and the Mt. Zirkel Wilderness Area. In summer, there is an emphasis on horseback riding, though your time may be spent hiking, fishing, whitewater rafting, hot-air ballooning or just enjoying the incredible views. Kids will love feeding and watering the barnyard chickens and gathering freshly laid eggs. In winter the ranch is used as a nordic center, getting 300-plus inches of snow. There are miles of groomed trails on the ranch and unlimited touring in the adjacent forest service terrain. Bring your own touring equipment.

Eight hand-hewn cabins are spread out among the aspen trees at Vista Verde. One-, two- and three-bedroom cabins offer the modern comforts of firm mattresses, private bathrooms and complete kitchens while retaining an entirely rustic feel. Each cabin is furnished with sturdy pine furniture, a wood stove and a distinct lack of anything unnecessary. The Brophys have "tried to stay away from becoming another resort," but recently made a very popular concession: a log-and-glass-enclosed spa with whirlpool, cold plunge, sauna and deck. "We tried to keep it in synch with the rest of the ranch," Frank said. By the way, a gourmet chef serves three heaping meals each day at the main lodge building. Meals are included in the weekly price; shorter stays can be arranged in the off-peak season. **PO Box 465, Steamboat Springs, CO 80477; toll free 1-800-526-RIDE or (303) 879-3858.**

Harbor Hotel — $$$

The Harbor Hotel is something of a landmark and, over the past 50 years, has attracted many stars. Mickey Rooney, Jack Dempsey and Shirley Temple have all stayed here, to name a few. All of the 61 rooms in the old hotel have been recently refurnished with English antiques. The character missing in newer hotels is provided by wooden and brass bedsteads, armoires, steamer trunks and creaky writing desks. Each of the rooms is simply and tastefully decorated; all come with private baths, cable TV and telephones. The honeymoon suite stands above the rest because of its large picture windows and a separate, elegant sitting room. Behind the original hotel, a separate building offers motel-type accommodations as well as plush condominiums. A health spa offers guests the use of two large hot tubs in addition to a sauna and changing room. In town. **703 Lincoln Ave., PO Box 774109, Steamboat Springs, CO 80477; (303) 879-1522;** call toll free **1-800-334-1012** in Colorado, or **1-800-543-8888** nationwide.

The Clermont Inn — $$ to $$$

An interesting facade and a bed and breakfast sign will draw your attention to the Clermont Inn. Once inside, the spacious lobby area is what you were hoping for, but the rooms are not. That is, unless you enjoy cramped and charmless quarters. Each room has a private toilet and sink, but a complex arrangement requires adjoining rooms to share one bathtub. Underneath it all, the Clermont is basically a motor lodge with a full breakfast served in the refurbished basement. In town. Located at **917 Lincoln Ave., PO Box 774927, Steamboat Springs, CO 80477; (303) 879-3083.**

Columbine — $$

During the Hahn's Peak gold strike in the late 1800s, the town of Columbine blossomed as a place for the miners and their families to live. The town and its residents lived fairly quietly until the mining petered out early this century. Like many other towns in Colorado connected with defunct mining areas, Columbine was soon abandoned, becoming a virtual ghost town.

In the early 1980s, the entire town, which consisted of the old general store and about a dozen cabins, was purchased and has been turned into a rustic getaway for those who don't mind stoking their own coal stove and walking down to the tiny sauna and shower building. The Columbine cabins have been fixed up and sparsely furnished with well-worn antiques. The view of nearby Hahn's Peak to the east conjures up old memories of the mining days gone by.

There is good fishing at Hahn's Peak Lake, Steamboat Lake and nearby streams. Columbine is located about 30 miles north of Steamboat Springs past Steamboat Lake on Elk River Rd. The cabins are available during the summer and into the fall. For information and reservations, contact Carl and Liz Hughes, **PO Box 716, Clark, CO 80428; (303) 879-7883** (summer) or **300 Leigh Circle, Hot Springs, AR 71901; (501) 321-9190** (winter).

Scandinavian Lodge — $ to $$$

Sven Wiik (see Colorado Profile section) and family opened this family-oriented lodge more than 20 years ago, and it has been a Steamboat Springs institution ever since. Nestled at the foot of Mt. Werner, the Scandinavian Lodge is a unique facility combining a nordic training center with an alpine lodge open to the public. Twice a year the US Olympic Nordic Ski Team comes here to train and ski the nearby terrain on Rabbit Ears Pass. The lodge encourages its guests to cross-country ski at the Steamboat Ski Touring Center and to attend clinics. If it's downhill skiing you want, fine. The Thunderhead ski lift is just 100 yards up the road. You can ski right from the mountain to the lodge.

Accommodations vary greatly from inexpensive dormitory beds to spacious apartments, some with their own fireplace. The hot tub tops off a day on the slopes or a summertime hike. With its own kitchen, the lodge offers three meals each day, highlighted by Scandinavian specialties served buffet style. The atmosphere is friendly, encouraging people to mix and swap stories of their day on the slopes and trails. This aspect of the stay is a reason many people return to the lodge year after year.

Buses to town leave six times daily from the lodge. On the mountain. For more information contact Margareta Olsson at **PO Box 774484, Steamboat Springs, CO 80477; (303) 879-0517.**

CAMPING

In Routt National Forest near Steamboat Springs—

Dry Lake Campground can be reached by heading 4 miles north of Steamboat Springs on Strawberry Park Rd., then east for 3.5 miles on Buffalo Pass Rd. There are eight sites and no fee. Another 8.5 miles up Buffalo Pass Rd. is **Summit Lake Campground**, located at the summit of the pass. Check to see if the road is open before planning a trip up here. There are 17 sites, and no fee is charged. From the summit of Buffalo Pass, **Granite Campground** can be reached by heading 5 miles south to **Fish Creek Reservoir**. You'll find six sites, and no fee is charged.

Hinman Campground can be reached by driving 18 miles north from Steamboat on Elk River Rd. to Glen Eden. Turn northeast on Seedhouse Rd. (Forest Rd. 400) for 6 miles. This campground on the Elk River has 13 sites, and a fee is charged. **Seedhouse Campground** is just another 3.5 miles up Forest Rd. 400 from the turn-off to Hinman Campground. Seedhouse has 24 sites, and a fee is charged.

Hahn's Peak Lake Campground is located 25 miles north of Steamboat up Elk River Rd. At the sign for the campground, turn left and proceed 2.5 miles on Forest Rd. 486. 26 sites; fee charged.

Heading southeast from Steamboat Springs on Hwy. 40 eventually leads you to **Meadows Campground,** 15 miles from town. It offers 33 sites, and there is a fee. Two miles farther up the road is **Walton Creek Campground,** which has 14 sites; a fee is charged. At the summit of Rabbit Ears Pass (22 miles from Steamboat), head north for a mile on the old Hwy. 40 road to **Dumont Lake Campground,** where 12 sites await; a fee is charged.

For other ideas for camping in Routt National Forest, talk to **Hahn's Peak Ranger District Office,** 57 10th St., Steamboat Springs, CO 80477; (303) 879-1870.

Private Campgrounds—
Fish Creek Campground—This campground claims to be the closest campground to a major ski area in the country. And who are we to question them? Sites for RVs and tents are available all year. Bathhouse, water, electric hookups and a game room are provided. Located just south of town on **Hwy. 40.** (303) 879-5476.

Strawberry Park Hot Springs—They offer secluded tent sites and the chance to awaken to a dip in the natural hot springs. See the Hot Springs section for more information.

WHERE TO EAT

Hazie's — $$$$

The experience of taking a gondola to the top of Thunderhead Peak for dinner is one to remember. Not many places can match Hazie's for atmosphere and spectacular views. What could be better than watching the sun set over the Yampa Valley while enjoying a candlelight dinner? Hazie's would be a natural hit, if only the food and service were more consistent. You might ask a few locals to learn the current status of dinner at Hazie's. A full meal and a round-trip gondola ticket are included in one package price. Winter hours: Open daily for lunch, 11:30 am–2:30 pm; dinner, one seating only, Tues.–Sat. 6:30–8 pm. During summer Hazie's is open only for Sat. dinner and Sun. brunch from 10:30 am–2 pm. Reservations required. On the mountain, at the top of the **Silver Bullet Gondola; 879-6111.**

L'Apogee — $$$

Muted pastels in this restaurant's dining room provide an elegant setting for a special night out. A small blackboard menu displays the nightly offerings of traditional French and nouvelle cuisines. Thankfully, the staff patiently translates dishes such as *entrecôte de boeuf aux trois poivres, côte d'agneau prisianne* and *canard rôti princesse.* L'Apogee has put together an award-winning wine cellar to complement the carefully prepared food of owner/chef Jaime Jenny. The wine list offers 450 choices; more than 40 selections are available by the glass. You may want to ask about their collection of single-malt scotch. Reservations recommended. Open from 5:30 pm. In town, **911 Lincoln Ave.;** 879-1919.

Mattie Silks — $$$

The highlight of any trip to Steamboat is dinner at Mattie Silks. This restaurant is named for the infamous Denver madam, who supposedly shot another woman in a pistol duel over a man. He must have been quite a guy! The split-level Victorian dining room is enhanced by a fabric-draped ceiling, soft music and fresh flowers on each table. There is an open courtyard view from the upstairs dining room. The owners and staff have worked side by side for years. Continental cuisine leaning toward French is prepared with an emphasis on freshness. A sampling includes roast rack of lamb, lemon pepper veal with brandy sauce, swordfish and trout amandine. Adjoining the restaurant is a lounge area with a backbar dating from the 1870s. Watneys and Heineken are on tap and more than 50 imported beers are chilled and ready. In winter, early reservations are a must. The restaurant is open 5:30–10 pm nightly; cocktails served 4 pm–2 am. On the mountain, **Ski Time Square; 879-2441.**

Old West Steak House — $$$

In cattle country, it's a good idea to follow the locals to the best steakhouse in town. The Old West is a no-nonsense eatery specializing in choice cuts of charbroiled beef. Prime rib, filet mignon and top sirloin are served, along with more exotic cuts of buffalo tenderloin and elk steak. If your taste leans toward seafood or chicken, there are several selections. We can attest to the fact that the owners, Barb and Don Silva, personally greet nearly every guest walking into their establishment. You may recognize Don: a few years back he was peering down from billboards across the country as the macho construction worker in a series of Winston cigarette ads. Don is also well traveled. When asked about his prime rib taco night (Wednesday evenings in the bar), he proclaimed, "I've eaten tacos all over the world and mine are the best." And we all know how tough it is to get a good taco in Bangkok. The upstairs bar menu offers a lighter version of the restaurant menu at much more affordable prices ($ to $$). Restaurant reservations recommended. Dinner served 5–10 pm nightly. A late-night bar menu is served until midnight. In town, **11th St. and Lincoln Ave.; 879-1441.**

5th Street Cafe — $$ to $$$

Opened in 1984, this restaurant is trying to become known as a place for breakfast, lunch and dinner. It seems to be working: opinions around town differ as to which of these meals is best at the 5th Street Cafe. Formerly a crepe shop, the new restaurant still serves great breakfast dishes, but the owner is pushing the idea of casual gourmet meals at affordable prices. The atmosphere is relaxed but tasteful, with oak trim and cabinetry, plants and local art on the wall from a gallery in town. Sidewalk seating is a big draw for the breakfast and lunch crowd. Inside there is a waiting area on the main floor with a wine cabinet built into the wall. Upstairs there are two dining rooms. The food is

sent up from the kitchen by dumbwaiter.

Crepes are still a favorite for breakfast, as well as omelettes and Belgian waffles. Specialty burgers are popular for lunch. For dinner try a daily seafood special such as salmon or yellowfin tuna. Lamb and beef dishes are also very good. The wine list is impressive, with Italian, French and domestics. Open seven days a week: breakfast served 7 am–2:30 pm, lunch 11 am–2:30 pm and dinner from 5:30–10 pm in summer; breakfast and lunch until 2 pm and dinner from 6 pm in summer. In town, **442 Lincoln Ave.; 879-4106.**

La Montaña — $$ to $$$

This restaurant offers table seating under a peaked solarium. The light southwestern feel goes well with the food. Unique and spicy concoctions range from lobster fajitas to more traditional enchilada and burrito dinners. Restaurant hours: 5:30–10 pm in winter, 5–9:30 pm in summer. Bar hours: 3:30 pm–midnight in winter; 4:30 pm–midnight in summer. On the mountain, **Après Ski Way** and **Village Dr.; 879-5800.**

Canton Chinese Restaurant — $$

What's this? The owner of a Chinese restaurant roaming the tables asking how the service and food are? And they have already been in business a few years. That's a welcome surprise. Formerly a Dairy Queen, the building underwent extensive changes when Ney Hoa Cheng and her husband, Siou Cheou, came in. Unfortunately, you can't order a Peanut Buster Parfait to go with your Peking duck. Business is booming and for good reason. The Cantonese and Szechuan items are delicious and affordable; the service is friendly. The decor does not evoke China but, hey, the food is the important thing. Try the curried chicken or Hunan beef. Wine and beer served, including Tsing-tao from China. Lunch specials ($) served 11:30 am–4 pm Mon.–Fri. Hours are Mon.–Fri. 11:30 am–10 pm, Sat.–Sun. 5–10 pm. In town, **720 Lincoln Ave.; 879-4480.**

Chelsea's — $$

An institution in the area? Well, maybe. Chelsea's, located in nearby **Oak Creek** (22 miles south), has been around since the late 1970s, when the town was enjoying a boom. A lot of young people lived here while working in Steamboat and at the nearby and now defunct Stagecoach Ski Area project. Due to the cost of living and lack of jobs, Oak Creek has seen many of its residents leave in the past few years, but Chelsea's remains.

People who live in Steamboat really like this place. We did too. Specializing in Szechuan Chinese food, Chelsea's is a small place with lots of character. Named after the owner's daughter, the restaurant is decorated with a mishmash of Chinese trinkets, including a kite and an ornate silk jacket. Rock music blasts from speakers and the atmosphere is very laid back. The menu is extensive and so is the beer list. Chelsea's T-shirts ($10) get the vote for the most creative design in Routt County. For an escape from Steamboat and a fun meal you might want to try it. Located on the main street in Oak Creek; **736-8538.**

Dos Amigos — $$

Since 1975 this restaurant has been a popular place for meeting friends and strangers alike. In summer, order a pitcher of margaritas and watch the people go by from the deck; during winter, the après-ski crowd is drawn inside for half-price appetizers and elbow-to-elbow company. Mexican dishes include combo plates, fajitas, chile rellenos and specials. Bar opens at 2:30 pm in winter, 3:30 pm in summer. Restaurant is open from 5 pm in winter and 5:30 pm in summer. On the mountain, **Ski Time Square; 879-4270.**

Cugino's — $ to $$

Asked what makes their Philly-style pizza so good, co-owner "Angie" Angelaccio hinted that it has something to do with the dough. Whatever it is, it keeps attracting locals. Angie and his cousin Henry own the place (*cugino's* means "cousin's" in Italian). This small, inexpensive restaurant has the feel of an East Coast pizzeria, with Italian travel posters, snapshots of Philadelphia on the wall and bottles of Chianti prominently displayed. The kitchen is easily visible from the tables, and you almost feel as though you are in there with them as they toss the dough and cook the spaghetti.

Cugino's does specialize in pizza, but they also are known for their strombolis, calzones and Philly steak sandwiches. A special board changes daily with dishes such as eggplant Parmesan, shrimp Alfredo and sauteed mushrooms with sausage. At lunchtime, pizza by the slice and small calzones are available. Along with wine, there is beer on tap and Moretti Italian beer in bottles. Open Mon.–Sat. 11 am–10 pm, Sun. 11 am–10 pm (in winter), Sun. 1–10 pm (in summer). Delivery available 5–9:30 pm. In town, **825 Oak St.; 879-5805.**

The Shack — $

Breakfast is served all day at this simple and dependable cafe. The Shack has been serving breakfast, under one name or another, for 25 years. It is also a good stop-off for a quick burger at lunch. Open 6 am–2 pm on weekdays, 6:30 am on weekends. In town, **8th St. and Lincoln Ave.; 879-9975.**

SERVICES

Alpine Taxi-Limousine Inc.—

A taxi/limousine service shuttles people back and forth from Stapleton Airport in Denver and other ski areas and Steamboat. **30670 Moffat Ave., Steamboat Springs, CO 80477; 1-800-343-RIDE** out of state, **1-800-232-RIDE** in state, **879-2800** locally.

Steamboat Springs Chamber Resort Association—

PO Box 774408, Steamboat Springs, CO 80477; 879-0880 locally, or **1-800-332-3204** in Colorado.

Grandkids Day Care Center—

80 Park Ave., Steamboat Springs, CO 80477; 879-5390.

COLORADO PROFILE—SVEN WIIK

Referred to by many as the "guru of American cross-country skiing" and "a legend in his own time," Sven Wiik observes, "those are slight exaggerations." Whatever the case, it's hard not to admire the contributions this man has made to the sport of cross-country skiing in America since he came over from Sweden in 1949. According to Wiik, he emigrated at a time when many Swedes were anxious to get out and see the world after being confined to their country during World War II.

Wiik landed a job at Western State College in Gunnison as the cross-country skiing coach for what he thought was going to be a year or two. His phenomenal success, however, made it difficult for him to leave, and he ended up coaching for 19 years. During that time, many of his skiers made the Olympic team, and Wiik coached various US teams from 1958 to 1966, including the 1960 Olympic team. He finally left coaching when he wasn't able to lead his skiers through the woods himself. When he couldn't keep up with his own athletes, "it wasn't any fun anymore." So Wiik, his wife, Birthe (pronounced "Bitty"), and their daughter, Birgitta, moved to Steamboat and built the Scandinavian Lodge and Mt. Werner Training Center for serious athletes. Still running today, it combines a lodge environment with the best of cross-country skiing teaching and training equipment, including Wiik's own invention, the Posi-Track computerized ski machine for year-round use.

Recreational cross-country skiers as well as Olympic athletes come to the lodge and training center to ski and learn from Wiik. He places a great deal of importance on learning to cross-country ski, especially for people who want to eventually learn to downhill ski. "Learning to downhill before you learn to tour is like trying to walk before you can crawl," he explains. When talking about the dramatically increasing interest in cross-country skiing in America, Wiik predicts that by the mid-1990s there will be two cross-country skiers for every downhiller. We'll see.

Summit County

Summit County sits high in the mountains 70 miles west of Denver. Taken as a whole, it's the undisputed king of recreation and winter resorts in Colorado. For sheer numbers of activities and visitors, forget Vail and Aspen. Summit County wins the prize. With four ski areas, numerous resorts and the beauty of the surrounding Arapaho National Forest, there is something to interest everyone.

The setting is spectacular. Towering mountains along the Continental Divide rim the east and south borders of the county, while the magnificent peaks of the Tenmile and Gore ranges lie to the west. Tenmile Creek, the Blue River and the Snake River all converge from different valleys at the focal point of the county—Dillon Reservoir. The dam that entraps this immense body of water was completed by the Denver Water Board in the early 1960s. From the reservoir, the Blue River meanders north to Green Mountain Reservoir, eventually dumping into the Colorado River after 36 miles.

Summit County didn't gain attention until settlements sprang up during the Breckenridge Gold Rush of 1859. Later, silver strikes near Montezuma in 1863 brought even more people to the area. After the mining boom petered out, towns died as people moved out, although some settlements, such as Breckenridge, Dillon and Frisco, hung on. With its unique charm, **Breckenridge** stands out above the rest. Streets in this Victorian town are lined with beautifully restored buildings from its former mining days, earning it a National Historic District designation.

With the development of ski areas and the completion of Dillon Reservoir, Summit County began to build a reputation as a great place to get away from it all. When Eisenhower Tunnel on Interstate 70 was completed in 1973, cutting the driving time from Denver by a half hour, many day visitors from the big city began to flock to Summit County.

Summit County is probably best known for its skiing. Four areas, each with its own personality, have much to offer. **Breckenridge** is the largest of the four, with diverse terrain on three separate mountains. The Victorian atmosphere in town, brought out by the mining history and restored gingerbread houses, adds a great deal of character, more so than the neighboring burgs. Steep terrain at **Arapahoe Basin**, one of the oldest ski areas in Colorado, complements the more easygoing hills at immaculate **Keystone**, just a few miles down the road. Keystone, a corporate-owned planned resort, stands out particularly for its fine accommodations, restaurants and first-class service. The other true planned resort in Summit County is **Copper Mountain**. Its amenities can't quite match Keystone's, but the ski mountain is superb and is considered by many to be one of the best-designed areas in the country—high praise indeed. In addition to downhill skiing, a number of nordic centers and dozens of backcountry trails attract many cross-country skiers.

142

When the snow melts and the wildflowers start to bloom, summer activity in Summit County comes close to matching that of the peak winter season. Hiking in the surrounding mountains, jeeping to old ghost towns and golfing on one of the exceptional courses are just some of the attractions.

There are about 8,000 full-time residents in Summit County. During the busy winter and summer seasons the county's population swells with vacationers. Clustered around Dillon Reservoir, the towns of **Frisco, Dillon** and **Silverthorne** can provide an escape from the resorts and their higher-priced accommodations. If you want a total escape from the adult-Disneyland atmosphere, you might also consider staying in one of the rustic lodges near the old mining town of **Montezuma**.

Summit County covers a huge area. Having spent a lot of time there over the years, we've narrowed the chapter down to include its "best" features. If you want more information, contact the **Summit County Chamber of Commerce** (see the Services section) or drop by their visitors center in Dillon or Frisco and sort through the walls of brochures and pamphlets.

HISTORY

Summit County history got rolling in August 1859 when a small group of prospectors found gold while panning along the Upper Blue River near present-day Breckenridge. Excited by their finds, the group spread out along the river and up French Gulch, looking for rich veins. Fearing an attack by the local Ute Indians, the group built a stockade and named it Fort Meribeh. During that first winter, prospectors made their first major discovery under eight feet of snow at Gold Run. Working with just a shovel and a pan, a prospector could extract up to $500 a day in this gulch.

Word got out and by spring the rush was on. When the town of "Breckinridge" was established that spring, it was the first permanent Colorado settlement on the Western Slope of the Continental Divide. Hoping to get a post office, the town fathers named it in honor of Vice President John C. Breckinridge. When the Civil War broke out, the townspeople were so angered by the vice president's support for the Confederacy that they altered the spelling to *Breckenridge*, changing the first *i* to an *e*. Over the next 40 years prospectors and mining companies used every conceivable method to extract gold and silver from surrounding streams and mountains, including panning, placer mining, loding and dredging. From 1898 to 1942, miles of streams and rivers were torn up by large dredging machines that gleaned gold from the sand while leaving ugly piles of rock in their wake. These rock piles are still very evident in the area.

Breckenridge grew quickly, experiencing economic ups and downs along the way. Perhaps the biggest shot in the arm came in 1882 when the Denver South Park & Pacific Railroad arrived in town via Boreas Pass. In

1897 a publicity boost came when miner Tom Groves unearthed "Tom's Baby," which at 13 pounds was the largest gold nugget ever discovered. (Tom, acting like a doting father, tenderly wrapped it in velvet before showing it off to the townsfolk.)

The town attracted its share of characters. Perhaps the best known was "Father" Dyer, the itinerant Methodist minister who traveled unceasingly to the surrounding mining camps, delivering the mail along with the word of God. His church still stands in Breckenridge. Another local character was "Captain" Sam Adams, who established the ill-fated Breckenridge navy. Adams, a real schemer, convinced the locals to supply him with four boats and a crew of 10 men to float down the Blue River to the Colorado River and eventually to the Pacific Ocean. The attempt failed miserably and Adams was run out of town.

Although Breckenridge was the largest and most successful mining region in Summit County, it was just a matter of time before settlers spread out into other parts of the county. In the 1860s, prospectors made rich silver strikes in the Montezuma mining district. Settlements such as Montezuma, Saints John, Peru, Chihuahua and Decatur yielded ore on and off through the turn of the century. In 1873 the town of Frisco got its start due to mining at nearby Mt. Royal. Frisco eventually grew as a central supply link and railroad stop between Georgetown and Leadville. As in other areas of Colorado that relied on mining, the 1900s brought hard times as most mines shut down and populations dwindled. But Summit County was perfectly suited for its 20th-century savior . . . skiing.

Skis were used for transportation in Summit County during the early mining days. However, it was not until after 1910 that skiing started being treated as a sport. A group of locals living in Old Dillon (now at the bottom of Dillon Reservoir) built a ski jump on which Anders Haugen, a Norwegian, set a world record in 1919. As downhill skiing caught on in the 1930s, people looked closely at Summit County for its potential ski area development. It wasn't until after World War II, however, that its first modern ski area took form—at Arapahoe Basin. Trails were cut, a lift was installed and the ski area was opened for business in 1948. Skiing's popularity increased, and the next area, Breckenridge, opened in 1962. With the completion of the Dillon Reservoir project in the early 1960s, Summit County really started to emerge as an important recreation area. The 1970s saw dramatic growth with the opening of Keystone Resort and Copper Mountain Resort in 1972. With the completion of the Eisenhower Tunnel in 1973, Summit County attracted more visitors than ever.

GETTING THERE

Summit County is located 70 miles west of Denver on Interstate 70. An ample number of van and limousine companies provide regular shuttle service between Denver's Stapleton International Airport and Summit County. If you get in a bind and have to catch a plane back to the real world, local taxi companies will also drive you to Stapleton. Greyhound Trailways Bus Lines makes a stop in Frisco.

FESTIVALS AND EVENTS

During winter and summer in Summit County there is a festival or an event going on most of the time. Complete listings of events throughout the year can be obtained by contacting the individual resorts or the **Summit County Chamber of Commerce** (see the Services section). Here are a few of the standout attractions.

Ullr Fest
late January
This week-long winter carnival in Breckenridge is one of the best in the state. In celebration of Ullr, the Norse god of winter, people really get into the party spirit. Ice sculptures line the Victorian streets of town. The infamous Ullr parade bonfire and dance can get very rowdy. The festival coincides with the Freestyle World Cup Championship, which includes exciting ballet, mogul and aerial ski competitions. For information contact the **Breckenridge Resort Chamber** at (303) 453-6018 or toll free in Colorado at 1-800-822-5381 and 1-800-221-1091 out of state.

Keystone Music Festival
throughout the summer
Keystone should be congratulated for developing such a wide reputation for its music festival in such a short number of years. Almost daily throughout the summer, the Summit Brass and the highly acclaimed National Repertory Orchestra perform concerts. Quite often they are joined by nationally known performers such as Doc Severinsen. Most of the concerts take place in the outdoor (but covered) Keystone Pavilion. For ticket information call **(303) 468-4294**.

Heeney Tick Festival
mid-June
This bizarre festival got its start in 1981 when a Heeney local recovered from a bout with tick fever. Friends decided this called for some sort of celebration. The first year's festivities consisted of miniature floats on a table. Big deal. But the celebration has expanded into a parade (about 10 minutes), a dance, food booths and the crowning of the annual Tick King and Queen. If you have nothing else to do, join in on this unique celebration of summer's arrival to the high country. Located 25 miles north of Silverthorne on Hwy. 9 at Green Mountain Reservoir. For more information, call **(303) 724-3812**.

Fourth of July
Celebrations take place throughout the county during the Fourth of July, including parades, dances, concerts, food booths and fireworks displays. The locals, being the patriotic bunch that they are, cut loose during this celebration of America. Call the **Summit County Chamber of Commerce** at **(303) 468-6205**.

Bach, Beethoven and Breckenridge
through July
This is another standout music festival in Summit County that attracts professional classical musicians from around the country who participate in workshops and performances. Music lovers can purchase tickets for the Festival Chamber Orchestra performances, as well as other events. Not all performances charge an attendance fee—a free concert is given on the Fourth of July at Carter Park and strolling musicians wander the streets throughout the month. For schedules and ticket information, contact the **Breckenridge Music Institute, PO Box 1254, Breckenridge, CO 80424; (303) 453-9142**.

No Man's Land Celebration
early August
In the early 1930s the federal govern-

ment learned that a tract of land, including Breckenridge, had accidentally been left off the map in several historic treaties. To commemorate this oversight, the town has been celebrating the "Kingdom of Breckenridge" for more than 50 years. The event is highlighted by a chili cookoff and an old-fashioned firemen's ball. For more information, call **(303) 453-6018**.

Summitfest
early August
The town of Dillon hosts this annual festival, which is highlighted by a 10K run, Colorado's largest sailing regatta, a food fair, fireworks and live music. For more information, call **(303) 468-2403**.

Montezuma Downs Horse Races
late summer
Don't let the name fool you. This is not an event where people dress up and sip mint juleps. It's much more down-home than that. Located in Montezuma, the event is highlighted by the quarter horse race down Main St. With that out of the way, folks can get down to the really important events, such as hay bale throwing, tobacco spitting and rifle shooting contests as well as activities that are a bit more off-the-wall. Call **(303) 468-5378** for more details.

Best of the West Fest
early September
Although this event is relatively new, it has enjoyed overwhelming success and rave reviews from Summit County residents. This tribute to the art, culture and music of the old and new West is highlighted by a dazzling display of southwestern art. Concerts also attract many folks. Native American artists come from many states in the region. Still searching for that perfect Navajo rug you've always wanted? This may be the place to look. Located at Copper Mountain. For information, call **1-800-458-8386**.

—— OUTDOOR ACTIVITIES ——

BIKING
MOUNTAIN BIKING
Dozens of old jeep roads and single-track trails provide anything from easy cruises to bone-jarring odysseys. The best areas to concentrate on are around Breckenridge and Montezuma. Please remember that the Eagles Nest Wilderness Area, to the west of Frisco and Silverthorne in the Gore Range, is off limits to bikes. For a complete rundown on various trail ideas in the area, drop by the visitors centers in Frisco and Dillon or the **Dillon Ranger District Office, 135 Hwy. 9, PO Box 260, Silverthorne, CO 80498; (303) 468-5400**.

Montezuma Helicopter Mountain Biking—
This may seem a bit extravagant, but what the heck. Rob Ilves will airlift you and your bike from his helipad in Montezuma and drop you off along the Continental Divide. Be sure to enjoy the views before starting down from the summit. Once you begin the ride down the mountain, your eyes will be glued to the trail—or at least they should be. Contact Ilves at **Box 30B, 501 Main St., Montezuma, CO 80435; (303) 468-5378**.

Bike Trails—
Argentine Pass—If you're looking for the ultimate mountain bike challenge, consider a frightening trip over 13,132-foot Argentine Pass. Needless to say, this is an extremely difficult trail that is only for expert bikers! Back in the 1800s a toll road crossed over Argentine Pass, connecting the Summit County area with Georgetown. The road has deteriorated since then and is only two feet wide in spots. As John Warner, a local biker, puts it, "One false move and you're hamburger." From Keystone head

up Montezuma Rd. about 3 miles and look for the Peru Gulch trailhead on your left. Park here and begin your ride up the trail, which gets increasingly steep and hazardous. From the summit of Argentine Pass, make your way northeast down to the ruins of Waldorf, an old ghost town from the silver mining days of the late 1800s. From here, the road takes you down to Guanella Pass Rd. and into Georgetown, but a shuttle is necessary to get back. Before attempting this trail, consult with the forest service at the **Dillon Ranger District Office** in Silverthorne. Be sure to carry good maps and supplies. Good luck.

Boreas Pass Road—This is a very easy 10-mile ride to the summit of Boreas Pass from Breckenridge. If you feel energetic you may want to continue down the other side of the pass to the town of Como. In summer, car traffic gets heavy. Ride in the morning or early evening to avoid eating dust. For a description and directions, see the Cross-Country Skiing section.

Deer Creek/Webster Pass Loop—This difficult 15-mile trail takes you to the Continental Divide, where you'll have views of the Tenmile and Gore ranges, Grays and Torreys peaks and sprawling South Park. In mid-summer, the tundra wildflowers are blooming in full force above 12,000 feet. The trail possibilities in this area are limitless—you may want to get maps at the **Dillon Ranger District Office** for more ideas. To get to the trail from Keystone, drive southeast on Montezuma Rd., 2.5 miles past the town of Montezuma. Deer Creek Rd. climbs up to the divide. From here, head east over to Radical Hill and down to Webster Pass Rd., which returns to Montezuma.

Peaks Trail—Intermediate riders can negotiate the uphill stretches and stream crossings required on this 9-mile ride along the Tenmile Range between Frisco and Breckenridge. From Frisco, head south on the bike path along Hwy. 9 for a mile or so and turn right on Rainbow Lake Rd. Pro-

ceed to Rainbow Lake and then south on the trail. You'll come out at the Breckenridge Ski Area.

Saints John—Near Saints John (an old town near Montezuma), a fantastic network of trails awaits. For information see the Saints John Lodge and Backcountry Trail System in the Cross-Country Skiing section.

Rentals and Information—

Antlers—Rent both mountain bikes and 10-speed touring bikes. Open 7:30 am–10 pm daily. 900 N. Summit Blvd., Frisco, CO 80443; (303) 668-3152.

Mountain Cyclery and Ski Exchange—Rent both mountain bikes and 10-speed touring bikes. Open 9 am–6 pm daily. 112 S. Ridge St., Breckenridge, CO 80424; (303) 453-2201.

TOURING

If you are planning a summer vacation in Summit County, strap your touring bike onto the car, because you're in for a treat. The area is a cyclist's dream. Miles of paved bike paths connect most of the towns in Summit County, including the 6-mile **Blue River Bikeway** between Frisco and Dillon, the 6-mile **Tenmile Canyon Bikeway** between Frisco and Copper Mountain and the 13.5-mile **Vail Pass Bikeway** between Copper Mountain and Vail. A Bike the Summit Trail Map showing the various routes in the area is available at local bike shops, visitors centers and at the **Dillon Ranger District Office** at **135 Hwy. 9 in Silverthorne; (303) 468-5400.** This is unquestionably one of the best ways to enjoy Summit County.

A special bikers/hikers-only campground has been set aside at the **Peninsula Recreation Area** on the south end of Dillon Reservoir. No motorized vehicles are allowed; very small fee.

Carpenter/Phinney Cycling Camp—

Connie Carpenter, an Olympic gold medalist, and Davis Phinney, her husband and fellow Olympic medalist, offer a special camp for serious recreational riders and racers. The camp is held at Copper Mountain and includes two one-week sessions. Videotape analysis, bicycle tuning, injury prevention and year-round training tips are just some of the things covered. Why not learn from the best? For information about the camp contact **Carpenter/Phinney Cycling Camp, PO Box 3001, Copper Mountain, CO 80443; (303) 968-2882 ext. 6301.**

FISHING

Blue River—

The Blue River begins its 45-mile run through Summit County (along Hwy. 9) from Hoosier Pass just south of Breckenridge. A number of small tributaries converge, and by the time the Upper Blue River reaches Breckenridge, the fishing can be pretty good. Downstream from Breckenridge the river runs through an area that was dredged during the mining days, which left large piles of boulders along the banks. Some fishermen who try their luck early in the season for rainbows, and in the fall for browns and brookies, end up with a full creel. Below Dillon Reservoir, the **Lower Blue River** is designated Gold Medal water; catch and release only. Many fishermen curse this stretch of the river, complaining that the fish are too hard to catch for it to be designated Gold Medal. There are plenty of places to park along Hwy. 9 as the river moves toward Green Mountain Reservoir. Try to fish the stretches that are as far away as possible from the road. Locals have had luck with No. 14 and 16 elk hair caddis flies for attracting rainbow, brook, cutthroat and brown trout.

Dillon Reservoir—

Dillon Reservoir is the focal point of Summit County, and many loyal fishermen see no need to look farther for good fishing. Casting from along the 24-mile shore is not quite as effective as fishing from a boat, but it can be worthwhile. There are boat launching ramps at **Frisco**

Bay, Frisco Marina, Blue River Inlet and **Peak 1 Campground.** Both the **Frisco Marina** and the **Dillon Yacht Basin** rent boats. A good time to fish for rainbow trout is in spring just as the ice recedes from the reservoir and after the lake has been stocked. Some four- and five-pounders have been reeled in at this time. Hog-sized brown trout cruise the waters, but are hard to catch. The reservoir is also stocked with small kokanee salmon and cutthroat and brook trout. Trolling slowly with a Kastmaster lure has been quite alluring to many species in the reservoir, but, of course, the time-tested worm will also do the trick.

Green Mountain Reservoir—

Although its waters yield many good-sized trout, Green Mountain Reservoir is best known for its excellent kokanee salmon. The kokanee are among the biggest in the state, weighing two pounds and up; snagging is permitted from Sept. 1 through Dec. 31. The water level at Green Mountain Reservoir fluctuates greatly throughout the summer. Boat ramps are available at the south end of the reservoir and at the town of Heeney. Ice fishing is popular in winter. Located 25 miles north of Silverthorne on Hwy. 9.

Mountain Lakes—

Dozens of lakes in Summit County offer good fishing. Some are right beside major roads, while others require a vigorous hike. **Mohawk Lakes** can be reached by heading west on Spruce Creek Rd., 5 miles south of Breckenridge on Hwy. 9. Drive up Spruce Creek Rd. about 3 miles and walk up to the three lakes (about 1 mile to the first lake and another mile to the others). Fairly sizeable cutthroat inhabit these lakes. **Officer's Gulch Pond,** located just off Interstate 70, 4 miles west of Frisco, is stocked with rainbow and brook trout. In the Eagles Nest Wilderness Area, **Salmon Lake** and **Willow Lakes** are 6- and 7-mile hikes, respectively. Although a bit hard to reach, the fishing can be quite good. Ten-inch cutthroats are the common catch with lures and flies. The trailhead begins up in

Wildernest, just west of Silverthorne. Stop in at the **Dillon Ranger District Office, 135 ·Hwy. 9, Silverthorne, CO 80498; (303) 468-5400** or see the Willow Lakes write-up in the Hiking and Backpacking section for exact directions.

Snake River—

Located east of Dillon Reservoir, the Snake River flows out of the Montezuma and Loveland Pass area of the Continental Divide and down through Keystone. As a result of recent development and mine runoff, fishing along the Snake River is not very good.

Tenmile Creek—

Tenmile Creek, which originates near Vail Pass west of Copper Mountain, has some reasonably good fishing between Frisco and Copper Mountain. The river follows along the east side of Interstate 70 and is especially good in fall when the browns are spawning.

FOUR-WHEEL-DRIVE TRIPS

The rule of thumb for four-wheelers in Colorado is that the more mining activity that went on in an area in the 1800s, the better the jeeping tends to be. Old wagon roads connecting the many mining settlements in Summit County provide great four-wheeling and offer historical glimpses into the past with spectacular backcountry scenery. No fewer than 11 major roads were built over high mountain passes in the area and many are open for jeepers today. Be sure to stay on the designated jeep roads, as cross-country driving, especially in the high alpine tundra, promotes erosion. For other trip ideas visit the **Dillon Ranger District Office at 135 Hwy. 9, Silverthorne, CO 80498; (303) 468-5400.**

Georgia Pass—

This was one of the first wagon roads built, connecting the Breckenridge mining district with South Park. At 11,598 feet, Georgia Pass presents great views of the Tenmile Range, Grays and Torreys peaks and South Park. To reach the pass road from Breckenridge, drive 4 miles north on Hwy. 9 to Tiger Rd. and turn right. Follow the road along Swan River past North Fork Rd. and keep bearing right. Follow the south fork of the river. You will pass through the remains of Parkville, which was the county seat back in the early mining days. One night, some residents of Breckenridge snuck into the county hall and stole the county records. Possession being nine-tenths of the law, the county seat was moved to Breckenridge.

The road along the South Fork of the Swan River eventually leads to the summit of Georgia Pass. From the pass, the road descends down into South Park along Michigan Creek, eventually reaching Hwy. 285 at the town of Jefferson. From Jefferson you can return to Breckenridge via Boreas Pass or Hoosier Pass (Hwy. 9).

Webster Pass—

Webster Pass is another old wagon road that was heavily used in the 1800s. It was built to connect the Montezuma mining district with the Eastern Slope of the Continental Divide. The road begins just above the town of Montezuma and heads up 4 miles to the pass at 12,108 feet. This section of the road is fairly easy to drive, but is usually snowed in until July. From the pass, the road descends the eastern side down Handcart Gulch into Hall Valley (see the Four-Wheel-Drive Trips section of the **South Park** chapter), but this side of the pass is very steep and is not recommended. To reach the road from Keystone, drive southeast on Montezuma Rd. through the town of Montezuma. The jeep road begins about 2.5 miles above the town.

Tours and Information—

Tiger Run Jeep Tours—Tiger Run Resort offers rather expensive guided tours from one to four hours in length. Located north of Breckenridge. **PO Box 1418, Breckenridge, CO 80424; (303) 453-2231 or (303) 453-9185.**

GOLF

The Summit County area, in keeping with its resort image, offers four fine golf courses which help lure out-of-state visitors as well as weekenders from the Denver area who want to escape the city.

Breckenridge Golf Club—

This young 18-hole course is the only public Jack Nicklaus-designed course in the world. True to the characteristic features of a course designed by Nicklaus, Breckenridge Golf Club is laid out following the natural contours and terrain of its surroundings. It plays through forests, valleys, mountainsides, streams and even beaver ponds. The course is owned by the town of Breckenridge. In June the Steve Watson Celebrity Classic offers a chance to see pro football stars and former stars such as Joe Namath hacking up the course. Tee times should be made at least two days in advance. Located at **720 Tiger Rd., Breckenridge, CO 80424; (303) 453-9104.**

Copper Creek Golf Course—

Located at Copper Mountain, this 18-hole course boasts the highest altitude of any PGA course in the country. Designed by Perry Dye, the course features great views of the Tenmile Range to the east. Trademark Dye railroad ties bulkhead the tees, lakes and greens. Resort guests get a break on the greens fees. Fees are reduced after Sept. 15. **122 Wheeler Pl., Copper Mountain, CO 80443; (303) 968-2339.**

Hikers can explore some of the rugged trails in the area (photograph by Bob Huestis).

Eagle's Nest Golf Course—

This challenging nine-hole course has a lot of hills, doglegs and narrow fairways. Set back from the Blue River Valley, it offers incredible views of the valley and the Gore Range. The final hole drops 150 feet from the tee to the green. Greens fees are lower before the end of May. Located in Silverthorne, 2 miles north on Hwy. 9 from the Silverthorne exit on Interstate 70. **305 Golden Eagle Rd., Silverthorne, CO 80498; (303) 468-0681.**

Keystone Ranch Golf Club—

Keystone Ranch is an excellent 18-hole course. Opened in 1980, it was designed by Robert Trent Jones, Jr., and offers a wide range of terrain and spectacular views. The front nine plays through trees; holes four through eight are patterned after old Scottish courses with lots of sagebrush and streams. The back nine is very open, with water hazards and few trees. The 60-year-old clubhouse (the old ranchhouse) is a beautiful facility with a fine pro shop and restaurant. Carts are required. Reservations for resort guests are required at least three days in advance; non-guests are given tee times on a space-available basis. The course opens at the end of May. Guests of the resort pay reduced greens fees. Located at Keystone Ranch, near Keystone Resort. **1437 Summit Co. Rd. 150, Box 38, Keystone, CO 80435; (303) 468-4250.**

HIKING AND BACKPACKING

It's hard to justify going to Summit County in summer and not getting onto one of the numerous trails into the backcountry. Hiking a trail through pine and aspen forests, fields of wildflowers or one of the many high alpine basins is one of the best ways to really see the area. Arapaho National Forest encircles the county, offering spectacular walking for the novice and experienced backpacker alike. To the west of Silverthorne, the Eagles Nest Wilderness Area straddles the lofty Gore Range, providing a quick escape from the crowds and condos of the resorts. Residents of the county are quick to share with you some of their favorite hiking trails. Stop in at the **Dillon Ranger District Office at 135 Hwy. 9, PO Box 260, Silverthorne, CO 80498; (303) 468-5400** for additional information. You might want to pick up a copy of Mary Ellen Gilliland's *The Summit Hiker* (Alpenrose Press, 1987). It is an excellent book containing details about dozens of hiking trails in the area as well as some interesting history. Topographical maps are available at many local sporting goods stores.

Argentine Pass—

In 1869, workers finally finished the dangerous wagon road over 13,207-foot Argentine Pass. Many lives had been lost in the process, but the much-needed link between the mines in Peru Gulch and Georgetown was complete. This 2.3-mile hike to the summit is difficult but worth the effort. The first part of the trail is very steep, but eventually mellows into a steady pitch. The rocky scree and talus slopes require that you wear a pair of sturdy hiking boots. From the summit on the Continental Divide you'll have views as far west as the Sawatch Range and east to Georgetown and Mt. Evans. To reach the trailhead from Keystone, drive 4.6 miles southeast on Montezuma Rd. and turn left onto Peru Creek Rd. Continue about 5 miles and park at the Shoe Basin Mine building on the right. Hike up the trail 0.3 miles to the Argentine Pass trailhead.

Masontown Trail—

This is an easy 1.4-mile hike (one way) that's great for the whole family. It starts near Frisco and climbs up the lower reaches of Mt. Royal. Along the trail, many old mining sites scar the forested slopes. Views of the Blue River Valley and Dillon Reservoir are superb. The trail ends at the battered remains of the old mining camp of Masontown. Specifics on the demise of Masontown are debatable, but local legend has it that on New Year's Eve, just after the turn of the century, the residents were down in Frisco whooping it up when an avalanche roared down the mountain, completely demolishing their small settlement. To reach the trailhead from the west end of Main St. in Frisco (near Interstate 70), head east into Frisco and turn into the public parking lot on the right. Cross the footbridge over Tenmile Creek and turn left onto the paved bike path. After a half-mile hike you'll see the Mt. Royal/Masontown trailhead on the right.

Mohawk Lakes—

This fine 2.8-mile day hike takes you past Mayflower Lakes and beyond to Lower and Upper Mohawk Lakes at 12,100 feet. Mining ruins abound. At Lower Mohawk Lake an old mill site still stands, with an aerial tram leading up the mountain above. Be sure to look for Continental Falls to the north above the old mill. Views from the lakes are spectacular. To reach the trailhead from Breckenridge, drive south on Hwy. 9 for 2.4 miles and turn right on Spruce Creek Rd. (just past the lake on your left). Drive 1.2 miles up to the trailhead. There is another trailhead 1.6 miles farther up the road that cuts the hike down to 1.2 miles, but to reach it you need a four-wheel-drive vehicle or at least one with high clearance.

Monte Cristo Gulch/Blue Lakes—

Although we suggest hiking through this steep-walled, mining-rich valley, you can cheat and drive almost all the way to the reservoir between Upper and Lower Blue Lakes. On the north side of the valley rises Quandary Peak (14,264 feet). The steep mountainsides are marked with remains of mine shafts and cabins built into seemingly vertical rock walls. It's a wonder the miners were able to get to the sites! For a short 1.1-mile hike, drive along the left fork in the road below the lower lake and park your car. Begin hiking along the trail on the south side of the lake, past a few old mine buildings (now inhabited), including the enormous Arctic Mine. With its five tunnels, tram and stamp mill, the Arctic was one of the biggest gold producers in the area and operated until 1936. The trail follows the lake shore and ends up at a cascading waterfall just below the upper lake.

To reach this valley from Breckenridge, drive south on Hwy. 9 for 7.5 miles and turn right onto Blue Lakes Rd. Drive 2.2 miles to the lower lake.

Quandary Peak—

Located near Breckenridge, Quandary Peak (14,264 feet) is one of the easiest 14,000-foot peaks to climb in the state. The peak supposedly got its name when a number of miners found some unusual rocks near the summit and were in a "quandary" to identify them. Mining was undertaken all over the mountain and many remnants are still visible, even near the summit. There are a couple of routes up the mountain, but the easiest is along the wide east ridge. To reach the trail from Breckenridge, head south on Hwy. 9 for 7.5 miles and turn right on Blue Lakes Rd. Drive about 0.5 miles and look for a trail on the right. Hike about 0.5 miles north and head left up the east ridge for 2 miles to the summit.

Ski Areas—Chairlifts to the Top—

For those uninitiated to the high altitude of Summit County, even a short hike can take your breath away (and we're not talking about a result from the beautiful scenery). Chairlift rides are available in the summer at Breckenridge, Copper Mountain and Keystone ski areas. Once at the top of the lift you have a number of options: hike up even farther, hike down to the bottom or enjoy a peaceful lunch and ride the lift back down. At Breckenridge the lift is open in summer from late June through early Sept., 10:30 am–3:30 pm daily. Tickets can be purchased at the base of Peak 8. From town, head west at the traffic light and up Ski Hill Rd. to the base of Peak 8. At Copper Mountain, E and F lifts are open daily from 10 am–4 pm July through Labor Day, and into the fall on weekends only. No fee. The gondola at Keystone is open daily throughout the summer from 9 am–3 pm. A small fee is charged for this ride.

Willow Lakes—

Located high in the Eagles Nest Wilderness Area, Willow Lakes can be a beautiful overnight getaway, but can get quite crowded on weekends and holidays. The 8.5-mile trail leads to a series of four lakes at about 11,400 feet. There is camping at the lakes, and fishing for small cutthroats can be good. You may want to stop in at the ranger's office in Silverthorne to get an idea of how crowded things will be at the lake. The trail begins at Mesa Cortina above Silverthorne and climbs up through dense forests of lodgepole pine. Game is plentiful up here; the last time we hiked this trail we saw a bear paw print. Above the lakes is a very steep, rocky trail to a saddle atop the Gore Range that offers fantastic views over into the Vail area. Firewood is limited, so packing a stove is a good idea. To reach the trailhead from Silverthorne, turn left off Hwy. 9 onto Wildernest Rd. (across from Wendy's). Go a short distance to a fork, turn right and then immediately left onto Royal Buffalo Dr. (No. 1240). Drive less than a mile and turn right onto Lakeview Dr. (No. 1245). Proceed to the fork with Aspen Dr. and turn left, negotiating the curve to the trailhead parking area. The trailhead is marked Mesa Cortina.

HORSEBACK RIDING

Be forewarned. Just because a horse stable happens to be conveniently located next to the visitors center at a resort doesn't mean the ride will be any good. If you want to ride a horse in Summit County, find out where rides are offered away from developed areas. One such company is **Alpine Adventures**. Though their headquarters are in Breckenridge, the trail rides begin up near Montezuma in Arapaho National Forest near the Continental Divide. Daylong breakfast and overnight rides are offered, as well as romantic rides in a hay wagon for an evening barbecue. Ride up into the high country and visit old ghost towns in the Montezuma mining district. For information, contact **PO Box 2620-B, Breckenridge, CO 80424; (303) 468-9297** or **(303) 453-0111.**

ICE SKATING

In winter **Keystone Lake,** in the middle of Keystone Village, is transformed into one of the largest outdoor, groomed skating rinks in the country. Lace up a pair of skates and give it a try. If you prefer the passive approach, sit at one of the nearby cafes and watch the action. A small fee is charged and rental skates are available. Open 10 am–10 pm daily. Call **(303) 468-2316** for more information. In Breckenridge, outdoor skating on **Maggie Pond** on the west side of **Bell Tower Mall** is also a good time, and skates can be rented. Open daily 9 am–9 pm; small fee charged. **West Lake Rink** in the village at Copper Mountain is outdoors, free and open daily 10:30 am–9 pm. Contact central reservations at Copper Mountain for more information.

RIVER FLOATING

Blue River—

Below Lake Dillon, the Blue River snakes its way 38 miles north, where it dumps into the Colorado River near Kremmling. The Blue River is not particularly well known to river floaters; Gold Medal fishing and Green Mountain Reservoir limit the navigable stretches, and the floating season is very short. If you visit Summit County during the floating season in June, there is one local outfitter that will attend to your needs.

Joni Ellis River Tours offers half-day trips on the Blue River and full-day trips on the Upper Colorado and Arkansas rivers. A lunch is provided on the full-day outings. **PO Box 764, Dillon, CO 80435; (303) 468-1028.**

SAILING

Lake Dillon, with its 26 miles of shoreline and views of the surrounding mountains, is one of the finest lake settings in the Rocky Mountains. **Dillon Yacht Basin** has launching facilities for boats up to three tons. They also rent sailboats, paddleboats and small motorboats for fishing. Evening dinner floats on the lake are available. Call

for hours. Located on **East Lodgepole St. in Dillon. PO Box 593, Dillon, CO 80435; (303) 468-2936.**

SKIING
CROSS-COUNTRY SKIING

Nordic skiers are not neglected in Summit County. In addition to four nordic centers, there are limitless trails into the backcountry at your disposal. If you want to get out on a trail in the backcountry, obtain information at the **Dillon Ranger District Office, PO Box 620, 135 Hwy. 9, Silverthorne, CO 80498; (303) 468-5400** or call their recorded message at **(303) 468-5434.** Information is also provided by the visitors centers in Frisco and Dillon (see the Services section). If you want to explore the backcountry with a guide, contact Rob Ilves at **Box 30B, 501 Main St., Montezuma, CO 80435; (303) 468-5378.**

Backcountry Trails—

Boreas Pass—Beginning just south of Breckenridge, the trail up Boreas Pass follows the old Denver South Park & Pacific Railroad bed, which connected Breckenridge to the outside world back in the mining days of the late 1800s. Views of the Tenmile Range from points along the trail are superb. The fairly easy trail follows Boreas Pass Rd. 3.5 miles up to Baker's Tank, which once stored water for railroad locomotives from 1882–1937. This is a great place for lunch. Ambitious skiers can continue up the trail another 3.5 miles to the summit of the pass. A settlement on the pass back in the late 1800s included the highest post office in the country. To reach the trailhead from Breckenridge, drive south on Hwy. 9 just past the Breckenridge Inn, then turn left and proceed about 3.5 miles to the end of the plowed road (Forest Rd. 223).

North Tenmile Creek—This often-steep 5-mile trail is not for beginners. Most of the way you are climbing through pine forests and meadows, but near the end of the trail, views west into the snow-covered Gore

Range are outstanding. The trail follows North Tenmile Creek the whole way. The first mile is a steep climb which then mellows somewhat. To reach the trailhead from Frisco, head west on Main St. under Interstate 70 and park your car just beyond the overpass. The trail heads up the valley to the west. Check avalanche conditions before attempting this trail.

Peru Gulch Trail—Beautiful high alpine views and old mining ruins highlight a trip up Peru Gulch Trail. It starts out as fairly easy terrain for the first 2 miles and then gradually climbs more steeply for 4 miles to the Pennsylvania Mine. Some skiers continue up from here through the ruins of the ghost town of Decatur and up into Horseshoe Basin, with views to Grays Peak (14,270 feet) and Argentine Pass. The avalanche danger can be high at the upper end of the valley. This trail gets a lot of use in winter. To reach the trailhead from Keystone, head east 4.6 miles on Montezuma Rd. and look for the trailhead and parking lot on the left.

Saints John Lodge and Backcountry Trail System—This area offers a little bit of everything. In a nutshell it's a backcountry lodging experience for mountain bikers, hikers and especially backcountry skiers.

Named for two saints, John the Baptist and John the Evangelist, Saints John is the locale of one of the first major silver discoveries in the Colorado Territory. In 1864 John Coley rigged up a primitive smelter, which was later replaced by a state-of-the-art version made with bricks imported from Wales. The townspeople of Saints John boasted that they had no bars (unheard of for a mining town), but they did maintain a fine library with more than 300 volumes of classics.

Abandoned since the early 1900s, the township (including three rundown buildings and the remains of the smelter) was acquired by Rob Ilves and his partners in 1988. The cabins recently underwent a renovation to provide spartan lodging ($ to $$) and meals for guests. Dorm space is

available and cabins can be rented by groups. In spite of its good points, the accommodations are not for everyone. If you are seeking creature comforts and privacy, don't bother showing up here. But if you don't mind using an outhouse and bringing your own sleeping bag, then you may like it.

Located within the Arapaho National Forest at 11,000 feet elevation, Saints John commands a fantastic view of Grays and Torreys peaks (both over 14,000 feet), Glacier Mountain and a number of nearby (and active!) avalanche chutes. The valley and the surrounding peaks and ridges are especially well set up for backcountry skiing. Ilves (pronounced something like Elvis) and the other owners have put up signs for nearby trails. There are almost 100 miles of trails in the area and most are on terrain that will require the ability to handle narrow downhill stretches. The proprietors are refurbishing a dozen or more huts that lie along the trails throughout the valley so they can be rented out for the night. The huts are rough, but provide good shelter and cost just a few dollars per night.

Trail use is free. Stop in at the main lodge for hot cider and trail information. The Wild Irishman Mine 2 miles above Saints John is a good place to eat lunch. A cabin here makes for good shelter. Ambitious skiers should be warned that the inviting bowl just above the Wild Irishman Mine is very susceptible to avalanches. Stay away from the steep walls.

Ilves, a helicopter pilot, is an accommodating innkeeper. He can take you helicopter skiing or mountain biking from the Continental Divide. How about a helicopter trip up to an old miner's cabin for a fresh lobster dinner? Use your imagination.

To reach Saints John from Keystone, drive 7 miles southeast on Montezuma Rd. to the town of Montezuma and park just off the road, on the right. You'll see the signs and the trail (a road in summer) heading up into the pines. In summer you can drive the remaining 1.4 miles up to the lodge with a four-wheel-drive vehicle. In winter you'll have to ski in, unless you want to pay extra for a ride in on a snowmobile. For more information contact **Box 30B, 501 Main St., Montezuma, CO 80435; (303) 468-5378.**

Webster Pass—This 4-mile trail is for intermediate and advanced skiers. It climbs up to the pass at 12,096 feet on the Continental Divide, providing a panorama of the jagged peaks of the surrounding Arapaho National Forest and a glimpse down into Hall Valley on the Eastern Slope. To reach the trailhead from Keystone, drive southeast on Montezuma Rd. about 2 miles past the town of Montezuma, up to where the road is unplowed. The trail follows the unplowed road to the summit.

Groomed Trails—

Breckenridge Nordic Ski Center—More than 30 kilometers of trails are available for track skiing and skating through the pines. The Breckenridge Nordic Ski Center is one of the oldest of its kind in Colorado, providing everything you need from rentals to lessons (individual or private). Guided skiing is available for the blind. Telemarking terrain and lessons are not provided, but are available at the Breckenridge Ski Area. Open daily from 9 am–4 pm. Located 1 mile west on Ski Hill Rd. from Main St. in Breckenridge. **PO Box 1776, Breckenridge, CO 80424; (303) 453-6855.**

Copper Mountain/Trak Cross-Country Center—This center has gained a reputation as one of the finest facilities of its kind in the state. Owned and operated by Copper Mountain Resort, it has more than 25 kilometers of machine-set tracks, skating lanes and rolling hills for more advanced cross-country skiers. The K lift takes skiers uphill for runs down challenging trails. A range of lessons is available, from beginning track skiing to telemarking (telemark lessons are given on the ski mountain). Clinics are offered throughout the winter on skiing techniques, waxing, snow safety and many more subjects. Rentals are avail-

able at the center. Hours are 8:30 am–3:30 pm daily. For more information, contact the **Copper Mountain/Trak Cross-Country Center** at PO Box 3001, Copper Mountain, CO 80443; (303) 968-2882 ext. 6342.

Frisco Nordic Ski Center—In a pine forest near the shores of Lake Dillon, skiers can explore 35 kilometers of set trails. The center, designed a few years ago by Olympic silver medalist Bill Koch, provides rentals and lessons. Open daily 9 am–4 pm. Located 2 miles south of Frisco along Hwy. 9; **PO Box 207, Frisco, CO 80443; (303) 668-0866.**

Keystone Cross-Country Center—More than 27 kilometers of set trails provide easy skiing around Keystone Resort. The center has a nordic ski school run by Jana Hlavati, a former US Olympic team member. Rentals are also available. Open 8 am–5 pm daily. Located 2.2 miles east of Keystone on Montezuma Rd., next to Ski Tip Lodge; **PO Box 38, Keystone, CO 80435; (303) 468-4275.**

Rentals and Information—

All of the nordic centers have rental equipment available, as do a number of area shops. Here are a few of them.

Mountain Cyclery & Ski Exchange—Touring, telemarking and track equipment are available along with good advice and trail ideas. **112 Ridge St., Breckenridge, CO 80424; (303) 453-2201.**

Mountain View Sports—Located 1 mile east of the Keystone stoplight in Keystone; **22869 Hwy. 6; (303) 468-0396.**

Wilderness Sports—Located across from Wendy's in Silverthorne. **171 Hwy. 9, Silverthorne, CO 80498; (303) 468-8519.**

DOWNHILL SKIING

Summit County's four ski areas host almost three million skiers each winter. More than 3,700 acres of slopes, 54 lifts and 255 trails should have the terrain you are looking for—whether it's easy ballroom skiing or steep, ungroomed mogul runs. Although tickets can be purchased at the individual ski areas, the Lake Dillon Resort Association, among others, offers daily discount tickets as well as four- and six-day Ski the Summit passes. These passes offer great savings and are interchangeable at all of the ski areas in Summit County. For more information contact the **Lake Dillon Resort Association** at **1-800-365-6365.** Or try **Ski the Summit, PO Box 267, Dillon, CO 80435; (303) 468-6607.** Front Range skiers should keep in mind that Summit County ski area tickets are sold at a discount by many outlets along the Front Range, including supermarkets.

Arapahoe Basin—

Open from mid-Nov. until June each year, Arapahoe Basin has one of the longest ski seasons in Colorado. The top of the mountain, perched at a lofty 12,450 feet, is the state's highest ski area summit. Of the four ski areas in Summit County, Arapahoe is the oldest, getting its start back in the 1940s when Max Dercum and a handful of cronies installed the first chairlift. Much of the equipment they used was army surplus, acquired from Camp Hale, near Leadville, where the 10th Mountain Division ski troops trained during World War II. Cables and pulleys were liberated from old mines around the state.

The area has come a long way since the early days, and now has more than 350 acres of skiable terrain. But it's not the best area for beginners. Only 10 percent of the mountain is for novices. However, intermediate and advanced skiers love it. The Pallavicini lift services a slew of black runs on the right side of the mountain—and they are steep! Every 20 minutes a shuttle bus leaves for Keystone. Lift tickets are good at both areas. Arapahoe Basin is located a few miles east of Keystone on Hwy. 6, at the western base of Loveland Pass. For information contact **Keystone Resort, Box 38, Keystone, CO 80435; (303) 468-2316.**

Breckenridge Ski Area—

The growth of Breckenridge, especially in the past eight years, has been phenomenal. The largest ski area in Summit County, at more than 1,500 acres, is comprised of three interconnected mountains, Peaks 8, 9 and 10, which offer plenty of terrain for skiers of all abilities. The lower part of Peak 8 and most of Peak 9 keep beginners and intermediates happy with well-groomed runs. Advanced skiers usually head to the back bowls of Peak 8 and to the exacting double black diamond bump runs on the North Face of Peak 9. Runs such as Devil's Crotch and Hades are extremely challenging. There are two main bases. The one at the bottom of Peak 9 is accessible right in town; the base at Peak 8 can be reached by a shuttle bus which runs every few minutes. Breckenridge's ample number of lifts, including several high-speed Superchairs, helps keep lift lines relatively short, even during peak season. On-mountain restaurants, such as the Vistahaus on Peak 9, have spacious sun decks and spectacular views of the Blue River Valley and the towering mountains to the east. If you are interested in snowboarding, Breckenridge is one of the ski areas in the state that is totally open to the sport; the World Snowboard Championships are held here in Jan. For more information, call **(303) 453-2368.**

Copper Mountain Resort—

Not only are the runs at Copper Mountain well designed, but geographically, the mountain is a natural. For the most part, beginner, intermediate and advanced terrain are separated into three distinct areas. This provides peace of mind to skiers who don't want to accidentally end up on a run that is either too easy or too difficult. Advanced skiers stick to the left (east) side of the area, which offers challenging bump runs and bowl skiing near the top of the mountain. Runs at Union Peak, on the right (west) side of the area, are well-groomed intermediate and beginner terrain. More than 20 lifts provide quick access to the many runs. Because of its fine reputation, Copper Mountain receives a lot of day skiers from the Denver area who are willing to drive just a bit farther. Some people grumble about the parking facilities at the resort, complaining that you have to walk up to a quarter of a mile. Our advice is to park in the east lot and take the shuttle to the mountain. Located about 10 miles southwest of Frisco on Interstate 70. For more information, call **(303) 968-2882.**

Keystone Resort—

Although Keystone hosted the second largest number of skiers in the state last year, it's not because they have a superior ski mountain. Their award-winning accommodations, facilities and excellent service can take most of the credit. In addition, sophisticated snow-making machines crank up in late Sept., allowing Keystone to open in Oct., much earlier than most other areas in the state. The area also offers **night skiing** on 40 percent of the runs, which keeps the slopes open for more than 13 hours a day.

Keystone is a mountain for beginners and intermediates. The runs are well groomed, providing worry-free skiing that is especially attractive for families. The teaching programs are first rate and include the Mahre Training Center. The Mahre twins (Phil and Steve), former world champions and Olympic gold and silver medalists, operate exclusively at Keystone, offering week-long lessons to teach you to ski like a champion. In the first 10 years of operation, expert skiers made jokes about the area because of its easy, boring terrain. To attract more advanced and expert skiers, Keystone purchased Arapahoe Basin and developed the challenging North Peak Mountain, which is accessible from the top of Keystone Mountain. Located about 10 miles east of Dillon on Hwy. 6. **Box 38, Keystone, CO 80435; (303) 468-2316.**

HELICOPTER SKIING

If you have an overpowering desire to ski untracked Colorado powder and are able to shell out a few hundred bucks, a day of helicopter skiing should be planned. Take off for thrilling runs down the snow-covered mountains in the surrounding White River and Arapaho national forests. This is the ultimate way to ski the Rockies.

Colorado Heli-Ski—

Skiers with at least an intermediate ability are welcome. The helicopter drops you off on a mountaintop and a guide leads you down. There is plenty of time to take in the views and snap a few pictures if you like. For more information, contact PO Box 64, Frisco, CO 80443; (303) 668-5600.

Montezuma Helicopter Service—

Rob Ilves whisks you from his helicopter pad to nearby peaks along the Continental Divide near Montezuma. Contact Ilves for details. Box 30B, 501 Main St., Montezuma, CO 80435; (303) 468-5378.

SLEIGH RIDES

Dinner in the Woods—

Looking for an elegant meal with a new twist? Try Dinner in the Woods at Copper Mountain. Taking off from Mountain Plaza, the sleigh makes its way along a torchlit trail to a tent in the woods where a gourmet dinner is served. The meal changes nightly. This is a guaranteed romantic outing—that is, unless you take the kids. Open Tues. and Fri. nights only, unless you're with a group of 18 or more. For reservations and information, contact **PO Box 1544, Silverthorne, CO 80498** (or the desk in the Mountain Plaza lobby); **(303) 468-2822.**

Two Below Zero Sleigh Rides—

Two mule-drawn sleighs depart nightly from the Frisco Nordic Center to a heated tent in the woods near Lake Dillon. Enjoy London broil with all the trimmings; vegetarian dinners are provided with advance notice. Closed Mon. Call or write for rates, times and reservations. **PO Box 845, Frisco, CO 80443; (303) 453-1520.**

TENNIS

Carter Park—

Four outdoor courts and a paddle

court. Free; lighted for night play. Located at the extreme south end of High St. in Breckenridge, 3 blocks east of Main St. There is a sign-up sheet at the park.

Copper Mountain Racquet and Athletic Club—

Year-round courts and lessons available; fee charged. Located at Copper Mountain. Open 6 am–10 pm Mon.–Fri., 8 am–10 pm Sat.–Sun. (303) 968-2882.

Dillon Public Courts—

Four outdoor courts are available at the park in Dillon on La Bonte St. Reservations can be made at **Town Hall** at **275 Chief Colorow**. Small fee charged between Memorial Day and Labor Day; free the rest of the year. For information, call **(303) 468-2403**.

Four Seasons Tennis Club—

Outdoor courts and lessons available; fee charged. In Breckenridge at **210 Park Ave.; (303) 453-2425**.

Keystone Tennis Center—

Open year-round; lessons available; fee charged. Located at Keystone; call for information. **(303) 468-4220**.

WINDSURFING

Each summer, after their skis have been put in storage, Summit County locals dust off their sailboards and head to **Green Mountain Reservoir**. (See the Fishing section for directions.) The fairly warm water of this reservoir attracts scores of windsurfing enthusiasts from around Colorado. The southeast end of the reservoir has sandy beaches, providing the best place to use as a base. A windsurfing concessionaire used to rent boards at the reservoir, but no longer does. Only recently, windsurfers were granted permission by the Denver Water Board to surf on **Lake Dillon**. However, you need to be a sailboard fanatic with a very thick wet suit. The water temperature is a full 10 to 15 degrees colder than Green Mountain Reservoir. One look at the snow-capped peaks will tell you why.

———— SEEING AND DOING ————

ALPINE SLIDE

On the **Super Slide** at Breckenridge you can glide down one of two tracks on Peak 8 in your specially designed sled. You control the brake lever so the ride can be as easy or as scary as you want. The sled is big enough for an adult and a small child. No. 5 chairlift takes you to the top of the track. One-ride tickets are available, as well as all-day passes. To reach the lift from the stoplight in town, head west up Ski Hill Rd. for about 1.5 miles. Open daily from late June through early Sept., 10 am–4:30 pm; weekends only in late Sept. Call **(303) 453-2368** for information.

CHAIRLIFT RIDES

During the summer, you can ride chairlifts up the mountains at Breckenridge, Copper Mountain and Keystone ski areas. See Hiking and Backpacking.

MUSEUMS AND GALLERIES

Frisco Historic Park—

Established in 1982, Frisco Historic Park consists of seven completely restored buildings from Frisco and the surrounding area. The Frisco Schoolhouse Museum, the largest of these, is located on its original site. It was first used as a saloon before becoming a schoolhouse. It now houses artifacts and information about the Ute Indians, mining and Dillon Reservoir. The other buildings include private residences and the old Frisco jail. Open Tues.–Sun. 11 am–4 pm in winter; Tues.–Sat. 11 am–4 pm in summer. No fee. Located at **120 Main St.** in **Frisco; (303) 668-3428**.

Summit Historical Society Tours—

The Summit Historical Society,

through local funding, has been able to restore a number of interesting historical sites around the county. Both self-guided tours and tours with a knowledgeable guide are available. For information, call **(303) 468-6079** or **(303) 453-9022**. Here are a couple of the more interesting tours:

Located near Breckenridge, the **Washington Mine** operated from 1880–1973. Visitors are led into the horizontal shaft with miner's candles. Many artifacts are on display to help you get a better understanding of gold and silver mining in Colorado. Tours begin June 1, Wed.–Sat. at 1 pm (Sat. in am) and run through the summer. A small fee is charged. The **Breckenridge Briggle House** is a fine Victorian home built in 1896. Its main attraction is an art collection that includes "hair" art. This unusual medium features small bobbles made from women's hair, which were popular accessories in the Victorian era. Open Wed.–Sat.; small fee charged. Tours begin at 10 am and last about 1 hour and 15 minutes.

NIGHTLIFE

Narrowing down the long list of nightlife options in Summit County is no easy task. Because it contains the largest collection of winter resorts in the country, Summit County offers an abundance of après-ski spots where people dance to live music into the wee hours. Briefly, here are the highlights.

Breckenridge—

For après ski, many people converge on the **Village Pub (453-0369)** and **Buffalo Flats Saloon & Grill (453-6767)**, both located in the Bell Tower Shops at **555 S. Columbine.** Across the street is **Mi Casa (600 Park, 453-2071)**. For dancing into the night try **The Mogul (109 S. Main St., 453-0999)** and **Shamus O'Tooles Roadhouse Saloon (115 S. Ridge, 453-2004)**. How about live theater? **The Backstage Theater (355 Village Rd., 453-0199)** gives evening performances in winter and summer. Call for reservations.

Copper Mountain—

Après ski kicks into high gear at **Farley's (968-2577)** and **The B lift Pub (968-2525)**, both located at the base of the B-lift. The **Liftside Lounge (968-2882 ext. 6505)** at **The Plaza** restaurant, at the Mountain Plaza, provides a soothing atmosphere with many hot drink specialties.

Frisco—

Along Main St. you'll find the **Moose Jaw, 208 Main (668-3931)**, for cheap beer and a game of pool. **Barkley's Basement Cafe, at 620 Main (668-3694)**, offers Mexican food, good Margaritas and live rock and blues.

Keystone—

The **Snake River Saloon** offers fine dining, and the rowdy bar in the next room has some of the best live music in the county. Built more than 25 years ago and originally called the Loveland Pass Bar, weary travelers, construction workers and miners used to frequent this popular night spot. It still rocks out late into the night. Located at **23074 Hwy. 6; 468-2788**.

Silverthorne—

The **Old Dillon Inn** was an institution in Summit County even before it was moved from the old townsite of Dillon, which was flooded by the reservoir in 1962. Both the restaurant (Mexican food) and bar pack people in like sardines for live music and a few cervezas and Margaritas. If you don't mind crowds, then give it a try. **321 Blue River Pkwy. (Hwy. 9); 468-2791**.

SCENIC DRIVES

Boreas Pass/Hoosier Pass—

From the comfort of your Chrysler or Ford, cross two of the most historic passes in the area, which were barely navigable by mule a century or so ago. Boreas Pass Rd. (Forest Rd. 223) begins near Breckenridge and heads southwest along the old Denver South Park & Pacific Railroad bed, which finally laid track to Breckenridge in

1882. The grade was so steep that the engine could only pull three cars at a time. One story has it that P.T. Barnum's circus train was on its way to Breckenridge when it started to stall. The elephants were let out of the cars and helped push the train to the summit. Historic sights along the way include **Baker's Tank** (a restored water tank) and the remains of a settlement on the 11,482-foot summit, which, at one time, had the highest post office in the country. When it was built, this line of train track was the highest in the country. The panorama of the Tenmile Range is spectacular along the way.

From the summit of the pass (10 miles from Breckenridge) continue down the other side of the Continental Divide and take in the views of the wide expanse of South Park. After about 13 miles you'll reach the old town of Como (see the **South Park and 285 Corridor** chapter). From Como, turn right on Hwy. 285 and head to Fairplay, then take another right onto Hwy. 9. The road almost immediately begins climbing northward to the 11,541-foot summit of Hoosier Pass. Homesick prospectors from Indiana gave the pass its name around 1860. From the summit, return to Breckenridge, about 10 miles north.

Loveland Pass—

It wasn't too many years ago that every motorist driving between Denver and Summit County had to ascend the skyscraping Loveland Pass. Since the completion of the Eisenhower Tunnel in 1973, people have forgotten how beautiful the views are from the summit of the pass. Granted, it takes longer to drive over the pass, but at the summit you can get out and walk along ridges of the Continental Divide. Views to both sides are spectacular. Visitors who want to see alpine tundra without having to walk up to it should make this drive. To reach Loveland Pass from Keystone, head east on Hwy. 6 past Arapahoe Basin Ski Area and follow the switchbacks to the summit. Either return the same way or descend the east side of the pass and return via Eisenhower Tunnel.

Ute Pass—

For one of the best overlooks of the Gore Range, try a trip up Ute Pass in the Williams Fork Mountains. This trip is especially nice in fall when the aspen turn gold. Ute Pass Rd. crosses at a summit of 9,524 feet and drops down to the Williams Fork River near the Henderson Mill. To reach the road from Silverthorne, head about 16 miles north on Hwy. 9 and turn right at the Henderson Mill sign (Forest Rd. 132). It's about 5 miles to the summit.

WHERE TO STAY

ACCOMMODATIONS

BRECKENRIDGE

The majority of Breckenridge accommodations are deluxe lodges and condominium rentals. At the base of Peak 9 the magnificent Breckenridge Hilton, Beaver Run Resort and the Village at Breckenridge all offer modern, luxurious rooms right at the ski mountain. Information and reservations for accommodations in Breckenridge can be arranged by calling **Breckenridge Central Reservations at 1-800-221-1091** out of state and **1-800-822-5381** in Colorado.

Ridge Street Inn — $$ to $$$

This quaint Victorian-style bed and breakfast was recently remodeled by the owner, Ed Mims. Four comfortable private rooms and a small dorm are available. Two rooms have private baths, while the others share bathrooms. Continental breakfast is served each morning. For reservations and information contact Mims at **212 N. Ridge St., Breckenridge, CO 80424; (303) 453-4680.**

Fireside Inn — $ to $$$$

Originally built in 1879, this home has

been added on to over the years, and the result is a charming, very popular inn. Rates vary quite a bit; there are four private rooms with baths and five dorm rooms. American Youth Hostel cards are honored, providing inexpensive lodging. The private rooms are furnished with some antiques, including brass beds. The Brandywine Suite is the finest room, with two queen beds and a living room. There used to be a decanter of fine brandy in the room, but it was removed after the maid kept getting bombed while cleaning! Downstairs, the living room with its cozy fireplace serves as a meeting place for guests. Continental breakfast comes with the room rate; full breakfast is available for a small fee. The hot tub soothes your muscles after a day on the slopes. **PO Box 2252, 114 N. French St., Breckenridge, CO 80424; (303) 453-6456.**

COPPER MOUNTAIN

Accommodations in Copper Mountain are mainly lodge rooms and condominiums. Specific descriptions and prices can be obtained by calling toll free **1-800-458-8386.**

Club Med — $$$$

This was the first Club Med in North America. Offering "the antidote to civilization," this glitzy international resort provides week-long vacation packages which include lodging in their lavish hotel, dining, cabaret entertainment and all the skiing you want. The only currency used is bar beads, which can be redeemed for drinks at the bar. Club Med at Copper Mountain is not strictly for swinging singles—programs for kids are provided. Transportation between Stapleton Airport in Denver and Copper Mountain is an additional charge. Open during winter only. Weekly rates per person are variable. **PO Box 3337, Copper Mountain, CO 80443; (303) 968-2161.**

FRISCO

With its location alongside Interstate 70, Frisco has quite a number of motel chains to choose from. In addition, condominiums and private homes can be rented. Call the **Lake Dillon Resort Association at 1-800-365-6365** (outside Colorado) toll free or locally at **(303) 468-6222** for information and reservations.

Twilight Inn — $$ to $$$

Of the many bed and breakfasts in Summit County, the Twilight Inn is a highlight. Only open since December 1987, this inn has already received rave reviews from travel magazines and major newspapers. Each of the 12 rooms is unique and carefully furnished. Eight have private bathrooms, while the others share baths. The largest room sleeps eight people. The library/TV room is an excellent place to relax and visit with other guests after a day of hiking or skiing. A hot tub and a steam room are also featured. The hosts, Rich Ahlquist and Jane Harrington, are great folks. Rich has lived in Summit County for 10 years and can provide a wealth of information about the area. Continental breakfast is included in the price—the zucchini bread is delicious. A comfortable, handsome and reasonably priced place, it's hard not to be impressed with the Twilight Inn. Reservations are recommended during the peak winter months and holidays. **PO Box 397, 308 Main St., Frisco, CO 80443; (303) 668-5009.**

Mardei's Mountain Retreat — $ to $$$

Ski maps and Victorian-era newspapers line the walls. Ski artifacts and a mishmash of other items shoved into nooks and crannies give visitors plenty to investigate when they enter Mardei's Mountain Retreat. The warmth of a ski lodge resonates at this old two-story home surrounded by pine trees two blocks off Main St. Five small rooms are affordable accommodations for people on a budget. Two rooms, the Columbine and the Pearly Everlasting, have private baths, while the other rooms share. The living room has a fireplace, a stereo, a TV, an organ and lots of games and reading material. A family-style breakfast is served each morning in the large dining room. **PO Box 1767, 221 S. Fourth Ave., Frisco, CO 80443; (303) 668-5337.**

GREEN MOUNTAIN RESERVOIR
Green Mountain Inn — $$

If the resort atmosphere and large numbers of people in the Lake Dillon area get to you, rustic cabins at the Green Mountain Inn await. The cabins are down the hill from the inn, by the reservoir. Three winterized log cabins come with baths and kitchen facilities and sleep up to four adults. The inn also has a restaurant (see the Where to Eat section). To reach the inn from Silverthorne, drive 23 miles north on Hwy. 9 to Heeney. Just follow the signs. **Blue River Rte., Box 82G, Dillon, CO 80435; 7101 Summit County Rd. 30, Heeney, (303) 724-3812.**

KEYSTONE

Accommodations at Keystone Resort are all handled through a central reservations number. You have three main choices—a room at Keystone Lodge in the village, a condominium or a luxury home rental. The central reservations numbers are **1-800-525-1309** outside Colorado and **1-800-222-0188** in state. For a charming, historic lodging opportunity, read on.

Ski Tip Lodge — $$$ to $$$$

If slick, modern accommodations are not what you are looking for, think about staying at Ski Tip Lodge. Located east of the ski area in an isolated pine forest, the lodge, without the distractions of telephones and TVs, is the perfect escape. The log building was a stagecoach stop in the 1880s. When Max and Edna Dercum bought the place in the 1940s, it became the first skiing guest ranch in Colorado. Max, an avid skier, developed Arapahoe Basin Ski Area just up the valley. Hosts and guests alike would ski all day and sit around the stone fireplace at night chatting and getting to know one another. The Dercums sold Ski Tip to the resort in 1983, but the charm lives on.

The lodge is decorated like a Swiss chalet, with colorful flowers blooming in window boxes in summer. The interior is complemented by hand-hewn wooden beams and ceilings. Accommodations are rustic but comfortable. Fourteen rooms are furnished with antiques, quilts and lace curtains. Some rooms have private baths while others share. Ski Tip Lodge is famous for its excellent food. In winter, lodging prices include breakfast and a four-course dinner. In summer, lodging includes breakfast only. For more information about the restaurant, see the Where to Eat section. In winter, bus transportation to Keystone is available every half hour. Reservations recommended in winter. **Box 38, Keystone, CO 80435; (303) 468-4202.**

MONTEZUMA

For a drastic escape from the pre-programmed accommodations and traffic of the main vacation centers of Summit County, stay in Montezuma. This sleepy old mining town is within striking distance of the major ski areas and has great cross-country skiing right at its doorstep. **Middle Earth Enterprises** is a local property management firm which books out private homes in the Montezuma area. Contact Steve and Bonita Hornback, **Box 9, Montezuma Rd., Dillon, CO 80435; (303) 468-8509.** Here are a couple of lodging ideas.

Saints John Lodge — $ to $$

For rustic (and we do mean rustic) accommodations in the backcountry see the Saints John Lodge and Trail System in the Cross-Country Skiing section of this chapter.

Skiota Lodge — $$

Located 8 miles up Montezuma Rd. from Keystone, Skiota looks like a bizarre wooden fortress complete with an observation deck on top. This unique, hand-crafted log home was built in 1976 by Larry Webb, the host. Logs from trees that were cut down to clear runs at Keystone Ski Area were used, as well as old wooden planks from buildings in the area. Inside, bookshelves, tables, etc., were all made by Larry. Though the interior is not spotlessly clean, the charm makes up for it. This small, rustic lodge is ringed by the beautiful 13,000-foot peaks of the Arapaho National Forest. Two rooms are available, as well as a nearby cabin that sleeps four people. Relax in the sauna and hot tub or sit around the kitchen table conversing with other guests and the hosts. Continental breakfast is included in the price. In winter, a car with good traction in snow is recommended for getting up the last 100 yards to the lodge. Due to the limited number of rooms, advance reservations are suggested. PO Box 234, Dillon, CO 80435; (303) 468-6851.

SILVERTHORNE AND DILLON

For arranging Summit County accommodations not connected with the ski resorts, contact the **Lake Dillon Resort Association** toll free at 1-800-365-6365 or locally at **(303) 468-6222.**

Alpine Hutte — $

When Fran Colson and her son, Dave, opened their low-cost lodge in the fall of 1987, they let out a sigh of relief—financing had not been easily obtained. As Fran puts it, "The bankers were trying to tell me tourists expected and wanted to spend a lot of money for lodging." Luckily, she convinced one bank otherwise. The result is a European-style lodge offering a startlingly low nightly rate for a bed. Fran got the idea for the lodge from her years traveling in Europe, Australia and New Zealand. The lodge sleeps 66 people in spacious rooms with four to eight bunks each and two large bathrooms on each floor. One of the bedrooms is equipped for handicapped visitors. Another room has a double bed but costs three times as much per night.

Downstairs, guests spend time either in the TV room or the main living room with its stone fireplace, dining room table and overstuffed sofas. For a very small fee, breakfast, lunch and dinner are offered. One drawback is that the bedrooms are closed for cleaning each day from 9:30

am–3:30 pm, but the downstairs rooms remain open. There is also an evening curfew. If you don't mind a few regulations, the Alpine Hutte is definitely worthwhile. American Youth Hostel members get a discount. Reservations are highly recommended. Contact Fran or Dave Colson at **PO Box 919, Silverthorne, CO 80498; (303) 468-6336.**

CAMPING

In Arapaho National Forest—

Lake Dillon—The national forest campgrounds at Lake Dillon are plentiful but extremely crowded during the summer months. Sites are available on a first-come, first-served basis. Stop in at the forest service office in Silverthorne to get an idea of where you'll have the best chance to find a site. **Heaton Bay Campground** (72 sites; fee charged), **Peak One Campground** (79 sites; fee charged), **Pine Cove Campground** (50 sites; fee charged) and **Prospector Campground** (108 sites; fee charged) are located along the northwest shore and along Hwy. 9 south of Frisco. Group camping is available at **Gold Pan Campground** (14 sites; fee charged) and **Windy Point Campground** (72 sites; fee charged). Reservations are required for these group campgrounds.

Blue River Campground (20 sites; fee charged) is located on the Blue River, 9 miles north of Silverthorne on Hwy. 9.

Green Mountain Reservoir—McDonald Flats Campground (44 sites; fee charged), **Prairie Point Campground** (39 sites; fee charged), **Elliot Creek Campground** (64 sites; fee charged) and **Cataract Creek Campground** (four sites; no fee) are located next to Green Mountain Reservoir, 25 miles north of Silverthorne on Hwy. 9.

Private Campground—

Tiger Run Resort—Believe it or not, as large as Summit County is, only one private RV campground exists. And it's pricey. Tiger Run, one of only a few five-star RV resorts in the country, offers RV sites, tennis courts, a large clubhouse, an indoor swimming pool, a hot tub, a laundry and a game room. Some RVs are available for rent. Tiger Run is located along Hwy. 9 between Frisco and Breckenridge. From Frisco, drive south about 6 miles and turn left at the Tiger Run sign. **Tiger Run Resort, PO Box 815, Breckenridge, CO 80424; (303) 453-9690.**

WHERE TO EAT

BRECKENRIDGE

Briar Rose Restaurant — $$$ to $$$$

In 1900, when the Briar Rose Mine up on Peak 10 was operating at full tilt, the miners stayed at the Briar Rose boardinghouse on Lincoln St. They raved about the food, and pretty soon people from around the area were making special trips into Breckenridge to dine there. After the mining days waned, the boardinghouse was abandoned and eventually burned down. In the early 1960s a new restaurant was built in tribute to the legacy of good food and drink at the Briar Rose. Both the fine food and the historic atmosphere make this a really fun place to eat. The dining area is decorated in Victorian style with antiques. The old wooden bar was moved from the Breckenridge Opera House, where for years it helped reluctant operagoers tolerate Madame Butterfly a little more easily. Game trophies line the walls and the portrait of a reclining nude behind the bar seems to fit perfectly.

Menu items range from steak to seafood; occasionally, game dishes such as elk, venison and buffalo are available. The prime rib has a good reputation around town. Pages of the menu are interspersed with an extensive wine selection, featuring straightforward descriptions of each vintage. Reservations are a good idea. Open daily in winter 5–10 pm, 6–10 pm Mon.–Sat. in summer. Located just off Main St. at **109 E. Lincoln St.; 453-9948.**

The Brown Hotel and Restaurant — $$$ to $$$$

This is perhaps the most charming of the Breckenridge restaurants that are housed in historic buildings. Upon entering the Brown Hotel and Restaurant, you are led through the front room to a Victorian dining area decorated in red and black. Many antiques grace the rooms. The building, which dates back to the 1860s, operated as a school in the 1880s, and later as a hotel run by Tom and Maude Brown. Because it housed the only bathtub in Summit County for quite some time, business was good.

The menu offers beef, lamb, chicken, duck, seafood and a daily chef's special. The sauces are prepared individually for each order. A full bar in a small side room is intimate and frequented by locals. Reservations recommended. Open in winter 5–10 pm daily; summer hours are 5:30–9:30 pm daily. **208 Ridge St.; 453-0084.**

Egil's — $$$ to $$$$

The intimate dining atmosphere and fine food at this quaint 100-year-old Victorian home are a highlight of eating out in Breckenridge. Hanging plants, fine wood trim, soft background music and lace tablecloths are all nice touches. A Scandinavian theme is obvious; paintings of Viking ships and skiing Vikings line the walls, and the entrée names range from Odin's Delight to Thor's Hammer. The food presentation is creative and the food is delicious. Choose from the small à la carte selection and four-course entrées. Variations of beef, game and seafood dishes change daily. Owner and chef David Arneson takes great care in personally preparing the entrées and delicious sauces. Reservations are recommended. Open 5:30–10 pm nightly in winter, 5:30 to late evening Tues.–Sat. in summer. **318 N. Main St.; 453-2871.**

Weber's Restaurant — $$$ to $$$$

This extremely popular German restaurant offers a warm European atmosphere and excellent food. Windows in the newly built Victorian-style building look to the ski slopes. Owner Richard Weber cooks all of the traditional German and American food and bakes the delicious rolls, pies and pastries. Weber learned how to cook the German fare from his grandparents who emigrated to Denver from Germany and ran the successful Weber's Restaurant in Denver for many years. Sauerbraten, wienerschnitzel and bratwurst highlight the German entrées with pork chops and Rocky Mountain trout as two of the American dishes. À la carte is available or try a full dinner with salad, spaetzle, dessert and coffee included. Be sure to check the chef's special of the day. Open in winter 5–10 pm daily; in summer it's open Wed.–Sun. 5–10 pm. **200 N. Main St.; 453-9464.**

El Perdido — $$ to $$$

El Perdido, meaning "the Lost One" in Spanish, was supposedly named when it was built in 1962 because of its backstreet location. But if you are looking for great Mexican food, the search for El Perdido will be rewarded. Many of the recipes on the menu are authentically Mexican, and contrary to the stereotype not all Mexican food is hot. Spicy dishes are offered, but so are items like Huachinango, a red snapper dish from Veracruz. El Perdido is a large restaurant that attracts a good crowd during ski season. Frank Walters, the owner, runs drink specials during the winter. When "Star Trek" comes on TV, 25-cent shots are offered each time "there is a Vulcan pinch, someone says 'beam me up' or Captain Kirk puts a lip lock on some beautiful alien." Be sure to try their house grog, a sweet eggnog-like drink called Rompope. Open daily for lunch from 11 am–4:30 pm and dinner from 4:30–10:30 pm. **306 N. French St.; 453-2928.**

Fatty's Pizzeria — $ to $$

If you're looking for a good pizza, look no farther. Fatty's serves up the best pizza in Breckenridge. You have the choice of white or whole wheat dough. This casual restaurant also offers five daily specials, such as beef stroganoff and Mexican dishes. Beer and wine are served. Open daily all year 11 am–10 pm. **106 S. Ridge St.; 453-9802.**

The Prospector — $ to $$

For the budget-conscious seeker of reasonably priced breakfasts, lunches and dinners, try the Prospector. The building dates back to 1892, when it was built as a private residence. For the last 50 years it has been a restaurant. It is a casual place with weathered wood walls, a cork ceiling and historic pictures of Breckenridge throughout. The restaurant also boasts a resident ghost, Sylvia, a lovely Victorian-era brunette with long flowing hair, who roams around upstairs dressed in a nightgown and occasionally floats through the front of the building, scaring the $#*! out of unlucky tourists. Breakfast specialties include huevos rancheros and blueberry pancakes; for lunch or dinner try homemade soup with a burger or chicken-fried steak. Takeout orders available. Open 7 am–9 pm daily. **130 S. Main St.; 453-6858.**

Tillie's — $ to $$

Known for its reasonably priced food and great atmosphere, Tillie's gets a high recommendation. The building is a very attractive neo-Victorian with a stamped-tin ceiling, lots of stained glass and a beautiful marble and wood bar. The restaurant is named after the owner's mother, who ran a restaurant in the Bronx for years. Homemade soups are offered, along with monstrous burgers, sandwiches and other dinner items. The appetizers are delicious; a heaping plate of nachos is a meal in itself. On Sun. mornings, Tillie's runs a breakfast special—if you buy a drink at regular price, you can get a plate of sausage, eggs and potatoes for 50 cents. What a deal. Whether you want a great meal or just want to belly up to the bar for a drink or two, try Tillie's. Open daily for lunch from 11 am–4 pm, dinner from 5–10 pm (11 pm in winter). **215 S. Ridge St.; 453-0069.**

The Gold Pan Restaurant — $

Recently voted by *Ski Magazine* as one of the top five restaurants in the country for local flavor, the Gold Pan is an experience. Built in 1906 and frequented by miners, this small place oozes history. At one time or another the building housed a nine-pin bowling alley, a funeral home and a buggy repair shop. The current layout features a saloon on one side with an ancient wooden bar. During Prohibition this bar was the only place in the state where a guy could get a drink (with a token purchased up the street). The restaurant decor is basic—wooden walls, tintype photos, mining relics and chairs that have been around since the 1930s. The Gold Pan is famous for its breakfasts, which are served all day. The specialties are the Mexican breakfast dishes with sauces (five kinds), beans, etc., prepared daily. Burgers and sandwiches are also served. Open 6:30 am–10 pm daily. **105 N. Main St.; 453-5499.**

COPPER MOUNTAIN
Farley's — $ to $$$$

An institution in Copper Mountain since 1973, Farley's excels in both its fine food and its après-ski entertainment. The restaurant gets its name from the owner's German shepherd, who's no longer with us. Fireplaces, beer kegs in the walls and vaulted ceilings characterize this comfortable place. Prime rib, steaks and fresh seafood highlight the menu. Appetizers, including barbecue ribs and artichoke parmesan, appease the après-ski crowd. Extensive wine list; Margaritas are quite good. Located at the base of the B lift, the tavern opens daily in mid-afternoon and closes at 2 am. Restaurant is open 5:30–10 pm daily. **Snowflake Building; 968-2577.**

DILLON
Ristorante Al Lago — $$$

Although newcomers to the Summit County area, the Ottoborgo family have wowed locals with their excellent northern Italian cuisine. After their highly praised restaurant in Berthoud Falls burned down a couple of years ago, the family moved to Dillon and opened Ristorante Al Lago. The father, Alessandro, is from Italy and spends most of his time tending bar. His son, Ivano, studied the culinary arts in Italy for a couple of years and picked up secrets from New York chefs. Ivano prepares everything from scratch and even cuts his own veal and fish. The veal entrées are creative and considered by many locals to be the restaurant's highlight. Also offered are chicken, fresh seafood and a daily special. Delicious bread and desserts round out the menu. The dining room is very comfortable with a stone fireplace, wood beams, brick floors, red tablecloths, candlelight and a spectacular view up to Buffalo Mountain. In the backyard, deer and chickens roam (the deer can be fed from the balcony). Open 5–10 pm Tues.–Sun. **240 Chief Colorow; 468-6111.**

FRISCO
The Blue Spruce Inn — $$$ to $$$$

Strangely enough, this old establishment has traveled through more of Summit County than many vacationers have. Opened 50 years ago as a roadhouse between Old Dillon and Breckenridge, the building was moved to Frisco in the 1960s to avoid the rising waters of the reservoir. Having come under the new ownership of Travis Holton and reopened in the fall of 1987, it continues to be one of the consistently fine restaurants in Summit County. The Blue Spruce Inn is cozy and intimate, with pine paneling, hanging plants and a lichen-covered stone fireplace. Specialties include slow-roasted prime rib, continental dishes and fresh seafood. Try their daily specials, such as poached salmon with tomato-hollandaise sauce or baked marlin with blackberry-hazelnut butter sauce. Service is superb. Dinners nightly 5–10 pm; call for reservations. **120 W. Main St.; 668-5900.**

The Spruce Restaurant — $$$ to $$$$

Chef/owner Jeff Worrell, formerly with the Blue Spruce Inn, recently set up shop down the street with many of his original staff and recipes. A good number of the local clientele also seem to have followed. And with good reason—Worrell can flat out cook. The whole family is involved and helps convey the feeling that you're eating in someone's home. A stone fireplace serves as the focal point; old wood on the walls was milled at the nearby mining town of Montezuma. Picture windows provide a great view of the Tenmile River. Creative beef, seafood and specialty entrées including the trademarked Scampi Blue Spruce and Spruce Ribs, highlight the menu. Be sure to make room for their delicious bread and fresh homemade pie. Joan Worrell has compiled an excellent wine list ranging in price from moderate to extravagant. For a special night out we highly recommend the Spruce Restaurant. In summer the hours are 7:30–11:30 am for breakfast, 11:30 am–3 pm for lunch and 5:30–10 pm for dinner; winter hours are 7:30–11:30 am for breakfast and 5–10 pm for dinner (no lunch). A special "summer fare" menu offers lower-priced entrées from 5:30–7 pm. Located at **Woodbridge Inn** at **450 W. Main St.** in west **Frisco; 668-5243.**

The Moose Jaw — $ to $$

Serving heaping baskets of burgers and fries, the Moose Jaw is a great place for a cheap beer and a game of pool. Primarily locals hang out here. It's not fancy, it's just an inexpensive alternative. Open noon–2 am Mon.–Sat.; until midnight on Sun. **208 Main St.; 668-3931.**

GREEN MOUNTAIN RESERVOIR
The Green Mountain Inn — $ to $$$

The restaurant at the Green Mountain Inn serves as the meeting place for locals in the Heeney area and we include it because of its atmosphere. Sit at the counter or in the dining room and listen to music on the old player piano, juke box or wind-up Victrola. Menu items are of the usual steak and fried chicken variety, but there are a few house specials you may want to investigate. Try a Heeney weenie, a cheesy Heeney beanie weenie or a "Dam" good sandwich, named for the water project just

down the hill. Be sure to ask about the Hiney Winery in Heeney, run by Thor Hiney and his mother, Ophelia Hiney. Open in winter 4:30–9 pm on weekdays, 9 am–9 pm on weekends; summer hours 4:30–9 pm weekdays and 7 am–9 pm weekends. Closed Mon. year-round. Located in Heeney, 23 miles north of Silverthorne on Hwy. 9. **7101 Summit County Rd. 30; 724-3812.**

KEYSTONE
Keystone Ranch — $$$$

When it closed down operations in 1972, Keystone Ranch had been a working cattle ranch for more than 30 years. The restaurant provides beautiful views of the Tenmile and Gore ranges, as well as some of the finest gourmet food in Summit County. The six-course meal changes nightly. Enjoy a cocktail in the living room beside the two-story stone fireplace. In summer, lunches ($$) are served on the terrace overlooking the golf course. There are two seatings nightly, from 5:45–6:45 pm and from 8:15–9 pm. Reservations recommended. Three miles from Keystone Village; **1437 Summit County Rd. 150; 468-4161.**

Ski Tip Lodge — $$$$

Located in a rustic cabin east of Keystone Ski Area, Ski Tip Lodge is well known for what many people consider to be the best food in Summit County. A stagecoach stop in the 1880s, the lodge has been operating as a ski lodge and restaurant since the 1940s. Enter the cozy restaurant and warm yourself by the stone fireplace before being seated in the dining room. Each evening a choice of meat, fowl or fish is offered, with items changing nightly. The sauces are wonderful. Four-course dinners are served 6–9 pm nightly with soup, salad and freshly baked bread. Lunches ($$) are served daily in winter from noon–2 pm and feature all the soup and bread you can eat. In summer, Sun. brunch ($$) is served from 10 am–1 pm. Reservations required. Call **468-4202.**

SILVERTHORNE
Old Dillon Inn — $$

The Old Dillon Inn has done its share of moving around. Built in 1869 in Montezuma, it was first moved to Old Dillon piece by piece. When Dillon Reservoir was completed in 1962, the building was loaded on a flatbed and moved to its present location. The owners supposedly had the kegs retapped before the beer had a chance to get warm. The Old Dillon Inn serves tasty New Mexican-style food; the specialty is blue-corn crab enchiladas. The nightlife here is locally famous and can get rowdy. Live music (usually country-western) plays Fri.–Sun., and solo artists perform Tues.–Thur. The Margaritas are excellent. Although the restaurant gets incredibly crowded, reservations are not accepted. Open for dinner only from 4:30–10 pm daily. Along Hwy. 9 in Silverthorne at **321 Blue River Pkwy.; 468-2791.**

SERVICES

Breckenridge Central Reservations—
1-800-221-1091 out of state and 1-800-822-5381 in state.

Breckenridge Resort Chamber—
555 S. Columbine, Box 1909, Breckenridge, CO 80424; (303) 453-6018.

Copper Mountain Resort—
PO Box 3001, Copper Mountain, CO 80443; 1-800-458-8386.

Keystone Resort—
Box 38, Keystone, CO 80435; 1-800-525-1309 out of state; 1-800-222-0188 in Colorado or (303) 534-7712 (toll free from Denver).

Lake Dillon Resort Association—
121 Dillon Mall, Suite 102, PO Box 446, Dillon, CO 80435; (303) 468-6222 locally, or toll free at 1-800-365-6365.

Summit County Chamber of Commerce—
Two visitors centers—one in Frisco and one in Dillon. Mailing address is **PO Box 214, Frisco, CO 80443; (303) 468-6205, (303) 668-5800 or 668-0376.**

Transportation—
Resort Express—Provides airport shuttles. **PO Box 1429, 273 Warren Ave., Silverthorne, CO 80498; (303) 468-7600.**

Summit Stage—This free public bus system provides wintertime transportation between all the resorts and major towns in Summit County. Pick up a schedule at a visitors center or wherever you're staying. For information call **(303) 453-1241** or **(303) 453-1339.**

Day Care—
Belly Button Bakery and Babies—Day care for kids two months and older. Reservations required. Located at **Copper Mountain; (303) 968-2882 ext. 6344.**

Keystone Children's Center—This 8,000-square-foot facility provides day care for infants up to 12-year-olds. Call **(303) 468-4182** for information.

Peak 8 Nursery—Day care in Breckenridge. **PO Box 1058, Breckenridge, CO 80424; (303) 453-2368, ext. 7227.**

Vail Valley

Considered by many to be the Colorado ski area with the finest snow conditions and most varied terrain, Vail has made quite a name for itself in a very short period of time. If it wasn't already, Vail Mountain became king of the ski hills in 1988 when a major expansion made it the biggest ski resort in North America, bigger in fact than the four ski areas in nearby Summit County combined. Located 100 miles west of Denver along Interstate 70, the town, which extends nearly 7 miles through the valley, offers 15 square miles of skiable terrain inside its boundaries. Although established in 1962, Vail really had its coming-of-age party in early 1989, when it played host to the World Alpine Ski Championships. Often called the Alpine Olympics, this biennial competition is the single most important event in alpine skiing. This was only the second time in the 60-year history of the event that it was held in the US.

There couldn't be a more worthy site for the championships than Vail. Tucked away behind massive Vail Mountain are the legendary back bowls, Colorado's own Shangri-La of schuss. The combination of sun, altitude and dry air on the back bowls is perfect for Dom Perignon powder. Recently four new bowls, not as steep as the others, have been added, opening the thrill of back-bowl skiing to intermediate skiers.

Beaver Creek, Vail's sister resort 10 miles west, adds over a square mile of terrain to the Vail Valley empire. (Lift tickets between the two areas are interchangeable.) Beaver Creek, sometimes called the "Last Resort," is Colorado's swankiest: "where the millionaires ski," comments one local observer.

Not to be ignored in all of the skiing hype is the beautiful backcountry of the White River National Forest, complete with two wilderness areas that flank Vail Valley. Within a cross-country run of Vail to the southwest is the popular Holy Cross Wilderness Area. To the north, at the heart of soaring Gore Range, lies Eagles Nest Wilderness Area. Sunsets in the valley turn the craggy range into a spectacular tangerine curtain. This national forest land contains an abundance of trails for hiking, mountain biking and cross-country skiing. Plenty of high mountain lakes and rushing streams await anglers.

Facing this striking alpine scenery in a front-row seat is the quaint Bavarian-style village of Vail itself. Skiers who prefer archrival Aspen call Vail a prefab storybook village with plenty of glitz, that lacks the historic charm of Aspen. And even Vail locals admit it can be a mountain Disneyland of sorts. But Disney does have its pluses—convenience, no cars in the center of town and five-star service. In addition, employees of Vail Associates, owner of the resort, have to attend Smile School in order to qualify for ski passes.

Yet the heart of a real town beats behind all the glamour. Vail now has its own library and cemetery, two symbols of civic maturity. There isn't a single stoplight, a fact that makes arriving in town a bit tricky. Don't try to navigate Vail in a car. Just park in structures at either Vail or Lionshead and walk or take the shuttle bus. Don't panic: what first seems a Tyrolean labyrinth of shops, lodges and eateries quickly reveals its meandering logic.

Spotting celebrities in Vail Valley isn't as popular as skiing, but it remains a favorite pastime. Former US president Gerald Ford and his wife, Betty, make their home in Beaver Creek. Ford hosts a celebrity golf tournament and a ski competition that draws many famous people. Clint Eastwood, Robert Redford, Connie Stevens and Henry Mancini all have homes in the area.

Perhaps the best day to ski Vail is Mar. 3—it has snowed on that date for 17 years. The best day to avoid snow is Apr. 15—records show it has snowed only once.

HISTORY

Vail is barely a baby boomer in Colorado history—many of its skiers are older than the 26-year-old area. But the narrow valley was home to the Ute Indians in the nineteenth century, before gold prospectors prompted their angry exit. As legend has it, the Utes set huge "spite fires" in their wake, burning thousands of acres of timber. The blazes turned out to be a blessing: the prized back bowls on Vail Mountain are said to be the result. Ironically, Utes later helped bring snow to those very bowls. On opening day of the new ski area in 1962, there was one problem: no snow. So the Utes were summoned back. Minnie Cloud led a ceremonial rain dance (renamed a snow dance for the occasion) on the deck of the new lodge at Vail. Within a week a blizzard hit, launching a successful season. By the way, the price of a full-day lift ticket back then was $5.

The first European to explore the vicinity of Vail Valley was, perhaps, Lord Gore, a wealthy baronet from Ireland. Gore decided in the mid-1850s to go on a massive, three-year hunting expedition in the wilds of America. So he assembled a veritable hunting army, with nearly 50 men, 100 horses, 50 hunting dogs, six wagons, 16 carts, a carpeted silk tent, a fur-lined commode, a few prostitutes and a three-month supply of trade whiskey (180-proof grain alcohol mixed with red pepper). Gore took along renowned mountain man Jim Bridger as a guide and the two exchanged stories along the way—Bridger's tales of the frontier for Gore's Shakespearean dramas. When they got into the mountains near Vail, Gore and his party proceeded to shoot every buffalo, deer and elk within range, killing literally thousands of them. Gore took a few trophies and left the rest to rot.

The trip finally came to an end after many misadventures in the Black Hills of South Dakota, when local Indians decided they'd had enough. Bear's Rib, an Uncpapa Sioux, and his war party surrounded Gore and his men, then stripped them of their horses, supplies and all their clothes. Gore was left wandering in the wild until friendly Hidatsa Indians took him in. Later, he quietly made his way back to Ireland. According to historians, Bridger came back afterward and named a mountain range and creek after Gore. Today the Gore name is attached to many land features in the area.

In 1873 William Henry Jackson brought early fame to the Vail area with his photographs of the long-rumored-to-exist Mount of the Holy Cross. Tales had circulated for years of lost travelers seeing the mountain's snowy cross and suddenly finding their way. One of Jackson's photos of the cross with clouds swirling around it inspired pilgrimages up the mountain, which continue today. Henry Wadsworth Longfellow saw the photo and penned a poem about the mountain. Making the pictures, however, was not easy, given the state of photography at the time. Jackson carrried his darkroom with him on mules.

In 1942 more than 15,000 men were stationed at Camp Hale, about 25 miles south of Vail, in preparation for winter fighting in Europe. After WWII, many of these 10th Mountain Division troopers became prime players in Colorado's burgeoning ski industry. Vail's modern history began with Pete Seibert, a 10th Mountain veteran.

Earl Eaton, who had been prospecting for uranium in Vail Valley, had met Seibert in Aspen. Eaton approached Seibert one day in Loveland (where Seibert worked) to tell him about a new prospect: the perfect ski mountain. Seibert took one look at the glorious slopes and agreed. They immediately began soliciting investors and, so as not to tip off anyone, formed the Trans Montane Rod & Gun Club to buy up land. Once permits were cleared and investors found, the ski area was built in a single year.

Vail got its name from Charlie Vail, chief engineer for Colorado's highway department in the late 1930s. Vail originally lent his name to present-day Monarch Pass, but locals who preferred Monarch protested. As a compromise, the moniker was transferred to the unnamed pass that is now Vail Pass.

Vail, which served as Gerald Ford's western White House during his presidency in the 1970s, celebrated its 25th birthday in 1987 as Colorado's, and America's, premier ski resort.

GETTING THERE

Vail Valley is 100 miles west of Denver on Interstate 70. Regular and chartered ground transportation is available directly from Denver's Stapleton International Airport via bus, taxi, limo and van. The resort area can be reached by air from Stapleton via Continental Express shuttle service to the Avon STOLport 7 miles west of Vail and 1 mile from Beaver Creek. There are seven flights a day; the shuttle flight would add only about $25 to the cost of a regular ticket to Stapleton.

FESTIVALS AND EVENTS

There's at least one special event every weekend in Vail. Some of the highlights:

Winterfaire
mid-January

Vail is spirited anyway during ski season, and during Winterfaire, it's just that much more so. Highlights of the annual winter carnival are the dog sled races and ice sculpture carvings around town. For information, call (303) 476-1000.

American Ski Classic
early March

Pros and amateurs descend on Vail for three events in a short period: the World Cup, the Gerry Ford Invitational Ski Classic and the Legends of Skiing, featuring the sport's greats. For a schedule, call (303) 476-1000.

VailAmerica Days
Fourth of July Celebration

This is one of Colorado's bigger celebrations of Independence Day. The festivities include the Vail Hill Climb and a mountaintop fireworks display. Contact (303) 476-1000 for more information.

Summer Sporting Events

In late July the annual **Beaver Creek Tennis Tournament** usually snares some big names: in 1988 it was Mats Wilander; and Jimmy Connors has been a regular attendee. Call **(303) 949-5750 ext. 4636** for more information. The **Gerry Ford Invitational Golf Tournament** gets underway in Aug. It attracts a slew of celebrity duffers, as well as some of the top pros on the PGA tour. The tourney is hosted by former president Ford at Vail Golf Club. Bob Hope and Jack Nicklaus are among the frequent returnees. Call **(303) 479-2260** for more information. In early Aug. the **Eagle County Rodeo** is usually kicked off with a bluegrass concert. In addition to events pitting cowboys against animals, competitions are held in horseshoe pitching, draft horse pulling and blindfolded tractor driving. For rodeo information, contact **(303) 328-7311 ext. 247.**

OUTDOOR ACTIVITIES

BIKING

MOUNTAIN BIKING

One of the world's premier mountain bikers, Mike Kloser, lives and trains in Vail Valley. That means Vail is a good place to two-wheel—good and tough. The steep valley makes for mostly challenging, uphill rides. For that reason, Vail's a little behind some of the other ski areas in promoting the sport. As of press time, there were no trail maps available and no marked trails. But Vail Mountain is open to mountain biking. Rentals are available at the top of the Lionshead Gondola at Eagles Nest every day during summer. Cyclists can take the gondola up and ride all the way down to return bikes in Lionshead. Bikes may also be taken up the gondola for a fee. On the way down the mountain, a helmet is a must. It's also a good idea to lower your seat so you won't fly over your handlebars.

Red Sandstone Road—

This is a moderate 12-mile ride north to scenic Piney Lake from Vail. The rocky road starts off steep, then levels out with plenty of stretches of downhill sprinkled amid the uphill. Especially fun is a roller coaster set of small hills near the end. At Piney Lake, you can claim your reward: a dramatic view of the full measure of Gore Range. Red Sandstone Rd. (Forest Rd. 700) leaves Vail's N. Frontage Rd. a mile west of the Vail Village exit from Interstate 70.

Shrine Pass Road—

See the Scenic Drives section for information.

Tigiwon Road—

For a taste of what a ride in the lunar rover must have felt like, try this bumpy 6-mile trail. The pitted road leads to the stone Tigiwon Hut south of Minturn. Most cyclists find this short ride more than enough. Depending on when the road was last graded, however, it's possible to continue another 2.5 miles to the edge of the Holy Cross Wilderness Area. But remember, mountain bikes aren't allowed in wilderness areas. To reach Tigiwon Rd. (Forest Rd. 707), drive or ride 2.8 miles south of Minturn on Hwy. 24 and turn right.

Vail Mountain—

A true fat-tire enthusiast will want to ride up the mountain on his or her bike rather than on the gondola to earn the trip down. A tough two-hour test is the dirt road from Vail Village to mid-Vail. Look for the road's start right behind the Vista Bahn lift. Taking a detour down a section of the ski hill when descending the road is discouraged by Vail officials (but there's nothing quite as frighteningly fun).

Vail Mountain Bike Tours—

An experienced guide will pick you up, equip you with a Cannondale bike and take you on a scenic ride down a back-road trail. Instruction and a gourmet lunch are included in the full-day tour. Half-day tours also are available. Since the rides are geared to any level of experience, it's great for families who have never tried mountain biking before. **PO Box 688, Vail, CO 81658; (303) 476-4520.**

Rentals and Information—

Christy Sports—For a good, varied supply of both mountain bikes and 10-speed touring bikes, check this place at **293 Bridge St.; (303) 476-2244.**

Custom Wheel Building—For advice and repairs, locals go to Custom Wheel Building just east of Vail Village at **302 E. Gore Creek Dr.; (303) 476-5311.**

TOURING

The 13.5-mile Vail Pass Bikeway from Vail to Copper Mountain and beyond has quickly become a favorite with cyclists of all abilities. But why ride a bike up a 10,666-foot pass, enduring a grueling hour or more of hairpin twists and killer inclines? For the thrill of speeding down the other side, of course. Tip: ascending the paved path from the Vail side (elevation gain: 2,206 feet) is a lot tougher than from the Copper Mountain side (elevation gain: 1,400 feet). For more information, see the Biking section of the **Summit County** chapter.

FISHING

Eagle River—

Although the once-proud Eagle River seems to be losing the battle to developers, there are still stretches of classic trout fishing to be found. The Eagle's main tributaries, the South Fork of the Eagle, which flows through Eagle Canyon near Redcliff, and Gore Creek, join near Minturn. From there Eagle River flows west down the valley between Hwy. 6 and Interstate 70 through ranches and pasture, where it is fed further by Brush and Gypsum creeks. Rainbow and brown in the 10- to 14-inch range can be found in the Eagle between its confluence with Gore Creek and Wolcott 14 miles downstream. The river is easy to get to from Hwy. 6, but stay off private land. Just below the confluence, you can fish on public water for about a mile. The fish seem to be a little bigger downriver near Eagle. Look for pools of deep, flat water. Locals recommend fly-fishing with streamers.

Gore Creek—

Gore Creek originates near Red Buffalo Pass in the Eagles Nest Wilderness Area, runs right through Vail and joins the Eagle River 2 miles northwest of Minturn.

Although much of it is surrounded by civilization and its trappings, the creek is still swimming with rainbow, brook, brown and cutthroat trout. In fact, within the town's borders (from Red Sandstone Creek to the Eagle River 3 miles downstream) the creek is designated Gold Medal water; flies and lures only. For a surprisingly natural setting in town, try fishing along the Vail golf course. The upper reaches of the creek in Eagles Nest Wilderness Area—north of Gore Creek Campground in East Vail—offer fishing away from the highway and condos.

Homestake Reservoir—

Though fishing is tricky because of steep, rocky banks, Homestake is a popular spot. There are rainbow, brook and cutthroat in this reservoir surrounded by the Holy Cross Wilderness Area. From Hwy. 24, 3 miles south of Redcliff, turn right onto Homestake Rd. (Forest Rd. 703) at Blodgett Campground and drive 11 miles up to the 300-acre reservoir. Controversy over the reservoir and an ongoing sister project, Homestake II, has resulted in a strange phenomenon: a lot of folks come up to see the area before it will be changed forever. Aurora and Colorado Springs owned water rights to much of Holy Cross before it was declared wilderness, so the dispute is not whether or not the water can be taken out of the area, but about the way it's being taken out. An ironic eyesore you'll see on the way up Homestake Rd. sums up the dispute—a large diversion pipe has Wilderness? gaudily painted on the side. Meantime, the fishing's great.

Mountain Lakes—

Near the summit of Vail Pass are the heavily fished **Black Lakes**. The two lakes, which feed into Black Gore Creek, are generally well stocked with rainbow and are easy to see from Interstate 70. **Lost Lake**, on the edge of the Eagles Nest Wilderness Area, is a popular lake in a beautiful setting at the headwaters of Red Sand-

stone Creek. Drive to the end of Red Sandstone Rd. off Vail's N. Frontage Rd. The short trail to the lake is right near the gate to Piney River Ranch. Folks there are glad to give directions. The upper three of the four **Missouri Lakes** in the Holy Cross Wilderness Area have brook and cutthroat trout. To reach the lakes from Redcliff, drive 3 miles south on Hwy. 24 and turn right on Homestake Rd. to Gold Park Campground. Follow the rough road southwest up Missouri Creek. The lakes are about a 3-mile hike from the end of the road. **Beaver Lake** on the upper reaches of Beaver Creek in the Holy Cross Wilderness Area also has a good supply of brook and cutthroat. Forest Rd. 738 follows the creek up from the Beaver Creek Ski Area to the wilderness boundary; then it's an easy half-mile hike.

Piney Lake—

This 60-acre lake about 15 miles north of Vail at the end of Red Sandstone Rd. (Forest Rd. 700) has fair to good brook trout fishing, with good to great views of the Gore Range. On the private, southwest side of the lake is **Piney River Ranch, (303) 476-3941,** which can provide canoes and other small craft for float fishing. Older folks especially love this gentle setting. The ranch also rents rods and waders. For information, contact **884 Spruce Ct., Vail, CO 81657.**

Guided Trips—

If the fishing budget is flexible, guided fishing trips are the way to go. Most trips feature transportation, guide, food, gear and instruction; many offer access to private land and little-known canyons otherwise inaccessible. **Vail Fishing Guides** has 8 miles of private water on the Eagle River for just such excursions. They may be reached at **American Angler, 225 Wall St., Vail, CO 81657; (303) 476-1477.** The tackle shop, Vail's oldest, also has all the equipment you'll need, and rents rods and waders.

FOUR-WHEEL-DRIVE TRIPS

Most of the back roads around Vail do triple duty as jeep roads and mountain biking trails in summer and cross-country ski routes in winter. For trip ideas, call or visit the **Holy Cross Ranger District Office** at **401 Main St., PO Box 190, Minturn, CO 81645; (303) 827-5715.**

Benchmark Road—

This drive, recommended by the forest service, is definitely advanced four-wheel driving. The route, which starts on the maintenance road that leaves from behind the Lodge at Vail, ascends through the ski area. Stay to the left as the road passes a gate about a mile up. Keep heading east up to the top of China Bowl and along the China Wall to 360° views of the surrounding ranges. The real jeeping begins on an old logging road that starts at another gate at about 10,500 feet. Drive until you can't go any farther. In winter, the challenging cross-country Commando ski run follows this road down. (See the Skiing section.) Allow for about a three-hour round trip.

Holy Cross City—

The former stage route from Gold Park Campground to Holy Cross City has a reputation as one of the best four-wheel-drive roads in the state. Rangers say people from across the country come to navigate the road's coils, which are spiced by plunging chasms below. One negative result of the popularity is a huge bog dug by stuck jeeps near the ghost town. In fact, some people come for the sole purpose of trying to get stuck. For that reason, the forest service may eventually have to close off the mudhole area. For historical information about Holy Cross City, see the Hiking and Backpacking section. To reach the road from Interstate 70, take the Minturn exit and drive 13 miles south on Hwy. 24. Turn right onto Homestake Rd. (Forest Rd. 703) and go 8 miles to the marked jeep road.

Rentals and Tours—

Timberline Tours—These folks offer guided backcountry trips in custom-built, off-road vehicles. In addition to half- and full-day trips, there are several variations on the theme: night tours, sunrise and sunset tours, and jeeping/caving or jeeping/rafting packages. **PO Box 3621, Vail, CO 81658; (303) 476-1414.**

GOLF

Four 18-hole public courses and one private course provide a good variety of high-altitude golfing in Vail Valley. All courses are long, narrow affairs due to the geography of the steep-walled valley. Most courses open mid-May and close in mid-Oct. But spring weather in Vail has on occasion allowed the ultimate recreational day: skiing in the morning and a round of nine in the afternoon.

Beaver Creek Resort Golf Club—

This course, designed by Robert Trent Jones, Jr., is preeminent among the links in the Vail Valley. It twists down the secluded Beaver Creek Valley from the foot of the ski mountain. Though not as long as the other courses in the area, rolling hills, large, irregular traps and undulating, basketball-court-sized greens promise a challenging round. Along the way are great views of the surrounding ranges in the White River National Forest. Many of the resort's multimillion-dollar homes line the fairways and an antique barn stands in the middle of the course. Greens fees for resort guests are less than those for non-guests; public tee times are limited. The course opens in mid-May. Located on the road up to Beaver Creek Ski Area, off the Avon exit on Interstate 70. **75 Offerson Rd., Beaver Creek; (303) 949-7123.**

Eagle–Vail Golf Course—

Designed by PGA pros Bruce Devlin and Bob Van Hagge, Eagle-Vail is a very challenging course wedged in between the Eagle River and White River National Forest. Along with the obvious river hazard, water holes and 60 sand traps wreak havoc on even the best hackers. This course, located midway between Vail and Beaver Creek, offers the best deals on golf in the valley, including bargain rate greens fees during spring and fall. The club features a pool and tennis courts as well as a driving range. The course usually opens in mid-May. Located just off Interstate 70 on Exit 171 at Avon. **0431 Eagle Dr., Avon; (303) 949-5267.**

Singletree Golf Course—

Singletree's location at the west end of Vail Valley, 7 miles from Beaver Creek, allows for a longer season than the other courses in Vail. Opening date in recent years has been Apr. 1. The course's rolling layout was designed in 1980 by Golf Force, formerly a Jack Nicklaus company. Like a Scottish course, there are few trees and many pot-hole-type traps. Tee times should be reserved 48 hours in advance. **1265 Berrycreek Rd., Edwards; (303) 926-3533.**

Vail Golf Club—

This 18-hole municipal course just east of Vail Village is the area's oldest, dating back to 1967, just five years after the ski area opened. Head pro Steve Satterstrom describes it as "a good test of golf," with fairways that dip in and out of the flanks of Vail Mountain and Golden Peak. Gore Creek cuts through the course, coming into play on over half the holes as do a number of sand traps. Nearly every tee has a view of the spectacular Gore Range. Among the several tournaments hosted by the club is the annual Gerry Ford Invitational, presided over by the former president himself, which draws a host of celebrities. The course opens around mid-May. Be sure to call for tee times. **1778 Vail Valley Dr.; (303) 479-2260.**

HIKING AND BACKPACKING

Patiently hunched around the glamorous town of Vail is some great hiking country known well by veteran hikers. Not 20 miles from the paparazzi, elk and marmots ply the Eagles Nest and Holy Cross wilderness areas. Holy Cross, which boasts over 100 miles of trails for hikers, is the second-most used wilderness area in the state. In fact, it used to be a national monument, but lost its designation in 1954 because of its poor accessibility and short summer season, according to rangers. Others say it's because the cross on the namesake mountain is crumbling. The enigmatic area remains popular, nonetheless, and the forest service is worried about overuse. Hikers and backpackers are asked to practice low-impact camping by staying on trails and using existing firepits.

Meanwhile, more and more hikers are discovering the terrain of the Eagles Nest Wilderness Area, which hunters once claimed as their own. Most hikes in this area have the stunning, 600-million-year-old Gore Range hanging above them like a curtain on a stage. For more information, stop in at the **Holy Cross Ranger District Office at 401 Main St., PO Box 190, Minturn, CO 81645; (303) 827-5715.** Or pick up *The Vail Hiker* (Alpenrose Press, 1988) by Mary Ellen Gilliland, the definitive guide for hiking and ski touring in the Vail area. For topographical maps, complete gear and sound advice, stop by **Vail Mountaineering, 500 Lionshead Mall; (303) 476-4223.**

Bighorn Creek and the Grand Traverse—

The 3.5-mile hike to the "Bighorn Hilton," an old homesteader's cabin, is less steep than many hikes near Vail. Wildflowers and a fern grove highlight the early part of this trail in the Eagles Nest Wilderness Area. At mile 2, it's hard to know what to look at first. Down the valley are views of Vail and Bighorn Creek. On the left wall is Bighorn Falls. From this point the trail takes a steep rise up a ridge. Shortly after, a level wooded trail brings you to the cabin. The structure, which serves as a storm shelter, makes a good turnaround point for the day hike. More seasoned hikers might continue on to the Grand Traverse along the 12,000-foot spine of the Gore Range.

Stay on the right fork of the creek and head straight northeast up through tundra and rocky slopes to the ridge. Experienced hikers will find this a rigorous climb with no marked trail. Since there aren't many places to camp, the forest service recommends completing it in a day (start before 8 am to get back before dark). To get to the trailhead, take the East Vail exit off Interstate 70 and drive east on S. Frontage Rd. to Columbine Dr. Turn left and go to the end of the pavement.

Booth Falls Trail—

Sixty-foot Booth Falls is a handsome reward for making this moderate 2-mile hike in the Eagles Nest Wilderness Area. The trail begins steeply, getting into the mountains quickly, but soon levels out to a wildflower meadow with columbines, mariposa lilies, shooting stars and great views back toward Vail. Hikers are treated to an uncountable number of waterfalls and Swiss Alps-like vistas along Booth Creek. Reach the trailhead by taking the East Vail exit off Interstate 70 and turn onto the frontage road on the north side of the highway. Drive a mile west and turn uphill on Booth Falls Rd. The trailhead is at the end of the road near the water gauging station.

Holy Cross City—

History buffs will enjoy this two-hour hike up an old stage route to the remains of Holy Cross City. The ruins of several cabins and other structures mark the treeline ghost town that had boomed and died by 1884. Shaft houses, the foundations of two ore mills and the skeletons of mines dot the mountainsides. During boom times, the Holy Cross Mill was connected to its sister mill in Gold Park by a 2.5-mile flume. From Interstate 70 take the Minturn exit. Follow Hwy. 24 south 13 miles to Homestake Rd. (Forest Rd. 703). Follow this gravel road 8.5 miles west to Forest Rd. 704 and turn right. Drive 2.3 miles to a "T" and turn right again. Go about 2 more miles, keeping to the right, and park in the level area just before the road turns into a very rough four-wheel-drive road. The trail starts on the four-wheel-drive road, quickly joining the historic Holy Cross City Rd. Look for a signed fork a little over 1.5 miles into the hike. Take the left fork and continue staying to the left to reach the city.

Mount of the Holy Cross—

Rangers say the climb up Mt. of the Holy Cross is the most popular hike in the Vail area. The trail up this 14er (barely, at 14,005 feet), about 6 miles each way, is usually climbed on an overnight trip. In the 1930s, a series of "hanky healing" pilgrimages were made up the mountain. People too ill to make the climb sent their handkerchiefs to a Denver pastor who promised to bless them on the peak and send them back. In 1932 the pastor received over 2,000 hankies, and two rangers had to help him carry them up the mountain. The trail starts off with a rugged, rocky climb to Half Moon Pass; hikers are rewarded by tremendous panoramas of the Gore and Mosquito ranges. The pass alone makes a good day's climb. After crossing the narrow path over the pass, the trail drops down to Cross Creek, which is a great place to see the aspen in fall. Most hikers camp here, so they can finish the ascent up Mt. of the Holy Cross before noon the next day to avoid electrical storms. After the trail crosses the creek and follows a series of switchbacks through the forest, its route is obvious: just follow the ragged edge of the Holy Cross Ridge to the summit. Start hiking up Half Moon Pass Trail, just to the right of the Fall Creek trailhead at the end of Tigiwon Rd. (For directions see Notch Mountain below.)

Notch Mountain—

Clergymen still lead pilgrimages up this 5-mile trail to see the giant cross of snow etched in Mt. of the Holy Cross to the west. A stone shelter was built on top of 13,100-foot Notch Mountain in 1924 to accommodate the hundreds of pilgrims. (When I was on the 35th switchback above treeline, it was hard to see how anybody brought materials up for such a structure.)

The fairly difficult hike starts off in a shadowy forest that soon opens up to a meadow. From there the trail clings to a steep valley wall until it gets to the posted fork for Notch Mountain at mile 2. After the killer switchbacks, the trail has an excellent ending: Mt. of the Holy Cross doesn't reveal itself until the final steps. Then the 1,500-foot-high cross is just sitting there, right in front of you as if on an easel. But alas, the cross' right arm isn't as prominent as it used to be because of erosion and avalanches. Perhaps a miracle will repair it one day. The best time to see the cross is between June 15 and July 10 when it's outlined with snow. To reach the trailhead from Vail, take the Minturn exit off Interstate 70. South of Minturn (2.8 miles) on Hwy. 24, turn onto Tigiwon Rd. (Forest Rd. 707). Drive 8.5 miles to the end of the road at Half Moon Campground. Take the Fall Creek Trail from there.

Ski Mountains—

Top-of-the-world views can be had without working up a sweat via gondola rides up Vail or Beaver Creek mountains. At the top of the Lionshead Gondola in Vail, seven easy hikes are laid out. The **Gore Range Loop** is a scenic mile walk to Eagle's View turnaround and back with no elevation gain at all. **Berrypicker Trail** is all downhill. Yes, it's lined with all sorts of berries, and it gets hikers back down the mountain to Lionshead in about two hours. Leave the car at the Lionshead parking structure west of Vail Village and walk to the gondola building. Trail maps are available there.

Two Elk Trail—

This 11-mile hike carries a National Scenic Trail designation, which means some past government official must have really enjoyed it. It's easy to see why: the summit of Two Elk Pass abounds with views of the Gore and Sawatch ranges and the many bowls on Vail Mountain's back side. A little farther along, the trail offers a peek at Mt. of the Holy Cross. But the best reason to hike the trail probably is to see its namesake—the elk. There's always a good chance of spotting some because they are boxed into the area by highways and towns. The best time to hear them bugling is Aug. and Sept. The hike can be done in one day, but is best as an overnighter. The trailhead begins in east Vail just south of the Gore Circle Campground on old Hwy. 6 at the closed gate. It ends in Minturn, making a car shuttle necessary. Drive the second car just past the forest service office in Minturn to the bridge over Eagle River. Cross the bridge and drive past the cemetery. Go right at the first fork and left at the second to the mouth of Two Elk Canyon, near the foot of Battle Mountain. The trail begins near Two Elk Creek.

HORSEBACK RIDING

Most trails in White River National Forest are open to horseback riding, so there are plenty of riding opportunities in the Vail Valley.

Beaver Creek Stables—

Here's where riders looking for more elaborate excursions should come. Among the variety of rides Steve Jones and his guides offer are breakfast and lunch rides, rides combined with fishing at Beaver Lake, sunset rides to Beano's Cabin for dinner, and overnighters to Trapper's Cabin with hiking sidetrips in the alpine meadows of McCoy Park. The stables are at Haymeadow, just above McCoy's restaurant in the Village Hall. **5344 Brush Creek, Eagle, CO 81631; (303) 845-7770.**

Piney River Ranch—

To really get away from the city and into the backcountry, drive out to this ranch at gorgeous Piney Lake about 15 miles north of Vail. The trails from the ranch lead into and around the Eagles Nest Wilderness Area, with the 13,000-foot Gore Range as a backdrop. Along with horseback rides, the ranch also offers boating, cookouts and fishing on the lake, making it a great destination for a day's getaway from Vail. The road to Piney Lake (Forest Rd. 700) leaves

Vail's N. Frontage Rd. a mile west of the Vail Village exit. The ranch is at road's end. **884 Spruce Ct., Vail, CO 81657; (303) 476-3941.**

Spraddle Creek Ranch—

This outfitter is conveniently located just across Interstate 70 from the four-way stop in Vail Village. Horses are available for one- to three-hour rides in the former Ute stomping grounds around Spraddle Creek and the lower reaches of Bald Mountain. The ranch is definitely geared toward families on day outings rather than serious trekkers out for longer trail rides. A pony ring on the ranch is ideal for young children. The ranch can accommodate groups of up to 25 people. **100 N. Frontage Rd. E.; (303) 476-6941.**

ICE SKATING

The John Dobson Ice Arena—

This arena, on the bus route between Vail and Lionshead, holds public skating sessions daily. Children under six are free but must be accompanied by an adult. Hockey and figure skates are available to rent. **321 E. Lionshead Cir., Vail, CO 81657; (303) 479-2270.**

RIVER FLOATING

Eagle River—

The floating season for the Eagle River is substantially shorter than many Colorado rafting rivers: mainly during spring runoff (May through July). During that period, however, the Eagle does churn up some pretty exciting white water on its upper reaches. It's one of the few free-flowing rivers left in the state. Families looking for more subdued trips will prefer the rides nearer Eagle on the lower reaches. With the icy-cold water, wet suits are a must in the early float season.

Vail's location near three of Colorado's most popular rafting rivers—the Eagle, the Colorado and the Arkansas—means there are plenty of outfitters to choose from. One suggestion is Raftmeister.

Raftmeister—

This local outfitter offers full- and half-day trips on the Eagle and the Colorado and full-day trips on the Arkansas. In addition, they arrange overnight trips and have a special early-morning wildlife tour on the Eagle. Kayaks and kayak instruction, and a special fly-and-float package, which combines hot-air ballooning and rafting, also are available. Meals provided. Located in the Gondola Building at Lionshead. **PO Box 1805, Vail, CO 81658; (303) 476-RAFT.**

SKIING
CROSS-COUNTRY SKIING

Nordic skiing hasn't gotten lost in the shadow of immense Vail Mountain. Besides two cross-country centers in Vail and one at Beaver Creek, there are a number of great backcountry trails throughout the Vail Valley and surrounding White River National Forest. For information on backcountry trails, contact the **Holy Cross Ranger District Office, PO Box 190, 401 Main St., Minturn, CO 81645; (303) 827-5715.**

Backcountry Trails—

Commando Run—This is Colorado's top-rated cross-country tour, a grueling 18 miles for advanced skiers only. Avalanche danger and tough-to-follow trails are only two of the formidable obstacles to completing this day-long trek. Two cars are required. Leave one in Vail and drive the other one to the Vail Pass rest area. The trail begins on the Shrine Pass Rd. and comes in three parts: The Shrine Pass–Lime Creek roads; Bowman's Shortcut to Two Elk Pass; and the descent to Golden Peak runs at Vail Ski Area. Magnificent views of Gore Range, Mt. of the Holy Cross, Notch Mountain and the Tenmile and Mosquito ranges will be seen along the way. But it's next to impossible to find the way without a topo map and detailed directions. Take along *Trails Illustrated*'s Topo map No. 108–Vail Pass, which has the run marked. It's best to ski it with someone who's done it before. Otherwise, *The Vail Hiker*, by Mary Ellen Gilliland, has the best directions for the trail we've seen.

Shrine Pass—This fairly easy 11-mile trail has a tried-and-true formula: 3 miles up, 8 miles down and Margaritas at Reno's (127 W. Water St. in Redcliff). No deviations allowed. Leave one car up Forest Rd. 709 from Redcliff and pile in the other car for the drive up to the rest area at the summit of Vail Pass. The trail starts on Shrine Pass Rd. with a moderate climb to Shrine Pass summit. After reaching the summit, the easy-to-follow road starts downhill to Redcliff, with a great view of Mt. of the Holy Cross along the way. Allow about 4–6 hours. For more information see Scenic Drives.

Tenth Mountain Trail Association Hut System—The system, organized in 1980 by the Tenth Mountain Trail Association, is named in honor of the members of the ski troops who trained in the area and fought in World War II. The trail system has been expanded to 10 huts, with plans for six more to eventually connect Aspen and Vail Pass. The Shrine Mountain Inn near the top of Vail Pass is one of the new additions. On this eastern end, the system now extends from Shrine Pass to Tennessee Pass near Leadville. The huts along the way sleep up to 15. Basics are supplied. For trail guides (a good idea for most people), see Paragon Guides listed under "Guided Tours." For hut reservations and other details, contact the **Tenth Mountain Trail Association, 1280 Ute Ave., Aspen, CO 81611; (303) 925-5775.** Detailed information on the Aspen-end of the system can be found in the Outdoor Activities in the **Aspen** chapter.

Tigiwon Trail (Tigiwon Road)—Beginning and intermediate skiers will like this 8-mile run up Tigiwon Rd. to Half Moon Campground. At mile 6 there's a stone hut to warm up in and views of the Gore Range and Vail's back bowls to warm up to. The lodge, built to house pilgrims on their way to Mt. of the Holy Cross, can be reserved (free) for overnight trips by calling the Holy Cross Ranger District Office at **(303) 827-5715.** Look for elk on the way since the trail crosses part of their winter range. The full 8 miles can take most of a day, but coming back down should only take a third as long. Tigiwon is a Ute word meaning friends—ironically, Tigiwon Rd. lets out near Battle Mountain, named for a notorious fight between Utes and Arapaho Indians in 1849. Tigiwon Rd. is 2.8 miles south of Minturn off Hwy. 24. Turn right and drive a half mile up the road, park and start skiing.

Groomed Trails—

Golden Peak Center in Vail—Vail's nordic center at the base of Chair 6 on the east side of Vail Village has 20 kilometers of trails. The center, open since 1968, specializes in backcountry tours, as well as short treks on Vail Golf Course. For the decadent nordic skier, there's the gourmet tour, including hot drinks, three appetizers, three entrées and three desserts served along the way. Reservations for the gourmet tour must be made a day in advance by 4 pm. Equipment rental, group lessons, private lessons, and telemark instruction are all available. **(303) 476-3239.**

McCoy Park at Beaver Creek—The spectacular groomed cross-country trails at the top of Chair 12 are a rarity: track skiing on top of a mountain. The top-of-the-world views make this the best place to ski groomed trails in Vail Valley. McCoy Park has 30 kilometers of trails, many named after mining claims made in the area in the late 1800s. Twenty percent of the terrain is beginner, 60 percent intermediate and 20 percent advanced. Telemarking lessons are given at the base of **Chair 12.** There's also a warming hut with hot drinks and boot lockers at the top of the lift. **(303) 476-3239.**

Vail Nature Center—The nature center has served as a nordic headquarters for East Vail since 1984. An 8-mile track with plenty of loops follows Gore Creek out from Golden Peak. Besides rental equipment and day tours, the center offers snowshoe walks and has exhibits on nordic skiing and natural history. The center is four blocks east of Golden Peak on Vail Valley Dr. Open daily Dec.–Mar. from 9 am–4 pm. **75 S. Frontage Rd., Vail; (303) 479-2261.**

Guided Tours—

Paragon Guides—These folks offer three- to six-day trips on the Tenth Mountain Trail Association Hut System between Vail and Aspen for experienced nordic skiers. See Backcountry Trails for more information. Contact Paragon at **PO Box 130, Vail, CO 81658; (303) 949-4272.**

Rentals and Information—

Vail Mountaineering—Guides for backcountry touring and rentals are available here. **500 Lionshead Mall, Vail; (303) 476-4223.**

Christy Sports—Located in Avon near Beaver Creek at **182 Avon Rd.; (303) 949-0241.**

DOWNHILL SKIING

Arrowhead—

Colorado's newest ski area is something of a David next to the Goliath of Vail. Pete Seibert, Jr., son of the founder of Vail, is at the helm of this upstart 12 miles west of Vail (2 miles west of Beaver Creek Resort). With one lift and six runs, Arrowhead plans to complement its giant neighbors rather than compete with them. The area is designed for families and those who want less demanding skiing away from the congestion of larger resorts. And lift tickets (at half the price of Vail's) aren't such a strain on the wallet.

The atmosphere is a refreshing counterpoint to Vail's glitz. The ticket office and ski shop are housed in a rustic ranch house, with two log houses on the slopes for picnics. In place of ski school, Arrowhead Alpine Guides will take small parties out for runs before or after the lifts open. The area also offers slopeside parking, a novelty in Vail Valley.

Arrowhead opened in 1988, 11 years after Pete Seibert, Sr., left the ski business during a corporate takeover of Vail. Arrowhead is linked up with the golf club of the same name in the Denver area, which Pete Sr. runs. With this kind of management legacy, the tiny area is bound to be a success. **PO Box 69, 0676 Sawatch Dr., Edwards, CO 81632; (303) 926-3029.**

Beaver Creek Ski Area—

"Like Tiffany's is to jewelry stores, like Gucci is to luggage, like Cadillac is to automobiles, that's what Beaver Creek is going to be to ski areas in this country." That's the way former Colorado governor Dick Lamm described Beaver Creek at the opening ceremonies in 1980. With something suspiciously like a guard tower on the road leading up to the area, it does feel a little like you're entering a members-only club. Beaver Creek was originally meant as the site for skiing events of the 1976 Olympics, which Colorado subsequently turned down. The area opened anyway in 1980. Its ski runs were designed with the help of a computer and the town was built after years of study on the best way to fit resort and nature together. Beginning skiers like the area because many of the easiest and most spectacular runs are concentrated at the top of the mountain. Experts like the gladed, narrow, double-diamond Birds of Prey, which is tougher than most runs at Vail. But most of Beaver Creek has a strange fall line that makes you feel like you are skiing at a slant. The skiers are less aggressive than those at Vail. At last report, the lift lines were still short. For more information, see page 169.

Vail—

"There is no comparison" is how master ski filmmaker Warren Miller refers to Vail's back bowls. This year there are four more reasons nothing else can compare. They are China, Tea Cup, Siberia and Mongolia bowls. With their opening, Vail has more than doubled its size. The new bowls collectively are bigger than any other ski area in the state. The back bowls are totally ungroomed, which can make for a variety of snow conditions. Mornings on fresh-snow days are heaven on skis. One tip for the next few seasons: the new, milder bowls undoubtedly will be crowded with skiers just because they are new. That means the older bowls might be left relatively uncrowded. Be forewarned: back bowls close at 3 pm, so don't get stuck at the bowl bottom at 3:30 pm or you'll have a long walk out!

The mountain now has four base areas—**Vail Village, Lionshead, Cascade Village** and **Golden Peak**. Vail can move 35,020 skiers an hour over a total of 3,787 acres of skiable terrain. Kids even have their own terrain at Golden Peak (renamed Whippersnapper Mountain). This area is strictly off-limits to adults.

The Vail Ski School is the largest in the world with 450 instructors. Special race classes provide technique evaluation; free "Meet-the-Mountain" tours give skiers a good idea of the immensity of this mountain. Call **(303) 476-3239.** For more information about the ski area, see the Introduction and History sections of this chapter.

SLEDDING AND TUBING

Head to Meadow Mountain, off the Interstate 70 exit to Minturn. No fee.

SLEIGH RIDES

Steve Jones Sleigh Rides—
Nightly rides leave between 4 pm and 8 pm during winter on Vail Golf Course. **(303) 479-2260.**

SWIMMING

Eagle–Vail Swim Club—
A fee is charged at this public pool. **0099 Eagle Dr., Avon, CO 81620; 949-4257.**

Vail Run Resort—
This sports center in Vail has a heated indoor pool open to the public. A fee is charged. **1000 Lionsridge Loop, Vail, CO 81657; 476-1500.**

TENNIS

Kiva—
During summers, there are four courts available at the Kiva. The courts are reserved for Beaver Creek Resort guests only. The activities desk can reserve a time for you. **135 Offerson Rd., Beaver Creek; 949-5750 ext. 4636.**

Public Courts in Vail—
During summer, there are 24 public courts available in Vail: nine at **Gold Peak;** six at **Ford Park** on S. Frontage Rd. just east of Vail Village; five at **Lionshead;** and four at **Booth Creek** in East Vail. Because it usually cools down too much at night to play, none of the courts are lighted.

Vail Run Resort—
Two indoor courts are open to the public at Vail Run Resort. Fees vary according to time of day. Open 8 am–11 pm daily. Be sure to call ahead for reservations. **1000 Lionsridge Loop, Vail; 476-1500.**

———— SEEING AND DOING ————

CHAIRLIFT RIDES

The Lionshead Gondola at Vail and the Centennial Express chairlift at Beaver Creek each have a lift open for sightseers and hikers daily during the summer and weekends in late spring and early fall. The barbecue is open daily for lunch during summer at the top of both mountains, weather permitting. Rides up the Beaver Creek lift are much cheaper than the gondola at Vail. For more details, see the Hiking and Backpacking section.

MUSEUMS

Colorado Ski Museum—

This compact museum showcases the history of skiing in the state, while the Colorado Ski Hall of Fame within honors Coloradans who have contributed to the industry. The museum, founded in 1976, is one of only a handful in the country dedicated to skiing. When Vail was chosen as the site, a few other ski areas grumbled that a history museum didn't belong in a place with no real history of its own. But Vail's central location in Colorado makes it ideal for visitors. One interesting exhibit shows the development of ski equipment over the years. Don't miss the 12-foot-long, two-inch-thick wood skis that look more like logs. There's also a theater inside that shows historical films about skiing. This free museum, on the bus route between Vail Village and Lionshead, is open 12–5 pm daily except Mon. Closed during May and Oct. 15 **Vail Rd., Vail; (303) 476-1876.**

Vail Nature Center—

This small natural history museum hosts guided nature walks and recreational activities in summer. In winter, the nature center becomes a nordic center and the trails become cross-country and snowshoeing treks. Knowledgeable guides run an interpretive center in a renovated farmhouse on the preserve. Inside are seasonal displays on the Vail Valley's flora, fauna and geography. The seven-acre preserve is on the southeast side of Ford Park just east of Vail Village. Open from 9 am–5 pm daily June–Sept., 9 am–4 pm Oct. and Dec.–Mar.; closed Apr., May and Nov. Hours vary. **75 S. Frontage Rd., Vail; (303) 479-2291.**

NIGHTLIFE

Avon—

If you need a break from Vail, head west—literally and figuratively—to the **Hole in the Wall, (303) 949-5463,** in Avon. This woody, Western-style bar has live music Fri. and Sat. night, and music on its enormous deck during summer.

Beaver Creek—

For après ski, folks gather at **Drink Water Park in Village Hall, (303) 949-5001.** The cafe is named for an elk and deer feeding ground on the mountain. Happy hour lasts from 4:30–6:30 pm. Whereas Vail is known for its nightlife, Beaver Creek is pretty quiet at night. So after 6:30 pm, head to Vail.

Vail—

For après ski if it's sunny, try the deck at either the **Lionshead Bar and Grill (303) 476-3060,** or **Pepi's, (303) 476-5626** at Gasthof Gramshammer in Vail Village. Ask for a toe-warming Snuggler—peppermint schnapps and hot chocolate—or a hot buttered rum with a cinnamon stick in it. If it's snowing, head for **Cyrano's, (303) 476-5551,** just below the lifts at Vail Village. During ski season the concept of weekend doesn't really exist in Vail—the joints are jumping every night. Each bar seems to have its designated night when it swells in popularity. If staying an entire week, you might try the following rotation:

Mon.: **Vendetta's, (303) 476-5070**—A newer bar upstairs from the restaurant with live music most nights of the week. Its location right in the thick of the village makes it easy to bounce around to several night spots.

Tues.: **Altitude Club, (303) 476-7810, ext. 23**—*The* disco spot, with revolving lights, glitzy dance floor and thundering pop music. Located in the Doubletree Hotel.

Wed.: **Hong Kong Cafe, (303) 476-1818**—This longtime reliable spot of Vail nightlife is still the sentimental favorite of locals. Bahama Mamas here are legendary. Jack Bone's Soul Show on Wed. packs them in.

Thur.: **Mickey's, (303) 476-5011, ext. 115**—This Vail institution features the pop and classical music of piano man Mickey Poage in the Lodge at Vail.

Fri.: **Cyrano's, (303) 476-5551**—Usually mentioned first when locals are queried about nightlife, Cyrano's has been *the* Vail night spot for several years. Rock and roll and blues are featured Tues. through

Sat. in an evolved fern bar/Jimmy Buffet lounge lizard sort of setting. During the summer, Friday Afternoon Club draws hordes.

Sat.: **The Club, (303) 479-0556**— Loud and young. Some local live musicians take the stage in the small, basement bar, which also features a big-screen TV. Generally the rowdiest crowd finds its way here.

SCENIC DRIVES

Red Sandstone Road—

Though probably a little rough for OldsmoBuicks and similar cars, this 30-mile round trip packs in quite a bit of scenery. And the end result—Piney Lake at the base of the Gore Range—is well worth the bumps. For more details and directions from Vail, see the Biking section.

Shrine Pass Road—

This route, once temporarily named Holy Cross Trail, was christened for its terrific view of Mt. of the Holy Cross. The route started out as an Indian trail when Utes hunted in the area. Indian campsites unearthed in the vicinity have been carbon-dated to 7,000 years ago. Before the Vail Pass Rd. was built in 1940, this road served as the major route between Denver and Glenwood Springs. Just east of the Vail Pass summit, turn off onto the Shrine Pass dirt road west of the interchange. The 11,000-foot summit is just 2.3 miles up, with wraparound views of Gore Range to the north, the Sawatch Range to the southwest, the Tenmile Range to the east and the Flat Tops in the far west. At mile 3.75 Mt. of the Holy Cross can be seen—look for the sign. The road continues down through the canyon to Redcliff, where it joins up with Hwy. 24 for a pretty drive on pavement past Battle Mountain and Minturn north to Interstate 70. Hwy. 24 south from Redcliff to Leadville makes a nice variation.

——————— WHERE TO STAY ———————

Most people come to stay in Vail for a week or more, so condos and lodges account for many of the rooms available. There's also a Marriott, a Westin, a Holiday Inn and a Raintree. Rates during the summer generally run about half of what they are in winter. For information on these and other hotels, condos and lodges, call the **Vail Resort Association** at **1-800-525-3875** nationwide; **(303) 476-1000** in Colorado. Renting a private home is another option. For information about renting a private home, contact the Vail Resort Association (number listed above) or Kathy Fagan at **(303) 949-1212**.

Right now, all rooms in Beaver Creek are in several self-contained condominium complexes or deluxe lodges. Most of the rooms are privately owned but are available to rent for about $100 a night and up, depending on the length of stay. The most convenient complex is **Village Hall**, the centerpiece of Beaver Creek village. **The Charter** nearby is also first-class. For information about renting these places, contact **Central Reservations, PO Box 7, Vail, CO 81658; 1-800-525-9132** nationwide; **1-800-525-2257 or (303) 476-1000** locally. There's also plenty of less expensive lodging in nearby Avon.

Gasthof Gramshammer—$$$ to $$$$

Proprietor Pepi Gramshammer is known locally as Mr. Vail; his lodge could just as easily be known as Hotel Vail. The lodge, born the same year as the town, epitomizes all that's good about Vail's transplanted Tyrolean charm. The Austrian word for it is *Gemutlichkeit*, which means something like friendliness and ambience. Pepi and his wife Sheika—both transplanted Austrians—are directly responsible for the cozy inn's charm. Pepi, a former Olympic skier, might turn up as your bellman, fix your TV or bus your table. Mrs. Gramshammer, an alumnae of Mt. Everest, travels to Europe four times a year to find authentic supplies for the lodge.

And the family dog, Tasso, Vail's most arrested canine, makes guests feel right at home.

The 27 European-style rooms and apartments come in color schemes of champagne, blue and rose. All feature fireplaces and down comforters. Warning: the rooms only rent out a week at a time (Sat.–Sun.) during ski season and are usually sold out a year ahead. Most guests are returnees. The hotel's restaurant, the Antlers Room, serves a Bavarian/continental menu, specializing in wild game. The adjacent deck is the best in Vail. **231 E. Gore Creek Dr., Vail, CO 81657; (303) 476-5626.**

The Lodge at Vail — $$$ to $$$$

This classic Bavarian lodge was Vail's first. The huge alpine chalet, which set the tone for architecture in the village, shows a seasoning and refinement well beyond its 26 years. The lodge's 225 paneled guest rooms include one-to three-bedroom suites and condos, all with flourishes such as marble baths and heated towel racks. The Lodge has an undeniably international feel—proprietor Hans Turnovszky can greet guests in five languages. Old Europe and the Rocky Mountain West are blended beautifully in the lobby, where a grand wooden stairway winds above a massive moss-rock fireplace. Also on the premises are a huge heated pool, jacuzzi, saunas and a small exercise room. The Lodge's position right at the base of the lifts at Vail Village means skiers can glide right up to the door. **174 E. Gore Creek Dr., Vail, CO 81657; (303) 476-5011.**

Sonnenalp — $$$ to $$$$

The Sonnenalp is a mountain hotel in three parts. The Bavaria Haus, the Austria Haus and the Swiss Chalet are all perched on the sunny side of Gore Creek in Vail Village. The separate houses allow this fairly large hotel to maintain a small-inn atmosphere. And this isn't imitation alpine: the Fassler family created the Sonnenalp idea at its resort near Oberstdorf, West Germany. Fourth-generation innkeepers Rosana and Johannes Fassler continue the tradition in Vail. A giant contingent of Bavarians was staying when we visited, and we were told that 50 to 60 percent of the guests are German, adding to the Bavarian ambience. The favorite of the three houses is the Swiss Chalet with its attention to detail. Second preference is Bavaria. All 178 rooms in the three houses are priced the same. Each features feather comforters and hand-crafted furnishings imported from Germany. The hotel has an elaborate spa even by Vail standards. Among its features are a cold dip—a narrow deep pool to plunge into before heading to the sauna or jacuzzi—and one of only 30 "hypotherapy" tubs in the country. It's necessary to book rooms at least three months in advance during ski season. **20 Vail Rd., Vail, CO 81657; (303) 476-5081.**

Roost Lodge— $$ to $$$

The Roost is like a Volkswagen bug: it isn't pretty but it's popular and reliable. This A-frame-style lodge has long been a favorite of the budget-conscious—it's the least expensive place to stay in the Vail Village vicinity. During ski season, it's about the only place to find a room available on fairly short notice for under $100. The 56 rooms are casually comfortable. Last time we visited, the pool area still doubled as a greenhouse. Roost Lodge is two miles from Vail Ski Area at the West Vail exit. A shuttle bus runs to the ski area hourly from 8 am to midnight. **1738 N. Frontage Rd., Vail, CO 81657; (303) 476-5451.**

Comfort Inn — $$

For skiers who like Beaver Creek but don't want to add too much more to their personal budget deficit, Avon's calling. Just a mile from the Beaver Creek Ski Area, in affordable Avon is the sturdy Comfort Inn. Inside are 150 good-sized rooms, all with double, queen or king beds. Amenities include a pool, jacuzzi, hospitality suites and free continental breakfast served in the wood-beamed Comfort Clubroom. Folks who have been in Avon in the past will remember this as the Wynfield Inn. It remains the best room deal in the Vail Valley. A bus leaves regularly from in front of the inn bound for both Beaver Creek and Vail. The Beaver Creek bus is free; Vail's charges a nominal fee. **0161 W. Beaver Creek Blvd., PO Box 5510, Avon, CO 81620; (303) 949-5511.**

Eagle River Inn — $$

Sante Fe in ski country? It's not a mountain mirage: this bed and breakfast inn on the bank of the Eagle River in Minturn was indeed reborn in 1987 as an adobe hacienda. Walk through a locally crafted portico and dispel all your doubts. A southwest-style beehive fireplace occupies a corner of the sitting room, which is filled with white-pine furniture. The 12 bedrooms have more of the same southwestern charms, including handcrafted headboards. The 7-mile drive to Minturn from Vail is just far enough so that it feels like a getaway, but not so far that it's inconvenient. Manager Beverly Rude equals the setting with a breakfast of fresh fruit and homemade yogurt and granola. Wine and cheese are served at 5 pm. **PO Box 100, 145 N. Main St., Minturn, CO 81645; (303) 827-5761.**

CAMPING

In White River National Forest—

Gore Creek Campground (17 sites; fee charged) is the closest to Vail and therefore the most popular in the area. It's 5 miles east of Vail Village, near the boundary of the Eagles Nest Wilderness Area. Take Exit 180 from East Vail onto Hwy. 6 and head east 2 miles.

Tigiwon Campground (nine sites; no fee) is 6 miles up Tigiwon Rd. off Hwy. 24, 2.8 miles south of Minturn. A stone lodge built as a restover for pilgrimages to Mt. of the Holy Cross is available to groups on a free reservation basis. **Half Moon Campground** (seven sites; no fee) is 2.5 miles farther up Tigiwon Rd. at two trailheads for Holy Cross Wilderness Area.

Hornsilver Campground (12 sites and a fee) is right off Hwy. 24, 1.5 miles south of Redcliff.

Blodgett Campground (six sites; fee charged) is just off Hwy. 24 on Homestake Rd. (Forest Rd. 703), 12 miles south of Minturn. **Gold Park Campground** (11 sites; fee charged), 10 miles farther up Homestake Rd., used to be an old gold mining camp. Jeep and hiking trails to Holy Cross City ghost town and the Holy Cross Wilderness Area leave from here.

——— WHERE TO EAT ———

At last count, Vail had more than 70 restaurants, and that's not including five on the mountain itself. Listed below are a few standouts.

Beano's Cabin — $$$$

Taking a moonlit sleigh ride to dinner is probably not something you do every day, so here's your chance. Beano's Cabin is a rustic log cabin in the Larkspur Bowl on Beaver Creek Mountain. Two 42-passenger sleighs leave the Inn at Beaver Creek twice nightly for a sumptuous western-style dinner at the cabin. During summer, guests ride horses up. Before boarding for either of the two seatings, one at 5:15 pm and another at 7:15 pm, diners are treated

to peppermint schnapps and hot chocolate. Be sure to make reservations in advance. Rides leave Wed. through Sun. **949-5750 ext. 4636.**

Mirabelle's — $$$$

This gourmet French restaurant has been referred to not only as the best restaurant at Beaver Creek, but as the best restaurant in the Rockies, period. It's housed in a gorgeous restored farmhouse that dates back to 1898, when it was the biggest residence in Avon. Inside are oak furnishings and etched glass. Entrées include salmon, trout, shrimp Provençal, veal, beef and lamb. The selection of wines is palate-boggling. No credit cards accepted. The restaurant is located right across from the reception house on the road up to Beaver Creek. Open for dinner 6–10 pm, Tues.–Sun. **55 Village Rd., Beaver Creek; 949-7728.**

The Left Bank — $$$ to $$$$

A host of restaurants in Vail seems to offer the same exclusive menu of French/ continental fare. Perhaps the Left Bank does it best. Co-chefs Liz and Luc Meyer apprenticed in France, where they also collected the restaurant's French country decor. The Meyers serve a variety of sea-food and game, specializing in veal, elk steaks and chicken prepared a different way each day. Though prices are high, the Left Bank is in demand. During ski season, reservations are necessary up to two weeks in advance. The Left Bank takes no credit cards. Open Thur.–Tues., 6–10 pm. Closed Wed. Located in the Sitzmark Lodge at **183 Gore Creek Dr., Vail; 476-3696.**

The Ore House — $$ to $$$

This Vail Village institution is still the most popular place to get a steak. The barn-wood walls and the smell of the grill put eaters immediately at ease. This is one of the few laid-back western eateries to be found in the Austrianized valley. Our waiter didn't have a specific specialty to recommend, but rest assured, the Steak Ore House is a treat for the taste buds. A filet is smothered with crabmeat, wrapped in bacon and topped with béarnaise sauce. A huge salad bar rounds out a menu of seafood, beef kabobs and chicken. The food doesn't seem to have faltered a bit in 10 years, and prices are still reasonable. Open daily 5:30–10:30 pm. **228 Bridge St., Vail; 476-5100.**

Sweet Basil — $$ to $$$

This sunny cafe is a lunch favorite of people who work in the village. One rea-son is that meals are served quickly, usu-ally in a half hour or less. But speedy service alone doesn't make a successful restaurant. The continental food is also delicious, rated four stars by the *Denver Post*. What struck us most was the variety

on the menu, from grilled duck breast sandwiches, to pizza, to chili with corn-sticks. The cooks outdo themselves with unusual garnishes, such as pink pepper-corn butter and cranberry mayonnaise. Don't leave too soon and miss the Sweet Basil forte—homemade desserts. The breezy interior is all wicker and chrome, and the works of local artists grace the walls. Though best at lunch (served daily from 11:30 am–2:30 pm), Sweet Basil also offers dinner from 6–10 pm. The Sweet Basil folks also operate a fish restaurant in Lionshead called Montauk. **193 E. Gore Creek Dr., Vail; 476-0125.**

Minturn Country Club — $$

No, it's not really a country club—just a great little restaurant with a good sense of both humor and food. The club truly believes in letting you "Have It Your Way": you're the chef here. Pick a steak, kabob, fish, or chicken from a meat case and toss it on the charcoal grill in the dining room. Sidelights include a 2-item salad bar, corn on the cob, baked beans, baked potatoes, and huge slabs of Texas toast you can swab with garlic butter and throw on the grill. We've heard the club is elbow to elbow for dinner during ski season. Don't bother scheduling tee times. The clubhouse is the old Minturn Post Office on Main St. Open daily from 5:30–10 pm. **131 Main St., Minturn; 827-4114.**

Alfie Packer's — $ to $$

There's a story told about the sentenc-ing day of legendary Colorado maneater Alferd Packer, for whom this restaurant is named. On that day, the judge told Packer that "there was only seven Dimmycrats in all of Hinsdale County, and you, . . . you eat five of 'em." Then the judge sentenced him to hang. There are no Democrats on the menu at Alfie's, but any restaurant named after a cannibal is guaranteed to be a fun place to eat. What the menu does have is a variety of tasty steak specials, plus prime rib, burgers and seafood. (Warning: the steak specials each have a Packer theme, including Adam's Rib and the Tender Loin.)

Alfie's draws a fairly lively crowd for après ski, mainly because of its enormous sun deck overlooking the bottom of Lionshead. The casual interior of the restaurant is timbered to feel like a mine shafthouse. Open for lunch from 11:30 am–3 pm; dinner is served from 6–10 pm. **536 W. Lionshead Mall, Vail; 476-2121.**

The Gashouse — $ to $$

When you've had a little too much overpriced French food, designer jeans and mink stoles, here's the perfect antidote. The only fur you'll see at the Gashouse is on the deer heads mounted on the log walls of this Conoco-station-turned-restaurant. This is where many locals run to escape the tourist blitz. Service can be a bit slow and indifferent, but the price is right. Beers are 50 cents a draw, and the Gashouse serves inexpensive hamburgers and bargain-priced, all-you-can-eat barbecue pork ribs on weekends. The Gashouse is 4 miles west of Beaver Creek on Hwy. 6. Open 11–2 am daily; until midnight on Sun. **34185 Hwy. 6, Edwards; 926-3613.**

Pizza and Pane — $ to $$

Pizza and Pane will take you back to your old neighborhood pizza pub, complete with loud, deliberately obnoxious cooks, loud red walls and low, low prices (by Vail standards). Pizza and Pane attracts a lot of college kids during spring and Christmas breaks, when the small restaurant can get pretty packed. The pizza doesn't suffer though. It comes in two

varieties: Sicilian or Neapolitan (thick or thin crust). The *pane,* meaning bread, also comes in the form of calzones and sausage bread. Pizza and Pane serves beer and wine, and has takeout. Hours are 11:30 am–11:30 pm daily. **122 E. Meadow Dr., Vail; 476-7550.**

D.J. McCadam's — $

Got a hankering for a hard-boiled egg at 9 pm? This is the place to go. D.J.'s in Lionshead serves breakfast and brunch 20 hours a day. Reasonably priced crêpes and omelettes are their specialties. Locals like to stop by at night for the decadent variety of dessert crêpes. Daring variations on the traditional breakfast theme are the breakfast burrito and the wicked chili cheese omelette. Be ready to crowd in: there's not a whole lot of room. Open 7–3 am. **616 W. Lionshead Cir., in Concert Hall; 476-2336.**

Leroy's — $

This Bennigan's-style restaurant serves up pretty inexpensive steak and seafood. Leroy's chief assignment at this meticulously planned resort is breakfast, including delicious eggs Benedict and omelettes. Later in the day, try the bar-menu appetizers, so popular in happy-hour haunts such as this. With its enormous patio and central location, Leroy's serves as a natural gathering place for après ski at Beaver Creek. Open from 7 am–10 pm. **46 Le Promenade in the Park Plaza, Beaver Creek; 949-5750 ext. 4508.**

SERVICES

Central Reservations–
Vail Resort Association—

Serves as chamber of commerce for both Vail and Beaver Creek, providing information about the ski areas. **PO Box 7, Vail, CO 81658; 1-800-525-9132 nationwide, 1-800-525-2257 in Colorado. (303) 476-1000 locally.**

Day Care—

ABC School Inc.—This preschool located in Vail will care for children 15 months to five years old. **149 N. Frontage Rd., Vail, CO 81657; (303) 476-1420.**

Vail Associates—Full-day care for children aged two months to six years is provided at Golden Peak in Vail and at Beaver Creek. In Vail, call **(303) 476-5601 ext. 5044;** in Beaver Creek **(303) 949-5750 ext. 4325.**

Vail Youth Center—The center has baby sitters available in the evenings as well as a teen hangout, cafe and activities for older children. Located in the Lionshead parking structure. **(303) 479-2292.**

Eagle Valley Chamber of Commerce—

PO Box 964A, Eagle, CO 81631; (303) 328-5220.

Transportation—

Vail's free bus system is second only in volume to Denver's. For schedule information, call **(303) 479-2172.**

Airport Super Shuttle—Offers 24-hour service and transport to Denver. **(303) 476-8008.**

Airport Transportation Service—Airport shuttles to Vail and Avon/Beaver Creek. **PO Box 2447, Vail, CO 81658; 1-800-247-7074 or (303) 476-7576.**

Continental Express—Air shuttle service from Stapleton Airport in Denver to Avon STOLport 7 miles west of Vail. **1-800-525-0280.**

It is somewhat unusual to see mountain goats, especially in heavily used areas, but there are those rare moments when one will strike a pose for anyone watching (photograph by David C. Holloway).

Winter Park and Middle Park

A dazzling array of peaks, many reaching above 13,000 feet, is situated around the perimeter of the Fraser Valley. The surrounding Arapaho National Forest is never far away as you visit the small towns anchored in a narrow procession along the Fraser River. At the head of the valley is **Winter Park**, a favorite ski destination for Front Range residents. A couple of miles north on Hwy. 40 is the neighboring town of **Fraser**. As the flat basin of the river valley widens into what is commonly known as **Middle Park**, the small towns of **Tabernash, Granby** and **Hot Sulphur Springs** make their entry.

Middle Park, unlike its northern and southern counterparts, offers a complexity of geologic terrain: faults, uplifts and overthrusts have been further altered by volcanic formations and erosion. The result of all this activity is a beautiful variety of mountainous landscape. Once a prized hunting ground of the Indians, today this region is a prized vacationing ground for people from around the country.

Winter Park is one of the state's most popular ski areas. With the addition of Mary Jane ski area in 1975, the combined resort can better accommodate the loads of people that flock in on weekends. Weekday skiing here, without crowds, is a great alternative. Once the snow has melted, people stay in the town of Winter Park as a base for hiking, mountain biking, golfing and just lazing around. Two miles north of the ski area, the town has developed in a haphazard fashion. A multitude of mini shopping plazas, restaurants and lodges is spread along both sides of Hwy. 40. The long town, split in half by traffic, is missing some of the intimacy of other ski villages. But what Winter Park lacks in city planning, it has gained back in personality. The people here know exactly how to have a good time, both on the slopes and in town.

"The coldest spot in the nation" is a phrase commonly associated with Fraser, Colorado. The ring of tall peaks around the town creates stationary pockets of frigid air. Sometimes the thermometer dips to more than 50 degrees below zero on winter nights. The masochists living here are actually proud of their self-proclaimed designation "Icebox of the Nation." The town has been locked in a running battle with International Falls, Minnesota, for the "Icebox" trademark. Fraser Mayor C. B. Jensen once explained to a reporter, "We don't have logging and railroading anymore, and Eisenhower doesn't fish here anymore . . . but, it's colder than hell."

The other towns down valley are small, ranching centers that are beyond the fray of the retail shops and restaurants in Winter Park and Fraser. A northwestern trip down Hwy. 40 takes you past prime ranchland to the Gold Medal trout water of the Colorado River and eventually to Hot Sulphur Springs. Though the hot mineral springs pools are unkempt, the old Riverside Hotel and the Grand County Historical Museum bring history to life.

HISTORY

Since the mid-1600s Middle Park has been a coveted Indian hunting ground because the large animal herds in the valley provided easy prey. Confrontations between Ute and Arapaho hunting parties were commonplace.

When the fur trade was booming in the 1820s, trappers came into the valley. These hardy mountain men had a practical knowledge of the park, but it was not until the expedition of John C. Fremont in 1844 that any maps of Middle Park existed. By 1850 trading in pelts had virtually stopped.

Irish nobleman Sir George Gore briefly visited Middle Park while on his legendary American hunting expedition, which lasted from 1854 to 1857. Traveling with a huge entourage, Gore singlehandedly killed thousands of bison and 40 grizzly bears and lost count of the elk, antelope and deer that he slaughtered. In the evening Sir St. George repaired to his green striped tents to sip vintage wines and enjoy the company of imported ladies of pleasure.

As the 1870s arrived, a smattering of whites had settled in Middle Park. Ute and Arapaho Indians continued to hunt in summer and did not appreciate the intrusion. By the time of the Ute massacre of whites in Meeker on Sept. 29, 1879 (see the **Meeker** chapter), tension was reaching new heights. It was a time of occasional violence and constant concern for the entire valley. A common white sentiment of the times was expressed by US Army Gen. Pope, who said the Utes were "worthless, idle vagabonds, who are no more likely to earn a living . . . by manual labor than by teaching metaphysics."

After the Indians were expelled from their homeland, sheep and cattle ranching took on primary importance in Middle Park. Many prospectors came into the area but left with little reward for their efforts.

Before the turn of the century, William Byers, owner of the *Rocky Mountain News*, had modest success in trying to lure wealthy vacationers to his latest purchase: Hot Sulphur Springs. Miners and lumberjacks appreciated the soothing vapor waters in greater numbers than the monied. Even though the natural springs beside the Colorado River were rumored to have healing powers, Byers's "spa" never really got off the ground. However, by 1911 Hot Sulphur Springs began attracting tourists to skiing events at its first annual Winter Carnival.

Winter has long been a popular season in the Fraser Valley. Skiers have streamed into the Winter Park area since completion of the Moffat Railroad Tunnel in 1927. The train would emerge from underneath the Continental Divide with eager skiers, ready to hike up the mountain with seven-foot wooden skis for a meager two runs per day. The first lift was a simple rope tow in 1935. Today the train still runs on weekends, but the facilities at the ski area have vastly improved. Under the stewardship of the city of Denver, Winter Park Ski Area has grown steadily into a major ski destination.

GETTING THERE

Winter Park is located 67 miles northwest of Denver. By car, the best route from Denver is via Interstate 70, west for 42 miles to exit 232. Then take Hwy. 40 over Berthoud Pass and drop into Winter Park at the head of the Fraser Valley. After Winter Park come the small communities of Fraser, Tabernash, Granby and Hot Sulphur Springs.

Several bus lines provide daily service to Winter Park from Stapleton Airport in Denver. Some lines provide service from downtown Denver.

On winter weekends and for special summer events, perhaps the best way to reach Winter Park from Denver is on the Rio Grande ski train. The scenery is fantastic as the train winds through South Boulder Canyon and passes under the Continental Divide by way of the historic Moffat Tunnel. The train has recently been refurbished, making the two-hour trip an even better one. For information call **(303) 290-8497**. There is also daily Amtrak train service to Winter Park from Chicago and San Francisco on the California Zephyr.

——— FESTIVALS AND EVENTS ———

Spring Splash
mid-April

The end of the ski season is ushered in with a splash. The highlight of the day-long party is a ski race down an obstacle course ending in a 40-foot long pool of cold water. Costumed skiers try to pick up speed so they can glide over the water, but many lose their momentum about halfway through. For more information, call **(303) 726-5514**.

High Country Stampede
Saturday nights from
mid-July to the end of August

In the rodeo grounds just west of Fraser, amateur riders and ropers display their skills in front of an enthusiastic crowd. Most of the contestants are local ranch hands; all are riding for their pride and a share of the purse. The popular event also coincides with a steak fry that is open to the public. For more information, contact the Winter Park/Fraser Valley Chamber of Commerce at **(303) 726-4118**.

——— OUTDOOR ACTIVITIES ———

BIKING

MOUNTAIN BIKING

"Life's too short to just ride paved roads!" Ranchers and loggers in this area have left behind a maze of dirt roads that are ideal for sturdy two-wheelers. Until re- cently, no one really cared about these rough roads; it wasn't until 1987 that the Winter Park Fat Tire Society (FATS) was formed to promote the burgeoning sport of mountain biking. This organization is responsible for a world-class trail system, featuring 500 miles of mapped trails and

200 miles of marked trails. Most of the trails follow roads cut by necessity over the past century.

The wide Fraser Valley is surrounded by a diversity of terrain that is easily accessible from downtown Winter Park. Trails wind their way through rolling hills, sprawling meadows and dense forests. According to FATS, there are enough trails for any skill level to ride for an entire week without repeating any of the rides. To find out more information about the trail system and for a free map, write to: **Winter Park FATS, PO Box 1337, Winter Park, CO 80482.** Or call the **Winter Park/Fraser Valley Chamber of Commerce** at **(303) 726-4118.**

Rentals and Tours—

Doesn't it seem as though there is always another hill to climb? A new company has taken some of the pain out of mountain biking: they will take you to the top of Mount Nystrom or Corona Pass so you can enjoy a continuous downhill ride. For more information call **Mad Mountain Bike Tours: (303) 726-5290.**

There is a proliferation of mountain bike shops in Winter Park. All are run by enthusiasts who are knowledgeable about the sport and nearby trails. If you plan on renting a bike for a long period of time, be sure to phone in an early reservation.

Ski Depot Sports—Located in **Park Plaza Shopping Center** on Hwy. 40; (303) 726-8055.

Sports Stalker—Located in **Cooper Creek Square** on Hwy. 40; (303) 726-8873.

Winter Park Sports Shop—Located in **Kings Crossing Shopping Center** on Hwy. 40; (303) 726-5554.

FISHING

Arapaho National Recreation Area—

Shadow Mountain Reservoir, Lake Granby, Grand Lake and Monarch Lake all offer excellent fishing in one of the most beautiful settings imaginable. Fishing for rainbow, brook, mackinaw and cutthroat trout should be enough, but there is also a large kokanee salmon population at several of the large lakes. See the Fishing section of the **Grand Lake** chapter for more information.

Colorado River—

After the Fraser River joins the Colorado River near Granby, the wide river is designated Gold Medal water. It is therefore a pity that, unless you are one of a privileged few, most of the river is off limits. Only 5 miles of the river between Granby and Kremmling remain unfenced. The river flows through sprawling cattle ranches, and permission is rarely granted to individuals. You might be able to gain access to private water by hiring a local outfitter who has already made arrangements with the landowner. Otherwise, your efforts are constricted. There is a good 2-mile stretch downstream from Hot Sulphur Springs in Byers Canyon. Fishing for large rainbows and browns is popular here, despite the fact that the river is closely paralleled by the road and the embankment is fairly steep. It is easier to wade this stretch than to try to fish it from the riverbank.

Fraser River—

Flowing down from the upper reaches of Berthoud Pass, the Fraser River can be worth your time and persistence. Upper portions of the river, near Winter Park Ski Area, offer a chance at well-stocked rainbows and brooks. The small river flows next to Hwy. 40 for much of its upper run. Access to the lower portions requires walking along the Denver & Rio Grande Railroad tracks north of Tabernash. Get permission to use their right-of-way and beware of the many trains still making runs. One mile downstream from Tabernash, until a mile or so above Granby, the river is designated Wild Trout water. As the river enters Fraser Canyon, the fishing for rainbows and browns is rated good. This was President Eisenhower's favorite place to fish. Although there are a few sections of private land, plenty of water remains open to the public. Popular flies include the Royal Wulff and gray caddis imitations on top; Hare's Ear and Stonefly nymphs under the surface. Mepps and Rapala lures tend to produce some bites.

Meadow Creek Reservoir—

As soon as the ice melts from this high mountain reservoir, the fishing gets hot for rainbows and brooks. There are a couple of campgrounds on the north shore. For a smaller, natural lake, try fishing at **Columbine Lake**, a 3-mile hike from above the reservoir. The high lake (11,100 feet) is a sure bet for pan-sized cutthroats. To reach this area, take Hwy. 40 to just east of Tabernash. Turn onto Forest Rt. 129, which winds northeast to the reservoir. Past the campgrounds, at the end of the road, is the trailhead for Columbine Lake.

Rio Grande Cutthroat

Williams Fork Reservoir—

This good-sized reservoir is locked between the high peaks of the Williams Fork and Vasquez mountains at an elevation of 7,800 feet. There are a lot of rainbow and brown trout, pike and even kokanee salmon swimming around in what will eventually be Denver's tap water. Though the water level fluctuates, this can be an excellent place to catch a stringer full of fish. A boat ramp and camping area are located on the west side. To get to the reservoir, take Hwy. 40 west of Hot Sulphur Springs 4 miles, to a point just east of Parshall. A good road branches south for the last few miles to Williams Fork Reservoir.

FOUR-WHEEL-DRIVE TRIPS

Rentals and Tours—

Mad Adventures—This Winter Park company offers a small selection of guided jeep tours in the area. One of the tours is along the Moffat Road to the top of Rollins Pass (described below). It is a three-hour jeep tour that dwells on the fascinating point-by-point history of the old railway. Reservations are required 24 hours in advance. **PO Box 650, Winter Park, CO 80482; (303) 726-5290, 1-800-451-4844** nationwide.

Rollins Pass Road (Corona Pass)—

This rough road follows the original path of the railway over the Continental Divide. The status of the road, once maintained as a passenger car route, has been difficult to assess since major rock slides in 1979 and 1982. It is therefore recommended to call the forest service office in Boulder— (303) 444-6001—to find out about current conditions. Passenger cars are known to make the drive from Winter Park to the top of the pass, but no farther. Last word was that the entire road is open to four-wheel-drive vehicles from the middle of July, as long as weather permits. The Boulder District Ranger strongly recommends four-wheel-drive vehicles for portions of the road near the top of the pass. Continued restoration work on the trestle and improvements to the road are planned.

Rollins Pass was used for 24 years as the main line of the Denver, Northwestern and Pacific Railway Company until the Moffat Tunnel was completed in 1927. The railway and namesake tunnel were both the brainchild of David H. Moffat. After he made his fortune in banking and mining, he set out to find a shorter passage to Salt Lake City and the West Coast. His idea for a line due west of Denver was a 175-mile shortcut to the established routes. The route over Rollins Pass was intended only as a stop-gap measure until the tunnel was completed. Built from 1923 to 1927, the 6.2-mile tunnel was finally completed at a huge cost: 19 lives and $18 million. At the Continental Divide the tunnel is bored a mile beneath the surface. The completion of the tunnel eliminated 23 miles and cut 2.5 hours of travel time off the "Hill" route.

From Winter Park, turn right (east) from Hwy. 40 onto Forest Rd. 149 and stay on the main road. As you continue toward the pass, the condition of the road gets worse. This drive is not recommended for passenger vehicles.

GOLF

Pole Creek Golf Club—

Considered by many to be one of the finest mountain courses in the state, Pole Creek is still coming into its own. Built in the early 1980s, the young 18-hole course makes for a very exciting round. Like other mountain courses, pines line the fairways on many holes and majestic mountain views can be distracting. Some holes are laid out Scottish-style with few trees and plenty of natural hazards. Colorado residents get quite a break on the greens fees. Pro shop, range and restaurant; club rentals and motorized carts available. Located 11 miles northwest of Winter Park on **Hwy. 40; (303) 726-8847.**

HIKING AND BACKPACKING

Arapaho National Forest surrounding the Fraser Valley provides a beautiful expanse for hiking and backpacking. Many backcountry trails weave their way through miles of high country. The popular Indian Peaks Wilderness Area, encompassed within the national forest, is situated on both sides of the Continental Divide. Because of heavy use, a permit is required for backcountry camping. Contact the Boulder District—**(303) 444-6003**—or the Sulphur District in Granby—**(303) 887-3331**—for reservations. If you are unable to plan your trip to the Indian Peaks ahead of time, there are a few last-chance permits issued by the district offices. Wilderness day use is not restricted by permit.

The Vasquez Mountains and the Fraser Experimental Forest are little-used forest areas to the west of Winter Park and Berthoud Pass. The experimental forest is not nearly as sinister as it sounds; new techniques of forest management are applied here. Christmas tree cutting permits are available during the Yuletide.

Byers Peak Trail—

This short, steep 2.5-mile hike leads to the top of Byers Peak (12,804 feet). Before reaching treeline the defined trail passes through tall stands of Engelmann spruce in the Fraser Experimental Forest. Nearly constant winds buffet the upper reaches of the peak. There are a couple of small lakes a short distance from the trail that are said to have good fishing. Once there, enjoy far-reaching views of the mountains and valleys of northern Colorado. To reach the trailhead, head west on County Rd. 73 from the Fraser Valley Market in Fraser toward Byers Creek Campground. After 4 miles, take a right at the Byers Peak signpost and continue along the dirt road for 4.5 miles to the Byers Peak Trail parking lot.

Caribou Pass Trail—

This trail offers a fairly difficult 4.4-mile hike to Caribou Pass (11,790 feet) and excellent views of the Indian Peaks. Those seeking a longer backpack trip can continue over Arapaho Pass to Monarch Lake. Be prepared for occasional muddy trail conditions as you set off on this trail. The first mile is on an old four-wheel-drive road (now closed to vehicles). As the trail tracks beside Meadow Creek, it passes a couple of crumbling log cabins that have seen better days. At a marked trail junction, follow the footpath that heads east from the Columbine Lake Trail (see below) and into a subalpine forest. For the next mile, the trail is a steep ascent through the trees, interspersed in places with flowering meadows. Caribou Pass is a tiring half-mile hike from treeline. Once at the top, the panorama to the east is inspiring: Apache Peak (13,441 feet), Navajo Peak (13,409) and down to Caribou Lake at the base of the pass. Another half-mile hike along the ridge to the north leads to the top of Satanta Peak (11,979 feet). A precarious half-mile cliff walk to the south leads to Lake Dorothy.

To reach the trailhead for Caribou Pass and Columbine Lake trails, take Hwy. 40 northwest almost to Tabernash. A half mile east of town, Forest Rd. 129 heads northeast to Meadow Creek Reservoir. The trailhead for both hikes is located above the reservoir at the parking area for Junco Lake.

Columbine Lake Trail—

This is a great half-day hike despite the fact that your feet will get wet while passing through a low meadow area. The nearly 3-mile trail uses the same route as Caribou Pass Trail (described above) for the first mile and a half. At a marked junction, Columbine Lake Trail continues south into a thick forest before heading to the top of a plateau. The trail passes through a couple of marshy meadows before reaching the lake at treeline. Along the trail the views to Winter Park Ski Area and the Fraser Valley are superb. Columbine Lake (11,060 feet) is a great place for picnicking and a chance at catching cutthroat trout. To reach Columbine Lake Trail, see the directions for Caribou Pass Trail above.

Corona Trail—

There are a couple of ways to reach Corona Trail, but the best is from the top of Rollins Pass at the Continental Divide. From there, the spectacular trail follows a level grade atop the divide for 6 miles. Since the trail is entirely above treeline it is wise to carry warm clothing and a full water bottle. Beware of incoming thunder- and snowstorms. Midway along the trail is Devil's Thumb Pass, where the finger-shaped rock of the same name is clearly visible. The thumb is a favorite technical climb. From the pass, Devil's Thumb Trail leads to the western and eastern sides of the divide. To reach Rollins Pass from Winter Park, take Forest Rd. 149 east of town. The road can be rough and the forest service does not recommend it for passenger cars, but many make it to the top without any problems.

Another access route to Corona Trail involves climbing 2,000 vertical feet in less than 2.5 miles before reaching the Continental Divide. This trail begins at Devil's Thumb Park at the junction of High Lonesome and Devil's Thumb Trail. Follow Devil's Thumb Trail to the divide. There

are good camping spots for backpackers after crossing to the east side of Devil's Thumb Pass, near Devil's Thumb and Jasper lakes. To reach the trailhead requires taking a four-wheel-drive road (Forest Rd. 128) east of Hwy. 40 at Fraser.

Monarch Lake Trailheads—

A number of excellent trails lead into the Indian Peaks Wilderness from Monarch Lake. Some of these hikes are described on page 195.

HORSEBACK RIDING

Since the Middle Park area was pioneered primarily by ranchers, it remains an excellent place to get back in the saddle. Several ranches can schedule trail rides of various lengths. Some rides include a meal on the trail, others are arranged by the hour. The following ranches and stables all have horses for the general public. Give 'em a call and see if you can wrangle some information.

Beaver Village—

Located on Hwy. 40 on the south end of Winter Park; (303) 726-5741.

YMCA Snow Mountain Ranch—

Located 12 miles northwest of Winter Park near Tabernash; (303) 887-2152.

RIVER FLOATING

The moderate 14-mile stretch of the **Upper Colorado River** from Kremmling down to State Bridge is one of the most popular day trips in the state. As many as 40 commercial outfitters make the trip.

Outfitters—

Mad Adventures—Call for reservations: (303) 726-5290 in Winter Park; 1-800-451-4844, nationwide.

Timber Rafting—Reservations can be made at **The Viking Ski Shop, (303) 726-8885;** or **Ski Depot Sports, (303) 726-8055.**

Rafting is an exciting way to spend some time in the summer on Colorado rivers (photograph by Frank Staub).

SKIING
CROSS-COUNTRY SKIING
Backcountry Trails—
Berthoud Pass—The top of the pass at Timberline Ski Area provides a great set-off point for skiers of all abilities. However, some of the slopes can be quite difficult. *A good map and an awareness of current avalanche conditions are essential for a safe backcountry trip.* Sevenmile Trail actually follows part of the old Berthoud Pass wagon road, which followed a route between Denver and Middle Park. To get the most out of this trail, leave a second car at the fourth switchback on the west side of Berthoud Pass. The trail begins at the top of the pass with a plummeting drop into Hell's Half Acre, which can be avoided by following down along Hwy. 40 to its first switchback. Eventually you will track out by your car on the west side of Berthoud Pass.

Groomed Trails—
Granby—SilverCreek Nordic Center maintains a selection of easy, well-groomed trails just outside of Granby. It has also become a popular place for telemarking on the downhill ski slopes. The trail fee at the Nordic Center includes a couple of rides on certain lifts. The views from the upper trails into the Fraser Valley are breathtaking, and a few of the descents will require all of your balance. You wouldn't want to end up doing a face plant on a run called Fay Splants! Rentals, instruction, restaurants and lodging are all available. For more information on the ski area, see below. SilverCreek Nordic Center is located 17 miles north of Winter Park on **Hwy. 40, (303) 887-3384.**

Tabernash—YMCA Snow Mountain Ranch/Nordic Center offers a 30-mile public trail system that stretches throughout their property. The Nordic Center at Snow Mountain Ranch has long offered equipment rentals, lessons and passes during its long winter season. Because the snow melts late in the year, the ranch trails are used extensively for training Olympic hopefuls. The employees have a refreshing, professional attitude about the sport. The trails range from beginner to expert. For more information on Snow Mountain Ranch see Where to Stay. Located 12 miles northwest of Winter Park; **(303) 887-2152.** Denver metro area **(303) 443-4743.**

Winter Park—Tour Idlewild is a complete nordic center that now operates out of the defunct downhill ski area of Idlewild. Over 18 miles of groomed trails are open to all abilities, and there is a good hill for practicing telemark turns. Ski rentals and lessons are available. Located a half mile east of Hwy. 40 from the town of Winter Park. The trail fee is also good for Devil's Thumb Ranch, making a total of 55 miles of trails available to cross-country skiers. For information, call **(303) 726-5564.**

DOWNHILL SKIING
SilverCreek—
    In the winter of 1982 Colorado skiing took a new turn with the opening of Silver-Creek. This compact ski area was designed

with families in mind. It's for people who are looking for a fairly gentle, uncrowded mountain and a reasonably priced ski vacation at a first-class resort. Despite the fact that you will see expert slopes at SilverCreek, the black-diamond designation here would indicate intermediate runs at other Colorado areas. Beginners have a separate learning area for making unsteady first turns without the intimidation of snickering experts. SilverCreek is becoming a haven for cross-country skiers; the Nordic Center has miles of groomed trails, and the ski mountain is an excellent place to learn telemark turns.

At the base area is a ski lodge with saloon, restaurant, ski-rental shop and nursery. The wide sun decks are a great place to watch returning skiers in the afternoon. Many condos are springing up at the bottom of the ski mountain. The Inn at SilverCreek ($$ to $$$, depending on the season) is a large, 342-room hotel complex with all the amenities just 2 miles away. Open year-round. For reservations, call 1-800-526-0590.

SilverCreek is located 17 miles north of Winter Park on **Hwy. 40.** There is daily train service on Amtrak's California Zephyr from the West Coast and some points east of Colorado. Daily bus service exists from Winter Park to SilverCreek each day.

Winter Park Resort—

"You could fit 2,500 football fields within its boundaries" says Gary McGraw, the director of operations. The ski area is actually made up of three interconnected mountains: Winter Park, Mary Jane and Vasquez Ridge. Mary Jane, with its own base facilities, is where advanced skiers head for deeply carved bumps on a mountain that was never meant for beginners. Powderhounds will be interested to note that weather patterns dump 100 inches more snow on Mary Jane each season than its skiable neighbors. If you are a novice or intermediate, there is a wide selection of groomed runs at both Winter Park and Vasquez Peak.

From the top of Winter Park Ski Area,

an incredible mountain panorama stretches out in front of you. Visible to the northeast on a clear day are the towering peaks of Rocky Mountain National Park and the nearby Indian Peaks Wilderness Area. The Continental Divide cuts a high route in front of your eyes. Besides all that, the skiing on the three mountains is consistently excellent. Since the area is easily accessible from Denver and a good value, expect some lift lines on the weekends.

Winter Park Handicapped Skiing— "I saw the joy on their faces when they moved on skis in a way they couldn't when they tried to walk," recalled Hal O'Leary, director of the Winter Park Handicap Ski Program. Since he founded the program in 1970, it has grown to be the largest of its kind. People with all types of disabilities, including blindness, amputation, mental retardation and multiple sclerosis, are given instruction and adaptive equipment at a nominal fee. In 1987 more than 14,000 lessons were given by hundreds of dedicated volunteers. For more information, call (303) 726-5514.

SWIMMING

If you really need to go for a dip, head for the indoor, Olympic-sized pool at the YMCA Snow Mountain Ranch. It's located 12 miles northwest of Winter Park on **Hwy. 40; (303) 887-2152.**

TENNIS

There are many courts spread out at lodging facilities in the Winter Park area. A couple of public courts are located at the Idlewild Lodge just east of the town of Winter Park. For information, call **(303) 726-5562.**

TUBING

Fraser—

At the **Fraser Valley** tubing hill you can enjoy the exhilarating feeling of jumping on a tube and gaining speed down the side of a snow-covered mountain. Kids and adults both seem to love the experience equally. A set hourly fee includes the rental of your own tube and as many rides up the rope tow as you can handle. The mountain is well lighted for frigid evening fun. If it gets too cold you can skip a run and go inside to a crackling fire and a cup of hot chocolate. Located on the south end of Fraser. Open Mon.–Fri. 4–10 pm and 10 am–10 pm on weekends. **(303) 726-5954.**

SEEING AND DOING

ALPINE SLIDE

Unlike the playground-variety slide we all grew up with, the longest slide in Colorado requires a chairlift ride to reach the top. The Alpine Slide is similar to a luge course in the way it twists down the ski mountain. High banked curves can be easily negotiated in a polyethylene sled equipped with wheels and brakes. Fun for a wide range of ages. Open from early June to Labor Day seven days a week from 9:30 am–5 pm. Open until 7 pm during most of July and Aug. Fee charged per ride. For more information, call **(303) 726-5514.**

MUSEUMS

Grand County Historical Museum—

The old Hot Sulphur Springs School, built in 1924, provides a perfect setting for recounting the long history of Grand County. The skiing exhibit is a revelation. Hot Sulphur Springs ski area was the first in Colorado; today it is just a clear swath of snow on the mountainside behind the museum. Looking through the old photos and ski memorabilia in the front room, you realize how much the sport has changed. Another section of the museum displays Indian artifacts from Windy Gap and more recent Indian history.

How many times have you heard the phrase, ". . . white man's settlement of the West?" The Grand County Museum doesn't forget that pioneer women also played an indispensable role. Other exhibits show the development of towns in Grand County including Fraser, Tabernash, Granby and Kremmling. The helpful staff can answer any questions you might have. Free admission, donations are accepted. Open in summer 10 am–5 pm daily. Winter hours are Wed.–Fri. 10 am–5 pm. and the first and third weekends of the month. Located at the east end of Hot Sulphur Springs on **Hwy. 40; (303) 725-3939.**

NIGHTLIFE

Crooked Creek Saloon (in Fraser)—

A young and very local crowd frequents this rowdy mountain bar. The floor starts to shake on weekends when the live rock or blues music begins. A full calendar offers specials to one group or another on every night of the week. The Crooked Creek is also a great place to eat hefty fatboy burgers, a plateful of pasta, stir fry or a 16-oz. T-bone steak. (They even serve full breakfasts, but the bar atmosphere and smoke never quite go away.) Check this place out. It's open every day of the week, from 7 am–2 am. **Hwy. 40, Fraser; 726-9250.**

The Derailer Bar—

Après-ski partying at the base of Winter Park Ski Area begins as soon as the lifts close. The Derailer Bar has live music Tues. through Sat. during the season. Appetizers are served. Open until 6:30 pm. **Winter Park base area; 726-5514, ext. 273.**

SCENIC DRIVES

Rocky Mountain National Park—

It is easy to forget that Rocky Mountain National Park is right around the corner from the Fraser Valley. The west entrance of the park is located north of Granby on Hwy. 34. Before reaching the park you will pass Lake Granby and Shadow Mountain Reservoir. If you have never driven over Trail Ridge Road don't miss this experience; open late-May to mid-Oct. For more information on Rocky Mountain National Park see the **Estes Park** chapter.

WHERE TO STAY

ACCOMMODATIONS

C Lazy U Guest Ranch — $$$$

Try not to look surprised when a bellboy picks up your luggage at the desk and leads you to your elegant accommodations. The mix of five-star luxury and dude ranch atmosphere is very popular among the selective crowd that frequents this large resort near Granby. Rooms can be booked either in individual cabins or in separate lodge buildings. Not only will you have your own horse for the duration of your week's stay, but you can keep your monogrammed C Lazy U pocket comb forever. The ranch is geared to horseback riding. You can participate in breakfast rides, afternoon rides or an evening steak fry. Other options might be to lounge by the pool, try your luck fishing in Willow Creek or play a game of racquetball or tennis. A trained instructor supervises all children's activities. In winter, guests take full advantage of 30 miles of groomed cross-country trails.

Three meals a day are served in the western-style dining room. In the early evening, many guests can be found in the cocktail lounge for hot hors d'oeuvres and conversation, followed by a gourmet dinner. A nightly meal might begin with bouillabaisse followed by veal scallopini, spinach souffles and, if you have room, delectable desserts. The average price is $900 per person, per week; $125 to $190 per day. The C Lazy U is open year-round except for the months of Oct./Nov. and Apr./May. Located **near Granby**. Reservations are a must. For information: **PO Box 378B, Granby, CO 80446; (303) 887-3344.**

Morningstar Ranch — $$

John Martling, the owner, builder and host of Morningstar, has a number of philosophies that make his small ski lodge a success. He strongly believes that "you should not pay more to sleep than to ski," and we agree! His 80-acre ranch is nestled in the woods 10 minutes away from Winter Park Ski Area—far enough from the bustle, yet close enough for easy access without a long drive. Each room feels homey without being cluttered. The rooms have a sink with hot and cold taps; clean bathrooms are located down the hall. You are not likely to become a room hermit because there are several attractive common areas open to guests. The upstairs lounge is the best place for après-ski conversation next to a log fire, while the downstairs rec room has an assortment of ski movies and classic videos. The morning meal includes fruit, juice and freshly baked muffins. Most guests at the Morningstar are singles and young couples (children are not encouraged). No walk-ins; call in advance for a reservation and directions. **Winter Park, (303) 726-8118.**

American Youth Hostel — $

Without a doubt, this is the cheapest place to stay in Winter Park. It is also a great place for a younger crowd to stay in basic, clean accommodations in six mobile homes. Rooms have two to four bunks or a double bed for couples (only two of these). Each of the trailers has its own kitchen and a common area for guests. Of course, the bathrooms and showers are shared. Reservations are necessary in winter. No curfew; no age restrictions; discount for AYH members. Located across the highway from Cooper Creek Square, behind the Conoco Station; **Winter Park, (303) 726-5356.**

Historic Riverside Hotel — $

In 1983 Abe Rodriguez took the bold step of restoring this vintage 1903 hotel in **Hot Sulphur Springs.** The clientele has shifted from railroad workers and lumberjacks to people in need of a break from the frenetic pace of city life. The preservation of the past is evident from the sturdy simplicity of the furnishings and the quiet ambience of the 21 rooms. Each room is complete with iron bedsteads, old-fashioned round sinks, oak dressers and, thankfully, the convenience of electric heat. Down the hallway are clean but charmless bathrooms. The downstairs public area has comfortable overstuffed chairs in front of a stone hearth. In a separate room, liquor is served from a mirrored cherrywood bar with a long brass footrest. See Where to Eat for information on the Riverside Restaurant. The Riverside is located 26 miles northwest of Winter Park by way of **Hwy. 40; (303) 725-3589,** or **(303) 725-9996.**

YMCA Snow Mountain Ranch — $ to $$$

In a spectacular mountain setting 14 miles north of the Winter Park Ski Area **near Tabernash** on Hwy. 40, a plethora of year-round activities are to be enjoyed by all. The ranch resort maintains a wholesome family environment and provides an excellent value. The Snow Mountain Ranch offers temporary memberships to all guests for the duration of their stay. This membership allows you all the privileges of a full member, except for one very important consideration—full members are given priority over the general public in reserving prime accommodations. Still, there are enough cabins and dorm rooms to take care of everyone for the majority of the year. The Aspen room is open year-round for inexpensive breakfasts and dinners. For more information and reservations: **PO Box 169, Winter Park, CO 80482; (303) 887-2152,** direct Denver line **(303) 443-4743.**

Cabins — $$$—Your best bet for a family vacation is to reserve a reasonably priced two- or three-bedroom cabin (the price goes up on larger cabins). Larger (from four- to seven-bedroom) cabins are available for family reunions. The well-equipped cabins come with refrigerator, range and telephone as well as kitchen implements. The rustic decor encourages gathering before a large moss rock fireplace or out on a wide balcony looking out to the Indian Peaks. Each cabin is a place where family memories are made.

Dorms — $ to $$—There are inexpensive lodge rooms available for families, groups and individuals in several room designs. Most rooms come with a private bathroom. The lodges are all very well kept with large common areas. The drawback of the various lodges is that you never know if you'll be sharing the same lodge with 200 screaming 13-year-olds.

Camping—During summer there are four campgrounds that cater to a segregated smattering of tents and recreational vehicles.

Recreation—Perhaps the single most outstanding aspect of the ranch is the extensive trail system stretching throughout the property. **The Nordic Center** offers equipment rentals, lessons and passes for 30 miles of groomed trails for beginner to expert cross-country skiers. Summer use of the marked trails revolves around hiking, mountain biking or horseback riding.

The ranch encourages its guests and members to use its many recreational facilities. A few seasonal activities include: swimming in the indoor pool, basketball, tennis, miniature golf and ice skating. If you didn't get enough bruises on your derrière while skiing at Winter Park, try strapping on some rollerskates.

CAMPING

In Arapaho National Forest—

Robbers Roost Campground is located 5 miles south of Winter Park on the east side of **Hwy. 40.** There are sites for both tents and trailers situated under the shadow of the Continental Divide. Ten sites; small fee.

Smack in the middle of the Fraser Valley is a small piece of national forest land almost entirely occupied by **Tabernash Campground.** The campground is located 3.5 miles northwest of Tabernash on **Hwy. 40.** It has 30 sites; handicapped facilities; small fee.

Meadow Creek Campground is located 3.5 miles northeast of Fraser on **Forest Rd. 129.** Five sites; small fee. Another campground of the same name is on up the road at **Meadow Creek Reservoir.** This is an ideal place to stay while hiking in the area. Both Caribou Pass Trail and Columbine Lake Trail leave from the reservoir.

In Fraser Experimental Forest—

There are many good places to primitive camp throughout the experimental forest. Please try to minimize your impact if you are camping outside of an organized campground. If your preference is a designated camping area, travel southwest on Forest Rd. 160 from Fraser. In 3 miles you'll come to **St. Louis Creek Campground.** There are 18 sites; drinking water; small fee. Another 3.5 miles down the road is **Byers Creek Campground.** Only 6 sites; drinking water; small fee.

Private Campground—

Elk Valley Ranch Campground in Granby—Laundry and showers, yes . . . but no pool. There are 30 campsites with full hookups. Located 5 miles southeast of Granby on **Hwy. 40; (303) 887-2380.**

WHERE TO EAT

Gasthouse Eichler — $$$ to $$$$

Hans and Hanna Eichler have a great reputation among locals for their authentic German food. This restaurant should be your first choice for a special meal in a classic European atmosphere. Sit in the bar area before dinner and sip on a German wheat beer (*weizen*) with a slice of lemon. The German specialties include rindsrouladen, wiener schnitzel, sauerbraten and kassler rippchen. For the gourmet, choose from veal dishes, lobster, scampi or Chateaubriand. Closed mid-Apr. to end of May. Open from 5:30 pm nightly. **Downtown Winter Park** on **Hwy. 40; 726-5133.**

Deno's — $$$

Deno describes his restaurant/sports bar as "unpretentious," and he's right. Crowded, loud and fun might be a few other appropriate adjectives. Low-priced light fare and appetizers are available in the bar. In the slightly more subdued restaurant area, the large selection of meals hinders classification. Decide from fettuccine Alfredo, crab legs, baby back ribs, chicken chardonnay, trout, veal scallopini, Greek salad and more. Lunch ($) consists of char-burgers, soups, salads and sandwiches. Dinner from 5 pm nightly. **Downtown Winter Park** on **Hwy. 40; 726-5332.**

Riverside Restaurant (in Hot Sulphur Springs) — $$ to $$$

The river room has a special feeling that comes from the owner's careful attention to every detail. Abe's philosophy of catering to the five senses is not immediately noticeable, but you gradually pick up on subtle and welcome differences. Clean white linens dress the tables; soft classical music reaches your ears; light is provided by small shaded lamps around the perimeter of the room; heat emanates from a freestanding wood stove; windows offer unobstructed views of the Colorado River; and the food is marvelous in taste, texture and value. The menu items, listed on a chalkboard, are sophisticated and downhome at the same time. Entrées include lemon pepper catfish, baked chicken, breaded pork chops and Canadian flounder. For information on the Riverside Hotel see Where to Stay. The Riverside is located 26 miles northwest of Winter Park by way of **Hwy. 40; 725-3589 or 725-9996.**

Crooked Creek Saloon — $ to $$$

See Nightlife section.

Hernando's Pizza Pub — $ to $$

Good pizza is found in abundance in **Winter Park,** but people tend to agree that Hernando's is the best. Tables are situated near a round fireplace in the center of the room, or you can take out. Served on white or whole wheat crust, with a variety of toppings. Also served are spaghetti, lasagna and antipasto salad. Full bar. **Near Kings Crossing Center; 726-5409.**

Carver Brothers Bakery—$

This place is so well known that, despite the hidden, off-Main Street location, there is plenty of business. Choose from a mouth-watering array of freshly baked pastries, including pecan rolls, cheese pockets and cinnamon raisin bagels. Take out or try to find a place at one of only seven tables. Reasonably priced full breakfasts include a light and tasty breakfast burrito and an assortment of egg dishes. Lunch items include savory homemade soups, salads, submarine sandwiches and daily specials. Open daily from 7 am; lunch is served 11 am–3 pm in summer, until 5 pm in winter. In winter dinner is served 5–9 pm. Located directly west behind **Cooper Creek Square; 726-8202.**

The Kitchen — $

A small, homey cafe with marvelous breakfasts. Get to this local favorite early or you'll have a long wait. If the tables are full, pour yourself a cup of coffee, sign in, put a number on top of your car and wait for a friendly tap at your window. Once inside, you will be treated to a real breakfast. Choose from a breakfast burrito, huevos rancheros, eggs Benedict or any number of "dishes for egg haters." No credit cards; smoking OK; no whining. Open 7:30 am–12:30 pm only. Located at the north end of Winter Park off **Hwy. 40; 726-9940.**

Trail Cafe (in Hot Sulphur Springs) — $

The sign says Hamburgers, Fries and Homemade Pies. We can only attest to a hearty breakfast, prices from a bygone era and a genuine smile from the cook/waitress/owner, who made us feel welcome. It was almost as if we were guests in her parlor. Located in **Hot Sulphur Springs** on the south side of **Hwy. 40.**

SERVICES

The Lift Bus Service—

Winter Park's free shuttle bus provides summer and winter transportation between town and the ski areas. During the peak hours of 8–10 am and 3–5 pm, there are frequent buses stopping along the length and breadth of the town.

Winter Park/Fraser Valley Chamber of Commerce—

PO Box 3236, Winter Park, CO 80482; **(303) 726-4118,** or **422-0666** in Denver.

Winter Park Children's Center—

Winter Park will take care of your youngster for the day, 8 am–4 pm. Minimum age is 1 year old. Kids from 3 to 13 can be taken skiing by specially trained children's instructors. For more information, call **(303) 726-5514.**

Winter Park Vacations Reservation Service—

(303) 726-9421 in Colorado; **825-0705** Denver direct; **1-800-228-1025** nationwide.

COLORADO PROFILE — CLARABELL AND RUDY JUST

Clarabell Just knows exactly what she means when she says, "A long time ago people lived off the land; now people live off one another." Her 80 years of ranching, wrangling, trapping and homesteading are belied by bright eyes and a tiny but strong five-foot frame; her mind is blessed with clear understanding and a sense of inner peace. Born in Oklahoma's Cherokee Nation of one-quarter Cherokee blood, Clarabell moved west with her family, including nine siblings, farm tools and animals, to Rifle, Colorado, in 1911. Eventually she made her own way by stagecoach to the Just Ranch, where she met her future husband, Rudy. He asked her to marry him because "she was too good a help to lose."

Rudy was born on land homesteaded by his mother and father in the 1890s. After Rudy and Clarabell were married, six kids were born, without complications, in their simple log cabin. This brings out another of Clarabell's philosophies: "Nature is not always right . . . but mostly." Their spread is now a living museum of the past. While we were visiting, Clarabell proudly displayed a large trunk of tanned pelts. Clarabell still shoots predators when they threaten the sheep grazing in a meadow below their cabin. She mentioned that her shot had improved greatly since her cataract surgery. The proud old couple have led pure lives that, according to Clarabell, " . . . didn't have no stress . . . we just did what we had to do."

Rudy Just died without suffering on Jan. 31, 1989.

The Female Short-Eared Owl

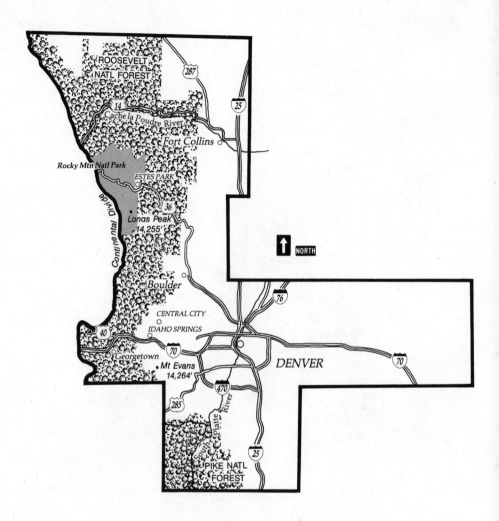

NORTH CENTRAL REGION

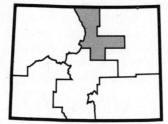

═══ Boulder ═══

Though Boulder is only a half-hour drive from Denver, it feels like a different world. From the moment you begin dropping into Boulder from the scenic overlook on the Boulder Turnpike (Hwy. 36), the view is enough to make you pull off and stare in awe at its beautiful setting—the Rocky Mountains shooting up to the west and the plains stretching east toward the horizon. Boulder's supreme location, at the base of the dramatic rock formations known as the Flatirons, is a major attraction.

For many people, Boulder is a utopia. *Healthy, young* and *educated* are the words that best describe the general mix of the population. Boulder is a thriving college community that retains the intimacy of a small town. It's also a major high-tech center, with computer and scientific institutions proliferating, sometimes in tandem with projects spawned at the University of Colorado's main campus. Fewer than 100,000 residents enjoy the quality of life Boulder has to offer, for which they pay a price—having to sustain an upscale economy and to endure Boulder jokes hurled by anyone who isn't lucky enough to live here.

Boulder doesn't fight its image as an idealistic bastion of free thought. The University of Colorado at Boulder, with more than 20,000 students, is the biggest but certainly not the only place to take classes. Alternative education flourishes at Naropa Institute (America's only Buddhist university), Hakomi Institute, Boulder College, Rolf Institute, Boulder Graduate School and the Boulder School of Massage Therapy.

Boulder is such an active town, with so many options, there's always the question of what to do next. The social and cultural offerings can fill anyone's calender. Music, lectures, theater and dance are just a sampling. A stroll down the Pearl Street Mall or through the beautiful University of Colorado campus are two things you shouldn't miss. Boulder Open Space land preserves spectacular views of the mountains and the wide-open prairies; 16,000 acres of open space is reserved solely for public recreational use. To the west, Roosevelt National Forest and Indian Peaks Wilderness Area provide unlimited opportunities for hiking, fishing, cross-country skiing and more.

The mountains west of Boulder are riddled with old supply towns and mining camps. Nederland, Ward and Gold Hill are still active today; countless other towns are nearly forgotten but still provide local color. Many old wagon routes are now traveled by car. Driving up any of the twisting canyons to the west of Boulder, emerging on the Peak to Peak Highway, and returning to town via another route, is a great way to spend a day in the beautiful high country of the Front Range.

HISTORY

In 1858 Capt. Thomas Aikins, an early prospector, said of the Boulder area: "The mountains looked right for gold and the valleys looked rich for grazing." Other settlers felt the same way. When the first gold strike was made on aptly named Gold Hill a few months later, the town of Boulder City sprang to life. Boulder was named for the numerous large rocks in the vicinity. *City* was added to the name in the hope it would actually become one someday; eventually the tag was dropped.

Early townspeople endured the elements in 70 dirt-floor log cabins built along Pearl St. Occupants used wool blankets to cover furnishings and supplies during rainy periods and slept under leaky roofs on mattresses made with pine needles and hay until enough straw could be grown. The newcomers had virtually no trouble with the Southern Arapaho Indians, who, under the leadership of Chief Niwot (Left Hand), let the settlers stay.

Although the town was built on a pile of rocks in the foothills, Boulder's fortune was not to be found in minerals, which is why it didn't fall victim to the same fate of the boom and bust mining towns. Instead, Boulder grew up as a supply and transportation center for the gold, silver and tungsten mining operations dotting the mountains to the west. It later served as a hub for farmers on the plains.

Boulder eventually found its future in education. In 1860 the young town opened the first schoolhouse in Colorado. By the time Colorado achieved statehood in 1876, the original University of Colorado building, Old Main, was under construction. The freshman class consisted of nine men and one woman in 1878. The university grew slowly with the town, until a dramatic leap in enrollment occurred after World War II as returning GIs took advantage of their educational opportunities.

It's hard to believe today, but Boulder was "dry" from 1907 until 1967. Absolutely no liquor was served (legally) until the Catacombs

Mining and miners were a vital part of Boulder in the late 1800s (courtesy of the Denver Public Library, Western History Collection).

opened in the Hotel Boulderado in 1969. Since then, a proliferation of night spots and quality restaurants has opened up in town.

GETTING THERE

Boulder is located less than 45 minutes from downtown Denver. To get there drive north on Interstate 25 until you reach the Boulder Turnpike (Hwy. 36), which leads 27 miles northwest to Boulder. Frequent daily Regional Transportation District (RTD) buses shuttle between Denver and Boulder.

MAJOR ATTRACTIONS

PEARL STREET MALL

You'll miss the essence of Boulder by neglecting to visit the Pearl Street Mall. Located in the center of the downtown business district, it's a place where the pulse of the city is out in the open air. The wide brick walkway is complemented by grassy areas, flowers and wooden benches; it's bordered on both sides by restaurants, shops, galleries, bars and outdoor cafes.

The mall is unquestionably one of the best people-watching places you'll ever visit. Fashion statements abound. Foreign accents hang in the air. The mood changes with the seasons, but there is always something happening.

On summer evenings, the atmosphere is fueled by free performances by jugglers, magicians, acrobats, musicians and mimes.

These often-professional acts attract large circles of curious people. If you are really interested in a show, the best time to visit is on Halloween night, when one big party of thousands of Boulderites promendades up and down the mallin full costume. The Halloween "Mall Crawl" sees the bars doing incredible business; the scene tends to get rowdy as the night wears on.

OTHER ATTRACTIONS

BOULDER BREWING COMPANY

Do you think beer has to be brewed in an oversized warehouse and that all beer tastes the same? The Boulder Brewing Co. breaks the mold by providing an array of tantalizing tastes in its porter, stout, extra pale ale and sport beer. This is the oldest micro-brewery in the US; it was started clear back in 1979. The original brew was made in a primitive building called the "Goat Shed," but its current brewery is up-town: beer is brewed in an attractive brick building with expansive views to the Flatirons. An award was given to the brewery for the "best view from a loading dock." Free brewery tours begin at 11 am and 1 pm, Mon.–Sat. in summer; 11 am only in winter. The tour ends with a free taste of some of the freshest beer you'll ever try. The Boulder Brewing Co. Tasting Room is open for lunch (see the Where to Eat section) from 11 am–2 pm Mon.–Sat.; tasting from 11 am–5 pm on weekdays and until 3 pm on Sat. **2880 Wilderness Pl.; (303) 444-8448.**

NATIONAL CENTER FOR ATMOSPHERIC RESEARCH (NCAR)

"Anyone curious about the air, sun and weather will find NCAR a fascinating place," according to Rene Munoz, education and tour coordinator. NCAR's scientists work on problems such as the greenhouse effect, windshear, global climate modeling and lightning. There are no classified secrets here. NCAR welcomes the public to take self-guided tours during regular hours. From June to Sept., hour-long guided tours begin at noon Mon.–Sat. Don't miss the interactive model of the sun or the two Cray supercomputers that can make nearly a billion calculations per second. A library and a cafeteria are also open to the public. Lunch is served from 11:30 am–1:30 pm. NCAR also has an art gallery on the second floor. A number of hiking trails lead into the Open Space land west of the facility.

Designed by noted architect I.M. Pei, NCAR commands an enviable mesa-top position overlooking Boulder. The unique building resembles the cliff dwellings of Mesa Verde; few modern structures commune in such a beautiful way with a natural setting. If you make the trip to NCAR you will surely see some deer. Open 8 am–5 pm Mon.–Fri., 9 am–3 pm weekends and holidays. Located at the west end of Table Mesa Dr., **1850 Table Mesa Dr.; (303) 497-1174.** Another stop on the science circuit is the **National Institute of Standards and Technology,** which has a number of lobby displays and guided tours on Thur. at 2 pm. No fee. **325 Broadway; (303) 492-3244.**

UNIVERSITY OF COLORADO, BOULDER CAMPUS

This is one of the most beautiful college campuses in the nation. Well into its second century, the campus reflects a stately maturity—even with occasional purple-haired students riding around on skateboards. Stone buildings with red-tile roofs are separated by open grassy areas. Wild animation prevails when a flood of students with 10 minutes to get to the next class is released. The University Memorial Center (UMC) serves as the nucleus of activity. An attractive fountain area is just outside the huge building; inside, cafes, restaurants, a video game room, a pool hall, a bowling alley and the all-important University Bookstore bustle with activity. Put on your walking shoes and take in all the beauty and energy that distinguish the University of Colorado campus.

FESTIVALS AND EVENTS

Conference on World Affairs
mid-April

Everything under the sun is analyzed by the experts who participate in panel discussions on the CU campus every spring. The audience is usually involved in question-and-answer periods after each presentation. You'll be able to mingle with government officials, CIA operatives, witches, cosmonauts, refugees, journalists and radical feminists—something for everyone. For schedule information, call **(303) 492-2525.**

Kinetic Sculpture Challenge
early May

This is a spectacle of huge proportions, with outrageous human-powered craft racing over land and water in front of a crowd of thousands. Imagine full-grown adults sitting inside a leg-powered toilet or crowded into a huge mud shark, spending a day competing for various titles at Boulder Reservoir. Ridiculous team names range from *A Streetcar Named Perspire* to *Gumby Goes Hawaiian*. The whole event is totally meaningless, which is a big part of what makes it so much fun. Beer and food are served, KBCO radio provides the music and the contestants provide the excuse for having a good time. A pre-challenge parade around the Pearl Street Mall allows spectators to catch a look at these wacky conveyances. Don't miss this one! Contact **(303) 444-5600** for more information.

Colorado Music Festival
late June through early August

Though not as well known as the Aspen Music Festival, this festival has everything going for it. Classical music concerts take place in the magnificent all-wood Chautauqua Auditorium, built in 1898. Under the direction of Giora Bernstein, musicians from symphonies around the world come together to play with renowned guest artists. Pre-concert picnickers cast a cheery array of color across the expansive lawns. If you prefer dining at a table, have dinner on the commodious porch of the Chautauqua Dining Hall and enjoy this quintessentially Boulder scene. (See the Where to Eat section.) Since 1976 the music festival has been an important part of summertime in Boulder. For more information, call **(303) 449-1397.**

Colorado Shakespeare Festival
early July through mid-Auguist

In a beautiful garden setting at the Mary Rippon Outdoor Theater on the CU campus, highly entertaining productions of Shakespeare are performed each summer. Talented company members are recruited through national auditions; well-known guest artists play a number of the major roles. This festival has been going strong since 1958 and is now considered one of the best in the country. Whether it is a joyful production of *A Midsummer Night's Dream* or a gruesome rendition of the *Tragedy of Titus Andronicus*, you will feel the timeless emotions only Shakespeare can evoke. For ticket information (after May 23), call **(303) 492-8181.**

Athletic Events
year-round

Boulder attracts many world-class athletes and this is mirrored in the large number of athletic events each year. The **CU Buffalos**, Big Eight football games at Folsom Field are always a raucous experience. Each game is preceded by Ralphie (a buffalo) making his traditional run around the football field. The **Bolder Boulder** is a 10K race that attracts some 20,000 runners every Memorial Day. Attending the **Jose Cuervo Doubles Volleyball Tournament** at the South Boulder Recreation Center is like going to a beach party. Call the **Boulder Chamber of Commerce** at **(303) 442-1044** for more information.

OUTDOOR ACTIVITIES

BIKING

MOUNTAIN BIKING

This sport has actually attracted too many people in the Boulder area. Due to the crush of riders in the past few years, bikes are now prohibited on most of the Boulder open-space trails. There are still some trails open, but riding is restricted to flat gravel roads. In Roosevelt National Forest, however, there are hundreds of miles of roads and trails open to mountain bikes. Eldora Mountain Resort has opened up 40 kilometers of cross-country trails to mountain bikers for a fee. Bring your own bike or rent one of theirs. Call **(303) 440-8700** in metro Denver or **(303) 258-7082** in Nederland.

Gold Hill—A ride up to Gold Hill via either Sunshine or Four Mile canyons should satisfy even the most avid riders. It's about a 10-mile uphill ride from the mouth of either canyon to this out-of-the-way hamlet. If you make the ride on a weekend, be sure to stop in at the Lick Skillet Cafe for breakfast or lunch (see the Where to Eat section). To get to Sunshine Canyon, ride west on Mapleton Ave.; to reach Four Mile Canyon ride west on Canyon Blvd. (Hwy. 119) for 2 miles, then turn right on County Rd. 118 and right again at the sign for Gold Hill.

Nederland—The area around Nederland is full of possible rides. At the windswept edge of treeline is the small ghost town of **Caribou**. There are a couple of ways to get to the townsite, which lies about 5 miles west of Nederland. Caribou Rd. is a wide dirt road offering the most direct route. A rougher way, with fewer competing autos, is to follow the old mining roads up Sherwood Creek. Eventually they funnel out to Caribou Rd. near the once-booming silver camp of Caribou. Another ride near Nederland is over **Rollins Pass**. If you are in good shape, consider an all-day trip via the pass to Winter Park; have someone meet you there or ride (gasp!) back over the next day.

TOURING

Just park your car and hop on a bike. You're in Boulder, the home of Olympic cycling champions Connie Carpenter-Phinney and Davis Phinney and Tour of Italy winner Andy Hamsted, to name just a few of Boulder's famous cyclist residents. It's easy to get around town, thanks to one of the best bike trail systems in the US. The number of people in Boulder who commute to work on bikes is 10 times the national average. Partly because there are so many bicyclists, the law is especially firm when it comes to violations. Please obey the rules and ride safely.

The **Boulder Creek Path** snakes through the city starting from Eban G. Fine Park at the west end of Arapahoe Ave. It leads east along the creek, crossing several bridges and ending east of 55th St. Bring your fly-fishing gear for some surprisingly good catch-and-release action. Other trails and designated bike lanes make up more than 50 miles of bikeway. Pick up a trail map at the **Boulder Chamber of Commerce** at **2440 Pearl St.; (303) 442-1044**.

Rentals and Information—
Cycle Logic—2525 Arapahoe Ave.; (303) 443-0061.

The Spoke—At two strategic locations in Boulder, the Spoke rents touring bikes and Rock Hopper mountain bikes by the day or by the hour. **1301 Pennsylvania Ave.; (303) 442-4086** and **637 S. Broadway, Unit P; (303) 494-0977.**

University Bicycles—These folks rent 10-speeds, three-speeds, tandem bikes and mountain bikes. **839 Pearl St.; (303) 444-4196.**

FISHING

Most fishing areas near Boulder receive heavy use as all of the lakes and streams are easily accessible to more than two million Front Range residents. A unique attraction in Boulder is the **Fish Observatory,** located on the bike path just behind the **Clarion Harvest House Hotel** at **1345 28th St.** In a park setting, four round windows are built into a subterranean wall bordering Boulder Creek. The windows provide an underwater view into the natural habitat of brown, brook and cutthroat trout. Look closely enough and you may learn something about their feeding patterns. Here are a few fishing ideas.

Barker Reservoir—

At the east side of Nederland, this popular fishing spot remains a consistent producer for stocked rainbow trout in the 12-inch range. No boats are allowed on the lake, though you may see a few facetious Nederland Yacht Club T-shirts. The water line at Barker Reservoir tends to fluctuate greatly.

Boulder Creek—

There are many sections of this small stream that are quite productive. **South Boulder Creek** flows down from the Continental Divide near Rollins Pass. The fishing on the South Fork can be good for smallish cutthroat trout all along Forest Rd. 149 near the East Portal of the Moffat Tunnel. At the tunnel, a smattering of small lakes—including **Arapaho Lakes, Crater Lakes** and **Forest Lakes**—are accessible by trail. Though they are heavily fished, there

is pretty good fishing for rainbow, brown and cutthroat trout. Fishing within the steep canyon below Gross Reservoir is excellent, but hard to reach.

Some good evening fly-fishing can be found within the Boulder city limits on Boulder Creek. It is all catch and release, and some of the trout—brook, brown and cutthroat—grow to large sizes.

Boulder Reservoir—

Warmwater fishing for species including crappie, catfish and largemouth bass can be good at this city-owned water supply. Unless you are a Boulder resident with a permit, boating is prohibited on weekends. For bank fishing try the deep water near the dam embankment. Take the Longmont Diagonal (Hwy. 119) east of Boulder and turn left on 51st St. Travel north for a couple of miles to the gatehouse. Fee charged; open year-round.

Brainard Lake—

Everyone likes to spend Sun. afternoons at Brainard Lake. A large campground is nearby, and the use is extremely heavy. The lake is in a beautiful setting just a few miles west of Ward. Fishing can be good for stocked rainbow and brown trout. A half mile up South St. Vrain Creek is **Long Lake**, which is limited to flies and lures. A 1-mile trail leads up above Long Lake to **Lake Isabelle**; flies and lures only.

FOUR-WHEEL-DRIVE TRIPS

Rollins Pass Road—

This classic drive was once open to passenger cars. Today a section of the historic route near the top of the pass is rough four-wheel-drive terrain, but the road may be improved for regular cars in the near future. For more information on the history of the road, see the Four-Wheel-Drive Trips section of the **Winter Park** chapter. To get to Rollins Pass from Boulder, drive west on Hwy. 119 to Nederland and then south on Hwy. 72 to Rollinsville. Follow the signs west from Rollinsville.

Switzerland Trail—

This rough four-wheel-drive road follows the path of the narrow-gauge railroad that once carried rich gold ore from the mines to the smelters. In the early 1900s, excursion trains also made this scenic trip into the high Front Range mountains. To reach this historic route, take Canyon Blvd. (Hwy. 119) west out of Boulder for 3 miles. Turn right on County Rd. 118, which leads into Four Mile Canyon. Stay on County Rd. 118 past Salina and Wallstreet until you reach Sunset, 17 miles from Boulder. From Sunset take a sharp right onto the Switzerland Trail, which climbs uphill, eventually emerging on County Rd. 52. From here you can pass through the old mining town of Gold Hill on the return to Boulder. Another segment of the Switzerland Trail can be reached by taking a left at Sunset. This four-wheel-drive road passes by Glacier Lake before joining Hwy. 72 between Nederland and Ward.

GOLF

Flatirons Golf Course—

This 18-hole course, with many lakes and mature trees, offers a true test of skills. All of the greens are exceptionally well kept and views of nearby mountains are excellent. This is one of the most popular courses in Boulder. Therefore, advance tee times are necessary in spring and summer. 5706 Arapahoe Ave.; (303) 441-7851.

Lake Valley Golf Course—

Located 5 miles north of Boulder, Lake Valley is an 18-hole course that has been challenging golfers since 1965. As the name implies, several lakes and other water hazards come into play. Tee times are taken two days in advance. Located east of Neva Rd. on Hwy. 36; (303) 444-2114.

HIKING AND BACKPACKING

Boulder lies flush against the dramatic rocky uplift of the Rocky Mountains. Just west of Boulder, possibilities for hiking and backpacking abound. Many residents can walk from their front doors and be on trails in minutes. Why sit back and look at the mountains from afar, when you are so close? This chapter could easily be expanded into a book of its own—instead, we have a scaled-back listing of some wonderful hiking options in the Boulder Open Space and the Indian Peaks Wilderness Area. Still other trails weave through Roosevelt National Forest west of Boulder. For more information and maps contact the **Boulder Ranger District Office, 2995 Baseline Rd., Boulder, CO 80303; (303) 443-5236**, or the **City of Boulder Open Space Department, PO Box 791, 1101 Arapahoe Ave., Boulder, CO 80306; (303) 494-2194**. Topographical maps, rental equipment, supplies and other information can be obtained at **Mountain Sports, 821 Pearl St.; (303) 443-6770**, and at **The Boulder Mountaineer, 1335 Broadway; (303) 442-8355**.

South of Rocky Mountain National Park, the Indian Peaks Wilderness Area straddles both sides of the Continental Divide. Dominant peaks, alpine tundra, colorful wildflowers and a smattering of lakes set a beautiful stage for hikers. Unfortunately, the area is so popular that backpacking access is limited by a permit system. Day hikers do not need a permit, but overnight camping permits are required from June 1–Sept. 15. They are available by reservation for a small fee and on a space-available basis the day before your trip begins at no charge. For more information, contact the **Boulder Ranger District Office, 2995 Baseline Rd., Boulder, CO 80303; (303) 443-5236**.

The hikes on the west side of the Continental Divide are discussed in the Hiking and Backpacking section of the **Winter Park and Middle Park** chapter.

Arapaho Glacier—

This day trip to Boulder's water supply begins at the same trailhead as hikes to Arapaho Pass (see next entry). Break right from the Arapaho Pass Trail (No. 904) onto Trail No. 905 1 mile after setting out. This

The magnificent scenery makes the Boulder area a favorite for hikers and backpackers (photograph by Bob Huestis).

strenuous 3.5-mile hike is above treeline for most of the way, ending at the glacier at 12,700 feet. Looking longingly up at Arapaho Peak (13,397 feet) from the glacier is irresistible. If you're a hardy hiker, go ahead and scramble to the top—the views are fabulous!

Arapaho Pass—

There are a number of exciting loop trips for backpackers in the Arapaho Pass area, all of which leave from the Fourth of July trailhead. The steady uphill trail (No. 904) begins at 10,121 feet and climbs 3 miles to the pass at 11,900 feet. It follows an old stagecoach route for part of the way, and close to treeline you'll see the remains of the Fourth of July Mine. From the pass on the Continental Divide, enjoy views to the tall peaks of Rocky Mountain National Park to the north and Middle Park down below to the west. Options from the top of Arapaho Pass include dropping down to the west to Caribou Lake, then continuing southwest over Caribou Pass to Columbine Lake. Another longer trip takes you all the way down to Monarch Lake. Come back over Pawnee Pass, ending at Pawnee Campground, which is north of where you began. If you choose this route, you'll need to arrange for transportation back to your other vehicle. To reach the Fourth of July trailhead, travel west from Nederland for about 12 miles on County Rd. 107, a rough dirt road.

Boulder Open Space—

This sweeping plot of open land encircles Boulder, offering some 100 miles of excellent hiking trails just outside the city. Since 1967 Boulder citizens have been paying a tax to preserve this land from development and to set aside more for the future. This foresight has allowed residents and visitors the luxury of hiking onto the eastern plains and into beautiful mountains to the west of Boulder. For a complete trail map to Boulder Open Space, drop by the **Boulder Chamber of Commerce, 2440 Pearl St.; (303) 442-1044,** or any local sporting goods store.

Trails lead away from Boulder in clusters from designated trailheads. **Chautauqua Park**, located on the west end of Baseline Rd., has a parking area at the start of a trail leading toward the Flatirons and Bluebell Shelter. Many trails pass near the stunning formations of the Flatirons. Technical climbers are often seen hanging on these vertical rocks; inexperienced climbers should stick to walking trails to avoid becoming statistics. Other trails lead away from **Sunrise Circle Amphitheater** near the top of Flagstaff Mountain. Still others lead from the National Center for Atmospheric Research, or NCAR (see the Other Attractions section), at the west end of Table Mesa Dr.

Some of the more popular trails include **Mesa Trail**, which leads from just below Bluebell Shelter on a beautiful 6-mile southerly course to Eldorado Springs. Have a car meet you in Eldorado Springs and you won't have to backtrack. The well-defined Mesa Trail provides sweeping views of the Front Range and the Flatirons while tracking through deep woods and grassy meadows. A highly recommended short hike begins on the Mesa Trail in a northerly direction from NCAR. Merge onto **Enchanted Mesa Trail**, which ends at Chautauqua Park. Another interesting hike, beginning at the west end of Mapleton Ave. (just past Boulder Memorial Hospital), is **Mt. Sanitas Trail**, which leads to the top of the 6,863-foot mountain. The round-trip hike provides great views of Boulder and can be completed in under two hours. This is a good hike early or late in the year because of its low elevation.

Isabelle Glacier Trail—

Each weekend hundreds of people take this hike—so if you want solitude, look elsewhere. Beginning at the ever-popular Brainard Lake, Trail No. 908 leads gradually uphill to Isabelle Glacier (12,000 feet) in 2 miles. A longer trail (No. 907) goes on up to Pawnee Pass at 12,541 feet. This 4.5-mile hike is particularly steep during the final 2 miles. If you're interested in a longer backpacking loop, head over the Continental Divide to Monarch Lake and return to the east side of the divide via Arapaho Pass (see entry above). To reach the trailhead, take County Rd. 102 west of Ward for 5 miles.

HORSEBACK RIDING

Broken Arrow Ranch—

Guided or unguided trail rides can be taken for an hourly fee. Also featured are breakfast and dinner barbecue rides. Lodging is available. Located 15 miles west of Boulder from the west end of Mapleton Ave.; **(303) 459-3460.**

Heil Valley Ranch—

Located northwest of Boulder in beautiful Left Hand Canyon, this ranch offers hourly trail rides, breakfast and dinner rides and overnight trips. **(303) 444-0238.**

LLAMA TREKKING

Timberline Llamas—

Wes and Mary Mauz run a complete llama packing company that will take you on an extraordinary summer excursion. The llamas carry your gear and provide an exotic aspect to your trip, which can last from two days to more than a week. Let the Mauzes know your interests or desires, and they will tailor a backcountry trip to your specifications. For more information contact Timberline Llamas at **30361 Rainbow Hill Rd., Golden, CO 80401; (303) 526-0092** or **American Wilderness Experience** (see the River Floating section).

RIVER FLOATING

Boulder is not a great place to do any serious floating. Many people, however, get a kick out of tubing down relatively calm stretches of Boulder Creek near town. There are a few companies that provide transportation, rafts, etc., for exciting whitewater runs in other parts of the state. To arrange a trip call one of the following.

American Wilderness Experience—

These folks offer combination horseback/float trips, llama trekking and a variety of rafting expeditions. **PO Box 1486, Boulder, CO 80306; (303) 444-2632.**

Don Ferguson's White Water Rafting—

This company takes most of its trips on the Arkansas River. **1280 Ithaca, Boulder, CO 80303; (303) 494-0824.**

SKIING
CROSS-COUNTRY SKIING

Boulder is a jumping-off point for miles upon miles of fantastic cross-country terrain. Whether you prefer a gentle trail or a plunging powder run with opportunities for telemark skiing, you'll find it here. For a map of marked backcountry trails, contact the **Boulder Ranger District Office,**

2995 Baseline Rd., Boulder, CO 80303; (303) 443-5236.

Backcountry Trails—

Brainard Lake Trail System—This area is closed to snowmobilers and is very popular among cross-country skiers, so having tracks to follow is seldom a problem. Fairly difficult marked trails lead to Long Lake and Lake Isabelle, as well as farther north on Blue Lake Trail. Be aware of avalanche areas, especially above Blue Lake and Lake Isabelle. An easy trail is the southern portion of the Walthrop Loop, which is a fairly level 5-mile round trip from Brainard Lake. More experienced skiers can make a hilly loop on Walthrop North Trail. Brainard Lake is located west of Ward. Drive in as far as possible on Brainard Lake Rd. and park on the side.

Lost Lake Trail— For people with some cross-country experience, this is an excellent half-day trip which leads up an unplowed road from the town of Eldora. The 6-mile round-trip route has an elevation change of 1,000 feet. A mile after setting out, take the left fork and ski up to the townsite of Hesse. Stay on the trail for 1.5 miles and take a left cutoff on Lost Lake Trail. The trail leads south to Lost Lake in just over a half mile. An option to turning left onto Lost Lake Trail is to continue straight on **King Lake Trail**; there is some avalanche danger as you come within a mile of King Lake. To reach the trailhead from Nederland, drive a half mile south on Hwy. 119. Take the right fork to a parking area at the west end of the town of Eldora.

Rainbow Lakes Road—This easy 4.5-mile trail works its way to Rainbow Lakes. The trail is better after a recent snow because it tends to become windblown and icy in spots. The lakes are half a mile beyond the campground. The return trip is a gradual downhill. From Nederland, drive 7 miles north on Hwy. 72. Turn left at a sign indicating the Colorado University Mountain Research Station and drive a little less than a mile to the fork in the road. Begin skiing on the unplowed left fork.

Groomed Trails—

Eldora/Rossignol Nordic Center—From the southeast side of the ski area parking lot, 40 kilometers of groomed and backcountry trails take off into the woods. The nordic center offers rentals as well as instruction in skating, telemarking and touring. For a longer trip, inquire about an overnight stay at Tennessee Mountain Cabin, which sleeps up to 12. A trail fee is charged; hours are 9 am–4 pm daily. Located 21 miles west of Boulder. Take Canyon Blvd. (Hwy. 119) west to a mile beyond Nederland and turn left at the Eldora turn-off. For more information, call **(303) 440-8700.**

Rentals and Information—

The Boulder Mountaineer—1335 Broadway; **(303) 442-8355.**

Chivers Sports—2000 30th St.; (303) 442-2493.

Eldora/Rossignol Nordic Center—At Eldora Mountain Resort; **(303) 440-8700.**

Mountain Sports—821 Pearl St.; (303) 443-6770.

DOWNHILL SKIING

Eldora Mountain Resort—

Only 30 minutes from Boulder, Eldora offers downhill skiing within reach of a short commute. The modest ski area, now under new management, appears to be back on the right track. Expanded skier facilities include five double chairlifts. Lift prices are reasonable and there is rarely a wait. Most of the terrain is intermediate, with some beginner and expert slopes. For the first time in many years the expert Corona Bowl, on the back side of the mountain, is open. Newly placed wind blocks should keep the snow here, so skiers can enjoy the steep pitch all winter long. Wind is the only nemesis at Eldora—toward the top it can be really gusty, though much of the mountain is protected by trees. More than half the mountain is lighted for night skiing, at a bargain price, from 3–9:30

pm Wed.–Sat. Snowboarders take note: there is a half pipe at Eldora. Rentals are available at the base. The lodge serves breakfast, lunch and dinner. Upstairs, the Alpenhorn is a great après-ski hangout.

Eldora is 21 miles west of Boulder. Take Canyon Blvd. (Hwy. 119) west to a mile beyond Nederland and turn left at the Eldora turn-off. There is RTD bus service five times daily (three times on Sun.) from Boulder. For more information, call **(303) 440-8700** in metro Denver.

SWIMMING

Boulder Reservoir—
It's not the prettiest beach in the world, but it is a beach. The "Res" is a fun place to swim and suntan; also available are boating, canoeing and windsurfing. Take the Longmont Diagonal (Hwy. 119) east of Boulder and turn left on 51st St. Travel north for 1.5 miles to the gatehouse; open Memorial Day–Labor Day; fee charged. **(303) 441-3468.**

Eldorado Artesian Springs—
Once a famed resort, Eldorado Artesian Springs has slipped a bit over the years. It is located just outside the entrance to Eldorado Canyon State Park. A day here can include swimming, hiking, picnicking and watching climbers hang on the canyon's sheer rock walls. The pool is naturally heated from geothermal waters more than a mile beneath the surface; the water is comfortably warm. Eldorado Springs is located 5.5 miles south of Boulder on Hwy. 93, then west on Hwy. 170 for 3 miles; open Memorial Day–Labor Day; fee charged. **(303) 499-1316.**

Scott Carpenter Pool—
This is a great outdoor pool that also boasts a 150-foot water slide. Open in summer only; small fee charged. **30th St. and Arapahoe Ave.; (303) 441-3427.**

TENNIS

Arapahoe Ridge—
Two courts; **1280 43rd St.**

Chautauqua Park—
One extremely scenic court. Everyone assumes that because there is only one court, it's always full. You'll never know unless you give it a chance. **9th St. and Baseline Rd.**

Martin Park—
Two courts; **36th St. and Dartmouth.**

North Boulder Recreation Center—
Four lighted courts. Fee charged only for reservations and lights. **3170 N. Broadway; 441-3444.**

South Boulder Recreation Center—
Four lighted courts. Fee charged only for reservations and lights. **1360 Gillaspie St.; 441-3448.**

WINDSURFING

Boulder Reservoir—
This is the place to learn how to windsurf or to show off your skills. Conditions are usually good, but at times the wind can be fierce. You can arrange lessons and rentals at the reservoir. Take the Longmont Diagonal (Hwy. 119) east of Boulder and turn left on 51st St. Travel north for 1.5 miles to the gatehouse; **(303) 441-3456.**

——— SEEING AND DOING ———

MUSEUMS AND GALLERIES

Boulder is a town of few museums and many galleries. Numerous galleries are located along the Pearl Street Mall. A standout is the **Boulder Arts & Crafts Cooperative**, featuring the works of 72 local artists. It is located at **1421 Pearl St.; (303) 443-3683.** For quality western paintings and sculpture, visit the **Leanin' Tree Gallery and Museum of Western Art, 6055 Longbow Drive; (303) 530-1442.** For southwestern art, see the **White Horse Gallery** on the Pearl Street Mall; **(303) 443-6116.** Another recommended stop is the **University Memorial Center** on campus, which features an ever-changing collection of art from nationally recognized artists as well as CU students.

Mapleton Hill Walking Tour—

See some of Boulder's grandest homes on this fine residential walking tour in a historic neighborhood. Pick up a self-guiding brochure at the **Boulder Chamber of Commerce, 2440 Pearl St.; (303) 442-1044.**

University of Colorado Museum—

This fine museum features subjects ranging from paleontology to anthropology and botany. Since the museum was established in 1902, it has grown to include a diversity of exhibits. Lectures, courses and special traveling exhibits are also offered at the museum. Located on campus at **15th St.** and **Broadway; (303) 492-6165.**

NIGHTLIFE

Boulder is bursting with nightlife. There is always something going on at the Pearl Street Mall (see the Major Attractions section) and at its many bars and cafes. Listed below are a few of the standout places that should stay in business for the foreseeable future. This is just a small sampling. For a more complete listing, check the *Colorado Daily* or the *Boulder Daily Camera* newspapers. The easiest way to get the latest happenings is to call the KBCO Entertainment Line at **(303) 444-5226** for a recorded message.

Boulder's Coast—

Every night something different is going on at Boulder's hottest dance club. Nationally known groups make this a regular stop on their circuit. Nightly themes include back-to-the-beach parties and skirt parties. Ladies' Nights have been ruled discriminatory in Boulder, so anyone in a skirt, male or female, can take advantage of cheap drinks. On Sat., Boulder's Coast is hopping till 2 am and at an after-hours party until 5 am with a free breakfast buffet. **2950 Baseline Rd.; 440-4399.**

Boulder Dinner Theater—

Since 1976 this dinner theater has provided complete evenings of dining and entertainment. A professional acting troupe with members from around the US puts on Broadway-style shows, including *Cabaret, West Side Story, A Chorus Line* and *Evita.* Unlike at some dinner theaters, the food here is chosen from a menu—prime rib, spinach lasagna and chicken teriyaki are a few of the entrées—and the performers also wait the tables. Our waiter, Jeff, played a domineering blonde female with a nasty disposition in *La Cage Aux Folles.* Yes, it was a shock! There isn't a bad seat in the house, but if you reserve early enough you can request a seat close to the stage. If a performance is sold out, go ahead and stop by. The theater will buy you a drink, and if there are any no-shows, you can buy their tickets. If no tickets become available, at least you've had a free drink. Open Tues.–Sun. **5501 Arapahoe Ave.; (303) 449-6000.**

Hotel Boulderado Mezzanine—

If you want a quiet, classy place to sink back into a comfortable chair and enjoy good conversation with a friend, head for the Mezzanine. On many evenings the Boulderado features subdued live music in its historic setting. The Mezzanine overlooks the lobby from the second floor and is topped by a magnificent stained-glass ceiling. See the Where to Stay section for more information on the hotel. **13th St.** and **Spruce; (303) 442-4344.**

The James Pub and Grille—

Just your neighborhood Irish pub. The James features live Irish music on weekends and good Irish beer all of the time. By dictate of the Guinness Brewery, "black and tans" are made from 100 percent Irish beer: Guinness Stout and Harp Lager (instead of the usual Watneys). An outdoor patio and a glassed-in greenhouse provide a wonderful atmosphere on summer evenings. The James is also a good restaurant (their specialty is corned beef and cabbage), with an excellent selection of appetizers. Open nightly. Located just off the mall at **1922 13th St.; 449-1922.**

Old Chicago—

So, you want to join the ranks of the elite members of the Beer Hall of Foam? Old Chicago offers a lengthy list of more than 100 beers from around the world; you can become a member by sampling one from each country. Old Chicago also serves legendary deep-dish pizza. For dessert or a late-night snack, try their deep-dish chocolate chip cookie with a scoop of ice cream; it's enough to keep four adults happy. **11th St.** and **Pearl St.; (303) 443-5031.**

West End Tavern—

This neighborhood tavern is a great place to hang out. The 100-year-old oak bar—brought to Boulder from Miss Kitty's Saloon in Nebraska—fits into its present home in the tavern with less than a quarter inch to spare. See the Where to Eat section for more information. Between **9th St.** and **10th St.** on **Pearl St.; (303) 444-3535.**

SCENIC DRIVES

Eldorado Springs—

Just south of Boulder at the base of a narrow, rocky canyon is the small community of Eldorado Springs. This town enjoyed a heyday in the early 1900s, when it became known as a fashionable spa. Warm artesian spring water was funneled into pools, and guests enjoyed comfortable rooms and a choice of restaurants. Today, the spa has lost its glossy image, but it is still a good place to swim (see the Swimming section).

Just beyond Eldorado Artesian Springs is Eldorado Canyon State Park. After buying an inexpensive parks pass at a self-serve station near the entrance, head into this land of sheer cliffs that reach for the

sky. Climbers from around the world come here for the challenge and joy of technical climbing. If you're not a climber, it's a great place to hike or relax and watch; bring along a picnic lunch. No camping is allowed. To reach Eldorado Springs, take Broadway south of Boulder for 5.5 miles. Turn right on Eldorado Springs Dr. (Hwy. 170) and continue 3 miles.

Flagstaff Mountain—

This is a quick, winding route up Flagstaff Mountain that overlooks Boulder from the west. The paved road has several pull-offs; after a few miles of continuous uphill driving there is a turn-off for the Sunrise Circle Amphitheater. Turn right and continue to a magnificent overlook of Boulder. At the amphitheater there are picnic tables and a trailhead for several hiking trails. There is also a nice view at night of the lights of Boulder. To reach Flagstaff Mountain, drive west on Baseline Rd. and keep going.

Peak to Peak Highway—

By taking any of the canyons west of Boulder, you'll soon end up on the spectacular Peak to Peak Highway. This road stretches all the way from Central City to Estes Park, with beautiful mountain scenery the whole route. In fall, the shimmering aspen stands provide a show of epic proportions.

A good loop trip from Boulder, saturated in history and natural beauty, begins at the west end of Canyon Blvd. (Hwy. 119). This old mining road was improved in 1915 by convict labor. The citizens of Boulder were so grateful, they put on a lavish luncheon for the prisoners at the Hotel Boulderado. After 8.5 miles on the twisting, paved road, there is a parking turnout on the left (south) side for **Boulder Falls.** Cross the highway and after a short distance you'll be face to face with North Boulder Creek cascading over wildly eroded rocks. It's a torrent during spring runoff. Another 8 miles west on Hwy. 119, the road comes out of the canyon at **Nederland.** This small town was born as a supply center to the nearby silver camp of **Caribou** a few miles to the west. In 1873 a few Dutch investors bought the Caribou Mine, which was producing $3 million a year by 1875. The glory years were short-lived, though, because of the demonetization of silver in 1893. Caribou is a ghost town today, but Nederland (named for the Dutch-owned mine) is still going strong. In town are a couple of restaurants, including the popular Pioneer Bar.

From Nederland turn right on Hwy. 72 (the Peak to Peak Highway), which provides stunning views on the way to **Ward**, 14 miles north. (A left would take you toward Rollinsville and eventually to Central City.) Ward is an old gold camp that has survived to accommodate a new generation of residents who prefer quiet and solitude. Situated in a narrow canyon, the town is one of the more beautiful near-ghost towns in the state. The schoolhouse and the church are two landmarks that survived a disastrous fire in 1900. Just north of Ward, a marked turn-off heads west for less than 5 miles to **Brainard Lake**. The view of the Indian Peaks from this popular mountain lake is astounding. For more information about some of the trails in the area, see the Hiking and Backpacking section. From Ward continue 27 miles north to **Estes Park** on Hwy. 7 (see the **Estes Park** chapter for more information) and loop back to Boulder on Hwy. 36. Or drop back toward Boulder via Left Hand Canyon.

WHERE TO STAY

ACCOMMODATIONS

Hotel Boulderado — $$$ to $$$$

This historic hotel opened with a bash on New Year's Day in 1909. It's a graceful brick hotel built with a style and elegance similar to that of the Brown Palace Hotel in Denver. A stained-glass mezzanine ceiling is clearly visible from the ornate lobby. The hotel thrived from day one; rooms were furnished in the finest style and equipped with both gas and electricity. Many famous guests stayed at the Boulderado, including Teddy Roosevelt (where didn't he stay?), Helen Keller, Louis Armstrong and Robert Frost. One controversial guest was traveling evangelist Billy Sunday who delivered his hell-fire sermons to the people of Boulder while staying at the Boulderado. He described the town as "a sinkhole of iniquity, crying for redemption."

The hotel declined dramatically during the 1960s and early 1970s, but was resurrected in the early 1980s. In 1985 a new expansion connected by a walkway added 61 rooms. Both the old and new portions of the hotel are reminiscent of the Victorian era. However, some of the "feel" of an old hotel, with its creaky floors and manual Otis elevator, is lost on the new side. Each of the rooms and suites has a unique personality; rooms on the upper floors have better views. Staying at the Boulderado entitles guests to a complimentary pass at a nearby full-service health club. Downstairs are three restaurants, three lounges and an oyster bar. **The Steak Porch** for dinner and the **Mezzanine** for cocktails couldn't be better. Reservations recommended. **2115 13th St., Boulder, CO 80302; (303) 442-4344 or 1-800-433-4344.**

Briar Rose — $$$

Hospitality is a genuine art and Emily Hunter, the owner of the Briar Rose, is a master artist. You will feel right at home in her immaculate 11-room bed and breakfast. The rooms are beautifully furnished in antiques, and the beds are topped with puffy feather comforters. Although it's in the heart of town, the Briar Rose is protected from the outside world by a dense shield of shrubbery and trees. An elegant continental breakfast is served each morning, in your room or out on the glass-enclosed sun porch. A common room open to all guests is filled with comfortable couches and chairs arranged around a fireplace; a decanter of sherry stands ready to be poured. Reservations encouraged. **2151 Arapahoe Ave., Boulder, CO 80302; (303) 442-3007.**

The Bluebird Lodge — $$

Built of rough-hewn logs in 1872 to accommodate travelers passing through the booming town of Gold Hill, the Bluebird Lodge invites guests to take a step back in time. You can also enjoy the present-day comforts of the outdoor hot tub and full complimentary breakfast served each morning in the formal dining room. The lodge is furnished with antiques that were stored in the attic for years. Each room features flowered quilts, antique bedframes (new mattresses) and no clutter. Nine rooms share four baths. As Barbara and Frank Finn, owners for the past 26 years, put it: "Our atmosphere is rustic and our ghosts are hospitable." Open in summer only. The Finns also operate the Gold Hill Inn, next door to the lodge (see the Where to Eat section). For information, contact the **Gold Hill Inn, Gold Hill, Boulder, CO 80302; (303) 443-6461.**

Foot of the Mountain Motel — $$

This motel, with its inordinate amount of charm, sits at the base of the mountains on the outskirts of Boulder. The convenience of the city blends well with unobstructed mountain views. Most rooms have bathtubs that offer spectacular window views up Flagstaff Mountain. The Foot of the Mountain conjures up the feeling of a mountain cabins with its rough bark exterior, bright red paint around the windowsills, blooming flower boxes and all-wood interior. All rooms are equipped with private baths, cable TV and small refrigerators. **200 Arapahoe Ave., Boulder, CO 80302; (303) 442-5688.**

Nederhouse Motel — $$

About a half hour from Boulder in the small community of Nederland you will find the Nederhouse Motel. From the outside it doesn't look like anything special, but all of the comfortable rooms are furnished tastefully in antiques. One recent guest said he liked everything about the Nederhouse "except the old furniture." Chances are you'll like something about this place. The Nederhouse is only 3 miles from Eldora Mountain Resort. Located on Hwy. 119 at the Eldora turn-off, **PO Box 220, Nederland, CO 80466; (303) 444-4705.**

CAMPING

Boulder Parks and Recreation—

Fourth of July Campground has only 10 tent sites, no water and no fee. It is a primitive campground reached by a rough dirt road. Its proximity to the Indian Peaks Wilderness Area trailheads is a major advantage. To reach the campground, travel west from Nederland on County Rd. 107 for about 12 miles.

In Roosevelt National Forest—

Located west of Boulder are a number of first-come, first-served campgrounds. Three miles south of Nederland on Hwy. 119 is **Kelly-Dahl Campground** with beautiful views of the Continental Divide. There are 48 sites and a fee. **Rainbow Lakes Campground** is reached by taking Hwy. 72 for 6.5 miles north of Nederland to a sign that reads Mountain Research Station. Turn left and continue on a rough dirt road for 5 miles. There are 18 sites, no drinking water and no fee. **Pawnee Campground** is 5 miles west of Ward on County Rd. 102. This extremely popular area near Brainard Lake has 76 sites and a fee.

To reach **Peaceful Valley Campground**, drive 15 miles west from Lyons on Hwy. 7 to the junction with Hwy. 72. Turn left and continue southwest on Hwy. 72 for 6 miles. There are 15 sites and a fee. **Camp Dick Campground** is located another mile west of Peaceful Valley. There are 34 sites and a fee.

Private Campground—

Boulder Mountain Lodge—Next to a gurgling creek, just five minutes away from Boulder, is a small RV and tent campground with a motel. The motel rooms ($$)

are clean and comfortable and some are equipped with kitchenettes. This is a really nice family place located at the former town of Ordell. The office is in the old narrow-gauge train depot. There are ma- ture trees, a small outdoor pool and a year-round hot tub. Kids will love fishing in the private pond. **91 Four Mile Canyon Rd., Boulder, CO 80302; (303) 444-0882.**

WHERE TO EAT

Flagstaff House — $$$$

Plan on arriving at Flagstaff House before dark so you can enjoy the commanding view of Boulder as dusk settles slowly over the valley. This restaurant, with tiered decks and glassed-in seating areas, virtually hangs from the side of Flagstaff Mountain. Once darkness takes over, the twinkling lights of Boulder are a beautiful accompaniment to your meal. The menu is not necessarily traditional—more than 40 entrées are served, including grilled rack of Colorado lamb, elk with ginger sauce, Maine lobster and pheasant breast. Flagstaff House is just about the only restaurant in Boulder where you must dress up. Valet parking; reservations requested. Open for dinner from 6 pm Mon.–Thur. and from 5 pm Fri.–Sun. To reach Flagstaff House, head west on Baseline Rd. and continue about halfway up Flagstaff Mountain and look for the sign. **442-4640.**

Red Lion Inn — $$$ to $$$$

Minutes from Boulder in a mountain setting, this wooden turn-of-the-century lodge has retained its original charm. The downstairs is dark and intimate, while the upstairs porch has a more casual feel. The Red Lion is known for wild game entrées such as buffalo and caribou; they also specialize in tableside service. It's always quite a show when someone orders a flambé dish, such as the Genghis Khan. The early bird specials (Mon.–Fri. 5–6:15 pm; Sat. 4:30–5:45 pm; Sun. 4–6:15 pm) are always real bargains. Reservations recommended. Open from 5 pm Mon.–Fri. and from 4:30 pm on Sat.; from 4 pm Sun. Located a couple of miles up Boulder Canyon (Hwy. 119); **442-9368.**

John's Restaurant — $$$

Since 1973 John Bizarro has been preparing European dishes at his own restaurant. His cooking has received wide acclaim for its balance, presentation and—most importantly—taste. After spending 20 years learning his trade in Italy and the US, Bizarro opened this tiny restaurant. It's formal yet comfortable. Linen tablecloths and fresh flowers adorn the tables. His dinner specials are unique creations that should be considered before looking at the regular menu. Nightly offerings include poached salmon in white wine, cream and dill sprigs, tenderloin of beef au poivre and chicken á la moutarde. The wine list is small but carefully chosen. For dessert, try homemade ice cream, a walnut fudge torte or Bizarro's caramel cheesecake. Reservations recommended; open each evening from 6 pm. **2328 Pearl St.; 444-5232.**

Gold Hill Inn — $$$

Barbara and Frank Finn operate this inn next door to the Bluebird Lodge in Gold Hill (see the Where to Stay section). Renowned for its delicious six-course dinners, there is a nightly choice of five or six entrées; virtually everything is homemade. Call ahead for special entrées and vegetarian dishes. Dinner by reservation only; closed in winter. For more information contact **Gold Hill Inn, Gold Hill, Boulder, CO 80302; (303) 443-6461.**

Brophy's Salmon Run — $$ to $$$$

Are we still in Boulder? This upscale eatery feels as though it belongs on the coast. The atmosphere is enhanced by three tremendous saltwater fishtanks built into the backbar. Watch exotic fish swimming around while you select from a menu that includes Maryland crab cakes, broiled shark teriyaki, poached salmon with hollandaise sauce and steamed clams. Also available are pasta and seafood combinations. Pete Brophy has been bringing fresh seafood to Boulder since 1973. Daily specials by chef Mark Shockley are served. Open for lunch from 11:15 am–3 pm Mon.–Fri.; dinner is served nightly from 5–10 pm. Closed Sun. **880 Walnut St.; 449-6565.**

Royal Peacock Cuisine of India — $$ to $$$

From the outside of this restaurant in a small shoppette, you'd never expect such a comfortable, classy interior. The muted wall colors are interrupted by colorful splashes of India, and the food is authentic. When Bombay resident Rajan Mehta says it's "the best Indian food in the USA," who are we to argue? Dishes such as lamb with lentils and a variety of northwest Indian specialties—tandoor, biryani and chapati—fill the menu. The weekday luncheon buffet gives you the chance to try a number of different items at one sitting. Full bar is available. Open for lunch from 11:30 am–2:30 pm Mon.–Fri.; dinner is served each evening from 5:30–10:30 pm; open at 5 pm on Sun. **5290 Arapahoe Rd.; 447-1409.**

Blue Parrot Cafe — $$

We hope the fire that closed the Blue Parrot for most of 1988 will not change the spirit of the place. Located in the small community of Louisville (residents pronounce the s), this landmark restaurant first opened in 1919. It has been treasured for years as one of the best places for down-home Italian cooking in the state. A plateful of thick homemade spaghetti and an extra pot of sauce is the main reason to eat here; top off your meal with some spumoni. Behind the restaurant the old guard passes time by playing the Italian game of boccie ball. This place is for real. In addition to serving lunch and dinner it is open for breakfast; if you like leftover pizza in the morning, you'll love the option of

ordering a side of spaghetti instead of potatoes. Open 6 am–9 pm Mon.–Thur., 6 am–10 pm Fri., 8 am–10 pm Sat., 8 am–8 pm Sun. **640 Main St., Louisville; 666-0677.**

Lick Skillet Cafe — $ to $$$

A beautiful 20-minute drive up Sunshine Canyon to Gold Hill will be further rewarded by a stop at the Lick Skillet. This small, personal restaurant features five-star food and service for breakfast, lunch and dinner. Owned and operated by former Flagstaff House chefs Eric Burson and Michael Thomas, the restaurant features exquisite cuisine in a causal atmosphere. A leisurely breakfast inside or on the patio is always special. Since reservations are not accepted for breakfast and lunch on weekends, the wait for a table is commonly more than an hour. Dinner at the Lick Skillet features artistically arranged food on oversized glass plates. The menu is brief, but the carefully prepared continental dishes are more than you could ever hope for in this log cabin village. *Breakfast and lunch are served on weekends only*; dinner is served Thur.–Sun. Call ahead for times. 10 miles west of Boulder in Gold Hill; **449-7775.**

Nancy's — $ to $$$

Nancy's does a wonderful job with breakfast, lunch and dinner—all served in a charming old house with a private outdoor patio. Over the past decade this small restaurant has become a local habit. For breakfast try a blintz, eggs Benedict or a bagel with lox and cream cheese. The lunch menu shifts toward a healthy blend of soups, salads, sandwiches and entrées. Vegetarians also have some choices here. Dinner selections include prime rib, veal picatta, chicken amaretto and tortellini. There is a full bar; fine coffees and espresso are served. Breakfast hours are 7–11:30 am Mon.–Fri., 7:30 am–2:30 pm weekends, lunch hours are 11:30 am–2 pm weekdays only; dinner is served 5:30–9 pm Tues.–Sat. **825 Walnut St.; 449-8402.**

Aristocrat Steak House — $ to $$

On weekends for the past 15 years,

customers have lined up outside this raucous breakfast and lunch joint. The cooks often holler at the top of their lungs, as if their verbal antics will cook the food faster. The restaurant is fairly small, but the portions are huge—just try to finish Nick's Special Omelette with six eggs, ham, cheese, peppers, onions and tomatoes. Did we forget to mention the heaping side of hashbrown potatoes that comes with every order? The best deal in town for lunch is the steak sandwich; other mid-day items include burgers, gyros and Greek salads. All items are also available for takeout. Open 7 am–3 pm Mon.–Fri.; until 4 pm on weekends. **2053 Broadway; 444-8688.**

Boulder Brewing Company Tasting Room — $ to $$

At the brewery's tasting room you can enjoy bratwurst simmered in their porter beer. Also served are soups, sandwiches and the freshest beer possible—only two days old. Try the extra pale ale, because it rivals the very best! See the Other Attractions section for more information. From the tasting room and the outdoor patio, enjoy an incredible view of the Flatirons. Open for lunch from 11 am–2 pm Mon.–Sat.; tastings are from 11 am–5 pm weekdays and until 3 pm on Sat. **2880 Wilderness Pl.; 444-8448.**

Chautauqua Dining Hall — $ to $$

The atmosphere on the porch of the historic Chautauqua Dining Hall is the main reason to eat here. A wide balcony overlooks grassy Chautauqua Park and offers wide mountain views. It's a good choice for breakfast, lunch and dinner. The food is traditional: omelettes and pancakes for breakfast, sandwiches for lunch and full entrées for dinner. On weekends there is usually a long wait for breakfast, but you can order coffee and banana bread and wait in the park for your turn: it's the most pleasant waiting room in Boulder. Chautauqua is also the perfect place to come for dinner before a festival or event at the drafty all-wood Chautauqua Auditorium, built in 1898. No reservations. *Open*

in summer only from 7 am–2 pm for breakfast, 11:30 am–2 pm for lunch, 5:30–9 pm for dinner. **Chautauqua Park, 900 Baseline Rd.; 440-3776.**

Dot's Diner — $ to $$

This is the ultimate dive restaurant. A gas station with working gas pumps and two bays shares space with a funky diner. If you can get a seat at a table or at the counter, you'll be treated to a great breakfast burrito, legendary huevos rancheros, homemade muffins or biscuits and gravy. In summer you can walk around back to a newly opened garden patio with five more tables. Open for breakfast and lunch from 7 am–2 pm Mon.–Fri., 8 am–2 pm on weekends. **799 Pearl St.; 449-1323.**

Lucile's — $ to $$

On a side street just off the Boulder Mall is the kind of restaurant you love to happen upon. Lucile's serves breakfast and lunch in the casual confines of an old house. The covered porch is the best place to sit on warm summer mornings; inside, the small rooms create a feeling of intimacy. For breakfast it is hard to imagine a tastier dish than the Cajun Breakfast—red beans, poached eggs topped with hollandaise sauce and served with grits or potatoes and a buttermilk biscuit. Spicy lunch dishes include gumbo, shrimp Creole and blackened red snapper. Open 7 am–2 pm weekdays, 8 am–2 pm weekends. **2124 14th St.; 442-4743.**

West End Tavern — $ to $$

"A stiff drink and a good portion of food for a reasonable price is what most people want," according to the owner of the new West End Tavern. "You can't finish what I serve you," he adds. The lunch and dinner menu (one and the same) has prices from a decade past. The food is nothing fancy, but it always tastes good, and the portions are huge. Choose from barbecue sandwiches, cheeseburgers, special hot dogs from Newark, New Jersey, and Jailhouse Chili with corn chips. When it's warm outside, make your way to the rooftop deck for a terrific view of the Flatirons. The only complaint about sitting inside at the West End is the thick cigarette smoke, otherwise unheard of in Boulder. Open from 11 am daily. Between 9th St. and 10th St. on **Pearl St.; 444-3535.**

Marie's Cafe — $

Rudy Bargak and his family came to America from Czechoslovakia one year after the 1968 rebellion was quelled by Russian tanks. "It was their tanks versus our tomatoes and eggs," he recalls. Instead of throwing eggs, Bargak now serves eggs with buttery hash browns and a kolacky— a delicious Czechoslovakian specialty. It's worth coming here just for a taste of this sweet-tasting roll filled with jam and cottage cheese. Lunch items include soups, sandwiches, diet plates and fish. For a touch of the Old World in a truly American shoppette, try this small restaurant. Open 7 am–2 pm daily. **2630 Broadway; 447-0320.**

Naoki's — $

If you are hungry for a quick, satisfying meal, stop by Naoki's. Japanese-style noodle dishes are served with only the freshest ingredients. Put your order in at the counter and don't forget the tip jar— it's actually a fund to "reorient some disoriented Orientals." This small restaurant has indoor and outdoor seating. Open Mon.–Sat. 11:30 am–8:30 pm; 5:30–8:30 pm on Sun. **1083 14th St.; 447-9837.**

Tra-Ling's Oriental Cafe — $

Another quick lunch and dinner spot on the hill is this bargain-priced Chinese restaurant. It offers your choice of entrée, rice and noodles for almost nothing. Open 11:30 am–9:30 pm Mon.–Fri.; Sat.–Sun. 4:30–9:30 pm. Free delivery. **1305 Broadway; 449-0400.**

SERVICES

Boulder Chamber of Commerce—

2440 Pearl St., Boulder, CO 80302; (303) 442-1044.

Transportation—

Boulder Airporter—One-way van service to the airport for a reasonable price. **(303) 499-1559.**

Boulder RTD Bus Service—For information on bus service in town and to Stapleton International Airport, call **RTD** at **(303) 778-6000** or stop by the Boulder Chamber of Commerce and pick up a free schedule (see listing above).

Boulder Yellow Cab—(303) 442-2277.

Day Care—

City of Boulder Child Care Support Center—Information and referrals for child care. (303) 441-3180.

YWCA and YMCA—Both of these organizations have referral lists of baby-sitters. The YWCA has emergency child care Mon.–Fri. (303) 442-2778.

Central City

As you drive up the mile-long road from Black Hawk to Central City and look at the many old houses perched on the steep mountainsides, it's easy to see how ill-suited the surrounding area is for a town. But early settlers had a very good reason for choosing this location. In the spring of 1859, gold strikes along Gregory Gulch fueled the first big rush to Colorado (at the time called Kansas) Territory. For years Central City and the surrounding mining camps captured the imagination of the nation, prompting droves of settlers to head west. Serving as a catalyst for settlement in Colorado, Central City was also the cultural center for the state. The town's tradition of theater and opera goes back to the 1860s. Today, many summer visitors to this Victorian mining town attend the renowned Central City Opera.

If you don't like opera, don't worry; there are plenty of other things to do. Visit one of the many interesting museums or investigate the stone buildings in the downtown area, which is now a National Historic District. A nice diversion might be spending some time at one of the many fine restaurants or historic bars, several of which boast decors and atmospheres that have remained unchanged for more than a hundred years. Or drive to some of the neighboring towns—say, Nevadaville or Apex—and to any number of old cemeteries. It's not a good idea to hike on the surrounding hills, due to hundreds of abandoned mines. Although the droves of visitors who flock here in summer have inspired a number of tacky tourist shops, a trip to Central City is an outstanding way to learn about a fascinating period in Colorado's history.

HISTORY

In the spring of 1859, when Georgia prospector John H. Gregory made his way up a side gulch of North Clear Creek, he couldn't possibly have known just how much gold he was about to find. At a spot between Central City and Black Hawk, he found what he was looking for at a place later called Gregory Gulch. The town of Mountain City grew around Gregory's claim, and by the end of the year thousands of residents were clamoring around the area. Colorado's first major gold rush was on, eventually producing more than a half billion dollars' worth of minerals. Many camps were established in the area, including Black Hawk, Gregory Point, Missouri City, Nevadaville, Hoosier City, Dogtown and, of course, Central City—so named for its central location in the gulch. Out of convenience, miners from the surrounding camps would meet here, and it quickly grew into the main supply center.

Placer strikes continued into the 1860s and many miners became rich. Central City continued to grow and for a few years rivaled Denver as the largest town in the territory. But by the mid-1860s the placer mining began petering out. No one doubted there was still plenty of gold left in the hills, but it was trapped in quartz formations, making it uneconomical to remove. In 1867 Prof. Nathaniel P. Hill came to the rescue. Hill, a chemistry professor from Brown University, had studied mining techniques on the East Coast and in Europe. He built the Boston-Colorado Smelter in Black Hawk, which could economically break down the refractory gold ore. That put the mining boom back on its feet. With the smelter and the arrival of the Colorado & Southern Railroad from Denver in 1872, Black Hawk grew into quite a town of its own.

Hardrock mining proceeded at a frenzied pace. On Quartz Hill, between Central City and Nevadaville, the Mammoth vein was discovered, over the years producing millions in gold, silver, lead and copper. The largest mine along the Mammoth vein was the Glory Hole, a highly profitable open-pit mine that helped the area around Quartz Hill to become known as "the richest square mile on Earth."

Aside from mining, Central City is well known for the cultural mark it left on the state. The area drew a diverse group of immigrant miners, including Chinese, Russians, Canadians, Scots and Englishmen. The Cornish miners from England had the greatest influence on the town. Their mortarless stone walls characterize both Central City and Black Hawk to this day. More importantly, they were active participants in and patrons of the opera and the theater. From the beginning, the community supported amateur shows performed in makeshift tents. In July 1862 the Montana Theatre opened. Its debut performance went on as planned, despite the fact that on the previous day George W. Harrison, the owner, fired 35 shots into local boxer Charlie Swits. His defense at the trial was that he "didn't like Swits." The jury must have agreed, because Harrison was acquitted. He eventually went on to become a state senator. The Montana Theatre played to packed houses until 1874, when a raging fire wiped out most of the wooden buildings and homes in Central City. Blame was placed on the Chinese, who were accused of allowing their joss sticks and incense to burn out of control during a religious ceremony.

Residents of Central City began to rebuild after the fire, using stone in place of wood to prevent further catastrophes. Evening entertainment resumed in 1875 with the completion of the new Belvidere Theatre, whose operatic and theatrical productions received rave reviews statewide. After a performance of *Bohemia Girl* brought down the house, townsfolk began planning a new opera house worthy of such quality performances. Twenty thousand dollars was raised, the Gilpin County Opera House Association was formed and construction of the impressive **Central City Opera House** began. As work progressed, the building's unique and beautiful architecture caught the attention of the Denver newspapers. In December of 1877 the *Rocky Mountain News* reported that the opera house construction was proceeding just fine and promised "the most beautiful auditorium to be found between Chicago and San Francisco." The opera house finally opened in the spring of 1878 to packed houses. Numerous dramas were also performed by famous thespians of the time, such as Sarah Bernhardt and Edwin Booth.

In the 1880s the Central City area experienced a decline in fortunes. With silver prices going up, the central economic focus of Colorado shifted from the dwindling gold fields of Central City to the booming silver town of Leadville. By 1890 many townsfolk had moved on. Along with a loss of local patrons, the Central City Opera House lost business when Tabor's Grand Opera House was built in Denver.

Although some mining continued well into the 1900s, Central City was on its way to becoming another ghost town. Peter McFarlane, who had taken over control of the opera house in 1896, kept it open despite consistent losses. In 1910 he began using the building to show the latest craze . . . motion pictures. This continued until 1927. Then, after staying closed for more than four years, the opera house experienced a rebirth, when the McFarlane family donated the building to the University of Denver. Funds were raised and restoration began. In the summer of 1932 the opera house reopened with the production of *Camille*, starring Lillian Gish. It was an immediate success and drew large crowds from Denver.

Today the summer opera performances are still going strong and are the main attraction of this small town. Periodically, some of the mines reopen, but the glory days of Central City are now only a memory.

GETTING THERE

Central City is located 30 miles west of Denver. From Golden, head west up Clear Creek Canyon on Hwy. 6 and then northwest on Hwy. 119 to Black Hawk. Central City is located 1 mile west of Black Hawk on Hwy. 279.

—— FESTIVALS AND EVENTS ——

Lou Bunch Day
third Saturday in June

Although Central City had very few brothels in comparison with many other mining towns in Colorado, each year the town holds a celebration in remembrance of their last madam—Lou Bunch, who left town in 1916. On Lou Bunch Day, the townsfolk dress up in period costumes (heavy on the garters) and have a brass bed race through town. In the evening, the Madams and Miners Ball takes place at the Teller House. All events are free except for the ball. For more information, call **(303) 582-5251** or toll free from Denver **573-0247.**

Summer Opera Festival
early July through mid-August

Since its grand reopening in 1932, the beautiful, historic Central City Opera House has been thrilling opera and theater lovers with its fine productions. Talented professionals perform in two or three different productions at the oldest summer opera in the country. See the History section for more information on the opera house. For ticket information, contact the **Central City Opera, 621 17th St., Suite 1601, Denver, CO 80293; (303) 292-6700 or (303) 571-4435.**

Central City Jazz Festival

third weekend in August

If you're a jazz lover, this international festival shouldn't be missed. Professional musicians (140 last year) from as far away as the Soviet Union converge on Central City for a long weekend of performances. With styles ranging from Dixieland to fusion, they play late into the night at local bars. On Sat. there is a parade through town. Expect a crowd if you come—Central City is gridlocked with cars and pedestrians during the festival. For information about ticket prices, call **(303) 582-5563.**

OUTDOOR ACTIVITIES

FOUR-WHEEL-DRIVE TRIPS

Central City to St. Mary's Glacier—

This 10-mile drive takes you west through magnificent country rich in mining history. For detailed directions, see the Four-Wheel-Drive Trips section of the **Georgetown and Idaho Springs** chapter.

HIKING AND BACKPACKING

Taking off on a hike around Central City is not such a good idea. Locals are very careful not to wander off established roads and trails because of the vast number of mine shafts nearby. Quite often a section of a shaft caves in, revealing a deep dark hole hundreds of feet deep. The following are a couple of safe bets.

Gilpin Gold Tram—

This unique trail follows a section of the old Gilpin Gold Tram rail bed. Built in 1887, the tram transported ore from the mines above Central City down to the mill in Black Hawk. By the 1890s the tracks stretched more than 26 miles up the valley through Central City, Nevadaville and to the mines near Quartz Hill. The tram made its last run in 1917. Today, the rock supporting wall of the tram is still visible along much of its route, but roads have obscured it in spots. To begin the hike, drive a half mile north of Black Hawk on Hwy. 119. If you look to the left you'll see the rock wall of the tram bed. Find a suitable parking spot and start hiking.

Golden Gate Canyon State Park—

See the Parks, Gardens and Recreation Areas section in the **Denver and Environs** chapter.

SEEING AND DOING

CEMETERIES

In the hills around Black Hawk and Central City there are more than 10 cemeteries, complete with ornate Victorian tombstones. That's a lot of cemeteries. A number of them, including the **Knights of Columbus, Masonic, Redmen Lodge** and **Oddfellows** cemeteries, contain plots of fraternal members and their families. Many miners (not just in Central City) joined lodges as a form of insurance—if a member miner died tragically in one of the far-too-common mining accidents, his wife and children would be taken care of. A couple of cemeteries can be easily reached from Central City by heading west on Eureka St. to the edge of town. You can't miss them. Please do not deface or remove any of the tombstones—you'll be slapped with a hefty fine if the locals don't lynch you first. For more information go to **City Hall at 117 Eureka St.; (303) 582-5251.**

MUSEUMS AND GALLERIES

Central City and Black Hawk are packed with museums and historic buildings. Many of them are open during summer months only. No matter what time of year you visit, be sure to pick up a self-guided map of Central City and take a walking tour. The free map has historical information about many of the buildings. You can pick one up at **City Hall** in Central City and at most restaurants.

Gilpin County Arts Association—

Since 1946, Gilpin County has helped sponsor the oldest juried art show in the state. An impressive display of work by Colorado artists includes everything from watercolor paintings to weavings. Whether you are interested in purchasing artwork or just want to look, there is no admission charge. The art show runs from early June through the second weekend in Sept. Open daily 11 am–5:30 pm. **Box 98, 117 Eureka St., Central City, CO 80427; (303) 582-5952** in summer; **(303) 582-5574** in winter.

Gilpin County Historical Museum—

Located in an old stone school building, this museum contains one of the largest historic collections around. The school was built in 1869 and classes were held until 1967. The Gilpin County Historical Society now owns the building and has packed both floors with displays of local memorabilia. Displays include a miner's Victorian home, a barber shop, a pharmacy, a law office and an extensive collection of dolls. The list goes on and on. Admission fee charged. Open Memorial Day–Labor Day, 11 am–5 pm daily at **228 E. High St., Central City, CO 80427; (303) 582-5283.**

The Lace House—

Built in 1863 by Lucien K. Smith, the Lace House is an excellent example of Carpenter Gothic architecture. Locals refer to it as the Gingerbread House. Ownership changed hands seven times until Evelyn Hume purchased it in 1943, intending to totally restore it. Hume wasn't able to accomplish the task, and after standing empty for a couple of decades, the Lace House was deeded to the town of Black Hawk in 1974. The town, with generous donations and grants from the Colorado Historical Society, restored the Victorian house and furnished it with period antiques. Admission fee is charged. Open May–Sept. 30, 11 am–5 pm; in winter by appointment only. **161 Main St., Black Hawk, CO 80422; (303) 582-5382** or **(303) 582-5251** in winter.

Lost Gold Mine—

Although it's somewhat of a tourist trap, complete with a gift shop and a singing ore cart at the entrance, the Lost Gold Mine does have some old mining equipment on display and you can walk 220 feet into the shaft. Part of the old National Bank Lode, the mine produced more than $56 million in gold beginning in 1860. Relics on display include drills, miners' hats and dynamite boxes. A fee is charged. Summer hours are 8 am–8 pm daily; winter hours are 10 am–6 pm daily. **231 Eureka St., Central City, CO 80427; (303) 582-5913** and in Denver at **(303) 642-7533.**

Teller House and Central City Opera House Tour—

When the railroad from Denver finally reached Black Hawk in 1872, construction had already begun on Central City's showpiece hotel—the Teller House. Built with local stone, the four-story masterpiece was furnished exquisitely, including luxurious carpeting in each of the 150 rooms. When President Ulysses S. Grant visited town in 1873, a special walkway was created out of silver bars, leading from his coach to the front door of the Teller House. In later years, other celebrities, including Mark Twain and P.T. Barnum, stayed at the hotel, but didn't receive quite the welcome Grant did.

Because it was built of stone, the Teller House survived the devastating fire in 1874 that ripped through Central City, destroying most of the buildings. For years, the hotel provided fine lodging and dining to people from around the world. When the adjacent opera house (see the History section) reopened in 1932, the Teller House and its famous bar also underwent a restoration. Twelve layers of wallpaper were peeled off the barroom walls, revealing the original murals. It was in 1936 that Denver newspaperman Herndon Davis painted the *Face on the Barroom Floor* while attending the summer opera with a lady friend. The face is still on the floor.

Today, the hotel's five dining rooms and the Teller House Bar are open daily to the public. (See the Where to Eat section for more information.) Tours of the Teller House and the opera house are conducted daily throughout the summer for a small fee. **Box 8, 120 Eureka St., Central City, CO 80427; (303) 582-3200.**

Thomas-Billings Home—

In 1892 newlyweds Ben Thomas and Marcia Billings moved into their home on Eureka St., which had been a wedding gift from her parents. Ben was a partner in the successful Sauer-McShane mercantile company until 1917, when he lost a great deal of money and had to leave town. The house was boarded up and, except for a visit every few years by relatives, remained closed until 1986 when it opened as a museum. From furniture to feather hats, all of the home's contents are still intact. It's very unusual to find so many household items untouched. Marcia was quite an artist, and many of her paintings and drawings are displayed. Ben brought home many items from his store, including a unique soda pop cooler and advertising art, which he framed. This is about the most authentic Victorian home tour you're going to find. Open daily year-round June 1–Aug. 3, 9:30 am–6 pm, Sept. 1–May 30, 11 am–4 pm. Admission fee charged. **209 Eureka St., Central City, CO 80427; (303) 582-5093 and (303) 582-5011.**

NIGHTLIFE

Gold Coin Saloon—

The sign behind the bar says Jack Brown . . . Service Without a Smile. The cranky bartender at the Gold Coin Saloon, known as Smilin' Jack, is considered to be the meanest bartender in the country. But locals say he really has a heart of gold. This hangout is a great place to belly up to the bar and get a feel for Central City. It's supposedly the oldest continuously operated bar in town (even during Prohibition), but you'll have to check this out yourself. For years women were not allowed past the swinging doors at the entrance, but they could purchase buckets of beer to take home to their husbands. Be sure to ask about the money on the ceiling and the origin of this custom. The Gold Coin serves breakfast, lunch and dinner daily ($ to $$), specializing in home-style and Mexican food. If you have too much fun at the bar, bed and breakfast rooms ($$) are available upstairs. The restaurant is open 8 am–9 pm daily in summer only; bar open year-round from 9 am–2 am (midnight on Sun.). **120 Main St., Central City, CO 80427; (303) 582-3300.**

Summer Opera—

See the Festivals and Events section.

Teller House Bar—

Visit this famous bar, which houses the *Face on the Barroom Floor*. For more information see the Teller House write-up in the Museums and Galleries section.

The Toll Gate Saloon—

For more than 100 years the Toll Gate Saloon (at least the building) has satisfied many thirsty clients at its wild bar. A sign boasts, "U.S. Grant Drank Here. He Drank Everywhere." This fun bar really gets rolling on weekends with live music and two gunfights daily (in the bar!). Lots of odds and ends cover the walls including many mounted animal heads. The second bar, in the basement, supposedly served as a mortuary for many years. The Toll Gate also serves lunch and dinner items ($ to $$), specializing in fried chicken. Open daily 11 am–2 am in summer; weekends only from noon–6:30 pm in winter. Located at the corner of **108 Main St.; (303) 582-5424** and **623-6743**.

RAILROAD

Black Hawk & Central City Narrow Gauge Railroad—

In a town where summer tourist attractions include gold panning and tours of old mine shafts, it was only a matter of time before someone started offering train rides. A couple of years ago, tracks were laid from the depot in Central City down the valley a mile or so along the old Colorado & Southern rail bed. The big attraction is the original Colorado & Southern steam engine No. 71, which pulls the cars along the track. Built in 1896, this engine was kept in service for 45 years, then sat on a local hillside collecting rust for another 46 years. It was then painstakingly restored for its return to the tracks.

Every 45 minutes, trips leave from the depot and head down the valley to the ghost town of Mountain City. Photo stops are made, and the crew provides plenty of historical information about the mining days and the train. Daily trips are offered Wed.–Mon. from the end of May through the first week of Sept. Weekend trips run through Oct. Open 11 am–5 pm. The depot is located at **220 Spring St.** in **Central City**. The mailing address for information is **PO Box 13558, Denver, CO 80201; (303) 629-1741** or in **Central City** at **(303) 582-5856**.

SCENIC DRIVES

**Oh My God Road
(Virginia Canyon)—**

A drive over Oh My God Road is highly recommended. It leads south from Central City over the mountains to Idaho Springs, 9 miles away. To reach the road, follow Spring St. south past the train station and keep driving. For more information about the road, see the Scenic Drives section in the **Georgetown and Idaho Springs** chapter.

WHERE TO STAY

ACCOMMODATIONS

The Golden Rose — $$ to $$$$

For a touch of class and history, look no farther. This is simply the finest hotel in Central City. Consisting of four impeccably restored historic stone buildings (the oldest was built in 1874), the Golden Rose is a great place to stay while taking in the opera or just poking around town for the weekend. The main building housed Goldman's saloon and delicatessen from 1877 to 1911. In 1917 it was converted into the Chain o' Mines Hotel, which expanded to include the building next door and the bank building across the street. When the current owners of the Golden Rose took over in 1981, they painstakingly restored the old hotel and opened for business in 1983.

The elaborately decorated lobby, with chandeliers, piano and other fine antiques has been featured in a number of travel magazines. Twenty-six rooms are filled with much of the restored, original furniture and bathroom fixtures from the Chain o' Mines Hotel. All but one room have just one double bed apiece, and some rooms share a bath. As an added bonus there is a hot tub, a sauna and a TV room for guests. **102 Main St., Central City, CO 80427-0008; (303) 582-5060** or in Denver at **(303) 825-1413**.

Raynolds Court — $$

Located on the second floor of the historic Raynolds home, a single room, furnished with a mix of fine antiques and modern pieces (including cable TV), provides a comfortable night's lodging. The room has a queen-sized bed, a shower and a separate entrance from the rest of the house. This building, built in 1863, survived the fire of 1874, which leveled most of Central City. Wet blankets were put on the roof and the sides of the house to save it from the flames. A full breakfast is served each morning downstairs in the dining room. If you admire old furniture, you'll love this place. There is also an antique shop on the premises. No children allowed. **132 Lawrence St., Central City, CO 80427; (303) 582-5046.**

The Shamrock Inn — $$

The Shamrock Inn is a good representation of an early miner's home. Built more than 125 years ago by a Cornish miner, the house sits just in front of his mine. Herb and Jeri Bowles renovated the place a couple of years ago, but made sure much of the original craftsmanship was kept intact. Some of the door jambs are crooked, for instance, because the original builder of the house had no square. The inn is decorated with a combination of antiques and newer furnishings; historical photos of the Central City area hang on the walls. On the main floor are the three guest rooms, one of which looks out on an impressive rock wall built by the original owner in the backyard. Head upstairs in the morning for a full breakfast served in the dining room. **351 Gregory St., Black Hawk, CO 80422-0137; (303) 582-5513.**

CAMPING

In Arapaho National Forest—

The closest campground to Central City is **Columbine Campground**, located 2.1 miles northwest of town on County Rd. 279. It has 47 sites and a fee. From Black Hawk, head 3 miles north on Hwy. 119 and 1 mile west to **Pickle Gulch Campground and Picnic Area**. This campground is reserved for groups only. There are 30 sites and no fee. For information call **(303) 567-2901.** Four miles north of Black Hawk on Hwy. 119 is **Cold Springs Campground and Picnic Area** with 47 sites and a fee.

Golden Gate Canyon State Park—

Located 7 miles north of Black Hawk on Hwy. 119 and 2 miles east on Gap Rd., **Golden Gate Canyon State Park** has 71 sites and a fee. There are also a few primitive campsites (no fee charged).

—— WHERE TO EAT ——

Black Forest Inn — $$ to $$$

Located conspicuously along the road in Black Hawk, this sprawling restaurant has become an institution among loyal locals and regular visitors from the Denver area. Since 1958 Bill Lorenz has been providing standout German cuisine that reflects his years of training in his home country. Numerous dining rooms disguise the actual size of this place. German music, paintings and even a cuckoo clock add to the atmosphere. Aside from the Hungarian goulash, the lunch menu features mainly American-style dishes, including fresh Baja avocado stuffed with assorted seafood, chicken salad, sirloin burgers and steaks. For dinner, start off with an appetizer, such as a Russian egg, topped with lox, capers and caviar. Then sink your teeth into wienerschnitzel, sauerbraten, a sea-

food dish or the game special (elk and goose the night we dined). Home-baked German sourdough rye bread goes well with all meals. Service at the Black Forest Inn is impeccable, and Lorenz often makes the rounds to talk personally with the customers—a really nice touch. A fine, reasonably priced wine list offers selections from Germany, France and the US. If you want a really special meal in the Central City area, we strongly suggest the Black Forest Inn. Open 11 am–9:30 pm, Mon.–Sat.; 11 am–8 pm on Sun. Located in **Black Hawk; 279-2333 or 582-9971.**

Gaslight Inn — $$ to $$$

As unbelievable as this sounds, there is another fine German restaurant in Central City. The Gaslight Inn is a much smaller, more intimate spot. Like a German *gast-*

haus, the atmosphere is less formal than the Black Forest Inn. Owner Jacob Forester is from Germany and used to be the chef at the Black Forest Inn. Menu selections at both places are similar; the Gaslight offers an evening special that changes nightly. Open in summer Tues.–Sun. 11 am–9 pm; in winter hours are Tues.–Sun. 11 am–8 pm Sun. **114 Lawrence St.; 582-5266.**

Mermaid Cafe — $$ to $$$

The restaurant has only been open since 1979, but the building has served, among other things, as an icehouse and a ham locker. Things were cool (even cold) around here in those early days, but today the spicy Mexican food that's served is definitely hot. Try a giant burrito, a cheese enchilada or a flauta. In addition to fine Mexican food, homemade soups, crisp salads and sandwiches round out the lunch menu. For dinner try a rib-eye steak, a salmon steak or chicken teriyaki, or one of the daily specials. Locals praise the Mermaid for its relaxed atmosphere and the fresh ingredients used in its menu items. Open daily Memorial Day–Labor Day from 11 am–10 pm; in fall Fri.–Wed. noon–9 pm. Closed Jan.–Apr. Open for dinners only in Nov., Dec. and May. **118 Spring St.; 582-5926.**

Teller House — $$ to $$$

This historic old hotel, located next to the opera house, has five dining rooms that all serve from the same lunch and dinner menus. Items include sandwiches, burgers and pizza for lunch; steaks, chicken and fish entrées dominate the dinner menu. A breakfast special is served during summer from 9 am–noon. Reports on dining at the Teller House are not all glowing. In summer when the opera is underway, all dining rooms are open and the atmosphere is lively. But quite often, many of the rooms are closed and service can be inconsistent. We recommend dining at the Teller House during the summer opera season—otherwise, try another place. For more information about the Teller House, see the Museums and Galleries section. **120 Eureka St.; 582-3200** or in Denver at **279-8306.**

Copper Broiler — $ to $$

The Copper Broiler is a comfortable little restaurant serving breakfasts and lunches. It has a homey feel, with wooden booths and table seating; chandeliers hang from the ceiling and the walls are covered with historical murals of Central City's early days. For breakfast, try one of their fresh cinnamon rolls; lunch items include sandwiches, homemade soups and salads and the well-known Yogyburger. Open daily from 8 am–6 pm. **109 Main St.; 582-5406.**

——— SERVICES ———

Office of Public Relations (Central City)—

For information about Central City and Black Hawk, go to City Hall in Central City, located across the street from the opera house. **PO Box 249, 117 Eureka St., Central City, CO 80427; (303) 582-5251** or **(303) 573-0247.**

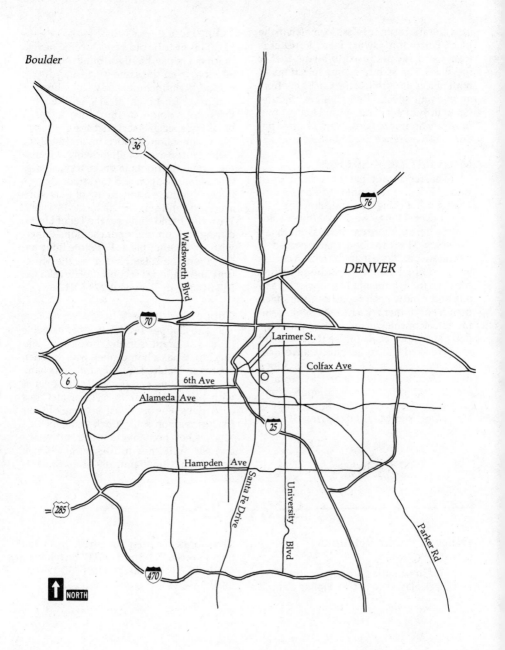

Denver and Environs

Most maps give you the impression that the Rocky Mountains rise abruptly about 100 yards west of the city. Actually, Denver proper is quite a number of miles from the mountains, located a mile above sea level, on the high, arid plains. From many points in the city, though, you can see the hills of the high plains break a bit, then the foothills, followed by mountains towering far in the distance—so large they sometimes seem to move like the clouds. On summer afternoons, thunderheads mix with the high peaks in a breathtaking display, dwarfing the city's downtown office towers.

Denver is the largest urban center within a 600-mile radius. Perhaps this is why, over the years, it seems to have had an inflated opinion of itself, readily acquiring names like Queen City of the Plains. Those unfamiliar with Denver tend to view the town between two vivid images: the dusty, riotous cow town and the glamorous snow-covered capital of the mountains. Both descriptions puzzle residents, who understand Denver is neither.

While Denver is extremely difficult to describe in a few words, it is, above all else, a very livable city, with a high quality of life difficult to find elsewhere. One of the best things about living here is the balance of a normal week, which often includes weekends at play in the nearby mountains: skiing, fishing, camping, hiking. The nearly two million Denver metro residents support more sporting goods stores per resident than anywhere else in the world. Denver also has the second highest number of college graduates per capita and, for some unknown reason, the highest movie attendance in the US. Most Denverites are staying on through the current economic slump, brought on by plummeting oil prices in the early 1980s. They envision a better future not far out of reach. As an important regional hub, Denver is a major transportation center. Stapleton International Airport is one of the five busiest in the world; in the early 1990s, an even larger airport will be opening.

Denver hosts a diverse ethnic population. You can find well-established Italian, Jewish, Greek and Japanese communities, usually in particular neighborhoods. The western part of the city reveals Colorado's Hispanic roots in its street names and large Hispanic population. Denver also has a very strong black community, centered in the old Five Points area northwest of downtown. Recent additions include the nationally recognized Black American West Museum and Heritage Center, which brings alive a long-neglected part of American history. Neighborhoods such as Park Hill have a 50-50 black and Anglo mix. Unfortunately, the Chinese presence in Denver dwindled after 1900 because of extreme prejudice against them. Now, however, Korean, Thai, Laotian and Vietnamese immigrants are building strong communities in the city. With its diverse neighborhoods, Denver enjoys a vitality unknown in racially homogeneous cities. Various festivals celebrate ethnic heritages.

The city's cultural diversions might not match those of Chicago, New York or Los Angeles, but there is still plenty to do within the city limits. More than 2,000 restaurants can be found throughout the city, accommodations are diverse and plentiful and the Denver Center for the Performing Arts (DCPA) has given the arts community something to sing about. There are tried-and-true tourist destinations in Denver—the gold-domed capitol, an odd granite miniature of the US Capitol; the US Mint with its bullion and machine-gun portals above a Florentine palace's passageways; or the Molly Brown House with its unusual style of western Victoriana. The abundant museums explain themselves for the most part, and serviceable bus tours leave no obvious stone unturned. But Denver also has other, hidden enjoyments. Therefore, our mission is to illuminate the unusual corners of Denver—places a Denver cousin would show to you only if you never betrayed her to the relatives. Denver's history is fascinating, and many of its lessons are relevant today.

HISTORY

In the spring of 1858, Georgia prospector William Green Russell and 12 companions found some gold dust on a tributary of the South Platte River, near present-day Englewood (a suburb of Denver). Though they were only panning $10 each per day and the gold soon ran out, news of a rich strike in the Rockies blew out of proportion and spread east. Enthusiastic miners began making their way west with the slogan "Pikes Peak or Bust."

When the gold played out on the Platte, members of Russell's party moved down the river to a grove of cottonwood trees at the confluence of Cherry Creek and the South Platte and erected a few cabins at Auraria (named after Russell's hometown in Georgia). Across the river from Auraria, the St. Charles Town Company, headed by Charlie Nichols, staked out another town. A group from Leavenworth, Kansas, led by Gen. William Larimer, jumped the St. Charles claim, infuriating Nichols. But Gen. Larimer and his Kansas group held firm, telling Nichols to quit complaining or they would use a noose on him. Since the area at the time was all part of the Kansas Territory, the group named their new town Denver City, after the Kansas territorial governor, James W. Denver, hoping it would stroke his ego enough to ensure their claim to the site. Circumstances surrounding the establishment of Denver angered the residents of Auraria, and an intense rivalry between the two towns lasted for years.

At this time a band of Arapaho Indians remained in the area, observing these strange newcomers who were trespassing on Indian land. Although the land around Denver had been guaranteed to the Arapaho in the Fort Laramie Treaty in 1851, the Indians remained friendly to the settlers for the first couple of years. Historian Thomas Noel recalls, "Arapaho warriors left their women and children in Denver while they made war on the Utes in the mountains. After returning, the

Arapaho invited white Denverites to their dog feasts and Ute scalp dances."

Miners arriving in 1858 and early 1859 were greeted with outrageously high prices for supplies and found no gold in the streams; many returned east in disgust. In the spring of 1859, however, a rich strike at Central City in the mountains west of Denver rekindled the rush to the area. This time it was real. Denver grew because it was a way stop for miners headed to the camps in the mountains. Those who decided to stay in Denver in these early days comprised a tough, independent group. A noteworthy representative was William Byers, from Omaha, Nebraska, who had written a guide book to the Pikes Peak region, compiled after hearing stories from miners returning from the Colorado gold fields. When Byers came to Denver, he brought his printing press with him. Quite aware of the feud between Auraria and Denver, Byers set up a newspaper office on the banks of Cherry Creek, between the two towns. His newspaper, the *Rocky Mountain News*, made an immediate impact on Denver when it first appeared on Apr. 23, 1859 and fueled further migration of people from the East.

As gold strikes in the mountains increased, Denver continued to grow. In these early years, Denver developed a reputation as a tough, dusty frontier town that disgusted many mannerly visitors. Horace Greeley, editor of the *New York Tribune*, wrote that in Denver there were "more brawls, more pistol shots with criminal intent . . . than in any other community with equal numbers on Earth."

In the early 1860s relations with the Arapaho and Cheyenne soured when the Indians refused to comply with terms of the new Fort Wise Treaty of 1861. The Indians attacked settlements on the plains and hindered freight shipments to Denver. This clash of Anglo and Indian culture culminated with the brutal massacre of peaceful Arapaho and Cheyenne at Sand Creek in 1864 (see the **Southeast Plains** chapter). When the territorial troops returned to Denver from the massacre site, the *Rocky Mountain News* reported, "Cheyenne scalps are getting as thick as toads in Egypt . . . everyone has got one, and is anxious to get another to send east." The Indians retaliated, once again attacking settlements on the plains and cutting off Denver's supply routes for a couple of months before troops squelched the uprisings once and for all.

In the mid-1860s the Union Pacific dealt Denver a severe blow when it chose to lay its transcontinental railroad tracks through Cheyenne, Wyoming, 100 miles to the north. Denverites believed their town was doomed without a railroad. Through the efforts of William Byers and

Gov. John Evans, $280,000 was raised by 1867 to finance a railroad spur to the railhead in Cheyenne. The Denver Pacific Railroad was completed in June 1870, followed by the Kansas Pacific, which had laid tracks across the prairie from Kansas. With efficient rail transportation, Denver's population soared from just over 4,000 to 35,000 in one decade. Along with the gold mining towns in the mountains, silver mining districts began to blossom—especially Leadville. Times were good in Denver; it was the major supply center not only for the mining towns, but also for the growing cattle industry of the plains and agricultural towns in the Platte and Arkansas river valleys. In the 1880s many rich miners and cattle barons built mansions in the Capitol Hill area of Denver. Their deep pockets and desire to out-do their neighbors spawned unique sandstone palaces characterized by turrets, bays, and leaded-glass windows. Many of these mansions still grace the neighborhoods of Denver.

Despite this new money and Denver's development, an unrefined image persisted. This wasn't helped by the town's notorious red light district on Market St., called "The Row." So seductive was this decadent area that one day, in June 1880, the town council didn't conduct any business—too many council members were attending the grand opening of a new house on "The Row."

In 1893 Denver's fortunes plummeted along with the price of silver. Many mines closed and 10 Denver banks went under. Denverites were confronted with a grim reality—their future was tied too closely with that of the mining industry. If Denver was to continue to grow and prosper, it needed to diversify its economy. In the second half of the 1890s, a huge gold strike at Cripple Creek gave another boost to the economy, but looking to the future, the town helped finance agricultural research and started to realize how well-suited it was for tourism. With constant reminders from a new paper in town—the *Denver Post*—about future possibilities, Denver entered a new era, overthrowing its dependence on mining. One of the first things Denver did was to clean up its act. The brothels were closed and, under the supervision of Mayor Robert Speer, parks (complete with statues and fountains) were built, streets were laid out and 18,000 trees were planted. When Speer died in 1918, Denver had undergone a remarkable transformation from a dusty cow town to a green, well-planned city.

Of course Denver's growth hasn't been a smooth, easy glide from 1918 to the present. Rather it has been somewhat lurching, sometimes complacent, but always optimistic. After World War II, Denver entered a new period of expansion—one that many felt was too fast. The tide turned in 1972 when the state resoundingly voted down a chance for Colorado to host the Winter Olympics. Residents were wary of overdevelopment, higher taxes and a change in their comfortable, uncrowded lifestyle. Times were good for most of the state, with Denver well on its way to becoming a major regional energy center. Vast oil and coal reserves attracted hundreds of small firms and many national giants. In the early 1980s new downtown office towers were going up at an incredible rate, with as many as six cranes dotting the skyline at once. Growth seemed to be its mandate as the city teemed with a too-good-to-be-true excitement. After the recent oil glut, it appeared as though Denver had once again made an error by putting all its eggs in one basket. Though the Mile High City still feels the effects of downturns in mining and energy, its role as a manufacturing and trade center as well as a transportation hub for the country keeps things rolling.

GETTING THERE

Stapleton International Airport is the fourth busiest in the country, fifth busiest in the world. There are direct and connecting flights to every major city in the US as well as flights to many towns and resorts around the state. The unusually convenient airport is only 15 minutes east of downtown. Greyhound Trailways Bus Lines maintains daily bus schedules from all parts of the country to Denver and several of the larger ski resorts. Their main terminal is in downtown Denver. For information about schedules and fares, call **(303) 292-6111**.

Denver's historic **Union Station** is still a railroad hub for AMTRAK. Six daily arrivals and departures serve Los Angeles, San Francisco, Seattle and Chicago. Trains also make daily stops in Winter Park, Glenwood Springs, Grand Junction and other Colorado towns. For train information, call **(303) 832-8000**. Denver can also be reached by car from New Mexico to the south and Wyoming to the north via Interstate 25; from Utah to the west and Kansas to the east via Interstate 70; and from Nebraska to the northeast via Interstate 76.

—— FESTIVALS AND EVENTS ——

The National Western Stock Show and Rodeo

mid-January

This one is big—really big. For two weeks cattlemen from around North America come to the largest livestock exhibition in the world. Stetsons and cowboy boots fill the town; horse trailers pull up to the doors of the Brown Palace Hotel and the doorman doesn't bat an eye. When the stock show is on, all other bets are off. Some of the events include pro and amateur rodeos, cattle competitions and horse shows. If you want to stay at a hotel in Denver during the stock show, make your reservations well in advance—no joke! For information about the schedule of events and tickets, call **(303) 297-1166**. All shows

take place at the **Denver Coliseum (4600 Humboldt St.)**, just off Interstate 70 at the Washington St. exit.

Capitol Hill People's Fair

late May

For one weekend each May over 100,000 punks, hippies, yuppies and average Joes flock to Civic Center Park to enjoy the People's Fair. The huge crowd, with a life of its own, ebbs and flows around the statues, past the four music stages and up and down the rows of over 500 booths. All Denver walks these aisles, sampling gyros and therapeutic teas, browsing through Krishna cookbooks and tomes on palmistry, signing petitions and greeting Broncos. You can discuss the intricacies of an embroidered dress with a seamstress and the virtues of Libertarianism with a true believer. Virtually every band in Denver spends an hour on a stage. It all happens between the Capitol and the City and County Building. Don't miss it, and bring an umbrella. For more information, call **(303) 892-1112.**

Cherry Blossom Festival
first weekend in June
Sakura Square, at 19th Ave. and Lawrence St. downtown, houses several Japanese shops, a Buddhist temple, a tea room and a high-rise apartment building. In early June, the Cherry Blossom Festival makes this place as crowded as Tokyo at rush hour. The festival revolves around the Buddhist temple, which contains a large collection of painted Buddhist statues and features several performances of the tea ceremony. The basement houses displays of bonsai, the delicate art of growing and pruning miniature trees, along with several other Japanese arts. In the monastery you will find an incredible array of Japanese foods, including sushi and chicken teriyaki. Music, plays, dances and martial arts demonstrations succeed one another in the square itself. Everything is authentic, especially the enthusiastic welcome you receive from the residents of Sakura Square. For information, call **(303) 295-0304.**

Festival of Mountain and Plain
Labor Day weekend
In 1895 Denverites got together to celebrate the recovery from the 1893 silver crash and to pay tribute to the strengthening economies of the mountains and plains. The week-long festival, patterned after Mardi Gras, was highlighted by a number of parades. Today the festivities last only a few days, but still draw a large crowd. Scores of arts and crafts booths line Broadway just west of the Capitol. The main attraction is the "Taste of Colorado," featuring food booths and free samples of dishes from the area's finest restaurants. Live local and nationally known bands perform throughout the festival. For information, call **(303) 295-7900, ext. 102.**

Broncomania and Other Sports Phenomena
Each Sun. afternoon in fall, Denver's shopping malls are deserted, streets are empty and the orange sunset over the mountains takes on a slightly brighter hue. What's going on? A Broncos football game, what else? Most Denver residents (or Colorado residents for that matter) have their eyes glued to the TV, while the lucky few (75,000) pack into Mile High Stadium to cheer the Broncos and jeer the opponents, creating ear-splitting decibel levels. Without question, Denver fans are the most rabid pro football fans in the country. The games at the stadium have been sold out for years, but people are usually selling extra tickets at the entrance gates. The **Denver Zephyrs** minor league baseball team takes to the field at Mile High Stadium in spring and summer. For ticket information, call **(303) 433-8645.** Just south of the stadium is McNichols Arena, home to the **Denver Nuggets** pro basketball team. Nuggets games run from Nov. to May; tickets are available at the box office, or by calling **(303) 893-3865.**

Other Festivals
There is always some sort of festival in Denver. **Cinco de Mayo** (5th of May) is one of the biggest celebrations in town, especially among the Hispanic community. The **Greeks** have theirs in June. **Old South Gaylord Street** celebrates in May, and **Oktoberfest** floods Larimer St. with beer in Sept. In fall the **Denver International Film Festival** draws large crowds, including critics and famous actors. The best source for week to week happenings in Denver is *Westword*, a free newspaper available virtually everywhere in town— look under the "Thrills" section.

Colorado Renaissance Festival

weekends in June to mid-July

At this re-creation of medieval England, a costumed lass or lad will ambush you for a kiss. As you approach the wooden fortifications surrounding King Hal's domain, be prepared to pay homage to His Highness as you quaff an ale and devour an enormous drumstick. And beware the fool, who makes quick work of anyone who challenges his wit. A host of merchants vie for your attention with wares from strange lands. The brave engage in feats of strength and the agile balance themselves on cunning rope contraptions. The festival runs on weekends only. Drive south on Interstate 25 for 25 miles to the town of **Larkspur; (303) 756-1501.**

OUTDOOR ACTIVITIES

GOLF

There are well over 20 public golf courses located in the Denver metro area. In winter Denver receives its share of snowfall, but much of it melts off rather quickly. Most courses stay open year-round, weather permitting. Here are five of our favorites.

Arrowhead Golf Club—

Located among the jutting cathedral-like red rocks near Roxborough Park, this course is an unforgettable golfing experience. Arrowhead was designed in 1970 by Robert Trent Jones, Jr., who considers the course among his favorite six in the world. The interesting layout snakes its way through the rocks and troublesome scrub oak following the natural contours of the land. It has 76 sand traps and six lakes to keep golfers challenged. The 13th hole is a standout—a par three that drops 95 feet to the green. Be sure to club down or you'll end up in the lake just behind the green. Reservations are a must. Pro shop, driving range and restaurant. Located southwest of Denver, south of Chatfield Dam. **10850 W. Sundown Trail, Littleton, CO 80125; (303) 973-9614.**

Hyland Hills Golf Course—

Hyland Hills is extremely popular, and with good reason. The challenging course is kept in great shape by the greens crew. Holes are long, with the lakes and ditches often coming into play. The eighth hole is particularly dangerous—a 526-yard straightaway is lined on the left by a lake and a ditch crosses the fairway just in front of the green. In addition to an 18-hole course, there's also a par three course. **9600 Sheridan Blvd., Westminster, CO 80030; (303) 428-6526.**

Meadow Hills Golf Course—

Meadow Hills is one of the finest all-around public courses in the Denver area. The course is very mature, with lots of cottonwood, pine and elms lining the fairways. Greens fees are reasonable to boot. With relatively few sand traps and three lakes, you can score well if you keep to the fairways. The resident Canadian geese, however, can be distracting and they don't show much fear. Located in Aurora, just east of Cherry Creek Reservoir. **3609 S. Dawson St., Aurora, CO 80014; (303) 690-2500.**

Riverdale—

Although Riverdale is considered part of the Denver metro area, it feels as if you're out in the country. Don't worry about distracting construction or traffic noise . . . there isn't any. Located near Brighton (northeast metro area), the two courses at Riverdale have developed quite a good reputation. A series of irrigation canals characterizes Riverdale's original Knolls course, and water comes into play on 13 holes. The newer Dunes course, finished in 1985, plays like the wide open Scottish links with rolling hills and natural grass roughs. On the Dunes, there are many water hazards; railroad ties border the greens and tee boxes. Located 8 miles southwest of Brighton next to the Adams County Fairgrounds. **13300 Riverdale Dr., Brighton, CO 80601; (303) 659-6700.**

Wellshire Golf Course—

Located in south Denver, Wellshire is another fine, mature course. One of the oldest in the city, it was a country club until the city of Denver purchased it in the 1940s. Wellshire plays long (6,592 yards), but the small number of lakes and traps helps your score. Trees are everywhere. Views west to the mountains accompany you on many of the holes. After your round, stop in at the pub or have a meal at the excellent Wellshire Inn restaurant (see the Where to Eat section). Try the unique driving range—you hit balls out into a lake at floating distance buoys. Located at the intersection of Hampden Ave. and Colorado Blvd. **3333 S. Colorado Blvd., Denver, CO 80210; (303) 757-1352.**

ICE SKATING

Evergreen Lake—

For decades, this lake has been popular for ice skating. At the skating center, you'll find a snack bar, rental skates and shelter from the cold. The lake usually opens for skating by Christmas on a daily basis and remains open afternoons, evenings and weekends after the holidays, weather permitting. A fee is charged. To reach Evergreen from Denver, head west on Interstate 70 about 20 miles to the El Rancho exit. From the exit, drive 8 miles south on Hwy. 74 to Evergreen. For information, call **(303) 674-2677.**

PARKS, GARDENS AND RECREATION AREAS

Cheesman Park—

Cheesman has the most unified and serene landscaping in the city park system, with a wonderful view of the mountains. It's probably the nicest spot within the city to attend a free summer concert. (For current schedules, call **331-4029.**) You owe yourself a stroll around the perimeter and a nice rest in the Greek-style pavilion, a remnant of the "City Beautiful" campaign launched early this century. You'll walk past some of Denver's most impressive houses, some of which open directly onto the park. Originally the city cemetery, this land was converted into a park in the 1890s. A massive project to re-inter the remains in other graveyards in town ensued, but sloppy workers desecrated many of the graves. To this day many of the surrounding homes as well as the park itself are believed to be haunted. Cheesman Park is located just north of **8th Ave.,** between **Humboldt** and **Race** streets.

Cherry Creek State Recreation Area—

"The Res" is one of Denver's most popular destinations, especially on scorching summer days. It is farther from the mountains but easier to get to than Chatfield Reservoir. For nature lovers it can't rival Chatfield, but it does offer all the water sports: good fishing (from the bank and from boats), windsurfing and water-skiing. Most people, however, come to this recreation area to hang out on a meager 250-yard strip of sand (some call it a beach) and dip their toes in the water. Families with small kids and teenagers ply the sandy northeast edge of the reservoir under the watchful eye of lifeguards. On summer weekends you start feeling like a human sardine. During the week though, this area can be a nearby peaceful getaway. Cottonwood trees protect 102 campsites in several designated campgrounds; all charge a fee. The east entrance to Cherry Creek Reservoir is 1 mile south from Interstate 225 on Parker Rd. For more information, contact **Cherry Creek State Recreation Area, 4201 S. Parker Rd., Aurora, CO 80014; (303) 690-1166.**

City Park—

The grounds of this large park contain the zoo, Natural History Museum, a golf course and three lakes. When it was completed in 1881, a buggy ride into the country was necessary to reach the park. The designer of the English Gardens in Munich and Hyde Park in London also laid out this Victorian idealization of nature, which has held up well, despite the expansion of the other facilities. Statues of Robert Burns and Martin Luther King show how much the park has stretched to contain the changing dynamics of Denver. On the west side people polish their cars, radios blasting, while on the east side, you can stroll through a large rose garden. Paddle boats can be rented at one of the lakes. Tall pine trees, grassy areas and views to the mountains make City Park a popular place for many residents. The park is located north of **17th St.**, between **Colorado** and **York** streets.

Denver Botanic Gardens—

The Denver Botanic Gardens offer more visual and olfactory pleasures than almost any other place in the city. You may recognize the futuristic buildings from Woody Allen's movie *Sleeper*. The enormous glass honeycomb of the conservatory dominates your initial view of the grounds. Under the enclosure grows a lush forest of carob, cocoa, banana and hundreds of other trees and shrubs. In winter, there is no better place to remember that spring is coming than in the orchid room, which catches the afternoon sun. If you walk to the far western end of the grounds, the Japanese garden, mountain flora path and alpine gardens offer wonderful contours, textures and scents—even in Feb. On a warm winter day (and such days are common), the goldfish swim below small stone shrines beside the shore of the lake in Shofu-en, the Garden of Pine Wind.

In summer, the Japanese garden is the most peaceful spot in Denver. The stream flows under a small wooden bridge, edged with irises in every shade. Bamboo spouts trickle water onto polished gray stones, and a family of ducks fights its way up a small waterfall. On occasion the Japanese tea ceremony is performed in the lovely teahouse near the east gate. The schedule is arcane, but worth inquiring about. A lin-

gering walk through the pine grove brings you to the alpine garden, which is particularly fine in May and early June. This is one of the most important and extensive collections of alpine plants in the world, with colors as vivid as any hybrid created with the gloved hand. You'll also see blossom-laden peonies, extensive rose beds, water lilies, a sensual garden of the plants of the Bible, an even more sensual herb garden, several well-conceived sculptures and fountains, and, from late May through July, an explosion of irises.

On many summer nights, KCFR, the local public radio station, hosts concerts in the amphitheater on the grounds. The gift shop has a fine selection of books and a wonderful collection of Chinese and Japanese porcelain. The gardens are open until dusk on Wed., Sat. and Sun., June through Aug. Otherwise, the hours are 9 am–4:45 pm daily. **1005 York St.; (303) 331-4010.**

Platte River Greenway and Confluence Park—

The Platte River winds a slow, meandering course through the heart of Denver. Until recently, it was nothing special to walk or bike along the Platte—in fact it was an eyesore. Since 1974, an extensive redevelopment has taken place, and today the river is traced by a well-used path. Several small parks are situated along its 11.5-mile route (several beavers had to be carted away because they were gnawing down newly planted trees). If you follow it from just west of Santa Fe Dr. on Evans Ave., the trail works its way to the inner city, eventually ending at the historic point of Confluence Park, where Cherry Creek and the South Platte merge. It was here that the first gold prospectors camped out. As the encampment grew into a tent city, Denver was born. It's because of the odd angle of Cherry Creek that the downtown grid runs frustratingly askew: the streets were originally laid out to run parallel to the creek, directly facing Longs Peak.

Confluence Park has grassy areas, cement paths and a tough river obstacle course that attracts urban kayakers. It's the best spot for a canoe run in Denver and a prime one for skateboarding. Of course, you could simply walk. Confluence Park is located just off **15th St.** and the Interstate 25 viaduct.

Washington Park—

Springtime brings Denverites outside in eager hordes to this favorite gathering place. Not only is it a beautiful park with mature trees and wide grassy expanses, there are also a couple of lakes—on the largest one you can rent a paddle boat by the hour for a mellow ride. The lakes provide fishing, and the old Denver Canal still flows here. Both kids and adults love all the diversions: two large playgrounds, an indoor swimming pool, several tennis courts and routes for walking. Bicyclists whir around and around the park road in their sinister black racing attire. If you are lucky, you can watch some of the world's most tenacious horseshoe throwers; most of the cunning participants throwing into sandy pits belong in the seniors division. Volleyball nets pop up by the tens as friends get together for an afternoon of fun in the sun. On the west side of the park, bordering Downing St., a barrage of flowers blooms in two intricately arranged gardens—one is a replica of George Washington's garden at Mt. Vernon. The park lies to the east of Downing St. between Alameda Ave. and Louisiana Ave.

NEARBY

Barr Lake State Park—

Twenty miles northeast of Denver, off Interstate 76, you'll find a haven for birds and birdwatchers. The manmade lake was constructed in the last century for the amusement of Denver weekenders. After it fell out of favor, the lake became a repository for all types of pollution. In 1965, however, the South Platte River flooded, "flushing the reservoir like a toilet," and since then it has been able to stay free of pollution. In 1977 Barr Lake opened as a state park—which is not to say it occupies a pristine wilderness setting. Rather, Barr Lake is a convenient sanctuary at the edge

of Denver that also happens to be on a major flyway. More than 300 species of birds have been spotted at the lake, including herons and cormorants, which nest in trees along the lake shore. Other common sightings include owls, falcons, geese and eagles. The nature/visitors center is a good place to find out what kinds of birds have been spotted recently.

A 9-mile trail encircles the lake and boardwalks extend out over the water to strategic birdwatching areas and observation blinds. As you walk (or cross-country ski) along the south shore, look for the great horned owl nest; the owls are usually happy to pose. Continue along the wooden walkway that takes you to a gazebo far out on the lake. This is a great place for a picnic, especially on a weekday when you can have the lake to yourself. At the north end of the lake, there is a boat ramp (sailboats, hand-propelled craft and boats with electric trolling motors are allowed). The warm-water fishing can be good for perch, bass and an occasional trout. To get here, take Interstate 76 northeast of Denver about 20 miles. **13401 Picadilly Rd., Brighton, CO; (303) 659-6005.**

Chatfield State Recreational Area—

This reservoir built along the South Platte River as a flood control effort offers every water sport except surfing. The Army Corps of Engineers didn't foresee how popular it would become with the boating set. Today there are 257 slips for people to park their yachts and sailboats. It's also a great place for swimmers, fishermen, scuba divers and windsurfers. Landlubbers enjoy the foothills location for hiking, biking, horseback riding (rentals available), sunbathing and birdwatching. Chatfield is one of the best bird habitats in the country—it's a veritable holy ground for birdwatchers. The nature trails are very nice, and the arboretum and heron rookery cement this lake's position as one of the best stops in the Denver area for nature lovers. Don't pass it up in winter either, especially for cross-country skiing and ice fishing. Stop by the visitors center for a look at the displays and a chance to learn more about the area. You might want to call the **Chatfield Livery Stables, (303) 978-9898,** or the **Chatfield Marina, (303) 791-7547.** For those of you prone to urban camping, 153 campsites are located along the shore; all charge a fee. To get here, drive south on Interstate 25 to C-470. Take C-470 west to the Wadsworth Blvd. (Hwy. 121) exit and go south on Hwy. 121 beyond the Army Corps of Engineers entrance to the park entrance. **11500 N. Roxborough Park Rd., Littleton, CO 80125; (303) 791-7275.**

Devil's Head—

Located in the Pike National Forest southwest of the Denver metro area, Devil's Head is a beautiful escape for city folk, especially in the fall. Although a lot of people choose to make a weekend out of it, Devil's Head is close enough to town to do in a day. Its craggy profile is easily visible along the Front Range. The main attractions are the huge rocks strewn about the forest, thick aspen groves and the easy 1.5-mile trail up to the Devil's Head Fire Lookout.

The well-marked trail begins at the Devil's Head Campground and climbs 948 feet through ponderosa pine and Douglas fir forests. Perched atop a giant granite outcropping at the summit is the fire lookout, an enclosed station that is the last of its kind along Colorado's Front Range. Visitors are welcome to climb the stairway and enjoy the spectacular 360° view from the lookout. Be sure to bring your camera.

Devil's Head Campground is a popular weekend destination, with 22 sites; a fee is charged. Some other campgrounds can be found in the area also. To reach Devil's Head from Denver, head south on Hwy. 85 from Littleton for 10 miles to Sedalia. At Sedalia, head west on Hwy. 67 for 9 miles and then left (south) on Rampart Range Rd. for 9 miles. Rampart Range Rd. is closed in the winter. For a scenic drive, continue south on Rampart Range Rd. to Woodland Park. From Woodland Park you can return to Denver by heading east on Hwy. 24 to Colorado Springs and then north on Interstate 25.

Golden Gate Canyon State Park—

For rugged mountains and dramatic rocky cliffs, this 8,500-acre park is lacking. But, within 45 minutes of Denver, you can surround yourself with beautiful, rolling, forested terrain—an ideal year-round escape from the city. Spring brings out a barrage of wildflowers in lush meadows, including columbine; fall is highlighted by golden hillsides of aspen. Roads traverse the outer portions of the park while the unspoiled interior can be reached only on foot or horseback. Fishing for rainbow trout on its well-stocked streams can be quite good. Nearly 60 miles of marked hiking trails wind through the park, providing perfect day outings. After winter storms, these trails are excellent, meandering cross-country ski routes. Stop by the visitors center (open daily from 8 am–4:30 pm, year-round), located on Golden Gate Canyon Rd. just inside the southeast entrance. Rangers can help you plan your visit and give you a trail map. There are exhibits on the ecology, geology and plant life of the park. In summer, a full-time naturalist leads walks and gives campfire talks.

Golden Gate Canyon State Park offers many planned campgrounds. All charge a fee, and they usually fill up on summer weekends; for an extra fee, reservations can be made by calling **(303) 671-4500.** **Reverends Ridge Campground** (106 sites), located in the northwest corner of the park, offers laundry and hot showers to campers. **Aspen Meadows Campground,** with 35 tent sites in the north-central portion of the park, is much smaller and less developed. There are 23 backcountry sites that appeal to hikers who want to get away from camping alongside the road—a permit must be obtained for these sites; no fires are allowed.

To get to the park from Denver, take Interstate 70 west to the Hwy. 58 exit. Stay on Hwy. 58 for 5 miles west to Washington Ave. (Golden exit). Turn right (north) for 1.5 miles to Golden Gate Canyon Rd. Turn left (northwest) and drive 15 miles to the park entrance. The visitors center is inside the park boundary along Ralston Creek.

For more information, contact **Golden Gate Canyon State Park, Route 6, PO Box 280, Golden, CO 80403; (303) 592-1502.**

Mount Falcon Park—

In the foothills just west of Denver, 1,400-acre Mt. Falcon Park offers easy day hiking. Almost 10 miles of hiking trails provide choice views of Denver, Red Rocks Park and Mt. Evans. But the park also has an interesting history.

It begins at the turn of the century with the story of wealthy dreamer John Brisben Walker, founder of *Cosmopolitan* magazine. Walker owned a 4,000-acre estate that included a stone castle on Mt. Falcon. His grandiose idea was to build a summer White House on Mt. Falcon for presidents to use. One source of funding included 10-cent donations from thousands of Colorado school children. Unfortunately, construction never got beyond the laying of the foundation and cornerstone. World War I caused delays, as did Walker's personal financial problems. The crushing blow came in 1918 when his own home was destroyed by fire. Walker died penniless in 1931 at age 83.

Remnants of his once-impressive home and the "Western White House" can still be seen along the hiking trails in the park. After a big snowstorm, Mt. Falcon is a great place to cross-country ski. To reach the park from Denver, head southwest on Hwy. 285 about 14 miles to the Indian Hills exit (Parmalee Gulch Rd.). Drive north for about 2.5 miles and turn right at the Mt. Falcon Park sign and proceed to the parking area. For more information about the park, contact **Jefferson County Open Space, 18301 W. 10th Ave., Suite 100, Golden, CO 80401; (303) 278-5925.**

Red Rocks Park—

Red Rocks Amphitheater, located in Red Rocks Park just west of Denver near the town of Morrison, is a sight to behold ... where else can you see golden and bald eagles perching where the Beatles once performed? This amphitheater, surrounded by towering 400-foot red rocks, was completed in 1941 by George Cranmer, Denver's legendary manager of improvements and parks. Nature had finished about three-quarters of the work in this natural bowl, but the 8,000-seat theater left something to be desired acoustically.

After a few years of dissonant complaints, Cranmer went to Germany at his own expense to consult with Wolfgang Wagner, son of the great Richard Wagner himself. Cranmer wanted to hear Richard Wagner's operas at Red Rocks, and he wanted to hear them right. Wagner came and adjusted the theater to the acoustic satisfaction of everyone, gallantly refusing to be paid.

These days, rock and roll, country and other popular music concerts pack the place every summer. Both musicians and spectators love the amphitheater for its unique location and the spectacular panoramic view of Denver spreading over the plains. Aside from the summer concerts, the amphitheater remains empty except for the Easter sunrise service that attracts thousands each year.

If you're not interested in seeing a concert, a number of fine hiking trails wind through the 2,700-acre park, and it's a great place for a picnic. Although it's tempting, stay off the rocks—park rangers are quick to dole out stiff fines to anyone challenging this rule. To reach Red Rocks Park from Denver, head west on Interstate 70 to the Morrison exit and drive south to the entrance to the park. Call **(303) 575-2637** for more information.

Roxborough State Park—

Spectacular razor-backed rocks march along the face of the foothills to join their brothers at Red Rocks. Miles of hiking trails take you through lush meadows and between rocks created over millions of years by stream-deposited sand, turned reddish from iron compounds. Both prairie and mountain species grow in this unique setting—aspen next to yucca and, in the spring, a diversity of flowers. Bobcats, deer and coyotes roam the hollows and eagles circle overhead when rainfall is short. There's no telling what the scrub oak hides from your view, but somewhere atop a red rock tower, you'll catch a glimpse of something that is seen only when it chooses to be seen.

One trail leads you to a small cabin built with hopes of turning this place into a resort four generations ago. Fortunately, the residents of Denver weren't quite up to making the trip on a regular basis. In another instance, a subdivision was planned amid the dramatic rocks, but as luck (and perhaps fate) would have it, the company went bankrupt before any houses could be built. Today everyone can enjoy the miles of nature trails in this dramatic environment; in winter Roxborough is a place of solitude and wonder. After a snowstorm, it's best explored on touring skis. The visitors center blends perfectly into the landscape—inside you can look at the exhibits and participate in educational programs. Rangers often lead trail hikes and interpretive nature walks. From Denver take Santa Fe Dr. (Hwy. 85) south to Titan Rd. Turn right and proceed 3.5 miles and left (still on Titan Rd.) another 3 miles to a marked entrance to the park. **4751 N. Roxborough Dr., Littleton, CO 80125; (303) 973-3959.**

Waterton Canyon—

This steep canyon, formed by the rushing waters of the South Platte River, has endured a number of major changes. The first was in 1877, when narrow-gauge tracks were laid through the canyon by the Denver South Park & Pacific Railroad. Then came Strontia Springs Resort, which catered to Denverites escaping the city for the weekend. The most drastic change occurred in 1983, when a large portion of the canyon was flooded by the Strontia Springs Reservoir. Though the reservoir has forever changed its character, Waterton Canyon remains an excellent recreation area that is close to the city.

Southwest of Denver, a dirt road leads 6 miles to the base of Strontia Springs Dam alongside the South Platte River. Fishing for large rainbow and brown trout in the tailwaters of the dam has been excellent.

The road into Waterton Canyon marks the start of the Colorado Trail, which leads 469 continuous miles to Durango in the southwestern corner of the state. This road ends at the former site of Stevens Gulch at the base of the dam. From here a 10-mile hiking (and horse) trail leads to the confluence of the North and South forks of the South Platte River (near the ghost town of South Platte). Along the way, watch for bighorn sheep. To reach the start of Waterton Canyon, drive south on Interstate 25 to C-470; west on C-470 to Wadsworth Blvd. Turn south on Hwy. 121. Continue past Chatfield Reservoir to the start of the service road (near the Martin Marietta plant).

At this confluence of the North and South forks, the controversial Two Forks Dam may be constructed, in effect flooding two mountain valleys. For now, at least, the South Fork of the South Platte flows through a beautiful, wide valley while providing some of the finest trout fishing in Colorado. A dirt road follows this fork of the river up the South Platte River Valley to the small town of Deckers; the entire valley is fairly heavily used with a lot of fishing, camping and hiking on public land. The South Platte River Valley can be reached from Denver by hiking the Colorado Trail up Waterton Canyon. Or drive south on Hwy. 285 for 32 miles to Pine Junction, then south on County Rd. 126 for 25 miles to Deckers.

SWIMMING

Celebrity Sports Center—

This indoor pool also features water slides. For more information, see the Amusements section.

Denver Parks and Recreation—

In parks around the metro Denver area, 37 recreation centers are open to the public. The centers don't all have pools, but there are 14 outdoor and eight indoor pools scattered around the city. For information on hours and exact locations, call **(303) 575-3043.**

TENNIS

Free courts can be found at parks throughout Denver. The city puts out a free listing of all public park facilities. For more information on tennis courts in Denver, call **(303) 295-4435** and talk with Jim Peros. Here are a few ideas.

City Park—

Six brand new, lighted courts have been added to the existing eight courts. Located at **E. 17th Ave.** and **Colorado Blvd.**

Crestmoor Park—

Four courts are located within this quiet park, and they are often open. **E. First Ave.** at **Monaco Pkwy.**

Huston Lake Park—

Play tennis next to a lake on one of four courts. **W. Kentucky Ave.** at **S. Vallejo St.**

Rosamond Park—

These four courts are usually open. The park is located in the vicinity of the Tech Center at **E. Quincy Ave.** and **S. Tamarac Dr.** If they happen to be full, travel south on Tamarac Dr. for a couple of miles to **Bible Park** where there are four more courts.

Washington Park—

The six lighted courts on the south side of the park are often crowded, but it's a great central location. **E. Louisiana Ave.** at **S. Downing St.**

———— SEEING AND DOING ————

AMUSEMENTS

Celebrity Sports Center—

This one building houses an 80-lane bowling alley, a billiard parlor, three large rooms filled with video games, three huge water slides, a swimming pool, bars and restaurants. There's probably more, but you get the idea. You'll even find free child care. The whole family can give in to a quarter-spending addiction. You may leave bleary-eyed, blinking at the sun like vampires who have made a dreadful mistake, but the kids will love it. **888 S. Colorado Blvd., Denver, CO 80222; (303) 757-3321.**

Elitch Gardens Amusement Park—

Elitch's has graced Denver since 1890, when the gardens were planted on the high plains northwest of town. Mary Elitch, whose husband died a year after the park opened, is one of Denver's heroines. She kept her prices low and her gardens inviting, offering a vast array of concerts and children's programs for free. She never forgot the children of the poor, as so many of the successful settlers did. Until recently, Elitch's Gaslight Theater housed one of the oldest summer stock theaters in America.

For a time in the 1900s Elitch's was the cultural center of Denver, providing the only access to classical music and light opera. Today, all your favorite rides are here, along with islands of flowers and a feeling that this is what amusement parks were meant to be. This is where banjos and straw hats belong. Ride the Twister, rated the sixth best roller coaster in the world by the planet's great roller coaster aficionados. The newer amusement parks around the country can't impart the same feeling of the good ol' summertime like Elitch's can. A variety of ticket options are available. Open May through Labor Day. **4620 W. 38th Ave., Denver, CO 80212; (303) 455-4771 or (303) 691-4705.**

Lakeside Amusement Park—

Yes, Denver has two very old amusement parks, and most Denverites would not choose a favorite. Smaller than Elitch's, Lakeside has some great attractions including the Cyclone Coaster and the funhouse. On the nearby lake, Lakeside features speedboat rides. They don't make amusement parks like this one any more. Open on weekends in May and then from 6 pm daily, June through Labor Day. Look for the high bell tower and the lake just south of Interstate 70 at Sheridan Blvd. **4601 Sheridan Blvd., Denver, CO 80212; (303) 477-1621.**

Water World—

Surfing in Colorado? It's possible at this monstrously large summertime hangout. Hundreds of sun and water worshippers turn out each day for rides down slides, through the innertube rapids and on the waves in the wave pool. "Wally World" provides a place for younger kids to play. Get into your suit, break out the suntan lotion and stop by for some good wet fun. Open Memorial Day through Labor Day, **1850 W. 89th Ave., Federal Heights, CO 80221; (303) 427-SURF.**

NEARBY

Tiny Town—

Tiny Town is back! Located on 20 acres in the mountains southwest of Denver, this unique place is just what the name implies . . . a tiny town. Miniature churches, fire stations, houses and schools line the streets, fascinating children and, yes, adults too. Started in 1915 by George Turner as a playground for his daughter, Tiny Town soon was attracting up to 25,000 visitors each summer. By the late 1940s, a series of floods, a fire and a rerouting of the highway had caused the town to begin crumbling. Attempts to resurrect it over the years failed—that is, until the summer of 1988. Thanks to community support, Tiny Town is going strong and plans to have its diminutive railroad running by summer of 1989. Small fee charged. Open on weekends in summer only. To reach Tiny Town from Denver, head southwest on Hwy. 285, about 5 miles past the Morrison exit and turn left onto **South Turkey Creek Rd**. You'll see the Tiny Town sign from the highway.

BREWERY TOURS

Coors Brewery Tour—

Each year 350,000 visitors head to Golden for a free, half-hour tour of the world's largest single brewing facility. Small groups of 14 people wander through, looking in awe at the 13,000-gallon copper kettles in which the beer is blended, heated and filtered. Coors beer is not heat-pasteurized but is made by a process that, according to their flavor experts, maintains a preferred taste. You'll also get a chance to look at the malting, quality-control and packaging departments. Saving the best part for last, the tour ends in the tasting room where visitors (of age) can sample a fresh, ice-cold glass of Coors on tap. With advance reservations, tours are available in foreign languages and for those with hearing and mobility limitations. Open from 10 am–4 pm Mon.–Sat. **13th St. and Ford St., Golden; (303) 277-BEER.**

BUFFALO HERDS

Once they numbered in the millions. After the white man made his way west and his 50-year slaughter ended, barely 1,000 of the furry beasts remained. Luckily, buffalo hunting was finally outlawed. Today their numbers have increased to more than 30,000 throughout the West. A couple of Denver mountain parks contain herds that are usually easy to see. The most accessible place is just off Interstate 70, 20 miles west of Denver at the Genesee Park exit. Daniel's Park, 20 miles south of Denver, has the largest herd. To reach Daniel's Park from Denver, head south on Interstate 25 to County Line Rd. and head west to Daniel's Park Rd. Turn left and proceed to the park.

HISTORIC BUILDINGS

Denver has a cache of historic buildings, hidden away on residential streets and garishly displayed on busy avenues. Just driving around isn't enough, so we suggest taking a tour with Historic Denver. You can select from a "Mansions and Millionaires" tour, or walk through Denver's 9th Street Historic Park. Van tours also are available. Call in advance to reserve a spot on the summer schedule or to arrange a custom itinerary with a historian. Fees are charged. Contact **Historic Denver Inc., Denver Union Station, 1701 Wyncoop St., Suite 200, Denver, CO 80202;** **(303) 543-1858.**

Colorado State Capitol—

It is not obvious that this building is modeled after the US Capitol. For one thing, its smaller dome is nicely plated with gold and, for another, the building is gray. The 13th step on the west side announces that it is precisely a mile high (a disputed measurement, by a few feet). Completed in 1908, the state capitol sits impressively on a hill overlooking Civic Center Park, commanding an excellent view of the mountains. As well it should—a law forbids high-rise buildings from blocking this view.

Inside, the workmanship is impeccable, with beautiful native marble, brass banisters and vaulted ceilings. Above the legislative chambers, stained-glass representations of surprisingly recent governors and early settlers illuminate the proceedings. The informative tours, which begin inside the west entrance, allow you to stand on the walkway at the base of the dome. But the best show is inside when the legislature is in session. In a small glassed-in room just off the senate floor, lobbyists vie for the attention of legislators. Or you can go into the cafeteria, where the governor tends to buy oatmeal cookies at about 9 am. Tours are given in summer on the half hour from 9 am–3:30 pm Mon.–Fri.; call ahead for winter hours. **1475 Sherman St., Denver, CO; (303) 866-2604.**

Governor's Mansion—

Walter Cheesman built this house for his family at the turn of the century. He died before its completion, but not before he had ensured that the grounds were terraced to rival the most innovative gardens in Europe. Cheesman, an early settler, was Denver's first pharmacist. At one time he owned the site of the future capitol, where he and his neighbors grazed their cattle. Cheesman was an opportunist whose name should not be attached to philanthropy— that was his wife's doing after he died.

Mrs. Cheesman and her daughter lived in the house until 1926, when they sold it to Claude Boettcher. Claude's father, Charles, had the foresight to bring a trunk full of sugar beet seeds home to Colorado after a trip to Europe, thereby founding the sugar beet industry in northern Colorado. From this enterprise he diversified into other businesses with incredible success. When Claude bought the Cheesmans' house, which promptly became known as the Boettcher house, he assured them that it would be maintained and that the collection of art inside would multiply. Most of the house remains as Cheesman designed it, including the large library and lounge off the main hall. Across the hall is an enormous dining room, which now suits the needs of Colorado's governors. The house has particularly striking pieces of oriental art. The chandeliers are superb works of crystal and porcelain.

The pride of the house, however, is the

The sights and sounds have changed in downtown Denver since R. C. McClure took this photograph in 1912 (courtesy of the Denver Public Library, Western History Collection).

60- by 70-foot Palm Room, added by Boettcher. Its white marble floor, white stone columns and white furniture give the room a feeling of great airiness. Palm trees accent the room; large windows open out to Cheesman's terraced garden. Free half-hour tours of the magnificent house are given on Tues. from 10 am–1 pm June through Aug.; call **(303) 866-3682** for information.

Grant-Humphreys Mansion—

In 1902 James B. Grant, a former governor, completed this 42-room mansion at a cost of $35,000. An Alabama boy, Grant wanted to live in an antebellum mansion. Since he had the money, he went ahead and built it here in Denver. The house is furnished with a billiard room, bowling alley, auditorium and an enormous ballroom. Mahogany ceiling beams adorn rooms up to 60 feet long. When Grant died in 1911, the house came into the hands of another southerner, Albert Humphreys. The new owner's family kept up the proud traditions of the house, though it never became the governor's mansion as Grant had hoped. Today it's all still there, including a grand staircase. Although much of the home is being used for office space, a tour of the mansion is worth your time. The house is open from 10 am–2 pm Tues.–Fri. Admission is charged. **770 Pennsylvania St., Denver, CO; (303) 894-2506.**

MUSEUMS AND GALLERIES

Black American West Museum—

Finally, the story can be told. Nearly one-third of all cowboys in the western US were black. This museum, located in the heart of Five Points, tells the history of blacks in the West in various roles as cowboys, doctors, barbers, legislators and teachers. It's a fine place to get a feel for this segment of our history, through artifacts, historic photos and, if you're lucky, through a real live legend. When we visited, Alonzo Pettie strode through the door. A spry 78 years old, decked out in a Levis jacket and cowboy hat, Alonzo told us his story, that of growing up in east Texas and breaking horses on a ranch. He didn't only break horses—while riding in various rodeos he broke his pelvis and crushed his knuckle. In 1929 he took first place for bullriding in an Odessa, Texas, rodeo with a broken shoulder. He participated in the first black rodeo in Denver in 1947. You may learn a lot if you stop by for a visit. Small admission fee. **608 28th St.** (at Welton, north of downtown); **(303) 295-1026.**

The Children's Museum—

If you don't have a child of your own, borrow one and go out for a great time at one of the best museums in town. Displays here are meant to be touched, prodded, pulled and played with, all with the purpose of teaching children (and adults) the inner workings of processes and machines. Shop at the smallest grocery store in the world, complete with automatic price scanner. (No coupons accepted!) Cover yourself in greasepaint at the circus tent or watch the youngsters shriek with delight while "dry swimming" in two rooms full of plastic balls. A child-sized house with its guts exposed shows the complete workings, including wiring and plumbing. Puppet shows are popular, as are various seasonal exhibits. Take the children yourself to see this museum—you'll enjoy the trip as much as they will. Open Sun. noon–5 pm, Tues.–Thur. and Sat. 10 am–5 pm, Fri., 10 am–9 pm, closed Mon. As you drive by on Interstate 25, you can't miss the museum, across the highway from Mile High Stadium; it's the brilliant green building with a pyramid roof. **2121 Crescent Dr., Denver; (303) 433-7444.**

Colorado History Museum—

Colorado's history really comes to life at this fine museum, run by the Colorado Historical Society. The well-organized museum is also home to many artifacts and great dioramas depicting Colorado's colorful history—from detailed and accurate Indian gatherings to a display of Denver's disastrous flood in 1864. There are photographs and artifacts of the Indian wars, the massacres, the pioneers and miners, the bars, brothels and early residents. It's as complete a gathering of state history as can be housed under one roof. Take your time and enjoy. Don't miss the fine book shop with a wide selection of Colorado books. Located in the wedge-shaped building just southwest of the State Capitol. Open Mon.–Sat. 10 am–4:30 pm, Sun. noon–4:30 pm. **1300 Broadway; (303) 866-3681.**

Denver Art Museum—

At first glance, this castle-like structure looks displaced among the office buildings and city hall. A castle it's not, but rather a great repository of artwork, including one of the finest Native American collections in the country. It's also home to a fine collection of Japanese and Chinese displays and a premier collection of Spanish American art. The American floor houses Thomas Cole's *Dream of Arcadia*, a masterpiece of the Hudson River School. Several Picassos, Monets and a Klee add strength to the European collection. Beware of Linda, resident art critic and patron—she's the lifelike sleeper/statue found on the floor of the contemporary section!

The museum hosts popular Wed. night parties, with music and open exhibits. Fashionable with the city's elite and singles, these gatherings provide a good time. A restaurant is open for lunch and, though service is not provided at lightning speed, the food is good. Try the chicken cashew salad! Open Tues.–Sat. 10 am–5 pm, Sun. noon–5 pm, closed Mon. **100 W. 14th Ave. Pkwy.; (303) 575-2793.**

Denver Firefighter's Museum and Restaurant—

One of the best-kept secrets in town, this place is unknown even to many natives. Learn about Denver's history as well as the history of firefighting. The museum houses old fire engines, fire equipment and a fairly good restaurant ($). Don't worry, you don't have to slide down the pole to the exit after lunch! Open Mon.–Fri. 11 am–2 pm. **1326 Tremont Pl.; (303) 892-1100.**

Denver Museum of Natural History—

The granddaddy of museums in Denver, this museum is probably best recognized for innovative, extensive dioramas of animals in their natural habitats. This was the first museum to use such displays (some of which were built in the 1930s as WPA projects). It holds the world's largest mammoth fossil, scaring small children and adults alike as they round the corner to a room filled with tusks and teeth. Dinosaur skeletons—especially that of Tyrannosaurus Rex—seem to roar in mid-stride at visitors, and a whale skeleton swims in dry air.

Ornithologists and butterfly enthusiasts will be delighted with the collection of North American birds and butterflies. A walk through the mineral collection mimics a journey into an underground cavern, complete with fluorescent rocks and samples from Colorado's richest mines and mills (be sure to look for "Tom's Baby").

The museum generally hosts several traveling exhibits (check the schedule for current offerings). There is a cafeteria, restaurant and gift shop. Admission fee charged. Open daily from 9 am–5 pm. **2001 Colorado Blvd.; (303) 370-6363.** The museum includes two other attractions that can make a visit here exceptional.

The **IMAX Theater**, located at the east entrance of the museum complex, is truly one of those places where the viewer becomes part of the film. The theater features a screen that is four stories tall with a state-of-the-art sound system. The screen can become the Grand Canyon, outer space, the stratosphere or Stonehenge. Go where the filmmaker wants to take you, and nobody will get hurt. Call **(303) 370-6300** for prices and show times.

Located on the west side of the building, the **Gates Planetarium** features traditional astronomical displays, including views of the night sky as it appears in all hemispheres and in all seasons. Occasionally, spectacular laser shows get the normally staid planetarium rocking to the music of Pink Floyd, U2, Led Zeppelin, the Beatles or whomever the laser projectionists are moved to feature. Call **(303) 320-0120** or **388-4201** for prices and show times.

Forney Transportation Museum—

A short walk from Confluence Park takes you to this impressive collection of antique cars, motorcycles, trains and planes. The museum is housed in the old powerhouse for the Denver Tramway, precursor to our current bus system. Older Denver natives mourn the demise of the trams, much as Brooklynites wish the Dodgers were still home . . . but the past can still be seen here at the museum. More than 300 vehicles fill the powerhouse and grounds outside, but the real darling of the collection rests on its own rail spur. The "Big Boy" is one of the few existing examples of the large steam locomotives that opened the West. Open in summer Mon.–Sat. 9 am–5 pm, Sun. 11 am–5 pm; in winter Mon.–Sat. 9:30 am–5 pm. Admission fee charged. To reach the museum, take Exit 211 off Interstate 25 or turn left off the 15th St. viaduct from downtown. **1416 Platte St.; (303) 433-3643.**

Mizel Museum of Judaica—

This small museum has a fine reputation for its fascinating changing exhibits. Anyone interested in Jewish artifacts from around the world should call ahead to see what the museum is exhibiting. Past displays have ranged from ancient Middle Eastern artifacts, to a wonderful collection of hats, to photos from the lost world of the European Jews. Open Mon.–Thurs. from 10 am–4 pm, Sun. from 10 am–noon. No fee is charged. **560 S. Monaco Pkwy.; (303) 333-4156.**

Molly Brown House Museum—

Built in 1889 by one of Denver's great architects, William Lang, this Colorado sandstone and lava stone home is a Victorian masterpiece. J. J. Brown, husband of one of the state's most colorful characters, Molly Brown, bought the mansion in 1894 with money made from his famous Little Johnny gold mine. Early in their marriage, J.J. accidentally burned up $300,000 in

$1,000 bills, which Molly had hidden in their pot-belly stove for safe-keeping. They later became more proficient in managing their money.

For years Molly sought acceptance by Denver's high society, but her image as a hell-raising country bumpkin worked against her. Her heroism during the sinking of the *Titanic* gained her international fame, the nickname "Unsinkable Molly" and acceptance in Denver.

Today, tours of the home are given by women dressed in turn-of-the-century costumes. Stone lions guard the entrance, and the interior is decorated in velvet, lace, beautiful dark wood and period furniture. Unfortunately, the Brown's personal furniture was sold at auction in the 1930s. At Christmas time, the decorations are enchanting, transforming the entire house into something more than a historical landmark. Open in summer Tues.–Sat. 10 am–4 pm, Sun. from noon–4 pm. In winter Tues.–Sat. 10 am–3 pm, Sun. from noon–3 pm. Admission fee charged. **1340 Pennsylvania St.; (303) 832-4092.**

Museum of Western Art—

Housing one of the finest Western art collections in the country, this museum is located downtown in the old Navarre Building. In the Gay Nineties, its convenient location across the street from the historic Brown Palace Hotel allowed it to serve beautifully as a high-class bordello and gambling house. Subterranean passageways between the two buildings assured "discretion in all transactions." The wonderful art includes more than 100 paintings and bronzes by the likes of Bierstadt, Moran, Remington and, in a more recent vein, paintings by Georgia O'Keeffe. It's difficult to imagine a better marriage of history and art. Open Tues.–Sat. 10 am–4:30 pm. **1727 Tremont Pl.; (303) 296-1880.**

United States Mint—

This building where US coins are made looks like a Florentine palace inside and out. Inside the mint you'll be treated to a guided tour that explains coin production and also stops before a stack of gold bullion—the mint is the third largest gold repository in the country. Near the end of the tour, the guide might point out the antiquated (we hope) machine gun turrets, installed after the stock market crash of 1929 to make sure things didn't get out of hand. Forever afterward you'll check for the little "D" below the date on your pennies. Open daily in summer from 8 am–3 pm; in winter from 8:30 am–3 pm. Located on the corner of **W. Colfax Ave.** and **Cherokee St.;** (303) 844-3582.

NEARBY
Buffalo Bill's Grave and Memorial Museum—

Perched atop Lookout Mountain, just west of Denver, you'll find the final resting place of William F. Cody, better known as "Buffalo Bill." Cody personified the Wild West, having been a pony express rider, scout for the cavalry and quite a buffalo hunter. Supposedly, he got his nickname from the thousands of buffalo he killed. In the late 1800s he achieved international fame with his Wild West show, which toured throughout the US, Canada and Europe. He died at his sister's home in Denver in 1917 and was quickly buried on Lookout Mountain, despite protests from Nebraska and Wyoming claiming Cody had wanted to be buried in their states. To make sure his grave wasn't robbed by miffed residents of either state, it was covered with concrete and reinforced with steel bars. When Cody's wife died, however, workers bashed away at the concrete in order to put Mrs. Cody's coffin on top of her husband's—quite an ironic end for a man who spent much of his life avoiding his wife!

Along with his grave is a museum containing much of Buffalo Bill's memorabilia. An observation deck on top of the museum gives you a great view of the mountains to the west and the Denver area to the east. Small fee charged. To reach the grave and museum from Denver, drive west on Interstate 70 about 15 miles and get off at Exit 256. Follow the signs up Lookout Mountain Rd. to the turnoff. If you continue on Lookout Mountain Rd. for about 7 miles you'll reach Golden. More scenic than the interstate, this road provides a spectacular bird's-eye view of Golden. Open May through Oct. 9 am–5 pm, Nov. through Apr. 9 am–4 pm. **(303) 526-0747.**

Colorado Railroad Museum—

Train buffs can get back on track at this large collection of trains scattered about a 12-acre yard. Some real gems are kept in this back lot—many of the silent trains are open for anyone to climb aboard and pretend. Take a close look at the D&RG Engine No. 346, the oldest operating locomotive in Colorado, or the Galloping Goose #2, a strange-looking contraption built with various parts from a Buick, Pierce Arrow, Ford truck and a railroad engine. Inside the re-created depot, old photos and exhibits of Colorado's railroad history are displayed. Downstairs, the scale model HO train running through a miniature world is a little boy's dream. Open from 9 am–5 pm daily. To get here, take exit 265 off Interstate 70 in Golden and follow the signs. **17155 W. 44th Ave., Golden; (303) 279-4591.**

NIGHTLIFE

Most visitors do not come to Denver specifically for its late-night and cultural diversions. Some travelers have been quick to decry the lack of big-city lights, and late-night (after 2 am) restaurants and bars. But, visitors generally will be pleased with Denver's ever-increasing diversity of places to eat, drink and "be happy." The jazz scene is flourishing and the Denver Center for the Performing Arts has added a vitality to the cultured side of this so-called "cow town." If you feel like a night of country-western dancing or comedy, there are a number of choices. For a complete listing of events and entertainment in the metro area, pick up a free copy of *Westword,* or consult either the *Rocky Mountain News* or the *Denver Post* Friday editions. Here are a few suggestions.

The Boiler Room—

Located in the old Tivoli Brewery, this is a beer lover's dream! For more information, see Tivoli Denver in the Shopping section.

The Burnsley Hotel—

For Denver's many talented jazz players, this is a favorite room. The mirrored walls allow you to watch the interaction of the players from several angles and to see the responses of other listeners to each nuance of the soloists. Live jazz with an "East Coast" flavor pervades the room and, better yet, there's no cover charge. Jazz performances 8:30–10 pm Tues., 5–9 pm Wed., 9 pm–1 am Thur.–Sat. **1000 Grant St.; (303) 830-1000.**

Casino Cabaret—

Originally opened in 1949 as a showcase for the big bands, this club now features nationally known acts and prominent local bands. Though not as posh as it was in its heyday, Casino Cabaret is still a good place to drink, listen to great rock, rhythm and blues or soul music and dance the night away on the large dance floor. In the heart of Five Points (one of Denver's inner-city neighborhoods), this place has an energy and excitement not found in suburbia. Check it out! It's a good idea to call ahead to find out which band is playing. Weekend nights only. **2639 Welton St.; (303) 292-9988.**

Comedy Works—

If you feel like some laugh therapy, stop by the Comedy Works, featuring local acts and national headliners nightly. New talent takes the stage on Mon. Located in Larimer Square at **1226 15th St.; (303) 595-3637.** If you are staying in the Tech Center area or the south part of town, consider the equally funny **George McKelvey's Comedy Club, 10015 E. Hampden Ave.; (303) 368-8900.**

Country Dinner Playhouse—

Located near the Tech Center, off Interstate 25 at the southern end of the metro area, this dinner playhouse is always consistent if not spectacular. A buffet dinner is followed by a full-scale musical production. After the "Barnstormers" perform some country music and square dance numbers, the stage descends from the ceiling. The acting and choreography are usually good, with some productions excelling each year. This is a great family outing. Reservations recommended. **6875 S. Clinton St., Englewood; (303) 799-1410.**

Denver Center for the Performing Arts—

Beautiful and functional, this impressive arts center has given Denver a cultural identity. Whether you are interested in theater, music, ballet or opera, this series of architecturally unique buildings in downtown Denver is the place to come. There are a number of nightly entertainment offerings. The acoustically acclaimed Boettcher Concert Hall is home to the **Denver Symphony Orchestra, (303) 592-7777;** since the 1930s this fine orchestra has been in Denver's limelight. **Stagewest, (303) 623-6400,** is a cabaret theater that has enjoyed a string of recent successes with lighthearted plays such as *Greater Tuna* and *Beehive.* For traditional and contemporary drama as well as musicals, contact **The Denver Center Theatre Company** at **(303) 893-4100.** National touring shows with huge casts play at the **Auditorium Theatre, (303) 893-4100,** as does the **Colorado Ballet, (303) 298-0677.** Whatever desire you may have for a night out, call one of these organizations first.

El Chapultepec—

No need to dress formally at this funky jazz dive. Small and unassuming, the smoky bar features some of the best bebop around. So, if you're into upright bass and sultry saxophone, stop by. El Chapultepec ("the grasshopper") is one of those places your mother probably warned you about. But never fear—the crowd won't bite. The Mexican food is hot and the jazz is cool. Open seven nights a week and never a cover. **1962 Market St.; (303) 295-9126.**

Herman's Hideaway—

Hot. Dark. Crowded. Smoky. What more could you ask for in a blues/rock club? In this small, informal setting, the music leaps out at you. Unless you want to stand, get here an hour or two before the bands start playing at 9 pm. There is also dancing (on a thimble-sized floor), pool and plenty of general overindulgence here. **1578 S. Broadway; (303) 778-9916.**

Muddy's Java House—

If you're wondering where the beret and bongo crowd hangs out in Denver, make a beeline for Muddy's. This coffee house/used bookstore provides a comfortable setting for people to hang out and explore the outer limits of their intellect— or at least make it appear that way. Order a decadent dessert and a cup of espresso and launch into a conversation that doesn't have to end anytime soon. Muddy's is open from 7 pm–2 am Mon.–Wed., 7 pm–4 am Thur.–Sat. **2200 Champa St.; (303) 298-1631.**

XXIII Parrish—

A taste of big-city nightlife has arrived in downtown Denver's warehouse district. Making an appearance at this multi-level, multi-theme nightclub is like walking into a very exclusive party. On the upper floor, various classy-looking rooms are created by painted canvas backdrops. Stop by for a drink on the patio, furnished with wicker chairs, or shoot some pool in the elegant billiard room. DJ-controlled dance music blares from above a large dance floor in one section (the ballroom) of the club. If you tire of the canned music and somewhat pretentious atmosphere upstairs, head down to the "garage," where local bands perform; have a snack and a cup of coffee in the quiet art deco room adjacent to the music room. If you can't seem to stop at 2 am, stay around for after-hours breakfast fare and a cappuccino. **2301 Blake St.; (303) 296-6628.**

Wynkoop Brewery—

In lower downtown, this brewpub not only offers a great room, but also a chance to taste various flavors of beer—brewed on the premises. Try the stout, wheat, amber ale or bitter brew. If you can't decide, try a reasonably priced, four-ounce sample of each. It's a comfortable place to knock down a couple and then sit down for a meal. The bangers and mashers (traditional English sausage simmered in stout beer and mashed potatoes) are tasty. Maybe you'd prefer black bean cakes and brown rice or one of the spicy Cajun specialties. Lunch served from 11 am–2:30 pm Mon.–Sat., dinner from 5–10 pm Mon.–Thur., until 11 pm on Fri.–Sat.; the bar stays open into the night. Closed Sun. **1634 18th St., Denver; (303) 297-2700.**

CONCERTS

For big-name concerts, Denver has three major venues: **Red Rocks, (303) 572-4704** (see the Parks, Gardens and Recreation Areas section for more information), and **Fiddler's Green, (303) 741-5000,** are outdoor theaters open in summer only; **McNichols Sports Arena, (303) 572-4703,** is open year-round. On a much smaller scale, **The Paramount Theatre, (303) 825-4904,** in downtown Denver and the **Arvada Center for the Arts and Humanities, (303) 431-3080,** both attract national acts. **The Botanic Gardens, (303) 331-4010,** also hosts summer concerts of the classical and jazz variety. It's a gorgeous place to hear music while sipping a glass of wine and polishing off a picnic dinner. For more information see the Parks, Gardens and Recreation Areas section.

NEARBY

The Buck Snort Saloon—

This is a great place for dancing, albeit in crowded quarters, to quality live rock bands on Fri. and Sat. nights. Located near **Pine Junction,** about an hour's drive from Denver. See the Where to Eat section for more information.

The Little Bear—

This rustic mountain bar in the town of Evergreen is known for providing wild nights of dancing to live music. The Little Bear attracts a diverse crowd—from bikers to bankers—and everyone seems to enjoy the contrast. Top local rock and blues bands play most often, with national acts frequently making one- and two-night stops. For local flavor and great music, "downtown" Evergreen is a favorite choice. **28075 Hwy. 74, Evergreen, CO; (303) 674-9991.**

Observatory Bar & Cafe—

Live jazz and light rock music are performed at the Observatory (Thur.–Sat. nights). The place doesn't look like anything special from the outside or, for that matter, from the inside—until summer nights when they roll back the roof so you can eat and drink under the stars. A large telescope is wheeled out for a closer look at the heavens. This small bar has a feel-good atmosphere that is tough to match; for nightlife it's a great choice. The Mexican food, however, is very ordinary. If you want a good meal, then go across the street to El Rancho, which is within walking distance (see the Where to Eat section for more information). From Denver, take Interstate 70 west 18 miles to the El Rancho exit. Cross over to the south side of the highway and look for the sign. **(303) 526-1988.**

SHOPPING

The Denver metro area, isolated from other major cities, attracts people from around the region for its extensive shopping network. More than 25 malls and shopping centers exhibit great appeal, but like any city, there are a few unusually good places to spend, spend, spend . . .

Cherry Creek Shopping Center—

While still under renovation as this book goes to press, the new Cherry Creek Shopping Center is already the talk of the town. This was the country's first shopping "mall," built by Denver's own Temple Buell. The renovation will mark it as home to some very upscale stores, including I. Magnin, Neiman-Marcus and, the current

anchor, May D&F. In addition to all of the stores in the main mall, the surrounding neighborhood is bursting with small shops, art galleries and restaurants. This is a great place to stroll around, window shop and peek into some of the city's best small businesses. Located at **E. 1st Ave. and University Blvd.**

Of course, no listing of Denver shopping would be complete without mention of, perhaps, the best bookstore in the region.

The Tattered Cover Bookstore—Denver's largest and best-known bookstore puts forth an offering of more than 175,000 books . . . probably more than were lost at the burning of the library in Alexandria. This is not a used bookstore. Even so, Joyce Meskis, the owner, encourages leisurely browsing and reading. Feel free to plop down in a comfortable stuffed armchair and leaf through a few interesting titles. You could easily spend hours wandering through the three-story assortment of books perched on tidy, well-stocked shelves. In a quandary about a gift? There is a solution here. The Tattered Cover also offers worldwide mailing and free gift wrapping. If they don't have it stocked, and the book is in print in the known world, the helpful staff has the best ability to retrieve it. Be sure to take a look at the selection of magazines, calendars, maps, globes and greeting cards. Free parking in the covered lot next to the store. Located in the **Cherry Creek Shopping Center at 2955 E. 1st Ave. (at Milwaukee), Denver; (303) 322-7727 and 1-800-821-2896** in Colorado.

Larimer Square—

In the historic 1400 block of Larimer St., this restored downtown area is a must visit in Denver. Housed in 1880s vintage buildings, a variety of distinctive shops, restaurants and bars line one of Denver's oldest and, at one time, seediest streets. In 1959 Kent Ruth, in his book *Colorado Vacations*, called Larimer St. "pretty much a skid-row slum." Today the mood is both romantic and exuberant, especially in the evening when twinkling tree lights and street globes cast a warm glow on the restored three-story, brick Victorians. During the Oktoberfest celebration, Larimer St. is blocked off and kegs are tapped; brass bands and lederhosen are nearly as common as jeans and T-shirts. The architectural integrity has been maintained, even though wares are displayed in a bold, modern manner. From the Market's excellent cappuccino to William Sonoma's exotic cookery utensils, Larimer Square is a treasure to be enjoyed.

The 16th Street Mall and the Tabor Center—

The tree-lined 16th Street Mall slices through the center of the downtown shopping district. Outdoor cafes, historic buildings, shops and restaurants can be found along its length; free shuttle buses run up and down the mall connecting the Market St. and Civic Center bus stations. The crown jewel of the mall is the Tabor Center, with 65 stores on three levels. This glass-enclosed galleria is home to Brooks Brothers and Sharper Image; a host of unusual items are sold from vendor carts throughout. Stop by for a shoe shine or ride the glass elevator to the third-floor food court, which will entice you with smells from around the world. In summer step on up to the rooftop patio. This may be the most dense concentration of shopping heaven anywhere in Denver. The Tabor Center is located at **16th** and **Lawrence** streets.

Tivoli Denver—

Just off the Auraria college campus, Tivoli Denver is a monument to ingenuity. After its last batch of beer was bottled in 1969, the old Tivoli Brewery stood idle for years, collecting dust and broken windows until recently re-emerging as a premier shopping and dining center. Scattered throughout the odd corners of the castle-like building are remnants of the brewing process—copper kettles, Tivoli beer logos and giant pieces of brewing equipment. If all this makes you thirsty, stop in at the Boiler Room where they have 20 beers on tap and more than 100 bottled selections from around the world. Many restaurants, including the Rattlesnake Club (see the Where to Eat section), a 12-screen cinema and numerous upscale shops are housed here. The Tivoli Trolley gives free rides between downtown and Tivoli Denver. Located at **9th St.** and **Larimer St.**

ZOO

Denver Zoo (City Park)—

Denver's zoo has consistently been one of the city's most popular attractions, with more than one million visitors each year. Generous donations by Denver residents have helped the zoo to continue offering better (not necessarily bigger) exhibits throughout the years. Include a visit to the dall sheep mountain and the "North Shores" exhibit where you can view polar bears and sea lions swimming underwater—but not in the same tank! The children's zoo allows kids to get close to many gentle animals; it also offers rides on a small train. Be sure to visit the animal nursery where there is usually a newborn receiving special attention. Many of the animals are fed in mid-afternoon. The zoo is open daily from 10 am–5 pm year-round. **E. 23rd St.** between York St. and Colorado Blvd.; **(303) 331-4110.**

—————— WHERE TO STAY ——————

ACCOMMODATIONS

Denver presents an overwhelming number of lodging choices to vacationers. First of all there is a choice of which part of the city to stay in: downtown, uptown, the Tech Center area, near the airport or near Interstate 70 for a quick exit to the looming mountains. Then there is the question of price and style. The **Brown Palace** is the best-known Denver hotel—and with good reason. For a non-stop row of inexpensive motels, take a cruise down E. Colfax Ave. (it's not the best part of town). Other possibilities include a number of new high-rise hotels, major chain and discount accommodations, bed and breakfast inns and a youth hostel.

We have gone into some depth in picking a range of places to stay in the central area. If, however, you are just passing through or you want to stay in a different part of town, the **Denver Metro Convention and Visitors Bureau, (303) 892-1112,** can help you make a selection. Or call **Denver Metro Central Reservations, (303) 863-8521.** Consider the following unique recommendations.

Brown Palace Hotel — $$$ to $$$$

Nowhere in Denver does history come more completely to life than at the Brown Palace Hotel. When the Brown opened in 1892, one year before the silver panic, it put the "Queen City" on the map. The hotel was such a monument to economic good times it helped create the expectations necessary for Denver to survive and flourish into the future. A stunning example of Victorian architecture, the Brown's triangular exterior is built of Colorado red granite and Arizona sandstone; hand-carved Rocky Mountain animals lie in wait above the arched seventh-floor windows. Though the hotel was originally built on the edge of the city, Denver has grown up around the Brown Palace and it now enjoys a downtown location.

Since day one, the magnificent interior lobby has left lasting impressions on visitors. Six stories of wrought iron balconies rise to a stained-glass ceiling; the spacious ground floor retains an intimate feel with red leather sofas and overstuffed chairs, arranged in small groups in the center of the room. Mon. through Sat., from 2–4:30 pm, the lobby hosts an elegant afternoon tea, served with sandwiches, scones and truffles. Around the perimeter of the room, a number of glass cases are filled with historical memorabilia. The hotel may sound a bit stuffy, but really it's not. Stop by during the National Western Stock Show in Jan. and you may see the tables moved aside to accommodate a prize bull. Unless you've got a Stetson and cowboy boots, forget about trying to fit in with the rest of the hotel guests.

Over the years, many famous guests have stayed at the Brown. Dwight D. "Ike" Eisenhower used the hotel for his presidential campaign headquarters in 1952. The biggest hubbub the hotel has ever seen was in 1964 when the Beatles stayed at the Brown while performing a concert at Red Rocks. Five thousand screaming fans crowded the streets to catch a glimpse of their favorite musicians. The Brown received hundreds of applications for employment from eager teenage girls. Alas, when the fab four arrived, almost none of their fans were aware of the secret back entrance to the hotel.

Each of the 230 rooms and 25 guest suites has its own unique personality, featuring a window view and the finest furnishings possible. Unlike some historic hotels, the Brown Palace is not tattered around the edges. Rather it is a solid, immaculately kept hotel. Many of the bathrooms are decorated in an art deco style and all come with Crabtree and Evelyn toiletries. After bathing, wrap yourself in a thick terry cloth robe. Indulge in 24-hour room service in your private, luxurious setting.

The Brown is also home to some of Denver's best known restaurants. Dine at the pub-like **Ship Tavern** with replicas of American clipper ships. Remember to wear a coat and tie to the formal dining room of the **Palace Arms**. It's decorated in a Napoleonic theme and contains a set of dueling pistols thought to have belonged to Napoleon. The classy setting of **Ellyngton's** is popular for all meals, including Sun. champagne brunch. **321 17th St., Denver, CO 80202; 1-800-321-2599** nationwide, **1-800-228-2917** in Colorado, **(303) 297-3111** in Denver.

The Burnsley Hotel — $$$$

This hotel is located on Grant St. in an area once bustling with prominent Denverites' mansions that have since fallen, one by one, to the shovels of progress. Now apartment buildings, including the one the Burnsley inhabits, have replaced many of those mansions. The hotel was constructed in the 1960s, a decade notorious for thoughtless "urban renewal" in Denver. Joy Burns redeemed this remnant of Denver's architectural dark age with a stunning renovation in 1985. The hotel is located conveniently near the heart of the city, and a walk to downtown will take you past some of the remaining Victorian houses, many now serving as offices.

Each of the elegant suites in this 82-suite hotel has a private balcony, some with views of downtown and to the mountains beyond. As luxury has its price, staying here is not for the weak of wallet. Your money will bring you unrivaled service and some of the most luxurious rooms in Denver. One of the hotel's proudest accomplishments is, perhaps, the finest jazz room in Denver (see the Nightlife section). **1000 Grant St., Denver, CO 80203; (303) 830-1000.**

The Oxford Alexis Hotel — $$$ to $$$$

To many, the Brown Palace Hotel alone represents the grand luxury of historic hotels in Denver. But that's not the case. When completed in 1891 (one year before the Brown Palace), the Oxford Hotel "sported the latest in gadgets and technology as well as Gilded Age opulence." Located next to Union Station, the Oxford stood for years as a standout luxury hotel that catered mainly to train travelers. Since its grand reopening in 1983, the hotel has regained its original richness along with all the modern-day conveniences.

Designed by architect Frank E. Edbrooke, who later went on to create his Brown Palace masterpiece, this five-story brick building has had quite a history. The interior, furnished with the finest oriental rugs, woodwork, marble floors and frescoed walls, reflected the profitable silver mining days Colorado was enjoying at the time. Private water closets, along with

electric and gas lighting, amazed guests. The Oxford also boasted the first elevator in Denver. When the silver market crashed in 1893 and many Denver businesses went bankrupt, the Oxford pressed on. In fact, business was so good that additions were built in 1902, 1906 and 1912. During the 1930s, the Oxford was remodeled and transformed into an art deco showpiece. With its proximity to the train station, troops during World War II packed the hotel from basement to ceiling. After the war, the hotel began a steady decline. Skid row crept into lower downtown Denver in the 1960s and 1970s and the Oxford deteriorated into a run-down flop house. But during these hard times many Denverites remember the Oxford for the great jazz, folk music and melodramas that packed the place in the evenings.

In 1979 the hotel was purchased by Charles Callaway. A three-year, $12 million restoration revealed the original luxury that had been hidden for so long. Today 82 rooms, a mezzanine, lobby and main-floor restaurants and bars are furnished with antiques. Rooms range from comfortable singles to palatial suites. In the lobby, Baby Doe Tabor's piano sits near the front door, and a fireplace beckons—coffee and complimentary sherry are served here. With **McCormick's Fish House and Bar** you don't even need to leave the building for dining and nightlife. Be sure to visit the **Cruise Room**, a restored art deco bar that opened in the 1930s. Wall carvings, expressing drinking cheers in many languages, were created to celebrate the end of Prohibition.

Guests at the Oxford Alexis also have free guest privileges at the adjoining health club. Special weekend packages offered for couples include a bottle of champagne in the room. This is Denver's "Grand Small Hotel." **1600 17th St., Denver, CO 80202; (303) 628-5400 or 1-800-228-5838.**

The Westin Hotel — $$$ to $$$$

Part of the Tabor Center in downtown Denver, the Westin is a beautiful art deco hotel done in peach tones with green and black trim. Elegantly decorated, you won't find a harsh shadow in the hotel. If you really want to live the posh life, be sure to get one of the rooms with a TV in the bathroom. Equally popular with investment bankers and paranoiac rock stars, the Westin is conveniently located in the heart of the city. The fourth floor features a well-equipped health club and special programs are made available to guests for the theater or other events. The hotel offers a romance package that includes a bottle of Champagne and breakfast. The spacious **Augusta Restaurant** inside the hotel is rapidly gaining renown as one of Denver's finest. The view is also exquisite, as the two-tier dining area looks out over the city. Hotel rates are half-off on weekends. **1672 Lawrence St., Denver, CO 80202; 1-800-228-3000** toll free out of state or **(303) 572-9100** in Colorado.

Loew's Giorgio Hotel — $$$

From the outside, the Giorgio looks amazingly like Darth Vader—you can almost hear it breathe. Don't let the ultra-modern exterior put you off—inside you will find exquisite northern Italian decor with pleasant, immaculate surroundings. Complimentary continental breakfast and access to the well-appointed **Sporting Club** are included. The restaurant features Italian cuisine, of course, and very good food at that. The dark one stands at **4150 E. Mississippi, Denver, CO 80222; (800) 345-9172** outside Colorado or **(303) 782-9300** in Colorado.

Queen Anne Inn — $$$

If you are looking for Denver's finest, most romantic bed and breakfast, look no further . . . the Queen Anne Inn is it. Although open only since 1987, the inn has already been praised in *The New York Times*, *USA Today* and countless other newspapers, magazines and travel guides. All this attention is deserved; owners Chuck and Ann Hillestad run a first-class operation.

Built in 1879, this three-story home was designed in the Queen Anne style by Denver's most famous architect, Frank E. Edbrooke. The neighborhood, located conveniently near downtown Denver, was scheduled for demolition until the Hillestads and other preservationists came in and refurbished the grand homes on this historic block, now known as the Clements Historic District.

The Queen Anne is impeccably decorated with fine antiques, fresh cut flowers and original artwork. Chamber music wafts through the hallways and each of the ten guest rooms—you can't change the station but you can turn down the volume. Each room has a private bath and unique decor. The Fountain Room on the second floor is the honeymooners' dream, with a queen-sized, four-poster bed, a sunken tub and large picture windows looking out at Benedict fountain across the street. The unusual Aspen Room on the third floor has a turret ceiling with a 360° aspen mural painted on the walls. You feel as if you're in an aspen grove. Each morning an excellent continental breakfast is served, including fresh-baked muffins and croissants, fruit and delicious coffee and tea. For reservations, contact **2147 Tremont Pl., Denver, CO 80205; (303) 296-6666.**

Holiday Chalet — $$

If you're looking for a unique, historic and generally comfortable place to stay without spending a fortune, this reasonably priced lodge fits the bill. Built in 1896 as a private residence for the Bohm family, it still retains much of its original charm. The Holiday Chalet is immaculately kept. Many stained-glass windows spread throughout add colorful touches; a Waterford crystal chandelier sways over the front entrance and sunny bedrooms all have odd little corners. Each room comes with a kitchenette, a telephone and a color TV. You'll get used to the pink decor in no time. You may hear some street noise from Colfax Ave., but thanks to 18-inch walls, you certainly won't hear your neighbor snoring. Another reason to stay is because innkeeper Margot Hartman makes you feel right at home—in the same house where she spent many years growing up. She is also extremely knowledgeable about what Denver has to offer. **1820 E. Colfax Ave., Denver, CO 80218; (303) 321-9975.**

Denver International Youth Hostel — $

If you want a cheap bed for the night, this is the place. For well under 10 bucks a night you can stay in a dorm at the youth hostel; a chore, however, is required. The doors are locked between 10 am–5 pm and again from 10:30 pm–8:30 am. For a small deposit you can have a key to the front door. At present there are about 30 beds available as well as kitchen and bathroom facilities. The hostel is located just east of downtown Denver. **630 E. 16th Ave., Denver, CO 80203; (303) 832-9996.**

WHERE TO EAT

Denver's restaurant market is, and has been for years, bursting at the seams. This narrowed-down list reflects the favorites of longtime Denverites, as well as some more off-beat eateries. It's a diverse collection of restaurants in various price ranges, ethnic styles and locations. Trust us—whether you're in the mood for fine French cuisine, raucous western dining, or an exotic Afghani meal, these places are good. As Denver has a large Hispanic population, you'll find a vast selection of excellent Mexican restaurants. For a more complete listing of restaurants, pick up a free copy of *Westword* newspaper.

AMERICAN

Cliff Young's — $$$$

Cliff Young's philosophy floats between the abstract and the concrete; the sumptuous food is both real and sublime. At the center of one of Denver's finest dining venues, on 17th Ave. just east of downtown, this restaurant manages to outshine other very bright lights. You needn't fear the standard failings of nouvelle cuisine here—the portions are large and the tastes are not forced together into a culinary shotgun wedding. The food looks even better in the classy environment in which it is served. Consider the separate Amethyst Room for a more relaxed atmosphere. For a special meal, Cliff Young's ambience and fine food is the perfect blend. Reservations recommended; valet parking. Open for lunch 11:30 am–2 pm Mon.–Fri. Dinner is served from 6–10 pm Sun.–Thur., 6–11 pm Fri.–Sat. **638 E. 17th Ave.; 831-8900.**

The Rattlesnake Club — $$$$

This very expensive restaurant has put Denver on the culinary map. Based on chef Jimmy Schmidt's expertise, the Rattlesnake has received wide acclaim for its fresh, imaginative cuisine. You might want to order swordfish with grapefruit and ginger sauce, venison medallions in a brandy sauce or chicken empanadas with a light bleu cheese dressing. The setting is hard to beat—a three-story tower of the old Tivoli Brewery (replete with copper brewing vats) enjoys a great view of the city lights. Frank Stella's mesmerizing geometrical studies in oscillating color grace the walls. One warning: the wines are much more expensive here than at other Denver restaurants with comparable selections. The formal dining room is open 6–9:15 pm Sun.–Thur., 6–9:45 pm Fri.–Sat. If you want to see the room without paying the prices, go to the **Rattlesnake Grill ($$)**, which features southwestern food. Though the food is inconsistent and the atmosphere isn't quite like the formal dining room, many people like it. The Grill is open from 11:30 am–10 pm Mon.–Thur., until 11 pm on Fri.–Sat. Both are located in the **Tivoli Shopping Center, 901 Larimer St.; 573-8900.**

The Buckhorn Exchange — $$$

Virtually everyone of any importance in the Old West has eaten here, including Ulysses S. Grant, Teddy Roosevelt and Ernest Hemingway. It looks much as it did then, complete with elk, deer, mountain sheep and other animal heads mounted on the walls. This is Denver's oldest continuously operated restaurant, first serving the wild and woolly public in 1895. After all those years, you can be assured that this place is part museum. The Buckhorn features buffalo, elk and alligator appetizers or the inevitable Rocky Mountain oysters (you needn't worry about shelling these oysters!). Their bean soup is legendary as are the steaks. That Denver cousin is almost obligated to take you here. If you just want to stop by for a drink, head to the upstairs bar, one of Denver's friendliest. Open for lunch 11 am–3 pm Mon.–Fri. Dinner is served from 5–10 pm Sun.–Thur., 5–11 pm Fri.–Sat. Located in an obscure off-downtown neighborhood at **1000 Osage St.; 534-9505.**

North Woods Inn — $$

This is the place to take the family for good steaks and prime rib in a less formal setting. Your first clue to the casual western atmosphere will be the peanut shells underfoot—which you are encouraged to throw on the floor. Once the main dish arrives you can be assured of having more in front of you than you can finish. Most diners leave with a "doggie bag." Be sure to order one of the side dishes—cottage cheese with caraway seeds is unusual and tasty! Noon–10 pm Mon.–Sat. noon–9 pm Sun. **6115 S. Santa Fe Dr., Littleton; 794-2112.**

The Paramount Cafe — $$

It's rock and roll all the way at this stop. In the heart of the 16th Street Mall, within the historic Paramount Theatre building, this is a high-energy setting. The prices are fair, and the burgers, sandwiches and daily specials are served in generous portions. The diverse beer selection is first rate, and the people-watching just doesn't get any better. If you can get a table for lunch (after 11 am there is usually a wait), you'll see power ties mingling with Lycra. This is a popular stop for downtown business people, as well as before and after concerts at the classic art deco Paramount Theatre. Open 11 am–midnight, Mon.–Sat. **511 16th St.; 893-2000.**

Bonnie Brae Tavern — $ to $$

You wouldn't expect great pizza at a tavern with a Scottish name, but the name is based on its location in the Bonnie Brae neighborhood, not the food. Established in 1934 by Carl Dire, this popular spot is now run by his two sons, Mike and Hank. Ever popular with singles, families and University of Denver students, the tavern offers what many consider the best pizza in town. It is a simple place with comfortable, low-slung booths, allowing everyone a good look around the room. A superb minestrone soup and regular specials of American and Italian food help round out the menu. Of course, a wide variety of beers is also available. You can expect a wait at this local favorite. Open from 10:30 am–11 pm (until 9 pm Sun.), closed Mon. **740 S. University Blvd.; 777-2262.**

Daddy Bruce's Bar-B-Que — $ to $$

No question, this is the least pretentious and best barbecue in town. Daddy Bruce Randolph, one of Denver's most dedicated philanthropists, donates hundreds of hours and dollars to provide holiday meals and clothing to the homeless. Bruce's Thanksgiving feeds provide meals to more than 20,000 people annually. Although in his late 80s, Bruce is as likely to be found working in the restaurant as out catering or organizing clothing and meals for the homeless. Though the neighborhood is not the best, and liquor is not served (you can step across the street and brown-bag your liquor), this place is invariably busy. The emphasis here is on great down-home barbecued ribs, chicken, sliced beef and pork. The sauce is the best part, although cornbread and beans are staples, too. Catfish and chitterlings are also available, but not nearly as popular. Desserts are also wonderful—try the peach cobbler or the sweet-potato pie. Open from 11 am–midnight (until 1 am Fri. and Sat.). **1629 E. 34th Ave. (now Bruce Randolph Blvd.); 295-9115.**

Spanky's Roadhouse — $

We're told the owner sometimes goes

by the name Spanky, but you'll have to ask him to be sure. This small, informal restaurant is simply a great value for large, juicy burgers, a variety of chicken sandwiches, delicious hot ("atomic") chicken wings and salads. Sit down at one of the counter seats or tables; in summer, umbrella-covered tables on the patio are popular. Since it's located just west of the University of Denver, you'll find a lot of students and professorial types stopping by for lunch or dinner. In the evening, Spanky's can get packed for the beer specials and excellent munchie food. They "do not take bad checks or stolen credit cards." Open from 11 am–10 pm Mon.–Thur., 11 am–midnight Fri.–Sat., closed at 9 pm on Sun. **1800 E. Evans Ave.; 733-6886.**

BREAKFAST

Dozens — $ to $$

This is a fun place to eat. Specializing in breakfast items (especially egg dishes), Dozens is located in a comfortable Victorian house with wood floors and high ceilings. The creative menu items all have a Denver or Colorado theme. Choose from a large selection of omelettes, scrambled egg dishes, or something lighter such as waffles or fresh fruit. Try one of their fresh-baked goods. Dozens attracts its share of business people who appreciate the telephones next to the table and the "power breakfast" entrée. Lunches feature sandwiches, but you can also have a breakfast item. A full bar is available. Hours are 6:30 am–2:30 pm daily. Dozens has two locations. Both are great, but the downtown restaurant has a bit more atmosphere. **13th St. and Cherokee St.; 572-0066 and 2180 S. Havana (in Aurora); 337-6627.**

Bud's—The Workingpeople's Cafe — $

As the name suggests, this is a haven for working people—especially for those rising before the sun each day. Treat yourself to friendly service in a casual setting that consists of a long Formica counter, comfy vinyl booths and plenty of calendars (William "Least Heat" Moon would

have loved it here!). Gigantic cinnamon rolls are Bud's trademark, but the egg dishes, pancakes and biscuits with gravy are all delicious. Though lunch and dinner are also served, breakfast is the real reason to come here. Open Mon.–Fri. 4:30 am–8 pm, Sat. 4:30 am–2 pm. **1701 38th St.; 295-2915.**

CONTINENTAL

The Normandy — $$$ to $$$$

At this longtime favorite, you can often hear patrons and waiters exchanging pleasantries and family news. The room is simple and unobtrusive, the food is distinctly French and the service could be the best in Denver. Heinz Gerstley, the owner, doesn't take his customers for granted, nor does he lose the edge to fine cooking as he never tires of exploring the world's richest culinary tradition. Favorite entrées include rack of lamb, fresh Rocky Mountain trout and medallions of veal Marie Antoinette. The fine wine cellar is stocked with a variety of rare vintages and reasonably priced bottles. Lunch is served from 11:30 am–2:30 pm Tues.–Sat. Dinner is served from 5–10:30 pm Tues.–Sun. Closed Mon. **515 Madison St.; 321-3311.**

Tante Louise — $$$ to $$$$

In a couple of unassuming houses linked together on Colfax Ave. and Cherry St. resides one of the city's better restaurants. Certainly it must be the coziest restaurant in Denver, with small tables in quaint nooks off the winding passageways and large tables beside roaring hearths. The decor has an Old World charm; the quality of food will have you returning often. Tante Louise, now in its second decade, has always had rave reviews for its fine French cuisine. The prices here are somewhat lower than at the other Denver restaurants of this quality, and the extensive wine list is reasonably priced. Open from 5:30–10:30 pm Mon.–Sat. Closed Sun. **4900 E. Colfax Ave.; 355-4488.**

Wellshire Inn — $$ to $$$$

An old English Tudor mansion on the

grounds of the Wellshire Municipal Golf Course is home to this appealing restaurant. Unobstructed views of the course and the mountains have made it a favorite among Denverites. One-hundred-year-old imported tapestries and paneling, in addition to leaded stained glass and Tiffany lamps, lend an air of sophistication to the atmosphere. The food is an interesting, delightful mix of continental, Polynesian and far eastern cuisine. Renowned chef Leo Goto ensures an excellent dining experience. This is also a good choice for Sun. brunch from 10 am–2 pm. Open for breakfast 6:30–10 am Mon.–Fri., lunch 11:30 am–2:30 pm Mon.–Fri. Dinner is served from 5:30–10 pm Mon.–Thur., until 11 pm, Fri.–Sat. 3333 S. Colorado Blvd.; 759-3333.

EXOTIC/MIDDLE EASTERN

Mataam Fez — $$$

The decor here could be straight out of the tales of 1001 Arabian nights—guests are seated on pillows and cushions in front of short tables and canopied ceilings. Shoes are removed, thick white towels are draped over the diners' shoulders and no utensils are to be found. It's all part of the dining ritual, along with ornately dressed waiters, belly dancers and sword dancers. Typical dishes are chicken with lemon and olives and lamb with apricots; curry dishes and fish are also available. This is a dining experience to be savored over the course of a few hours. Do not schedule a concert or theater show after the meal, unless you want to watch the midnight show. Open for dinner seven nights a week from 6 pm until the last customer leaves. 4609 E. Colfax Ave.; 399-9282.

Khyber Pass — $$ to $$$

There is something clandestine about dining in one of the small square rooms, three feet above the main floor of the restaurant, behind a small, curtained entrance. The unique atmosphere, enhanced by a lighted, tile fountain, is just part of the appeal. Exotic food will throw a curve on your flavor expectations. Afghan specialties include kabobs, lamb, lentil soups and pasta. One of the most unappealing but best-tasting appetizers is lamb's brains. Other Afghan dishes have more pleasant origins, with the curried dishes especially interesting. When the food is gone, you can join the international crowd in the bar for a night of belly dancing. Open Mon.–Thur. 5:30–10:30 pm, Fri.–Sat. 5:30–11 pm. The lounge is open until 2 am. 720 S. Colorado Blvd.; 692-8500.

Ethiopian Restaurant — $ to $$

This cuisine is based on a sourdough bread, about the size of a large pancake, which is baked to a spongy consistency. Tear off a piece of bread to scoop up various stews. The restaurant offers wonderful spicy concoctions of lamb, beef and chicken, and some especially good vegetarian dishes. Try them with a glass of honey wine. The front room is steamy and small, while the back room displays Ethiopian art and a scattering of tables. Special tables are available for large parties out for a feast. You'll often see visiting foreigners here; large groups of African men chat over cups of rich Ethiopian coffee. Open daily from 11 am–3:30 pm for lunch; 4:30–10:30 pm for dinner. 2816 E. Colfax Ave.; 322-5939.

ITALIAN

Little Pepina's — $$

Good, plentiful, flavorful Italian food. This is the kind of food that makes you feel fulfilled—while you're eating and afterward. All the standard Italian classics are served just like Mama used to make. The only reason not to visit is if you're on a low-carbohydrate diet. Located in northwest Denver, the original home of Denver's Italian immigrants, this restaurant is very popular. Lunches offered 11:30 am–2 pm Mon.–Fri. Dinner served from 5–10 pm nightly. 3400 Osage St.; 477-3335.

Pagliacci's — $$

You can't miss this restaurant at night, and if you've seen the opera I Pagliacci, you'll know why the owners have a lighted neon clown on top of the building. Traditional Italian food has been offered here since 1944. Featuring homemade pasta and sauces, this busy place is a true classic. The food is tasty, plentiful and reasonably priced. Dinner from 5–10 pm nightly. **1440 W. 33rd Ave.; 458-0530.**

MEXICAN
Casa Bonita — $$

The decor is so well done, you almost believe that former Disney employees came to Colorado to open a Mexican restaurant. While the food has never surpassed the atmosphere or entertainment, a trip to Casa Bonita is still a must, especially for families with small children. While you relax over your meal, the kids will be turning their heads crazily, trying to see what's going to happen next. Let them roam into the caverns near the pool, where the green beads of bats' eyes gleam, or the skeleton of an unfortunate miner awaits discovery in an abandoned shaft. Adults and children alike watch in rapture as cliff divers plunge 30 feet from craggy peaks past waterfalls and into a small pool. Watch the deadly gunfight between Black Bart and the sheriff, or listen to strolling mariachis and other entertainers. Dining is never dull here. If you can possibly eat another helping of your all-you-can-eat combo plate or drink a refill of your Margarita, just raise the service flag at your table; be sure to save room for a sopapilla. Open Sun.–Thur. 11 am–9:30 pm, Fri.–Sat. 11 am–10 pm. Look for the pink tower at **6715 W. Colfax Ave.; 232-5115.**

Las Delicias — $

If you are one of those people on a continual hunt for an inexpensive and authentic Mexican cafe, then be sure to come here. Unless you are fluent in Spanish, don't even try to pick up the banter between the service staff; even the jukebox offers only Spanish tunes. This is not a contrived place in the least. A series of rooms, linked by archways, is decked in fake brick wallcovering. As you may have guessed, the real reason to come here is the food—mouth-watering burritos, tacos and enchiladas will keep you utterly happy. "Las D" is a favorite with the downtown

crowd for lunch. A full bar is available. Open daily 9 am–9 pm. **439 E. 19th Ave.; 839-5675.**

ORIENTAL
CHINESE
VIETNAMESE/THAI
The House of Hunan — $ to $$$

We have scientific verification that this is Denver's finest Chinese restaurant: every visitor from mainland China we have ever encountered has declared this to be the most authentic Chinese cooking in the city. The restaurant is unhappily located in a Target store parking lot, which ruins the effect of what would have been impressive guardian lions at the door. Inside, however, the place is as spacious and luxurious as you could hope. The friendly service is helpful, which is a relief, because some of the dishes require explanations. Excellent dim sum gave the House of Hunan its first loyal customers, but as Denver palates have become more accustomed to the taste of real Chinese food, they have ventured into gung bao ro-din, sputtering rice dishes and many legendary dishes of Hunan and Szechuan. Open Sun.–Thur. 11 am–10 pm, Fri.–Sat. 11 am–10:30 pm. **440 S. Colorado Blvd.; 329-9955.**

T-Wa Inn — $$

A section of S. Federal Blvd. has been transformed into a strip of Vietnamese shops and restaurants. This was one of the first Vietnamese restaurants in town. The food reflects a delicate balance of tastes, borrowing from both Chinese and French cuisines and featuring many traditional specialties. T-Wa boasts an extensive menu of exotic hot and spicy dishes and wonderful seafood. Order something from the excellent selection of appetizers! It has very moderate prices for the quantity and quality of food. Open for lunch and dinner, seven days a week from 11 am–9 pm. **555 S. Federal Blvd.; 922-4584.**

The Erawan Cafe — $ to $$

If not for the colorful green sign, it

would be easy to pass by this little cafe. It's a favorite of doctors and nurses working across the street at the CU Medical Center. Pull up a chair at one of the few tables or choose counter seating. Some of the best Thai food in town is ordered for you by Linda (voted 1988 "Best Jewish Mother Working at an Oriental Restaurant" by *Westword* newspaper). She knows exactly what you need, and you'll be pleased with her selection. Open for lunch Mon.–Sat. 11:45 am–3 pm, dinners served Mon.–Sat. 5:30 pm until the last customer leaves, **3919 E. 8th Ave.; 388-3226.**

VEGETARIAN/HEALTH
Gemini I & II — $ to $$
The look is early 1970s fern bar, but don't let that keep you from enjoying some excellent food. The Gemini restaurants specialize in wonderful vegetarian concoctions, but carnivores are also kept happy by a few meaty dishes. For breakfast, you can order fluffy scrambled eggs with a variety of ingredients, pecan waffles or frozen raspberry yogurt. For lunch and dinner they serve an incredibly good black bean soup as well as vegetarian chili. Soups, salads and casseroles are all well prepared and tasty. Be sure to save enough room for something sweet (or, at least carry some out!). The baked goods—pies, cheesecake, carrot cake, carob brownies and "blondies"—are all delicious. Open daily 6:30 am–10 pm. **4300 Wadsworth Blvd., Wheat Ridge; 421-4990 and 5056 S. Wadsworth Blvd., Littleton; 972-0210.**

The Harvest Restaurant & Bakery — $ to $$
What used to be a small restaurant in Boulder, called the Good Earth, has flourished in Denver. Featuring vegetarian and meat dishes, the Harvest stresses freshness and will not serve food containing additives. Breakfast items include buttermilk pancakes and omelettes. You can't really go wrong for lunch, or dinner either—especially if you enjoy a homemade roll or muffin with a steaming bowl of soup or a fruit shake or smoothie for dessert. Service

is fast and the prices are still reasonable. If you're dining alone, you may wish to eat at the community table—where single diners can enjoy a meal together. **430 S. Colorado Blvd.; 399-6652.**

NEARBY
El Rancho — $$$ to $$$$
For 40 years, people have been pulling off Interstate 70 at El Rancho restaurant as a matter of tradition. Dinner always begins with a relish tray followed by a basket of homemade cinnamon rolls, salad, soup, entrée and chiffon pie or ice cream. Entrées include rock lobster, buffalo steak, roast prime rib or roast turkey with all the trimmings (year-round). Don't be discouraged if there is a short wait—just pull up a comfortable chair in one of the lounge areas and have a cocktail. The views from nearly everywhere in El Rancho are spectacular and, in winter, any or all of the seven fireplaces may be burning. Open every day of the year for lunch 11:30 am–2:30 pm, 5–10 pm for dinner Mon.–Sat.; brunch is served on Sun. from 10:30 am–1:30 pm, dinner from 2–8 pm. Located 18 miles west of Denver on Interstate 70 at the **El Rancho exit (No. 252); 526-0661.**

The Fort — $$$ to $$$$
The Fort is one of the most popular places near the metro area to go for a special occasion, especially when out-of-town visitors show up. Views of Denver from the dining room are wonderful. The restaurant is a reproduction of Bent's Fort, one of the first trading posts in the Colorado Territory (see the **Southeast Plains** chapter). The atmosphere of Colorado's early days permeates this large restaurant; mandolin-playing musicians rove between the tables on weekends and all employees dress in frontier costumes. And they get into character . . . when we visited, one waitress dressed as an Indian maiden whacked the top off a champagne bottle with a tomahawk.

Even so, the most unique thing about the Fort is the food. Owners Sam and Carrie Arnold have diligently researched old frontier recipes for food and drink, updated slightly for modern tastes. The fare is made exclusively with ingredients from the American Southwest. Before dinner try some buffalo sausage, Rocky Mountain oysters or buffalo tongue. Entrées include large steaks as well as buffalo, quail, elk and fish. Specialty drinks with names such as the Hailstorm, Jim Bridger and Bear's Blood conjure up images from the early days. Reservations recommended for groups over 6. Open Mon.–Fri. 6–10 pm, Sat. 5–10 pm, Sun. 5–9 pm. Located west of Denver just off Hwy. 285. **19192 Hwy. 8, Morrison; 697-4771.**

The Buck Snort Saloon — $ to $$$

In an out-of-the-way location near Pine, Colorado, the Buck Snort has no equal. Menu items include the messiest, sloppiest half-pound burger you'll ever see, smothered burritos, and their wurst sandwich. The menu reminds you that "Tipping is not a town in China" and encourages you to go to McDonald's if you're in a hurry. Their sense of humor blends into the rustic, let-it-all-hang-out atmosphere. The reputation of the Buck Snort Saloon far outpaces their available room—especially on Fri. and Sat. nights, when live music keeps the place jumping. If you are anywhere close to Pine Junction on Hwy. 285 (some 32 miles southwest of Denver), pull off and make your way 6 miles south to Pine on County Rd. 126. Then you'll have the pleasure of negotiating your way on the marked, but very rough 1.5-mile road to the Buck Snort Saloon at Sphinx Park. It's an adventure. Open 4 pm till the last person leaves, Wed.–Fri., noon–midnight Sat.–Sun. Closed Mon.–Tues. **15921 Elk Creek Rd., Pine; (303) 838-0284.**

Morrison Inn — $ to $$

Simply put, this is a fun place. Located west of Denver at the foot of the mountains in the small community of Morrison, the inn specializes in Mexican food and good times. You'll see the adobe-colored build-ing with green awnings and trim on Main St. Favorite meals include spinach enchiladas, fajitas and pork barbacoa. Don't expect authentic Mexican food—but you should be ready for incredible taste sensations. A major point in their favor is that they don't use pre-mix for their custom-made Margaritas. They're great! Open Sun.–Thur. 11:30 am–10 pm, Fri.–Sat. 11:30 am–11 pm. Located in the middle of Morrison. **301 Hwy. 74; 697-6650.**

Whippletree — $ to $$

Located in Bergen Park near Evergreen, the Whippletree serves up some of the best Mexican food around. In the front room there is a rustic bar and a pool table. Have a plate of nachos and a Margarita before attacking one of their spicy dishes. More seating is located in back. The atmosphere is laid-back and the attire is come-as-you-are. The Whippletree serves a great breakfast on the weekends. Open Mon.–Fri. 11 am–10 pm, weekends from 8 am–10 pm. **1338 County Rd. 65, Evergreen; (303) 674-9944.**

Coney Island — $

Located along Hwy. 285 about 20 miles southwest of Denver, the Coney Island is hard to miss. Just look for the giant pink hot dog with all the trimmings. Walk inside this hot dog and order up (you guessed it) a hot dog, Coney Island or corn dog. Hamburgers, fries and ice cream are also available. Tack your business card up on the wall, if you can find any room. Picnic tables out on the sun deck provide the best seating at this unusual place. Vervea Goodwin, the owner, said the building used to sit on Colfax Ave. in Denver until it was moved by flatbed to Conifer in 1969. It's now one of the best moneymakers in the area. It's worth a visit if you're in the neighborhood. Like we said, you can't miss it. If you have an aversion to greasy food, however, keep driving. Located in **Conifer; 838-4210.**

SERVICES

Denver Metro Convention & Visitors Bureau—

The visitors center's knowledgeable staff can answer all your questions about attractions, events, shopping, etc. Open in winter Mon.–Fri. 8 am–5 pm, Sat. 9 am–1 pm. Summer hours are Mon.–Fri. 8 am–5 pm, Sat. from 9 am–5 pm. **225 W. Colfax Ave., Denver, CO 80202; (303) 892-1112.**

The Greater Denver Chamber of Commerce—

1600 Sherman St., Denver, CO 80203; (303) 894-8500.

Day Care—

Mile High Child Care Association—They have nine centers located around Denver. **1510 High St., Denver, CO 80218; (303) 388-5700.**

Mile High United Way Child Care Resource and Referral Service—Free referrals for more than 3,000 child care centers around the Denver metro area. **(303) 433-8900.**

Transportation—

Metro Taxi Company—24-hour service; 333-3333.

RTD (city bus service)—For maps and route information, call **(303) 778-6000.**

Yellow Cab—24-hour service; 777-7777.

Estes Park

As you drive into Estes Park, the eastern gateway to **Rocky Mountain National Park**, it's not the town that immediately strikes you, but the surrounding craggy peaks—especially 14,255-foot-high Longs Peak, which dominates the scene. Upwards of three million visitors pass through Estes each year. Most people coming to this area spend as much time as possible exploring the beautiful high alpine country of the national park, returning to town in the evening for accommodations and meals.

Dropping into town from Hwy. 36 can be a bit disappointing, because the first thing you see is a mass of high-tension power lines and a power plant. But don't let that deter you. This little burg, just a bit farther down the road, is waiting to take care of your every need—whether you want to gorge yourself at one of the many candy shops, play golf or tennis, sail, ride a horse or explore the incredible backcountry on foot. During the peak summer season it can be circus-like. Multitudes of visitors descend, and the crass display of commercialism on Elkhorn Ave. rankles many people. Still, beneath the hubbub, lurks the heart of a real town. If you want to get a better feel for Estes Park, visit in the off-season in June and Sept., or in winter when it's blissfully quiet.

Estes Park is lucky to be here at all. In the summer of 1982, a mountain dam broke, causing a torrential flood to follow the path of the normally quiet Fall River. The disastrous flood killed four people in its wake and ripped through the business district, inflicting massive damage on the center of town. Everyone pulled together in the aftermath, and now Estes has regained its luster. One of the best attributes of the town is its residents (7,950 year-round and 13,000 during the summer), who are genuinely friendly despite the crowds.

HISTORY

"The cattle should do fine here." With those words uttered by Joel Estes in 1859, Estes Park was on its way to being settled. Estes and his family moved to the valley in 1860. Visitors to the homestead were few; mountain men, Indians and explorers were long gone. In 1864, however, the challenge of climbing Longs Peak attracted William Byers, editor of the *Rocky Mountain News*. Byers and his two companions stayed with the Estes family while attempting to climb the peak. Byers was so enamored with the scenery, he wrote a story in the *News* and proclaimed the area Estes Park, in honor of his host.

After the bitterly cold winter of 1865–1866, Estes was disgusted. Despite his proclamation upon first seeing the valley, the cattle hadn't done as well as he had hoped. Sixty-year-old Estes decided it was time to move on. So he sold out for either $50 or a yoke of oxen (nobody knows for sure). The following year his property changed hands several times, until it was purchased by Griffith Evans. Evans liked beauty and solitude and wanted to keep everyone else away from his personal paradise. To his dismay, Byers was back in Aug. 1868 to climb Longs Peak, and this time he conquered it with his companion, Maj. John Wesley Powell. Byers's resulting story in the *News* brought hunters, mountaineers and tourists to Estes Park. Evans soon found he was running a makeshift hostel and was making good money at it, and his desire for solitude vanished.

In 1871 Evans's business was doing so well he built cabins and expanded his thriving operation into a full-scale dude ranch. The following year, the Earl of Dunraven (a wealthy Irishman) visited Estes Park after hearing about the excellent hunting. He liked the area so much he decided he had to own it—all of it. Being a foreigner, he was forbidden from homesteading, but Dunraven wasn't going to let a little thing like legality stand in his way. He simply hired an agent to find men—mostly loafers and down-on-their-luck drifters from Denver—to buy 8,200 acres of land for him. He gained control of another 7,000 because of the lay of the land, bringing the total under his control to more than 15,000 acres. Even Evans is said to have sold his land to the earl.

Though he tried, Dunraven couldn't keep the people away. An increasing number were streaming in, and soon his beloved valley was crisscrossed by homesteaders' fences. Famous landscape artist Albert Bierstadt was captivated by the area and his evocative paintings brought in even more people (one especially fine painting of Longs Peak still hangs in the Western History Department of the Denver Public Library).

As homesteading opportunities diminished, newly arrived ranchers and homesteaders began contesting the earl's land claims. After Dunraven left, his personal agent, Theodore Whyte, hid the earl's substantial stock of whiskey in a cave for safekeeping. He rolled a boulder in front of the cave, then promptly forgot where it was. The cache may still be there, just waiting for a connoisseur of perfectly aged, single-malt whiskey.

In 1903 a man of vision entered the picture—F.O. Stanley, inventor of the Stanley Steamer. He had just been diagnosed as having tuberculosis and was given only a short time to live. Along with his wife, Stanley immediately planned a trip to Estes Park, hoping the dry mountain air would help his illness. Confounding doctors, Stanley recovered from the tuberculosis and, in 1907, went into partnership to buy Dunraven's remaining land. He also built the famous Stanley Hotel (see the Where to Stay section) and an electric power plant. The hotel opened in 1909 and was booked solid the entire first summer—partly because the inventor used his fleet of Stanley Steamer Mountain Wagons to bring his guests to the hotel from the railhead at Lyons. With his flowing white hair and beard, Stanley became known as the Grand Old Man of Estes Park. He made large contributions to the town and was instrumental in reintroducing herds of elk. F.O. Stanley died in Newton, Massachusetts, at the ripe old age of 91.

When Congress established Rocky Mountain National Park in 1915, Estes Park was well on its way to becoming a center for visitors to the area.

GETTING THERE

From Denver take Interstate 25 north to Hwy. 36 (the Boulder Turnpike). Follow Hwy. 36 through Boulder, Lyons and into Estes Park. The 65-mile drive takes about an hour and a half.

MAJOR ATTRACTIONS

ROCKY MOUNTAIN NATIONAL PARK

Rocky Mountain National Park is one of those places that must be seen to be experienced—even photos only scratch the surface. The park straddles the Continental Divide for 40 miles and is without question the showpiece of Colorado's public recreation lands. Each year, millions of visitors make their way through the park to see some of the most spectacular high mountain scenery in the Rockies. Its eastern side is characterized by steep, glaciated valleys and cirque lakes, carved out by the ice floes that once dominated the surroundings. On the western side of the Continental Divide, the land is more gentle, with lush pine forests covering much of the terrain. But all of this terrain takes a back seat to the 79 peaks over 12,000 feet. The largest of these is famous Longs Peak (14,255 feet), which dominates the Front Range skyline and is visible from more than 100 miles away. Wildlife abounds throughout the park, which serves as a sanctuary for elk, deer, bears, bighorn sheep, mountain lions and raptors such as bald eagles and hawks.

There are numerous ways to experience the park. Whether you choose a strenuous, multi-day backpack trip into the park's remote areas or a leisurely drive over Trail Ridge Rd., you'll remember a trip to Rocky Mountain National Park for years to come.

History—

In the early 1900s, a conservationist movement in Estes Park developed. Overuse of land by individuals and businesses in what is now Rocky Mountain National Park galvanized a push to protect this uniquely beautiful area from further damage. Many preservationists were happy when the federal government set aside a large part of the land as a national forest, but others felt that wasn't enough. Another movement to create a national park began, despite opposition from forest service officials who thought they were the best ones to oversee the land. Some private landowners also posed opposition, fearing they would lose their land. On Jan. 26, 1915, President Woodrow Wilson ended all the debate by signing the bill creating Rocky Mountain National Park.

Controlled development of the park really started in 1920 when Fall River Rd. opened, helping more than 250,000 people gain better access to the beautiful areas. By the 1950s, the incredible popularity of the park began to work against it—overcrowding and serious damage to the vegetation (especially the high alpine tundra) were apparent. As a result of all this, protective restrictions were imposed, still leaving ample room for all visitors to enjoy the park to its fullest. Today this beautiful area remains much as it was when Joel Estes first settled here in the 1860s. With proper management, officials hope to keep it that way.

Getting There—From the east, Rocky Mountain National Park can be reached via Hwy. 34 or Hwy. 36 from Estes Park. Once inside the park, Hwy. 34 (Trail Ridge Rd.) crosses the Continental Divide 50 miles to Grand Lake on the Western Slope.

Visitor Information—

Visitors to Rocky Mountain National Park must comply with regulations that have been established to preserve the natural beauty. Stop in at one of the visitors

View of the north face of Hallett Peak from Dream Lake in Rocky Mountain National Park.

centers or at Park Headquarters, where questions can be answered about picnicking, hiking, fishing, wildlife and most anything else. **Park Headquarters Visitors Center, (303) 586-2371,** is located just inside the east boundary of the park on Hwy. 36. Visitors entering the park from the west side at Grand Lake can stop in at **Kawuneeche Visitors Center, (303) 627-3471,** just inside the park boundary. **Alpine Visitors Center,** located at the top of Trail Ridge Rd., can also be a good place to visit if you have any questions. For additional information any time of year, contact **Rocky Mountain National Park Headquarters, Estes Park, CO 80517-8397; (303) 586-2371.**

RECREATION INFORMATION

Biking—

Mountain Biking—Since off-road biking is not allowed in the park, the mountain bike trail possibilities are limited to the existing roads. For a challenging dirt road, see the Fall River Rd. write-up in the Scenic Drives section of Rocky Mountain National Park.

Touring—Touring on the roads in Rocky Mountain National Park provides some of the most spectacular high mountain scenery you'll find anywhere. There are quite a few challenging uphill stretches, so you should be in pretty good physical shape for most of the rides. Be careful when riding, however, since most routes are heavily traveled by cars.

Bear Lake Road is a strenuous 10-mile tour that climbs 1,500 feet. For information about the road, see Scenic Drives.

Trail Ridge Road, the 50-mile road between Estes Park and Grand Lake, is one of the toughest and most rewarding bike tours in Colorado. It crosses over the Continental Divide at 12,183 feet and provides incredible, high alpine scenery. If you pedal the entire distance, you'll probably be too tired to return the same day. Stay a night in Grand Lake and return the next day. See Scenic Drives for more information about Trail Ridge Rd.

Fishing—

Fishing within Rocky Mountain National Park is fairly sporadic, but patient anglers can be successful. Your chances of catching a trophy-sized trout in the icy waters isn't too good, but if you hit it just right, you can catch a creel full of smaller ones. Even though this is some of the most beautiful fishing country anywhere, surprisingly few visitors to the park ever throw a line. Some of the prime spots require hiking, but there are several lakes and streams alongside the roads. Some of the lakes have paved pathways around them to enable access for handicapped anglers. It would be wise to pick up a copy of the park rules. One important rule allows only artificial flies and lures, and many stretches are limited to catch and release fishing. Of special note is the growing population of the rare greenback cutthroat trout. If you ever hook one of these odd-looking trout, return it to the water immediately!

Big Thompson River—Surrounded by high peaks, this river ambles northeast through the park before flowing to the town of Estes Park and eventually onto the plains. On its upper reaches, you'll find mainly brook trout with a few browns and rainbows thrown in for good measure. Most of the trout are fairly small, eight- to 10-inch fryers. From Estes Park drive west on Hwy. 36 to the Beaver Meadows Entrance Station. At the first intersection after the entrance, turn left (south) on Bear Lake Rd. After 1 mile turn right (west) onto Moraine Park Rd., which follows the Big Thompson for 2.7 miles to the Fern Lake trailhead. You can either fish the water along the road or follow the rough trail up into the higher country.

Peacock Pool—Plan a day's outing for this combination hiking/fishing trip. Once you complete the 5-mile hike to this little lake, chances are you'll catch many smallish (eight-inch) brook trout. The "pool" is filled by a splashing waterfall in a picture-perfect setting at the base of Longs Peak.

The hike, beginning at the East Longs Peak trailhead, is not a cakewalk, so don't attempt it unless you're in pretty good shape. About 4 miles up the trail a spur leads to Peacock Pool (11,360 feet in elevation), offering tremendous views along the way. If you want to complete the hike to **Chasm Lake**—another 1.5 miles from Peacock Pool—you may be able to catch a large cutthroat in the lake's very deep water. The lake is located under the diamond face of Longs Peak. To get to the East Longs Peak trailhead from Estes Park, head 9.2 miles south on Hwy. 7 and turn right at the sign.

Sprague Lake—This shallow, picturesque lake at the east edge of the park yields many brook trout in the 10-inch range. Because it's right next to the road and has a trail all the way around its shore, use is fairly heavy. To get there from Estes Park, drive west on Hwy. 36 to the Beaver Meadows Entrance Station. At the first intersection after the entrance, turn right (south) and continue on Bear Lake Rd. for about 6 miles.

Thunder Lake—Once again the fishing may not be spectacular, but the scenery makes up for it. Fishing here is reasonably good for rainbow and brook trout. For more information see Hiking and Backpacking.

West Rocky Mountain National Park—For information about some of the excellent fishing near the park's western boundary, see the Fishing section of the **Grand Lake** chapter.

Hiking and Backpacking—

Getting into the backcountry is what Rocky Mountain National Park is all about. Most of the park is accessible only by hiking trails. Backcountry permits are required for any overnight stays. These free permits can be picked up at Park Headquarters near Estes Park or at Kawuneeche Visitors Center near Grand Lake. During the summer, backcountry permits can be reserved by writing the **Backcountry Office, Rocky Mountain National Park, Estes Park, CO 80517**. Reservations can be made for the off-season (from Oct.–May) by calling **(303) 586-4459** or **(303) 586-2371** or writing Park Headquarters (office is open year-round). No pets are allowed on trails and in most places camping is allowed in designated areas only. For handicapped visitors, Handicamp, a special backcountry camping area, is accessible to wheelchairs. For more information call **(303) 586-2371**.

For topographical maps, equipment and information, talk with Rob Mardock at **Colorado Wilderness Sports, 358 E. Elkhorn Ave., Estes Park, CO 80517; (303) 586-6548**. His shop is open all year.

An excellent book with a wealth of information about hiking in the park is *Rocky Mountain National Park: Classic Hikes & Climbs* (Fulcrum, 1988) by Gerry Roach.

Dream Lake Trail—Heading west from Bear Lake, this trail climbs gently up to three lakes—Nymph, Dream and Emerald. It's a popular and easy hike that can be done in a couple of hours. The distances are short (a half mile to Nymph, 1 mile to Dream and just under 2 miles to Emerald) and the scenery, dominated by Hallett Peak, is magnificent.

Fern Lake/Odessa Lake Trail—There are two routes into these lakes, but no matter which trail you take, the scenery is incredible. Perhaps the best starting point is from the trailhead at Bear Lake, which is 1,300 feet above Fern Lake and provides a downhill hike for most of the way. To find the trailhead at Bear Lake, walk up Flattop Trail for about 1.5 miles. At a trail junction you'll find a sign pointing the way to Fern and Odessa lakes. From Bear Lake it's about 4.7 miles to Fern Lake. Along the way you'll pass over a saddle between Joe Mills and Notchtop mountains. The trail, which hugs the mountainside, climbs up to 10,500 feet and affords magnificent views of the surrounding peaks as well as of the valleys in the park. From Fern Lake it's another 3.8 miles to the Fern Lake trailhead (located 2.7 miles west on Moraine Park Rd. from Bear Lake Rd.). If you have someone to pick you up, you can start at one trailhead and finish at the other.

Flattop Mountain/North Inlet Trail—If you feel like taking a long hike, you can follow this trail all the way (16 miles) to Grand Lake. From Bear Lake you will climb west about 2.5 miles to the summit of Flattop Mountain (12,324 feet). This mountain is aptly named, having the roomiest summit of any in the park. From there, it's a relatively easy 16-mile, downhill hike southwest along North Inlet Trail through pine forests to Grand Lake. This hike (at least the hike to the summit of Flattop) is very popular in summer, so expect to see some other folks. After crossing over the Continental Divide and beginning your descent to Grand Lake, you'll be in pretty remote country until the last few miles.

Longs Peak Trails—This is the peak that has inspired poets, painters and assorted adventurers since explorers first sighted it in the mid-1800s. The challenge of reaching the summit is as exciting today as it was

when the 14,255-foot peak was first scaled in 1868 by William Byers and John Wesley Powell. It's not only the tallest and most dominant peak in the park, it's also the northernmost 14er in Colorado (or the Rocky Mountains for that matter).

Following are two hikes up the peak. If you plan to climb Longs Peak, it's recommended that you start very early and try to be off the summit by noon to avoid the all-too-common afternoon lightning storms. Both hikes are considered difficult and are not recommended for novices. If you want to make it an overnighter, there are places to camp along the way, but remember that you need a camping permit.

North Longs Peak Trail is reached from the Glacier Gorge trailhead, just before reaching Bear Lake on Bear Lake Rd. It's the longer of the two routes, but it's also less crowded. Start hiking south on Loch Vale Trail. After a mile take the left fork and climb southeast for 5 miles until the trail joins East Longs Peak Trail at the 11,900-foot summit of Granite Pass. From there it's another 2.5 miles to the summit. The round trip takes about 17 hours. To get to the trailhead, drive up Bear Lake Rd. to Glacier Gorge Junction. The marked trailhead is on the left.

East Longs Peak Trail starts at the Longs Peak trailhead and climbs 7.5 miles to the summit. The first 6 miles to the boulder field is on a good trail. From the field the trail climbs to the Keyhole, where the route traverses a steep ledge system across the west face. From there the trail heads up the Trough, then across ledge system called the Narrows and finally up the Homestretch to the summit. The route from the Keyhole to the summit is marked with yellow and red bull's-eyes. The round trip from the ranger station at the trailhead takes about 15 hours. To get to the trailhead from Estes Park, head south 9.2 miles on Hwy. 7. Turn right and drive about a mile to the trailhead.

Thunder Lake/Wild Basin—The 7-mile hike to Thunder Lake is an easy to moderate outing, depending on whether you decide to do it all in one day. The main trail follows the St. Vrain River, where you'll be treated to lots of waterfalls and cascades. The upper part of the trail moves through the trees to 10,500 feet, breaking out onto promontories overlooking the valley and the Continental Divide—this scenery is all postcard material. There is fishing in the lake and the stream below it. Plan on catching rainbow and brook trout in the 10-inch range.

The hike to Thunder Lake takes four to five hours, and the return trip takes about three and a half hours. To get to the trailhead, take Hwy. 7 south from Estes Park about 13 miles. Turn right and drive a quarter mile to Wild Basin Lodge. Just past the lodge, turn right and follow the road past the ranger station for 2 miles to the trailhead.

Tonahutu Creek—See the Hiking and Backpacking section of the Grand Lake chapter.

Horseback Riding—

Almost all the outfitters in Estes Park have rides venturing into the park. There are also stables at two locations within the park.

High Country Stables—Two-hour, half-day and all-day rides are available at High Country's two locations. Both are located close to Estes Park, at Glacier Basin and at Moraine Park. Numbers change from year to year so call Park Headquarters at **(303) 586-2371** for information and reservations.

Scenic Drives—

Bear Lake Road—From the Beaver Meadows Entrance Station, it's a 10-mile drive up this heavily traveled, winding road to Bear Lake at 9,475 feet. Along the way you'll have a chance to see deer, elk and other wildlife, as well as views of the surrounding peaks. If you just want to look at the scenery, take one of the free shuttle buses, which leave from Glacier Basin Campground about halfway up the road. At the end of the road, Bear Lake Trail takes you a couple hundred yards to the

pine-clad shores of the lake. Chances are you've seen a picture of the often-photographed Bear Lake with its unforgettable mountain backdrop.

Fall River Road—This was the first auto route over the Continental Divide in this part of the state, and it played a big part in the tourist boom of the early 1920s. The first 2 miles are paved and open to two-way traffic. After that, it's a narrow, one-way gravel road, which climbs 11 miles before joining Trail Ridge Rd. at the summit of 11,796-foot Fall River Pass along the Continental Divide. The route is described by park officials as a "motor nature trail," so stop often to enjoy the scenery as the terrain turns from sub-alpine forest to alpine tundra. The route doesn't offer the spectacular vistas of Trail Ridge Rd., but does provide shelter from the harsh wind and closer contact with the wilderness. It is closed in winter. To reach Fall River Rd. from Estes Park, drive west on Hwy. 34 to the Fall River Entrance Station. Proceed 2 miles from the entrance and turn right onto Fall River Rd. Trailers and other RVs are prohibited from driving the road due to narrow switchbacks.

Trail Ridge Road (Highway 34)—No question about it, a drive over Trail Ridge Rd. is a must for visitors to the park. You'll see an incredible amount of scenery in a short span of time. The narrow, winding 50-mile ribbon of asphalt stretching between Estes Park and Grand Lake is the highest continuous highway in the US. More than 200 men braved the elements to build Trail Ridge Rd., which opened in 1932. Paving and other final touches continued for another 10 years.

The landscape transition along the way is remarkable. The road heads west and climbs through meadows, spectacular mountain valleys and over the Continental Divide on an 13-mile stretch of alpine tundra that's similar to the arctic. From the 12,183-foot summit, the road drops down the Western Slope of the Continental Divide along the North Fork of the Colorado River. Along the drive there are numerous pullouts and informational signs. Take the time to stop and read the signs, as they provide excellent information about the changing ecosystems along the way. Near the top, at the junction with Fall River Rd., you'll find the Alpine Visitors Center. The center has exhibits on this fragile tundra environment; knowledgeable rangers are on duty to answer your questions. There is also a snack bar and a souvenir shop.

Plan on spending three to four hours on the way to Grand Lake. The road is usually open from May–Oct., depending on snow conditions. To get to Trail Ridge Rd. (Hwy. 34), enter the park at either Beaver Meadows or Fall River, and follow the signs.

Skiing (Cross-Country)—

The best cross-country skiing in the Estes Park area is in the national park. Due to snowfall and blowing snow, ski conditions change quickly in this area. Before heading out on a backcountry trip, be sure to check avalanche conditions at Park Headquarters. The rangers can also give you a number of good trail ideas.

If you're a novice, **Glacier Basin Campground** is a good place to get the exhilarating feel of cross-country skiing. The main trail leaves the campground and heads southwest on easy terrain for 1 mile to Sprague Lake. There are also a multitude of trails in and around the campground. Glacier Basin Campground is located about 5 miles up Bear Lake Rd.

Black Lake offers a moderately difficult 8-mile round trip that takes you into some of the most spectacular country in the park. It's especially beautiful under a thick blanket of snow. The trip starts at the Glacier Gorge Junction parking lot and follows the signs southwest toward Alberta Falls and Loch Lake. Just past the intersection of Icy Brook and Glacier Creek, turn south and follow Glacier Creek to Mills Lake. After passing Mills and Jewel lakes, continue along the creek through the forested drainage. When you break out of the trees, proceed up the open slope to Black Lake. The view from the lake is spec-tacular, with Longs Peak to the east, McHenrys Peak to the west and Chiefs Head Peak to the south. When you're ready, take the same route back. Glacier Gorge Junction parking lot is located about 11 miles up Bear Lake Rd.

For rentals and information, see the Cross-Country Skiing section in Outdoor Activities.

Camping—

Camping is allowed in the park at five designated drive-in campgrounds. All charge a fee. During the summer, all offer nightly campfire programs. Guided nature hikes and walks are provided by rangers at **Aspenglen, Glacier Basin** and **Moraine Park** campgrounds. For a schedule of events, check with the office at each campground, the ranger stations or the visitors centers. Advance reservations for Aspenglen and Glacier Basin campgrounds can be made year-round by writing **Ticketron at Dept. R, 401 Hackensack Ave., Hackensack, NJ 07601.** During the summer, reservations can be made by calling your nearest Ticketron. The other campgrounds are on a first-come, first-served basis. Camping is limited to seven days parkwide from June 1–Sept. 30. **Longs Peak Campground** has a three-day limit. No hookups are available. Camping is also available in the backcountry (see Hiking and Backpacking in this section for more information).

Aspenglen Campground is located 5 miles west of Estes Park off Hwy. 34 just past the Fall River entrance to the park. With 61 sites (water in summer), it's open all year.

Glacier Basin Campground is located 9 miles west of Estes Park. Enter the park on Hwy. 36 and turn south on Bear Lake Rd. This 150-site campground is closed in winter.

Longs Peak Campground is a 28-site campground that's set up for tents only. It's located at the Longs Peak trailhead and is open all year. To get there from Estes Park, drive south on Hwy. 7 for 9.2 miles and turn right (west) to the Longs Peak Ranger Station. Follow the road 1 mile to the campground.

Moraine Park Campground (247 sites) is located 3 miles southwest of Park Headquarters Visitors Center. Drive west into the park, turn left on Bear Lake Rd. and proceed 1.3 miles to Moraine Park Rd. Turn left and proceed to the campground. It's closed in winter.

Timber Creek Campground, with 100 sites, is located 7 miles inside the west entrance to the park near Grand Lake.

FESTIVALS AND EVENTS

Fourth of July Celebration

Independence Day

It seems all the mountain towns celebrate July 4th with wild abandon. But not too many towns can boast a skydiving demonstration that has parachutists landing in a lake—Lake Estes, to be precise. A day of varied entertainment includes an outdoor barbecue and a concert with John Philip Sousa music at the Stanley Hotel. It all ends with a stunning display of fireworks over Lake Estes. For more information call **(303) 586-4431.**

Rooftop Rodeo and Western Week

mid-July

Estes Park celebrates its western heritage with the Rooftop Rodeo and Western Week. The main draw is the rodeo, which has cowboys competing for various titles. Other events include a parade, a mountain man rendezvous and an arts and crafts fair. This annual rodeo has been going on for more than 60 years, so you can be assured there will always be one next year. For information call **(303) 586-6104.**

Scottish Highland Festival

mid-September

Long, long ago in Scotland, clan members competed in curious contests of strength and stamina to prove themselves as capable soldiers. The ways of the Celts have crossed the Atlantic, and now this annual event in Estes Park provides a weekend of fun and sport. The traditional sporting events include the hammer throw and the caber toss—a caber, by the way, is a tree trunk, averaging 19 feet in length and 120 pounds. Other activities include Scottish bagpipe and drum-major competitions, a highland dance and sheepdog contests. The highlight of the celebration is the Tattoo, a performance of light and sound that has evolved over 300 years. This festival draws people from all over Colorado and the Rocky Mountains. Call **(303) 586-2132** or **(303) 586-4431** for more information.

OUTDOOR ACTIVITIES

BIKING

MOUNTAIN BIKING

Roosevelt National Forest offers many challenging trails suitable for mountain biking. Backcountry trail riding is not allowed in Rocky Mountain National Park. One possibility is Fall River Rd. (listed under Scenic Drives in the Rocky Mountain National Park section).

Crosier Mountain Trail—
This difficult ride provides stunning views of the surrounding mountains. See the Hiking and Backpacking section.

Lion Gulch Trail—
This is a relatively strenuous ride. For details see the Hiking and Backpacking section.

Rentals and Information—

Larry Wexler, owner of **Colorado Bicycling Adventures,** can set you up with all the equipment you'll need to take off and do some exploring. If you don't feel like taking off on your own, Wexler also provides guided mountain bike tours, including an overnighter in Colorado State Forest. Open year-round. **184 E. Elkhorn Ave., Estes Park, CO 80517; (303) 586-4241.**

TOURING

For information about touring in the national park, see the Major Attractions section.

CLIMBING

Colorado Mountain School—

If you want something a little more challenging than hiking, then you should check out the **Colorado Mountain School.** Owner Mike Donahue will teach you the ropes. A one-day introductory class will have you ready to take to the field with experienced guides. Everything from one-day climbs to extended international expeditions is offered. If you have an itch to climb a challenging route up Longs Peak, this is your chance. Guided hikes and equipment rentals are also available. Open year-round. **PO Box 2062, 351 Moraine Ave., Estes Park, CO 80517; (303) 586-5758 or 1-800-444-0730** outside Colorado.

FISHING

There are several opportunities for angling just outside of Estes Park. If you are interested in fishing within Rocky Mountain National Park, see the Major Attractions section. The local fishing authority is Scot Ritchie at **Scot's Sporting Goods.** He can direct you to the hot spots as well as set you up with tackle. Located 1.5 miles west of Estes Park on Hwy. 36 at **870 Moraine Ave., Estes Park, CO 80517; (303) 586-2877.**

Big Thompson River—

After gaining strength in Rocky Mountain National Park, the Big Thompson River flows through spectacular Big Thompson Canyon on its way to the plains. There is a good quality section of river (flies and lures only) starting about 5 miles downstream from Lake Estes. The best spot on this stretch is 8 miles downstream from the lake, just below a place called Grandpa's Retreat. To help nurture the primarily pan-sized rainbow and brown trout that call this stretch home, the Colorado Division of Wildlife and the National Forest Service have created several deep holes. The Big Thompson is parallel to Hwy. 34 for much of its length, and small parking areas are located along the shoulder. This good stretch of water extends 5–9 miles down this heavily traveled, steep-walled canyon. It's hard to realize today, but in 1976 a disastrous flood roared through this area, killing many people.

Lake Estes—

Located on the east side of town, Lake Estes offers an easy-to-get-to spot for anglers who may not have time to search out more secluded areas. The Colorado Division of Wildlife regularly stocks the lake with eight- to 12-inch rainbows. Though the fishing pressure is heavy, an occasional lunker-sized German brown is caught. For best results use worms or salmon eggs on No. 8 and No. 10 hooks. Mepps lures at a quarter of an ounce or less are also effective. The **Lake Estes Marina** sells fishing tackle and rents boats by the hour. **1770 E. Big Thompson Ave.; (303) 586-2011.**

Marys Lake—

Marys Lake is like Lake Estes in almost every way except for its location. Try fishing the lake's inlet where the fish tend to congregate and feed. Take Hwy. 36 to the west end of Estes Park to Marys Lake Rd. (it's the only stoplight). Turn left and drive 1.5 miles to the small lake.

FOUR-WHEEL-DRIVE TRIPS

If you want to get away from the crowds, a sure way to do it is in a four-wheel-drive vehicle. For more information and maps contact the **Estes Park Office of Roosevelt National Forest** at **161 Second St., Estes Park, CO 80517; (303) 586-3440.**

Pole Hill Road—

From Estes Park, drive 3 miles southeast on Hwy. 36 to the top of Park Hill. Turn left onto Pole Hill Rd. (Forest Rd. 122) at the sign for Ravencrest Chalet. Drive another mile and enter Roosevelt National Forest. There are numerous loop options with a variety of terrain in this area. One short circle tour starts when you take the first left after entering the national forest. You'll pass an observation platform in this area referred to as The Notch. The platform affords excellent views of the Estes Valley, the Mummy Range to the north and Flattop Mountain and Hallett Peak west along the Continental Divide.

Brook Trout

Twin Sisters Road—

This beautiful, albeit short four-wheel-drive road can be taken in a loop from Estes Park. Drive 10 miles south on Hwy. 7 and turn left into the Meeker Park area. After 1.5 miles take another left onto Twin Sisters Rd. Look for the Pierson Park sign. This road takes you through a beautiful valley bordered by Twin Sisters Peaks to the west and House Rock, Pierson Mountain and Lion Head to the east.

Rentals and Tours—

American Wilderness Tours—With their six-wheeled trucks that look like they could go anywhere, these folks will take you to spots you may never see otherwise. You'll pass through beaver country, deep forests and meadows laden with wildflowers on the way to far-reaching views of the Rockies. Open during the summer season only (specific dates vary), Mon.–Sat., with Sun. tours available by reservation. **481 W. Elkhorn Ave., Estes Park, CO 80517; (303) 586-4237.**

GOLF

Estes Park Golf Club—

Although only 6,000 yards long, low scores are hard to come by on this difficult mountain course. Grainy greens make putting a real challenge. Be sure to keep in mind the location of Fish Creek while putting—the ball will invariably break that direction. Several of the par fours are pretty short, but the difficult par three fifth, 10th and 15th holes more than make up for them. The views are tremendous and the clubhouse personnel are quite friendly. The course is usually open from Apr. through Oct., but is in its best condition from July 1 through Oct. 15. Located about 2 miles south of downtown Estes Park on Hwy. 7. **1080 S. St. Vrain Ave., Estes Park, CO 80517; (303) 586-8146.**

Lake Estes Executive Course—

Open all year, this challenging nine-hole course requires complete concentration if you expect to brag in the clubhouse afterwards. In addition to the 186-yard, par three ninth hole, which crosses over the Big Thompson River, water comes into play on many of the other holes. The course is relatively flat, with views of the mountains to the west and Twin Owls rock to the north. Located next to Lake Estes on Hwy. 34. **690 Big Thompson Ave., Estes Park, CO 80517; (303) 586-8176.**

HIKING AND BACKPACKING

Granted, the scenery from Estes Park is hard to beat, but you owe it to yourself to get out on a trail and escape the crowds, to see deer munching grass in an alpine meadow or the burst of wildflowers as you round a corner. Trails in Rocky Mountain National Park and nearby Roosevelt National Forest cover the spectrum from easy day hikes to challenging high alpine backpacking trips. The **Estes Park Office of Roosevelt National Forest** can provide maps and more information about hiking opportunities in the area. Their address is

161 Second St., PO Box 2747, Estes Park, CO 80517; (303) 586-3440. For hikes in Rocky Mountain National Park, stop by the visitors centers at the east and west entrances to the park, or contact **Rocky Mountain National Park, Estes Park, CO 80517-8397; (303) 586-2371.**

For topographical maps, equipment and information, talk with Rob Mardock at **Colorado Wilderness Sports at 358 E. Elkhorn Ave., Estes Park, CO 80517; (303) 586-6548.** His shop is open year-round.

Crosier Mountain Trail—

This moderately difficult 8-mile round-trip hike starts at 7,200 feet and ends up at the 9,250-foot summit of Crosier Mountain. From the summit and various vantage points along the trail, you'll have fantastic views of the high peaks along the Continental Divide to the west in Rocky Mountain National Park. On your way to the summit you'll pass through lush aspen groves and meadows with ruins of settlers' homesteads. Keep an eye out for mule deer and take the time to enjoy the abundant and beautiful wildflowers. To get to the trailhead from Estes Park, take Devil's Gulch Rd. northeast about 8 miles (about a mile beyond Glen Haven). There will be a large gravel cut on the right (south) side of the road. Pull in and park. The trailhead is just up the hill from a gate. After going through the gate be sure to close it.

Lily Mountain Trail—

Lily Mountain is one of the easiest climbs in the Estes Park area. The trail starts at 8,800 feet and climbs 1.5 miles and 986 vertical feet to the summit. Along the way you'll have numerous opportunities for incredible views down to the Estes Valley. From the summit, enjoy the panorama of the Mummy Range to the northwest, Longs Peak to the south and the Continental Divide to the west. Many boulders near the top provide challenging scrambling, if you like that kind of thing. The trail is well marked for the entire route and makes an ideal half-day trip. To reach the trailhead from Estes Park, take Hwy. 7

about 6 miles south. Just before the 6-mile marker there is a small turn-off on the right and a parking area by the trailhead sign.

Lion Gulch Trail—

This fairly easy trail starts at 7,360 feet and climbs 1,000 feet, taking you into Homestead Meadows, where remains of homesteaders' ranches dating back to 1889 dot the valley floor. Some ranch houses, corrals, outhouses and other log buildings are still standing. A series of trails crisscrosses the area and is readily accessible after you've made the 2.5-mile trip to the meadows on Lion Gulch Trail. You can easily spend an entire day exploring the ruins and perhaps pondering what it would have been like to live in these buildings in the early days. The area is an excellent spot for a picnic and the views won't disappoint you. To reach the trailhead from Estes Park, head southeast on Hwy. 36 to mile-marker 8. The trailhead is on the right side of the road.

Rocky Mountain National Park—

See the Major Attractions section.

HORSEBACK RIDING

If you've got a yearning to saddle up and hit the trail, you've come to the right place. Estes Park is home to numerous outfitters offering everything from pony rides for the kids to all-day and overnight rides. Most rides head for trails within Rocky Mountain National Park. If you can't get a reservation, check the Yellow Pages for a complete listing.

Elkhorn Stables—

Located just west of downtown, they specialize in breakfast steak-fry rides. **PO Box 2111, 650 W. Elkhorn Ave., Estes Park, CO 80517; (303) 586-3291.**

Sombrero Stables—

Only a couple of miles east of Estes Park on Hwy. 34. **PO Box 1735AC, Estes Park, CO 80517; (303) 586-4577.**

LLAMA TREKKING
KL Ranch—
KL Ranch offers llama hikes with their "boys," Keno, Cashew, Sergio and Polo. Not only will you be treated to exotic companionship, but you'll learn about the history, and flora and fauna of the Estes Park area. One of the treks includes a lunch cookout. Call ahead for reservations. **PO Box 2385, Estes Park, CO 80517; (303) 586-2827 or (303) 586-5994.**

RIVER FLOATING
Feeling the exhilaration of having just negotiated a tough stretch of white water is something you won't soon forget—you can give it a try on a couple of rivers near Estes Park. The Cache la Poudre River north of Estes Park is run by rafters and some kayakers, but most kayakers prefer the more challenging Big Thompson River.

Cache La Poudre River—
See **Fort Collins and West** chapter.

Big Thompson River—
This river, which runs out of Rocky Mountain National Park through Estes Park and east to Loveland, has become a hot spot for kayakers. During runoff, from mid-Apr. to mid-July, the river offers enough challenge for expert kayakers, while some calm stretches can be navigated by novices. If you are a beginner and want to run the Big Thompson, check with Colorado Wilderness Sports about lessons (see listing below).

Outfitters—
Colorado Wilderness Sports—Along with raft trips on the Cache la Poudre, excursions to the Arkansas and Colorado rivers are also offered. Trips up to five days are available. Owner Rob Mardock gives kayak lessons on the Big Thompson and will have you doing Eskimo rolls like a pro in no time. Reservations recommended. **358 E. Elkhorn Ave., Estes Park, CO 80517; (303) 586-6548.**

Estes Park Adventures Limited—These folks specialize in half-day to two-day trips. **401 E. Elkhorn Ave., Estes Park, CO 80517; (303) 586-2303.**

Rapid Transit Rafting—The drive over Trail Ridge Rd. through Rocky Mountain National Park will keep you interested on the way to this outfitter's favorite spot—the Colorado River. **PO Box 4095, Estes Park, CO 80517; (303) 586-8852 or 1-800-367-8523 outside Colorado.**

SKIING
CROSS-COUNTRY SKIING
See Skiing (Cross-Country) in Rocky Mountain National Park.

Rentals and Information—
In addition to equipment and information, **Colorado Wilderness Sports** offers guided backcountry tours. **358 E. Elkhorn Ave., Estes Park, CO 80517; (303) 586-6548.**

Colorado Mountain School is a unique operation that can supply any equipment you need. They also lead backcountry tours and snow school courses. **351 Moraine Ave., Estes Park, CO 80517; (303) 586-5758.**

Ski Estes Park has a full range of rental equipment.

DOWNHILL SKIING
Ski Estes Park—
This small family resort is the only ski area in Colorado that's located in a national park. Offering 27 uncrowded trails, the ski area is equally divided into runs for novice, intermediate and advanced skiers. Trail Ridge Rd. runs right through the area, with most of the advanced terrain up above the road. To reach the advanced terrain from the main lodge you need to take a shuttle bus, which runs back and forth several times daily, from the lodge. Up on top of the advanced section (11,500 feet), the runs are in open bowls and are exposed to the wind. The lower runs are sheltered in a pine forest. A ski school,

equipment rentals, a children's center and a cafeteria are available at the base lodge. There is also a special Never Ever Skied bargain package that includes lift ticket, rental and lesson. The ski area is located 10 miles west of Estes Park via Hwy. 34 or Hwy. 36. For information contact **PO Box 1379, Estes Park, CO 80517**, or call **1-800-345-2361** in Colorado, **1-800-334-3708** out of state, or **(303) 586-8173** locally.

SWIMMING

Estes Park Aquatic Center—

This indoor/outdoor pool is open all year. Small fee charged. Located just south of Lake Estes at **660 Community Dr.; (303) 586-2340.**

Lake Estes—

There are several beach and picnic areas, but the lake is ver-r-r-y cold. The **Lake Estes Marina, (303) 586-2011,** also rents boats, windsurfers and wet suits by the hour. Located just east of downtown on Hwy. 34.

TENNIS

Estes Valley Recreation and Park District—

Six courts are just waiting for you in Stanley Park. Playing is free unless you want to reserve a time. Located on Community Dr. just south of Lake Estes; **(303) 586-8191.**

———— SEEING AND DOING ————

MUSEUMS

Estes Park Area Historical Museum—

The emphasis at this museum is the heritage of Estes Park and the surrounding area. Exhibits include a shiny Stanley Steamer automobile, a homestead cabin and numerous smaller displays relating the colorful history of the people who settled Estes Park. No admission fee, but donations are accepted. Open 10 am–5 pm Mon.–Sat. and 1–5 pm Sun. May–Sept.; 10 am–5 pm Tues.–Sat. the rest of the year. **200 Fourth St. (at Hwy. 36), Estes Park, CO 80517; (303) 586-6256.**

MacGregor Ranch Museum—

In 1872 Alexander MacGregor visited Estes Park on a camping trip and fell in love with the land. That same year the Earl of Dunraven came to the valley and decided he wanted to own every acre. MacGregor helped lead the fight against Dunraven's claims, and the museum contains all the documents telling the story of the land battle. You can also see ranch equipment and household items from the years 1870 to 1950. More than 50 paintings by western artists, including Charles Partridge Adams, are displayed. The collection of antiques, china and silver would make any collector envious. There are marked walking trails around the ranch property. Admission is free. Open from 11 am–5 pm Tues.–Sat., Memorial Day–Labor Day. Located half a mile north of Estes Park on Devil's Gulch Rd. at **180 MacGregor Ln., Estes Park, CO 80517; (303) 586-3749.**

NIGHTLIFE

The nightlife in Estes Park is somewhat limited, but with all the activities available while the sun shines, you might look upon this as a blessing. If you feel like going out on the town, don't despair. Several bars on Elkhorn Ave. feature live music. If you're looking for something more exceptional, read on . . . .

Barleen Family Country Music Dinner Theater—

The Barleen family, featuring three generations of singers, musicians and comedians, has been entertaining folks for 10 years. The shows are a blend of country-western favorites along with pop music. Open mid-May through Sept. Located a half mile south of the Holiday Inn on Hwy. 7. **1110 Woodstock Dr.; (303) 586-5749.**

Stanley Hotel Theatre/
Fine Arts Series—

Every year the Stanley presents a year-round series of theater and fine arts performances. The hotel boasts that it puts on more theater and classical concerts than any other private property in the western US. It's a great setting! See the Where to Stay section. Check with the Stanley to find out the current schedule. 333 Wonderview; (303) 586-3371.

SCENIC DRIVES

Fall River Road—

See the Major Attractions section.

Lyons Loop—

After you've driven across Trail Ridge Rd., other scenic drives pale in comparison. Even so, if you are interested in a beautiful 60-mile loop trip from Estes Park, consider this drive to Lyons and back. There are two fine restaurants along the way— The Fawn Brook Inn in the town of Allenspark and La Chaumiere in the community of Pinewood Springs (see the Where to Eat section). You may want to start out in the glow of late afternoon and stop for dinner as darkness descends.

The scenery is equally spectacular going either direction on the loop, but we'll start out south on Hwy. 7 under the craggy summits of Battle Mountain, Mt. Meeker, Longs Peak and Horsetooth Peak. By far the most impressive are 14,255-foot Longs Peak and 13,911-foot Mt. Meeker. You'll pass the Twin Sisters and a variety of lower peaks that lie to the east. About 11 miles from Estes Park be sure to stop at the St. Catherine's Chapel or "Chapel on the

Rock." This place of worship, built in 1935, looks like it grew out of the massive rock on which it sits. Located at the base of Mt. Meeker, this is a beautiful picture-taking spot. After Allenspark, Hwy. 7 takes an eastern tack and enters a canyon with steep rock walls. The South St. Vrain Creek will be your traveling companion along this part of the drive. More spectacular scenery is in store as you hit Lyons and take Hwy. 36 back to Estes Park.

A highly recommended option: the Peak to Peak Highway is a magnificent drive to the south of Allenspark. It's especially colorful in autumn when the shimmering aspen groves are at their peak. To link up with this scenic highway, turn right (south) on Hwy. 72, 4 miles east of Allenspark. For detailed information, see Scenic Drives section of the **Boulder** chapter.

Trail Ridge Road—

Don't miss this one! See the Major Attractions section.

TRAMWAY

Aerial Tramway—

This tram will take you to the summit of 8,896-foot Prospect Mountain, which is virtually surrounded by the town of Estes Park. From the top you'll be treated to a great view of Longs Peak and the Continental Divide. Once at the summit you can stay until the last tram runs back down to town. Yes, they have a souvenir shop and a snack bar available while you are captive atop the mountain. Open mid-May to mid-Sept. 420 E. Riverside Dr., Estes Park, CO 80517; (303) 586-3675.

———— WHERE TO STAY ————

ACCOMMODATIONS

Estes Park sports a multitude of lodging choices ranging from the plush Stanley Hotel to a Holiday Inn and right down to the most rustic of log cabins. Here are a few that have something special going for them.

The Aspen Lodge — $$$ to $$$$

This four-season resort is something like a guest ranch, but you can stay any amount of time you wish, and meals are optional. The flexibility is a terrific plus. Activities include horseback riding, wildlife tours and children's programs. In winter, you can cross-country ski, snowmobile and take a sleigh ride. (All activities are open to the public for a fee.)

As you walk into the open lobby you will be awed by the huge fireplace and monstrous log beams. The entire building is constructed of log and stone, and although new, it comfortably blends in with the older lodges and cabins. The main lodge is built of 2,500 lodgepole pine logs, with the resort's longest being 30 inches in diameter and spanning 56 feet. Rooms in the main lodge have a true western feel and are the nicest accommodations. Most of the cabins are small but comfortable duplexes. The Aspen Lodge is located 8 miles south of Estes Park on Hwy. 7. **6120 Hwy. 7, Estes Park, CO 80517; (303) 586-8133; (303) 440-3371** in metro Denver; **1-800-332-6867** toll free.

The Stanley Hotel — $$$ to $$$$

At its grand opening in 1909, this elegant hotel was said to rival anything of its size in the world. Inventor F.O. Stanley and a partner began building the hotel in 1906. Horse teams moved supplies 22 miles to the site on roads built especially for the purpose. At its ideal hilltop perch, the hotel is now listed on the National Register of Historic Places.

When patrons arrived by Stanley Steamer from the railhead in Lyons, they walked into a lobby that stretched 80 feet on either side of the main desk. A mirrored, ornate brass elevator took them to their rooms, which were color coordinated to the red and yellow exterior (a hideous but popular color scheme patterned after European mountain resorts). Rooms were furnished with the finest furniture of the era, including four-poster and brass beds. This type of luxury sounds commonplace today, but in 1909 Colorado, this was indeed a spectacular establishment. A private horse stable and a nine-hole golf course were maintained for guests. In the evenings, bowling, billiards, dinner dances, theater productions and golf putting contests in the lobby provided the entertainment. For those with "new-fangled horseless carriages," there was a fully equipped garage.

Over the years the hotel has played host to such notables as John Philip Sousa, Theodore Roosevelt, "Unsinkable" Molly Brown and, more recently, Stephen King. King was so impressed with the hotel that he drew upon its ambience and history for the setting of his horror classic *The Shining*. Contrary to popular belief, the hotel wasn't actually used in the film version of the book. Director Stanley Kubrick tried, but a lack of snow and the proximity of the town made it impossible.

For all its grand past, the hotel ran into problems in the late 1970s, when it was poorly managed. The Stanley, however, has undergone a renaissance that would have made F.O. proud. The exterior has been painted white, and the rooms have been completely redone with original furnishings wherever possible. Some of the elegant rooms once again feature canopied, four-poster beds and claw-foot bathtubs. The corner rooms provide magnificent views of the mountains and town. An excellent kitchen staff serves food sure to please the palate in the still-impressive MacGregor Room and Dunraven Grille. The veranda is a perfect spot to take in the beauty of the area. Be sure to ask about the evening concert series. The hotel is open year-round. During summer weekends, reservations must be made for at least two nights. **333 Wonderview, Estes Park, CO 80517; (303) 586-3371.**

RiverSong Bed and Breakfast — $$$

You'll find yourself never wanting to leave this cozy, romantic hideaway, which is situated on 27 wooded acres next to the Big Thompson River. RiverSong Bed and Breakfast offers a gazebo by the river, a pond and hiking trails complete with stone benches for rest stops. Elk, deer, eagles, owls, chipmunks and squirrels are just a few of the animals you may see on the grounds.

The living room features large picture windows with an impressive view of the mountains. Sit back in the big circular sofa next to a crackling fire after choosing a book from the well-stocked library. Grab a cookie from the cookie jar—it's always full. When it's time for bed, retire to a room decorated with antique furniture, or maybe you would prefer one with a private sauna and a huge sunken bathtub. Consider staying in the Cowboy's Delight; it's a large rustic room in the carriage house with its own deck, woodburning stove and queen-sized four-poster bed. All of the rooms have unique themes and six of the eight have private bathrooms.

Wake up at a leisurely hour for a gourmet breakfast you won't soon forget. Wrap up in one of their thick terrycloth robes and enjoy. RiverSong is popular and fills up fast, so make reservations as far in advance as possible. Open year-round; kids over 12 are welcome. **PO Box 1910, Estes Park, CO 80517; (303) 586-4666.**

Wind River Ranch — $$$

Owners Rob and Jere Irvin have worked hard to preserve the history of this 110-acre ranch homesteaded in 1876. Limited to 55 guests, this is a place where you can get away from the crowds and enjoy the stunning scenery in an unstructured, relaxed atmosphere. Take in the views of Longs Peak and Mt. Meeker from atop a trail-wise horse or from the ranch's heated pool. Log cabins create a rustic atmosphere without neglecting the modern comforts. The main living room projects a comfortable atmosphere, with its large stone fireplace, beamed ceilings and walls lined with bookshelves. Sit down and enjoy a chat with other guests. This ranch is noted for its fine food. With delicious buffets, hearty steak dinners, filet mignon, shrimp scampi, special pastries and patio picnics, you'll never go hungry. A minimum stay of three days is required. The ranch is located at the top of Wind River Pass, 7 miles south of Estes Park on Hwy. 7. **PO Box 3410-CG, Estes Park, CO 80517; (303) 586-4212.**

Glacier Lodge — $$ to $$$

Twenty cabins at this resort are nestled along the banks of the Big Thompson River. Some of the cabins are so close to the river you can fish from their front porches. Other cabins are located up on the hill, or you can stay in a lodge room. Glacier Lodge lives up to its western atmosphere, offering guests horseback rides from the stable, fishing and a western cookout every Mon. during summer. There is a heated swimming pool. Kids love the Soda Saloon, where they can meet others of the same age. Jim and Penny Ranglos have gone out of their way to provide a variety of accommodations, from rustic to brand new. Many of the cabins have fireplaces and all are equipped with full kitchens. Open year-round. There is a minimum two-day stay, unless they happen to have an opening between reservations. **2166 Hwy. 66, Estes Park, CO 80517; (303) 586-4401.**

YMCA of the Rockies — $$ to $$$

This family-style resort, sprawling over 1,400 forested acres, is virtually a small town. Once you get there, you may decide you don't need to go anywhere else. For those traveling with children, there are a variety of scheduled activities. You can drop off the kids for swimming, roller skating, basketball, tennis, horseshoes, volleyball, miniature golf, horseback riding and hayrides, to name just a few of the summer activities. In winter, the sledding hill is an unforgettable experience, and there's always ice skating, snowshoeing and cross-country skiing. A rental shop can take care of all your equipment needs. Also available at this "town" are a church, a restaurant, a grocery store, a library, a museum, a gift shop and a gas station.

The resort has more than 200 cabins with a variety of features. Most have fireplaces and all have refrigerators, stoves, telephones and at least one full bedroom. Whether you stay in the most rustic or the most luxurious cabin, you'll have all the modern conveniences along with spectacular views of the surrounding peaks. Some 500 lodge rooms, catering primarily to groups, offer motel-style accommodations. Low-priced YMCA temporary memberships are granted for the duration of your stay. Open year-round. For reservations and information, contact: **Estes Park Center/YMCA, 2515 Tunnel Rd., Estes Park, CO 80511-2800; (303) 586-3341;** Denver metro area **(303) 623-9215;** toll free in Colorado **1-800-228-3947.**

CAMPING

In Rocky Mountain National Park—
See the Major Attractions section.

In Roosevelt National Forest—
Olive Ridge Campground (56 wooded campsites and a fee) is open all year. Located 13 miles south of Estes Park on Hwy. 7.

Private Campgrounds—
Estes Park Campground—This campground has 65 sites and hot showers, but there are no RV hookups. Open June–Sept. To get there from Estes Park, head west on Hwy. 36 and then left for 3 miles on Hwy. 66. **PO Box 3517, Estes Park, CO 80517; (303) 586-4188.**

KOA Campground—Twenty-five tent sites and plenty of RV hookups await. There is also a laundry room, a game room and general store. Open Mar. 15–Nov. 1. Located 1 mile east of Estes Park on Hwy. 34. **D.G. Rt., Estes Park, CO 80517; (303) 586-2888.**

Spruce Lake RV Park—This RV-only campground is open all year with 110 sites. Amenities include a rec room, a swimming pool, a laundry room, etc. Lake and stream fishing are also available. **1050 Marys Lake Rd., PO Box 2497, Estes Park, CO 80517; (303) 586-2889.**

WHERE TO EAT

La Chaumiere — $$$$
The rather plain exterior of this small restaurant successfully disguises the excellent food to be had within. A father and son team, Heinz and Andy Fricker, are your hosts. They specialize in French cuisine, which Heinz regards as an art form. He will delight you with an array of masterpieces such as roast duckling with wild rice and corn pancakes, poached salmon with herbed hollandaise, and roast lamb with rosemary sauce. The menu changes weekly and the restaurant is open all year. Reservations are recommended. Hours vary depending on the season. Located in Pinewood Springs, 12 miles southeast of Estes Park on Hwy. 36; 823-6521.

Black Canyon Inn — $$$ to $$$$
If you're looking for the most romantic dinner spot in the area, this is it. A huge stone fireplace dominates a room rich with hunting and skiing lore. Moose, elk and buffalo heads share the walls with antique cross-country skis and snowshoes. The three-story, log-beamed dining room plays host to chef Carlo Castiglione's most popular dishes, including veal chausseur and rack of lamb Provençal. Scallops and pasta Santa Cruz are also favorites among regulars. Lunch is generally served from 11:30 am–2 pm; dinner service from 5:30–9 pm. Hours and days vary with the season. Reservations recommended. **800 MacGregor Ave.; 586-8113.**

The Fawn Brook Inn — $$$ to $$$$
Some locals say this intimate restaurant has the best food in northern Colorado. Located in the sleepy village of Allenspark, this gourmand's delight is also known for its fine service and excellent views. Select from a menu that specializes in fish, veal, lamb, steak and duck. While you're waiting for a table, relax in front of the stone fireplace. Reservations are recommended. Open from Memorial Day through Labor Day for dinner Tues.–Sat. 5–9 pm; Sun. hours for lunch from noon–2 pm and dinner from 4–8:30 pm. Winter

hours vary. To reach the restaurant, drive 15 miles south from Estes Park on the Hwy. 7 business loop in Allenspark; 747-2556.

The Dunraven Inn — $$ to $$$

Sit back and enjoy the dark, romantic atmosphere and the fine Italian cuisine at this very popular restaurant. House specialties include lasagna, veal parmigiana, eggplant parmigiana marinara and chicken cacciatore. The walls of the lounge are covered with dollar bills—customers write notes on the bills and tack them to the walls. A great selection of Italian wines and cocktails is available in the dining room and the lounge. You'd better make reservations or be ready for a two-hour wait during the summer. Dinner is served nightly from 5 pm. Open year-round. 2470 Hwy. 66; 586-6409.

The Old Plantation Restaurant — $$ to $$$

The Old Plantation was founded in 1931 by Thelma Burgess and is still owned by her family. The dining room is dotted with antiques and the walls show off works of early western artists. The trout and duck entrées seem to be the most consistent menu items, but the outstanding desserts are what attract most people. Sample one of the seven kinds of pies as well as cheesecake and cobbler, and you'll know why this has been a local favorite for over 50 years. Reservations recommended. Open daily from Memorial Day–Oct., 11:30 am–9 pm. 128 E. Elkhorn Ave.; 586-2800.

La Casa — $ to $$$

In summer head straight to the pretty outdoor garden at this Mexican/Cajun-style restaurant. It may sound like they specialize in conflicting types of food—that is, until your palate is dazzled by a taste of blackened shrimp, voo doo chicken, a spicy beef burrito or their family specialty, the Estorito. They even have Margaritas on tap. Live entertainment nightly. Open from 11 am–10 pm year-round. 222 E. Elkhorn Ave.; 586-2807.

SERVICES

Estes Park Chamber of Commerce—

500 Big Thompson Ave., Estes Park, CO 80517; (303) 586-4431 or 1-800-44Estes

Estes Park Central Reservations—

This office can help you book almost any accommodation. 481 W. Elkhorn Ave., Estes Park, CO 80517; 1-800-762-5968 toll free; in Estes Park call (303) 586-4402 or (303) 586-4237.

Transportation—

Rocky Mountain Park Tours—If you want to concentrate on the scenery and leave the driving to someone else, contact this outfit for a bus tour of the local surroundings. 401 E. Elkhorn Ave., Estes Park, CO 80517; (303) 586-8687.

Estes Park Bus Co.—This company also offers a variety of bus tours of the local scenery. 205 Park Ln., Estes Park, CO 80517; (303) 586-8108.

The Estes Park Trolley—1773 Wildfire Rd., Estes Park, CO 80517; (303) 586-8866.

Fort Collins and West

Fort Collins, which labels itself variously as "The Fort," or "Fort Fun," is characterized by a mix of the old and young, the progressive and the provincial, topped off by the love of a health-conscious lifestyle. You can't help but notice walkers, bicyclists and joggers of all ages on the roads and trails. You'll also notice Fort Collins keeps a tight leash on smokers. The city was one of the first in the nation to pass a tough smoking ordinance— you're not supposed to light up in any public building except in designated areas.

The town's progressiveness comes from its diverse population, mellow lifestyle and the presence of Colorado State University (CSU), which is the area's largest employer. Out of the 90,000 residents, more than 19,000 are students who attend the university. In a fine location on the plains just east of the mountains, Fort Collins retains the feel of a much smaller town. Some first-time visitors are surprised by the city's central area; it's not much larger than the downtowns of some midwestern towns that have one-third the population. One particularly nostalgic section of Fort Collins is Old Town. In the early 1980s, this original business section of town was restored. It stands as a picturesque reminder of Fort Collins' earlier days and boasts a very pleasant array of up-scale shops and restaurants. Another small-town touch is the sight of trains chugging through and across the main streets. While some citizens aren't amused by the delays or the train noises in the middle of the night, others retain a sense of humor. One deli near the railroad tracks offers "train specials"—discounts on sandwiches and beer if you're in the store when a train goes by.

Fort Collins is more aptly described as a gateway for vacationers than as a vacation destination in itself—it offers quick access to some of Colorado's best recreation lands. Just west of town, Roosevelt National Forest with its four wilderness areas provides ample opportunities for hiking, mountain biking, fishing and cross-country skiing among other things. The Cache la Poudre River barrels out of the mountains through the beautiful Poudre Canyon just west of town. The river alone keeps many a sightseer, camper, fisherman and rafter happy.

HISTORY

The name of the city notwithstanding, there is no military base here. In fact, there hasn't been a fort in Fort Collins since the 1860s.

The mountainous area west of modern-day Fort Collins was well known to Indians, fur traders and trappers who passed through and camped under tall cottonwoods, long before any permanent settlement was established. Traders and Indians peacefully co-existed in the Cache la Poudre area. The Cache la Poudre ("hide the powder") River receives its name from a party of French trappers who stashed their heavy barrels

291

of gunpowder at the river's edge to make traveling through deep snow less burdensome. In 1844 life there was so good for one trader that he described the area, with its mild climate, rugged landscape and teeming buffalo herds, as "the loveliest spot on earth."

In the late 1850s gold discoveries in the Rockies prompted a number of fortune hunters to pour into the Cache la Poudre area. Few people found any gold to speak of, but some of the discouraged prospectors set up farms and ranches. In 1871 Camp Collins, a short-lived military encampment, was established to protect the Overland Trail and the few farms and ranches nearby, but it was soon abandoned simply because it wasn't needed. A couple of years later lots were offered for sale in an agricultural colony modeled after the successful Union Colony at Greeley, just to the east. No ruffians applied as the lots were sold only to temperate people of "high moral character."

The survival of Fort Collins was not assured in its early days, as it had a population of only a few hundred people. In September 1879 the Agricultural College of Colorado opened its doors to five students. Experiments at the college resulted in improved farming and ranching techniques. In the early 1900s the state's sugar beet industry and other agricultural pursuits helped the young town continue a slow but sustained growth. The agricultural college eventually grew into Colorado State University, which still maintains a highly regarded agricultural program.

GETTING THERE

Fort Collins is located 60 miles north of Denver on Interstate 25. It's also 45 miles south of Cheyenne, Wyoming off Interstate 25. The mountainous area to the west of Fort Collins is accessible almost solely from Hwy. 14. Stapleton International Airport in Denver is well served by shuttle vans to Fort Collins. Contact **Airport Express** in Fort Collins for reservations and information at **(303) 482-0505**. Greyhound Trailways Bus Lines makes five daily trips between Denver and Fort Collins.

———— FESTIVALS AND EVENTS ————

Fort Collins has a number of small festivals. If you happen to be in town you might want to stick around for one of the following.

Fort Collins Flying Festival
late September
This spectator event features everything from kite flying to hot-air balloon races. Since the Fort Collins area is known for excellent wind currents, this is a perfect place for all kinds of aerial sports. For more information contact the **Fort Collins Chamber of Commerce** at **(303) 482-3746**.

International Invitational Poster Exhibit
(in odd years during fall)
This major event comes only every other year, but it's worth the wait. Outstanding posters from around the world

are displayed and judged by a panel of experts. Several visiting artists personally take part in the show. After the show in Fort Collins, the exhibit travels to a few other cities. For more information, contact **Colorado State University** at **(303) 491-6444**. (You might also ask about upcoming lectures and concerts on the university events calender.)

OUTDOOR ACTIVITIES

BIKING

MOUNTAIN BIKING

Colorado State Forest—

A network of gravel and four-wheel-drive roads wind together in many loop combinations providing a perfect destination for mountain bikers. The best way to reach the majority of these trails is through the main entrance to the forest, located 2 miles beyond the town of Gould on the north side of Hwy. 14 (75 miles west of Fort Collins). Check in at the park entrance station for a map of recommended bike rides. The remote and beautiful scenery along the roads warrants the extra effort of getting here.

Never Summer Nordic Yurt System—

A yurt provides sleeping space for six people in a more comfortable environment than a tent. It's a great way to see the Medicine Bow mountain range without carrying a lot of extra weight on your bike. At the park entrance, be sure to pick up a trail map. From here, bikers can take the **Grass Creek Loop**, a difficult 16-mile round trip, which goes past North Michigan Reservoir, 10,000-foot Gould Mountain and finally out to Hwy. 14. This ride takes you past the **Grass Creek Yurt**, 1 mile from the trailhead. The most remote yurt, called the **North Fork Canadian Yurt**, can be reached by taking a trail north past Bull Mountain (3 miles). Then head north on the **North Fork Trail**. Total round-trip mileage on this ride is about 19 miles. This is a good place to spot moose and elk. The third yurt is located on Ruby Jewel Rd., a four-wheel-drive road that heads to Ruby Jewel Lake. For more information see the Cross-Country Skiing section.

Horsetooth Mountain Park—

This mountain park, on the western side of Horsetooth Reservoir, as well as **Lory State Park** provide miles upon miles of terrific mountain biking trails. See Parks and Recreation Areas for information.

Rentals and Information—

Dirtmasters specializes in mountain bikes, including day tours. They can help you find some great trails near town. They also sell maps (pick up the mountain bike trail map) and mountain biking equipment. It's located at the shopping center on the corner of Shields and Drake streets; **(303) 226-DIRT**.

Another mountain bike rental shop is Adventure Quest, which is open in spring and summer only. **Adventure Quest, 822 S. College Ave.**

TOURING

Fort Collins has an extensive bike trail system within the city. Bicycle shops in town carry a supply of "Tour de Fort," a free map with 56 miles of local bike trails, lanes and routes. One especially nice ride is the snaking trail which runs alongside the Cache la Poudre River in northern Fort Collins. Not only is it relatively flat and very scenic, but it is accessible from several points in the city. Bingham Hill and Cache la Poudre Canyon are also a couple of longer trips in the mountains to the west of Fort Collins.

Bingham Hill—

To get to Bingham Hill, ride north on Overland Trail Rd., a main north-south artery that lies just west of the city. Once on Overland Trail Rd., continue north past W. Vine Dr. and Lake Lee on the right. About

5.5 miles from downtown Fort Collins, turn left (west) onto Bingham Hill Rd., marked by a sign to Lory State Park. The road is somewhat steep, but you'll enjoy a far-reaching view out to the plains. You'll see many other bicyclists on the Overland Trail and Bingham Hill route.

Cache la Poudre Canyon—

About 10 miles northwest of Fort Collins, Hwy. 14 leads west into the spectacular Poudre Canyon as it heads toward North Park. Go as far as you want alongside the crashing river, but beware of motorists on this narrow, winding route. It's basically uphill but it tends to be gradual unless you go all the way to Cameron Pass (70 miles west of Fort Collins). Of course, if you go that far, you probably are a skilled rider with little concern about hills anyway.

Rentals and Information—

Adventure Quest will supply touring rentals. Stop by **822 S. College Ave. Recycled Cycles** will rent you any of their used touring bikes for a most reasonable price; they also have weekly rates. Recycled Cycles is located south of town. **6024 S. College Ave.; (303) 223-3300.**

FISHING

The Fort Collins area presents an unusual combination of stream trout fishing and warmwater lake fishing. In addition, an abundance of tributaries, small lakes and beaver ponds in the high country west of Fort Collins have trout. This water often presents challenging, uncrowded fly-fishing for smallish (eight- to 10-inch) brook trout or cutthroats. Stop by any local fishing store for information about current conditions; fly fishermen should check in with the folks at **Garrett & Duffey, No. 17 Old Town Sq.; (303) 224-9744.**

Cache la Poudre River—

The Poudre offers long stretches of accessible water along its rush east from the high reaches of Rocky Mountain Na-

tional Park. Much of the river parallels Hwy. 14 as it flows easterly toward Fort Collins. Though the Poudre has a predominant brown and rainbow trout population (average size is about 11 inches), it's also home to a number of ugly whitefish. Actually, the whitefish are strong fighters and surprisingly good to eat. Fly-fishing is the most effective way to take Poudre River trout, but fishermen occasionally do well with lures, worms or salmon eggs. One warning for bait anglers: the Poudre has several Wild Trout sections in which bait is not allowed. One section is in the lower Poudre; the others are farther upstream near the town of Rustic. The Poudre River is scenic, easy to reach from Fort Collins, and as a result, heavily fished. There are campgrounds, picnic grounds, resorts and frequent turn-offs along Hwy. 14. Try fishing the Poudre in the area near Long Draw Reservoir just as the river comes out of Rocky Mountain National Park. To get there from Fort Collins, head 10 miles northwest on Hwy. 287 and then 53 miles west on Hwy. 14. Turn left (south) on Long Draw Reservoir Rd. (Forest Rd. 156). The best time to fish the Poudre is Sept.–Oct. and prior to runoff in the spring. If you only take one fly along to fish the Poudre, make sure it's a Hare's Ear nymph (size eight to 12 hook).

Horsetooth Reservoir—

See the Parks and Recreation Areas section for fishing information.

Laramie River—

In the Chambers Lake area, the Laramie can be good fishing for small rainbow, brown and cutthroat trout. The narrow stream flows north through the Rawah Wilderness Area, and eventually into Wyoming with many beaver ponds along the way. To get here from Fort Collins, drive northwest on Hwy. 287 for 10 miles and then west on Hwy. 14 for 52 miles. Turn right (north) on Laramie River Rd.

Red Feather Lakes—

Red Feather Lake is only one of 14

lakes in the Red Feather region, about 50 miles northwest of Fort Collins. Six of the lakes are open to public recreation with fishing as the main attraction. The fishing can be good whether you're in a boat or fishing from the shore. You can use flies, lures or bait, except on Parvin Lake, which is restricted to flies and lures only. Red Feather Lakes can be reached from Fort Collins by taking Hwy. 287 north and then west for 22 miles. Turn left onto Red Feather Lakes Rd. (the old North Park freight trail) at the Forks Cafe and continue about 30 miles to the lakes. Red Feather Lakes are also accessible from Poudre Canyon via Forest Rd. 162 at Rustic.

Watson Lake/Poudre River—

Watson Lake, which has plenty of parking and some picnic tables, is stocked regularly with trout. The north end of Watson is a Wild Trout area that is open only to fly or lure anglers. The Poudre flows by Watson and is also stocked. Fishing pressure on both Watson Lake and the Poudre River is pretty heavy. If you come up empty, however, you can always stop by the hatchery on the way out and see thousands of trout. Watson Lake is about 8 miles northwest of Fort Collins. To get here take Hwy. 287 to Rist Canyon Rd., a mile past La Porte. At the junction, turn left onto Rist Canyon Rd. (at a marked turn for the Bellvue Fish Hatchery) and continue about a mile to the lake.

FOUR-WHEEL-DRIVE TRIPS

Green Ridge Trail—

This is a scenic, moderately difficult, 17-mile round-trip drive. Special attractions include challenging, narrow sections of road and a lot of mud holes. The drive starts at about 9,400 feet and passes Lake Laramie and Twin Lakes before ending at Deadman Rd. (10,200 feet). Just before reaching Deadman Rd., the trail goes through thick stands of lodgepole pine to Nunn Creek Basin. To the west from Nunn Creek Basin are sweeping views of Medicine Bow Range. To reach Green Ridge Trail, take Hwy. 14 up Poudre Canyon for 52 miles. Turn right on the Laramie River Rd. (Forest Rd. 190) and drive for about 1.5 miles to Lost Lake parking lot. The trail, marked with a sign, starts at the north end of the parking lot.

Kelly Flats—

This rugged road receives low use and has steep hills and some challenging stream crossings—good ground clearance is a must. The 9-mile round trip leads to the top of Wintersteen Mesa, which provides a panorama of Poudre Canyon and parts of Rocky Mountain National Park to the south. If the gate is not locked at the top of the mesa, it's possible to continue west to Manhattan Rd., which runs north and south between the town of Rustic and Red Feather Lakes. To reach the road, take Hwy. 14 west up Poudre Canyon for 20 miles to Kelly Flats Campground. Turn right onto Forest Rd. 162, just past the campground, and head north. The first 1.5 miles is a steep climb which drops off into a drainage, then climbs for another 2 miles before leveling off in a grassy meadow.

Roach Area—

Another popular area for four-wheel-drive vehicles is in the Roach area near the Wyoming border. Many old logging and mining roads crisscross this remote region. You should definitely take along a Roosevelt National Forest map to help you navigate these back roads. To reach Roach from Fort Collins, head west on Hwy. 14 for 52 miles to Chambers Lake and turn right (north) on Laramie River Rd. (Forest Rd. 190). Proceed north for 29 miles and turn left to Hohnholz Lakes. Continue west past the lakes and choose a road.

GOLF
Collindale Golf Course—

This fine 18-hole course is the first choice of locals. Characterized by many mature cottonwood trees, a number of creeks and carefully maintained fairways, Collindale is open all year, weather permitting. Unless there has been a lot of rain, the greens are usually very fast. So that you don't end up breaking your fairway wood across your knee on the very first hole, be forewarned: there is a large hidden lake to the front right of green No. 1. You'll find all of the services you expect at a course including a very good snack bar. **1441 E. Horsetooth Rd.; (303) 221-6651.**

Ptarmigan Golf and Country Club—

Though this is a new course, you can be sure of having a memorable and challenging round—it was designed by Jack Nicklaus. In true Nicklaus fashion, the course follows the natural contour of the rolling terrain, rather than trying to dominate it. And it's tough. Long water hazards, lots of trees and monstrously large sand traps come into play on just about every hole. One of the sand traps is as expansive as a California beach, complete with a grass island in the middle. The back nine is considerably more hilly than the front. Ptarmigan is a country club and is currently rounding up enough memberships so they can go private—so don't waste any time. Located southeast of Fort Collins, just east of the Windsor exit off Interstate 25. **5412 Vardon Wy.; (303) 226-6600.**

HIKING AND BACKPACKING

Within the Roosevelt National Forest to the west of Fort Collins, four wilderness areas including the Cache la Poudre, Neota, Comanche Peak and Rawah provide varied terrain ranging from easy, low altitude hikes to multi-day backpack trips. Two of the most spectacular areas are Rawah and Comanche Peak with pine forests, alpine tundra, barren rock formations, high peaks, cirque lakes and moraines, trout streams, and an abundance of wildlife. Both have extensive, interconnecting trail systems. These areas deserve more than just a peek.

For more specific details about the wilderness areas and other parts of Roosev-

elt National Forest, stop in at the **Estes–Poudre Ranger District Office** at **148 Remington St., Fort Collins, CO 80524; (303) 482-3822.** For information on the northern section of the forest, near the Wyoming border, contact the **Red Feather Ranger District Office at 1635 Blue Spruce Dr., Fort Collins, CO 80524; (303) 224-1375** or **224-1362.** Either office can supply you with pamphlets and maps of the forest area. *Open Space and Trails Guide*, a pamphlet offered free of charge by the city of Fort Collins, shows short hikes in town and the foothills. Further information, maps and rental equipment may be picked up at **The Mountain Shop at 632 S. Mason; (303) 493-5720.**

Browns Lake Trail—

This beautiful 4-mile (one way) hike in the Comanche Peak Wilderness Area, at altitudes between 10,000 and 12,000 feet, illustrates up close what the term "treeline" means. The area around the lake is heavily wooded, and in summer, many colorful wildflowers line the trail. The mountain tops, however, are devoid of trees or much growth of any type. To reach the trailhead, head up Poudre Canyon on Hwy. 14 for 26 miles to Pingree Park Rd. (Forest Rd. 131) and turn left. Take Pingree Park Rd. 4 miles and keep right at Crown Point Rd. (Forest Rd. 139) for another 12 miles. The trail is on the left.

Cache la Poudre Wilderness Area—

This wilderness ranges in altitude from a little more than 6,000 feet to 8,600 feet, but it does not have the overwhelming beauty of some of the higher mountain areas. The trade-off is that the steep, rugged terrain within this small wilderness area is seldom traveled. **Mt. McConnel Trail** is the only maintained trail in the wilderness area. It's a 5-mile loop climbing through juniper, fir and pine to the summit. Once there, eat lunch at the flat rock while enjoying the views. Other parts of the wilderness area are accessible, if you don't mind bushwhacking. Your efforts will be rewarded with solitude, thick forests and a chance to glimpse some of Colorado's more exotic fauna—bear, mountain lion and the endangered peregrine falcon. The South Fork of the Cache la Poudre River flows through the west-central part of the wilderness, so there is a chance for fishing as well. From Fort Collins, head northwest on Hwy. 287 for 10 miles and then west on Hwy. 14 for 22 miles to Mountain Park Campground. The wilderness area is south of the river (you'll see the Mt. McConnel trailhead).

Colorado State Forest—

This 28-mile strip of remote land runs along the western edge of the Medicine Bow Range. Because it's sandwiched by Roosevelt National Forest, Rocky Mountain National Park and the Rawah Wilderness Area, the Colorado State Forest is often overlooked. But you'll find some standout hiking here. The state forest is characterized by miles of streams and thick pine forests. The southern tip of the forest offers a seldom-used access (Thunder Pass Trail) to Rocky Mountain National Park. From this area there are also trails leading to Lake Agnes, Nokhu Crags and the barren summit of Mt. Richtoffen. From Fort Collins drive northwest on Hwy. 287 for 10 miles and then west on Hwy. 14 for 60 miles to 10,200-foot Cameron Pass. As you drop down the south side of the pass, you'll be in the state forest. For more information, contact the **Colorado State Forest** at **Star Route, PO Box 91, Walden, CO 80480; (303) 723-8366** or **(303) 866-3437** in Denver.

Backpackers who are interested in something a little different might want to check with **Never Summer Nordic** about their yurt system located in the Colorado State Forest. These backcountry huts provide great shelter on multi-day hikes. For more information see the Biking and Cross-Country Skiing sections.

Greyrock Trail—

Greyrock is perhaps the best known and one of the most often recommended day hikes in the Fort Collins area. It's a fairly steep 3-mile (one way) hike but the reward comes at the 7,500-foot summit where you'll have views west to higher mountains and east to the plains and Fort Collins. You might even catch sight of a bobcat or a black squirrel. Local hikers rate Greyrock as a much better experience during spring or fall than in summertime, when it is less crowded and cooler. The Greyrock Trailhead is located 9 miles west up Poudre Canyon on Hwy. 14. You'll see it on the right side of the road.

Lory State Park—

More than 30 miles of hiking trails attract many people to this nearby park, only 20 minutes from Fort Collins. The elevation is low enough that you can hike all year, though there are a few snowstorms in winter. One suggested hike is **Arthur's Rock**. Trail maps are available at the park entrance. See the Parks and Recreation Areas section for directions.

Mirror Lake—

The trail to this high alpine lake at 11,000 feet takes you through a beautiful section of Rocky Mountain National Park. It's a tough, 7-mile hike over steep terrain

Backpacking and hiking trails lead to unusual and beautiful terrain in Colorado's high country (photograph by Bob Huestis).

through pine and fir to the glacial moraine which holds Mirror Lake. You'll also pass a waterfall on the way. There are two forks along the trail: at the first fork, head right and keep left at the second one. To reach the trailhead from Fort Collins, head northwest on Hwy. 287 for 10 miles and then west on Hwy. 14 for 53 miles. Turn left on Long Draw Reservoir Rd. (Forest Rd. 156). Continue for 8 miles and look for the parking area on the left side of the road. The trail begins by following Corral Creek.

Rawah Lakes Trail—

This 10-mile hike into the heart of the Rawah Wilderness Area makes a great overnighter. It's a fairly steep hike, climbing 2,100 feet through aspen and pine forests, eventually giving way to spruce and fir. From Rawah Lakes there are spectacular views of surrounding peaks in the Medicine Bow and Mummy ranges. The lakes even yield an occasional trout. To reach the trailhead from Fort Collins, drive 10 miles northwest on Hwy. 287 and then 52 miles west on Hwy. 14. Turn right (north) on Laramie River Rd. (Forest Rd. 190). Continue about 12 miles to the trailhead near Rawah Ranch. Start hiking west.

HORSEBACK RIDING

Fort Collins has a long tradition of interest in horses. Indeed, as far back as the 1880s, the town was home to a two-story livery stable, which was widely admired. Today, CSU has a nationally known equine sciences program and Fort Collins is undeniably western in its outlook. It's a great place to get back in the saddle.

Double Diamond Stables—

Located within Lory State Park west of town, Double Diamond offers miles of uncrowded trails over rolling and uncrowded terrain and rents mainly Tennessee walkers that are easy on the back if you haven't been on a horse in a while. Double Diamond also has breakfast and dinner rides, hayride parties, western entertainment and guided tours. During winter,

sleigh rides are offered. Call ahead for reservations and information. (303) 224-4200.

Sno-Cap Stables—

These stables also offer hayrides, guided trips and mountain horses for hunting and fishing expeditions. Sno-Cap Stables can be found in Glacier View Meadows at Livermore, about 35 miles northwest of Fort Collins. Call (303) 482-4784 for information.

ICE SKATING

Edora Pool Ice Center—

Skate year-round at this excellent indoor arena. Rentals, changing room, lessons and a snack bar are all available. 1801 Riverside Dr.; (303) 221-6679.

PARKS AND RECREATION AREAS

Horsetooth Reservoir—

Named after a nearby rock that looks vaguely like a horse's tooth, this body of water just west of town attracts hordes of people for water recreation as well as hiking, mountain biking and horseback riding. Many dirt roads and trails wind through the land surrounding Horsetooth Reservoir providing scenic, hilly tours on foot or mountain bike. Horsetooth Mountain Park and Lory State Park, adjacent to the reservoir, offer wide stretches of public land. Horsetooth Reservoir has almost 4,000 acres of water and attracts people from much of northern Colorado. There are picnic and camping areas as well as several marinas. Horsetooth sometimes gets very crowded with swimmers, boaters, waterskiers, windsurfers, etc., so it is vitally important to pay attention to water safety and etiquette.

The first choice of many fishermen in this area is Horsetooth Reservoir. Horsetooth has kokanee salmon, various species of trout (including Mackinaw up to 30 pounds), bass, walleye and panfish. You can fish Horsetooth by boat or from the shoreline. Because the shoreline at Horsetooth drops off quickly, it's possible to fish very deep water from the bank; the problem is that most of the reservoir's shoreline is composed of large boulders and smaller rocks that make moving around kind of tough. Horsetooth has a reputation of being either hot or very slow. Fish can be taken with lures or bait. A map of the reservoir from HydroSurveys Inc. (available at area sporting goods stores) is extremely handy because it shows water depth as well as other pertinent information.

More information about Horsetooth is available from the **Larimer County Parks Department** at **(303) 226-4517**. To get to the reservoir from downtown Fort Collins, drive west on virtually any road until reaching Overland Trail Rd. at the edge of town. Turn left and drive to County Rd. 42C at the south end of town. Then turn right (west) and continue to the reservoir.

Lory State Park—

Lory State Park borders the west side of Horsetooth Reservoir in a space of land which lies between the prairie and foothills. The transitional environment is remarkably rugged and scenic: there are rolling hills, tall grasses, wide sculpted valleys and sharply uplifted rock formations to the west. Though close to town, this secluded area will make you feel as though you can really get away from it all. The park attracts people for its 30 miles of hiking trails, backcountry camping, rock climbing, picnicking, horseback riding **(Double Diamond Stables, 303-224-4200)** and mountain biking—an easy gravel road travels through the center of the park. Fishing in the coves from the west shore of Horsetooth Reservoir can be quite good. In winter, after a snowstorm, it's an ideal place for cross-country skiing.

Wildlife is abundant in the park and visitors frequently spot deer, rabbits and many birds; occasionally, there are sightings of prairie rattlesnakes, bear and bobcat. To reach the park from town drive west to Overland Trail Rd. Turn right (north) and continue past W. Vine Dr. and Lake Lee on the right. Turn left (west) onto

Bingham Hill Rd., marked by a sign, to Lory State Park. Turn left again at the T intersection leading 3 miles to the park entrance. Stop by the park office just 300 yards beyond the entrance for information, maps and advice.

RIVER FLOATING

For river floating in the Fort Collins vicinity the choice is obvious—the **Cache la Poudre**. As the only designated Wild and Scenic river in Colorado, it's definitely one of the state's hot spots for both rafters and kayakers. The river gets its start high in Rocky Mountain National Park and works its way 25 miles northeast before turning abruptly east. For the next 40 miles the river twists down a deep canyon that it has slowly scoured out of the granite. Spilling out onto the plains, the Poudre loses its fight and flows gently into the Platte River.

Kayakers are particularly attracted to the Poudre; it offers some serious whitewater stretches rating up to Class IV and Class V. The problem is that the river can only be run in short sections as a number of suicidal boulder-clogged rapids are feared by even the finest rafters and kayakers. The Poudre Canyon stretch can be easily scouted from Hwy. 14 which follows alongside; a number of picnic areas and campgrounds provide easy access. If you are going to arrange your own raft or kayak trip, be sure to check with the forest service or an outdoor shop in Fort Collins about the dangerous sections and how to avoid them. Also be sure to pick up a free copy of the informative *Poudre Profile*, a pamphlet that is available at the forest service office and at businesses around town. If you want to leave the worries to an experienced guide, then contact one of the following.

Adrift Adventures—This outfitter specializes in half-day family runs down the Poudre on paddle rafts. They also run trips to the Arkansas and Green rivers. Advance reservations are a must. **1816 Orchard Pl., Fort Collins, CO 80521; 1-800-824-0150 or (303) 493-4005.**

Wildwater Inc.—Although they offer trips around the state, their Poudre runs are definitely the most popular. The "Poudre Wildwater" trip is a half-day run that anyone can handle, while the "Poudre Wild and Scenic" offers some very tough white-water stretches. Trips run from May into Aug. Call for reservations and details. **317 Stover St., Fort Collins, CO 80524; (303) 224-3379.**

SKIING

CROSS-COUNTRY SKIING

Although Fort Collins is a long way from the major downhill skiing areas, locals get their skiing fix on a multitude of cross-country ski trails. Opportunities abound. Whenever there is enough snow, skiers take to nearby areas, such as Fort Collins City Park or Lory State Park. Because of the relatively mild climate, however, cross-country skiers from Fort Collins most often head for the high country. Cameron Pass is perhaps the most popular area. The district offices for **Roosevelt National Forest, Estes–Poudre Ranger District Office at 148 Remington St.; (303) 482-3822** and the **Red Feather Ranger District Office at 1635 Blue Spruce; (303) 224-1375** or **224-1362** have information and maps.

Backcountry Trails—

Blue Lake Trail—This moderately difficult 6.5-mile trail offers very diverse terrain, from steep, uphill sections to level glides through meadows. On the whole, the trail climbs steadily uphill from 9,500 feet to 10,800 feet. Panoramic views of the Mummy Range and Rocky Mountain National Park await you at the lake, but there is also plenty of scenery along the way, too. To reach the trailhead from Fort Collins, drive 10 miles northwest on Hwy. 287 and then 53 miles west on Hwy. 14 to the trail parking lot. The trail begins on the right side of the highway, across from Long Draw Reservoir Rd. (Forest Rd. 156). By the way, the road up to Long Draw Reservoir also provides some good cross-country skiing.

Never Summer Nordic Yurt System—Cross-country skiers interested in comfortable huts on a multi-day backcountry trip definitely should check out Never Summer Nordic. Actually, they aren't huts . . . they're *yurts*—round, portable dwellings used by nomadic Mongols and Turks in central Asia. Located in the Colorado State Forest (70 miles west of Fort Collins), this yurt system offers great skiing and a comfortable night's stay along the trail. Not quite as rustic as their Asian cousins, these yurts are supported by wood-lattice and have waterproof walls and roofs. Each one sleeps six and is equipped with bunk beds and foam mattresses, a cook stove, lantern, utensils, firewood and a sun deck. During the winter, nightly rates are $75 per group Fri.–Sun. and $55 during the rest of the week. (The yurts rent for $35 per group Fri.–Sun. or $25 all other nights during the summer.) Reservations are a must. For more information, contact **Never Summer Nordic, PO Box 1254, Fort Collins, CO 80522; (303) 484-3903.**

Upper Michigan Ditch—Although this trip is very easy if you follow the regular trail, side gulches along the way can provide some very challenging downhill runs. Upper Michigan Ditch Trail is located at the top of Cameron Pass. The route contours gradually uphill through the valley, alongside the Michigan River. Once you reach the old, rundown cabins you'll have gone a mile and a half. The trail continues up the ditch if you're so inclined. To reach the trailhead from Fort Collins, head 10 miles northwest on Hwy. 287 and then 60 miles west on Hwy. 14 to Cameron Pass. Pull into the parking lot on the northwest side of the highway. The trail begins across the highway to the southeast.

Zimmerman Lake Trail—This very popular well-marked trail is moderately difficult. It climbs a mile and a half up along an old logging road to Zimmerman Lake. Once at the lake, you can enjoy plenty of off-trail skiing. Winter is indeed a great time to be at the lake—the views of the Medicine Bow Range and Poudre Canyon are spectacular. This high-altitude trail starts at 10,000 feet and climbs to almost 10,500 feet. To reach the trail from Fort Collins, head northwest on Hwy. 287 for 10 miles and then west on Hwy. 14 for 58 miles. The parking lot is on the left, just past Joe Wright Reservoir.

Groomed Trails—

Beaver Meadows—This resort has more than 20 miles of maintained trails, some of which are groomed. Terrain varies enough to challenge even the best nordic skiers. Located northwest of Red Feather Lakes, Beaver Meadows' trails are on national forest and private land. The ski shop on the premises provides rentals and lessons. In addition to cross-country skiing, there are a variety of other winter activities as well as fine accommodations (see the Where to Stay section). To reach Beaver Meadows from Fort Collins, drive northwest on Hwy. 287 for 22 miles and turn left on the Red Feather Lakes Rd. Drive to Red Feather Lakes and turn north on Creedmore Rd. Proceed 6 miles to the Beaver Meadows sign. For more information, call **(303) 482-1845**.

Rentals and Information—

The Mountain Shop—This shop rents equipment for any kind of cross-country skiing, whether it is for groomed trails or backcountry telemarking. **632 S. Mason; (303) 493-5720.**

SWIMMING

Edora Pool Ice Center—
This facility offers a large indoor pool that has a handicap ramp. **1801 Riverside Dr.; (303) 221-6679.**

Fort Collins Community Pool—
Open year-round. Call for times. **424 S. Sherwood; (303) 221-6659.**

TENNIS

Rolland Moore Racquet Center—
There are eight lighted courts at this outdoor complex which is open from Apr.–Nov. For reservations during prime times (4–10 pm Mon.–Fri.), call ahead. **2201 S. Shields; (303) 221-6667.**

Warren Park—
Five courts with lights are located at this park. **Lemay St.** and **Horsetooth Rd.**

WINDSURFING

Horsetooth Reservoir is the obvious place for this sport. Beware however: Horsetooth can get very crowded with speedboats. For more information on the reservoir see the Parks and Recreation Areas section. For information, rentals, lessons and supplies, check in with **Outpost Sunsport** at **622 S. College, Fort Collins; (303) 482-1069.**

———— SEEING AND DOING ————

BALLOONING AND OTHER AERIAL PURSUITS

Many businesses around Fort Collins are waiting to take you for a ride in a hot-air balloon. Floating high above the Front Range allows a wonderful perspective of the Rockies, but it's not cheap. Most companies offer hour-long balloon rides with catered breakfast or brunch and, of course, the traditional bottle of champagne.

Fred Herr Sport Aviation Inc.—
In addition to ballooning, Herr also offers aerial tours in a powered sail plane. Call for reservations and information at **(303) 226-0671.** If they don't have any room, consider a ride with **Dragon Fire Ltd., (303) 226-4465.**

Owl Canyon Gliderport—
Because favorable wind currents come off the mountains, Fort Collins is an excellent place for gliders. If your idea of a good

time is to take a ride in a motorless airplane with one wheel and no propeller, check in with the gliderport. They offer lessons, tows and individual 20- to 30-minute flights north of Fort Collins. The best seasons for gliding are fall and winter. For information call **(303) 568-7627.**

BREWERY TOUR

Anheuser Busch Brewery—

A relatively new attraction has bubbled up on the outskirts of Fort Collins. Anheuser Busch has built what is currently the fastest producing brewery in the world, with a top capacity of 2,200 cans of beer per minute. Beer started rolling from the plant in spring of 1988. The brewery's hospitality center, scheduled to open by Memorial Day 1989, will offer free tours and tastes of beer. The walking tour of the huge facility will include stops at the **Clydesdale Hamlet** (stables) and the gift shop. Located north of Fort Collins (Exit 271 from Interstate 25), on Busch Dr. **PO Box 20000, Fort Collins, CO 80522; (303) 490-4500.**

MUSEUMS AND GALLERIES

Colorado State University has five art galleries that feature a variety of media styles. The **Curfman Gallery** in the Lory Student Center is the main gallery on campus; **Duhesa Lounge** on the second-floor corridor of Lory specializes in Native American arts; **Hatton Gallery** in the Visual Arts Center on campus features works by the university's art students, faculty and visiting artists; **Direction Gallery**, also in the arts center, usually features exhibits by the faculty; finally, **Gustafson Gallery** in the Gifford Building is home to clothing and textile exhibits. All of these are free and open to the public. Contact the information desk at Lory Student Center. **(303) 491-6444.**

The Fort Collins Museum—

This rather small museum specializes in displays focused on Fort Collins history.

The museum complex also includes restored and preserved buildings from early Fort Collins. Perhaps its real claim to fame is one of the most extensive collections of Folsom points outside the Smithsonian Institution in Washington, DC. These prehistoric spear points were collected in the 1920s and 1930s at the Lindenmeier site, near the Wyoming border north of Fort Collins. Open Tues.–Sat. 10 am–5 pm, Sun. 12–5 pm. **200 Mathews St.; (303) 221-6738.**

Historic Buildings—

An interesting tour of the town's historic buildings is highlighted by the **Avery House** at **328 W. Mountain Ave.** This elegant, custom-built Victorian home also hosts many special events, including a Christmas open house in early Dec.—Victorian-style Christmas wrapping paper, ornaments, note paper and cookies are for sale. For more information on the Avery House, call **(303) 221-4448.** A brochure that outlines a tour of other historic buildings in Fort Collins is free at the **Visitors Bureau** in **Old Town.** As an aside: if you miss the good old days, visit the **Woolworth's** at **107 N. College Ave.** "Woolies" is like the old time five-and-dime stores, complete with soda fountain and lunch counter.

NIGHTLIFE

Though Fort Collins is definitely not one of the nation's hot spots for nightlife, there is enough going on to keep most normal people occupied. If it's nostalgia you're after, try College Ave. from Mulberry St. to Maple St. on Sat. night. The cruising in souped-up cars is just like the '50s—no kidding!

Beethoven's—

Most people are skeptical about heading to the Holiday Inn on Fri. night, but in Fort Collins a somewhat bizarre crowd turns out. Beethoven's is a good place to dance to canned music and watch videos on eight monitors. If the music gets too loud on a Fri. or Sat. night, step next door to **Fountain Court**, a piano lounge that caters to more mature musical tastes. Both places are located at the **University Park Holiday Inn, 425 W. Prospect Ave.; (303) 482-2626.**

Comedy Works—

So, you think you're warped? Coming to Comedy Works is perfect therapy for putting out-of-kilter minds at ease. Every week local and national comedians vie for audience guffaws. **7 Old Town Sq.; (303) 221-5481.**

Fort Ram—

Where do the college students go? They head directly to the largest dance floor and, as you may have guessed, the cheapest drinks. This is a great place to meet people and dance to rock and roll. **450 N. Linden St.; (303) 482-5026.**

Lincoln Center—

Lincoln Center is the city's performing and visual arts center. The center plays host to live theater, concerts, the Fort Collins Symphony, Larimer Chorale and art exhibits. Some of the more unique features include a mini-theater with its intimate performance area and **The Terrace,** a sculpture and performance area complete with flower gardens and plants. Step across the street to **Marsanne's,** a restaurant that caters to the arts crowd and others who like homemade soups and desserts; **(303) 484-6744.** The Lincoln Center is at **417 W. Magnolia St.; (303) 221-6735,** box office **(303) 221-6730.**

Mishawaka Inn—

Located about 25 miles from Fort Collins, this bar and restaurant really gets shaking on weekends to live country rock music. The old place was built in 1901 with the help of convict labor. Nationally known musicians, such as Jerry Jeff Walker and Commander Cody, often play on summer weekends. You might also want to stay for a juicy steak or rainbow trout. A deck next to the Poudre River allows a close feel of the mountains without having to travel very far. Sometimes the view includes bighorn sheep that come down to drink in the river. Open Nov.–Feb. Thur.–Sun., Mar.–Oct. seven days a week. To get here from Fort Collins drive 10 miles northwest on Hwy. 287 and then 15 miles west on Hwy. 14. **13714 Poudre Canyon Hwy.; (303) 482-4420.**

Wine Cellar—

Come here for good drinks, a great selection of wine by the glass and live jazz in an intimate atmosphere. See the Where to Eat section for more information.

SCENIC DRIVES

Poudre Canyon/Red Feather Lakes—

This three-hour loop will take you into some beautiful mountainous country west of Fort Collins. Start by heading northwest out of Fort Collins on Hwy. 287. When you get to the town of La Porte stop off at Vern's restaurant for a gargantuan cinnamon roll. From La Porte continue northwest on Hwy. 287 and then turn left (west) onto Hwy. 14. This highway proceeds into a narrow rocky canyon, next to the Cache la Poudre River as it tumbles east to the plains. You may be wondering how this unique name was given to a river in a territory not settled by the French. In Nov. 1836 a trapping party from the Hudson Bay Trapping Company was making its way up the Poudre Canyon when it became mired in deep snow. To lighten their load, it is said, these men stashed their heavy barrels of gunpowder and any unnecessary provisions near the banks of the river—so came the river's name, which means "hide the powder."

As you're driving upriver, you can almost feel the intense force of the water, especially during spring runoff. Keep an eye out for bighorn sheep along the higher reaches of the canyon walls. The exceptional Poudre is the last free-flowing river along the Front Range. You may see cars with a bumper sticker reading, "Don't Damn the Poudre." Today the age-old conflict of growth versus environment remains. Thankfully, the Poudre has been designated Wild and Scenic, which should keep it from being dammed—at least for the near term. An excellent source of information on the entire Poudre Canyon area is contained in a publication called *Poudre Profile*. Free copies are on the publications rack at the **Estes–Poudre Ranger District Office** at **148 Remington St.** in Fort Collins, and at most businesses in the canyon.

Take Hwy. 14 through Poudre Canyon for 31.5 miles to Rustic. Turn right at Rustic onto Forest Rd. 162 which leads north to Red Feather Lakes. This series of small lakes can provide excellent fishing. It's also a good place to picnic. To complete the loop trip take Red Feather Lakes Rd. east to Hwy. 287 and then right (southeast) back to Fort Collins.

WHERE TO STAY

ACCOMMODATIONS

Except for a couple of bed and breakfast inns, Fort Collins is strictly a motel town. Most national chains have motels here (Holiday Inn has two). In the mountains west of town, however, there are a number of cabins and resorts stretched out along the banks of the Poudre River and in more secluded areas such as Red Feather Lakes.

Beaver Meadows — $$$

Located 55 miles northwest of Fort Collins in the Red Feather Lakes area, this ranch/resort is best known for its cross-country skiing and easy access to 20 miles of marked trails in the Roosevelt National Forest including some maintained and tracked trails. Along the backcountry trails, you are invited to stop in a warming hut for snacks and spirits. During the summer, Beaver Meadows features horseback riding, a kids' fishing pond and, for more serious anglers, fishing in the North Fork of the Poudre. Accommodations are either in condos, mountain homes or cabins; all come equipped with kitchens. If you don't feel like cooking, stop by the restaurant that is open daily. Live entertainment is featured on Fri. and Sat. nights. There is not a minimum stay, but weekly packages are offered. For more information and reservations, contact **PO Box 2167, Fort Collins, CO 80522; (303) 482-1845.**

Helmshire Inn — $$$

The Helmshire Inn is actually a hybrid, produced by crossing a bed and breakfast concept with a small hotel. Inside are 27 beautifully decorated rooms, each with a unique, almost contemporary feel. Each immaculate room has a private bathroom as well as the convenience of a refrigerator and microwave. A stay at the Helmshire comes with a breakfast that is anything but ordinary: fresh fruit and juice, your choice of delicious baked goods and a blintz or quiche for the entrée—all served in the dining room from 7–9 am each morning. Dinner is also served on request. Since the Helmshire is located just across the street from the CSU campus, you are likely to run into students' families and visiting professors. **1204 S. College Ave., Fort Collins, CO 80524; (303) 493-4683.**

Sylvan Dale Ranch — $$ to $$$

Located 7 miles west of Loveland (which is 15 miles south of Fort Collins on Hwy. 287) this ranch has a "bunk and breakfast" arrangement. All of the accommodations have private bathrooms; nine cottages are also available. You are free to participate as much as you want in maintaining the working ranch aspect of this operation: stack hay or brush the horses. Enjoy the luxury of the heated pool or play a set of tennis. Stay over Fourth of July weekend and you can get involved in the cattle drive. There are no telephones or TVs here. The Jessup family has been operating this ranch for more than 40 years. For a few extra dollars you can sign up on the full American plan and savor Tillie Jessup's wonderful, country-style meals. Kids love all of the activities and the change of pace of being out in the country. **2939 N. County**

Rd. 31 D, Loveland, CO 80537; (303) 667-3915.

Elizabeth Street Guest House — $$

Staying at this charming three-room bed and breakfast is akin to being welcomed into a friend's home. The comfortable rooms each have their own sink, but bathrooms are shared. A homey atmosphere is created by plentiful antiques, old quilts, handmade items, leaded windows and oak woodwork. Breakfast, served as late as 10 am, may include homemade pastries or a unique specialty called "Scotch eggs"—we won't spoil the surprise, but they are delicious. All breakfasts come with juice, tea or coffee. A big plus is the excellent location of this four-square brick-style home, just one block from the university. 202 E. Elizabeth St., Fort Collins, CO 80524; (303) 493-2337.

Never Summer Nordic Yurt System — $

See the Cross-Country Skiing section for information.

CAMPING

Campers should be utterly pleased with the Fort Collins area—there are 26 maintained campgrounds with more than 500 campsites.

In Colorado State Forest—

The state forest not only charges a fee for admission to its land but also to stay at one of its four maintained campgrounds (104 sites) or rustic cabins. To reserve a campsite or cabin in advance call the **MISTIX Corp.** in Denver at **(303) 671-4500** or call **1-800-365-2267.**

All four campgrounds in the state forest are accessible via Hwy. 14 west of Fort Collins. Some 66 miles west of Fort Collins (15 miles past Chambers Lake) the twisting road to **Crags Campground** takes off from the left side of the road. Crags, in a beautiful forest setting, has 27 campsites (no RVs or trailers should attempt the road). Four miles farther west on Hwy. 14 is

Ranger Lakes Campground (25 sites). To reach **North Michigan Campground** (24 sites) turn right off Hwy. 14, 2 miles beyond Gould, at the official entrance to the state park. This is a heavily used campground since boating is permitted at North Michigan Reservoir. To reach **Bockman Campground** (28 sites), continue east for just over a mile on the road past North Michigan Reservoir.

In Roosevelt National Forest—

The Poudre River has a cache of campgrounds conveniently located just off Hwy. 14 west of Fort Collins. Access to the stream from each of these campgrounds is easy, but the campsites often fill up by early afternoon and even earlier on weekends and holidays. Seven campgrounds are bunched together within about a 15-mile stretch between Poudre Park and Kelly Flats. The first is **Ansel Watrous Campground** (19 sites; fee charged), which is about 23 miles west of Fort Collins. **Stove Prairie Campground** is 3 miles farther west offering 7 sites and no fee. A mile beyond, you'll reach **Upper Landing Campground** with five sites and no fee. Virtually next door is **Stevens Gulch Campground** with four sites and no fee. Three miles west is the **Narrows Cooperative** with four units and no fee. **Mountain Park Campground** is 3 miles down the road with 45 sites and a fee, followed by **Kelly Flats Campground** 2 miles farther (23 sites; fee charged). Kelly Flats and Stevens Gulch campgrounds have handicapped facilities.

Still rolling west on Hwy. 14, 49 miles west of Fort Collins you will arrive at **Big Bend Campground** with nine sites and a fee. Travel another 4 miles and come to **Sleeping Elephant Campground** with 15 sites and a fee.

Four public campgrounds are located in the vicinity of Red Feather Lakes. To get here from Fort Collins drive 22 miles northwest on Hwy. 287 to the Forks Cafe. Turn left and drive 30 miles west on Red Feather Lakes Rd. **Dowdy Lake Campground** (52 sites; fee charged) is located 1.5 miles east of Red Feather Lakes Village on Forest Rd.

218. Dowdy has campsites designed for handicapped use. **West Lake Campground** (30 sites; fee charged) is 2 miles east of the village on Forest Rd. 200. To reach **Bellaire Lake Campground** (seven sites; fee charged) take Forest Rd. 162, 5 miles south of the village toward Rustic. **North Fork Poudre Campground** (nine sites; no fee) is located 6.5 miles west of Red Feather Lakes Village on Forest Rd. 162.

From Fort Collins, drive 10 miles northwest on Hwy. 287 and then 52 miles west on Hwy. 14. Turn right on Laramie River Rd. (Forest Rd. 190). There are three campgrounds along this road. The first, **Skyline Campground** (six sites; no fee), is located 3 miles north of Hwy. 14. **Tunnel Campground** (49 sites; fee charged) is another 2.5 miles north on Laramie River Rd. And **Brown's Park** (28 sites; no fee) is 14.5 miles north near Glendevey.

A couple of other campgrounds are located on the northern edge of Rocky Mountain National Park. To reach **Long Draw Campground** (25 sites; no fee) drive 10 miles northwest of Fort Collins on Hwy. 287 and then west on Hwy. 14 for 53 miles to just past Chambers Lake. Then turn left onto Long Draw Rd. (Forest Rd. 156) and continue 9 miles to the campground. Continue another 4 miles on Forest Rd. 156 and you'll arrive at **Grand View Campground** (10 sites; no fee).

Private Campgrounds—

Glen Echo Resort—Located in the Poudre Canyon with good fishing available. To get here drive 41 miles west of Fort Collins on Hwy. 14. **31503 Poudre Canyon Dr., Bellvue, CO 80512; (303) 881-2208.**

KOA Mile High—With a swimming pool and full hookups this campground gets plenty of use. To get here, drive 10 miles northwest of Fort Collins on Hwy. 287, just opposite the turn-off for Hwy. 14. **6670 Hwy. 287N, PO Box 600, La Porte, CO 80535; (303) 493-9758.**

WHERE TO EAT

Fort Collins offers a good selection of restaurants, and, like any college town, keen competition is the rule. New restaurants rise and fall with amazing regularity; some just change their name, cuisine or owners. We've done our best to select restaurants that appear to be entrenched in the market.

Cuisine! Cuisine! — $$$

This is one of the consistently better restaurants in Fort Collins. It features regional American as well as international specialties for lunch and dinner. The diverse menu, which is posted daily on an outdoor chalkboard, gives you a chance to sample different cuisines, including southwestern, Cajun, French, nouvelle ... it's the perfect place to come when you are part of a group that can't decide what to eat. Cuisine! Cuisine! is also known for its excellent desserts, especially cheesecake. Open for lunch from 11 am–3 pm Mon.–Fri., until 2 pm on Sat., dinner is served from 5–9 pm Tues.–Sat. Closed Sun. **130 S. Mason St.,** across from the courthouse; **221-0399.**

Hemingway's — $$$

Friendly, intimate and charming describe Hemingway's. Located within a converted house, there is no pretentious or contrived atmosphere. For lunch you might select a sandwich, salad, crêpe or pasta or try one of the southwestern specialties for any meal. On a warm summer night, the patio is the place to be. The extensive beverage menu includes many beers and wines as well as almost a dozen coffee drinks. If you have to pick just one restaurant in Fort Collins, this should be it. Open from 11:30 am–2 pm, 5:30 pm–9 pm Mon.–Sat. Not open for lunch on Sat. Closed Sun. Located across from the city library at **400 E. Olive; 484-8447.**

Wine Cellar — $$$

When the Wine Cellar is "on," the food can be very good indeed. As the name implies, there is an outstanding selection of wines and you can order many of them by the glass. The staff is unusually knowledgeable about which wine will go well with specific entrées. Dinner specialties include veal, seafood and tender beef Wellington. The atmosphere is low-key, but classy. Stick around after dinner for some live jazz in the lounge. Open from 11 am–2 pm and 5 –10 pm Mon.-Sat., 5–9 pm on Sun. Not open for lunch on Sat. **400 S. College Ave.; 226-4413.**

Charco Broiler — $$ to $$$

Feel like having a slab of steak cooked to perfection over an open flame? Fort Collins locals go straight to the Charco Broiler's lived-in setting. You'll know why it's crowded nearly all the time as soon as your meal arrives. Try to save some room for a slice of homemade pie. This is also a good choice for your basic American breakfast and bottomless cup of coffee. Keep in mind—no reservations and no credit cards. Open Mon.-Thur. 6 am–11 pm, Fri-Sat. 6 am–midnight, Sun. 11 am–10 pm. **1716 E. Mulberry** (Hwy. 14, east of Fort Collins), **482-1472.**

Cafe Français — $$

Genuine European-style pastries at this classic cafe are a delightful way to start the day. An outdoor seating area provides a comfortable place to linger over a cup of capuccino. Fresh breads, chocolates and other temptations are offered for take-out. The manager swears that Cafe Français has the best French bread in town, and we are inclined to believe her. The lunch and dinner menu embraces lighter dishes such as quiches and generous salads, as well as more elaborate roast duck or fondue. Open Mon.-Tues. from 8 am–7 pm, Wed.-Thur. 8 am–8 pm, Fri.-Sat. 8 am–9 pm, Sun. 8 am–5 pm. **11 Old Town Sq.; 221-0931.**

Young's Cafe — $ to $$$

Don't let the name fool you. Young's is much more than an ordinary "cafe." With outstanding Vietnamese cuisine, this fairly new restaurant already has a loyal following. The atmosphere is elegant and carefully prepared meals tease tastebuds you never knew existed. The house specialties are highly recommended as are their Vietnamese "creations," in which you select your favorite seafood or meat to go with a special sauce. This is also a good choice for vegetarians. At Young's there is a strong emphasis on fresh ingredients. Lunch is a bargain. Carry out is available. Open from 11:30 am–3 pm weekdays; dinner is served from 4:30–9:30 pm Mon.-Thur., from 4:40–10:30 pm Fri.-Sat., 4:40–9:30 pm Sun. In the Crystal Gardens at **3307 S. College Ave.; 223-8000.**

Silver Grill Cafe — $

This well-known breakfast spot provides good food at reasonable prices. It retains some of the feel of old Fort Collins, even though it has recently been remodeled. Their claim to fame is the giant cinnamon rolls for $1 each and the cinnamon roll toast. They also serve up all of the other breakfast standards. Open daily from 6 am–2 pm. **218 Walnut St.** in **Old Town; 484-4656.**

NEARBY

Bruce's — $ to $$$

East of Fort Collins, in the almost empty town of Severance, a totally unique dining experience awaits. Fort Collins residents often make a special trip here when entertaining out-of-town guests. For detailed information on Bruce's, see Where to Eat in the **Northeast Plains** chapter.

The Pied Woodpecker

SERVICES

Fort Collins Chamber of Commerce—

Located at **225 S. Meldrum St., Fort Collins, CO 80522; (303) 482-3746.**

Visitors Center/Chamber of Commerce—

If you're going to be around the area for a few days, be sure to stop in at **No. 9 Old Town Sq. (Walnut St., Suite 101); (303) 482-5821.**

Transportation—

Buses—Transfort, the Fort Collins bus system, serves most of the major areas of the city from 6:30 am–6:30 pm. Schedules are widely available. **6570 Portner Rd.; (303) 221-6620.**

Taxi—Call **Shamrock Taxi (303) 224-2222** or **Yellow Cab (303) 493-8200.**

Trolley—It doesn't go very far, or very often, but if you're in Fort Collins from Mar. through Oct., check out the trolley. It runs from City Park to W. Mountain Ave. and back, from noon–6 pm Sat., Sun. and holidays.

Georgetown and Idaho Springs

About 30 miles west of Denver, Interstate 70 drops down from Floyd Hill and makes its way along Upper Clear Creek through one of the oldest historic areas in the state. Gold strikes in 1859 brought thousands of fortune hunters to this high mountain valley rimmed by soaring rocky peaks. Even if you are just driving through in a car, views from the highway suggest the mining legacy that's so deeply entrenched in this area. Old mine shafts and tailing piles on the nearby mountainsides and the long-established towns of **Georgetown**, **Idaho Springs** and **Silver Plume** all serve as reminders of the bygone glory days. Idaho Springs was the first settlement in the valley, but Georgetown and Silver Plume evoke the most vivid image of the mining days. Once the third largest town in Colorado, Georgetown is full of impeccably restored Victorian homes and buildings, making it an exceptional National Historic District. History also comes to life on a trip along the recently refurbished Georgetown Loop Railroad. This engineering wonder snakes its way up to nearby Silver Plume, offering a ride as memorable today as it was 100 years ago.

With its easy access along Interstate 70, many skiers and summer visitors stop in Georgetown and Idaho Springs for a look around or to have a meal at one of the many fine restaurants. But don't let the accessibility lead you to believe the area is overdeveloped—lots of remote country surrounds the valley and it's common to catch a glimpse of a bighorn sheep among the rocky crags on the mountainsides.

Ghost towns and old mine ruins are scattered throughout the canyons and mountains in the Georgetown and Idaho Springs area. Many old mining roads, including Waldorf Rd. and the precipitous Oh My God Rd., cut through backwoods sites once teeming with miners. Another road not to be missed is Mt. Evans Hwy., one of the world's highest paved roads. It climbs 14 miles up 14,264-foot Mt. Evans, providing views of the surrounding mountain ranges that are hard to match.

Encompassing most of this area, heavily used Arapaho National Forest attracts many outdoor enthusiasts, especially for its great hiking and cross-country skiing. Mt. Evans, like numerous other 14,000-foot peaks in Colorado, can be climbed in a day, and the Mt. Evans Wilderness Area provides a secluded getaway. In winter, many cross-country skiers converge on the area and fan out on the snow-covered roads and trails. Loveland Ski Area, 10 miles west of Silver Plume on Interstate 70, attracts many day skiers, especially from Denver, with its relatively inexpensive lift tickets and light powder snow.

HISTORY

In January 1859 George Jackson, a prospector on a hunting trip, made his way to what is now Idaho Springs. The story goes that as he trudged through the snow over a hill, he saw haze in the distance that he believed to be smoke from an Indian camp. What he found instead were natural hot springs. More importantly, just up the valley near the confluence of Clear Creek and Chicago Creek, he found some rocks that he believed contained gold. Returning the next spring with a few comrades, Jackson confirmed his belief when they panned and placered $1,500 in gold the first week. Soon, thousands of miners and merchants poured into the site known at the time as Jackson's Diggins. Eventually the name was changed to Idaho Springs, due largely to the importance of the hot springs, which later lured many visitors for medicinal purposes.

Shortly after Jackson's big discovery, two brothers, George and David Griffith, made a historic strike. After leaving their home in Kentucky and heading west to Denver in 1858, the two brothers followed the masses up to Central City. Since most of the good mining claims were taken, they set off to explore Upper Clear Creek Canyon upstream from Jackson's Diggins. Quickly they struck rich gold ore, established their claims and built a cabin. Other miners soon followed, and soon the mining camp was named Georgetown, after the elder Griffith brother. Although Georgetown miners were initially drawn to the gold, by the mid-1860s it was apparent that silver mining held the future for the camp. Silver ore abounded in the mountains around Georgetown and its sister mining camp, Silver Plume, 2 miles up the valley. Soon more silver was being produced here than in any other district in the world until the great Leadville strike in 1878. It's estimated that more than $200 million in silver was mined near Georgetown during these early days.

Georgetown boomed and by the 1870s had more than 5,000 residents. Unlike other mining towns in Colorado, Georgetown was settled by families with relatively upstanding morals. Many fine and substantial homes were built, showing off a variety of architectural styles popular in that era. Georgetown was very proud of its volunteer fire department, which kept the town from burning down (the fate of most other towns during this period). Thanks to the fire department's commitment, more than 200 of Georgetown's original buildings still stand today.

As mines in the valley and surrounding mountains grew in number, locals anxiously awaited the Colorado Central Railroad, which eventually reached Georgetown in 1877. But it was not until 1884 that the famous Georgetown Loop Railroad, stretching from Georgetown to Silver Plume, was finished. When the Argentine Central Railroad was built from Silver Plume to the mines up near Waldorf, silver ore could be more economically shipped to the mills and smelters.

When the silver market crashed in 1893, most of the mines around Georgetown and Silver Plume closed, and the mining population began to dwindle. Although some mines continued to produce gold, copper and other minerals, the boom days were over. By 1910 the 22,000-foot Argo Tunnel was completed from Idaho Springs under the mountains to Central City. The Argo connected many existing tunnels and provided easy access between the two mining towns. (For information about Central City, see the **Central City** chapter.) In 1913 the Argo Gold Mill was completed in Idaho Springs. The finest mill of its kind in the country, it supplied much of the gold for the Denver Mint. Due to increased mining costs, most of the area's mines are closed these days. Plenty of gold and silver still remain in the hills around Idaho Springs and Georgetown, but until mining becomes more profitable, the minerals will remain in the ground.

GETTING THERE

Idaho Springs is located 32 miles west of Denver on Interstate 70. A more scenic route is up Lower Clear Creek Canyon from Golden on Hwy. 6, which follows the old Colorado Central Railroad bed. Georgetown is located 14 miles west of Idaho Springs along the interstate.

MAJOR ATTRACTIONS

GEORGETOWN HISTORIC DISTRICT

What separates Georgetown from many other historic mining districts in Colorado is the sheer number of old Victorian homes still standing and the heartfelt dedication of its citizens to preserving and restoring these buildings. The Georgetown Society (a local historical preservation group) has spearheaded the painstaking restoration of many homes, buildings and shop fronts. Visitors need only walk or ride through the streets of town to get a feel for the way things were a century ago.

Many of the buildings in town are on the National Register of Historic Places, including two museums, the Hamill House and the Hotel de Paris (see the Museums and Galleries section for details). There are many beautifully restored homes to see. One of the finest examples of residential architecture is the Maxwell House, stunningly painted in shades of pink and cream. It is, however, a private home. Stop by the Episcopal church, which houses the oldest pipe organ in the state. You can still see the bell tower that blew off with the roof in a big wind of 1867, the year the church was built. During summer pick up a historical buildings map at the Community Center on 6th St. (across from the post office) and take a self-guided walking or driving tour of the sites.

GEORGETOWN LOOP RAILROAD

If you want to get from Georgetown to Silver Plume, everyone knows that the 2-mile stretch of Interstate 70 will whisk you there in a matter of minutes. But what's the fun of that? If you climb aboard the Georgetown Loop narrow-gauge railroad, however, the trip to Silver Plume takes on a whole new meaning. This historic 3-mile stretch of tracks, once called the Scenic Wonder of the West, was quite an engineering feat when it was built more than a century ago. Today, passengers can take a

trip back in time while learning about the railroad and mining history of the area.

History—

During the booming silver mining days in Upper Clear Creek Canyon, getting the ore down out of the mines to the mills by wagon was extremely difficult. A railroad line to the upper end of the valley was greatly needed. Building a railroad to Georgetown presented the usual construction problems, but extending the tracks to

Silver Plume was a real nightmare. The situation seemed insurmountable—Silver Plume was only 2 miles away, but stood a full 700 feet above Georgetown. Conventional railroad locomotives would not be able to climb the grade, which averages 6 percent.

An engineer for the Union Pacific Railroad, Jacob Blickensderfer, spent a couple of years studying the problem and offered this solution: by using a system of curves and bridges, the average grade could be reduced to 3 percent. The planned route included three hairpin curves and four bridges. At Devil's Gate, the valley's narrowest spot, the track looped over itself by a 300-foot-long bridge that passed 75 feet above the track below. The Georgetown Loop was completed in 1884. From Silver Plume, tracks were laid on up the valley to Greymont and Bakerville.

After silver prices crashed in 1893, there was little ore for the railroad to carry, so it shifted its focus to tourists. The engineering feats of the Georgetown Loop were known throughout the world, and soon as many as seven trains a day made the trip between Georgetown and Silver Plume. Passengers seeking further adventure opted for a trip up from Silver Plume to Pavilion Point on the Argentine Central Railroad. Later, as automobile routes were built into the mountains, train travel began losing its glamour, and the tourist trade faded. In 1939 the railroad tracks on the Georgetown Loop were torn up and sold for scrap. But the story has a happy ending. Thanks to help from the Colorado Historical Society and generous benefactors, the Georgetown Loop was restored and reopened in 1984, 100 years after its inception.

Facts—

Today the Georgetown Loop Railroad offers trips from the station at the west edge of Georgetown to the restored Silver Plume Depot up the valley. Both depots offer free slide shows and ticket servicing. The Silver Plume Depot also has a number of railroad exhibits. Trips on the railroad begin from either end. The round-trip ride takes about an hour, but we strongly recommend you stop along the way to take a tour of the 1870s Lebanon Mine, accessible only by train (for a small additional charge). Put on a hard hat and enter the old silver mine with a guide who will fill you in on its history and explain early mining techniques.

The train makes frequent runs daily from Memorial Day through Labor Day; through Sept. the train runs on weekends only. For information, contact **Georgetown Loop Railroad, PO Box 217, Georgetown, CO 80444; (303) 279-6101.** For reservations, call **(303) 569-2403** or in Denver at **(303) 670-1686.**

—— FESTIVALS AND EVENTS ——

The Silver Plume Melodrama

weekends in April

Each April the Plume Players perform melodramas on the weekends to raise money for historic preservation in Silver Plume. Encore performances are given on one weekend in May and on July 3. The shows are great fun and usually receive good reviews. A sandwich buffet and dessert are served; bring your own beer and wine if you wish. Reservations should be made well ahead of time. Call **(303) 569-2023** or in Denver at **(303) 893-2333.**

Biennial Summer Victorian House Tour

August

Every two years in Aug., many magnificent private Victorian homes and gardens in Georgetown are opened up for this one-day tour. If you are interested in history and architecture, don't miss this opportunity. For information and tour times,

Victorian Home (sketch by Michael A. Darr).

call the Georgetown Society at **(303) 569-2840** or in Denver at **(303) 674-2625**.

Christmas Market
first two weekends in December

The Christmas season gets into full swing at Georgetown's Christmas Market in Strousse Park. Food booths offer home-baked goods from many nations of the world. Homemade crafts are also on display, and folk singers, dancers and carolers provide the entertainment. The shops in town are decorated for the occasion. Open 10 am–5 pm. Contact the **Georgetown Society** at **(303) 569-2840** or in Denver, **(303) 674-2625**.

OUTDOOR ACTIVITIES

BIKING
MOUNTAIN BIKING

There is no organized mountain biking in the area, but plenty of hiking trails and old mining roads provide exciting rides if you seek them out. Check the Hiking and Backpacking, Scenic Drives and Four-Wheel-Drive Trips sections for ideas. For additional trail ideas, contact the **Clear Creek Ranger District Office**, one block south of Interstate 70 on Hwy. 103, in Idaho Springs. **PO Box 3307, Idaho Springs, CO 80452; (303) 567-2901** or **(303) 893-1474**.

Rentals and Information—
Virage Ski and Sports—These folks offer mountain bike rentals and repair, maps and advice. **1410 Argentine St., PO Box 1021, Georgetown, CO 80444; (303) 569-2754**.

FISHING

There are many places to fish in the Georgetown and Idaho Springs area but, overall, the fishing is not much to speak of. Mine runoff has made fish in many of the streams unfit to eat; overfishing has also taken its toll. Following are some of the better opportunities.

Bard Creek—
This small stream flows into the West Fork of Clear Creek at the town of Empire. Many ponds along the stream provide pretty good fishing for small brook and rainbow trout. To reach the creek, turn south on the road just past the Hard Rock Cafe along Hwy. 40 in Empire.

Clear Creek—
The Clear Creek headwaters begin up near the Continental Divide at the Eisenhower Tunnel and flow east through Georgetown, Idaho Springs, Lower Clear Creek Canyon and eventually Golden. The stretch of water from the junction of Hwy. 40 and Interstate 70 down to Idaho Springs provides reasonably good fishing for rainbows and browns. A paved frontage road provides the best access. Fishing on Clear Creek below Idaho Springs is not worthwhile; mine runoff has killed or contaminated many of the trout along this stretch. The South Fork of Clear Creek cascades north to Georgetown from Guanella Pass. The best place to fish the South Fork is at the beaver ponds above Lower Cabin Creek Reservoir. Fishermen have pretty good success reeling in small brookies and rainbows. The West Fork of Clear Creek, which

flows down through Berthoud Falls and Empire along Hwy. 40, has some small rainbows but the fishing is mediocre.

Fall River Reservoir—

This is not a bad place to catch brook, brown and cutthroat trout, but the reservoir is very heavily fished. To reach the reservoir, take the Fall River Rd. exit on Interstate 70 (about 2 miles west of Idaho Springs). Follow the road 5.5 miles and turn left onto the dirt road just at the base of a steep switchback. Follow the dirt road 3 miles, keeping to the right.

Georgetown Lake—

Located at the east end of Georgetown along Interstate 70, Georgetown Lake is well stocked with rainbow and cutthroat trout. Though the pressure is heavy, fishing can be rewarding.

Silver Dollar Lake—

To reach this high mountain lake from Georgetown, head 8.5 miles south on Guanella Pass Rd. just beyond Guanella Pass Campground and turn right at the sign for Naylor and Silver Dollar lakes. The road climbs steeply for half a mile to a trailhead for Silver Dollar Lake. The hike into the lake is about a mile, and fishing can be good for 12-inch cutthroat trout.

FOUR-WHEEL-DRIVE TRIPS

Jones Pass—

This 3.3-mile jeep road heads up to the Continental Divide, offering views north to the Indian Peaks, south to Loveland Pass and west to the Gore Range. The west side of the 12,451-foot pass is closed, so you'll have to turn around at the summit. To reach Jones Pass from Idaho Springs, head west on Interstate 70 for about 5 miles and get off at the Hwy. 40 exit to Berthoud Pass. Drive through the towns of Empire and Berthoud Falls for about 7.5 miles to the Henderson Mine turn-off on the left. Proceed to the Henderson Mine guardhouse, where Jones Pass Rd. (Forest Rd. 144) takes off to the right.

St. Mary's Glacier to Central City—

The backcountry between Silver Lake (near St. Mary's Glacier) and Central City is a great place for jeeping, but a few words of advice are necessary. Many four-wheel-drive roads crisscross the area, and a patchwork of private mining claims prevents access to many of them. Be sure to have a topographical map of the area and follow the brown markers posted by the forest service. When you get up on the high alpine meadows, don't create your own road —this kills the fragile plant life and promotes erosion, requiring decades for recovery. Enough said. This 10-mile (one way) drive offers beautiful alpine scenery, wildflowers, historic mines and old cemeteries.

To reach the road from Idaho Springs, head west on Interstate 70 for about 2 miles and get off at the Fall River Rd. exit. Drive 9 miles to the end of Fall River Rd. at Silver Lake. Turn right and after a short distance turn left on Forest Rd. 175 up a hill to Yankee Hill. Stick to this route for about 4.5 miles and you'll reach Pisgah Lake. Another mile past the lake brings you to the junction with Forest Rd. 273.1. Turn left here and proceed 2 miles to Bald Mountain Cemetery. From the eastern end, turn left (north) and follow the road to Boodle Mill just west of Central City.

HIKING AND BACKPACKING

The territory covered in this chapter offers an excellent array of alpine hikes. Although a large number of hikers from Denver invade this area in summer, the beauty of the country overrides the sometimes-crowded trails. A vast majority of the land is within Arapaho National Forest, including a large part of the Mt. Evans Wilderness Area south of Idaho Springs. Many of the hikes around Idaho Springs, Georgetown and Silver Plume are accented by old ghost towns and mining sites. *We must caution you to not explore the old mines*

... they are extremely dangerous! For hiking ideas and information about Arapaho National Forest, visit the **Clear Creek Ranger District**, one block south on Hwy. 103 from Interstate 70 in Idaho Springs, **PO Box 3307, Idaho Springs, CO 80452; (303) 567-2901** or **(303) 893-1474.** For equipment, maps and advice, talk with Kelly or Jennifer Babeon at **Virage Ski and Sports, 1410 Argentine St., PO Box 1021, Georgetown, CO 80444; (303) 569-2754.**

Chicago Lakes Trail—

This 4-mile trail, which leads up to Chicago Lakes in the Mt. Evans vicinity, gets quite a bit of traffic from day hikers and backpackers, but it scores a 9 on the scenic meter. The trail begins at heavily used Echo Lake. It winds around to the south end of the lake, where heavily trampled ground makes it difficult to follow the main trail—look for blazes on the trees. From the lake, the trail heads southwest for 1.7 miles to Idaho Springs Reservoir and then up through the Chicago Lakes Burn, where 400 acres went up in flames in 1978. Though the trees are not much to look at, the wildflowers are beautiful. Eventually you reach the spectacular Chicago Lakes Basin, which is surrounded by the looming cliffs of the Mt. Evans Massif. To reach the trailhead at Echo Lake, drive 14 miles south from Idaho Springs on Hwy. 103 and park just inside Echo Lake Campground. Walk across the Mt. Evans Hwy. (Hwy. 5) and look for the trailhead under the power lines.

Grays and Torreys Peaks Trail—

These twin peaks, called the Ant Hills by the Ute Indians, are anything but. Standing 14,270 feet and 14,267 feet, respectively, Grays and Torreys were at one time as well known as Longs Peak and Pikes Peak. When Georgetown and Idaho Springs were booming back in the late 1800s, it was very fashionable to hike the 4.5-mile trail to the summit of Grays and traverse the half-mile ridge over to Torreys. Even Victorian ladies, delicate creatures that they were, would adjust their skirts and ride horses

sidesaddle up the mountains.

These days the beautiful hike, with spectacular views from the top of the peaks, is still very popular. Beginning at 11,200 feet, the trail crosses Quayle Creek and heads up the valley to the southwest, eventually beginning a steep ascent up Grays Peak. Be sure to take a camera, as this is a good area to spot bighorn sheep and mountain goats. To reach the trailhead from Georgetown, head west on Interstate 70 for 6.5 miles and get off at the Bakerville exit. From Bakerville, proceed south up Stevens Gulch Rd. for 4 miles to the parking area near Stevens Mine.

The Griffin Monument Trail—

In the late 1860s an Englishman named Clifford Griffin struck a rich vein of ore high above Silver Plume and named his mine the Seven-Thirty. It produced both gold and silver and Griffin went on to become one of the wealthiest miners in the region, but this didn't make him happy. Locals learned that Griffin had left his homeland shortly after his bride-to-be died on the eve of their wedding. He never got over his heartache. Griffin built a cabin next to his mine, and in the evening after a hard day's work, he would play melancholy tunes on his violin. The strains of his sad music would drift down the deep canyon to the town below, causing residents to come out and listen.

The story goes that on a spring evening in 1887, after Griffin had finished his evening recital, he shot himself in the heart and fell dead into a grave he had dug in front of his cabin. He left instructions to be buried there. The townsfolk were so moved that they not only honored the sad miner's wishes to remain on the mountain, but also erected a granite monument at the spot.

The monument still stands today, about 1,300 feet above Silver Plume. A fairly steep 2-mile trail leading from town takes you to the monument, where you get a spectacular view of the valley and surrounding mountains. The trail begins near the intersection of Silver St. and Main St. next to the K-P Cafe. For more information about the hike and Clifford Griffin, visit the George Rowe Museum. (See the Museums and Galleries section.)

Herman Gulch Trail—

Each day thousands of people whiz by this trailhead alongside Interstate 70 with no idea that a beautiful, secluded valley is just a short hike away. This moderately difficult 2.5-mile trail climbs almost 2,000 feet up through thick stands of pine, eventually coming out into an alpine meadow where wildflowers (especially columbine) grow abundantly in mid-July. The trail heads up to Herman Lake at 12,000 feet, which is a good place for lunch. If you still have the drive, climb the saddle above the lake for views south to the east portal of the Eisenhower Tunnel. To reach the trailhead from Georgetown, head west on Interstate 70 for 9.5 miles to Exit 218. Park on the south side of the highway, walk over to the north side and then head east a couple of hundred yards to the trailhead near the highway department sandpiles.

Mount Bierstadt Trail—

This 14,060-foot peak, Mt. Bierstadt, deserves mention for its spectacular high-altitude beauty and easy accessibility (the trail to the summit is a mere 2.5-mile climb). From the top of Guanella Pass the mountain and its long jagged north ridge tower to the east. It's an impressive sight and quite often you'll find a painter or two sitting by the road getting the scene down on canvas. Routes to the summit of Mt. Bierstadt are numerous, but take this hard-earned advice... begin the hike by heading far right to avoid the boggy meadow and a bushwhack through wet alder and willow bushes. You don't want to be soaking wet during the climb. After getting around most of the bushes and the bog, head east up the gradual ridge to the summit. To reach the trailhead at the summit of Guanella Pass Rd., drive south 11 miles from Georgetown.

Mount Evans (Rest House Trail and Summit Lake Trail)—

Yes, we know, you can drive to the summit, but that's not quite as rewarding as doing it the old-fashioned way. This 12-mile route from Echo Lake Campground to the summit is challenging, beautiful and, at times, even eerie. The trail winds through a number of burn areas complete with charred pine trees which can make parts of the hike look like a forest out of *The Wizard of Oz*.

From Echo Lake Campground, begin hiking southeast on Rest House Trail (Forest Service No. 57). This 6.5-mile section of the trail crosses over a couple of ridges before entering an area of forest near Lincoln Lake that burned in 1968. After 5 miles you'll reach a fork in the trail—the right fork leads 1 mile to Lincoln Lake. This lake lies just below Mt. Evans Rd. (6 miles up from Echo Lake Campground). If you want to knock a few miles off the hike to the summit, consider beginning the hike from the road at Lincoln Lake. Meanwhile, back at the fork, continue on the left trail another 1.5 miles to the remains of the Mt. Evans Shelter House, which burned in 1962. There are a number of good campsites in this area, but be sure to bring a stove, as firewood is scarce. From here, you'll need to head right, connecting with the Summit Lake Trail (Forest Service No. 82), which begins a 4.7-mile climb to Summit Lake at 12,830 feet. The last 2 miles of this stretch can be wet and sloppy in early to midsummer, so consider yourself forewarned. From Summit Lake, you'll have to scramble the remaining distance (less than a mile) to the summit—unless you want to hitch a ride along the road. To reach the trailhead at Echo Lake Campground, drive 14 miles south from Idaho Springs on Hwy. 103. For more information about hiking trails in the Mt. Evans area, visit the **Clear Creek Ranger District Office,** one block south of Interstate 70 on Hwy. 103 in Idaho Springs, **PO Box 3307, Idaho Springs, CO 80452; (303) 567-2901.**

Pavilion Point—

This is more of a historic walk than an actual hike. A short trail (1 mile, tops) follows a section of the old Argentine Central Railroad bed to Pavilion Point.

When the railroad was built in 1905 to transport ore from the Argentine Mining District at Waldorf down to Silver Plume, it was the highest steam railroad track in the country and remained so until it was dismantled in 1920. Although it was built to haul ore, tourists eventually became its bread and butter. Hordes of visitors would board at Silver Plume and ride up to Pavilion Point for picnics and spectacular bird's-eye views down to Silver Plume and Georgetown. (For information about the Argentine Central Railroad, see the Waldorf Rd. write-up in the Scenic Drives section.)

These days a stone chimney is all that remains of the pavilion, but you still have the great views. In summer, with good timing, you can look down on the Georgetown Loop train as it chugs up the valley to Silver Plume. To reach the trail from Georgetown, drive south on Guanella Pass Rd. for 2.5 miles to Waldorf Junction (Forest Rd. 248). Turn right and proceed 1.2 miles to the fourth switchback and park your car. The trail heads off to the north. An alternate route begins in Silver Plume on the south side of Interstate 70. After heading under the highway bridge, turn right, head up the road and turn south up the old Argentine Central rail bed for about 3 miles to the pavilion.

St. Mary's Glacier—

See the Fall River Rd. description in the Scenic Drives section.

SKIING
CROSS-COUNTRY SKIING

When snow falls on the mountains and in the valleys around the Georgetown and Idaho Springs area, summertime jeep roads and hiking trails are transformed into wonderful trails for cross-country skiing. The forest service has done a good job of marking many trails and providing information and maps for the many skiers coming here each winter. Snow conditions and trail ideas are available at the **Clear Creek Ranger District Office** (closed on weekends in winter). **PO Box 3307, Idaho Springs, CO 80452; (303) 567-2901 or (303) 893-1474.**

Backcountry Trails—

Butler Gulch—This 3-mile trail (one way) leads up into a snow-covered bowl just below the Continental Divide. Due to its quick access from Denver, many skiers come here on weekends. The trail begins next to the Henderson Mine property. Begin skiing up the Jones Pass Rd. After about a quarter mile, take the left fork over a good bridge and start your climb through the forested valley. The skiing along most of the trail is fairly easy, but there is a steep, narrow section about halfway up that can be a bit tricky for beginners. When you reach a series of switchbacks, the pine trees begin to thin out. Once up in the high open area you can choose your own trail, but be sure to stay clear of the avalanche chutes along the steep walls to the left. Return on the same trail or choose your own route down through the steep, dense forests along the gulch. To reach the trailhead from Idaho Springs, head west on Interstate 70 to the Hwy. 40 turn-off. From Empire drive along Hwy. 40 about 7.5 miles to the Henderson Mine turn-off on the left. Proceed about a mile and a half along this road to the ski parking area next to the mine.

Chicago Lakes Trail—This is a moderately difficult trail. See the Hiking and Backpacking section for details.

Loveland Pass—If you don't want to spend time skiing uphill, consider a few runs down Loveland Pass. This is a great place to practice telemark turns. You need to shuttle cars between the pass and Loveland Valley Ski Area. From the summit of the pass, pull off to the right side of the road and ski along the contour to the west into a wide open bowl and start skiing down the steep drainage heading north. After a half mile, you'll run into Hwy. 6. Cross the road and continue skiing down the drainage on easier terrain, where you'll meet up with the runs at Loveland Valley Ski Area. You can't beat the price.

Mount Evans Road—Beginning at Echo Lake, the gradual 14-mile-long road up Mt. Evans (Hwy. 5) provides a scenic ski trip. On the way down you may want to bypass some of the switchbacks near the bottom by breaking your own trail through the pine glades. The powder can be exceptionally light! For details about the Mt. Evans Rd. see the Scenic Drives section.

Waldorf Road—Located just 2.5 miles south of Georgetown on Guanella Pass Rd., this fairly easy 6-mile trail leads to the old ghost town of Waldorf. For information see the Scenic Drives section.

Rentals and Information—
Virage Ski and Sports—Kelly and Jennifer Babeon rent downhill and cross-country ski equipment and offer a wealth of information about trails in the area. Open daily in winter from 7 am–7 pm. **1410 Argentine St., PO Box 1021, Georgetown, CO 80444; (303) 569-2754.**

DOWNHILL SKIING
Loveland—
Nestled just below the Continental Divide 12 miles west of Georgetown on Interstate 70, Loveland is primarily a day ski area. The majority of visitors come from the Denver metro area and enjoy Loveland's excellent skiing without the extraneous trappings of a major resort. Two connected ski areas, the easy rolling Loveland Valley and the larger, more challenging Loveland Basin, provide a wide variety of terrain and snow conditions.

The first rope tows were installed in 1938, and the ski area has since grown to include seven lifts. With a top elevation of 12,230 feet, the area has become well known for its fluffy powder. Most of the runs have a protected northern exposure, but some of the snow on the slopes with a southern exposure can turn into heavy slop after a few hours in the sun. Winds often kick up, blasting snow off some of the higher slopes (this is the Continental Divide, after all). The season at Loveland is quite long, running from mid-Oct. to mid-May.

Loveland Valley is connected to the main base at Loveland Basin by a long chairlift. It's an excellent place for novices and is very popular with families. Loveland Basin is serviced by five lifts, which whisk skiers up to runs that are primarily intermediate and advanced. The diversity of runs—including glade skiing, bowl skiing and steep bump runs—is a big part of Loveland's appeal.

The base facilities include a restaurant, a bar, a nursery, a rental shop and a ski school. In addition to a daily ski school, Loveland occasionally offers special clinics for advanced skiers who want to work on mogul and powder technique. For more information about Loveland, contact **PO Box 899, Georgetown, CO 80444; (303) 569-2288** or in Denver at **(303) 571-5580.**

SEEING AND DOING

CEMETERIES
Alvarado Cemetery—
Take time to visit the old Alvarado Cemetery, located 3.5 miles east of Georgetown on the Interstate 70 frontage road. Ornate Victorian-era tombstones dot this burial ground, including that of Louis Dupuy, founder of the Hotel de Paris.

HOT SPRINGS
Indian Springs Resort—
If you've had a long day on the ski slopes and want to soothe your tired body, consider a soak at Indian Springs hot springs. Many skiers returning to Denver on winter weekends avoid the traffic jam by stopping in at the springs until the traffic dies down. Not a bad idea!

Indians, who first used the springs, had a unique arrangement—the springs were a no man's land where all tribes could enjoy the hot water. Supposedly, after George Jackson discovered the springs in 1859, local miners enjoyed the luxury of soaking after their long workdays. By the late 1860s the first resort development began. Touted as the Saratoga of the Rocky Mountains, Indian Springs attracted quite a few famous visitors, including Walt Whitman and Teddy Roosevelt.

Today this sprawling resort offers a number of spa experiences that turn many people off—the facilities are a bit grimy and rundown. The swimming pool is covered by a translucent bubble and surrounded by a botanic garden of ferns, palms and other tropical plants—a bizarre sight in winter. Downstairs, hot mineral baths and vapor caves are accessible from the men's and women's locker rooms. For an extra price, try a massage or a dip in Club Mud, an eight-foot-square by one-foot-deep pool of mud. Hey, it's supposed to be good for you!

Overnight accommodations, though not recommended, are available in the 120-year-old lodge (bathrooms down the hall) and newer units across the road (private baths and TVs). The lodge rooms ($$) are very dingy, but if you're just too relaxed after a soak it may not matter. Indian Springs also has a lounge and a restaurant ($ to $$$), serving breakfast, lunch and dinner. The complex is located about 100 yards up Soda Creek Rd. from Idaho Springs. **PO Box 1990, 302 Soda Creek Rd., Idaho Springs, CO 80452; (303) 567-2191** or in Denver at **(303) 623-2050.**

MINE TOURS

The Edgar Mine—

In the 1870s this hardrock mine produced large amounts of silver, gold, lead and copper. Today it serves as a research area and classroom facility for future mining engineers from the Colorado School of Mines in Golden. Students use the latest in high-tech mining equipment on site to gain the valuable experience they'll use after graduation. Tours last from 45 minutes to an hour and are available throughout the year to the general public. There is a small fee. From mid-June through late Aug. no advance warning is necessary . . . just show up for a tour. Open Tues.–Sat. 8 am–4:30 pm. During the rest of the year, reservations are necessary. Located just outside Idaho Springs. Head north for a quarter of a mile on 8th St. and follow the signs to the mine. **(303) 567-2911** or in Golden at **(303) 273-3701.**

Lebanon Mine Tour—

This fascinating tour is accessible only by the Georgetown Loop Railroad. See the Major Attractions section for details.

MUSEUMS AND GALLERIES

Argo Gold Mill and Museum (in Idaho Springs)—

Opened for business in 1913, the Argo Gold Mill processed rich ore from mines in the area, much of it delivered via the 22,000-foot Argo Tunnel. The mill was shut down in 1943 and has since been added to the National Register of Historic Places. Currently it processes tourists instead of ore. A section of the old mill with much of its original machinery intact is open for self-guided tours (for a rather hefty price). Mining relics, such as ore cars and parts of a stamp mill, are strewn about the grounds. Adjacent to the mill, gunfights (don't worry folks, they're only blanks) take place four times daily at a "re-created" Old West town. For an additional charge, you can take a jeep ride up a nearby mountain to the Double Eagle Gold Mine.

The museum is open from May through mid-Oct., 9 am to 30 minutes before sundown. Located in Idaho Springs on the north side of Clear Creek at **2350 Riverside Dr.; (303) 567-2421.**

George Rowe Museum (in Silver Plume)—

Located in an old schoolhouse built in 1894, this museum contains a number of interesting historical artifacts, as well as a completely restored old-time schoolroom. The museum is a step back in time that's worth a look if you're in town. This is also the place to pick up Colorado history books and maps for a historic walking tour of Silver Plume and nearby hiking trails. Open daily from Memorial Day through Labor Day 10 am–4 pm and weekends in Sept. Fee charged. **95 Main St.; (303) 569-2562.**

Georgetown Galleries—

The restored buildings lining the streets of Georgetown house many shops and galleries. **Saxon Mountain Gallery** at **408 6th St., Georgetown, CO 80444; (303) 569-3186** or in Denver at **674-0353**, is owned by Bill Alexander, nationally known for his impressive watercolors of mountain snow scenes (especially downhill skiers). Alexander has been in Georgetown for almost two decades. The gallery has a large display of his prints and paintings, along with artwork by other Colorado artists.

Georgetown Gallery at **710 6th St., Georgetown, CO 80444; (303) 569-2218,** is a cooperative with works from various Colorado artists and craftsmen. It features watercolors, oils and pastels as well as pottery.

Hamill House—

Completed in 1879, this elegant Victorian mansion was home to William Hamill, a local silver magnate, politician and civic leader. At the time it was considered one of the finest homes in the state. Today it's owned by the Georgetown Society, which provides tours. The exquisite interior serves as a reminder of just how much money some of the mine owners made! Marble fireplaces, walnut and maple woodwork, a curved-glass conservatory and diamond-dust mirrors show off the superb craftsmanship of the era. Be sure to pay a visit to the elegant three-seat, cupola-covered outhouse. Catch a glimpse of how the upper crust used to live. A fee is charged. Summer hours (Memorial Day–late Sept.) are 9 am–5 pm daily; winter hours are 1–4:30 pm Mon.–Fri., noon–4 pm Sat.–Sun. **305 Argentine St., Georgetown, CO 80444; (303) 569-2840** or in Denver at **(303) 674-2625.**

Hotel de Paris—

Perhaps the most famous of Georgetown's grand old buildings, the Hotel de Paris served for years as the social center of town and was the talk of the nation. The hotel was built in 1875 by Louis Dupuy, "the mysterious Frenchman," so called because locals disagreed over just who he was, where he came from and, perhaps more importantly, what he may have done. But evidence suggests he was a French army deserter. Guests at this magnificent two-story hotel were attracted by discussions about art and literature with Dupuy who was a philosopher and a scholar as well as a gourmet cook. But without a doubt, this plush hotel's main attractions were the fine furnishings, the cuisine and the French wines.

Today the hotel has been faithfully restored to its former grandeur by the National Society of Colonial Dames of America, and tours are offered. The stone and stucco building is complete with cast-iron decorations and pressed-metal trim. Many of the original furnishings and decorative art objects fill the hotel. The resplendent dining room and the famous kitchen with its antique stove and accessories highlight the tour. Open daily from late May–late Sept., 9 am–5 pm; winter hours are Tues.–Sun., noon–4 pm. Located at Taos St. and 6th St. in Georgetown, **409 6th St.; (303) 569-2840** or in Denver at **(303) 674-2625.**

Silver Plume Depot—

This is the restored, original depot for the historic Georgetown Loop Railroad. It serves as a ticket office for the train and has a number of original rooms, including a telegraph office. The railroad yard displays a number of engines and cars. There is also a gift shop and a free slide show about the train. For more information about the Georgetown Loop Railroad, see the Major Attractions section. The depot is located on the south side of Interstate 70 at Exit 228 (Silver Plume).

Underhill Museum
(in Idaho Springs)—

This small mining museum is especially interesting because it's located in the town assay office. Assayers were a vital element in the mining communities—they analyzed the ore to determine its mineral content. Assaying equipment as well as other artifacts are on display. Small fee charged. Open Memorial Day–Labor Day and for special events during the rest of the year. Located in the 1400 block of Miner St. in Idaho Springs.

NIGHTLIFE

Buffalo Bar (in Idaho Springs)—
See the Where to Eat section.

Marti's Crazy Horse Saloon
(in Georgetown)—
See the Where to Eat section.

Plume Saloon (in Silver Plume)—

Locals crowd into this rustic night spot for a bite to eat and a drink to take the edge off. Part of the building is more than 100 years old, while other sections have been added over the years. Warm up by the potbellied stove in the corner. Over the mantelpiece of the stone fireplace hangs a portrait of Frances Willard, president of the Women's Christian Temperance Union at the turn of the century. Devilish locals are fond of toasting her as they quaff their drinks. This place is especially lively when local folk musicians wander in. Open year-round Wed.–Fri. 4 pm–midnight, Sat.–Sun. 11 am–midnight. Located next to the Brewery Inn in Silver Plume. **238 Main St.; 569-2277.**

SCENIC DRIVES

Fall River Road—

Drive up this 9-mile road along the Fall River through aspen and pine. Enormous rock outcroppings hang from the valley walls. About 7.5 miles up the road is a turn-off to the ghost town of Alice. If you continue ahead on Fall River Rd. for about a mile, you'll see the trailhead for the short half-mile hike to St. Mary's Glacier. A beautiful lake awaits, as well as the glacier. To reach Fall River Rd. from Idaho Springs, head west on Interstate 70 for about 2 miles and look for the Fall River Rd. exit.

Guanella Pass Road—

Guanella Pass is a very popular scenic drive and for good reason. Pine forests and shimmering aspen line the road most of the way. At the 11,669-foot summit, the above-treeline view east to Mt. Bierstadt is quite a sight. The road is open year-round, but the best time to go is in late fall when the aspen are turning. Begin the trip from Georgetown by driving south on Guanella Pass Rd. (Hwy. 118). After 5 miles you'll reach the Cabin Creek pumped storage hydroelectric plant, owned by the Public Service Company of Colorado. Power is generated during peak power-usage periods by releasing water from the upper reservoir down a 4,300-foot tunnel, where it turns two turbines. When power demand decreases, the turbines are reversed, pumping the water back up to the reservoir. Continue on the road for 6 miles to the summit. From here you drop south over the pass about 15 miles to the intersection with Hwy. 285 at the town of Grant.

Loveland Pass—

The pass is located 11 miles west of Georgetown on Interstate 70. Instead of driving through the Eisenhower Tunnel, turn left onto Loveland Pass Rd. (Hwy. 6) for a fantastic drive over the top of the Continental Divide. See the Scenic Drives section of the **Summit County** chapter for more details.

Mount Evans Road—

This has to be one of the most underrated attractions in Colorado. The paved Mt. Evans Rd. snakes its way 14 miles to the summit of Mt. Evans (14,264 feet). Although only 35 miles from Denver, many residents are amazed to find out this road exists.

Mt. Evans was first named Mt. Rosalie

by the famous landscape painter Albert Bierstadt, in honor of his wife. In 1863 he was also the first person on record to climb the peak. In 1870 the peak was re-named in honor of the second governor of the Colorado Territory. A primitive road was built up the mountain in the early 1930s and was improved for regular passenger cars in 1939. The road begins at Echo Lake, 14 miles south of Idaho Springs on Hwy. 103. It climbs up to treeline after about 3 miles and eventually leads to Summit Lake, where picnic tables and restrooms are available. There is also a short trail, which climbs about 600 vertical feet to the summit. If you continue on the road from Summit Lake, a tight series of switchbacks will lead you to a parking area just below the summit. Along the way is the Denver Cosmic Ray Research Lab, built in 1936, which attracts famous scientists from around the country for atmospheric research. The 360° view from the summit is something you'll just have to see for yourself. Be sure to watch out for approaching lightning storms and get to your car if you spot one. Ralph Reiner, a meteorologist who lives at Echo Lake, recounted to us in graphic detail the stories of unfortunate victims struck by lightning on the mountain. Mt. Evans Rd. (Hwy. 5) is open in summer only; the stretch up to Summit Lake is usually open by Memorial Day.

Oh My God Road—

Although there are a couple of steep drop-offs, this drive up Virginia Canyon isn't nearly as intimidating as the name implies. The 9-mile road connects Idaho Springs with Central City and is open year-round to all vehicles. Mine shafts dating back to the 1860s can be seen along the road. There are superb views to the south across Clear Creek Canyon to Chief Mountain and Squaw Mountain. Once over the top of the hill, descend through the remains of the Russell Gulch townsite and into Central City. This drive begins in Idaho Springs at the intersection of Canyon St. and Placer St. and heads north on Virginia Canyon Rd. Stay on the main road or you

may have the same nightmare that a recent visitor had—he drove off on a side road and plunged his new Blazer into an abandoned mine shaft! For a self-guided map, stop in at the visitors center (open daily) in Idaho Springs at 2200 Miner St.

Waldorf Road—

Although this road is not bad enough to require a four-wheel-drive vehicle, your vehicle should have good ground clearance (RVs can forget it!). Located near Georgetown, the road leads up to the old ghost town of Waldorf, which was quite a booming silver and gold mining area when rich ore was found in the 1860s. Just southwest of Waldorf, a stage route crossed over 13,207-foot Argentine Pass, providing transportation to the early mining camps in Summit County. In 1905, Edward John Wilcox, owner of the prosperous Waldorf Mining & Milling Company, built a 16-mile stretch of railroad track connecting mines in the area with Silver Plume in the valley far below. The Argentine Central Railroad ended up making much more on tourism than it ever did hauling ore. Until ceasing service in 1920, it was the highest railroad in the world. Part of the road to Waldorf follows along the old rail bed. Not much is left of the town, as scavengers have stripped the buildings down to the foundations, but with a vivid imagination you can picture what life must have been like for the hundreds of miners who lived there. To reach Waldorf from Georgetown, head south on Guanella Pass Rd. for 2.5 miles and turn right onto Waldorf Rd. (Forest Rd. 248). Continue about 6 miles to Waldorf.

The Racoon

WHERE TO STAY

ACCOMMODATIONS

Georgetown Resort Service — $$ to $$$$ (rates based per home)

Perhaps the most intriguing lodging possibility in Georgetown is to rent a historic Victorian home. Working through the Georgetown Resort Service, choose from many of Georgetown's fine gingerbread homes or simple miners' cabins. A minimum stay of two nights is necessary, and some require a stay of one week. Advance reservations are required. This can be a great mountain rendezvous for two, but family reunions, celebrations and large meeting groups are also encouraged. PO Box 247, Georgetown, CO 80444; (303) 569-2665.

The Hardy House — $$ to $$$$

Relax in this red Victorian home which was built in 1877 by Georgetown's blacksmith. The three guest rooms at the inn are the Ruby Room, Under the Eaves (two-room suite with two baths) and the romantic Victoria Suite, which features a private bath and a potbellied stove. The Hardy House's comfortable 19th-century furnishings add a real charm; spend some time in the parlor by the potbellied stove. Full breakfast is served each morning and four-course candlelit dinners are available upon request for an additional charge. Reservations necessary. PO Box 0156, 605 Brownell St., Georgetown, CO 80444; (303) 569-3388.

Brewery Inn — $$ to $$$

If you want to stay in Silver Plume, this is the place—it's also the only place. This Victorian bed and breakfast was built in the 1890s and is filled with antiques. The house sits on the site of the old Bush Brewery, which burned in 1889 and should not be confused with the Busch Brewery in St. Louis. You'll find no Clydesdale horses around, but if you look up on the rocky cliffs north of town, chances are good that you'll see a bighorn sheep. The old spring pump house, which was the water source for the brewery, still operates, and the water flows by the house, under the gazebo in the backyard and down to nearby Clear Creek. Four guest rooms are available—the suite on the first floor has a private bath and the three upstairs rooms all share a bathroom downstairs. A continental breakfast is included. Advance reservations are recommended, especially during ski season. PO Box 473, Silver Plume, CO 80476; (303) 569-2277 or in Denver at (303) 674-5565.

The Peck House — $$ to $$$

James Peck was a successful Chicago merchant who came west in the Pikes Peak gold rush of 1859. A year later, he built the Peck House as his private home in the little town of Empire. It wasn't until 1872 that Mrs. Peck opened her doors to overnight guests, and soon the home became a regular stagecoach stop for travelers over Berthoud Pass. As the oldest hotel in Colorado, the Peck House still carries on in a grand Victorian tradition.

A wide veranda stretches along the front of the building, with views across the valley. Inside, the mood is created by a large parlor with comfortable antique furniture, historic photos, red velvet curtains and a full bookcase available to guests. The owners, Gary and Sally St. Clair, have done a tremendous job in catering to all of your wants. A hot tub and downstairs ski lockers are a couple of nice touches. Eleven smallish rooms are elegantly appointed with period antiques and a constant supply of fresh flowers; nine of the rooms have private bathrooms. The Peck House is well known for its fine dining and Sun. brunch (see the Where to Eat section). Located along Hwy. 40, 2 miles from Interstate 70. 83 Sunny Ave., PO Box 428, Empire, CO 80438; (303) 569-9870.

Indian Springs Resort — $$

This Idaho Springs resort offers fairly rundown accommodations, but the hot springs are a big plus. See the Hot Springs section for details.

CAMPING

In Arapaho National Forest—

From Georgetown, there are two national forest campgrounds located up Guanella Pass Rd. Drive south on Guanella Pass Rd. (Forest Rd. 118) about 4 miles to Clear Lake Campground. There are eight sites and no fee. Another 4 miles south of Clear Lake Campground is **Guanella Pass Campground** with 17 sites and a fee.

About 8 miles west of Empire on Hwy. 40 toward Berthoud Pass is **Mizpaw Campground**. It has 10 sites and a fee.

Southwest of Idaho Springs are two other campgrounds. From Idaho Springs drive southwest on Hwy. 103 to the intersection with Forest Rd. 188. Turn right onto Forest Rd. 188 and proceed to **West Chicago Creek Campground** (12 miles from Idaho Springs). It has 11 sites and a fee. If you continue on Hwy. 103 for 14 miles from Idaho Springs you'll reach **Echo Lake Campground** with 16 sites and a fee.

Private Campgrounds—

Indian Springs Resort—Full hookups right next to the hot springs pool. Located a couple hundred yards up Soda Creek Rd. from Idaho Springs. **PO Box 1990, 302 Soda Creek Rd., Idaho Springs, CO 80452; (303) 567-2191.**

Mountain Meadow Campground—This place offers plenty of RV hookups and tent sites. Located 2 miles west of Empire on Hwy. 40. **PO Box 2, Empire, CO 80438; (303) 569-2424.**

———— WHERE TO EAT ————

The Peck House — $$ to $$$

The ambience of the Peck House, built in 1860, is only part of the dining experience—the fine food is the real attraction. Empire is a little out of the way, but it is worth the trouble to make your way to the Peck House for lunch, dinner or Sun. brunch. Located within the Victorian confines of a fine inn (see the Where to Stay section), the ground floor dining room is set with red linen tablecloths, and a crackling fire is often burning. Dinner prepared by owner Gary St. Clair is a tasty menu of steaks, fowl and seafood selections; nightly specials during our visit included baked, stuffed rainbow trout. Hearty appetizers such as escargot, shrimp and baked French onion soup are served nightly. Also offered is an extensive wine list. On Sun., the champagne brunch features menu items such as quail and eggs, eggs Benedict and salmon Napoleon. In summer, the covered porch with stunning mountain views is open for meals. Lunch hours are 11 am–4 pm Mon.–Sat., June–Sept.; Sat. only, Oct.–May. Dinner hours year-round are 4–9 pm Sun.–Thur., 4–10 pm Fri–Sat. Sun. brunch is served year-round from 10 am–2 pm. **83 Sunny Ave., Empire; 569-9870.**

The Ram — $$ to $$$

By many accounts this is the finest restaurant in Georgetown. Lunches and excellent dinners are served in this historic brick building, which served as the Bank of Clear Creek County when it was built in 1888. After the silver panic in the 1890s the bank went broke. For years it housed the Pease Grocery Store, until the present restaurant moved in during the early 1960s. The elegant dining room features an exposed brick wall, a crystal chandelier and a stained glass depiction of a bighorn sheep. The large saloon in front of the dining room has been a local watering hole for 25 years. The lunch menu includes a daily Mexican special, sandwiches and burgers; dinner highlights are tournedos, filet mignon, fettucini, veal à la Marsala and an all-you-can-eat spaghetti special on Wed. Meals are also served in the bar. Open weekdays (except Tues.) 11 am–9 pm, Sat.–Sun. 11 am–10 pm. Bar is open until 2 am (midnight on Sun.). **606 6th St., Georgetown; 569-3263.**

The Renaissance — $$ to $$$

People don't come to the Renaissance for the atmosphere and decor because, to be quite honest, it's lacking. What draws the large clientele to this Georgetown restaurant is the exquisite northern Italian cuisine that chef/owner Paul Dufka meticulously whips up back in the kitchen. The dishes are accented by Dufka's delicate sauces and fresh ingredients. Lunches include popular linguini dishes, chicken Vesuvio, quiches and fresh salmon. For dinner, veal, chicken, fish and beef dishes come with soup, Caesar salad, homemade bread and a side of pasta. Take a look at the fine wine list. Be sure to show up with a large appetite—you'll probably still leave with a doggie bag. Reservations recommended. Open Wed.–Sun. 11 am–3 pm (lunch), 4–10 pm (dinner), closed Mon.–Tues.; in winter lunches served only on weekends. **1025 Rose St., Georgetown; 569-3336.**

Beau Jo's — $ to $$$

Beau Jo's is probably better known for its pizza than any other restaurant in Colorado. That's quite a statement, but true nonetheless. In the early 1970s this Idaho Springs restaurant got its start with a seating area for 15 customers; today they can seat 300. The reason for their huge success is the creative pizzas they prepare with a mind-boggling array of choices. Select from five thicknesses of crust (made with either sesame wheat, whole wheat or white) and 25 toppings. The thick-crust mountain pies come with honey to use on the leftover crust for dessert. Specialty pizzas include Thai pie and tofu pizza (that's right, tofu). Beau Jo's also serves sandwiches, but to order one would be a sin. The restaurant has a comfortable decor and a wild napkin art display near the entrance. Open daily from 11 am–9 pm Sun.–Thur. and until 9:30 pm Fri.–Sat. **1517 Miner St., Idaho Springs; 567-4376.**

Buffalo Bar — $ to $$$

Located in a brick building on Miner St. that's been a watering hole since 1885, the Buffalo Bar in Idaho Springs reeks of history. The layout is very inviting, with its wooden bar and mirror, exposed brick, high ceilings and the buffalo head on the wall. Very Old West. The Buffalo Bar opens its doors early in the morning when it starts serving its famous breakfast, which includes trout and eggs, breakfast burritos and numerous omelettes. The lunch and dinner menus offer specialty sandwiches, buffalo burgers, steaks, seafood and popular Italian calzones. A nightly dinner special is also offered. The nightlife here gets hopping during the summer and during winter ski season. If you just want a light snack with your drink, try an appetizer or a salad. Open year-round Sun. 7 am–midnight, Mon. 11 am–midnight, Tues.–Thur. 8 am–midnight, Fri.–Sat. 7 am–2 am. **1617 Miner St., Idaho Springs; 567-2729** or **595-9018 in Denver.**

Marti's Crazy Horse Saloon — $ to $$$

The Crazy Horse in Georgetown features a full menu of sandwiches, burgers, great Mexican food, seafood and steaks, but the real reason to come here is for the cozy pub atmosphere. Marti's is especially popular with skiers driving back to Denver after a day on the slopes. A large fireplace, dark wood-paneled walls, Victorian chandeliers and a pool table provide the character. In summer, outside seating is available. It's a great place to visit with a few good friends. Open daily from 11 am–10 pm; the bar stays open until 1:30 am (midnight on Sun.). **1211 Argentine St., Georgetown; 569-2475.**

The Happy Cooker — $ to $$

Located in an old, restored Victorian home set back off a street in Georgetown, the Happy Cooker serves up some of the tastiest and most creative breakfast and lunch items around. This upbeat place is decorated with turn-of-the-century antiques, and the walls are covered with art-work for sale from the Georgetown Gallery. Menu favorites are quiches, Belgian waffles, homemade bread and soups. If you are on your way to the ski slopes, stop in for a hearty breakfast. Open daily in winter from 8 am–4 pm, in summer Mon.–Fri. 8 am–5 pm and Sat.–Sun. 8 am–6 pm. 412 6th St., Georgetown; 569-3166.

Hard Rock Cafe — $ to $$

This small Empire cafe with vinyl booths and counter seating was founded in 1932. No, it's not part of the international chain that sells the popular Hard Rock Cafe T-shirts. Named for hardrock mining in the area, the cafe serves full breakfasts and lunches. It is a great place to stop on the way to Winter Park for a day of skiing. Fill up on homemade cinnamon rolls, biscuits and gravy, bacon and eggs or French toast. Lunch items include burgers and pizza. Open Thur.–Tues. from 7 am–2 pm. Located on Hwy. 40 in Empire; you can't miss it. 18 E. Park Ave.; 569-2061.

SERVICES

Georgetown Chamber of Commerce—

PO Box 444, Georgetown, CO 80444; (303) 567-4844 or in Denver at (303) 674-9813.

Georgetown Information Center—

Located on 6th St. across from the post office. Open Memorial Day–Labor Day.

The Georgetown Society—

This group is involved in the historic preservation of Georgetown. They offer information about tours and events. PO Box 667, Georgetown, CO 80444; (303)

569-2840 or in Denver, (303) 674-2625.

Idaho Springs Information—

For information on Idaho Springs, stop by the visitors center at 2200 Miner St. (next to the statue of Steve Canyon). Or contact PO Box 97, Idaho Springs, CO 80452; (303) 567-4382 or (303) 567-4844.

Silver Plume Information—

In the summer months, information is available at the George Rowe Museum in Silver Plume at 95 Main St; (303) 569-2562. Also try the Silver Plume Town Hall at 285 Main St., Silver Plume, CO 80476.

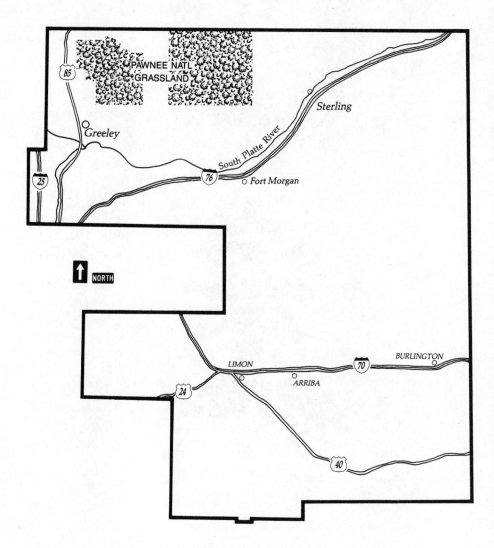

NORTHEAST REGION

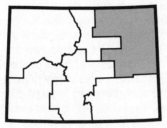

Northeast Plains

The plains—a huge, rolling expanse of irrigated fields and grasslands, plotted dirt roads, wide swaths of fenced-in space, silent oil pumps and an occasional town—have an image problem. The truth is, unless you slow down and pull off the highway, these characteristics are all you'll have a chance to see.

A fascinating history can be found along the routes of trappers, traders and homesteaders in the northeast plains; several towns preserve this history in excellent museums. Other attractions are usually passed, but they provide the essence of the "Other Colorado." Feel like something to eat? Drovers and Bruce's, located in Brush and Severance, respectively, are two unique restaurants you won't find anywhere else. Consider a cushy, overnight stay at Tarado Mansion bed and breakfast in the hamlet of Arriba—it would be tough to match, even in the most sophisticated city. And a ride on the turn-of-the-century carousel in Burlington will make you appreciate the craftsmanship of another era. Most important, what the plains may be lacking in drama and excitement, its people make up for in old-fashioned hospitality.

One of the major influences in the settling of the northeast plains was (and still is), the accessibility of water flowing down from the Rocky Mountains. The South Platte, the largest and most crucial river in northeastern Colorado, marked a route for explorers and was life-sustaining to settlers. In its own right, however, it wasn't very impressive—especially compared to the Mississippi. When Mark Twain saw the South Platte, he wrote in *Roughing It*, it's "a melancholy stream straggling through the center of the enormous flat plain, and only saved from being impossible to find with the naked eye by its sentinel rank of scattering trees standing on either bank . . . the Platte was 'up' they said which make me wish I could see it when it was down, if it could look any sicker and sorrier."

Homesteads over one hundred years old can also be recognized by sudden, dense clumps of trees on the barren prairie. Some homesteads are thriving farms today, while many others have faded or disappeared altogether. Most residents of northeastern Colorado still work on large farms and ranches. It's these people, more than the landscape, that make this corner of Colorado an interesting place. Close-knit communities are situated along historic migration routes, now paved highways. Their sense of community is strong, but unless you are able to attend a high school football game or town festival, you probably won't see it.

A vast diversity of birdlife draws many people to northeastern Colorado. Audubon Society members enjoy gazing quietly into binoculars and identifying species, while hunters prefer aiming their rifles for good shots at low-flying pheasants. No one, however, will pull a trigger at frequently sighted sandhill cranes, white pelicans or blue herons. Keep your eyes peeled for a glimpse of these large birds while driving down those long straightaways—and consider taking some side roads, especially during the spring and fall migrations.

HISTORY

When Maj. Stephen Long passed through Colorado's northeastern plains, he proclaimed that the region "would never be fit for human habitation other than by the nomad races." He also reported, it "should forever remain the unmolested haunt of the native hunter, bison and jackal." We're sure the predominant Arapaho and Cheyenne Indians who lived on the plains would have agreed, but by the 1820s traders and trappers began trickling through. An abundance of beaver was the primary attraction for the newcomers; soon trading posts were springing up along the South Platte corridor. At one time there were four trading posts (Fort Lupton, Fort Vasquez, Fort Jackson and Fort St. Vrain) within a 15-mile radius. The well-fortified posts did a thriving trade with Anglos as well as Indians, especially when inhibitions loosened after a few swigs of potent "Taos Lightning."

Just when trading had almost dried up, the 1859 gold strikes in the Colorado mountains lured a new wave of people across the plains. The vast majority were passing through, but some discouraged miners settled near the South Platte River, taking advantage of the fertile bottom land.

Almost coinciding with the gold strikes, the short-lived Pony Express established a mail stop in Julesburg, in the far northeastern corner of the state. (It wasn't until 1862, however, that mail was carried regularly along the South Platte route to the burgeoning town of Denver.) A transcontinental railroad was the next big step. Union Pacific rails reached Julesburg in 1867, causing a population explosion and earning this wild town the nickname, "wickedest city in the West." Four thousand gamblers, speculators, prostitutes, outlaws and road agents poured into Julesburg, forming a ramshackle village that featured 22 saloons and five dance halls. At this stage of development, there was no law and order—murder by six-shooter occurred at the least provocation. Though the first railroad across America stopped in Julesburg, it passed for the most part above present-day Colorado.

The influx of new settlers wreaked havoc on the Indians' way of life, especially their hunting. The Indians began to strike back as a last resort when the herds of buffalo were depleted. In one incident, just southeast of Denver, the entire Hungate family was murdered and scalped by unknown Indians. The mutilated bodies were displayed in Denver, and residents were in a frenzy, fearful of a full-scale Indian attack. Territorial troops struck first, however, when in 1864 about 100 peaceful Arapaho and Cheyenne, primarily women and children, were killed at the Sand Creek Massacre on the Colorado plains (see the History section of the **Southeast Plains** chapter). The final engagement on the eastern plains came a year later, at the Battle of Summit Springs (located between Sterling and Akron).

The open range had been used for years as pasture, but a long drive was necessary to get the beef to the railheads. With the Indians removed and the arrival of trains to Colorado, cattle barons were enjoying their zenith. John Iliff was the biggest of them all, owning much of the northeastern part of the state. Sheep ranching was to follow, but cattlemen never liked the woolly beasts—one line of a poem recalls, "A sheep just oozes out a stink, that drives a cowman to drink!" Or was that just an excuse?

In the spring of 1870 the Union Colony agricultural cooperative, under the steadfast direction of Nathan C. Meeker, founded a town named after Meeker's boss Horace Greeley (owner of the *New York Tribune*). This group of greenhorn easterners came west with inflated expectations of paradise—including waterfalls, which were not to be found on the barren prairie of northeastern Colorado! Water, however, was plentiful, and the town of Greeley was platted at the confluence of the South Platte and Cache La Poudre rivers. With the help of irrigation canals, the fertile soil produced successful crops. The newcomers had their share of problems, but liquor wasn't one of them—Meeker had brought only temperate colonists. One of the enforced rules of the young town was, "Thou shall not sell liquid damnation within the lines of the Union Colony." This rule had an adverse effect by prompting the success of several small establishments that sold booze just outside the city limits.

One nagging problem in Greeley was the trampling of crops by roaming cattle; settlers solved it by stringing up a 50-mile-long, $20,000 fence around the crops. Their neighbors scoffed at them, saying the fence was erected to keep out "godless" cowmen. But it worked and the town achieved unprecedented agricultural success. Just when things were going well, Meeker was forced by money matters to leave Greeley and take a job at the White River Indian agency in northwestern Colorado. Meeker went down in history in 1879 when he was murdered by Ute Indians who didn't appreciate his efforts to transform them into farmers. The Meeker Massacre caused the entire tribe to be removed to distant reservations (see the History section in the **Meeker** chapter).

In retrospect, it seems not much has changed in terms of the plains economy: crops are more diverse and methods for planting and picking have been modernized, but agriculture and ranching are still the mainstays. Though a flurry of activity in the 1970s caused oil wells to sprout up, the prehistoric-looking machinery now lies dormant.

Interstate 76 and Interstate 70—

Since the northeast plains is not a destination as such, we have organized this chapter based on attractions along the major interstates, focusing on interesting diversions along the way. The main arterial roads passing through the northeast plains from the east are Interstate 76 and Interstate 70. Most people will be coming into the state on these roads. If you happen to be traveling from west to east, turn to the end of the write-up on each highway route, and work through the chapter backward.

———— INTERSTATE 76 ————

This highway leads into the extreme northeast corner of Colorado from Nebraska, ending in north Denver. We are fudging the borders a bit to let you know about a beautiful diversion, as you come into Colorado from the east.

OGALLALA, NEBRASKA

Lake McCanaughy—

This long, slender reservoir, filled by waters from the South Platte River, is located about 30 miles over the Nebraska border. Along the northern shore, several roads make their way down to a wide sandy beach. This gorgeous beach, in an unlikely western-Nebraska location, really makes you feel as if you're on the coast—except you can see across the lake. Find a shaded camping place under a cottonwood tree or take your boat to the middle of the lake and drop in a fishing line. Go for a run on the beach or play in the sand. Windsurfing

Pelican soaring on the winds of the northeastern plains (photograph by David C. Holloway).

here is extremely popular—people from as far away as Denver make a special trip. Lake McCanaughy is on the migratory route of many birds, including sandhill cranes.

STERLING

The small town of Sterling, in the midst of irrigated farm country, is an attractive regional hub. It's a good place to pull off the road for a quick meal at one of a dozen fast-food places on Main St. or to spend the night at one of many AAA-rated motels. While driving about, keep your eyes open for "living trees" sculptures. These detailed works of art, scattered around town, include a clump of giraffes, a mermaid and a golfer. By the way, there are four golf courses here. Jumbo, North Sterling and Prewitt reservoirs provide good warm water fishing and boating. A number of campsites can be found at water's edge. If you're just dying for a change of scenery, drive north on N. 7th Ave. to County Rd. 70 and then west for 8 miles to Chimney Canyons with its 250-foot chalk cliffs. For more information on Sterling, stop in at the **Overland Trail Museum's Visitor Information Center** (see entry below for directions).

Overland Trail Museum—

It is well worth your while to stop and take a look inside this excellent regional museum, named for the well-trod route pioneers followed on westerly journeys. The grounds offer shaded picnic tables; a large plot is planted with several types of prairie grasses, identified by small markers; and there are tree-trunk-sized pieces of petrified wood scattered about. The museum is housed inside a stone reproduction of Fort Sedgewick, established on the Overland Trail in the early 1860s to quell Indian problems. Once inside, take a leisurely look at the branding iron collection, horse-drawn machinery, the one-room schoolhouse and geological displays. Wildlife exhibits include rattlesnakes and a buffalo. Lots of interesting stuff can be found here—and it's free! Open from May to Sept. 30. Mon.–Sat. 9 am–5 pm, Sun. 10 am–5 pm. Located conveniently at the intersection of Interstate 76 and Hwy. 6 just east of Sterling; **(303) 522-3895.**

BRUSH

In the 1860s John Iliff and Jared Brush contracted to sell beef to Army troops; thus began a cattle empire reaching from Jules-

burg to Greeley. In the early 1900s farmers were given incentives to plant sugar beets. Today the beets are such an important crop that the high school football team goes by the name "Beetdiggers." This little town with its wide, tree-lined streets is an agricultural and ranching center. Main St. features a Duckwalls five-and-dime store. If you are passing through Brush on July 2, 3 or 4th, stop in for the Brush Rodeo. The long tradition of rodeo continues as 450 top amateur cowboys and cowgirls compete. Other events include wild cow milking and a 3.1-mile run. On Independence Day, the town comes out for a pancake breakfast, a parade and, when it gets dark, a fireworks display.

Drovers Restaurant — $ to $$

If you grew up in rural America, Drovers will be like a homecoming; if you're a "city slicker," it will be a fascinating eye-opener. To a casual observer, Drovers may seem like nothing special, but because of its setting, 1950s prices and genuinely friendly waitresses, it's worth going a few miles out of your way. Sit at the counter or find an unoccupied table. Most of the clientele comes in from outlying ranches to do some business, or meet with friends over a cup of coffee (it only costs a dime) and a slice of lemon meringue or cherry pie. The menu varies from traditional breakfasts to burgers, barbecue beef sandwiches and T-bone steaks. You can bet the beef is good, because, just outside Drovers, thousands of penned-up cattle are ready for auction. Open from 5:30 am–8 pm daily. **28601 Hwy. 34; (303) 842-4218.**

Across the hallway from the restaurant is the sale barn: a small auction house with spittoons placed all about for the bidding, tobacco-chewing ranchers. If you show up on a Thurs. or Fri., you can witness an auction (lasting from noon into the night). The western-wear store in the same building is one of the best places around to buy a pair of cowboy boots, a hat or a plaid shirt—it's not meant for urban cowboys and, accordingly, the prices are fair.

FORT MORGAN

This agricultural and ranching center is the Morgan County seat. It's a quiet, small town with some beautiful houses. Just northeast of Fort Morgan is Jackson Reservoir, with excellent warmwater fishing in the spring and early summer.

Fort Morgan Museum—
The displays of this tidy museum cover the history of Morgan County. Permanent exhibits include information on the life of Glenn Miller (who attended high school here) and an old soda fountain from the Hillrose Drugstore. Unfortunately, cold drinks or ice cream are not served at the fountain any longer. (However, in Akron, 32 miles west of Fort Morgan, you can visit a similar working fountain right on Main St.) Also displayed is a collection of Plains Indians artifacts. A large room is reserved for traveling exhibits that change every two to three months. When we visited in Sept., there was an excellent collection of Charles Russell's western paintings and sculptures as well as some of his personal letters. Open year-round, Mon.–Fri. 10 am–5 pm, Sat. 1:30–4:30 pm. **414 Main St., Fort Morgan, CO 80701; (303) 867-6331.**

Sherman Street Historical District—
Four magnificent homes, lined up in a row on Sherman St., represent distinctive styles of historical development. The **Warner House, 508 Sherman St.** (built in 1886), **Curry House, 404 Sherman St.** (built in 1916), **Graham House, 428 Sherman St.** (built in 1914) and **Bloedorn House, 440 Sherman St.** (built in 1926) are unique in their quality of architecture and fine state of preservation. They are all privately owned, but the view from the quiet street is worth checking out. The Fort Morgan Museum can furnish you with more information on the history of each house, if you're interested.

Pawnee Buttes—
Exceptions to a landscape virtually devoid of unique features are these two 300-foot-tall sandstone towers. Once called White Buttes, these primitive monuments rise from the expanse of the Pawnee National Grasslands having withstood the erosion that affected the surrounding landscape. Get out of your car and take a walk on 4-mile Pawnee Buttes Trail. It's like revisiting the Old West while letting your senses adjust to the solitude and comfort of the prairie. Silence is interrupted only by the wind and by a surprising number of songbirds and raptors. Stories of rattlesnakes hold some truth, so be aware of where you sit down for a break or a picnic. The best times to visit Pawnee Buttes are in spring and fall when the scorching heat isn't so intense, or in early morning or evening when shadows lengthen and a colorful sky brings added contrasts to the sandstone monoliths.

To reach the trailhead from Fort Morgan, drive north on Hwy. 52 for 25 miles to Raymer. Turn left onto Hwy. 14 and continue about 10 miles to County Rd. 390. Turn right, proceed north for 14 miles and then turn right again onto County Rd. 112. Drive east for 6.5 miles to a "T" intersection where you'll take a left on a marked road leading shortly to the Pawnee Buttes Trail. The parking area is located next to a large windmill.

GREELEY

Founded by the Union Colonists in 1870, Greeley has enjoyed steady, sustained growth. Today, it's the largest town in this part of the state, with a population of 70,000. The town's wide streets are shaded by trees, many of which were planted by settlers in the 1870s; cattle and crops are still the moving forces behind the town's economy. History is perhaps the reason to come to Greeley. James Michener lived here while writing *Centennial*. You can visit several excellent museum collections in town.

Centered in Greeley, the University of Northern Colorado is well known for its education and music programs. The town has a brand new performing arts center, **Union Colony Civic Center, (303) 356-5555,** that hosts a number of plays and

Grand Victorian house on a Greeley side street (photograph by Bruce Caughey).

concerts. Its schedule includes an impressive line-up of local and national talent. Another Greeley attraction is the **Denver Broncos Training Camp.** You can watch practices and scrimmages each July and Aug. as the Broncos prepare for yet another NFL season. Quite a number of hotels, motels, restaurants and bars are available if you are passing through. For more information, contact the **Greeley Convention and Visitors Bureau, 1407 8th Ave., Greeley, CO 80631; (303) 352-3566.**

Centennial Village—

The history of the plains is vividly told through the chronological reconstruction of old buildings from the years 1860–1920. Hour-long tours are given through the Centennial Village grounds by enthusiastic, knowledgeable guides. You'll see various building materials such as rock, wood, adobe and sod, which were used to construct living quarters. Some highlights along the way include the wagon house (built in 1917, the predecessor to the modern-day Winnebago) and a Swedish-Ameri-

can Stuga home. At the end of the tour, a firehouse and a blacksmith's shop prove especially fascinating for kids. If you visit only one museum on the northeastern plains, it should probably be this one. Open Memorial Day through Labor Day, Mon.–Fri. 10 am–5 pm, Sat.–Sun. 1–5 pm. The last tour leaves one hour before closing time. Reduced hours from mid-Apr. through mid-Oct. **14th Ave.** and **A St., Greeley, CO; (303) 350-9224.**

Fort Vasquez—

Built in 1835 by a few hard-core mountain men, Fort Vasquez capitalized on the trade routes along the South Platte River. Twelve-foot-high adobe walls had rifle ports and two corner towers. The merchandise available at the fort in the early days included ivory combs, silk handkerchiefs, brass tacks and kettles, and, of course, the key ingredient—"Taos Lightning," a potent alcohol that flowed freely to facilitate amenable trading by Indians and mountain men. An ill-fated attempt was once made to ship 700 buffalo robes and 400 buffalo tongues from Fort Vasquez to St. Louis via the South Platte River. After 69 days of pushing, pulling and occasionally floating a flat-bottomed boat, the tired crew arrived in St. Louis with the news that the South Platte was not a navigable stream.

Fort Vasquez crumbled to the ground many years ago, but the WPA reconstructed an identical structure in the 1930s. Today the State Historical Society runs a visitors center next to the fort with information and displays on the fur trade and Plains Indians. The friendly staffers are extremely knowledgeable about the history of the area. Walking around Fort Vasquez provides a glimpse of how life might have been in the early 1800s—except for the cars zooming by on the nearby highway. Open Memorial Day through Labor Day, Mon.–Sat. 10 am–5 pm, Sun. 1–5 pm. Located 17 miles south of Greeley (1 mile south of Platteville) on **Hwy. 85; (303) 785-2832.**

Meeker Home Museum—

Nathan Meeker, founder of the Union

Colony at Greeley, was a fascinating man. You can visit his well-preserved two-story adobe home that has survived the past 100-plus years in good stead. Filled with many of the Meeker family's personal artifacts, it gives an excellent idea of life in the 1870s. If you want to learn every conceivable detail about Meeker's life, you'll find the information here. For casual visitors, however, the personal tour can be too in-depth and, therefore, lengthy. The Meeker Home's future opening hours are uncertain due to city budget cuts. As it stands now, the museum is open Memorial Day through Labor Day, Mon.–Sat. 10 am–5 pm. **1324 9th Ave., Greeley, CO; (303) 350-9221.**

WHERE TO STAY

Plenty of motels are spread throughout Greeley, including most of the national chains. For a unique night's lodging, try this new bed and breakfast listed below.

Sterling House
Bed and Breakfast — $$

The Sterling House, built in 1886, has only two rooms, but they are sunny, fresh and immaculate with 12-foot ceilings, fresh flowers by the beds and spacious private baths. If you enjoy Victorian elegance (no TVs) and being surrounded by antiques, then this is the place. The parlor, with its gold-print wallpaper and antique furniture, is centered around a porcelain-tile fireplace. The woodwork throughout the old house is stunning. Full breakfasts are served on china plates at a linen-draped dining room table; specialties are apple pancakes and crêpes. Dinners may be arranged by request. Why not rent both rooms with some friends and have the whole house to yourselves? No children under 10; smoking on the enclosed porch is OK. Reservations recommended. **818 12th St., Greeley, CO 80631; (303) 351-8805.**

WHERE TO EAT
Bruce's — $ to $$$

Located in Severance, about 10 miles north of Greeley, this restaurant has an unusual theme. Their logo is a bull standing up on two legs with a picket sign saying unfair—Bruce's specialty is Rocky Mountain oysters. The owner Bruce Ruth says "bull fries are my ace in the hole." For those of you still in the dark about this unique product, you'll just have to go to this popular restaurant and ask. Tender turkey oysters, steaks and seafood are also served. You can get a juicy hamburger for a mere $2. The casual setting in the former Severance Recreation Hall is created with four long tables, each seating about 20 people, in the center of the room and booths running down both sides. The down-home atmosphere encourages people to laugh easily, carry on and have a genuinely good time. On weekends, live country and western bands play from 8 pm to closing. Make a special trip to this restaurant! The restaurant and bar are open seven days a week: 10 am–10 pm Mon.–Thur., 10–2 am on Fri.–Sat., and 10 am to midnight on Sun. Located in **Severance; (303) 686-2320.**

Potato Brumbaugh's — $ to $$$

Named after a character in Michener's *Centennial*, this restaurant received rave reviews from virtually everyone we talked with in Greeley. The atmosphere is classy; tables are set with linen tablecloths and napkins as well as pewter hot plates. Meals are, appropriately, of the meat and potato variety. Specialties include slow-roasted prime rib and steak Centennial, which is topped with a large shrimp, broccoli and Béarnaise sauce. Also offered are lobster, prawns and several enticing chicken dishes. Lighter meals are also available. Open for lunch 11:15 am–2 pm Mon.–Fri., dinner served from 5–10 pm Mon.–Sat. Located in Cottonwood Square shopping plaza, **2400 17th St.; 356-6340.**

Lance's Chuckwagon — $ to $$

This local truckstop has friendly service and low prices. Lance's is located a few miles south of Greeley in La Salle. Breakfast dishes range from pork chops and eggs to an omelette or breakfast burrito. All bread and pastries are homemade. For dinner try a cut of elk, venison or buffalo; maybe you'd prefer roast beef or seafood. The prices are reasonable and what the Chuckwagon lacks in atmosphere it makes up for in tasty food. Open Sun.–Thur. 5 am–10 pm, Fri–Sat. open 24 hours. **316 2nd St. (Hwy. 85), La Salle, CO; 284-5158.**

INTERSTATE 70

Interstate 70 is the most heavily used route into Colorado, entering from Kansas in the east-central part of the state. The highway passes several interesting places as it makes a beeline west for Denver and the mountains.

BURLINGTON

The first thing to do when arriving at Burlington is stop in at the **State Welcome Center**, just off Interstate 70; **(719) 346-5554**. The center, staffed by knowledgeable travel counselors, can help you plan your Colorado vacation, and you can pick up armloads of brochures from around Colorado. Burlington offers many fast-food restaurants and inexpensive places to spend the night. About 22 miles north of town, **Bonny State Recreation Area** boasts great warmwater fishing, windsurfing, boating and birdwatching; four campgrounds at the reservoir have a total of 159 sites (fee charged). Following are a couple of attractions you shouldn't miss.

Kit Carson County Carousel—

This fully restored, handcarved wooden merry-go-round, built in 1905, is a designated National Historic Landmark. Climb onto one of several life-sized horses or maybe you'd prefer a more exotic camel, zebra, giraffe, deer or lion. Take a while to observe the incredible detail of the snake curling around the giraffe's neck and the various prancing positions of each animal. These proud animal figures march to the music of a 1909 Wurlitzer Monster Military Band Organ—one of only two of this particular vintage in existence today. On the outer rim of the carousel, three tiers of oil paintings portray various subjects of the time. Admission for a ride and a tour is only a quarter. Open from late-May through mid-Sept. during afternoons and evenings. At the Burlington Fairgrounds, **15th St. and Lincoln Ave., Burlington; (719) 348-5562.**

Old Town—

This outstanding collection of 1900s buildings, with rooms full of antiques and exhibits, re-creates a historic atmosphere. Tour guides patiently explain the implements of the blacksmith, newspaper and harness shops. The spacious grounds also feature a western saloon, where you can witness can-can shows and staged gunfights. Special on-site craft demonstrations are continuous. Be sure to take a wagon ride from Old Town to the Kit Carson County Carousel (see previous entry). In a monstrous red barn with a 45-foot-high roof, a troupe performs melodramas, providing a family night of cheering the heroes and hissing the villains. Melodramas are staged from June through mid-Aug. at 7 pm nightly (except Mon.); they are free of charge with a tour ticket. Old Town is open year-round: Memorial Day–Labor Day 9 am–9 pm; the rest of the year from 9 am–5 pm. **420 S. 14 St., Burlington, CO 80807; (719) 346-7382.**

ARRIBA

Tarado Mansion — $$$ to $$$$

Until recently, the only reason to pull off the interstate in the small farming community of Arriba would be to escape a blinding snowstorm. Now the luxurious confines of this Greek-revival mansion give you a better reason to stop for the night or at least for a guided tour. The massive front of the building appears like a mirage as it rises from the flat farmland. Inside, beautiful furnishings represent an extensive collection of antiques from around the world.

A harp once belonged to Gen. George Custer's wife; several porcelain figures were hand-sculpted in Italy in the 1700s. Oriental pieces from China, Japan and Korea add an exotic touch—some of the Chinese pieces date back to the Ming Dynasty. The rooms will give you some indication of how royalty must have lived: a chandelier over the bed, Priscilla curtains with swagged valance, print wallpaper and plush Victorian-era furniture. No detail has been overlooked. Christmas is extra special—a towering tree is decorated with antique ornaments and hundreds of lights and candles are placed throughout the mansion. Next door to Tarado, a small store sells antiques and crafted Christmas items. If you're really lucky, there may be a concert or a dance in the **Lamplighter Ballroom** (formerly the high-school gym). Advance reservations required. **Rt. 1, Box 53, Arriba, CO 80804; (719) 768-3468.**

GENOA

Genoa Tower—

If you're into two-headed calves and things from Grandma's attic, then you'll probably get a kick out of the Genoa Tower. Like a bad commercial, it makes itself known from the interstate. Actually, after a long drive across the high plains, this is a good place to stretch your legs. The Genoa Tower has one of the largest collections of curiosities to be found anywhere: Indian artifacts, hundreds of branding irons, antique guns, mutated animals—the list goes on and on. Some of the pieces are really crazy, but locals warned us not to believe everything we encountered. Of course, the jackalopes are authentic.

The view from the top of the tower is impressive. On a clear day you can see into six states, a fact that got this place a mention in Ripley's *Believe It or Not.* One part of the museum has a display of old-time gadgets—if you can guess what any 10 of them were used for, your modest admission fee will be refunded. Enjoy. Open year-round, 8 am–8 pm. Located in Genoa, just off Interstate 70 at Exit 371; **(719) 763-2309.**

The Pheasant

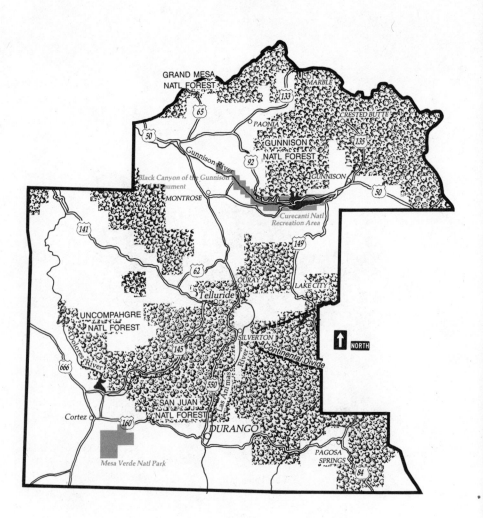

GRAND MESA
NATL FOREST

MARBLE

133

CRESTED BUTTE

65

PAONIA

50

Gunnison River

GUNNISON
NATL FOREST

135

92

GUNNISON

Black Canyon of the Gunnison
Monument

50

MONTROSE

Curecanti Natl
Recreation Area

149

62

UNCOMPAHGRE
NATL FOREST

OURAY

LAKE CITY

Telluride

NORTH

Dolores River

145

SILVERTON

Continental Divide

666

550

Las Animas River

SAN JUAN
NATL FOREST

160

Cortez

DURANGO

PAGOSA
SPRINGS

Mesa Verde Natl Park

84

SOUTHWEST REGION

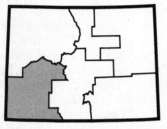

Black Canyon Country

This intriguing area of western Colorado, which we refer to as Black Canyon country, is seldom seen by residents, let alone out-of-state visitors. That it is overlooked and underdeveloped is a major part of its appeal. Black Canyon country encompasses a large area with deep canyons, lush valleys, towering mountains and far-reaching views.

The focal point of this area is the **Black Canyon of the Gunnison National Monument**, one of the most magnificent canyons in the world. As deep as 2,900 feet and as narrow as 1,300 feet, this snaking 50-mile-long chasm draws hundreds of thousands of visitors each year, many of whom take a brief look and then move along to another part of the state. But the Black Canyon is not something to see in a hurry. So take the time to camp overnight or to do some hiking, perhaps down one of the steep trails to the river far below.

The waters of the Gunnison River flow north, eventually emerging from the Black Canyon and Gunnison Gorge to be joined by the North Fork of the Gunnison, which flows out of the beautiful North Fork Valley to the east. Ranches and fruit orchards are spread throughout the valley; Grand Mesa to the north and the West Elk Mountains to the southeast provide an unbelievably picturesque setting. The small towns of Crawford, Hotchkiss and Paonia are great jumping-off places for fishing, hiking and river floating. Or you may want to just sit around and enjoy the views.

West of the Black Canyon lies the Uncompahgre Plateau and the fairly large towns of Montrose and Delta. Both towns are good way stations along Hwy. 50 and offer plenty of motels. Your best bet, however, would be to camp at the monument or to drive to the more scenic towns in the North Fork Valley.

HISTORY

Into the 1880s, Ute Indians hunted plentiful game and foraged in the area around the Black Canyon and the North Fork Valley. A Ute trail that came down out of the Uncompahgre Plateau to the west went through present-day Delta and up to Grand Mesa to the north. The Ute council tree, an ancient cottonwood tree that still stands in north Delta, was a famous meeting place for the Indians.

The first Europeans in the area were probably Friars Dominguez and Escalante, who passed through in 1776. Hwy. 92, between Delta and Hotchkiss, is lined with numerous historical markers where the two men camped. Trappers entered the area in the 1820s, but did not leave much of a record of their findings. French trapper Antoine Roubidoux built a trading post just west of Delta in 1830 and named it Fort Uncompahgre. He was successful until the Utes burned it down in 1837.

By 1880 the Anglos' desire for the mineral-rich country of the San Juans became too great and the Utes were pushed off their land, which included Black Canyon country. Following the miners were cattlemen and farmers, who quickly began to settle the land from Montrose north to Delta and up the North Fork Valley. The original ranchers moved their herds from Gunnison to the hills just north of Crawford, which is still a cattle town. Today, a ride along Hwy. 92 near Crawford may be interrupted by a herd of cattle being driven down the road.

Pioneers Sam Wade and Enos T. Hotchkiss were some of the first settlers to introduce fruit trees to the North Fork Valley. For years the produce of the valley consistently won competitions at the World's Fair. Although a vicious frost in 1912 killed most of the productive orchards in Hotchkiss, today the fruit has made a comeback. Paonia, 10 miles up the valley from Hotchkiss, was spared the devastation of 1912 because of its Million Dollar Wind, which blows in early morning and late afternoon, preventing serious frost damage. Today, Paonia is famous for its sweet cherries as well as pears, peaches, apricots, plums and grapes. Paonia once made it into *Ripley's Believe It or Not* for having more churches per capita than any other place in the country.

GETTING THERE

From Denver, Black Canyon country can be reached several ways. The quickest way may be heading 250 miles west on Interstate 70 to Grand Junction and then south on Hwy. 50 for 40 miles to Delta. A scenic alternative from Denver is to turn south (left) off Interstate 70 at Glenwood Springs onto Hwy. 82 and drive 12 miles to Carbondale. At Carbondale, turn onto Hwy. 133, which takes you up the Crystal River Valley past Redstone, over McClure Pass and down into the Upper North Fork Valley above Paonia. Both Montrose and Delta are serviced by

Greyhound Trailways Bus Lines. Montrose has one of the finest airports in western Colorado, with daily flights from Denver.

MAJOR ATTRACTIONS

BLACK CANYON OF THE GUNNISON NATIONAL MONUMENT

Wallace Hanson, a US geologist who surveyed the Black Canyon in the 1950s, had this to say:

Several Western canyons exceed the Black Canyon in overall size. Some are larger; some are deeper; some are narrower; and a few have walls as steep. But no other canyon in North America combines the depth, narrowness, sheerness and somber countenance of the Black Canyon.

Most visitors to the Black Canyon agree with these sentiments. The unassuming 6-mile drive on the road to the south rim of this spectacular canyon gives no indication of what awaits. Suddenly you're looking down into the yawning chasm of the Black Canyon. Sheer, shadowy rock walls drop more than a half mile down to the Gunnison River, one of the last protected stretches of river in western Colorado. Entering the deep, narrow passage to the east, the river snakes its way northwest for more than 50 miles before making its way to open country.

Along the deepest, most spectacular 12 miles of this canyon, the Black Canyon of the Gunnison National Monument allows visitors a glimpse at one of the most awesome geologic sites in the world. You can visit the canyon from either the south rim or the north rim. Most people choose the easily accessible (and often crowded) south rim, though some prefer the other, which is more remote and less developed.

Geology—

Many people who see the Black Canyon wonder how it could ever have been sliced through the surrounding gentle countryside. The answer is erosion. More than 2 million years ago, volcanic debris from the West Elk Mountains to the east and the San Juan Mountains to the south accumulated in the Black Canyon area. The ancient Gunnison River, making its way west, began cutting through the soft debris, eventually hitting the harder and much older rock of the Gunnison uplift. Since the river's course and steep banks had already been established, all it could do was wear away at the harder, underlying rock.

History—

The Ute Indians dared not enter the Black Canyon of the Gunnison. Calling the area *Tomichi*, meaning "land of high cliffs and plenty water," they preferred instead a view from the rim. Game was plentiful, and the Utes hunted buffalo and deer by driving them into traps or over some smaller cliffs in the area. On the north rim of the Black Canyon some of these old traps and pits can still be found. The first documentation of the river was given in 1853 by the Gunnison party that was scouting a transcontinental railroad route. In the 1880s, a survey crew for the Denver & Rio Grande Railroad was the first to bring up an intriguing possibility—diverting some of the water from the Gunnison River to irrigate the arid Uncompahgre Valley to the west by tunneling through the rock.

With this idea in mind, people began to talk of its possibilities, though most thought it was absurd. In order to irrigate the valley, a 9-mile tunnel would have to be drilled with pinpoint accuracy through solid rock. If the dream were to become reality, an accurate survey of the "impassable" canyon would be necessary.

In September 1900, William W. Torrence and four other men set off in two wooden boats on a 30-mile journey through the canyon, expecting to emerge four or five days later. Wrong. The second day out they lost one of the boats, which contained most of their food and survey equipment. After three long weeks the weary crew had made it only 14 miles. Finally they reached a narrow section of the canyon where 60-foot-high boulders and cascading waterfalls blocked their way. Unable to portage around the boulders or to turn back, they were forced to climb the dangerous 2,000-foot-high cliffs. After 12 hair-raising hours they reached the rim, but Torrence was more determined than ever to complete his mission. The next year he returned with A.L. Fellows. The two men set out in rubber rafts. The accounts of this voyage are intriguing. At one point they had lost the last of their food but somehow managed to corner a mountain goat; Torrence held onto it while Fellows killed it. Finally they made it through the canyon, and Fellows's notes provided the information needed to begin the routing of the diversion tunnel. The project began in 1903, but it was not easy—workers cursed the dense rock, staggering heat, scalding hot springs and poisonous gas pockets. Not surprisingly, everyone cheered when the tunnel was completed in 1909. President Taft presided at the opening ceremony.

In 1933, President Hoover declared the most spectacular 12 miles of the canyon a national monument. Although three dams—Blue Mesa, Morrow Point and Crystal (see Major Attractions in the **Gunnison and Crested Butte** chapter)—have reduced the flow of the mighty Gunnison through the canyon, it is a compelling, pristine area that should not be missed.

Getting There—To reach the south rim from Montrose, head east on Hwy. 50 for 8 miles and turn left. Drive the 6-mile paved road to the monument boundary. The north rim can be reached from Hotchkiss by heading southeast on Hwy. 92 for 13 miles to Crawford Reservoir. Turn right at the sign and continue 11 miles on the dirt road. The North Rim Rd. is closed in winter.

RECREATION INFORMATION
Camping—

South Rim Campground has 102 sites. **East Portal Campground**, along the river at the bottom of East Portal Rd., has 12 tent sites. **North Rim Campground** has 13 sites. A fee is charged at each of these campgrounds; all are closed in winter.

Fishing—

Lower Gunnison River—From both the north and south rims, several difficult trails descend on steep grades to the Gunnison River far below (see page 347). If you can make it down to the river's edge, chances are you'll be rewarded. Deep pools and large trout, many in the five-pound range, are lurking within the canyon—and because the river is so hard to reach, the fishing pressure is fairly light. In some places there is room to pitch a tent and fish for a few days at the bottom of the spectacular canyon. Flies and lures only. Try a large, weighted wet fly or nymph: Stone Fly, Woolly Worm or Muddler Minnow; on top a 12 to 16 Royal Wulff or an Adams are local favorites. The Panther Martin lure works wonders.

Just south of the monument boundary on the south rim, the steep and twisting East Portal Rd. leads down to the river's edge below Crystal Reservoir. It's good fishing from the bank, and there is a small campground (no RVs). Fishing in the Gold Medal water downstream from the monument can be great (see page 346 for more information).

Hiking and Backpacking—

Into the Canyon—Anyone thinking about hiking down to the river from the rim should keep this in mind—the trails are very rough, tiring and can be dangerous. It's also easy to lose your way as the trails are not well marked. Campsites along the river are very limited, but the fishing is superb. In summer, be on the lookout for tall poison ivy plants, which are found along most of the trails and along the river. All backpackers heading down one of the trails need to register with the park ranger.

Listed below are the trails from the south rim:

Tomichi Trail drops 1,800 feet and takes about one hour (ascent is three hours). Two campsites are available along a half-mile stretch of river. **Gunnison Point Trail** drops 1,800 feet and takes an hour and a half to descend (ascent is three hours). Three campsites are located along a 0.75-mile stretch of the river. **Warner Point Trail**, the longest route to the inner canyon in the park, drops 2,660 feet and takes two and a half hours (ascent is five hours). Five campsites are located along a 1.5-mile stretch of river.

Trails accessible from the north rim are as follows: **S.O.B. Draw** is well named and drops 1,800 feet, taking two hours (ascent is four hours). There are six campsites along a 2-mile stretch of the river. **Long Draw** is a straight shot, 1,800-foot drop, taking one and a half hours (three-hour ascent) with many loose rocks and large boulders along the way. There is only one campsite on a quarter-mile stretch of the river. **Slide Draw** drops 1,600 feet, takes one and a half hours (ascent is four and a half hours) and has two campsites along a 0.75-mile stretch of the river.

On the Rim—Stop in at the visitors center at the south rim for a map of short hiking trails that provide great views of the canyon. On the north rim, the quarter-mile **Chasm View Trail** heads from the campground to a great canyon observation point. Take the time for a hike—it's the best way to see the wildlife of the canyon. Golden eagles, mule deer, mountain lions and even black bears make their home here.

Scenic Drives—

In the Monument—The roads running along both the south and north rims within the monument offer great views of the canyon and the surrounding area. **South Rim Dr.** has pull-offs with views from Tomichi Point and a spectacular view across the canyon to Painted Wall, the highest rock cliff in the state. If you look closely you may see climbers on the wall, making their way very slowly to the top. Pick up a pamphlet at the visitors center, which provides more information about sites along the drive. Just outside of the southern monument boundary, a very steep paved road winds its way down to the East Portal of the irrigation tunnel, just at Crystal Dam. No RVs are allowed on the road and regular cars should have good brakes. **North Rim Dr.** also provides a number of good views.

Scenic Highway 92—From the north side, consider a longer but spectacular drive along Hwy. 92, which heads southeast along the canyon and Curecanti National Recreation Area. From Hotchkiss, head southeast on Hwy. 92. The road extends 52 miles, providing great views of the far-off San Juan Mountains and Curecanti Needle before joining Hwy. 50 at Blue Mesa Reservoir. From the junction at Hwy. 50 you head west to Montrose and then north to Delta and east on Hwy. 92 back to Hotchkiss.

Visitors Center—

Located at the south rim, the visitors center is open from Memorial Day through Labor Day. There are exhibits on the history, flora, fauna and geology of the canyon. Daily programs, guided walks and demonstrations are given. Open Memorial Day to mid-Sept. 8 am–8 pm daily. Closed the rest of the year.

For More Information—

Contact the **Black Canyon of the Gunnison Park Superintendent** at PO Box 1648, 2233 E. Main St., Montrose, CO 81402; (303) 249-7036.

The Squirrel

FESTIVALS AND EVENTS

Crazy River Raft Race
mid-June
This event is wild. Individuals and groups build "crazy" rafts and float them down a 7-mile stretch of the Gunnison River below the Black Canyon. Dozens of prizes are given out to the contestants, but most people are there for a good party. Festivities kick off with a Saturday morning parade of the crews and their rafts. For more information, contact the Delta Chamber of Commerce, 301 Main St., Delta, CO 81416; (303) 874-8616 or 1-800-228-7009.

Paonia Cherry Days
early July
This three-day festival, celebrating the cherry harvest, has been a tradition for years. A parade, a barbecue, a talent show, crafts, games, fireworks and the crowning of the Cherry Day Queen pack people in from miles around. And, of course, there are plenty of cherries and cherry pies to eat. Call (303) 527-3886 for more information.

OUTDOOR ACTIVITIES

FISHING
Crawford Reservoir—
This popular recreation area has good fishing for 10-inch rainbows and some warm-water species, especially perch. The catfish here can get really big—some over 15 pounds. Crawford Reservoir also has a campground, a swimming beach and boat ramps. There is a fee to get to this large reservoir. Located a mile south of Crawford on Hwy. 92.

Curecanti National Recreation Area—
Curecanti encompasses the reservoirs on the Gunnison River above the national monument. Fishing on Blue Mesa, Morrow Point and Crystal reservoirs can be very good. For more information see the Major Attractions section in the Gunnison and Crested Butte chapter.

Lower Gunnison River—
Don't miss fishing this Gold Medal stretch of the Lower Gunnison as it flows out of the Black Canyon of the Gunnison National Monument down to the confluence with the North Fork. It contains some of the finest trout water in Colorado. Recently, a Division of Wildlife employee estimated there were more than 10,000 trout larger than six inches in each mile of the Lower Gunnison. A good road provides fairly easy access to the river from the north. From Delta drive 14 miles east on Hwy. 92 to a sign marked Gunnison Forks Wildlife Management Area River Access. Turn right and head a mile south to the confluence of the North Fork and the Gunnison River. Cross the North Fork on a footbridge and walk up the Gunnison River on a 4-mile trail leading up to the Smith Fork. The fishing all along this stretch is excellent for large trout. Since this is the easiest access to this prime portion of the river, the fishing pressure is fairly heavy.

It is possible to reach the Gunnison River above the Smith Fork, but getting there is involved. The water just below the monument in the Gunnison Gorge is best fished from a boat with a guide. Several companies offer this service. The one with the most experience is Hank Hotze of Gunnison River Expeditions, PO Box 604, Hotchkiss, CO 81419; (303) 527-3648. If you want to head down on your own to try some bank fishing or wading, there are four trails leading to the water's edge from the plateau on the west side of the river. It takes a high clearance vehicle to reach the trailheads. For more information on the specific routes, see the Gunnison Gorge

Trails in the Hiking and Backpacking section.

Lower Gunnison River within the National Monument—

See the Major Attractions section.

Sweitzer Lake—

Fishing for warm-water species can be good, but the fish are inedible due to a high selenium content. To reach the reservoir head 1.5 miles south from Delta on Hwy. 50 and then east for a half mile on Park Entrance Rd.

HIKING AND BACKPACKING

Hiking and backpacking in the Black Canyon area are very diverse. Trails leading down into the Black Canyon and the Gunnison Gorge provide access to excellent fishing and to the river ecosystem with its multitude of wildlife. To the east of the Black Canyon, Gunnison National Forest offers pine and aspen forests as well as high alpine scenery. For information about hiking and backpacking opportunities in the area contact the **Delta Ranger District Office** at 2250 Hwy. 50, Delta, CO 81416; (303) 874-7691, or the **Paonia Ranger District Office** at PO Box 1030, N. Rio Grande Ave., Paonia, CO 81428; (303) 527-4131.

Black Canyon of the Gunnison National Monument Trails—

See the Major Attractions section.

Curecanti Trail—

This 10.5-mile trail heads up Curecanti Creek through aspen and spruce fir and into mountain grasslands. The creek has created a canyon with many unusual rock formations and spires. The trail eventually reaches Curecanti Pass after an elevation gain of 1,600 feet. From Crawford, head south on Hwy. 92 for 25 miles to the Curecanti Creek crossing, turn left onto Forest Rd. 720 and proceed 8 miles to the trailhead.

Gunnison Gorge Trails—

Located just downriver (north) of the monument boundary, this section of the Gunnison River offers beautiful scenery and Gold Medal fishing. There are four trails that lead down to the river from the west rim. Be on the lookout for river otters and bighorn sheep, which were reintroduced to this area in the last few years. Access to the trails is possible from Hwy. 50 between Montrose and Delta. From Montrose, head north on Hwy. 50 for 6 miles and turn right on Falcon Rd. Proceed 3.6 miles to Peach Valley Rd. and turn northeast. From Peach Valley Rd. there are four roads that break off to the east, leading to four trailheads.

After 1.5 miles, the first access road (four-wheel-drive vehicle recommended) heads right for 10 miles down to the **Chukar Trail** trailhead. Chukar Trail drops 500 feet in a 1-mile hike to the river.

Another 2.1 miles down Peach Valley Rd. the second access road (four-wheel-drive vehicle recommended) turns right and heads a mile and a half to **Bobcat Trail**. Bobcat Trail drops 800 feet to the river in 1 mile.

Following Peach Valley Rd. for another 1.4 miles leads you to the third access road (four-wheel-drive vehicle recommended) on the right, which winds 2 miles to **Duncan Trail**. This steep 1-mile trail drops 900 feet to the river.

Two more miles along Peach Valley Rd. lead you to the last access road (four-wheel-drive vehicle recommended), heading right and continuing 2.5 miles to **Ute Trail**. Ute Trail descends 1,200 feet to the river in 4.5 miles.

Gunnison National Forest—

Three Lakes Trail—This easy 3-mile loop takes you to a waterfall and provides impressive views into the West Elk Wilderness Area. As the name indicates, there are also three lakes along the way with pretty good fishing. To reach the trailhead from Paonia, head northeast on Hwy. 133 and then right on Hwy. 12. Drive about 14 miles to Forest Rd. 706 and turn right.

Proceed 2 miles to the trailhead at Lost Lake Campground.

HORSEBACK RIDING

Needle Rock Ranch—

Located on the western boundary of the West Elk Wilderness Area, Needle Rock Ranch provides good trail horses and access to the wilderness area. Full- and half-day rides are offered Mon.–Sat. during the summer and into the fall. To reach the ranch from Crawford, head east on the road between the church and the post office, then follow the signs. **4345 F Rd., PO Box 305, Crawford, CO 81415; (303) 921-3050.**

LLAMA TREKKING

Backcountry Llamas—

One great way to experience the beauty of the West Elk Wilderness Area of Gunnison National Forest is by taking a llama trek with Backcountry Llamas. Working out of Paonia, Paul and Fran Cranor run trips into the wilderness area from a number of trailheads. Hike along the trails while the llamas carry most of your supplies. Treks from a half day to four nights are offered. Be sure to set up a trek well in advance, as there are a limited number each season. Special dietary requirements are no problem. Contact Paul and Fran Cranor at **PO Box 1287, Paonia, CO 81428; (303) 527-3844.**

RIVER FLOATING

The Lower Gunnison—

Although it's hard to believe, there are some expert kayakers who run the river through the 12-mile stretch of the Black Canyon of the Gunnison National Monument. This is the canyon the Utes feared and early settlers said could never be navigated. Nonetheless, each year determined kayakers run the Class IV and Class V rapids, portaging around drop-offs as high as 17 feet. A lot of planning is necessary for this section. Most kayakers put in at the East Portal, which they reach via the steep road just outside of the monument boundary on the south rim.

Below the monument, the canyon opens up a bit into the Gunnison Gorge, a stretch of river that offers excellent floating. This section of the river is home to many species of birds, including golden eagles, red-tailed hawks, prairie falcons and great horned owls. Currently, a plan to dam this section of the river threatens to flood this last free-flowing section of the Black Canyon below the monument. There are no roads into this 16-mile stretch of the river down to the North Fork confluence—most boaters carry their crafts in on the 1-mile Chukar Trail. For directions to Chukar Trail see the Hiking and Backpacking section. Rafters take out at the campground next to Hwy. 92 at the Gunnison–North Fork confluence. From here down through Delta the river is calm.

Below the confluence with the Uncompahgre River at Delta, the Gunnison cuts through the maroon and purple Morrison strata, eventually reaching the exposed red sandstone of Dominguez Canyon. Within the canyon walls are many unusual rock formations—one resembles a profile of Richard Nixon. This 39-mile stretch between Delta and Whitewater is fairly calm but beautiful.

Outfitters—

Gunnison River Expeditions—Hank Hotze began running river trips down the Gunnison River in the 1970s, and today his operation has been outfitting river runners longer than any other in the area. The main stretch he runs is the Gunnison Gorge, which combines great rafting, Gold Medal fishing and plentiful wildlife. For more information contact Hotze at **PO Box 604, Hotchkiss, CO 81419; (303) 527-3648.**

Dvorak's Kayak & Rafting Expeditions—One of the most respected outfitters in the state. Offers multi-day expeditions on the Gunnison and other Colorado rivers. **1-800-824-3795** toll free.

SEEING AND DOING

FISH HATCHERY

Hotchkiss National Fish Hatchery—
Located 3 miles southwest of Hotchkiss (1 mile south of the small town of Lazear), the Hotchkiss National Fish Hatchery is a main supplier of rainbow trout for reservoirs in western Colorado and New Mexico. Millions of eggs are hatched in the controlled ponds, and when the hatchlings are the right size (three to nine inches) they are shipped to various reservoirs in special trucks resembling aquariums on wheels. The public can tour the facility year-round from 7:30 am–4 pm daily, free of charge. There are a few picnic tables nearby. From Hotchkiss, head west on Hwy. 92 for 2 miles and turn left (south) to Lazear. **(303) 872-3170.**

MUSEUMS

Ute Indian Museum—
Dedicated to Ouray, the chief of the Southern Ute Tribe, and his wife, Chipeta, this museum provides information and displays about the Ute Indians of Colorado. Artifacts (many of which belonged to famous Utes such as Ouray, Ignacio, Colorow and Buckskin Charlie), dioramas and other information help you to gain insight into traditional Ute culture, which ended so tragically. A large collection of ceremonial and traditional artifacts were provided by Thomas McKee, a local photographer who lived with the Utes beginning in the 1880s. Just next to the museum building is Chipeta's grave. A fee is charged. Open Memorial Day–Labor Day, Mon.–Sat. 10 am–5 pm, Sun. 1–5 pm. Located at the southern end of Montrose, just off Hwy. 550. **17253 Chipeta Dr., Montrose, CO 81401; (303) 249-3098.**

NIGHTLIFE

Thunder Mountain Lives Tonight!—
If the kids get restless consider taking them to "the greatest outdoor show west of the Mississippi." Thunder Mountain Lives Tonight! is an extravaganza spiced with music, humor and a cast of 60 people. It recreates many historical episodes of Delta County, with Thunder Mountain (Grand Mesa) in the distance. Started in 1986 to help out the faltering local economy, the show has received rave reviews from magazines, newspapers and even NBC's "Today Show." It's an entertaining way to learn about Indian culture and the life of pioneers in the area. There is a fee charged, but a discount is given if you buy your tickets in advance. The show runs from late June until early Sept., Tues.–Sat. 6–8 pm. Located at the Delta Roundup Club Arena, 4 miles east of Delta off Hwy. 92. For reservations and information contact the **Delta Chamber of Commerce** at **301 Main St., Delta, CO 81416; 1-800-228-7009** toll free or **(303) 874-8616.**

SCENIC DRIVES

Black Canyon of the Gunnison—
For information see the Major Attractions section.

Escalante Canyon—
Located northwest of Delta, this starkly beautiful and historic canyon drive is worth a look. The road follows Escalante Creek up toward the Uncompahgre Plateau. Within easy access are a couple of rocks displaying Ute petroglyphs and an area where dinosaur digs have been conducted. Many old homesteads remain in the area. One in particular is very interesting—Capt. Smith's Cabin. In 1907, Capt. H.A. Smith, at the age of 67, moved into the canyon and built a fascinating stone house. One wall is built into a solid slab of rock while the other three were made from rough-cut stones. This ex-Union Army officer was a skilled stonemason who claimed to have learned his techniques from Indians. In the cabin, a six-foot-long sleeping area was cut into the rock, as well as a small niche for a bedside pistol. Remember, this was the

Wild West.

To reach Escalante Canyon, head northwest from Delta on Hwy. 50 toward Grand Junction and turn left onto County Rd. 650. Follow the road down to the river and across the bridge. There are a number of side trips you can make from here. A well-marked signpost gives directions and information about the different sites. If you need more information about this area, visit the **Delta Chamber of Commerce, 301 Main St., Delta, CO 81416; (303) 874-8616.**

Kebler Pass—

See the **Gunnison and Crested Butte** chapter.

WHERE TO STAY

ACCOMMODATIONS

Both Montrose and Delta are large towns with plenty of motels along the main thoroughfare for people just passing through. The unique lodging opportunities listed here are located up the North Fork of the Gunnison, near Hotchkiss and Crawford. They're a bit off the beaten track but are worth the drive.

Saddle Mountain Guest Ranch — $$ to $$$

Located 6 miles east of Crawford in Gunnison National Forest, Saddle Mountain has to be one of the most accommodating guest ranches around. If you want to stay one day or one month—fine. If you want to take part in planned activities or prefer keeping to yourself, that's OK, too.

This 250-acre spread is less than a mile from the West Elk Wilderness Area. Horses are available at the ranch for an additional charge if you want to explore the area on a saddle. A large lake on the property is stocked with rainbow, brown and cutthroat trout and the Smith Fork River, which runs through the property, is stocked by the forest service. In winter, you can cross-country ski in the rolling hills around the ranch and then relax in the hot tub.

Accommodations include 11 rooms at the main lodge, three cabins and an old ranch house with five quaint bedrooms upstairs. The Watsons, owners of the ranch, serve delicious down-home meals in the dining hall. The food has a good reputation in the area and many people from nearby Crawford call ahead for dinner. Saddle Mountain Guest Ranch is out of the way and reasonably priced. If that's what you're looking for, then we recommend a stay. Be sure to call ahead for lodging or dining reservations. To reach the ranch from Hotchkiss, head 11 miles southeast on Hwy. 92 to Crawford and turn left on the road between the church and the post office. Drive 3 miles, turn right and proceed another 3 miles to the ranch. **4536 E. 50 Dr., Crawford, CO 81415; (303) 921-6321.**

Campstool Ranch Bed and Breakfast — $$

George and Winnie Tracy are hosts at this peaceful getaway. Located on a working cattle ranch on the north side of the Black Canyon, Campstool Ranch Bed and Breakfast is a good jumping-off place for activities in the area. This comfortable stone home was built in 1912 and has three rooms available with a shared bath. Continental breakfast is included in the room rate, but for a small additional charge Winnie will fix you a Rancher breakfast guaranteed to fill you up. Open year-round. Located in Maher, 5 miles south of Crawford on Hwy. 92. **PO Box 14, Maher, CO 81421; (303) 921-6461.**

Ye Olde Oasis — $$

This peaceful, restored farmhouse in the middle of the orchards of the North Fork Valley is a perfect place to get away from the tempo of the city. Built in 1907, Ye Olde Oasis is full of restored antique furniture and country knickknacks. Dwight and Rose Ward have only been operating the bed and breakfast since 1986, but the response from guests has been tremendous.

When you get here you'll feel like family in no time. Every morning, fresh eggs collected from the hen house are prepared with toast, bacon or sausage, coffee and juice. Rose will also make picnic lunches or serve a special dinner with some advance notice (extra charge). Mick, Scout, Ranger and Heidi, their well-behaved shelties, will work their way into your heart—unless you're allergic to them. **3142 J Rd., PO Box 609, Hotchkiss, CO 81419; (303) 872-3794.**

CAMPING

Black Canyon of the Gunnison National Monument—

For information on camping on the north and south rims of the Black Canyon, see the Major Attractions section.

Crawford State Recreation Area—

Located a mile south of Crawford on Hwy. 92 at Crawford Reservoir. There are 61 sites and a fee is charged. Open all year.

In Gunnison National Forest—

Smith Fork Picnic Ground offers four campsites for free camping. To reach it, head southeast from Hotchkiss on Hwy. 92 to Crawford and turn left onto Forest Rd. 712. Proceed about 7 miles east to the picnic ground. **Erickson Springs Campground** is located in the upper North Fork Valley. From Paonia, head northeast on Hwy. 133 for about 12 miles and turn right on County Rd. 12. Proceed 6 miles to the campground. There are five sites and no fee is charged. From Erickson Springs Campground head up Hwy. 12 another 7 miles to Forest Rd. 706, turn right and

proceed about 2 miles to **Lost Lake Campground**. This campground has heavy use in summer; there are 15 sites and no fee is charged. **McClure Campground** is located on McClure Pass, 12 miles north of Paonia Reservoir on Hwy. 133. There are 19 sites and a fee is charged.

Paonia State Recreation Area—

Located about 16 miles northeast of Paonia on Hwy. 133 at Paonia Reservoir. There are 23 sites and a fee is charged.

Private Campgrounds—

Crystal Meadows Ranch—Crystal Meadows Ranch, with its gorgeous location at the base of Kebler Pass, has plenty of RV hookups and tent sites. Other attractions include a fishing lake, laundry facilities, a restaurant and showers (extra charge). Located just out of Somerset in the North Fork Valley. From Hotchkiss, drive 17 miles northeast on Hwy. 133. **30682 County Rd. 12, Somerset, CO 81434; (303) 929-5656.**

Delta/Grand Mesa KOA Campground—This is one of the best-equipped RV campgrounds available, with complete RV hookups and tent sites. Full amenities include showers, a store and even a swimming pool. Located a mile east of Delta on Hwy. 92. **1675 Hwy. 92, Delta, CO 81416; (303) 874-3918.**

The Hangin' Tree RV Park—RV hookups, tent sites, showers and everything else you could possibly expect to find at an RV park. Located 2 miles south of Montrose on Hwy. 550 (across from the Ute Indian Museum). **17250 Hwy. 550 S., Montrose, CO 81401; (303) 249-9966.**

WHERE TO EAT

The Glenn Eyrie Restaurant (in Montrose) — $$ to $$$

Located in an old farmhouse surrounded by stately trees, the Glenn Eyrie was a pleasant surprise when we visited in the spring. Inside, the atmosphere is very

comfortable and homey. Lunches and dinners are served at tables out on the lawn or at the more formal tables inside. The food is excellent. Owner and chef Johannes "Steve" Schwathe is from Austria, where he studied in Vienna under the watchful eye of a master chef. The ambitious menu selection is impressive, with entrees ranging from lamb kebab and Chateaubriand Bouquetière to Steak Diane. An entrée with a local twist is the crab-stuffed Colorado trout. The fine wine list is reasonably priced. Reservations are recommended. If you're staying in Montrose or just passing through, stop in for a great meal. Open 11:30 am–2 pm and 5–9 pm Mon.–Sat. in summer; 5–8 pm Mon.–Sat. in winter. **2351 S. Townsend Ave.; 249-9263.**

Sakura (in Montrose) — $$ to $$$

Yayoi Corder has lived in Montrose for more than 20 years and when she opened this restaurant in 1985 people thought she was crazy. A Japanese restaurant in Montrose?! You bet, and it's a good one, too. People from as far away as Telluride rave about it and make the long drive for a plate of her sushi or tempura. The decor is very Japanese, including an intimate tatami room. Great lunch specials ($) and dinners are served. Try the teriyaki chicken and bee. The green tea ice cream is delicious. Imported Japanese beer and saki, as well as a full bar, are available. Lunch is served Mon.–Fri. 11 am–2 pm, dinner Mon.–Sat. 5–9 pm; closed Sun. **411 N. Townsend Ave.; 249-8230.**

Zack's Trading Post
(in Hotchkiss) — $$ to $$$

Zack's is known throughout the area for its succulent barbecued ribs, beef, chicken and ham. Breakfasts are also served. Open 6:30 am–9 pm in summer, 6:30 am–8 pm in winter. Located at the east end of **Bridge St.** in Hotchkiss; **872-3199.**

Boardwalk Restaurant and Lounge (in Crawford) — $ to $$

With its home-cooked meals at very reasonable prices, the Boardwalk deserves a special mention. This restaurant serves great breakfasts and dinners including T-bone steaks for under $10! Well, this is ranch country. Homemade baked goods including their special wheat bread are served with all meals. Dinners come with potato or rice and salad bar or vegetable of the day; fresh bread and rolls are also served. Open 7:30 am–8 pm Thur.–Tues., closed Wed. Located on the main street in Crawford; **64 Hwy. 92; 921-4905.**

Little's Brewery Restaurant (in Paonia) — $ to $$

Finally—a brew pub in Colorado. In Little's basement, Fire Mountain beer is made from scratch; upstairs, fresh kegs are tapped for patrons of the restaurant and bar. Little's amber beer is a good-tasting, distinctive home brew that is also distributed throughout the Western Slope. Hand-hewn wooden ceiling beams and a huge round fireplace adorn the restaurant's interior. It's a comfortable place to kick back and relax while the chef prepares your meal. Dishes include chili beer shrimp, Cajun grilled salmon, chili verde enchiladas and pasta primavera. Kids will love the Jedi burger; both parents and kids will love a slice of coconut cheesecake to top off the meal. Open seven days a week for lunch and dinner from 11 am–10 pm. Just west of Paonia on **Hwy. 133; (303) 527-6141.**

—————— SERVICES ——————

Delta Chamber of Commerce—

301 Main St., Delta, CO 81416; (303) 874-8616.

Hotchkiss Chamber of Commerce—

PO Box 727, Hotchkiss, CO 81419; (303) 872-3226.

Montrose County Chamber of Commerce—

550 N. Townsend Ave., Montrose, CO 81401; (303) 249-6360.

Paonia Chamber of Commerce—

PO Box 366, Paonia, CO 81428; (303) 527-3886.

Cortez

Southwestern Colorado should be the destination of anyone interested in learning about the culture of the prehistoric Indians called the *Anasazi*— a Navajo word meaning "Ancient Ones." This area was once alive with Anasazi settlements until their civilization vanished mysteriously about AD 1300. Today, this corner of the state continues to be an important location for exploration, excavation, study and interpretation by archaeologists. Most visitors coming here blast their way to Mesa Verde National Park. Mesa Verde, with its wondrous cliff dwellings, is the most popular site, but only scrapes the surface when it comes to learning about what this area has to offer. Consider staying for a few days to understand more about the Anasazi far off the beaten track.

The hub for the area is the town of Cortez, lying in the Montezuma Valley where the San Juan Mountains and the high desert come together. With a population of 8,000, Cortez is basically a sleepy agricultural center, though it has recently been awakened by a tourism boom.

The surrounding area is as diverse as it is beautiful. As the soaring peaks of the San Juans descend to the desert, the Colorado Plateau marks the transition with weirdly eroded canyons, pine-clad mesas and rolling foothills. Southwest of Cortez is the ever-present Sleeping Ute Mountain. Entangled in Ute legend, the prominent slopes of the mountain clearly show the outline of a sleeping Indian with his arms folded across his chest. It is said that the sleeping Ute is a great warrior god who fought a fierce battle with the powers of evil. He once lay down to rest and the blood pouring from his wounds turned into water for all creatures to drink.

There are fantastic options for fishing and hiking in San Juan National Forest. The newly completed McPhee Dam, near the small town of Dolores, has created a number of recreational opportunities, from water skiing to fishing to canoeing in a "wakeless zone." The reservoir's constant supply of irrigation water means that pinto beans and a few other crops can better survive the long, dry summers, but the pristine Dolores River Canyon and a multitude of Anasazi artifacts have been lost forever.

HISTORY

Some 2,000 years ago, nomadic Indians roamed southwestern Colorado while gathering plants and hunting game. There was no written history and, consequently, what is known about these people today is sketchy and speculative. Archaeologists agree, however, that the Indians settled in the mesa lands and began primitive farming of beans, corn and squash in the rich red soil of the valleys and eventually on the mesa tops. These early inhabitants lived in shallow caves and wove baskets. By AD 450 these Basket Makers had also learned how to make pottery and crude pit dwellings. Also around this time, the bow and arrow replaced the primitive atlatl spear thrower.

Experiencing dramatic cultural advancements, the Basket Makers emerged as a Pueblo culture around AD 750. It is likely that the Pueblo period was influenced by more advanced cultures from the south. Many rich and varied cultural traits can be traced to this period of development. At this time, mesa-top homes built of stone and masonry replaced the subterranean pit houses. Underground rooms (kivas) were reserved solely for ceremonial purposes. Cotton weaving and fire resistant pottery also improved the quality of life.

The Anasazi gradually sought refuge beneath overhanging cliffs, including the ones we know as Mesa Verde. Reasons for this move are unclear, but accepted theories suggest the cliffs provided protection from the elements as well as from hostile Indians. Many archaeologists believe these ancient people moved there to be closer to natural spring water. By AD 1000 they had developed masonry houses built into the cliffs and a sophisticated artistry, which is aptly demonstrated in their delicate clay pottery. Other groups near Mesa Verde chose to remain closer to their fields by living atop the mesas. The final period of development, after AD 1000, featured fine pottery craftsmanship.

By 1300 the Anasazi had disappeared from Mesa Verde and the Four Corners area for reasons that have never been fully explained. It was not a spontaneous exodus, but rather a gradual migration over the course of many years. Like gypsies, the Anasazi spread out in small groups, eventually losing their cultural identity. The two generally accepted theories are that the Anasazi left because of a prolonged drought and/or were driven out of the area by a hostile force. Other theories suggest that a cooling of the climate, soil depletion and a lack of burnable wood may have contributed to their disappearance. After their departure, their cliff houses and mesa-top communities stood empty, even though Ute tribes lived in the area.

GETTING THERE

Located in southwestern Colorado near the Four Corners, where Utah, Colorado, Arizona and New Mexico converge at one point, Cortez acts as a gateway to traffic coming into the state from the south on Hwys. 160 and 666. From Denver (377 miles to the northeast), Cortez can be reached via Interstate 25 south to Walsenburg and then west on Hwy. 160.

──── MAJOR ATTRACTIONS ────

MESA VERDE NATIONAL PARK

Mesa Verde is a dramatic introduction to the ancient Anasazi culture. With its twisting canyons, panoramic views and outstanding archaeological remains, Mesa Verde continues to fascinate visitors from the US and abroad.

History—

During the apex of the Anasazi civilization—between AD 1000 and 1300—advances in masonry skills allowed the Indians to build huge 100- to 200-room cliff houses, some four stories high. Hundreds of years after the Anasazi disappeared, Ute Indians moved into the Mesa Verde area. They knew about the empty cliff dwellings, but kept away, believing the ancient cities to be haunted. Spanish explorers and settlers looked around the area for many years before white trappers, prospectors and settlers entered the region, but they never saw the ruins. Abandoned for almost 600 years, the interconnected settlements at Mesa Verde were finally rediscovered in December 1888.

While looking for stray cattle during a snowstorm, ranchers Richard Wetherill and Charlie Mason stumbled upon Cliff Palace, one of the largest sites in Mesa Verde with more than 200 rooms and 23 kivas. It was after this discovery that word of the incredible cliff dwellings became common knowledge. In the 1890s, many people flocked to the area to collect artifacts. In 1906, due to persistent lobbying by some Coloradans, the US Congress passed a bill creating Mesa Verde National Park. It was this unusual foresight that helped create the first park in the country set aside exclusively for the preservation of archaeological artifacts.

Getting There—The entrance to the park is located 10 miles east of Cortez on Hwy. 160 halfway to Mancos. From there a narrow paved road snakes its way up the mesa to the south for about 21 miles. The ruins are located in two main areas: Chapin Mesa and the recently opened Wetherill Mesa.

Facts About the Park—

Mesa Verde National Park is well maintained and equipped with facilities to make a visit there convenient and comfortable. There is an extensive network of designated hiking trails in the park. Due to the large number of visitors each year and the potential damage to the artifacts and the environment, straying off the trails is forbidden.

The park is open year-round, but some of the sites are closed during the winter months. For more information, contact: **Mesa Verde National Park, CO 81330; (303) 529-4465 or (303) 529-4475.**

Archaeological Museum—

A visit to the Archaeological Museum will reveal the fascinating history of the Anasazi Indians. Allow plenty of time for this museum before going to look at the major cliff dwellings. In addition to a bookstore, it contains exhibits and artifacts about the Anasazi. Open 8 am–6:30 pm daily; 8 am–5 pm in winter. Free admission.

Helicopter Rides—

For an aerial view of some of the ruins at Mesa Verde and within the Ute Mountain Tribal Park to the south, try a helicopter ride that takes off from Soda Point. For information about the helicopter rides contact **Four Corners Helicopters, Inc., 7553 County Rd. 25, Cortez, CO 81321; (303) 882-4966.**

Mesa Verde is one attraction that should not be missed when visiting this area (sketch by Michael A. Darr).

Lodging and Camping—

The park is close enough to Durango and Cortez to be a day trip, but consider an overnight stay. Waking in the early morning to the intense colors of the rock walls makes it well worth your time. There are two options for staying in the park:

The rooms at the comfortable **Far View Lodge** feature balcony views of the park and the far-off mountains. The lodge also has a restaurant and a lounge. Advance reservations are highly recommended. The lodge is closed from Oct. to May. For reservations and information write: **Far View Lodge, Mesa Verde, c/o PO Box 277, Mancos, CO 81328; (303) 529-4421.**

Located 4 miles from the park entrance, **Morefield Campground,** with its 490 sites (showers available and fee charged), offers the only camping in the park. No reservations are necessary, but camping is on a first-come, first-served basis. Nearby is a general store, a gas station, a gift shop, a snack bar and laundry and shower facilities.

Visitors Center—

There is a visitors center 15 miles from the park entrance that offers information, maps and modern southwestern Indian exhibits. Hours are 8 am–5 pm daily; closed in winter.

OTHER ANASAZI CULTURE SITES

In addition to the spectacular cliff dwellings at Mesa Verde, there are several other places to visit for a more complete understanding of the Anasazi culture, without the frustration of crowds. While wandering in near-solitude around the ruins of Hovenweep or Lowry Pueblo, it is easier to feel the pure isolation of the remote Anasazi villages. On the Ute Mountain Tribal Park Indian Reservation, a Ute guide will take you on a backcountry excursion to out-of-the-way ruins. Or, by taking a tour led by the Cortez Center to a current dig at the town of Yellow Jacket, you will gain a better knowledge of how archaeologists work their magic. Better yet, participate in an excavation at the Sand Canyon archaeological site under the guidance of professional archaeologists. (See the Crow Canyon Archaeological Center section below for more information.) There are many ways of gaining a more complete picture of what this peaceful culture was all about.

ANASAZI HERITAGE CENTER

This excellent archaeological museum, which opened in the summer of 1988, provides an excellent background for understanding the ancient Anasazi culture. Ironically, this facility is a result of the highly controversial McPhee Dam and Reservoir project. To mitigate the damage brought by the reservoir, the federal government was required to contribute 4 percent of the total cost of the dam project toward the preservation and study of Anasazi artifacts found in the area. This included funding the museum, as well as digs in the area now covered by the water of McPhee Reservoir.

In 1977, the Dolores Archaeological Program got underway, discovering 1,600 Anasazi sites, only 125 of which were extensively excavated, sampled and tested before the reservoir was filled in 1986. The museum houses more than 2 million artifacts from these digs, with some of the most outstanding pieces displayed for the public. The "discovery" section of the display room gives people a chance to learn about the Anasazi through hands-on experience: you can grind corn with a stone grinder, examine grains with a microscope and watch a weaver using a loom. Traveling exhibits (some from the Smithsonian) change at least yearly. Be sure to see the eerie three-stage hologram depicting what these ancient people looked like.

Group tours of the Anasazi Heritage Center are available through prior arrangement with the museum staff. This fascinating museum is well worth a look. Open year-round, admission is free. Mon.–Sat. 9

am–5 pm, Sun. 10 am–5 pm. Located just west of the town of Dolores. **27501 Hwy. 184, Dolores, CO 81323; (303) 882-4811.**

Next to the museum are the **Dominguez** and **Escalante** ruins, named for the Franciscan friars who passed through the area in 1776. They were the first white men to document a sighting of Anasazi ruins in Colorado. The Escalante ruins can be reached from the center by a half-mile path.

CORTEZ CENTER

The University of Colorado initiated this nonprofit center in 1987 to help preserve the Anasazi heritage of the Cortez area. The newly refurbished facility has a small museum displaying artifacts from Yellow Jacket and other sites in the area. The exhibits will give you a better understanding of Anasazi culture in areas besides Mesa Verde. An archaeological lab on the premises is staffed by students from the university. Twice a week in summer the museum hosts evening lectures on subjects of interest, including archaeology, astronomy and Native American culture. The museum is open Mon.–Sat. 9 am–5 pm in summer and on a limited basis during the rest of the year. Free admission.

In addition to the museum there are guided half-day and full-day tours of current excavations in the vicinity. The tours leave at 8:30 am and 1 pm in summer only; reserve one day in advance. A fee is charged. All tours leave from the museum. **25 N. Market St., PO Box 1326, Cortez, CO 81321; (303) 565-1151.**

CROW CANYON ARCHAEOLOGICAL CENTER

Entering through a locked door we looked with amazement at row after row of carefully reconstructed ceramic pots and mugs once used by the Anasazi. Sandy Thompson, director of the Crow Canyon Archaeological Center, explained how many of them were unearthed by people on one-week "archaeological vacations." That's right, people from all walks of life come together for one-week sessions of on-site digging, sweating and learning. The

successful privatization of archaeological research through this nonprofit center is a boon to knowledge of the Anasazi.

Participants in the program, operated under the careful supervision of professional archaeologists, are currently excavating a five-acre site called Sand Canyon. After some classroom training, eager volunteers lay out grids and remove dirt inch by inch with trowels, chisels, toothbrushes, buckets and brooms. All of the finds are numbered, catalogued and set aside for further study in the slow winter months. Eventually, all of the finds will be moved to the Anasazi Heritage Center near Dolores. In addition to the digs, volunteers have time to study and test ancient technologies, such as throwing a spear with an atlatl, flint knapping and fire building.

Crow Canyon offers a meaningful vacation alternative to lying around on a beach. All participants receive one week's lodging (shared quarters) and meals, in addition to the planned activities. For prices and more information, contact **Crow Canyon Archaeological Center, 23390 County Rd. K, Cortez, CO 81321; 1-800-422-8975 or (303) 565-8975.**

Self-Guided Tour of the Sand Canyon Pueblo—

A half-hour walk around the Sand Canyon archaeological site under current excavation will add to your appreciation of the science of archaeology. A free trail guide can be picked up at the center near Cortez. **(303) 565-8975.**

HOVENWEEP NATIONAL MONUMENT

Established as a national monument in 1923, Hovenweep (a Ute word meaning "deserted valley") stands as one of the most impressive Anasazi ruins in the Four Corners area. Although the culture of the Hovenweep people was similar to that at Mesa Verde, the structures at Hovenweep are different and are characterized by tall stone towers, some as high as 20 feet.

Looking out across the inhospitable landscape at Hovenweep, it's hard to imagine that prior to AD 1300 the inhabitants planted terraced fields in this dry, rocky landscape. Near the end of their habitation here, they moved from smaller scattered pueblos to larger settlements at the heads of the canyon. It is thought they did this to protect their water sources and fend off invaders.

Facts About the Park—

Hovenweep National Monument straddles the Colorado–Utah border west of Cortez. There are six main sites—**Square Tower** and **Cojon** ruins in Utah, and **Holly, Hackberry Canyon, Cutthroat Castle** and **Goodman Point** ruins in Colorado. Square Tower Ruins is the best preserved of the six sites and the only one that can be reached by car. The others involve a hike. But if you enjoy desert canyon hiking, Hovenweep should not be missed. The square, oval and circular towers are especially spectacular at sunset, and this time of day makes for great photos.

There are a ranger station and a campground near Square Tower Ruins on the Utah side of the border. The campground has no water and charges a fee. The monument and the campground are open year-round.

If you are staying in the Cortez area, a scenic driving loop with stops at Hovenweep and Lowry Pueblo (see below) is highly recommended. From Cortez, head southwest of town for 3 miles on Hwy. 666 and turn right on McElmo Canyon Rd. Drive up this beautiful slickrock canyon over the border into Utah, following the signs to Hovenweep. After 39 miles you arrive at the monument headquarters, where the ranger station, the campground and Square Tower Ruins are located. After spending all the time you want here, drive northeast 25 miles, which takes you back into Colorado. This road brings you near Lowry Pueblo and back to Hwy. 666, 20 miles northwest of Cortez. Along the way you have panoramic views of many Four Corners landmarks—Sleeping Ute Mountain, Mesa Verde Plateau and the La Sal Mountains in Utah. Be sure to inquire locally about road conditions because these rough dirt roads can be impassable after storms.

For more information about Hovenweep, contact the park superintendent at **Mesa Verde National Park, CO 81330; (303) 529-4465.**

LOWRY PUEBLO

Lowry Pueblo, located northwest of Cortez, was built about AD 1000 and inhabited by 100 Indians. It is best known for its large kiva, one of the biggest yet discovered in the American Southwest. The ruins were first excavated in 1928, restored in 1965 and dedicated as a National Historic Landmark in 1967. To reach Lowry Pueblo from Cortez, drive northwest on Hwy. 666 for 20 miles to the town of Pleasant View. Turn left (west) and proceed 9 miles to the site.

UTE MOUNTAIN TRIBAL PARK

In an isolated setting just south of Mesa Verde National Park on the Ute Mountain Indian Reservation are spectacular remains of the Anasazi Indians. The Ute Mountain Tribal Park encompasses these ruins and offers an opportunity for individuals or groups to explore hundreds of ancient cliff and mesa dwellings as well as the unrelated and more recent Ute rock art. Emphasis is placed on experiencing Anasazi ruins within a natural setting. Hiking into the remote sites for a few hours or a few days is a welcome change from the masses of people at Mesa Verde. The Ute Mountain Tribal Park was set up by the tribe to preserve the culture of these ancient people. Stretching over 125,000 acres, centered along a 25-mile stretch of the Mancos River, the park is operated primarily as a primitive area offering no developed amenities—you even have to bring in your own water.

For more information about the Ute Mountain Tribal Park, contact: **Art Cuthair, Ute Mountain Tribal Park, Towaoc, CO 81334; (303) 565-3751, ext. 282.**

Overnight Camping—

Rumor has it that camping is available in the park, down by the banks of the Mancos River. One thing is certain: if you are allowed to camp overnight in the park, you'll need a permit. Check with the tribe for details.

Tour Information—

Because the Anasazi ruins cannot be reached by road, good weather is essential for an enjoyable hike. Tours are usually available by June 1 and continue into autumn on a limited basis, depending on the weather. The tribe asks that visitors to the park make reservations at least three days in advance. All tours are led by an Indian guide and start at the Ute Mountain Pottery Plant, located 12 miles south of Cortez on Hwy. 666. A full-day tour begins each morning at approximately 8 am. *If arranging a tour, be sure to call and reconfirm the tour and what time it begins!* You need to bring your own lunch, water and car. Make sure the car is gassed up before starting the 50-mile drive inside the park.

One- to four-day guided backpacking trips are also available. Starting at the campground, a tribal guide will take you to the most remote parts of the park. You must bring your own equipment and food and be in pretty good shape to consider one of these backpacking trips.

EVENTS

Indian Dancing
summer

During June, July and Aug., Ute danc-ers perform Mon.–Thur. evenings at 7 pm in **Cortez City Park**; no fee charged. For more information call the **Cortez Visitors Center** at **(303) 565-3414**.

OUTDOOR ACTIVITIES

FISHING

For information, tackle, supplies and bait, visit **Outfitter Sporting Goods** in **Dolores**. 410 Railroad Ave.; (303) 882-7740.

Disappointment Creek—
Can't you take a hint?

Dolores River—

McPhee Dam has tamed the river into a top-producing site for rainbow, cutthroat and brown trout. Of course, the catch and release designation for the 12-mile stretch downstream from the dam to Bradfield Bridge is meant to keep it that way. Whatever your opinion of McPhee Reservoir, the tailwaters from the new dam are rich in nutrients, and the fish there are thriving. Because of the controlled water flow, the river no longer dries up in late summer. From Cortez head north on Hwy. 666 for 21 miles to just beyond Pleasant View, then turn right (east) onto County Rd. DD. Drive 1 mile to County Rd. 16, then 3 miles north to an access road for Bradfield Bridge. Once there, take Lone Dome Rd. (County Rd. 504), which follows along the Dolores River for 12 miles southeast to the dam.

Groundhog Reservoir—

The fish population is on the rebound from a complete draining a few years ago, but many fishermen seem to have forgotten about Groundhog Reservoir. The fishing can be excellent for 12- to 14-inch trout, especially from a boat. The reservoir has an assortment of brown, brook, rainbow and cutthroat trout. There are four rental cabins, a small store and boat rentals available. Call Jim or Louanne Wagoner at **(303) 882-4379** for more information. To reach the lake from Dolores, take 11th St. (which turns into Forest Rd. 526) north for 27 miles until the road splits. Take the right fork and continue 5 miles on Forest Rd. 533 to the reservoir.

McPhee Reservoir—

Filled completely for the first time in 1987, McPhee Reservoir is now one of the largest bodies of water in the state. The sloping, timbered shoreline creates an interesting vista and the fishing can be superb. However, it has also been inconsistent and may take a few more years to stabilize. For each of the past three years, the Colorado Division of Wildlife has stocked this newly made reservoir with 450,000 three- to five-inch McConaughy-strain rainbows. While this is the main thrust of the stocking program, large- and smallmouth bass, bluegills and crappies can be found in abundance. Since McPhee is a flooded river canyon with the deepest section in the middle, fishing is better from a boat. At the upper end of the lake are two boat ramps. To reach McPhee Reservoir from Cortez drive 8 miles north on Hwy. 145, then 4 miles northeast on Hwy. 184. There is a marked access road from there.

Navajo Lake—

This backcountry lake at the foot of El Diente Peak (one of the toughest 14ers in the state to climb) provides a spectacular location for dropping in a line. The lake receives heavy pressure from fishermen, however, and the brook trout are not as plentiful as they once were. The fishing is generally best in early July when the ice has just melted. Navajo Lake (11,154 feet in elevation) can be reached by a 5-mile trail that winds alternately through forest and open meadows. The trailhead leaves from Burro Bridge Campground (see the Camping section).

West Fork of the Dolores River—

The angling for small rainbow, brown and cutthroat trout is normally quite good on the West Fork. Some 8 miles of the river are posted against fishing, but there is still plenty of public water. The small stream is paralleled for 30 miles by a well-main-

tained gravel road in an exceptionally beautiful, thickly wooded area in the San Juans. The drive is incredible in late Sept. when the scrub oak and aspen change colors. To reach the West Fork of the Dolores River from the town of Dolores drive 15 miles northeast on Hwy. 145 to a marked turn-off for Dunton Rd. (Forest Rd. 535). The road follows the stream for 30 miles, ending up back on Hwy. 145 north of the town of Rico.

GOLF

Conquistador Golf Course—

This 18-hole public course offers great views of the surrounding peaks and mesas in the Cortez area. Green fees are reasonable. The course is open from mid-Mar. to mid-Nov. Located in northeast Cortez just off Hwy 145. **2018 N. Dolores Rd., Cortez, CO 81321; (303) 565-9208.**

HIKING AND BACKPACKING

Hiking near Anasazi sites in the canyons and along the mesas in the Cortez area is hard to beat. Hiking trails at Mesa Verde, Hovenweep and the Ute Mountain Tribal Park take you through juniper and pinon pine and over slickrock to Indian ruins. See the Major Attractions section for more information.

From Hwy. 145, east of Dolores, there is some excellent high country waiting to be explored. Fourteen-thousand-foot peaks, fields of wildflowers, abandoned mine buildings and abundant wildlife characterize the alpine country of the San Juan and Uncompahgre national forests reached from the Upper Dolores River area. For more trail ideas or information, contact the helpful folks at the **Dolores Ranger District Office, PO Box 210, 100 N. 6th St., Dolores, CO 81323; (303) 882-7296.** Read on for some trail ideas.

Calico/Fall Creek/Winter Trail Loop—

This 14-mile loop begins at the new

Calico trailhead, above the small town of Dunton. Calico Trail climbs southwest, following a ridge between the Dolores River and the West Fork of the Dolores. Along the route you have spectacular 360-degree views of the surrounding mountains. The trail begins in a vast mountain meadow and rises through Engelmann spruce and subalpine fir before reaching treeline and, eventually, the summit of 11,866-foot Papoose Peak. The trail then drops down to the intersection with Fall Creek Trail, 6 miles from the start of the hike. Turn right and follow Fall Creek Trail for 4 miles to Dunton at 8,800 feet. From Dunton, turn northeast (right) onto Winter Trail to complete the loop. Winter Trail is an old wagon road used to move supplies between Rico and Dunton in the early 1900s. Mail was delivered over this road in winter by skiing mailmen. The 4-mile trail climbs sharply the first mile and then levels off for the remainder.

To reach the trailhead from Dolores, drive east on Hwy. 145 for 12.5 miles and turn left onto West Fork Rd. (Forest Rd. 535). Drive about 25 miles to an area called the Meadows above Dunton, then turn right onto Forest Rd. 471. Drive to the trailhead.

Geyser Spring Trail—

This easy 1.25-mile trail ends up at a small pool of water fed by the only true geyser in the state of Colorado. The frequency of eruptions varies, but one usually occurs about every half hour. It's not exactly Old Faithful, but the geyser bubbles for about 15 minutes, emitting a strong-smelling sulphur gas. The trail begins 2.2 miles south of Dunton. From Dolores, drive east on Hwy. 145 for 12.5 miles and turn left onto Forest Rd. 535. Follow this road for 23.3 miles (a half mile beyond **Paradise Hot Spring**, which is closed to the public) and look for the trailhead on the right. The gradual hike up to the geyser takes you through aspen forests and small meadows.

Navajo Trail—

Navajo Trail, which begins about 2 miles north of Dunton on Forest Rd. 535, takes you into the heart of the Lizard Head Wilderness. From the trailhead, follow the trail 5 miles up steep switchbacks through open meadows and forests to Navajo Lake in Navajo Basin. This is the source of the headwaters of the West Fork of the Dolores River. Navajo Basin is also a good place to be if you like to climb 14ers—El Diente, Mt. Wilson and Wilson Peak are all within striking distance. This is the most heavily used area in the West Dolores area—so if you don't want to run into other hikers, try another area.

HORSEBACK RIDING

The Trappers Den—

Trail rides from an hour to overnight pack trips in the Mancos Valley are available through the Trappers Den. They have horses for beginners as well as experienced riders. Yes, they have campfire cookout rides with "wieners and marshmallows for the kids." Located 1.25 miles east of the Mesa Verde turn-off east of Cortez on Hwy. 160; **(303) 533-7147.**

RIVER FLOATING

Dolores River—

Considered by many floaters to be the most beautiful river in the west, the Dolores is one of the best rivers for an overnight trip in North America. With its sandstone canyons and Anasazi artifacts, it features more of a desert Southwest flavor than do most of the other major rivers in Colorado. Plan an early trip (mid- to late Apr. through June), because the Dolores peaks sooner than almost any other river in the state.

The **Upper Dolores**, a 37-mile stretch from Rico down to the town of Dolores, drops an average of 50 feet per mile through shady pine forests and ranch property. Kayaks are the best bet for this section.

Aside from the already apparent reduction of water flow on the desert canyon section of the Dolores, other long-term effects of the newly completed McPhee Reservoir remain to be seen. Running this

171-mile section of the river can be done in one week, but a lot of people choose leisurely weekend snippets. Highlights of this section include **Ponderosa Gorge, Dolores Canyon** (offering wild rapids including the famous **Snaggletooth,** which many prudent rafters choose to portage), **Little Glen Canyon, Slick Rock Canyon, Paradox Canyon, Mesa Canyon** and **Gateway Canyon.** For up-to-date flow information or other questions about the river, call the **Bedrock Store, Bedrock, CO 81411; (303) 859-7395.**

Outfitters—

Peregrine River Outfitters—PO Box 808, 447 Grand Ave., Mancos, CO 81328; (303) 533-7235.

Humpback Chub River Tours—202 S. 4th St., Dolores, CO 81323; (303) 882-7940.

Dvorak's Kayak & Rafting Expeditions— One of the most respected outfitters in the state, offering extended day trips down the Dolores. **1-800-824-3795.**

SKIING
CROSS-COUNTRY SKIING

Backcountry Trails—
Dunton—Hopefully, the hot springs at Dunton will be back in operation and open to the public by the time this book hits the shelves, but for now you're out of luck. Too bad, because a hot soak would be just the thing after a day of cross-country skiing. Located 12.5 miles east of Dolores on Hwy. 145 and then 20 miles up West Fork Rd. (Forest Rd. 535), Dunton offers some of the best intermediate touring and views in the southwestern part of the state.

Just above Dunton the road is not plowed. A mile after setting out on skis, you'll reach the fork of Forest Rds. 611 (left) and 535 (right). The left fork leads up a road through aspen and eventually a meadow, coming out at Groundhog Stock Driveway, 2 miles from the fork. This is a good area for telemarking. The right fork (Forest Rd. 535) leads up past Burro Bridge

Campground, over Burro Bridge and past the Navajo Lake trailhead. After about 5 miles, the trail leads into high meadows with good views of Mount Wilson, Wilson Peak and El Diente Peak to the northeast. This route is not for beginners.

Take note, the West Fork Rd. into Dunton can be very slippery—four-wheel-drive vehicles are suggested. Check road conditions before the trip.

Lizard Head Pass—A bit farther up Hwy. 145 from Dolores (47 miles), is 10,250-foot Lizard Head Pass, which offers excellent cross-country skiing. Heavy snows, open meadows and great views of surrounding peaks (especially Lizard Head Peak to the north) make this a popular area with nordic skiers. From the summit of the pass there are a number of directions in which to ski. Try the south side of the highway and ski southwest for 2 miles down fairly easy slopes, in and out of trees. On the north side of the highway, many advanced skiers head north toward Lizard Head Peak and the Lizard Head Wilderness Area for some great tree skiing. Trails can be difficult to follow in winter, so topographical maps and a compass are recommended. Be sure to stay clear of avalanche-prone areas.

Mesa Verde National Park—Inside the park, the eastern loop of Ruins Rd. is not plowed in winter. Although it's usually only skiable for a few days after a snowfall, it can be one of the most memorable ski tours you'll ever take. Like the men who first discovered Mesa Verde during a snowstorm in 1888, you'll be awed by the haunting dwellings at Cliff Palace and other sites along the way. The east loop is an easy, 6-mile ski trail. Be sure to check on snow conditions at the park before driving up there. If they give you the thumbs up, drive 10 miles east from Cortez on Hwy. 145 to the park entrance and turn right (south). Drive 20 miles to where Ruins Rd. forks— the left fork is the east loop. Please park well off the road. For more information about skiing in the park, contact the park supervisor at **Mesa Verde National Park, CO 81330; (303) 529-4465 or (303) 529-4475.**

SWIMMING

There is a 50-meter municipal swimming pool open to the public in **City Park**. Small fee. Open Memorial Day through Labor Day. Located in Cortez, next to the visitors center. **830 E. Montezuma Ave; (303) 565-7877.**

TENNIS

Four lighted courts are open to the public in **City Park**; no fee. Located in Cortez, next to the visitors center.

SEEING AND DOING

HOT SPRINGS

Dunton Hot Springs—

As of this printing, the popular, out-of-the-way Dunton Hot Springs are closed to the public. Located in a beautiful mountain valley on the West Fork of the Dolores, the springs were run for years as a laid-back resort. Rumor has it they may be reopening soon. If you are interested, inquire locally.

MUSEUMS AND GALLERIES

Anasazi Museums—

See the Major Attractions section.

Galleries and Shops—

A proliferation of Indian pottery shops and the like has sprouted on the main streets of Cortez. Some of them offer carefully worked Indian crafts, while others have cheap (but often pretty) imitations. If you'd like to take a look at some fine arts and crafts to judge the other shops by, visit **Toh-Atin Gallery** 1 mile east of Cortez on Hwy. 160; **(303) 565-0105.** Another gallery of note is the **Ute Mountain Pottery Plant**, located on the Ute Mountain Indian Reservation 15 miles south of Cortez on Hwy. 666; **(303) 565-8548.**

SCENIC DRIVES

Cortez/Hovenweep Loop—

See Hovenweep in the Major Attractions section.

Dolores/Dunton Loop—

This drive takes you through the wide spectrum of terrain southwestern Colorado has to offer: from juniper and pinon pine of the redstone canyon country to shimmering aspen and mountain wildflowers of the high San Juan Mountains. This drive is especially beautiful in fall when the colors change. From Dolores, head east up Hwy. 145 along the Dolores River for 12.5 miles to the junction with West Fork Rd. (Forest Rd. 535). Turn left onto the West Fork Rd. and proceed up along West Fork of the Dolores River. The fishing along this stretch can be quite good for cutthroat trout.

About 20 miles up West Fork Rd. is the old gold and silver mining town of Dunton. Known these days for its hot springs (closed to the public at this time) and access to the beautiful Lizard Head Wilderness Area, Dunton is definitely worth a visit. Driving on from Dunton, look off to the northeast to see the looming, snowcapped El Diente Peak (14,149 feet) and Mount Wilson (14,246 feet). The road eventually turns east and then southeast, meeting up again with Hwy. 145. Turn right and drive through the town of Rico on your way back to Dolores. A booming mining town back in 1879, Rico is now struggling to keep from becoming another Colorado ghost town.

WHERE TO STAY

ACCOMMODATIONS

For the most part, lodging opportunities in Dolores and especially Cortez are predictable. The main street through Cortez is lined with motels ranging from high to low end. Many major motel chains are present as well as other independent motels, including several with Indian themes such as the Arrow Motel and Tomahawk Lodge. During the summer it's highly recommended to make reservations in advance because lodging gets surprisingly tight. For information and help securing motel reservations, contact the **Cortez Visitors Center, PO Box 968, Cortez, CO 81321; (303) 565-3414.** Out in the countryside there are several unique lodging opportunities.

Stoner Lodge — $$

The attractive Stoner Lodge is set in a beautiful valley with aspen-cloaked mountains and red rock formations. Located at the defunct Stoner Ski Area, the lodge stays open year-round even though the lifts no longer run (closed in 1985). Value is the word that immediately comes to mind when thinking about this lodge. The prices sounded good even before we learned breakfast was included. Rooms sleep from two to eight people; some have private baths, while others share bathrooms. There are good views, and the lodge is far enough away from the highway to buffer the noise. A comfortable common room with a pool table and a full-service restaurant and bar are located downstairs. Some telemark skiers are willing to climb the 1,200-foot ski runs behind the lodge for a powder run. There is easy access to other cross-country skiing as well. Located 14 miles northwest of Dolores. **25134 Hwy. 145, Dolores, CO 81323; (303) 882-7825.**

Kelly Place — $$

Located on 100 acres in beautiful McElmo Canyon about 15 miles west of Cortez, Kelly Place not only offers unique, affordable lodging, but also involves visitors in the archaeology and early history of the area. Smack dab in the middle of Anasazi country, the Kelly property has ancient ruins where guests can lend a hand excavating artifacts while learning about the Anasazi culture. Guests may also weave and throw pottery in the same style as the Anasazi. Tours to the major sites in the area (Mesa Verde, Hovenweep, etc.) are available year-round.

Kelly Place is also set up to educate visitors in the farming techniques of Colorado pioneers. Draft horses are used to plow fields and a number of crops are grown year-round. Weaving, canning and quilting as well as tanning and blacksmithing are taught. This hands-on approach helps the guests acquire an appreciation for the archaeology and the history of southwestern Colorado.

Guests can stay from one night to as long as six weeks. Five rooms with private baths can each accommodate as many as six people. Groups of up to 24 people can be accommodated. Breakfast is served each morning in the guest house. Kelly Place accepts reservations only. **14663 County Rd. G, Cortez, CO 81321; (303) 565-3125.**

CAMPING

Anasazi Areas—

McPhee Reservoir—McPhee Recreation Site has 80 sites and a fee. From Dolores head west on Hwy. 145 for 5 miles and turn right at the reservoir entrance. Drive 1 mile to the campground. The other campground at McPhee is **House Creek Campground**, with 46 sites and a fee. To reach House Creek Campground, drive about 1 mile east from Dolores on Hwy. 145 and turn left onto Forest Rd. 526. Drive 6 miles and turn left onto Forest Rd. 528 and proceed 5 miles to the campground.

Morefield Campground—See Mesa Verde in the Major Attractions section.

Ute Mountain Tribal Park—See Ute Mountain Tribal Park in the Major Attractions section.

In San Juan National Forest—

There are a number of campgrounds east of Dolores. **Forks Campground** (6 sites), **Mavreeso Campground** (14 sites), **West Dolores Campground** (13 sites) and **Burro Bridge Campground** (15 sites) are located up the beautiful West Fork Rd. (Forest Rd. 535) along the West Fork of the Dolores River. Each campground has a fee. To get there, head east from Dolores on Hwy. 145 for 12.5 miles and turn left onto Forest Rd. 535. Forks Campground is at the junction; Mavreeso, West Dolores and Burro Bridge campgrounds are 5, 7 and 24 miles up the road.

From the junction of Hwy. 145 and Forest Rd. 535 (12.5 miles east of Dolores) head east on Hwy. 145 for 11 miles to **Priest Gulch Campground** with 12 sites and a fee. Continuing another 30 miles east on Hwy. 145 will take you by **Cayton Campground** up near Lizard Head Pass. It has 27 sites and a fee.

Heading east on Hwy. 160 from Cortez, there are a couple of campgrounds. **Transfer Campground** is located 9 miles north of Mancos on Forest Rd. 561. It has 13 sites and a fee. **Thompson Park Campground** is located along Hwy. 160, 5.5 miles east of Mancos. There are 51 sites and a fee.

Private Campgrounds—

Cortez KOA Campground—Plenty of RV hookups, laundry facilities, showers, etc. Located just east of Cortez on Hwy. 160. **PO Box 1257, 27432 Hwy. 160, Cortez, CO 81321; (303) 565-9301.**

Dolores River RV Park—Situated along the Dolores River, 2.5 miles east of Dolores on Hwy. 145, this place has hookups, tent sites and everything else you could possibly need. **18680 Hwy. 145, Dolores, CO 81323; (303) 882-7761.**

Priest Gulch Ranchcamp—Located 35 miles northeast of Cortez on Hwy. 145. Full hookups and tent sites. Laundry, store, playground, etc. **26750 Hwy. 145, Dolores, CO 81323; (303) 562-3810.**

WHERE TO EAT

Stromsted's — $ to $$$

Not too long ago, Todd Stromsted had something happen that most restaurant owners only dream about. Late one afternoon, two hang gliders walked into the restaurant and announced they had just flown from Flagstaff, Arizona, setting a world hang gliding distance record. They had heard Stromsted's was the place to eat in Cortez and we have to agree. Todd Stromsted's slick, well-run establishment gets an almost unanimous thumbs up from locals. Stromsted's specializes in steak and fresh seafood entrées flown in daily. The downstairs bar has an inexpensive menu. In summer the outside deck offers beautiful views toward Mesa Verde and Sleeping Ute Mountain; Wed. through Fri. a barbecue grill churns out tasty, reasonably priced food for the deck crowd. The inside dining area is very comfortable with subtle colors and some interestingly curved wooden booths. Be sure to check out the diorama of Mesa Verde near the entrance. The bar opens at 4:30 pm daily; dining from 5:30–10 pm. **1020 S. Broadway; 565-1257.**

Francisca's — $ to $$

Excellent Mexican food is served at reasonable prices at Francisca's. Try the stacked enchiladas, stuffed sopapilla, chile rellenos or a chimichanga. For those not hungry for Mexican food there are a few burgers and steaks. When we asked the owner, Pedro, if we could take a menu for reference, he immediately thought we were spies from another restaurant—his food probably is the best! Thanks to a couple of large white gazebos and many hanging plants, the restaurant always feels like an outdoor patio in summer. Open from 11 am–10 pm Mon.–Sat. **125 E. Main St.; 565-4093.**

Bob's Drive In — $

In a hurry? Need a quick, filling meal? Stop in at Bob's for a "chez" burger with all the fixins. Bob Cowan, the owner, boasts that his burgers are less fatty than those at many other burger joints. Hot dogs, burritos, fish and chicken sandwiches and pizza pockets round out the menu. If you still have room, get an ice cream cone to go. Hours are 10 am–6 pm Mon.–Sat.; closed Sun. Located next to the Rust mobile home park. **610 N. Broadway; 565-3911.**

M&M Truckstop and Restaurant — $

With rows of Phillips 66 gas pumps out front, this full-service restaurant is a great place for sandwiches, burgers, steaks and tacos. But their best meal of the day is undoubtedly breakfast (served 24 hours a day). The coffee keeps coming just as soon as you find a seat, pancakes are piled five high, the service is fast and friendly and the majority of the clientele are wearing plaid flannel shirts. In this part of the state, refried beans are an option with your eggs. When we asked people in town where they go for breakfast, there was a unanimous reply, "M&M's." Open 24 hours a day, seven days a week. **7006 Hwy. 160; 565-6511.**

SERVICES

Cortez Visitors Center—

PO Box 968, 928 E. Main St., Cortez, CO 81321; (303) 565-3414.

Durango

"Durango is out of the way and glad of it," Will Rogers wrote after a visit to southern Colorado. His statement still reflects the virtues of a town that once had visions of surpassing Denver as the wealthiest city in the state. These expectations went up in a non-existent puff of smoke as the railroad discontinued service and the rich gold and silver mines faltered.

Nestled between reddish sandstone bluffs, Durango occupies a spectacular position in the Animas River Valley. *El Rio de las Animas Perdidas,* "the River of Lost Souls," is bordered by more than 2 million acres of awesome scenery, dotted with the jagged peaks of San Juan National Forest. The changing seasons prove this to be a region of infinite variety. A shimmering grove of aspen trees, a light-falling snow and a colorful blanket of wildflowers all enhance the ageless natural beauty of the San Juans.

Durango is blessed with a bounty of historic landmarks and has managed to retain a feeling of the frontier West. A whistle blast from the restored Durango & Silverton Narrow Gauge Railroad's black steam engines recalls a past era. The aura of 19th-century prosperity accompanies you on a memorable journey upriver to Silverton on the train's well-maintained passenger cars.

The influence of the Spanish, Indian and Anglo populations has permeated the town, creating a unique spirit. As you walk through the streets of Durango, the melding of cultures is apparent, not only in the faces of the residents but also in the surroundings. The choice of Mexican restaurants, Indian art galleries and stately hotels built from mining profits all contribute to the town's unique heritage.

Much of Durango's draw is the diversity of recreational possibilities: golf and tennis, hiking and mountain biking, fishing and horseback riding, skiing or simply enjoying the mountain scenery of the area. A visit to this southwestern corner of the state embodies the best of what Colorado is all about.

HISTORY

In 1868 the United States government granted Chief Ouray and the Ute Indians a tract of southwestern Colorado that encompassed nearly a quarter of the territory. Almost as soon as this huge tract of land was assigned, rich gold and silver strikes in the San Juan Mountains drew a legion of miners seeking fortunes into the area. Under the terms of the 1868 treaty, the government should have protected the rights of Utes against the intruding prospectors. The mood of the day, however, ensured only the miners' "destiny" and, by 1873, Ouray had relinquished 6,000 square miles of mineral-rich land. The Meeker Massacre of 1879 in northwestern Colorado (see the **Meeker** chapter) provided the excuse to remove the Southern Ute Indians to a reservation in southern Colorado and New Mexico. This removal coincided conveniently with the early growth of a railroad center named Durango.

A great need for efficient transport of the tons of ore generated by the mines prompted the Denver & Rio Grande Railroad to extend its tracks from the eastern plains to the Animas River Valley. A railroad center was needed, and the logical location was the small farming community of Animas City (two miles north of present-day Durango). But the town declined the offer, refusing to have its solitude destroyed. By snubbing the railroad, Animas City sealed its destiny as one more western ghost town.

A railroad town was still needed, so consequently, a group of investors formed the Durango Trust to provide money for a new townsite. A city plan was drawn up in 1880, and Durango sprang into being, with the railroad providing the basis for prolonged future growth.

By 1881 the mining boom was in full swing in the nearby mountains, and so were the related problems of public drunkenness, prostitution and gambling. Most of the growing pains subsided as Durango came into its own. The largest industry of the decade was the smoke-belching smelter that refined the rich ore transported from the nearby mines.

When mine production began to wane in the early 1900s, Durango fell on hard times. Gradually, the scope of the local economy shifted from the centrally located smelter to another mother lode: tourism. Now visitors come from across the US to enjoy the scenic beauty, history and recreational diversity that Durangoans are blessed with year-round.

GETTING THERE

To reach Durango from Denver, take Hwy. 285 south to Monte Vista and then head west on Hwy. 160. This is a very scenic 332-mile drive. The other route is via Interstate 25 to Walsenburg and then Hwy. 160.

Several airlines now offer daily service to Durango from various parts of the country, with the majority of flights connecting in Denver. Air access has closed the time gap between Denver and Durango, making short trips possible without the long drive. Car rentals are available from several Durango companies.

———— MAJOR ATTRACTIONS ————

MESA VERDE NATIONAL PARK

Within striking distance of Durango is Mesa Verde, site of the world's largest Indian cliff dwellings. Once home to as many as 50,000 inhabitants, it is a must-see stop for anyone visiting southwestern Colorado. See Major Attractions in the **Cortez** chapter for information.

NARROW-GAUGE RAILROAD

During the summer season in Durango (early May to late Oct.) the relative tranquility of the town is briefly interrupted each morning and evening by the lonesome whine of a train whistle: the Durango & Silverton Narrow Gauge Railroad. For almost as long as Durango has existed, the narrow gauge train has been making its 45-mile trip north to the well-preserved mining town of Silverton (see the **Silverton** chapter). Each year more than 200,000 passengers pile on board one of the four daily trains to enjoy a trip that hugs hair-raising cliffs while crossing and recrossing the raging Animas River. To experience the unique beauty and history of the San Juans, there is no better way than a trip along the tracks of the narrow-gauge railroad.

History—

In the fall of 1881 the Denver & Rio Grande Railroad (D&RG) broke ground for a stretch of track linking Silverton to the eastern plains. The route was completed the following summer and was used for shuttling passengers and supplies in and out of this remote area. More importantly, it transported an estimated $300 million in gold and silver out of this rich mining town. In 1921 the D&RG emerged from receivership as the Denver & Rio Grand Western (D&RGW). In the late 1960s, the tracks between Antonito and Durango were abandoned, cutting off Durango and Silverton from the rest of the present-day D&RGW rail system.

The railroad between Durango and Silverton was purchased from the D&RGW in 1981 by a Florida orange grower. The new owner changed the name of the train to the Durango & Silverton Narrow Gauge Railroad Co. (D&SNG). Stressing authenticity, he poured money into refurbishing the train, including open and closed coach cars and the old Alamosa parlor car. The Alamosa, built in 1880, is a first-class, 28-passenger car equipped with an ash wood bar serving the only liquor on the train.

Further Information—

A round trip on the D&SNG takes eight hours (three hours getting to Silverton, two hours in town and three hours back to Durango). Many passengers, young and old alike, who have ridden the full-day round trip suffer from track burnout.

Although most people do make the round-trip journey in one day, there are options. You can stay a night or two in Silverton before returning to Durango. Bus transportation is also available between the two towns, making it possible to take the train one way and to return via Hwy. 550 over scenic Molas Pass. If you have a car and are with a group, consider splitting up: half can drive to Silverton while the other half take the train. Then switch for the return trip.

Handicapped Facilities—

One train each day is equipped with lifts, spacious seating and adequate restrooms.

Reservations—

Reservations for a trip on the D&SNG are strongly recommended. Advance purchases must be made 30 days prior to the date of the train's departure. No credit cards are accepted and personal checks are accepted only with a check guarantee card. Although groups can be accommodated, there are no group rates. For additional information contact: **Durango & Silverton Narrow Gauge Railroad Co., 479 Main Ave., Durango, CO 81301; (303) 247-2733.**

RailCamp—

Billed as a "wilderness recreational vehicle," RailCamp functions as an RV on train tracks to bring groups into the remote Weminuche Wilderness Area of San Juan National Forest. It is offered for people who wish to camp out but still enjoy the creature comforts of home. RailCamp is a rail car equipped with four bunk beds, a bath, running water, a kitchen with a propane stove and refrigerator, utensils and cooking necessities. What, no cable TV?! RailCamp rents by the week (Mon.–Fri.) from late May through late Sept. Reservations are required. For further information contact: **Durango & Silverton Narrow Gauge Railroad Co., 479 Main Ave., Durango, CO 81301; (303) 247-2733.**

Wilderness Access—

The D&SNG train makes daily stops in the Weminuche Wilderness Area at Needleton and Elk Park. Backpackers may get on and off the train at these points. For more information, see the Hiking and Backpacking section.

UTE MOUNTAIN TRIBAL PARK

In an isolated setting just south of Mesa Verde National Park on the Ute Mountain Indian Reservation, you can see other spectacular Anasazi remains. See Major Attractions in the **Cortez** chapter for information.

—— FESTIVALS AND EVENTS ——

Ute Bear Dance
late spring

"Leave your troubles behind and start your life anew. . ." is the philosophy behind the Ute Bear Dance. With the coming of spring the Southern Ute Indian Tribe in Ignacio awakens from the long winter as if coming out of hibernation. The happy festival dates back to at least the 15th century according to reports from Spanish explorers. Today the Bear Dance is still an important rite of spring and everyone is invited to take part. Ute women lead the dance and upon asking men to join them, the gentlemen have absolutely no way of saying "no." All of the Utes are dressed in traditional finery. The dance involves exaggerated swaying movements that mimic the way a bear would dance. Everyone is encouraged to join in on the weekend celebration.

Consider staying in Ignacio (a half-hour's drive southeast of Durango) at the **Sky Ute Lodge** ($). For more information on the Bear Dance or other Southern Ute Indian events, contact the **Tribal Affairs Building, PO Box 737, Ignacio, CO 81137; (303) 563-4525.**

Iron Horse
Bicycle Classic
Memorial Day weekend

World-class cyclists are pitted in a grueling road race against the Durango & Silverton Narrow Gauge train. Taking place during **Narrow-Gauge Days**, this 50-mile race ends in Silverton and is a unique tribute to the long history of the train. Throughout the long weekend there are several other touring and mountain-bike races. Other Durango events during the festival include a street dance, a parade and a rodeo in addition to kayak races and footraces. For more information, call **(303) 247-0312.**

Animas River Days
last weekend in June

Whitewater enthusiasts from around the country converge on Durango for a weekend of competitions on the Animas River. Watch as participants maneuver canoes, rafts and kayaks through specially designed courses. One highlight is the all-out race down a swift 4-mile stretch. In addition to events, there are several instructional clinics. For more information, call **(303) 247-0312.**

Colorfest
mid-September to mid-October

The Four Corners area celebrates the arrival of autumn's colors with a variety of events. Each year from mid-Sept. through mid-Oct., when the aspen turn gold and red, Colorfest happenings fill the calender. The area's brilliant colors highlight a vintage automobile show, workshops, art shows, fishing contests, raft races, hang gliding and more. For information, call **(303) 247-0312.**

Snowdown—
A Celebration of Winter
late January

Durango has found a way to shake off the wintertime blues. For the past decade a collection of fun events, from the serious to the slightly crazy, has entertained locals and visitors alike. A couple of past themes have been "Romancing the Snow" and "Still Crazy After All Ten Years." Among the activities are snow and ice sculpturing, kids' games, tug-of-war championships, an ice-fishing derby, a broomball tournament and a film festival. For more information, call **(303) 247-0312.**

——— OUTDOOR ACTIVITIES ———

BIKING
MOUNTAIN BIKING

Durango hosts a lion's share of bicycle events and has become a natural hub for the sport. Mountain bike enthusiasts have found the area ideal, as the nearby trail possibilities are endless. Another reason for the popularity of mountain biking is that the current national champion, Ned Overend, is from Durango. If you didn't bring a bike, don't sweat it. There are several local shops with rentals, tour recommendations and maps. Even the bicycle carrying rack for your car can be rented on a daily basis.

Colorado Trail—
This fairly narrow, single-track trail is great for more experienced riders. See the Hiking and Backpacking section for more information.

Hermosa Creek Trail—
This has become one of the more popular half-day rides in the Durango area. It's a fairly advanced 21-mile ride with a couple of stream crossings (dangerous during spring runoff) and a 2,000-foot change in elevation. The rough trail passes through beautiful wooded terrain near Hermosa Creek—bring your fishing equipment along! Most people prefer a one-way route. This requires leaving a car at the lower trailhead located 11 miles north of Durango on Hwy. 550 and a mile up County Rd. 201. The upper trailhead where you will begin the ride is near Purgatory Ski Area, 28 miles north of Durango on Hwy.

550. From the ski area parking lot, stay right and follow the signs on Forest Rd. 528 to Sig Creek Campground. Continue for 2 miles past the campground and turn left on a road that leads to the trailhead.

La Plata Canyon Road—
A maze of dirt roads dotted with remains of old mining camps provide a great day of mountain biking. For more information, see the Four-Wheel-Drive Trips section.

Mountain View Crest—
North of Durango, this dirt road leads to the edge of the Weminuche Wilderness Area. The last section is particularly beautiful and rough. For information, see the Hiking and Backpacking section.

Rentals and Information—
Hassle Free Sports—The people at this shop are knowledgeable about the area and the sport. They rent mountain bikes on a per day basis with discounts for longer terms. Open Mon.–Sat. 8:30 am–6 pm. **2615 Main Ave.; (303) 259-3874.**

FISHING

A bounty of brook, rainbow and cutthroat trout, pike and kokanee salmon can be reeled in from the area's many streams, lakes and reservoirs. Listed below are public access fishing areas. There are several private lakes and streams that may be fished by arrangement with outfitters and guest ranches in the area. For further fishing information and supplies, call on

Duranglers Fly Shop, 801-B Main Ave., Durango, CO 81301; (303) 385-4081.

Animas River—

This is a highly fished river, but rest assured that large trout can be pulled from inside the Durango city limits. Generally the best fishing on the Animas is south of town or from Devils Falls downstream to the Takoma power plant.

Dolores River—

This has been called the best public access trout stream in the state. It is worth the trek from Durango to fish the water between the newly created McPhee Dam (10 miles northwest of Dolores) south to Bradfield Bridge. See the Fishing section of the **Cortez** chapter for more information.

McPhee Reservoir—

See the Fishing section of the **Cortez** chapter for information on fishing this new reservoir.

Piedra River—

See the Fishing section of the **Pagosa Springs** chapter for more information.

Vallecito Reservoir—

The surrounding snowcapped peaks of San Juan National Forest help attract visitors to this heavily used area. Rainbow and German brown trout, northern pike and kokanee salmon round out the fishing possibilities. There are several boat ramps and docks along the 22-mile shoreline. Boat rentals and fishing supplies are available. Vallecito Reservoir is located 23 miles northeast of Durango. Take County Rd. 240 out of town. Stay to the right on 240 at the junction of County Rd. 243. Turn left on County Rd. 501 and continue along the Los Pinos River to the lake.

FOUR-WHEEL-DRIVE TRIPS

Durango is close to the Silverton and Ouray area, often touted as the greatest jeeping in the world. Serious jeepers can take day trips on these scenic and treacherous roads by heading north out of Durango on Hwy. 550 over Molas Pass. See the Four-Wheel-Drive Trips section of the **Silverton** chapter for more information.

The area immediately surrounding Durango is not known as a jeeper's mecca, but there are some interesting ghost towns and old mining roads close by.

Around Durango—

A great day trip combining remnants of old mining towns and a far-reaching view of the La Plata Mountains is up **La Plata Canyon**, just west of Durango. Head west on Hwy. 160 to the town of Hesperus, then north on La Plata County Rd. The road is paved up to the small community of **Mayday**, near the site of **Parrott City**. Once a gold placer camp and miner's supply town, Parrott City was the county seat in 1876. A cluster of old white frame buildings with red trim stands out on the west side of the main street. The first is the old saloon brought down from **La Plata City** by Billy and Olga Little. Twenty-seven bullet holes were found in the wall behind the bar. Must have been a pretty wild place on Saturday nights!

From Mayday/Parrott City the road turns to dirt and is rough going without a four-wheel-drive vehicle. Four miles up the road is what's left of La Plata City, an old mining camp. You will pass the old schoolhouse on the west side of the road. Continue to the end of the road at the 12,000-foot mountain summit for great views of the La Plata Mountains, Junction Creek Canyon, the Animas River Valley and Durango.

Another backroad possibility is E. Animas Rd. Though not actually a four-wheel-drive road, it's worth a look. From Durango, head east to the end of 32nd St. and then turn north on E. Animas Rd. (County Rd. 250). The road hugs the cliffs and offers a beautiful view of the Animas River Valley. Follow E. Animas Rd. 11.7 miles to a series of winding turns leading to the one-lane Baker's Bridge, which spans a deep chasm of the Animas. This is the site of Animas City No. 1, the original settlement in the area that once had 300 residents eager to cash in on the new mining boom. Baker's Chasm is also a worthwhile stop for movie buffs. It is the location of the famous jump-off-the-cliff-into-the-river scene from the 1969 classic, *Butch Cassidy and the Sundance Kid*.

GOLF

Hillcrest Golf Course—
This well-kept 18-hole course offers a far-reaching view of the La Plata Mountains. Also available at the course are a snack bar and a driving range in addition to practice greens and a sandtrap. There are several summer tournaments, the most well-known being the Ken Stabler Sports Classic. This tournament is packed with stars and professional athletes competing on the links for the benefit of The Durango/Purgatory Handicapped Sports Association. On the Fort Lewis College mesa, east of town; **2300 Rim Dr.; (303) 247-1499.**

Tamarron Resort Golf Course—
One of Colorado's finest resorts, Tamarron lies in a once-wild cross-section of thick ponderosa woodland and sharp rock bluffs. Guests and members staying at Tamarron have first choice of tee times on this classic 18-hole course. Non-lodging golfers cannot reserve advance tee times, making play in the peak summer season close to impossible. Green fees are expensive. Located 18 miles north of Durango on Hwy. 550; **40292 Hwy. 550 N; (303) 259-2000, ext. 422.**

HIKING AND BACKPACKING

There are few places better than the Durango area for experiencing Colorado's outdoors. Whether you are interested in a half-day hike in the La Plata Mountains near town or a week-long trip deep into the Weminuche Wilderness Area, your satisfaction is assured.

Snowfall in the San Juans is heavy.

During normal years snow cover remains at the higher elevations (above 11,000 feet) until July. Many folks choose to take backcountry trips in early fall when the aspen are turning color. This is a spectacular time to see the San Juans, but be prepared for snow, as storms are not uncommon in Sept. Visitors can also expect afternoon and evening rainstorms in July and Aug.

Forest service maps, brochures and friendly advice about hiking in the Durango area can be obtained at the **Animas Ranger District, 701 Camino del Rio, Room 301, Durango, CO 81301; (303) 247-4874.** Topographical maps are available at local sporting goods stores.

Colorado Trail (Junction Creek)—
For hikers interested in exploring the southwest end of the 469-mile Colorado Trail, this is the place. To reach the trailhead, head west on 25th St. from north Main Ave. in Durango. At a cattle guard about 3.5 miles up the road is the San Juan National Forest boundary. Proceed from here about 100 feet and look for the trailhead on the left. For more information about the Colorado Trail, check in at the Animas Ranger District in Durango and refer to page 17.

Goulding Creek Trail—
Another good day hike, the Goulding Creek Trail is especially nice in Sept. and Oct. when the aspen groves are shimmering gold. It's a moderately difficult 6-mile round-trip hike that climbs up above Hermosa Cliffs near Tamarron. Three miles up the trail is a spot that offers a view into the secluded Hermosa Creek Roadless Area, one of the best elk summering grounds in southwestern Colorado. The trail begins 17 miles north of Durango on the west side of Hwy. 550, a half-mile north of the main entrance to Tamarron Resort.

Mountain View Crest—
Though a bit harder to get to from Durango, this scenic area offers spectacular views of Pigeon Peak, Turret Peak and Chicago Basin, all located deep within the

Weminuche Wilderness Area. To reach these great views, it's necessary to plan a full day (9 to 10 miles round trip). The hike is moderately difficult and rises to 12,998 feet. From Durango, head east to the end of 32nd St. Turn north on E. Animas Rd. and proceed 9.5 miles to Missionary Ridge Rd. Take a right and go 19 miles to where Henderson Lake Rd. turns right. Follow it 4 miles to the wilderness barrier and park your car. The last 4 miles may require a four-wheel-drive vehicle. From the wilderness barrier, hike north along the east side of Lima Mesa past Silver Lake and on up to the summit of Mountain View Crest.

Perin's Peak—

From the summit, look to the La Plata Mountains while enjoying a bird's-eye view of Durango. Perin's Peak is a difficult, 5-mile round-trip hike through pine forests. The peak is characterized by a sharp, pointed cliff that must be scaled at its easiest point—a 10-foot rock wall. It can be done, however, and the view from the top is worth it! This hike is possible in wintertime. To reach the trailhead from town, take 22nd St. west from Main Ave. Follow 22nd St. up Crestview Mesa, where it turns west and becomes Montview Pkwy. At the west end of Montview Pkwy. turn left on Highland Ave. to Leyden St. Head right on Leyden to the dead end and park there.

Twin Buttes—

From the top of Twin Buttes (7,737 feet) the view of the surrounding La Plata Mountains is beautiful. It is an easy 4-mile round-trip hike that can often be done in winter, depending on snowfall. To reach the trailhead, take Hwy. 160 to a road 1.3 miles west of the Animas River Bridge (south end of Durango). Turn right and follow the road as it winds north and then west to where it starts climbing a steep hill. You can park there and begin the walk.

Weminuche Wilderness Area—

Deep valleys, jagged peaks, beautiful blue lakes and raging rivers characterize the Weminuche. Named for the band of Ute Indians that once inhabited the area, the Weminuche was granted wilderness designation by President Ford in 1975, making it one of the largest wilderness areas in the country. Here are some ways to gain trail access to the area.

Via the Narrow-Gauge Railroad—One of the most exciting backpacking adventures possible is a trip into the Weminuche Wilderness Area via the narrow gauge railroad. Starting each day from both Durango and Silverton, as many as 20 to 40 backpackers ride the train to and from the isolated stops at Elk Park and Needleton. From these locations they begin their trips up the extensive trail system. The quick transition from the civilized world of the train to primitive wilderness is striking. One minute you are surrounded by laughing, shouting passengers drinking Pepsi and eating potato chips; the next minute they have traveled on and you are left standing by the train track, surrounded by jagged mountains, miles from the nearest road, with no sounds but the crashing water of the Animas River and the wind in the pines.

The **Needle Creek Trail**, starting in Needleton, heads up into the breathtaking Chicago Basin, home to Mt. Eolus (14,084 feet), Sunlight Peak (14,059 feet) and Windom Peak (14,087 feet). **Elk Creek Trail** begins in Elk Park and climbs east up into the Elk Creek River Valley and eventually to the Continental Divide.

Backpacking into the Weminuche via the narrow-gauge railroad has become very popular. Unfortunately, signs of heavy use are apparent. The forest service has been forced to consider limiting use of the area. By practicing low-impact camping (use of existing fire pits, packing out all trash and staying on designated trails when possible), visitors can ensure that this plan of action does not become a reality. For Durango & Silverton Narrow Gauge Railroad information see the Major Attractions section.

Via Vallecito Reservoir—Both the **Vallecito Trail** and the **Pine River Trail** are heavily used and provide access to the Weminuche Wilderness Area. They are fine for both day hikes and extended trips. This is a popular access for horseback riders. See the Camping section for directions.

Via Purgatory Campground—Located 26 miles north of Durango on Hwy. 550. On the east side of the highway **Cascade Creek Trail** begins, crossing Purgatory Flats before dropping 4 miles down to the Animas River. From there you can hike another 7 miles upriver on the **Animas River Trail** to Needleton for access to the wilderness area. Many people find the 8-mile hike down to the river and back a good day trip.

HORSEBACK RIDING

One of the best ways to enjoy the astounding beauty of the San Juans is from the saddle of a horse. Riding the trails, as the pioneers and Indians once did, will spur your imagination. Hang on tight and enjoy a two-hour tenderfoot ride or an early morning breakfast trip. Why not an overnight pack trip? Several local outfitters offer a variety of long and short trips.

Purgatory Resort—
Call to arrange from several local outfitters at **(303) 247-9000.**

Southfork Riding Stables—
Six miles east at **28481 Hwy. 160; (303) 259-4871.**

RIVER FLOATING

"Water is God in southwestern Colorado," says Walt Werner of the National Forest Service in Durango. Diverting the water for irrigation and damming it for hydroelectric power are necessary in this arid landscape. However, this "progress" has certainly taken a toll on the rivers by reducing the natural water flow. Dams like McPhee Reservoir (near Dolores) have not only buried Anasazi Indian artifacts but also have forever altered the natural features of the rivers in the Durango vicinity. Despite a controlled water flow, when the heavy winter snows of the San Juan Mountains begin melting in springtime, the swollen rivers offer some of the most hair-raising rapid rides in the state. The Animas River upstream from Durango is claimed by locals to have some of the wildest stretches in the world. Whether you are looking for a bone-jarring adventure or just a leisurely float with the family, it can be found on the rivers of southwestern Colorado.

Animas River—
Many a kayaker and rafter has wondered if the River of Lost Souls wasn't a name conjured up for those crazy enough to float the 28-mile stretch of the **Upper Animas.** From Silverton down to the town of Rockwood, the river drops an average of 85 feet per mile and offers water that is isolated and beautiful, rugged and dangerous. To attempt this section of the river you should be in good physical shape and an expert kayaker. Be sure to get out at Rockwood because the river then enters a boxed-in, churning chasm lasting 3 miles. Floating this section would have an effect on your body not unlike what the average carrot experiences going through the puree cycle in a Cuisinart.

Closer to Durango, beginning near Trimble Hot Springs (6 miles north of Durango off Hwy. 550), there is a tranquil 10-mile stretch of the river that drops only five feet per mile. This section is best for canoes and those who shuddered while reading the previous paragraph.

Downstream from Durango, the **Lower Animas** has some good rapids but is a bit more sedate. Especially exciting for novices and intermediates, the Lower Animas winds its way 20 miles south through the Southern Ute Indian Reservation. The river drops an average of 24 feet per mile and can be floated by kayaks, rafts and canoes. The Lower Animas can be floated into autumn. Permits are needed to enter the Indian reservation.

Dolores River—
This river is one of the most beautiful

floats you could imagine. See the River Floating section of the **Cortez** chapter for more information.

Piedra River—

Intersecting Hwy. 160 between Durango and Pagosa Springs, this is a river that more and more serious whitewater enthusiasts are discovering. See the River Floating section of the **Pagosa Springs** chapter for more information.

Outfitters—

Durango suffers no shortage of rafting outfitters offering guides, equipment, supplies and transportation to the rivers. Most of them stop offering services after spring runoff while a few others stay open into the fall. Listed below are some of the outfitters.

Durango Rivertrippers—Promising "miles of smiles," these folks offer safe trips for the family. Located at **720 Main Ave., Durango, CO 81301; (303) 259-0289.**

Big Tujunga River Tours—3533 N. Main, PO Box 2814, Durango, CO 81302; (303) 385-4675. Off-season (303) 259-0665.

Four Corners Marine—This outfitter offers kayak lessons on the San Juan, Dolores and Colorado rivers. PO Box 379, Durango, CO 81302; (303) 259-3893.

SKIING

CROSS-COUNTRY SKIING

If isolation and natural beauty are what you're after, this is the ideal place. Due to the abundant snowfall in the San Juans, the ski season is lengthy, but avalanche danger can run high. Backcountry skiers should use good judgment. To find the best snow consider the higher elevations to the north of Durango off Hwy. 550. Take a glance at the Hiking and Backpacking section for some more trail ideas.

Backcountry Trails—

Haviland Lake—Several easy routes take off from Haviland Lake Campground, 17

miles north of Durango via Hwy. 550. After a recent snow, this is an excellent area to come for the day. Beginners can practice by skiing around the unplowed campground on gentle terrain.

A 3-mile route follows a roller coaster trail on an old wagon road from the campground. The route is marked with blue signs with a distinctive XC. The trail eventually comes out on Forest Rd. 166 (Chris Park Rd.). Look for a historical marker at this point before you complete the loop to Haviland Lake Campground. Another marked 2-mile cross-country loop begins just after turning off Hwy. 550 toward Haviland Lake. The trail heads into the forest to the right (south) just before you reach Forest Rd. 166 which leads to Chris Park Campground.

Molas Pass—See the **Silverton** chapter.

Groomed Trails—

Purgatory Ski Touring Center—This established cross-country trail system is ideal thanks to a stunning location in the San Juan National Forest. More than 15 kilometers of trails are designed to accommodate all abilities. Instructors are available for touring and telemark lessons. Rental equipment; small trail fee. Located across the highway from Purgatory Ski Area on Hwy. 550; (303) 247-9000, ext. 3196.

Ski Rentals and Information—

Pine Needle Mountaineering—Anything you want to rent. **835 Main Ave.; (303) 247-8728.**

DOWNHILL SKIING

Purgatory Ski Area—

You already know what a thrill it is just to look at the San Juans. . . . Now it is time to buckle your boots and experience them. Sunshine and plenty of powder snow are perfect partners in making Purgatory's 35 miles of slopes desirable in the dead of winter. Once there, cruise the vertical drop of 1,750 feet down the varied trails that receive an average of 300 inches of dry powder each year. The area is located 28 miles north of Durango, yet convenient because the Durango Lift provides bus service to and from the area. The resort village at the base of the slopes is growing steadily, providing a range of services as well as condominium units. **PO Box 166, Durango, CO 81302; (303) 247-9000.**

Or consider spending a day of skiing at the nearby areas of **Telluride** and **Wolf Creek.** See the **Telluride** and **Pagosa Springs** chapters, respectively, for information.

SWIMMING

Durango Municipal Swimming Pool—

A public outdoor pool located at **2400 Main Ave.** next to Durango High School. Open daily in the summer from 1:30–6 pm for a small fee.

Fort Lewis College Natatorium—

An indoor pool located on campus. Open to the public from 7–9 pm Mon.–Fri., 1–5 pm Sat. and Sun. A small fee is charged.

Trimble Hot Springs—

For information see the Hot Springs section.

TENNIS

Durango High School—
2390 Main Ave. Six courts.

Fort Lewis College—

Overlooking Durango from the mesa. Twelve courts are open unless scheduled for lessons or tournaments.

Mason School—
12th St. and **E. 3rd Ave.** Two courts.

—— SEEING AND DOING ——

HOT SPRINGS

On December 13, 1883, the *Durango Herald* proclaimed **Trimble Hot Springs** as "The Favorite Health and Pleasure Resort of the San Juans." The irrepressible (and some say healing) hot water still bubbles forth despite devastating fires that destroyed three separate resorts over the course of the past 100 years.

The area is now enjoying a rebirth with the help of Ruedi and Leith Bear. The Bears's 1988 renovation of Trimble Hot Springs allows guests full use of a new bathhouse, snack bar, nursery and locker rooms. The main attractions are the Olympic-sized outdoor pool (150 feet x 50 feet), the smaller outdoor pool with massage jets and two private tubs. The source water is heated far beneath the La Plata Mountains, arriving through a fault at Trimble at a piping hot 119° F. The hot mineral source water is mixed to a tolerable 104° F in the small pool, while the large pool is cooler and more suited to swimming. Behind the pools is a landscaped park with picnic tables, outdoor grills and a volleyball court. Trimble Hot Springs is open in summer from 7 am–10 pm daily; 8 am–11 pm in winter. Admission fee. Located just 6 miles north of Durango via Hwy. 550 at the junction of Trimble Ln. and County Rd. 203; **6475 County Rd. 203; Durango, CO 81301; (303) 259-0314.**

MUSEUMS AND GALLERIES

Animas School Museum—

Time stops as you enter a turn-of-the-century schoolroom furnished with small wooden desks, heavy blackboards and a faded 46-star flag. Can you name the last four states to join the Union? Upstairs is a photographic history of Animas City and Durango. Also displayed are artifacts from the Basket Maker Anasazi Indians and opium pipes found below a once-active(!) Chinese laundry in the area. It is a small museum that is worth a few moments to those interested in the lively history of

Durango. Open in summer from 10 am–6 pm. **31st St.** and **W. 2nd Ave.; (303) 259-2402.**

Southwest Book Trader—

This small shop reflects the enthusiasm of the owner, George Hassen. He clearly enjoys his job of sorting through old books and gleaning out the best. The feel of an amply stocked attic is complemented by a number of collectibles that are scattered about the crowded space. This shop is worth a look! **175 E. 5th St.; (303) 247-8479.**

Toh-Atin Gallery—

Intricate Navajo rugs, sculptures and Indian jewelry of the highest quality are sold in a harmonious setting. There is no pressure to buy, and the looking doesn't get much better. Items range from the contemporary jewelry of US Congressman Ben Nighthorse Campbell to affordable prints and posters. Authenticity is guaranteed on each handmade Indian item. Located one block west of Main Ave. at **145 W. 9th St.; (303) 247-8277.**

NIGHTLIFE

Now Magazine, a supplement to the Thursday *Durango Herald*, provides current information about nightlife and leisure pursuits on a weekly basis. To learn about nocturnal activities such as live music, theater presentations and dancing, pick up a free copy at your hotel, motel, lodge or condominium. Listed are a few of the more unique night spots around town.

Diamond Circle Theatre at the Strater Hotel—

Hisssss the villain and cheer the hero during a Victorian melodrama presentation. The whole family will enjoy this entertainment in a period setting of red velvet curtains, checkered tablecloths and brass chandeliers. During a break in the show, the actors and actresses serve refreshments from the bar. According to *Time* magazine the Diamond Circle Theatre is

"one of the top three Gay-Ninety theaters in the United States." **699 Main Ave.; (303) 247-4431.**

Farquahrts—

Live rock and roll or blues music is the rule for the lively crowd at this popular spot. The small dance floor in front of the stage encourages rubbing elbows while enjoying a great view of the band. (See the Where to Eat section.) **725 Main Ave.; (303) 247-5440.**

Kiva Theatre–
Rocky Mountain Jamboree—

"We really want to stress the family aspect of the show," says Patti Belle, co-host of the Jamboree. The show features a contemporary country sound mingled with inoffensive comedy geared to the kids. The two-hour show begins at 8:30 each evening. In Durango you'll be bombarded with pamphlets and advertisements for the Jamboree. In our opinion, for the quality, the entertainment is overpriced. Open May to Oct. Closed Mon. Corner of **8th St.** and **Main Ave.; (303) 259-1290.**

SCENIC DRIVES

You just need to hop in the car and go. The Durango area offers spectacular scenery and history, particularly to the north of town.

Molas Pass—

At 10,910 feet this pass offers a high route to the town of Silverton. Proceeding from there will take you over the Million Dollar Highway and on to Ouray (see the **Ouray** chapter for more information). From Durango, the well-maintained road follows high above the tracks of the narrow gauge railroad, but offers much of the same scenery. The grand view of the Needles Mountains towering above the Animas River Valley will force you to stop and linger awhile. In fall, riding above a carpet of golden aspen will make the drive even more beautiful. Molas Pass is 40 miles north of Durango via Hwy. 550.

WHERE TO STAY

ACCOMMODATIONS

There is a wide spectrum of lodging opportunities awaiting the visitor to Durango. The list contains hotels with Victorian refinement, typical roadside motels, guest ranches and continues from there. We were utterly surprised to see a local bed and breakfast (Mountain Memories) offer rooms above animal pens! Rustic cabins along the beautiful shoreline at Vallecito Reservoir are available by the week or weekend. An intriguing possibility involves taking a specially converted railcar up a seldom-used narrow gauge track in the Weminuche Wilderness Area. (See RailCamp in the Durango & Silverton Narrow-Gauge Railroad section.)

For inexpensive motel accommodations simply follow Main Ave. to the north end of town. Both sides of the street offer ample lodging choices, but in high season neon No Vacancy signs begin flickering in early evening. Here are a few choices for a memorable stay in the Durango area.

Tamarron Resort — $$$ to $$$$

Perched on a sandstone bluff overlooking a highly respected 18-hole golf course is a three-story lodge built of stone and wood. Townhouses with a number of options, some with full kitchens, may also be rented. This self-sufficient resort offers a cartload of amenities to the discriminating visitor, including several dining choices, boutiques and a healthy variety of recreational opportunities. Tamarron is an ideal place to stay in winter, due to its closeness to Purgatory Ski Area. In summer there is much more to do than golf: fishing, horseback riding, swimming, hiking and jeeping round out the possibilities. Tamarron offers several enticing packages for guests in the off-season; some include use of the health spa, tennis courts and platform tennis courts at no extra cost. Located 18 miles north of Durango on Hwy. 550. **PO Box 3131, 40292 Hwy. 550 N., Durango,** CO 81302-3131; 1-800-678-1000 or (303) 259-2000.

The General Palmer Hotel — $$$ to $$$$

Named for the cavalry general who was farsighted enough to push for railroad service into southern Colorado. The hotel, built in 1898, successfully blends Victorian elegance with modern conveniences. Enjoyable personal touches include chocolates by the bed and a toiletry basket in the bath. Complimentary fresh muffins are served with juice and coffee each morning in the meeting room. Adjacent is the Old Muldoon Saloon with plush velvet couches and a long bar. Reservations are essential. **567 Main Ave., Durango, CO 81301; 1-800-523-3358** nationwide, **1-800-824-2173** in Colorado, or **247-4747** locally.

The Jarvis Suite Hotel — $$$

This historic hotel was built inside a 100-year-old theater, but was converted into contemporary suites with skylights, kitchens and modern furnishings. It is a welcome experiment in contrasts of style, form and function. Offered in summer is a deluxe three-night package (two nights in Durango sandwiching a night at a hotel in Silverton), including lodging, narrow gauge train tickets and breakfast for two people. Called "the sentimental journey," it is an exceptional weekend escape during the summer at a reasonable cost. In winter the Durango Lift extends doorstep bus service to Purgatory and the airport. Prices vary considerably, depending on season and room design. **125 W. 10th St., Durango, CO 81301; 1-800-824-1024** nationwide, **1-800-228-9836** in Colorado, or **259-6190** locally.

The Strater Hotel — $$$

Some 100 years ago at the seemingly exorbitant cost of $70,000, Henry H. Strater built the hotel that was to become his legacy. Durango was in need of a first-class operation to demonstrate that the burgeoning community was worthy of the title Denver of the West. The 93 rooms are tastefully decorated in restored antiques; each is different and has its own bath. Despite the modern amenities of telephone and color television in every room, the Victorian grandeur of the red brick hotel is retained by antique walnut furniture, lace curtains and old-time light fixtures.

Located within shouting distance of the comfortable hotel lobby are Henry's Restaurant, the Diamond Belle Saloon and the Diamond Circle Theatre with its outstanding melodrama. Room rates vary according to season, but are generally moderate to expensive. Reservations recommended. **699 Main Ave., Durango, CO 81301; 1-800-247-4431** nationwide, or **247-4431** locally.

Durango Hostel International — $

So it's slightly run down. This AYH-approved house is the cheapest place to stay in town. Open 7–10 am, 5–10 pm; doors closed at all other times. Use back entrance. **543 E. 2nd Ave., Durango, CO 81301; (303) 247-9905.**

CAMPING

In San Juan National Forest—

The closest campground to Durango is **Junction Creek Campground**, located about 4 miles away. 34 sites; fee charged. Head west on 25th St. from north Main Ave. and follow the road up into the national forest.

Lemon Reservoir—Located 17 miles northeast of Durango. Follow County Rd. 240 out of town. Turn north on County Rd. 243 and follow it to the reservoir. There are three campgrounds: two located north of the reservoir and one on the east shore. Fee charged; total of 62 sites.

North toward Purgatory—Traveling north out of town on Hwy. 550 leads you to **Haviland Lake Campground** just north of Tamarron. 43 sites; fee charged. Stay on Hwy. 550 north for another 7 miles to reach **Purgatory Campground**. 14 sites; fee charged. For a more remote location try **Sig Creek Campground.** Nine sites; small fee. Situated 28 miles northwest of Durango on Hermosa Park Rd. From Hwy. 550, turn into the ski area and stay right above the parking lot. Just follow the signs.

Vallecito Reservoir—This popular area, located 23 miles northeast of Durango, can be reached by taking County Rd. 240 out of town. Stay to the right on 240 at the junction of County Rd. 243. Turn left on County Rd. 501. Vallecito Reservoir boasts five campgrounds with 116 sites by the reservoir and one (**Vallecito Campground,** 88 sites) just to the north on Vallecito Creek. Fee charged.

Private Campground—

KOA Campground—For folks looking for electrical and water hookups, showers and the like, the KOA Campground is located east of Durango at **30090 Hwy. 160, Durango, CO 81301; (303) 247-0783.**

——— WHERE TO EAT ———

Ariano's — $$$

The owner and chef, Vince Ferraro, has created a menu loaded with northern Italian specialties. He assured us that his pastas and ravioli are made fresh daily in the restaurant. Milk-fed veal, ginger shrimp, steaks and specials round out the menu. An extensive Italian wine list com-

plements the full bar. In the words of one longtime Durango resident, "If I could go to any restaurant in Durango, it would definitely be Ariano's." Open nightly from 5:30 pm. **150 E. 6th St.; 247-8146.**

The Ore House — $$ to $$$

Nothing too fancy graces the menu of

Durango's most popular steakhouse. All of the beef at the Ore House is aged in an on-premises cooler and is hand-cut daily; try a generous rib-eye cut or a 16 ounce T-bone steak. Also offered are fresh seafood items ranging from scallops to Australian lobster. The decor is rustic with barn-wood walls and old mining implements throughout. Voted best steakhouse by readers of the *Durango Herald*'s *Now Magazine*. Good wine cellar. Bar open at 5 pm; restaurant open from 5:30–11 pm nightly. **147 6th St.; 247-5707.**

The Edgewater Dining Room at the Red Lion Inn — $$ to $$$

Look out the large picture windows from your table to the rushing Animas River below as ecstatic rafters float by. A trip to the Edgewater's extensive salad bar can be a complete lunch. Or come by in the evening for more elaborate and expensive ($$$) fare. The dinner menu includes a good selection of steaks and seafoods. The soups and appetizers will make your mouth water: baked French onion soup, brie soup, stuffed mushrooms, escargot or oysters casino. What are you waiting for? Their Sun. brunch ($$) is considered by many locals to be the best in town. Open Mon.–Sat. 6 am–2 pm, 5–10 pm; Sun. 6–10 am, 10 am–2 pm (brunch) and 5–10 pm. **501 Camino del Rio; 259-6580.**

Henry's at the Strater Hotel — $$

Sunday brunch is served from 10 am to 2 pm at a lavishly appointed buffet. Omelettes are made to order. Try the seafood crêpes or perhaps fresh Belgian waffles. The relaxed Victorian setting and the fine food blend into a true Durango experience. If you can't make the Sun. brunch, Henry's is also open for lunch daily ($$) from 11 am–2 pm and dinner ($$$) from 5:30 pm nightly. Four dinner specials are served each evening. During summer there is an all-you-can-eat prime rib buffet, including a salad bar and two other entrées. **699 Main Ave.; 247-4431.**

Farquahrts — $ to $$

Voted the best pizza in town by the *Durango Herald* readers, but there is much more. The interior decor is rustic and inviting; a turn-of-the-century portrait of a nude woman gazes down upon a long bar at one end of the room. Antique signs form a shield of armor on the walls, and ceiling fans are forever circling overhead. It tends to attract a college-age crowd, especially after 9 pm when live rock and roll or blues begins. Open 11 am–10 pm, Mon.–Sat.; 4–11 pm on Sun. **725 Main Ave.; 247-5440.**

The Durango Diner — $

A sure sign of value is the large number of locals rubbing elbows at the long counter in this unpretentious diner. Huge portions are served up as you catch the latest goings-on around town. Hash browns are a favorite of the house; large peeled potatoes are shaved onto the grill and may be smothered with melted cheddar cheese and green chilies. There is little room left on your plate for the bacon and eggs. Other breakfast specialties are flapjacks, biscuits and gravy, and omelettes. Lunch items are added to the menu and served until closing at 2 pm. Open Mon.–Sat. from 6 am, Sun. from 7 am. **957 Main Ave.; 247-9889.**

Griego's — $

The only drive-in Mexican restaurant in Durango is housed in a former A&W franchise. The likeness is obvious until you bite into a smothered burrito, taco or combination plate. Order anything smothered in green chili and a smile will break across your face about the same moment sweat rivulets appear on your forehead. However, no alcoholic beverages are served to help you cool down. Top off your authentic meal with a homemade sopapilla dipped in honey. Open 10 am–9 pm Mon.–Sat. **2603 Main Ave.; 259-3558.** If you're looking for a plush atmosphere or a Margarita, skip Griego's and head into town to **Francisco's ($$),** open Mon.–Sat. 11 am–10 pm, Sun. brunch 10 am–4 pm. **619 Main Ave.; 247-4098.**

The Meeting Place — $

Creative homemade foods and smoke-free dining are the obvious attributes of the Meeting Place. Traditional omelette and egg varieties share the menu with whole wheat pancakes, breakfast shakes and homemade bread. The food is good for you! Lunches feature crêpes and brown rice, which share the menu with a variety of soups, salads and pasta dishes. Alcohol-free beverages are served. The Meeting Place is open daily from 7 am–2 pm, closed Wed. 6th St. and E. 7th Ave.; 247-5322.

SERVICES

Bus Transportation—

The Durango Lift provides daily bus service to and from Purgatory during ski season from several pickup spots in Durango; reservations recommended.

Bus service is available in and around Durango for a small fee.

The historic Durango mini-tour is a one-hour self-guided tour of historic Durango. Check with your hotel/motel for more information, or call 259-LIFT.

Central Reservations—

Durango Area Chamber Resort Association—Call toll free nationwide 1-800-525-8855, in Colorado toll free 1-800-358-8855.

Purgatory/Durango Central Reservations —nationwide 1-800-525-0892.

Durango Area Chamber Resort Association—

PO Box 2587, 111 S. Camino del Rio, Durango, CO 81302; (303) 247-0312.

Day Care—

Peter Pan Pre-School—750 E. 4th Ave., Durango, CO 81301; (303) 247-5954.

Gunnison and Crested Butte

The Gunnison area is quintessentially western, its character having been molded by Indians, miners, ranchers and railroads. Located in the fertile Gunnison Valley at the confluence of the Gunnison River and Tomichi Creek, Gunnison is one of the most purely outdoor-oriented destinations in this book. To the north are the snow-capped Elk Mountains and Taylor Park, to the east are the Sawatch Range and the Continental Divide, and to the west is Curecanti National Recreation Area.

Once a center for ranchers and miners, Gunnison now serves as a jumping-off point for vacationers who come to enjoy the expanse of spectacular country surrounding the town. The town itself is *not* a draw. But nearby Gunnison National Forest, encompassing 1.6 million acres, offers hiking, skiing, fishing and hunting—some of the best in the state. More than 750 miles of teeming trout streams and a number of productive reservoirs continue to draw avid fishermen from all around the country. In addition, exploring the back roads and old ghost towns in the Gunnison area can comprise a whole vacation in itself.

Gunnison locals appear proud of the fact that chilling winter temperatures in the Gunnison Valley are often the coldest in the country. Up at **Crested Butte**, about 30 miles north of town, the temperatures are a bit warmer and the skiing is hot. During winter, exceptional powder snow challenges downhill and cross-country skiers. Crested Butte offers a tremendous variety of year-round activities and is widely considered to be the mountain biking capital of Colorado. Any time of year, Crested Butte locals are friendly and perfectly willing to share their version of paradise.

Crested Butte will never take on a contrived feeling. This well-preserved Victorian mining town has always charmed visitors with its weathered wooden buildings, isolated setting and laid-back atmosphere. Undoubtedly, you'll be awed by the sweeping ring of peaks that encircles the century-old town.

The old and the new come together at Crested Butte without colliding, thanks in part to the 2-mile distance between the old town and the modern ski resort at Mount Crested Butte. This short distance has alleviated many conflicts by separating the luxury condos and multi-level hotels from the historic district. Each town complements the other without crowding or creating aesthetic confrontations. Most of Crested Butte's accommodations are located at Mount Crested Butte; the majority of fine restaurants—there are many—can be found in the old town.

HISTORY

As early as the mid-1600s, the Gunnison area was a primary Ute hunting ground for buffalo, deer and other game. In 1853 a famous expedition, led by Capt. John W. Gunnison, passed through the area in an attempt to find a suitable transcontinental railroad route. Gunnison and his men had a very successful expedition until they reached Utah, where all but four members of the party were brutally killed by a band of Paiute Indians. Capt. Gunnison was shot with 15 arrows and then his arms, tongue and heart were removed. The least that could be done was to name a town after the man.

After the Ute Indian Treaty of 1868, an Indian agency in the Gunnison area was opened at Los Piños. Under treaty, the Utes had to move west, vacating the Gunnison valleys. It wasn't long before some whites began arriving. Though the few settlers were relatively safe, some prospectors pushed their luck by venturing into the Elk Mountains of the Ute reservation, usually with severe consequences. Rich mineral strikes further to the west in the San Juan Mountains put pressure on the Utes to renegotiate the treaty, further reducing their territory. In 1873 the Brunot Treaty forced the Utes to cede more land to the US and relocate in the Uncompahgre area to the west.

In 1874 the town of Gunnison got its start when farmers and cattle ranchers settled land in the valleys. Five years later the Gunnison area came to life when many miners struck rich gold and silver deposits. With the mining boom in full swing, Gunnison became a very important place to come for supplies and a little hell-raising. The town also became an important transportation center. Demand from mining towns in the area and from cattle ranchers eager to send their stock to outside markets prompted both the Denver & Rio Grande Railroad (D&RG) and the Denver South Park & Pacific Railroad (DSP&P) to extend service to Gunnison in the early 1880s.

Gold and silver strikes up Tomichi and Quartz creeks, in Taylor Park and in the Elk Mountains, spurred the growth of many mining towns such as Pitkin, Tincup and Gothic. But in 1893, as in so many other mining areas across the state, the demonetization of silver proved catastrophic to these boom towns. Many of them became ghost towns immediately, while others lingered on, dying slow deaths. The town of Gunnison, with its cattle industry and its role as supply center for the area, emerged unscathed from this period of economic upheaval. So did another nearby town—Crested Butte.

During the mining boom of the early 1880s, Crested Butte was in a good location to provide its rich neighbors with supplies and cut lumber. It wasn't long before residents discovered that Crested Butte was situated on a deposit of high-grade coal. In 1881 Crested Butte was connected to the outside world by the Denver & Rio Grande Railroad, which was transporting 1,000 tons of coal per month by 1884.

Coal fueled the economy in Crested Butte, and by the 1890s the young town had 1,000 residents, 13 saloons and one minister. As the boom towns in the nearby Elk Mountains began to wither away, Crested Butte became a company town under the guiding hand of Colorado Fuel & Iron (CF&I). The town prospered until 1952, when the Big Mine finally closed. In 1953 the *Denver Post* published a fallacious article on Colorado's "newest ghost town."

It was only 10 years later that skiers were challenging the slopes of Crested Butte Mountain (12,162 feet). Resort developers were on target when they started cutting runs and building a planned community at the base area. Today, the delightful allure of Crested Butte has allowed the town to escape "ghost town" classification.

GETTING THERE

Gunnison—Located 196 miles southwest of Denver, Gunnison can be reached on Hwy. 285 to Poncha Springs, then west over Monarch Pass on Hwy. 50. Monarch Pass can be slow going in the winter. Check for road conditions if it is snowing. Greyhound Trailways Bus Lines services Gunnison from points east and west.

Getting to Gunnison by air is easy. In winter, direct flights are available from Dallas on American Airlines, from Chicago on United and Denver on Continental Express. In summer, United Express and Continental Express fly in daily from Denver.

Crested Butte—Located 30 miles north of Gunnison on Hwy. 136. It takes about 40 minutes to make the trip from Gunnison to Crested Butte.

———— MAJOR ATTRACTIONS ————

CURECANTI NATIONAL RECREATION AREA

Blue Mesa Reservoir and much of the **Black Canyon of the Gunnison** are encompassed by Curecanti National Recreation Area and its breathtaking scenery. A series of dams have altered the natural path of the Gunnison River on its course through the ancient Precambrian stone of the Black Canyon. Blue Mesa Dam, at the head of the Black Canyon, created the first and largest of three reservoirs. It has transformed the semi-arid landscape into an area especially well suited to boating, fishing and windsurfing.

Downstream from Blue Mesa is the dramatic beauty of Morrow Point and Crystal reservoirs. The mixture of jutting rock and calm water in the abyss of the canyon is reminiscent of the Norwegian fjords. Below Crystal Dam, the Gunnison River flows freely through the deepest and narrowest section of the Black Canyon of the Gunnison. This area has been preserved as a national monument (see the **Black Canyon Country** chapter).

History—

The namesake of Curecanti was former Ute Chief Curecata, who was known for directing the Ute Bear Dance with his twin brother, Kanneatche. The Ute Indians once hunted wild game in the dry hills around the Gunnison River. When trappers and traders began exploring the area in the mid-1800s, the rugged canyon terrain was viewed as an obstacle. Nonetheless, in 1882 the Denver & Rio Grande Railroad was able to complete its narrow-gauge Scenic Line of the World through the upper part of the canyon, which left lasting impressions on its passengers. In 1899 English author Rudyard Kipling wrote the following description about the passage:

We seemed to be running into the bowels of the earth at the invitation of an irresponsible stream. The solid rock would open up and disclose a curve of awful twistfulness. Then the driver put on all steam, and we would go round that curve on one wheel chiefly, the Gunnison River gnashing its teeth below.

The route climbed out of the canyon in the vicinity of Crystal Reservoir and continued to Cimarron and Montrose. The railroad operated until 1949, with a pyramid-shaped Curecanti Needle as its logo. The track bed is now submerged by Morrow Point and Blue Mesa reservoirs.

Facts About the Recreation Area—

Blue Mesa Reservoir is 20 miles long, offering a wide expanse of clear water for sailing, windsurfing and fishing. Narrow arms reach out from the main body of water, making boat exploration the best way to get into remote areas. The two other smaller reservoirs are more difficult to reach, but the beauty of the canyon makes it worth a hike. Hwy. 92 follows the northern rim of the Black Canyon, offering several dramatic overlooks down to Morrow Point and Crystal reservoirs. Several hiking trails wind their way down to water level; only hand-carried watercraft are allowed on the smaller reservoirs.

Camping—

There are a number of developed campgrounds situated, for the most part, around the perimeter of Blue Mesa Reservoir. The major campgrounds are at **Elk Creek, Lake Fork, Cimarron** and **Stevens Creek**. For a smaller, less developed area, try camping at **Red Bridge** or **Gateview**. All campgrounds are first come, first served. There are more than 350 sites; all charge a fee.

Elk Creek Marina—

Tackle, gas, a convenience store, boat rentals and tours can all be found here. Located off Hwy. 50 on the north shore near the midpoint of the Blue Mesa Reservoir. **(303) 641-0402.**

Elk Creek Visitors Center—

A good place to begin your visit to the recreation area is at the park headquarters/visitors center. Several exhibits, a slide presentation and printed information tell the story of the Curecanti area. Rangers will inform you of any interpretive programs and of the many recreational possibilities in the area. Open from mid-May to late Sept. Located on the north side of Blue Mesa Reservoir off Hwy. 50. For more information, contact: **Superintendent, Curecanti National Recreation Area, 102 Elk Creek, Gunnison, CO 81230; (303) 641-2337.**

Fishing—

Curecanti National Recreation Area provides excellent fishing on three reservoirs: Blue Mesa, Morrow Point and Crystal. **Blue Mesa** is by far the largest and most popular, with 96 miles of shoreline. It accommodates heavy use from both bank and boat anglers. Shore fishing is best when the water level is low. More than 30 streams flow into Blue Mesa, providing numerous channels and inlets. Rainbows are the most frequent catch, although brown, mackinaw and brook trout and kokanee salmon are also caught in quantity. The reservoir is stocked with hundreds of thousands of trout and salmon each year. The best fishing is early and late in the day. Snagging for kokanee begins in Oct. In winter, many fishermen drive out onto the ice from the boat ramps around the reservoir. Iola Basin is a favorite for ice fishing.

Handicapped Access—

The East Elk Creek Visitors Center, as well as the Lake Fork, Cimarron and East Portal information centers are all wheelchair accessible. Most of the campgrounds can accommodate handicapped persons.

Hiking—

A number of hiking trails leave the roadside and twist their way down inside the Black Canyon. **Neversink Trail**, at the eastern tip of Blue Mesa Reservoir, is a half-mile walk through a lush bird habitat. Several other trails leave the north side of the reservoirs from Hwy. 92 and offer dramatic views.

For a water-level view of Morrow Point

Reservoir and the Curecanti Needle, try **Curecanti Creek Trail**. This 2-mile trail rapidly descends 1,000 feet from the rim of the Black Canyon of the Gunnison down to the water level of Morrow Point Reservoir. It would be wise to save some time and energy for the walk back up. The trail is well maintained, with bridges and even a few steps in places. The route follows the path of turbulent Curecanti Creek, which looks more like a waterfall than a creek due to the steep grade. Once at the bottom, the view up the canyon walls and across the water to Curecanti Needle is fantastic. There is room for a couple of tents on a sandy bank at the bottom of the trail. Fishing is usually good in the deep water where Curecanti Creek flows into the reservoir.

Morrow Point Reservoir Boat Tours—

From within the deep canyon walls you will find a new appreciation for the beauty of the Black Canyon. Once you are on the small tour boat, an interpreter will relate the history of the lake as you ride toward a water-level view of the Curecanti Needle.

Before embarking on a boat tour, you must first take a mile-long hike down Pine Creek Trail. For reservations and more information call the **Elk Creek Marina; (303) 641-0402.**

Water Sports—

Sailing, motorboating and windsurfing are popular activities on Blue Mesa Reservoir. There are many boat ramps situated around Blue Mesa for easy entry into the water. Windsurfers prefer the warmer waters of East Elk Creek Bay. Morrow Point and Crystal reservoirs are restricted to hand-carried crafts because of the surrounding canyon walls. Fluctuating water levels at the two smaller reservoirs cause some boating hazards. Check with rangers at the Cimarron Information Center for information and advice.

FESTIVALS AND EVENTS

Cattlemen's Days
mid-July

Gunnison cuts loose each year during Cattlemen's Days, the state's oldest rodeo celebrating the ranching heritage of the area. Held annually since 1901, the rodeo features stock shows, horse races, a barbecue and pro rodeo events. If you want to get a good feel for the area and its people, work this rodeo into your schedule. Call the **Gunnison County Chamber of Commerce** for more information at **(303) 641-1501.**

Aerial Weekend
last weekend of July

For 15 years this ultimate spectator event has filled Crested Butte's skies with a colorful rainbow of hot air balloons. As many as 50 balloons participate in the annual event. The graceful balloons are visible from practically anywhere in the wide valley. The aerial excitement also includes sky divers, hang gliders, a stunt pilot and games in the town park. For more information, call **(303) 349-6438.**

Fat Tire Bike Week
mid-September

This Crested Butte celebration originated in 1975 when a few locals decided to ride one-speed Schwinn klunkers over 12,705-foot Pearl Pass to Aspen. The hapless riders made the trek, but only by pushing their bikes most of the way. Today, riders have mountain bikes equipped with 18 gears, lightweight alloy frames and cantilever brakes to assist them. Fat Tire Bike Week mingles pro racing events with tours for riders of all abilities. The Pearl Pass Classic is the perfect culmination to the festivities. Hundreds of riders camp below Pearl Pass for a night of music, bonfires, food and fermented hops. At first light everyone heads over the rough pass to Aspen in a boisterous reenactment of the first ride in 1975. For more information call **(303) 349-6438.**

--------- # OUTDOOR ACTIVITIES ---------

BIKING
MOUNTAIN BIKING

Crested Butte is fat-tire paradise. With only one paved road leading into town, it's obvious why the locals' favorite mode of travel is on sturdy mountain bikes. If you have never tried a mountain bike, take one for a spin. The bikes are not only comfortable and stable, but are designed for abuse and quick braking. Single-track trails and jeep roads provide varied terrain for all abilities. Because there are so many backcountry trails, there are no conflicts among hikers, horseback riders and mountain bikers.

Cement Creek Trail—

A country dirt road passes through the valley next to Cement Creek. You can take this road all the way to the base of Italian Mountain or you can take a turn-off leading to the many trails snaking up the sloping valley walls. Walrod Gulch is a steep four-wheel-drive road. For single tracking on a rough trail, try Trail 409, leading the way to Farris Creek Rd. and a loop back to town. For access to Cement Creek, see the Hiking and Backpacking section.

Crested Butte to Marble—

You can't use this route until late summer due to the heavy snowpack before then. It's a long ride unless you have arranged for someone with a vehicle to pick you up in Marble. Maybe you like long rides? Anyway, this arduous route passes through Gothic, over 10,707-foot Schofield Pass, past the Devils Punchbowl, on through the pristine ghost town of Crystal, finally ending in Marble. Once in Marble you can either turn around and return to Crested Butte or ride an exhausting loop over McClure and Kebler passes.

Rentals and Information—

Before heading out on a fat-tire bike excursion, check with one of the following mountain bike shops for trail maps, advice and rentals.

Bicycles Etc./The Alpineer—419 6th St., PO Box 813, Crested Butte, CO 81224; (303) 349-5210.

Paradise Bikes and Skis—224 Elk Ave., PO Box 1460, Crested Butte, CO 81224; (303) 349-6324.

The TuneUp—222 N. Main St., Gunnison, CO 81230; (303) 641-0285.

FISHING

The Gunnison and Crested Butte area is an excellent base for a fishing vacation. Reservoirs, streams, creeks and clear alpine lakes are all good providers. In the drainages above the major rivers are countless smaller creeks alive with many small brook trout. The natural beauty will keep you smiling even if you're skunked. If you need advice or tackle, stop in at **Gene Taylor's Sporting Goods** in **Gunnison:** 201 W. Tomichi Ave.; (303) 641-1845.

Blue Mesa and Morrow Point Reservoirs—

See the Major Attraction section.

East River—

Unfortunately, much of the East River below its headwaters at Emerald Lake flows through private land. Permission to fish some of the best stretches requires an OK from landowners. Public access is downstream from Crested Butte, adjacent to the Roaring Judy Hatchery. The water above and below the hatchery bridge is designated Wild Trout water. Your chance for hooking a large rainbow, brown, brook or cutthroat is excellent on this section. Only flies are permitted; catch and release all trout.

Emerald Lake—

This high-country lake is best known for its rainbow trout and a beautiful location just below Schofield Pass. An elevation of 10,445 feet makes the fishing a bit sporadic, though the trip is worthwhile. Emerald Lake is located 4.5 miles north of Crested Butte on Forest Rd. 317.

Gunnison River—

At the town of Almont, where the East and Taylor rivers join, the Gunnison River is born. Stretches of this legendary trout stream are easily considered some of the very best in the state.

For 3 miles downstream from Almont, there is good fishing in public water. Beyond that point the river flows through mostly private property until passing the Neversink Picnic Area a couple of miles below the town of Gunnison. From Neversink down to the inlet of Blue Mesa Reservoir is a popular public fishing area. The length of the section below Neversink fluctuates between 5 miles and a half mile, depending on the water level of the reservoir. Try a weighted Hare's Ear, a Stone Fly or a Woolly Worm in the deep pools near the banks; Mepps and Rapala lures are favorites.

As you follow downstream, the Gunnison flows into a series of three reservoirs: Blue Mesa, Morrow Point and Crystal.

The **Lower Gunnison River** below Crystal Reservoir is difficult to reach, but worth it. The Gunnison River below surpasses all other rivers in the state for sheer numbers of trout per mile of river. See the **Black Canyon Country** chapter for more information on the Gold Medal water and the spectacular scenery of this area.

Roaring Judy Ponds—

Don't be too skeptical about pulling trophy-sized fish from a couple of small ponds beside the East River. Alan Schnei-der, a student at Western State College in Gunnison, pulled a record 30 lb., 8 oz. brown trout from one of the ponds in March 1988. The ponds are connected by drainages to the hatchery, but the state wildlife officer swears the record-breaking fish did not come from there. At any rate, the ponds are fed by warm spring water and do not freeze during winter. Fishing for small rainbows is generally quite good. From Hwy. 135, cross the East River at the Roaring Judy Hatchery and follow the signs.

Taylor Park Reservoir—

If a beautiful location is any consideration, you should definitely try fishing here. Located in the shadow of the jagged Sawatch Range, Taylor Park Reservoir is best fished early and late in the season. Catch rainbows, browns, mackinaws and even kokanee salmon. Rental boats and supplies can be found at the Taylor Park Boat House.

The Taylor River—

Runoff from the Elk Mountains is stored in Taylor Park Reservoir and escapes ice-cold from the bottom of the dam. The Taylor River above the reservoir is literally full of rainbows, brooks and browns to 10 inches. Forest Rd. 742 follows the Taylor upstream for 22 miles. Below the reservoir wading is difficult, even dangerous at times, because the river bottom consists of smooth, round rocks and sudden, deep pools. More than half of the land below the reservoir is public. Fishing for browns, brooks and rainbows can be good with large nymphs and select lures. Try throwing a line in the large pools near the bridge just below Taylor Park Dam. Nine campgrounds line the Taylor River between Almont and Taylor Park Reservoir.

FOUR-WHEEL-DRIVE TRIPS

Schofield Pass—

See the **Redstone and Crystal River Valley** chapter.

Taylor Pass—

This is a quick, very scenic way to get over to **Aspen** and the **Roaring Fork Valley**. It can be treacherous and snow-covered, so be sure to get updated conditions (try the forest service office in Gunnison).

Taylor Pass, at 12,400 feet, was used as a supply route to the Aspen area in the 1880s. The views north to the Roaring Fork Valley and Hunter Fryingpan Wilderness Area are almost as awe-inspiring as the view back south to Taylor Park.

To reach the pass from Gunnison, head north on Hwy. 135 for 11 miles to Almont and then turn left on County Rd. 742, which heads up the Taylor River. Follow the road to Taylor Park Reservoir. A mile or so beyond Lakeview Campground, turn left, following the reservoir shoreline and heading upriver all the way to Dorchester Campground. The road gets rough from here. Once to the summit of Taylor Pass, follow Express Creek to Ashcroft in the Castle Creek Valley. Head down the road about 15 miles to Hwy. 82 near Aspen. For a scenic return to Gunnison, turn left on Hwy. 82, and proceed to Carbondale, then head up the Crystal River over McClure and Kebler passes to Crested Butte and back to Gunnison.

GOLF

Dos Rios Golf Club—

Dos Rios is a semi-private club located at the confluence of the Taylor River and Tomichi Creek. It's a great setting. Water is the key to this course—it comes into play on 17 holes. Especially tough is the relatively young front nine, which will take a few years to fill in. Open in summer only. Greens fees are moderate. Pro shop; carts; club rentals. Located 2 miles west of Gunnison, just south off Hwy. 50; **(303) 641-1482.**

Skyland Resort—

Designed by Robert Trent Jones, Jr., this fine 18-hole course has a short history and a long reputation. Open since 1984, Skyland is already considered one of the best courses in the state. The mountain views from its position at the base of Mount Crested Butte are spectacular. Keep out of the numerous sand traps and you may be able to enjoy the scenery. Besides a pro shop and a restaurant, Skyland features a full health club with indoor tennis and racquetball facilities. Club and power cart rentals are available. Located at the base of Mount Crested Butte. **Country Club Dr. #1, Crested Butte, CO 81224; (303) 349-6129.**

HIKING AND BACKPACKING

Deep canyons, lush meadows, streams, lakes and ghost towns can be easily found in **Gunnison National Forest**. Narrowing down the long list of hiking possibilities is especially difficult, simply because there are good trails crisscrossing virtually the entire county.

For maps and further information about hiking in the Gunnison and Crested Butte area, visit the **Taylor River/Cebolla District Forest Service Office, 216 N. Colorado St., Gunnison, CO 81230; 641-0471.**

Cement Creek Trail—

This excellent, short hiking loop begins on Trail 409, only a mile up the Cement Creek Valley. The trail leads quickly uphill toward a large rock outcropping with a couple of deep caves. Just above the caves, the trail splits in two. The right fork leads east across the forested mountainside, eventually reaching Walrod Gulch. Walrod is a seldom-driven four-wheel-drive road that heads back down to Cement Creek. Upon reaching Cement Creek, walk downstream and back to your starting point. The left branch of the trail (back by the caves) continues uphill to an aspen-cloaked ridge and a number of longer trail possibilities.

A veritable trail system leads away from different points along Cement Creek and into the mountains of this little-known mountain valley. Cement Creek is located 7 miles south of Crested Butte off Hwy. 135. Turn east onto Cement Creek Rd., which leads up the valley to a number of trail access points and a shaded campground. Trail 409 begins directly across from the Cement Creek Guard Station, 1 mile from Hwy. 135.

Conundrum Trail—

This trail has it all: beautiful scenery, a ghost town, natural hot springs and, consequently, heavy use. If your goal is to get away from other humans, try someplace else. A full-day hike or perhaps an overnight stay would be the best way to experience Conundrum Trail. It is quite possible to hike to Conundrum Hot Springs one day and on to Aspen the next. To reach the trail, drive to Crested Butte Ski Area and continue 6 miles to the ghost town of Gothic (see page 394). From Gothic follow Copper Creek Rd. (four-wheel-drive vehicles only) 4 miles to the north. Hike for half a mile up Copper Creek Trail to reach a junction just before Copper Lake. The right fork is Conundrum Trail; the left fork heads over East Maroon Pass toward Colorado's best-known mountains.

Curecanti Creek Trail—

See the Hiking section under Major Attractions.

Mill Creek Trail—

This short 1.5-mile trail cuts between steep valley walls and through a thick conifer forest before ending in a grassy meadow at the West Elk Wilderness Area boundary. The watery sounds of Mill Creek provide a soothing background for a picnic or a nap. Bring along your fishing pole.

For serious backcountry exploration of the West Elk Wilderness Area, the Mill Creek Trail provides a little-used access. The trail continues from the wilderness boundary into a scenic area, with views to the volcanically formed Castles and to West Elk Peak (13,035 feet). A 14-mile route takes you over Storm Pass (12,440 feet), which is steep going on both sides. On an autumn hike you'll be able to enjoy the changing colors, but wear bright clothing and beware of hunters. From Gunnison, drive 17

miles north up the Ohio Creek Valley on Forest Rd. 734 to the Mill Creek turn-off. Turn left and follow Mill Creek 4 miles on a fairly good dirt road (two-wheel-drive vehicles are fine) until the road reaches a dead end and the trail begins.

Timberline Trail—

Enjoy superb views of Taylor Park Reservoir while hiking on a level contour averaging over 10,000 feet in elevation, just beneath the snow-streaked peaks of the Sawatch Range. This is a perfect trail for extended trips. The trail is fairly easy and it passes many small lakes and streams along its route. Be sure to bring your fishing gear! There are a number of marked access points for Timberline Trail because it traverses several roads. From Taylor Park Reservoir take Cumberland Pass Rd. southeast to the ghost town of Tincup. Follow E. Willow Creek Rd. 2 miles east to Mirror Lake. The trailhead begins just below Mirror Lake Campground. Another good idea would be to pick up Timberline Trail as it crosses Cottonwood Pass Rd.

RIVER FLOATING

The character of the rivers flowing into the Gunnison Basin has been altered forever by several monolithic reservoirs. Nonetheless, there are excellent stretches, enticing you to bring out your raft or kayak for a short run. A couple of river outfitters in the area will take you on a quiet family float or a whitewater odyssey.

Lower Gunnison—

See the **Black Canyon Country** chapter.

Upper Gunnison—

One mile downstream from Almont, all types of watercraft—open canoes, rafts and kayaks—put in for the fairly gentle trip. The wide river flows unobstructed through the town of Gunnison, all the way to the fringe of Blue Mesa Reservoir. The only rapids in this mild stretch are the result of the spring thaw early in the season. The river passes through a rural setting of pasturelands and country homes. Unfortunately for river enthusiasts, the free-flowing water doesn't last long enough. Beginning 5 miles below the town of Gunnison, large dams force the water into lakes for the next 45 miles.

Taylor River—

The water rushing out of Taylor Park Dam tumbles downstream through a deep, flat-bottomed canyon. The fast water is ideal for experienced kayakers who can handle Class II to Class V water. The path of the river is followed by Hwy. 306; many developed campgrounds and access points can be found along its entire run from the dam to Almont. The dam tends to lengthen the season by holding water back during runoff and slowly releasing it into the fall.

Outfitters—

C.B. Rafting—309 Gothic Rd., Crested Butte; (303) 349-7423.

Scenic River Tours—703 W. Tomichi Ave., Gunnison; (303) 641-3131.

SKIING

CROSS-COUNTRY SKIING

Whether you are into telemarking or just gliding along in solitude, there are any number of trail choices available. Mount Crested Butte is known for its throngs of devoted telemark skiers. Several broad alpine valleys leading from Crested Butte provide safe and easy passage. More adventuresome skiers can test their limits on the ridges and slopes. Supposedly, nordic skiing at Crested Butte started back in the 1880s when a skiing mailman, Al Johnson, covered his rugged mail route by way of 15-foot birch skis and one long pole. The good old days are remembered by a unique tribute: the Al Johnson Memorial Uphill Downhill. This race pits expert telemark skiers against each other on a race up the steep 1,500-foot slope of the North Face, and then back down.

Backcountry Trails—

Gothic—Tracks are set each year to the ghost town of Gothic (see the Scenic Drives section). It is an easy 8-mile tour, with tremendous views for the duration. Ski tracks usually continue beyond Gothic and into the upper valley.

Pearl Pass—Skiing over Pearl Pass to Aspen has long been a favorite of experienced skiers. This route is strenuous, isolated and exceptionally beautiful. The Braun Hut System allows for a warm overnight stay during the long trek (see the Aspen chapter). Check with the folks at the Alpineer for more information.

Groomed Trails—

Crested Butte Nordic Ski Center—Located at the Crested Butte Athletic Club in the downtown historic district. This is a complete facility, offering rentals, lessons, advice, a 9-kilometer groomed track and, most importantly, a hot tub and a sauna. Open daily 9 am–4 pm. 2nd and Whiterock Ave.; (303) 349-6201.

Ski Rentals—

Paradise Bikes and Skis—224 Elk Ave., Crested Butte; (303) 349-6324.

The Alpineer—419 6th St., Crested Butte; (303) 349-5210.

DOWNHILL SKIING

Crested Butte —

Soaring above its namesake town, Crested Butte Mountain appears as an intimidating pinnacle. As you near the base lifts, the mountain reveals its true diversity of terrain. It can be a wonderful place to learn the sport. In fact, Crested Butte has a "kids ski free" policy. Though there is plenty of intermediate terrain, only true experts can take advantage of the entire mountain. As one local said, "Crested Butte has all the expert terrain that a sane person needs." Experts flock to the double black diamonds of the North Face, which offer some of the best "steep and deep" powder in the state. The area gets an abundance of snow that doesn't melt quickly because the temperatures stay cold. For information contact **Crested Butte Mountain Resort, 12 Snowmass Rd., PO Box A, Crested Butte, CO 81225; (303) 349-2333.**

Snowcat Skiing—2,000 feet of untracked powder await you on the ridge behind the Irwin Lodge (see the Where to Stay section).

SWIMMING

Dos Rios Golf and Swim Club—
Pool, restaurant, bar and golf course

are open to all visitors during summer. Follow the signs from Hwy. 50 just west of Gunnison; **(303) 641-1482.**

Gunnison Sport and Fitness—
A large pool is open to the public. Located a half mile north of Gunnison off Hwy. 135; **(303) 641-3751.**

TENNIS

Crested Butte—
In the center of the town park there are three outdoor courts (not lighted). No fee.

—————— SEEING AND DOING ——————

MUSEUMS

The Pioneer Museum in Gunnison—
One thing to be said about this museum is that there are a lot of big exhibits. Big, you ask? Yeah, big. How about the first post office in Gunnison, a schoolhouse built in 1909, the Denver & Rio Grande Railroad depot, Narrow Gauge Railroad Engine #268 and the old Mears Junction water tank. The Pioneer Museum also displays old photos, furniture and other artifacts that sufficiently convey life as it was when the pioneers were in the valley. Open Memorial Day through Labor Day, Mon.–Sat. 9:30 am–5 pm, Sun. 1–5 pm. Located at the east end of Gunnison on Hwy. 50; **(303) 641-9963.**

NIGHTLIFE

Kochevar's—
So, you want to boogie? There are a number of Crested Butte night spots with live music, but it is hard to beat Kochevar's for a lively crowd, good bands and reasonable prices. And besides, with pool tables, dart boards and a shuffleboard table, there is something for everyone. This place has enjoyed a long history of illicit entertainment as you can see by the turn-of-the-century gaming tables and slot machines;

the upstairs was once a notorious bordello. Watney's and Heineken are on tap. A bar menu is served from 10 pm–midnight with food from Karolina's Kitchen (see Where to Eat section) next door. **127 Elk Ave.; (303) 349-6745.**

The Rafters—
The Rafters has become the place to be seen at the mountain. Don't miss the great happy hour that starts just as the lifts begin closing. On sunny days the deck stays crowded from lunch till dusk. Each night during ski season, live bands get the house rockin' at a high energy level on the large dance floor. Pool and foosball tables are available. Sandwiches, salads and soups are served until 9 pm. Located in Crested Butte right at the base of the ski area in the upper level of the **Gothic Building; (303) 349-2299.**

The Wooden Nickel—
A great place for an après-ski drink in a traditional Crested Butte hangout. The Wooden Nickel is a long and narrow room with a mirrored wooden bar down one side and tables on the other. It has the feeling of an upscale Old West saloon. A fire is often roaring under the huge brass mantel. Hungry? Try the half-pound bur-

gers, sandwiches, prime rib and nightly seafood specials. Live lobster on Fri. **222 Elk Ave.; (303) 349-6350.**

SCENIC DRIVES

Alpine Tunnel—

The Alpine Tunnel, constructed by the Denver South Park & Pacific Railroad in 1881, is an engineering marvel. The 1,800-foot-long tunnel was bored through the Continental Divide in a race with the Denver & Rio Grande Railroad to provide railroad service to the Gunnison area. Working conditions were miserable, and the labor turnover was rumored to have totaled more than 10,000 men. The tunnel proved very expensive to maintain, and the DSP&P railroad abandoned the line in 1910. Even though the west portal of the tunnel caved in a number of years ago, remnants of many buildings and a water tower remain along the drive. Just above the water tank is what's left of Woodstock, a train workers' boardinghouse destroyed in an 1884 avalanche that killed 13 people.

To reach the Alpine Tunnel from Gunnison, head east on Hwy. 50 for 12 miles to Parlin. Turn left, heading north up along Quartz Creek to Ohio City and then Pitkin. About 3 miles beyond Pitkin, the marked road to the Alpine Tunnel turns off to the right. Follow this rough dirt road about 10 miles up to the west portal of the tunnel. A passenger car with good ground clearance can make the trip.

Black Canyon of the Gunnison—

See the **Black Canyon Country** chapter.

Cottonwood Pass—

See the **Upper Arkansas Valley** chapter.

Cumberland Pass/Taylor Park Loop—

For a firsthand look at Gunnison area history and some outrageous scenery, take this drive. You'll visit Quartz Creek, Tincup and Taylor Park mining districts, all of which brought settlers into the area in the late 1870s. Cumberland Pass, at just over 12,000 feet, is one of the highest dirt roads in the state and can be easily driven in a passenger vehicle.

The loop starts from Gunnison and can be done in one day, but you may want to take a few days and camp along the way. Head east on Hwy. 50 from Gunnison for 12 miles to Parlin, then north on the road leading up Quartz Creek. The first big area of interest is along Quartz Creek. **Ohio City** and **Pitkin** were centers for two large silver strikes in 1879 and 1880. Cumberland Pass Rd. begins climbing north out of Pitkin to its orange-colored summit. Built as a pack trail in 1880 to connect Tincup with the Quartz Creek camps, the pass has seen a lot of use over the years. From the summit you can look out on the massive, steep mountains of the Sawatch Range to the east and beyond Taylor Park to the north.

When you've seen enough, head down the pass to **Tincup.** Now a peaceful summer residence for a lucky few, Tincup was once a rough mining town that saw seven sheriffs killed within a period of a few months. Gunfights were a very common way to settle arguments here. The origin of Tincup's name is not completely clear, but many believe it comes from one of the original miners here who sifted through the gold-flaked gravel of the stream with his tin cup. People began prospecting here as early as 1859, but things didn't get hopping until 1879 when Tincup became the leading silver producer in the area.

Continuing north from Tincup, the road leads to **Taylor Park Reservoir** in Taylor Park. There are plenty of campgrounds in the area and the trout fishing in the creeks and reservoir can be great. From the reservoir, follow the Taylor River southwest through Taylor Canyon, eventually intersecting Hwy. 135, 11 miles north of Gunnison at Almont.

Gothic—

A trip to Gothic is easily worth the minimal effort it takes to get there. Located 7 miles north of Crested Butte, this silver camp once boasted a population of thousands. Rich pockets of silver created much excitement but small returns. In 1880 the town received a visit from President Grant, who wanted a firsthand look at some Rocky Mountain mining camps. He traveled with Gov. Frederick Pitkin and ex-Gov. John Routt by mule team from Gunnison. Grant distrusted mule drivers and therefore insisted on holding the reins for most of the trip.

By 1885 the Sylvanite Mine could no longer stay open and Gothic began to wither away. Most of the old buildings are gone, but the site receives a lot of use in summer and fall from students of the Rocky Mountain Biological Laboratory. Gothic is also a jumping-off point for many popular hikes in the Maroon Bells–Snowmass Wilderness Area. To reach Gothic, drive to Mount Crested Butte and continue north on scenic Forest Rd. 327 above the East River.

Kebler Pass—

In fall this is the ultimate foliage drive, highlighted by mountainsides of golden aspen. A graded dirt road winds past alpine meadows covered with wildflowers and dense forests; the West Elk Mountains and the Raggeds rise all around. With an elevation of about 10,000 feet, Kebler Pass never rises above treeline, but the views are far reaching at times. About 7 miles after reaching the summit, a left turn onto Forest Rd. 706 will land you at Lost Lake. The road can be rough, but is passable by all vehicles. Lost Lake is ideal for a lazy afternoon picnic or an overnight stay at the small campground.

To reach Kebler Pass from Crested Butte, take County Rd. 12 from the west end of town. The road continues for about 24 miles before intersecting Hwy. 133 at Paonia Reservoir. From here you can take a right and drive over McClure Pass (8,755 feet) before dropping into the beautiful Crystal River Valley.

Lake City—

The 55-mile drive south to Lake City on Hwy. 149 gets progressively more beau-tiful after you pass through the barren hills near Blue Mesa Reservoir. Soon, the San Juan Mountains introduce themselves dramatically as the road continues beside the Lake Fork of the Gunnison. Situated in the narrow river valley is the small town of Lake City, named for its setting only 2 miles from spectacular Lake San Cristobal. The area is better known for the grotesque antics of cannibal Alferd Packer. For more information on the Lake City vicinity, see the Major Attractions section of the **Creede** chapter.

Marshall Pass—

One of the lowest passes over the Continental Divide, Marshall Pass was the route the Denver & Rio Grande Railroad chose when extending service to the Western Slope. Tracks were laid over this 10,846-foot pass in 1881. A train robbery took place at the pass in 1902. The inept outlaws couldn't blow open the safe (they blew up just about everything else), so they robbed the passengers, though not before the travelers were able to hide most of their valuables under seats and in petticoats. The railroad is long gone, but the dirt road follows the railroad grade up and over the pass.

From Gunnison, head east on Hwy. 50 for 32 miles to Sargents. An old stagecoach stop, Sargents was later a railroad depot for cattle and ore from mines in the area. Just east of the town's gas station, the Marshall Pass road turns right. Once at the summit of the pass, continue on the road past O'Haver Lake to Hwy. 285. Turn left at the highway, heading north over Poncha Pass to the intersection with Hwy. 50 at Poncha Springs. From here, turn left on Hwy. 50 and head over Monarch Pass back to Gunnison.

Rainbow Trout

WHERE TO STAY

ACCOMMODATIONS
CRESTED BUTTE

Irwin Lodge — $$$

This 22-room self-contained lodge offers a perfect means to experience the isolated beauty of the Elk Mountains. Located a scant 12 miles from Crested Butte, it remains a world away. Irwin Lodge is a year-round destination offering as much to guests in summer as in winter.

An average year drops over 30 feet of snow on the lodge. Since the nearest plowed road is 10 miles away, the only way to reach Irwin Lodge in winter is over the snow: by snowcat, snowmobile or skis. The downhill skiing on the ridge behind the lodge is spectacular. Take the lodge's snowcat to the ridge for the chance of a lifetime: 2,000 vertical feet of virgin powder. Cross-country trails start at the front door.

Once there you'll take advantage of the comfortable lobby with its massive fireplace and heavy wooden beams. A family-style restaurant, a bar and a hot tub round out the lodge amenities. For reservations and information: **PO Box 457, Crested Butte, CO 81224; (303) 349-5308.**

Christiana Bed and Breakfast — $$

A casual atmosphere pervades this 20-room ski lodge. Built with comfort in mind, there are many common areas to enjoy. Perhaps the best feature of the lodge is the outdoor hot tub with views to Mount Crested Butte. The rooms are basic and clean; each has a private bath. **621 Maroon Ave., PO Box 427, Crested Butte, CO 81224; (303) 349-5326.**

The Claim Jumper — $$

The Victorian parlor of this small bed and breakfast makes it easy to imagine Crested Butte in the late 1800s. Soaking your tired bones in the redwood hot tub, or sweating it out in the wet sauna will snap you back to the comforts of today. The Claim Jumper is a pleasant mix of old and new. Oh-Be-Joyful is the largest of the three guest rooms and the only one with a private bath. Each of the rooms, including Poverty Gulch, has a queen-sized brass bed, period antiques and a supply of complimentary brandy. For rentals of a week or more, a rustic two-bedroom, three-story condominium ($$$$) accommodates as many as eight guests. A basket of hot biscuits with butter and jam, cereal, juice and coffee are served each morning in a sunny room just off the parlor. The owners, Jim and Nancy Harlow, will make you feel right at home, as will their friendly springer spaniel, Weaver. Make reservations in advance; no smoking allowed; no credit cards. **704 Whiterock Ave., Crested Butte, CO 81224; (303) 349-6471.**

The Nordic Inn — $$

At the base of the mountain is a 25-room inn that aptly reflects the warmth of the owners. Each room has two double beds, cable TV and a private bathroom. It is the common room that really shines at this Norwegian-style lodge. Chairs are grouped around the fireplace, providing a relaxing après-ski environment. Kids stay free. **PO Box 939, Crested Butte, CO 81224; (303) 349-5542.**

GUNNISON

Unfortunately, there are no historic hotels or cozy bed and breakfasts to recommend in Gunnison. The town offers a number of roadside motels, but to stay in a really special place you'll have to leave the immediate vicinity. Listed are a couple of the better motels in Gunnison.

Best Western Tomichi Village — $$

This exceptionally clean and well-kept motel is located 1 mile east of town. Enjoy all the amenities: restaurant, heated pool, sauna and whirlpool. Each of the 49 rooms has air conditioning and cable movies. One mile east on **Hwy. 50; PO Box 763, Gunnison, CO 81230; (303) 641-1131.**

Comfort Inn Water Wheel — $$

There are 65 rooms at this comfortable motel. Half of the rooms have air conditioning; all have cable movies. A tennis court and an exercise room are available for guest use. Take Hwy. 50 west of town for 1.5 miles; PO Box 882, Gunnison, CO 81230; (303) 641-1650.

Cattlemen Inn — $

If you are on a tight budget and just want a place to sleep, try the low-cost rooms at the Cattlemen Inn. The rooms are simple, small and stuffy. With the money you save, you can buy a steak at the restaurant just down the hall. 301 W. Tomichi Ave., Gunnison, CO 81230; (303) 641-1061.

CAMPING

In Gunnison National Forest—

Crested Butte Area—Cement Creek Campground can be reached by heading 7 miles south of Crested Butte on Hwy. 135. Turn east onto Cement Creek Rd. and travel 4 miles up the valley to the shaded campground. Thirteen sites; no fee. Irwin Campground enjoys a beautiful location west of Crested Butte. Take Hwy. 2 for 7 miles west of Crested Butte to the Lake Irwin turn-off and proceed north on Forest Rd. 826. There are 32 tent and trailer sites; no fee. Avery Peak Campground is located just north of Gothic, 7.4 miles north of Crested Butte by Forest Rd. 317. Ten sites; no fee. Gothic Campground is another half mile up the road. Four sites; no fee.

Lake Fork of the Gunnison—Campgrounds south of Hwy. 50 get much less use than those areas to the north. To reach Red Bridge and Gateview campgrounds drive 25 miles south on Hwy. 149 from the eastern end of Blue Mesa Reservoir, to a turn-off with a sign noting Red Bridge 2 miles. Keep an eye peeled for bighorn sheep during the short drive. Red Bridge Campground has 12 sites and no fee. Another 5 miles down a rough dirt road through a narrow canyon is Gateview Campground. There are five well-placed tent sites above the road and no fee.

Taylor River Area—North of Gunnison there are a dozen popular campgrounds from Almont, upstream on Taylor River Rd., to Taylor Park Reservoir. Well known among trailer and RV campers, these areas fill up early. The camping areas are scattered along the shaded river banks and up above the reservoir.

Curecanti National Recreation Area—

See the Major Attraction section.

Private Campgrounds—

Gunnison is truly RV heaven, with six private campgrounds offering hookups, showers, etc. There are no private campgrounds in Crested Butte.

KOA Gunnison—Get comfortable at this cushy campground near the Gunnison River. One mile west of town on Hwy. 50, turn south and follow the signs for a half mile. (303) 641-1358.

WHERE TO EAT

CRESTED BUTTE

For a small mountain town, Crested Butte has a fantastic array of restaurants to suit every mood and pocketbook. Though there are many restaurants at Mount Crested Butte, the ones with character, variety and great food are located on historic Elk Ave. in the old part of town. Most

of the restaurants have been around for awhile, and stay surprisingly busy year-round (excluding the spring mud season and late fall when many close). Nearly all restaurants cater to the hearty appetites of skiers and mountain bikers by heaping food on every plate. You will not go away hungry.

Soupçon — $$$$

High expectations should accompany you upon entering this small log cabin on a back alley behind Kochevar's. Once inside, you will join a lucky group of people about to sample exceptional French food. The casual atmosphere belies the careful preparation in the kitchen. The menu is spelled out on a chalkboard; innovative poultry, lamb, beef and fish entrées are offered. On our visit a sampling of appetizers included duckling mousse, escargot Monaco, and fresh scallops in caviar cream. This smoke-free restaurant is open nightly from 6–10 pm. Reservations are a must. In the alley just behind Kochevar's Bar at **2nd St. and Elk Ave.; 349-5448.**

Le Bosquet — $$$ to $$$$

For 11 years this fine French restaurant has served consistently excellent food with polished service. Le Bosquet is the place to enjoy a special meal in an elegant setting. The featured entrees come with complex and creative sauces. A few tempting dishes are: grilled duck breast in a minted raspberry sauce, elk filets in a Bordelaise sauce, veal with a Roquefort basil sauce, and fresh salmon with a ginger glaze. A selection of appetizers and salads is also available. Reservations requested. Luncheon menu 11:30 am–2 pm during summer; dinner served nightly from 5:30 pm. **2nd St. and Elk Ave.; 349-5808.**

Slogar Bar and Restaurant — $$$

The fried chicken at Slogar's is darn good. Skillet-fried chicken is served family style with a relish tray, cole slaw, mashed potatoes and gravy, fresh biscuits with honey butter and sweet creamed corn. Steak dinners are also served. That's it—a hearty meal for one reasonable price. Open nightly 5–9 pm. Reservations recommended. **2nd St. and Whiterock Ave.; 349-5765.**

Angello's — $$

Pizza, pasta, meatball sandwiches and antipasto salads are the order of the day at Angello's. The restaurant has recently expanded into the shop next door, to satisfy even more hungry customers. The dinners come in full and half portions, including salad and homemade bread. Garlic bread with melted cheese is the perfect appetizer. Delivery during winter. Open daily from 5–9 pm. **501 Elk Ave.; 349-5351.**

Donita's Cantina — $$

At the slightest thought of Mexican food, you should head straight to Donita's. Your hunger will be satisfied with enormous portions of spicy fare. If you're not very hungry, order a la carte. Specials of the house are beef or chicken fajitas, dinner quesadillas with shredded beef, chicken or veggies, and camarones (Gulf shrimp) sautéed in butter and garlic. Everything, including the sauces and salsa, is made fresh daily. The margaritas are excellent. Open seven nights a week 4:30–9:30 pm. Reservations are not accepted. **330 Elk Ave.; 349-6674.**

Karolina's Kitchen — $$

Though the restaurant is new, the Kochevar building has enough history to fill this book. Take a look around the dining room at the various antique contraptions. The still in the far back provided jugs of moonshine for the valley during Prohibition. Large sandwiches, salads and homemade soups make up the bulk of the menu. Also served are pork chops, peel-and-eat shrimp, knackwurst and sauerkraut, and a 24-ounce rustler's T-bone ($$$$). Open daily from 11 am–midnight. **127 Elk Ave.; 349-6756.**

Penelope's — $$

Penelope's greenhouse is a perfect place to enjoy a slow-paced gourmet breakfast or brunch. The greenhouse is an addition to a lovingly restored Victorian home with all the complements of a fine restaurant. The superb breakfasts are served on weekends only: Sat. 7:30 am–noon; Sun. 7:30 am–1 pm. Dinner is served nightly from 5:30–10 pm. **120 Elk Ave.; 349-5178.**

The Bakery Cafe — $

Select from a long list of fresh-baked goods for a quick take-out or enjoy a leisurely cappuccino while poring over the morning paper. The blackboard menu offers cinnamon rolls, quiches, various croissants and delicious homemade soups and sandwiches. This corner cafe gets hectic during the lunch rush in winter, but the food is worth the wait. Open daily 7:30 am–5 pm and until 8:30 pm during ski season. **302 Elk Ave.; 349-7280.**

GUNNISON

The Gold Creek Inn — $$$ to $$$$

You wouldn't expect to find a five-star gourmet restaurant in a community of 44 people, but that's exactly what awaits in Ohio City (24 miles east of Gunnison). Built in an 1890s general store, the Gold Creek Inn has a tiny, fireside dining room. Chef/owner Joe Benge was trained at New York State's Culinary Arts Institute—and you can watch him work his magic. The flexibility of a chalkboard menu assures the freshest of ingredients are used for each dish. In the cozy atmosphere of the restaurant, the succulent food seems to taste even better.

This restaurant is worth going out of your way for—but be sure to reserve well in advance because Joe is often booked solid. Sunday brunch, served on a deck overlooking Gold Creek, is a memorable affair if you can get a table. Dinner is served from 5:30–10 pm Wed.–Sat.; Sun. brunch 10 am–3 pm. As a quiet bed and breakfast alternative, consider staying overnight in one of his two guest rooms ($$). It's quite nice. To get here from Gunnison, drive 12 miles east on Hwy. 50 to Parlin. Turn left and follow Quartz Creek Rd. 12 miles to Ohio City. **Box HH, Ohio City, CO 81237; (303) 641-2086.**

The Trough — $$$

As you may have gathered by the name, this is the place in Gunnison to "pig out." This spacious, rustically tasteful restaurant and bar is known for monstrous slabs of prime rib, steak and beef ribs. Kevin Brown, the manager, assures us the large variety of seafood is flown in every other day. Try the pork Hawaiian, the shrimp and other surf and turf items. The not-so-ugly-duckling is served with the Trough's special *l'orange* glaze. In winter there is an all-you-can-eat pork and beef rib special. The lounge and bar area really hop during the winter and summer peak seasons; live rock and roll thunders Wed. through Sun. nights. The lounge, open from 3 pm–2 am daily, offers a small sandwich menu. The restaurant is open 5:30–10:30 pm during the week and 5:30–11 pm on Fri. and Sat. One mile west of Gunnison on **Hwy. 50; 641-3724.**

Hunan Chinese Restaurant — $$

It's a long journey to Gunnison from Qingdao, the Chinese port city north of Shanghai, but the Liu family and their superior recipes made it intact. Open since 1985, this Chinese restaurant has built a good reputation and even draws people away from the posh restaurants in Crested Butte, 30 miles north of town. The menu offers a reasonably good selection of Chinese fare, especially Hunan, Szechuan and seafood dishes. Try the house duck plate. Full bar. The lunch menu ($) is offered until 3:30 pm each day. Hours are 11:30 am–9:30 pm Mon.–Thurs., 11:30 am–10 pm Fri.–Sat., noon–9:30 pm Sun. **405 W. Tomichi Ave.; 641-3600.**

Mario's Pizza — $ to $$

Mario's serves great pizza on white or whole wheat, thick or thin crust. You'll probably end up with enough left over for breakfast. The kitchen also prepares pasta dishes, calzones and a long list of reasonably priced sandwiches. Eat in the restaurant or take advantage of free delivery. Open seven days a week 11 am–11 pm. **213 W. Tomichi Ave.; 641-1374.**

The Sidewalk Cafe — $

With breakfast and lunch items at reasonable prices, the seats are usually filled at this attractive little cafe. Lots of windows, plants and an outdoor wooden deck add considerably to the meal. For breakfast, egg dishes as well as pancakes are the specialties; sandwiches and burgers for lunch. An all-you-can-eat soup and salad bar is available. Open Mon.–Fri. 5 am–3:30 pm, Sat. 5 am–2 pm, closed Sun. **113 W. Tomichi Ave.; 641-4130.**

Sundae Shop — $

Contrary to its name, this small restaurant is a good place to get a traditional breakfast of eggs, bacon and hash browns. Also served are pancakes, omelettes and breakfast sandwiches. The booths are filled with locals and the service is snappy. An inexpensive lunch and dinner menu is also served each day. Top your dinner off with a mouth-watering hot fudge parfait or a banana split. Open daily from 7:30 am–8 pm. **901 W. Tomichi Ave.; 641-5051.**

SERVICES

Crested Butte Central Reservations—
    Box A, Mount Crested Butte, CO 81225; 1-800-525-4220.

Day Care—
Butteopia Children's Program—They will take care of kids from ages 6 months to 6 years while you are on the slopes. A baby-sitting referral list is available. Located in the Wetstone Building, PO Box A, Crested Butte, CO 81225; (303) 349-2209.

**Gunnison County
Chamber of Commerce—**
    500 E. Tomichi Ave., PO Box 36, Gunnison CO 81230; (303) 641-1501.

**Crested Butte
Chamber of Commerce—**
    The Old Town Hall, PO Box 1288, Crested Butte, CO 81224; (303) 349-6438.

Taxi—
Just Horsin' Around—29 Whiterock Ave., Crested Butte, CO 81224; (303) 349-5765.

Ouray

To get out and see the rugged, beautiful country around Ouray, the town mayor, Bill Fries (better known as country-western singer C.W. McCall), lays out three possibilities: "You can hike it if you've got the legs, ride it if you've got the horse, and jeep it if you have the nerve." One look at the mountains around town and you'll know what Fries is talking about. Ouray is a quiet little Victorian community wedged tightly into a nook of the Uncompahgre River Valley. To the east and the west, colorful rock walls shoot hundreds of feet skyward; to the south, the famous Million Dollar Highway clings to a cliff high above the river, snaking its way up to Red Mountain Pass. This stretch of road defies gravity and ranks as one of the most scenic and hair-raising in the state.

Ouray's roots go back to the mining days of the 1870s, when rich deposits of gold and silver were discovered. Hardrock miners have left behind more than 10,000 tunnels, cuts and abandoned shafts within a 10-mile radius of Ouray. Dozens of old wagon roads lead to many of the mines, giving rise to another of Ouray's claims to fame—fantastic jeeping. Drives over narrow, rough roads such as Engineer Pass, Imogene Pass and Black Bear Pass are not soon forgotten.

Summer is the big tourist season for Ouray, and a number of curio and souvenir shops on the main street suggest as much. Jeeping, hiking and camping are big draws. During the winter, when the San Juans are covered with a heavy blanket of snow, shops in Ouray close and the day-to-day pace winds down. But winter is a great time to be in Ouray. Cross-country skiing on Red Mountain Pass is hard to beat, especially when followed by the activity Ouray is perhaps best known for—soaking in a hot springs pool. The hot springs are soothing any time of year, but in winter, when steam rises from the water, the soak is just a bit more relaxing. Four lodges in town have hot springs facilities; the town pool offers an outdoor soak with spectacular views of the surrounding mountains. Eight miles downriver, Orvis Hot Springs features more of the same in a very quiet, relaxing environment.

For its small size, Ouray offers plenty of great lodging. Several well-kept Victorian homes have been converted into bed and breakfasts, and other places to stay are generally very good. Unfortunately, the enormous old Beaumont Hotel, built in 1887, is boarded up; let's hope it will someday be back in business, offering guests a trip back to the grand, prosperous mining days.

HISTORY

Long before prospectors led their heavily laden mules into Ouray, the Ute Indians cherished this spot on the Uncompahgre River for its hot springs. The town's namesake, Chief Ouray, spent much time here. White settlers named the town in honor of this great Ute who, through

401

his wisdom, almost singlehandedly averted inestimable bloodshed between whites and Utes during the twilight of the tribe's claim to western Colorado.

Mineral strikes in the Ouray area began in 1875. Although most of these early mines produced silver, one aptly named mine, the Mineral Farm, yielded large chunks of gold that were extracted from the ground using nothing more than hoes and shovels. The very first building in town was a saloon that did a hopping business. As with other mining settlements in the San Juans, Ouray's growth was hampered by its isolated location and the astronomical cost of transporting the ore. This problem was solved when Otto Mears built a cliff-hanging toll road up the wall of Uncompahgre Canyon to Red Mountain Pass south of town, connecting Ouray with Silverton. Wagons replaced mules for transporting ore, and Ouray began to boom. The first railroad arrived in Dec. 1887, further reducing shipping costs. Ouray became a crucial trading and transportation center for the surrounding mining camps and even then was attracting tourists. One of the town newspapers, the *Solid Muldoon*, was widely read and frequently quoted around the state. Its unusual format and sarcasm prompted even Queen Victoria of England to send for a subscription!

When the silver crash hit in 1893 and many mines closed down, Ouray lost its stride. But in 1896 an Irishman by the name of Thomas Walsh put Ouray-area mining back on track. Walsh had arrived in Ouray after suffering a huge loss in Leadville in 1893. He began to inspect the discarded piles of rock at local silver mines and discovered they were full of gold. This "dump grabber," as he was known to some, bought up a number of claims near Yankee Boy Basin, west of Ouray, and named them Camp Bird. Camp Bird went on to produce $20 million in gold before Walsh sold it in 1902 to an English group. Walsh moved to Washington, DC, and gradually became part of the high society. His daughter, Evalyn Walsh McLean, talked her father into buying her the famous (but cursed) Hope diamond. The diamond's curse proved true when McLean lost her 9-year-old son in an auto accident and her 25-year-old daughter to a drug overdose. On top of all these tragedies, her husband was an adulterous alcoholic who eventually went insane. But we digress.

Mining and tourism have successfully sustained Ouray's economy, but fluctuating mineral prices currently have most miners looking for another line of work. The silver crash in the early 1980s, brought on by the efforts of Texas' Hunt brothers to corner the market, prompted one local miner to tell us his one big wish is to see the formerly wealthy brothers lynched.

GETTING THERE

Ouray is located 320 miles southwest of Denver. Travel west on Interstate 70 to Grand Junction, then south on Hwy. 50 to Montrose. Continue south on Hwy. 550 to Ouray.

FESTIVALS AND EVENTS

Cabin Fever Days
Presidents Day weekend
A fun way to shake off the winter blahs is to join the Ouray locals for this homegrown festival. One of the highlights is the Chili Cookoff. Anyone can enter a favorite recipe, to be judged by an expert panel of chili connoisseurs. Recipes are rated on the basis of aroma, appearance, flavor and afterburner. Kiddy events are held at the local ski hill, and there is usually a cross-country ski race for adults. For more information call **(303) 325-4746.**

Culinary Art Show
mid-September
The Culinary Art Show coincides with many Colorfest events. Colorfest is an autumn festival celebrated throughout the Four Corners area. Ouray hosts some of the finest chefs in the region for a noncompetitive display of epicurean talents. The free event kicks off with beer tasting before moving into other culinary areas. Come celebrate excellence in food with a variety of expert demonstrations and seminars. The art of fine food manifests itself in the unmatched setting of Ouray.

OUTDOOR ACTIVITIES

BIKING
MOUNTAIN BIKING
Although mountain biking is not as formally developed in Ouray as it is in other parts of the state, there certainly are plenty of roads and trails to peddle on. Many old mining roads with beautiful scenery await your tracks. See the Four-Wheel-Drive Trips section for more ideas. At present, rentals in Ouray are hard to find, but **Big Horn Mercantile at 609 Main St., (303) 325-4257,** has a few bikes.

FISHING
The streams near Ouray rush out of the mountains and join the Uncompahgre River on its way north. Between Ouray and Montrose the river flows through private land, but much of the fishing there is slow anyway. There are some good high-country lakes discussed in the **Silverton** chapter. You might try **Silver Jack Reservoir** northeast of Ouray. Silver Jack provides pretty good fishing for rainbow, particularly in the spring and fall. No boats are allowed on the water. Take Hwy. 550 for 12 miles to just beyond Ridgway. Turn east on Owl Creek Rd. (Forest Rd. 858) and continue to Silver Jack. The reservoir catches water from the West, Middle and East forks of the **Cimarron River,** which can be good for brook and cutthroat in addition to rainbow.

FOUR-WHEEL-DRIVE TRIPS
"Ouray is to jeepers what Oahu is to surfers" states a newspaper article tacked to the wall in the San Juan Scenic Jeep Tours office in Ouray. And how true it is. For visitors to Ouray, especially those coming for the first time, a jeep trip on the network of old mining roads is a must. Via these exciting roads, often cut into cliffs with sheer drops of hundreds of feet, history comes to life and the scenery can't be beat. But as scary as a jeep trip can be on these roads, nothing compares to the danger encountered by travelers back in the early days. Rev. J.J. Gibbons, who arrived in Ouray in 1888, relates many experiences on these roads in his journal, *In the San Juan.* One occurred while he was returning from a particularly frightening trip over Imogene Pass in winter. After making his way over, he warned an oncoming traveler of the danger, but his advice went unheeded. He recounts:

I looked back and saw the young man close to the top of the range, making slow progress. The horse was slipping, and I sat upon a rock to watch the developments. When within ten yards of the pass the horse fell, rolled off the trail and shot down the mountain like a rocket. The young man threw up his hands in terror and it was well for him that he was not in the saddle at the time. The horse must have tumbled for a quarter of a mile among the jagged rocks, and I presume every bone in his body was broken. I continued my journey, having learned a useful lesson, never to ride a poor horse, or one not properly shod.

Black Bear Pass—

See the Four-Wheel-Drive Trips section in the **Silverton** chapter.

Corkscrew Road—

Drive south from Ouray on Hwy. 550 up to Ironton just before the summit of Red Mountain Pass. Turn left and follow the road south as it starts up Corkscrew Gulch. The narrow road winds up to the summit, which is covered with the same red soil as nearby Red Mountain. From the summit you can return on the same road, or work your way east and then south near the ghost town of Gladstone and along Cement Creek Rd. (County Rd. 110), ending in Silverton. Return to Ouray on Hwy. 550.

Engineer Pass—

See the Four-Wheel-Drive Trips section in the **Creede** chapter.

Ophir Pass—

See the Four-Wheel-Drive Trips section in the **Silverton** chapter.

Poughkeepsie Gulch—

Drive south from Ouray on Hwy. 550 for 4 miles and turn left on Engineer Mountain Rd. Three miles up the road, turn right and drive up through a basin and across rock outcroppings on the way to Lake Como.

Yankee Boy Basin/Governor Basin—

This is one of the best drives in the area, as it goes by mines, towering mountains and fields of wildflowers. The road begins just south of town on Camp Bird Rd. (County Rd. 361). Follow the road southwest up the valley through aspen and pine. After about 4 miles the road takes a frightening curve along a ledge blasted out of the canyon's rock wall. Another mile up the road, the famous Camp Bird Mine can be seen on the left (see the History section for more information). Follow the dirt road up to the old townsite of Sneffels. There is a fork here, the left being Imogene Pass Rd., which goes over to Telluride (see the Four-Wheel-Drive Trips section in the **Telluride** chapter). Stay right past the Sneffels townsite and follow the steep, winding road up past Twin Falls and into immense Yankee Boy Basin. Mt. Sneffels is directly to the north and can be climbed fairly easily via the ridge on its east side.

From Yankee Boy Basin a road heads off to the left, up a set of tight switchbacks into Governor Basin, site of the well-known Virginius Mine. The dramatic spires of St. Sophia Ridge are just to the southwest.

Rentals and Tours—

San Juan Scenic Jeep Tours—In business for more than 40 years, these folks are the ones to do your driving if you aren't up for it. They offer half- and full-day trips on some of the toughest roads around. For reservations and information, contact the office at **PO Box 290W, 480 Main St., Ouray, CO 81427; (303) 325-4444** or **(303) 325-4154.**

Switzerland of America Jeep Rentals—If you have experience operating a four-wheel-drive vehicle and want to rent a jeep, contact Switzerland of America. Open from June through Sept., they have jeeps seating from two to five people. Jeeps may be picked up the night before you leave. **PO Box 367, 226 7th Ave., Ouray, CO 81427; (303) 325-4484.**

HIKING AND BACKPACKING

Rugged trails, wide open mountain meadows, towering peaks, aspen glades, beautiful waterfalls and crashing streams; all of this and more awaits hikers and backpackers interested in getting out in the country surrounding Ouray. Uncompahgre National Forest encircles the town. Mountains rise to the west, leading into the Mt. Sneffels Wilderness Area, which straddles the Sneffels Range. To the east, the Big Blue Wilderness Area offers beautiful hikes in valleys seldom used by other hikers. South of town, trails climb up into the heart of the old mining country. Many shafts, buildings and even an occasional aerial tram indicate the extent of activity that went on here 100 years ago. *As in other areas of the San Juans, caution should be used when near mine sites. PLEASE stay out of the mines!!*

A good map of hiking trails in the Ouray area can be picked up at the visitors center next to the Ouray Hot Springs Pool. Topographical maps of the area are available at **Big Horn Mercantile** at **609 Main St., (303) 325-4257.** The Uncompahgre National Forest near Ouray is under the jurisdiction of the **Ouray Ranger District Office, 2505 S. Townsend Ave., Montrose, CO 81401; (303) 249-3711.**

Bear Creek Trail—

This is one of our all-time favorite trails in the state. It begins south of town and heads up along Bear Creek, on an old road that was built by miners with diggings in the area. The trail is cut into the rock wall of the steep canyon high above the raging water. Mining history is so pervasive along the trail that you almost expect to see a miner coming around the next corner followed by a burro weighted down with a load of ore. Volcanic intrusions are also visible from the trail. After some initial switchbacks, the trail traverses high above the creek. The Grizzly Bear Mine is visible after 2.5 miles and the Yellow Jacket Mine after 4.2 miles. At the Yellow Jacket Mine the trail forks, the left heading up to Ameri-can Flats where you can take Horsethief Trail northwest, eventually ending up north of Ouray near the Bachelor-Syracuse Mine. The right fork heads up Bear Creek for 3 miles to the summit of Engineer Pass. From here you can turn around or try to bum a ride from a jeeper.

The views on this hike are beyond description. Parents should think twice about taking this trail with small children—the drop-offs to the creek along the first few miles of the trail are substantial, so why tempt fate? To reach the trailhead, drive 4 miles south on Hwy. 550 to the first tunnel. The trail begins on top of the tunnel.

Blue Lakes Trail—

This trail leads into the beautiful Mt. Sneffels Wilderness Area and can be approached from two directions. Perhaps the most popular route is from the Dallas Divide. It's about a 4-mile hike to the lakes. From Ouray, drive north to Ridgway and turn left onto Hwy. 62. Proceed about 5 miles and turn left onto East Dallas Creek Rd. (County Rd. 7). Go almost 9 miles to the gate at the wilderness area boundary and begin hiking south. A sign marks the trailhead.

The other approach is just south of town on the road to Camp Bird Mine. You can drive up to the mine with a regular passenger car, but if you have a four-wheel-drive vehicle it's possible to continue an additional 3 miles up into Yankee Boy Basin. From there hike up the basin to the northeast for 2 miles to the lakes.

Box Canyon Falls and Park—

Off Hwy. 550 just southwest of Ouray is a torrent of water falling 285 feet into a narrow box canyon. The magnificent falls rushing through a fault in the quartzite rock are quite a sight. There is a rickety wooden pathway providing easy access to a misty viewpoint near the base of the falls. Allow about 15 minutes for a short but steep walk to a rocky overlook with a 1900s-era steel bridge spanning a narrow gap high above the waterfall. The view from atop the falls is wonderful. The city owns the land and access to this unusual geologic showpiece. Covered picnic tables and restrooms are available, but no overnight camping is allowed. Small fee. Open officially from mid-May to mid-Oct. For more information call **(303) 325-4464.**

Lower Cascade Falls Trail—

This is a good hiking introduction for people not yet used to the high altitude of Ouray. Starting at the east end of 8th Ave., the trail climbs a half mile up to the impressive Lower Cascade Falls. The water has cut deep into the sandstone, as you can see at the top of the falls. There are a couple of picnic tables along the way.

Upper Cascade Falls Trail—

Beginning at Amphitheater Campground just south of town, this trail (No. 213) heads 2.5 miles and 1,500 vertical feet up a series of switchbacks. The last half mile traverses the rock walls east of town, eventually crossing over Cascade Creek just below the falls. Just beyond the falls are the remains of the Chief Ouray Mine's boardinghouse and machine shop. The views down onto town and of the surrounding mountains make the steep climb worth it. To reach the trailhead, drive south on Hwy. 550 to the entrance to Amphitheater Campground. A sign marks the trailhead.

Wetterhorn Basin Trail—

Located in the heart of the Big Blue Wilderness Area, Wetterhorn Basin Trail is a 5-mile hike that stays above treeline most of the time. The views to Wetterhorn Peak (14,015 feet) and Coxcomb Peak (13,656 feet) are spectacular.

To reach the trailhead from Ouray, head north on Hwy. 550 a couple of miles past Ridgway and turn right on Owl Creek Pass Rd. After crossing the summit of Owl Creek Pass, turn right on Forest Rd. 860 and proceed 5 miles to the trailhead (you will need a four-wheel-drive or high-clearance pickup truck for the last 1.5 miles).

HORSEBACK RIDING

San Juan Mountain Outfitters—

This thoroughly professional outfit will take you on short backcountry rides into the San Juan Mountains. Hour rides are not available but half-day, full-day and overnight trips leave regularly during summer. The outfitters provide raincoats, water and snacks on morning and afternoon rides. Lunch is added on full-day rides. On overnighters, they not only take care of dinner, next day's breakfast and the campsite, but encourage fishing on a private pond (gear is furnished). All you have to do is wear a shirt, shoes and full length pants—and keep your body weight under 225 pounds. Reservations required. **2882 Hwy. 23, Ridgway, CO 81432; (303) 626-5360.**

ICE CLIMBING

When the large number of waterfalls in the Ouray area freeze in winter, out of the woodwork appear droves of that strange breed of winter recreationist...ice climbers. Converging on the Ouray area, these serious thrill seekers search for an iced-over waterfall and, with pterodactyl-like axes in each hand and ice screws on their belts, they start their ascents. It's exciting to watch; if you want a lesson, inquire at the visitors center in Ouray.

LLAMA TREKKING

Llama Tours of Ouray—

Bill Crawford, a Ouray native, knows the mountains around Ouray like the back of his hand and is now offering llama treks to some of his favorite spots. Half-day, full-day and overnight trips allow you to experience the San Juans in a unique way. It's not cheap, but it's memorable. Bill's two llamas, Sneffels and Doolittle, carry the fixings for a gourmet lunch including wine, cheese, pasta salad, meat, etc. and music to enhance your enjoyment of the mountains. Half-day trips leave at 8 am and 2 pm; full-day trips leave at 7 am; overnights leave at noon. For information, call **(303) 325-4875.**

SKIING

CROSS-COUNTRY SKIING

The magnificent backcountry skiing around Ouray is getting better known each year. West of town toward the Mt. Sneffels Wilderness Area are a number of fine trails offering good views and very few people. Although avalanches are a serious consideration, the basins around Red Mountain Pass provide an almost limitless amount of ski terrain. As one Ouray local puts it, "Backcountry skiing around Red Mountain Pass is like playing on a 1,000-hole golf course—every hole is different, so just tee off and enjoy." If you are unfamiliar with the area and want to try skiing on Red Mountain Pass, be sure to inquire locally about avalanche danger. Trail guides for the Ouray area are available in town.

Backcountry Trails—

East Dallas Creek Trail—This easy trail heads south, winding its way up 7 miles to the northern boundary of the Mt. Sneffels Wilderness Area. The lofty Sneffels Range (including Mt. Sneffels at 14,150 feet) is laid out in front of you while you ski in through pinon and juniper and eventually spruce and fir forests. Private property lines the road for the first 5 miles, so stay on the trail. To reach East Dallas Creek Trail from Ouray, head north on Hwy. 550 for 10 miles to Ridgway and turn left on Hwy. 62. Drive about 5 miles, turn left again onto County Rd. 7 and follow the signs to Uncompahgre National Forest. Start skiing where the plows stop.

Miller Mesa Trail—A good route for beginners to intermediates, Miller Mesa Trail rises above Ridgway, providing views of both the Sneffels Range and the Uncompahgre Valley. The trail heads south and then east up the mesa for 5 miles. From Ouray, drive north on Hwy. 550 to Ridgway and turn left on Hwy. 62. At the west end of Ridgway turn left onto County Rd. 5, which is marked by a sign to the Girl Scout Camp. After a quarter mile, turn right and drive about 5 miles to Elk Meadows. Park where the plowing has stopped.

Red Mountain Pass—At the summit of the pass many people choose to ski the trees on the west side of the road. There are a number of small lakes in the area. On the east side of the pass, US Basin offers what one Ouray local calls "the best backcountry skiing with road access in the country." Up near the basin is the St. Paul Lodge, run by Chris and Donna George. Chris, an avalanche expert, offers cross-country ski lessons and fairly rugged accommodations. For more information about the lodge and other skiing opportunities on Red Mountain Pass, see the Outdoor Activities section in the **Silverton** chapter.

Rentals and Information—

Big Horn Mercantile—A large assortment of cross-country skis, boots and poles, including sturdy telemark equipment, is rented throughout the winter at **609 Main St.; (303) 325-4257.**

TENNIS

Two public courts are located at the northwest end of town, adjacent to the hot springs pool. No lights and no fee.

———— SEEING AND DOING ————

HOT SPRINGS

The healing waters of the area's natural hot springs were well known to Chief Ouray for their spiritual and medicinal qualities. After Chief Ouray and the Utes left the area, the town became known for its "radioactive" hot springs. Don't worry, the water isn't really radioactive, but geothermal waters continue to boil to the surface from deep inside the earth. Some are diverted to the large Ouray Hot Springs Pool, while others are used at several smaller hotel/spas. Unfortunately, it is no longer possible to walk up Canyon Creek for a soak in a natural hot pot.

Orvis Hot Springs—

A word of advice, whether you are looking for a relaxing soak in a hot pool or just want a unique place to stay the night: get to Orvis Hot Springs. Originally known for the Orvis Plunge pool built in 1916, Orvis Hot Springs now offers four private indoor pools (102–108° F) and a large outdoor pool (103–104° F); bathing suits are optional. Another, smaller outdoor pool is currently under construction. The views of the Sneffels Range from the outdoor pool make Orvis Hot Springs a highly recommended stop. If you want to spend the night, there are six spacious rooms that share two bathrooms. For overnight guests, there is no fee for use of the hot springs. Massage therapists are available. The pools are open to the public daily from 10 am–10 pm; there is no curfew for guests of the hotel. Open since fall 1987, we can only hope this reasonably priced San Juan highlight stays in business. Located 9 miles north of Ouray on Hwy. 550 (1.3 miles south of Ridgway). **1585 County Rd. 3, Ridgway, CO 81432; (303) 626-5324.**

Ouray Hot Springs Pool—

Life somehow makes sense while you're soaking in this hot spring's shallow 104° F pool and gazing up at the surrounding peaks. For swimming laps or cooling off, dive into the larger of the two pools. In winter, large snowflakes fill the air and steam billows off the water, creating an almost mystical atmosphere. The hot springs entry fee is good for the whole day, provided you get a hand stamp. After a fire in 1988, a complete workout room and new locker-rooms were built. Also available are picnic tables, a playground and a running track. Kids love searching in the murky goldfish pond for crawdads. Open from 9 am–9 pm Mon.–Sat. and 9 am–7 pm Sun. in summer; 11 am–9 pm Sat.–Sun. and 1–9 pm, Thur., Fri. and Mon. in winter. Located on the north end of town just off Hwy. 550; **(303) 325-4638.**

Wiesbaden Hot Springs—

A recent addition to this well-known spa is a private outdoor tub with a roomy deck, enclosed by a redwood fence. Natural hot water cascades over a gentle rock waterfall before reaching the contoured Fiberglas tub. Day or night, it is a complete escape from the rest of humanity—unless of course you'd like to go there with a special friend. Controls for whirlpool jets and lights are easily reached from the tub. The tub is reserved by the hour and is open to the public; there is a significant discount for Wiesbaden guests. See the Where to Stay section for more information. **(303) 325-4347.**

MINE TOUR

Bachelor-Syracuse Mine Tour—

A sure-fire way to get a feel for what brought people to the San Juan area more than 100 years ago is to take a tour of the Bachelor-Syracuse gold and silver mine. Featured in a recent issue of *National Geographic*, this mine tour could easily be the best in the state. Ride the "trammer" 3,350 feet back into this hardrock mine, first worked in 1884 by three bachelors. Closed after the silver crash in the early 1980s, the mine now offers daily tours during the summer months. A real miner acting as tour guide accompanies you deep into the mountain; the jokes are as stale as the air, but who said miners have to be funny?

Actually, the hour-long tour is fascinating. You stop at a work site where the guide describes the whole hardrock mining process, from drilling holes for the dynamite to hauling the ore out of the mine by trammer. He also compares today's sophisticated mining to the rudimentary methods and extremely dangerous conditions endured by miners in the 1800s. The tunnel is well-lighted and ventilated. Be sure to bring a coat, as the temperature in the mine is a brisk 52° F. The mine site also offers a gift shop, gold panning and the "miner's outdoor cafe." A fee is charged. Be sure to take the tour before silver prices go back up and the mine re-opens for the real thing. Open daily mid-May to mid-Sept., 10 am–4 pm, mid-June to Sept. 1 from 10 am–5 pm. Closed July 4. To reach the mine, drive a mile or so north from Ouray on Hwy. 550. Turn right onto County Rd. 14 and follow the signs. **PO Drawer 380W, Ouray, CO 81427; (303) 325-4500.**

MUSEUMS AND GALLERIES

Nava—

This undersized gallery features traditional and contemporary Native American arts and crafts. Fine rugs, baskets and Doug Nava's own jewelry are tastefully displayed throughout. Located on 6th Ave. half a block east of Main St., **308 6th Ave.; (303) 325-4850.**

Ouray Historical Museum—

There is a lot to do in Ouray without heading inside to the confines of a museum. This is a special place, however, that can give you a historical perspective while visiting room after room of quality displays. Victorian-era items rekindle the town's heyday: guns and bullets from the 1890s, Edison phonographs, bar tokens and hotel log books—even a piano with worn ivory keys from the Gold Belt Theatre. Since the ivory is worn through only in the key of C, it can be assumed that most patrons played by ear.

Upstairs are several re-created hospital rooms, a general store and a legal office. Stop off between the first and second floors in a sunny sitting room with a black and white photo album of grizzled faces from Ouray's early years. There is more downstairs! A fine collection of mining tools, including bellows, an ore train and tongs, is displayed next to the assayer's office. Outside are a couple of restored cabins from the town's early years.

The museum is located inside the former St. Joseph's Hospital, which opened in 1887. Open daily from 9 am–5 pm May–Oct. Minimal admission fee. **5th St.** and **6th Ave.; (303) 325-4576.**

NIGHTLIFE

San Juan Odyssey—

If you are looking for something to do in Ouray at night, consider the San Juan Odyssey. It's an impressive computerized slide show of the San Juan Mountains done with 15 projectors, five screens and surround-sound. The London Symphony Orchestra performs the soundtrack. The show was put together by Ouray mayor and country singer, C.W. McCall. He personally narrates the show and even sings one of his rip-roaring songs, such as "Wolf Creek Pass" or "Convoy" to loosen up the audience. Most of the inspiring photos were taken by McCall and his family on their many trips around the San Juans. There is one show nightly at 8:30; a fee is charged. The box office, which opens at 8:15 pm, is at the old Ouray Opera House at **5th St.** and **Main St.** in Ouray where the show is held. For information about group rates or special showings call **(303) 325-4607.**

SCENIC DRIVES

Dallas Divide—

This 25-mile stretch of road between Ridgway and Placerville is one of the most photographed in Colorado. From the summit of the divide, views to the Sneffels Range and Uncompahgre and Wetterhorn peaks are stunning. To reach the Dallas Divide from Ouray, head north on Hwy. 550 to Ridgway and turn left onto Hwy. 62.

Million Dollar Highway—

Try as you will, there is absolutely no better vantage point for an auto trip deep into the San Juans than the Million Dollar Highway. This road winds up a glacial valley past once-thriving mines to the 12,217-foot summit of Red Mountain Pass. Towering peaks, elephantine mountain slopes, sheer cliff walls and thick stands of aspen and pine dominate the scenery.

The road was the result of Otto Mears's foresight. He understood that most counties were too poor to build roads to provide crucial economic links between the mining towns. So he took it upon himself to build this road to connect Ouray with Ironton Park, and in time completed the route over Red Mountain Pass to Silverton. The narrow road had a tollgate located atop Bear Falls, which charged $3.75 per vehicle and $.75 per horse. (One-and-a-half miles south of Ouray there is a turnout to view the 227-foot waterfall.)

The debate continues as to the origin of the name Million Dollar Highway. It is true that gold tailings were used in the original construction, but certainly not a million dollars' worth. Though the highway is said to have cost $40,000 per mile to build in 1883, a million-dollar price tag for the entire project would be too high. Another possibility involves a woman who traveled the road by stagecoach back in its early days. She exclaimed, "I wouldn't go back over that road for a million dollars!"

Lastly . . . the most probable and least colorful explanation is that it cost approximately $1 million to improve the road so it could be used by automobiles. At any rate, you'll enjoy million-dollar views for the duration of this scenic drive.

To encourage people to board a stage taking the toll road from Ouray to Ironton, a publicity sheet once proclaimed that the stagecoach could carry passengers with "celerity, certainty and safety." It goes on: "Rarely does an accident happen on this, the most remarkable highway in the world." The stagecoach is long out of service, but the Million Dollar Highway remains a breathtaking adventure. Take the 22-mile drive south on Hwy. 550 out of Ouray to the top of Red Mountain Pass, which eventually drops into historic Silverton. The entire route is easily completed in a passenger car.

WHERE TO STAY

ACCOMMODATIONS

Ouray may be the perfect place for people to own and operate bed and breakfasts. There are an abundance of large Victorian homes just crying for someone to renovate them and put them back in service. Many people have done just that, and a recent smattering of bed and breakfasts have opened up in town.

Which one should you stay in tonight? For a personal touch, in addition to a breakfast that draws rave reviews, try **The Kunz House ($$), 723 4th St., Box 235, Ouray, CO 81427, (303) 325-4220.** At the **Ouray 1898 House ($$),** each room has its own bathroom and is furnished in antiques. For reservations, contact the **Ouray 1898 House, 322 Main St., PO Box 641, Ouray, CO 81427; (303) 325-4871.** How about a Victorian-style suite with a fully equipped kitchen? The **Main Street House ($$$)** has two suites with exterior decks. There is a courtyard with a large playground for kids. **Main Street House, 334 Main St., Ouray, CO 81427; (303) 325-4317.**

San Juan Guest Ranch — $$$$

Set in the Uncompahgre Valley just 4 miles north of Ouray is a small ranch steeped in the western tradition. The intimacy of the ranch is its highlight. Located in the midst of working ranches, the San Juan Guest Ranch fits in well with the rest. All of the buildings appear weathered and well used from the outside, but comfortably modern from within. Horseback riding on spectacular trails in the San Juan Mountains is the underlying emphasis at this ranch. You'll also be treated to a balloon ride, a jeep tour and a soak in the Ouray Hot Springs Pool. Consider staying here for a fall photo workshop or for cross-country skiing in winter. **2282 Hwy. 23, Ridgway, CO 81432; (303) 626-5360.**

Wiesbaden Hot Springs Spa and Lodgings — $$$

Follow a stairway from the glass-enclosed lobby into the geothermal wonders of a hot mineral water vapor cave below. Guests receive free, unlimited use of the vapor cave, hot mineral outdoor pool, sauna and universal weight room. Available for guests at reduced fees is a private outdoor tub (see the Hot Springs section) and services such as professional massage, reflexology, acupressure treatment and facials. The rooms in the L-shaped motel are fairly standard, though some are equipped with kitchenettes; rooms in the main lodge building take on fanciful designs. The central lobby has a common seating room and free coffee and tea. For a special retreat ask about renting the rustic cabin on the hill above the lodge. It is heated by a wood stove and the small porch offers a spectacular panorama of the surrounding mountains. The Wiesbaden offers special winter discounts. **Box 349, Ouray, CO 81427; (303) 325-4347.**

St. Elmo Hotel — $$ to $$$

Built by Kitty Heit in 1898 as a boardinghouse for miners, the St. Elmo has been transformed into a first-class bed and breakfast. The turn-of-the-century ambience is tastefully preserved in each of the 11 uniquely furnished rooms. Period antiques, touches of polished brass and stained glass are in abundance throughout the hotel. Some rooms come with elegantly appointed sitting rooms; families may reserve separate sleeping rooms linked by a common bath; for special occasions, the genteel refinement of the presidential suite is at your disposal. Light breakfasts are served in the sunny Kitty Heit Room. The caring attitudes of Sandy and Dan Lingenfelter are warmly reflected in their well-run hotel. **426 Main St., PO Box 667, Ouray, CO 81427; (303) 325-4951.**

Western Hotel — $$ to $$$

Established in 1891, this three-story whitewashed structure sports an elaborate wooden facade that has somehow been spared from the ravages of fire. After a long trail of owners, the Western Hotel has now returned to much of its former grandness. These days, room rates are a bit higher than the 1899 rates of $1.25 per day, and meals currently go for more than a quarter.

The character of the hotel is revealed through slanted floors, smallish rooms, antique bedframes, claw-footed bathtubs (down the hall), and views to the once-active cribs (small, one- or two-girl houses of ill repute) on the street below. There are a couple of large corner rooms with private bathrooms. Since there is no heat, the hotel is open only in summer. The proprietress, speaking of the hotel in terms of European-style lodging says, "It's inexpensive, old-fashioned and comfortable." Downstairs there is a casual restaurant (see the Where to Eat section) and 17-ounce Margaritas in a small, lively bar. **210 7th Ave., Box 25, Ouray, CO 81427; (303) 325-4645.**

Orvis Hot Springs — $$

See the Hot Springs section for information.

The Adobe Inn — $ to $$

This small lodge is well named. Tile floors, adobe-style archways and wooden ceilings and furniture give the Adobe Inn a distinctive southwestern feel. Passive solar helps heat the place. Three private rooms are available, as well as an eight-bed dorm room for those traveling on tight budgets. Bathrooms are shared by all guests. Opened in 1987 by Joyce and Terre Bucknam, the Adobe Inn is a good value. Continental breakfast is served each morning. See the Where to Eat section for details about their fine restaurant. Located 10 miles north of Ouray in Ridgway. **651 Liddell Dr., Ridgway, CO 81432; (303) 626-5939.**

CAMPING

In Uncompahgre National Forest—

Just a mile south of Ouray on Hwy. 550 is the turn-off for one of the most popular national forest campgrounds in the state—**Amphitheater Campground.** With fantastic views of the Sneffels Range and the Uncompahgre Valley, people don't want to leave. There is a seven-day limit and a fee is charged; 30 sites.

The other national forest campgrounds in the Ouray area are located quite a few miles northeast, near Silver Jack Reservoir. Drive about 2 miles north of Ridgway on Hwy. 550 and turn right on Owl Creek Pass Rd. (Forest Rd. 858). After crossing the pass, follow the road north along the Cimarron River to **Silver Jack Campground** at Silver Jack Reservoir. There are 60 sites and a fee is charged. Handicapped facilities are available. Continuing north on Forest Rd. 858 for 1 mile brings you to **Beaver Lake Campground** with 11 sites and a fee. Another half mile north is **Big Cimarron Campground** with 16 sites and no fee.

Private Campgrounds—

KOA Ouray—Located away from town in a quiet setting, KOA Ouray offers RV hookups, tent sites, a store and even jeep rentals. Open during summer only. To reach the campground from Ouray, drive 4 miles north on Hwy. 550 and turn left onto County Rd. 23. **Box J, Ouray, CO 81427; (303) 325-4736.**

Polly's Campground—Operating in conjunction with a motel, this campground offers all of your favorite amenities. Located just north of town on Hwy. 550. **Box 342, Ouray, CO 81427; (303) 325-4061.**

WHERE TO EAT

Bon Ton Restaurant — $$$

Carefully prepared northern Italian cuisine is the specialty of this highly regarded restaurant. The inception of the Bon Ton Restaurant dates back to the 1880s. The long history is still evident in the Victorian atmosphere of its intimate surroundings. Cut-glass booth dividers and exposed brick walls create personal spaces for all diners. Indulge in a rich pasta entrée of linguini with clam sauce, tortellini carbonara or fettuccine verde alfredo. House specialties include beef Wellington and a selection of veal dishes. For a special treat we urge you to eat champagne brunch ($$) at the Bon Ton on Sun. beginning at 10 am; dinner is served each evening from 5 pm. Reservations are recommended. **426 Main St.; 325-4291.**

The Outlaw — $$ to $$$

When the overpowering urge to savor a perfectly cooked steak comes over you, as it does with alarming frequency in the San Juans, head to the Outlaw. Choice cuts of aged Colorado beef are charbroiled and accompanied by salad, hot rolls, baked potatoes, seasonal vegetable and your choice of coffee or tea. Other entrées include rainbow trout Almaden, Alaskan king crab, red snapper, shrimp and Aus-

tralian lobster tails. Hefty portions are served in a casual western atmosphere with red checkered tablecloths, antique junk hanging on the walls and a pressed-tin ceiling. Hats hang everywhere—it all started when "the Duke" left his here after a day of filming *True Grit*. The Outlaw offers a special outdoor chuckwagon barbecue cookout during the summer for a limited number of reservations. Serving dinner nightly from 5 pm. **610 Main St.; 325-9996.**

The Western Hotel — $$ to $$$

After whetting your appetite with a 17-ounce Margarita, there are plenty of Mexican and southwestern dishes to fill up on. Chili rellenos, crab enchiladas and seafood tostadas are just a few of the spicy entrées served in this tastefully renovated hotel. The comfortable setting of the Monte Alta room is casual and the service attentive. An exquisite combination is the grilled Rocky Mountain trout garnished with citrus salsa and jalapeno mayonnaise. The restaurant also serves exotic cuts of buffalo, elk and venison. You won't be disappointed. Weather permitting, lunch ($) is served on the outdoor deck from 11 am–3 pm. Open nightly for dinner from 5–9:30 pm. **210 7th Ave.; 325-4645.**

The Adobe Inn — $$

Joyce and Terre Bucknam serve up some of the most delicious and creative Mexican food you'll find anywhere in Colorado. Southwestern decor and South American music add rich atmosphere as you look out the windows at the surrounding mountains. If you are looking for that perfect Mexican meal and/or Margarita, this is the place. Entrées include enchiladas served six different ways, chimichanga de carne and chimichanga de Jaiba (spiced crab, nuts, chili verde, etc.). Each dinner comes with chips and salsa, refried beans and tomal en elote (corn casserole). The Adobe Inn also has a good selection of Mexican beers. During summer, lunches ($$) are served on the patio from 11:30 am–1:30 pm. Dinners are served from 5:30–9:30 pm; closed Nov. and Dec. Located 10 miles north of Ouray in Ridgway. **651 Liddell Dr., Ridgway; 626-5939.**

Pricco's — $

A classy yet casual feel invades this popular lunch and breakfast spot. The same family has owned the historic Pricco building since the late 1800s. Today, the exposed brick is juxtaposed with an airy skylight and dark green tablecloths. A large selection of omelettes and egg dishes stands out on the breakfast menu. For lunch, try a hoagie sandwich, a Philly cheese steak or a Rueben. For a full meal, combine a sandwich with homemade soup and top it off with a fresh dessert. Beer and wine are served. Breakfast served daily from 8–11 am, lunch from 11 am–4 pm . **736 Main St.; 325-4040.**

Silver Nugget Cafe — $

Each mountain town has a cafe that attracts a local crowd by worrying more about the food than the decor. The Silver Nugget has an open kitchen and counter seating, as well as table service. The country-style food is served in generous portions for breakfast, lunch and dinner. Open year-round from 6 am–9 pm daily. Closed at 8 pm in winter. **740 Main St.; 325-4100.**

SERVICES

Ouray County Chamber of Commerce—

An excellent visitors center is located next to the Ouray Hot Springs Pool at the north end of town. **Box 145, Ouray, CO 81427; (303) 325-4746.**

COLORADO PROFILE — OTTO MEARS

The profits made in the vast San Juan mining district would not have been nearly as substantial if it weren't for a man whose name is unknown to many these days... Otto Mears. Born in Russia in 1841, Mears emigrated to California with his parents in 1854. He joined the First California Volunteers and later served with Kit Carson. Mears arrived in Colorado in the 1860s and opened a store in Saguache. He began farming wheat, which he ground in a grist mill. Having trouble finding a market for his grain in the San Luis Valley, he looked north to the boom town of Leadville, located over Poncha Pass. Not willing to let a rugged pass stand between his grain and a good market, Mears built a crude road over the pass, which not only got his wheat to market but also allowed him to charge tolls to anyone wanting to use the road. He went on to build more than 300 miles of roads in the San Luis Valley, which greatly contributed to the fast pace of settlement in the area.

Mears was also involved with Indian affairs. He was responsible for handling the relocation of Utes to a reservation in Utah, as well as negotiating a treaty to provide them with more territory in the western part of the state.

But more road building was in his future. Mears saw great opportunity for profits in the San Juans, where steep mountains made travel between the isolated mining camps very difficult. In less than 10 years, Mears built more than 450 miles of toll roads in the San Juans, including many that engineers said couldn't be built. Two of his greatest accomplishments were Ophir Pass Rd. and the road south of Ouray now known as the Million Dollar Highway. In the early 1880s, Mears agreed to build a rail bed for the Rio Grande Southern Railroad to connect the booming towns of Rico and Telluride with the outside world. This line of narrow-gauge track went over Lizard Head Pass and featured the Ophir Loop, with its 100-foot-high trestles. The most amazing aspect of Otto Mears's accomplishments was that he never had any formal geological or engineering training. Mears died in Pasadena, California, in 1931.

Pagosa Springs

An author who visited Pagosa Springs in 1924 called the area a "Shangri-la...a great retreat from the speakeasies, jazz and stock market of the real world." Today the stress factors of the "real world" are somewhat different (except for the stock market), but the sentiments still ring true. Pagosa Springs is a good place to get away from it all.

This little town is located in southwestern Colorado, surrounded on three sides by the San Juan Mountains. From the Continental Divide to the northeast, the San Juan River crashes down out of alpine country, making its way through Pagosa Springs and then down to Navajo Reservoir on the New Mexico border. From anywhere in town you have a fantastic mountain panorama.

San Juan National Forest near Pagosa Springs offers many outdoor recreational opportunities. The fishing and hunting are outstanding. Countless hiking trails crisscross their way through low valleys and up into the high country of the Weminuche Wilderness Area and the Continental Divide. In winter, rolling, forested hills are ideal for cross-country skiing. Wolf Creek Ski Area has reached legendary status for its short lift lines and heavy snowfall, quite often the deepest of any ski area in the state.

Pagosa, a Ute word meaning "healing waters," gets its name from the hot mineral springs that were long coveted by the Indians in the area. Over the years the springs have never achieved the success of other resorts such as Glenwood Springs and Ouray. But unlike other towns with hot springs, Pagosa uses the geothermal water to heat many of its buildings.

Most people familiar with Pagosa Springs think of it as a place they pass through on their way to somewhere else. If you want to spend a vacation eating at fine restaurants, visiting exceptional museums and enjoying a hopping nightlife, Pagosa is not the place. To escape hectic schedules—and for that matter, hectic vacation spots—consider Pagosa Springs.

HISTORY

In 1859 when Capt. J.N. Macomb, a surveyor for the US government, arrived at Pagosa Springs, he described the location as "... the most beautiful hot springs in the world. There is scarcely a more beautiful place on the face of the earth." The Utes and Navajos probably agreed with these sentiments, as they sporadically fought with each other for centuries over control of these springs. The largest spring (Great Pagosa) measured 75 feet across, and even today its water comes out of the rocks at a scalding 153° F. More than one Indian brave attempted to show his courage by trying to swim across this seething cauldron; the results were grim.

415

In 1866 the Utes and Navajos agreed to decide once and for all which tribe would lay sole claim to the coveted springs. One brave from each tribe was to be chosen for mortal combat, and the winner would claim the springs for his people. Unexpectedly, the Utes chose a white man, Col. Albert Pfeiffer, an Indian fighter and a friend of Kit Carson. Pfeiffer, a short, stocky Dutchman, was haunted by the murder of his wife by Indians in New Mexico. He had spent a few years with Kit Carson's battalion, fighting Apaches and Navajos. Pfeiffer had gained respect from the Utes and was honored to be chosen by them for the chance to do in another Navajo. Pfeiffer chose knives as the weapon for the fight. Close accounts of this showdown indicate that both men ran toward each other, then Pfeiffer stopped, raised his knife and threw it into the Navajo's heart, killing him instantly. The Utes finally had possession of the springs.

But the possession was short-lived, as white settlers, miners and lumbermen began crowding into the area. In 1878 Fort Lewis was established to deal with the growing controversy between the settlers and the Utes. In 1880 the town was established and the Utes were pushed aside. Not long after, the Denver & Rio Grande Railroad arrived when it extended service to the nearby San Juan mining district. Ranches and lumbermills sprang up. At one time, the Pagosa Springs area was the largest lumber-producing area in the state, but it didn't take long before much of the good timberland was destroyed. Although a number of spas were started, none really took hold. A travel brochure from the early 1900s pushed the town as "a wonderful place to recuperate." Perhaps the image of dozens of sickly people sitting in the hot springs kept many vacationers away.

GETTING THERE

Pagosa Springs is situated along Hwy. 160 in the southwestern part of the state, 60 miles east of Durango. From Denver, Pagosa Springs is 265 miles southwest via Interstate 25 south to Walsenburg, then west on Hwy. 160. Bus service is available daily. Air connections can be made at Stevens Field, just 2 miles from Pagosa Springs.

——— OUTDOOR ACTIVITIES ———

BIKING

MOUNTAIN BIKING

Pagosa Springs has yet to attract a crowd of mountain bikers or, for that matter, even a place to rent the darn things. The area offers jeep roads and single-track hiking trails that should interest those with their own bikes.

Trails—

The forest service recommends a 16-mile loop ride beginning at the Red Ryder Rodeo Grounds at the east side of Pagosa Springs on Hwy. 84. Head north on Hwy. 84 before turning right on Hwy. 160, then continue 3 miles toward Wolf Creek Pass to the graveled Fawn Gulch Rd. Turn right and continue uphill for about a mile past two cattle guards. Just past the second cattle guard, turn right on an unmarked two-track dirt road. The road leads generally downhill through Willow Draw, with stunning views of the San Juan Mountains. You may need to ford Mill Creek. After crossing, turn right onto Mill Creek Rd. and ride east into town.

FISHING

Echo Lake—

"It's the most underrated lake in Colorado," says one Pagosa resident. The lake is well stocked with rainbow trout, largemouth bass and yellow perch. Many rainbows over five pounds have been taken from the deep, unassuming lake. Trout take lures, flies and the sure-fire worm; bass rise to surface lures; catfish respond to cut bait. Echo Lake is known to have good ice fishing for trout and bass. Located 4 miles south of Pagosa Springs on Hwy. 84.

Lake Capote—

Good-sized rainbow and cutthroat trout are regularly pulled from this spring-fed lake on the Southern Ute Indian Reservation. Fishing the lake does not require a Colorado fishing license, but you must obtain a permit from the tribe. A fee of $5 entitles you to a four-fish limit. Lake Capote is regularly stocked with catchable trout in the 12- to 14-inch range. At the lake there are boat rentals, a store and a campground with 25 sites (fee). Lake Capote is located 17 miles west of Pagosa Springs at the junction of Hwys. 160 and 151.

Navajo Reservoir—

The northern third of Navajo Reservoir is located in Colorado, while the remainder of this large body of water lies in northern New Mexico. The reservoir contains both warm- and cold-water species. Millions of rainbow trout, kokanee salmon and largemouth bass have been stocked since the dam was dedicated in 1962. Pike, crappie and perch can also be caught. To fish the Colorado side of the reservoir, only a Colorado license is required,

even though it lies in the Southern Ute Indian Reservation. If you cross the border to fish, you'll need a New Mexico fishing license. At Arboles there is a visitors center, camping and a large boat ramp. The reservoir can be reached by taking Hwy. 160 west from Pagosa Springs for 17 miles and then south on Hwy. 151 for 35 miles.

Piedra River—

With its headwaters in the Weminuche Wilderness Area and its lower waters on the Southern Ute Indian Reservation, the Piedra River has 40 miles of good trout water in between. The upper tributaries that flow into the Piedra are quite good for small cutthroat trout. Below these upper tributaries, in the stretch of water from First Fork down to Lower Piedra Campground (just north of Hwy. 160), only artificial flies or artificial lures may be used. Try gray and brown nymphs below the surface, or the current hatch on top. Travel upstream (north) from Hwy. 160, 22 miles west of Pagosa Springs. Turn right and follow Forest Rd. 622 just east of the river into a box canyon. The farther upstream you go, the better the fishing.

San Juan River—

Ten miles north of Pagosa Springs, the East and West forks of the San Juan River join. Along the length of the river are many stretches of public fishing, primarily for small rainbow and brown trout. The river flows through Pagosa Springs; below town there are rumored to be larger trout. Eventually the San Juan flows into the Southern Ute Indian Reservation and Navajo Reservoir.

Below the reservoir, the San Juan River has many posted rules. Fishing is allowed only with artificial lures and flies with barbless hooks; you may keep only one trout over 20 inches. The most important rule is that you must have a New Mexico fishing license.

North of Pagosa Springs, the West Fork of the San Juan can be reached by driving a mile on a rough dirt road from West Fork Campground (see the Camping section) to Born's Lake. From there a trail follows the river for a dozen miles up into the Weminuche Wilderness Area. Stretches of the river flow through a canyon with deep pools and some hard-to-reach places. The West Fork is wadeable except during runoff. When the river calms down in July, the fishing really picks up. The East Fork of the San Juan flows out of Crater Lake (good fishing for cutthroat) and is paralleled for most of its 10-mile run by Forest Rd. 667. To reach Forest Rd. 667, take Hwy. 160 for 10 miles northeast of Pagosa Springs and turn right. The East Fork has mostly pan-sized rainbow. The river remains murky until early July and after heavy rains. Quartz Creek flows into the East Fork about 8 miles upstream from East Fork Campground and is paralleled for 5 miles by a rather steep trail. The creek is known for fairly large cutthroat trout.

GOLF

The Fairfield Pagosa Golf Club—

Located at the plush Fairfield Pagosa Resort, the 18-hole Pines and the newly opened nine-hole Meadows courses have what you are looking for if you're a golfer. The setting among the pine trees is beautiful, but unless you're a guest of the resort, the green fees are high. Resort guests are entitled to reduced fees. The price includes a cart. Fairfield Pagosa Resort is located 3.5 miles west of Pagosa Springs on Hwy. 160. For more information call **(303) 731-4141**.

HIKING AND BACKPACKING

For information, maps and trail ideas in the Pagosa Springs area, stop in at the **Pagosa Ranger District Office** at the corner of 2nd and Pagosa St. **PO Box 310, 180 2nd St., Pagosa Springs, CO 81147; (303) 264-2268.** If you are interested in getting in-depth information about hiking possibilities in the Weminuche Wilderness Area, consider picking up a copy of the fine *Backpacking Guide to the Weminuche Wilderness Area* by Dennis Gebhardt (Basin Repro-

duction Co., 1976), available at bookstores in Pagosa and at the Chamber of Commerce visitors center at 342 Hermosa St.

Fourmile Falls—

This is an easy 3-mile hike (one way) that follows Fourmile Creek up between Pagosa Peak and Eagle Mountain, both over 12,000 feet. The falls are on the left. From there, you can take the trail up another 4 miles to **Fourmile Lake.** After about 2 miles there is a fork in the trail; the left fork goes to the lake and the right fork goes on to Turkey Creek Lake and over the Continental Divide into the Creede area. To reach Fourmile Falls Trail from Pagosa Springs, head north out of town on Fourmile Rd. (Forest Rd. 645) and drive to the end of the road about 14 miles from town. The trailhead is at the end of the road.

Poison Park Trail—

Poison Park Trail, located near Williams Creek Reservoir, gets pretty heavy horse traffic, but it leads into the spectacular Weminuche Wilderness Area, where you can branch off in many directions. Talk to the folks at the Pagosa Ranger District Office for trail ideas via Poison Park Trail. The Weminuche Wilderness Area has few equals for extended backpacking trips. Towering peaks, crystal clear mountain lakes, wildflowers and thick forests await. To reach Poison Park Trail from Pagosa Springs, head west 2.5 miles on Hwy. 160 and turn right on Piedra Rd. Drive 22 miles and turn right on Williams Creek Reservoir Rd. (Forest Rd. 640). Drive in a few miles and turn left on Forest Rd. 644 and follow it to the end. The Poison Park Trail heads off to the northwest.

Rainbow Hot Spring—

See the Hot Springs section.

Treasure Pass—

Treasure Pass is located up near the summit of Wolf Creek Pass. The wildflowers and views are incredible. To reach the trailhead from Pagosa Springs, head northeast on Hwy. 160 to the summit of Wolf

Creek Pass. A trail heads south to the top of a bowl. From there, Treasure Mountain is on the right. You need to head for the saddle on the left side of Treasure Mountain. From the saddle you can return to Hwy. 160 on Wolf Creek Rd. (Forest Rd. 725) or continue southwest on Treasure Mountain Trail for about 4 miles and take the right fork onto Windy Pass Trail, which continues for 3 miles to Hwy. 160 near Treasure Falls. If you choose this route, a car shuttle or hitchhiking is necessary unless you want to hike back up the pass to your car.

HORSEBACK RIDING

San Juan National Forest north of Pagosa Springs is beautiful country for horseback riding. There are a number of outfitters who can take you out for an hour-long trail ride or a 10-day pack trip.

Sundown Outfitters—

David and Jane Cordray provide just about every horse-related service imaginable within reason. They specialize in extended fishing and hunting trips up into San Juan National Forest but also offer trail rides. Drop camps or full-service camps are available. For more information, contact: **PO Box 261, Pagosa Springs, CO 81147; (303) 264-2797.**

Wolf Creek Outfitters—

Working out of the Bruce Spruce Ranch, Wolf Creek Outfitters provides mainly short rides on an hourly basis, but also offers full-day and overnight pack trips. They are open into the fall for rides up in the golden aspen glades. Located 15 miles northeast of Pagosa Springs on **Hwy. 160; (303) 264-5332.**

RIVER FLOATING

Piedra River—

Increasing numbers of whitewater enthusiasts are discovering this river, which intersects Hwy. 160 between Durango and Pagosa Springs. The Piedra, currently under consideration for membership in the National Wild and Scenic River System, offers challenging, steep rapids as well as tame, meandering sections.

The Upper Piedra is a difficult 20-mile section, beginning at the Piedra Rd. Bridge 10 miles north of Pagosa Springs on Piedra Rd. The stretch ends at Hwy. 160. This narrow, deep river runs through canyons with steep rock walls that can make portages impossible. The Upper Piedra peaks early and should be run in May and June. It is recommended for upper intermediate and expert kayakers. The Lower Piedra, a 10-mile section, can be done by rafters, kayakers and canoers of all abilities. It winds its way through cottonwood trees and ranches, dropping 20 feet per mile before reaching Navajo Reservoir.

San Juan River—

The headwaters of the San Juan River are just northeast of Pagosa Springs. By the time the river gets to town, there is enough water during runoff for kayaking and raft trips. Inner-tubing is also possible, but the water is very cold. The San Juan River is not particularly difficult to float and is very relaxing.

Outfitters—

Pagosa Rafting Outfitters—These folks offer trips down the San Juan River and the Piedra River for a half day to three days. **PO Box 4040, Fairfield Pagosa Resort, Pagosa Springs, CO 81157; (303) 731-4141,** or out of state at **1-800-523-7704.**

SKIING
CROSS-COUNTRY SKIING

Pagosa draws a lot of cross-country skiers in winter because the terrain is so varied. Just out of town, mellow, fairly level trails please beginners and novices. On the other end of the spectrum, backcountry skiers enjoy challenging, steep trails, excellent snow conditions and inspiring views—especially in the Wolf Creek Pass area. Rentals are available at the **Pagosa Pines Touring Center.** (See the Groomed Trails write-up in this section.) For maps and avalanche information, contact the **Pagosa Ranger District Office** in **Pagosa Springs** at **(303) 264-2268.**

Backcountry Trails—

Chimney Rock—This is an excellent 3-mile ski up to the Chimney Rock Archaeological Area. Along the way there is an excellent chance to see elk and deer as well as peregrine falcons and a bald eagle or two. The trail can be skied by beginners. To reach the trailhead, drive west from Pagosa Springs on Hwy. 160 to Hwy. 151 and turn left. Drive about 3.5 miles and be looking for the snowed-in road up to Chimney Rock on the right. It may be hard to find a place to park off the road. The snowed-in road winds its way up through pine and aspen, eventually terminating just below the summit of Chimney Rock. Make your way up to the summit from here. Please respect the wishes of the forest service: look at the Anasazi ruins but don't climb around on them. For more information about Chimney Rock see the Anasazi Ruins section.

Williams Creek Reservoir—This is a beautiful and fairly easy trail, which winds its way through pines and meadows with mountain views all around. To reach the trailhead from Pagosa Springs, drive 2.5 miles west on Hwy. 160 to Piedra Rd. and turn right. Follow Piedra Rd. for 22 miles to Williams Creek Reservoir Rd. and park the car. Begin skiing on the snowed-in road. You will pass Williams Creek Campground and then Teal Campground after about 2 miles. From here it's another 3 miles up to Cimarrona Campground.

Wolf Creek Road—This 4-mile trail is not for beginners. From the summit sign at the top of Wolf Creek Pass on Hwy. 160, look to the south. You should see an open bowl. Begin skiing toward its summit (11,600 feet) through the trees. Be sure to stay to the right, as the left side can be struck by avalanches. From the summit, traverse down, heading south and slightly west. On your left is the Continental Divide and to the right is Treasure Mountain. You need to get to the saddle between them. Once at the saddle, you are on Wolf Creek Rd. From here, turn right and ski 2.5 miles back to Hwy. 160, about 2 miles below the pass. Hitch a ride or leave one car here and one at the trailhead. Topographical maps are highly recommended.

Groomed Trails—

Pagosa Pines Touring Center—This touring center, located on the golf course at the Fairfield Pagosa Resort west of town, is exceptionally well maintained. Twelve kilometers of groomed trails are perfect for beginners to intermediates. To the east you get good views of the mountains at the Continental Divide. The touring center rents and sells cross-country equipment. Instruction and backcountry guides are available. A fee is charged for use of the trail system. The touring center is open from Nov. 1 to the end of Mar. To reach the touring center, head west on Hwy. 160 from Pagosa Springs for 3 miles and turn right onto Piñon Causeway just past the Fairfield lodge. Continue on to Pines Club Place. The clubhouse is on the right. **PO Box 4040, Pagosa Springs, CO 81157; (303) 731-4141 ext. 2021.**

DOWNHILL SKIING

Wolf Creek—

The daily snow reports in the newspaper provide ample proof: Wolf Creek has the highest average snowfall in the state. The ski area receives 450 inches of snow in a normal year! There is no better place to learn to ski powder, because the mountain rarely gets "skied off." Besides great snow, Wolf Creek has one of the least expensive lift tickets in the state. The base area sits at 10,600 feet, atop the Continental Divide, and rises to 11,775 feet at the summit. As one of the oldest ski areas in Colorado, Wolf Creek has had a rope tow in place since 1938. Expansion has been gradual, and in 1988 a second triple chair was added, opening up 20 acres of new trails. Even though the vertical drop at Wolf Creek is nothing spectacular, the skiing is. And there is more than enough skiing for all abilities.

Wolf Creek is remote, and there is no resort development at the base—just a cafeteria and a rental shop. If you want to stay in the area, the closest pillow is in Pagosa Springs or on the other side of the pass at South Fork. Wolf Creek is located about 20 miles northeast of Pagosa Springs on Hwy. 160. For more information, contact **PO Box 1036, Pagosa Springs, CO 81147; (303) 731-5605.**

SNOWCAT SKIING

The Water Fall area at Wolf Creek Ski Area will be serviced by lift in the future, but for now this expert terrain is only accessible by snowcat. The deep powder is tough to beat, and only a few skiers at a time are lucky enough to be in the area. A snowcat will shuttle you out from the bottom of the sparse pine forest. Sign up at the top of the Treasure Triple Chairlift. Snowcat skiing is not included in the price of a lift ticket. Contact Wolf Creek at **PO Box 1036, Pagosa Springs, CO 81147; (303) 731-5605.**

SEEING AND DOING

ANASAZI RUINS

Chimney Rock Archaeological Area—

Known as the Machu Picchu of America, Chimney Rock, with its towering structure and mountain setting, slightly resembles the lost city of the Incas in South America. Occupied 1,000 years ago by as many as 2,000 Anasazi, Chimney Rock was supposedly the northernmost outpost of the Chaco Canyon Anasazi, who were mostly concentrated to the south in New Mexico. The Anasazi at Chimney Rock were farmers who lived in pueblo villages on ridges along the Piedra River and on the high mesa tops. The most impressive remains of these ancient people are the large pueblo ruins located just below the two rock pinnacles at the summit.

Chimney Rock Archaeological Area came into being in 1970 when the federal government set aside more than 3,000 acres, which is under the watchful eye of the National Forest Service. The area is also home to the endangered peregrine falcon, which is protected in its natural habitat. Other wildlife, including elk and deer, also thrive here. Visitors are allowed to enter the site only with guided tours. Daily tours for no more than 30 people are given by the National Forest Service in summer (tours can be requested in winter, weather permitting). The tours are free, but reservations are necessary. For more information contact the **Pagosa Ranger District Office** in Pagosa Springs at **(303) 264-2268.** Tours begin at the Chimney Rock entrance, located 17 miles west of Pagosa Springs on Hwy. 160 and 3 miles south on Hwy. 151. The Southern Ute Indian Reservation also provides tours of the area for a small fee. For information about the tribal tours, which are arranged at Lake Capote, contact Tom and Linda Rohde at **Box 81, Chimney Rock, CO 81127; (303) 731-5256.**

HOT SPRINGS

In Town—

It's about time Pagosa Springs developed one of its best resources: natural hot springs. Except for heating some public buildings, the town has not really capitalized on the geothermal activity it is sitting on. For many years there has been talk about building a large public pool in a natural setting. At this point, all Pagosa has in the way of a public facility is the small concrete pool and indoor bathhouses at the Spa Motel. The somewhat rundown facilities are open to the public for a fee. See the Where to Stay section for more information. For a natural hot spring, read on.

Rainbow Hot Spring—

This is undoubtedly one of the best undeveloped and undisturbed hot springs in the state. Should we tell you where it is? After some mental grappling we've decided to spill one of Colorado's prime secrets, but only because it's a 5-mile hike to get there. The natural hot water pours from between a crack in a massive rock wall, collecting in a gorgeous pool on the banks of the West Fork of the San Juan River. It all happens in a particularly lush setting. The source water is just over 100°, providing an idyllic soaking temperature. And if you get too warm, just step out of the natural tub and plunge into the frigid waters of the West Fork. To reach the trailhead from Pagosa Springs, drive northeast on Hwy. 160 toward Wolf Creek Pass. After 13 miles (1 mile before reaching the Treasure Falls turnout) turn left on Born's Lake Rd. Continue about 3 miles to the trailhead. Rainbow Trail sets off through private property, eventually leading into the Weminuche Wilderness Area and on to this undisturbed spring. Please leave it in as good or better condition as you find it.

MUSEUMS AND GALLERIES

Fred Harmon Art Museum—

This museum captures the lifework of one man from Pagosa Springs: Fred Harmon. Not everyone remembers his comic strip, *Red Ryder and Little Beaver*, but at one time the strip appeared in more than 750 newspapers on three continents. Later, Red Ryder and his buddy Little Beaver were seen in films. Fred Harmon was a gifted artist who never had any formal training. He once said, "I wasn't a born artist—I was born with a husky pair of lungs and a liking for hair and rawhide." In his later years, Harmon devoted his life to capturing the spirit of the West with oil on canvas. Small fee charged. Open 10:30 am–5 pm Mon.–Sat., 12–4 pm Sun. Two miles west of Pagosa Springs on **Hwy. 160; (303) 731-5785.**

Upper San Juan Historical Museum—

Inside this false-fronted museum building, you'll be treated to an array of historical knickknacks. The many displays include items such as Angora goat chaps, worn saddles, a one-horse open sleigh and an old barber's chair; there is also a re-created blacksmith shop and a schoolroom (circa 1900). Since the historical society is located in the same building, chances are you will be able to talk with a knowledgeable person about the area. No fee, but donations are accepted. Open from Memorial Day to Labor Day, Mon.–Sat., 10 am–5 pm. **1st St.** and **Pagosa St.; (303) 264-4424.**

TOURS

The Pagosa Springs Area Chamber of Commerce has organized a variety of area tours given on a daily basis. The two-hour tours are led by local volunteers who introduce visitors to everything from alpine wildflowers to the workings of a sawmill. The tours are free and can be very interesting. For more information contact the **Chamber of Commerce** at **(303) 264-2360.**

———— WHERE TO STAY ————

ACCOMMODATIONS

Fairfield Pagosa — $$$

Anyone visiting Pagosa Springs will inevitably hear about or see the sprawling Fairfield Pagosa Resort just west of town. Although it functions primarily as a retirement community with time-share condominiums, the complex also features a large 100-room lodge and a number of condo-miniums for vacationers. The place is particularly suited to families—the resort provides a large number of activities including many for the kids. A fine golf course, tennis facilities, indoor swimming pool, ballooning, cross-country skiing, snowmobiling and many other diversions make it tempting to never leave the grounds during your stay. If you like the self-enclosed, all-inclusive type of resort vacation, you'll like Fairfield Pagosa.

Many people comment on the beautiful views of the surrounding mountains that you have at the resort. Luxurious accommodations are complemented by a family-style restaurant and the Southface (a gourmet restaurant). Special summer golf packages and winter ski packages make a stay here more affordable for the masses. Located 3.5 miles west of Pagosa Springs on Hwy. 160. **PO Box 4040, Pagosa Springs, CO 81157; 1-800-523-7704** out of state and **(303) 731-4141** in state.

Echo Manor Inn — $$ to $$$

Echo Manor Inn, referred to as "the castle" by the locals, looks very out of place in Pagosa Springs. It's so unusual that many people driving by actually slam on their brakes and stare at the extraordinary structure. Ginny and Sandy Northcutt, the owners, recall one day when an entire busload of people was outside taking pictures of their place.

This sprawling inn, with more than 10,000 square feet of space, enjoys a setting with a spectacular view to Wolf Creek Pass. Although the structure was originally a small A-frame, the first owner, upon returning from Disneyland, began building additions that were inspired by Fantasyland. Each of the comfortable rooms is individually named and decorated. The Royal Suite includes a basket of fruit and complimentary champagne. The Sir Francis Drake Room, which adjoins the Princess Di Room, will be renamed shortly to avoid scandalizing any British visitors. The Dungeon, located in the basement (where else), can accommodate up to 12 people and has its own kitchen facilities.

Guests not staying in the Dungeon are treated to Ginny's enormous breakfast, which will keep you full for most of the day. The breakfast table, set with 100-year-old crystal, offers great views. Be sure to make time for the hot tub on the back porch, and check out Sandy's Game Room, where he has a large collection of game trophies mounted on the walls.

The Echo Manor Inn is located 3 miles

south of Pagosa Springs on Hwy. 84 on the left side of the road across from Echo Lake. You can't miss it. **3366 Hwy. 84, Pagosa Springs, CO 81147; (303) 264-5646.**

Davidson's Country Inn — $$

Staying at Davidson's will provide a simple, country experience that is particularly well suited to families. The three-story log inn has 10 individually decorated rooms with country touches that will appeal to many. Except for the Mountain Man Room (with a waterbed and a glass rifle case), the rooms are of the dainty sort. Kids will love the solarium filled with pint-sized toys; older kids (up to age 90) can make use of the pool and Ping-Pong tables, horseshoes and table games. Evelyn and Gilbert Davidson will make you feel right at home as soon as you walk in the door. Evelyn loves to bake and included in the price of a room is a full homemade breakfast at their dining room table. On request she'll make a box lunch for anyone heading out on a hike or a fishing trip. No smoking inside. Davidson's Country Inn is located 2 miles northeast of Pagosa Springs on Hwy. 160. **PO Box 87, Pagosa Springs, CO 81147; (303) 264-5863.**

Spa Motel — $$

This is a very ordinary motel with an important exception: it's one of the best places in Pagosa to splash around in the natural hot springs. A large outdoor pool and segregated (male/female) indoor bathhouses are free to motel guests (charge for non-guests). The bathhouses have a long list of rules—no smoking, no alcohol, no suits, no children, no soap, etc. Staying at the Spa Motel is definitely not a luxurious getaway, but the rooms are inexpensive and the water is great. There are several picnic tables and a grill in a central grassy area. **317 Light Plant Rd., PO Box 37, Pagosa Springs, CO 81147; (303) 264-5910.**

CAMPING
In San Juan National Forest—

Camping opportunities are numerous

in the San Juan National Forest around Pagosa Springs.

Blanca River Campground, located 13 miles south of Pagosa Springs on Hwy. 84 and 2 miles east on Forest Rd. 656, has 18 sites and no fee. **East Fork Campground, Wolf Creek Campground** and **West Fork Campground** are located about 12 miles northeast of Pagosa Springs on Hwy. 160 heading toward Wolf Creek Pass. They have between 25 and 28 sites each and a fee charged. **Bridge Campground** is 17 miles northwest of Pagosa Springs on Piedra Rd. (Forest Rd. 631). It has 19 sites and a fee. Another 2.5 miles up the road brings you to **Williams Creek Campground** with 67 sites and a fee. **Teal Campground** (16 sites) and **Cimarrona Campground** (21 sites) are a couple more miles up Piedra Rd. A fee is charged at both. Heading west on Hwy. 160 from Pagosa Springs to the Piedra River and then north a mile on Forest Rd. 621 brings you to **Lower Piedra Campground,** with 17 sites and no fee.

Navajo State Recreation Area—

Ninety campsites await you at Navajo Reservoir. This state-run area also offers showers. A fee is charged. From Pagosa Springs, drive 17 miles west on Hwy. 160 and turn left on Hwy. 151. Proceed about 15 miles, turn left on County Rd. 982 and drive 2 miles.

Private Campgrounds—

The Pagosa area has more than its share of private RV campgrounds equipped with everything from showers to laundry facilities. The ones with the best surroundings are located east of town on Hwy. 160 toward Wolf Creek Pass. Here are a few of them.

Bruce Spruce Ranch—Located 16 miles northeast of Pagosa Springs on Hwy. 160, this place offers cabins and a trailer park. Not open in winter. **PO Box 296, Pagosa Springs, CO 81147; (303) 264-5374.**

Elk Meadows Campground—Located 5 miles east of town, Elk Meadows entices visitors by its alluring invitation, "Sleep to the sound of the ol' San Juan River!" Open from June to Nov. **PO Box 238, Pagosa Springs, CO 81147; (303) 264-5482.**

KOA Pagosa—Open year-round, the KOA Pagosa is located 1.5 miles east of Pagosa on Hwy. 160. **PO Box 268, Pagosa Springs, CO 81147; (303) 264-5874.**

WHERE TO EAT

Old Miner's Steakhouse — $$ to $$$

The weathered barnwood walls create the feeling of a mine shaft, and privacy is guaranteed by low lighting and tables that are tastefully partitioned from one another. Even the waiting room is something special—so comfortably appointed that it's as though you are waiting in the owner's living room. The food gets rave reviews! Most of the entrées are charbroiled steaks, but there are also seafood, pork and chicken dishes. The menu also promises "Grub served with hot bread and your 'pickins' from the salad bar." No alcohol is served and no smoking is allowed. Open for lunch from 11:30 am–1:30 pm Mon.–Fri., dinner from 5:30 pm Mon.–Sat.; call for winter hours. Three and a half miles northeast of town on **Hwy. 160; 264-5981.**

The Elkhorn Cafe — $

For a great Mexican-style breakfast, lunch or dinner, stop in at the Elkhorn Cafe. Located downtown, this one-room Mexican restaurant opens early, serving both Mexican and American entrées. For breakfast try the huevos rancheros or the green chili cheese omelette. Lunch and dinner specialties include the Elkhorn stuffed sopapilla and the combination plate. No alcohol. The Elkhorn opens at 6 am Mon.–Sat., 7 am Sun., and closes at 9 pm daily. **438C Main St.; 264-2146.**

Rocky Mountain Pie Company — $

For an inexpensive breakfast or lunch, this is a good choice. The cinnamon and caramel pecan rolls are massive; other breakfast items include biscuits and gravy and Belgian waffles. For lunch there is a list of sandwiches—ham, beef, pastrami, vege-tarian, turkey—all served on homemade cracked-wheat buns. Soups and chili are also served. When you're finished, order homemade pie by the slice or by the pie. Open Mon.–Sat. 7:30 am–6:30 pm; closed Sun. Off **Hwy. 160; 140 Piedra Rd.;** 731-4004.

SERVICES

Pagosa Central Reservations—

PO Box 1534, Pagosa Springs, CO 81147; (303) 731-2215.

Pagosa Springs Area Chamber of Commerce—

PO Box 580, 342 Hermosa St., Pagosa Springs, CO 81147; (303) 264-2360.

Silverton

The ornate Victorian buildings in Silverton are a true reflection of the millions of dollars in gold and silver brought up during the mining heyday of the late 1800s. Though mining continues to play a big part in the area, the town, designated a National Historic Landmark, appears as if it were frozen at the turn of the century. The population of 800 lives in a movie-set world, surrounded by the opulent, many-windowed Grand Imperial Hotel, the pretentious gold-domed courthouse, false-fronted buildings, magnificent Victorian homes and small, restored miners' cabins. Silverton once played host to as many as 32 gambling halls, saloons and what were affectionately known as the Blair St. "sporting houses." It's easy to imagine the bawdy nature of the establishments on Blair, thanks to a couple of female mannequins peering out of second-story windows.

The only reason Silverton exists is because of its proximity to the rich gold and silver mines in the San Juan Mountains. Located in a high valley at 9,303 feet, the town is surrounded by four towering peaks. North of town, Storm Peak is the tallest at 13,487 feet. There is not one acre of tillable land within the boundaries of San Juan County. Rhubarb is the one garden crop that survives a growing season rumored to last only "14 days . . . and not 14 in a row." Winter is undoubtedly the longest season at this altitude.

In summer the Durango & Silverton Narrow Gauge Railroad pulls into Silverton several times a day, letting off its passengers for a couple of hours of poking around town. The spawning of T-shirt, candle and curio shops attests to the forced speed of most purchases by the train crowd. Understandably the locals are glad to have a captive audience of train travelers during high season, but it is a love-hate relationship. One restaurant worker said, "We've got four trains and 2,000 people and two hours to get rid of them." Two hours is really not enough time to get to know Silverton. If you arrive on the train, consider spending a night or two. The town and its residents take on a more genuine and relaxed personality after the last train of the day departs for the journey back to Durango. Besides, to get a complete picture of the area's rich history, you should do some further exploring.

Isolation and supreme natural beauty make this area an excellent choice for backpacking trips and cross-country skiing. The town is located in the midst of hundreds of square miles of the San Juan, Uncompahgre and Rio Grande national forests. Another popular pastime is jeeping to ghostly mining camps, as well as to towns such as Ouray, Telluride and Lake City.

HISTORY

The commonly accepted legend is that Silverton got its name from an early miner who bragged, "We may not have gold here, but we have silver by the ton." The first attempt at prospecting came in 1860 when Charles Baker led a party of men over the Continental Divide to the site of Silverton. Baker seemed to know there was gold in the hills, and despite meager finds he kept coming back to the vicinity of the Upper Animas River (referred to at that time as Baker's Park). After a short stint in the Confederate Army during the Civil War, Baker returned to the area in 1865, only to be killed by Ute Indians.

Once the exclusive domain of Utes, all of San Juan County was officially granted to them in an 1868 treaty. Gold fever set in a few years later and a steady stream of miners poured into the area. There was a short, bitter struggle for the land, and the Utes, under the direction of Chief Ouray, soon surrendered 3 million acres of mineral-rich mountains to the US government.

With the Indian trouble resolved, Silverton boomed in a hurry. In 1875, settlement began in earnest when a crude mountain road connected Durango and Silverton. That same year a newspaper known today as the *Silverton Standard and The Miner* printed its first issue. Soon Otto Mears connected Silverton to his system of toll roads in the San Juans. Since transportation of supplies, mail and tons of high-grade ore was crucial for the town's survival, everyone celebrated when the Denver & Rio Grande Railroad pulled into Silverton in 1882. Over the next decade Silverton's population grew to more than 2,000 residents and the young town became the terminus of three other railroads. From 1880 until the end of the century, nearby mines took minerals worth millions every year from the surrounding mountains.

Growing pains accompanied the early years. Vigilante groups took care of law control and did fairly well at keeping the local peace. After a police force evolved, it was sometimes used as a tool for ethnic suppression. White merchants, tired of the proliferation of Chinese businesses, called on the police to "raid the Mongolians." In 1891 a Chinese Endeavor Society was formed to "convert the Chinese and to induce them to handle soiled linen and red checks with more Christian charity," according to an article in the *Silverton Standard*.

The demonetization of silver in 1893 and, later, the nationwide financial panic of 1907, effectively stopped the growth of the town. Mining was still the bread-and-butter industry, but tourism and occasional moviemaking gradually entered the fray. The "mining town that wouldn't quit," however, still largely sustains itself by income from the Sunnyside Mine. Silverton remains a snapshot of another era, with a core community of people who truly appreciate a simple and isolated lifestyle.

GETTING THERE

Silverton is located 343 miles southwest of Denver. For those arriving from the southwest, Silverton is located 49 miles north of Durango on Hwy. 550 over Coal Bank and Molas passes. Many people who visit Silverton do so by riding the Durango & Silverton Narrow Gauge

Railroad from Durango. From Ouray it is an unforgettable 22-mile drive over Red Mountain Pass on the "Million Dollar Highway." (See the Scenic Drives section of the **Ouray** chapter for more information.) For more information on the train, see the Major Attractions section of the **Durango** chapter.

MAJOR ATTRACTIONS

DURANGO & SILVERTON NARROW GAUGE RAILROAD

Riding the Durango & Silverton Narrow Gauge Railroad is the best way to relive the history of the area. On its 45-mile route to Durango, the vintage train passes through some of the most beautiful terrain imaginable. See the Major Attractions section of the **Durango** chapter for more information on the train. There are packages available including one-way ridership with bus return, and layovers in Durango or Silverton. In Silverton, call **(303) 387-5416**. In Durango, call **(303) 247-2733**.

FESTIVALS AND EVENTS

Gunfight
summer

Each day at 5 pm at Blair St. and 12th St. there is a reenactment of a gunfight. The actors have as much fun as the visiting crowd as they run around shooting blanks at each other. The Wild West returns!

Hardrockers Holidays
mid-August

Some people expect to see leather-clad teens slam dancing to the blaring rock guitar of Twisted Sister when they first hear of Hardrockers Holidays—a first impression that couldn't be more wrong. This is a time for miners from across the state to prove their mettle (so to speak) in events ranging from machine drilling to mucking. It's a fun way to learn about what normally goes on deep in the mines. The miners also create an exciting atmosphere in town. For more information, call **(303) 387-5654**.

Brass Band Festival
third weekend in August

Since 1981 musicians from around the world have converged on Silverton to make music at the Great Western Rocky Mountain Brass Band Festival. Melodic strains of John Philip Sousa music fill the thin mountain air. Outdoor concerts held in Memorial Park are free (a donation bucket is passed afterwards) and open to the public. This is no ordinary pickup band! For more information call **(303) 387-5654**.

The narrow-gauge train (sketch by Michael A. Darr).

OUTDOOR ACTIVITIES

BIKING

MOUNTAIN BIKING

If you are an advanced mountain biker you will appreciate the selection of long and grueling trips over rough jeep roads. One thing in the Silverton area should be remembered: there are only two ways to go from Silverton—up or down. It is not a good area for mellow rides, unless you limit yourself to staying in the valley.

Trails—

One suggested tour from Silverton involves riding over **Ophir Pass** and on to Telluride. Spend the night there and cross over **Imogene Pass** to Ouray on the next day. Then spend a day recovering and soaking in the hot springs pool before considering a route back to Silverton. Consult the Four-Wheel-Drive Trips section for information on routes in the area.

Information—

Triangle Conoco—Make your way to the Conoco station at the south end of town for advice on mountain biking in the area. They also have parts and tools for most repairs. **9th St. and Greene St.; (303) 387-9990.**

FISHING

The streams near Silverton do not provide good angling because of fast currents and high mineral content. The Durango area offers a number of fishing possibilities only a short distance away.

There are, however, a number of high lakes near Silverton that are hopping with small but feisty trout. Just 6 miles south of Silverton on Hwy. 550 there are three popular lakes: **Molas, Little Molas** and **Andrews.** Another area abounding with small alpine lakes can be reached by taking Hwy. 550 northwest for 2 miles and then 5 miles southwest on Forest Rd. 585. At South Mineral Campground there is a good trail following the South Fork of Mineral Creek to **Ice Lake, Little Ice Lake, Fuller Lake** and **Island Lake.** The fishing for cutthroat is usually good. Since access is on foot, the fishing pressure is usually minimal. You can also take Forest Rd. 815 (four-wheel-drive) from the campground for about 2 miles to **Clear Lake,** which is also a good place to catch cutthroat trout.

FOUR-WHEEL-DRIVE TRIPS

Silverton was the first mining area worked in the San Juan boom of the late 1800s. As a result, it's connected all around by roads leading to other mining towns, including Lake City, Creede, Ouray and Telluride. Jeeping is highly recommended in this area.

Black Bear Pass—

This is probably the most frightening and dangerous pass in the state and perhaps in the country. Still interested? If you are, then you're in for a thrill. Black Bear Pass Rd. begins near the summit of Red Mountain Pass and heads west up to the summit of Black Bear Pass. North of the road is the old Black Bear Mine. The road was built to deliver ore from the mine to Ouray and Silverton via the Million Dollar Highway. (See the Scenic Drives section of the **Ouray** chapter for more information about the highway.) From the summit of the pass things get rough. The switchbacks descending the mountain are so tight that many jeepers choose to drive forward down one and in reverse down the next to save a turn. Below the worst of the switchbacks, the road arrives at the hydro station at the top of Bridal Veil Falls. This is a good place to stop and collect your thoughts and let your adrenalin level return to normal. From the falls, drive down the remainder of the road past the Liberty Bell Mine and into Telluride. From Telluride return to Silverton via Imogene Pass or drive around to Ridgway and Ouray on the highway.

Cement Creek/Corkscrew Road—

See the Four-Wheel-Drive Trips section in the **Ouray** chapter.

Engineer Pass/Cinnamon Pass—

These two passes, located northeast of Silverton, connect with both Ouray and Lake City. The historic sites of Animas Forks, Mineral Point, Rose's Cabin, Capitol City and Sherman lie along the way. High alpine views of the surrounding peaks and basins attract a large number of jeepers each year. To reach these two roads from Silverton, head east from town on County Rd. 110 along the Animas River. For more specific information see the Four-Wheel-Drive Trips section in the **Creede** chapter.

Ophir Pass—

As far as four-wheel-drive roads go, Ophir Pass is fairly easy, but it can be a bit hairy in spots. From the 11,750-foot summit, enjoy great views of the peaks around Red Mountain Pass to the east. To the west, a spectacular view awaits of Mt. Wilson, Wilson Peak and El Diente Peak, as well as the deep valley of Howard Fork with the towns of Old Ophir and New Ophir. According to some old-timers, the name *Ophir* came from an early resident of the area, Lt. Howard, who stumbled upon a huge cave and exclaimed, "O fer God's sake, lookit that hole!" However, in all probability the name is a biblical reference to King Solomon's mines. A toll road was built by Otto Mears over Ophir Pass in 1881, connecting Telluride with Silverton.

To reach the pass road from Silverton, drive 5 miles north on Hwy. 550 toward Red Mountain Pass and turn left onto the Ophir Pass Rd. Follow the road as it drops down over a bridge before climbing about 4 miles to the pass. From the pass, the road descends sharply on a shelf road that cuts across a rock slide. It eventually enters a forest of pine and aspen just above Old Ophir. Before reaching Old Ophir, you may want to visit the old cemetery up the hill on the right. Old Ophir, 3.5 miles from the pass, was once a thriving mining town.

Today people still live there, braving the monstrous avalanches that thunder down steep chutes and pummel the valley floor in winter. About 2.5 miles below Old Ophir you will arrive at the remains of New Ophir, established mainly as a stop for the Rio Grande Southern Railroad next to the Ophir Loop. From here you can return to Silverton by heading north on Hwy. 145 to Telluride and over Imogene Pass or just continue northwest and around to Ridgway and Ouray and over Red Mountain Pass.

Stony Pass—

The road over Stony Pass was built as a crucial supply route between Silverton and settlements to the east in the San Luis Valley. It's a very rough road that crosses over the Continental Divide, dropping into the Rio Grande drainage at the headwaters of the Rio Grande. It passes by Rio Grande Reservoir and eventually comes out on Hwy. 149 between Creede and Lake City. To reach the road from Silverton, head east on County Rd. 110 to Howardsville. In its day Howardsville was quite a town; it was once the county seat, and the residents supported many saloons, a livery stable and even a meat market. Turn right at Howardsville and head up the Cunningham Gulch Rd. Drive about 2 miles and be looking for Stony Pass Rd. on the left.

Rentals and Tours—

Silver Lakes Campground Jeep Rentals— Located on the northeast end of town, this campground rents jeeps for half- and full-day trips. Reservations are strongly urged in July and Aug. **PO Box 126, Silverton, CO 81433; (303) 387-5721.**

Silverton Guided Jeep Tours—The office is located in the Wyman Hotel on Main St. Full- and half-day trips are offered. Inquire at the **Wyman Hotel** or contact **PO Box 780, Silverton, CO 81433; (303) 387-5372 or (303) 387-5336.**

Triangle Service Station Jeep Rentals— Open-top Jeep Wranglers and four-door Jeep Cherokees rent for full or half days.

864 Greene St., Silverton, CO 81433; (303) 387-9990.

HIKING AND BACKPACKING

Silverton is surrounded by three national forests; to the north is the Uncompahgre, to the west is the San Juan and to the east is the Rio Grande. No matter which direction you go, high mountains, raging rivers and ghost towns await, providing great hiking and backpacking. The area on the Continental Divide to the east of town provides excellent hiking on rolling hills once you're up on top. For hiking information try the visitors center, **PO Box 565, Silverton, CO 81433, (303) 387-5654,** on the west end of town but your best bet is to stop into the **San Juan National Forest Headquarters** in Durango at **701 Camino del Rio, Room 301, Durango, CO 81301; (303) 247-4874.**

The Durango & Silverton Narrow Gauge Railroad offers a unique service. The train, which travels along a remote section of the Animas River, drops off and picks up hikers daily at Elk Park and Needleton during its runs between Durango and Silverton. From Silverton you can catch an afternoon train on it's return to Durango and get off at a trailhead leading into the Weminuche Wilderness Area. Morning trains bound for Silverton will pick you up. For specific train schedules, fares and policies for hikers, contact the **Durango & Silverton Narrow Gauge Railroad** office in Silverton at **(303) 387-5416,** or in Durango at **(303) 247-2733.**

Continental Divide Trail—

Silverton is an excellent jumping off point for some great backpacking in the Weminuche Wilderness Area. South of town, the Weminuche straddles San Juan and Rio Grande national forests, providing access to miles of trails and dozens of rugged peaks. Many sheep graze here, so be sure to treat your water. The Continental Divide runs through the wilderness area. A trail along the divide offers high alpine hiking and opens up quite a few possible trips. To reach the Continental Divide Trail, follow the directions to Highland Mary Lakes (see below). From Highland Mary Lakes, hike southeast and then south along the divide. About 4 miles south on the divide, a trail switchbacks down into the Elk Creek Valley to the right (west). There is a mine shack just down from the divide that makes a fine place to spend the night. If you follow the trail down Elk Creek for 9 miles, you'll end up in Elk Park, where you can catch the train back into Silverton.

Many hiking trails take off from the Continental Divide Trail. Obtain some topographical maps (the Storm King Peak, Howardsville, Rio Grande Pyramid and Needle Mountains quadrangles) to devise your own route.

Highland Mary Lakes Trail—

This is a fine day hike that takes you into the upper reaches of Cunningham Gulch, a heavily mined area with many fascinating relics still in place. Near the trailhead the famous Highland Mary Mine can be seen high up on the right. The trail heads due south, climbing up along Cunningham Creek for 2.5 miles to the lakes. To reach the trailhead from Silverton, drive east for 5 miles to Howardsville, then turn right on Forest Rd. 589 and head up Cunningham Gulch. Proceed about 4.5 miles to the end of the road. Along the drive you will see many mine sites that still remain high up on the mountainsides. Aerial trams with rusty cables still hang hundreds of feet above the valley floor.

Ice Lake Trail—

Beginning at South Mineral Creek Campground, this trail climbs west up the valley for 3 miles to Ice Lake. Along the way you will see a waterfall, ruins of old mining camp buildings and fields of wildflowers. Just north of Ice Lake is US Grant Peak. A nice side trip is to Island Lake, about a half mile northeast of Ice Lake. Island Lake is well named, with a small bit of land in its center. Some people try to reach the island by hopping over the ice floes that remain until late summer, but this is not recommended. To reach the trailhead from Silverton, drive 4 miles northwest on Hwy. 550 and turn left onto Forest Rd. 585. Proceed 5 miles, until just past the campground, and look for the trailhead climbing into the forest on the right.

Molas Pass Trail—

Although only a 3-mile hike, this trail drops over a thousand feet on its way down to Elk Park, along the Animas River. It's very steep and you should have on a good pair of tightly laced hiking shoes to prevent blisters. The trail begins beside Molas Lake, about 5 miles south of Silverton on Hwy. 550. Park at the lake. The trail begins by dropping through spruce and fir forests. The west wall of the river valley is lined with high rock walls. Stunning views southeast to the Grenadier Range in the Weminuche Wilderness Area highlight this hike. Once down to the river, the trail runs parallel to it and then crosses a bridge. Just downriver from here along the train tracks is a fine camping area. A stove would be a good idea, as this area gets high use and firewood is scarce. The train stops here each morning on its way to Silverton if you want to catch a ride.

ICE SKATING

The ballfield at the southwest end of town is flooded during winter, forming a town ice rink. There is a small supply of rental skates at the public library.

RIVER FLOATING

Expert kayakers consider the Upper Animas an excellent but treacherous stretch of whitewater. See the River Floating section of the **Durango** chapter.

SKIING

CROSS-COUNTRY SKIING

No question about it, the Silverton area is a great place to strap on skinny skis and head into the backcountry. Numerous trails extend into nearby valleys and basins from town. The terrain can be quite difficult and unstable—many avalanche paths are visible from the highway. For knowledgeable and experienced skiers the routes are unlimited. Mountaineering skiing is an especially appropriate way to get the most out of a day of skiing. Anyone wishing to learn more about avalanche safety should consider a three-day workshop at **Silverton Avalanche School.** The course is attended by ski-patrol members, highway workers and recreational skiers. For more information contact the **Silverton Chamber of Commerce** at **418 Greene St., Silverton, CO 81433; (303) 387-5654.**

Backcountry Trails—

Molas Pass—Cross-country skiing from the top of Molas Pass (10,910 feet) allows for unimaginably beautiful views to the rocky spires of the Needles and to the summit of Snowdon Peak (13,077 feet). Many easy backcountry routes can be taken across rolling hills that were cleared by a forest fire over a century ago. Sparse groves of lodgepole and spruce are the result of a reforestation effort. Skiers wanting to sample a few short downhill runs can find many opportunities in deep, untracked powder. The avalanche danger is low in most of the area. A number of routes leave from points along Hwy. 550, near the top of the pass heading away from the road. Little Molas Lake is a bit over a half mile from the highway. The route leaves Hwy. 550 from the west side of the road, just before reaching the summit of Molas Pass, some 6 miles south of Silverton. Andrews Lake Rd. is an easy climb from the left side of the highway, about a mile after the Molas Pass crossing. The road reaches Andrews Lake in a half mile; there is more challenging terrain beyond the lake. One route makes a steep ascent to the top of a knoll (11,290 feet) from the west end of Andrews Lake.

Ophir Pass—Intermediate and advanced skiers may want to ski up the eastern side of the pass (a 1,700-foot gain in elevation) and return on the same route from the 11,789-foot summit. A ski down the other side to the town of Ophir would be foolish because of high avalanche danger. As it is you'll be crossing several avalanche slide paths; the 9-mile route should not be attempted during avalanche warnings. To reach the Ophir Pass Rd. take Hwy. 550 northwest for 4.6 miles, to a marked forest road (No. 679) on the left.

Red Mountain Pass—The St. Paul Lodge (see the Where to Stay section) offers unique access to some of the finest backcountry skiing imaginable. The rustic lodge, which sits at an elevation of 11,400 feet, provides ski touring equipment as well as tours guided by avalanche expert, Chris George. Though George is unchallenged by the telemark turn, he swears he can "teach you to telemark in 20 minutes." This technique is extremely useful for the terrain and conditions in US Basin and on McMillan Peak. There are gentle routes as well as steep, wide-open slopes to choose from.

South Mineral Creek—This easy half-day excursion involves skiing along a level forest road in a wind-protected valley. Oftentimes there are tracks leading the way. All in all the area is fairly safe, but there is some danger of a natural snow release from above due to avalanche slide paths. You should inquire about snow conditions before setting out. To get there head northwest on Hwy. 550 for 2 miles and park at the head of the valley. Forest Rd. 585 leads about 5 miles southwest, ending at South Mineral Campground.

Groomed Trails—
Purgatory Ski Touring Center—See the Outdoor Activities section of the **Durango** chapter.

Rentals and Information—
The French Bakery—This full-service bakery undergoes a complete metamorphosis in winter, when it turns into a full-service cross-country ski rental shop. The people there can give you a quick rundown of trails in the area. **1250 Greene St.; (303) 387-5423.**

DOWNHILL SKIING
Purgatory—
This respected downhill resort is situated midway between Durango and Silverton. Staying in Silverton would be a pleasant alternative while skiing in Purgatory. The end-of-the-day drive back to Silverton is virtually devoid of traffic and the scenery is tough to beat. For more information on Purgatory see the Outdoor Activities section of the **Durango** chapter.

TENNIS
There are a couple of public courts located in Memorial Park on the northeast end of Silverton.

SEEING AND DOING

HOT SPRINGS
The Ouray hot springs are only a short distance away. See the **Ouray** chapter for more information.

MUSEUMS
**San Juan County
Historical Museum—**
Located in the old San Juan County Jail, this museum provides historical information and interesting relics from surrounding mining camps. The jail operated from 1902–1931, and the sheriff and his family lived here; one of the sheriff's babies was born in the women's cell. Open 9 am–5 pm daily from June 1 to mid-Sept., 10 am–3 pm daily until mid-Oct. Small fee. Located next to the courthouse on **1567 Greene St.; (303) 387-5838.**

SCENIC DRIVES

The **Million Dollar Highway** is a beautiful and historically fascinating drive (see the Scenic Drives section of the **Ouray** chapter for more information). The trip to Durango over **Molas Pass** is another worthwhile drive and will take you over an even higher route than that traveled by the narrow-gauge train (see the Scenic Drives section of the **Durango** chapter).

———— WHERE TO STAY ————

ACCOMMODATIONS

St. Paul Lodge — $$$

From the summit of Red Mountain Pass, a cross-country ski trail works its way up to the rustic confines of the St. Paul Lodge at 11,400 feet. Since 1974 Chris and Donna George have been housing groups of skiers in an old tipple house, originally built in the 1880s over the main shaft of the St. Paul Mine, where the ore was cleaned and loaded into carts. Using an eclectic hodgepodge of recycled materials, including lumber from abandoned mine buildings and solid oak paneling from a Denver church, the couple have created a warm environment for up to 22 skiers at a time. The lodge is not for everyone—it is, for the most part, a rough and basic environment. There are small upstairs dormitory rooms and an indoor outhouse, but also a redwood sauna and hot showers. For many the St. Paul Lodge is the perfect escape from an orderly world. Enjoy the kerosene light, woodstove heat, and unique access to some of the best high alpine skiing anywhere (see the Outdoor Activities section for more information). Staying at the lodge includes three meals a day; Chris is a trained chef as well as an Outward Bound instructor and avalanche specialist. Open in winter only. **St. Paul Lodge, PO Box 463, Silverton, CO 81433; (303) 387-5494.**

Grand Imperial Hotel — $$ to $$$

It would be nice to be able to recommend this landmark hotel as a wonderful place to stay. Built in 1882, it is a fine example of Victorian architecture, but the people running the place are rude to all comers: guests, writers and even townspeople. Ask what the rooms are like and you'll have some Polaroid snapshots thrust in front of you. You might take a look at the gorgeous lobby, with its fine leather couches, pressed tin ceiling and portrait of the town sweetheart, Lillian Russell, over the piano. Adjacent to the lobby is a separate barroom with a stunning backbar made of heavy columns of cherry wood with intricate carvings and even a bullet hole. The bar doesn't get too wild anymore—it closes at 3 pm daily. The hotel is open in summer only. **1219 Greene St., Silverton, CO 81433; (303) 387-5527.**

Wingate House — $$

A block off the town's main thoroughfare, this carefully restored Victorian "gingerbread" house provides an authentic setting to transport yourself back to Silverton's heyday. Built in 1886, the Wingate House features handcrafted, queen-sized four-poster beds, antique fixtures and a full breakfast served a block away at the French Bakery. Look past lace curtains to far-reaching views of 13,000-foot peaks and back down to the compact town. The common parlor has a TV, and the kitchen is open to guests. The covered porch is a great place to spend a relaxing summer's afternoon. No smoking inside; open year-round. **1045 Snowdon St., Silverton, CO 81433; (303) 387-5713.**

The Wyman Hotel — $$

If you feel like an "Accidental Tourist," this should definitely be your choice for lodging. Yes, each room has a Beautyrest mattress and a private bathroom with individually wrapped Neutrogena soap. Each room is equipped with a VCR, and you may choose two movies each night from a video library at no extra charge. The plush rooms are large, tastefully decorated and clean. No smoking is allowed. **14th and Greene St., Silverton, CO 81433; (303) 387-5336.**

Teller House Hotel — $ to $$

The smell of baking bread wafts into open windows at the Teller House—it is located atop the French Bakery restaurant. Full breakfast at the bakery is included in the price of your room. Once a boarding-house for hard rock miners, the Teller House still has a lot of character. The rooms are situated around the outside of the upper floor, with windows facing both inside to a common area and out. The comfortable rooms have high ceilings and are furnished with oak dressers; one room has an upright piano and another a comfortable couch. The clean bathrooms down the hall are large and luxurious. The Teller House is an inexpensive and enjoyable lodging alternative. Men's and women's dorm rooms are available; if you have an American Youth Hostel card the rates are reduced.

1250 Greene St., Silverton, CO 81433; (303) 387-5423.

CAMPING

One of the most beautiful areas near Silverton to camp is **South Mineral Campground**. To get there, head northwest on Hwy. 550 for 2 miles, and then southwest on Forest Rd. 585 for 5 miles. There are 23 sites; a fee is charged. **Purgatory Campground** is located 22 miles southwest of Silverton near Hwy. 550. There are 14 sites; a fee is charged. To reach **Sig Creek Campground** take Hwy. 550 for 21 miles southwest of Silverton and then proceed 6 miles west on Forest Rd. 578. There are 9 sites and a small fee.

Private Campgrounds—

Silverton Lakes Campground—Just northeast of town, not far from the Animas River, is this full-service campground. Hookups, groceries, laundry, hot showers and jeep rentals are available. **PO Box 126, Silverton, CO 81433; (303) 387-5721.**

WHERE TO EAT

Romeros — $$

Nearly 20 years ago, George Romero came out of the mines and opened up this small Mexican restaurant on Silverton's main street. The narrow room has a mural down one long wall and metal mine tools, irons and general knickknacks hanging on the other. The family-run institution is known equally for its smothered burritos and its silky smooth Margaritas. George makes 150 Margaritas each day (more than 1,000 per week) during the summer rush. The special blend is a family secret—you won't see any pre-mix here. Romeros was open-year round until 1988. George's semi-retirement means summer hours only from 10 am–10 pm daily. **1151 Greene St.; 387-9934.**

The French Bakery Restaurant — $ to $$

Opened in 1917, this distinctive glass-fronted building was once a meat market and grocery store. The ground floor level of the Teller House Hotel is now an enjoyable full-service restaurant. As the name implies, the bakery on the premises makes fresh goodies daily. For breakfast, standard eggs and bacon or omelette dishes are cooked to perfection. Starting mid-morning consider picking something from a large variety of baked goods lining the glass case. In winter the bakery side of the restaurant converts to a ski rental shop. Soup and salad are served daily for lunch; dinner is available three nights a week (Fri., Sat. and Mon.). Open year-round from 7–11 am for breakfast, 11 am–3 pm for lunch, 5:30–9 pm for dinner. **1250 Greene St.; 387-5423.**

SERVICES

Silverton Chamber of Commerce—
PO Box 565, Silverton, CO 81433; (303) 387-5654.

The Walsh House, Animas Forks, Colorado (sketch by Michael A. Darr).

Telluride

Whether you are looking for a plush ski vacation and nights out at fine restaurants or a week of backpacking in the high mountains of the San Juans, we highly recommend Telluride. Squeezed into a box canyon along the San Miguel River, Telluride could easily be the most beautiful spot in Colorado. Surrounding this Victorian town of 1,300 full-time residents are lofty, jagged peaks—many approaching 14,000 feet in elevation. Once a thriving mining town where Butch Cassidy pulled his first bank job, Telluride is now a year-round vacation destination offering some of the best skiing, hiking and jeeping to be found anywhere.

The mining legacy of Telluride is one of great wealth and prosperity—$60 million in gold and silver were mined in the first 30 years alone. But slowed by steadily declining profits in the 1900s, the mines began closing one by one. Today, abandoned mine shafts and buildings are scattered throughout the nearby mountains, and Telluride's bread and butter has shifted to tourism, especially skiing.

It's claimed by some locals that Telluride skiing really started back in the mining days. On payday at the Tomboy Mine, located 3,000 feet above Telluride, the Finns and the Swedes would beat everyone else to the brothels in town by skiing down from the site. Today, skiers take advantage of 735 pristine acres of groomed slopes at Telluride Ski Area—including the Plunge, the longest, steepest mogul run in the US. After a day on the slopes, head into town for the après-ski scene.

During summer the surrounding Uncompahgre National Forest offers some of the state's best opportunities for exploring nature. Cascading waterfalls, rushing streams, soaring mountains, wildflowers and, in the fall, golden aspen are enough to justify spending an extended period of time here.

But the town has an additional drawing card in summer with its numerous festivals, running from June through Sept. The excellent bluegrass, jazz, wild mushroom, film and hang gliding festivals, among others, attract many people who come for the event and leave town completely in love with the beauty of the area. Actually, many people who visit decide to make it their home.

Telluride is very concerned about its future. Because of its obvious appeal, debates rage on between developers and those wanting slow growth. It seems as if everyone who lives here, from an unemployed miner to John Naisbitt, author of *Megatrends*, has his or her own vision of the town's future. In the meantime, Telluride retains its authentic Victorian charm. The downtown area has been declared a National Historic District; any building plans are closely scrutinized by the town's architectural review committee. Modern lodges and homes occupy the area west of town and up at the sizeable Mountain Village at the ski area base.

HISTORY

A handful of eager prospectors first climbed into Telluride from over the towering mountains to the east in 1875. Their efforts were rewarded when they found rich deposits of gold and silver, causing a rush to the area. Successful mines, including the Liberty Bell, the Union, the Tomboy, the Pandora and the Gold King, began producing. In 1876, J.B. Ingram discovered through careful research that two adjacent mines had overextended their claims by 500 feet. He filed a claim and set up shop between the other two mines, naming his the Smuggler. The Smuggler was sitting on a rich silver vein. Ingram went on to expand his operation, which eventually became one of the richest mines in the state.

In the 1880s, Telluride, originally known as Columbia, underwent a name change after a rare sulphurous element, tellurium, occasionally was found in local gold deposits. Isolation plagued Telluride through the 1880s. The high cost of transporting the ore to faraway smelters and mills prevented an all-out mining boom. A solution appeared in 1890 when Otto Mears's amazing pathfinding skills brought the Rio Grande Southern Railroad into town, connecting the mines with the outside world. The boom was on, but was interrupted briefly in 1893 when the silver market crashed. Soon, however, rich gold strikes brought the town back to life.

From the beginning Telluride had a reputation as a hell-raising mining town, with an infamous gambling and red-light district on Pacific Ave. By 1891 the 4,000 residents supported 26 saloons and 12 bordellos. Supposedly, this immoral section of town and the harsh natural conditions prompted warnings of "to-hell-u-ride" to people bound for this area. Decent people turned a blind eye to this decadence; the bordellos were fined $250 weekly, which is said to have almost singlehandedly financed the town government!

During the 1890s Telluride prospered. In 1895 the New Sheridan Hotel was built, rivaling the finest hotels in Denver with its accommodations and gourmet dining. But at the turn of the century, the boom days began to wane. Intense labor wars at the mines began in 1901 when union miners struck, protesting a new contract work policy that decreased their wages substantially. Scab labor was brought in and violence erupted. A brief, uneasy peace hung over the valley until 1903, when more trouble erupted. This brought the national guard to town in the winter of 1903–1904 (see Imogene Pass in the Four-Wheel-Drive Trips section). Decreasing profits from mining, coupled with labor problems, brought the mining industry in Telluride to its knees. It has never recovered. Most of the mines as well as the Bank of Telluride had closed by 1930, and the population dwindled to 500. Telluride was saved from becoming a complete ghost town when the Idarado Mining Company bought up the existing mines in the area in 1953 and began operation. Idarado connected all of the mines with a 350-mile network of tunnels, one of which extended 5 miles through the mountains to a point just south of Ouray. Idarado mined millions of dollars worth of copper, lead, zinc, silver and gold before closing in 1978.

During the slow decline of mining in the area, the idea of turning Telluride into a ski resort was kicked around by a few locals. In 1945 a rope tow was constructed at Town Park, but it operated for only two years. It was brought back to life in 1958, when $5 season passes were offered. But in 1968, skiing in Telluride went from the minor leagues to the big time when Beverly Hills entrepreneur Joe Zoline visited town and launched plans for a major ski resort. In 1971 ground was broken for the Telluride Ski Area, which today ensures prosperous times ahead for a town that the *Denver Post* once called "doomed."

GETTING THERE

Telluride is located along the San Miguel River 327 miles southwest of Denver. The quickest route to Telluride from Denver is southwest on Hwy. 285 to Poncha Springs, west on Hwy. 50 to Montrose, south on Hwy. 550 to Ridgway, west on Hwy. 62 to Placerville and then southeast on Hwy. 145. The Telluride Regional Airport, located 5 miles west of town, is serviced year-round by Continental Express and Mesa Airlines. It's the highest commercial airport in the country and can be a bit intimidating for squeamish fliers. Perched on a mesa high above the valley floor, the runway was described by one pilot as looking "somewhat like an aircraft carrier." Most flights arrive from Denver and Albuquerque. Rental cars and bus transport are available from the airport into town. Shuttle buses in Telluride run every 12 minutes between town and the Mountain Village. For further information, call **Telluride Central Reservations** at **1-800-525-3455** (outside Colorado) or **(303) 728-4431** (within Colorado).

FESTIVALS AND EVENTS

As if there wasn't already enough to do in Telluride ... every summer there is a procession of festivals that attracts a diverse crowd to the area. Many of the festivals are yearly events with loyal followings. The rocky peaks forming the box canyon around this picturesque mountain town provide one of the most dramatic backdrops imaginable. Come to Telluride for the well-known bluegrass, jazz or chamber music festivals, or the rather obscure wild mushrooms, ideas or ethnopoetics festivals. For more information and a complete schedule of events, call the festival hotline at **(303) 728-6079**.

There is not enough space to give a complete listing of all the happenings, but here is a sampling.

Telluride Bluegrass Festival
late June

Esquire magazine proclaimed recently that "Telluride has established itself as the country's premier progressive bluegrass event," and after experiencing a few of them we have to agree. Each summer the town gears up for its biggest event, which runs Wed. through Sun. Since 1973 the country's best bluegrass musicians have been performing at the festival, including the New Grass Revival, David Bromberg, David Grisman and "Colorado's own" Hot Rize. Amateur mandolin, banjo, flat-picking guitar and band contests begin on Wed. and run through Fri. morning. The main acts play Fri. through Sun. night. All concerts take place at Town Park. On the weekend some of the musicians play until the wee hours of the morning at local bars. Workshops for those interested in everything from banjo picking to clogging are offered during the festival. For more information about the Bluegrass Festival contact the **Telluride Festival Company** in Boulder at **(303) 449-6007,** or in **Telluride** at **(303) 728-3041.**

Telluride Jazz Festival
mid-July
The outdoor stage in Telluride's Town Park provides a 360° view of the scenery—a perfect accompaniment to a weekend of cool jazz. Since 1976 the festival has attracted well-known musicians in traditional as well as nontraditional jazz styles. After the sun sets, the music comes indoors to local bars and the Sheridan Opera House. **(303) 728-6079.**

Telluride Film Festival
early September
Whether you are a filmmaker or a film lover, this late-summer event will appeal to your cinematic instincts. Since 1973 the film festival has been attracting attention as a lesser-known American counterpart to Cannes. Free showings of premieres and foreign films take place nightly in an outdoor theater. Animation and innovation are topics at daily seminars, and private showings around town are hot tickets. **(303) 728-6079.**

Telluride Hang Gliding Festival
mid-September
Just as the chill of fall enters the high country, professional hang gliders send more chills through the crowd by performing high altitude acrobatics. There are also flying competitions between some of the top-ranked hang gliders in the world. It's a wonderful time of year to come to Telluride for this incredible spectator event. **(303) 728-6079.**

—— OUTDOOR ACTIVITIES ——

BIKING
MOUNTAIN BIKING
From Telluride you can leave town on a mountain bike and enter another dimension in about five minutes—a dimension without cars, houses and people. Mountain biking is catching on in Telluride as it is in other mountain towns. The terrain is perfect for riders of all abilities and there is even a hut to hut system available for an extended ride from Telluride to Moab, Utah (see San Juan Hut Systems in this section).

Bear Creek Trail—
A quick morning or evening ride up to Bear Creek Falls can be taken right out of town. See the Hiking and Backpacking section for more information.

Ophir Pass—
Known to many as a great four-wheel-drive shortcut from Telluride to Silverton, the Ophir Pass road also offers an interesting road to negotiate on a mountain bike. See the Four-Wheel-Drive Trips section in the **Silverton** chapter for more information.

Rentals, Tours and Information—
Olympic Sports—101 W. Colorado Ave.; (303) 728-4477.

Paragon Ski & Sport—213 W. Colorado Ave.; (303) 728-4525.

San Juan Hut Systems—This first-of-its-kind operation will sound compelling to anyone who can appreciate the idea of spending a week riding a mountain bike through beautifully diverse backcountry. Mike Turrin, co-owner of the hut system, is excited about the scenery, describing it as "a continuously unfolding transition, up and down, through the various climatic, geologic and vegetative zones." The 210-mile ride starts in the high alpine setting of Telluride and works gradually down from the Uncompahgre Plateau to the deserts of Utah's canyon country, ending at Moab.

The trek should appeal to riders of all abilities, as long as they are reasonably fit. Advanced mountain bikers can leave the main route and take single tracks over more difficult terrain. Even novices can complete the ride. The huts are spaced an average of 30 miles apart—far enough for a good five hours of riding each day. They are basic, yet have everything you'll need, including wood stoves and ample wood.

The long ride would be a weighty effort if you had to set up camp and carry your food for each night. Let someone else take care of the details. For a small nightly fee you can stay in the huts and take the ride on a self-guided basis. Another few dollars and you will have a couple of wool blankets and a sleeping pad waiting for you at each hut. Three basic meals a day are available for a very reasonable fee. Groups of seven or more must have a guide (additional charge). If you can't devote an entire week, think about doing a two- or three-day stage of the route. **San Juan Hut Systems, Box 1663, Telluride, CO 81435; (303) 728-6935.**

Telluride Sports—226 W. Colorado Ave.; (303) 728-3501.

FISHING

The fishing around Telluride can be good, but you won't hear tales about huge trout coming from area water. This is a good place to learn how to fish and to have fun catching smaller trout. You may want to enroll in the **Telluride Whitewater Fly-fishing School** for one- to three-day classes with on-stream instruction, in addition to classes on fly casting techniques, entomology, fly tying and reading the water. A six-day class includes a three-day float down the Gunnison River. For information: **PO Box 685, 224 E. Colorado Ave., Telluride, CO 81435; (303) 728-3895.**

Dolores River—

This Gold Medal river is one of the hottest in the state. See the Fishing section of the **Cortez** chapter.

San Miguel River—

This fast-moving river is stocked with rainbow trout up to about 12 inches. While catching trout in the San Miguel below Telluride, remember that the water has become highly mineralized from all of the mining operations. You may want to catch and release all fish. After heavy summer rains, the river becomes a useless, muddy flow; when the water is clear, try fishing in the morning and evening with small, brightly colored dry flies. Fishing with black caddis and hares ear nymphs is also recommended. The San Miguel River below the town of Norwood offers poor fishing.

Town Park Lake—

Kids 12 and under can fish at Town Park Lake at the east end of town. The kids love it and can usually catch trout on whatever bait they use.

Trout Lake—

If beautiful scenery is part of the fishing experience for you, then you should make an effort to drive to Trout Lake. The fishing is inconsistent, but can be quite good for smallish rainbows and brooks. Boat rentals are available, and there is a national forest campground nearby. There is even a gazebo for picnicking. Trout Lake is located about 12 miles south of Telluride on Hwy. 145.

Woods Lake—

Nestled at the base of three 14,000-foot peaks (Mt. Wilson and El Diente and Wilson peaks), Woods Lake enjoys a spectacular location away from any major roads. Artificial flies and lures only are permitted. The lake is well stocked with rainbow trout, and an occasional brook or cutthroat can be caught. To get to Woods Lake take Hwy. 145 northwest for 10 miles (just beyond the town of Sawpit). Turn left and head south on Fall Creek Rd. (Forest Rd. 618), which winds its way to Woods Lake in 9 miles.

FOUR-WHEEL-DRIVE TRIPS

Life for the miners in early-day Telluride was not only tough while working underground, but also when they tried to go anywhere. Steep, treacherous mountains proved difficult but conquerable obstacles for road builders. Mining camps in the San Juans, including Ouray, Lake City, Silverton and Telluride, were eventually connected by frighteningly steep wagon roads. Today, those with courage (in some cases, stupidity) and a reliable four-wheel-drive vehicle can navigate these rough roads. Old mining camps and spectacular views make this part of the state the jeeping capital of Colorado. Jeep rentals are available in Telluride, but people with no four-wheel-drive experience should seriously consider arranging a trip with a tour company.

Black Bear Pass—

Black Bear Pass is etched into the west side of Ingram Peak at the east end of the valley above Telluride. Looking from town, the road zigzags up what seems to be a vertical wall. Black Bear is a one-way road that begins near the summit of Red Mountain Pass, heads west and eventually ends in Telluride. For specifics on the pass see the Four-Wheel-Drive Trips section of the **Silverton** chapter.

Imogene Pass—

Built back in the 1870s to transport ore from the Tomboy Mine over to Ouray, Imogene Pass is one of the toughest jeep roads in Colorado. Locals strongly urge that only experienced drivers attempt this frightening and dangerous road. The view from the summit will make the drive worthwhile, except for vertigo-prone passengers. Imogene begins in Telluride. From the north end of N. Oak St., turn right onto the pass road (Forest Rd. 869). As the road climbs up, it offers a great view of Telluride and the east end of the valley, including Ingram Falls, Black Bear Pass Rd. and Bridal Veil Falls. Five miles up the road you'll arrive at the Tomboy Mine site. When the Tomboy was in full operation during the late 1890s, hundreds of men living at the mine camp enjoyed such unusual luxuries as tennis courts, a bowling alley and a YMCA. Today the Tomboy is nothing but ruins. Above the mine it's another 1.5 miles of tough switchbacks to the summit at 13,509 feet.

Just after the turn of the century, Telluride mines were hit with serious labor disputes that eventually built up into a long strike in 1903. The national guard was called in. They loaded the union "agitators" on a train and shipped them out of town with orders never to return. Just to make sure they didn't return via the "back door" to Telluride, the guardsmen erected Ft. Peabody on the summit of Imogene Pass and manned it through the winter of 1903–1904.

On the other (east) side of the pass, the road winds down a steep section into Imogene Basin. From the pass it's about 11 miles to Ouray. For more information about the Ouray side of the pass, see the Four-Wheel-Drive Trips section in the **Ouray** chapter. From Ouray you can return to Telluride via Ridgway and the Dallas Divide or try another jeep road such as Ophir Pass.

Ophir Pass—

This is a fairly safe four-wheel-drive road that can be reached just south of Telluride. Head south on Hwy. 145 for about 10 miles and turn left to the pass on Forest Rd. 630. *The road is very narrow and vehicles traveling uphill have the right of way.* For more information about the pass from the Silverton side see the Four-Wheel-Drive Trips section in the **Silverton** chapter.

Tours and Rentals—

Big Red Jeep Tours—Big Red offers half-day trips leaving at 8:30 am and 1:30 pm daily during the summer. The tour office is located at the **Victorian Inn, 401 W. Pacific Ave., PO Box 217, Telluride, CO 81435; (303) 728-6601.**

Telluride Whitewater—Take a full-day or a half-day trip on some of the wild roads near Telluride. Trips depart at 9 am daily in the summer. Rentals are also available if you want to drive yourself. Jeeps and Chevy Blazers are available for half or full days. You can pick up your vehicle the night before. **PO Box 685, 224 E. Colorado Ave., Telluride, CO 81435; (303) 728-3895.**

HIKING AND BACKPACKING

When talking about what the Telluride area has to offer visitors, it's difficult to not use superlatives. Hiking and backpacking opportunities are no exception. Just out of town await beautiful forests and high alpine basins covered with wildflowers. Dozens of abandoned mines expose hints of the long-gone days when men scoured the area in their search for gold and silver. Many of the old mining buildings are still standing, and some overnight backpackers use the structures for shelter from summer storms. It should be kept in mind that many of the mining claims in the mountains around Telluride are private property and the owners' wishes should be respected. *And by all means, stay out of the mine tunnels—they can be death traps!*

West of Telluride is the Lizard Head Wilderness Area of Uncompahgre National Forest. It straddles the San Miguel Mountains and is characterized by many glacial cirque lakes, roaring streams, spruce and fir forests and jagged mountains, including some 14,000-foot peaks.

The visitors center in Telluride (666 W. Colorado Ave.) has very good information concerning trails in the area. Topographical maps and information are also available at **Telluride Sports, 226 W. Colorado Ave.; 728-3501.** The national forest area around Telluride is under the jurisdiction of the **Norwood Ranger District Office** at **1760 Grand Ave., PO Box 388, Norwood, CO 81423; (303) 327-4261.** To reach Norwood from Telluride drive 33 miles northwest on Hwy. 145. The following are some standout trail ideas.

Bear Creek Trail—

This trail is a beautiful 2-mile hike that starts in town and leads south to an impressive waterfall. The trail through this deep valley offers great views of the surrounding jagged peaks. At one point it crosses over an avalanche slide area, showing vividly why cross-country skiers avoid the valley in winter. The trailhead begins at the south end of Pine St.

Bridal Veil Falls, near Telluride (photograph by Ingrid Lundahl).

Bridal Veil Falls—

Although this is a short hike, it is steep and can catch the unacclimated by surprise. If you are new to the high altitude, take it slow and easy. From Telluride, drive to the end of the canyon and begin hiking up the jeep road. Views of Ingram Falls on the left and impressive Bridal Veil Falls on the right make this a highly recommended 1-mile hike. At the top of the falls, hanging over the 480-foot cliff, is the old Smuggler-Union hydroelectric plant. Built in 1904, the structure is a National Historic Landmark. Views back down the valley to Telluride are stunning.

Hope Lake Trail—

From the Hope Lake trailhead, this is a gradual 3-mile hike up to 12,500 feet. Many families like this hike, which offers impressive views. There are fish in the lake, but fishing is usually poor. Hope Lake is located above Trout Lake and was built as a reservoir for the Ames hydroelectric plant. To reach the trailhead from Telluride, head south about 12 miles on Hwy. 145 to Trout Lake. Turn left onto Trestle Rd. (Forest Rd. 626) and drive 1 mile to the intersection with Hidden Lake Rd. (Forest Rd. 627). Turn left again and drive to the parking area 2.5 miles up the road.

Silver Pick Basin/Navajo Basin Loop—

This has to be one of the most exciting and beautiful backpacking areas in the state. Old mine buildings, snowfields and rugged mountains are all around you. The trail (No. 408) begins on the north side of the Lizard Head Wilderness Area and heads south into Silver Pick Basin. It climbs out of the forest and up into a rocky area where a lot of old mining claims dot the mountainside. At the top of the basin a saddle allows access to Navajo Basin to the southwest. From the saddle, Wilson Peak, Gladstone Peak, Mt. Wilson and El Diente Peak loom from left to right. Wilson Peak is a fairly easy climb but the others are very difficult. Just below the south side of the saddle is an old building that many hikers sleep in.

If you drop down from the saddle into Navajo Basin and follow the drainage west, you will come to Navajo Lake. Below the lake the trail splits. The left fork (Navajo Lake Trail) heads toward Dunton and Woods Lake (see the Hiking and Backpacking section of the Cortez chapter). The right fork climbs northwest and then down to another fork. From this new fork, head to the right on Trail No. 407, which will take you back to the start of the loop. To

reach the trailhead from Telluride, head northwest on Hwy. 145 for about 7 miles and turn left onto Big Bear Rd. (Forest Rd. 622). Follow the road south for 5.5 miles and begin hiking up the jeep road to the wilderness area boundary.

Ski Mountain—

The ski mountain at the Telluride Ski Area is a very popular hiking spot with spectacular views. The Coonskin Chairlift is open in summer Wed.–Sat. 10 am–2 pm. For a small fee you can ride to the top and hike down. If you're feeling ambitious, forget the chairlift and hike to the top. Be sure to call (303) 728-3041 for information. Located on the west end of town.

Wasatch Trail—

Starting from town, this 10-mile loop trail is one of the most scenic in the Telluride area. Many people hike it in a day, but it also makes a good overnighter. The trail follows Bear Creek up to the falls and then climbs up to 13,000 feet at a divide between Bear Creek and Bridal Veil Creek. From Telluride follow the trail from the south end of Pine St. up to the falls and look for the Wasatch Trail (No. 414) on the right. It climbs steeply for the first mile to La Junta Basin and then gradually climbs to the divide. Follow the trail northeast as it drops down to Bridal Veil Creek then follow the trail down past Bridal Veil Falls and back into town.

HORSEBACK RIDING

D&E Outfitters—

This outfit offers one-hour, full-day and overnight horseback rides. There are also barbecue dinner rides and horse-drawn wagon rides through town. 805 W. Pacific Ave.; (303) 728-3200.

RIVER FLOATING

San Miguel River—

Much like the Upper Dolores, the San Miguel River flows west out of the San Juans, cutting a deep valley and exposing red rock walls. From Telluride the river meanders west for about 3 miles before plunging 400 feet in a half mile, then flowing into the South Fork. From here on down the floating can be good in May through June depending on the runoff. At high water, this section of the San Miguel can be dangerous due to huge waves. Be careful. From its confluence with the South Fork, the San Miguel can be run 54 miles down to the bridge at Naturita.

Upper Dolores River—

See the River Floating section in the **Cortez** chapter.

Outfitters—

Telluride Whitewater—Based in Telluride, Telluride Whitewater has experienced river guides who lead one- to six-night trips on the San Miguel, Gunnison, Dolores and upper Animas rivers. They can also cook a pretty mean river meal. For information, contact them at **224 E. Colorado Ave., Box 685, Telluride, CO 81435; (303) 728-3895.**

SKIING
CROSS-COUNTRY SKIING
Backcountry Trails—
Lizard Head Pass—See the **Cortez** chapter.

San Juan Hut Systems—Though this hut system is primarily used by mountain bikers in the summer, it makes for an excellent backcountry ski trip in winter. Take off from Telluride on old mine roads and backcountry trails for 6 miles a day with a cozy mountain hut waiting at the end. There are three huts in this self-guided system. The trails, designed for beginner to intermediate skiers, wind through spectacular territory in Uncompahgre National Forest, with views of the Sneffels Range. All skiers should have a basic knowledge of changing mountain weather conditions and preparedness. The nightly fee is quite reasonable. For more information: **San Juan Hut Systems, Box 1663, Telluride, CO 81435; (303) 728-6935.**

Groomed Trails—
Telluride Nordic Center—About 10 miles of groomed trails meander through aspen groves and open meadows with fabulous views to the nearby peaks. The Telluride Nordic Center offers primarily hilly terrain that varies from moderately challenging to easy. Guided backcountry trips, telemark skiing and skating are all options. There are plans for an extended trail system at the top of lift No. 10 for more experienced skiers. Special three- to five-day nordic packages include track, telemark and guided backcountry skiing. Rentals are available at the base lodge; trail fee. The nordic center is located at the Mountain Village at the Meadows Base (free shuttle). **(303) 728-3856.**

Town Trail—This informal, mile-long trail is popular among locals wanting to stretch out a bit. Located along the south edge of town, the trail loosely follows the course of the San Miguel River.

Rentals and Information—
There are numerous places to rent skis in town, including the Telluride Nordic Center in the Mountain Village; **(303) 728-3856.** All of the shops should have current knowledge of avalanche conditions in the area.

Olympic Sports—101 W. Colorado Ave.; **(303) 728-4477.**

Paragon Ski & Sport—213 W. Colorado Ave.; **(303) 728-4525.**

Telluride Sports—226 W. Colorado Ave.; **(303) 728-3501.**

DOWNHILL SKIING
Telluride Ski Area—
Telluride Ski Area has a wide reputation for having some of the longest, steepest, nastiest bump runs in the country. It's all true, but there is also a gentle, more sunny side to the mountain that towers over town. The back side of Telluride, with its southern exposure, is a paradise for

non-expert skiers. Not only is the skiing great, but the views to the 14,000-foot summits of the San Miguel Mountains, the odd rock of Lizard Head Peak and the distant La Sal Mountains in Utah will stop you in your tracks. But Telluride is still the consummate expert mountain. The shaded front side of the mountain offers soft snow nearly all of the time since it hardly ever melts and re-freezes. The Spiral Stairs run has a 40° slope near the top and keeps going for what seems like forever. From the expert front side of the mountain, the dramatic view down into town and around the edge of the box canyon will take your breath away—as if that's what you need at 11,000 feet! If the 3,145-foot vertical drop of the mountain isn't long enough, there are walk-up runs from the top of Gold Hill. Someday the steep slopes of Bear Creek and Delta Bowl, known to a select group of expert skiers, will be serviced by lift.

On the mountain, Gorrono Ranch is a mid-point restaurant, accessible by skiers of all abilities. Built among the weathered buildings of an old homestead, it looks rustic on the outside, but once in the plush facility you may not want to leave. All of the mountain restaurants have a specialty, so those skiing for a week (or longer) won't get tired of the food.

The ski mountain is accessible both from town and from Telluride Mountain Village—a recent development of hotels, condominiums and restaurants. It takes some determination to get to Telluride. Once there, you will be greeted by short lift lines and some of the best conditions imaginable. For information, contact **Telluride Ski Resort, PO Box 307, 562 Mountain Village Blvd., Telluride, CO 81435; (303) 728-3856.**

TENNIS

There are two free tennis courts at Town Park, located at the east end of town.

SEEING AND DOING

BALLOONING

San Juan Balloon Adventures—
Year-round early morning balloon rides take off from Telluride and float down the valley, offering spectacular views of the surrounding mountains. The traditional champagne toast takes place at the end of the flight. Reservations are required. Contact San Juan Balloon Adventures at **PO Box 2458, Telluride, CO 81435; (303) 728-3895.**

CHAIRLIFT RIDES

In summer, rides up the Coonskin Chairlift are available Wed.–Sat. 10 am–2 pm. From the top of the mountain at 10,500 feet, there are spectacular views of the surrounding peaks including the La Sal Mountains in Utah. Food is available at a snack bar, or bring your own picnic lunch. A small fee is charged, but children under 6 years old ride free if accompanied by an adult. Located at the west end of town. For more information, call **(303) 728-3041.**

HOT SPRINGS

See the **Ouray** chapter.

MUSEUMS AND GALLERIES

San Miguel County Museum—
Take some time to wander around the interesting collection at this small historical museum. All of the objects, when taken together, create a fine reflection of life in early Telluride. Old black and white photos of a raucous saloon are displayed with beer tokens, old pool balls and gaming tables. There is a barber's chair with leather handstraps—from times when barbers were the ones to pull teeth or do minor surgery. In the kitchen are handwritten cookbooks, old calendars and an assortment of gadgets for the time. Don't miss the pipe racks with clever sayings, such as "Don't croak, better smoke." Small fee; open from Memorial Day to mid-Oct. 10 am–5 pm daily. **317 N. Fir St.; (303) 728-3344.**

Telluride Gallery of Fine Art—

Work from national and international artists is displayed in a beautiful environment. The gallery is often home to many touring exhibitions. When we visited there were display cases of wearable art from Holland. This is a very low key place considering the high quality (and prices) of the artwork. Feel free to roam around and look at the contemporary oil paintings, jewelry, basketry and other media. Open daily from 10 am–6 pm in summer; 10 am–9 pm in winter. **130 E. Colorado Ave.; (303) 728-4242.**

NIGHTLIFE

Fly Me to the Moon Saloon—

This is the one and only consistent venue for live music in Telluride. Downstairs in a narrow underground room, the major attraction is a stage, a spring-loaded dance floor that absorbs shocks from frantic dancing and a well-stocked bar. The bands usually play danceable rock, reggae or blues music. During ski season or large festivals, Fly Me to the Moon can get packed. Cover charge when there is a live band. **132 E. Colorado Ave.; 728-6666.**

Last Dollar—

This local hangout is just a good place to go for a beer and a game of pool or darts. A stone fireplace keeps things warm in the winter months. Open until 2 am (midnight on Sun.). Located at the **corner of Pine St. and Colorado Ave.; 728-4800.**

Mountain Splendor—

If you aren't able to get out into the surrounding mountains and forests for yourself, or you just appreciate quality nature photography, set aside time to attend Mountain Splendor. The changing seasons in the San Juans are brought to life in Jack Pera's well-done computer-synchronized slide show. Pera, a Telluride native, speaks before the slide show, which features 25 years' worth of his wildlife and wildflower slides taken in the San Juan area. A photo gallery of Pera's work is displayed in the lobby; framed photos are available for purchase. Mountain Splendor is shown at 8:30 pm nightly in the Masonic Lodge Hall. The box office opens at 8:10 pm. A fee is charged. **200 E. Colorado Ave.; 728-3632 or 728-4132.**

Sheridan Bar—

There is no better place to imagine how Telluride looked and felt at the beginning of the century. After all, it was only a block away from here that Butch Cassidy made his very first unauthorized bank withdrawal in 1889. Located just off the lobby of the New Sheridan Hotel, this bar is a happening spot for locals and visitors. It's a casual place with a stamped tin ceiling and well-worn hardwood floors. The massive, cherry wood backbar is stocked to the hilt and there are darts and foosball games for those inclined to test their motor skills. Open daily until 2 am (midnight on Sun.). **225 W. Colorado Ave.; 728-3626.**

SCENIC DRIVES

If you want to get out on the road and see some spectacular scenery, it's hard to go wrong in the Telluride area. Everywhere you can go is beautiful and historic. The following are a few of the best choices for passenger cars.

Alta—

Located a short 12 miles from Telluride, Alta provides great views of Ophir Needles to the south, Lizard Head Peak, Mt. Wilson and Wilson and El Diente peaks to the west. The development of the rich Gold King Mine in 1877 enabled the mining community of Alta to boom into the 1890s. Mining in the Alta area produced gold, silver, copper and lead, and continued sporadically until the mid-1940s. Today a few buildings remain, including the old boardinghouse for Gold King miners. The site is privately owned by a mining company, but visitors are allowed as long as you stay out of the buildings and don't destroy anything. To reach Alta from Telluride, head south on Hwy. 145 for about 5 miles to Boomerang Rd. (Forest Rd. 632) on the left. From here the drive to Alta is 4 miles.

Last Dollar Road—

This dirt road travels past old ranch properties with weathered buildings and provides excellent views to the west end of the Sneffels Range. Last Dollar Rd. heads north from Telluride and comes out near the Dallas Divide on Hwy. 62. The road traverses Hastings Mesa and is a good shortcut between Telluride and Ouray. Passenger cars can drive Last Dollar Rd. when it's dry, but it would be a good idea to inquire locally before heading off. To reach the road from Telluride, drive west 3 miles and look for Last Dollar Rd. (Forest Rd. 638) on the right.

Lizard Head Pass—

Lizard Head Pass is only about 15 miles from Telluride, but there is a lot of spectacular scenery packed into this short drive. Heading south on Hwy. 145 takes you by the town of Ophir (about 10 miles from Telluride). This was the location of the legendary Ophir Loop, an impressive 100-foot-high trestle for the Rio Grande Southern Railroad. The railroad, built by Otto Mears, connected Telluride with the smelters in Durango and the rest of the outside world via Lizard Head Pass. Continuing on the highway from Ophir for another 3 miles takes you to Trout Lake, one of the most beautiful lakes in the state. Towering above the lake to the south are Yellow Mountain, Vermillion Peak and Sheep Mountain. Trout Lake was built as a reservoir for the historic power plant downriver at Ames, which in 1891 generated the world's first commercial AC power. It generated power for the Gold King Mine up in Alta. Trout Lake is privately owned, but fishing is allowed. On the south end of the lake, an old, rickety Rio Grande Southern Railroad trestle stands ready to topple any day. See it while you can.

From Trout Lake continue on Hwy. 145 up to the summit of Lizard Head Pass for views west down Upper Dolores River Valley and north to the eerie-looking Lizard Head Peak. From the top of an already-tall peak, this 400-foot spire of crumbly rock is an inspiring sight, as well as what many rock climbers consider to be the most difficult technical climb in the state.

WHERE TO STAY

ACCOMMODATIONS

Telluride has a lot to offer when it comes to accommodations. If you would like to stay in a historic hotel or bed and breakfast, there are a number of choices. Listed below are the best choices at the time this book was written, but the situation is changing fast. At present there are five small bed and breakfast inns under construction in town; at the Mountain Village, a couple of miles away, plans for future expansion are rapidly coming to pass. If you prefer a modern condominium with all the amenities, call **Telluride Central Reservations** at **1-800-525-3455** (outside Colorado) or **(303) 728-4431** (in Colorado).

Skyline Guest Ranch — $$$ to $$$$

Just 8 miles south of Telluride off Hwy. 145, Skyline Guest Ranch sits on what could very possibly be the most beautiful property in the Colorado Rockies. Nestled at 9,600 feet in a mountain meadow, the ranch is surrounded by towering peaks, most notably Mt. Wilson and Wilson Peak (both over 14,000 feet) just to the west. In the summer, wildflowers bloom, covering the fields with every color under the sun. In the fall, golden aspen groves present an almost overwhelming beauty—compelling many visitors to snap roll after roll of pictures.

Years ago Skyline Ranch was a logging camp that used water to run the mill. For a few years in the 1950s it was run as a guest ranch. Dave and Sherry Farney, the current owners and hosts, purchased the ranch in 1968, which for many years served as a base camp for their well-known Tellu-

The Alta Lakes, with views of peaks in the San Miguel Range.

ride Mountaineering School. Today the ranch provides guests the opportunity to experience the San Juan Mountains and share the love of nature and people that Dave and Sherry so enthusiastically impart.

Accommodations at the ranch include 10 guest rooms in the main lodge and half a dozen private cabins nearby. Exquisite meals are served in the main lodge, accented by the famous "Sherry" bread. The atmosphere in the lodge and the diverse group of guests encourage everyone to get to know one another. Those staying in the cabins can opt to cook their own meals.

Dave and Sherry go out of their way to help guests get the most out of their stay—whether they want to go climb a mountain or just lounge around the ranch. Up the hill from the main lodge is a lake stocked with brown, brook and Tasmanian rainbow trout. A string of excellent horses allows you to ride to your heart's content. After a day of hiking you can relax with a cold beer or head to the sauna and the wood-fired hot tub.

Skyline Ranch is open June to Oct. and from Thanksgiving to Apr. It's hard to imagine a better ranch experience. A week-long minimum stay is required in summer. In winter, cabins and rooms in the lodge ($$$) are available and rates are figured on a daily basis. **Box 67, Telluride, CO 81435; (303) 728-3757.**

Dahl House — $$ summer, $$$ winter

Back in the 1890s the Dahl House was a boardinghouse for miners. Today the small size of the rooms in the Victorian-era house hasn't changed much, but the quality has. A smattering of antiques and lightly patterned wallpaper have given the bed and breakfast a period charm. The top floors are reached by climbing up a steep, narrow stairway. Eight rooms share three bathrooms (an occasional wait) and one room has a private bathroom. The downstairs common area is a good place to kick back and watch cable TV or get to know the other guests. Each morning a continental breakfast is served for one-and-a-half hours at a long dining room table. **PO Box 695, 122 S. Oak St., Telluride, CO 81435; (303) 728-4158.**

New Sheridan Hotel — $$ to $$$

In 1895 two enterprising men, Gus Brickman and Max Hippler, decided to stop their search for riches in the mountains around Telluride and build a fine hotel for the town. Despite a burgeoning population of 2,000, Telluride lacked quality accommodations. The first guests in the hotel were treated to well-appointed rooms and a lavish dining room with a Japanese chef and an opulent bar.

In 1902 perennial presidential hopeful William Jennings Bryan made a speech from a large wooden stage erected at the front of the landmark three-story hotel. As the mining town declined, the hotel followed, eventually closing in 1925. In 1977 the resilient hotel reopened after extensive renovations and today is back in the limelight. The rooms range from the merely comfortable to the plush William Jennings Bryan Suite, with its expansive views and period antique furniture. Many rooms are not equipped with private baths, but the "club" baths are clean and numerous enough. All rooms have color TVs and phones. Just off the first-floor lobby is Julians Restaurant (see the Where to Eat section), the Sheridan Bar (see the Nightlife section) and the Sheridan Opera House. **231 W. Colorado Ave., Telluride, CO 81435; (303) 728-4351.**

The Victorian Inn — $$ to $$$

Though built in 1976, the Victorian Inn does have some of the charm that its name implies. And the rates for its 26 rooms are very reasonable. Located in the center of town, this inn offers rooms with both private and shared baths. Each room has cable TV and a phone. The sauna and hot tub help ease stiffness after a day on the slopes. Continental breakfast (included in the price of the room) features delicious homemade stone-ground wheat muffins. **401 W. Pacific Ave., PO Box 217, Telluride, CO 81435; 1-800-537-2614 nationwide or (303) 728-6601.**

Oak Street Inn — $$

Built originally as a Methodist church, the Oak Street Inn now caters to a congregation of budget travelers. A younger crowd frequents this informal hostelry, which offers fairly basic rooms at low prices (discounts to American Youth Hostel cardholders staying in a dorm room). A number of different room designs accommodate from two to six people. Only a couple of rooms have private baths. For taking the kinks out, there is a coed sauna. Upstairs is a TV lounge that offers free tea and coffee in the morning. **134 N. Oak St., Telluride, CO 81435; (303) 728-3383.**

CAMPING

Town Park Campground, on the east end of town, is very popular in the summer, with its 28 sites, restrooms and shower facilities. During peak summer times, such as the Bluegrass Festival, the sites are taken quickly. The campground's beautiful location in the trees along the San Miguel River and its proximity to town make it a great spot. There are no RV hookups; a fee is charged.

In Uncompahgre National Forest—

Sunshine Campground possesses what is certainly one of the most spectacular views of any national forest campground in the state. Located 8 miles southwest of Telluride on Hwy. 145, Sunshine has a larger-than-life view west to Mt. Wilson and Wilson Peak in the Lizard Head Wilderness Area. There are 15 sites and a fee is charged. Two miles farther southwest on Hwy. 145 is **Matterhorn Camp-ground** with 24 sites; a fee is charged. The view from Matterhorn is also a standout.

A few primitive camping areas are nearby. On Hwy. 145 between Sunshine and Matterhorn campgrounds, Boomerang Rd. (Forest Rd. 632) heads east for 3 miles to Alta Lakes, where there are some places to camp; no fee is charged and water is not available. Camping at **Woods Lake** is also possible. It's located 17 miles west of Telluride—drive northwest on Hwy. 145 past Sawpit and turn left on Fall Creek Rd. (Forest Rd. 618). Follow the road south to Woods Lake; there is no pump water and no fee charged. Campsites are also available along **Illium Valley Rd.** (Forest Rd. 625) just west of Telluride. The road can be reached from Telluride by driving northwest on Hwy. 145 for about 5 miles. Look for the turn-off for Illium Valley Rd. on the left. There are no facilities and no fee charged.

WHERE TO EAT

Julians — $$$

The northern Italian cuisine at Julians has long been a local favorite. The owners are involved in the day-to-day operation of the restaurant, and their attention to detail is what makes it a choice for a special meal. Choose your dinner from a menu that includes a number of pasta dishes, such as baked cannelloni stuffed with veal, chicken and spinach. Or you may want to try a boneless chicken breast filled with mushrooms and a sausage mixture flavored with Marsala wine. The walls in the restaurant's bar area were painted with a large mural of playful nudes for the filming of a movie about Butch Cassidy. The cozy restaurant area has a much more subdued decor. The carefully selected wine list provides a welcome addition to the meal and it's "user-friendly": hidden in back of the list there is a brief description of the character of each wine. Call ahead for reservations. Located on the first floor of the New Sheridan Hotel. Open daily from 6–10 pm in summer, 5:30–10 pm in winter (they will seat until 10 pm). **231 W. Colorado Ave.; 728-3839.**

La Marmotte — $$$

La Marmotte is new in town, but has received consistently high praise from the locals—quite a testimony. It's a special place for a fine meal. Offering classic and country-style French cuisine at reasonable prices, owners Bertrand and Noelle Lepel-Cointet have hit on a restaurant formula that works well. La Marmotte is located in the old town icehouse down in the warehouse district. Exposed brick and weathered wood dominate the decor of this small, intimate place. The menu offers interesting entrées ranging from pasta to steak du jour. The wine list is a fine selection from French and California vineyards. Sun. brunch is also served at the restaurant (not a buffet). Reservations recommended during the busy winter months. Hours at La Marmotte are 6–10 pm nightly; Sun. brunch from 10 am–2 pm in summer only. **150 W. San Juan Ave.; 728-6232.**

Leimgrubers Bierstube & Restaurant — $$ to $$$

Christal Leimgruber brings a genuine warmth and lively spirit to her relatively new Bavarian restaurant. Raised in East Berlin, Leimgruber made it across the border to the West just two years before the raising of the Berlin Wall. We're glad to have her here! She has brought the Old World to Telluride, and local support has been tremendous. The basic formula of the small restaurant works—the service is friendly, the portions are generous and the beer is good. Menu entrées include bratwurst, wienerschnitzel and Kassler—smoked pork tenderloin with champagne sauerkraut. Choose from a wide selection of German beer, including three different shades of draft Pauliner and wheat beer, as well as a good selection of wines and liquors by the glass. Bavarian music and a collection of beer steins give the restaurant a distinctly European feel. There is also deck seating. Leimgrubers serves breakfast in winter and gets packed and wild for après ski. Open for dinner from 5:30–9:30 pm Tues.–Sat. during summer; in winter the restaurant is open from 3–10 pm daily. **573 W. Pacific Ave.; 728-4663.**

Floradora Saloon — $$

Although the Floradora Saloon serves everything from huevos rancheros to steak dinners, it is best known for its salad bar and tasty ground-sirloin burgers. The oldest singly owned eating establishment in Telluride, Floradora gets its name from two voluptuous ladies of the evening, Flora and Dora, who worked the red light district during the mining days. During the busy winter season and summer festivals, this place can get pretty crowded. But be patient—it's worth the wait. The Floradora bar is a great spot to belly up for a beer. Box lunches and takeout orders are available. Open 11 am–10 pm daily. **103 W. Colorado Ave.; 728-3888.**

Sofios — $$

Mexican food with a southwestern slant fills the menu at this busy eatery. Enchiladas, burritos and tacos come in traditional and jazzed-up versions. Enchiladas Especial comes with large chunks of chicken layered with Monterey Jack cheese and blue corn tortillas smothered in salsa verde, all topped with sour cream. Smaller appetites may order à la carte ($). You'll be served in a two-tiered room with exposed brick walls and a pressed tin ceiling. A southwestern feel comes from the few white stucco archways and several hanging strands of red chili peppers. Sofios is also a good place to come for breakfast, which includes egg dishes, pancakes and waffles. Breakfast served daily from 7–11:30 am (noon on Sun.), dinner from 5:30–10 pm. **110 E. Colorado Ave.; 728-4882.**

Eddie's — $ to $$

Eddie's has one of the best sun decks in town, and it definitely has the best pizza. From your table you have great views of the ski mountain and up and down the valley. In addition to pizzas made with the usual toppings, specialty pizzas with ingredients such as capers, calimari and artichoke hearts can satisfy even the most adventuresome. Pasta specials, sandwiches and appetizers round out the menu. The bar has Coors, Anchor Steam and Watneys on tap. Orders to go and deliveries are available. Eddie's is open from 11 am–11 pm daily. Located on **Colorado Ave. next to Elk's Park; 728-5335.**

The Excelsior Cafe — $ to $$

It's hard to say whether this popular restaurant serves a better breakfast or lunch, but both are excellent. Located in a building that was a bowling alley in the 1890s, the Excelsior Cafe is a fun place to eat. Exposed brick walls, pressed tin on the ceilings and a spiral staircase leading to upstairs seating give this place its charm. The restaurant has an open-space feel, with a patio, high ceilings and the grill near the front door so customers can watch the cook do his thing. Owner Peter Muckerman calls the restaurant's layout a "theater-in-the-round style." Breakfast highlights include the Eggs Excelsior; the coffee here is great. Lunches include Filé Gumbo, Cobb salad and the renowned Colorado Plateau chili. A special board changes daily, offering breakfast and lunch items. Open daily from 7:30 am–mid-afternoon. **200 W. Colorado Ave.; 728-4250.**

Skeeter's — $ to $$

Chances are that this restaurant will make you feel like you're eating in a *Town & Country* feature photo spread. Skeeter's is decorated in what you might call Pennsylvania Dutch or French Country, and the food is definitely down-home. Reasonably priced dinners include steaks, pork chops, trout, spaghetti and burgers. On Tues. and Thur. the fare is Mexican, and the owners often bring in their talking macaw parrot (it can quack like a duck) to add to the atmosphere. Wine and beer are served. Open from 5–10 pm Tues.–Sat. Skeeter's is also open for full breakfasts from 7–11 am Tues.–Sat. Located 10 miles northwest of Telluride on Hwy. 145 in the community of Sawpit; 728-3608.

Baked in Telluride — $

A mouth-watering array of croissants (plain or filled with fruit or various meat and cheese combinations), rolls, donuts, bagels and brownies keep people coming back to this full-service bakery. There is also fast counter service for deli sandwiches and pizza by the slice. A great alternative to restaurant dining is to take out some freshly baked goods; in summer find an outside bench or bring your food up on the first chairlift ride in winter. You may also want to find a spot at one of the few inside tables or on the small covered porch. Open from 5:30 am–10 pm daily. **127 S. Fir St.; 728-4775.**

SERVICES

Telluride Central Reservations—

Call **1-800-525-3455** (outside Colorado) or **(303) 728-4431** (in Colorado).

Telluride Chamber
Resort Association—

The visitors center is located on the west end of town at **666 W. Colorado Ave., Box 653, Telluride, CO 81435; (303) 728-3041.**

Telluride Taxi—

Twenty-four hour-taxi service is available with Telluride Taxi at **(303) 728-6667.**

Telluride Transit—

Chartered bus/van transportation to and from the Telluride, Montrose and Grand Junction airports can be arranged 24 hours in advance by calling **(303) 728-4105.**

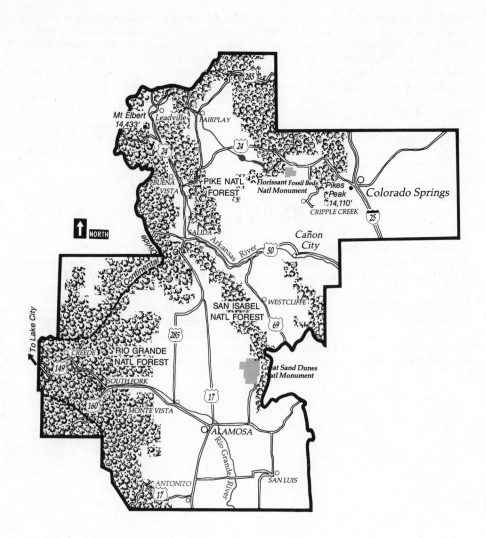

SOUTH CENTRAL REGION

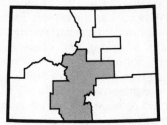

Cañon City

By itself, Cañon City is not a traditional destination for vacationers. But if you find yourself in the area, there are a number of enticements. The Royal Gorge is the most well-known attraction. Over 1,000 feet deep and eight miles long, the gorge is an awesome sight, especially when viewed from the world's highest suspension bridge: examples of nature and human engineering at their best. A float trip down the Arkansas River can be a mellow family excursion or a rough ride in the rapids. There are a number of little-known mountain parks in the surrounding foothills.

Cañon City's 12,000 residents enjoy a protected, natural setting that buffers the town from harsh weather. A well-preserved five-block stretch of Main Street has been named to the National Register of Historic Places. Though Cañon City is best known as the home of the state penitentiary, it is really just a quiet town with an intriguing history.

HISTORY

Cañon City was a favorite camping area for Ute Indians, but it also served as a war line between the mountainous domain of the Utes and the territory of the eastern plains Indians. Sporadic tribal fighting kept permanent settlers away in the early 1800s. Several US Army explorations headed by the well-known soldiers Lt. Zebulon Pike and Maj. Stephen Long passed through the area. Their travels in the early 1800s helped chart the territory acquired in the Louisiana Purchase of 1803.

It was the gold rush that eventually brought settlers to Cañon City in 1859. People came not for mining per se, but to build a trading center for supplies and provisions needed by miners in the mountains to the west. The town grew quickly and within two years there were 900 residents.

Cañon City hit the skids by 1863 as the men rode wagons east to join either the Union or the Confederate side in fighting the Civil War. The Anson Rudd family was nearly the only one to stay behind. By autumn of 1864 a few families had begun to return to occupy vacant homes and begin a town revival.

In 1868 Golden and Denver were vying to be named the seat of the territorial government. Just as the heated political battle appeared dead-locked, Cañon City lined up the support of a block of southern Colorado legislators to name Cañon City as the capital. Even though Cañon City had no possibility of winning, it now had enough clout to make a deal. During some backroom wheeling and dealing, Denver enlisted the support of Cañon City. Soon Denver was named the capital and, in return, Cañon City was given the choice of building the university or the penitentiary. A territorial prison was built in 1871 after the townspeople decided the prison would provide a steady economic base. And besides, no one would have to put up with all-night fraternity parties.

In the early 1900s Cañon City was a prime location for movie making. Spectacular scenery provided the backdrop for local cowboy Tom Mix, the hero of many silent Westerns. But the spotlight was short lived. Grace McCue, a popular leading lady of the times, was swept away and drowned in the Arkansas River during filming, and the tragedy pro-voked damage suits that forced the Colorado Motion Picture Co. into bankruptcy. Recently, films such as *Cat Ballou, Continental Divide* and *The Dutchess and the Dirtwater Fox* were made in the Cañon City vicinity.

Cañon City had the dubious honor of being state headquarters for the Ku Klux Klan in the mid-1920s. The Klan published a small newspa-per and eventually controlled many county and civic offices as well as the school board. They even operated a Klan bank in the Hotel St. Cloud for five years. Thankfully, the hateful ideals of the Klan were short lived.

Due in large part to the prison system, slow, steady growth has provided residents with jobs over the years, without depriving them of small-town status. Cañon City is a quiet town that has developed into a favored place to retire, partly because of its mild climate and lack of big-city problems.

GETTING THERE

Cañon City is located 115 miles south of Denver, or 38 miles west of Pueblo. To get there from Denver, drive south on Interstate 25 for 68 miles to Colorado Springs. Angle southwest on Hwy. 115 for 36 miles, then turn right (west) on Hwy. 50 for the last 11 miles into town.

MAJOR ATTRACTIONS

ROYAL GORGE

Three million years of the Arkansas River's cutting through solid granite has formed this spectacular 1,053-foot-deep chasm. Known to early explorers as the Grand Canyon of the Arkansas, the Royal Gorge has astonished travelers for generations. Despite overcommercialization, the gorge remains a magnificent sight to anyone willing to look over its edge.

History—

In 1806 Lt. Zebulon Montgomery Pike camped near the eastern portal of the canyon, but his scouting party determined that it would be impossible to get through the gorge. It took 70 years and the promise of profits from the silver boom to inspire the railroads to chisel a way through the narrow canyon. When the Leadville silver rush was in full force, two railroad companies started laying tracks in different sections of the gorge, and a bitter right-of-way struggle ensued. There was room in the narrow canyon for only one track, and both companies desperately wanted the route. By 1878 the "war" between the Denver & Rio Grande (D&RG) and Santa Fe railroads escalated to the point of gunfire and frequent sabotage. Somehow, no one was ever killed. Ultimately, a lease through the gorge was granted to the D&RG by the courts.

In 1929 the world's highest suspension bridge was built across the Royal Gorge more than 1,000 feet above the Arkansas River. The bridge is still the best way to get an unobstructed view of the river—that is, unless you attach yourself to a bungicord and hurl yourself over the edge, as four daredevils did in 1980. Other reasonable ways to experience the gorge are via the aerial tramway, the steep-incline railway to the bottom or a "multi-media slide presentation." All of this costs money: from $5–$7, depending on which combination of rides and attractions you choose. Also available are restaurants and curios by the armload. Open during daylight hours year-round. **(719) 275-7507.**

It doesn't cost a thing if you simply want a view of the gorge and bridge from afar. Drive along the road toward the north rim toll booth, then pull off to the side and walk over to the rim. The view is a little sweeter without the entrance fee.

Getting There—The gorge is located 8 miles west of Cañon City, off Hwy. 50. Beware of tame deer on the winding road as you near the entrance. Unfortunately, during the short drive from Cañon City to the gorge entrance, you can't avoid the tacky shops and numerous massive billboards spouting all manner of means for lightening your wallet. For an unspoiled alternate route to the gorge via the south rim, see the Temple Canyon description in the Scenic Drive section.

FESTIVALS

Blossom Festival

first weekend in May

The biggest event in Cañon City attracts thousands to a colorful spring get-together. For 50 years Fremont County residents and visitors have gathered to celebrate the cherry and apple blossoms in the surrounding orchards. High school marching bands come from across the country to parade down historic Main St. alongside many floats. The weekend features an art show, a craft fair and carnival rides. For more information, call **(719) 275-7411.**

OUTDOOR ACTIVITIES

BIKING

MOUNTAIN BIKING

Mountain biking is the best way to go in this area due to rough road conditions on most of the scenic routes. The Scenic Drives section provides many ideas near Cañon City that are perfect for sturdy two-wheelers.

FISHING

Want to hear the latest on fishing in the Cañon City area? Talk with Jimmy at **Jimmy's Sport Shop** on Main St. He has been handing out advice and selling tackle, bait and licenses for 42 years. **311 Main St.; (719) 275-3685.**

Arkansas River—

It's possible to catch trout within the Cañon City limits, but the best fishing on the Arkansas is west of town. Actually, for a great day of fishing on the Arkansas, head to the Gold Medal trout water below **Salida** (see the Fishing section of the **Upper Arkansas Valley** chapter). Large brown trout can be pulled from the roily water. The river is not wadeable, forcing most fishermen to approach from the highway side.

Lake DeWeese—

Beware of this warmwater reservoir. You'll reel in a sucker nine out of 10 times, even though the lake has been stocked with rainbows.

Texas Creek—

Twenty-six miles west of Cañon City, Texas Creek flows into the Arkansas River. Next to the creek, Hwy. 69 follows south into the high country along the east side of the Sangre de Cristo Mountains. This road provides access to a number of small streams and lakes. Fishing can be good for brown trout in Texas Creek.

GOLF

Shadow Hills Golf Course and Country Club—

This nine-hole, 36-par golf course has been at its present location since 1949. Two sets of tees help to make the "back nine" marginally different from the front. Shadow Hills is a mature course with great views and, as the name implies, lots of rolling hills. The course is open to the public with a couple of exceptions. Before 3 pm on weekends you must play with a member to get on the course. At other times, you may play without a member, but for a slightly higher greens fee. Advance tee times are required. The course is just south of town on 4th St. **1232 County Rd. 143; (719) 275-0603.**

HIKING

Cañon City is a good area for short hikes and picnics. **Red Canyon Park, Temple Canyon** and the **Royal Gorge** provide miles of trails for easy walks. For longer, more strenuous backcountry trips in the area, we suggest reading the Hiking section in the **Wet Mountain Valley** chapter.

RIVER FLOATING

Along with the Royal Gorge Bridge, the biggest draw to the Cañon City area is the Arkansas River with its scenic canyons and treacherous rapids. Raft and kayak trips along the Upper Arkansas offer, according to many serious river floaters, perhaps the best water in the state of Colorado. The Royal Gorge section is one of the hairiest rapid stretches in the West. In addition to exciting floating, the river is very accessible as Hwy. 50 snakes alongside all the way to Salida, 44 miles upriver.

Downriver from Salida to the Royal Gorge entrance, the river travels through the Arkansas River Canyon, past cottonwoods and rock walls, offering nothing too difficult. Just below Texas Creek there is a rapid rated Class III. Just beyond that, Spike Buck and The Tube rate Class IV and Class III, respectively. *Warning: Be sure to take out above Parkdale or you will end up entering Royal Gorge!*

The Royal Gorge section, beginning at Parkdale, is a 7-mile journey of churning, dangerous rapids. Enclosed within the towering rock walls, the river sees sunlight only during a short period each day. This stretch of river has killed many people over the years. If you are not an expert rafter or kayaker, sign up with an outfitter to do this stretch.

For information about the Upper Arkansas River from Salida upriver to Granite, see the River Floating section of the **Upper Arkansas Valley** chapter.

Outfitters—

Upriver, along Hwy. 50 from Cañon City to Salida, dozens of raft outfitters have hung up signs and are peddling their expertise and guided trips down the river.

Outfitters are open for business from May through Sept., but the fastest water is, of course, during the spring runoff. The following are a few reputable outfitters that have been doing business for quite a while.

Arkansas Adventures—PO Box 1359, Cañon City, CO 81212; (719) 269-3700 or toll-free in Colorado at **1-800-892-8929.**

Arkansas Valley Expeditions—Located in Salida, these folks concentrate on half-day and full-day trips along the Arkansas. **944 E. Hwy. 50, Salida, CO 81201; (719) 539-6669** or toll free at **1-800-833-RAFT.**

Brown's Royal Gorge Rafting—Offering half-day and full-day trips on the Arkansas. Located 7 miles west of Cañon City on Hwy. 50. Open seven days a week. **(5045 US Hwy. 50, Cañon City 81212; (719) 275-5161.**

Lazy J Rafting, Inc.—PO Box 85, Coaldale, CO 81222; (719) 942-4274.

———— SEEING AND DOING ————

AMUSEMENTS

Buckskin Joe Theme Park—

You won't miss the signs for Buckskin Joe's on the drive to the Royal Gorge. It is a re-creation of an Old West town, made of 100-year-old log buildings from ghost towns around the state. Used frequently as a movie set, it has a print shop, a blacksmith shop, a livery stable, a barn and H.A.W. Tabor's general store. Gunfights on Main Street are acted out several times a day. There are also many shops, a few saloons and the Gold Nugget restaurant— fun for families and for burned-out parents who want to drink a yard of beer. Admission fee; kids under 4 are free. Open May–Oct. 8 am–dusk. **(719) 275-5149.**

MUSEUMS

Cañon City Municipal Museum—

This museum features displays of

Indian artifacts and big-game trophies. Anson Rudd's small stone house, built in 1860, is just behind the museum; inside are furnishings of the late 1800s. Look for the bear trap, handmade by the blacksmith in the nearby town of Silver Cliff. Free admission. Open daily, May–Aug. 8 am–5 pm, Sept.–Apr. 1–5 pm. In the municipal building at **6th St.** and **Royal Gorge Blvd.**

Colorado Territorial Prison Museum—

Restores and preserves the history of the state prison system. Open daily May–Sept., 10 am–5 pm; Oct.–Apr., 10 am–5 pm, Wed.–Sun. **1st St.** and **Macon Ave.; (719) 269-3015.**

SCENIC DRIVES

The Cañon City area is beautiful, relatively undiscovered and perfect for taking

460 SOUTH CENTRAL REGION

scenic backcountry drives. With a little effort, you can be cruising along in a surprising number of completely different natural settings. Most of the roads are dirt, but well graded. Two-wheel drive and steady nerves are all that is required.

Oak Creek Grade (State Road 143)—

Heading southwest from Cañon City is a spectacular road leading toward the Wet Mountain Valley. After crossing over the hump of a small pass, the panorama of the Sangre de Cristo Mountains will take your breath away. Crestone Needles, Kit Carson and Humboldt peaks are only a few of the 14ers in this dramatic range. Stay right at the major forks and the dirt road will take you to Silver Cliff/Westcliffe in the Wet Mountain Valley. To reach State Rd. 143 from Royal Gorge Blvd. turn south on 4th St. and cross over the Arkansas River. Keep going.

Phantom Canyon Road—

Drive along an old D&RG railbed that twists its way to the historic mining towns of Victor and Cripple Creek. The scenery is awesome as the dirt road passes through granite tunnels and between sheer cliff walls. The narrow, winding road is not recommended for large recreational vehicles. The 35-mile, one-hour trip begins 8 miles east of Cañon City on the north side of Hwy. 50.

Red Canyon Park—

Red sandstone rocks shoot up the valley in dramatic formations. The contrast of immense red rocks against the lush green of the pine forests is striking. This beautiful park is a hidden gem, well worth the short drive from Cañon City. Many hiking trails provide access to secluded portions of the park. There are several designated picnic areas with grills and tables. To reach Red Canyon Park, head north on Field Ave. until you reach the park 12 miles north of Cañon City.

Skyline Drive—

This one-way lane threads its way along the narrow spine of the hogback northwest of Cañon City. Look down on the town and prison from 800 feet above. The 3-mile drive was built by convict labor in 1906. It takes a strong stomach and a steady hand on the wheel to negotiate this road. You've never seen one like it before. To reach Skyline Dr., head west on Hwy. 50 out of town. About 3 miles after the highway turns north, you'll see the sign for Skyline Dr. Turn right, pass under a rock archway on the east side of the highway and head on up the hill.

Temple Canyon—

From town, a dirt road meanders past arroyos, up and down rolling, rocky hills covered with pinon pine, juniper and an occasional yucca plant. The closer you get to this city-owned park, the better the scenery. Temple Canyon picnic ground is a pleasant area to enjoy the unique rock formations in the park. A one-hour walk from the picnic ground will take you to an ancient place of Indian worship. Follow the trail to a natural temple of rocks that closely resembles an amphitheater. Another nice spot for a picnic is at a grassy area near Grape Creek.

To reach Temple Canyon, head south across the Arkansas River on 1st St. at the west end of Cañon City. The road winds its way for a few miles to the park entrance. Continue through the park and you will intersect a paved road. A right turn will take you to the south rim of the Royal Gorge; in summer, an entrance fee will allow crossing of the suspension bridge and a loop back to Cañon City. A left on the paved road will take you around to Parkdale, a few miles upriver from the gorge on Hwy. 50.

Tunnel Drive—

A short drive through three tunnels in what was originally intended to be a water project. Convict labor blasted through solid granite to create this interesting road that dead-ends near the Arkansas only a short distance from the Royal Gorge. Catch Tunnel Dr. opposite the penitentiary on the west end of town. Tunnel Dr. begins near the banks of the Arkansas River as

Hwy. 50 rounds a large bend and heads north.

WHERE TO STAY

ACCOMMODATIONS

Best Western Royal Gorge Motel —$$$

The 68-room motor inn has a trout pond and a heated pool (not one and the same!). Also available are a whirlpool, air conditioning, cable TV and movies. One mile east of downtown Cañon City on **Hwy. 50; (719) 275-3377,** or toll free **1-800-528-1234.**

The Hotel St. Cloud — $$$

If you want to experience a piece of history in the best location in Cañon City, stay at the St. Cloud, which has been accommodating guests in this location for more than 100 years. And yet this proud old hotel had a previous life! It was originally built in Silver Cliff, in the Wet Mountain Valley, during the boom days of the late 1870s. For more than a decade the St. Cloud had a thriving business there, until 1886 when the silver mines around Silver Cliff dried up. Then, instead of boarding up the hotel, each brick was numbered and moved to Cañon City via the D&RG Railroad. Once all the materials were in place, it was painstakingly rebuilt at its present location on 7th St. and Main St.

The hotel recently underwent a major restoration, and the owners are trying hard to please a new generation of guests. Though the rooms are comfortable, the hotel is a bit rough around the edges: for instance, the water flows a bit slowly and the floors are no longer plumb, so they tend to creak. Each room has a TV, tele-

phone and private bath (some with original fixtures). On the second floor there is a wide, outdoor deck overlooking historic Main St. Off the downstairs lobby is a restaurant and the Silver Lining Saloon, with its long, hand-carved oak bar. **631 Main St., Cañon City, CO 81212; (719) 275-2335.**

Quality Inn — $$$

Boasts 104 rooms with all the amenities: heated pool, six mineral whirlpools, putting green, exercise room, coin laundry, air conditioning and cable TV. Two dining rooms and a nightclub. Two miles east of downtown Cañon City on **Hwy. 50; (719) 275-8676.**

CAMPING

In San Isabel National Forest—

Oak Creek Campground is located 15 miles southwest of Cañon City. For directions see Scenic Drives: Oak Creek Grade. Only six sites; no drinking water at the campground and no fee. Forest Service phone: **(719) 275-4110.**

Private Campgrounds—

Royal Gorge KOA Kampground—Full and partial hookups with tent sites. Signs will direct you from Royal Gorge Rd. **(719) 275-6116.**

Royal View Campground—Many secluded tent sites and 31 RV hookups. Go 1.5 miles west of the Royal Gorge exit on **Hwy. 50. (719) 275-4369.**

WHERE TO EAT

Merlino's Belvedere — $$ to $$$

Opened in 1946, this restaurant has a solid reputation that goes far beyond the borders of Cañon City. Italian dinners,

including ravioli, cavatelli, manicotti and spaghetti, are all homemade from family recipes. If you are not in the mood for fresh pasta, order from a long list of steak, seafood or chicken dinners. Sandwiches and soup are available. Open Mon.–Thur. 5–10 pm, Fri. and Sat. 5–11 pm, Sun. noon–8 pm. Reservations available for groups of 12 or more. Located 2 miles south of Cañon City on **Hwy. 115; 275-5558.**

Bavarian Inn — $$ to $$$

Owners Henry and Anita Keaferlein came to America 35 years ago from Munich, so Bavarian specialties come easy to them. Sauerbraten, wienerschnitzel and bratwurst are served in addition to American dishes, including steaks, shrimp and trout. Ever have the urge to bite into a buffalo burger? Try one here. The Bavarian Inn offers a wide selection of German beer and wine. Open daily from May–Sept. 11 am–9 pm; Oct.–Apr. Fri.–Sat. 5–9 pm, Sun. 11am–8pm.Eight miles west of Cañon City at **Hwy. 50** and the Royal Gorge turn-off; **269-3594.**

Burger Baron — $

No Arches, No Clown . . . Just the Best Burgers in Town reads the sign at this walk-up, drive-in burger hut. They aren't kidding. Large, perfectly cooked burgers with a bag of onion rings will fill almost any appetite. Very reasonable prices. Outdoor seating consists of a few picnic tables on the asphalt. Open daily 11 am–11pm. in summer; 11 am–9 pm in winter. **1006 Royal Gorge Blvd.; 275-8513.**

Ortega's — $

Patsy Ortega knows how to cook authentic, homemade Mexican food. Since she opened the small restaurant on a shoestring 16 years ago, her business has boomed. Hand-dipped whole chilis are used for their chili rellenos. Taquitos, smothered burritos and other traditional favorites are made fresh each day. The decor is simple and unobtrusive. Patsy studied for a week in Mexico learning how to mix the perfect margarita. Mexican beer and cocktails are also served. Open Thur.–Mon. 11 am–9 pm in summer; 11 am–8 pm, Thur.–Mon. in winter. **2301 E. Main St.; 275-9437.**

Waffle Wagon Restaurant — $

Go where the locals go for a full breakfast. Homemade biscuits and gravy, breakfast burritos, pecan and blueberry waffles and egg dishes are among the choices at this crowded restaurant. Closed Mon. and Tues., open at 6 am Wed.–Fri., open at 6:30 am weekends. Open for lunch 11 am–2 pm Wed.–Sat. **315 Royal Gorge Blvd.; 269-3428.**

SERVICES

Cañon City Chamber of Commerce—

1032 Royal Gorge Blvd., Cañon City, CO 81212; (719) 275-2331.

Colorado Springs

When Katharine Lee Bates wrote "America the Beautiful," she was looking out upon Colorado Springs, and the "purple mountain majesties" in the anthem refer to the perch that inspired her: Pikes Peak. It's quite a legacy to live up to, but Colorado Springs and its famous mountain manage to do so beautifully.

Colorado's second largest city sits on a high plateau right in the shadow of the 14,110-foot peak. Crammed into the area are a lion's share of the state's most popular attractions. In addition to Pikes Peak are the red sandstone towers of Garden of the Gods, Seven Falls, popular Cave of the Winds and scenic Cheyenne Canyon. But nature doesn't get all the credit: the Pikes Peak area is also home to the US Air Force Academy, the renowned Broadmoor Hotel resort, quaint Manitou Springs, the Olympic Training Center and the country's only mountain zoo. Nearby are Florissant Fossil Beds National Monument and the mining-town relics of Cripple Creek and Victor. In a few years Colorado Springs will also be home to the Olympic Hall of Fame.

The concentration of manmade and natural treasures and the city's central location make Colorado Springs one of America's most popular vacation destinations. In that lies a pair of warnings—squadrons of people in touring formation sweep through each summer, and there's plenty of fool's gold in them thar hills. Some of the scores of area attractions, though amazingly popular, stretch the imagination in terms of audacity and sheer cheesiness. For example: cliff dwellings have been moved here 350 miles from their natural home, and the North Pole now rests at the foot of Pikes Peak.

But Colorado Springs does have it all. And with a little forethought and a bit of extra effort, ways can be found to see the worthwhile sights far from the mad-dashing crowd.

HISTORY

Years before Zebulon Pike spotted his namesake peak in 1806, the Ute Indians hunted the area below what they called "The Long One." Pike first saw the peak from near present-day Las Animas, where he recorded, "it appeared like a small blue cloud." Pike tried to christen it Grand Peak or Blue Peak, but his name stuck.

Fifty years later, in 1859, the mountain gained its enduring place in history thanks to the gold rush: thousands of fortune hunters headed west in Conestoga wagons with Pikes Peak or Bust emblazoned on the sides. Although most of the gold actually was found 100 miles to the north, near Central City, Pikes Peak proved to be a magnet for would-be millionaires.

That same year, prospectors staked out a town named El Dorado (now known as Colorado City) at the base of the Ute Pass Trail. Wedged between Colorado Springs and Manitou Springs, this area served as the territorial capital of Colorado before Denver's rise.

The city of Colorado Springs was conjured up by a lovestruck general for his thankless queen in the early 1870s. The general was William Jackson Palmer, a Civil War hero who founded several southern Colorado cities as part of his Denver & Rio Grande Railroad empire. Colorado Springs was to be the posh resort home for his blue-blood bride, Queen Mellen, complete with a castle of her own. But she stayed at the estate only a year, running home to the safe civility of the East and, later, of England. It's ironic that many of the attractions that draw visitors to Colorado Springs today went unappreciated by the person for whom they were intended.

Palmer's vision was to make the town a genteel place for well-to-do people. The name Colorado Springs was chosen by an early publicist because of its "rich eastern spa sound," as historian Marshall Sprague puts it. The actual springs referred to are the ones at Manitou Springs.

The city soon became better known as "Little London" because of the number of Englishmen and other tea drinkers brought in by Palmer. The resort didn't really take off until a second gold rush in 1891, this time closer by in Cripple Creek. By 1900 the population of the region had swelled to over 50,000. Over the next 10 years, thanks to tycoons who had invested in Cripple Creek mines, Colorado Springs was the richest city per capita in the country.

Guided and goaded by tycoons such as Spencer Penrose, founder of the Broadmoor Hotel, Colorado Springs thrived for the next few decades as a tourist and retirement center. During World War II the military's omnipresence began. In 1942 Camp Carson, now Fort Carson, was built, followed quickly by Peterson Air Force Base and later by the North American Aerospace Defense Command (NORAD). In 1955 Colorado Springs struck gold again, this time by landing the US Air Force Academy. It's now the state's most popular manmade tourist attraction. Today the area is home to almost as many generals as the Pentagon. Recently Colorado Springs became headquarters for the US Space Command, which will oversee all space-based defense activities, including the Consolidated Space Operations Center now being built east of the city. CSOC will control all military space missions. With stars in their eyes, some city officials predict Colorado Springs will soon surpass Houston as a space center. Perhaps astronauts will be signing off with a "Roger Colorado" before long.

GETTING THERE

Colorado Springs is located 65 miles south of Denver on Interstate 25. The town is a major bus hub; there are frequent daily buses between Denver and the Springs.

Colorado Springs Municipal Airport handles over 100 direct flights per day and is served by most major carriers, including American Airlines, America West, Continental, Delta, TWA and United. Other airlines connect out of Denver. An expansion of the airport will be completed by 1992.

MAJOR ATTRACTIONS

AIR FORCE ACADEMY

The US Air Force Academy, training center for America's future Air Force officers, receives more than a million visitors annually, making it Colorado's third most popular attraction after Rocky Mountain National Park and Denver's Museum of Natural History. Although much of the stunning 18,000-acre campus at the foot of the Rampart Range is off limits, most of the manmade facilities are free and open to the public. An easy way to see the grounds is to take a self-guided tour using the "Follow the Falcon" brochure available at the visitors center. Not to be missed are the soaring 17-spire Cadet Chapel and the great square just below it, where you can see Colorado's version of the changing of the guard. At around noon Mon. through Fri. during the academic year, most of the 4,400 cadets parade across the square to lunch. The campus is also a game refuge, so watch for deer and wild turkeys on the road.

The new **visitors center**, open daily from 9 am–5 pm, features a gift shop, displays about cadet life and films on the history of the Air Force. A short nature trail leads to the chapel.

Getting There—Exit 156B off Interstate 25 north of Colorado Springs; **(719) 472-4515.**

GARDEN OF THE GODS

Red sandstone formations that jut out at wild angles, thousand-year-old juniper trees, twisting needles of rock sculpted by wind—all these make this Colorado Springs city park truly a "garden fit for the gods."

Dedicated in 1909, the 1,350-acre park at the foot of Pikes Peak has since become a Registered National Landmark. Most visitors take a quick drive through the park—maybe with a stop to pretend to hold up Balanced Rock—then leave and think they've seen it all. A better way is to park your car and take a walk on one of the many trails, several of which are accessible to the handicapped. Or find a rock perch from which to watch the technical climbers, or do some bird watching, or scramble in between two pinnacles to take a unique nature photo. Picnicking and guided horseback riding are also popular (see the Horseback Riding section).

Geology—

A half day in Garden of the Gods is probably the equivalent of a semester of geology. About 300 million years ago, Frontrangia, part of the ancestral Rocky Mountains 30 to 50 miles west of the modern-day Rockies, stopped growing. Ancient rivers began to carry rocks and debris from the shrinking mountains and spread them out over the Colorado Springs area in hundred-foot-thick alluvial fans. Balanced Rock and Steamboat Rock are evidence of these deposits. A great sea covered Colorado for the next 150 million years; then, about 60 million years ago, the Rockies began to rise again. As a massive dome grew at the site of Pikes Peak, it vertically tilted the horizontal rock layers along its edges. Wind and water finished the job, stripping away the less resistant rocks while carving the tougher ones into the towers and spires that make up Garden of the Gods.

The formations are as whimsical as their names: Three Graces, Kissing Camels, Weeping Indian, Rocking Chair. An early publicist for the area, W. E. Parbor, lost his job when he dubbed one formation Seal Making Love to a Nun. The name was changed to Seal and Bear.

Getting There—From Interstate 25, go west on Hwy. 24 to the Ridge Rd. exit, which enters the park from the south.

HIDDEN INN

Right in the center of things, the Hidden Inn has a free lookout tower for photographers, snack bar, gift shop, maps and information. It's usually packed with tourists. Hours are 8:30 am–7 pm in summer; 9:30 am–4:30 pm in winter.

HIGH POINT

The best vantage point in the park. There's also a gift shop and a "camera obscura" here—a 16th-century invention that provides a 360-degree panoramic view from inside a darkened chamber. Located on Ridge Rd. near the south entrance to the park.

TRADING POST

Built in the late 1920s to resemble the home of Pueblo Indians, the post is the largest gift shop in the Pikes Peak region. It includes a Southwest Indian art gallery with paintings, rugs, crafts, pottery and jewelry. Located near Balanced Rock on the west edge of the park. Also has patio dining. Open year-round.

VISITORS CENTER

Located on the park's southeast boundary, the visitors center is a good place to start and usually not as crowded as the Hidden Inn. Hours are 9 am–5 pm.

PIKES PEAK

Pikes Peak is America's Mountain, the best-known peak in the country. This isn't because it's the highest (30 other peaks surpass it in Colorado alone) or the most beautiful, but because it rears out of the plains apart and alone, dominating the landscape around it.

History—

A small expedition headed by Lt. Zebulon Pike came to within 15 miles of the summit on Nov. 27, 1806, when Pike declared "I believe no human being could have ascended to its pinnacle." The first ascent came just 14 years later, by Dr. Edwin James, a botanist with the Long expedition. In 1929, a Texan, Bill Williams, pushed a peanut to the top with his nose. He wore out 170 pairs of pants during the 20-day trek. Today there's a cog railroad and a toll road to the summit.

In 1873 the US Army Signal Corps built a weather observatory on the summit. The station was manned year-round by a lone enlisted man. The most notorious of these early weathermen had to be Sgt. John O'Keefe. He collaborated with journalist Eliphalet Price to concoct stories about what was then the most remote, intriguing spot in the country. His most in-famous tall tale told of man-eating rats. As the story goes, rats devoured O'Keefe's baby, "leaving nothing but the peeled and mumbled skull." The Denver papers picked up the yarn, and consequently it ran in papers as far away as Turkey. O'Keefe appeared in a photo beside a tiny headstone with little Erin O'Keefe's name on it. In truth, however, O'Keefe had neither wife nor child—his black cat was named Erin. He received a reprimand from army headquarters for the stunt.

A whale was reported on the summit in 1923. When journalists investigated, they found a 40-foot wooden frame with a notorious public relations man inside spraying seltzer through a blowhole.

Today die-hard runners race up and down the peak every August in one of the most rigorous marathons on the planet. It's also the nation's second oldest. In winter, a local club trudges up through the snow to set off midnight fireworks marking the New Year.

Facts About Pikes Peak—

The view from the summit is well worth the trip. From there you can look straight down on Colorado Springs, see Denver 70 miles to the north, the spiny

Sangre de Cristo Mountains to the south, and the snowcapped Collegiate Range to the west. The summit itself is windswept and barren, except for the summit house, and anywhere from 10 to 30 degrees colder than Colorado Springs. Take a coat. The summit house features a gift shop, snack bar and incredibly good hot chocolate and donuts. Ask one of the workers to tell you stories about living at the top (especially during lightning storms).

Getting There—To reach the Pikes Peak Hwy. from Colorado Springs, head west for 10 miles on Hwy. 24. Look for the signed exit.

BARR TRAIL

There are several hiking routes to the summit of Pikes Peak, and Barr Trail is the most commonly used. The trail, about 13 miles each way, starts just off Ruxton Ave. above Manitou Springs, near the cog railway station. Fred Barr built the trail between the years 1921 and 1923 with a pick, shovel and dynamite. The trail has since made Pikes Peak one of the state's longest but easiest 14ers, and its most-ascended. Probably the best way to make the hike is a two-day trip with a stopover at the Barr Camp 6.8 miles up. At treeline (about 8.5 miles up) is a lean-to that can also be used as a stopover. For a slightly shorter hike, ride up the Mt. Manitou Incline and take Incline Trail over to Barr Trail. For more information, see the Mt. Manitou Incline entry in the Other Attractions section. For a one-day trip, it's possible to take the cog railway or hitchhike to the summit and hike down. For information on other routes, call **(719) 520-6375.**

COG RAILWAY

Zalmon A. Simmons decided to build a cog railroad up Pikes Peak after a painful ride to the top on a mule. His goal, says historian Marshall Sprague, was no less than "to alleviate the suffering of the soft-bottomed human race." The railroad, which first made it to the top in 1891, is still the quickest and easiest way up the mountain.

Swiss-made diesel trains have long since replaced the old angled steam engines, but one relic still sits at the station. Trains depart regularly from the depot. Round trip is three hours. Advance reservations are advised. Open May through Oct., but trains don't always make it all the way up in May because of snow. **515 Ruxton Ave., Manitou Springs; (719) 685-1045.**

PIKES PEAK HIGHWAY

Although Pikes Peak has been tamed by a highway, the road itself is anything but tame. The 38-mile round trip is said to take six months off the life of your car. The drive includes 156 often harrowing turns along a nearly 7,000-foot climb. The original carriage road was built in 1868–88 and the first car reached the summit in 1901. The present highway was built in 1915–16 for $500,000. Great panoramas of the Continental Divide appear along the way, and you might even spot bighorn sheep, deer

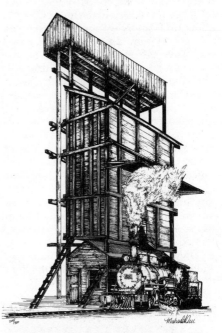

The old steam engines were required to take on fuel and water at various stops (sketch by Michael A. Darr).

or elk. The road is paved for the first 7 miles and improved dirt the rest of the way. Open seasonally, May through Oct. Toll fee is charged. **(719) 684-9383.**

PIKES PEAK HILL CLIMB

For information on this spectacular car race to the summit of Pikes Peak, see the Festivals and Events section.

OTHER ATTRACTIONS

CAVE OF THE WINDS

Although it has sacrificed something to commercialization, such as rocks that sing in the parking lot and colored lights that enhance the formations' natural beauty, Cave of the Winds is still worth seeing. Discovered in 1880 by children playing, the mile-long cavern gets its name from winds that used to blow through it. Alas, the magical sound has since been silenced by the need for a new entrance.

The cave is known for its dazzling samples of stalactites and stalagmites. (Okay, which one hangs from the ceiling?) A new 60-foot-long, 40-foot-wide, 35-foot-tall room was added to the tour in 1988, lit up by 10,000 more watts of colored lights.

The 40-minute guided tour on paved walkways can make you feel a bit like you're on a conveyor belt. For a true taste of spelunking, call ahead to make reservations for the so-called wild tour of the Grand Caverns. This is a muddy two-and-a-half-hour plunge into the deepest pockets of the cave. One highlight is crawling on your belly under Fat Man's Misery, where Gen. Palmer, on his first visit, was said to have gotten stuck and ordered part of the ledge to be sawed off. On the wild tour, old clothes and a flashlight are required. Light jacket recommended for all tours. Admission fee charged. The cave is located 6 miles west of Colorado Springs off **Hwy. 24** above **Manitou Springs**. Open 9 am–9 pm during summer; 10 am–5 pm during winter. **(719) 685-5444.**

CHEYENNE MOUNTAIN ZOO

Clinging to the side of Cheyenne Mountain, this zoo's setting has to be one of the greatest. What the zoo lacks in size it makes up for in unique animal habitats. It's also a bastion for endangered species, more than 100 of which are represented in the over 800 animals at the zoo. These include orangutans, Asian lions and a huge collection of giraffes. Some of the better exhibits are the birds of prey and the monkey house.

Just above the zoo stands the **Will Rogers Shrine of the Sun**, a tribute to the famed American humorist. Admission to the zoo also includes the shrine, which is worth a quick drive. Open year-round, the winter months are less crowded. Hours are 9 am–5:30 pm in summer, 9 am–4 pm in winter. To reach the zoo from Interstate 25, head south on Nevada Ave. (which turns into Hwy. 155). Turn right on Lake Ave. and proceed to the Broadmoor. Then turn right and follow Mirada Rd. up to the zoo. **(719) 475-9555.**

GLEN EYRIE

Colorado Springs' own castle, Glen Eyrie, is a well-kept secret mainly bypassed by the hordes of summer tourists. The reason is that it's privately owned by the Navigators, a Christian group, which permits limited tours but doesn't generally encourage them. It's best to call ahead.

Built by Gen. Palmer in 1904 for his wife, the Tudor-style castle testifies to Palmer's European tastes and high standards of architecture. Mrs. Palmer eventually spurned the nest, though it's difficult to see why. The estate is practically a city unto itself, with greenhouses, stables, nine reservoirs, a dairy, schoolhouse, pool, bowling alley and Turkish bath. The castle, listed on the National Register of Historic Places, sits at the entrance to Queens Canyon, which has some of the same stunning rock formations found in Garden of the Gods.

Glen Eyrie makes for a good bicycle ride from Colorado Springs. Located just north of Garden of the Gods on 30th St.; **(719) 598-1212.**

MANITOU SPRINGS

Colorado Springs was named for the mineral springs that are actually located in Manitou Springs. Ute Indians used this area on the west edge of Colorado Springs as one of their favorite hunting grounds. They probably used the springs for their medicinal value. *Manitou* is in fact an Indian word meaning "Great Spirit," but the town's name actually comes from a reference to a spirit in Longfellow's poem "Hiawatha."

Manitou became nationally known in 1877 for "the water cure," said to remedy almost any illness. Later, as hospitals began to take over its role, this Victorian town evolved into a tourist center and has been designated a National Historic District. The 26 springs still bubble, and samples are available in many restaurants and stores.

Today Manitou is home to artists, crafts people and even a couple of witches' covens. Many knickknacks, antiques and original works of art can be found in the quaint shops crammed into a few blocks. There's also a charming outdoor arcade, including what has to be one of the few penny arcades left in the country.

Most visitors to the Pikes Peak area end up in Manitou because of its proximity to many of the most popular attractions. If you do find yourself here for a day, get off the main road and walk through the Queen Anne homes that crawl up either side of the canyon. There are plenty of the expected tourist amusements in Manitou, like a combination mini-golf/water park. Be sure to stop by **Patsy's Candies** at 930 **Manitou Ave.** for some saltwater taffy. One quick and different way to see the town is by horse-drawn carriage. **2 K Enterprises** provides both the horse and the carriage and leaves from **404 Manitou Ave.**

and **925 Manitou Ave.; (719) 685-5089.** For lodging and restaurant information see the Where to Stay and Where to Eat sections.

MIRAMONT CASTLE

Stair-stepping up Mt. Manitou is the eccentric castle Father Jean Baptiste Francolon had built for his mother and himself in 1895. Its name means "look at the mountain." The structure is a fantastic, rambling hodgepodge of nine different styles of architecture, from Byzantine to Romanesque. Inside are 46 rooms, a Victorian Life Museum, a miniature model of Colorado Springs in the 1888 "Little London" days and, as sort of an added bonus near the end, a model railroad display. The castle was built by Francolon after he was sent to Manitou to avail himself of the mineral waters for his health. Over the years it has been a sanatorium run by the Sisters of Mercy and an apartment complex in which bannisters and furniture are said to have been used by apartment dwellers as firewood before the castle was added to the National Register of Historic Places in 1977. Admission fee charged. Open daily Memorial Day through Labor Day, 10 am–5 pm; tearoom and soda fountain, 11 am–4 pm. **9 Capitol Hill Ave., Manitou Springs; (719) 685-1011.**

MOUNT MANITOU INCLINE

This ride, straight up the side of 9,000-foot Mt. Manitou at a 68-percent grade, offers spectacular views of the city and the prairie stretching out to the east. Once at the summit, hike to excellent overlooks or hike back down to the bottom (one-way tickets are available). Those wishing to hike up Pikes Peak can reach the Barr Trail from the top of the Incline, saving themselves a climb of at least 2,000 vertical feet. There are also picnic areas, a snack bar and a souvenir shop at the top. Go up at twilight to see the city lights. Open daily May, June, Sept., 9:30 am–5 pm; July–Aug. 9:30 am–9 pm. **508 Ruxton Ave., Manitou Springs; (719) 685-9086.**

NORAD

The North American Aerospace Defense Command, though not exactly open to the public, does host some tours. A visit to the underground fortress is unforgettable. Buried deep inside Cheyenne Mountain behind 25-foot-thick doors, NORAD is an entire city on metal springs, built to withstand nuclear attack. Within the complex, sharp, serious GIs keep watch over the world's airspace. Every Saturday the Air Force takes 15 people through. The tours are usually booked far in advance, sometimes as much as six months. For information contact: **NORAD Public Affairs, Attention Tours, Peterson AFB, CO 80914-5001; (719) 554-3841.**

OLYMPIC TRAINING CENTER

Each year this 36-acre complex plays host to thousands of athletes training for the Olympics in the thin mountain air of Colorado Springs. The center is also home to 20 of the 38 national governing bodies for amateur athletics. Although the facilities themselves aren't much to see (mostly old army barracks), it's worth an afternoon stop to watch athletes work out. There are also regularly scheduled competitions. The visitor's center features a gift shop and a 90-minute Olympic film. Open Mon.–Sat.

9 am–4 pm, Sun. noon to 4 pm. **1776 E. Boulder St.; (719) 578-4500.**

SEVEN FALLS

Billed as "The Grandest Mile of Scenery in Colorado," the concentration of beauty in Seven Falls and South Cheyenne Canyon is both a blessing and a curse. Indian tribes used to trap animals in the box canyon by stampeding them into its dead end. Although truly spectacular, this area can still feel like a trap as some 300,000 visitors a year cram in.

Seven distinct but connected falls splash 300 feet down a black granite wall and are accessible by two sets of stairs. One set leads to Eagles Nest platform, which offers a good view of the falls; another goes to a mile-long trail ending at an overlook of the city. But for the best view of the falls, consider going up North Cheyenne Canyon, rather than south, and walking up the never-crowded Mt. Cutler Trail. It's an easy 2-mile round trip and it's free. Seven Falls and South Cheyenne Canyon charge admission. The falls are open year-round; from mid-May to mid-Sept. the canyon is illuminated by over 1,000 multicolored lights. It's the only completely lighted canyon in the world. Seven Falls is at the west end of Cheyenne Blvd. in southwestern Colorado Springs. Open daily 9 am–4 pm year-round, except during May 15– Sept. 15 hours are 8 am–11 pm. **(719) 632-0741.**

——— FESTIVALS AND EVENTS ———

Springspree Street Festival
late June
Many locals turn out for this festival, which features a 10K run and bed races down Pikes Peak Ave. (the Air Force Academy team always wins). Music and merriment spread throughout downtown and in adjoining Monument Valley Park. **(719) 635-1632.**

Colorado Opera Festival
summer
Many of the country's best directors

and artists are in residence in Colorado Springs for this annual summer series. Operas are always in English and range from rare to contemporary. **(719) 473-0073.**

Pikes Peak Hill Climb
mid-July
Every summer race-car drivers take to the highway in the Race to the Clouds. It's the second oldest auto race in America and without a doubt the most grueling. Bobby and Al Unser, Mario Andretti and Rick and Roger Mears have all won the event.

The best vantage points include Devil's Playground or Crystal Creek; Halfway Picnic Grounds and Glen Cove aren't bad either. Many people drive up the night before and stake out a camping site near the best viewing areas. There is a charge for both camping and the race. For more information call **(719) 634-7470.**

Pikes Peak or Bust Rodeo
mid-August

As the state's largest outdoor rodeo, this event attracts the country's best professional cowboys and cowgirls. Taking place just after the adults' rodeo is the National Little Britches Rodeo for youngsters. Little Britches pits kids 8 to 18 years old in the national finals later on in Aug. The city kicks things off with a free pancake breakfast downtown and a parade. Both rodeos

are held at Penrose Stadium. **(719) 635-1632.**

International Balloon Classic
Labor Day weekend

More than a hundred hot-air balloons take off from Memorial Park at sunrise each of the three days, making for spectacular photo opportunities. Accompanied by parachuting displays and other aerial events, the classic seems to increase in popularity every year. Worth waking up for. **(719) 635-1632.**

Olympic Trials

Several national and international events are hosted yearly by the Olympic Training Center. Call for schedules. **(719) 578-4500.**

———— OUTDOOR ACTIVITIES ————

BIKING
MOUNTAIN BIKING

The best places to try are off Gold Camp Rd. and Rampart Range Rd. (see the Scenic Drives section for directions). Check with Criterium Bike Shop (see Touring) for more information.

To rent a mountain bike, try **Backeddy Boating** at 1326 Pecan St.; **(719) 520-0066.**

TOURING

Bicycling has taken off in Colorado Springs, which recently was the first US city to host the World Cycling Championships. Most of the races were held at the new 7-Eleven Velodrome in Memorial Park, where speed records continue to be set thanks in part to the area's thin air. A popular trail right in the heart of the city follows Monument Creek through Monument Valley Park. Destinations for longer rides include: Garden of the Gods, Air Force Academy, Black Forest, Woodland Park.

The folks at **Criterium Bike Shop** can provide maps, trail information and excellent repair service. They're located across

from the Colorado College campus near downtown. **829 N. Tejon St.; (719) 475-0149.**

FISHING

Elevenmile Canyon and Reservoir—
See the **Cripple Creek** chapter.

Manitou Lake—
Locals suggest using salmon eggs and worms to snag the rainbow trout at this ideal family spot. Seven miles north of Woodland Park on Hwy. 67.

Rampart Reservoir—
This out-of-the-way reservoir provides 10 miles of excellent shoreline for fishing. The difficulty of getting to this reservoir means the angling is usually uncrowded. No fishing is allowed Dec. 2 through Apr. 30. Rampart Reservoir is located 8 miles east of Woodland Park on Rampart Range Rd.

GOLF
PRIVATE COURSES
Air Force Academy—
Retired or active military are invited to play the two 18-hole courses at the academy. The Blue is a Robert Trent Jones course with long, narrow fairways, and The Silver is a mountainous course with shorter holes demanding a bit more precision. The courses lie directly across from the cemetery on Parade Loop. Call one day in advance for tee times. **(719) 472-3456.**

Broadmoor Golf Club—
The courses at the Broadmoor are considered by many to be some of the finest in the state. This is where Jack Nicklaus got his start with a win in the US Amateur. The three 18-hole courses provide three good reasons to stay at the Broadmoor Hotel, since they're reserved for members and hotel guests only. Pines and scrub oak dot the rolling fairways, which all have Cheyenne Mountain as their backdrop. Greens fees are moderately expensive if you are a guest and pricey for friends of hotel guests. Cart required. **(719) 634-7711.**

PUBLIC COURSES
Patty Jewett Golf Course—
Built in 1898, this course was the first set of links west of the Mississippi. The tall trees and mature greens make Patty Jewett the best public course in Colorado Springs. Its 27 holes are in central Colorado Springs with a view of Pikes Peak. **900 E. Espanola St.; (719) 578-6825.**

Valley Hi Municipal Golf Course—
This 18-hole course has one distinctive draw: great views of Cheyenne Mountain and Pikes Peak from every hole. The 30-year-old par 71 is relatively flat with plenty of lakes. **610 Chelton Rd.** in east Colorado Springs; **(719) 578-6351.**

HIKING AND BACKPACKING
Colorado Springs' proximity to the mountains is such that its city parks are full of great hikes. The treks range from hour-long strolls to two-day climbs above treeline. The visitors bureau provides a reasonably good list of hiking trails in the area. For hikes in nearby Pike National Forest, contact: **Pikes Peak Ranger District Office, 601 S. Weber St., Colorado Springs, CO 80903; (719) 636-1602.**

Barr Trail—
See the Pikes Peak entry in the Major Attractions section.

Bear Creek Regional Park—
Five miles of easy trails, with access for the handicapped. An ecologist's dream, the park also contains a nature center that can guide and educate. **Bear Creek Rd.** in west Colorado Springs. **(719) 471-5437.**

The Crags—
See the Hiking and Backpacking section in the **Cripple Creek and Victor** chapter.

Mount Cutler Trail—
See the Seven Falls entry in the Other Attractions section.

North Cheyenne Canyon Trail—
This 5-mile loop has an easy grade, passes three springs and provides widespread views. The trail begins just past the entrance to the canyon, on the left side of the road. To reach Cheyenne Canyon, head west on Cheyenne Blvd. from Colorado Springs.

Old Ute Trail—
Centuries old, this 4-mile trail was first used by the Ute Indians and later traveled by miners and trappers. The trailhead begins near the Mt. Manitou Incline on Ruxton Ave. and ends up on Hwy. 24 near Cascade. Easy grades.

St. Mary's Falls Trail—
This 4-mile trail begins at the top of Helen Hunt Falls and leads to St. Mary's

Falls. Cross the bridge and follow the path on the far side of the stream. Expect a half day there and back. Bring a lunch and enjoy great glimpses of Colorado Springs. To reach the trailhead at the far western end of North Cheyenne Canyon, head west on Cheyenne Blvd. from Colorado Springs.

Waldo Canyon—
A staircase leads up to a 7-mile loop. The views of Colorado Springs are especially great at dusk. Look for the trailhead on the right side of Hwy. 24 between Manitou Springs and Cascade.

HORSEBACK RIDING

Academy Riding Stables—
This stable rents horses for one- and two-hour guided tours through Garden of the Gods. Seeing the park from a saddle is a good way to avoid the many carloads of visitors. Reservations urged. **(719) 633-5667.**

The Mark Reyner Stables—
Horses are rented by the hour in Palmer Park. Ride in this unspoiled mountain oasis surrounded by the city in northeast Colorado Springs. **3254 Paseo Rd.; (719) 634-4173.**

ICE SKATING

Broadmoor World Arena—
The aging but still world-class ice rink at the Broadmoor hosts many skating championships, ice shows, curling, speed skating and hockey. Numerous Olympic hopefuls have trained here. For public skating sessions, call **(719) 634-7711, ext. 5795.**

Plaza Ice Chalet—
Downtown in the Plaza of the Rockies, this urban rink is surrounded by shops in an enclosed atrium. Small fee charged; lessons offered. Open for public skating from 10 am–10 pm. **111 S. Tejon St.; (719) 633-2423.**

SKIING
CROSS-COUNTRY SKIING
The Crags—
The best cross-country skiing in the Pikes Peak area lies about 30 miles away at The Crags. See the Outdoor Activities section in the **Cripple Creek** chapter.

Rampart Reservoir—
Located about 8 miles east of Woodland Park on Rampart Range Rd. The 13-mile Lakeshore Trail around the lake makes for a good day's worth of cross-country skiing. Although it's possible to drive all the way from Colorado Springs to the reservoir on Rampart Range Rd., the road is often blocked in winter. It is wiser to take Hwy. 24 west to Woodland Park and then backtrack 8 miles to the reservoir.

Rentals and Information—
Mountain Chalet—This shop in downtown Colorado Springs rents touring equipment and can point skiers in the right direction. **226 N. Tejon St.; (719) 633-0732.**

DOWNHILL SKIING
Ski Broadmoor—
Located just up the road from the Broadmoor hotel, this one-slope area requires constant snowmaking but is conveniently located. This tiny area offers night skiing and lesson packages. **(719) 578-6056.** For real skiing, Breckenridge to the north and Monarch to the south are less than two hours away.

SWIMMING
Manitou Springs Public Swimming Pool—
This indoor pool is open year-round. 202 Manitou Ave., Manitou Springs; (719) 685-9753.

Monument Valley—
Open only during summer. Set in a beautiful park next to Monument Creek. (719) 578-6636.

Prospect Lake Beach—

This roped-off swimming area is open only during summer in the lake adjacent to Memorial Park. Located in central Colorado Springs. **(719) 578-6637.**

TENNIS

Bear Creek Park—

Eight new, lighted courts are set right in the foothills. At the corner of Argus and 21st streets.

Memorial Park Tennis Center—

Twelve new courts (eight lighted) and a club house. The park hosts several tourneys during summer. East Pikes Peak Ave. and Hancock St.; **(719) 578-6676.**

Monument Valley Park—

Eight courts (six lighted) within walking distance of downtown. Courts are located near Cache La Poudre Ave., next to Monument Creek.

—————— SEEING AND DOING ——————

AMUSEMENTS

North Pole/Santa's Workshop—

Most people probably don't realize it, but the North Pole isn't on some remote ice floe above the Arctic Circle; it's perched conveniently on the flank of Pikes Peak! It's always Christmas at the region's only amusement park, where you'll find brightly garbed elves, reindeer, plenty of rides, magic shows, Christmas gift shops and of course Santa himself (real beard). Kids who still believe love the place. Open mid-May through Christmas Eve. Summer hours are 9 am–6:30 pm. Closed Thurs. in May, and Wed. and Thurs. Sept. through Dec. Located 10 miles west of Colorado Springs on Hwy. 24 at the entrance to the Pikes Peak Hwy. **(719) 684-9432.**

MUSEUMS AND GALLERIES

American Numismatic Museum—

Numismatic is probably a word only coin collectors know, and this is a museum probably only coin collectors will love. Operations for the American Numismatic Association are headquartered here, so this is the big time of coin collecting. The museum houses one of the most extensive collections of coins, paper money, tokens and medals in the United States. Open Tues.–Sat. 8:30 am–4 pm. **818 N. Cascade Ave.** near Colorado College; **(719) 632-2646.**

Fine Arts Center—

The city's art museum is composed of several galleries, including the **Taylor Museum**, which houses a fairly good collection of Indian and Hispanic art. Well known for its traveling exhibits, the Fine Arts Center also hosts art performances in its theater and weekly wine-tasting parties in its outdoor sculpture garden. Open Tues.–Sat. 10 am–5 pm; Sun. 1–5 pm. Free document tour on Sun. at 1:15 pm. **30 W. Dale St.; (719) 634-5581.**

Hall of Presidents—

This museum contains more than a million dollars' worth of wax figures from the renowned studio of Madame Tussaud of London. All of the presidents from Washington to Reagan are among the 100 figures from American history. Each one features real hair and actual dentures, and is dressed in period clothing in a historically accurate diorama. Highlights include Thomas Jefferson writing the Declaration of Independence and Lincoln on his deathbed. Smack dab in the middle of the historical scenes—as sort of a bonus for kids—is a fairyland section with storybook figures such as Snow White (see her heart actually beat), Pinocchio and Peter Pan. Admission fee charged. Summer hours are 9 am–9 pm daily; 10 am–5 pm in winter. **1050 S. 21st St.** just south of Hwy. 24; **(719) 635-3553.**

Manitou Cliff Dwellings Museum—

If you want to see Indian cliff dwellings in their natural setting, you'll have to go to Mesa Verde in southwestern Colorado. None of the cliff dwellers lived within 350 miles of Manitou Springs. The 40-room dwelling here is a reconstruction of prehistoric basketmaker apartment houses in a convenient sandstone overhang above Manitou. It was built in 1906 after the stones were hauled from a private ranch near Mesa Verde by concerned Manitou citizens seeking to preserve pieces of the ancient Anasazi culture and make them easily accessible to the public. The museum provides a good introduction to the Anasazi culture, but pales in comparison to the real thing. Admission fee charged. Hours are 9 am–6 pm during summer; 10 am–5 pm in May, Sept. and Oct.; **(719) 685-5242.**

May Natural History Museum—

The giant beetle outside welcomes visitors to one of the world's outstanding collections of arthropods. Bugs, that is. Some 8,000 of them are on display, collected by James May over a period of 63 years. Don't miss the tarantula locked in a death grip with a hummingbird, and the Colombian beetles so big they are said to have knocked people over with speeds of 40 miles per hour. The center also has 5 miles of nature trails and a new National Museum of Photography. Take the Hercules turn off Hwy. 115, 9 miles south of Colorado Springs. Admission fee charged. Open 8 am–5 pm in May; 8 am–9 pm June–Sept. 30. Closed in winter. **710 Rock Creek Canyon Rd.; (719) 576-0450.**

McAllister House—

Maj. Henry McAllister, "born friend" of Colorado Springs founder Gen. William Jackson Palmer, came out to Colorado Springs in 1872. He built the first brick house in Colorado Springs. After one of the area's infamous chinook winds blew a train off its track, McAllister ordered 20-inch-thick walls to withstand all the elements. His unique house opened as a museum in 1961. Guided tours give a taste of Colorado Springs in its "Little London" era. Summer hours are 10 am–4 pm Wed.–Sat., noon–4 pm Sun.; winter hours are 10 am–4 pm Thurs.–Sat. Admission fee. **423 N. Cascade Ave.,** near downtown; **(719) 635-7925.**

Michael Garman Galleries—

Even if you're not planning to buy sculpture, this gallery is worth a stop. The studio is dominated by "Court and Darby Street," a miniature 24-foot-long city scene, and contains other of Garman's unique urban miniatures and realistic figures. Garman makes originals for the figures out of sculptor's wax. Then a mold is made of latex rubber, and the pieces are cast out of a type of cement. A variety of pieces are for sale at reasonable prices. **2418 W. Colorado Ave.; (719) 471-1600.**

Pioneer's Museum—

To see the way Colorado Springs was, visit this museum in the old El Paso County Courthouse. The building, a registered National Historic Landmark, is worth the stop in itself. Inside, among other things, is the house and furnishings of writer and poet Helen Hunt Jackson. Other tidbits of Pikes Peak history include historic photos, turn-of-the-century toys and Indian artifacts. Hours are 10 am–5 pm Tues.–Sat., 2-5 pm Sun. Free admission. **215 S. Tejon St.; (719) 578-6650.**

Prorodeo Hall of Champions—

This is the rodeo hall of fame. The young museum is also a monument to the legacy of the American cowboy. A visit begins with two multimedia shows: one on the history of the Old West, another that recreates the feel of being a cowboy. After that, Heritage Hall traces the development of cowboy gear. The Hall of Champions showcases the trophies, belt buckles and other paraphernalia of the rodeo greats. Where do Brahma bulls retire? Right here at the mini-rodeo arena—at least one especially mean-looking one has. Altogether, this is one of the best designed museums in Colorado Springs. Open 9 am–5 pm year-round; closed Mon. during winter. Admission fee. Take exit 147 west off Interstate 25; **(719) 593-8847.**

Space Command Museum—

Exhibits on the history of flying in Colorado Springs, concentrating on the Air Force and space. Aviation, art, historic uniforms and model aircraft make it the perfect museum for aviation buffs. It features a fascinating film on the history of the North American Aerospace Defense Command and a sample of 3.9-billion-year-old moon rock. An accompanying air park is brimming with aerial hardware. Admission is free. Hours are 9 am–5 pm Mon.–Fri., 10 am–5 pm Sat. Closed Tues. from Dec. 1 to Feb. 28. Located on **Peterson Air Force Base** in east Colorado Springs.

Van Briggle Pottery—

Artus Van Briggle came to Colorado Springs in 1899. Trained in the East and in Paris, this supremely accomplished artist won more awards in his life than any other American potter. Most of his original designs still are made in Colorado Springs. The studio used to be an old roundhouse and still has some of its feel. The free tour ends at the showroom, where finished works can be bought. Open daily 8:30 am–5 pm except Sun., all year. **600 S. 21st St.; (719) 633-7729.**

Western Museum of Mining and Industry—

Before heading to the mining country up around Cripple Creek and Victor, think about stopping by this gem of a museum. Visitors can learn how the mines were worked and what to look for when sightseeing. See a host of mining machines in operation and learn how to pan for gold. Tours include a multimedia show, a blacksmith shop and a reconstructed mine. Admission fee. Open daily 9 am–4 pm. Take the Gleneagle Dr. exit off Interstate 25 at the North Gate to the Air Force Academy; **(719) 598-8850.**

World Figure Skating Hall of Fame and Museum—

Displays memorabilia of skating champions, including the Broadmoor's own Peggy Fleming, and a history of the sport. The museum includes what is billed as the finest collection of skating art in the world and also has a gift shop. Free admission. Located on the Broadmoor campus at **20 First St.; (719) 635-5200.**

NIGHTLIFE

For a full list of nighttime activities, consult an issue of *Springs* magazine or a *Gazette-Telegraph* "Scene" section on Fridays. Or call the FunFone Events Line at **(719) 635-1732.**

The Cadillac and Lake City Railway's Showtrain—

Looking for a totally unique place to eat dinner and spend an evening being entertained? We've found it. Board the Cadillac and Lake City Railway's Showtrain in Falcon. Eat a delicious dinner and relax as the train chugs its way through rolling hills and the high eastern plains to the small town of Ramah. Once in Ramah, you'll be treated to a melodrama or mystery at the American Legion Hall. You need to be geared up for this, because audience participation is a must. On the return trip to Falcon, dessert is served.

Although the train has been operating for only a couple of years, its popularity is growing rapidly. Unlike most of the train rides offered in Colorado, this one is not on a turn-of-the-century narrow gauge but, rather, just a regular train. Most of the cars were built in the last 40 years and one was built in 1912. If you really want to splurge you can reserve the parlor car, where you dine at an oval table with a white tablecloth.

The train leaves at 6:30 pm from Falcon, 12 miles northeast of Colorado Springs on Hwy. 24, and returns about 12:40 am. For reservations and more information contact **The Cadillac and Lake City Railway, PO Box 2415, Colorado Springs, CO 80901; (719) 495-2223.**

Cruising—

Depending on your mood, Nevada Ave. on Friday and Saturday nights could be a good place to take a drive back in time. Or it could be a place to avoid at all costs. The approximately 10-block-long section of the parkway that cuts through downtown has to be one of the last great cruising strips in the West. Hundreds of "cherried-out" cars, from vintage Chevys to low riders and the latest sports cars, extend bumper to bumper along Nevada Ave. Most cruisers drive a loop that starts around Colorado Ave. to the south, eventually wrapping around the statue of Gen. Palmer to the north. But if you are in a hurry to get somewhere, take Cascade Ave. or Interstate 25.

The Golden Bee—

Walking into the Golden Bee, the curators like to say, is like pulling on a familiar sweater—you feel right at home. The Bee is an authentic English pub brought over from London and reassembled in the basement of the International Center at the Broadmoor. The infectious piano tunes and wide variety of English ales make this small room one of the best night spots in Colorado Springs. The entire pub sings along to the ragtime piano music, often led by a baritone named Gary. But don't worry about knowing the words—the Bee has its own hymnal. Another tradition that shouldn't be missed is the quaffing of a 38-ounce yard of ale. The record for polishing off a full yard stands at about seven seconds. The Bee's farcical Organization of Sportsmen includes luminaries such as Arnold Palmer and, at one time, John Wayne and Liberace. Warning: waiting in line is often part of visiting the Bee, but there is a tangible reward—nary a patron is allowed to leave without a woven bee stuck to his or her lapel. Beef and kidney pies are served, as well as complimentary cheese and crackers. Located at the Broadmoor; 11:30 am–2 am Mon.–Sat.; Sun. 11:30 am–midnight. **1 Lake Ave.; (719) 577-5776.**

The Iron Springs Chateau—

The emphasis is on audience participation at this comedy melodrama. Things get under way at 6 pm with an all-you-can-eat meal of barbecue beef and country-fried chicken. The curtain goes up at 8:30 pm, with ample opportunity for cheers and jeers. A rousing sing-a-long olio and dancing in the lounge round out a hilarious night. Open Wed.–Sun.; dinner served from 6–7 pm. Located in Manitou Springs across from the Cog Railway Station; **(719) 685-5104.**

Old Colorado City—

A registered National Historic District, the 1858–59 buildings also house a few of the best bars in the city. **Thunder and Buttons**—named for the two bull elk ridden by Laura Belle, an early-day madam of some repute, and her escort Prairie Dog O'Byrne—has dancing and live country/rock bands Mon.–Sat. 11:30 am–2 am; Sun. 10 am–midnight. **2415 W. Colorado Ave.; (719) 636-5088.**

Just across the street is **Meadow Muffins**, covered with memorabilia. Its dance floor features pop and rock. Theme nights every night. Mon.–Sat. 11 am–2 am; Sun. 11 am–midnight. **2432 W. Colorado Ave.; (719) 633-0583.** For a step into the Old West, step into **Roger's Frontier Bar** down the block. A little seedy at night, but serves up great chili, country dancing and pool. Open Mon.–Sat. 6 am–2 am; Sun. 8 am–8 pm. **2520 W. Colorado Ave.; (719) 634-9882.**

SCENIC DRIVES
ROADS TO CRIPPLE CREEK AND VICTOR

Three scenic drives lead from Colorado Springs to the historic mining towns of Cripple Creek and Victor. A combination of two makes for a great 70-mile round trip.

Through Florissant—

This route works best for stops at Florissant Fossil Beds National Monument. Take Hwy. 24 to Florissant, turn south on County Rd. 1 into the monument. About 5 miles past the monument the road turns to dirt, climbs up past Mt. Pisgah and then descends into the Cripple Creek basin.

Gold Camp Road—

Teddy Roosevelt took this ride along Gold Camp Rd. by train. But without the tracks the scenery is just as stunning. The sometimes harrowing drive is open late spring to early fall. It's quite a show in late September when the aspen are turning.

Go up North Cheyenne Canyon and follow the signs on the left for Gold Camp Rd. On the way to Cripple Creek the dirt road wraps around Cheyenne Mountain, with views of Colorado Springs, then plunges through seven tunnels still etched with the soot from Short Line locomotives. Since the road is often in poor condition and very narrow, the 30-mile trip can take hours. RVs and trailers are not recommended.

Highway 67—

This is the most traveled and fastest route to Cripple Creek, but that doesn't mean the drive is any scenery slouch. After winding up Ute Pass to the town of Divide on Hwy. 24, take Hwy. 67 south through great stands of aspen and a one-way tunnel. You might consider this paved route for a speedy return trip.

HIGH DRIVE

A quick, cliff-hugging drive with a tremendous panorama of the Broadmoor, Cheyenne Canyon and Colorado Springs. Drive up North Cheyenne Canyon to the end of the pavement at the Gold Camp Rd. crossroads. Follow the signs to the right for High Drive or Lower Gold Camp Rd., both of which eventually feed into Hwy. 24, without ever really having left the city.

PIKES PEAK HIGHWAY

See the Pikes Peak entry in the Major Attractions section.

RAMPART RANGE ROAD

The scenery along this road starts off auspiciously in Garden of the Gods and never really quits. The road actually goes north through Pike National Forest and all the way to Hwy. 67 northwest of Castle Rock, but the Woodland Park turn-off is usually far enough for the shock absorbers of most vehicles—and riders. Beware of boulders in the middle of this roller-coaster dirt road. Taking Hwy. 24 back to Colorado Springs from Woodland Park makes for an adventurous half-day trip.

WHERE TO STAY

ACCOMMODATIONS

Colorado Springs is home to plenty of well-known first-rate hotels including a Clarion, a Hilton, a Red Lion Inn, a Sheraton, an Embassy Suites Hotel, two Holiday Inns, two Ramada Inns and three Raintree Inns. There's also a healthy representation of national bargain chains, many campgrounds, and a sprinkling of bed and breakfast inns, dude ranches and cabin-type motels. It's easiest to find a bed by calling the **Colorado Springs Visitor's Center** at **1-800-88-VISIT.** Below are some of the more unique and indigenous places to stay in the area.

The Broadmoor — $$$$ and up

A destination in itself—worth visiting even if you're not staying. This resort at the foot of Cheyenne Mountain is one of only eight in America to be awarded Mobil's five-star rating. The complex contains three hotels, three championship golf courses, 16 tennis courts, a carriage museum, a small ski area, a movie theater, several restaurants, three spring-fed pools, a shooting grounds, a "Fifth Avenue" row of shops, and an ice arena where Olympic figure skaters train. Separating the modern Broadmoor West from the two older hotels is an idyllic lake graced by a variety of waterfowl. Don't miss the black swans, which are native only to Australia. One of the most pleasant ways to spend an hour in Colorado Springs is to stroll around the shoreline path.

A casino originally stood where the main hotel now stands. After it burned down, Spencer Penrose, who had made his fortune in gold and copper, bought the property in 1916 and opened the luxury resort two years later.

If you see the Broadmoor logo you will notice that the "A" is raised. There are a number of stories as to why this is. The most commonly told tale is that Penrose was so disappointed after a night at the rival Antlers Hotel, he decided to build his own resort and raise the "A" as play on the Antlers. But according to historian Marshall Sprague, the truth is that Penrose raised the "A" as a trademark, since the word *Broadmoor* itself could not be copyrighted.

Staying here can be an expensive proposition. Room prices start at a little over $100 a night and go all the way up to $1,000. Check-out time is as it should be: 2 pm. **1 Lake Ave., Colorado Springs, CO 80901; (719) 634-7711.**

Cheyenne Mountain Inn — $$$$

This luxury resort holds its own against the formidable competition from the nearby Broadmoor resort by offering many modern amenities. The inn's 216 rooms are spread throughout several buildings in a condominium-like setting. The resort also has its own 18-hole golf course, three swimming pools and a nearby lake with fishing and sailing. Its two restaurants include five-star Remington's. This hotel was built for conferences and offers good prices on weekend packages. Some rooms can accommodate as many as 10 people. **3225 Broadmoor Valley Rd., Colorado Springs, CO 80906; (719) 576-4600.**

Antlers Hotel — $$$

There's been an Antlers in downtown Colorado Springs since 1883, when Gen. William Jackson Palmer built the original. He named it the Antlers because the hotel seemed a good place to store the deer and elk trophies a friend kept bringing from Manitou Park. The original burned down in 1898 and was replaced by a larger, fireproof one by 1901. The demise of that hotel in favor of today's steel and concrete version is still mourned by some, but on the inside the Antlers still maintains its sure and quiet elegance.

The hotel has a swimming pool and offers golf and tennis privileges at Broadmoor South, which can be reached by a shuttle. The fierce rivalry between Colorado Springs' two leading hotels is no more: the Antlers is operated by the Broadmoor Management Company. The hotel is downtown. **4 S. Cascade Ave., Colorado Springs, CO 80903; (719) 473-5600 or 1-800-232-2323** outside Colorado.

Hearthstone Inn — $$$

This has to be one of the premier B&Bs in Colorado. The inn is actually two sister Victorians in a row of similar mansions on serene Cascade Ave. near downtown Colorado Springs. Inside are three floors of 25 sumptuous, sometimes eccentric rooms. Each chamber has its own theme, such as the Gable Room, the Author's Den and the Billiard Room. Most have baths or showers, some have antique fireplaces and one boasts its own breakfast terrace. But none has a TV or telephone, as it should be in this 19th-century setting.

Half the fun of staying at the Hearthstone is exploring the other rooms. Puzzles, games and a piano in the homey lobby encourage guests to revive the art of conversation. Just behind the inn is Monument Valley Park, with a jogging trail, tennis courts and swimming pool. Breakfast is easy to miss at 8 am, but don't. **506 N. Cascade Ave., Colorado Springs, CO 80903; (719) 473-4413.**

Grays Avenue Hotel — $$ to $$$

Tom and Lee Gray run this Queen Anne–Victorian-style hotel right in the historic Manitou Springs district. Sightseers couldn't ask for a better location. Built in 1885, this is one of Manitou's original seven hotels. It's graced with antiques and a distinctive floor plan that winds around a central staircase. There are 10 rooms, some with private baths. Each includes breakfast on the front porch. Great deals for families. **711 Manitou Ave., Manitou Springs, CO 80829; (719) 685-1277.**

Holden House — $$

This restored 1902 Victorian offers all the comforts of home without any dishes to do. Sallie and Welling Clark have filled the home with family heirlooms, including a tremendous quilt made by Sallie's great-grandmother. The three rooms are all named for gold-rush towns and all have private baths. Two come with queen beds, one with a double. The Cripple Creek room has a view of Pikes Peak. Sunday's champagne breakfast on the veranda is worth the stay in itself. No pets allowed; children aren't encouraged. The home is located in a shady residential neighborhood near Old Colorado City at the corner of 11th St. and Pikes Peak Ave. **1102 W. Pikes Peak Ave., Colorado Springs, CO 80904; (719) 471-3980.**

Outlook Lodge in
Green Mountain Falls — $$

This former parsonage for traveling Congregational ministers sits on a steep hill behind the Little Brown Church in the Wildwood. Hosts Rodney and Sherri Ramsey take great pains to keep things Victorian in this mountain lodge. One way they do it is with marshmallow roasts at the grand fireplace in the lobby. The lodge is too close to Pikes Peak for a view. Nearby is a small lake with a bandstand on an island. Eleven rooms are open in summer, only four during winter months. Homemade breakfast included. Located about 15 miles west of Colorado Springs off Hwy. 24; in Green Mountain. **(719) 684-2303.**

American Youth Hostel — $

The Colorado Springs AYH shares facilities with Garden of the Gods Campground near Manitou Springs. Twelve cabins, with four bunk beds in each, at $7 a night. No restrooms in cabins, but campground facilities are accessible. It's a good idea to call ahead. **3704 W. Colorado Ave.; (719) 475-9450.**

CAMPING

In Pike National Forest—

North of Woodland Park via Hwy. 67 are several good campgrounds. The first campground, 5.8 miles north of Woodland Park, is **South Meadows Campground** with 56 sites; fee charged. Another mile up the road is **Colorado Campground** with 63 sites; fee charged. Farther up the road are **Big Turkey Campground** (10 sites and fee charged), **Painted Rocks Campground** (15 sites and fee charged) and **Trail Creek Campground** (seven sites and fee charged). They're usually filled by early afternoon in summer.

For more information, maps, and campground vacancies, stop by the **Pike's Peak Ranger District Office** in Colorado Springs at **601 S. Weber St.; (719) 633-7619.**

Private Campground—

Garden of the Gods Campground—Conveniently located near the south entrance to Garden of the Gods, this RV heaven includes 250 campsites, complete with heated pool, jacuzzi and grocery store. Tours and Jeeps available as well. Open Apr. 15–Oct. 15. **3704 W. Colorado Ave.; (719) 475-9450.**

WHERE TO EAT

Charles Court at the Broadmoor — $$$$

This elegant restaurant decorated in the style of an English country manor is the Broadmoor's most exclusive. The food is superlative but the prices are even more stunning. Charles Court is in the modern Broadmoor West and has a wonderful lake view. Serving breakfast, Sunday brunch and dinner. Sunday brunch is unsurpassed in the Springs. Reservations recommended. Open 6–9:30 pm daily. Coat and tie required, dresses or suits for women. **1 Lake Ave.; 577-5774.**

Flying W Ranch — $$$

This working cattle and horse ranch north of Garden of the Gods is part restaurant, part tourist attraction. Keep a tight rein on your money, pardner, as you visit 14 different museum buildings and gift shops. All meals include the campfire western show featuring the Flying W Wranglers. Chuckwagon suppers are held mid-May through mid-Sept. Festivities start about 5:30 pm, and reservations are necessary. As many as 1,400 can be seated. Take Garden of the Gods Rd. west off Interstate 25 to 30th St. and turn right. The ranch is on the left at **3330 Chuckwagon Rd.; 598-4000.**

Penrose Room at the Broadmoor — $$$

The Penrose Room tries to reflect the Edwardian era with both its decor and its menu. The European cuisine is served nine stories up at the top of Broadmoor South, with a view of Cheyenne Mountain to the west and Colorado Springs to the east. Coat and tie required for dinner (the maitre d' has ties available). Open Sun.–Fri. 6–9 pm; Sat. 6–9:30 pm. **3 Lake Ave.; 577-5773.**

The Stagecoach Inn in Manitou Springs — $$$

This former stagecoach stop, built in 1880, is on the route between Colorado Springs and Cripple Creek. It was the summer home of poet and Indian rights activist Helen Hunt Jackson. The trout amandine is a favorite of Manitou folks. Lunch is served from 11 am–3 pm Mon.–Sat., dinner from 5–9:30 pm. Champagne brunch on Sun. served from 10:30 am–2:30 pm. **702 Manitou Ave.; 685-9335.**

The Sunbird — $$$

Perched on a bluff high over Colorado Springs, the Sunbird provides the pleasure of dining in the mountains without having to leave the city limits. The restaurant features great margaritas and adequate steak and seafood. But the premier item on the menu is the view, best enjoyed from one of the four outdoor patios. Happy hours, on Thurs. from 4–7 pm and on Fri. from 4–9 pm, are the best times to be here. The hosts lay out a tasty buffet of hot dogs, corn on the cob, veggies, chips, dips and more—and it's free. Otherwise the Sunbird serves lunch from 11 am–3 pm, dinner starting at 5 pm, and a champagne brunch on Sun. **230 Point of Pines Dr.; 599-8550.**

Zeb's — $$$

Named after Zebulon Pike, this restaurant lives up to its name with Pikes Peak-sized portions. Prime rib is a sure bet, as are the baby back pork ribs, which are baked during the day, then put on the grill at night. Dinner is served with a great view of the mountains. Open Sun.–Thurs. 6–10 pm, Fri.–Sat. 5:30–11 pm. **945 S. 8th St.** in south-central Colorado Springs; **473-9999.**

Giuseppe's Old Depot — $$

This restored Denver & Rio Grande train station specializes in spaghetti and other Italian dishes. Great salad bar, too. Relax at the comfortable tables and watch the freight trains go by. Meals arrive on plates rimmed with train track. Kids who are into model trains go ape. Open Sun.–Thurs. 11 am–10 pm; Fri. and Sat. 11 am–11:30 pm. **10 S. Sierra Madre; 635-3111.**

Luigi's — $$

The Luigi family has operated this small, inconspicuous restaurant for 29 years with their priorities solidly in place: good food comes first. From the outside it doesn't look like much, but once you're inside, the pasta will transport you straight to Rome. Homemade manicotti is featured on Fri. nights, lasagna on Wed. Open from 4:30 pm nightly; closed Mon. **947 S. Tejon St.; 632-0700.**

Michelle's — $

The Micopolous family makes its own ice cream in the basement, then serves it in style upstairs, where pastoral Greek scenes adorn the walls of this vintage soda fountain. Once featured in *Life* magazine, Michelle's serves about 14 flavors of ice cream and frozen yogurt and scores of candies. The truffles are delicious. Special coffees. The Believe-It-or-Not sundae serves 22 people and sells for about $60. Sandwiches also served. Open daily from 9 am–midnight. Two locations, but go to the one at **122 N. Tejon St.; 633-5089.**

Red Top — $

This Colorado Springs institution made its name with larger-than-life burgers—six inches around and weighing half a pound. One of these hamburgers is, as the owners say, indeed a meal. And the malts here are like the unforgettable, rich, thick ones of the 1950s (the campy decor is 1950s-like, too). Red Top has expanded to three locations, but the south Nevada restaurant is the one with the 1950s ambience. Open Mon.–Thurs. 11 am–9 pm; Fri.–Sat. 11 am–9:30 pm and Sun. noon–9 pm. **1520 S. Nevada Ave.; 633-2444.**

Wade's Pancake House — $

Wade's is a local legend. Breakfast is served any time in this most democratic of restaurants. Wade's cooks up 25 varieties of pancakes and waffles. The Ranchman's breakfast is the best bet on the menu: eggs, bacon and all the flapjacks you can eat for under $5. Why not try to beat the pancake-eating record set years ago by Colorado College student John Wilbur? He munched 69 in one sitting. For brave stomachs, the chili cheese omelette is unbeatable. Hours: 6 am–8 pm. Wade's has two locations, but the old one near downtown has the atmosphere. **16 S. Walnut St.; 635-4150.**

SERVICES

TOURIST INFORMATION

Stop by the visitors bureau in the Sun Plaza building in lower downtown for more information and free itinerary planning. **Suite 104 S. Cascade Ave.; (719) 635-1632** or **1-800-88-VISIT.**

Colorado Springs Chamber of Commerce—

PO Drawer B, Colorado Springs, CO 80901; (719) 635-1551.

Manitou Springs Chamber of Commerce—

354 Manitou Ave., Manitou Springs, CO 80829; (719) 685-5089.

Pikes Peak Country Attractions Association—

354 Manitou Ave., Manitou Springs, CO 80829; (719) 685-5854.

Creede

Creede is isolated and strikingly picturesque. Nestled in the Rio Grande Valley in a compact side canyon, this small town has none of the trappings of a full-service resort. The San Juan Mountains provide a spectacular and imposing backdrop, even though no jagged 14ers mark the immediate landscape. Historic Creede Ave., lined with shops and a few restaurants, leads directly into a sharply cut ravine behind town. Continuing into the ravine, this road works its way near the town's original settlement, which is now called North Creede, soon arriving at the mines that have pulled out 80 million troy ounces of silver in the past century.

Creede residents are friendly and helpful without having lost their integrity to quick-buck tourist shops. Though incomes are seasonal and many people are lacking money, especially since the Homestake Mine closed, an independent spirit lives on. Fortunately, Creede is in no danger of becoming a ghost town. People choose to live here, in spite of a few sacrifices, because of the dramatically beautiful environment and the low-key atmosphere. Creede is also the kind of place that sets your mind whirling back to the wide-open history of a century ago.

Rio Grande National Forest, as well as the Weminuche and La Garita wilderness areas, provides enormous enticement for people who like to explore the backcountry without crowds. Take a hike to the stunning formations at the Wheeler Geologic Natural Area. In winter, after the hunters have left the valley, locals reclaim a sense of quiet and solitude. Very few visitors come through Creede after snow has fallen, but cross-country skiing here remains an excellent way to enjoy the surroundings.

Creede, in its remote section of southwestern Colorado, seems an unlikely place for a renowned repertory theater. But in the center of town, at the Creede Opera House, you can watch plays throughout the summer. Outside of Creede, in the Upper Rio Grande Valley, a huge number of guest ranches cater to people searching for rustic vacations.

The town, isolated on a long stretch of Hwy. 149, is located between **South Fork** and **Lake City**. Since the late 1800s, South Fork (to the southeast) has been a logging and lumbering community. Located at the foot of Wolf Creek Pass, South Fork is not an especially attractive town, as it has developed along the highway. Nevertheless, because of its proximity to a wealth of year-round recreational possibilities, it offers a variety of restaurants and motels. South Fork is a convenient place to stay while skiing the deep powder at Wolf Creek Ski Area. Lake City sports an entirely different history, remaining a charming little community deep in the San Juan Mountains northwest of Creede (see the Major Attractions section).

HISTORY

"Holy Moses!" shouted Nicholas C. Creede when he discovered the area's first silver lode in 1889. Within a few months, the Holy Moses, Ethel, Amethyst and Last Chance mines were producing fantastic quantities of high-grade ore. A latecomer to the silver bonanza, the new town of Creede was soon attracting 300 newcomers a day and nearing a population of 10,000. During the boom, a seething mass of humanity became locked in a struggle for huge stakes. With land selling for exorbitant prices, some new arrivals built shanties on wooden supports laid across Willow Creek; later, outhouses were built across the creek, which "flushed" away the sewage.

This reckless growth contributed to Creede's reputation for nonstop nightlife. In 1892 Cy Wyman penned a famous poem about the town—the last verse reads, "It's day all day in the daytime, and there is no night in Creede." On April 29, 1892, the *Creede Candle*, one of the town's five newspapers, reported, "Creede is unfortunate in getting more of the flotsam of the state than usually falls to the lot of mining camps."

Soapy Smith, a strongman con artist from Denver, ran nearly all of the gambling in town from his Orleans Club. Smith once claimed he discovered a petrified man in the mud near town at Farmer's Creek. He cleaned it for display at the Vaughn Hotel and charged a quarter admission. Soon enough, however, the so-called petrified man's cement skin began to flake off, and the scam was forced to move to a new location. Smith eventually resurfaced in Skagway, Alaska, where he was gunned down in 1898.

Boomtown status attracted a special breed of men and women whose names have survived the passage of time. Bat Masterson was the marshal of Creede for a short while. Bob Ford was another of Creede's residents—famous only because he killed Jesse James with a shot to the back. Ford operated a saloon in Creede until Ed O'Kelly gunned him down with a double-barreled shotgun. Champagne, wine and song flowed freely at Ford's funeral. He will be forever remembered in a ballad as "the dirty little coward." The flourishing trade of ladies of the night had a queen named Slanting Annie. Calamity Jane and her friend Poker Alice Tubbs were a couple of other well-known locals.

Though Creede was once the leading producer of silver in the state, the repeal of the Silver Act in 1893 caused the area economy to collapse. Boom had turned to bust in less than five years. On top of that came catastrophic fires in 1892, 1895, 1902 and 1936. A number of flash floods nearly completed the picture of destruction, and today many of the town's grand buildings are only memories.

Even with all this adversity, the town was able to rebuild and, over the years, it has attracted an eclectic bunch of locals. For awhile, a volatile combination of hippies and rednecks flocked to the area—very gradually, the distinction has become blurred. Today the town is a relaxed haven for writers and artists as much as it is for retired people and outdoorsmen.

GETTING THERE

Creede is located between South Fork and Lake City on Hwy. 149. The town is about 300 miles southwest of Denver. The easiest route from Denver is on Interstate 25 south for 160 miles to Walsenburg, then head west on Hwy. 160 for 120 miles to South Fork. Turn right onto Hwy. 149 for the remaining 22 miles to Creede. A more scenic route from Denver is via Hwy. 285.

MAJOR ATTRACTIONS

LAKE CITY

The colossal peaks of the San Juans dwarf this already-little town to even smaller proportions. Tucked into a grassy canyon at the confluence of Henson Creek and the Lake Fork of the Gunnison, Lake City is one of those Colorado secrets that only a few lucky people know about. Most of the people living in and around Lake City are not Coloradans, but Texans and Oklahomans who have been coming here for years. In the 1920s and 1930s, when Lake City was on the verge of becoming a ghost town, a rash of visitors from the south discovered its air-conditioned summer weather at 8,663 feet. This perfect getaway rebounded as miners' houses were repaired for summer residence. A soft Texas drawl is commonly encountered in this southern enclave. An early promotional brochure even reads: "Hey, Pardner—I'm a Goin' to Lake City."

Not everyone is happy about the tourism boom. One aged resident remarked, "The tourism business has ruined Lake City. It was better when we had the mines and the railroad; in those days I could catch all the fish I wanted!" Despite such scathing comments, good fishing is still a major draw to the area. Many small alpine lakes, spectacular Lake San Cristobal and hundreds of miles of streams, including the popular Lake Fork of the Gunnison River, are productive reminders of the good old days. Other favorite pastimes are hiking in the nearby Rio Grande, Uncompahgre, Gunnison and San Juan national forests, as well as exploring the backcountry by jeep. A regular passenger car can also take you to some incredible scenery: Lake San Cristobal, Slumgullion Earthflow and Windy Point Overlook are all located within 10 miles to the southeast of Lake City.

In summer all of the town's shops, restaurants and lodges are open, and many people roam the streets, which are shaded by ancient cottonwood trees. Winter, however, brings forth a quiet side as visitors leave and the population dwindles, though the area has become a very popular destination for snowmobiling and cross-country skiing.

For more information on Lake City and its outlying areas, stop by the **Visitor Information Center** on Silver St. in downtown Lake City. Or contact the **Lake City Chamber of Commerce at PO Box 430, Lake City, CO 81235; (303) 944-2527.**

History—

Many years before Creede hit its heyday in the late 1880s, this San Juan mining camp had already gone through a few booms and busts. Before 1874, Ute Indians prevented any permanent settlements from cropping up in the Lake City area. But after pressure from the government, the Utes ceded most of the San Juan territory, and rumors of gold inspired prospectors to come into the area. When Enos Hotchkiss made a major strike in 1874, a rush of prospectors started arriving. Within two years, the young town of Lake City had a population of 1,000 and supported two banks, five blacksmith shops, seven saloons, two breweries, the *Silver World* newspaper and four Chinese laundries.

The first church on the Western Slope of Colorado was built at Lake City in 1876. Today this pretty, white-frame church still stands at 5th St. and Gunnison Ave.

Because it was difficult to get ore out of this hard-to-reach valley, Lake City's initial boom died down by 1880. The town experienced periods of exaltation and discouragement until 1889, when the Denver & Rio Grande Railroad laid 38 miles of track from Sapinero (north of town) to Lake City. The railroad became a stabilizing force in the economy for years to come.

Compared with other mining towns, Lake City was a rather calm place to live. There were a few lynchings and, of course, the requisite bordello district (called Hell's Acres), but most hoodlums moved on to other camps.

One particularly gruesome exception to law and order occurred the winter before Lake City was established. In January 1874, when Alferd Packer and some companions showed up at a Ute encampment near present-day Delta, they were warned not to continue because of deep snow and severe weather. Though Packer knew nothing of the San Juans, he claimed expertise, and five eager prospectors hired him as their guide. They set out on the dangerous passage into the snow-covered mountains with only enough provisions to last 10 days. Six weeks later, Packer showed up at the Los Piños Indian Agency 76 miles northeast of Lake City—all alone, with a beard and long hair, but appearing well-fed.

He claimed to have endured the below-zero weather by eating rose pods and roots. Packer then stupidly turned down something to eat and soon went on a drinking binge in Saguache, paying for drinks with money from several wallets. This suspicious behavior raised a few eyebrows, especially when Indians, walking along the same trail Packer had taken, found strips of human flesh. It wasn't until late summer that five partially decomposed bodies were discovered a few miles south of Lake City on the northeast side of Lake San Cristobal (the area is now called Cannibal Plateau). Four of the men had been murdered in their sleep with an axe to the head and the fifth, found nearby, was shot to death. Chunks of flesh had been cut from the men's chests and thighs.

Packer sensed something was awry and managed to escape from detention in a Saguache jail. Nine years later he was discovered in Wyoming living under the assumed name of John Schwartz. On April 13, 1883, Packer was sentenced to hang at the Lake City courthouse. The embellished version of the sentencing, which is now folk history, was actually made up by an Irish barkeep in Lake City. According to his story, presiding Judge Melville Gerry shouted, "Packer, ye man-eatin' son of a bitch, they was seven dimmycrats in Hinsdale County and ye eat five of 'em, God damn ye! I sentins ye to be hanged by the neck until ye're dead, dead, dead ...."

Gallows were constructed, but because of a technicality, Packer's trial was declared unconstitutional. He was given a new trial, convicted of manslaughter and sentenced to 45 years of hard labor at the Cañon City Penitentiary. However, as his last act, Colorado Gov. Charles Thomas pardoned Packer, who was released after serving only five years. He died of natural causes in 1907 and is buried in Littleton under the misspelled name Alfred Packer.

Each Sept., Lake City remembers its famous cannibal during the Alferd Packer Jeep Tour and Barbecue. For information contact the chamber at **(303) 944-2527.**

Getting There—Lake City is located 50 miles northwest of Creede on Hwy. 149; it's also 55 miles southwest of Gunnison on Hwy. 149. This is a beautiful drive no matter which direction you're coming from.

RECREATION INFORMATION
Mountain Biking—
San Juan Mountain Bikes—A great way to experience the country around Lake City is from the seat of a mountain bike. These folks will rent you a bike or arrange a guided tour of the area for you. Choose your terrain, from mellow dirt roads to steep, single-track trails. **PO Box 524, Hwy. 149 N., Lake City, CO 81235;** no telephone.

Fishing—

Lake Fork of the Gunnison—The Lake Fork headwaters begin in the mountains far above Lake San Cristobal. Some good public fishing for smallish rainbow and brook trout can be found in a mile-long stretch, 1.5 miles below Lake San Cristobal. The water, accessible from Hwy. 149, offers some nice riffles for dry fly-fishing. This little-known area receives relatively light use.

Within Lake City town limits, some good holes attract many anglers in the summer months. The water is stocked, and occasionally some very large trout are pulled out on nymphs, flies and lures. Below Lake City, the river flows through mostly private property until reaching Gateview. Below Gateview, at Red Bridge Campground, the river is entirely public, offering some prime trout water. With waders, this 30-foot-wide stream is easily fished. Along the stretch between Gateview Campground and Blue Mesa Reservoir, the water and the bank are strewn with debris from the reservoir, making the area unattractive and difficult to fish.

Lake San Cristobal—This lake, the second largest natural lake in Colorado, was formed about 800 years ago when the Slumgullion Earthflow blocked the valley. It is rimmed by high, snowcapped peaks, and in fall the area becomes a golden carpet of aspen. Most fish in the lake are rainbows and browns, but every now and then someone pulls out a 20-pound Mackinaw. In spring, just as the ice is receding from the banks, is the best time to catch one of these hogs. Bank fishing and boat casting are both popular at this crowded, easy-to-reach destination. The mossy upper end of the lake is the best place to fly-fish from the bank. Many people do very well by throwing lures or baiting with eggs, cheese or worms. To get there, drive 2 miles south of town on Hwy. 149, turn right on County Rd. 30 and proceed 1.5 miles to the lake.

Four-Wheel-Drive Trips—

Engineer Pass/Cinnamon Pass Loop—This 49-mile round trip can be taken just as easily in either direction, but we will start out by heading over Engineer Pass. A highly recommended detour—not included in the mileage—involves a short drive to Silverton. Various trips can be taken to the other surviving San Juan boom camps: Ouray and Telluride (see the Four-Wheel-Drive Trips sections of those two chapters for route information). From the south end of Lake City, a green sign directs you toward Engineer Pass. The road soon climbs uphill alongside Henson Creek, reaching a T intersection at Capitol City after 9 miles. This ghost town was named in an attempt to compete with Denver for the state capital—good thing it lost! Turn left and drive 4.5 miles over fairly rough road to Rose's Cabin, which is a good place to lock in your hubs. Bear right here at the sign indicating Ouray/Silverton and in a half mile take another right. This road leads above treeline to the summit of Engineer Pass (13,100 feet), which offers fantastic views of the San Juans.

The main road then drops over the other side of the pass and comes around the west side of Engineer Mountain before descending into a valley. (A couple of miles after the pass, Mineral Point Rd. leads off to the right for 7 miles to the Million Dollar Highway just south of Ouray.) Some 5.5 miles after the summit, you arrive at a marked turn-off for Cinnamon Pass, a moderately steep jeep road that breaks off to the left. This road goes over the pass and then winds downhill, passing many mine ruins along the way and reaching Lake City in 24 miles. Back at the marked turn-off for Cinnamon Pass, consider going straight (past the ghost town of Animas Forks) for 13 miles to Silverton.

Rentals and Tours—So you feel like negotiating the spine-tingling roads yourself? **Rocky Mountain Jeep Rental** is the place to rent your own jeep and to find out about routes in the area. For reservations, call **(303) 944-2262.**

Hiking and Backpacking—

Lake City is virtually surrounded by national forest land and awesome 14,000-

foot peaks. It's a good base for taking off into the Big Blue, La Garita and Weminuche wilderness areas. *However, please be aware of the dangerous pits and traps that miners inadvertently set a century ago. For your safety, stay out of old mines.* For information on hiking in the area, consult the **Ouray, Silverton** and **Gunnison and Crested Butte** chapters. Other nearby hikes are discussed in the Hiking and Backpacking section under Outdoor Activities.

Where to Stay—

A number of small cabins and quasi-ranches are available during the summer season. Many of these places rent by the week or by the season. The **Lake City Chamber of Commerce** can provide a complete listing: **PO Box 430, Lake City, CO 81235; (303) 944-2527.**

The Crystal Lodge — $$$—A couple of miles south of Lake City, in a beautiful location not far from Lake San Cristobal, this exceptional lodge caters to all guests' needs. Built of wood and decorated in natural colors, it blends well with the environment. Fourteen spacious rooms and four small cabins are available. All have private bathrooms but no TVs. But who needs the drone of a TV when each room has a deck with a far-reaching view to the San Juans? Fishing on the Lake Fork of the Gunnison is only steps away from the front door. Outside, a heated pool and a wide deck provide a leisurely escape. Don't miss the Crystal Lodge restaurant. The home-cooked food is created by the skilled hands of Caryl Rudofsky. Her evening dishes include stir-fry vegetables, tender steaks and herb chicken with fresh pasta—all come with homemade bread. Try to save room for something sweet, such as her acclaimed hot apple cake with caramel-rum sauce.

Brown Trout

No credit cards are accepted. Open year-round except when Harley and Caryl are on vacation—it's a good idea to call ahead. Located 2 miles south of Lake City on Hwy. 149. **PO Box 246, Lake City, CO 81235; (303) 944-2201.**

Camping in Gunnison National Forest—South of Lake City, not far from Lake San Cristobal, are a couple of prime campgrounds. Drive 2 miles south of Lake City on Hwy. 149, turn right and continue 6 miles to reach Williams Creek Campground (25 sites; fee charged).

Slumgullion Campground (21 sites; fee charged) is located 6.5 miles southeast of Lake City on Hwy. 149. From just west of the campground, Forest Rd. 788 heads northwest from Hwy. 149 to a number of campgrounds. After turning, drive 2.5 miles to **Deer Lakes Campground** (12 sites; fee charged). In another 4.3 miles you'll come to **Hidden Valley Campground** with six sites and no fee. Continue another 1.5 miles to **Spruce Campground** (eight sites; fee charged) and soon after **Cebolla Campground** (five sites; fee charged).

Big Blue Campground is located 10 miles north of Lake City on Hwy. 149, then 10 miles northwest on rough Forest Rd. 868. It has 11 sites and no fee.

Private Campgrounds—Woodlake Campground has shaded, grassy campsites and RV hookups. It also offers fishing on its private stretch of river. Located just 2.5 miles south of Lake City on Hwy. 149. Contact Latella Smith at **PO Box 400, Lake City, CO 81235; (303) 944-2283.**

Where to Eat—

There are several restaurants in Lake City. Nothing really struck us as being worthy of special mention—but this isn't to say you should starve yourself. Nearly all of the restaurants close up during the off-season. If you are in search of an excellent meal in a comfortable setting, stop by the **Crystal Lodge** (see the Where to Stay section above) 2 miles south of Lake City on Hwy. 149.

OTHER ATTRACTIONS

CREEDE REPERTORY THEATER

Since 1966, the old Creede Opera House has been a perfect setting for popular musicals, historical dramas and light comedies. The plays are performed on a rotating schedule, with a new one each night of the week. It's a fun evening for people who come from miles around to enjoy the energy and excitement of the show. The nonprofit theater recruits performers from across the country to its remote downtown Creede location. Check this place out! Reservations are required; many plays are sold out early in the season. **Creede Ave.** in downtown Creede; **PO Box 269, Creede, CO 81130; (719) 658-2540.**

FESTIVALS AND EVENTS

Rio Grande Raft Races
early June

Since 1959 wild raft races on the Rio Grande, between Creede and South Fork, have been a summer highlight. Various race categories provide a weekend of excitement, including money and prizes for contestants. The Hooligan Race is the most fun to watch; all of the crafts are judged on originality—entries may be anything that floats, except for boats. The Elks Lodge in Creede puts on a Sat. night dance as this small town kicks into high gear. For more information, contact the **Creede/Mineral County Chamber of Commerce, PO Box 580, Creede, CO 81130; (719) 658-2374.**

Days of '92
Fourth of July weekend

Creede Ave. turns into an open market as vendors sell snake oil, jewelry and crafts. Everyone turns out for the parade (more marchers than spectators) and soon afterward the mining contests get underway. Fiercely competitive miners test their skills in events such as single-jack drilling, machine drilling and hand mucking. At the end of the festivities, an impressive fireworks display lights up the sky. For more information call **(719) 658-2374.**

OUTDOOR ACTIVITIES

BIKING
MOUNTAIN BIKING

The Creede area offers as much good terrain for biking as you could ever explore in an entire summer of riding. And, for the first time, quality rental bikes are available at **San Juan Sports**, on **Creede Ave.; (719) 658-2359.** Check with the folks at this shop for trail ideas and maps, or consider some of the roads in the Four-Wheel-Drive Trips and Scenic Drives sections. A highly recommended ride is on the rough road to the stunning formations at Wheeler Geologic Natural Area (see the Hiking and Backpacking section).

FISHING

If vast opportunities for good fishing in spectacular scenery mean anything to you, come to the Creede/South Fork area. We've outlined a few of the better possibilities, but there are literally hundreds of miles of streams and dozens of brimming lakes and reservoirs in this part of the state. For more information on local conditions, stop by the **Ramble House on Creede Ave.; (719) 658-2482.** Talk with Alton Cole and take a look at his excellent selection of flies and lures.

High-Country Lakes—

In the mountains around Creede and South Fork, innumerable lakes situated in gorgeous locations provide excellent fishing. Spend a morning on the trail and an afternoon throwing a line. Fern Creek Trail (see the Hiking and Backpacking section) leads into the Weminuche Wilderness Area west of Creede. After a few miles, the trail comes out at **Little Ruby Lake, Fuchs Reservoir** and **Ruby Lake**. Of the three, Ruby Lake is the deepest and most consistent. The most common catch is pan-sized rainbow and brook trout. Shelter at a few tumble-down cabins is available on the lakeshore. If you continue up the trail toward the Continental Divide, you will reach **Trout Lake**. This high lake can be good for cutthroat trout in mid-summer and fall.

Rio Grande River—

The Rio Grande headwaters lie 30 miles to the west of Creede above Rio Grande Reservoir. Fed by a number of tributaries, the river gains strength as it flows east. From the reservoir down to Creede, several patches of public water offer excellent fishing for German brown trout as well as a few rainbows and brooks. The runoff usually calms down in early July. Twelve miles east of Creede (6 miles west of South Fork), a 15-mile stretch of Gold Medal water, beginning at Collier Bridge, entices anglers. Many lunker trout can be caught on flies and lures. The land along this stretch is mostly public, arranged through a series of leases and buy-outs. Please observe and obey posted signs. The Gold Medal water is easily wadable, with many of the larger trout staying low near the banks.

Rio Grande Reservoir—

Thirty miles west of Creede, this long reservoir offers good fishing for trout from boats and from the shore. This is the place to skewer a worm and wait for a tug on your line while enjoying the scenery. The northern shore is traced by Forest Rd. 520, while the steep southern shore is the boundary for the Weminuche Wilderness Area. Several campgrounds and picnic areas are available near the reservoir. To get there from Creede, drive west on Hwy. 149 for 21 miles and then turn left on Forest Rd. 520, which reaches the reservoir in 9 miles.

Rio Grande Tributaries—

Between Creede and South Fork an incredible number of productive tributaries flow into the Rio Grande from the nearby mountains. A wide variety of fishing challenges can be found on national forest land. Starting at the west end of Rio Grande Reservoir, a trail follows **Ute Creek** into the Weminuche Wilderness Area. This small creek is a good place to catch small cutthroat; a large brook trout population inhabits the higher elevations. About 6 miles from the reservoir, Ute Creek forks into **West, Middle and East Ute creeks**; trails follow each tributary to popular high-country lakes with good-sized cutthroat and rainbow trout. Just below the east end of Rio Grande Reservoir, **Little Squaw Creek** flows down from the Weminuche Wilderness Area, entering the Rio Grande at River Hill Campground. This creek is small, but boasts a population of large cutthroat trout. There is no good trail along the lower portions, but you can fight your way upstream. Fern Creek Trail (No. 815) provides good access to the upper reaches of Little Squaw Creek. The trailhead is at Thirtymile Campground at the east end of the reservoir.

Road Canyon Reservoir—

Just 5 miles east of Rio Grande Reservoir, this smaller fishery offers a chance for big fish. And these fish are big, meaning up to six-pound rainbow trout and two-pound brookies. The long, western shore of Road Canyon Reservoir is easily accessible for bank fishing. Boats at wakeless speeds are allowed. Road Canyon Campground is located at the southwest end of the reservoir. Follow the directions to Rio Grande Reservoir (see above) and you'll pass Road Canyon Reservoir 4 miles after turning off Hwy. 149.

South Fork of the Rio Grande—

The South Fork of the Rio Grande converges with the Rio Grande at the community of South Fork, 22 miles southeast of Creede. A major tributary of the Rio Grande, the South Fork is about 18 feet wide and is paralleled for many miles by Hwy. 160. The stream is pretty good for brown, rainbow and brook trout. A trail from Big Meadows Campground (14 miles southwest of the town of South Fork) follows the upper reaches of the South Fork to some small lakes near the Continental Divide.

FOUR-WHEEL-DRIVE TRIPS

East Willow Creek Loop—

The beautiful aspen-cloaked mountains north of Creede are strewn with mine remnants. Drive through this area on an easy four-wheel-drive road that makes a 7-mile loop. Drive north on Creede Ave. into the sharp ravine at the end of town. After 0.6 miles, turn right at the fork leading to North Creede. Thousands of miners lived here in 1890, but today North Creede is home to only a few hardy souls who love the isolation and the beauty of the area. Follow the road up the west wall to the vicinity of the top-producing Solomon–Holy Moses vein. Both sides of the road are littered with old mine buildings and shafts. The road switches back down to West Willow Rd. Just north of where the road crosses East Willow Creek, a hiking trail leads up into the unspoiled Phoenix Park area. Take West Willow Rd. back down to Creede or continue past the Midwest Mine to the townsite of Bachelor (see the Scenic Drives section for more information on this route).

Stony Pass—

This is a stunning ride over a rough and, as you may have guessed, stony road. Take time to enjoy the scenery as you angle toward the Continental Divide among high 13,000-foot peaks. To reach Stony Pass Rd., drive west on Hwy. 149 for 21 miles. Turn

left onto Forest Rd. 520, which passes Rio Grande Reservoir and circumvents Pole Creek Mountain (13,716 feet) on the 30-mile route to the summit of Stony Pass. Once there, enjoy the views before continuing down the other side. The road eventually leads down Cunningham Gulch, ending at a T intersection at County Rd. 110. A left turn will land you in the National Historic District of Silverton (see the Four-Wheel-Drive Trips section of the **Silverton** chapter for more information on the history of this area and for connecting routes). A right turn on County Rd. 110 takes you through Animas Forks and over Cinnamon Pass (see the Major Attractions section) to Lake City. Return to Creede on Hwy. 149.

HIKING AND BACKPACKING

Surrounded by Rio Grande National Forest and the La Garita and Weminuche wilderness areas, Creede offers a slew of remote hiking options. You'll be satisfied with the area whether you are interested in hiking for days along the high reaches of the Continental Divide or are looking for a shorter day hike near town. Also, since these wilderness areas receive relatively little use, it isn't difficult to get away from crowds. This is horse country, though, and you will find traces of the lovable beasts wherever you go. For more information on area trails, contact the **Creede Ranger District, PO Box 270, Creede, CO 81130; (719) 658-2556.** For topographical maps, advice and supplies, stop by **San Juan Sports** on **Creede Ave.** in the **Elks Building; (719) 658-2359.**

Whenever you are in the backcountry, beware of remnants of old mine buildings and mine shafts. *Besides being privately owned, the mines are often filled with "bad air," rotten timbers and unstable soil—stay out of them!*

Continental Divide Trail (in the Weminuche Wilderness Area)—

Along the 80-mile length of the Continental Divide Trail from Stony Pass to Wolf Creek Pass, you'll find some incredibly beautiful backcountry. But this underused area offers a special set of worries for avid hikers. For one thing, most of the trail is above treeline, making hikers susceptible to lightning strikes. Another consideration is the sheer elevation, which can even tire and disorient hikers in top condition. *If you are considering the entire trek, remember you must bring enough supplies for a week to 10 days.* Pick up topographical maps, because the trail can be difficult to find—especially between Stony Pass and Weminuche Pass—and you may need to change your route at the last minute. Despite all the necessary precautions, this is a prime route that we highly recommend. There isn't enough room here to detail the passage along the Continental Divide. If you want a good description of the route, pick up a copy of *A Backpacking Guide to the Weminuche Wilderness* by Dennis Gebhardt (Basin Reproduction Co., 1976).

Fern Creek Trail—

This may not be the most beautiful trail in the wilderness, but its destination at the shores of Little Ruby Lake, Fuchs Reservoir and Ruby Lake is enticing. The fishing is quite good at Ruby Lake and the reservoir. At Ruby Lake, a couple of drafty cabins are available for overnight use on a first-come basis. Many fishermen make the 3.5-mile trek up Fern Creek Trail. Often used as a stock driveway, the trail climbs steadily to the lakes. In early summer, fields of wild iris take over the grassy meadows, providing a pretty purple haze. To reach the trailhead from Creede, take Hwy. 149 southwest for 17.5 miles to Fern Creek Rd. (Forest Rd. 522). Turn left and drive for about 2 miles to the trailhead.

Rio Grande Pyramid—

In 1874 when the Wheeler Survey came through the area, William Marshall called the then-unnamed Rio Grande Pyramid "one of the handsomest and most symmetrical cones in Colorado." It hasn't changed much since then. A hike to the 13,821-foot summit is an invigorating experience. In a day, it's a very long 20-mile round-trip hike with a 4,500-foot elevation gain. In two days, you'll be able to stop and smell the flowers: columbine, Indian paintbrush and alpine sunflowers, among others. There are many picture-perfect campsites at the midpoint near Weminuche Pass.

The trail begins at Rio Grande Reservoir and reaches the summit of Weminuche Pass after about 5 miles. From the pass, which sits atop the Continental Divide, continue south for a mile to a split in the trail. Take the right fork up Ricon La Vaca ("Valley of the Cow"). In a short while the trail emerges above treeline, with an awesome view to the landmark Rio Grande Pyramid and, just south of the summit, the window—a 150-foot-deep cut in the ridge. Shepherds used to call it the devil's gateway. Stay on the trail until it veers sharply south away from the peak. From here the trail disappears, but the obvious route up the east flank of the peak is square in front of you. From the top it's hard to imagine a better view of the San Juans.

To reach the trailhead from Creede, drive west on Hwy. 149 for 21 miles and then turn left on Forest Rd. 520, which leads to Thirtymile Campground (at the eastern end of Rio Grande Reservoir) after 9 miles. The forest service trail (No. 818) heads west along the southern shore of the reservoir before turning south to Weminuche Pass.

Wheeler Geologic Natural Area—

Reminiscent of Bryce Canyon, Utah, the weird rock formations at Wheeler Geologic Natural Area will stand out in your memory long after you see them. Outcast Ute Indians used the area as a hideout, calling the configurations "sand stones." Actually, most of the eerie rock spires, canyons and domes are volcanic in origin and have been formed by erosion. The site, which has been called the City of Gnomes, can be reached on foot in three to four hours over an extremely rough 7-mile four-wheel-drive road. To reach the trailhead, drive east of Creede on Hwy. 149 for 7.3 miles. Turn left on Pool Table Rd. (Forest Rd. 600) and proceed 10 miles to a sign marking what's left of Hanson's Mill. Park your car and start walking on the jeep road.

Try this shortcut if you don't mind getting your feet wet: A quarter mile after setting out, take the left (west) fork and continue for a mile down to East Bellows Creek. Ford the creek and pick up the trail on the other side. In 4 miles the trail rejoins the jeep road leading to the formations.

HORSEBACK RIDING

Broadacres Guest Ranch—
These folks have the largest stable near Creede. If you are considering a trail ride or an overnight pack trip, they would be the best ones to contact. **PO Box 39, Creede, CO 81130; (719) 658-2291.**

LLAMA TREKKING

Lost Trails Ranch—
Carol Ann Getz and her son Bob raise llamas at their ranch 30 miles west of Creede near Rio Grande Reservoir. For a scenic trip into the wilderness without the burden of a heavy pack, contact them about a tailor-made adventure. Whether you are interested in a long overnighter or just a day trip into the hills—they can fix you up. They take loop trips into undiscovered areas, and last year every llama tour came within close range of elk or mountain sheep. Bring your camera along! **5224 E. 3 South Rd., Monte Vista, CO 81144; (719) 852-2036 or (719) 852-5737.**

RIVER FLOATING

Floating on the Rio Grande has long been a pastime of residents—especially during the maniacal annual raft races from Creede to South Fork. Many good stretches of water can be found on the "Grand River from the North," and several professional outfitters can make your trip a pleasant one. If you sometimes dream about fishing and floating at the same time, this is an ideal place.

Rio Grande River—
The Rio Grande begins its nearly 2,000-mile journey to the Mississippi River above Rio Grande Reservoir in the mountains west of Creede. The water exits the dam and rushes into a narrow box canyon accessible only by boat. The fishing in this 5-mile stretch is excellent and there are many secluded campsites along the way. Since the river drops fairly rapidly, there are many good Class III and Class IV rapids. After the river emerges from the canyon, it meanders into the wide Rio Grande Valley. The best put-in for a trip into the box canyon is a couple of miles below Rio Grande Reservoir at River Hill Campground (see the Camping section). Take out at the Fern Creek Rd. Bridge.

Down below Wagon Wheel Gap, southeast of Creede, is the most popular of all Rio Grande runs. Good fishing and a few rapids make this float down to South Fork a memorable one. Good places to put in along Hwy. 149 are at Phipps Bridge and Goose Creek Rd. Bridge. Soon after setting out, beware of a steel bridge with rather closely spaced supports (dangerous to rafters). Otherwise, enjoy the ride!

Outfitters—
Mountain Man Rafting Tours—Take a guided float down the Upper Rio Grande or just rent all the gear you need and go by yourself. This established company is run locally by Greg Coln—you can trust his advice and experience. If you are in the mood for something a little different, he can take you on a kayak run down the tumbling waters of the Lake Fork of the Gunnison. For reservations and information contact **Mountain Man Rafting Tours at Box 11, Eagles Nest, Creede, CO 81130; (719) 658-2663 or (719) 658-2843.**

SKIING

CROSS-COUNTRY SKIING

When the snow comes down, most of the people in the Rio Grande Valley are long gone, with the exception of a few hardy locals and travelers who can appreciate the change of seasons. Skiing is a great way to explore the gently rolling terrain that lies around the edge of the valley. Investigating old townsites and experiencing the peace and quiet of the high country is what it's all about. The higher elevations always have enough snow and, at times, even the valley floor can be a good place to ski. Some people prefer snowmobiling, but with so few people and so much space, you will not come across them often while skiing.

Backcountry Trails—

Spar City Trail—This is one of the best tours in the valley. It's a 5-mile loop trail that is well marked by blazes. Working its way on an easy grade to the ghost town of Spar City, this trail is normally well packed, except after recent storms. In 1892, 300 people lived in Spar City while working the nearby silver mines. The town once had a host of buildings, including a jail, a dance hall, a newspaper office (the *Spar City Candle*), a sawmill and a lumberyard. On the way to the townsite, the trail offers great views to the Bristol Head Cliffs before heading deeper into a mixed forest of pine and aspen. To reach the trailhead, drive south and west of Creede on Hwy. 149 for 7 miles to Sevenmile Bridge (at Marshall Park Campground). Turn left and continue to the trailhead.

West Willow Canyon—Right outside of town is one of the area's best possible ski trips. Up an unplowed road (if the mines are being worked, it's occasionally plowed) that begins at the north end of town, this route heads up to the townsite of Bachelor (see the Scenic Drives section for more information). This 11-mile loop trip over varying terrain is not recommended for beginners. If you want an even more difficult and longer trip, head up past the Equity Mine and to the Continental Divide. This route follows a jeep trail up West Willow Creek from a sharp switchback at the northern extreme of the loop. To reach the trailhead, drive, walk or ski north from Creede until the road is no longer plowed (see the Scenic Drives for specific directions).

Wheeler Geologic Natural Area—The four-wheel-drive road that winds its way to this former national monument is now maintained by local snowmobilers. Because the site was so remote and could not be reached by passenger car, its designation was changed in 1933. The route makes a great ski trip, especially during the week when you are less apt to come across snowmobilers. There are also many places to take shortcuts or different routes altogether. See the Hiking and Backpacking section for more specifics and directions to the trailhead.

Guided Tours—

Lost Trails Ranch—Bob Getz will take you on guided backcountry ski tours in the Weminuche Wilderness Area above Rio Grande Reservoir. He also specializes in winter survival courses for those souls hardy enough to stand the bitter cold at this high elevation. While on a tour, you can also take up residence in one of the ranch's winterized cabins, which are heated but have no running water. Reservations required. For reservations and information, contact Getz at **5224 E. 3 South Rd., Monte Vista, CO 81144; (719) 852-2036.**

Rentals and Information—

San Juan Sports—Before setting out into the backcountry, stop by this full-service shop for trail ideas, topographical maps and the latest on avalanche conditions. The shop stocks rentals for touring and mountaineering skiing, as well as incidental items such as gaiters. Located in the **Elks Building** on **Creede Ave.; (719) 658-2359.**

DOWNHILL SKIING

Wolf Creek —

This rather small ski area is renowned for the huge quantity of light powder snow it receives each year. It is located about halfway between Pagosa Springs and South Fork at the summit of Wolf Creek Pass along Hwy. 160. For more information on Wolf Creek Pass see the Outdoor Activities section of the **Pagosa Springs** chapter.

SEEING AND DOING

GALLERIES

The Horn Hut—

This place is a tacky testimony to the multitude of wildlife in the vicinity. Walk under an archway of antlers and into a small room crowded with trophies of elk, mountain sheep and mule deer. The shop specializes in items made from deer and elk antlers. Pasted on the walls are photos of massive fish caught nearby. The owner, who lives in a trailer next to his shop, is full of tales and information about the area. Open 8 am–8 pm daily, year-round. **7th St. and Creede Ave.; (719) 658-2382.**

SCENIC DRIVES

Creede's Historic Silver Mining District—

This circle tour, a little over 11 miles long, takes you past some famous mines in a beautiful area north of Creede. Head into the aspen-covered hills by driving north from Creede Ave. into the narrow canyon. The first notable sight is not a mine but Creede's firehouse—or should we say fire cave—blasted 120 feet back into a solid rock wall. A half mile after setting out, the road splits. Take the left fork up West Willow Rd. Very soon after the fork, on your left, is the stone foundation to the

Humphry's Mill, which was a large gravity ore concentrator. The road follows the creek up to the Commodore Mine along a steep 2.5-mile stretch called the Black Pitch. (If the pitch is too extreme for your car, consider starting your trip at the other end of the road and coming down this section.) The Commodore Mine tapped the southern portion of a huge amethyst silver vein. A mile farther along the road are the stables for the sturdy mules that once carried the heavy ore. When the road practically doubles back on itself at the Midwest Mine, be sure to stay left. Keep left again as the road crosses Willow Creek.

The road eventually passes the Bachelor townsite. Now only a deserted meadow with a few foundations, it was once home to 1,000 people. In 1893 the town was booming with mines such as the Bachelor, the Spar, the Cleopatra and the Sunnyside, all located on Bachelor Mountain. It also supported as many as a dozen saloons. The views from the road down to the Rio Grande Valley are tremendous. On the way back to Creede the road passes the Sunnyside Cemetery, with gravestones dating to the 1880s.

Lake City—

See the Major Attractions section.

WHERE TO STAY

ACCOMMODATIONS

The Rio Grande Valley is home to a quantity of guest ranches and lodging establishments. Many families from Texas, Oklahoma and other southern states flock to the higher elevations of southern Colorado during the summer to escape the oppressive heat of their homelands. No matter where you're from, an extended stay is recommended. Right in the town of Creede the choices are extremely limited; South Fork hosts a number of motels and is a convenient home base while skiing at

Wolf Creek Ski Area. For a more complete listing of accommodations, contact the **Creede/Mineral County Chamber of Commerce** at **PO Box 580, Creede, CO 81130; (719) 658-2374.**

Wason Ranch — $$ to $$$

Just 2 miles southeast of Creede on the banks of the Rio Grande, Wason Ranch rents modern cabins of various sizes. The ranch owns 4 miles of riverfront property with excellent fishing (guests only) for good-sized German browns. The cabins are equipped with kitchenettes, furnishings and baseboard heat. The larger three-bedroom cottages down by the river come with fully loaded kitchens, fireplaces and, most importantly, unobstructed views out picture windows. In summer, guided river trips are available; in winter the ranch hosts a large number of skiers and snowmobilers. Very reasonable prices; discounts for longer stays. For reservations contact Rod and Marilyn Wintz, **Box 220, Creede, CO 81130; (719) 658-2413.**

Wetherill Ranch — $$ to $$$

The combination modern / rustic one-, two- and three-bedroom cabins at Wetherill Ranch are situated well off Hwy. 149, 17 miles southwest of Creede. Private fishing on the ranch's stretch of river and easy access to the Weminuche Wilderness Area make this a popular place to stay. The staff will be happy to arrange a private outfitter to take you on horseback into the wilderness for some great fishing. The all-wood cabins feature kitchens—but if you don't feel like cooking, the ranch restaurant serves up delicious steaks and "East Coast seafood" each night. Reserve early for the peak summer season. **Wetherill Ranch, PO Box 370, Creede, CO 81130; (719) 658-2253.**

Creede Hotel — $$

In 1890 there were 100 places to stay in Creede. Today this five-room bed and breakfast is virtually the only option. The Creede Hotel is not for everyone, but if you appreciate rustic charm and owners who are low-key and friendly, stop by. In their first year of operation, Rich and Cathy Ormsby are constantly renovating the historic hotel. It's certainly not finished at this point, as the wallpaper is tattered and some walls are covered with burlap—but the place has character! Each room is sparsely furnished with an iron bedframe, a dresser and a chair. Breakfast is always a wonderful homemade concoction: it may be an egg and sausage casserole, salsa eggs or creamy oatmeal with homemade muffins. The hotel is officially open in summer only; if you

want to stay in winter, try to catch the owners. See the Where to Eat section for information on the restaurant. Rich and Cathy Ormsby, **PO Box 284, Creede, CO 81130; (719) 658-2608.**

CAMPING

In Rio Grande National Forest—

There are several nice campgrounds near the town of South Fork. To reach **Beaver Creek Campground** (20 sites; fee charged) and **Upper Beaver Campground** (12 sites; fee charged) drive 2.5 miles southwest from South Fork on Hwy. 160. Turn left on Forest Rd. 360 and continue for 3 and 4 miles, respectively. From Upper Beaver Campground drive another 2 miles on Forest Rd. 360 to **Cross Creek Campground,** where there are nine sites and fee.

Five miles southwest of South Fork on Hwy. 160 is **Highway Springs Campground** with 11 sites and a fee. **Park Creek Campground** (10 sites; fee charged) is located 9 miles southwest of South Fork on Hwy. 160. Ten miles northwest of South Fork on Hwy. 149 is **Palisade Campground** with 13 sites and a fee.

Closer to Creede, a number of campgrounds await. **Marshall Park Campground** is located 6 miles southwest of Creede on Hwy. 149. There are 15 sites and a fee. To reach **Rio Grande Campground** from Creede drive 10 miles southwest on Hwy. 149. It has four campsites and a fee.

A grouping of campgrounds is located farther southwest of Creede via Hwy. 149. To reach **South Clear Creek Campground** drive 23 miles southwest of Creede on Hwy. 149. Turn right on Forest Rd. 510 and continue for 0.3 miles. There are 11 sites and a fee. **North Clear Creek Campground,** with 22 sites and a fee, is located another 1.8 miles up Forest Rd. 510. **South Clear Creek Falls Campground** is located 24.5 miles southwest of Creede on Hwy. 149. It has 11 sites and a fee.

To get to **Road Canyon Campground** (five sites; no fee), drive 21 miles southwest of Creede on Hwy. 149 and turn left on Forest Rd. 520. The campground is located on the southern end of Road Canyon Reservoir. Another 3.5 miles down Forest Rd. 520 will take you to **River Hill Campground** with 20 sites and a fee. Continue another 1.5 miles to **Thirtymile Campground** on the eastern end of Rio Grande Reservoir. There are 33 sites and a fee. **Lost Trail Campground** is located on the northwestern end of the reservoir another 5.5 miles down Forest Rd. 520. It has seven sites and a fee.

Private Campgrounds—

This remote area of Colorado is truly RV heaven. Every time you come around a bend in the road it seems as if there are a dozen happy RV owners at an organized campground. It is vaguely reminiscent of wagons pulling up in a circle for protection at night. Here are just a few ideas from the many choices available.

Broadacres Travelin' Tepee—This ranch/trailer park has 20 full hookups on a prime location beside the Rio Grande (and away from the highway). Bring your fishing pole! Located 5 miles southwest of Creede on Hwy. 149. **PO Box 39, Creede, CO 81130; (719) 658-2291.**

KOA South Fork/Rio Grande—This is one big campground. More than 100 sites are nestled in a tree-lined meadow between the Rio Grande and the highway. Full hookups are offered at a third of the sites. In summer, free movies are shown in the laundry/recreation room. Located just east of South Fork. **26359 W. Hwy. 160, Del Norte, CO 81132; (719) 873-5500.**

Riverbend Resort RV Park—Just over 50 sites are available, some with full hookups. This RV park is located along a 1-mile stretch of the South Fork of the Rio Grande. To get there from South Fork, drive 3 miles southwest on Hwy. 160. **PO Box 129, South Fork, CO 81154; (719) 873-5344.**

WHERE TO EAT

The Bristol Inn — $$$

Located in an out-of-the-way corner of the woods southwest of Creede, the Bristol Inn has a loyal following. The atmosphere is casual, with an elegant touch. Only the freshest ingredients are used in the kitchen; the homemade bread is made from fresh stone-ground flour. Chicken, beef and fish entrées are served. The service has a professional flair, even though tips are not accepted. From Mother's Day through the end of Sept. the restaurant is open for dinner from 5–9 pm Wed.–Sat.; their famous Sun. buffet is open 11 am–3 pm and should not be missed. The restaurant also houses an art gallery, so you'll be able to browse before or after your meal. Reservations are strongly recommended. Located 18 miles southwest of Creede on Hwy. 149; **658-2455.**

Creede Hotel — $$

Since there is no set menu, you can be assured of the freshest quality ingredients. Each day there are two entrée selections; special dishes include grilled tamari honey chicken and mouth-watering lasagna. The restaurant is small and homey. It tends to fill up before plays next door at the Creede Repertory Theater. If you would like to stay at the Creede Hotel, see the Where to Stay section for more information. **Creede Ave.** in downtown Creede; **658-2608.**

Golden Nugget — $ to $$

Your choice of restaurants in downtown Creede is limited, but the Golden Nugget is a place that residents feel good about. The comfortable atmosphere in the old building is created by exposed brick walls, overhead ceiling fans and a pressed-tin ceiling. The dinner menu is basic: miner's stew, chicken-fried steak, trout, chili and a salad bar. Don't miss the Griffen B. Hardy ice cream, scooped in a dish or on a cone. Full breakfasts are served from 7:30–11 am, lunch from 11 am–2:30 pm, dinner from 5–9 pm. The staff is friendly and knowledgeable about the area. Creede Ave. in downtown Creede; **658-2385.**

SERVICES

Creede/Mineral County Chamber of Commerce—
PO Box 580, Creede, CO 81130; (719) 658-2374.

Lake City Chamber of Commerce—
PO Box 430, Lake City, CO 81235; (303) 944-2527.

South Fork Chamber of Commerce—
PO Box 312, South Fork, CO 81154; (719) 873-5512.

Cripple Creek and Victor

Although not known to many Americans these days, the gold-hearted mining town of Cripple Creek was once a household word throughout the country. The Cripple Creek district has produced more than $600 million in gold—more than any other single geological deposit on earth. That's 12 billion in today's dollars. The streets in Cripple Creek are literally paved with gold—gold ore, that is. A very low grade.

And the gold isn't gone. Some local miners say 80 percent of the gold in the area is untapped. But today most of the claims are owned by international companies that are keeping the mines dormant until gold prices go up.

Cripple Creek sits in the crater of an extinct volcano, which created the gold fields. Although the district is scarred by mines and nearly barren of trees, it's ringed by tremendous views of Pikes Peak to the north and the Sangre de Cristo Mountains to the south. The thing to do in Cripple Creek is mingle among its ghosts and its mine skeletons to get a sense of its glorious past. But a word of caution: *most of the mine shafts in the district are death traps just waiting to happen.* Stay on the roads.

Cripple Creek is a tourist center, with shops, a famous melodrama, a narrow-gauge railroad and crowds. But nearby Victor is where most of the gold mining took place, and it's still a mining town, its hills and yards perforated with famous mines like the Ajax, the Independence and the Portland. Victor, once known as the "City of Gold," remains much more like it was originally than does Cripple Creek. The town is named after an early settler, Victor Adams, but its most famous resident was Lowell Thomas (1892-1981), the world's first news commentator.

HISTORY

As the story goes, according to a local miner, the town was named the day an early settler's son fell off the house they were building and broke a limb. That same day a calf broke its leg jumping over a high-banked stream nearby. The settler's comment: "This sho is some Cripple Creek."

It took drunken cowpoke and erstwhile rancher Bob Womack (known as "Crazy Bob") to transform a barren cow pasture he called "Poverty Gulch" into the "the world's greatest gold camp." There was no reason for people to believe his claims of riches: the geology was all wrong, and the man drank himself into a stupor regularly. In fact, Womack could lean down from his saddle while riding at full gallop and scoop up a bottle of whiskey.

The beginning of the country's last major gold rush was delayed even further by false reports. In 1884, two charlatans salted a vein with gold in Cripple Creek. Hundreds of prospectors rushed to the area, only to discover the hoax after about a month of digging. In 1891 however, Womack finally convinced a few people to believe him, and gold fever rose faster and higher than ever before. Unfortunately, Womack was left out: soon after he found his first gold, he got drunk again and sold his claim for $500. The mine went on to produce hundreds of thousands of dollars of the precious metal.

Within a year of the find, 2,500 people were living in Cripple Creek. The first train reached the town in 1894, and the city installed its own nickel-a-ride trolley. That same year, three stock exchanges were trading in Colorado Springs thanks to the influx of Cripple Creek gold.

The rush made millionaires out of at least 30 people, and the town got a taste of fame. The Wright brothers won an auto race from Cripple Creek to Colorado Springs, and Groucho Marx once delivered groceries between Cripple Creek and Victor. For a while, boxer Jack Dempsey lived in Cripple Creek, mining during the day and boxing at night.

In April 1896, fire broke out in a Cripple Creek dance hall and burned down most of the town. Another blaze five days later nearly finished the job, leaving 5,000 people homeless. But Colorado Springs and Victor came to the rescue with a trainload of supplies. Within days the town was rebuilding, with brick this time. Three years later an eerily similar fire destroyed 12 blocks and 200 buildings in Victor.

By 1900, 25,000 people lived in Cripple Creek, making it the state's fourth largest city at the time. The district boasted 150 saloons (70 on notorious Myers Ave. alone), 90 doctors, 34 churches and 15 newspapers (priorities were in order). At the height of the rush the Continental Hotel was so busy the silverware at the restaurant wasn't washed between meals.

Myers Ave. was also home to plenty of brothels, or "pleasure palaces," as they were known. Some of the more illustrious ones in the district were Bucket of Blood, Crapper Jack's Great View, Iron Clad and the Red Onion.

Labor strife broke out in 1903, leading to sabotage and several murders. In one period, 400 to 500 miners just disappeared off the streets. The violence came to a head in 1904 when a railroad station at Independence (just north of Victor) was dynamited, killing 13 non-union workers and maiming many more. Riots followed, and the state militia finally came in and broke the union by deporting members to Kansas and New Mexico.

As gold prices fell, the boom declined as quickly as it had surged. By 1912 most of Cripple Creek's 475 mining companies had folded. By 1920 only 40 of the original 500 mines were working. Bob Womack, the spark of the rush, died penniless in Colorado Springs. But the atmosphere of the boom days is still in evidence, including a herd of donkeys (like those used to haul gold ore) that roams the streets.

The beginning of gold mining in the town of **Victor** had ironic origins. Two promoters, Frank and Harry Woods, advertised the town in 1893 by saying that on every lot was a gold mine. The promotional gimmick turned out to be true as homesteaders began pulling gold out of their backyards. When grading for a hotel, the Woodses discovered an 18-inch vein and decided to build a mine there instead. Within a year the Gold Coin Mine was turning out $50,000 a month. Frank, who had a penchant for luxury, built stained-glass windows in the mine's shaft house, lined it with marble and laid down carpeting.

Lowell Thomas is remembered everywhere in Victor. The author, radio announcer and lecturer began his journalism career as a paper boy for the *Victor Record* and went on to travel around the world. The Lowell Thomas Museum tells his story and is worth a brief stop.

GETTING THERE

From Denver, drive 65 miles south on Interstate 25 to Colorado Springs and then west for 25 miles on Hwy. 24 to the town of Divide. From Divide, drive south (left) on Hwy. 67 for 20 miles to Cripple Creek.

——— MAJOR ATTRACTIONS ———

FLORISSANT FOSSIL BEDS NATIONAL MONUMENT

Palm trees in Colorado? Once upon a time—about 36 million years ago—yes. Also thriving in the Florissant area were enormous redwoods, a thousand species of insects, including tsetse flies common to South Africa, giant katydids and an incredible variety of plants and animals. Thanks to a once-raging volcano field nearby, these remnants of the Oligocene epoch have been preserved better than any other ecosystem in the world.

The fossil bed formed when volcanic eruptions sent lava and mud into the Florissant Basin, creating a large lake. Continued eruptions sent more ash and dust over the lake, taking insects, leaves and fish to the bottom with it. Over a 500,000-year period the sediment formed shales. Mud flows eventually covered and protected these future fossil beds, and recent erosion led to their discovery.

Facts About the Monument—

Florissant ("flowering" or "blooming") was named for the abundant wildflowers in the area. But the rest of the scenery is subtle. At first sight the park appears to be an empty valley, the grassy pit of an extinct lake. Stop by the visitors center for an introduction to spotting fossils and then head off on two or three of the many hiking trails. The Petrified Forest Loop is the best. Don't miss the Trio (three petrified redwood trunks sharing a root system) and Rex Arborae ("King of the Forest"), a petrified stump 14 feet tall and 74 feet around. Scientists guess the tree was once up to 350 feet tall—one of the biggest sequoias ever found. An admission fee is charged. Open daily in summer 8 am–7 pm; during the rest of the year hours are 8 am–4:30 pm. **PO Box 185, Florissant, CO 80816; (719) 748-3253.**

Getting There—To get to the fossil beds, take Hwy. 24 west from Colorado Springs for 35 miles to Florissant. Turn south on County Rd. 1. The monument entrance is about 5 miles up the road on the right. From Cripple Creek, head northwest on County Rd. 1 for 15 miles to the monument entrance.

OUTDOOR ACTIVITIES

BIKING

MOUNTAIN BIKING

With hidden mine shafts sunk all over the area, Cripple Creek is a dangerous place to go off-road. Many mines cave in. If you want to ride in this area, stay on the roads. See the Scenic Drives section for some ideas.

FISHING

Elevenmile Canyon—

Plenty of brown and rainbow trout inhabit the tumbling waters of the South Platte River in this narrow, scenic canyon about 40 miles west of Colorado Springs. The river comes out of Elevenmile dam and flows northeast through the canyon for 10 miles. Since the water flow coming out of the dam fluctuates, so does the quality of the fishing. When the water is high, try fishing with nymphs near the banks of the river. The Elevenmile stretch is stocked regularly. To reach Elevenmile Canyon from Cripple Creek, head north on Hwy. 67 to Hwy. 24 at Divide and turn left. Drive to Lake George and look for the canyon turn-off on the left.

Elevenmile Reservoir—

This reservoir 8 miles southwest of Lake George is known for its bountiful mackinaw trout, kokanee salmon and pike. The largest kokanee in Colorado are often caught at Elevenmile Reservoir. The good fishing prompts lots of fishermen to come out and try the reservoir, both from boats and from the shore. From Cripple Creek, head north on Hwy. 67 to Divide and turn left on Hwy. 24. Drive to Lake George and look for the road sign to the reservoir at the west edge of the town. Ironically, the reservoir can't be reached from Elevenmile Canyon.

HIKING AND BACKPACKING

The Crags—

Located on the west slope of Pikes Peak, this is a relatively undiscovered hiking area. Trails spread out over the back side of Pikes Peak and through the granite formations that give the area its name. Day hikes and backpack trips are possible in this beautiful section of Pike National Forest. From Cripple Creek, head north on Hwy. 67 for about 15 miles and turn right (east) onto Forest Rd. 383. Drive 3.5 miles to the trailhead at the end of the turn-around near the Crags Campground.

From Colorado Springs, head west 25 miles on Hwy. 24 to Divide and turn left onto Hwy. 67. Drive about 4 miles and turn left onto Forest Rd. 383.

SKIING

CROSS-COUNTRY SKIING

The Crags is a raved-about but still secluded area packed with good winter touring trails, from beginner to advanced. Skiing up through the Crags (dramatic granite formations) is beautiful just after a snowfall. From Cripple Creek head north on Hwy. 67 for 15 miles and turn right onto Forest Rd. 383. Proceed about 3 miles (as far as you can).

From Colorado Springs, head west 25 miles on Hwy. 24 to Divide and turn left onto Hwy. 67. Proceed about 4 miles to the Crags turn-off on the left (Forest Rd. 383).

SEEING AND DOING

GOLD PANNING

Why not try a little prospecting? If old-timers say 80 percent of the gold is still left, maybe you'll stumble onto a vein during your visit (but don't count on it). **Trego's Emporium** in town can outfit you to pan for gold. Or rent a metal detector and scour some of the ghost towns for precious metal. Some miners were said to have thrown away now-valuable coins each time they got out of jail. The best ore in Cripple Creek's boom produced about an ounce of gold per ton.

MUSEUMS

Victor–Lowell Thomas Museum—
This interesting museum is worth a quick look if you're in town. The main floor displays relics of Victor's early days, including mining equipment, antique furniture and even a slot machine. The upstairs floor is devoted exclusively to Victor's most famous son—Lowell Thomas. The first news commentator, he was also a prolific writer. Thomas memorabilia, re-creations of rooms in his house and all of his books are displayed. Open daily 10 am–5 pm, May 1–mid-Oct. Located in Victor at **3rd** and **Victor** sts.; **(719) 689-3211.**

NIGHTLIFE

Imperial Melodrama Theatre—
One of the main attractions at the Imperial Hotel is the melodrama theater—the nation's oldest. *Time* magazine has called the thespians here the "Old Vic" of modern melodrama. Delicious dinners are served by the actors in character. Open June through Labor Day; show times are 2 and 8:30 pm Tues.–Sat., 1 and 4:30 pm Sun. For information, contact **PO Box 400, Cripple Creek, CO 80813; (719) 689-2992** or **(719) 471-8878.**

RAILROADS

**Cripple Creek &
Victor Narrow-Gauge Railroad—**
Ride this train and get a literal feel for the Old West—by the seat of your pants. A 15-ton 0-4-0 engine (0 front wheels, 4 in the middle, 0 in the back) follows the three-foot-wide narrow-gauge tracks of the Old Midland Terminal Railroad on a 4-mile round trip past some great mountain scenery, historical sites and mines. Along the way you'll stop to take plenty of photos and hear a bit about Cripple Creek's history, in which trains played a huge role. Fifty-five locomotives used to stop in Cripple Creek daily, hauling ore out and passengers in. The ride's great fun for kids, but it's too bad the train doesn't go all the way to Victor. Open Memorial Day–mid-Oct. 10 am–5 pm. The train leaves every 45 minutes from Midland Station at the end of Bennett Ave., next to the Cripple Creek Museum at the north end of town. **PO Box 459, Cripple Creek, CO 80813; (719) 689-2640.**

SCENIC DRIVES

Take a self-guided car tour on some of the district's back roads, using the ghost town map available at most shops in town. It is very helpful.

Cripple Creek/Victor—
From Cripple Creek make sure to drive to Victor along Hwy. 67, which goes past some of the larger mines in the region. Also consider driving half of this 12-mile round trip via **Range View Rd.** This dirt road leaves Cripple Creek just north of the Molly Kathleen Mine, climbs around Battle Mountain and connects with Diamond Ave. in Victor.

Gold Camp Road—
This beautiful and historic back road follows the path of the railroad, which used to connect Cripple Creek with Colorado Springs. An *excellent* drive. See Gold Camp Rd. in the Scenic Drives section of the **Colorado Springs** chapter.

Phantom Canyon—
This road begins in Victor and snakes its way through a narrow canyon to the south along an old stagecoach line. See the Scenic Drives section of the **Cañon City** chapter.

TOURS

Ghost towns, mines and history are the reasons for a trip to Cripple Creek, not the souvenir shops in the commercialized center of town. That poses a question: how is it possible to step out of one's sightseeing shoes into those of a miner? Put another way: how can visitors live a bit of history? Suggested below are a couple of the best ways to experience the fascinating history of the area.

Molly Kathleen Mine—

Ride the "skip" down 1,000 feet into the Molly Kathleen Mine for a taste of the subterranean insides of a mountain. Although it looks touristy from the outside, don't be put off: this is a full-fledged tour led by miners through the inner workings of an actual mine. The Molly first opened in 1892 and was active until 1961. This is one of the few places where you can see a bit of what was Cripple Creek's reason for being—gold. A display shows all the forms found in Colorado and what to look for if you happen to be out prospecting yourself. Open 9 am-5 pm May through Oct. An admission fee is charged. The Molly's just north of town off **Hwy. 67; PO Box 339, Cripple Creek, CO 80813; (719) 689-2465.**

Tours by Miners—

Stop by the little red caboose at the north end of Cripple Creek and arrange for a guided tour of the ghost towns and mines by the people who knew them—the miners. One colorful prospector, Dale Weaver, gives an incredible, funny tour with plenty of personal flourishes. What sets these van tours apart is the book *The Last Gold Rush*, provided for passengers. The pages are full of reproductions of antique photos to compare with the view, so riders get a before-and-after perspective to make sense of the ruins. After the tour return to the caboose for yet more insights where you're bound to find either Raymond Drake or Bill Grimstad, the book's authors. Tours start at 8:30 am and continue until about 5 pm. A fee is charged. **(719) 689-3000.**

WHERE TO STAY

ACCOMMODATIONS

The Imperial Hotel — $$

The Imperial Hotel is the only one of Cripple Creek's original brick hotels still standing. Staying here is like taking a trip back to the "Gay 90s": most of its furniture dates to that rich period, as do the antiques and paintings. Some of the rooms have private bathrooms with clawfoot tubs and others have just a corner-mounted sink (use a bathroom down the hall). One of the best things about the hotel is that the 30 rooms are all reasonably priced. Other highlights include the Red Rooster Bar, which is packed with roosters of all kinds—stone, wood, metal, etc. Customers bring them here from all around the country! There are three choices for dining within the grand old hotel: the Imperial dining room (see the Where to Eat section), the Carlton Room and the Red Rooster lounge. Reservations recommended. **123 N. 3rd St., Cripple Creek, CO 80813; (719) 471-8878.**

CAMPING

The Crags—

Located on the west side of Pikes Peak, the Crags Campground has 17 sites, and no fee is charged. An abundance of good hiking trails is nearby. This lightly used area is a great spot to camp, though the access road is not very forgiving to RVs. Take Hwy. 67 north from Cripple Creek for 13.5 miles, then turn right (east) on Forest Rd. 383. Drive 3.5 miles to the campground.

Elevenmile Canyon—

This scenic canyon has six campgrounds with a total of 91 campsites (fee charged). The road in the canyon is slim and twisting, so large trailers and RVs are advised to stay near the entrance. To get to the canyon take Hwy. 24 west out of Colorado Springs to the Elevenmile Canyon turn-off (Forest Rd. 245) to the left (south) at the town of Lake George. Great fishing.

Elevenmile State Recreation Area—

The campground at the recreation area can be reached from Hwy. 24 at the west end of Lake George. Turn left on Forest Rd. 247 and proceed to the recreation area where 137 sites (fee charged) await. Some sites are on the shore.

Private Campground—

Lost Burro—"Wilderness camping with modern conveniences" says the Lost Burro literature. They offer electric hookups, restrooms, showers and picnic tables. Tent sites. Located 4 miles northwest of Cripple Creek on County Rd. 1. **(719) 689-2345.**

WHERE TO EAT

The Imperial Hotel — $$ to $$$

The five dining rooms at the Imperial Hotel serve up the best meals in town. All meals are served buffet style. The dining rooms are best known for their dinner items, highlighted by glazed duck, prime rib and chicken curry. Leave enough room for chocolate mousse or any of the other rich desserts. The Imperial is open daily from May 15–Oct. 1. Breakfast is served 7–10 am; lunch from 11:30 am–2:30 pm; dinner from 5:30–9 pm. **123 N. 3rd St., Cripple Creek, CO 80813; 689-2713.**

Red Lantern — $$

This is where the Cripple Creek locals eat, mainly because of the heaping portions and the location just off the main drag. The Red Lantern dishes up great barbecue in a roadhouse setting; the chicken plate can match the biggest of appetites. **353 Myers Ave., Cripple Creek, CO; 689-2519.**

Zeke's — $

The chili at Zeke's is probably the best reason to drive to **Victor**. Some Colorado Springs residents make the 60-mile trip often for just that reason. The bearded "Zeke"—third in the bar's history—generally finds time to regale all comers with his colorful stories and off-color language. In keeping with Zeke's personality, the walls of this wooded saloon are papered with pin-up girls and the likes of Elvis and Marilyn. The beers are cheap and there's a pool table, too. Open year-round, 7–2 am (till midnight on Sun.). **108 S. 3rd St.,** between Victor and Portland aves. in Victor. **(719) 636-3091**

SERVICES

**Cripple Creek
Chamber of Commerce—**

PO Box 650, Cripple Creek, CO 80813; **(719) 689-2169.**

Victor Chamber of Commerce—

PO Box 83, Victor, CO 80860; **(719) 689-3072.**

Leadville

Everywhere you turn in Leadville, there are reminders of its yesteryears. Though paved streets have replaced dirt roads, and cars have replaced horse-drawn wagons, many Victorian-era buildings and mining sites still stand as tarnished mementos of the silver boom. In 1880 Leadville was the second largest city in Colorado, bursting with a population of more than 24,000; today it is a quiet community of 3,000 with a profound sense of history. The town has been designated a National Historic District and eight museums attempt to preserve the memory of the town's prosperous early days. After visiting, you'll agree with author Carlyle Channing Davis, who in 1916 wrote, "There has been but one Leadville. Never will there be another."

The area surrounding Leadville has produced gold, silver, zinc, molybdenum, manganese and turquoise. It is, without question, one of the most highly mineralized areas in the world. Just east of town, mines at California Gulch and Carbonate, Fryer and Iron hills provided the source of Leadville's birth and livelihood for many decades. Driving the "routes of the silver kings" is an excellent way to relive the mining history of the area (see the Scenic Drives section).

Located high in the Arkansas Valley at an elevation of 10,152 feet, Leadville is said to have 10 months of winter and two months of late fall. It is hemmed in by the Sawatch Mountains (*Sawatch* is a Ute word meaning "blue earth") to the west and the Mosquito Range to the east. From within the glacially formed Sawatch Mountains, Colorado's two highest peaks, Elbert (14,433 feet) and Massive (14,421 feet), dominate the town. The Colorado Trail tracks along the base of these peaks (see the Hiking and Backpacking section). There are also a number of walking routes to the summits—literally at the top of Colorado. In winter, Leadville is at a ski crossroads: in 20 minutes you can be on the slopes at Ski Cooper; in less than an hour you can be skiing at six other areas. Cross-country skiing on miles of groomed and backcountry trails is excellent.

A visit to Leadville creates feelings of nostalgia and an urge to romanticize the beauty and excitement of "the good old days." However, day-to-day life for thousands of miners and millworkers in the 1800s meant long hard hours for paltry wages of about $2.50 a day. Still, vast fortunes were made and, nearly as often, squandered. Representative of Leadville's opulent history are the twists and turns of Horace A.W. Tabor's fate.

HISTORY

A Vermont stonecutter named H.A.W. Tabor and his wife, Augusta, came west during the Pikes Peak gold rush of 1859. After many years of chasing his fortune from one Colorado gold camp to another, he eventually settled in Oro City (2.5 miles from present-day Leadville) where he was involved in mining and running a small general store. Not long before Tabor arrived, Oro City had boomed when gold deposits were discovered in California Gulch in 1860. But the deposits were not big producers and a heavy black sand made it difficult to isolate the gold ore. Within a few years, much of the population, which had swelled to 5,000, left to seek fortunes elsewhere.

Tabor also left Oro City for another more promising town—Buckskin Joe. He lived there with Augusta and their young son for seven years. When the claims at Buckskin Joe appeared to be played out, Tabor once again packed the family belongings and returned to Oro City, where he took on the tasks of shopkeeper and postmaster. He stayed on, hoping his luck would change as Oro City gradually decayed around him. It wasn't until 1875 that William Stevens and his partner A.B. Wood, a metallurgist, reworked some of the abandoned mines and discovered that the heavy black sand clogging the gold sluicing operations had a high silver content. Working quietly to discover the source, Stevens and Wood staked out claims that eventually netted them millions. After this initial success, miners began prospecting to the north and west on Iron and Carbonate hills. But it wasn't until George Fryer discovered a rich body of ore, on what is now called Fryer Hill, that the camp sprang to life.

Meanwhile Tabor had moved his fledgling store down the road to the exciting town of Leadville. Not long after he had reestablished his operation in its new location, he was hounded by two poor German shoemakers with no money or mining experience. In an effort to get rid of them so that he could tend to his busy store, Tabor grubstaked George Hook and August Riche in return for a one-third interest in their claim on Fryer Hill. As luck would have it, the inexperienced miners soon hit a 30-foot-thick silver vein, some 29 feet below the surface. A month later their Little Pittsburg Mine was producing $50,000 worth of ore per month.

Tabor became the talk of the state and was soon commissioned to purchase a claim for a Denver wholesaler. Hearing of Tabor's commission, a man named Chicken Bill salted one of his unproductive claims with silver dust and duped Tabor into buying the mine. When the Denver wholesaler learned of the swindle, he refused to give Tabor any money for the worthless mine. Tabor was the laughingstock of the town, but somehow he felt lucky enough to continue mining at the site. He hired a group of miners to deepen the shaft and soon they discovered the famous Chrysolite lode. In less than two years, the former stonecutter was Leadville's first multimillionaire.

The valley flooded with fortune hunters. Oro City was overtaken by the new town of Leadville due to the swarm of miners who were seeking fortunes from the carbonate ores of lead. Smelters were built and operated day and night. A quarter mile of saloons, brothels, wine-theaters and gambling halls sprang up along State St. (now Second St.), giving Leadville an uninhibited atmosphere.

By 1880 Leadville had gone from a camp of 200 to a rip-roaring city of 24,000. Each transaction and discovery intensified the excitement as the population swelled beyond capacity. Houses, hotels, banks and saloons were filled with humanity. As many as 500 workers at a time paid 50 cents each to sleep for an eight-hour shift in a circus tent that was erected at the southern end of town. Saloons sold sleeping spaces on the floor for 25 cents up to a dollar for a heated spot. A law of survival ruled the streets, and hundreds of unfortunates died of starvation and exposure.

The town, crammed with homeless workers, and the mining hills, riddled with overlapping claims, became lawless. Claim-jumpers and squatters brought violence. Mine owners hired guards for protection. The court dockets were filled with suits and countersuits. William Stevens said that of the first $11 million he took from his Iron Hill mine, he spent $9 million in litigation just trying to hang on to it. Even so, back on Fryer Hill, extraordinary transactions of mining properties brought quick profits. Unproductive claims were snatched up by rich bonanza kings trying to consolidate their mining efforts and to keep clear title on the ore bodies. Stockholders reaped enormous profits.

Lucky miners and stockholders were not the only ones to profit from the phenomenal growth. Merchants were able to charge four times the Denver price for supplies; a barrel of whiskey could reap a $1,500 profit. Inflated prices could be charged because of Leadville's isolation and the difficulty of getting the goods to market. Freight rates were exorbitant. It wasn't until 1880 that the first train tracks were laid; even so, harsh winters and deep snow often stopped the train short of town.

It wasn't long before Tabor and the other bonanza kings tried to civilize the city with gracious Victorian homes, hotels and even the Tabor Opera House. Great fortunes were made. Many who got their start in Leadville are well remembered today, such as Meyer Guggenheim, Marshall Field and David May (May D&F). Sidewalks lined the gaslit streets, and Harrison Ave. was paved with black slag. (Today, a huge mound of slag—not coal—is piled next to the highway at the south end of town.) The mountains around Leadville were left bald from the frenzied construction of mine shafts as well as the extraction of charcoal for the smelters and city buildings.

In the scandal of the era, H.A.W. Tabor divorced his stoic wife, Augusta, to marry the young divorcee, Elizabeth "Baby Doe" McCourt, who shared his passion for a flamboyant lifestyle. He married Baby Doe in a lavish Washington, DC, ceremony that was attended by President Chester Arthur. Baby Doe's wedding dress alone cost thousands of dollars and was covered with pearls and diamonds.

By 1880 Leadville was a fabulous camp producing nearly $12 million of silver a year. The two biggest mines, the Robert E. Lee and the Little Pittsburg, held a contest to see which could produce the most silver in a 24-hour period. Working three shifts around the clock, the miners hardly stopped for food and drink. The Robert E. Lee Mine won by producing a quantity of silver worth $118,500 at a meager cost of $300.

The decade of the 1880s brought a period of settling in and shed new light on Cloud City, as Leadville was sometimes referred to. While law and order were restored to the streets, new troubles arose. Big mines nearing the end of their ore borrowed heavily to pay stockholders. When their insider secrets were discovered, stocks fell and overextended banks began to falter. There were other troubles too, such as mine disasters and labor strikes that closed some of the best mines. The final blow occurred when the Sherman Silver Purchase Act was repealed, causing the great silver panic of 1893. Leadville's glory days were over forever.

Tabor's fortunes continued to mirror those of Leadville as he lost virtually everything he owned. Though he eventually moved to Denver and pushed his way into political office as high as US Senator, Tabor died there a penniless postmaster in 1899. While on his deathbed, he told Baby Doe to "hang on to the Matchless." For 36 years Baby Doe lived in a cabin next to the Matchless Mine above Leadville, until she froze to death one winter evening. With the irony of a Greek tragedy, only Augusta Tabor, who preferred to live simply, died a millionaire.

In the winter of 1895, the Ice Palace, a vast entertainment center, was built to revitalize the fledgling economy. As luck would have it, the temperatures that season were unusually warm and the 50-foot-high Norman structure with 8-foot-thick ice walls melted away faster than anticipated. During its short life, the Ice Palace covered five acres and contained a skating rink, a ballroom, a restaurant and curio shops.

Just before the turn of the century, James J. Brown (husband of the *Titanic* heroine, "unsinkable" Molly Brown) sank a deep shaft into the Little Johnny Mine just east of the city and discovered a huge gold vein. This discovery revitalized Leadville enough for it to be established as a permanent mining town.

Around 1900 zinc was discovered to have value. Previously a byproduct that had clogged the silver sluicing operations, it was now being taken from the abandoned silver mines. Lead and manganese deposits were also worked profitably. A huge body of molybdenum was discovered in 1918 at Fremont Pass. Until fairly recently, the Climax Mine near Leadville accounted for as much as 80 percent of the total world production of this steel-hardening mineral. Now the Japanese have developed new synthetic compounds that accomplish the same thing, and molybdenum is usually sold as a byproduct. At present, Climax is closed except for reclamation of the tailings ponds. With the closing of Climax, another chapter has closed on Leadville's mining era.

In 1942, 15,000 men in the 10th Mountain Division were stationed at Camp Hale, 18 miles north of Leadville just over Tennessee Pass. In white camouflage uniforms, the army troops practiced alpine combat maneuvers in the area before heading to Europe for battle. Camp Hale was nicknamed Camp Hell by men forced to endure the high altitude, the harsh weather and the rigorous training regimen. Near Tennessee Pass, a 20-foot slab of granite is etched with the names of nearly 1,000 of these men who lost their lives in WWII. A number of their fellow veterans went on to make a huge impact on the ski industry in Colorado. Locally, Ski Cooper is a direct result of the efforts of former 10th Mountain members.

GETTING THERE

Leadville is located 103 miles southwest of Denver. To get there take Interstate 70 west to Copper Mountain. Turn south on Hwy. 91 and continue 24 miles to Leadville.

———— FESTIVALS AND EVENTS ————

Oro City

summer weekends from late June to mid-July

In Apr. 1860, Oro City sprang up near present-day Leadville, and by July of the same year there were 5,000 inhabitants. More than 120 years later, there is an annual re-creation of this mining camp, including tents, false-front buildings and log cabins manned by a bunch of locals dressed up in period clothes. They provide demonstrations of gunsmithing, gold panning, sluicing and even breadmaking. As the saloon becomes filled with camera-laden tourists in plaid shorts, it gets a little tough to imagine the Wild West, but it is good fun nonetheless. Admission fee. For more information call **(719) 486-3900.**

Leadville Music Festival

mid-July through early August

Opera, Dixieland jazz, chamber music and Jolson are all performed by topnotch university musicians at the Leadville Music Festival. The summer program was initiated in 1986 by Loyola University of New Orleans and it has grown each year. Concerts take place in various halls around Leadville; all are open to the public for a small admission fee. For more information call **(719) 486-3900.**

Boom Days

early August

During Leadville's main summer bash, you'll have no trouble imagining what the town was like during the real silver boom. The streets are once again filled with tough looking hardrock miners, dancing girls, brass bands and burros. The weekend kicks off with a parade down Harrison Ave. and ends with a burro race over Mosquito Pass. In between, there are mining events such as hand mucking (loading broken rock by hand) and jackleg drilling (drilling with a jackhammer). Carnival rides accompany the carnival atmosphere. The Lions Club sets up a traditional beer garden every year. For more information call the **Leadville/Lake County Chamber of Commerce** at **(719) 486-3900.**

Tomato War

early September

For one weekend each Sept., the Twin Lakes area, as local Ray James puts it, "runs red with the gore of war." Tomato war, that is. The annual Colorado vs. Texas Tomato War features state-to-state combat between armies of soldiers armed only with boxes of rotten tomatoes. Since the first war broke out in 1982, battle tactics have become more sophisticated, including the use of camouflage and homemade tanks. With battle cries of "Drink beer, hit a Texan!" waves of Colorado troops attempt to storm the heavily fortified Tomalamo, a plastic fort atop a ridge, which is valiantly defended by visitors from the Lone Star State. Once a participant is pelted by one of the messy vegetables, he or she is out of the battle. The point (if there is one) of all this is to have a good time—and everyone does. An official invitation has been sent to the governor of Texas for next year's competition—"Remember the

Tomalamo!" For more information, call **(719) 486-0440.**

OUTDOOR ACTIVITIES

BIKING

MOUNTAIN BIKING

Leadville is starting to become recognized as a haven for mountain bike enthusiasts. The maze of old mining roads around town provides a limitless area for exploring via mountain bike. Some particularly good roads are just east of town on heavily mined Fryer Hill. Stop by the **Leadville/ Lake County Chamber of Commerce** at **809 Harrison Ave.** for a booklet with a map and a historical description of the "routes of the silver kings." Another excellent ride is up and over Mosquito Pass, ending in South Park (see the Four-Wheel-Drive Trips section). In addition, a number of marked cross-country ski trails set off from the western side of Tennessee Pass for riders who want to find single-track trails.

Rentals and Information—
10th Mountain Sports—This shop not only rents and repairs bikes, it also offers van service to the top of Mosquito Pass so you can enjoy the ride down. The shop also offers guided mountain bike trips. **112 E. 7th St.; (719) 486-2202.**

FISHING

Arkansas River—
The heavily mined mountains around Leadville have created a toxic imbalance in the Arkansas River near Leadville. The fishing improves markedly below Twin Lakes, where some Bureau of Land Management land is open to the public. See the Fishing section of the **Upper Arkansas Valley** chapter.

Crystal Lakes—
Stocked with rainbow and cutthroat trout, these lakes are usually hopping with feeding trout in early evening. From the

shore, small dry flies are effective on top; many fishermen cast hardware and bait into the middle where larger trout enjoy the deep water. This easy-access fishing area is only 3.5 miles south of Leadville on Hwy. 24.

Halfmoon Creek—
Directly beneath the tallest peaks in Colorado, Halfmoon Creek offers many pools and eddies to the diligent angler. It is stocked with rainbow trout, but browns and brookies can also be caught. To reach Halfmoon Creek travel west on Hwy. 24 for about 2 miles. Continue west on Hwy. 300 instead of following Hwy. 24 around a wide bend in the road. Stay on Hwy. 300 for a mile before turning south on Halfmoon Creek Rd. (Forest Rd. 110). After a couple of miles the creek parallels the path of the dirt road for 4 miles to Halfmoon Campground.

Upstream from Halfmoon Campground, the creek is paralleled by a jeep road that disintegrates into a trail. It is possible to hike all the way up to **North Halfmoon Creek**, which is good for small brook trout.

Turquoise Lake—
At nearly 10,000 feet in elevation, this large lake offers some of the best fishing in the Leadville area—only 3 miles west of town. Good fishing combined with a beautiful location make it a heavily used recreation area; eight campgrounds are located around the lake. Fishing from a boat or from the shore will yield brown, rainbow and cutthroat trout. There are other species in the lake, including stocked kokanee salmon. Turquoise Lake is known for its excellent ice fishing. Hiking trails lead from Turquoise Lake to high alpine lakes, including several good producers just inside

Holy Cross Wilderness: **Timberline Lake, Galena Lake** and **Bear Lake**. To reach Turquoise Lake, drive west on 6th St. to the edge of town. Turn right (northwest) on Turquoise Lake Rd. and continue 3 miles.

Twin Lakes Reservoir—

So, you want to catch a mackinaw (lake trout) in the 30-pound range? Twin Lakes, at the foot of Independence Pass, will give you the chance, but you can only keep one and it must exceed 20 inches. In addition to large lake trout, Twin Lakes Reservoir is stocked with rainbow and cutthroat trout. Good fishing opportunities exist from the shore. Many fishermen, however, prefer trolling for mackinaw; boat ramps are located on the north side of the lake. There are several picnic and camping areas, making this lake an extremely popular destination. From Leadville follow Hwy. 24 south for 14 miles until reaching Hwy. 82. Turn right and head west on Hwy. 82, which follows along the north shore.

FOUR-WHEEL-DRIVE TRIPS

There are untold numbers of four-wheel-drive roads in the mountains around Leadville. This is a great place to explore because the mines have left so many visible traces. If you don't have a jeep, contact **Sugar Loafin' Campground** at **(719) 486-1031** for information on their group tours.

Halfmoon Drainage—

Up above Halfmoon Campground, Forest Rd. 110 gets progressively rougher, eventually phasing from a four-wheel-drive road to a hiking trail. The road leads around behind Mt. Elbert (14,433 feet) next to Halfmoon Creek. Two miles beyond the campground, a left fork leads along South Halfmoon Creek. There are many traces of mining in the area, as well as an old mill. To reach Halfmoon Campground, head west on Hwy. 24 for about 2 miles. Turn right and continue west on Hwy. 300 instead of following Hwy. 24 around a big bend. Stay on Hwy. 300 for a mile before turning left

on Halfmoon Creek Rd. (Forest Rd. 110), then continue for 6 miles.

Mosquito Pass—

This wagon road that connects the mining camps of South Park with Leadville and the Arkansas Valley was completed in 1879. But it was only in service for a short time—in 1880 the train arrived in Leadville, making the wagon road obsolete. Today, this moderate four-wheel-drive road leads over the summit of Mosquito Pass. The road reaches an elevation of 13,188 feet, making it the highest through road in North America. The rough dirt road offers wide vistas of the Sawatch Mountains as it rises quickly to the summit. At the summit, a stone marker refers to the mail-carrying Father John Dyer as the "snowshoe itinerant." He not only held services for many mining camps, but also carried the mail over several high passes on 10-foot wooden skis. Every summer during Boom Days, a 23-mile pack burro race takes place on Mosquito Pass.

From Leadville take 7th St. east from Harrison Ave. The road leads into the Fryer Hill mining district as it follows Evans Gulch up toward the pass. Stay on the main road past the Matchless Mine. About 4.5 miles after starting out, Mosquito Pass Rd. breaks off to the left. From here, the road leads over the summit and drops down to the town of Fairplay in 18 miles. Instead of returning on the same route, come back to Leadville via Weston Pass, located 5 miles south of Fairplay on Hwy. 285 (see the Scenic Drives section).

GOLF

Mount Massive Golf Club—

At 10,200 feet, this nine-hole course is billed as the highest in the world. The claim is disputed, but the beauty of the course is not. The well maintained greens are located along gentle slopes at the base of Mt. Massive (14,421 feet). Since the course is surrounded by a thick forest of lodgepole pines, it is not uncommon to see deer and elk wander onto the links. Advance tee times are normally unnecessary. Located 3.5 miles west of town on **Turquoise Lake Rd. (County Rd. 4); (719) 486-2176.**

HIKING AND BACKPACKING

The Leadville area offers some of the most spectacular mountain terrain imaginable—and hiking is perhaps the best way to get out and enjoy it. The town is surrounded on three sides by San Isabel National Forest and hemmed in from the west by Colorado's two highest peaks: Mt. Elbert (14,433 feet) and Mt. Massive (14,421 feet). Hiking to the top of either peak is an accomplishment that lasts a lifetime. At lower elevations a web of trails meanders through ponderosa forests, wildflowers, meadows and crumbling remnants of the mining boom. Several great hikes near the Leadville area are discussed in the **Vail** and **Upper Arkansas Valley** chapters. For trail information and maps, contact the **Leadville Ranger District Office, 2015 N. Poplar St.; (719) 486-0749.** For topographical maps and outdoor equipment try **Bill's Sport Shop** at **225 Harrison Ave.; (719) 486-0739,** or **Buckhorn Sporting Goods** at **616 Harrison Ave.; (719) 486-3944.**

Colorado Trail—

Hike for as long or short a distance as you wish on a segment of the Colorado Trail, which stretches 469 miles from Denver to Durango. Passing just to the west of Leadville, the trail offers access to spectacular scenery: thick woods, trout streams and historic mining areas. Consider leaving a second car at a pickup point near the trail and taking a one-way backpacking trip for a few days. The stretch near Leadville between Tennessee Pass and Twin Lakes is gorgeous. A hike up Mt. Elbert or Mt. Massive could be easily taken (without pack) from the Colorado Trail. For more information on the Colorado Trail, contact the **Leadville Ranger District Office.**

Leadville National Fish Hatchery—

Beginning near the teeming cement fish tanks of the hatchery is a nature trail with 15 numbered stations along its 1-mile route. The walk takes about an hour and is in a beautiful area near the base of Mt. Massive. At a midpoint between the three Evergreen Lakes is a picnic area. Pick up a trail guide at the visitors center. To reach the hatchery take Hwy. 24 west of Leadville for 2 miles to Hwy. 300. Turn right and drive a couple more miles to the historic hatchery, built in 1899.

Mount Elbert—

A hike up Colorado's tallest peak requires a degree of strength, stamina and common sense. Be sure to bring enough water and to watch for telltale signs of altitude sickness. This is a popular hike that can be done in one day. The first part of the hike is heavily wooded and provides the best chance for sighting mule deer and other wildlife. After you leave the trees behind, colorful alpine tundra takes over the ground. Please stay on the trail, as this plant life is easily damaged. In early summer the trail passes over snowfields close to the top. When you make it to the summit, the views are astounding in all directions.

North Mt. Elbert Trail begins at an elevation of 10,100 feet and climbs 4.5 miles to the summit. Since this is just about the shortest route, it receives very heavy use. To reach the trailhead, head west on Hwy. 24 for about 2 miles. Continue west on Hwy. 300 instead of following Hwy. 24 around a wide bend. Stay on Hwy. 300 for a mile before turning south on Halfmoon Creek Rd. (Forest Rd. 110). Continue 6 miles on the dirt road to Halfmoon Campground. The trail leaves from just above the campground, which has a parking area.

South Mt. Elbert Trail is longer, but receives less use. The trail begins at 9,600 feet and climbs 6 miles to the summit. The trailhead is located at Lake View Campground near Twin Lakes.

Yet another approach to the summit of Mt. Elbert is on **Black Cloud Trail.** This is the least used of all the routes and is a truly beautiful way to the top. Even if you don't have the urge to conquer a 14er, this can be an excellent short hike—just return when you feel like it. The elevation gain on Black Cloud Trail is nearly 5,000 feet in 5.5 miles. The steady uphill pull is rewarded by the view from the top. To reach the trailhead travel south on Hwy. 24 for 14 miles to Hwy. 82. Turn right and drive past Twin Lakes to a half mile beyond Twin Peaks Campground. The trail leaves from the north side of the highway.

Mount Massive Trail—

Even though Mt. Massive is 12 feet shorter than Mt. Elbert, its trail is quite a bit longer—from Halfmoon Campground it is 7 miles to the summit, with an elevation gain of almost 4,500 feet. It is a long day hike that is fantastic if you're in good shape. The trail begins on the Colorado Trail and tracks north along the base of the peak for 3 miles. At a marked junction with Mt. Massive Trail you take the left fork and head sharply uphill toward treeline. Once above the trees, views to Leadville and Mt. Elbert are incredible. It gets even better once you are on the summit! To reach the trailhead see the entry on South Mt. Elbert Trail. Both hikes begin just above Halfmoon Campground.

HORSEBACK RIDING

Pa and Ma's Guest Ranch—

Sign up for an all-you-can-eat breakfast or dinner ride—or rent a horse by the hour up to a full day. The ranch also runs historical tours of Leadville in a horse-drawn surrey, beginning in front of the Leadville/Lake County Chamber of Commerce at 809 Harrison Ave. Open 9 am–5 pm daily in summer. Pa and Ma's is located 4 miles west of town on **Hwy. 24** at E. **Tennessee Rd.; (719) 486-3900.**

RIVER FLOATING

The Upper Arkansas River is renowned for giving rafters thrilling, whitewater rides. A slew of outfitters make the run, but most are based near the town of Buena Vista. The **Upper Arkansas River,**

including Brown's Canyon, is discussed in detail in the River Floating section of the **Upper Arkansas Valley** chapter. Only one local outfitter makes the trip from Leadville: **10th Mountain Sports, 112 E. 7th St., Leadville, CO; (719) 486-2202.**

SKIING
CROSS-COUNTRY SKIING

Leadville is at the center of a cross-country skier's paradise. Miles of backcountry trails weave through the lower reaches of the Sawatch Mountains. In addition, groomed trail systems leave from the base of Ski Cooper and from the Colorado Mountain College campus. All in all, the snow conditions at this altitude are excellent, the views are beautiful and the avalanche danger is low. For maps and information about trails in San Isabel National Forest, contact the **Leadville Ranger District Office, 2015 N. Poplar St.; (719) 486-0749.**

Backcountry Trails—

Leadville National Fish Hatchery—A marked system of looping trails for various abilities leads away from the fish hatchery at the base of Mt. Massive. The area is stunning in its natural beauty. A good half-day trip is on the Highline Trail Loop or the more difficult Kearney Park Loop. More information is posted at the hatchery. To get there, travel west from town on Hwy. 24 for about 2 miles. Continue west (right turn) on Hwy. 300 instead of following Hwy. 24 around a big bend. The hatchery is 2 miles ahead on the left side of the road.

Silver City Trail—Skiing through Leadville's historic mining district is one of the best ways to get a feeling for the lifestyle of the miners. Back when the mines were operating year-round, however, men working the mines in winter never saw the sun. Today, miles of unplowed mining roads weave past the abandoned mine buildings that litter the countryside. Dangerous pits and holes abound off the roads. A map with a key to the markers on the "routes of the silver kings" is available at the **Leadville/Lake County Chamber of Commerce, 809 Harrison Ave.; (719) 486-3900.**

Tennessee Pass—Just west of the summit of Tennessee Pass on Hwy. 24, a number of trails head off into the woods. Some of the trails follow the old Denver & Rio Grande Railroad beds. The Mitchell Creek Loop begins on the even grade of a railroad bed for 2.5 miles before getting a bit tougher. The entire loop is slightly over 7 miles long. More difficult tours include the Powder Hound Loop and the Treeline Loop. Views of old mine buildings accompany nearly every tour. This is the area where the 10th Mountain Division trained before heading off to Europe in World War II. All of the trails are marked; maps are available from the **Leadville Ranger District Office, 2015 N. Poplar St.; (719) 486-0749.**

Groomed Trails—
Ski Cooper Nordic Center—Thirty-five kilometers of maintained trails leave from the base of Ski Cooper. Many of the trails are loops of varying length and difficulty. Reasonable trail fees make the terrain accessible to all skiers. Cross-country rentals and instruction can be arranged at the nordic center. For those interested in telemark skiing, 302 acres of lift-served slopes at the ski mountain are perfect (telemark clinics and rentals available). Located 10 miles north of Leadville on **Hwy. 24; (719) 486-2277.**

Rentals and Information—
Ski Cooper Nordic Center—The nordic center offers excellent telemark and cross-country equipment. See the entry above for information. Located 10 miles north of Leadville on **Hwy. 24; (719) 486-2277.**

10th Mountain Sports—This full-service sporting goods store offers guided backcountry tours as well as rental equipment. **112 E. 7th St.; (719) 486-2202.**

DOWNHILL SKIING
Leadville is not a resort community—you won't find condo developments or a large, well-known hotel in its low-key setting. But Leadville is simply a great place to be in winter, and there are plenty of unique places to stay. In about 20 minutes you can be on the slopes at Ski Cooper; other areas, such as Copper Mountain, Breckenridge, Vail, Beaver Creek or Keystone/Arapahoe Basin, can be reached in under an hour. Ski Cooper is the only area discussed in detail in this chapter.

Ski Cooper—
One of Colorado's best-kept secrets is located astride the Continental Divide at the summit of Tennessee Pass. Low-priced lift tickets, no lines, good snow and a casual atmosphere are trademarks at Ski Cooper. The mountain does not have the intimidating runs of some larger areas, making it perfect for most families. Since the base elevation is at 10,500 feet, the snowfall (250-inch average) is normally dry and powdery. The base lodge has a cafeteria, a rental shop and a nursery, but no overnight accommodations are available at the ski area. Located 10 miles north of Leadville on **Hwy. 24; (719) 486-2277.**

SWIMMING
Lake County Intermediate School Recreation Complex—
An indoor Olympic-sized pool, full gym facilities and a 22-person whirlpool spa are all open to the public for reasonable fees. Don't forget to ask about "dive-in movies"! Hours vary daily, so call for information. **6th St. and McWethy Dr.; (719) 486-2564.**

TENNIS
Four public courts are located at **City Park** just west of **W. 5th St. and Leiter Ave.**

SEEING AND DOING

MUSEUMS

Shed some light on Leadville's colorful past by spending some time in a museum, or two, or eight for that matter. That's right, this small town has a host of eight museums and was recently selected as home of the National Mining Hall of Fame. Each delves into the history of the area from a different perspective. We have discussed some of the best museums. "The Earth Runs Silver," a multi-image slide show with narration, is a good place to get an overall view of Leadville before heading to your museum of choice. In summer the show runs on the hour, inside the old church next door to the **Leadville/Lake County Chamber of Commerce.** For tickets and information stop by **809 Harrison Ave.; (719) 486-3900.**

Healy House and Dexter Cabin—

Take an outstanding "living tour" of the Healy House, an elaborate Victorian built in 1878. Knowledgeable guides dressed in period costumes assume the roles of Victorian boarders in the year 1898. "No questions after 1899, please." The house was originally a single-family residence, but from 1897 to 1902 was used as a boardinghouse. Five of the residents in 1898 were female schoolteachers. In those days, schoolteachers were required to wear seven undergarments at all times and take examinations twice a year. For their troubles they were paid $40 per month; $30 was for the rental of cramped quarters in the Healy House.

Dexter Cabin looks like any primitive log miner's cabin, until you get inside. The builder of the small structure was James Dexter, who made a pile of money in mining and investments. Dexter Cabin was never used as a residence; rather, it was for members of an exclusive poker club. The cabin's interior, furnished with the finest woods, is an example of pure luxury. The museum complex is open from Memorial Day through Labor Day, 10 am–4:30 pm

Mon.–Sat., 1–4:30 pm Sun.; shorter hours in Sept. Fee charged. **912 Harrison Ave.; (719) 486-0487.**

Heritage Museum—

The Carnegie Library, built in 1904, was turned into a historical museum in 1977. Inside you'll find mining implements, dioramas of mining activity and placards describing the exciting history of the area. Upstairs are museum exhibits from Leadville's heyday as well as a gallery featuring the work of Colorado artists. Small admission fee. Open 9 am–6 pm Memorial Day through Labor Day; 10 am–5 pm from Labor Day to the end of Oct.; winter hours are limited. **102 E. 9th St.; (719) 486-1878.**

Matchless Mine—

The headlines around the country screamed "Queen of Colorado's Silver Boom Perishes" and "Baby Doe Freezes To Death While On Guard At Matchless Mine." It was a tragic end to a life of incredible swings of fortune. Baby Doe Tabor, second wife of mining magnate H.A.W. Tabor, was true to her husband even after his loss of fortune and death. On his deathbed, Horace Tabor whispered to Baby Doe, "Hang on to the Matchless." Baby Doe moved into a shack at the mine and became a recluse. She died in squalor in 1935 after a 36-year vigil.

The Matchless has been preserved, and tours of the property are given, including the exterior workings of the mine. Follow E. 7th St. east of town for 1 mile to the mine entrance. Small admission fee. Open from June–Labor Day 9 am–5 pm.

Tabor Opera House—

Built in 1879 by H.A.W. Tabor to provide Leadville with culture and entertainment, this opera house is a dazzling relic, with its original stage, dressing rooms and wrought-iron seats with red velvet cushions. Originally the theater was a complex with retail stores on the ground level, a saloon in the rear and a five-room suite on the upper floor. The Claredon Hotel, built adjacently, was joined by a walkway on the upper level so the Tabors and other hotel guests could enjoy private access. Baby Doe and Horace had a private curtained booth close to the stage.

Even today, it isn't hard to imagine the theater on opening night. Surprisingly, the very first show was not a sellout. Despite high expectations from early-day citizens, the mood of the town was still somber from the previous night's hangings of two outlaws. Their bodies were still swaying in the wind in front of the courthouse just up the street.

For quite a time, the Tabor Opera House was touted as the best theater west of the Mississippi. Several of the greats appeared on its stage, including John Philip Sousa, Harry Houdini (note the trap door on the stage), Lillian Russell and Oscar Wilde. In all, the theater still provides an intimate setting, with good acoustics from its original canvas ceiling (see the Nightlife section for more information). For a small fee, self-guided, tape-narrated tours can be taken in summer from 9 am–5:30 pm Sun.–Fri. **815 Harrison Ave.**; no telephone.

NIGHTLIFE

Silver Dollar Saloon—

Very few saloons in Colorado are entering their second century of operation. The Silver Dollar is one of them. The first drink was pushed across the bar in 1879 when it opened under the name the *Board of Trade*. The stunning white oak backbar was shipped in by wagon from St. Louis, Missouri. It is a remarkable piece of work, inlaid with a 0.75-inch-thick diamond-dust mirror. There is also an oak windbreak as you enter the bar; some say it was placed there to protect men from the prying eyes of their wives. During Prohibition the bar remained active, with a trap door mounted beneath the bar for quick disposal of moonshine. Today the bar retains the feel of boomtown Leadville. **315 Harrison Ave.; 486-9914.**

Tabor Opera House—

An Icicle Pickle, or How to Stay Cool as a Cucumber While Your Frozen Assets Thaw was the title of last year's theater production at the Tabor Opera House. The melodramatic comedy was based on events surrounding the 1896 Leadville Ice Palace. Every year a new play by the Crystal Comedy Company breathes life back into the historic theater. And what a setting! (For more information see the Museums section.) The reasonably priced family entertainment starts in mid-June and lasts through Labor Day. Shows only on Wed., Thur. and Sat. nights at 8 pm. Tickets may be purchased the day of the show. The Tabor Opera House is located at **815 Harrison Ave.**; no telephone.

RAILROADS

Leadville, Colorado & Southern Railroad—

In 1988, after a 50-year silence, a passenger train once again began arriving and departing from Leadville. Pulled by a strong locomotive, the open passenger cars on the standard-gauge railroad provide expansive views during the entire traverse up to treeline. The scenic ride ends at a roundhouse just before reaching the boundary of the Climax Mine at an elevation of over 11,000 feet. Stephanie and Ken Olsen made the bargain of a century when they purchased two 1,750 horsepower engines, eight flatcars, five cabooses, 13 miles of track and a roundhouse for $10—less than it costs for a ticket to ride the train today. However, they have poured a lot of money into the operation to make it a worthwhile venture. The train departs from the Leadville depot two times daily from Memorial Day through Labor Day; weekend trips continue until the fall colors are gone. The ride takes about two-and-a-half hours including a short break at the water tower. Reduced tickets for children and seniors. **326 E. 7th St., PO Box 916, Leadville, CO 80461; (719) 486-3936.**

SCENIC DRIVES

Independence Pass—
During the summer and fall, this beautiful drive leads to Aspen over a narrow, twisting road. For more information see the Scenic Drives section of the Aspen chapter.

Routes of the Silver Kings—
Driving among the decaying wooden mine structures and piles of yellowed mine tailings is a fascinating way to get a true picture of the once-booming industry. Good dirt roads thread their way between famous mines on Fryer Hill and California Gulch. Several round-trip auto tours leave from Leadville and snake their way into the mountains. Along the roads, numbered route markers are placed at points of historical interest. Each marker corresponds with a description in a booklet that can be purchased at the **Leadville/Lake County Chamber of Commerce at 809 Harrison Ave.**

Weston Pass—
This old wagon road connects South Park with Leadville and the Arkansas Valley. The washboard road will shake your car, but high clearance is not necessary to complete the scenic trip. Following the South Fork of the South Platte River, the road winds its way up to an elevation of 11,921 feet. The route goes between Weston Peak (13,572 feet) to the north and Marmott Peak (13,326 feet) to the south. To reach Weston Pass Rd. from Leadville take Hwy. 24 for 6 miles south to the marked turn-off. Turn left and drive over the pass, eventually reaching Hwy. 285 south of Fairplay.

———— WHERE TO STAY ————

ACCOMMODATIONS

Hilltop House — $$ to $$$
Looking down on Harrison Ave. from a hilltop perch is the kind of house dreams are made of. A sweeping lawn, encircled by a white picket fence, leads up to the stately Queen Anne-style home. A spacious porch wraps around the front of the house. It's a great spot to sit on a rocking chair and read a book. Dick and Cheryl Cleveland bought the Hilltop House in 1987 and have turned it into a small bed and breakfast. At present there are only two guest rooms sharing one bathroom. But the couple plan to expand to more rooms in the near future and are working hard to accomplish their goals. Dick commutes to Vail each day to work as a general contractor and private eye; Cheryl works a night shift at Vail Valley Medical Clinic a few times every week. Somehow, after working their other jobs, they have enough energy left to be charming hosts. Full breakfasts and candlelight dinners (with advance notice) are meticulously prepared. No smoking allowed; children under 10 are not encouraged. 100 W. 9th St., Leadville, CO 80461; (719) 486-2362.

Club Lead — $$
"Lodging like a west Texas bunkhouse!" exclaims owner Jay Jones when asked about Club Lead. After looking through the large house, we can assure you it isn't quite that rough. Club Lead offers dorm accommodations with queen-sized beds, to individuals and groups. Breakfast is included in the price. Jones is in the process of adding more rooms, but it's hard to say when the work will get done—this man is going in 10 directions at once. He is in the process of integrating his 10th Mountain Sports store with a unique lodging concept. Geared to the active traveler, Club Lead is into everything from whitewater rafting to mountain biking to cross-country skiing. Jones will tailor a vacation to your interests. It's a great idea, but may take a few years to really work. 500 E. 7th St., Leadville, CO 80461; (719) 486-2202.

Delaware Hotel — $$
By 1888 the Delaware Block was com-

pleted, with 50 upstairs offices and bedrooms. Named for the first owners' home state, the Delaware Hotel originally featured the conveniences of steam heat and hot and cold water, but had only four bathrooms for the entire complex. The exterior similarities between the Delaware and the defunct Tabor Grand/Venodome Hotel across the street can be attributed to a common architect—George E. King. For a long time the venerable Delaware operated as the Crew Beggs Dry Goods Company, but recently returned to service as a hotel.

A nice touch at the Delaware Hotel is that you can choose a room that fits your mood. Each room is slightly different, and interested parties can wander through the hotel's wide upstairs hallways and glance into all of the vacant rooms. Climb the steep stairway and you'll get a feel for the old hotel beyond its worn wood floors. The careful renovation is not overdone or cutesy. Every room has a handmade quilt on the wall and furniture from the late Victorian period; many have the nice touches of exposed brick and brass beds. All have plush carpet, or hardwood floors and beautiful rugs. With the exception of the suites, the rooms are on the small side—shall we say cozy? The two-room suites are a bargain for four people—my personal favorite was the suite tucked into the western corner on the third floor. A night's stay in any room at the Delaware includes a full breakfast. Dinner on the second floor of the hotel, at Le Grande Cafe, is an intimate dining experience featuring continental and Italian cuisine. **The Delaware Hotel, 700 Harrison Ave., PO Box 960, Leadville, CO 80461; (719) 486-1418.**

Matchless Properties — $$

This property management company can rent you a Victorian house or even a cabin. The completely furnished homes can accommodate large or small groups. **700 Harrison Ave., PO Box 971, Leadville, CO 80461; (719) 486-3030.**

Mountain Mansion Bed and Breakfast — $$

Ana Maria Nezol, from Argentina, runs this unique bed and breakfast in the center of Leadville. Traditional South American breakfasts are served each morning, or if you prefer, bacon and eggs. If you don't mind a house that is far from immaculate, this may be a good place for you. Once the home of Colorado Governor Jess McDonald, who served from 1905–1907, the large house contains a haphazard collection of rooms and suites; some are charming reminders of the Victorian era, with private fireplaces and period antiques. Others appear unfinished, with different shades of wallpaper and a rather tattered appearance. Nezol will let you walk through the vacant rooms to help you decide which one you want. On a special note: singles can cut the cost of bed and breakfast if they don't mind sharing a room with a stranger. **129 W. 8th St., Leadville, CO 80461; (719) 486-0655.**

CAMPING

In San Isabel National Forest—

Eight campgrounds (368 campsites) are situated around the perimeter of Turquoise Lake. This is a heavily wooded area that offers hiking, fishing and boating. The **Belle of Colorado Campground**, on the east end of the lake, is the only walk-in campground and is limited to tents. All campgrounds charge a fee and have water and toilets. Turquoise Lake is located 3 miles west of Leadville.

South of Leadville, under the towering summits of Mt. Elbert and Mt. Massive, are the nicely wooded **Halfmoon** (24 sites) and **Elbert Creek** (17 sites) campgrounds. A fee is charged at both. Since a trailhead for climbing Elbert and Massive takes off from the area, use is heavy, especially on weekends. To reach the campgrounds travel west from town on Hwy. 24 for about 2 miles. Continue west on Hwy. 300 instead of following Hwy. 24 around a big bend. Stay on Hwy. 300 for a mile before turning south on Halfmoon Creek Rd. (Forest Rd. 110). Continue 6 miles on the dirt road to the campgrounds.

In the Twin Lakes Reservoir area there are five large campgrounds. From Leadville follow Hwy. 24 south for 14 miles until reaching Hwy. 82. Turn right and head west on Hwy. 82, which skirts the north side of the reservoir. After 3 miles you'll reach **Dexter Point Campground** beside the lake. There are 26 sites, and a fee is charged. Another 2 miles down Hwy. 82, turn left onto Forest Rd. 125 and continue to **Lake View Campground**. As the name suggests, the view to Twin Lakes is beautiful. There are 59 sites and a fee is charged. Past Lake View Campground you can proceed west along Hwy. 82 to **White Star**

(64 sites), **Perry Peak** (26 sites) and **Twin Peaks** (37 sites) campgrounds. All charge a fee.

Private Campgrounds—

Sugar Loafin' Campground—Not far from **Turquoise** Lake is this scenic campground. Full RV hookups and tent sites. Amenities include hot showers, laundry and, listen up—ice cream socials! Located 3.5 miles northwest of Leadville on **County Rd. 4; (719) 486-1031.**

WHERE TO EAT

The Prospector — $$$

Leadville residents frequently take the short 3-mile trip out of town to this special restaurant. From the outside it looks as if it were someone's log cabin. Pass through the stone entrance and once inside you'll be treated to a friendly, family atmosphere. A large picture window offers a beautiful view to the south. Full portions of steak and seafood take up most of the menu at the Prospector. The food is excellent and carefully prepared. Start off with a trip to the full salad bar and soup tureen. When we visited in Aug., the fresh peach pie in a crumbly homemade shell was delicious. Open from 5–9 pm Mon.–Thur., 5–9:30 pm Fri.–Sat. Closed Sun. Located 3.5 miles north of Leadville on **Hwy. 91; 486-2117.**

The Garden Cafe — $ to $$

There is no garden here; in fact, there isn't even one outdoor table. Despite misguided expectations, the Garden Cafe is a great breakfast spot. Occupying a tiny house in an off-Main St. location, this restaurant is a good find. Many of the breakfast dishes are of the ham and eggs variety. But you can also order waffles, huevos rancheros or hash brown supreme—with lots of veggies and melted cheese. The French toast can be topped with blueberries, bananas, sunflower seeds, walnuts and yogurt. The European-blend coffee is refreshingly strong. Breakfast is served from 7–11 am daily. The Garden Cafe is

also open for lunch from 11 am–2 pm daily; Italian-style dinner is served from 5:30–9 pm, Wed.–Sun. **115 W. 4th St.; 486-9917.**

The Golden Burro — $ to $$

Good old American food and lots of it. If you are in the mood for a hot meatloaf sandwich or a chicken-fried steak platter, this is the place. Also served are rainbow trout grilled in butter, fried chicken and liver smothered in sauteed onions. Most of the dishes are meat and potatoes; the only item that would make it to a health food menu is the chef's salad. There are booths and tables as well as counter service. The Golden Burro is one of the few buildings in Leadville that attempted to modernize its storefront—back in the 1950s. Hours are 6 am–10 pm daily in summer; 7 am–9 pm in winter. **710 Harrison Ave.; 486-1239.**

The Grill — $ to $$

It's tough to single out the best Mexican restaurant in Leadville, partly because there are four good ones. However, local opinion tilted the balance to the Grill and La Cantina—both run by cousins in the Martinez family. The Grill was our personal favorite. It has white stucco walls covered with colorful sombreros, shawls and oil paintings. Slip into a red vinyl booth and enjoy a Margarita or a Mexican beer and complimentary chips before choosing from the menu. Lunch and dinner choices come either à la carte or as a combination meal. The burritos and enchiladas are better when topped with a side of green chili. Try a sopapilla stuffed with chicken or beef, topped with a thick layer of sour cream and green chili. It's a slightly funky and immensely popular place with locals. Open 11 am–10:30 pm daily. Located south of town, one block from Hwy. 24. **715 Elm St.; 486-9930.**

La Cantina — $ to $$
 Chili rellenos, stuffed sopapillas and pork tamales are all popular entrées at La Cantina. All of the dishes are based on a southwestern style of cooking from northern New Mexico. The main dining room has a feeling of openness and is banked along one side by deep wooden booths. Some weekends all of the chairs and tables are pushed aside in favor of Spanish music and dancing. A pool table fills the area in front of the bar. Open daily 11 am–10 pm in summer; 4–10 pm in winter. One mile south of Leadville. **1942 Hwy. 24; 486-9927.**

SERVICES

Leadville/Lake County Chamber of Commerce—
 PO Box 861, 809 Harrison Ave., Leadville, CO 80461; (719) 486-3900.

San Luis Valley

High in the mountains of southern Colorado lies an often overlooked, oval-shaped alpine treasure—the San Luis Valley. Its rich and fascinating cultural heritage and extensive history combine with natural surroundings as beautiful as any area in the state, making the region worth considering for an extended stay. Ranging in elevation from 7,000 feet on the valley floor to the 14,345-foot summit of Blanca Peak, the geography is impressive. At 125 miles long and 50 miles wide, it's one of the largest valley basins in the world. To the east and south, the valley is bounded by the mighty Sangre de Cristo (Blood of Christ) Range, which is dominated by the Sierra Blanca Massif. Nestled up against these mountains are the ever-shifting Great Sand Dunes, perhaps the most unusual (and popular) geographical feature in the valley. To the north and west, the valley is enclosed by the San Juan, La Garita and Conejos-Brazos mountains. The Rio Grande originates in the nearby mountains and runs west through most of the valley on its way to New Mexico.

Long a buffer zone between New World colonial settlements, the valley has a history spiced with Indian, Anglo and particularly Spanish influences. The Hispanic culture is etched deeply in the valley even today; examples surface frequently in Spanish architecture (particularly in the Catholic churches), arts and crafts, local folklore and the pure Castillian dialect, which has changed little since the 16th century. Most of the towns, rivers, peaks and valleys have Spanish names.

The people in the San Luis Valley are some of the friendliest in the state. You'll find few pretensions, a lot of wholesome values and a relaxed attitude toward everyday life. The town of **Alamosa** is set in the center of the valley and, mainly for this reason, it's the area's largest community. It has served as a main shipping point for valley products to outside markets since its founding in 1878, when the Denver & Rio Grande Railroad arrived. Adams State College is located here, boasting an outstanding cross-country running team. From Alamosa, communities in the valley spread out in all directions.

Northeast of Alamosa, situated against the jutting Sangre de Cristo Range, lies the intriguing little settlement of **Crestone**. Originally a stage stop and mining area, the town has long been a summer getaway. More recently it has become a haven for the spiritual community. Apparently, Crestone was once a sacred Indian site where lines of planetary energy are said to converge. Today many people, from Tibetan monks to Shirley MacLaine, are snapping up real estate in the area.

West of Alamosa lie **Monte Vista** and **Del Norte**; both were early stage stops and trading towns and are agricultural areas today. To the east, the **Fort Garland Museum** remains a vivid example of life in frontier Colorado.

The vibrant Hispanic community of Colorado's oldest town, **San Luis**, evokes an atmosphere reminiscent of John Nichols's *Milagro Beanfield*

War. Located in the southern part of the valley at the foot of 14,047-foot Culebra Peak, this town has one of the last commons (*vegas*) in the country outside of the Boston area. The San Luis vega is an 860-acre tract of land that the entire community uses for grazing and crops. Culturally, the people of San Luis and the neighboring villages of adobe structures are more connected to New Mexico than to Colorado.

West of San Luis, the small town of **Manassa** was settled by Mormons who thought the local Indians were descendants of Manasseh, son of Joseph. It's also the birthplace of ex-heavyweight boxing champion Jack Dempsey (a.k.a. the "Manassa Mauler"). At the extreme south end of the valley, near the New Mexico border, **Antonito** acts as the depot for one of the best narrow-gauge railroad trips you can take in the country—the **Cumbres and Toltec Scenic Railroad**. Antonito was a railroad town built to house Anglos who were less than willing to assimilate into the much older Hispanic settlement of **Conejos**, a mile or two north of town. Our Lady of Guadalupe Church in Conejos is considered to be the oldest in the state, although residents of San Acacio beg to differ.

HISTORY

The Ute Indians controlled the San Luis Valley for hundreds of years before Europeans ever set foot in the area. Called the Blue Sky People by other tribes, the Utes followed herds and hunted throughout this territory.

Although some speculate that Spanish explorer, Francisco Coronado entered the San Luis Valley in 1540, the first recorded European visit to the valley was by another Spaniard, Don Diego de Vargas, in 1694. Eighty-five years later, the governor of New Mexico, Juan Bautista de Anza, passed through the San Luis Valley on a vengeful search for Comanche Indians who had raided northern New Mexico settlements. De Anza noted both the Rio Grande and Cochetopa Pass, a well-traveled crossing over the Continental Divide in the northwest section of the valley.

In the first half of the 1800s, Mexican government officials were anxious for settlers to populate what was then the Mexican frontier. They awarded large sections of land (known as land grants), much of it in what is now northern New Mexico and southern Colorado, to men who planned to develop the area. However, it was not until after the Mexican War that the first permanent settlement appeared in what eventually became the state of Colorado. In 1851 a group established the town of **San Luis**. A number of Hispanic settlements soon followed San Luis' lead. By that time the United States had gained possession of southern Colorado, and one of the responsibilities that beset the new government was protecting these frontier settlements from marauding Utes and other Indians from the south. In 1852 Fort Massachusetts was built, then replaced six years later by Fort Garland, which helped stabilize the valley until the fort was abandoned in 1883.

Rich mineral strikes in the valley at Summitville and Kerber Creek and in the San Juan mining district to the west helped bring about a rail connection with the Front Range by way of La Veta Pass in 1878. **Alamosa**, a railroad town and former stage stop, literally sprang up in a few days when most of the buildings were shipped in by flatcar as the railroad arrived. *Alamosa*, which means "cottonwood grove" in Spanish, was well named—a large number of cottonwood trees awaited the settlers. A particularly large tree by the Rio Grande served as the town gallows; early train passengers were frequently greeted by a corpse swinging from this giant cottonwood.

During the 1880s much of the valley along the Rio Grande was irrigated by canals, turning the naturally arid land into rich farmland especially suited to growing potatoes. Today the valley is used primarily for farming and ranching.

GETTING THERE

The San Luis Valley is located in south central Colorado. Alamosa is located 212 miles from Denver via Interstate 25 south to Walsenburg, then west on Hwy. 160 over La Veta Pass. The valley can also be reached via Hwy. 285 from the Upper Arkansas River Valley to the north. Buses service most towns in the valley with frequent stops in Alamosa.

The Alamosa Municipal Airport is serviced by Continental Express from Denver. Call 1-800-525-0280 for information and reservations.

—— MAJOR ATTRACTIONS ——

CUMBRES AND TOLTEC SCENIC RAILROAD

This narrow-gauge train is irresistible. The wail of the whistle, the hiss of the steam and the pungent aroma of coal smoke will linger in your memory long after your adventure. An added bonus is the lush, rolling countryside and inspiring rock formations along the way. The Cumbres and Toltec, America's longest and highest narrow-gauge railroad, begins its 64-mile journey to Chama, New Mexico, from the small burg of Antonito, Colorado. Its serpentine path takes you through Toltec Gorge of the Los Piños River and up to the 10,015-foot summit of Cumbres Pass, a pass once used by the Spanish to enter the San Luis Valley as early as the 16th century. From the summit, the train drops down a steep 4-percent grade into Chama. Along the way, the train crosses the Colorado–New Mexico border seven times!

This scenic railroad, now a National Historic Site, should not be missed if you are spending any time in the San Luis Valley.

History—

Tracks between Antonito and Chama were originally laid down in 1880 by the Denver & Rio Grande Railroad to connect their line to the rich mining camps in the San Juan Mountains of southwestern Colorado. After the gold and silver mining petered out in the San Juans, the need for the train fizzled, and eventually the route was discontinued by the railroad. In the late 1960s, a determined group from Colorado and New Mexico set out to fix the track. Volunteer gangs and train crews worked more than 2,000 hours fixing tracks and clearing obstacles. In September 1970 the refurbished track from Antonito to Chama was opened, and the train made its run.

Facts About the Train—

The Cumbres and Toltec Scenic Railroad is jointly owned by the states of Colorado and New Mexico. The train runs daily from mid-June through mid-Oct. The trip to Chama takes all day, stopping at the halfway point (Osier), where lunch is served for an extra charge. Afterward, many people take the train that returns to Antonito, while others push on to Chama and return to Antonito by van, which takes about an hour and a half.

Reservations are highly recommended. Overnight lodging packages in either Chama or Antonito can also be arranged. Group rates are available, and the caboose can be reserved for special parties. Cars equipped with wheelchair lifts are available for the handicapped, but reservations and notification must be made at least seven days in advance of the trip. **PO Box 668, Antonito, CO 81120; (719) 376-5483. In Chama, PO Box 789, Chama, NM 87520; (505) 756-2151.**

GREAT SAND DUNES NATIONAL MONUMENT

These sand dunes never cease to amaze visitors to the state and Coloradans alike. Like a piece of the Sahara Desert grafted onto the side of the snowcapped Sangre de Cristo Mountains, Great Sand Dunes National Monument looks out of place—almost inappropriate. The 50 square miles of dunes rise as high as 700 feet, and are one of the most visited places in the state during summer. Thanks to the hard work of valley residents, the Great Sand Dunes were proclaimed a national monument by President Hoover in 1932.

Providing all of the information you need for a stay at the monument, the visitors center has exhibits explaining the natural and human history of the area. Ask about walks, talks and campfire programs with rangers in the summer months. There is also a good bookstore here. Open Memorial Day to Labor Day 8 am–8 pm, winter 8 am–5 pm. Closed for federal winter holidays.

Getting There—From Alamosa, head east on Hwy. 160 for 14 miles to Hwy. 150. Turn left (north) and drive 16 miles to the monument entrance. **Great Sand Dunes National Monument, 11999 Hwy. 150, Mosca, CO 81146; (719) 378-2312.**

Geology—

There are many colorful explanations as to why the sand dunes exist, but the real reason is not nearly so interesting. Water and wind scour the surrounding mountains, breaking much of the rock down into sand. The sand is blown or carried by rivers down into the valley. Once in the valley, prevailing winds carry the sand northeast to where the Sangre de Cristos rise 4,000 feet from the valley floor. Acting as a natural trap, these mountains create such a high barrier that the wind loses its punch, dropping the sand and thus forming the dunes.

CAMPING

Within the monument, **Piñon Flats Campground** is the only camping area. It's open from Apr. to Oct. on a first-come, first-served basis. Fee charged. Pay for the campsite at the entrance station in summer and at the visitor's center in winter. **Great Sand Dunes Oasis and RV Park**, located just outside the monument entrance, offers hookups, showers, etc. See the Camping section for more information.

FOUR-WHEEL-DRIVE TRIPS

Medano Primitive Rd. follows Medano Creek up along the edge of the dunes for a few miles. Four-wheel-drive vehicles can follow the road, but are not allowed to drive off it. Because the sand creates traction difficulties, air needs to be let out of the tires. Near the campground there is an air hose for refilling tires. The road is open from May through Sept. Trips are offered by the **Great Sand Dunes Oasis Campground and RV Park** located just outside the monument entrance. Contact **Great**

Sand Dunes Oasis, Mosca, CO 81146; (719) 378-2222.

HIKING AND BACKPACKING

The sand dunes' location next to the Sangre de Cristos makes for some unique hiking and backpacking opportunities. Permits are free but are required for all backcountry camping. Pick them up at the visitors center. No open fires are permitted in the backcountry.

For additional information about hiking and backpacking in and around the monument, contact the visitors center.

On the Dunes—

The beckoning power of the dunes is amazing. As soon as many people pull into the parking lot, an overpowering desire to conquer the sand overtakes them. During the midst of tourist season, visitors dressed in Bermuda shorts wade across Medano Creek and scamper all over the dunes, lost in their own thoughts about Lawrence of Arabia and the French Foreign Legion. From the top of the dunes, there are spectacular views of the San Juan Mountains to the west and the Sangre de Cristos to the east. The problem is that many people don't realize what hot and thirsty work dune trekking can be. *Be sure to take something to drink and bring along shoes, sunscreen and a hat.* Even worse, many people don't realize how vulnerable they are up on the dunes. The dunes do get violent thunderstorms: proof positive is on display at the visitor's center, where you can see exhibits of sand that has been fused into big globs

by lightning. *If you are up on the dunes and a thunder-storm is approaching, get off them.*

When Bruce and I were up on the highest dune, we saw a storm approaching from the southwest. It looked ugly. We got down as fast as we could, encountering people who were on their way up, oblivious to the danger and unwilling to take any friendly advice. When we got to our car the storm hit, bringing lightning and marble-sized hail. Where do you hide from pelting hailstones when you are on the dunes? I guess you can bury your head in the sand like an ostrich.

Along Medano Creek—

Flowing out of the Sangre de Cristos from the east, Medano Creek makes its way down a river valley and runs into the dunes. The creek then angles left, paralleling the edge of the dunes all the way past the picnic area and campground, eventually disappearing into the dry soil of the San Luis Valley.

When you approach Medano Creek you will notice a rather unusual phenomenon—waves come down the creek about every 30 seconds! These "bores" are created by sand build-up on the bottom of the creek, forming anti-dunes. The water pressure builds up, the anti-dunes break and water comes gushing downstream.

A primitive road follows the creek upstream along the dunes and then up into Rio Grande National Forest, passing numerous old log cabins along the way. Eventually the road reaches Medano Pass, where views back down to the dunes are spectacular, as are those of the Wet Mountain Valley to the east.

Mosca Pass—

A 3.5-mile trail heads up to the summit of Mosca Pass, providing great views of the San Luis Valley and the Wet Mountain Valley. This is the pass Lt. Zebulon Pike used when he crossed over into the San Luis Valley for the first time in 1807. The trail follows Mosca Creek up through juniper and piñon pine. Look for the trailhead on the right side of the road near the first picnic area.

FESTIVALS AND EVENTS

Sunshine Festival

early June

This is a two-day festival held in Cole Park along the Rio Grande in Alamosa. Arts and crafts booths are set up; food, music and dance highlight the festivities. The Sunshine Festival could be a nice chance to see some of the valley weavings, but don't plan your vacation around it. **(719) 589-3681.**

Ski-Hi Stampede

end of July

An annual event, this three-day pro rodeo has been a tradition since 1921. Chuck wagon dinner, carnival and rodeo events. **835 1st Ave., Monte Vista; (719) 852-2055.**

San Luis Valley Renegade Rendezvous

early August

In the tradition of the mountain men of the early 1800s, modern men (and women) don their buckskin outfits and coonskin caps, pick up their muzzle loaders and hatchets and head for the rendezvous in Del Norte. The rendezvous gets modern-day Jim Bridgers together for events like muzzle loading and knife and tomahawk throwing. Fiddlers encourage people to dance around the fire; booths display cottage industry crafts and offer "mountain man" food. Camp out and enjoy the activities at a festival you definitely won't find in New Jersey. For information call **(719) 657-3113** or **(719) 657-2845.**

OUTDOOR ACTIVITIES

BIKING

MOUNTAIN BIKING

As of this guidebook's publication date, there is no organized mountain bike trail system in the San Luis Valley or the surrounding Rio Grande National Forest. But this is not to say there aren't any good trails; the southwestern section of the forest (west of Antonito in the Cumbres Pass area and up the Conejos River) has several. For more information about Rio Grande National Forest trail possibilities, talk to the **Rio Grande National Forest Headquarters, 1803 W. Hwy. 160, Monte Vista, CO 81144; (719) 852-5941.**

For bike rentals and trail information, go to **Kristi Mountain Sports** and ask for Allen McFadden or Eric Burke. **7565 Hwy. 160, Alamosa; (719) 589-9759.**

FISHING

Conejos River—

Meaning "rabbits" in Spanish, this stream flows southeast through the beautiful Conejos Valley from Platoro Reservoir (good fishing, boat rentals available) to Antonito, eventually merging with the Rio Grande southeast of Alamosa. The best and most scenic water west of Antonito is paralleled by Forest Rd. 250 within the boundaries of Rio Grande National Forest. The stream is about 50 feet wide and is best fished with chest waders. On the upper Conejos you'll catch good-sized brown trout for the most part; the lower areas east of Antonito are flanked by cottonwoods and can be good for rainbows, browns and even an occasional northern pike. After runoff this clear-running stream can provide excellent dry fly-fishing. When it is running murky your best bet is a caddis fly or stone fly imitation. Many excellent tributaries flow into the upper Conejos from the south; trails provide good fishing access to Elk Creek and the South Fork of the Conejos and on up to high lakes.

La Jara Reservoir—

Several small streams flow into La Jara Reservoir, helping it maintain a population of small, pan-sized brook trout. Motorboats are allowed on the rather large reservoir and provide the best way to get around. No rentals; primitive campsites. La Jara Reservoir is located 13 miles south of Alamosa on Hwy. 285.

Rio Grande—

The Rio Grande, at 1,887 miles long, is the second longest river in the country. It is also a diverse river system offering good fishing during its flow through Colorado. The stretch from just above the town of South Fork downstream to Del Norte has been given a Gold Medal designation. Only one-third of this 22.5-mile stretch is open to the public. It can be the inspiration for a good float trip, with large brown trout feeding near the banks. For more information, see the **Creede** Fishing section. Between Monte Vista and Alamosa, a large population of northern pike provides a lot of excitement. They like the slow water near weeds and other obstructions and feed on both flies and lures. Pike have razorlike teeth, so be sure to use a steel leader or 50-pound test nylon tippet and use care in removing the hook.

Colorado
Squawfish

Sanchez Reservoir—

This reservoir, 5 miles south of the town of San Luis, has been gaining the respect of many skeptics. The fishing has improved markedly in recent years, especially for 30- to 40-pound northern pike. Check out the freezer at Alamosa Sporting Goods for a firsthand look at some recent catches. There are also some walleye and yellow perch, but no trout. Boat ramp available; primitive camping by the shore.

FOUR-WHEEL-DRIVE TRIPS

The valley is not well known for four-wheel-drive roads, however, there is a worthwhile route in Great Sand Dunes National Monument (see the Major Attractions section). Also, see the **Creede** chapter for some great nearby ideas and the Hayden Pass write-up in the **Upper Arkansas Valley** chapter.

HIKING AND BACKPACKING

Blanca Peak—

The Mount Blanca Massif, located in the Sangre de Cristo Range northeast of Alamosa, is the dominant feature in the San Luis Valley. Without many foothills around it, the mountain shoots up thousands of feet from the valley floor, providing a stunning view that has held Indians, Hispanics and Anglos spellbound for centuries. Blanca Peak is such a big mountain, at 14,345 feet, that it's hard to believe it is only the fourth tallest in the state. Alamosa radio announcer Donald Bennet was so convinced that the peak was the tallest, he began crazy promotional stunts to get the state to re-evaluate Blanca's ranking. In 1935–36, Bennet led a group of determined locals to the summit of the peak through waist-deep snow for an Easter service. He also tried erecting a 50-foot pole on the summit, but that project failed miserably.

The actual climb up the peak is not that difficult for an average person, but the trail takes a bit of effort to reach. Unless you have a good four-wheel-drive vehicle and a full day, you will need to camp along the way. From Alamosa, head east on Hwy. 160 for 14 miles to the road to the sand dunes, then turn north (left). Proceed about 3.2 miles to a dirt road heading off to the right, up into the mountains. Turn onto the dirt road and drive about 1.5 miles northeast to a parking lot. Passenger cars should park here—the road ahead is not maintained and is extremely punishing even for four-wheel-drive vehicles. From the parking lot it's about 4.5 miles up to Lake Como. From Lake Como the easy trail crosses alpine tundra to Blue Lakes and then to Crater Lake, just a half mile above Blue Lakes. From Crater Lake the trail starts climbing a rocky slope up to the saddle between Ellingwood Point and Blanca Peak. From the saddle, head straight up to the 14,345-foot summit of Blanca Peak. *Hike early to avoid afternoon thunderstorms.*

Crestone Trails—

To explore the northeastern part of Rio Grande National Forest in the Sangre de Cristo Range, there is no better jumping-off point than the town of Crestone. From town, head north for a mile, then northeast on the dirt Forest Rd. 950 past North Crestone Creek Campground and begin hiking up along the creek. After a couple of miles there is a fork in the road. The left fork heads up to Groundhog Basin and Venable Pass for views of the San Luis Valley and east down into the Wet Mountain Valley. The right fork (Trail No. 744) turns southeast and heads about 3 miles up to North Crestone Lake. To the south 13,900-foot Mt. Adams blocks the view of Crestone Peak and Crestone Needle, two of the most treacherous 14,000-foot peaks in the state.

Rio Grande National Forest—

This part of the forest does not get a lot of use, but it offers worthwhile hiking and backpacking opportunities. Easily accessible from Del Norte, Monte Vista and Antonito, this area boasts rolling hills, river canyons and thick forests of pine and aspen. Altitudes are comparatively low, with the larger peaks reaching only 12,000 feet. The Continental Divide forms the western edge of the forest, with San Juan National Forest just over the divide. A trail follows the divide from just north of the Tierra Amarilla Grant, past Wolf Creek Pass. Access to the under-used South San Juan Wilderness Area is fairly easy from the Rio Grande side of the divide.

For more information about these areas of Rio Grande National Forest and other trail possibilities, contact: **Rio Grande National Forest Headquarters, 1803 W. Hwy. 160, Monte Vista, CO 81144; (719) 852-5941** or the **Conejos Peak Ranger District Office at 21461 Hwy. 285, La Jara, CO 81140; (719) 274-5193.**

Sand Dunes National Monument—

For information about hiking on the dunes and up Medano Creek to Medano Pass and up Mosca Pass, see the Major Attractions section.

RIVER FLOATING

The upper Rio Grande offers some floating. See the River Floating section in the **Creede** chapter for more information.

SKIING
CROSS-COUNTRY SKIING

For the most part, the San Luis Valley offers much less in the way of organized cross-country trail systems than do many other parts of the state. Though this is not the best place to plan a cross-country ski vacation, there are some trails that can be good, depending on the snow.

Bonanza—

Located in the extreme northern part of the valley, the Bonanza area is a great wintertime ski-touring destination. Fairly flat terrain and numerous stands of aspen and pine accent this old mining area. Many small summer cabins have been refurbished in this settlement, which was founded in 1865 by soldiers from Fort Garland and later became a mining camp in the 1880s. The population of the Bonanza district is reported to have been between 10,000 and 40,000 in its prime.

To reach the area from Alamosa, head north on Hwy. 17 for 55 miles to Villa Grove and turn left onto the dirt road to Bonanza. Drive about 25 miles to Bonanza and proceed up above the settlement for a couple more miles. For specific trail ideas and snow conditions, contact the **Saguache Ranger District Office, PO Box 67, Saguache, CO 81149; (719) 655-2553.**

Cumbres Pass—

From Antonito, Hwy. 17 snakes its way 39 miles over La Manga and Cumbres passes to the New Mexico border, offering some pretty good areas to cross-country ski. The snowfall is not much, but it does sustain interest among people in the region, both from northern New Mexico and southern Colorado. The terrain between the two passes is perfect for ski touring, made especially good as a result of a forest fire in 1879 that left the area open and now dotted with spruce trees. *Avalanches can be a problem so use extreme care.* Trujillo Meadows is an excellent area to focus on; see Camping section. For maps and trail information, contact the **Conejos Peak Ranger District Office, 21461 Hwy. 285, La Jara, CO 81140; (719) 274-5193.**

Rentals and Information—
    Kristy Mountain Sports rents cross-country equipment in winter. **7565 Hwy. 160, Alamosa; (719) 589-9759.**

DOWNHILL SKIING
For information on the nearby **Wolf**

Creek Ski Area, see the **Pagosa Springs** chapter.

SWIMMING
Splashland—
    Though it resembles a regular pool found in Anytown, USA, Splashland is actually fed by geothermal water. This water flows continuously through the pool, providing a complete changeover every eight hours. Showers, rental suits and towels. Wading pool for the kids. This is a great place to cool off after a trip to the sand dunes. Small fee. Hours are Sun. 12–6 pm, Mon.–Tues. 10 am–6:30 pm, closed Wed., Thurs.–Sat. 10 am–6:30 pm. One mile north of Alamosa on **Hwy. 17. (719) 589-6307.**

—— SEEING AND DOING ——

HOT SPRINGS
Valley View Hot Springs—
    During weekdays this recently opened series of natural mineral pools provides a relaxing soak to anyone interested (members only on weekends). Locals in the valley rave about it, but the bashful should be warned: bathing suits are optional. Valley View Hot Springs is located in the upper end of the valley, northeast of the now-defunct Mineral Hot Springs. At one time a going concern of its own, Mineral Hot Springs had a curse put on it by the Ute Indians, who forewarned that the springs would never make any money. The springs have since dried up. Let's hope a similar fate does not await Valley View, with its prime location against the west slope of the Sangre de Cristo Mountains. You can soak in the large developed pool or hike up the mountainside to a smaller tub. Overnight accommodations ($) are available in a dorm room or private cabin. Bring your own sleeping bag. To reach the hot springs from Alamosa, drive 50 miles north on Hwy. 17 to where it meets with Hwy. 285. At this junction, turn right on the dirt road and head east toward the mountains for 8 miles.

Small fee charged. Open 7 am–11 pm daily. **PO Box 175, Villa Grove, CO 81155; (719) 256-4315.**

MUSEUMS AND GALLERIES
ALAMOSA
Rio Grande Art Market—
    There is no better gallery that exhibits and sells traditional as well as contemporary arts and crafts of the San Luis Valley. Pottery, jewelry, traditional Hispanic wood carvings and fine weavings highlight the works on display. Wool rugs woven by nationally renowned Eppie Archuleta and her family perhaps draw the most people to the gallery. Many of the traditional arts and crafts are in danger of dying out, due to rapid social changes in the 20th century and shrinking numbers in the small villages of the valley. Do your part to preserve these priceless aspects of the valley's cultural heritage by visiting the gallery and buying something that catches your eye. Hours are Mon.–Sat. 10 am–8 pm. On the corner of **Main St.** and **State Ave., Alamosa; (719) 589-5557.**

DEL NORTE
Rio Grand County Museum and Cultural Center—

Moved recently from its previous home at the county courthouse, the Del Norte Museum houses some fine historic relics. One highlight is the display of rock art along with background information. Throughout the summer months, regional and local artists are in residence; every two weeks lectures are given on the valley's wildlife and social history. Open 10 am–5 pm Mon.–Sat., May–Sept.; open part time during the rest of the year. **580 Oak St., PO Box 430, Del Norte, CO 81132; (719) 657-2847.**

FORT GARLAND
Fort Garland Museum—

Twenty-six miles east of Alamosa on Hwy. 160 sits Fort Garland, one of the most famous outposts on the frontier and now a museum run by the Colorado Historical Society. It should not be missed.

As settlers pushed into the San Luis Valley from the south, protection from the Indians and a strong military presence in the area became priorities of the US military. In 1852 Fort Massachusetts was built a few miles north of the present site of Fort Garland. Fort Massachusetts proved vulnerable to attack, and the swampy area it occupied made everyone ill, so in 1858 Fort Garland was built to replace it.

During the Civil War, Union soldiers from Fort Garland were sent south into New Mexico, where they had a bloody battle with Confederate troops at Glorietta Pass. The Union side won, and their victory essentially eliminated any serious threat to the American West by the rebels.

Life in the valley became difficult for the settlers in 1863 when two Mexican brothers, the "Bloody Espinozas," began a murderous reign of terror. Supposedly, the older of the two brothers was inspired by the Virgin Mary in a dream to go out and make life hell for the "gringos." A $1,500 reward was offered to put an end to the killings. Tom Tobin, a local army guide and mountain man, along with a few soldiers, set out from the fort and in no time tracked down and killed the older Espinoza brother and his cousin (the younger brother had already been killed). Feeling a need for proof of his kill, Tobin cut off Espinoza's head, took it back to the fort and threw it at the feet of the commander. When informed that he needed to wait until the Colorado General Assembly reconvened in order to collect his reward, Tobin put the head in a jar of alcohol so it would keep. Thirty years went by before Tobin finally collected his reward.

Following the Civil War, only a volunteer regiment was retained at the fort. Kit Carson commanded the fort in 1866, but left only a year later. The fort continued to play a crucial stabilizing role in Colorado's history until 1883, by which time the Utes had been relocated to reservations in southwestern Colorado and northeastern Utah.

Today the reconstructed fort is a fascinating place to visit and get a feel for Colorado history. Anglo, Indian and Hispanic artifacts fill the many rooms, much as they did during the days when the fort was considered the Siberia of US Army outposts. One visitor to the fort in the 1860s said he was "struck with commiseration for all the unfortunate officers and men condemned to live in so desolate a place." Believe me, it's not that bad now. Be sure to check out the old stagecoach and the list of rules posted by the Barlow and Sanderson stage company that serviced the San Luis Valley before the train arrived. Tips like "spit with the wind, not against it" and "no hogging the buffalo robes" prove that some people in the Wild West cared about manners.

Open Memorial Day to Labor Day; Mon.–Sat. 10 am–5 pm, Sun. 1–5 pm. Small fee charged. **PO Box 368, Fort Garland, CO 81133; (719) 379-3512.**

MANASSA
Jack Dempsey Museum—

Every little town in America dreams of a local boy (or girl) going out into the world and making good, putting the town on the map. A local boy from Manassa,

Colorado, did just that. Jack Dempsey, born in Manassa in 1895, went on to become the heavyweight boxing champion of the world. At age 14, Jack began fighting at mining camps under the name "Kid Blackie." When he was 24, he took the heavyweight crown from Jess Willard. In 1950 the Associated Press voted the "Manassa Mauler" the best heavyweight of the first half of the 20th century. Until Jack's death in 1983, he kept in close touch with his family and friends in Manassa.

The pride of the community shows itself in the Jack Dempsey Museum, a one-room log cabin sitting near the spot where Jack grew up. Boxing mementos and pictures donated by locals and the Dempsey family are on display. Be sure to take a look at the old postcards that have been on the display rack since the place opened in the mid-1960s. Located in downtown Manassa, across the street from the post office. Open daily 9 am–6 pm from the end of May through Sept. **PO Box 130, Manassa, CO 81141.**

SAGUACHE
Saguache County Museum—
If you are passing through Saguache, you should visit this museum which houses a little of everything, including what is said to be the largest Indian artifact collection in the country. You will feel as if you're rummaging around in someone's attic. Established in 1959, it is sprawled out in the old town jail and the schoolhouse next door. The jail cell holds the Alferd E. Packer display, in honor of this notorious cannibalistic Coloradan who was held briefly in Saguache in 1874. (He escaped from the jail.) Small fee. Open Memorial Day through Labor Day, 10 am–5 pm daily. Located 35 miles north of Monte Vista.

SANFORD
Pike's Stockade—
In the winter of 1806–1807, Lt. Zebulon Pike and his men came west over Mosca Pass down into the San Luis Valley at the sand dunes. From there the weary group made their way south to what Pike thought

was the Red River of Texas. They built a stockade nearby, raised the American flag and settled in for the remainder of the winter. However, Pike, the Inspector Clouseau of American explorers, had made a major navigational error—what he thought was the Red River was really the Rio Grande. He had built a fort and raised the American flag on Mexican soil (Spanish at that time). It was not long before a detachment of Spanish troops arrived, arrested Pike and his men, and escorted them to Santa Fe and later all the way down to Chihuahua. Pike and his men were eventually released at the US border with the promise that they never set foot in Mexico (New Spain) again.

In the early 1960s the Colorado Historical Society built a re-creation of Pike's stockade on the land where the original once stood. You would have to be a truly diligent historian to make a trip here worth your while. It's very run-down and the site is infested with mosquitos and snakes. In addition, it is almost impossible to find, as the roads are not marked and the signs to the stockade were taken down years ago. At this point, the best we can say is that it is located about 5 miles northeast of Sanford. Drive to Sanford and ask directions.

SAN LUIS
San Luis Museum, Cultural and Commercial Center—
Hispanic culture of southern Colorado comes to life in this excellent museum in Colorado's oldest town. The building's 17th-century New World Spanish architecture blends with solar technology as an example of old ways coming together with new. The museum contains a wonderful collection of santos (Hispanic religious items), including wood carvings and, most notably, a morada (where the Penitentes gathered for meetings and worship). Downstairs, the award-winning exhibit La Cultura Constante de San Luis vividly conveys the Hispanic culture of southern Colorado, especially that of the San Luis Valley. Open Memorial Day–Labor Day Mon–Fri. 8:30 am–4:30 pm, Sat–Sun 11

am–5 pm. Closed weekends the rest of the year (open Sat. until the end of Oct.). **402 Church St., San Luis, CO 81152; (719) 672-3611.**

ROCK ART

There are a number of places in the San Luis Valley where ancient Indians left their mark in the form of rock art. Many of them are on private property. An impressive wall of pictographs located on La Garita (L-Cross) Ranch is worth a look. If you are interested, the gate key and directions to the ranch can be obtained at La Garita Store in, as you may have guessed, La Garita. By the way, the store serves great hamburgers. North of Monte Vista, **(719) 754-3755.**

SCENIC DRIVES

Alamosa–Monte Vista National Wildlife Refuge—
See the Wildlife section.

Cochetopa Pass—
Used by the Indians, mountain men and early settlers as an easy crossing of the Continental Divide, Cochetopa Pass can be driven today by passenger cars. Cochetopa (an Indian word meaning "buffalo crossing") rises to 10,022 feet, crossing to the west, then eventually branching north to Gunnison or southwest over Los Piños Pass to Lake City. Capt. John Gunnison crossed Cochetopa Pass in 1853 on his expedition to search for a transcontinental railroad route. The Los Piños Indian agency was established on the west side of the pass in 1868 and for years served as the central government post for dealing with the Utes. To reach Cochetopa Pass from Alamosa, drive 17 miles northwest on Hwy. 160 to Monte Vista, then head north on Hwy. 285 for 35 miles to Saguache. From Saguache, head west on Hwy. 114 (North Pass Rd.) until you see the sign for the Cochetopa Pass turn-off on the left. Open in summer only.

Cumbres Pass—
Roughly following the route of the Cumbres and Toltec Scenic Railroad, Hwy. 17 over Cumbres Pass is a beautiful drive, especially in the fall when the aspen turn color. The road passes through rolling hills and the Conejos River Valley of Rio Grande National Forest. To reach the road from Alamosa, drive 28 miles south on Hwy. 285 to Antonito and then 35 miles west on Hwy. 17 to the summit.

WILDLIFE
Alamosa–Monte Vista National Wildlife Refuge—
Birders will be pleased to know that the San Luis Valley is one of the best bird habitats in the state. Canals and marshland near the Rio Grande make this area a popular place for many migratory birds, such as whooping cranes, sandhill cranes, avocets and teals. In winter many hawks, bald eagles and golden eagles make their home here.

The US Fish and Wildlife Service oversees two large tracts of land, offering a self-guiding loop drive through the refuge complex during winter, spring and summer. Headquarters are located at the Alamosa unit, 4 miles east of Alamosa on Hwy. 160 and 2 miles south on El Rancho Ln. The Monte Vista unit is located 6 miles south of Monte Vista on Hwy. 15. For more information contact **Refuge Manager, Alamosa–Monte Vista National Wildlife Refuge, PO Box 1148, Alamosa, CO 81101; (719) 589-4021.**

WHERE TO STAY

ACCOMMODATIONS
ALAMOSA

Alamosa is by far the largest town in the valley and serves as a major intersection for traffic heading to all four points on the compass. So, naturally, there are quite a few motels to choose from. Every major chain appears to be represented. (Warning: the Holiday Inn has its lobby next to the indoor pool, and the smell of chlorine is almost overpowering.)

Cottonwood Inn — $$

This charming bed and breakfast was a welcome surprise, found while poking around Alamosa. Owners Julie Mordecai and George Sellman opened for business in the summer of 1988 after painstakingly refurbishing this fine old corner-lot home. The handsome wood trim, local art and tasteful antiques all accent the comfortable feel inside. There are currently five rooms available, two of which have have private baths. The parlor is equipped with a VCR and a movie library. Julie and George, both teachers, are quite knowledgeable about the San Luis Valley and can offer very good advice. A stay at the Cottonwood is highly recommended. Full breakfasts made from local products are health oriented or traditional. No smoking or pets. Ten percent discount for bicyclists, seniors and groups. **123 San Juan Ave., Alamosa, CO 81101; (719) 589-3882.**

DEL NORTE
Windsor Hotel — $$

According to the current owners, this is the oldest operating hotel in the state. Built in 1872 as a "Gentlemen's Hotel," the Windsor has recently undergone a massive restoration that isn't quite complete. Locals marvel at the fact that the new owners have been able to accomplish what they've done, which has included a six-month stripping and refinishing of the wooden floor downstairs. At one time or another the hotel housed a mortuary, a liv-ery stable, a slaughterhouse, a barber shop and a bordello. A stairway leading up from the back alley provided a discreet entrance to Madame Pulaski's Massage Parlor. Currently, eight rooms upstairs are available to guests, with more to be opened soon. Thirteen-foot-high ceilings and many original fixtures give the rooms a rustic charm. Full breakfast is served each morning and it's included in the room price. **605 Grand Ave., PO Box 762, Del Norte, CO 81132; (719) 657-2668.**

MONTE VISTA
Monte Villa Inn — $$ to $$$

Squeaky clean, a place made for the white-glove test, Monte Villa Inn offers spotless rooms for reasonable prices. Built in 1929, this restored, 40-room hotel features rooms with king-, queen- and double-sized beds, each room a little different in size and color from the next. Be sure to ride the original cage-style elevator. Though this place is so clean you could probably eat off the floor, why bother? Downstairs there is a breakfast room/dining room and lounge. The owner of the hotel assured us, "The dining room serves the best Mexican food and the best steaks in the state and the lounge serves the best margarita in the state." You'd "best" decide for yourself. Ask about the bed and breakfast package and group rates. **925 First Ave., Monte Vista, CO 81144; (719) 852-5166.**

Movie Manor — $$

Ever enjoyed a drive-in movie from the comfort of your own motel room? I didn't think so. George Kelloff's Movie Manor is Americana gone crazy. "It's the only one of its kind in the world," George beamed. So unique is it that it was included in a PBS special. Two and a half miles west of Monte Vista, Kelloff's Drive-In has been showing movies on its big screen since 1955. Back in the early days, when the Kelloff family lived over the snack bar, George and his wife would tuck the kids in and scoot their beds over to the window so they could see the movie. As George explained, "I started thinking, hey! Why not build a motel at the back of the drive-in so everybody can do this?" The rest is history.

The first addition of this two-story motel was completed in 1964 and has been added on to more than once since then. The rooms are comfortable (Best Western Motel), and every window looks out at the big screen. A speaker is built into the ceiling and it's free with the room. Unfortunately, double features ceased a few years ago because, as George put it, "The locals [watching the movies from their cars] got a little liquored up and this disturbed the guests." Movies are not shown in winter. There is also a lounge and the Academy Award Dining Room on the premises. If unique is what you seek, look no further. **2830 W. Hwy. 160, Monte Vista, CO 81144; (719) 852-5921.**

SAN LUIS
El Convento Bed & Breakfast — $$

Built in 1905 as a school and then used as a convent, this building has recently undergone a complete restoration and is open for business as one of the most interesting bed and breakfasts in the state. Under the direction of Father Pat Valdez of the Sangre de Cristo Catholic Church, El Convento ("the convent" in Spanish) offers four upstairs bedrooms with a kiva fireplace in the corner of two of the rooms. Thick adobe walls and 10-foot-high ceilings give the place a homey and roomy feel. Downstairs is an artists' center where local artisans practice and sell their works. Breakfast is served in the dining room each morning. For a quiet, slightly different overnight experience in the state's oldest town, try a night at El Convento. **PO Box 326, San Luis, CO 81152; (719) 672-3685.**

CAMPING

For some reason (maybe it's our imaginations) there seem to be a lot of private campgrounds in the San Luis Valley. KOA and KOA-clone road signs pop up all over the place. It's truly an RV heaven. In addition to the impressive representation of private campgrounds, Rio Grande National Forest offers numerous possibilities.

In Rio Grande National Forest—

In the southwest section of the national forest there are a number of campgrounds. Forest Rd. 250, which is the major access road to this area, heads west along the Alamosa River 12 miles south of Monte Vista from Hwy. 15. Thirteen miles up Forest Rd. 250, just past Terrace Reservoir, is **Alamosa Campground** at 8,600 feet, with 10 sites and no fee. Another 21 miles up the road is **Stunner Campground** at 10,000 feet, with 10 sites and no fee charged.

From Antonito, head west into Rio Grande National Forest on Hwy. 17 for 15 miles to **Mogote Campground** at 8,400 feet, with 20 sites (fee charged). Eight miles farther up Hwy. 17 is where Forest Rd. 250 heads off to the right (northwest), reaching **Elk Creek Campground** at 8,700 feet. There are 14 sites, and a fee is charged. Five more miles up Forest Rd. 250 is **Spectacle Lake Campground**, with 24 sites and a fee charged. Another mile will take you to **Conejos Campground**, with 16 sites and a fee. **Lake Fork Campground** is yet another 9 miles up Forest Rd. 250. At 9,500 feet it has 10 sites and charges a fee. **Mix Lake Campground** at Platoro Reservoir is another 5.5 miles up the road. Boats are available. There are 22 sites, and a fee is charged.

Near the top of Cumbres Pass (about 35 miles west of Antonito on Hwy. 17), turn right onto the Trujillo Meadows Rd. and proceed about 4 miles to the **Trujillo Meadows Campground**. There are 25 sites; a fee is charged. Trujillo Meadows Reservoir has a boat ramp.

Two miles south of Monte Vista on Hwy. 15, and then right on Forest Rd. 265 for 13.5 miles, will lead you to **Rock Creek Campground** and **Comstock Campground**, offering eight sites and 13 sites respectively. No fee.

Up in the northeastern part of the valley near Crestone is **North Crestone Peak Campground**. There are 13 sites, and a fee is charged. From Crestone head 1.5 miles northeast on Forest Rd. 950. This is a great place to watch for bighorn sheep. They have been reintroduced to various parts of Rio Grande National Forest and are doing well. Look for them up on top of the rocky canyon walls.

Great Sand Dunes National Monument—
See Major Attractions.

San Luis Vicinity—
Rito Seco Park is a piece of land donated to the people of San Luis by the Forbes Ranch. There is primitive camping available and no fee. Located 7 miles northeast of San Luis (Hwy. 150 to County Rd. 1690; turn right). **Sanchez Reservoir**, located 7 miles southeast of San Luis on Hwy. 242, has 28 primitive sites for year-round camping; no fee.

Private Campgrounds—
Located 21 miles east of Alamosa on Hwy. 160, **Blanca RV Park** has full hookups, showers and a laundromat. **Blanca; (719) 379-3201.**

Located just outside the entrance to Great Sand Dunes National Monument, **Great Sand Dunes Oasis and RV Park** offers RV hookups, cabins, showers and other services, including four-wheel-drive trips into the monument. **Sand Dunes Rd., Hwy. 150; (719) 378-2222.**

The **KOA Kampground** in Alamosa offers full hookups and showers. **6900 Juniper Ln., Alamosa; (719) 589-9757.**

WHERE TO EAT

ALAMOSA
Out House 'N' — $$ to $$$
Anyone in the restaurant business who calls themselves the "Out House 'N' " and still manages to pack in the customers must be doing something right. Located on the east end of Alamosa, this restaurant has the best pizza in town. You may also want to try their steak and seafood meals. Out House 'N', as you may have guessed, has a very rustic, western atmosphere. Reservations are probably not necessary but can be taken after 4 pm. Open Tues.–Thurs. 4–10 pm, Fri.–Sat. 4–10:30 pm, Sun. 4–10 pm, Mon. closed. **12536 Hwy. 160, Alamosa; 589-4708.**

Lara's Soft Spoken Restaurant — $$
Lara's is a very popular lunch spot and also a fine dinner choice. Jumbo salads and sandwiches keep the locals coming in for a quick midday bite. The dinner menu is highlighted by surf and turf entrees and Italian dishes such as fettucini and chicken parmesan. The obligatory Mexican food is available. Mark Lara, the owner, recently completed an outside beer garden, which is a bit unusual juxtaposed with an Italian restaurant. But when you're served a cold brew here on a hot afternoon, who cares?

As for the origin of the restaurant's name, Mark says it is in honor of his mother, who died when he was very young. She was said to have been a very soft-spoken woman. The name has attracted business from curious tourists wondering about the name; some think it's a play on "Speakeasy." Mark has fun with visitors, telling some of them that "Soft Spoken" was an Indian princess (among other stories). Open Tues.–Sat. 9 am–9 pm, Sun. 9 am–3 pm, Mon. 11 am–2 pm. **801 State Ave., Alamosa; 589-6769.**

Bauer's Campus Pancake House and Restaurant — $
This is the breakfast hangout for the locals. There are no frills at the Campus—just good pancakes and waffles; gigantic cinnamon rolls and egg dishes smothered with green chili are also standouts. If you are accustomed to saying grace before eating, you can choose from among three prayers printed on the menu. Locals meet for breakfast and sit around for an hour or two, chatting at their tables as the ceiling fans slowly rotate above. The Campus is also open for dinner; meals include down-

home specials like veal, chicken, roast beef and liver and onions. Discounts for seniors. Open daily 5 am–2 pm. **431 Poncha Ave., Alamosa; 589-4202.**

El Charro Cafe — $

El Charro Cafe is a standout Mexican restaurant in an area that has many to choose from. It's a small, intimate place with quick service. Neon lights around the windowsills, small orange booths and a jukebox are about the only adornments. You get the feeling from the food and the people who run the place that they really take pride in what they do and what they serve. For over 50 years Ike Lucero's family has run El Charro Cafe, and they have it down to a science. The chili rellenos are delicious and HOT! Also consider the chorizo Mexicano con huevos or an enchilada. Alcohol is not served here. For a margarita or a cold cerveza try the better known Oscar's on the main street. El Charro Cafe's hours are Tues.–Thurs. 11 am–11 pm, Fri.–Sat. 11 am–3 am, Sun. 11 am–11:30 pm. **421 6th St., Alamosa; 589-2262.**

CENTER
Farmer's Buffet — $

Many valley locals head to the Farmer's Buffet for the beef entrees and, especially, for the acclaimed Mexican food. It's a bit out of the way but worth it if you like large portions and highly seasoned food. Located 12 miles north of Monte Vista, then 2 miles east. Open Tues.–Thurs. 7 am–8 pm, Fri.–Sat. 7 am–9 pm. Closed Sun.–Mon. **213 S. Worth; 754-3477.**

CRESTONE
The Bistro — $$

This place is well known for its pastries and wholesome "holistic" food. Located in Crestone, The Bistro is especially popular during good weather when customers can enjoy the sun deck. Be sure to take a look around this peaceful little community while you have the chance. Open in summer Mon., Thurs.–Sat. 9 am–2 pm and 6–8:30 pm; Sun. 10 am–2 pm. Winter hours are Thurs.–Sat. 11 am–2 pm, 6–8:30 pm and on Sun. 10 am–2 pm. To reach The Bistro from Hwy. 17 (running north from Alamosa), turn east at Moffat and drive about 12 miles to Crestone. At the junction just before town, turn right. **256-4114.**

ROMEO
Abe's Cafe — $

Put a tune on the jukebox and enjoy an authentic Mexican meal at Abe's. On one side is a restaurant, on the other a bar (food is served at both). The menu is not fancy, but neither are the prices. Abe, a miner by trade, got into the restaurant business a number of years back. He's very easy-going and makes this an enjoyable alternative to eating in Alamosa. So play some pool, eat a couple of chili rellenos and relax. Open daily 9 am–10 pm. Sunflower mural on the outside of the building. **110 Main St., Romeo; 843-9902.**

SAN LUIS
Emma's Hacienda — $

Keep in mind that even though you can count the places to eat in San Luis on one hand, Emma's standout Mexican food would get rave reviews no matter where it was located. In business since 1949, Emma still oversees the restaurant and personally takes orders. Menu notables include Emma's Special (a little of everything), enchiladas and the S.O.B. burger smothered with green or red chili. Try a slice of homemade pie for dessert. It seems fitting that in this laid-back town the restaurant should keep non-specific hours. But it's usually open for business (how's that for vague?). **San Luis; 672-9902.**

SERVICES

Alamosa Chamber of Commerce—
Cole Park, Alamosa, CO 81101; (719) 589-3681.

Antonito Chamber of Commerce—
PO Box 427, Antonito, CO 81120; (719) 376-5441.

Del Norte Chamber of Commerce—
PO Box 148, 1160 Grand Ave., Del Norte, CO 81132; (719) 657-2845.

Monte Vista Chamber of Commerce—
1125 Park Ave., Monte Vista, CO 81144; (719) 852-2731.

Sangre de Cristo Chamber of Commerce—
PO Box 307, San Luis, CO 81152; (719) 672-4441 or 672-3346.

COLORADO PROFILE — PENITENTES

One of the most fascinating and mysterious sects of the Christian faith once thrived in southern Colorado, playing an integral part in the history and culture of the Hispanic communities. The Penitentes began as an off-shoot of the Catholic faith in 13th-century Europe as a society honoring St. Francis of Assisi. They practiced self-flagellation as a way to prove their devotion, but eventually the practice died out everywhere in Europe except for Spain. It is commonly believed that when the conquistadors came to New Mexico, the Penitentes (los Hermanos) came with them. Beginning about 1810 in the isolated communities of northern New Mexico, the Penitentes thrived and eventually spread north into southern Colorado. Since many of the small villages did not have a regular priest, the Penitentes filled a spiritual void and satisfied a desire for ritual.

Many men in the communities joined los Hermanos and met at their moradas or lodges. Self-torture was a part of their practice, but more impor-tantly, the men quite often helped bind together the community, taking on charitable work that no one would do. The Penitentes continued to obey the Catholic church, adhering to all of its precepts except during Holy Week. During this time, the brothers dressed in black hoods and white breechcloths and re-enacted Christ's capture, trial and crucifixion. Whipping themselves with cactus leaves, they climbed a hill on which one of the members was tied (and, some say, even nailed) to a cross and left until he fainted. Because of the high number of injuries and the mock crucifixions, the Catholic church finally outlawed the Penitentes. The Penitentes did not disband, but instead became secretive and did not allow outsiders to visit their moradas or witness their rituals.

Well into the 1900s there were still hundreds of practicing moradas spread throughout southern Colorado. Today, however, these numbers have dwindled to just a few, but many deserted moradas can still be seen in and around the small Hispanic villages of southern Colorado.

South Park and 285 Corridor

At the center of Colorado, the high grassland basin of South Park lies undiscovered. Displaying its beauty in a different way than mountain resorts, the entire 30- by 40-mile park is virtually devoid of commercialism. Partly because of this lack of development, many people drive through South Park without slowing to enjoy a plethora of scenery and activities. You won't have a chance to be slowed by a stoplight either—there isn't one in the entire county.

Fairplay, the largest town in South Park, will charm you with its obvious ties to history. At an elevation of almost 10,000 feet, this one-time gold mining camp is now home to only 450 permanent residents. Of particular interest in town is the South Park City Museum, a reconstructed 19th-century mining town. Some 30 buildings, containing more than 50,000 historic objects, were carted here from around Colorado. Fairplay also has two historic hotels, several local restaurants and a patrol car with a very active radar gun (the speed limit is 25).

Around the perimeter of the park, the Mosquito, Park and Tarryall mountain ranges offer unlimited terrain for hiking and cross-country skiing. Hundreds of thousands of acres are set aside for public use in Pike National Forest, including the Lost Creek Wilderness Area. The aspen-cloaked mountains are dotted with ghost towns and weathered remnants of gold mines; when exploring away from designated roads or trails, beware of open shafts and pits. At the base of several 14,000-foot peaks north of Fairplay, the Bristlecone Pine Scenic Area boasts 2,000-year-old trees growing in beautiful wind-twisted forms. Gushing tributaries from the surrounding mountains form the headwaters of the South Platte River, then find their way to the valley floor, which is laced with miles of streams and many reservoirs.

Hwy. 285 leads to South Park from Denver. This route was established, in succession, by Ute Indians, covered wagons, the narrow-gauge Denver South Park & Pacific Railroad (DSP&P) and cars. Today, it is a smooth, paved road, plying a winding route past the communities of Bailey, Shawnee and Grant before angling southwest over Kenosha Pass (10,001 feet) and dropping into South Park. The area included in this chapter, from Bailey to the top of Kenosha Pass, we refer to as the 285 corridor. This time-honored route follows the North Fork of the South Platte River up through a pine-clad valley on its southwestern voyage. The memory of the far-reaching view into South Park from the summit of Kenosha Pass will stay with you for years.

HISTORY

Long before Spanish explorers came to South Park, Ute Indians were ensconced in the area. Vast game reserves provided the Utes easy hunting grounds for herds of deer, elk, antelope and buffalo. Other tribes learned about the fine hunting and came to South Park. Because the area was worth fighting for, frequent skirmishes erupted.

One notable battle, in the spring of 1852, was not the usual spontaneous ambush, but a carefully organized challenge for control over the park between the Utes and the Comanches. With a stream as the dividing line between the warring tribes, one tribe would be declared victorious if it could force the other back to a nearby ridge. Kit Carson witnessed the fight and very wisely decided not to take sides. Soon after the war cries sounded, blood started flowing and scalps were claimed. Volleys of arrows and hand-to-hand combat inflicted heavy losses on both tribes. After three exhausting days (both tribes would break for dinner and a night's rest), the Comanche tribe managed to push the Utes back to the ridge. The Utes left after the fight, but never fully relinquished South Park. It wasn't long, though, until the white influx wrested control over the park from all of the tribes.

White trappers were attracted to the park, primarily for beaver but also for the boundless game. It wasn't until the gold rush in 1859 that settlement of towns began. In July of that year, a few straggling prospectors crossed Georgia Pass and started prospecting north of present-day **Como** at the north end of the park. Their gold pans revealed an exciting strike and, within two weeks, hundreds of prospectors were staking out claims and panning for gold. After only a couple of months, the town of Tarryall ("Let's tarry, all," said one early miner) was in place and all of the claims had been taken. Disgruntled late arrivals dubbed the town Graball and founded a new town called Fair Play on the banks of the South Platte River. Prospecting fell into a deep freeze with the arrival of winter. But by the summer of 1860, 11,000 miners were swarming over the surrounding hills and establishing gold camps with names like Buckskin Joe, Hamilton, Montgomery and Sacramento.

South Park was known to many as "Bayou Salado" because of its plentiful natural salt springs. In 1864 the Colorado Salt Works, located just north of Antero Junction on Hwy. 285, started evaporating brine into usable salt. To accomplish this task, the company imported 18 cast-iron kettles and heated them over a fire. When the saltworks were operating at capacity, 4,000 pounds of salt could be recovered in 24 hours. The salt was used primarily for refining gold ore, but it also found a place on many dinner tables. The saltworks operated successfully for three years until other suppliers came into the area. A few other attempts were made to find a stronger brine, but no one made enough money to stay in business for long.

Silver Heels is a name that conjures up images of South Park's heyday. As the legend goes, Silver Heels was the most beautiful woman ever seen at Buckskin Joe . . . a dance-hall girl whose beauty went far beneath her skin, to the depths of her soul. When a terrible smallpox epidemic broke out, the people who had not contracted the disease left immediately. Silver Heels, however, stayed behind to help stricken miners, and eventually she too became sick. When the epidemic had run its course, she mysteriously disappeared. Many years later, a silent woman was seen visiting the cemetery in Alma, paying her respects to victims of the disease. She always wore a veil over her face, it was said, to hide scarring pockmarks; the townsfolk seemed to know who the mystery lady was. Grateful miners honored her by naming the beautiful Mt. Silverheels (13,822 feet) in her memory, sometime before 1870.

By 1879 the Denver South Park & Pacific Railroad finally completed the route from Denver to Como. A tent city with more than a thousand residents sprang up at the Como terminus of the railroad, where a roundhouse was built. From Como, people often transferred onto a stagecoach to complete the trip west over Mosquito Pass to the booming town of Leadville. Eventually the rail line was completed over Boreas Pass to Breckenridge and on to Leadville. In the 1880s Como became known for its coal reserves, and lumbering began in the vast forests around South Park. Ranchers fenced in the prime grazing land, and it wasn't long before large herds of sheep and cattle flourished.

The trains provided exciting weekend excursions for people from Denver as well as a means to move goods. But due to limited demand, the railroad was abandoned in 1938. Without the train, Como began to decline, while the rest of the park remained aloof from much of the development happening in other parts of the state. With mixed blessings, South Park remains a quiet place—much as it was a few decades ago.

GETTING THERE

The town of Fairplay, situated in the middle of South Park, is located 80 miles southwest of Denver on Hwy. 285.

—— FESTIVALS AND EVENTS ——

Old Fashioned Fourth of July Celebration

This is a major event for the folks in Como. A lot of time goes into planning the festivities, which include a chili cookoff, a watermelon eating contest and a staged shootout by the notorious Reynolds gang (this outlaw gang used to hide out near Como). Crafts booths are set up in town and everyone is encouraged to wear period dress. The evening highlight is still the fireworks. For more information contact

Vicky Portice at **(719) 836-2403.**

Burro Days
last weekend in July

You don't want to miss the "world championship" pack burro race. Determined men and women are pitted not only against Mosquito Pass, but also against the iron will of their burros. This fun event has contestants racing to the top of the pass and back to Fairplay. When the racers are out of town, you'll have time to concentrate on the food booths and the arts and crafts displays in town. The new pack llama race is a sign of the times. Stick around for a parade and dancing into the night. For more information, call Al at the J Bar J Ranch; **(719) 836-9971.**

—— OUTDOOR ACTIVITIES ——

BIKING

MOUNTAIN BIKING

With varied terrain in South Park and the surrounding mountains, this area attracts many mountain bikers. Since there are no places to rent bikes, you must bring your own. There is no organized trail system, but the mining roads and hiking trails extending from the park are endless. Take a close look at the Four-Wheel-Drive Trips and Hiking and Backpacking sections for trail ideas. For more information contact the **South Park Ranger District Office** at the junction of Hwys. 285 and 9, **PO Box 219, Fairplay, CO 80440; (719) 836-2031.**

TOURING

Many riders from Denver make the arduous (one could say dangerous) journey up narrow Hwy. 285 to South Park. The park itself is a wonderful, flat expanse, but it invariably seems as if you are working against a headwind. Why not stay the night in Fairplay or Como and return the next day?

FISHING

Elevenmile Reservoir—

For catching trophy-sized trout, Elevenmile State Recreation Area, at the south end of the park, is an excellent choice. For specific fishing information, take a look at the Fishing section of the **Cripple Creek and Victor** chapter.

Jefferson Lake—

At the headwaters of Jefferson Creek northwest of Kenosha Pass, this popular lake provides quality fishing. Early and late in the day, fly-fishing for rainbows can be excellent from the northeast side. Many boaters ply the water for a diversity of Mackinaw, brook and rainbow trout. Jefferson Lake receives heavy fishing pressure but is also frequently stocked. From the small town of Jefferson in the northwest corner of South Park, head north and west on Forest Rd. 400. After a couple of miles, turn right (north) on Forest Rd. 401, which leads to the campgrounds and to the lake within Pike National Forest.

South Platte River—

Each fork of the South Platte offers a variety of fishing. The headwaters lie northwest of Fairplay in the Mosquito Range. Most of the land surrounding the South Platte as it runs through the park is private. (The best public fishing is actually in the Deckers area and below Cheesman Reservoir—an area that may someday be flooded by the massive Two Forks Dam project.) For some good public water closer to South Park, try fishing the Middle Fork of the South Platte above the Montgomery Reservoir inlet (on Hwy. 9 north of Fairplay). The Middle Fork flows south from the reservoir to Fairplay between piles of displaced river rock from dredging operations, but can still be good for small rainbow and brown trout. The South Fork of the South Platte merges with the Middle Fork just above the town of Hartsel in the center of South Park, creating the South Platte River. Above Hartsel, some Division of Wildlife leases are open to public fishing. Another public stretch is located 5 miles northwest of Hartsel on Hwy. 9, within the Tomahawk State Wildlife Area. The North Fork of the South Platte flows east from Kenosha Pass toward Denver. Located right next to Hwy. 285, the river is heavily fished with fair results.

Spinney Mountain Reservoir—

This fairly new reservoir has only been open for public fishing since 1983, and those who appreciate feisty cutthroat trout keep returning. Partly because no overnight camping is allowed, the fishing pressure is fairly light. The city of Aurora owns the reservoir and charges a small fee to fish the nitrogen-rich water. The South Fork of the South Platte fills the reservoir, but the land upstream from Spinney Mountain is private; downstream can be good, but it is closed from Sept. through Nov. On the north shore, a boat ramp and a small picnic area are available. From Fairplay, drive 23 miles south on Hwy. 9 and follow the signs.

Tarryall Creek—

On the east side of South Park, Tarryall Creek exits from Tarryall Reservoir. A challenging and often good stretch of water for brook and rainbow trout exists between the reservoir and Lake George. A few miles of water above the confluence with the South Platte are designated Wild Trout water. Though the creek is fairly narrow, the fish often grow to lunker sizes. To reach the creek from Jefferson (northeast corner of the park), take Hwy. 77 southeast for about 20 miles.

FOUR-WHEEL-DRIVE TRIPS

Mosquito Pass—

This classic four-wheel-drive road is the highest road over a pass in the country. It leads west over the Mosquito Range to Leadville. The area is saturated in mining history. For details see the Four-Wheel-Drive Trips section of the **Leadville** chapter.

Webster Pass—

A narrow, rough road leads up beautiful Hall Valley from the east side of Kenosha Pass. After passing Handcart and Hall Valley campgrounds, the road gets extremely rough and steep as it heads through thick groves of aspen to the summit of Webster Pass (12,108 feet). Try this four-wheel-drive tour in autumn and you'll be treated to quite a show. On the opposite side of the pass, the former wagon road switchbacks down to Montezuma (see the **Summit County** chapter for more information). To reach the road from the town of Grant, drive 3 miles southwest on Hwy. 285. Turn right and head basically west on Forest Rd. 120.

HANDICAPPED RECREATION

Wilderness on Wheels—

For people confined to wheelchairs, this is a totally accessible wilderness area designed for special needs. A wooden boardwalk, wide enough to allow two wheelchairs to pass, has been constructed for 1,000 feet along the banks of Kenosha Creek. Campsites, prime fishing spots and a nature trail are just the beginning. Campsite reservations can be made by calling ahead; no fee is charged. Restroom and shower facilities are available. In addition, a 7-mile trail to the summit of Twin Peaks (12,300 feet) is currently in the works. Volunteer labor and donated lumber have made this excellent program possible. Many more hours are needed to complete ambitious future plans. For more information on the area and how you can help out, contact **7125 W. Jefferson Ave., Suite 455, Lakewood, CO 80235; (303) 988-2212.** Wilderness on Wheels is located 15 miles west of Bailey on Hwy. 285.

HIKING AND BACKPACKING

The varied terrain of the mountains around South Park is perfect for long backpacking trips and short walkabouts. Miners have left traces of their work all around, but instead of appearing as ugly scars, the kingdom of abandoned mines and mining camps leaves the hiker with a profound sense of history. If you visit in fall, a barrage of colors, unequalled on Colorado's Eastern Slope of the Continental Divide, will make your backcountry experience even better. For more information on hiking and backpacking, contact the **South**

Park Ranger District Office at the junction of Hwys. 285 and 9, **PO Box 219, Fairplay, CO 80440; (719) 836-2031.**

Colorado Trail—

From South Park and the 285 corridor, it's easy to reach the Colorado Trail. The moderately steep trail offers hikes as long or short as you wish through beautiful and surprisingly uncrowded terrain. Plan a two- or three-day backpacking trip by leaving a vehicle at a pre-arranged point along the trail. A good place to get on the trail is just south of the town of Bailey on Forest Rd. 543 near Wellington Lake. Another easy place to start or stop a hike is at Kenosha Pass Campground on Hwy. 285. From Kenosha Pass, the well-defined trail heads west past the Jefferson Creek Recreation Area and then over Georgia Pass toward Breckenridge. Several campgrounds are near the route; primitive camping can be done anywhere except in the Jefferson Creek area, where designated campgrounds are the rule.

Limber Grove Trail—

This nice 1-mile round-trip hike heads into the woods only to emerge on a rocky slope above treeline. The trail leads to one of the best areas for viewing gnarled bristlecone and limber pine groves. Some of the bristlecone trees date back 2,000 years, and the views of the Mosquito Range and South Park are tremendous. Limber Grove Trail begins at Horseshoe Campground (see the Camping section for directions).

Lost Creek Wilderness Area—

Within the Tarryall Range to the east of South Park, the Lost Creek Wilderness Area offers spectacular scenery with easy access. The wilderness is known for its unearthly granite rock formations, grottos and large herds of bighorn sheep. As the name implies, the creek disappears for a mile or so as it works its way under a rocky hill. There's an excellent trail system, including a 25-mile loop, which circles through the southern section of the wilderness. Lost Creek is a very popular area and can get quite crowded in the summer. Since most of the trails are below 10,000 feet, you can hike in early spring and into the fall. Here are a few of the trailheads.

From Hwy. 285, 1 mile northeast of Jefferson, turn east onto Lost Park Rd. (Forest Rd. 127). The dirt road leads to Lost Park Campground in 20 miles. The campground serves as a trailhead for the **Brookside-McCurdy Trail** (No. 607) and the **Wigwam Trail** (No. 609). Ranchers have grazing rights around this section of the wilderness, so you'll probably see some cattle. Be sure to purify your drinking water. Another trailhead can be reached by driving southeast from Jefferson on Tarryall Rd. (County Rd. 77) for about 20 miles to Tarryall Reservoir. Continue another 4 miles to the **Ute Creek Trail** on the left (northeast) side of the road. The trailhead is marked, and there is a parking area.

Perhaps the most popular access to the wilderness area is **Goose Creek Trail**. This section of the wilderness area features some of the most beautiful rock formations. Fishing for small trout along Lost Creek is not bad either. It can be reached by continuing about 16 miles southwest on County Rd. 77 from the Ute Creek Trailhead to Forest Rd. 211. Turn left (northeast) on Forest Rd. 211 and follow it 12 miles to Forest Rd. 558. Turn left and continue about 1 mile to the trailhead. For specific information about the Lost Creek Wilderness Area, visit the South Park Ranger District Office at the junction of Hwys. 285 and 9 in Fairplay; **(719) 836-2031.**

Mounts Democrat, Lincoln and Bross—

Bagging three 14ers in a long day of hiking is ambitious but entirely possible in the Mosquito Range towering just above Alma. Because of the mountains' proximity and connecting saddles, climbing all three together is easier than one at a time. All in all, the elevation gain is about 3,600 feet, and the loop trail is just over 6 miles. Of course, hiking to the summit of the first mountain (14,148-foot Democrat) is enough for many hikers. The trail to Democrat leads northwest from Kite Lake, which is above treeline, passing some exposed mining shacks on the way to the summit. From the top, views to the Sawatch, Gore, Tenmile and Elk ranges are tremendous.

If you are still energetic enough to continue, walk back down to the saddle (which you passed on the way up) between Democrat and Lincoln. The trail leads 2 miles northeast to the summit of Lincoln (14,286 feet), passing Mt. Cameron along the way. Mt. Cameron is a mountain in its own right, but it's actually considered a part of Mt. Lincoln. From Lincoln, head back down to Cameron and then hike 1 mile southeast to the broad summit of Mt. Bross (14,169 feet). Hiking down from Bross to Kite Lake is a bit tricky, but very doable.

To reach the trailhead from Fairplay, follow Hwy. 9 northwest for 7 miles to the town of Alma. In Alma, turn left on an unmarked dirt road that breaks away from Main St. across from the Texaco station. Follow the rough dirt road 7 miles up Buckskin Gulch to Kite Lake. Don't try this last bit in a passenger car if it has been raining. High clearance vehicles are better suited to this road in all types of weather. The road passes many old mines along the way to the trailhead at Kite Lake.

HORSEBACK RIDING

Wade's Stables—

For an hourly ride on a meandering trail, pull off Hwy. 285, 2.5 miles west of Bailey; **(303) 838-7993.**

SKIING

Fairplay is located on heavily used Hwy. 9, a half hour away from several popular Summit County ski areas. Many people blast through Fairplay without a second glance on their way to the slopes at Breckenridge, Keystone, Arapahoe Basin and Copper Mountain. Why not consider stopping off for a less-expensive night in Fairplay? The ski area at nearby Geneva Basin will remain closed for the foreseeable future.

Cross-country skiing in the South Park area (photograph by Bob Huestis).

CROSS-COUNTRY SKIING

Many avid cross-country skiers are discovering the wealth of backcountry trails in the South Park area. With the addition of the groomed trails at Fairplay Nordic Center, this is becoming a touring oasis. For more information on backcountry skiing, contact the **South Park Ranger District Office** in Fairplay at the intersection of Hwys. 285 and 9; **(719) 836-2031.**

Backcountry Trails—

Bristlecone Pine Scenic Area—This 7-mile trip is a backcountry highlight. Allow about six hours round trip, over varied terrain, to complete this beautiful and historic tour. There is little avalanche danger, as the trail follows a road to nearly 12,000 feet in elevation—a gain of 700 feet. The trail passes mining sites from the 1860s, ending on a ridge among bristlecone pine trees dating to the birth of Christ. To reach the trail from Fairplay, drive 6 miles northwest on Hwy. 9. Turn left (west) in Alma at the Texaco station and continue on the road for 3 miles to the Paris Mill. The road isn't plowed beyond this point—begin skiing here.

Tie Hack Trail—This 5.5-mile ski loop is well marked by forest service blazes. It follows a fairly difficult route that is best skied after a snowstorm. Tie Hack Trail is steeped in history: the trail follows an old stage road to the defunct mining camps of Sacramento and Horseshoe, passing through aspen groves and wide-open meadows. Several stretches of downhill cruising help make this a fun tour. By the way, tie hacks were men who cut timber

and worked it into usable railroad ties. To reach the trailhead from Fairplay, drive south on Hwy. 285 for a quarter mile to County Rd. 18, marked by a Forest Access sign. Turn right (west) and drive 3.5 miles to the trail, which follows a jeep road from the right side of the road.

Groomed Trails—

Fairplay Nordic Center—Even though South Park can get very windy, the Fairplay Nordic Center enjoys a protected setting with 15 kilometers of groomed trails. In fact, it is on the lee side of a ridge and the wind sometimes drops powder on the trails, even on sunny days. This new center is experiencing rapid growth under the direction of its owner, Gary Nichols. Not only does the center offer touring lessons and rentals, but there is a series of lectures and seminars on relevant topics throughout the winter. This is a beautiful area of the state, so stretch out and try the trails before they become known to all. Ask about bed and breakfast ski packages. To get to the center, turn north on Fourth St. in Fairplay (at the Fairplay Family Store) and continue north for four blocks to Bogue St. Turn left and continue on a gravel road 1.8 miles. **PO Box 701, Fairplay, CO 80440; (719) 836-2277.**

Rentals and Information—

Fairplay Nordic Center—This is the only place to rent skis without going over Hoosier Pass. Talk with Gary Nichols about backcountry skiing routes and avalanche conditions (see entry under Groomed Trails).

—————— SEEING AND DOING ——————

MUSEUMS

South Park City—

South Park City puts history in context. More than 30 buildings from crumbling mining towns in the area have been moved to a central location where a period town—circa 1870–1900—has been re-created. Filled with room settings, dioramas

and exhibits, this museum vividly shows how life was a century ago. South Park City has been open as a private nonprofit enterprise since 1959, attracting thousands of visitors each year. You'll see a simple trapper's cabin, a mercantile, the South Park Lager Beer Brewery, the old Bank of Alma and a stage stop from the top of

Mosquito Pass. One display shows the heavy equipment used in hydraulic and hardrock mining; in front of the railway station lies a narrow-gauge engine with several cars and a caboose. A slide show on the history of South Park is shown daily on the half hour from 10:30 am–3:30 pm at the stone brewery building.

To be honest, we were anticipating this would be a tacky tourist trap. After two fascinating hours of walking into creaky old buildings, we learned South Park City is anything but a trap. Admission fee charged. Open May 15–Oct. 15: 9 am–7 pm Memorial Day through Labor Day; 9 am–5 pm from May 15 to Memorial Day and from Labor Day to Oct. 15. Follow the signs from the center of Fairplay; **(719) 836-2387.**

SCENIC DRIVES

Boreas Pass/Hoosier Pass—

The connecting routes between the mines in South Park and Summit County provide both history and beauty. Hwy. 9 over Hoosier Pass can be taken right out of Fairplay to Breckenridge; Boreas Pass is a graded dirt road heading north from Como with spectacular scenery on the route to Breckenridge. For more information on Boreas Pass, see the Scenic Drives section of the **Summit County** chapter.

Bristlecone Pine Scenic Area—

This short drive leads into one of the few areas in Colorado where ancient, wind-twisted bristlecone pines can be seen. This type of tree is believed to be the world's oldest living thing—one tree in Nevada is thought to be 4,500 years old. New branches grow only on the leeward side of trees, as new buds are quickly blown off the windy side. The trees somehow survive at exposed elevations as high as 12,000 feet. This scenic area, at the foot of 14,169-foot Mt. Bross, can be seen from a car. From Fairplay drive 6 miles northwest on Hwy. 9. Turn left (west) in Alma at the Texaco station and continue up Buckskin Gulch until reaching a marked turn-off.

Guanella Pass—

For an exciting drive with a beautiful view of Mt. Bierstadt from the summit, head north on Guanella Pass Rd. from Grant. For details see the Scenic Drives section of the Georgetown chapter.

Weston Pass—

This road, which crosses the Mosquito Range, can get pretty rough, but it should be OK in the family car. Originally an Indian trail, the road became a wagon route crossing the 11,945-foot pass in 1860. The road still provides exceptional scenery. On the west side of the pass, it descends south of Leadville. To reach Weston Pass Rd. from Fairplay, drive 11 miles south on Hwy. 285 to the marked turn-off. Take a right and begin the odyssey.

———————— WHERE TO STAY ————————

ACCOMMODATIONS

Hand Hotel — $$$

Jake Hand built this hotel in the early 1930s, but today the look of the place is more akin to the 1890s. You're easily transported back in time at this upscale bed and breakfast on historic Front St. The plush lobby has chairs and couches situated around a large mantel. Upstairs, 11 rooms are tastefully furnished in period antiques. All of the rooms are equipped with private bathrooms and, true to the 1890s, have neither TVs nor telephones. One of the most unique aspects of the Hand Hotel is the period furnishings—and you can purchase any of the antiques you see in the rooms. Each of the rooms, from the Miss Silver Heels Suite to the Outlaw Room, has a distinct personality. On a summer afternoon there is no better place to enjoy a view of the Mosquito Range than from the upstairs deck. After a day of hiking or skiing be sure to take a long soak in the hot tub.

Breakfast, lunch and dinner are served in the downstairs dining rooms. (See the Where to Eat section for more information.) **531 Front St., Fairplay, CO 80440; (719) 836-2277.**

The Depot Hotel — $$

The restored Depot Hotel used to fill up with guests when the narrow-gauge train made its runs from Denver to South Park in the early 1900s. After the train stopped service, the hotel shut down until 1978, when it was reopened by Jo and Keith Hodges. It was the first business in Como in 25 years. Now the small town has a centerpiece bed and breakfast and restaurant. Four upstairs rooms are simple, clean reminders of the past. One room, decorated in pastel blues, sleeps three to four guests and has a fireplace. All rooms share a bathroom down the hall, equipped with a claw-foot bathtub. It's nothing fancy, but this friendly place exudes the colorful history of Como. There are no TVs or telephones. The downstairs restaurant has an excellent reputation among locals in Como and Fairplay and is open from 8 am–8 pm daily, except Tues. (See the Where to Eat section.) The hotel and restaurant are closed in Jan. and Feb. For more information or reservations, contact: **The Depot Hotel, Box 648, Como, CO 80432; (719) 836-2594.**

Fairplay Hotel — $$

Twenty-six rooms are spread out on the upper floor of the historic Fairplay Hotel. They are simple reminders of a western past and can be a nice place to spend the night. About half of the rooms come with a private bathroom. There is a comfortable lobby area with couches situated around a stone mantel adorned with a huge elk trophy. One word of advice . . . unless you plan on staying up till 2 am, request a room that is not above the raucous Silver Heels Bar. **500 Main St., Fairplay, CO 80440; (719) 836-2565.**

Glen Isle — $$

Since 1900 Glen Isle has been a rustic retreat. It is located halfway between Bailey and Grant on Hwy. 285. The first guests arrived on the narrow-gauge train. Thankfully, few changes have been made to the outward appearance of Glen Isle over the years. And the sure-fire hospitality of the owners is as strong as ever. An incredible doll and artifact collection adds to the character; don't miss the octagonal fish tank (made in 1875) in the dining room with live trout inside!

Cabins for two to eight people are available, as well as comfortable lodge rooms with a bathroom down the hall. During the summer season, Glen Isle operates as a resort with three meals a day (optional) and activities during the week. You may want to participate in the all-day picnic or the chuckwagon dinner and square dance. Kids love fishing in the private pond (an ice rink in winter), and the resort is hemmed in by plenty of national forest terrain. Though Glen Isle doesn't have any horses, you can rent by the hour at a stable a quarter mile up the road. For families, this is a low-priced alternative to guest ranches; the minimum stay is two nights. Reserve early in summer, because by June most of the best times are taken. In winter the lodge and restaurant are closed, but the cabins remain open. Gordon and Barbara Tripp, **PO Box 128, Bailey, CO 80421; (303) 838-5461.**

CAMPING

In Pike National Forest—

Beginning on the east side of Kenosha Pass on Hwy. 285 at the town of Grant, take Guanella Pass Rd. (Forest Rd. 118) north. After 2.5 miles you'll reach **Whiteside Campground** (five sites; no fee). Another 2.5 miles up the road is **Burning Bear Campground** (13 sites; fee charged). Continue 2 miles to reach **Geneva Park Campground** (26 sites; fee charged).

Take Hwy. 285 west of Grant for 3 miles to the Hall Valley turn-off. Head northwest on rough and narrow Forest Rd. 120 for 5 miles to reach **Handcart Campground** (10 sites; no fee). Virtually at the same point on the road is **Hall Valley**

Campground (nine sites; fee charged). After the campgrounds, this road gets even rougher as it leads over Webster Pass (see the Four-Wheel-Drive Trips section).

Popular **Kenosha Pass Campground** is at the top of Kenosha Pass on Hwy. 285, between Grant and Jefferson (25 sites; fee).

On Hwy. 285 west of Kenosha Pass, turn northwest on Forest Rd. 400 at Jefferson. Continue 2 miles and turn right (north) on Forest Rd. 401. After 1.5 miles you'll come to a succession of campgrounds. The first one is **Lodgepole Campground** (35 sites; fee charged), followed by **Aspen Campground** (12 sites; fee charged) and **Jefferson Creek Campground** (17 sites; fee charged). Bring your fishing pole along and try your luck at Jefferson Lake. If you continue on Forest Rd. 400 for 6 miles past Jefferson, you will reach **Michigan Creek Campground** (13 sites; fee charged).

From 1 mile northeast of Jefferson, head southeast on Forest Rd. 127 for about 20 miles. This will take you to the edge of the Lost Creek Wilderness Area and **Lost Park Campground** (10 sites; no fee). Back in Jefferson, take Hwy. 77 south for approximately 30 miles to **Spruce Grove Campground** (28 sites; fee charged).

From Como, take Boreas Pass Rd. (Forest Rd. 404) northwest for 7 miles to a turn-off for **Selkirk Campground** (15 sites; no fee).

Beaver Creek Campground (three sites; no fee) is located 4 miles north of Fairplay on Forest Rd. 413.

To reach **Kite Lake Campground** (seven sites; no fee) from Fairplay, follow Hwy. 9 northwest for 7 miles to Alma. In Alma, turn left on an unmarked dirt road that breaks away from Main St. across from the Texaco station. Follow the rough dirt road 7 miles up Buckskin Gulch to Kite Lake, which is above treeline. The road is especially rough for the last mile. You may want to walk, unless you have a jeep.

From Fairplay you can easily reach **Fourmile** (14 sites; no fee) and **Horseshoe** (seven sites; no fee) campgrounds. Drive south on Hwy. 285 for 1.5 miles, turn right (west) on Forest Rd. 421 and continue for 7 miles.

Five miles south of Fairplay on Hwy. 285 is a turn-off for Weston Pass Rd. Turn right (southwest) and drive 11 miles to Weston Pass Campground (14 sites; no fee). Fifteen miles south of Fairplay on Hwy. 285, take a right turn (west on Forest Rd. 431) and drive for 0.5 miles to **Buffalo Springs Campground** (17 sites; no fee).

WHERE TO EAT

Silver Tip Lodge — $$$

This location along the 285 corridor used to be a stop for the stagecoach and later for the narrow-gauge train. The old Silver Tip Lodge burned down in the 1930s, but this newer lodge still serves as a way station for travelers along Hwy. 285. Elegant meals are served in the comfortable dining room with a lakeside view. An acclaimed dining experience, the Silver Tip features on its menu steaks up to 16 ounces, shrimp scampi, crab legs and chicken in a light orange sauce. On Sat. nights, the separate bar area features live country-western music. Closed Mon. and Tues.; open for lunch from noon–2 pm and dinner from 5–9 pm Wed.–Fri. and until 10 pm on Sat. and Sun. nights. Located between Grant and Shawnee on Hwy. 285; **(303) 838-6450.**

The Depot Hotel — $ to $$$

Gather around the fireplace at this local favorite and enjoy a down-home meal. This historic hotel located in the town of Como has a relaxed setting and excellent food. The menu will satisfy your desires for anything from a simple quarter-pound hamburger to 14 ounces of prime rib or salmon steak. Try their Mexican specialties. The Depot Hotel is also open for breakfast, offering pancakes, chicken-fried steak and eggs as well as sweet rolls. Open from 8 am–8 pm daily except Tues. For information on staying at the Depot Hotel, see the Where to Stay section. Closed in Jan. and Feb. The restaurant is located in Como; **(719) 836-2594.**

Fairplay Hotel — $ to $$$

This has long been the restaurant of choice for a filling breakfast before heading out for a day of skiing. The cozy dining room of the hotel has a warm ambience. It's open for breakfast, lunch and dinner. Breakfast is the standout: omelettes, eggs, home fries and, especially, gigantic cinnamon rolls. For lunch try a burger, fried chicken or a bowl of homemade soup. Dinners include reasonably priced fish, chicken and beef dishes. For more information on the Fairplay Hotel, see the Where to Stay section. Open daily from 7 am–9 pm Sun.–Thur., until 10 pm on Fri. and Sat. nights. (The restaurant closes one hour earlier in winter.) **500 Main St., Fairplay; (719) 836-2565.**

Hand Hotel — $ to $$$

Both of the historic hotels in Fairplay offer good meals at fair prices—after all, they are in Fairplay! The Hand Hotel, in particular, has a wonderful dining environment, with a glassed-in extension on the back of the dining room. There is also a smaller, more casual cafe at the front of the hotel. Breakfast, lunch and dinner are served at the Hand. The dinner menu is varied, with seafood and steak dishes sharing space with burritos and spaghetti. Breakfast offerings range from bacon and eggs to a breakfast burrito and hot cakes. A bottomless cup of coffee costs only a quarter. For more information see the Where to Stay section. Open daily from 7 am–2:30 pm for breakfast and lunch; dinner is served from 5–8 pm Sun.–Thur., until 9 pm on Fri. and Sat. nights. **531 Front St., Fairplay; (719) 836-2277.**

Carlos O'Briens — $ to $$

The atmosphere is nothing fancy, but the Mexican food, prepared by owner Betty Vigil, is authentic and delicious. Despite a rather remote location, Carlos O'Briens can get really busy. Instead of blowing by on Hwy. 285, stop in for a meal. Try the chili rellenos, stuffed sopapillas or chimichangas. An American food menu is also available, but most people prefer to cross the border. Also open for breakfast, with egg dishes, pancakes and other items available. Open from 7–11 am for breakfast; lunch and dinner are served from 11 am–10 pm. In a separate bar area, there is an odd-looking pool table with snarling lions sculpted below the corner pockets. The place can get hopping. Look for the sign 11 miles west of Bailey, near Grant.

SERVICES

Platte Canyon Chamber Visitors Center—

Located 6 miles east of Bailey on Hwy. 285. Open from 1–5 pm on Fri.; 10 am–6 pm on Sat.–Sun. **66803 Hwy. 285, PO Box 477, Bailey, CO 80421; (303) 838-7487.**

Regional Tourism Office—

PO Box 701, Fairplay, CO 80440; (719) 836-2771, ext. 203.

Upper Arkansas
Valley

Throughout the years the Upper Arkansas Valley, stretching 45 miles north from Salida to the small town of Granite in southcentral Colorado, has hosted people "just passing through." Early on, wagon roads and rail lines crisscrossed the valley, providing routes over the Continental Divide to the west, over Poncha Pass to the south, across Trout Creek Pass to South Park and alongside the Arkansas River. Today the Upper Arkansas Valley still suffers somewhat from an unfair "nondestination" stigma; many motorists fill up their tanks at local gas stations and peruse road maps, calculating how far they still have left to travel to wherever they are going. And that's too bad, because if you enjoy the Colorado outdoors, this area is hard to beat.

The Arkansas River, one of the longest in North America, flows through the valley before entering Upper Arkansas Canyon on its way to the eastern plains at Pueblo. In recent years the river has attracted increasing numbers of rafters and kayakers (well over 100,000 per year) who seek the thrill of shooting some of the finest rapids in the West.

Along the western edge of the valley, the lofty Sawatch mountain range angles skyward, providing a memorable view, especially to first-time visitors. More 14,000-foot peaks are packed into this small area than anywhere else in North America. The Sawatch, within San Isabel National Forest, offers fantastic recreational possibilities, especially if you like to climb peaks. Monarch, at the southern end of the range, is a fine small ski area.

Mining history can be relived by a visit to one of the many ghost towns in the region. Though some require a four-wheel-drive vehicle, many others can be reached in the family car. But the ghost towns are not the only places to get a sense of the Upper Arkansas Valley history. **Salida**, located in the southern end of the valley, still reflects its railroad legacy. The turn-of-the-century brick buildings in downtown Salida make up a very large National Historic District. This town of 4,600 residents, along with smaller **Buena Vista**, located 25 miles up-valley, offer the majority of accommodations, restaurants and other services.

HISTORY

Before settlers entered the scene, the Upper Arkansas area was the domain of Indian tribes, especially the Utes. Semi-permanent villages were occupied by the Utes along the Arkansas River near Buena Vista and, farther upriver, by the Comanche. When the Indians began using horses and could travel much farther to hunt, habitation in the valley declined. Lt. Zebulon Pike, who passed through the area in 1806, found an old Indian camp in which he believed 3,000 natives had once lived. By the time settlers entered the area in the 1860s, few Indian villages were in evidence, though curious, friendly Utes made occasional visits.

It was mining that first drew large numbers of settlers to the Upper Arkansas. In 1860 gold was discovered at Kelly's Bar near Granite, 20 miles upriver from Buena Vista. Eager to strike it rich, placer miners spread out along the Arkansas and up the side valleys and gulches. Though some decent mines were worked in the 1860s and 1870s, this area paled in comparison to strikes upriver at Oro City, near present-day Leadville. By the 1880s, better roads and improved mining techniques contributed to successful mines throughout the area, including those up Clear Creek Canyon and Chalk Creek Canyon. Vibrant towns like Winfield, Vicksburg and St. Elmo grew and prospered along with the mines in these two canyons.

Meanwhile, down along the Arkansas River, hay farmers and ranchers moved in. By the end of the 1870s, cattle were grazing on most of the land throughout the valley. Buena Vista grew as a supply town for the mines and ranches, as well as a transportation center for those making their way upriver to Leadville (Oro City). By 1880 Buena Vista had grown large enough to be voted the new county seat. Townsfolk in Granite, the prior county seat, did not take kindly to the news, refusing to relinquish the county records. Buena Vista residents took matters into their own hands by sneaking into the courthouse in Granite late one night and stealing all the county records. The next day, county business went on as usual, but from Buena Vista.

The railroads finally came to the Upper Arkansas Valley in 1880, when Gen. Palmer's Denver & Rio Grande Railroad made its way upriver to South Arkansas (later named Salida). This town grew quickly as a rail hub and smelting and supply center, much to the consternation of residents of Cleora, a couple of miles downriver. Miffed that the Denver & Rio Grande did not choose their town as a rail center, the townsfolk fired off a protest letter to the governor in Denver. He quickly replied, "God Almighty made some townsites and Salida is one of them!" Though these words from the governor were not popular in Cleora, they settled things once and for all. From Salida, the Denver & Rio Grande extended tracks up the valley through Buena Vista and on to Leadville. They also ran a line up Poncha Pass and over Marshall Pass to the Western Slope near Gunnison. Shortly after, the Denver South Park & Pacific arrived in the valley. Its major achievement was the Alpine Tunnel at the upper end of Chalk Creek, which was bored through the Continental Divide in a race with the Denver & Rio Grande to reach Gunnison. When the Colorado Midland Railroad reached the valley in 1887, both Salida and Buena Vista were rip-roaring towns. Buena Vista was especially rowdy, with 36 bars and a hanging judge (Judge Lynch). Quite often visitors to town would be greeted by bodies strung up in the trees. Two of Colorado's most notorious madams operated in these towns. Cockeyed Liz ran her "Palace of Joy" in Buena Vista for years until marrying at the age of 40. Laura Evans, who lived to the ripe old age of

90, ran a bordello in Salida from 1896 until 1950.

With the demise of the mining industry and railroads, most area residents make their living ranching, farming or in tourism. Tourism is the bread-and-butter industry, especially with the incredible growth of commercial rafting on the mighty Arkansas River during summer months.

GETTING THERE

Buena Vista is located 117 miles southwest of Denver via Hwy. 285. Another approach from the east is along the Arkansas River from Pueblo to Salida—a beautiful 97-mile trip on Hwy. 50. Bus service is available to Salida.

FESTIVALS AND EVENTS

FIBArk

mid-June

FIBArk (meaning First In Boating on the Arkansas) brings many visitors to Salida for a long weekend of good fun. Music, craft booths, a bed race, a parade and many boat races provide the entertainment. The featured event is the 26-mile kayak race from Salida down to Cotopaxi, touted as the oldest and longest whitewater kayak race in North America. For more information, write **FIBArk, PO Box 762, Salida, CO 81201; (719) 395-6612.**

Folklife Festival

mid-July

Anglo, Hispanic and Indian folk traditions are kept alive at this annual event in Buena Vista through arts, crafts, dancing and music. Festivities begin with a Western-style barbecue dinner followed by a square dance. Mountain dulcimer and fiddle competitions as well as traditional American, Spanish and Indian dancing highlight the weekend. For information, call **(719) 395-6612.**

OUTDOOR ACTIVITIES

BIKING

MOUNTAIN BIKING

Although there are not any organized mountain bike trail systems, many opportunities await. For a description of some jeep roads in the area, see the Four-Wheel-Drive Trips section. An excellent route is from Buena Vista west over Cottonwood Pass and down into Taylor Park (see the Scenic Drives section). For maps and other trail ideas, visit the **Salida Ranger District Office, 230 W. 16th St., Salida, CO 81201; (719) 539-3591.**

Colorado Trail—

The Colorado Trail (No. 1776) cuts north/south along the eastern edge of the Sawatch Range. It's a well-maintained trail,

providing challenging terrain. Access points lie along Cottonwood Pass Rd., Chalk Creek Rd. and Hwy. 50 (toward Monarch Pass).

Rainbow Trail—

Beginning up at the Continental Divide, southwest of Poncha Springs, the well-maintained Rainbow Trail (Trail No. 1336) stretches 100 miles along the north and east side of the Sangre de Cristo Range, ending in the Wet Mountain Valley. The trail travels through a wide variety of terrain from flat open meadows to steep, forested stretches. Many other side trails lead off from the main one, providing unlimited exploring if you're up for it. Access points to the trail are numerous; many lie along Hwy. 50, east of Poncha Springs.

Visit the forest service office in Salida for maps.

Rentals and Information—
Trailhead Ventures supplies trail ideas, maps and rental mountain bikes. **707 N. Hwy. 24, Buena Vista, CO 81211; (719) 395-8001.**

FISHING

For many years, the Upper Arkansas Valley has been well known for its excellent fishing. Countless anglers have reeled in lunker browns and other trout from stretches along the Arkansas River; the multitude of streams and lakes in the mountains to the west has yielded ample numbers of smaller brookies, cutthroats and rainbows. For the time being, however, fishing opportunities on the Upper Arkansas River and its lower tributaries are in a holding pattern. In Aug. 1988, an attempt by the Division of Wildlife to kill suckers in Clear Creek Reservoir north of Buena Vista ended in catastrophe—the chemical used was accidentally released into the Arkansas River, killing about 60,000 trout between the reservoir and Salida. Locals are still steaming over the mistake, with good reason. It may take a few years for the fishing to get back to the quality it was before the kill. Through a heavy restocking program and the passage of time, area fishing is sure to rebound.

In the meantime, the tributaries along the Arkansas and high lakes provide adequate fishing. If you plan to fish in the area, your best bet is to consult with locals for up-to-date information on where the fish are biting. **Bob's Hackle & Tackle Shop, 329 Ponderosa Pl., Buena Vista, (719) 395-2623,** has tackle for sale or rent and will give you ideas for good fishing spots. You might also try visiting the **Division of Wildlife Office** in Salida at 7405 Hwy. 50; **(719) 539-3529.**

FOUR-WHEEL-DRIVE TRIPS

Aspen Ridge/Bassam Park—
Located in the rolling Mosquito Hills on the east side of the Arkansas River, this route runs 28 miles north/south between Buena Vista and Salida. With thick stands of aspen trees and occasional views west to the magnificent Sawatch Range, we highly recommend this drive, especially in autumn. Much of the route, including the popular picnic area at Bassam Park, is accessible by regular passenger cars but if you drive the entire way you'll need a four-wheel-drive vehicle.

To reach the road from Salida, head northwest on Hwy. 291, 1 mile past the traffic light at First and F streets. Turn right onto County Rd. 153, cross the river and turn right on County Rd. 175 (Ute Trail). About 7.5 miles from the highway, turn left onto County Rd. 184 and proceed 1.5 miles before turning right onto County Rd. 185. Here the aspen get thick. After a few miles you'll pass through Calumet, an old Colorado Fuel & Iron Co. town and mine. Continue on County Rd. 185 to Bassam Park, where it joins up with County Rd. 187. Keep going north on County Rd. 185 until reaching junction County Rd. 307. Turn left and proceed 1.4 miles to Hwy. 285/24, about 7 miles east of Johnson Village.

Hayden Pass—
This road crosses over the Sangre de Cristo Range, southeast of Salida, dropping into the upper San Luis Valley near Valley View Hot Springs (see the Hot Springs section of the **San Luis Valley**

Deserted farmstead in a high mountain valley (sketch by Michael A. Darr).

chapter). A very rough road near the summit, it offers a spectacular bird's-eye view of the San Luis Valley and surrounding mountains. To reach the pass from Salida, drive east on Hwy. 50 for 20 miles to Coaldale and turn right on County Rd. 06. After 4 miles you'll pass Hayden Creek Campground. Proceed another 4 miles to the pass at 10,709 feet. From the pass, descend into the San Luis Valley and drive to the town of Villa Grove, along Hwy. 285 (about 7 miles from the summit of Hayden Pass). Return to Salida by turning right at Villa Grove on Hwy. 285.

Tincup Pass—

Stretching from St. Elmo over the Continental Divide to the ghost town of Tincup, this rugged road provides sweeping views from its 12,154-foot summit. To the west, the West Elk Mountains are an impressive backdrop to Taylor Park. Before the Denver South Park & Pacific Railroad built the Alpine Tunnel under the divide, Tincup Pass was an important stagecoach and freight supply route for settlements such as Gunnison and Tincup on the Western Slope. From St. Elmo, the road can be reached by crossing the bridge in town and turning left. Tincup Pass Rd. starts climbing through a thick aspen forest. The pass is about 8 miles up the road. From the summit, descend about 7 miles, past Mirror Lake to Tincup. For information about Tincup, see the Scenic Drives section of the **Gunnison and Crested Butte** chapter. From Tincup, an interesting return trip to the Upper Arkansas area is over Cottonwood Pass. Drive north from Tincup to Taylor Park Reservoir and then east over Cottonwood Pass to Buena Vista. For more information about Cottonwood Pass, see the Scenic Drives section.

Rentals and Tours—

Overland Jeep Tours—This outfit offers two-hour jeep tours up into the Sawatch Range from Buena Vista. Call for information about other tours, too. **300 Cedar, PO Box 926, Buena Vista, CO 81211; (719) 295-2888.**

Shawano Motel/Jeep Rental—Half-day and full-day jeep rentals get you to those hard-to-reach spots in the backcountry. Reservations are a good idea. Located along Hwy. 50 in Salida. **525 W. Rainbow Blvd., Salida, CO 81201; (719) 539-6689.**

GOLF

Collegiate Peaks Golf Course—

This nine-hole course offers great views of Mt. Princeton and other mountains in the Sawatch Range. Large cottonwood trees dot the course with a creek and several small lakes coming into play. To reach the course from the center of Buena Vista, turn west at the stoplight and continue 1.3 miles. Turn right at the green-and-white sign for the golf course. **28775 Fairway Dr., PO Box 533, Buena Vista, CO 81211; (719) 395-8189.**

Salida Golf Club—

Built in the 1920s, the nine-hole course at the Salida Golf Club offers a challenging round to even the best golfers. With narrow fairways on many of the holes, accuracy is necessary to avoid the thick, troublesome roughs. The par-3, number-8 hole is particularly difficult with a pond guarding an elevated green. Located at the corner of **Crestone St.** and **Grant St.** in **Salida; (719) 539-6373.**

HIKING AND BACKPACKING

If you enjoy putting on a pack and getting out into the backcountry (especially high alpine country), the Upper Arkansas Valley region is for you. When you get your first glimpse of the towering Sawatch Range, you'll know why. There are many trails, from easy mile-long jaunts to long, steep ascents of 14,000-foot peaks. In the Upper Arkansas area, 12 14ers are easily accessible, but not necessarily easy to climb. They include La Plata Peak, Huron Peak, Missouri Mountain, Mt. Belford, Mt. Tabeguache, Mt. Shavano, Mt. Antero and the Collegiate peaks Oxford, Yale, Princeton,

Harvard and Columbia. *If you plan to hike in the high country, remember to get an early start to avoid frequent afternoon thunderstorms.*

Information for many hiking trails can be obtained at the **Salida Ranger District Office, 230 W. 16th St., Salida, CO 81201; (719) 539-3591.** Trail maps, equipment rental, information or whatever you need can be supplied by **Trailhead Ventures, 707 N. Hwy. 24, Buena Vista, CO 81211; (719) 395-8001.**

Brown's Creek Trail (Mount Antero)—

This 11-mile trail begins in the valley at 9,000 feet and climbs west along Brown's Creek, eventually reaching the summit of 14,269-foot Mt. Antero. It provides outstanding scenery from ponderosa and lodgepole pine, mountain meadows and spruce forests to the far-reaching views from the summit of Mt. Antero. Except for the final push up the peak, the trail climbs easy terrain. To reach the trailhead from Hwy. 285 between Buena Vista and Poncha Springs, head west on County Rd. 270 for 1.5 miles and then straight on County Rd. 272 for 2 miles. At the intersection, turn left and proceed 1.5 miles to the trailhead.

Mt. Antero can also be accessed via a four-wheel-drive road that begins on Chalk Creek Rd. (County Rd. 162). From Nathrop drive west up Chalk Creek about 11 miles and turn left on the Baldwin Gulch Rd. This rocky road takes you about 6 miles, up near the gem field, about a mile south of the Mt. Antero summit. If you are climbing the peak, this route is the quickest.

The Colorado Trail—

The 469-mile Colorado Trail, stretching from Denver to Durango, makes its way through the Upper Arkansas area, skirting the eastern edge of the Sawatch Range. Terrain varies from relatively low-altitude sections through ponderosa pine groves to high alpine meadows. Access to the trail is possible from numerous roads that head west along Hwy. 285 (between Poncha Pass and Buena Vista) and from Hwy. 24 (north of Buena Vista).

Mount Tabeguache/ Mount Shavano Trail—

This fairly difficult day hike climbs up the southwest ridge of 14,155-foot Mt. Tabeguache and then follows a saddle over to the summit of 14,249-foot Mt. Shavano. On Shavano's east side, an unusual snow formation known as the "Angel of Shavano" is visible in May and early June, depending on the snowfall. Many legends exist concerning the "angel"—one explains that a mischievous Indian princess so angered the gods that they turned her into ice and put her on the mountain. When a drought struck the valley below, the princess redeemed herself by crying. Her tears became the melted snow, which ended the drought.

Begin the 5-mile hike to Tabeguache's summit by going north along Jennings Creek and then angling northeast to the ridge on Tabeguache's southwestern side. Follow the ridge up to the summit. Cross over to Shavano's summit and then return by traversing below the summit of Tabeguache. A topographical map is suggested for this hike. To reach the trailhead from Poncha Springs, drive west on Hwy. 50 for 6 miles and turn right onto County Rd. 240. Drive about 3.8 miles to Angel of Shavano Campground and continue 1.7 miles up the road to the trailhead at Jennings Creek.

Ptarmigan Lake Trail—

Beautiful Ptarmigan Lake is a popular destination for hikers. Fishing at the 11-acre lake has been very good for small cutthroats. Views of the surrounding peaks are perhaps the biggest attraction. The moderately difficult 3.3-mile trail begins at 10,670 feet and climbs to 12,132 feet. The forest service asks that you camp and collect firewood well away from the lake. To reach the trailhead from Buena Vista, drive about 14 miles west on Cottonwood Pass Rd. (County Rd. 306). The trailhead is on the left side of the road.

Rainbow Trail—

See the Biking section.

Tunnel Lake Trail—

This trail traverses the Continental Divide beginning at the east portal of the Alpine Tunnel (see the Scenic Drives section in the **Gunnison and Crested Butte** chapter for information). The 7.5-mile trail begins at the Hancock townsite, an old settlement that serviced area mines and housed Alpine Tunnel workers. Hike 2.5 miles up the jeep road (No. 298) to the tunnel. On top of the tunnel, the trail (No. 1439) heads north through alpine meadows and willow fields. Alpine Lake can be seen below. The trail intersects Tincup Pass Rd., 4 miles above St. Elmo. To reach the trailhead from St. Elmo, drive (or walk) southwest on County Rd. 295 for 5.5 miles to the ghost town of Hancock.

HORSEBACK RIDING

With a rich ranching history in the valley and a vast amount of nearby public land, horseback riding is very popular in this part of the state. Many companies provide anywhere from hour-long trail rides to multi-day hunting trips into the mountains.

Gunn's Livery Stables—

Guided trail rides head into San Isabel National Forest, BLM land and the old Hutchison Homestead, one of the original ranches in the valley. Gunn's also features breakfast and dinner wagon rides, certainly a unique option to a cafe in town. Reservations for the meals and overnight pack trips are necessary. Located just east of Poncha Springs on Hwy. 50. **PO Box 171, Poncha Springs, CO 81242; (719) 539-3213.**

Horn Fork Guides—

Horn Fork is the company to contact if you're looking for an extended pack trip into the remote mountains of San Isabel National Forest. Fishing and hunting expeditions are their specialty. For information about available trips, contact Glen Roberts at **29178 County Rd. 361, Buena Vista, CO 81211; (719) 395-8363.**

Mount Princeton Hot Springs Stables—

Located up Chalk Creek Rd. above Mt. Princeton Hot Springs Resort, these folks offer trail rides up into the surrounding mountains of the Sawatch Range. **15870 County Rd. 162, Buena Vista, CO 81211; (719) 395-2447.**

RIVER FLOATING

Of the many large rivers originating in Colorado, none is run by more rafters, kayakers and canoers than the Upper Arkansas River. Heavy use is related not only to the ample rapid sections, but also to the fact that so much of the river is accessible from major highways. When the spring runoff begins, river rats flock to the area; scores of outfitters offer float trips throughout the summer.

Upper Arkansas River—

Forty-seven miles of the Upper Arkansas, from Granite down to Salida, provide a full range of water. Running parallel to Hwy. 24 between Granite and Buena Vista, the infamous "Numbers" rapids, rated Class IV to Class V, are too treacherous for many river runners. This is perhaps the most technical stretch on the Arkansas. Below Buena Vista, at Ruby Mountain Recreation Area, boaters put in for the most popular river run in the state— Brown's Canyon. From Ruby Mountain, the first 2 miles are relatively mild until the river drops into the granite canyon. Boulder fields abound during low water; they are transformed into standing waves at high water. Most rafters and kayakers conclude this exciting section by taking out at Hecla Junction Campground at the Hecla Junction Recreation Area to avoid the nasty Seidel's Suckhole (a churning spot a half mile downriver that flips many boats). Below Seidel's Suckhole, the river flows 12 miles to Salida, offering less hair-raising water.

Below Salida, the river enters the narrow Arkansas River Canyon and eventually the frightening Royal Gorge, 44 miles downstream. For information about this part of the river, see the River Floating section of the **Cañon City** chapter.

Permits are not needed to run the river if you have your own raft or kayak. Be aware that 60 percent of the land along the river is private, so please respect the landowners' rights by staying off their property. Maps of the river, showing put-in and take-out spots, are available at many river companies in the valley and at the Chamber of Commerce visitors centers in Salida and Buena Vista. Currently, there is a push to turn the Arkansas River corridor into a state recreation area, which will provide better access and riverside facilities, as well as signs posting private property. An excellent book that's worth picking up is *Upper Arkansas River* by Frank Staub (Fulcrum, 1988). It contains a mile-by-mile description of the river including geology, wildlife and a compelling history.

Outfitters—

There are more than 70 licensed river outfitters in the Upper Arkansas Valley; you can't help but run across them if you're anywhere near the river. The outfitters vary in quality and type of service provided. The following are a few of the most reputable businesses in the area.

American Adventure Expeditions—Located in Johnson Village, 2 miles south of Buena Vista, American Adventure Expeditions offers anything from half-day trips to overnighters on the Arkansas. They also run trips on other rivers in Colorado as well as out of state. **PO Box 1549, Buena Vista, CO 81211; (719) 395-2409.**

Arkansas Valley Expeditions—Billy Mansheim and Pam Green have been running the Arkansas longer than most other outfitters in the area. They specialize in exciting day trips with an emphasis on having a good time. Floats on relatively calm water are offered along with more challenging runs through the Numbers, Brown's Canyon and the Royal Gorge. For

a first time on the river, these folks are highly recommended. **944 E. Hwy. 50, Salida, CO 81201; (719) 539-6669** or toll free at **1-800-833-RAFT.**

Dvorak's Kayak & Rafting Expeditions—Perhaps the most respected outfitter in Colorado, Dvorak's specializes in expedition-type boating. In addition to trips down the Arkansas, they run extended trips on other major rivers in Colorado (including the Gunnison and Dolores rivers) and in foreign countries. Kayak lessons are offered. **17921-B Hwy. 285, Nathrop, CO 81236; (719) 539-6851** or **1-800-824-3795** toll free.

Moondance River Expeditions—These folks offer moonlight floats and quarter-day to five-day trips down the Arkansas. Their trips are more suited for people looking for a rafting vacation and an outdoorsy experience. Contact Nonny and "Bear" Dyer at **310 W. First St., Salida, CO 81201; (719) 539-2113.**

ROCKHOUNDING

Attention geologists and weekend rockhounds! Rock formations in the Upper Arkansas River area yield an incredibly diverse assortment of minerals and gems. Armed with rock hammers, hordes of people scour the mountains and valleys each year, but plenty of specimens still lay unclaimed. Be sure to stay off private land unless you have permission from the landowner. Information about where to spend your time looking can be obtained at the Buena Vista Chamber of Commerce visitors center. Here are a couple of the most famous sites.

Mount Antero—

The gem field at the top of Mt. Antero (14,245 feet) is the highest one in the country. If you take the trouble to climb this high peak, you may be rewarded with aquamarine crystals, bright blue beryl and phenakite crystals, all of which can measure up to two inches in diameter. Smoky quartz and beryllium minerals are also found. For directions to the summit, see the Hiking and Backpacking section.

Ruby Mountain—

Located along the east side of the Upper Arkansas River, Ruby Mountain has long attracted seekers of small crystals of spessartite garnet, yellow topaz and marekanite obsidian pellets in a rhyolite formation. Small amounts of canidine crystals and smoky quartz have also been found here. To reach Ruby Mountain from Buena Vista, drive 5.7 miles south on Hwy. 24/285 to Fisherman's Bridge and turn left. Proceed a half mile, turn right and continue 2.5 miles.

SKIING

CROSS-COUNTRY SKIING

With the large number of national forest hiking trails and backcountry jeep roads in the Upper Arkansas Valley area, it makes sense that much of the terrain is used for cross-country skiing in winter. Although snowmobiles compete for many of the trails, you can find secluded areas away from the whine of their engines. Valley locals and the San Isabel National Forest Headquarters have done plenty to accommodate cross-country skiers by marking trails well and providing services in the towns. For avalanche information, maps, etc., contact the **Salida Ranger District Office, 230 W. 16th St., Salida, CO 81201; (719) 539-3591** or **Trailhead Ventures, 707 N. Hwy. 24, PO Box 2023, Buena Vista, CO 81211; (719) 395-8001.**

Backcountry Trails—

Cottonwood Pass Road—From the trailhead near Rainbow Lake, this trail follows the easy grade of Cottonwood Pass Rd. for 10 miles to the summit at 12,126 feet on the Continental Divide. Pine and aspen line the road up to treeline. On a clear day you'll have views west to Taylor Park, the Elk Mountains and other mountain ranges. To reach the trailhead from Buena Vista, head west on County Rd. 306 to where the plowing ends near Rainbow Lake.

Evans/Rush Memorial Trail—This fairly easy 3.25-mile loop trail is named in memory of two men killed in a nearby avalanche in 1975. But don't worry, if you stick to the trail, you won't meet a similar fate. The entire loop is marked with blue diamonds. To reach the trailhead from Buena Vista, drive about 10 miles south on Hwy. 285 to County Rd. 270 and turn right. Proceed 1.5 miles to County Rd. 272 and follow it to the parking area.

Old Monarch Pass Road—Located just west of the Monarch Ski Area on Hwy. 50, Old Monarch Pass Rd. takes off to the right. The first 1.5 miles to the summit have set tracks. From the summit of the pass, take time to enjoy the views of the surrounding mountains. The trail descends to the west for 7 miles through pine forests. Be sure to save enough energy for the return trip.

Tincup Pass Road—The road up to the summit of Tincup Pass at 12,154 feet makes a fantastic ski trip, but it can receive heavy snowmobile traffic on weekends. This intermediate trail starts at St. Elmo. Cross the bridge over Chalk Creek, turn left and begin skiing up the trail through the trees. It's steep for the first half mile but gradually mellows for the remaining 7.5 miles to the summit. To reach the trailhead from Buena Vista, drive south on Hwy. 285 for about 10 miles and turn right on Chalk Creek Rd. (County Rd. 162). Drive about 15 miles to St. Elmo.

Groomed Trails—

Monarch Ski Area—A number of groomed trails are available for no charge at Monarch Ski Area. The nearby Old Monarch Pass Rd. is also groomed for 1.5 miles to its summit on the Continental Divide. Rentals and cross-country lessons are available. To reach the ski area from Salida, drive west on Hwy. 50 for 21 miles.

Rentals and Information—

Trailhead Ventures—This shop rents everything from telemark skis to gaiters. **707 N. Hwy. 24, PO Box 2023, Buena Vista, CO 81211; (719) 395-8001.**

DOWNHILL SKIING
Monarch Ski Area—

Major ski magazines and other national ski area reviewers have long sung the praises of Monarch. Located along the Continental Divide near the summit of Monarch Pass, the ski mountain is a natural. A basin traps more than 300 inches of light, fluffy powder snow each winter—who needs snowmaking machines? The runs are laid out so you can reach any one of the four lifts from any place on the mountain. A major attraction here is Monarch's diversity of terrain—beginners, intermediate skiers and experts can find challenging runs from the top of all the lifts. This is especially appealing to families: one parent can take the kids down an easy bunny slope while the other hits the mogul run; everyone can meet at the bottom for another ride up the lift. Although the vertical drop is only 1,000 feet, you'll get as much skiing in (if not more) than at a much larger area. Monarch's appeal to many skiers is its laid-back atmosphere. Lift-ticket rates are reasonable to boot.

The day lodge at the base offers a cafeteria and the Sidewinder Saloon where happy hour begins at 4 pm (quite often there is live music). Ski school and rentals are also available. Three miles down the road you can stay at the reasonably priced Monarch Lodge (see the Where to Stay section). Located 16 miles west of Poncha Springs on Hwy. 50. **Hwy 50 W., Garfield, CO 81227; (719) 539-3573.**

SWIMMING
Salida Hot Springs—

See the Hot Springs section.

TENNIS
Centennial Park Courts—

In Salida, there are four courts at Centennial Park, next to the Chamber of Commerce visitors center. Reservations are not taken.

Town Park Court—

One court is located in the park on the west side of Hwy. 24 at the traffic light in Buena Vista. Just show up and play.

—— SEEING AND DOING ——

HOT SPRINGS
**Mount Princeton
Hot Springs Resort—**

Don't miss a soak in one of the two large swimming pools or one of many rock pools down along Chalk Creek. For information, see the Where to Stay section.

Salida Hot Springs—

Hot mineral water is piped from 8 miles away to Salida Hot Springs Pool, the largest indoor hot springs pool in Colorado. Built as a WPA project in 1937, this well maintained facility is worth a stop. Take a swim in the 25-meter lap pool or a hot soak in the 18-inch wading pool or 4-foot-deep shallow pool. Private hot tubs are available for an additional charge. Summer hours are Tues.–Sun. 1:30–9 pm, winter hours are Tues.–Fri. 4–9 pm and Sat.–Sun. 1:30–9 pm. Located next to the Chamber of Commerce at Centennial Park. **410 W. Rainbow Blvd., Salida, CO 81201; (719) 539-6738.**

MUSEUMS
Buena Vista Heritage Museum—

Located in the old Chaffee County Courthouse, built in 1882, this museum features period clothing displays, a school room and a mining and ranch room packed with historical artifacts. Railroad buffs will be particularly interested in the scale layout of the three major narrow-gauge railroads that chugged their way through the Upper Arkansas Valley in the 1880s. Be sure to examine the re-creation of the Denver South Park & Pacific's amazing Alpine

Tunnel, which ran under the Continental Divide. Open Memorial Day through Labor Day, 1–4:30 pm. Fee charged. **511 E. Main St., Buena Vista; (719) 395-8458.**

Salida Museum—

The Salida Museum houses the usual mining, railroad, pioneer and Indian artifacts as well as the unusual. Displayed prominently is a horse-skin coat made by an early Salida resident after his favorite horse died—what a tribute! The museum is open Memorial Day through Labor Day, 11 am–7 pm. Small fee charged. Located next to the Chamber of Commerce at **406 W. Rainbow Blvd.**

Winfield School Museum—

If you drive up Clear Creek Canyon to the ghost town of Winfield, visit the museum located in the old school building. Old worn desks and other memorabilia are on display. Maintained by the Clear Creek Canyon Historical Society, the museum is open in summer only. To reach Winfield from Buena Vista, drive 16 miles north on Hwy. 24 to Clear Creek Canyon Rd. (County Rd. 390) and turn left. Drive about 13 miles. No fee charged.

NIGHTLIFE

You must be kidding. For the most part, sidewalks roll up by 9 pm in Buena Vista and Salida throughout the year. During the ski season Monarch Lodge and the lounge at Monarch Ski Area are hopping. In addition, here are a couple of places that can get rolling, especially on weekends.

The Bar'n—

You'll find live country-and-western music on weekends in this big building that used to serve as a horse motel. Open Sun. noon–midnight, Mon.–Sat. 2 pm–2 am. Located just west of Salida. **7870 Hwy. 50, Salida; 539-6545.**

Victoria Hotel & Tavern—

Very popular among Salida locals, the Vic is a great place to unwind and listen to live rock and blues music. Open Sun. noon–midnight, Mon.–Sat. noon–2 am. **143 N. F St., Salida; 539-4891.**

SCENIC DRIVES

Clear Creek Canyon Road—

A drive up Clear Creek Canyon is highly recommended for its beautiful scenery and history. Beginning in 1867, prospectors made their way up this canyon and surrounding gulches while looking for gold and silver. Known as the La Plata Mining District, many successful mines led to the founding of a number of settlements, including Beaver City, Vicksburg and Winfield, by the 1880s. The largest of these towns was Winfield, which had a population of more than 1,500 by 1890. Today quite a few buildings remain at these sites— many are used as summer homes. Winfield Cemetery serves as the final resting place for more than 25 of the early residents, many of whom died from gunfights, avalanches, fire and lightning.

Clear Creek Canyon serves as a jumping-off point for trails up many of the 14,000-foot peaks in the area, including Mt. Oxford, Mt. Belford and Missouri Mountain. To reach the road from Buena Vista, drive about 16 miles north on Hwy. 24 and turn left on County Rd. 390. A few cabins remain at Vicksburg, 8 miles up the road. You'll reach Winfield in another 4 miles.

Cottonwood Pass—

This is one of the best all-around drives in the state. Views from the 12,126-foot summit on the Continental Divide are spectacular. There is good camping along the way, with plenty of side roads to explore. Cottonwood Pass Rd., which opens fairly early in the summer, can be easily driven in a regular car.

Before Independence Pass Rd. was built, the route over Cottonwood Pass served as a vital supply link not only to the mining camps of Tincup and Pitkin in Taylor Park on the west side of the Continental Divide, but also to Ashcroft and Aspen via Taylor Pass (see the **Gunnison** and Crested Butte chapter). Built as a toll road in 1880, the road climbs through pine forests, aspen groves and eventually into alpine tundra where wildflowers, especially columbine, can be seen flourishing into mid-Aug.

To reach the pass from Buena Vista, head west for 28 miles up Cottonwood Creek on County Rd. 306. Be sure to stop on the summit for great views in all directions, especially the Three Apostles to the north. Continue down the west side 12 miles to Taylor Park Reservoir. From here you can turn around and return to Buena Vista or return via Gunnison or Tincup and Cumberland Pass, eventually heading back east over Monarch Pass on Hwy. 285.

Marshall Pass—

See the Scenic Drives section of the Gunnison and Crested Butte chapter.

Midland Tunnels Road—

If you are heading north from Buena Vista, consider this scenic alternative to Hwy. 24. This road parallels the Arkansas River on the east side for about 10 miles before rejoining Hwy. 24. From the stoplight in Buena Vista, head east on Main St. for a couple of blocks and turn left at the Colorado Highway Department building. This road takes you north out of town. You'll drive through a series of four rock tunnels, blasted out of the mountainside over 100 years ago by the Colorado Midland Railroad. Since the Denver & Rio Grande already had its tracks laid down by the river, the Colorado Midland had no alternative but to blast the tunnels through this narrow section of the valley. A local claims this was the only stretch of railroad track in which one train could be in four tunnels at once. After making your way through the tunnels, be on the lookout for Elephant Rock, which is hard to miss.

St. Elmo—

St. Elmo is the typical Old West ghost town. Weathered false-front buildings line the main street, resembling something out of a Western movie set. Originally settled

in 1880, St. Elmo served as a supply center and hell-raising Sat. night town for the mines around the area. The biggest mine was the Mary Murphy, which produced millions in gold until closing in 1926. In 1881 the Denver South Park & Pacific Railroad started construction of the Alpine Tunnel just a few miles above town (for information see the Scenic Drives section of the Gunnison and Crested Butte chapter). By the mid-1880s, St. Elmo was home to more than 2,000 residents, however, by 1890 its inevitable decline began. A fire in 1890 destroyed the two main blocks in town, including the post office. The postmaster valiantly saved the mail from going up in flames, but was harrassed for failing to rescue the liquor and cigar supply.

To reach St. Elmo from Nathrop (8 miles south of Buena Vista), head west up Chalk Creek on County Rd. 162. St. Elmo lies about 15 miles up the valley. Along the way you'll notice the white Chalk Cliffs to the right on the southeast side of Mt. Princeton. A popular legend claims that Spanish conquistadors stashed two bags of gold and silver at the base of the cliffs while being chased by Indians. Many treasure hunters have lost their lives over the years climbing these limestone cliffs looking for the booty. Keep your eyes peeled for the herd of bighorn sheep that is frequently spotted near the cliffs. The scenery along the drive is especially striking when the aspen turn colors in fall.

TRAMWAY

Monarch Aerial Tramway—

Take a ride up the highest gondola in the United States to the Continental Divide for incredible views of the surrounding Colorado mountain ranges. The gondola whisks you up to an enclosed observation tower that is equipped with maps and telescopes. Many fairly level hiking trails branch away from the tower for hikes at 13,000 feet. Located near the summit of Monarch Pass, the tram runs from May 15 through Oct. 15; open daily from 9 am–5 pm. From Poncha Springs, drive west on Hwy. 50 for 16 miles. Call **(719) 539-4789.**

WHERE TO STAY

ACCOMMODATIONS

With emphasis on the outdoors and camping, unique lodging opportunities are few and far between in the Upper Arkansas Valley. With main highways passing through most of the towns, many motels line the main streets, especially in Buena Vista and Salida. The following are a few standouts.

The Adobe Inn — $$ to $$$

The Adobe Inn looks a bit out of place in Buena Vista. This distinctly Southwestern-style inn is something you'd expect to find in Santa Fe. The building is more than 100 years old, but since the owners, Paul and Marjorie Knox, remodeled it a few years ago, it is nothing like its former self. A solarium with Mexican tiles, a large adobe fireplace and southern-facing windows make for a cozy place to relax and read or chat with other guests. Three guest rooms, each with a private bath, represent the cultures of the Southwest. The Antique Room is equipped with antique oak furniture and a brass bed. The Mexican Room features hand-carved Mexican furniture; the Indian Room comes with a hand-carved headboard, a loft and a kiva-style adobe fireplace in the corner. In an adjacent house, the Wicker Suite and Mediterranean Suite are tastefully furnished, providing additional sleeping space for larger groups. Breakfast is served each morning, quite often including eggs with chili, fruit and coffee or Mexican hot chocolate. You may also want to get into the Southwestern spirit by eating lunch or dinner at the Knoxes' **Casa del Sol** restaurant, located next to the inn. The small (and pricey) restaurant features "gourmet Mexican" food; no liquor is served. Reservations are advised. Located at **303 N. Hwy. 24, PO Box 1560, Buena Vista, CO 81211; (719) 395-6340.**

Blue Sky Inn — $$ to $$$

With its exceptional views west to the Collegiate Peaks and location along the Arkansas River, the Blue Sky Inn is a great alternative to a night in a motel. From the breakfast room or the patio, watch rafters and kayakers make their way downriver through the white water. Many guests use the inn as a base for day trips around the area, while others just relax in the spacious living room by the river stone fireplace or play croquet on the lawn. Upstairs, two suites (each with two bedrooms) provide great views. Additional space in the main house next door is available for larger groups. Country breakfast, with eggs, sausage and homemade bread, is served each morning. For reservations and directions to the inn, contact Hazel Davis at **719 Arizona St., Buena Vista, CO 81211; (719) 395-8862.**

Monarch Lodge — $$ to $$$

Located just 3 miles down the road from Monarch Ski Area, Monarch Lodge has comfortable accommodations no matter what time of the year you visit. Each of the 100 rooms has modern furnishings, a bathroom and a TV. If you want to cook your own meals, choose one of the 16 rooms that come with a kitchenette. Balconies look out to the South Arkansas River and the surrounding forest (if you get a room on the south side).

Monarch Lodge's additional features include an excellent fitness center with Nautilus machines, indoor tennis and racquetball courts, a heated pool, jacuzzi and sauna. There are also a restaurant and two lounges. In winter, free shuttle buses run between the lodge and ski area. In summer, special weekend packages are phenomenally low-priced. Contact the lodge for specifics. Located in Garfield, 13 miles west of Poncha Springs on **Hwy. 50 West, Garfield, CO 81227; 1-800-332-3668** in Colorado or **1-800-525-9390** outside Colorado.

Mount Princeton Hot Springs Resort — $$ to $$$

Sandwiched between Mt. Princeton and Mt. Antero along Chalk Creek Gulch, this resort is the pride and joy of many valley residents. The resort has three outstanding features: comfortable accommodations, fine dining and, of course, hot springs pools. Early settlers wasted no time in constructing bath houses by the 1870s. Improvements were made to the facilities, climaxing with the completion of the imposing Antero Hotel in 1917. This elegant four-story resort, with its large veranda, served as host to the rich and famous until the stock market crash of 1929 prompted a slow decline. The hotel was torn down in 1950; over a million board feet of lumber was salvaged and shipped to Texas.

A newer lodge has since been built and the current owners are constantly expanding the facilities. Nine rooms in the main lodge and 20 motel units are spacious and modern with TVs and private baths. For people on a budget, nine rustic rooms in the upstairs of the old stone bath house offer shared baths, kitchen facilities and a balcony view of Chalk Creek and the upper valley.

The biggest draw the lodge has are its hot springs. There are three large outdoor swimming pools, a couple of private indoor hot tubs and numerous rock pools down by the creek. Jess Ayers, the manager, admits that he was amazed by the popularity of the rock pools, which were built in 1987 by a group of 70 guests who stayed at the resort for a week during the harmonic convergence. All guests of the lodge have free use of the hot springs; a reasonable fee is charged to others.

The restaurant and lounge in the main lodge are very popular with area locals. For information about the restaurant, see the Where to Eat section. To reach Mt. Princeton Hot Springs from Buena Vista, drive south on Hwy. 24/285 to Nathrop and turn west on County Rd. 162. Proceed 5 miles to the lodge. **15870 County Rd. 162, Nathrop, CO 81236; (719) 395-2447.**

Sweet Adeline's — $$ to $$$

Staying at Sweet Adeline's is a bit like spending a night at Granny's house. Located in a quiet, old residential neighborhood in Salida, this Queen Anne-style home was built in 1900. Adella and Bob Schulz opened for business in 1986 after a speedy but well-done restoration. Three guest rooms are decorated with antiques and Adella's needlework. The Briar Rose Room has a private bath, while the other two share a bath. Guests can spend time by the fireplace, on the porch swing or sing along with the player piano. A full breakfast is served each morning, including egg dishes, homemade rolls and bread, just to name a few. Candlelight dinners are available upon request for an additional charge. The Schulzes really try to accommodate your every wish. No smoking, pets or children under eight years old. Reservations are strongly recommended, especially since the inn is closed for a few months in winter. **949 F St., Salida, CO 81201; (719) 539-4100.**

The Poor Farm Country Inn — $$

When the Chaffee County Poor Farm was built in 1892, little did anyone know that one day visitors would flock happily to its doors. Until 1945, the Poor Farm provided housing to those who were out of luck and money. The current owners, Herb and Dottie Hostetler, first saw the three-story brick structure in 1982, when they decided to buy it and turn it into a bed and breakfast. What a task that was! The building had been abandoned for 20 years, and though structurally sound, the inside was a mess. The front room on the main floor had even been used as a chicken coop. With Herb's general contracting background and Dottie's knack for interior decorating, the Poor Farm was open for business within six months.

On the second floor, there are five separate bedrooms and four baths. Up on the third floor, 12 dorm-style bunks provide inexpensive accommodations for individuals and groups on a budget. Downstairs there is a library and TV room for guests' use. Each morning guests gather round the breakfast table for fruit, coffee or tea and Dottie's special Belgian waffles. The Poor Farm sits in the country outside of Salida with fantastic views west to the

Sawatch Range. It's a good idea to call ahead for directions and reservations. **8495 County Rd. 160, Salida, CO 81201; (719) 539-3818.**

Vista Court — $$

The cluster of cabins that comprise Vista Court allow for privacy at a reasonable price. Each of the eight cabins has a private bath, kitchenette and cable TV. Four of the cabins have two bedrooms. Sit back in the jacuzzi on the front lawn while looking off at Mt. Princeton. The current owners, Ginger and Grover Horst, have put extensive work into these rustic cabins and are eager to make your stay enjoyable. Located a half mile west of the traffic light in Buena Vista on Main St. **1004 W. Main St., PO Box 3056, Buena Vista, CO 81211; (719) 395-6557.**

CAMPING

The vast majority of visitors to the Upper Arkansas Valley choose to camp out. Plenty of campgrounds in San Isabel National Forest as well as private campgrounds meet these needs.

Hecla Junction Recreation Area—

About 9 miles north of Poncha Springs on Hwy. 285, turn right (east) on County Rd. 194 and proceed about 3 miles to the undeveloped Hecla Junction Recreation Area along the Arkansas River. This is a popular take-out spot for rafters and kayakers coming out of Brown's Canyon. There are a number of places for primitive camping. No fee.

Ruby Mountain Recreation Area—

About 5.7 miles south of Buena Vista on Hwy. 285, turn left at Fisherman's Bridge, drive a half mile, turn right and proceed another 2.5 miles to Ruby Mountain Recreation Area. This scenic spot down along the Arkansas River offers a number of primitive campsites. No fee.

In San Isabel National Forest—

West of Buena Vista along Cotton-wood Pass Rd. (County Rd. 306), there are two campgrounds. Driving 7 miles west of town and then south on County Rd. 344 leads to **Cottonwood Lake Campground**. Located along the shores of beautiful Cottonwood Lake, the campground offers 28 sites; a fee is charged. Driving 11 miles west of Buena Vista on County Rd. 306 leads to **Collegiate Peaks Campground**, with 45 sites; a fee is charged.

From Nathrop (8 miles south of Buena Vista on Hwy. 285), Chalk Creek Rd. (County Rd. 162) heads west to four campgrounds; all charge a fee. Driving 7 miles up County Rd. 162 leads to **Mt. Princeton Campground** with 17 sites. Another mile up the road is **Chalk Lake Campground** with 21 sites. Still another mile up the road is **Cascade Campground** with 23 sites. **Iron City Campground**, located 15 miles west of Nathrop on County Rd. 162, offers 17 sites.

Heading west from Poncha Springs on Hwy. 50 toward Monarch Pass will take you to four more campgrounds. Six miles west of Poncha Springs at Maysville, turn right on County Rd. 240 and proceed 4 miles to **Angel of Shavano Campground** with 20 sites; a fee is charged. Another 6 miles up County Rd. 240 is **North Fork Reservoir Campground** with eight sites and no fee. Thirteen miles west of Poncha Springs on Hwy. 50 is **Garfield Campground** with 11 sites; a fee is charged. Another 2 miles west on Hwy. 50 brings you to **Monarch Park Campground** with 38 sites; a fee is charged.

O'Haver Lake Campground, located southwest of Poncha Springs, has 24 sites; a fee is charged. To reach the campground from Poncha Springs, head south on Hwy. 285 for 5 miles and turn right (west) on County Rd. 200 for 2.3 miles and then right on County Rd. 202 for 1.5 miles.

About 20 miles east of Salida on Hwy. 50 and right (southwest) for 3 miles on County Rd. 06 leads to **Coaldale Campground**. It offers 11 sites and no fee is charged. One mile farther up County Rd. 06 is **Hayden Creek Campground** with 11 sites and no fee.

If you just want to primitive camp on national forest land, drive up Clear Creek Canyon Rd. (County Rd. 390). To reach the road from Buena Vista, head north on Hwy. 24 for about 16 miles and turn left on County Rd. 390 toward **Clear Creek Reservoir.** Along the road, which continues 12 miles to Winfield, there are plenty of places to camp.

Private Campgrounds—
Buena Vista Family Campground and Resort—Located 2.5 miles southeast of Buena Vista on Hwy. 24, this well-equipped RV campground offers, among other things, a large recreation room and free movies nightly. Tent sites are also available.

27700 County Rd. 303, Buena Vista, CO 81211; (719) 395-8318.

Four Seasons Campground—Amenities include a TV room and a laundromat. Tent sites are available as well as hookups for RVs. Located 1.5 miles east of Salida. **4305 E. Hwy. 50, Salida, CO 81201; (719) 539-3084.**

Heart of the Rockies KOA—Heart of the Rockies offers plenty of RV hookups and tent sites by the stream. A heated swimming pool helps provide a comfortable stay. Located 5 miles west of Poncha Springs on Hwy. 50. **16105 Hwy. 50, Salida, CO 81201; (719) 539-2025.**

WHERE TO EAT

Fine dining is not a strong suit of this area. Many restaurants rely heavily on fried foods with an astronomical calorie count. One Buena Vista local said the best place to eat in the valley was at the barbecue pit in his yard. Whether that's true or not, we can recommend a few other places.

Grimo's — $$ to $$$
The casual atmosphere of Grimo's belies the excellent Italian food served up nightly. Start off with a drink from the bar or a game of pool before dinner. Veal, chicken and pasta dishes dominate the menu. The specialty of the house is baked eggplant parmigiana. Seafood plates include scallops sauteed in wine and baked with mushrooms and cheese. Open 4–9 pm; closed Mon. **146 S. Main, Hwy. 285, Poncha Springs; 539-2903.**

Delaney's Depot — $ to $$$
Conspicuously located along Hwy. 24 in Buena Vista, Delaney's does a booming business. Large portions of down-home food and fast service keep the place packed with locals and vacationers stopping in for a quick bite. In keeping with the railroad theme, a train whistle blows when orders are ready in the kitchen. Breakfast items

are fairly standard, except for the "whistle stopper" steak and egg plate. A salad bar is available for lunch and dinner to go along with burgers, soups, ribs, steaks, chicken and fish. Open in summer Mon.–Sat. 7 am–9 pm, Sun. 7:30 am–9 pm; in winter closing time is one hour earlier. **605 Hwy. 24, Buena Vista; 395-8854.**

First Street Cafe — $ to $$$
A bit off the main drag, the First St. Cafe is worth a stop whether you want a meal or a freshly ground cup of coffee. Located in one of the oldest brick buildings in Salida, the cafe is decorated with hanging plants and unique wood paneling. There is a large fish tank in the bar area. For breakfast, try stuffed French toast, a breakfast burrito, an omelette or quiche. Lunch is the most popular meal here for salads, sandwiches and stir-fry. Dinners feature steaks, lemon garlic chicken and pan-fried trout topped with almonds. Open in summer Mon.–Sat. 8 am–10 pm; in winter Mon.–Thur. 8 am–7 pm and Fri.–Sat. 8 am–10 pm. Closed Sun. **137 E. First St., Salida; 539-4759.**

Gourmet Chef — $ to $$$
Although most Salida locals said the

Gourmet Chef served the best Chinese food in the area, we were skeptical. After all, it serves the *only* Chinese food in the valley. But after eating there, we have to agree—it is good and reasonably priced. Located along Hwy. 50 in Salida, the Gourmet Chef is owned and operated by a family from Taiwan, so they should know what they are doing. Along with a bar, the dining area has booths, tables and subdued lighting. Lunch specials are offered; main dishes include specialties from many different regions of the Chinese mainland. Open Mon.–Sat. 11 am–9:30 pm for lunch and dinner. **710 Milford St., Salida; 539-6600.**

Princeton Club Restaurant & Lounge — $ to $$$

The Princeton Club is as well known for its attractive dining environment and sweeping views as it is for its fine food. Located in the main lodge at Mt. Princeton Hot Springs Resort, the attractive restaurant is accented by a large stone fireplace and local artwork hanging on the walls. Large picture windows provide views west to the Chalk Cliffs of Mt. Princeton. Breakfast items include omelettes and spicy huevos rancheros and eggs bayou. Sandwiches and salads are featured for lunch. For dinner, the Princeton Club is especially well known for its fine Cajun and vegetarian dishes, although the steaks and seafood are also quite good. You might want to take a soak in the hot springs while you're here. Open 7:30 am–9 pm nightly; the bar is open until 10 pm (11 pm on weekends). To reach the lodge from Buena Vista, drive south on Hwy. 24/285 to Nathrop and turn west on County Rd. 162. Drive about 5 miles to the lodge. **15870 County Rd. 162, Nathrop, CO 81236; 395-2447.**

The Windmill — $ to $$$

When you first step into this false-front building, you'll think you're in an old country store. But don't be fooled, this is a restaurant and a very good one at that. Knickknacks, including many old signs, line the weathered wood walls. Behind the counter of the gift shop near the front door, an old pharmacist's wooden display shelf is filled with antique packaged medicines. Owner Clifton Jones thanks his dad for most of these relics: "He's a real antique buff." The building used to house a Ford car dealership, so there is plenty of room. The lunch and dinner menus are extensive. Burgers, specialty salads and Tex-Mex dishes are lunch highlights. For dinner, try a rib-eye steak or the popular chicken-fried steak. Soup, salad bar and potato come with all dinners. The Windmill has a good selection of beer and a separate bar area. Hours are 11 am–10 pm daily. **720 E. Hwy. 50, Salida; 539-3594.**

El Duran Y Miguel — $ to $$

This laid-back restaurant stands out as the best all-around place to go in the valley for Mexican food. Mexican music blasts from the jukebox and sombreros and blankets hang from the walls. Sip a Margarita or order from their selection of Mexican beers. Owner Frank Duran prepares green chili from his secret recipe; his mother is in charge of red chili. The menu includes chimichangas, stuffed sopapillas, fajitas and the enchilada supreme (portions are large). For dessert, try a sopapilla delight, topped with ice cream, strawberries and whipped cream. Open daily in summer 11 am–10 pm and in winter 11 am–9 pm. **301 E. Main St., Buena Vista; 395-2120.**

Evergreen Cafe — $

Sit down at the counter or find a table at this reasonably priced diner. The Evergreen offers lighter meals than you'll find at many other places in the valley. For breakfast, create your own omelette, enjoy a breakfast crêpe or choose a breakfast shake made with milk, egg, yogurt, banana, pineapple and orange. Lunch dishes include burgers, sandwiches, soups and salads. Try a slice of homemade pie or cake for dessert. Open daily from 6:30 am–2:30 pm. Located at the north end of Buena Vista. **418 Hwy. 24, Buena Vista; 395-8984.**

SERVICES

Buena Vista Chamber of Commerce—
343 S. Hwy. 24, PO Box P, Buena
Vista, CO 81211; (719) 395-6612.

Salida Chamber of Commerce—
406 W. Rainbow Blvd., Salida, CO
81201; (719) 539-2068.

Wet Mountain Valley

Though the phrase "off the beaten path" gets too much use these days, it does seem appropriate when describing the Wet Mountain Valley. This beautiful, remote location in the southern part of the state, wedged between the Wet Mountains to the east and the jagged peaks of the Sangre de Cristo Range to the west, remains unknown among many Coloradans. Quite a few people, however, find the valley by accident and end up returning by design. The surrounding San Isabel National Forest gets year-round use by fishermen, horseback riders, cross-country skiers and hikers. Steep trails into the Sangre de Cristos on the western side of the valley lead along many streams and high alpine lakes. Some of the state's most rugged 14,000-foot peaks, including Crestone Needle, await those who want a difficult climbing challenge.

Though cattle ranching and farming are the mainstays in the area, it was the silver boom in the late 1800s that attracted thousands of folks to the valley. Today **Silver Cliff**, the dominant mining town during the boom days, and nearby **Westcliffe**, the original rail town in the valley, are the supply centers providing the few services the area has to offer. Although tourism is gaining importance in the valley, many locals cherish the lack of development, doing whatever it takes to eke out a living. Many artistic, individualistic people are attracted here by the beauty and the simple, unadorned lifestyle that prevails. One local told us his biggest problem was the noise a herd of elk made while bugling out on his front lawn. We should all have such problems.

HISTORY

Along with documented facts, many legends animate the early history of the valley. One, concerning a lost gold mine, has turned out to be partially true. Spanish conquistadors, while exploring the region from their territory to the south, discovered a gold mine in a deep cave located high on a mountain in the valley. The cave's entrance was reportedly marked with a Maltese Cross. In the late 1920s the existence of the cave was officially confirmed. Now known as Marble Cave or "La Caverna del Oro," it is located high up on Marble Mountain, southwest of Westcliffe. A number of speleologists have explored the vertical shafts, finding evidence of mining but, so far, no gold.

Ute Indians who inhabited the Wet Mountain Valley came into contact with trappers in the first half of the 1800s, but nothing changed much until the 1870s. In 1870 a group of 400 German immigrants arrived in the valley to establish Colfax, an ill-fated agricultural co-op, about 7 miles south of present-day Westcliffe. As it turned out, many of the colonists did not find communal living to their liking. On top of that, the cows ate garlic, which ruined the cheese! Within a few years many members of the group had left the valley; those remaining split up the land and started farming and cattle ranching.

About the time of Colfax's demise, interest of a much larger magnitude focused on the valley—the silver mining boom. In winter of 1872–1873, Richard Irwin discovered rich silver deposits, and the rush was on to the new camp Rosita. For a short time, Rosita received recognition for being what the *Pueblo Chieftain* called "the liveliest mining town in the territory." Aside from another strike at Querida in 1877, the real glory days in the valley began when horn silver was discovered in 1878—these chunks of black, greasy rock from a nearby cliff melted down to 75 percent silver. Thousands poured into the area and established the town of Silver Cliff. And what a town it was! Many considered it to rival Leadville as the wildest town in the state. When the decision was to be made concerning the location of the state capital, Silver Cliff was in the running along with Denver and Golden.

Hopes soared for the town in 1881 when the Denver & Rio Grande Railroad announced plans to lay tracks from Cañon City up Grape Creek to the area. But, much to the irritation of Silver Cliff residents, the train tracks stopped a mile from town—and as it had done so many other times throughout the state, the Denver & Rio Grande built its own community. Westcliffe became more important than Silver Cliff. When mining activity waned, prosperity in the valley took a sharp downturn and the Denver & Rio Grande Railroad discontinued service. Ranching and farming then became the dominant industries. When the Denver & Rio Grande Railroad laid tracks to the valley again in 1900, development and prosperity seemed a sure thing. But alas, the Denver & Rio Grande Railroad continued to lose money and ended service to Westcliffe in 1937, this time for good.

Today, cattle ranching and wheat, hay and barley farming are very important to the area's economy, as is ever-increasing tourism.

GETTING THERE

Westcliffe is located 150 miles southwest of Denver. From Denver, drive south on Interstate 25 to Colorado Springs and take Hwy. 115 from the south end of town. Drive to Florence and head south on Hwy. 67 and then west on Hwy. 96.

——— FESTIVALS AND EVENTS ———

Rainbow Trail Mountain Bike Race

late July

Among serious mountain bike racers, this race is considered one of the finest of its kind. Riders take off from the starting line in Westcliffe for a grueling loop ride south on the Rainbow Trail. For informa-tion about entering the race, contact the Westcliffe Chamber of Commerce at (719) 783-9163.

Jazz in the Sangres

second weekend in August

Come to Wet Mountain Valley for a weekend of great jazz performed by some of the best musicians in the Rocky Mountain West, including some nationally known performers. Styles range from fusion to blues to big band. This festival, which got its start in 1984, has been developing quite a reputation among jazz lovers in the region. But you don't have to be a jazz lover to have a good time here. Shows run during the day Sat. and Sun.; at night performers appear at local restaurants and bars. Make sure to book accommodations well in advance of the festival, unless you want to camp out. For information or advance ticket purchases, contact **PO Box 327, Westcliffe, CO 81252; (719) 783-9141** or **(719) 783-9145.**

──── OUTDOOR ACTIVITIES ────

BIKING

MOUNTAIN BIKING

Wet Mountain Valley offers many places to explore on a mountain bike. On the west side of the valley, jeep roads and national forest trails are everywhere. There are no rental shops in the area, however. For information about trail possibilities, inquire locally and refer to the Hiking and Backpacking and Scenic Drives sections.

FISHING

There are many worthwhile fishing spots in the Wet Mountain Valley area, although it's not exactly a fisherman's paradise. Streams running down out of the Sangre de Cristos are, for the most part, steep and fast-moving. Most people have luck fishing the beaver ponds along smaller tributaries. For tackle and advice about where the fish are biting, stop in at **F&S Hardware Plus, 111 2nd St., Westcliffe; (719) 783-9111.**

De Weese Reservoir—

Beware of this warmwater reservoir: according to many reports, you'll reel in a sucker nine out of 10 times, despite repeated attempts to stock the lake with rainbows.

Grape Creek—

Fishing along Grape Creek, just below De Weese Reservoir, can be good for rainbow and brown trout. The water runs through state-owned and BLM land, so access isn't a problem. To reach the creek from Westcliffe, head 4 miles north on County Rd. 241. The creek begins at the northeast end of the reservoir.

Hermit Lake/Horseshoe Lake—

See Hermit Pass in the Four-Wheel-Drive Trips section.

Lakes of the Clouds—

To reach three lakes at an 11,200-foot elevation, you'll need a four-wheel-drive vehicle or else you'll be in for a 5-mile hike. Below the lakes there are beaver ponds that yield brook and cutthroat trout. The upper lake offers good rainbow and cutthroat fishing; the lower lake has mostly cutthroat. Don't bother with the middle lake because it's too shallow and often has winterkill. To reach the lakes from Westcliffe, head north on Hwy. 69 for about a mile and turn left on County Rd. 170. Proceed about 8 miles. From here, either continue in your jeep or start hiking.

Lake Isabel—

Lake Isabel, heavily stocked with rainbow and brook trout, is accessible by car. There are also a few browns in the lake that grow up to 15 pounds. A boat ramp is available. Many people try their luck ice fishing here in winter. To reach the lake from Westcliffe, drive east on Hwy. 96 and turn south on Hwy. 165 for 25 miles. The lake is on the right side of the road.

Middle Taylor Creek—

See Hermit Pass in the Four-Wheel-Drive Trips section.

FOUR-WHEEL-DRIVE TRIPS

Hermit Pass—

From the 13,000-foot summit of this road high in the Sangre de Cristo Range, you'll have beautiful views of the expansive San Luis Valley to the west and Wet Mountain Valley to the east. The road travels up Middle Taylor Creek past beaver dams, Hermit Lake and Horseshoe Lake; all provide decent fishing for brook, rainbow and cutthroat trout. To reach the road from Westcliffe, head west on Hermit Lake Rd. and keep going.

Medano Pass—

Once a route used by the Indians and even a few Spanish conquistadors, 9,950-foot Medano Pass Rd. is a spectacular way to cross the Sangre de Cristos. From the summit of the pass, the road drops 6 miles along the Medano River to Great Sand Dunes National Monument (see the Major Attractions section of the **San Luis Valley** chapter). When you reach the dunes, it's a 4-mile drive to the visitors center. You may want to let some air out of your tires to help you drive across the sand and refill at the air hose available at the visitors center. To reach Medano Pass from Westcliffe, drive south on Hwy. 69 for 24 miles and turn right (west) on County Rd. 17. The summit of the pass is 9 miles west of Hwy. 69.

HIKING AND BACKPACKING

Although Wet Mountain Valley remains undiscovered by many residents of the state, it's fairly well known among active hikers and backpackers, especially those who like steep, challenging terrain. The Sangre de Cristo Range, which runs along the western edge of the valley, matches any mountain range in the state for rugged, high-altitude hikes—Crestone Needle, Crestone, Humboldt and Kit Carson peaks all top out above 14,000 feet. Among them, only Humboldt is considered a fairly easy climb; the other three

have claimed their share of lives over the years. This eastern slope of the Sangre de Cristo Range, and much of the rolling Wet Mountains on the east edge of the valley, lie within San Isabel National Forest. Many well-marked trails crisscross the forests and valleys, but you should take along a good topographical map of the area in which you're hiking. For specific information about trails in San Isabel National Forest, check with the **San Carlos Ranger District Office, 326 Dozier St., Cañon City, CO 81212; (719) 275-4119.**

Comanche/Venable Loop Trail—

Although this trail can get crowded in summer, the beauty of the area makes it worth trying. The fairly difficult, 10.5-mile loop begins at Alvarado Campground. Start the hike up the Comanche Trail (No. 1345). You'll climb steeply through the pine and aspen, eventually paralleling Hiltman Creek up to Comanche Lake. From the lake, the trail switchbacks up to the crest of the Sangre de Cristo Range, well above treeline. Many people continue west, down the western slope of the mountains to Crestone Creek for extended trips. If you're not interested in this option, head north from the crest along the trail, which eventually drops down to Venable Lake and Venable Creek. Be on the lookout for the waterfall along Venable Creek, about 1.5 miles below the lake. Eventually, you'll run into Rainbow Trail, a half mile north of your starting point. There is great camping and pretty good fishing along the entire route. To reach the trailhead from Westcliffe, head south on Hwy. 69 for 3 miles and turn right on Schoolfield Rd. Proceed 7 miles to Alvarado Campground.

Rainbow Trail—

This 100-mile-long trail is also very popular, with few uphill stretches. For the most part, it traverses the eastern slope of the Sangre de Cristos from Music Pass, about 15 miles southwest of Westcliffe, north by northwest to the Continental Divide near Marshall Pass. Take off for a day hike or a longer trip. There are many places to reach the trail; it is well marked with trail signs. One of the easiest accesses from Westcliffe is at Alvarado Campground. See the previous entry for directions.

LLAMA TREKKING

Mountain Odysseys—

Have you ever taken a llama to lunch? Well, you can, on a day trip with Mountain Odysseys. In the nearby Wet Mountains, trips leave each morning at 10 am and return at 3 pm. The llamas carry all of the supplies, so you can have a relaxing hike without any weight on your back. Although you won't have lunch served on fine china, the food is better than you'd be able to rustle up out of a backpack. Lunch usually includes home-baked sourdough croissants or muffins with cold cuts and fresh fruit, served with lemonade or wine. In addition to the lunch trip, Mountain Odysseys can take you out in the mountains for an extended llama trek—from one night to a week. For prices and other information, contact **PO Box 295, Rye, CO 81069; (719) 489-2864.**

SKIING

CROSS-COUNTRY SKIING

Cross-country skiing opportunities in the Wet Mountain Valley vicinity abound. Many trails lead up into the Sangre de Cristo Range west of Westcliffe. For information about trail possibilities, contact the **Custer County Chamber of Commerce, PO Box 81, Westcliffe, CO 81252; (719) 783-9163.** Additional information can be obtained at the **San Carlos Ranger District Office, 326 Dozier St., Cañon City, CO 81212; (719) 275-4119.**

Backcountry Trails—

Hermit Pass Trail—Many local cross-country skiers wax their skis and head for the Hermit Pass Rd. A popular jeep road in summer, this road winds its way up Middle Taylor Creek, past Hermit Lake to the summit of the pass, just over 13,000 feet. From the summit, views west into the San Luis Valley and east to Wet Mountain Valley are stunning. To reach the trailhead, head west from Westcliffe on Hermit Lake Rd. Drive to where the plowing stops and begin skiing up the road. The trail is about 5 miles long.

Rainbow Trail—Stretching almost 100 miles along the eastern slope of the Sangre de Cristo Range, Rainbow Trail (No. 1336) provides excellent cross-country skiing in winter. Fairly easy rolling terrain through lodgepole pine, douglas fir and aspen combined with far-reaching views of the valley make this a highly recommended trail. The easiest access point from Westcliffe is at Alvarado Campground. From town, drive south on Hwy. 69 for 3 miles and turn right (west) on Schoolfield Rd. Just follow the signs to the marked trailhead.

DOWNHILL SKIING

Conquistador—

This small ski area, located 5 miles west of Westcliffe against the Sangre de Cristos, attracts a lot of day skiers from Pueblo and Colorado Springs. Since its beginning in 1966, the area has expanded to 10 runs serviced by four lifts. Although Conquistador has snowmaking equipment, inadequate snow cover quite often can be a problem.

At the base lodge, there are a cafeteria, a ski rental shop and a ski school. Conquistador is currently for sale. The new owners should have the area ready to go for the 1989–1990 ski season, unless they rip out the equipment and lease the water rights. Contact the **Custer County Chamber of Commerce** at **(719) 783-9163** for the latest on the Conquistador saga.

SEEING AND DOING

CEMETERIES

Silver Cliff Cemetery—

One night, in 1882, as four drunken miners were walking by the Silver Cliff Cemetery, they saw blue lights darting around the gravestones. At first, no one in town believed the stories of mysterious lights. Eventually many townsfolk also saw them. Over the years, locals and visitors alike claim to have seen these lights at the graveyard. The phenomenon even attracted the attention of *National Geographic.* Whether you go to the graveyard at night to see the ghostly blue lights or roam around during the day to see this Victorian burial site, it's worth a trip. To reach the cemetery from Silver Cliff, head south on the road next to Clever's along Hwy. 96.

MUSEUMS AND GALLERIES

Bishop's Castle—

About 27 miles southeast of Westcliffe, located among the thick pine trees of the Wet Mountains, lies one of Colorado's most bizarre attractions. Since 1969, Jim Bishop has been working single-handedly on his colossal stone and iron castle, which so far is a cross between Camelot and the Eiffel Tower. Not many who see it would argue Bishop's claim that the structure, billed as a monument to hard-working people, is the country's biggest one-man, physical project. Jim describes it as "building by coincidence rather than design," which makes it more art than architecture. At the moment, it consists of three stories of hand-set stone, topped with ornamental iron arches and an assortment of other wrought-iron flourishes. Other features include a 58-foot tower (which will reportedly reach 130 feet), flying buttresses and a spiral stone staircase to the top. On the front gable is perched a metal dragon whose nose serves as a chimney for a wood stove on the third floor.

As Bishop's wife Phoebe says, "The castle and Jim are one and the same." Despite his devotion, Bishop is the first to admit that the project may never be finished, but he adds, "It ain't important that I get it done; it's important that I'm doing it." Future plans include a roller coaster mounted on the outer wall and an onion dome, like the one on Saint Basil's Basilica in Russia, on top of the castle tower. "Maybe people will think I'm a communist or something," Bishop laughs.

Admission is free but donations are appreciated. Visitors are free to explore the castle, if they sign an insurance waiver. To reach Bishop's Castle from Westcliffe, drive 16 miles east on Hwy. 96 and turn right onto Hwy. 165. Proceed about 11 miles and look for the signs on the right side of the road. **HCR 75, Box 179, Rye, CO 81069.**

Silver Cliff Museum—

Get a feel for the history of the valley at this small museum. Exhibits are housed in the old Silver Cliff Town Hall and Fire Station, which operated from 1879 to 1959. The museum, open daily from Memorial Day through Labor Day, is worth a look if you're in the area. Located on **Hwy. 96** in **Silver Cliff.**

NIGHTLIFE

Silver Dome Dance Hall and Saloon—

Good times kick into high gear at this strange-looking geodesic dome, especially on weekends when live acoustic country as well as rock music is performed. Relax on one of two levels inside and choose from six beers available on tap. Full bar service and munchies are also offered. Open Mon.–Sat. 11 am–2 am; Sun. from noon to midnight. Located on **Hwy. 96** in **Silver Cliff**—you can't miss it.

SCENIC DRIVES

**Oak Creek Grade
(County Road 143)—**

This scenic road heads northeast to

Cañon City. To reach the road from Silver Cliff, drive east on Hwy. 96 for about 5.5 miles and be looking for the road on the left. For more information, see the Scenic Drives section of the **Cañon City** chapter.

Rosita/Junkins Park—

For spectacular scenery and a look at historical settlements around Wet Mountain Valley, take time to drive this 40-mile loop. From Westcliffe, head east for 16.2 miles and turn right on County Rd. 358. It takes you through Junkins Park with its interesting rock formations and remains of old cabins built by Czechoslovakian settlers. After passing through Junkins Park, you'll drop down a hill to Blumenau, origi-nally settled in the late 1800s by German immigrants. The view of the Sangre de Cristos is fantastic from here. Further on you'll reach an intersection. County Rd. 347 heads to the right, back to Hwy. 96. County Rd. 328, on the left, leads to Rosita, which was the original silver mining town in the valley. Many old buildings still stand, including the general store and the Wet Mountain Rosita Fire Station. If you continue west from Rosita, you'll drive by Rosita Cemetery on the left. Established in 1870, there are still old tombstones as well as recent ones. From here, proceed west to Hwy. 69, turn right and head back to Westcliffe.

———— WHERE TO STAY ————

ACCOMMODATIONS

There are a few motels in Westcliffe and Silver Cliff as well as some cabins located on the outskirts and in the surrounding hills. During the jazz festival and hunting season, many of the accommodations are booked. The rest of the year you shouldn't have any trouble finding a place. For a complete rundown on all lodging opportunities in the area, contact the **Custer County Chamber of Commerce, PO Box 81, Westcliffe, CO 81252; (719) 783-9163.** Here are a couple of possibilities.

Alpine Lodge — $$

For a more rustic stay in Wet Mountain Valley, consider staying in one of the cabins at the Alpine Lodge. Located at the base of the Sangre de Cristos, the small, cozy cabins have kitchenettes and sleep up to four people comfortably. Instead of cooking in your cabin, you may want to eat at the fine restaurant at the lodge (see the Where to Eat section). Alpine Lodge is located 10 miles west of Westcliffe on Schoolfield Rd. **6848 County Rd. 140, Westcliffe, CO 81252; (719) 783-2260.**

Antler Motel — $

If it's low-budget accommodations you're looking for, go straight to the Antler Motel in Westcliffe. The rooms are nothing much to look at, but they are clean. Each has a telephone and cable TV. Located next to the Antler Liquor Store. **102 S. 6th St., Westcliffe, CO 81252; (719) 783-2426.**

Malachite School — $

In these days of runaway environmental problems, rampant consumerism and giant agri-business, a visit to Malachite School is a refreshing break. Located in the Huerfano River Valley, with a spectacular view up the valley to Blanca Peak, this 260-acre nonprofit school "practices, teaches and searches for respectful and sustainable ways of living and farming that are community responsible and environmentally sound," according to director Kent Mace. Malachite focuses on family farm stays and college-credit programs. By experiencing one of the programs, you can develop the skills to become more self-sufficient, and you will be more aware of our fragile green world.

Participate in plowing with draft horses, organic gardening, beekeeping and farm shop, which teaches you how to repair farm equipment, household items, etc. Families can spend a night or a week in this beautiful valley, join in with farm chores, take a hay ride or go hiking. Most visitors to the farm camp out in tents, but beds are available in a solar-heated dorm room. Farm-fresh meals are provided three times a day. If you just want to stop by for a visit and take a tour, that's fine, too—just call ahead. A visit to Malachite is a rejuvenating experience. For more information about programs, costs, etc., contact **Malachite School, ASR Box 21, Gardner, CO 81040; (719) 746-2412.**

CAMPING

In San Isabel National Forest—

Alvarado Campground, located in the foothills of the Sangre de Cristo Range, is 10 miles from Westcliffe. From town, head south on Hwy. 69 and then west on Schoolfield Rd. There are 47 sites and a fee is charged. **Lake Creek Campground** is located 12 miles northwest of Westcliffe on Hwy. 69 and 3 miles west from Hillside. It has 11 sites and a fee is charged.

In the Wet Mountains southeast of Westcliffe are a number of other campgrounds. From Westcliffe, drive east on Hwy. 96 and turn south on Hwy. 165 for 18 miles to **Ophir Campground**. It has 31 sites; a fee is charged. A couple of miles further south on Hwy. 165 takes you to **Davenport Campground** with 15 sites; a fee is charged. Five miles south from Davenport is the **Lake Isabel Recreation Area**. It has three campgrounds, including **Southside Campground** (eight sites), **St. Charles Campground** (15 sites) and **Cisneros Campground** (25 sites). All charge a fee.

Private Campgrounds—

Lea's Haven—Plenty of hookups for RVs. Located at the west edge of Westcliffe; **(719) 783-2242.**

WHERE TO EAT

Dining opportunities in this remote valley are limited. On top of that, there is a high turnover rate. Aside from a number of cafes in Silver Cliff and Westcliffe, here are a couple of current standouts.

Alpine Lodge — $$ to $$$

Located among the pines, 10 miles southwest of Westcliffe, the lodge offers the finest dining in the area. The rustic lodge provides a comfortable dining atmosphere. Look out at the Wet Mountain Valley while enjoying one of the fine steak or seafood entrées. The Alpine Lodge has nightly specials, including prime rib every Sat. Salads, sandwiches and homemade soups round out the lighter side of the menu. If you're not counting calories, try a slice of their excellent homemade pie. Open Wed.– Sat. 5–9 pm, on Sun. from 4–8 pm. **6848 County Rd. 140, Westcliffe, CO; 783-2260.**

Clever's Cafe & Mountain Tavern — $ to $$$

A friendly atmosphere and pretty good food await at Clever's. It's located in one of the oldest buildings in Silver Cliff. This turn-of-the-century brick building had been a bank, an assay office and a grocery store/post office before it was renovated as a restaurant a few years ago. An antique bar and a few tables occupy the original room. An adjacent dining room has an exposed brick wall, a wood stove in the corner, skylights and a great view of the Sangre de Cristo Range. Lunch specialties include burgers, sandwiches and Mexican dishes. For dinner, try a large steak or stuffed trout. Locals like to hang out in the bar; there is a happy hour Mon.–Fri. from 4–6 pm. Plunk a quarter in the jukebox and relax. Open for lunch and dinner daily from 11 am–10 pm. The bar remains open until 2 am (midnight on Sun.). Located along **Hwy. 96 in Silver Cliff; 783-9986.**

SERVICES

**Custer County Chamber
of Commerce—**
    PO Box 81, Westcliffe, CO 81252; (719)
783-9163.

Deserted barns and homesteads add a rustic beauty to the countryside (sketch by Michael A. Darr).

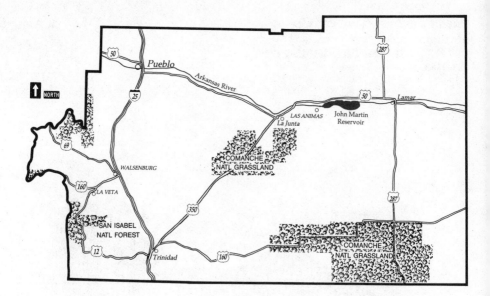

SOUTHEAST REGION

Cuchara Valley

It's surprising that most Coloradans are unfamiliar with this little valley in the southern part of the state. Vacationers from Texas and Oklahoma have been coming to the Cuchara Valley since 1906, discovering early on what many natives continue to overlook. Nestled between the eastern slope of the southern Sangre de Cristo Range and the looming Spanish Peaks, the Cuchara Valley offers plenty of outdoor beauty along with an interesting history and a mix of Hispanic and Anglo cultures. Originally part of a Spanish land grant, the valley retains an Hispanic feel. In addition, working ranches give Cuchara a western flair. Texas longhorn cattle still graze in some of the pastures along the road.

The expansive San Isabel National Forest runs through the central part of the valley, stretching west to east from the top of the Sangre de Cristo Range to the twin Spanish Peaks. These twins dominate the surrounding landscape, towering 7,000 feet above the nearby prairie. The national forest offers a number of outdoor activities, most notably hiking and skiing.

At the northern entrance to the valley, La Veta, a quaint, undiscovered little mountain town, serves as sentinel. An eclectic citizenry made up of seniors, alternative lifestyle advocates and expatriate southerners will make you feel relaxed, no matter how long you plan to stay. If you're a golfer, a round at the Grandote Golf Club may cause you to stay longer than you thought. The Cuchara Valley is definitely worth looking into for its peace and quiet and stunning scenery.

HISTORY

Right from the beginning the Spanish Peaks have been inexorably tied to the history of southern Colorado and the Cuchara Valley. Called *Huajatolla* ("Breasts of the Earth") by the Plains Indians, these two mammillary peaks were a source of significant religious wonder and, perhaps, mineral wealth. Gold on Aztec shrines in present-day Mexico was said to have come from "a double mountain far to the north." Despite reported sightings of ancient mines on the mountains, no significant mineral strikes have ever been recorded at the Spanish Peaks.

The Santa Fe Trail, which brought settlers across the prairie in the first half of the 1800s, relied heavily on the Spanish Peaks as a landmark. In 1862, the first settlement in the Cuchara Valley sprang up at the present site of La Veta. Col. John M. Francisco, with the help of Henry Daigre and Hiram W. Vasquez, built a fort that took on the name *Fort Francisco* and later *Francisco Plaza*. Francisco and his associates started a large sheep and cattle ranch, thereby enticing many sheep ranchers into the area in the next few years. But like many settlements in this part of the country, the real boost came in 1876 when the Denver & Rio Grande Railroad came to town on its way west. Farming and coal mining became the prominent industries for quite a while, but they eventually bowed to the rise of tourism.

GETTING THERE

From Denver, the Cuchara Valley and the town of La Veta can be reached by driving 160 miles south on Interstate 25 to Walsenburg and then turning west on Hwy. 160. Drive about 11 miles to Hwy. 12, heading off to the left. The town of La Veta is 3 miles down the road at the base of the Cuchara Valley.

Daily bus service is available from Colorado Springs and Denver. Commercial airlines fly into Cuchara Valley Airport from Colorado Springs.

——— OUTDOOR ACTIVITIES ———

GOLF

Grandote Golf and Country Club—
Named for the Tarahumare Indian prophet who led his people to the Spanish Peaks from the south, this young but fine course commands an excellent view of the nearby Spanish Peaks. Opened in the spring of 1986, this 18-hole course was designed by Tom Weiskopf. It has been planned in conjunction with a real estate development and eventually may go private, though, reportedly, that won't be for at least five years.

Water hazards, including the Cucharas River and two lakes, come into play on 10 of the holes. The front nine is still open, but the back nine, with plentiful aspen and pine, looks much more mature than it really is. Moderately priced fees. Open May 1 to mid-Oct. Cart and club rentals available; full pro shop. **5540 Hwy. 12, PO Box 506, La Veta, CO 81055; (719) 742-3123.**

HIKING AND BACKPACKING

The southernmost parcel of land in San Isabel National Forest encompasses the Cuchara Valley and the immediate mountains in the area, providing relatively undisturbed hiking and backpacking possibilities. The Spanish Peaks Wilderness Study Area protects the two famous mountains that have long helped explorers, pioneers and hikers find their way. There are a number of fine trails near these peaks.

North Fork Trail—

Beginning near Trinchera Peak and angling southeast, this is a 4.5-mile hike ranging in altitude from 9,800 to 10,800 feet. It begins at the four-wheel-drive road to Trinchera Peak near **Bear Lake Campground** (see Camping section) and ends at **Purgatory Campground**.

Peaks/Wahatoya Trail—

This highly recommended 10-mile hike takes you along the southern edge of the Spanish Peaks and then north through the saddle between the two peaks. Be on the lookout for the deer and wild turkeys that thrive in this area. Reach the trailhead by taking the Cordova Pass Rd. (see Scenic Drives section). After crossing over the pass, continue down to the **Apishapa Creek Picnic Ground**. Look for the trailhead on the left side of the road.

West Peak Trail—

Starting at about 11,000 feet, this trail is fairly easy up to treeline, then it's a steep rock scramble to the 13,626-foot summit of West Spanish Peak. Be sure to watch for thunderstorms. To reach the trailhead, drive to the top of **Cordova Pass** (see Scenic Drives section) and look on the left for the 2.5-mile trail.

SKIING

CROSS-COUNTRY SKIING

There are a number of good places to go cross-country skiing in the Cuchara Valley. Although there are no groomed, tracked trails, **Cuchara Valley** Ski Area has a trail system (small fee) and provides lessons. If you want lessons, but in a more backwoods locale, contact the **Adobe Arch Trading Post, Box 488, La Veta, CO 81055; (719) 742-3042**. They offer cross-country ski guides throughout the winter.

For those who like to go out on their own, the San Isabel National Forest hiking trails make for good cross-country skiing in the winter. Try the trails near the summit of **Cordova Pass** (see Scenic Drives). Another standout trail in winter is the **Old La Veta Pass Road**. A narrow-gauge railroad was built over the pass in the 1870s. A 3-mile ski up to the summit leads to a number of old buildings, including the old depot, listed on the National Register of Historic Places. To reach the trail (road) from La Veta, take County Rd. 450 northwest for about 3 miles to **Hwy. 160** and turn left. About 4 miles up the highway, turn left onto **Old La Veta Pass Rd. (County Rd. 443)**.

DOWNHILL SKIING

Cuchara Valley Resort—

As the name implies, Cuchara Valley strives to be known as a resort destination, not just a ski area. Although it's not in the league with powerhouses like Steamboat and Vail, Cuchara Valley does have its own appeal. Small crowds, relatively inexpensive lift tickets and lodging, and a general low-key atmosphere help keep the place going. The resort caters mainly to southerners, spawning such ski trail names as *El Tejano* (Spanish for "Texan") and *San Antonio*.

Located just 25 miles from New Mexico, Cuchara Valley Resort is the southernmost ski area in Colorado. Its southern latitude is not a factor in winter snow depths, as the ski area averages over 200 inches annually. However, wind is a factor; it can whip the snow off a trail right down to the rock. Wind aside, the mountain, with its evergreen- and aspen-covered slopes, is a very pleasant place to ski. It features mainly beginner and intermediate terrain with a couple of expert runs thrown in for good measure.

Located at the base of the mountain is the Baker Creek Village complex, offering shops and a restaurant. Adjacent to the base area is the condominium complex, with the only lodging at the mountain. About a mile north of the ski area on Hwy. 12, the Cuchara Inn offers quality hotel ac-commodations. Ski lessons and rentals are available.

To reach the ski area, head south on Hwy. 12 from La Veta about 12 miles to the ski area entrance on the right. For infor-mation about the ski area and its accom-modations, contact **Cuchara Resort, PO Box 3, Cuchara, CO 81055; (719) 742-3163** in Colorado, **1-800-227-4436** out of state.

SEEING AND DOING

MUSEUMS

Fort Francisco Museum—

For such a small town, La Veta has put together an impressive museum that looks back nearly 130 years to the days of the first pioneers. The museum is located at the site of the original Francisco Plaza, built in 1862 by the original La Veta settler, Col. John M. Francisco. The land and building were donated to the town in 1957. Some of the original fort structures contain the museum displays. Two main buildings have theme rooms, including Clothing, Pi-oneer Ranching, Indian Artifacts and Fur-niture. Each room is packed full of an eclec-tic assortment of items, most of them do-nated locally. Read through letters written by settlers to the territorial governor in 1873 appealing for protection against the Indians. One letter was written in 1853 to a local attorney from another attorney in Springfield, Illinois—Abraham Lincoln. Allow plenty of time to examine the large collection.

Also inspect the blacksmith shop, sa-loon, post office and schoolhouse that were all moved to the grounds from within the area. Admission fee is minimal. Open daily from Memorial Day through Labor Day 9 am–4:30 pm. Located in the center of La Veta just off **Hwy. 12** (west side).

SCENIC DRIVES

Cordova Pass—

This drive is probably the most beauti-ful in the area. Paralleling the Spanish Peaks along their southern sides, Cordova Pass winds a serpentine course to its summit at 11,000 feet and then down to the town of Aguilar near Interstate 25. Along the way, aspen groves and spectacular, unob-structed views of the adjacent Spanish Peaks vie for your attention. Just up the road a few miles is a fantastic quarter-mile wildflower identification trail, best seen in July and Aug. A brochure that will help you identify the flowers is available at the forest service office in La Veta.

Cordova Pass was originally known as Apishapa Pass. Apishapa means "stinky water" in Apache, apparently named after the nearby river which takes on a strong smell during the dry part of the year. The road over the pass was built in 1934.

To reach the pass, drive south from La Veta on Hwy. 12 to **Cucharas Pass**. Just at the summit, turn left on the **Cordova Pass Rd. (Forest Rd. 415)**. After reaching the summit of Cordova Pass Rd. you drive through a tunnel blasted through one of the rock dikes radiating from the Spanish Peaks. In addition to a picnic area, there are a number of good hiking trails along the road (see Hiking and Backpacking for some ideas).

Highway 12 south from La Veta—

Along this highly scenic route (known as the "Highway of Legends"), enjoy green pastures with grazing longhorn cattle, as-pen and evergreen stands, and far-reach-ing views to the Spanish Peaks and their incredible geology. The two mountains are lava formations that popped up millions of years ago, causing cracks in the sedimentary layers on the surface. Lava flowed into these cracks, causing igneous intrusions. These intrusions, much more resistant to erosion than the surrounding sedimentary layers, remain now as lava dikes, radiating from the two peaks like bicycle spokes from a wheel. An amazing sight, many of them can be seen from Hwy. 12. Some of these dikes run unbroken as long as 13 miles, rising as high as 100 feet. Some of the

better known dikes along the highway are Devil's Stairstep, the Gap and Profile Rock (the profiles of George and Martha Washington and an Indian).

About 15 miles from La Veta, the highway reaches the summit of Cucharas Pass. From here you can turn left up Cordova Pass (see previous entry) or continue down south, eventually reaching Trinidad.

WHERE TO STAY

ACCOMMODATIONS

The 1899 Inn — $$

Re-opened for business in 1980, this old stone home (actually built in 1909, not 1899) has seen a lot of changes over the years. Marilyn Schwarz Hall, the innkeeper, told us the building began as a residence, then was a hospital, a boarding house and finally a bed and breakfast. Hall, a New Englander, has renovated all the rooms and furnished them with antiques. With 18-inch-thick walls, the place is well insulated. Five bedrooms are available, some with private bath. In winter, Hall offers a special cross-country skiing package, including ski rentals, a guide if needed and accommodations. Breakfast on Sun. includes popovers and eggs. No smoking. The 1899 Inn is located in La Veta next to the Fort Francisco Museum. **314 South Main St., La Veta, CO 81055; (719) 742-3576.**

Yellow Pine Ranch — $$

A working ranch since 1896, Yellow Pine raises longhorn cattle in its pastures. Just 2 miles north of the Cuchara Valley Resort, the ranch offers very affordable rustic cabins, available year-round. Eight cabins are equipped with modern conveniences, but no TV or phones. The idea here is to relax; there are no planned activities, but fishing on two ponds and a mile of river await you on the property. Autumn is an especially beautiful time to visit, when the aspen are turning gold. A

minimum stay of two nights is required. To reach the ranch, head south 11 miles on Hwy. 12 from La Veta. **Cuchara Rt. Box 20, La Veta, CO 81055; (719) 742-3528.**

CAMPING

Four San Isabel National Forest campgrounds can be reached from Hwy. 12, starting just 2 miles south of the Cuchara Valley ski area turn-off. Turn right onto Forest Rd. 413, which follows Cucharas Creek up to Bear Lake and Blue Lake, nestled at 10,500 feet on the eastern flank of the Sangre de Cristo Range. The first campground is **Cuchara Campground**, with 31 sites; a fee is charged. Farther up Forest Rd. 413 are **Bear Lake Campground** (14 sites) and **Blue Lake Campground** (15 sites); fees are charged at both. Good views from these campgrounds southwest to 13,500-foot Trinchera Peak. Back on Hwy. 12, continue south over Cucharas Pass down to North Lake and turn right (west) onto Forest Rd. 411. Follow this road about 4 miles to **Purgatory Campground**; 23 sites, no water and no fee.

WHERE TO EAT

The Streamside — $$ to $$$

Serving fine northern Italian entrées, The Streamside is a favorite among locals and skiers staying in Cuchara. This charming wooden building boasts a comfortable dining room with windows looking out on the Cucharas River. For a romantic dinner this is the place. Open Mon.–Sat. 5–10 pm (bar opens at 4 pm). Located about 12 miles south of La Veta on Hwy. 12 at the covered bridge. **16984 Hwy. 12; 742-3434.**

Covered Wagon — $ to $$$

Arguably the best steak house in the valley. Rib eyes, sirloins and large hunks of New York strip are "consistently good," according to many locals we talked to. I was drawn to the baked trout stuffed with crab. Daily dinner specials including ribs, chicken-fried steak and poor man's lobster are a good deal. The Covered Wagon is open for breakfast, lunch and dinner. The breakfast menu offers no surprises, just big portions. Lunch items include mainly sandwiches and burgers, including the Wagon Supreme. Complete wine list.

Breakfast from 7–11 am Wed.–Sun., lunch during weekdays 11 am–3 pm, dinner served Mon.–Sat. 4–10 pm, Sun. 11 am–9 pm. **205 Main St., La Veta; 742-3679.**

The Bank — $ to $$

If the bankers who worked here from 1906 to 1921 could see what's going on in the bank now, they probably wouldn't believe it. This combination cafe and gallery features local handicrafts and delicious wholesome food. Pat McMahon, the owner, has been in the area since 1968, when she lived in a tepee and got interested in cottage industry. The importance she places on *homemade* shows through in her support for local artists' work and in her cooking. Everything is made from scratch. For breakfast try a blintz, huevos rancheros or pancakes. At lunchtime, her sandwiches are scrumptious, served on her stone-ground wheat bread. The Chocolate Sin Pie is well named. Sidewalk seating available. Open for breakfast and lunch daily. Hours vary. **222 Main St., La Veta.**

SERVICES

La Veta/Cuchara Chamber of Commerce—

PO Box 32, La Veta, CO 81055; (719) 742-3676.

Pueblo

Once the butt of many jokes about its heavy industry and shabbiness, this town along the Arkansas River at the east edge of the Rockies has come a long way toward changing its image. Pueblo now has plenty of things to attract vacationers who previously had little or no reason to come. Completion of the beautiful Pueblo Reservoir, significant tapering off of pollution from the steel plant smokestacks, and a tenacious commitment to improving the economy have all helped to boost Pueblo's quality of life. These efforts have paid off. Recently, Pueblo was voted the best place to live in the United States by a University of Kentucky research team.

It's still debatable whether you will want to spend your precious vacation time in Pueblo. But by taking a few minutes to exit Interstate 25, you might be surprised by what you find. Pueblo has an amazing number of old neighborhoods with rows of nicely restored Victorian homes. At least drive by the immense Rosemount Victorian House Museum. You might even want to stop for a tour.

Pueblo's people leave a lasting impression on any first-time visitor. Community pride and traditional hard-working ethics surface in everything from completed community projects to conversations in the local pubs. A diversity of ethnic groups, particularly Hispanics, populate the town. Up until the end of the Mexican War in the 1840s, the Arkansas River, which runs through the middle of town, was the border line between the United States and Mexico.

HISTORY

Over the years, Pueblo has been a natural crossroads for Indians, Spanish troops, traders/trappers and gold seekers, due to its prime location on the Arkansas River along the Front Range of the Rockies. Ute Indians long used the area as a camp when they traveled up the Arkansas Valley into the mountains. The first recorded visit to the Pueblo site was by Juan de Ulibarri, a Spaniard who came up from Santa Fe in 1706 looking for escaped Indian slaves.

In 1806 Capt. Zebulon Pike led an expedition into Colorado from St. Louis to "ascertain direction, extent, and navigation of the Arkansas and Red Rivers." As the result of some pretty bad information, Zeb wasn't too successful in finding the Red River (due to the minor fact that it's located in Texas, a few hundred miles to the south). But he did manage to find the Arkansas River and follow it west to the present site of Pueblo. Here he erected a log fort, supposedly the first structure built by Americans in Colorado. It was from here that he set out on an unsuccessful attempt to scale the mountain that bears his name.

In 1822 fur trader Jacob Fowler and his party built a house on the Mexican side (south) of the Arkansas River. Twenty years later, Jim Beckwourth, mountain man and "White Chief" of the Crow Indians, helped establish Fort Pueblo. It was a trading center for the mountain men and Indians. The fort was crude but relatively peaceful until the Christmas massacre of 1854, when 100 Utes and a few Apaches led by Tierra Blanca were allowed into the fort by a settler drunk on "Taos Lightning." The Indians nearly wiped out the entire settlement, sparing only a young Mexican woman, two children and a man named Rumaldo. Rumaldo lived long enough with a bullet hole through his tongue to tell the story, using Indian sign language.

Fort Pueblo remained largely uninhabited for the next few years. According to Lt. E.G. Beckwith, who passed by Fort Pueblo in 1855, mountain men avoided the site entirely, "because it was believed to be haunted by headless Mexican women." Others were concerned about the slightly more substantial threat of additional Indian attacks.

In 1858 prospectors began to enter the area, establishing Fountain City near Pueblo. The large gold strikes in the mountains the following year lured many a miner to the Pueblo area. In 1860 Pueblo City was established, absorbing the Fountain City overflow. Pueblo really picked up when the Denver & Rio Grande Railroad rolled into town in 1872. The railroad connection to the gold and silver mines in the mountains, along with access to nearby coal deposits at Trinidad, made Pueblo the perfect workshop for the mines. Between 1870 and 1880 Pueblo's population grew by leaps and bounds, increasing eightfold to 24,588.

The Colorado Coal & Iron Company, later the Colorado Fuel & Iron Company (CF&I), opened its first blast furnace in 1881. Other companies opened smelters in 1882 and 1888. Workers were needed in these plants. European immigrants, Mexicans and blacks responded by making Pueblo their home, giving the town a melting-pot image.

Early explorers had conflicting ideas about the agricultural potential of the Pueblo area. Ulibarri, the early visitor from Santa Fe, praised the valley for its beauty and fertility. But Maj. Stephen Long, whose expedition in 1820 brought him through the Pueblo area, had another opinion. He referred to the surrounding land as "dreary and disgusting, almost wholly unfit for cultivation." Ulibarri was closer to the mark, because in the late 1800s farmers moved into the valley in droves. With the help of irrigation, the land east of Pueblo soon became an agricultural center. Ranches also sprang up. Charles Goodnight, a pioneer of the range cattle industry who blazed 2,000 miles of cattle trails from Texas to Wyoming, headquartered his operation near Pueblo. Today the Pueblo State Recreation Area and the zoo are located on parts of his ranch.

By 1902 CF&I steelworks was the biggest employer in town, and it continued to be for decades. As recently as the 1940s, Pueblo was the second largest town in Colorado. Unfortunately, in 1982, due to an industry downturn, CF&I was forced to lay off 4,000 workers. It was a devastating blow to the Pueblo economy. But in some ways it was a blessing in disguise. By shutting down the smokestacks and ridding itself of its steel-town image, Pueblo has been successful in attracting new industry.

GETTING THERE

Pueblo has always been easy to get to. It's located 110 miles south of Denver on Interstate 25. The town is serviced by Greyhound Trailways Bus Lines. America West flies into the Pueblo Memorial Airport from Phoenix, Las Vegas and multiple destinations in California. Continental offers a Denver/Pueblo connection at no extra charge for Denver flights. For airline schedule information in Pueblo, call **(719) 544-0035.**

———— MAJOR ATTRACTIONS ————

PUEBLO RESERVOIR

Located upriver on the Arkansas a few miles west of Pueblo, at the **Pueblo State Recreation Area**, this reservoir is in a beautiful setting. Semi-arid plains surrounded by limestone cliffs and buttes contrast with mountain views of Pikes Peak to the north and the Wet Mountains to the west. This manmade reservoir is the pride of the Colorado State Recreation Areas, not to mention the town of Pueblo, and with good reason. Cool, clean water, reasonably good fishing and fantastic sailing are just a few of the reasons more people visit this recreation area than any other in the state.

In the planning stages for decades, the dam was finally completed and operational by the early 1970s. The water is intended for agricultural irrigation and municipal use in Pueblo and Colorado Springs.

Facts About the Reservoir—

There are over 60 miles of twisting shoreline at the reservoir. Most of the northern shoreline is accessible by road, whereas getting to most of the southern shore involves a hike. You have to pay an entrance fee. Here are some things to do once you get there.

Camping—

The recreation area has 270 sites available and a fee is charged. Reservations can be made up to 120 days in advance, but during most of the year they may not be necessary at all. Modern toilets, showers and trailer hook-ups available.

Handicapped Facilities—

The Rock Canyon Area, just below the dam, offers accessible fishing, camping and swimming areas as well as a half-mile, level nature trail suited for wheelchairs.

Horse Trails and Rentals—

Located near the south entrance by park headquarters.

Reservoir Fishing—

Most of the boats plying the waters of Pueblo Reservoir are for fishing purposes. People fish the reservoir year-round. Trout (up to six pounds) are best caught in spring and fall. Walleyes strike often in winter; crappie, small- and largemouth bass, white bass and sunfish feed in the spring and summer. Tackle and minnows are available at the north and south marinas.

Swimming—

Swimming in the reservoir is not allowed. There is, however, a swimming area located just below the dam. A sandy beach down by the river is protected by limestone bluffs and shady cottonwood trees. Rock Canyon Swim Area has lifeguards. There is a small fee. Open in summer only.

Watersports—

Boat ramps allow easy launching for power boats and sailboats. Two marinas offer boat slips and boat rentals. Wind at the reservoir is consistently strong in springtime, and the sailboaters and windsurfers love it. If you plan to windsurf, remember that the water in the reservoir comes from snow melt-off in the mountains. It's really cold in springtime. Most windsurfers wear a wet suit until at least mid-May. Although windsurfing is allowed all over the reservoir, a special beach is set aside for the sport on the north shore. Rentals and instruction are available.

Wildlife—

A wildlife habitat is located in the northwest corner of the recreation area.

Here you can observe deer, wild turkeys, quail, hawks, golden eagles and bald eagles. Below the dam to the east are the **Pueblo Nature Center** and the **Raptor Rehabilitation Center.** You can hike down from the reservoir or drive from town. For more information see the Riverfront section of Seeing and Doing.

For More Information—

Contact the **Pueblo State Recreation Area, 640 Pueblo Reservoir Rd., Pueblo, CO 81005; (719) 561-9320.**

EVENTS

Colorado State Fair
August

Each year at the end of August, Pueblo cuts loose when it hosts the Colorado State Fair. The town had its first annual fair way back in 1872 and has been going strong ever since. Cowboys and city slickers alike crowd into the fairgrounds for the 10-day

event which features stock shows, fiestas, top rock and country music groups and, of course, a rodeo. It's hard not to have a good time no matter what your interests are. Be sure to make advance hotel reservations during the fair, as space gets very tight. The fairgrounds are located at the corner of Prairie and Arroya aves.; **(719) 561-8484.**

OUTDOOR ACTIVITIES

GOLF

The sun shines 73 percent of the year in Pueblo, making it a great climate for golfing. This town has the courses you're looking for. The best course in the area is the **Pueblo West Golf Club,** located about 8 miles west of town. It's rated 73.5, making it the second most challenging course in the state. To reach it, head west on Hwy. 50 to McCulloch Blvd. then turn left. **201 S. McCulloch Blvd.; (719) 547-2280.** In town, try **City Park Golf Course,** located in City Park at **3900 Thatcher Ave.; (719) 561-4946.** Both courses are open all year.

RIVER FLOATING

The Arkansas River flowing through town is one of the most popular floating rivers in the state—though if you're a

whitewater aficionado it isn't for you, because by the time the Arkansas exits its steep mountain canyon and arrives at Pueblo, most of its fight is gone. If you like tranquil water, rent a canoe at the Pueblo Nature Center. For a more secluded float, head upriver on Hwy. 50 to **Swallow's Canyon,** just below the town of Portland. This 10-mile stretch of the Arkansas is a mellow, peaceful float that snakes along through cottonwood groves. Look for blue herons, ospreys and eagles. It's perfect for an open canoe. You can float all the way down into the reservoir and get out at the Oasis Marina on the north shore or stop before the reservoir at any one of a number of fishing access roads.

For more challenging rafting and kayaking water, see the River Floating section in the **Cañon City** chapter.

SEEING AND DOING

MUSEUMS AND GALLERIES

El Pueblo Museum—

The main attraction at this museum is the re-creation of Fort Pueblo, which is especially popular with school kids, who come from all over the state to take tours. Historical information about Pueblo and the Arkansas River is available as well as some interesting artifacts. One exhibit displays metal chest armor worn by a Spanish conquistador. Overall, the quality of the museum exhibits is above average. The admission fee is minimal. Between Memorial Day and Labor Day the hours are Tues.–Fri. 10 am–5 pm; Sat. 10 am–4 pm; during the rest of the year Wed.–Sat. 10 am–3 pm. Located behind the fairgrounds at **905 S. Prairie Ave.; (719) 564-5274.**

Fred E. Weisbrod Aircraft Museum—

This collection of vintage military aircraft is still getting off the ground. Climb inside and inspect fighters, missiles, research vehicles and support equipment, like the 1942 Ford Refueler. Located 6 miles east on Hwy. 50 at the **Pueblo Memorial Airport, 31475 Bryan Cir.** Open daily from 9 am to sunset. For special tours, call Lt. Col. William Feder at **(719) 547-2285.**

Rosemount Victorian House Museum—

This palatial 24,000-square-foot mansion is easily one of the finest Victorian homes in Colorado. Rosemount was contracted in 1890 for John A. Thatcher, founder of the First National Bank of Pueblo, and was completed three years later. Serving as a monument to the finest designers and craftsmen of the era, Rosemount was built for less than $100,000, an extravagant sum by Victorian standards. Thirty-seven rooms, 10 fireplaces, dual gas and electric lighting, a 1,500-gallon copper-lined tank in the attic for pressurized water, stunning woodwork throughout—it really has to be seen and experienced to be appreciated.

John Thatcher's son, Raymond, lived in the house until his death in 1967, at which time it was willed to the city of

Built for John A. Thatcher in the early 1890s, the 37-room mansion is one of the finest examples of Victorian architecture in the state (courtesy of the Rosemount Victorian House Museum).

Pueblo. Most of the original furniture and carpets remain. The mansion was named after Mrs. Thatcher's favorite flower. A rose theme appears in almost every room: from ceiling frescos to patterns on chamber pots. Even if you are just driving through Pueblo, make time to stop in for a tour. Knowledgeable guides are happy to take you on an hour-long tour through the mansion and fill you in on all the details. Special tours can be arranged.

Hours are June 1–Sept. 1: Mon.–Sat. 10 am–4 pm, Sun. 2–4 pm; Sept. 1–June 1: Tues.–Sat. 1–4 pm, Sun. 2–4 pm. Closed Mon. and Jan. Small admission fee charged, discount for seniors and children. Kids under 5 accompanied by an adult are free. **419 W. 14th St.; (719) 545-5290.**

Sangre de Cristo Arts & Conference Center—

Located downtown, the arts center includes a permanent western art display, three galleries with changing exhibits, a theater for performing arts and the hands-on, participatory Children's Museum. On Fri. afternoons in summer, live music, food and good times can be had on the front steps. Galleries are free, and the Children's Museum admission is inexpensive. Open 11 am–4 pm Mon.–Sat. **210 N. Santa Fe Ave.; (719) 543-0130.**

NIGHTLIFE

Pueblo's bars are a great place to get the local perspective on the town, the world—or anything else for that matter. Hopping night spots featuring live music as well as neighborhood pubs pack in the people. Supposedly, there are more liquor licenses per capita in Pueblo than in any other town in the state. Here are a couple of suggested spots where you can go to take the edge off.

The Gold Dust Saloon—

Just down the street from Savoy (see below), this place is a bit more subdued. It's a corner bar with hanging plants, big windows, high ceilings and posters on the walls. Lunch is served from 11 am–4 pm. The Gold Dust is a fun bar where you can throw peanut shells on the floor and sit back in an old barber's chair while the bartender fixes you up with a kamikaze or an upside-down Margarita. You get the picture. Open until 2 am (midnight on Sun.). **130 S. Union Ave.; (719) 545-0741.**

Savoy—

Located on historic Union Ave., this is a fun, lively bar attracting a younger crowd. An eclectic bunch of stuff hangs on the walls and from the ceiling—like a torpedo, a punching bag and a gas pump. The front end of an old Lincoln Continental sticks out of the wall. Live rock and roll or jazz fusion gets this place hopping nightly, especially on the weekends. Lunch and light dinner menus offer sandwiches, salads, burgers and the house spaghetti dinner. Sundaes are a specialty. Serving food from 11–1 am Mon–Sat. Closed Sun. Located at **229 S. Union Ave.; (719) 545-6761.**

THE RIVERFRONT

Trails for hiking and bicycling follow the river through Rock Canyon, connecting 16 miles of trails in the Pueblo State Recreation Area with those in town. The meandering river is lined with tall cottonwood trees and limestone bluffs. This place where Indians used to camp is now a peaceful escape from town.

Pueblo Nature Center—

The center offers nature trails and year-round events intended to educate children and adults alike about the prairie, desert and river valley ecosystems. It's a great place for family picnics. Bicycle and canoe rentals are available. Reach the Nature Center on foot by following the river trail just west of Pueblo Blvd. By car, turn west off Pueblo Blvd. onto W. 11th St. Follow past the entrance to the Raptor Rehabilitation Center to the end of the road. Open seven days a week, 9 am–5 pm. **5200 W. 11th St., Pueblo, CO 81003; (719) 545-9114.**

Raptor Rehabilitation Center—

One of very few centers in the country that rehabilitates birds of prey and returns them to the wild. Located next to the Pueblo Nature Center. Open daily 9 am–5 pm. **(719) 545-7117.**

Zoo at City Park—

Located just east of Rock Canyon, this is a great place to take the kids. The zoo has regular exhibits as well as a children's section called Happy Time Ranch—a farm re-creation complete with goats, chickens, Shetland ponies and even an outhouse. Across from the zoo entrance is a recently restored carousel, built originally in 1911. After a trip to the zoo and a ride on the carousel, your kids will be so grateful they might even start eating their beets. Small fee. Zoo hours are Apr.–Sept. 10 am–6 pm, Oct.–Mar. 9 am–5 pm. **(719) 561-9664.**

WHERE TO STAY

In 1863 the first hotel was built in Pueblo. This log structure was described at the time as being "a hospitable old caravansary with a great, comfortable fireplace and a sufficient force of sleek, well-fed bedbugs." Lodging opportunities have changed a bit since then. The original hotel is long gone and, unfortunately, so is the possibility of staying at any historic hotels. Lodging in Pueblo is limited to well-known motel/resort chains offering the latest in cable TV hook-ups and other comforts.

The only bed and breakfast stops in the Pueblo area lie 26 miles west of the city in Beulah Valley. Located on the eastern flank of the Wet Mountains, Beulah has long been a cool summer escape for Pueblo residents and a scenic detour for visitors to the area.

Settled in the 1850s, the valley was first known as Mace's Hole, after Mexican outlaw "Don" Juan Mace who regularly hid out here. His fabricated stories of having many fellow desperadoes living with him were lies that probably helped keep him alive until 1863. That's when local settlers finally put an end to Mace's cattle rustling by catching him alone on the plains and riddling his body with bullets.

In 1876 the valley was renamed Beulah. It quickly became a resort when word spread about the mineral springs in the area, and many summer homes were built. Unfortunately, the site was abandoned in the 1920s after blasting for water supply lines dislocated the water source.

The two bed and breakfast houses in Beulah still make the valley the perfect hideout.

BEULAH

The Beulah House — $$$

Proprietors Ann and Harry ("Mama and Papa") Middelkamp strive to make the Beulah House a home to their guests. This homey, informal inn hidden in the pines offers nine rooms, five in the main house and four in the nearby clubhouse. The clubhouse, reached by a path that parallels a creek, is usually rented to groups. The best thing to do here is nothing. However, there are a sauna and two hot tubs, one of which is out in the trees where a herd of deer often gathers. Breakfast is served on the stone patio.

Harry's wit and tall tales are part of the charm. Be sure to ask to see his golf course, but don't expect Pebble Beach. With the money from room rentals going to charity, the Middelkamps don't actively attempt to keep the rooms full, so if you show up without a reservation, chances are you'll get a room. **8733 Pine Dr., Beulah, CO 81023; (719) 485-3201, (719) 543-3362.**

K.K. Ranch — $$

Retired Navy Capt. Kay Keating runs a delightfully tight ship at the K.K. Ranch in Beulah. The guest house, an impeccably restored 1870s farmhouse, typifies the picture most travelers conjure up when they think of bed and breakfasts: a quaint, cozy Victorian, brimming with antiques and heated by wood stoves. Keating is in business mainly for the company. International guests will feel at home here: she speaks fluent Japanese and some German and French, learned in her sailing days. "I spent 30 years in the Navy, traveled all over the world and never found as nice a place as Beulah," she says.

What gives K.K. its flair is Capt. Keating's avocation of restoring antique carriages. At the moment she owns 15 of the museum-quality vehicles, including a stagecoach and an eerie-looking hearse. She also restores antique sleighs, which she usually puts out in winter for dashes through nearby Pueblo Mountain Park.

Accommodations include three bedrooms upstairs and one bedroom downstairs. A hearty continental breakfast is served. Reservations through Bed and Breakfast Colorado required; (303) 494-4994. To reach K.K., turn left at the fork just east of Beulah at the Host Restaurant. Proceed to the sign to Pueblo Mountain Park and take a right on Mountain Park Rd. Take a quick right at the red barns. 8987 Mountain Park Rd., Beulah, CO 81023.

PUEBLO

Best Western—The Inn at Pueblo West — $$$

Located north of Pueblo Reservoir in the planned community of Pueblo West, 10 miles west of Pueblo. Restaurant (popular Sun. brunch), cocktail lounge, room service, 80 rooms. The inn arranges tee times for guests at the nearby Pueblo West Golf Club. 201 S. McCulloch, Pueblo West, CO 81007; (719) 547-2111.

Holiday Inn — $$$

Boasting the only full-service hotel in Pueblo, the Holiday Inn offers 193 rooms, indoor pool, lounge and dining room. Free movies. 4001 N. Elizabeth, Pueblo, CO 81008; (719) 543-8050.

Best Western Town House Motor Hotel — $$

Centrally located in town. 88 rooms. Pool is open in summer. 730 N. Santa Fe Ave., Pueblo, CO 81003; (719) 543-6530, toll free 1-800-528-1234.

Youth Hostel — $

Located at the University of Southern Colorado dorms on the east side of town, the youth hostel is open only June through Aug. TV, gym facilities and a washroom are offered. 2200 Bonforte Blvd., Pueblo, CO 81001-4901; (719) 549-2601.

———— WHERE TO EAT ————

Let's put it on the table from the start—Pueblo has some great Mexican food. After all, the south end of town (south side of the Arkansas River) used to be part of Mexico. The Hispanic community is large and offers local restaurants with food so authentic it will make your eyes water. For continental dining, however, try La Renaissance.

La Renaissance — $$$

La Renaissance is definitely a Pueblo dining highlight. Located in an old church built in the 1880s, the restaurant has been in operation since 1974. High ceilings and, of course, lots of stained glass provide a unique interior design element. The menu is primarily continental, offering prime rib, steaks, chicken and tempting seafood entrées. These are five-course dinners, so come hungry. A good selection of imported wines and beers awaits you. The lunch menu ($ to $$) contains sandwiches, seafood and salads. There is also a dessert cart. Compared to restaurants in Denver, La Renaissance is a good value. Lunch served Mon.–Fri. 11 am–2 pm, dinner Mon.–Sat. 5–9 pm. 217 E. Routt Ave.; 543-6367.

DJ's Steak House — $$ to $$$

If Charles Goodnight, the famous local cattle rancher, were alive today, he'd probably be eating his steak at DJ's. The restaurant has built up a good reputation among the townsfolk for large portions of high-quality beef at reasonable prices. The prime rib is especially good. Seafood is also featured, as well as surf and turf combos. Open daily from 4:30–10 pm. **4289 N. Elizabeth; 545-9354.**

Lindy's at Rosemount — $$

This unique little lunch spot is located in the old carriage house at the Rosemount Victorian House Museum. Dine in a quiet, relaxed atmosphere with fine woodwork throughout. Sandwiches, salads and soups are served. Half portions are available for children under 12 years. Combine lunch at Lindy's with an afternoon tour of the mansion. Open Mon.–Fri., 11 am–2 pm. **419 W. 14th St.; 544-9593.**

Do-Drop-Inn — $ to $$

Ask the locals where the best pizza in town is and you'll get the Do-Drop-Inn for an answer. And it's great! They have recently installed a new oven, which will cut down the waiting time that can stretch out to as long as an hour and a half on a busy night. It's a small, very casual downtown bar that also serves up sandwiches and a pretty decent margarita. Belly up to the bar or sit in a booth. Take-out orders are available (add $1 per order). This joint is strictly cash-and-carry (no checks and leave your Gold Card at home). Open 11 am–2 am, Mon.–Sat.; 2 pm–10 pm on Sun. **117 N. Main St.; 542-0818.**

Nachos — $ to $$

Nachos is more comfortable than Jorge's (see below), and they serve great margaritas, frozen or on the rocks. Their guacamole dip is delicious and so is the Ultimate Burrito. Open Mon.–Thurs. 10 am–9 pm; Fri. 10 am–midnight, Sat. 9am to midnight; Sun. 9 am–9 pm. Located at **215 N. Main St.; 544-0733. Nacho's Fireside ($$)** is their newer, slightly more upscale restaurant with an expanded menu. Hours are Tues.–Thurs. 11 am–10 pm, Sun. 11 am–9 pm. **801 Hwy. 50 W.; 542-4557.**

Jorge's — $

For authentic food cooked from scratch at a very reasonable price, this is the place to go. Their menu is fairly extensive, though subject to seasonality; many of the items may not be available. Whatever is offered on the Special of the Day board, posted on the wall by the kitchen, may be worth trying. It's usually cheap and delicious. House specialties include chorizo, enchiladas and Jorge's burrito. The jukebox has a good mix of Spanish and "American" music. If your tastebuds haven't had enough of a workout by the end of the meal, there is a Hot Tamale candy dispenser by the door. No alcohol served. Open Wed., Thurs. and Sun. 9 am–9 pm. Open Fri. and Sat. 9 am–3 pm. Closed Mon. **314 W. Northern Ave.; 564-6486.**

Liz's Old Town Cafe — $

This take-out Mexican cafe opens at 5 pm and delivers anywhere in Pueblo until 4 am! Open daily. **1550 E. Evans Ave.; 564-5476.**

SERVICES

The Pueblo Chamber—
302 N. Santa Fe Ave., Pueblo, CO 81003; (719) 542-1704.

Southeast Plains

The southeastern section of Colorado with its miles of windswept plains isn't exactly a garden spot. Jackrabbits and rattlesnakes outnumber tourists by dizzying numbers. These high, barren plains, however, slope down to the fertile Arkansas Valley, which is one of the most intensely farmed areas in the state. For 150 miles, from Pueblo to the Kansas border, the Lower Arkansas River makes its way east across the plains through this lush bottomland dotted with farms and ranches. The produce from this area, especially the melons, is some of the best in the country.

What the southeast plains lack in tourist appeal is more than made up for by its fascinating history. The Indian, Hispanic and Anglo cultures have all left an indelible imprint on this part of Colorado. The Santa Fe Trail, which brought so many pioneers west from Missouri in the 1800s, traveled right through the heart of the Arkansas Valley before angling southwest at La Junta. Today Hwy. 50 follows the Santa Fe Trail as it moves west from the Kansas border through the Arkansas Valley. Along the way you'll find a number of farming and ranching communities that offer accommodations, restaurants and a few attractions worth your time. One big draw to this corner of the state is the outstanding bird hunting, especially for geese and pheasants.

HISTORY

After Mexico declared independence from Spain in 1821, the Santa Fe Trail was established as a trade route between St. Louis, Missouri, and Santa Fe, Mexico. Along the mountain branch of the trail, near present-day La Junta, Bent's Fort was established in 1833 and for years served as the most important trading center for the American western frontier (see page 597). Along with mountain men and travelers passing by on the Santa Fe Trail, the fort attracted the attention of Plains Indians. From the north side of the Arkansas River, bands of Arapaho and Cheyenne camped near the fort and traded their buffalo robes for food and trinkets. Other tribes, such as the Kiowa, Prairie Apache and Comanche, camped along the south side of the river, also trading at the fort.

In the late 1840s, US troops spent time in the area during the war with Mexico. After the US victory, land south of the Arkansas River that had been previously claimed by Mexico became part of the US. With this part of Colorado (then the New Mexico Territory) under US jurisdiction and the allure of gold strikes in the Colorado mountains, white settlers poured west along the Santa Fe Trail. Because of this huge influx, relations with the Plains Indians inevitably deteriorated.

In 1861 the Treaty of Fort Wise required the Plains Indians to cede much of their land in eastern Colorado. The Arapaho and Cheyenne refused to honor the treaty. After a band of renegades attacked the Hungate Ranch south of Denver in 1864, and white settlers called for massive retaliations against the Indians, a group of Arapaho and Cheyenne, under the leadership of Chief Black Kettle, sued for peace. The Indians met with Gov. Evans in Denver and then traveled to Sand Creek, near Fort Lyon, where they were to be under the protection of US troops. Gov. Evans dispatched a battalion of Colorado Volunteers to southeastern Colorado, where the Indians were camped. What ensued was one of the most tragic episodes in Colorado history.

The volunteer soldiers, led by Col. John M. Chivington, traveled to Fort Lyon, where they were told the Indians' location. They then traveled north to Sand Creek and, on the morning of Nov. 29, 1864, attacked the Indian camp. Here is Chivington's report on what happened: "I, at dawn this morning, attacked a Cheyenne village of one hundred and thirty lodges, from nine hundred to one thousand warriors strong. We killed Chief Black Kettle, White Antelope and Little Robe, and between four and five hundred other Indians. . . . " Later it was discovered that only about 150 Indians were in the camp and of them approximately 120 were killed—mostly old men, women and children. Although anti-Indian sentiments ran high during this era, settlers were outraged with Chivington's act. The Sand Creek Massacre dealt one of the most serious blows to the Plains Indians and eventually they were relocated at reservations in other states.

By 1870 cattlemen began to move into southeastern Colorado. The Chisholm, National and Goodnight trails brought huge herds of Texas longhorns up from the Lone Star State for summer grazing on the high grassy plains. Many head were sold to Colorado ranchers. One of the most lively cattle towns was Trail City, located near the Kansas border. Edward Bowles, a rancher in northeastern Colorado, visited the town as a boy and recalls, "It was the toughest town God ever let live; nothing there but saloons and gambling houses, hotels and corrals." The Santa Fe Railroad arrived in the valley by the mid-1870s and proved to be a crucial link for getting cattle (and, later, produce) to market back east. Cattle barons ruled this part of the state for a number of years, until encroaching homesteaders changed the balance of power. Agricultural land in the Arkansas Valley was quickly snapped up by farmers eager to carve a niche in this wild country. Once irrigation canals were in place, land in the valley became immensely productive. Large crops of vegetables and, especially, melons became well known throughout the country.

Today, this part of the state is still dominated by ranching and agriculture.

Highway 50—

This chapter describes towns that lie along Hwy. 50, beginning near the Kansas border and then heading west.

LAMAR

Known as the Goose Hunting Capital of the Nation, Lamar rolls out the red carpet each fall for hunters who arrive here from all around the country. Established in 1887, the town was named after L.Q.C. Lamar, the secretary of the interior under President Grover Cleveland. By naming the town in his honor, early developers hoped to sway the secretary to install the headquarters of the area land office in Lamar. He must have had a big ego, because the townsfolk got their wish.

In the 1890s, Lamar suffered the devastation of a prolonged drought, a major fire and a catastrophic invasion of jackrabbits. The gentle beasts were eating up the farmers' crops, and finally action was taken. More than 100 hunters encircled a large area of land and converged on the horde of rabbits. When the dust cleared, more than 4,700 rabbits had been shot or clubbed to death. The rabbits were then strung up on wire for the whole town to see. This annual harvest went on for a few years until the problem was under control.

Today Lamar serves as a trade center for the region and boasts the Neoplan factory, which builds buses for many cities around the world. There are plenty of services for travelers cruising through the area.

Big Timbers Museum—

This museum takes its name from the 45-mile stretch along the Arkansas River where enormous cottonwood trees (some 18 feet in circumference) once lined both banks of the river. Indians, trappers, traders and pioneers traveling the Santa Fe Trail used to camp in Big Timbers, which provided a lush, wooded area in an otherwise barren region. William Bent (of Bent's Old Fort fame; see the Las Animas section) maintained a couple of trading stations here. Eventually, virtually all of the trees were cut down by settlers for building material and fuel. Many of the area's original buildings were constructed with this wood.

Housed in the museum is a collection of pioneer memorabilia, including a kitchen display, farm implements and period clothing. There is also an interesting collection of historic photos. No admission fee. Open 1:30–4:30 pm daily. Located just north of Lamar. **7515 Hwy. 50, Lamar, CO 81052; (719) 336-2472.**

Comanche National Grassland—

Flat expanses of prairie, twisting rocky canyons and scorching heat: All of these ingredients make up the harsh country in the Comanche National Grassland. Located in two separate sections of land (one is 50 miles south of Lamar and the other is southwest of La Junta on Hwy. 350), this barren country was the territory of the Comanche Indians until the early 1800s. When cattlemen entered southeastern Colorado in the 1870s, they allowed their herds to overgraze the fragile land. Eventually, most of the land was taken over by homesteaders. As required by the government, each homesteader farmed at least 40 acres of his 160-acre tract. The dry soil was unfit for cultivation, but the farmers persisted with poor results. Problems caused by the destruction of the natural ground cover came home to roost in the Dust Bowl days of the 1930s. Beginning in 1938, the federal government began buying back the land to retire it from cultivation.

Though the forest service has successfully reintroduced vegetation to the majority of these grasslands, on the whole they constitute a hot, dry, inhospitable region that is rarely visited. Archaeologists are an exception. Several prehistoric Indian campsites and rock art provide fascinating clues about early Colorado residents. Recently, some archaeologists have hypothesized that strange lines carved in a local cave are symbols similar to a form of writing used by the ancient Celts of Ireland. Could it be that Europeans visited the New World hundreds of years before Columbus?

The grasslands also hold an appeal for those who enjoy desert hiking and wildlife. Some of the animals that inhabit the grasslands are antelope, mule deer, coyotes, badgers, foxes, raccoons and jackrabbits. Among the bird life, the endangered lesser prairie chicken can be spotted occasionally. If you visit the grasslands in summer, be sure to bring drinking water. For maps and information, stop in at the **Comanche National Grassland Office, 46 miles south of Lamar on Hwy. 287. 27162 Hwy. 287, PO Box 127, Springfield, CO 81073; (719) 523-6591.**

Cow Palace Inn — $$$

Lamar's activities seem to center around this large motel, which caters to goose hunters, vacationers and businessmen. It also doubles as a popular place for local wedding receptions. Ninety comfortable rooms come with color TVs, king- and queen-sized beds and direct-dial phones. The motel has an indoor pool and a courtyard dining area with many tropical plants. The restaurant ($$ to $$$) is well known for its excellent steaks and salad bar. **1301 N. Main St., Lamar, CO 81052; (719) 336-7753.**

Queens State Wildlife Area—

Located about 15 miles north of Hwy. 50 on Hwy. 287 are four reservoirs, all within a 5-mile radius of each other. Nee Noshe, Nee so Pah, Nee Grande and Nee Shaw provide good waterfowl hunting (especially for pheasants and geese) and excellent warmwater fishing in the spring. During hunting season, goose pits are available on a first-come, first-served basis. Fishing these waters can yield walleye, perch, crappie, northern pike, channel catfish and bass. Nee Noshe is especially well known for excellent bass fishing. Boat ramps are available at every reservoir except Nee so Pah.

LAS ANIMAS

Founded in 1869 at the junction of the Arkansas and Purgatoire rivers, Las Animas was originally an important cattle grazing area. The largest business was the Prairie Cattle Co., an English outfit that grazed 50,000 head of longhorn in the early 1880s. By 1916 the last major roundup was held. Today, Las Animas serves as a trade center for farmers and ranchers. Accommodations and restaurants can be found in town.

Bent's Old Fort—

When Mexico seceded from Spain in 1821, trade began between this newly created nation and the US. In 1833–34, brothers William and Charles Bent and Ceran St. Vrain completed a trading post along the Arkansas River in southeastern Colorado. It quickly became the most important hub for US trade with Mexico and the western territories all the way to the Pacific Ocean. Traders moved American-made goods along the Santa Fe Trail from Missouri to Santa Fe, where they traded for Mexican products to be brought back east. Bent's Fort became an important depot for the mountain men who traded beaver pelts in exchange for the supplies they needed to survive in the wilds.

The Bent brothers and St. Vrain were also very adept at trading with the Plains Indian tribes. Since the fort was located on southern Cheyenne hunting grounds, good relations with this tribe were especially important. To secure harmonious relations, William Bent married Owl Woman, the daughter of a Cheyenne priest, in 1837.

Bent's Fort was an immensely profitable venture that thrived until the late 1840s. William Bent abandoned the fort after Charles was killed in the Taos Revolt of 1848 and a cholera epidemic swept into the area from Missouri a few years later.

Today the fort is a national historic site, that has been reconstructed to look exactly as it did in the 1840s when the Bents and St. Vrain were at their height of power. The immense adobe structure is furnished with antiques and reconstructions of other items used at the fort. Costumed employees provide a wealth of information about the history of Bent's Old Fort and what life was like in those times. This is a highly recommended stop for anyone interested in the history of Colorado and the American West. Small fee. Open daily 8 am–6 pm Memorial Day through Labor Day and 8 am–4:30 pm during the rest of the year. Located 15 miles west of Las Animas (8 miles east of La Junta) on Hwy. 194. **35110 Hwy. 194 E., La Junta, CO 81050-9523; (719) 384-2596.**

John Martin Reservoir State Wildlife Area—

Surrounded by flat, treeless terrain, John Martin Reservoir is definitely not one of the most scenic bodies of water in the state, but it is one of the biggest. Located along the Arkansas River between Lamar and La Junta, it has a whopping capacity of 618,660 acre-feet, but is usually at about 15,000 acre-feet. Even at this level, the reservoir provides enough water to support an impressive waterfowl population. Hunting can be quite good for geese, ducks and especially pheasant. Birdwatchers can be treated to sightings of white pelicans in summer and bald and golden eagles in winter.

In the past few years, the reservoir has also become a warmwater fishing destination. The waters have been stocked with channel catfish, largemouth and smallmouth bass, crappie, walleye and sunfish. A couple of boat ramps are available at the east end of the reservoir.

Adjacent to John Martin's eastern border is **Hasty Lake**, a springfed, warmwater lake that's stocked with yellow perch, crappie, smallmouth and white bass, channel catfish, walleye and northern pike. There is also a campground at Hasty Lake.

To reach John Martin Reservoir from Las Animas, head east on Hwy. 50 for about 15 miles to the town of Hasty and turn south on Hwy. 260. Proceed about 5 miles to the reservoir entrance.

LA JUNTA

La Junta, which is Spanish for "the junction," was named for its location at the convergence of the Santa Fe and Navajo trails. Today Hwys. 50 and 350 follow these same routes. Since the Santa Fe Railroad arrived in 1875, La Junta has been the transportation hub for the lower Arkansas Valley. Today the town is home to the largest airport in southeastern Colorado. Amtrak trains also make daily stops. Produce and cattle are shipped by train to every part of the country. For its setting on the windswept plains, La Junta is an attractive town, with parks and focal points, such as the Santa Fe Plaza and Otero Junior College, to highlight its appearance. Alhough its population is predominately Anglo, the Hispanic influence is apparent. La Junta has a number of places to stay the night, along with a couple of good steak houses and Mexican restaurants.

Koshare Indian Museum—

What started as a Boy Scout troop's project in 1933 has grown into a nationally known Indian dance group and an excellent Indian museum. "Buck's Brats," as they were known for years, developed quite a reputation for their authentic Native American dances. Today the Koshare Indian Dance Group, from Explorer Scout Post 230, performs around the country as well as in their kiva at this museum. Though it takes a few minutes to get used to these youngsters with blond crew cuts, they really can dance. Generous donations have helped finance the attractive museum, which houses $5 million worth of Indian artifacts and art. The Koshare collection is magnificent and beautifully displayed. If you're interested in Native American culture, dance and history, make a point to stop by. Open daily 9 am–5 pm June through Sept. and noon–5 pm during the rest of the year. Dances are performed Sat. during summer at 8 pm. For Christmas holiday performances and other selected show times, check with the museum. Located on the Otero Junior College campus at **115 W. 18th St., PO Box 580, La Junta, CO 81050; (719) 384-4801.**

Otero Museum—

Displays and artifacts of life from 1875, when the Santa Fe Railroad arrived, until the present are the focus of this fine historical museum in the Arkansas Valley. Housed in the old Sciumbato Grocery Store, the building dates back to the early 1900s and is listed on the National Register of Historic Places. Exhibits include early grocery store items, farming and ranching equipment, histories of the local sugar beet factories, and a Santa Fe Railroad room. The number of artifacts crammed into this place is impressive. Don't miss the old chuckwagon, the 1903 REO roadster and the 1857 stagecoach in which Horace Greeley is said to have traveled part of his famous journey west. Admission fee charged. Open daily from 1–5 pm June through Sept. Located **one block south of Hwy. 50** at **2nd** and **Anderson** streets at the west end of La Junta; **(719) 384-7406** or **(719) 384-7121.**

ROCKY FORD

This small farming community gets its name from early pioneers who crossed the Arkansas River at this safe point in order to avoid quicksand along many other sections of the river. Rocky Ford really should be remembered for being the site of the first community irrigation canal in the lower Arkansas Valley. In 1874, settler George Swink convinced his neighbors to help dig a ditch. When it was finished, their hard work helped produce fantastic crops. Swink went on to develop the sweet, juicy Rocky Ford cantaloupe, which is known throughout the country. If you are travelling through the area in Aug. or Sept., stop by one of the many roadside produce stands for a taste of this delicious treat as well as other fruit from the valley.

Arkansas Valley Fair
mid-August

Coinciding with the melon harvest, this multi-day gathering of Arkansas Valley residents features events such as horse races, livestock shows, a carnival and a rodeo. Special theme days include Fiesta Day, which celebrates the area's Hispanic culture. You'll eat enough on Watermelon Day to keep you away from melons for a year. For more information about this annual event, contact the **Rocky Ford Chamber of Commerce, 105 N. Main St., Rocky Ford, CO 81067; (719) 254-7483.**

SERVICES

La Junta Chamber of Commerce—
PO Box 408, La Junta, CO 81050; (719) 384-7411.

Lamar Chamber of Commerce—
17 S. Main St., Lamar, CO 81052; (719) 336-4379.

Las Animas/Bent County Chamber of Commerce—
511 Ambassador Thompson Blvd., Las Animas, CO 81054; (719) 456-0453.

Rocky Ford Chamber of Commerce—
105 N. Main St., Rocky Ford, CO 81067; (719) 254-7483.

Trinidad

Located just off Interstate 25, Trinidad is a mere 19 miles away from the New Mexico border. The Spanish influence on Trinidad is still palpable today: cobblestones line the hilly streets of old downtown, and the Baca House, an early Hispanic residence, is a major attraction. Located under the shadow of Fisher Peak, this small industrial city of about 10,000 inhabitants has a history dating back to the arduous path of the Santa Fe Trail. Though you'd hardly want to spend your entire vacation in Trinidad, it remains a good place in which to occupy an afternoon at some fine museums.

HISTORY

The site of Trinidad at the confluence of the Purgatoire River and Raton Creek has always been a favored camping place—first for nomadic Indian tribes and then for white trappers and traders. In the 1800s, many canvas-covered wagons passed through present-day Trinidad, heading south over Raton Pass on the "Mountain Branch" of the Santa Fe Trail. The trail provided a fairly direct route between Santa Fe and trading centers along the Missouri River. The first record of permanent settlement was made in 1859, when Gabriel Gutierrez and his nephew built a cabin. As the town slowly grew, it maintained a tough reputation. Men of Spanish and Mexican descent mingled uncomfortably with those arriving from the eastern states. Fistfights were common, and tension reached a violent height on Christmas Day 1867, when a friendly wrestling match turned into a free-for-all riot. Several were killed during the "Battle of Trinidad," which was fought along racial lines.

The Trinidad area was a part of the Territory of New Mexico from 1850 until the Territory of Colorado usurped the land in 1861. The town was officially established in 1877. Over the years it grew steadily as a sheep center and then a cattle center, until vast deposits of coal were mined from the nearby hills. For decades coal mining was the main source of employment for the people of Trinidad. Though coal production has virtually reached a standstill, the innocents killed in the nearby Ludlow Massacre on April 20, 1914, will never be forgotten (see page 602).

GETTING THERE

Trinidad is located 197 miles south of Denver on Interstate 25. Getting there by automobile requires absolutely no turn-offs.

—————— **SEEING AND DOING** ——————

MUSEUMS

A. R. Mitchell Memorial Museum and Gallery—

Maybe this is just a romantic impulse to try to recreate the past of my own forebears . . . a world of horses and horsemen, big skies, and the great unfenced outdoors.

Arthur Roy Mitchell was one of the leading western-style painters of our century. During his lifetime (1889-1977) he painted more than 160 cover illustrations for popular "pulp" Westerns. In his later years he concentrated on painting accurate representations of early western life, gathering many awards for his style and expertise. Some 250 of his originals are on display in this large collection of western art. The gallery is also home to many other artists in the same genre. One part of the museum is dedicated to the Hispanic folk art of Colorado and New Mexico. Rare *bultos* (wooden sculptures) and *retablos* (wooden altar pieces) are displayed in addition to a small replica of a *morada*—the meeting house of the Penitente religion. A gift shop sells, among other items, jewelry, rugs and original paintings of southwestern artists. Free admission. Open Apr.–Sept., 10 am–4 pm daily, except Sun. and holidays. **131 West Main St.; (719) 846-4224.**

Baca House, Bloom Mansion and the Pioneer Museum—

This fascinating museum complex represents a decade-long span of tremendous change in the Colorado of the 1870s: from territory to state, from Sante Fe Trail to railroads, from sheep to cattle ranching, from natural gas to electricity, from adobe to brick Victorian. Side by side these imposing domiciles allow you to trace this dynamic phase of history. A knowledgeable tour guide in period dress will take you around. Small fee charged. Open 10 am–4 pm Mon.–Sat., 1–4 pm Sun., Memorial Day to Sept. Off-season open by appointment. **300 East Main St.; (719) 846-7217.**

Baca House—Built of adobe bricks in 1869 by John Hough, a merchant from Pennsylvania, this house was undoubtedly the finest in Trinidad at that time. It was purchased for $7,000 by Don Felipe Baca in 1870, complete with furnishings and dishes. Baca was a prosperous Spanish-American rancher and freighter who preferred a lifestyle of simplicity. Uneven wooden floors are covered by handwoven rugs, and the pie safe is built from recycled tins. Looking out of the second-floor windows you can see the path of the Santa Fe Trail (now Main St.) through distorted hand-rolled glass. There are numerous treasures of the times spread throughout.

Bloom Mansion—In 1881 the Victorian-styled Bloom Mansion was built next to the Baca House for Frank Bloom, a Colorado cattleman, merchant and banker. The differences between the two are startling. First off, the opulent Bloom Mansion was built for a mere $3,000, thanks to the establishment of the railroads and the accompanying infusion of cheap labor. Conveniences from the eastern United States were built into the elaborate three-story setting. The parlor features combination gas/electric fixtures, high ceilings, tasseled draperies and ornately carved furniture. The upstairs bedrooms all have massive bedsteads, quilts and lace curtains. On the top floor are the servants' quarters. Behind the house, where a brick barn once stood, you'll enjoy a stroll through a carefully tended **Victorian Cutting Garden**, enhanced by the accompaniment of a splashing waterfall.

Pioneer Museum—Behind the Baca House, in the adobe carriage house and sheepherders' quarters, are rooms full of interesting items from Trinidad's early days. Kit Carson's buckskin coat is displayed, along with many Indian artifacts. Don't miss the bear trap, old photos of Bat Masterson and Doc Holliday and a gun collection dating from 1870. Every room has something new to offer. Outside, several horse-drawn carriages appear ready to be hitched.

Louden-Henritze Archaeology Museum—

Our expectations were not exactly soaring as we proceeded to the ground floor of the Trinidad State Junior College library for a look at this museum. So it was a pleasant shock to be given a personal tour through the small but excellent collection of exhibits. The highlight was a diorama of nearby Trinchera Cave, which was occupied for thousands of years by prehistoric man. Other items range from fossilized shark teeth to an amazing collection of arrowheads. In 1962, before the construction of Trinidad Reservoir, there was a hurried excavation of more than 300 sites. The excavation was done under the direction of the college, and now there are many artifacts on display at the museum, including a complete skeleton inside a bell-shaped burial pit. Trivia buffs may be interested to know that the now-defunct archaeological program at Trinidad State Junior College was initiated by Hal Chase in 1951. Chase was a friend of Jack Kerouac, William Burroughs and Allen Ginsburg and is mentioned in Jack Kerouac's *On the Road* as a character named Chad King. Free admission. 9:30 am–1:30 pm Mon.–Fri., May to early Sept. **Freudenthal Memorial Library, Trinidad State Junior College; (719) 846-5508.**

Ludlow Monument—

Twelve miles northwest of Trinidad, on April 20, 1914, a battle between striking coal workers and militiamen ended with the tragic deaths of several miners and 15 citizens. Seven months before the "Ludlow Massacre" took place, the United Mine Workers had encouraged the miners to strike for better working conditions and pay. Workers moved out of company-owned camps and established tent colonies to wait out the struggle. On the Ludlow prairie, not far from the mines, hundreds of miners and their families took residence.

Sporadic violence at Ludlow caused Gov. Elias Ammons to call out the state militia to quell the rising emotions. It might have been a good move, except that the militia was infiltrated with coal company strongmen. The "peacekeepers" were armed to the teeth, and it didn't take long for an accidental shot to prompt a volley of bullets. On April 20 several miners, along with an 18-year-old-passerby and a young boy, were killed by gunshot. During the same day, 11 children and two women were suffocated to death while taking refuge in a makeshift cellar underneath a tent that went up in flames. This violent story from the annals of the American labor movement is preserved in a granite monument erected by the United Mine Workers. To reach the monument, take Interstate 25 12 miles northwest to the Ludlow exit.

RECREATION AREA

Trinidad State Recreation Area—

Only 4 miles west of Trinidad is a pleasant area for water sports, hiking and camping. Trinidad Lake covers a coal-mining area that was heavily populated for decades around the turn of the century. Trinidad Lake is now open for boating, water skiing and fishing. The large lake is stocked with rainbow trout, but largemouth bass, catfish, walleye and crappie can also be caught.

Bonytail Chub

A couple of short hiking trails lead into the surrounding hills, with excellent views of Fisher Peak. On the north side of the lake are 62 campsites in a developed campground providing flush toilets and showers. Trailers and tents are accepted. Fee charged. To reach Trinidad State Recreation Area, take **Hwy. 12** west of Trinidad for 4 miles.

SERVICES

Colorado Welcome Center—

This is a great source of information for vacationers. You'll see the signs on Interstate 25. **309 N. Nevada Ave., Trinidad, CO 81082; (719) 846-9512.**

INDEX